Killer Windows 95

Glenn Fincher
Ewan Grantham
Robin Hohman
Yvonne Johnson
Bill Lawrence
Gordon Meltzer
Benjamin F. Miller
Gregory J. Root
Clayton Walnum
Allen L. Wyatt
Martin R. Wyatt

que®

Killer Windows 95

Copyright© 1995 by Que® Corporation.

All rights reserved. Printed in the United States of America. No part of this book may be used or reproduced in any form or by any means, or stored in a database or retrieval system, without prior written permission of the publisher except in the case of brief quotations embodied in critical articles and reviews. Making copies of any part of this book for any purpose other than your own personal use is a violation of United States copyright laws. For information, address Que Corporation, 201 W. 103rd St., Indianapolis, IN 46290. You may reach Que's direct sales line by calling 1-800-428-5331.

Library of Congress Catalog No.: 95-078885

ISBN: 0-7897-0001-8

This book is sold *as is*, without warranty of any kind, either expressed or implied, respecting the contents of this book, including but not limited to implied warranties for the book's quality, performance, merchantability, or fitness for any particular purpose. Neither Que Corporation nor its dealers or distributors shall be liable to the purchaser or any other person or entity with respect to any liability, loss, or damage caused or alleged to be caused directly or indirectly by this book.

97 96 95   6 5 4 3 2

Interpretation of the printing code: the rightmost double-digit number is the year of the book's printing; the rightmost single-digit number, the number of the book's printing. For example, a printing code of 95-1 shows that the first printing of the book occurred in 1995.

All terms mentioned in this book that are known to be trademarks or service marks have been appropriately capitalized. Que cannot attest to the accuracy of this information. Use of a term in this book should not be regarded as affecting the validity of any trademark or service mark.

Screen reproductions in this book were created by using Collage Plus from Inner Media, Inc., Hollis, NH.

Credits

President and Publisher
Roland Elgey

Associate Publisher
Joseph B. Wikert

Editorial Services Director
Elizabeth Keaffaber

Managing Editor
Sandy Doell

Director of Marketing
Lynn E. Zingraf

Senior Series Editor
Chris Nelson

Title Manager
Bryan Gambrel

Acquisitions Editor
Lori A. Jordan

Product Director
Stephen L. Miller

Production Editor
Mike La Bonne

Editors
Judy Brunetti
Elizabeth Bruns
Tom Cirtin
Susan Shaw Dunn
Patrick Kanouse
Susan Ross Moore
Caroline D. Roop

Assistant Product Marketing Manager
Kim Margolius

Technical Editors
Kyle Bryant, Russell Jacobs

Technical Specialist
Cari Skaggs

Acquisitions Coordinator
Angela C. Kozlowski

Operations Coordinator
Patricia J. Brooks

Editorial Assistant
Michelle R. Newcomb

Book Designer
Barbara Kordesh

Cover Designer
Dan Armstrong

Copywriter
Jennifer Reese

Production Team
Steve Adams, Angela Bannan, Claudia Bell, Lisa Daugherty, Chad Dressler, DiMonique Ford, Amy Gornik, John Hulse, Darren Jackson, Brian-Kent Proffitt, Bobbi Satterfield, Susan Springer, Michael Thomas

Indexers
Kathy Venable, Debra Myers

Composed in *Utopia* and *MCPdigital* by Que Corporation.

About the Authors

Glenn Fincher has worked in the computer industry for the last 12 years. Working in the fast-moving electronic manufacturing industry, Glenn spent the early years of his career in Test Engineering at SCI Systems, Inc., the world's largest computer contract manufacturer. Spending the bulk of the SCI years in component, board, and unit testing, he became intimately familiar with the building blocks of today's computer technology. Joining Intergraph Corporation in 1991 as a Customer Support Analyst, he has applied his wealth of computer knowledge to providing Intergraph's customers with quality, timely, and accurate support for the MicroStation CAD product. Leading the software certification efforts for the successful release of MicroStation 5.0, he continues to be involved in the day-to-day world of Intergraph's partner Bentley Systems MicroStation product. Sharing the knowledge gained in the experience of these years in the industry has always been a priority, so it is no surprise that he is in demand as a speaker, writer, and presenter throughout Intergraph. With his present involvement in Intergraph's WWW effort as Webmaster for Intergraph's Software Solutions, Glenn continues to remain at the leading edge of this industry. Continually seeking to stay on this edge has required both the support and understanding of wife Jan and their three children, Ashely, Will, and Aimee, without whom this and all his other endeavors would have been a lonely journey indeed. Glenn can be reached by electronic mail at gtfinche@ingr.com.

Ewan Grantham's main work is as a consultant specializing in building GUI front-ends for client/server systems, and creating multimedia presentations and training for clients. Equally adept at changing diapers (three kids under the age of 4) and changing jumpers on his IDE controller, he also finds time to work with Visual C++, MS Access, MS Help, and a monthly column on multimedia in *Windows 95 Journal*. Ewan can be reached on CIS at 74123,2232 or through the Internet at 74123.2232@compuserve.com.

Robin Hohman has been writing about computers and other subjects for more than 10 years. Her articles have appeared in newspapers, magazines, and books. She also survived a stint as a writer/producer in television news, and she refuses to be cowed by even the most obstinate computer software.

Yvonne Johnson has been involved in teaching and writing about PCs since they first came into use. For 12 years she owned and operated a successful computer training school. During that time she authored all the training material for the school and wrote several books published by Que and other publishers. She sold the school and now devotes more of her time to writing, consulting, and programming. Her training and writing background has made her exceptionally well-versed in database, word processing, graphics, spreadsheet, presentation, integrated, and publishing software. She holds a BA degree from Centre College of Kentucky with a major in education and English. She did her post-graduate work at the University of South Florida.

Bill Lawrence started using NetWare in 1983, when the software was called ShareNet and was delivered on five low-density diskettes. He is part of the team that manages a 3000-node network for a major western utility, and writes and speaks extensively about networking issues. He is the author of Que's *Using Novell NetWare 4*, which covers NetWare 3.x.

Gordon Meltzer has been teaching himself about computers since they were made with vacuum tubes. Recently, Gordon designed and built workgroup networks for a music marketing division of Time-Warner and several New York City law firms. He is a consultant on computing issues to NBC Post Production in Manhattan. Gordon has produced a number of jazz records for people like Miles Davis, Michel LeGrand, Al Di Meola, and Wallace Roney, and has a special interest in using computers on the business side of the music industry.

Benjamin F. Miller is a features editor at *PC/Computing Magazine,* and has written on Windows 95 and the Internet. He regularly contributes articles on multimedia and application development.

Gregory J. Root started his work with computers when TRS-80s were in style and 16K of RAM was equivalent to infinity. He has worked for Northern Trust Bank and Follett Software Company. He also has made part of his living as a computing consultant for lawyers, churches, and a government contract. Throughout his career he has administered and installed peer-to-peer and server-based networks, developed applications using FORTRAN and Visual Basic, and managed software development projects. He lives in Lake in the Hills, Illinois, with his beautiful wife and lifelong companion, Tracy.

Clayton Walnum has been writing about computers for a decade and has published more than 300 articles in major computer publications. He is the author of several books, covering such diverse topics as programming, computer gaming, and application programs. His most recent book is *Creating Turbo C++ Games,* also published by Que. His earlier titles include *Borland C++ Object-Oriented Programming, Borland C++ Power Programming,* and *QBasic for Rookies* (Que); *PC Picasso: A Child's Computer Drawing Kit,* and *The First Book of Microsoft Works for Windows* (Sams); *PowerMonger: The Official Strategy Guide* (Prima); and *C-manship Complete* (Taylor Ridge Books). Walnum is a full-time freelance writer and lives in Connecticut with his wife and their three children.

Allen L. Wyatt, a recognized expert in small computer systems, has been working in the computer and publishing industries for over 15 years. He has written more than 30 books explaining many different facets of working with computers. These books have covered topics ranging from programming languages to using application software to using operating systems. The books he has written and worked on have helped millions of readers learn how to better use computers.

Allen is the president of Discovery Computing Inc., a computer and publishing services company located in Sundance, Wyoming. Besides writing books, he helps further the computer book industry by providing consulting and distribution services. With his wife and three children, he lives on a 350-acre ranch just outside of town, on the edge of the Black Hills. In his spare time he tends his animals, has fun with his family, and participates in church and community events.

Martin R. Wyatt has been hooked on microcomputers for almost as long as he can remember. In fact, troubleshooting PCs and consulting (and an occasional game or two) have long been a favorite hobby. Only recently, however, has he been able to really earn a living from it. Currently, Marty works at Discovery Computing Inc., in Sundance, Wyoming, where he helps his brother, Allen Wyatt, author books. In his spare time, Marty prepares for those calm Wyoming winters.

We'd Like to Hear from You!

As part of our continuing effort to produce books of the highest possible quality, Que would like to hear your comments. To stay competitive, we *really* want you, as a computer book reader and user, to let us know what you like or dislike most about this book or other Que products.

You can mail comments, ideas, or suggestions for improving future editions to the address below, or send us a fax at (317) 581-4663. For the online inclined, Macmillan Computer Publishing now has a forum on CompuServe (type **GO QUEBOOKS** at any prompt) through which our staff and authors are available for questions and comments. The address of our Internet site is **http://www.mcp.com** (World Wide Web).

In addition to exploring our forum, please feel free to contact me personally to discuss your opinions of this book. You can reach me on CompuServe at 76103,1334, or through the Internet at slmiller@que.mcp.com.

Thanks in advance—your comments will help us to continue publishing the best books available on computer topics in today's market.

Stephen L. Miller
Product Development Specialist
Que Corporation
201 W. 103rd Street
Indianapolis, Indiana 46290
USA

Contents at a Glance

Introduction   1

Part I Setting Up and Interfacing with Windows 95
1   The Windows 95 Interface   15
2   Under-the-Hood Improvements   43
3   New Windows 95 Tools   65
4   Installing Windows 95   87
5   Installing Windows 95 on a Laptop   127
6   Troubleshooting Windows 95 Installation and Startup   159

Part II Hardware Issues
7   How Windows 95 Interacts with Your Hardware   175
8   Examining the Hardware You Need for Windows 95   199
9   Exploiting Memory, Space, and Resources   213
10   Optimizing Your Disk Drives   227
11   Video Cards, Drivers, and Monitors   257
12   Using Mice and Other Pointing Devices   287

Part III Software
13   How Windows 95 Interacts with Software   311
14   Tailoring Windows 95 and the Registry   325
15   Taking Control of Windows 95 Startup   373
16   Installing Windows Applications   395
17   Fine-Tuning Windows 95 for Your Windows Applications   409
18   Installing DOS Applications   421
19   Fine-Tuning Windows 95 for Your DOS Applications   437

Part IV Output
20   Managing Your Printers   461
21   Printing from Windows 95   501
22   Working with Fonts   523
23   Handling Graphics   545
24   Getting the Most from Your Printer   559

Part V Multimedia

25 Adding Multimedia Capability to Your Computer	577
26 Using Multimedia on Your Computer	603
27 Getting the Most out of Multimedia	615
28 Understanding Full-Motion Video	639
29 Fine-Tuning Your Windows 95 Sound Card	663

Part VI Communications

30 Using OLE to Communicate with Other Applications	681
31 Serial Communications Basics	713
32 Communicating with a Modem	767
33 The Microsoft Network	791
34 Using Microsoft Exchange	821
35 Internet Communications	859

Part VII Networking and Remote Computing

36 Communicating with a Network	891
37 Using Windows 95 on a Network	923
38 Setting Up Remote Computing	943
39 Seamless Remote Computing	967

Part VIII Optimizing Performance

40 Operating in Windows 95 DOS	1001
41 Monitoring Your Windows 95 Vital Files	1051
42 Dealing with Viruses and Security	1063

Part IX Microsoft Plus!

43 System Agent	1101
44 DriveSpace 3 and Compression Agent	1125
45 Desktop Additions	1147
46 Internet Explorer and Jumpstart Kit	1169

Appendixes

A Adding and Removing Windows 95 Components	1193
B Installing the Killer Windows 95 CD-ROM	1205

Index	**1213**

Contents

Introduction 1
  Who Needs This Book? 2
  What Is in This Book? 2
    Part I—Setting Up and Interfacing with Windows 95 3
    Part II—Hardware Issues 4
    Part III—Software 5
    Part IV—Output 6
    Part V—Multimedia 7
    Part VI—Communications 8
    Part VII—Networking and Remote Computing 9
    Part VIII—Optimizing Performance 9
    Part IX—Microsoft Plus! 10
    Appendixes 11
  The Companion CD 11
  Conventions Used in This Book 12

1 The Windows 95 Interface 15
  Booting Windows 95 16
  New Desktop Icons 17
    My Computer 18
    Network Neighborhood 19
    Recycle Bin 20
    Microsoft Exchange 22
  New Windows Design 23
  The Taskbar 24
    The Start Button 26
      The Programs Menu 27
      The Documents Menu 28
      The Settings Menu 29
      Other Start Button Capabilities 31
    Switching to Other Tasks 32
  Getting Help 33
    Tips 34
    The Help System 34
      The Contents Tab 35
      The Index Tab 35
      The Find Tab 36
      Viewing Help Documents 38
    Wizards 39
  Context Menus 40

2 Under-the-Hood Improvements 43
A Full-Blown Operating System 44
Preemptive Multitasking 45
Better Reboot Support 46
Long File Names 47
Traditional FAT Directory Entries 48
Windows 95 Directory Entries 50
Alias File Names 53
Improved 32-Bit Architecture 54
The Kernel 55
File Access 55
TrueType Font Engine 55
Printing and Spooling 56
Device Drivers 56
Better Resource Management 57
Built-In Networking 58
Plug-and-Play Support 59
What Is Plug and Play? 60
Hardware Devices 60
The BIOS 61
The Operating System 63
How Does Windows 95 Support Plug and Play? 64

3 New Windows 95 Tools 65
Using the Explorer 66
Starting the Explorer 66
Understanding the Explorer Window 67
The Menu 67
The Folder Window 67
The Contents Window 68
Other Explorer Features 70
Putting the Explorer to Use 74
Managing Files and Folders 74
Sorting the Contents Window 75
Creating Associations 76
Using Quick View 79
Understanding Shortcuts 82
Creating a Shortcut 82
Renaming a Shortcut 83
Deleting a Shortcut 83
Searching for Files 84
Entering Your Criteria 85

Starting a Search	85
Saving Your Search Criteria	86

4 Installing Windows 95 87

The Different Types of Systems	88
What Is a Home Computer?	88
What Is an Office Computer?	89
What Is a Network Workstation?	90
System Requirements to Install Windows 95	90
Before You Install	91
Checking Your Media	91
Defragmenting Your Hard Disk	91
Backing Up Your System	92
Disabling Your Swap File	92
Checking Your Disk Compression	94
Disabling Programs	94
Dual-Booting	95
Installing Windows 95	96
Starting Setup from MS-DOS	97
Starting Setup from Windows	97
Choosing a Setup Type	104
Choosing a Network Installation	109
Installing on a Client/Server Network	109
Running a Server-Based Setup	110
Defining Home Directories for Shared Files	113
Creating a Batch Script	114
Running Setup from a Workstation	116
Running Setup from the Server	117
Using Novell NetWare Servers	118
Limitations with a NetWare Server	119
Creating Directories on a NetWare Server	119
Setting the Appropriate Access Levels	120
Assigning Drive Letters Using Login Scripts	121
Providing a Drive Letter for the Installation Directory	121
Providing a Drive Letter for a Shared Copy of Windows 95	122
Connecting to the Server	123
After You Install	123
Installation Problems	124
Using the Emergency Startup Disk	125
Changing Your Windows Configuration	125

5 Installing Windows 95 on a Laptop 127
What Is a Portable Computer? 128
System Requirements to Install Windows 95 129
Before You Install 130
    Checking Your Media 130
    Defragmenting Your Hard Disk 131
    Backing Up Your System 131
    Disabling Your Swap File 132
    Checking Your Disk Compression 133
    Disabling Programs 134
Dual-Booting 134
Installing Windows 95 135
    Starting Setup from MS-DOS 136
    Starting Setup from Windows 136
    Choosing a Setup Type 143
After You Install 147
Special Portable Features 148
    Power Management 148
    PC Card (PCMCIA) Properties 149
        Inserting a PCMCIA Card 151
        Removing a PCMCIA Card 152
    Off-line Printing 154
    Off-line E-mail 156
Installation Problems 157
    Using the Emergency Startup Disk 157
    Changing Your Windows Configuration 157

6 Troubleshooting Windows 95 Installation and Startup 159
Troubleshooting the Installation 160
Troubleshooting Startup 161
    Isolating a Startup Problem 162
        Is It a Hardware or Software Conflict? 162
        Is It a Driver Conflict? 163
        Are You Running Low on Hard Disk Space? 163
        Are Files Corrupted? 163
        Is the Hardware Malfunctioning? 164
    Checking for Driver Conflicts 164
    Using Safe Mode Startup 166
    Using Command Line Switches 168
    Using the Startup Disk 169
    Using BOOTLOG.TXT 170
Hardware Troubleshooting 171

7 How Windows 95 Interacts with Your Hardware 175
  Understanding Hardware Properties 177
  Using the Device Manager 178
    Inspecting Settings 179
    The Device Manager and Adding New Hardware 181
    Deactivating a Device 183
    Printing Resource Information 185
    Removing Hardware 186
  Setting Up Hardware Profiles 188
    Defining a Hardware Configuration 189
    Deleting a Hardware Configuration 191
  Using the Add New Hardware Wizard 191
    Legacy Devices with Jumpers 192
    Legacy Devices Without Jumpers 195

8 Examining the Hardware You Need for Windows 95 199
  Evaluating Hard Drive Space 200
  Evaluating Graphics Capabilities 200
  Improving Hardware for Windows 95 201
  Getting Your Computer Ready for Windows 95 202
    Adding RAM 204
    Replacing Your Hard Drive 205
      Types of Hard Drives 205
      Controller Cards 207
    Adding a CD-ROM Drive 208
    Installing Graphics Cards and Monitors 208
  Checking System Compatibility 209
  Plug-and-Play Equipment 211

9 Exploiting Memory, Space, and Resources 213
  Understanding System Memory 214
    Understanding Conventional Memory 216
    Using Expanded Memory 217
  Understanding Virtual Memory 217
    Changing Virtual Memory Settings 218
    Disabling Virtual Memory 220
  Optimizing Virtual Memory 221
  Understanding the TEMP Setting 226

10 Optimizing Your Disk Drives 227
  Working with Caches 228
    Examining RAM 228
      Understanding Page Mode RAM Design 229

	Understanding Interleaved RAM Design	229
	Effects of RAM Design	230
	Understanding RAM Caches	231
	Understanding Disk Caches	234
	Software Caches	234
	Adjusting Caching Parameters	235
	Using SmartDrive	239
	Write-Behind Caching	241
	Hardware Caches	242
	Using Compression Software	243
	Using Swap Files	245
	Defragmenting Your Disk Drive	247
	Surviving with a Small Hard Drive	250
	Using Low-Level Formatting	250
	Adjusting the Interleave	251
	Cleaning Up Your Drive	252
	Considering Hard Drive Upgrades	252
11	**Video Cards, Drivers, and Monitors**	**257**
	Video Cards	258
	Types of Video Cards	258
	Graphics Accelerators	260
	Understanding Busses	261
	VL-Bus	263
	PCI Bus	265
	Monitors	266
	Screen Size	267
	Dot Pitch	269
	Screen Curvature	271
	Refresh Rate	271
	Interlacing	272
	Multisync Monitors	273
	Video Drivers	273
	Selecting a Monitor Type	276
	Changing Video Parameters	278
	Speeding Up Your Video	280
	Using Fewer Display Colors	281
	Configuring Your Software	281
	Installing Graphics Accelerator Cards	283
	Buying a Faster Computer	285

12 Using Mice and Other Pointing Devices 287
Using a Mouse 288
Understanding Mouse Sensitivity 289
Using Mouse Shortcuts 290
Choosing a Pointing Device 291
Getting Your Money's Worth 293
Understanding Connections 293
Examining Different Types of Mice 294
Considering Mouse Alternatives 297
Trackballs 297
Pens 298
Touch Tablets 298
Pointing Devices for Portable Computers 299
Installing Your Pointing Device 301
Selecting the Correct Driver 304
Troubleshooting Pointing Device Problems 306
Pointing for Physically Impaired Users 307

13 How Windows 95 Interacts with Software 311
Understanding the Virtual Machine 312
Process Scheduling 313
Cooperative Multitasking 314
Preemptive Multitasking 314
Memory Paging 316
MS-DOS Mode 317
Different Types of Software 318
Removing an Application 320
Removing a Win32 Program 320
Removing a Win16 Program 322
Removing an MS-DOS Program 323

14 Tailoring Windows 95 and the Registry 325
Using This Chapter 326
Understanding the Registry 327
How the Registry Works 327
Changes to the Registry 330
Manually Editing the Registry 331
Finding Information in the Registry 332
Editing Value Data 333
Adding Keys or Values 336
Deleting Keys or Values 336
Importing and Exporting the Registry 337
Emergency Registry Recovery 337

Accessing a Registry on a Remote System 339
Tailoring Windows 95's Appearance 339
    Video Card and Monitor Settings 340
    Modifying Your Background 342
    Changing Windows Colors and Styles 343
        Working with Schemes 344
        Changing Item Color and Size 346
        Changing Font Color and Size 349
    Configuring the Screen Saver 350
        Activating the Screen Saver 351
        Setting the Screen Saver's Options 352
        Using Password Protection 353
    Setting the Date and Time 355
    Configuring the Mouse 356
        Setting the Mouse Double-Click Speed 357
        Enabling Pointer Trails 358
        Setting Mouse Acceleration 358
        Changing the Mouse Driver 360
    Configuring Your Keyboard 361
        Controlling the Cursor Blink Rate 362
        Configuring the Keyboard Speed 362
        Picking a Type of Keyboard 363
    Controlling Application Icons and Folders 363
        Automatically Arranging Icons 364
        Controlling Program Applets 364
Tuning Windows Configuration 365
    Choosing Startup Preferences 365
    Reorganizing Program Groups 366
    Assigning Sounds to Windows Events 368
    Defining File Associations 370
    Changing the Name of the StartUp Folder 372

15 Taking Control of Windows 95 Startup 373
Controlling the Startup Process 374
    Understanding the Startup 374
    Modifying the Startup 375
    Startup Option Keys 377
    Changing Startup Options 378
Controlling Menus 380
    Changing the Start Menu 381
    Changing the Programs Menu 384
    Changing the Documents Menu 385

	Automatically Running Programs	387
	Using a Wizard to Change the StartUp Folder	388
	Manually Changing the StartUp Folder	390
	Conserving System Resources	391
16	**Installing Windows Applications**	**395**
	Installing with a Wizard	396
	Running the Installation Wizard	396
	Installation Wizard Problems	398
	Installing Manually	399
	32-Bit versus 16-Bit Windows Programs	400
	Preemptive Multitasking	401
	Threaded Operation	402
	Separate Message Queues	402
	Flat Address Space	403
	Memory Protection	403
	Long File Name Support	404
	16-Bit Application Problems	405
	User Interface Problems	405
	Undocumented Features	406
	Version Number Errors	406
17	**Fine-Tuning Windows 95 for Your Windows Applications**	**409**
	Changing Your Environment	410
	Improving Video Performance	410
	Improving Disk Performance	412
	Defragmenting Your Drives	412
	Changing Your Disk Cache Size	412
	Disabling Disk Compression	413
	Improving CD-ROM Performance	414
	Working Directories	415
	16-Bit Program Performance	417
	System Resources	417
18	**Installing DOS Applications**	**421**
	Installing a Program	422
	Using the Wizard	422
	Manually Installing	424
	After Installation	425
	The Application Information File	426
	The [PIF95] Section	426
	The Applications Sections	428
	AppHack	430

BatchFile 430
Disable 430
DPMIMem 432
EMSMem 432
Enable 432
LowMem 433
Params 433
XMSMem 434
The [Strings] Section 434

19 Fine-Tuning Windows 95 for Your DOS Applications 437
What About the PIF? 438
Program Initialization 439
   Changing the Environment Variables 439
   Setting the Path 441
      Globally Setting the Path 441
      Temporarily Setting the Path 442
   Setting a Working Folder 442
Fine-Tuning Memory 443
   Conventional Memory 444
   Expanded Memory 445
   Extended Memory 445
   DPMI Memory 446
   Video Memory Use 447
Fine-Tuning the Screen 448
   Changing Fonts 449
   Text-Mode Lines 450
   Adjusting Screen Size 451
Other Fine-Tuning 453
   Adjusting Multitasking 453
   Using a Mouse Under DOS 455
   Shortcut Keys 456
MS-DOS Safety Tips 458
   The Registry 458
   Disk Utilities 459

20 Managing Your Printers 461
Using the Printers Folder 462
   Understanding Printer Drivers 463
   Adding a Printer 464
      Picking a Type of Printer 466

Picking a Printer Port	467
Configuring Your Printer Port	468
Finishing the Installation	471
Adding a Network Printer	472
Understanding Printer Compatibility	474
Understanding Printer Icons	476
Setting Up Your Printer	476
The General Tab	478
The Details Tab	479
Adding Ports	480
Picking a Printer Driver	481
Mapping Ports	481
Timeout Settings	482
Spool Settings	483
Port Settings	483
The Device Options Tab	483
The Fonts Tab	484
The Graphics Tab	485
The Paper Tab	486
The PostScript Tab	487
PostScript Output Format	488
PostScript Header	489
PostScript Errors	490
Advanced Settings	491
The Sharing Tab	492
Deleting a Printer	493
Special Network Considerations	494
Sharing a Printer	494
Network Printer Properties	496
Tuning Printing Performance with Shared Printers	497
When to Bypass the Local Print Spooler	497
When to Use the Local Print Spooler	498
Network Responsibilities	498

21 Printing from Windows 95 501

Using the Print Spooler	502
How the Print Spooler Works	503
Controlling Print Spooling	504
Creating a Print Job	507

Managing Your Print Jobs 510
    Pausing Print Jobs 511
    Resuming Print Jobs 513
    Deleting Print Jobs 514
Printing to a File 515
    Changing the Output Device 515
    Copying a Disk File to a Printer 516
Printing on a Network 517
Point-and-Print Capabilities 518
Printing from a DOS Application 520

22 Working with Fonts 523
What Are Fonts? 524
Purposes for Fonts 525
    Printer Fonts 526
    Display (Screen) Fonts 526
Types of Fonts 527
    Bitmap Fonts 527
    Outline Fonts 528
        TrueType Fonts 529
        True Type Fonts Are Embedded into the File 530
        Printing TrueType Fonts 530
    PostScript Fonts 531
    Other Types of Fonts 532
Installing Fonts 532
Controlling How TrueType Fonts Print 535
    TrueType Printer Options 537
    PostScript Font Substitution Table 538
    Sending TrueType Fonts to a PostScript Printer 539
Changing the Fonts Used by Windows 542
Changing Fonts in Applications 543

23 Handling Graphics 545
Properties for Graphics 546
System Properties for Graphics 547
Types of File Formats 548
    Raster Graphics 548
    Vector Graphics 549
Setting Associations for Graphics Files 551
The Graphics Tab for Printing 552
Using Windows 95 Paint 554

24 Getting the Most from Your Printer 559
- Speeding Up Your Printer 560
  - The Windows 95 Side of the Fence 560
  - The Printer Side of the Fence 562
  - Your Computer's Role 564
- Troubleshooting Common Problems 565
  - Driver Problems 566
  - The Wrong Font Prints 567
  - TrueType Fonts Won't Print 568
  - You Can't Print in an MS-DOS Window 570
  - Your Print File Is Too Big 571
  - Incomplete Printing 572
  - Your Print Job Disappears 573
  - Printing Is Slower Than Normal 573
- Using the Print Troubleshooter 574

25 Adding Multimedia Capability to Your Computer 577
- Understanding the Multimedia PC 578
- Upgrading Your Hardware to MPC Standards 579
  - The Level-1 Multimedia Standard 579
  - The Level-2 Multimedia Standard 580
  - Beyond Level-2 581
  - Getting the Top of the Line 582
  - Upgrading an Existing System 583
- Learning About Sound Cards 585
  - Sound Blaster Compatibility 586
  - Sound Cards and Windows 586
  - Sampling Quality 587
  - FM Synthesis versus Wavetable Synthesis 588
  - General MIDI MPU-401 588
- Adding a Sound Card to Your PC 590
  - Plug-and-Play Sound Cards 590
  - Jumperless Sound Cards 592
  - Sound Cards with Jumpers 592
  - Adding New Hardware 595
  - Testing Your Sound Card 598
  - Troubleshooting Your Sound Card 599
- Installing a CD-ROM Drive 601

26 Using Multimedia on Your Computer 603
- Assigning Sounds to Windows Events 604
  - Understanding the Sounds Properties Sheet 604

Contents **xxiii**

  Viewing, Selecting, and Listening to Sounds 605
  Saving Sound Schemes 606
 Playing an Audio CD with CD Player 607
  Creating a Play List 608
  Accessing CD Player's Toolbar 611
  Setting CD Player's Options 612
  Setting CD Player's Preferences 613

27 Getting the Most out of Multimedia 615
 Understanding the Multimedia Properties Sheet 616
 Setting Audio Properties 617
 Setting Video Properties 621
 Setting MIDI Properties 623
 Setting CD Music Properties 630
 Using the Advanced Page 631
 Using Volume Control 632
 Configuring a Joystick 633
 Checking CD-ROM Settings 636

28 Understanding Full-Motion Video 639
 Video for Windows 640
 Video Hardware 641
 Video Software 642
 Video for Windows 642
 Compression Schemes 643
  Cinepak 644
  Intel Indeo R3.1 and R3.2 644
  YUV9 645
  RLE 645
  Video 1 645
 MPEG-1 645
  MPEG-2 647
  MPEG-3 648
  MPEG-4 648
 Windows 95 Codecs 648
 Viewing AVI Files 650
 Media Player 651
 Scale: Frames 652
 Scale: Time 652
 Playing the File 653
  Selection Points 653
 Properties 654

OLE	658
Options	661
DCI	661

29 Fine-Tuning Your Windows 95 Sound Card 663

Using Volume Control	664
Choosing Which Channels to Display	665
Mixing Sound	666
Setting Record Levels	667
Accessing Volume Control from the Taskbar	670
Setting Recording Quality	671
Recording Sound	673
Editing Sounds	676
Creating a MIDI Configuration	678

30 Using OLE to Communicate with Other Applications 681

Understanding OLE	684
Understanding Linking	685
Understanding Embedding	691
Choosing Between Linking and Embedding	694
Understanding Packaging	695
Creating and Managing Links	697
Creating Links Between Windows Applications	698
Editing Linked Documents	699
Opening Documents that Contain Links	700
Editing Multiple Links	701
Controlling Update Frequency	701
Choosing Manual Updating	702
Updating Manual Links	702
Breaking the Link	703
Restoring a Broken Link	704
Embedding Objects	704
Choosing the Correct Embedding Procedure	706
Creating an Embedded Object	707
Starting from the Server Application	707
Starting from the Client Application	709
Editing Embedded Objects	710
Deleting an Embedded Object	710
Canceling Embedding Without Deleting the Object	711

31 Serial Communications Basics 713

Understanding Serial Communications	714
Understanding Modems	715

  Analog and Digital Signals 715
  Modem Speed 718
  Modulation Standards for Modems 720
  Hayes-Compatible Modems 722
  Error-Control 723
  Data Compression 724
  External Versus Internal Modems 725
  Telephone Line Requirements 727
 Understanding Serial Ports 728
  Adding a 16550A UART 730
  The Serial Connector 730
  Asynchronous and Synchronous Transmissions 731
  Data Bits 732
  Parity Checking 733
  Interrupt Request Lines 734
  Base Addresses 738
 Understanding Communications Software 739
  Understanding Terminal Emulation 739
  Transferring Files 741
   Sending or Receiving a File 741
   Understanding File-Transfer Protocols 742
   Understanding XMODEM 745
   Understanding YMODEM 746
   Understanding ZMODEM 746
   Understanding KERMIT 748
   Transferring Files on CompuServe 748
 Setting Up Your Modem in Windows 95 748
  Selecting a Modem 749
  Configuring Your Modem 752
  Configuring Dialing Properties 757
   Dialing Locations 758
   How Calls Should Be Placed 759
   Using Calling Cards 760
  Checking Out Your Modem 764

32 Communicating with a Modem 767
 The Basis of Communications in Windows 95 768
 Setting Dialing Properties 768
 Using Phone Dialer 773
  Opening the Phone Dialer 773
  Dialing a Number 774
  Storing a Number on a Speed Dial Button 774

Editing Speed Dial Buttons 775
Using the Call Log 775
Using HyperTerminal 776
Starting the HyperTerminal Program 777
Making a Connection with a Remote Computer 777
Disconnecting and Saving a Session 779
Making a Connection with a Saved Session 780
Chatting 780
Saving or Printing the Text of a Session 780
Sending a File 781
Receiving a File 781
Using Terminal Emulation 782
Using Third-Party Communications Software 785
Understanding Online Services 785
Using Microsoft Exchange 787
Starting Microsoft Exchange 788
Reading Mail 789
Composing and Sending Mail 789

33 The Microsoft Network 791
Connecting to and Disconnecting from MSN 792
Becoming a Member of MSN 792
Connecting to MSN 795
Changing Your Password 797
Disconnecting from MSN 798
Exploring MSN Central 798
MSN Today 798
E-Mail 799
Favorite Places 799
Member Assistance 799
Categories 799
The Menu Bar 800
The Toolbar 800
Navigating the Network by Using My Computer 801
Navigating the Network by Using the Explorer 805
Getting General Information about Forums and Services 807
Getting There the Fastest Way 807
Adding to Favorite Places 808
Creating a Shortcut 808
Using a Go Word 809
Setting Up MSN 809
Exploring Kiosks 810

Contents **xxvii**

Exploring Bulletin Boards 811
    Reading Messages 811
    Replying to a Message 814
    Posting a New Message 814
    Downloading Files 814
    Setting Options for Downloading 815
Exploring Chat Rooms 815
    Setting Chat Options 817
    Saving a Chat 817
    Scheduled Chats with Famous People 818
Sending E-Mail 818
Finding Topics of Interest 818
Problems You Might Encounter 819
Checking Your Bill 819

34 Using Microsoft Exchange 821
Setting Up the Microsoft Exchange Postoffice 822
    Creating the Postoffice 823
    Sharing the Folder That Contains the Postoffice 824
Setting Up Profiles for Users 825
Specifying Internet Mail Properties 826
Specifying Microsoft Fax Properties 828
    The Message Page 828
    The Dialing Page 829
    The Modem Page 831
    The User Page 833
Specifying Microsoft Mail Properties for Local Use 834
    The Connection Page 834
    The Logon Page 834
    The Delivery Page 836
    The LAN Configuration Page 836
    The Log Page 837
Specifying Personal Address Book Properties 838
Specifying Personal Information Store Properties 838
Specifying Microsoft Network Online Service Properties 839
Configuring the Options of Microsoft Exchange 839
    The General Page 840
    The Read Page 841
    The Send Page 842
    The Spelling Page 844
    The Services Page 844
    The Delivery Page 844

The Addressing Page	846
Using Microsoft Exchange More Efficiently	847
Using a Personal Address Book	847
Selecting a Name from a PAB	848
Adding a Name to a PAB	848
Keeping the PAB Up-to-Date	850
Using the Personal Information Stores	850
Adding Personal Folders	851
Arranging and Finding Messages	852
Selecting the Columns of Information That Are Viewed	853
Sorting the Information	853
Finding Messages	854
Attaching Files, Messages, and Objects to Messages	855

35 Internet Communications 859

What Can You Do on the Internet?	859
E-Mail	860
Newsgroups and Mailing Lists	861
World Wide Web	862
Gopher	863
FTP Sites	864
Telnet	865
WAIS	865
Connecting to the Internet	866
Network Connection	866
SLIP/PPP Connection	866
Online Connection	868
Connecting to the Internet with Windows 95	868
Installing and Configuring TCP/IP	868
Understanding the Properties of TCP/IP	870
IP Addresses	870
DNS Server	871
Subnet Mask IP	871
Gateway IP	872
Configuring TCP/IP	872
Configuring DNS	872
Configuring the IP Address	874
Additional TCP/IP Settings for a Network	874
Configuring the Gateway	875
Configuring the WINS	875
Installing and Setting Up Dial-Up Networking	875
Installing Dial-Up Networking	876

Creating a Connection	876
Configuring Encrypted Passwords	877
Connecting to the Internet through PPP	878
Configuring and Using SLIP	880
Specifying a Terminal Window after Dialing	881
Specifying the Server Type	881
Connecting to the Internet through SLIP	881
What to Do Once You Get Connected	882
Using FTP	882
Common Commands	882
Disconnecting and Exiting FTP	884
Using a Web Browser	884
Using a Windows Gopher	886
Using Telnet	887
Using Archie	888
Using WAIS	889

36 Communicating with a Network 891

Understanding Network Components	892
Your Initial Network Configuration	894
The Purpose of Bindings	896
Changing Your Network Configuration	897
Adding Network Components	897
Adding Clients	898
Adding Adapters	899
Adding Protocols	900
Adding Services	901
Removing Network Components	902
Changing Bindings	902
File and Print Sharing	905
Your Primary Network Logon	906
Network Identification	907
Access Control	909
Configuring Your System for a Microsoft Network	911
Setting the Primary Network	911
Specifying Domain and Network Drive Information	912
Running Windows 95 on a Novell Network	914
Choosing the Right NetWare Client	914
The Microsoft NetWare Client	915
Novell's NetWare Client	916
Configuration Options for the Microsoft Client for NetWare	918

Understanding the PROTOCOL.INI File 919
    The [protman$] Section 921
    The [NETBEUI$] Section 921
    The [nwlink$] Section 922
    The [EPRO$] Section 922

37 Using Windows 95 on a Network 923
Sharing Information 924
Sharing Folders 924
    Naming a Shared Folder 926
    Setting Access Rights 926
    Determining Who Can Do What 927
    Changing What Is Shared 927
Accessing Other People's Data 928
    Mapping a Drive 928
    Disconnecting a Network Drive 931
Printing in a Networked Environment 932
    Adding Separator Pages 932
    Customizing Separator Pages for NetWare Printers 934
    Using Fonts 934
Managing the Network 936
    Managing a Peer-to-Peer Network 937
        Network Printers 937
        Centralized Files 938
        Workgroup Standards 939
    Managing a Client/Server Network 940
        Setting Up User Privileges 941
        Managing User Accounts 941
        Using Resources on a NetWare Server 942

38 Setting Up Remote Computing 943
Advanced Power Management (APM) 944
    Showing the Battery Meter 946
    Enabling Suspend Mode 949
Preparing to Connect a Laptop to a Desktop 952
    Installing Remote Networking 952
    Serial and Parallel Connections 956
    Installing Microsoft Briefcase 957
Deferring Communications on a Portable Computer 959
    Deferred Printing 960
    Deferred Electronic Mail 961

39 Seamless Remote Computing 967
Establishing the Remote Connection 968
Choosing the Right Protocols 970
    What's a Protocol? 970
    Remote Access Configurations 971
Installing a Protocol 972
Dial-Up Networking 974
    Creating the Connection 976
    Specifying a Server Type 977
    Establishing the Connection 980
    Transferring Your Deferred Communications 981
Direct Cable Connections 983
    Setting Up the Host Computer 984
    Setting Up the Guest Computer 988
    Using Direct Cable Connection 988
    Changing from Guest to Host 990
    Troubleshooting a Direct Cable Connection 991
Hot-Docking 991
Using Briefcase 992

40 Operating in Windows 95 DOS 1001
DOS Commands No Longer Available 1002
    Disk Commands 1002
    File Commands 1004
    Memory Management 1005
    Printer Management 1006
    Device Drivers 1006
    Miscellaneous Commands 1008
New Commands 1009
    Network Commands 1010
        NET CONFIG 1011
        NET DIAG 1012
        NET HELP 1012
        NET INIT 1013
        NET LOGOFF 1013
        NET LOGON 1013
        NET PASSWORD 1014
        NET PRINT 1015
        NET START 1016
        NET STOP 1017
        NET TIME 1017
        NET USE 1018

NET VER	1019
NET VIEW	1020
NETSTAT	1020
NBTSTAT	1021
TCP/IP Commands	1022
ARP	1023
FTP	1024
PING	1028
ROUTE	1029
TELNET	1030
TRACERT	1032
The Start Command	1033
Using the Command Line	1034
Using a DOS Window	1034
How DOS Windows Work Under Windows 95	1035
Controlling the Appearance of the DOS Window	1035
Jumping to the Command Line	1037
DOS Window Properties	1038
The Program Tab	1039
The Font Tab	1043
The Memory Tab	1044
The Screen Tab	1045
The Misc Tab	1046

41 Monitoring Your Windows 95 Vital Files ... 1051

Windows 95 Vital Files	1052
Boot Files	1052
Common MSDOS.SYS Elements	1054
Needing Your CONFIG.SYS and AUTOEXEC.BAT Files	1055
Setup Information in INF Files	1056
The Registry Files	1056
Using REGEDIT to Copy the Registry to a Text File	1057
Restoring the Registry	1060
Still Needed DOS and Windows 3.x Files	1061
Application INI File Considerations	1062

42 Dealing with Viruses and Security ... 1063

Windows 95 Virus Software	1064
Dealing with Viruses and Security	1065
Understanding the Computer Virus	1066
Understanding the Windows 95 Boot Sequence	1069

Boot-Sector Viruses	1071
Understanding Trojan Horses	1073
Understanding File Viruses	1074
Using Effective Antivirus Strategies	1075
Current Virus Technology	1075
Current Antivirus Technology	1076
Antivirus Scanning	1077
Monitoring Antivirus	1077
Inoculation or Integrity Method	1078
Rule-Based Antivirus Checking	1078
Controlling the Portals of Entry to Your Computer	1079
Watching Out for Dangerous Floppy Disks	1079
Protecting Your Network from Viruses	1080
Knowing the Risks of Downloaded Software	1086
Online Sources for Antivirus Information	1087
Designed for Windows 95—An AntiVirus Example	1088
Backing Up Your System	1091
43 System Agent	**1101**
Exploring System Agent's Files	1103
Understanding the System Agent File Functions	1104
The SAGE.XXX Files	1105
The SYSAGENT.XXX Files	1105
Working with System Agent's Defaults	1106
Working with Low Disk Space Notification	1106
Changing the Schedule	1107
Changing the Settings	1109
Changing the Low Disk Space Notification	1109
Low Disk Space Notification Output	1110
Working with ScanDisk for Windows	1112
ScanDisk in Standard Configuration	1112
ScanDisk in Thorough Configuration	1112
Advanced ScanDisk Options	1113
Working with Disk Defragmenter	1116
Settings and Thresholds	1117
Scheduling Options	1119
Interruptions and Restarts	1119
Output and Logging	1119
Working with System Agent Options	1120
Running a Scheduled Program Now	1120
Disabling a Scheduled Program	1120

	Removing a Scheduled Program 1121
	Suspending System Agent 1121
	Stopping System Agent 1122
	Scheduling a New Program 1122
	Backup Programs 1123
	Communications Programs 1123
	System Agent and Portable Computers 1123

44 DriveSpace 3 and Compression Agent 1125
Understanding Drive Compression Compromises 1126
Features of DriveSpace 3 1126
    DriveSpace 3 Performance Features 1127
    DriveSpace 3 Convenience Features 1129
Installing DriveSpace 3 1129
Configuring DriveSpace 3 1130
    Running DriveSpace 3 on an Uncompressed Drive 1131
    DriveSpace 3 Compression Information Screens 1133
    Running DriveSpace 3 on a Drive
        Compressed with DriveSpace 1135
Adjusting DriveSpace 3's Settings 1136
    Adjusting Free Space 1136
    Creating an Empty Compressed Drive 1138
    Choosing the Type of Compression 1140
Working with Compression Agent 1140
    Compression Agent Exceptions 1142
    Advanced Compression Agent Settings 1144
Running Compression Agent for the First Time 1145
Scheduling Compression Agent 1145
Understanding DriveSpace 3's Memory Requirements 1145

45 Desktop Additions 1147
Installing Desktop Additions 1148
Visual Enhancements 1149
    Full-Window Drag 1149
    Font Smoothing 1150
        How Font Smoothing Works 1152
    Enhanced MS-DOS Font 1154
    Animated Pointers 1154
    High Color Icons 1157
    Large Icons 1158
    Taskbar Auto Hide 1160
    Wallpaper Stretching 1161

Desktop Themes 1161
    Starting with Themes 1162
    Previewing Theme Elements 1164
    Running the Theme 1165
    Screen Saver Hot Spots 1165
3D Pinball 1166

46 Internet Explorer and Jumpstart Kit 1169

Using the Internet Setup Wizard 1170
    Connecting to the Internet Through Microsoft Network 1171
    Connecting to the Internet Through a Service Provider 1173
    Connecting to the Internet Through a Network 1177
Working with the Internet Explorer 1178
    Tips on Using the Internet Explorer 1179
    Setting Options 1181
    Favorites and Shortcuts 1185
Internet Explorer and Microsoft Network 1187
Internet Explorer and the Right Mouse Button 1189
Some Things to Remember While Surfing the Web 1190

A Adding and Removing Windows 95 Components 1193

Understanding the Windows 95 Components 1194
Adding and Removing Components 1195
Removing Windows 95 from Your Computer 1197
    Boot to DOS 1199
    Delete All Directories Associated with Windows 95 1199
    Remove System Files 1200
    Copy MS-DOS Files to DOS Directory 1202
    Transfer System Files 1203

B Installing the Killer Windows 95 CD-ROM 1205

Starting the Killer 95 CD-ROM Setup Program 1206
    Starting the Killer CD-ROM with AutoPlay 1207
    Starting the Killer CD-ROM Manually 1207
The Different Killer Program Categories 1208
Installing the Individual Killer Programs 1208
Quitting the Killer CD Setup Program 1211

Introduction

by Allen L. Wyatt

The Windows phenomenon continues, sparked this time by the release of Windows 95. This operating system (and it really is an operating system this time around) has gone through more development and more testing than any other operating system in the history of computers. You are the beneficiary of that Herculean effort—and this book can make all the difference between merely using Windows 95 and making it the most productive partner you've ever had on your computer.

Windows 95 is quite a bit different from the previous versions of Windows. In fact, an entirely new user interface breaks with tradition and provides new ease of use, less learning time, and greater productivity. As you work with Windows 95, don't let the ease with which you are able to perform tasks fool you—this is the most powerful operating system you can place on your desktop.

Who Needs This Book?

So do you need this book? Well, that depends. If you can answer *yes* to any of the following questions, then *Killer Windows 95* is definitely for you:

➤ Do you need to get a head-start on putting Windows 95 to work on your system?

➤ Do you want to learn more than just the "bare essentials" about Microsoft's newest operating system?

➤ Do you want a complete reference that will stay with you for months, if not years?

➤ Do you want to benefit from the combined expertise of a number of Windows 95 experts?

➤ Do you want the best Windows value between two covers?

➤ Are you tired of the marketing hype surrounding Windows 95, and you're ready to "get down to brass tacks"?

➤ Are you ready to get your hands on powerful Windows 95 software right away?

Killer Windows 95 has been developed over the past 18 months while Windows 95 was developed. It represents a phenomenal amount of work on the part of a lot of people—and you will be impressed with the results.

What Is in This Book?

Killer Windows 95 definitely provides more information about Windows 95 than you can get from any other single volume. If you doubt this statement, take a look at the extensive table of contents, as well as the thorough index. Every topic has been carefully researched, organized, documented, and conveyed in a plain and clear manner.

Part I—Setting Up and Interfacing with Windows 95

Part I, "Setting Up and Interfacing with Windows 95," introduces you to the new world of Windows 95. You learn about the new interface, what has been changed, what new tools are available, how to install Windows 95 on different configurations, and where Windows 95 is heading.

Chapter 1, "The Windows 95 Interface," teaches you how to start Windows 95 and how to use the new interface. You learn about the principles behind the design, how to use the taskbar, and how to get help when you need it.

Chapter 2, "Under-the-Hood Improvements," takes a peek beneath the surface of Windows 95. You learn what makes this operating system so robust. You learn how 32-bit performance can increase your productivity, as well as information about using networks. You also learn exactly what all the excitement is concerning Plug and Play.

Chapter 3, "New Windows 95 Tools," introduces you to the new tools provided with Windows 95. You get a guided tour of the Windows Explorer and the Quick View feature. You also learn how to create shortcuts and search for files on your system or over the network.

Chapter 4, "Installing Windows 95,"explains how to install Windows 95 on three different types of systems: a home computer, an office computer, and a network workstation.

Chapter 5, "Installing Windows 95 on a Laptop," examines the unique features provided by Windows 95 for portable computer users. You learn not only how to install, but also how PCMCIA cards work in Windows 95.

Chapter 6, "Troubleshooting Windows 95 Installation and Startup," discusses the common problems you may face either when installing Windows 95 or when you first power up your system. You get answers that will get you up and running with a minimum of inconvenience.

Part II—Hardware Issues

Part II, "Hardware Issues," takes an in-depth look at the many facets of hardware in your system. You learn what hardware you need for your Windows 95 system. You also examine memory, hard drive space, your video system, and peripherals such as mice and joysticks.

Chapter 7, "How Windows 95 Interacts with Your Hardware," looks at how Windows 95 views hardware. You learn about hardware properties, using the Device Manager, configuring your system with multiple hardware profiles, and how you can easily add new hardware to your system.

Chapter 8, "Examining the Hardware You Need for Windows 95," looks at the stated hardware requirements for Windows 95 and then tells you what you *really* need. Compatibility is addressed, as is the wisdom of looking for Plug-and-Play equipment.

Chapter 9, "Exploiting Memory, Space, and Resources," teaches you how Windows 95 views memory. Gone are the hodgepodge days of multiple types of memory. Instead, you learn about system memory and virtual memory in your system. You also learn how to configure memory use for your various needs.

Chapter 10, "Optimizing Your Disk Drives," unleashes the power of the most important component in your system. You learn about disk caches, RAM disks, compression software, and swap files. You also discover how to use the disk defragmenter and what to look for in a hard drive upgrade.

Chapter 11, "Video Cards, Drivers, and Monitors," teaches you what you need to know to make the most of your video system, including your video card and monitor (as well as the drivers that are used between them). You can greatly affect system performance by applying the information in this chapter.

Chapter 12, "Using Mice and Other Pointing Devices," discusses the various types of pointing devices you can use with Windows 95. You learn not only about mice, but also about other pointing devices such as joysticks, trackballs, and glidepoints.

Part III—Software

Part III, "Software," provides all the information you need to make your software really hum under Windows 95. You learn how Windows 95 interacts with software, how to "tune up" your system, how to manage the startup process, and how to install both Windows and DOS software on your system. You also learn how to fine-tune Windows 95 for your software after it's installed.

Chapter 13, "How Windows 95 Interacts with Software," gives a complete overview of how Windows 95 manages the software in your system. You learn about the Virtual Machines created by Windows, and what type of software you can run in those VMs. You also learn how to remove an application from your system.

Chapter 14, "Tailoring Windows 95 and the Registry," is an in-depth examination of how you can configure Windows 95 to your liking. Not only do you learn how to modify the appearance of your system, but also you learn the power and sensibility of the Registry, Windows' new consolidated configuration database.

Chapter 15, "Taking Control of Windows 95 Startup," discusses the startup process and how you can modify it to fit your needs. You learn how to control which programs run when you start Windows 95, as well as how you can modify the system menus according to your needs.

Chapter 16, "Installing Windows Applications," provides guidance on how to successfully install Windows software. You also learn how Windows 95 interacts with the different types of Windows software (16-bit and 32-bit) you can install.

Chapter 17, "Fine-Tuning Windows 95 for Your Windows Applications," examines what you do after you've installed your Windows software. You learn how to affect the software environment, how to create working folders for your software, and how to improve 16-bit program performance.

Chapter 18, "Installing DOS Applications," discusses the ins and outs of installing DOS-based software in a Windows-based environment.

You also get an in-depth glimpse at how Windows 95 automatically knows the configuration needs of over 400 DOS-based programs.

Chapter 19, "Fine-Tuning Windows 95 for Your DOS Applications," teaches you how to completely control the Virtual Machine that Windows 95 creates for your DOS program. You learn the fine points of fine-tuning program initialization, memory use, your screen display, and a host of other items.

Part IV—Output

Part IV, "Output," takes an in-depth look at getting information out of your system in the form of the printed page. You learn how Windows 95 manages the print process, how to control printing, how fonts are handled, the best way to print graphics, and how you can improve printing performance.

Chapter 20, "Managing Your Printers," provides the information you need to successfully set up printers with Windows 95. You learn what printer drivers are and how to install them. You also learn about configuring your printer and removing it, if necessary.

Chapter 21, "Printing from Windows 95," delves into the internals of the Windows 95 print system. You learn about the spooler and how it works with your printer drivers. You also learn how to use the spooler to your advantage, for both local and network printers.

Chapter 22, "Working with Fonts," examines the improved font management capabilities of Windows 95. You learn the basic differences between all types of fonts—bitmapped, TrueType, and Adobe. Discussions center around successfully installing fonts in your system, controlling how they're handled on a printer, and how to use fonts in your applications.

Chapter 23, "Handling Graphics," looks at how Windows 95 can be optimized for printing graphics. You learn the details you need to successfully print graphics on virtually any type of printer.

Chapter 24, "Getting the Most from Your Printer," examines how you can improve the performance of your printer. You find out what is necessary to both speed it up and troubleshoot problems you may encounter.

Part V—Multimedia

Part V, "Multimedia," jumps into the wild world of multimedia with both feet. You learn how to install multimedia components, how to use multimedia on your system, and how to optimize your system for multimedia. You also learn about full-motion video (new in Windows 95) and how to fine-tune your sound cards for peak performance.

Chapter 25, "Adding Multimedia Capability to Your Computer," looks at what you need to bring the world of multimedia to your desktop. You examine the different components of a multimedia system and discover what is recommended for use with Windows 95.

Chapter 26, "Using Multimedia on Your Computer," teaches you how to put multimedia to work right away. You learn how sounds can be used at both a system and application level. You also learn what MIDI is and how your system can be configured for MIDI.

Chapter 27, "Getting the Most out of Multimedia," covers what you can do to improve the performance of your multimedia system. You learn the tricks that can make the difference between a "run of the mill" system and one that is truly impressive.

Chapter 28, "Understanding Full-Motion Video," provides a full discussion of how you can use full-motion video on your system. The inclusion of Microsoft Video for Windows opens up exciting new possibilities in multimedia.

Chapter 29, "Fine-Tuning Your Windows 95 Sound Card," looks at the special needs and requirements of your sound system. You examine how to get the most out of your 8-bit, 16-bit, or 32-bit sound card.

Part VI—Communications

Part VI, "Communications," provides the information you need to "get connected." You learn how OLE allows applications to communicate with each other, as well as how you can connect your computer to other computers all over the world.

Chapter 30, "Using OLE to Communicate with Other Applications," discusses the expanding world of OLE (object linking and embedding). You learn the details that make it work, as well as how you can put it to work in your system.

Chapter 31, "Serial Communications Basics," introduces you to a sometimes difficult and mystifying area of computing. You learn, in plain English, how serial communications works. You also explore different types of communications software and how you can set up your modem in Windows 95.

Chapter 32, "Communicating with a Modem," provides all the information you need to use your modem to connect with other computers. You learn about dialing properties, the phone dialer, HyperTerminal, and various third-party software packages. You also learn about the world of online services such as CompuServe, Prodigy, and America Online.

Chapter 33, "The Microsoft Network," teaches you what you need to know to take advantage of Microsoft's newest commercial venture. You learn how to set up your Windows 95 system to take full advantage of the network, as well as what you can expect after you're connected.

Chapter 34, "Using Microsoft Exchange," explores the "communications command center" on your desktop. You learn how to use Microsoft Exchange to send and receive both electronic mail and faxes.

Chapter 35, "Internet Communications," looks at the fast-expanding world of the Internet. Windows 95 provides everything you need to get connected, and shows you how to do it. Coverage of dial-up Internet accounts, using both SLIP and PPP, provides you the understanding you need to make the most of your Internet experience.

Part VII—Networking and Remote Computing

Part VII, "Networking and Remote Computing," examines the specifics of networking your system with Windows 95. You learn how Windows 95 views networks, as well as how to put your network to use right away. You also learn what special features are provided for remote computing, and you learn what is needed to stay connected with your office when you're away.

Chapter 36, "Communicating with a Network," covers the specifics of installing a network on your system. You learn about the different Windows 95 network components and how they work together, as well as how you can configure your network for your needs. Both Microsoft and Novell networks are covered.

Chapter 37, "Using Windows 95 on a Network," teaches you how you can put your network to use. You learn how to share information over the network, how to print in a networked environment, and how you should manage your network installation.

Chapter 38, "Setting Up Remote Computing," discusses how you can configure your system for your needs while you're on the road. You learn how to set up both remote e-mail and the Briefcase utility.

Chapter 39, "Seamless Remote Computing," shows you how to put your system to work on the road. Here you learn how to use remote network access to get your e-mail while away from your desk, how to use Briefcase to synchronize your files, and how to manage deferred printing.

Part VIII—Optimizing Performance

Part VIII, "Optimizing Performance," provides the information you need to fully exploit the power of Windows 95. You learn how the DOS command line has changed, how to manage the important files in your Windows 95 system, and how to improve your system security.

Chapter 40, "Operating in Windows 95 DOS," takes an in-depth look at the changes in the DOS command line. Gone are the days when DOS was king; DOS now plays a more subservient role, and the command structure has changed accordingly. You learn what commands have been dropped and which ones have been added. You also learn how to change the properties of a DOS window.

Chapter 41, "Monitoring Your Windows 95 Vital Files," teaches you how to protect the files at the heart of Windows 95. You learn how to both prevent and recover from disasters that may befall your system.

Chapter 42, "Dealing with Viruses and Security," discusses how you can make your system more secure. You learn how to effectively create backups, how to provide security in remote networking, and how user profiles can increase system security.

Part IX—Microsoft Plus!

Part IX, "Microsoft Plus!," looks at this powerful add-on to Windows 95. You examine each part of the product and discover how it can enrich your use of Windows 95.

Chapter 43, "System Agent," discusses how you can use this tool to improve your productivity. The System Agent provides an easy way to run common system management tasks at regular intervals so you can make sure that your system is in top-notch condition.

Chapter 44, "DriveSpace 3 and Compression Agent," examines the more powerful features this element adds to the DriveSpace component of your system. You learn about the newest innovations in disk compression and how they can benefit your system.

Chapter 45, "Desktop Additions," looks at the new customization features provided by Microsoft Plus!. You learn about the Desktop Themes program, the Multimedia Pinball, full-window dragging, and font smoothing.

Chapter 46, "Internet Explorer and Jumpstart Kit," provides the information you need to enrich your Internet experience. Learn about the tools provided in Microsoft Plus! that open the Internet to your view—tools like the Web browser, mail reader, and a collection of powerful shortcuts.

Appendixes

The two appendixes provided with *Killer Windows 95* provide information on how you can add and remove Windows 95 components, and how you can install the Killer Windows 95 companion CD-ROM.

The Companion CD

Putting Windows 95 to work right away often involves having the proper type of software utilities to take advantage of the new operating system. The companion CD-ROM included at the back of this book provides just that—a wide selection of software that you can put to work right away to enrich your use of Windows 95.

The CD-ROM contains the following utilities, just to name a few:

- **WinZIP** brings the convenience of Windows to the use of ZIP files. TAR, gzip, Unix compress, LZH, ARJ, and ARC files are also supported. WinZip features an intuitive point-and-click interface for viewing, running, extracting, adding, deleting, and testing files in archives. Optional virus scanning support is included. Extract an archive to any directory through drag-and-drop without leaving the Explorer. Use the right mouse button to drag and drop a ZIP from an Explorer window to any directory, then choose "Extract to" from the context menu.

- **InfoSpy** is a Windows utility that interrogates and lists the various items within your Windows environment, including global heap, active windows, Windows tasks, loaded modules, open files, memory information, and DOS information. InfoSpy also acts as a real-time monitoring utility, allowing you to monitor Windows messages and serial communications.

➤ **PolyView** is a multithreaded 32-bit application that provides viewing and image manipulation support for JPEG, GIF, photo-CD, and Windows and OS/2 8- and 24-bit BMP files.

➤ **TextPad** is a fast and powerful text editor. Key TextPad features include huge file support (up to the limits of virtual memory), multiple simultaneous edits with up to two views per file, OLE 2 drag-and-drop editing for copying and moving text between documents, unlimited undo/redo capability, and much, much more.

➤ **Easy Icons** is a complete icon management system. Here are just a few of the features: extract or view all icons from virtually any file, save any icon as a separate ICO or BMP file, and create and maintain icon libraries with simple drag-and-drop operations.

Also included are many more useful and fun utilities that will help you get even more out of Windows 95.

All in all, *Killer Windows 95* provides the information you need to make the most of using Windows 95 on your system. With the information in this book at your disposal, you might not become an expert overnight, but you'll have all the information you need to eventually get there.

Conventions Used in This Book

The conventions used in this book have been established to help you learn quickly and easily how to use Windows 95. Instructions in this book emphasize use of the mouse to do tasks (to accomplish commands, to make choices in dialog boxes and sheets, and so forth).

Windows 95 lets you use the keyboard and the mouse—although the mouse is the preferred method—to select menu and dialog box or sheet items: you can press a letter (or number), or select an item by clicking on it with the mouse. The letter or number you press to select many items is underlined; for example, choose the P̲rint command from the F̲ile menu by typing **P**. If you use a mouse with Windows 95, you place the mouse pointer on the relevant menu or dialog box or sheet item and click with the left mouse button to make your selection.

Uppercase letters are used to distinguish file names, such as MYFILE.DOC. In most cases, the keys on the keyboard are represented as they appear on your keyboard (for example, J, Enter, Tab, Ctrl, Insert, and Backspace). For keystrokes separated by plus signs, such as Alt+F4, which closes the active application or window, hold down the first key (in this example, Alt) and press the second key (in this example, F4) to invoke the command. When a series of keys is separated by commas, press and release each key in sequence.

Text you're asked to type appears in **boldface**. On-screen messages from Windows 95 and its applications appear in a special font: `[Left Tab]`. Special words or phrases defined for the first time are introduced in *italic*.

Conventions Used in This Book   **13**

The Windows 95 Interface

by Allen L. Wyatt

At the root of any operating system or any application program lies the user interface—the conventions and methods used to communicate with the software. Windows 95 is no exception; it includes a user interface based on the graphical presentation of information. The user interface provided with Windows 95 is different from that used in previous versions of Windows. Some differences are cosmetic, while others are quite substantial.

In this chapter, you'll learn how you can best use the new Windows 95 interface. Much of the information in this chapter is essential to using Windows 95 effectively. If you're a "dive-in-the-deep-end-of-the-pool" type of person, you may be able to bypass much of this chapter. You'll still need to grapple with and learn the information, however. Even the most die-hard Windows aficionado will benefit by at least scanning through this chapter.

Booting Windows 95

When you first sit in front of a system on which Windows 95 has been installed, you may be tempted to believe there's no difference between the new operating system and your previous DOS- and Windows-based systems. This is both true and false. In reality, there is quite a bit of difference, but you'll also find many similarities between Windows 95 and older Windows systems.

Perhaps the first thing you'll notice is that when you turn on your computer, you no longer see the DOS prompt. This may be disconcerting to some users, while others may notice very little that's odd about this. For instance, if you're used to doing all your work in Windows, you probably configured your computer to automatically start Windows whenever you started your computer. Windows 95 takes this process one step further—you actually boot directly into Windows 95, bypassing DOS altogether. You'll learn more about this in Chapter 2, "Under-the-Hood Improvements."

So what happens when you first start your computer? The booting process has three distinct steps:

1. Initial testing.
2. Windows 95 startup screen.
3. Log-in process, if required.

Step one should look familiar; done on any computer, it involves initial system testing. Copyright notices are displayed, memory is tested and counted, and other components are tested.

After testing is complete, you quickly see the Windows 95 startup screen. While this screen is displayed, Windows 95 is going through a loading and testing process to make sure that everything is in order. The length of time required for this booting step depends on the configuration of your computer. The more resources (memory, disks, and so on) you have and the slower your computer, the longer this startup phase will take.

Finally, you're asked to log in to Windows 95. If you've previously used Windows for Workgroups, this step looks very familiar. Logging in is done so that Windows 95 can identify who is using the system and make sure that you're an authorized user. Generally, all you need to do is type your password. If you have trouble with this, you should talk to your network administrator or whoever installed Windows 95 on your system.

> **Note:** If Windows 95 has already been installed on your system and you aren't connected to a network, you aren't asked to log in to Windows 95.

New Desktop Icons

Once you log in, you see the Windows 95 desktop, as shown in figure 1.1. This desktop looks a bit different from the Windows desktop you're already familiar with. You may have noticed right away that the traditional Program Manager is missing. Instead, everything is done directly from the desktop, without the need for an explicit Program Manager. Rather than have to go through the Program Manager—and program groups—to get to the program you want to start, the program can sit right on the desktop for easy access.

The Windows 95 desktop has six primary parts:

- My Computer icon
- Network Neighborhood icon (optional)
- Recycle Bin icon
- A Microsoft Exchange (InBox) icon
- The Microsoft Network icon (optional)
- The taskbar

These elements are present in a full Windows 95 installation; your system might not have all of them. For instance, you might not see the Network Neighborhood icon if you aren't connected to a network. If your system has been used by someone else, it's also possible that additional elements are on the desktop. This is natural, since Windows 95 allows you to completely customize your working environment right on the desktop.

Fig. 1.1 The Windows 95 desktop appears different from previous Windows desktops.

The next several sections describe each standard element of your desktop.

My Computer

If you double-click on this icon, a window appears with icons that represent the structure of your local computer. Figure 1.2 shows what you typically see if you open this icon.

Fig. 1.2 The My Computer window displays information on your local computer.

Notice that this window contains icons for each disk drive on your system (including any CD-ROM drives), as well as the Control Panel, Printers folder, and a Dial-Up Networking folder. (The names of some items, such as the Control Panel, should be familiar if you've used older versions of Windows.) The exact contents of the window will vary, based on the configuration of your local computer. For instance, there is a very good chance you won't have the Dial-Up Networking icon shown on your system. (Dial-Up Networking is an optional feature of Windows 95 that allows you to connect your computer to remote computer networks, including the Internet.)

Primarily, you use the My Computer icon to browse through the contents of your system. For instance, if you double-click a disk drive, the contents of that drive are displayed in another window. You can continue to browse through different folders, or you can double-click a program or document to work with it.

Network Neighborhood

Just as the My Computer icon allows you to browse through your local system, the Network Neighborhood icon allows you to browse around a network. (Remember that this icon is available only if your system is connected to a computer network that Windows 95 can recognize.) Figure 1.3 shows what you might see if you double-click on this icon.

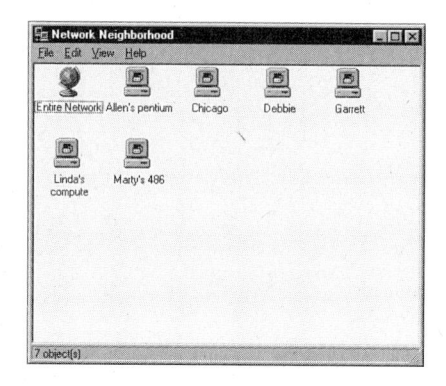

Fig. 1.3 The Network Neighborhood window displays information on networks that you're connected to.

The actual contents of this window vary, depending on the composition of your network. Again, you can browse through the network by choosing different connections or folders.

Recycle Bin

The Recycle Bin icon looks like a wastebasket with an ecological recycling symbol on the front of it. The Recycle Bin is a new addition in Windows 95 and represents a new way to manage the files you've deleted.

As you work with files, sometimes you'll want to delete them. For instance, you could be browsing through My Computer to examine files on a disk drive. If you highlight the icon for a document file and then press the Delete key, the icon is removed. The file hasn't been permanently deleted, however. It has been moved to the Recycle Bin, where it can still be recovered before it's completely deleted.

Look again at the Recycle Bin icon. If the wastebasket looks empty, no files are in the bin. If it looks as though it has paper in it, it contains files. Double-clicking the Recycle Bin displays the files it contains. Figure 1.4 shows an example of how the Recycle Bin window appears.

Fig. 1.4 The Recycle Bin allows you to manage the deletion and recovery of files.

After the Recycle Bin window appears, you can select files and then permanently delete them or recover them (move them back out of the Recycle Bin).

> **Tip:** If you're running low on disk space, you should periodically empty the Recycle Bin. This is done by choosing File, Empty Recycle Bin in the Recycle Bin window.

When you delete a file and it is moved to the Recycle Bin by Windows 95, it stays there until one of three events occur:

1. You recover the file by moving it out of the Recycle Bin and back into another folder on your system.

2. You permanently delete the file by selecting it and pressing the Delete key.

3. You have deleted enough newer files to cause Windows 95 to delete this file automatically.

Once any of these conditions is met, the file no longer is shown in the Recycle Bin. If these conditions are not met, then the file stays there, even from one Windows session to the next.

Microsoft Exchange

If your computer is attached to a network, it's possible that you'll see an icon for Microsoft Exchange. This icon could be named Microsoft Exchange on some systems, but more than likely it's called Inbox. Regardless of the name, this icon allows you to quickly access network-related and communications-related features such as e-mail and faxing. Microsoft Exchange is actually an optional part of Windows 95 and does not appear unless you specifically choose it when you install your system. In many environments where Windows 95 is used, such as a large office, the operating system comes already installed and configured on your machine. In such a case, there is a very good chance that Microsoft Exchange is already installed for you.

Assuming you have Microsoft Exchange installed on your system, when you double-click this icon, its window appears similar to what figure 1.5 shows.

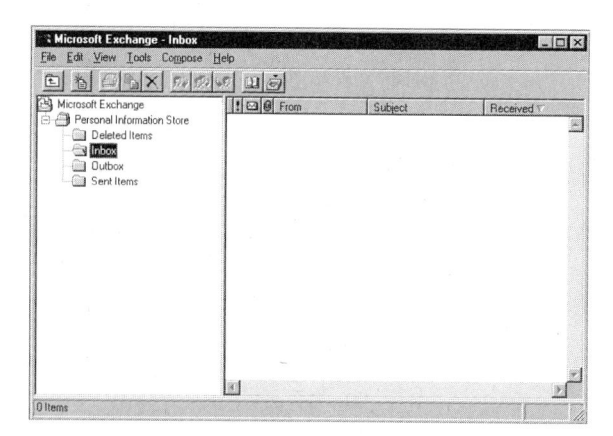

Fig. 1.5 The Microsoft Exchange is an integrated communication center for your computer.

The exact features provided in Microsoft Exchange depend on how your system is configured. It can be used for communication needs as diverse as e-mail on your local network, to faxes, to Internet e-mail, or

22 Chapter 1: The Windows 95 Interface

to CompuServe. Since the uses of Microsoft Exchange are so diverse, you'll find information about this area in many different chapters of this book.

New Windows Design

By now you've probably already noticed that the actual windows displayed in Windows 95 are different from their predecessors in older versions of Windows. Most of these changes are cosmetic in nature, which can lead to a momentary sense of disorientation as you first use Windows 95. This quickly passes, however, and you're shortly faced with more substantial changes.

Most of the substantive changes are visible in the title bar of any window. Gone are the old-version window-control buttons. In their place are new window-control buttons at the right side of the title bar (see fig. 1.6).

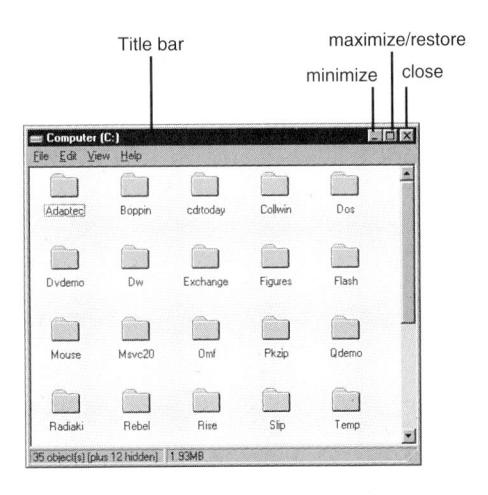

Fig. 1.6 The windows used in Windows 95 appear a bit different from those used in previous versions.

Notice that three window-control buttons are visible on all windows in Windows 95, even for programs you previously used in Windows and DOS. One button has an image that looks like a bar, another has a window image, and the third contains an ×. The button that contains a bar serves the same purpose as the minimize button in older versions of Windows. Rather than minimize the window to an icon, however, it minimizes it to a spot on the taskbar. (The taskbar is discussed fully in the next section.)

The window button serves the same purpose as the maximize and restore buttons in older versions of Windows. If the window doesn't currently occupy the entire screen, clicking this button maximizes it so that it's as large as possible. If the window has already been maximized, clicking the window button restores the window to an open but less-than-full-screen size.

Finally, the button that contains an × is used to close the window. This has the same effect as double-clicking the control menu icon in earlier versions of Windows. If a program was running in the window, the program is ended. If the window contained a data file, the file is closed.

While the new window-control buttons may appear different at first, they do offer greater and more intuitive functionality than what was available in older versions of Windows. You should be able to get used to them within a day of starting to use Windows 95.

> **Tip:** As you're getting used to the new window-control buttons, take a moment to look at them before you click on them. If you go by position alone, you'll easily confuse them with the button that occupied that position in older versions of Windows.

The Taskbar

While the concept behind icons, folders, and other desktop objects is (by this point) intuitive to anyone who has previously used Windows, Windows 95 includes a new desktop feature that's an entirely new departure from previous Windows versions—the taskbar. Depending on how your system is configured, the taskbar can be at the left, right, or bottom of your desktop. (In most systems it is at the bottom.) You can recognize the taskbar because it has the Start button at the left side, as shown in figure 1.7.

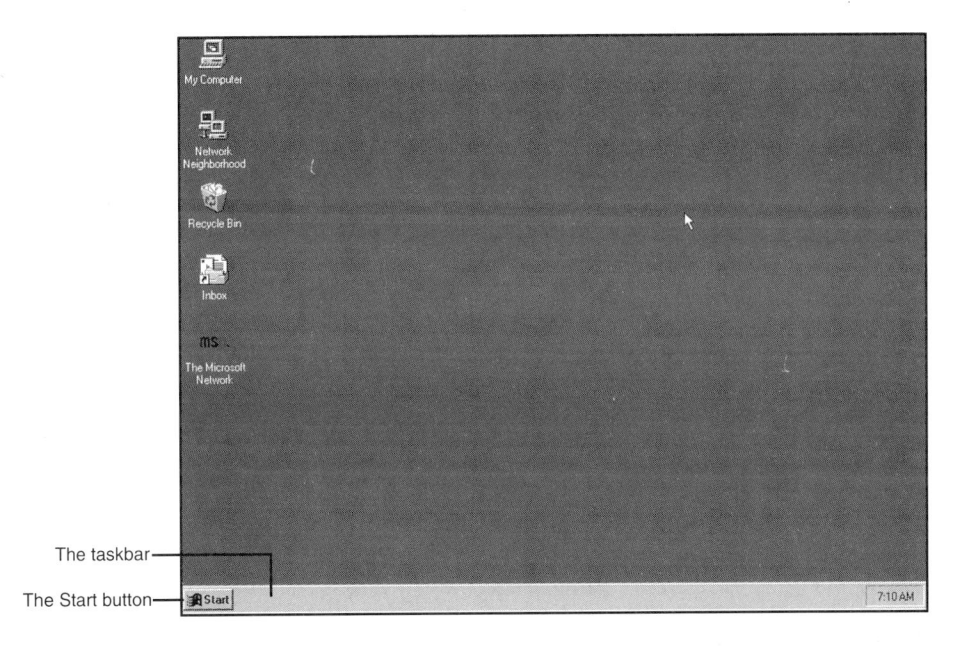

Fig. 1.7 The newest addition to the Windows 95 desktop is the taskbar.

The primary purpose of the taskbar is to quickly and easily allow you to switch between applications on your system. Think of the taskbar as a "command center" for Windows 95. It's analogous to the Task List displayed in older versions of Windows when you pressed Ctrl+Esc. The only difference is that the taskbar can be available all the time. If you prefer not to use the taskbar, you can also turn it off or control how it appears on your screen. (How you do this is covered later in this book.)

The Start Button

At the left side of the taskbar is the Start button. Clicking this button provides a shortcut to access quickly and easily any part of your Windows 95 system. If you click the Start button, you see a series of choices that you can make. These choices are presented in a menu, as shown in figure 1.8.

Fig. 1.8 A menu appears when you click the Start button.

Notice that choices can appear on a menu in three ways:

- *Triangles.* Highlighting a menu choice that has a triangle to the right of it displays another menu.

- *Ellipsis.* Selecting a menu choice that's followed by three dots (an ellipsis) displays a dialog box.

- *Regular.* Selecting a menu choice that has no triangles or ellipses opens a folder, starts the indicated program, or loads the document.

To use a menu, all you need to do is use the mouse pointer to highlight a menu choice. As you position the pointer over a menu choice, the choice is automatically highlighted in around half a second. If another menu is associated with the choice (if there's a triangle to the right of the choice), the menu is displayed automatically—you don't even need to click on the choice. For instance, if you use the mouse pointer to highlight the Programs option, you see another menu, as shown in figure 1.9.

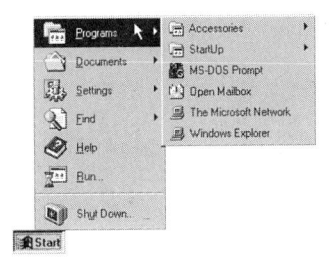

Fig. 1.9 Highlighting the Programs option displays the Programs menu.

To select any other menu choice, all you need to do is highlight it and click the mouse button. The next several sections describe the purpose of each menu option on the Start button menu.

The Programs Menu

If you highlight the Programs option from the Start button menu, you see the Programs menu (refer to fig. 1.9). The Programs menu displays the contents of the Programs folder. Thus, the Programs menu contains an Accessories folder, a Startup folder, the MS-DOS prompt, the Open Mailbox program, the Microsoft Network program, and the Windows Explorer.

Accessories is a menu choice that has another triangle to the right of it. If you highlight it, you see many different accessory programs you can use right away (see fig. 1.10).

The Accessories menu is merely the contents of the Accessories folder, presented in menu format. Many of these accessories should look familiar to you if you've used older versions of Windows.

The StartUp option displays programs that are started whenever Windows 95 is started. Again, this menu lists the contents of a folder (the StartUp folder). If you change the contents of the folder, you automatically change what's displayed in the menu.

The Taskbar **27**

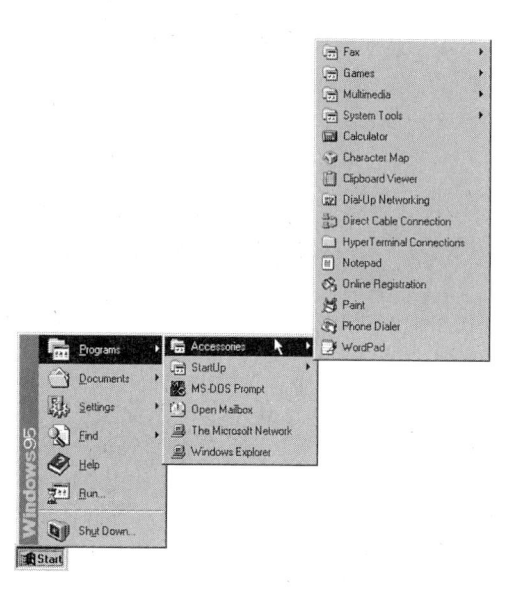

Fig. 1.10 Highlighting the Accessories option displays the Accessories menu.

More information about the other other Programs menu items is discussed later. The Windows Explorer is explained in Chapter 3, "New Windows 95 Tools," and the MS-DOS prompt (probably familiar to anyone who has used an older version of Windows) is covered in Chapter 40, "Operating in Windows 95 DOS."

The Documents Menu

Documents are nothing but data files that are associated with a program. This means that documents are not just things such as memos, reports, or book chapters, but also can be files containing your appointments, a database, or a spreadsheet. Windows 95 keeps track of what program created which document, and then makes those documents accessible through the Documents menu. Figure 1.11 shows an example of how the Documents menu could look.

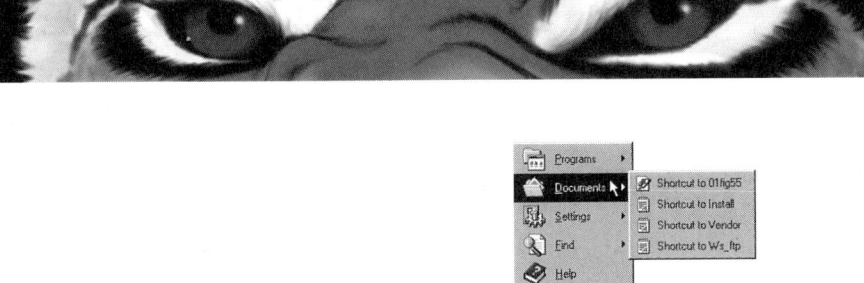

Fig. 1.11 The Documents menu allows quick access to the documents you used most recently.

Exactly how the documents window appears depends on the type and number of documents you've created in your system. To use a document, all you need to do is select it from the menu. Windows 95 starts the program associated with the document and displays it.

The Settings Menu

When you highlight the Settings option on the Start menu, you see three other options (see fig. 1.12). Each option allows you to change settings used to control Windows 95. The Control Panel option displays the Control Panel, a concept that should be familiar to anyone who has used an older version of Windows.

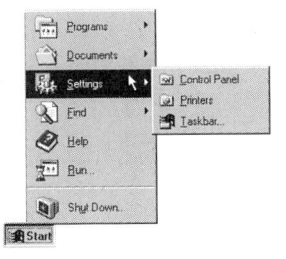

Fig. 1.12 The Settings menu is used to control the appearance of Windows 95.

The Printers option on the Settings menu displays a folder that indicates all the printer drivers you've installed for use with Windows 95

The Taskbar **29**

(see fig. 1.13). This folder also contains an option that allows you to add new printer drivers, as desired. Printer drivers are used by Windows 95 to control your printer. You learn how to add printer drivers in Chapter 20, "Managing Your Printers."

Click here to add a printer driver

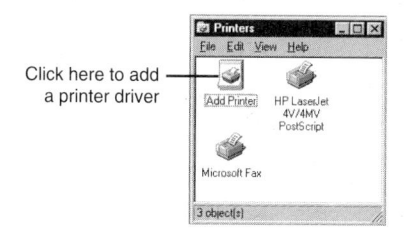

Fig. 1.13 The Printers folder contains icons for the printer drivers you've installed.

The final option on the Settings menu is Taskbar. If you choose this option, you can modify some of the aspects (properties) of the taskbar. Figure 1.14 shows the dialog box displayed when you choose this option.

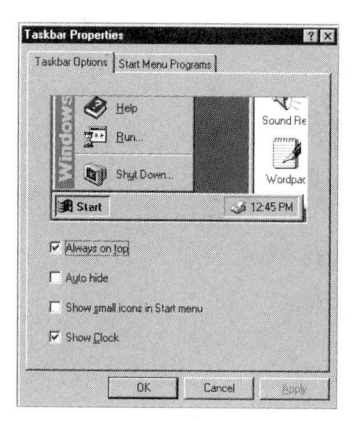

Fig. 1.14 Windows 95 allows you to change the properties of the taskbar.

The Start Menu Programs tab allows you to change the menu options used on the actual Start and Programs menus. The Taskbar Options tab is used to modify what's shown on the taskbar.

Other Start Button Capabilities

The Start menu presents you with several other options as well. The Find option is used to find files, folders, or resources on your computer. (This option is explained in more detail in Chapter 3, "New Windows 95 Tools.") The Help option is covered later in this chapter, in the section titled "The Help System."

If you choose the Run option from the Start menu, you can run a program directly. Users of previous Windows versions will recognize this option as the same as choosing File, Run from Program Manager.

The Shut Down option allows you to end your session with Windows 95. If you choose it, you're given four options (see fig. 1.15). You should choose the option that best describes the type of shutdown you want to perform, and then choose Yes.

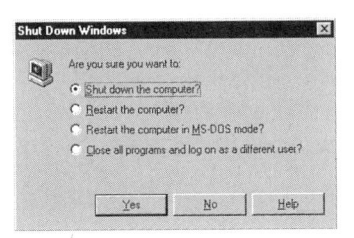

Fig. 1.15 You can select four options when shutting down the computer.

Tip: If you choose Shut Down by mistake, you can stop the shutdown process by choosing No from the Shut Down Windows dialog box.

Using the Sh_ut Down option is the best way to end your computer session. By choosing this option, in effect you give Windows 95 a warning that you're done using it. This allows files to be closed and devices to be shut down in an orderly manner. If you simply turn your machine off, you could loose data that might be important. Sh_ut Down precludes such an event from happening.

Switching to Other Tasks

To the right of the Start button you may see other buttons, each of which represent active tasks you can use. For instance, if you choose a program or option from the Start menu, you see that program or option appear on the taskbar. Figure 1.16 shows an example.

Fig. 1.16 The options on the taskbar represent programs now running.

You can switch to different programs by clicking the taskbar button for that program. For instance, if you choose the Programs button, the Programs folder is displayed. To later minimize a window, use the window-control buttons in the upper-right corner of the window. You've already learned that if you click the button with the bar-shaped image, the window is minimized to the taskbar. Once a window is minimized, the task represented by the window is still running, but it isn't actively displayed.

As you add more and more tasks to your Windows 95 session, these tasks are added to the taskbar. Every time you start a program or open a resource, the taskbar appears. When you close a program or resource, the corresponding task button is removed from the taskbar. If you open more tasks than can be fit across the taskbar, the buttons for all the tasks are made smaller so they can all fit.

The number of task buttons that will fit across your screen depends on the resolution of your screen. For instance, at 640 × 480 resolution, you can fit 19 task buttons, but you can fit 25 at 800×600 resolution. When the maximum number of buttons is passed, Windows still creates a task button for each new task, but these new buttons are not immediately visible. Instead, scroll controls appear at the right side of the task bar, and you can use them to display additional lines of the task bar. If you want to display all the task bar at once, you can increase the size of the task bar by using the mouse to drag the top border of the task bar so it covers a larger area of the screen. For instance, figure 1.17 shows an example of a two-line task bar on the screen.

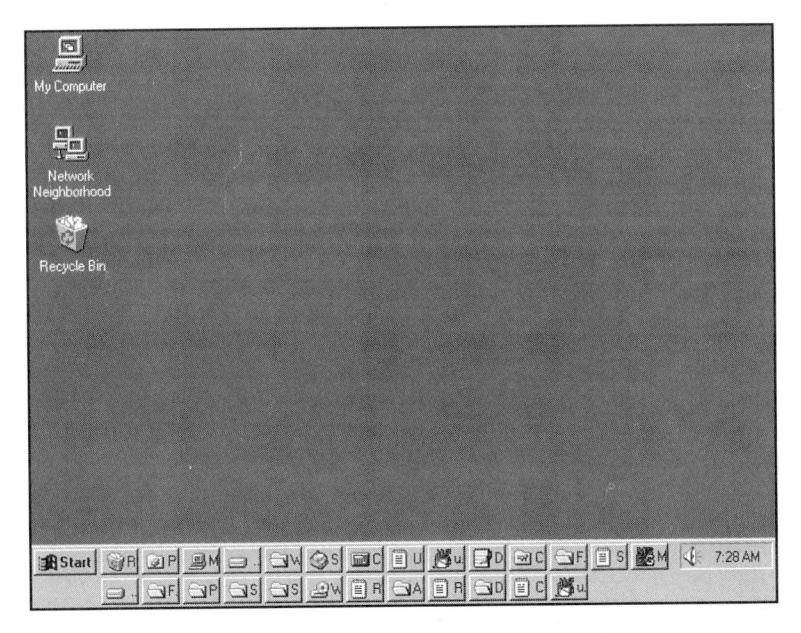

Fig. 1.17 The task bar can use multiple lines on the screen.

Getting Help

Getting help in Windows 95 is easier than in previous versions of Windows. Helpful information is continually presented while you're using Windows 95, and you can quickly and easily get help on a variety of topics. The help available from Windows 95 is presented by using the following features:

- Tips
- The Help system
- Wizards

Tips

If you move the mouse pointer over an object in Windows 95, you may see a tip about that object appear just below the mouse pointer. This is true whether the object is part of the operating system itself (for instance, a button on the taskbar) or part of a program (see fig. 1.18). This helpful information is designed to jog your memory about what a particular object is for.

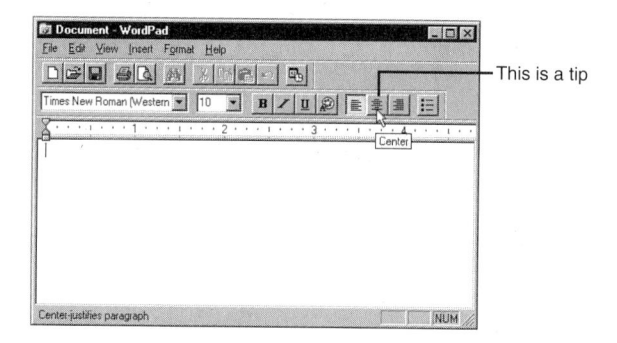

Fig. 1.18 Helpful tips are common in Windows 95.

Tips, as a form of help, are becoming more pervasive in the Windows 95 environment. They're available in many different programs and different parts of Windows 95 itself.

The Help System

Windows 95 features a new and improved Help system that uses an entirely new user interface. The easiest way to access the Help system is to choose Help from the Start menu; you can also start the Help system by pressing F1 at any point while you're using Windows 95. Either way, you then see the dialog box shown in figure 1.19.

Fig. 1.19 The Windows 95 Help system allows you to quickly gain assistance on a variety of topics.

Notice that the Help Topics dialog box contains three tabs: Contents, Index, and Find. Each of these represent different ways you can find information in the Help system.

The Contents Tab

The Contents tab shows you the major help topics available in the Help system. Three types of icons can be used in the Contents list:

- *Closed Book*. Double-click the book to see more detail on the topic. You can also click the topic and select the Open button.

- *Open Book*. Double-click the open book to show less detail on the topic. You can also click the topic and choose the Close button.

- *Document*. Double-click the document to display the actual help information. You can also select the topic and click the Display button.

The Index Tab

While you can select a general help topic from the Contents screen, it's often more productive to jump directly to the topic you want to view. This is done by selecting the Index tab. When you do, the Help Topics dialog box changes to look like figure 1.20.

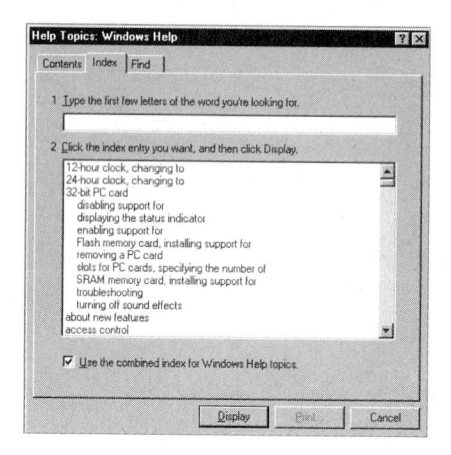

Fig. 1.20 With the Index tab selected, you can use the Help Topics dialog box to search for topics on a particular subject.

With the Index tab selected, the Help Topics dialog box is divided into two sections. In the top section, you can type the name of the subject you want to view. In the bottom section is a list of Help system topics. You can scroll through the list of topics, or you can start typing the name of the topic you want to view. As you type, Windows 95 displays the topics that match what you've typed. When you see a desired topic displayed, highlight it and click the Display button.

The Find Tab

The Contents and Index tabs allow you to quickly find your way through the major headings in the Help system. There are times, however, when the headings just won't do. For instance, you may want to look at documents that contain all occurrences of a particular word or phrase—and that word or phrase isn't included in a major topic heading. The Find tab provides this detailed search capability. When you click this tab, what you see depends on whether you've used the Find tab before.

If you haven't used the Find tab before, Windows 95 needs to make a detailed index of the words in all the topics in the Help system. This can take a while, as indicated in figure 1.21.

Fig. 1.21 The first time you use the Find tab, Windows 95 needs to create a detailed index you can use.

In most instances, you'll want to use the default choice (Minimize database size). Click on the Next button, and then click on Finish. The Help system files are examined and the necessary index is compiled. Shortly, the Help window changes to a form you can use to actually locate words (see fig. 1.22).

Fig. 1.22 With the Find tab selected you can search by any word in the Help system documents.

The dialog box is divided into three sections. In the top section, you can type the word or words you want to locate. In reality, all you need

Getting Help **37**

to do is type the first couple of letters of the words. You can narrow this search down in the second part of the window by selecting the exact matching words. Finally, the third part of the window (at the bottom) displays a list of Help system topics that contain the selected words. When you see a desired topic displayed, highlight it and click the Display button.

Viewing Help Documents

Regardless of how you locate the topic you want displayed (using the Contents, Index, or Find tabs), when you finally locate the topic on which you want help, Windows 95 displays a document containing the help information. These documents are displayed in a Help window (see fig. 1.23).

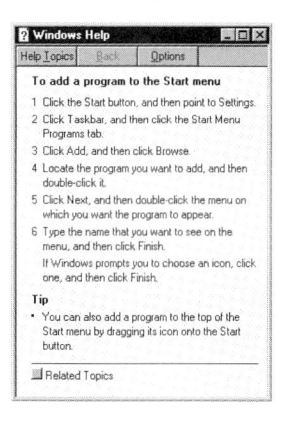

Fig. 1.23 Informational documents are displayed in the Help window.

This window is much simpler in nature than the Help windows used in earlier versions of Windows. It contains only three choices on the button bar: Help Topics, Back, and Options. The first button displays the same Help system dialog box you used to access this topic (the Contents tab, the Index tab, or the Find tab). The second button (when available) allows you to step back through previous help screens you've viewed. The final button is used to change how the help screen is displayed or to print the information in the Help window.

Chapter 1: The Windows 95 Interface

Wizards

A *wizard* is the name used to identify a step-by-step procedure to accomplish a task. Wizards have been used for some time in Windows programs, such as Excel. They lead a user through what might otherwise be a complex set of steps.

Windows 95 provides several wizards for your use. For instance, the process of creating a Find tab index in the Help system (described in the previous section) uses a wizard. You can see another example of a wizard if you open the Control Panel by selecting it from the Settings menu (which is available from the Start menu). The Control Panel should appear as shown in figure 1.24.

Fig. 1.24 The Control Panel contains many familiar icons.

Notice the icon titled Add New Hardware. You can't necessarily tell it by looking at the icon, but when you double-click it, a wizard is started. Go ahead and start it now. You then see the window for the Add New Hardware Wizard (see fig. 1.25).

Wizards always have a series of buttons that control the steps you perform. These buttons, located at the bottom of the window, are fairly standard, regardless of the wizard. They include the following:

➤ *Hint*. Displays a hint about what can be done at the current time within the wizard.

➤ *Cancel*. Ends the task without making any changes.

Getting Help **39**

➤ *B*ack. Backtracks to the previous step of the task.

➤ *Next.* Proceeds to the next step of the task.

➤ *Finish.* Completes the task by using the information provided so far, along with default information for the steps not yet completed.

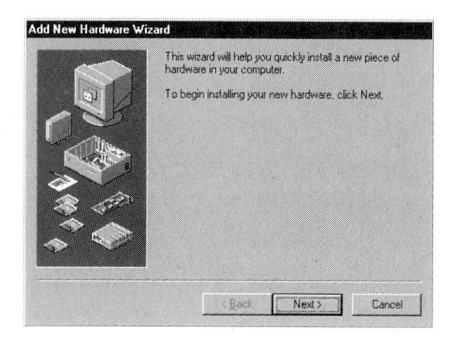

Fig. 1.25 The aim of the Add New Hardware Wizard is to help you configure Windows 95 for new hardware.

To use a wizard effectively, all you need to do is answer the question posed in the present screen, or make a selection when prompted and then click Next. If you make a mistake but don't realize it until you've clicked Next, you can click *B*ack to return to the previous step. The exact steps presented in a wizard depend on the wizard's purpose. Working through concise steps in this manner, however, allows you to complete tasks that otherwise have the potential of being difficult to perform.

Context Menus

A *context menu*, sometimes called a *pop-up menu*, is used to display a series of options applicable to a particular object. You display a context menu by pointing to an object (such as an icon, the desktop, a menu item, a title bar, or a window) and then clicking with the right mouse button. For instance, figure 1.26 shows the context menu displayed when you click the right mouse button while pointing to a disk drive.

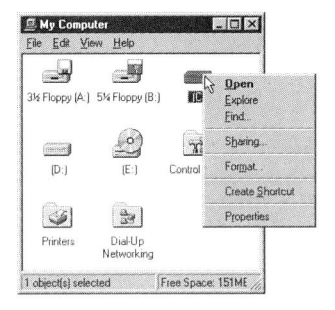

Fig. 1.26 Context menus display options applicable to objects on the desktop.

Once a context menu is displayed, it behaves like any other menu. You can select items and accomplish tasks by selecting options from the menu.

Context Menus **41**

Under-the-Hood Improvements

by Allen L. Wyatt

In Chapter 1, you learned about the new Windows 95 interface. However, Windows 95 is more than just a pretty face. There are many new improvements to the operating system that you may never see because they function completely behind the scenes or, "under the hood," so to speak. You reap the benefits of the improvements through a more robust and responsive operating system.

In this chapter, you learn about these improvements in Windows 95 and also learn about the following:

➤ How multitasking has been improved in Windows 95

➤ How long file names are implemented in the existing file structure

- What benefits are introduced by the new 32-bit architecture
- How improved resource management leads to a more stable environment
- What networking features have been improved
- How the Plug-and-Play specification is supported

A Full-Blown Operating System

Windows 95 is a full-blown operating system, in its own right. Previous versions of Windows have sometimes been referred to as an operating system, but this definition has been a very loose application of the term. This is because previous versions of Windows functioned on top of the DOS platform. Windows 95, however, replaces DOS entirely. Instead, many DOS functions now operate in an environment controlled by Windows. Thus, Windows and DOS have traded places; Windows 95 now provides the base platform on which other services are built.

You already know that Windows takes full advantage of your computer hardware. One of the advantages used fully is called *protected mode operation*. Protected mode is an operational mode that has been available on Intel CPUs since the 286, but has not been used by DOS. In protected mode, a program can address large amounts of memory quickly and easily, and provide protection for different programs running in your system. This protection means that if one program in your system begins acting erratically, that behavior has less effect on the other programs in your system.

Many of the components of Windows have been completely rewritten to take advantage of operating in protected mode. Later in this chapter you will learn what this means in terms of actual use of Windows.

Because Windows now is the controlling force in your computer system, Windows 95 can offer many improvements not available in previous versions. These improvements include preemptive multitasking, better reboot support, and long file names. Some of these features you may have heard of; others may be new to you. Each of these features is explained fully in the following sections.

Preemptive Multitasking

Multitasking is the ability to apparently perform more than one task at a time. This ability has been a feature of Windows for many years, but it has been a feature lacking in many areas. You need to understand these shortcomings to appreciate the improvements in Windows 95.

In previous versions of Windows, users implemented multitasking through a method called *cooperative multitasking*. This method worked fine as long as all the applications behaved well. When an application was functioning under Windows 3.1, for example, it periodically needed to relinquish control of the system so that other programs could run; this voluntary relinquishment is the cooperative part of multitasking. As long as a program gave up control periodically, other programs could use their fair share of time, and everyone was happy.

The problem, however, was that not all programs would give up their fair share of control. If you've used Windows for a while, you're probably familiar with the situation where a program is busy, the mouse cursor changes to an hourglass, and you're stuck waiting for the program to finish before you can do something else. This feature is the downside of cooperative multitasking.

Multitasking in Windows 95 is different and much improved. It uses a method referred to as *preemptive multitasking*. This method means that the operating system itself exercises complete control over what program gets what attention. No longer can a program hog resources, giving them up when it voluntarily decides to. Instead, Windows 95 decides which program gets attention and when. The term *preemptive* means that the operating system can preempt the executing program in favor of another program that may need more attention. This preemption occurs based on internal algorithms that determine when a certain program has had control long enough, although other programs can request control of the CPU earlier by generating system interrupts.

What is the result of this preemptive feature? Basically, you can reliably run historically intensive operations simultaneously. For instance, you can format a floppy disk under Windows 95 at the same time you're downloading a file from the Internet and composing a letter. If you tried that under Windows 3.1, you would never get to second base; you would be stuck waiting for the floppy disk to finish formatting before you could do anything else.

Better Reboot Support

Rebooting your computer has always been an action of last resort. To programmers, it has been a frightening consideration because users could decide to reboot at any time. Rebooting means that critical data might not be saved before the computer wipes the slate clean. (When you reboot, the contents of your computer's memory is erased, thereby wiping out any data contained therein.)

Windows 95 solves this problem completely. Now when you attempt to manually reboot your system (by pressing Ctrl+Alt+Del), Windows grabs control and displays a Close Program dialog box that asks you what you want to do. For instance, you might only want to end the current program, not the three or four programs running in the background. This is a big change from earlier versions of Windows, and a big advantage to using Windows 95.

Stepping in and moderating the reboot process allows Windows to make sure that rebooting is not done at an inopportune time, as far as the operating system is concerned. This moderating capability means there is less chance of corrupting your Windows files by rebooting. However, you can still mess up files maintained by applications running under Windows. For instance, if you choose to terminate a program by pressing Ctrl+Alt+Del, you're asked to confirm your action. If you cancel the reboot, no harm is done. If you end an application, it is terminated immediately—Windows 95 assumes you know the consequences of your actions. If you reboot the entire system, then any unsaved data in all your running programs could be lost. Again, Windows assumes that you have fully thought through the consequences and want to reboot anyway.

The bottom line is that even though it is possible to reboot your system under Windows 95, the way in which rebooting is handled by the operating system is much more stable than in previous versions of Windows. This stability means you have less chance of inadvertently losing data (you have to *really* want to lose it now) and have one less thing to worry about.

Long File Names

Windows 95 supports long file names. Many people tout this achievement as the single biggest improvement in the operating system. (In fact, as you are learning, it is only one of several major improvements.) It is true that Windows 95 does away with the need to limit files to the "eight dot three" convention of naming files. Now you can provide descriptive names that really mean something. File names can be up to 255 characters long, yet you can still refer to the same file by using a shortened alias that passes as a traditional file name.

The caveat in long file names is that they are based on the historically significant FAT file structure. FAT is an acronym for *file allocation table,* and refers to the file structure used in the DOS operating system. This vestige of DOS is a necessary admission that most people are migrating to the Windows 95 environment from a DOS environment, and those people are happiest when the files they have accumulated over the past 15 years are still accessible.

So how does Windows 95 do it? How does it allow you to create long file names by using the FAT file structure, which is synonymous with short, cryptic file names? The answer is simple, really—it cheats. It exploits quirks in the FAT structure definition to achieve the benefits.

To fully understand how long file names are implemented in Windows 95, you need to understand more about the file structure used. Fair warning—this means you need to understand what may appear to be technical information, but the benefit is that you can wow your friends and always have something to discuss at cocktail parties. The following sections address the technical aspects of long file names; when you understand this information you will understand exactly how long file names work.

Traditional FAT Directory Entries

At the heart of the FAT file structure is what is referred to as a *directory entry*. Traditionally, directory entries maintain the following information about a file:

➤ File name and extension

➤ Type of file

➤ Time of last update

➤ Date of last update

➤ Location on disk

➤ Size of file

In the FAT file structure, this information is contained in a 32-byte record. Table 2.1 shows the structure of this record, indicating how the directory information is stored.

Table 2.1 Layout of Traditional Directory Entries in the FAT File System

Byte Offset	Length in Bytes	Purpose
0	8	File name
8	3	File extension
11	1	File attribute
12	10	Unused
22	2	Time of last update
24	2	Date of last update
26	2	Beginning disk cluster
28	4	Bytes in file

Chapter 2: Under-the-Hood Improvements

Everything in the directory entry is fairly straightforward, although there are a few nuances to understanding how the directory entry is actually interpreted. For instance, the first character of the file-name entry has special significance. Normally, the file name is composed of ASCII character values that represent the file name. However, if the ASCII value of the first character is 0, then the directory entry has never been used before. If the first character has an ASCII value of 229 (E5 in hexadecimal notation), then the directory entry represents a file that has been deleted. Finally, if the directory entry begins with the value 46 (2E in hexadecimal), the entry represents a subdirectory. Any other value is interpreted as part of a valid file name.

The file attribute byte at offset 11 may need some explaining, as well. The eight bits that make up this byte have special meaning, and indicate the type of file represented by this directory entry, or possibly the file's status. Table 2.2 shows the meaning of the bits in this attribute byte.

Table 2.2 Meanings for File Attribute Bytes in a Directory Entry

Bit Position	Meaning If Set
0	Read-only file
1	Hidden file
2	System file
3	File name is really a volume label
4	File is really a subdirectory
5	File has been updated since the last backup
6	Unused
7	Unused

Many of the bits in the attribute byte can be combined for a cumulative effect. For instance, a file can be set as read-only and hidden, in which case both bits 0 and 1 would be set.

Windows 95 Directory Entries

To implement long file names, Windows 95 takes advantage of previously unused combinations of information in the directory entry, as well as allows directory entries to be chained together. This chaining of directory entries implies several things. First, there is an initial directory entry which signals Windows that there are additional entries. Second, the initial directory entry is somehow different from subsequent directory entries for the same file.

To understand how this all works, take a look at table 2.3. This table shows the layout for the initial directory entry for a file.

Table 2.3 Layout of an Initial Directory Entry in Windows 95

Byte Offset	Length in Bytes	Purpose
0	8	File name
8	3	File extension
11	1	File attribute
12	6	Unused
18	2	Last access date
20	2	Exclusive access handle
22	2	Creation time
24	2	Creation date
26	2	Beginning disk cluster
28	4	Bytes in file

Notice that the directory entry layout for Windows 95 is essentially the same as the traditional layout, except for three differences. First, four bytes beginning at offset 18 are now used in what was previously unused and reserved space. Now two additional fields are stored in this area. The first is an indication of the date when the file was last accessed, and the other is a handle to be used when the file is being exclusively accessed by a process. Second, the purpose of the time and date fields at offsets 22 and 24 has changed. Third, now the time and fields are used to indicate the time and date the file was created, not the time and date of last access.

So how does Windows 95 indicate that a file name occupies additional directory entries? This is done through use of the attribute byte. If you refer to table 2.2, you'll recall the traditional meanings of the bits in the attribute byte. You also learned that it's possible for the bits to be treated cumulatively—for instance, to note a file that is both read-only and hidden.

Some attribute combinations are illogical, however, and therefore not allowed in the traditional FAT environment. One of these illogical combinations is used by Windows 95 to signal that the directory entry is the first in a series of directory entries. If the bits 0 through 3 are set (meaning the file is read-only, hidden, system, and a volume label—an impossible combination in normal use), then Windows 95 recognizes the directory entry as the first in the series.

Once the first directory entry is detected, the next directory entry is read and the long file name is concatenated. The structure of these secondary directory entries is shown in table 2.4.

Table 2.4 Layout of Secondary Directory Entries Under Windows 95

Byte Offset	Length in Bytes	Purpose
0	1	Sequence
1	10	File name
11	1	File attribute
12	1	Type
13	1	Checksum
14	12	File name
26	2	Unused (set to 0)
28	4	File name

A Full-Blown Operating System

Notice that there are 26 bytes in each of the secondary directory entries that can be used for a file name, but that these bytes are not contiguous. Instead, they are divided by information used internally by Windows. The sequence number and checksum bytes are used to ensure the long file name (the entire sequence of directory entries) has not somehow been corrupted.

The type byte (at offset 12) is used to indicate exactly what type of information this directory entry contains. Long file names can use secondary directory entries for continuations of the file name, as well as for class information. This information can be used by object-oriented programs to further manipulate the file, as an object. If the type byte indicates the directory entry contains class information, then the information in the entry follows the layout shown in table 2.5.

Table 2.5 Layout of the Class Information Secondary Directory Entry

Byte Offset	Length in Bytes	Purpose
0	1	Sequence
1	10	Class information
11	1	File attribute
12	1	Type
13	1	Checksum
14	6	Class information
20	6	Reserved
26	2	Unused (set to 0)
28	4	Reserved

Notice that the class information can occupy only one directory entry for any given file. This information is included in the sequence of long file name entries, as indicated by the sequence byte at the beginning of the entry.

Chapter 2: Under-the-Hood Improvements

You probably already know that the PC relies on the ASCII character set to represent information. ASCII uses eight bits (a byte) to define individual characters. Windows 95 uses ASCII as well, but not when storing a long file name. Instead, it uses the Unicode character set, which uses 16 bits (two bytes) to represent a single character. Thus, a file name that is 255 characters long actually occupies 510 bytes of data. Because each secondary directory entry can contain 26 bytes (refer to table 2.4), it takes 20 directory entries to accommodate a full-length file name.

Taken in total then, there is a primary directory entry, up to 20 secondary directory entries, and a single directory entry for class information. Thus, the longest a directory entry chain under Windows 95 can be is 22 entries.

Alias File Names

To maintain compatibility with older programs, every file that has a long file name also has a short file name. In Windows 95, the long file name is called the *primary file name,* and the short file name is called the *secondary file name,* or *alias.* This short file name is automatically created by Windows, based on the long file name you use. It's stored in the primary directory entry for the file, using the older eight-dot-three naming convention. This alias is put together by shortening the primary (long) file name in the following manner:

- Historically illegal characters (except spaces) are replaced with underscores
- Spaces are removed to pack the name together
- The name is truncated at six characters
- The two characters ~1 are appended to the file name
- The file name is converted to uppercase
- If a file already exists with the resulting eight-character name, the number at the end of the name is incremented. The name is checked again; if a conflict still exists, the number is incremented again and repetitive checks are made.

A Full-Blown Operating System   **53**

For example, assume you have a spreadsheet file that has the following name:

```
Tests, showing initial data.xls
```

This is the primary file name. The alias for this file would be the following:

```
TESTS_~1.XLS
```

If there were successive files that shared the same initial characters, they would become the following:

```
TESTS_~2.XLS
TESTS_~3.XLS
TESTS_~4.XLS
TESTS_~5.XLS
TESTS_~6.XLS
TESTS_~7.XLS
TESTS_~8.XLS
TESTS_~9.XLS
TESTS~10.XLS
TESTS~11.XLS
```

Improved 32-Bit Architecture

Earlier in this chapter, you learned that Windows 95 fully exploits the protected mode of your computer. One advantage of protected mode operation is that programs can run faster because they can use 32-bit data access techniques. Traditionally, programs have accessed data either 8-bits or 16-bits at a time. The CPUs used in today's computer systems are optimized for 32-bit operations, however. Windows 95 fully exploits this capability, and allows your programs to do the same.

Many parts of Windows 95 have been rewritten in 32-bit code. This means that these components can operate more efficiently and process data more quickly than was previously possible. The following sections describe the major parts of Windows 95 that benefit from 32-bit operations.

The Kernel

The kernel is the heart of Windows. It is the part of the operating system that remains in memory at all times, providing basic functions that form the core of what Windows does. In Windows 95, the kernel provides memory management, file management, and task management functions.

Windows 95 has a new and improved kernel. Earlier in this chapter, you learned about the improved multitasking capabilities of Windows 95; these are part of the kernel. This portion of the operating system has been completely rewritten in 32-bit code that operates entirely in protected mode. Thus, operations occur more quickly and with higher security and stability than in previous versions of Windows.

File Access

You already know how Windows 95 interprets the FAT file structure to implement long file names. Along with rewriting the kernel in 32-bit code, Windows 95 also includes improved 32-bit file management routines that allow enhanced file access. This means that files can be accessed more quickly than was previously possible, even though the file itself has not been changed. Instead, the way in which the files are accessed is modified. This is analogous to using better equipment to dig a hole—the dirt and rock are not changed, you use more powerful equipment. (If the traditional file access routines are a shovel, Windows 95 has replaced them with a back hoe.)

TrueType Font Engine

TrueType fonts were introduced with Windows 3.1. As you'll learn in Chapter 22, "Working with Fonts," these fonts allow precise correlation between what you see on-screen and what you see on your printed output. Windows 95 includes a new TrueType rasterizer (often called a font engine) that provides the following benefits:

- Faster manipulation of fonts
- Faster font loading
- Better output at high resolutions
- Easier handling of complex fonts

The font engine has been written in 32-bit code and was adapted from the engine used in Windows NT. Because manipulating fonts involves heavy use of mathematics, the 32-bit code allows greater precision and accuracy than was previously available. This means crisper output and better support for high-resolution displays and printers.

Printing and Spooling

One of the frustrating parts of dealing with Windows in the past is printing. The output you got was pretty good, but the way in which the printing process was managed many times seemed backward or awkward.

The entire print management system in Windows 95 has been rewritten. No longer do you set up printers under the Control Panel and manage print jobs from the Main program group. Now all printing functions are managed by using the consistent interface of the Printers folder. Combining 32-bit code with preemptive multitasking also means that print jobs are processed smoother and with fewer delays. The result is faster printing to either a local printer or across a network.

Device Drivers

Device drivers control how Windows 95 interacts with equipment you have connected to your system; this basic fact is no different than in previous versions of Windows. The differences in device drivers under Windows 95 are two-fold: quantity and quality.

Windows 95 directly supports many more devices than previous versions of Windows. Most devices are detected either when Windows 95 is installed or when you change the device, and the appropriate driver is loaded from the installation disks or CD-ROM. While you may still need to contact a vendor for device drivers for new or esoteric equipment, the frequency of doing this is diminished greatly.

The quality of the included device drivers is significantly improved. 32-bit device drivers are necessary to work seamlessly with the improved Windows 95 kernel. All of the device drivers distributed with Windows 95 have been rewritten in 32-bit code, which provides faster, more robust throughput.

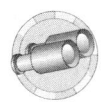

> **Note:** Windows 95 still supports 16-bit device drivers. The disadvantage to using them is that they are inherently slower than 32-bit device drivers. If you have an option, make sure you use a 32-bit device driver designed for use with Windows 95.

Better Resource Management

The other part of the kernel that has been rewritten involves resource management. Resources are components of your computer that can be used by Windows 95 to accomplish a task. For instance, memory is a resource, as is disk space, or a device such as a printer.

In previous versions of Windows, resource management was shaky, at best. This shakiness was due to several factors. First, Windows was built on top of DOS. This meant that many limitations inherent to DOS needed to be compensated for. Because Windows 95 replaces DOS, these limitations are no longer a problem; resources can be directly controlled and accessed by Windows instead of using DOS as an intermediary. Another factor is that Windows did not operate entirely in protected mode. Because some operations were handled outside of protected mode, the resources were open to corruption or compromise during those times.

Windows 95 includes improved resource management routines that have been rewritten from the ground up. These routines affect the operating system in the following areas:

Better Resource Management **57**

- ➤ *The heap.* This is a memory area used to hold and manipulate objects in the Windows environment. In the past, the heap was limited to a single 64K area; in Windows 95 the 64K heap still exists but has been supplemented by a 32-bit memory pool used for the more memory-intensive objects. The result is less chance of exhausting system resources (as was common for many users in Windows 3.1).

- ➤ *Memory management.* When Windows was operating as an add-on to DOS, it still needed to be concerned with (and constrained by) different types of memory. For example, if too much conventional memory was used before Windows even started, then performance could be seriously impaired. Windows 95 removes traditional memory constraints, treating the memory in your system as a single, contiguous linear space. This means that memory operations can occur more quickly, and program throughput can be faster.

- ➤ *The Registry.* Much of the configuration information previously stored in WIN.INI and SYSTEM.INI files has been moved to the Registry. This is a special database that provides a consistent and secure way to store configuration information.

The result of better resource management is a more stable system that better responds to changing program needs.

Built-In Networking

There is a good chance that you are already familiar with Windows for Workgroups, a networking version of Windows 3.1. Windows 95 does away with the networked and non-networked versions of Windows. Instead, networking is built in, from the ground up. You saw evidences of this in Chapter 1, "The Windows 95 Interface." There you learned about the Network Neighborhood icon and how you can use it to explore a network.

Windows 95 includes the following networking improvements:

- ➤ *Wider network support.* Besides the Microsoft peer-to-peer network, Windows 95 also supports third-party networks such as Novell, TCP/IP, and Banyan Vines. Extensions are provided so that other networks can interface with Windows 95, as well.

- ➤ *Easier network access.* The result of networking being an integral part of Windows 95 is that you can easily access network resources. You already know about the Network Neighborhood icon, but you can also access the network through virtually any other Windows 95 application program. You can also access dial-up networks quickly and easily.

- ➤ *More tools.* Network management is easier than in earlier versions of Windows due to tools included with Windows 95. Tools are provided that allow you to manage connections, resources, and users.

Plug-and-Play Support

One of the major features that Windows 95 boasts is the ability to support the Plug-and-Play standard. Essentially, the Plug-and-Play standard allows you to insert a new device into your computer and the system will automatically recognize the device and go through the configuration process for you, thereby saving you time and headaches.

How many times have you tried to install a modem in your computer only to discover that your mouse stopped working? Or, have you tried installing a CD-ROM and suddenly your system doesn't boot up? Traditional installation of devices such as video or sound cards, network adapters, CD-ROMs, and even additional serial ports requires a major investment of time and frustration. But even this investment doesn't guarantee it will work when you are finished. At the least, the trial-and-error method of changing jumper settings, installing device drivers, and editing the configuration files makes most users anxious.

What Is Plug and Play?

Although Plug and Play is a hardware specification, it is also a concept. This concept is nothing new, either. In the 1980s, IBM introduced the PS/2 with its Micro Channel architecture. Several years later, the EISA bus was also introduced. Both busses included auto-configuration capabilities, but neither bus really took hold; the ISA bus was too firmly entrenched in the market.

As hardware and software have evolved, it seems that the complexity of both has grown exponentially. Because of the drawbacks and problems associated with the traditional ISA bus (including IRQ conflicts, DMA configurations, and manual jumper settings), Plug and Play is an architecture designed to take care of the configuration for you and eliminate the typical bother associated with installing hardware.

Whether you are installing a sound card, a modem, a disk drive, or any other device, Plug and Play will detect and configure your equipment for you automatically. Suppose you want to add a modem to your system. Plug it in, turn on the computer, and after some time for auto-configuration, it works. While this may sound too good to be true, it is possible based on the components you have in your system. Basically, you need three elements to have a true Plug-and-Play system:

- Plug-and-Play hardware devices
- Plug-and-Play BIOS (Basic Input/Output System)
- Plug-and-Play operating system (such as Windows 95)

A true Plug-and-Play system requires all three elements, but you can get similar Plug-and-Play functionality if one of the latter two is missing. Take a quick look at these elements and how each contributes to the overall Plug-and-Play system.

Hardware Devices

The base component of Plug-and-Play architecture is the Plug-and-Play device. A device can be a card, peripheral, or other internal part that interfaces with the computer. Compared to the traditional ISA device, the Plug-and-Play device can "communicate" with the BIOS, the operating system, or both to configure itself automatically. As you can see in figure 2.1, from the moment you power on the system, these devices interact with the BIOS by reporting their presence through a special built-in identifier called *resource data*. If the BIOS is not Plug-and-Play compatible, then the operating system communicates with the devices instead.

Notice the sequence of how Plug-and-Play hardware and the BIOS, and/or the operating system, interact. First, the BIOS and/or the operating system isolate one device. It then reads the card's resource data and configures its resources accordingly. If necessary, the operating system then obtains a driver for the device either by finding it somewhere in the system, or by requesting it through a floppy disk from you.

Don't worry about your current non–Plug-and-Play devices. The Plug-and-Play standard takes into account that you already have existing computer equipment. To maintain compatibility with existing hardware, Plug and Play does not strictly rely on each of these components (although having each would be ideal). In fact, Plug-and-Play components will function alongside regular ISA devices without any problem. The only limitation you might notice when using both together is that the configuration process will not be fully automatic. In such instances, you install the device as-is—that is, plug it into the computer by using its default settings. From that point, either the BIOS or the operating system will configure the other Plug-and-Play devices around the existing components.

The BIOS

The Plug-and-Play BIOS also plays a major role. When you first flip the switch to start your system, the BIOS is the first part of your computer system to obtain control, so this is a natural place to incorporate control for the Plug-and-Play system. The Plug-and-Play BIOS communicates very quickly with each Plug-and-Play device, in turn. It first assigns the device a handle and then reads the resource data. Once this takes place for all components, the BIOS verifies that none of the devices conflict with each other. If there is a conflict, the BIOS quickly communicates with all the devices and alters handles until there are no conflicts.

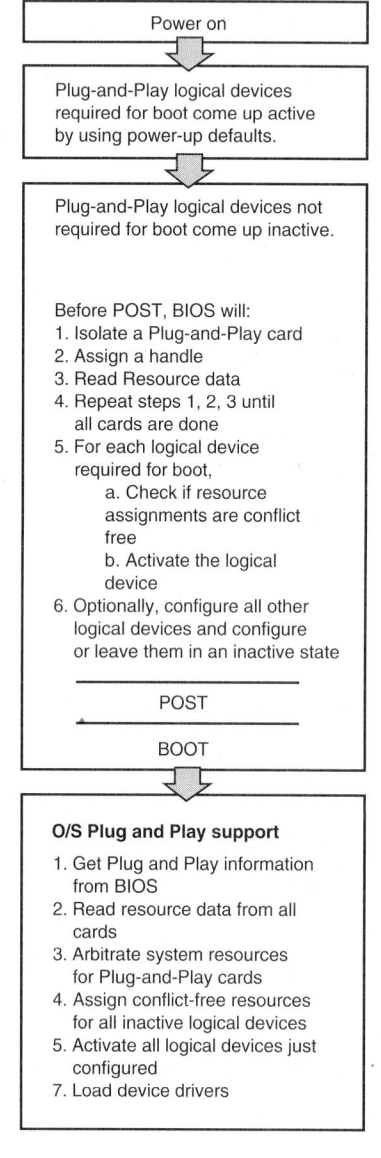

```
                    ┌─────────────────┐
                    │    Power on     │
                    └─────────────────┘
                             ⇩
         ┌──────────────────────────────────────┐
         │ Plug-and-Play logical devices        │
         │ required for boot come up active     │
         │ by using power-up defaults.          │
         └──────────────────────────────────────┘
                             ⇩
         ┌──────────────────────────────────────┐
         │ Plug-and-Play logical devices not    │
         │ required for boot come up inactive.  │
         │                                      │
         │ Before POST, BIOS will:              │
         │ 1. Isolate a Plug-and-Play card      │
         │ 2. Assign a handle                   │
         │ 3. Read Resource data                │
         │ 4. Repeat steps 1, 2, 3 until        │
         │    all cards are done                │
         │ 5. For each logical device           │
         │    required for boot,                │
         │       a. Check if resource           │
         │          assignments are conflict    │
         │          free                        │
         │       b. Activate the logical        │
         │          device                      │
         │ 6. Optionally, configure all other   │
         │    logical devices and configure     │
         │    or leave them in an inactive state│
         │  ─────────────────────               │
         │          POST                        │
         │          BOOT                        │
         └──────────────────────────────────────┘
                             ⇩
         ┌──────────────────────────────────────┐
         │ O/S Plug and Play support            │
         │ 1. Get Plug and Play information     │
         │    from BIOS                         │
         │ 2. Read resource data from all       │
         │    cards                             │
         │ 3. Arbitrate system resources        │
         │    for Plug-and-Play cards           │
         │ 4. Assign conflict-free resources    │
         │    for all inactive logical devices  │
         │ 5. Activate all logical devices just │
         │    configured                        │
         │ 7. Load device drivers               │
         └──────────────────────────────────────┘
```

Fig. 2.1 The sequence of events when booting a Plug-and-Play system involves well-defined steps.

If your BIOS does not support Plug and Play, don't worry. You can probably upgrade your BIOS. If not, you can still use a Plug-and-Play operating system (such as Windows 95) and devices that support the Plug-and-Play standard. Of course, you lose some functionality and benefit of Plug and Play, namely the ability to let your computer automatically configure all the devices, but it's still better than nothing.

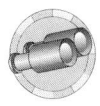

> **Note:** For a computer system to receive the Windows 95-compatible logo, it must have a Plug-and-Play BIOS version 1.0a (or later) installed on the motherboard.

The unique advantage of incorporating the Plug-and-Play BIOS is that, among other things, it tracks each installed device and allows the operating system to retrieve and update detailed information about each device. It resolves conflicts with hardware that ultimately prevent the system resources from being over-allocated by the operating system.

The Operating System

The operating system, Windows 95 in this case, works in harmony with the Plug-and-Play BIOS and continues the automatic configuration process.

Every time your system boots up, Windows 95 builds and keeps a diagram of the system configuration, called a *hardware tree*. As you make changes, Windows 95 compares the hardware tree with the most recent configuration and, if it finds a change, modifies the configuration files, IRQs, and other related parameters accordingly. Such a system certainly relieves you of the configuration woes that come when you change, add, or remove hardware.

After it reads the BIOS, the operating system mimics the same steps as originally followed by the BIOS. First, it reads the resource data from all the cards and portions out resources accordingly. Then it activates the devices and loads their corresponding device drivers. During the system's up-time, the operating system and BIOS maintain a close connection, watching all device activity.

If you don't have a Plug-and-Play BIOS, as described earlier, you can still obtain most of the benefits of Plug and Play. In such a case, the operating system takes over the responsibility of the BIOS and configures system resources.

Eventually, all PCs will be manufactured with hardware and software that employs the Plug-and-Play standard. Most hardware vendors want to service the needs of their customers and will therefore offer the simplest solution to configuring a system—Plug and Play.

How Does Windows 95 Support Plug and Play?

Windows 95 is the first operating system for the PC to support the Plug-and-Play specification. Because Windows 95 is designed from the ground up to be a Plug-and-Play operating system, it is far more advantageous than other operating systems (such as DOS), which would need to use OS extenders to provide Plug-and-Play compatibility.

When a system is first powered on, the BIOS performs its functions, finally checking all the available devices. That information is retained in the BIOS and is later requested by Windows 95 to continue in the regulation of the system. After the BIOS is finished examining the system, it proceeds with the power-on self test (POST) and boots Windows 95.

During the loading process, Windows 95 performs a series of routine steps, which are supervised by the Configuration Manager. This Windows component communicates with the BIOS and responds to dynamic changes in the system since the last boot. Next, under direction of the Configuration Manager, a new hardware tree is drawn and stored for future reference. Once these steps have been performed, the Configuration Manager works silently in the background, monitoring any changes in the configuration that may occur.

If a device is removed, drivers are instantly removed from memory and resources are freed for use by other system processes.

New Windows 95 Tools

KILLER 3 WINDOWS 95

by Allen L. Wyatt

Virtually every tool available in previous versions of Windows has been redesigned for Windows 95. Also, several new tools provide a wider degree of control over your computer system. This chapter describes several of the new tools available within Windows 95, particularly those you'll probably use every day:

- The Explorer
- Quick View
- Shortcuts
- Finding Files

Using the Explorer

Perhaps the most powerful new tool in Windows 95 is the Explorer. This tool is meant to replace the File Manager available in previous versions of Windows, as well as some aspects of Program Manager. The Explorer allows you to view, change, and manage the contents of your disk drives. If you have the proper security permissions, you can perform the same functions on disk drives over the network.

Starting the Explorer

You can start the Explorer in two ways:

➤ Open the My Computer or Network Neighborhood icons, and then choose a drive. Then choose File, Explore.

➤ Perhaps the simplest method of starting the Explorer is to click the Start button and then choose Programs, Windows Explorer.

Either way, the Explorer window appears (see fig. 3.1).

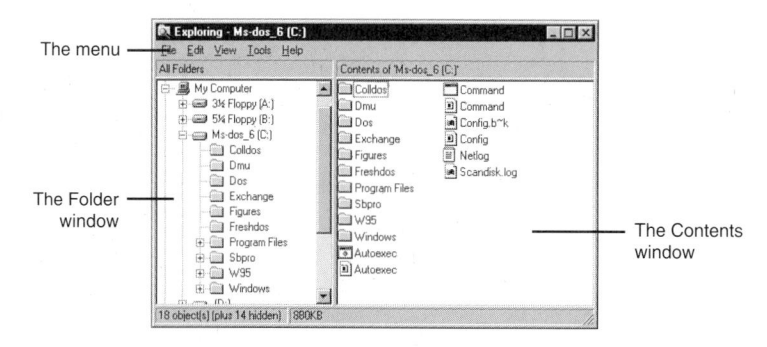

Fig. 3.1 The Explorer window looks different from the previous Windows File Manager.

Understanding the Explorer Window

There are three main parts to the Explorer window: the menu, the Folder window, and the Contents window. The following sections explain each part.

The Menu

Explorer has a menu with five choices. These menus function in the same manner as any other Windows 95 menu; you click the menu desired and then choose an option.

The actual options available on the menus combine the functionality available in Program Manager and File Manager in previous versions of Windows, along with some new features. Many of the menu options are explained later in this chapter.

The Folder Window

The left side of the Explorer window, referred to as the Folder window, is used to show the organization of your system. The format used for this depiction is sometimes called a *tree,* although you can think of it as an outline of your system. For example, if you look at figure 3.2, you can see that the various disk drives (A, B, C, and so on) are directly under the My Computer icon. This is because they're part of your computer, not some other part of your system (such as the network). Under each disk drive, you can also see other subdivisions, such as folders and files.

Take another look at figure 3.2. Notice that many branches in the tree have a small box next to them that contains a plus or a minus sign. This indicates whether more detail is available for a particular branch. If you click a plus sign, the branch is expanded; clicking a minus sign collapses a branch. If there's no plus or minus sign, there's no additional detail for the branch.

Using the Explorer

The Folder window ———

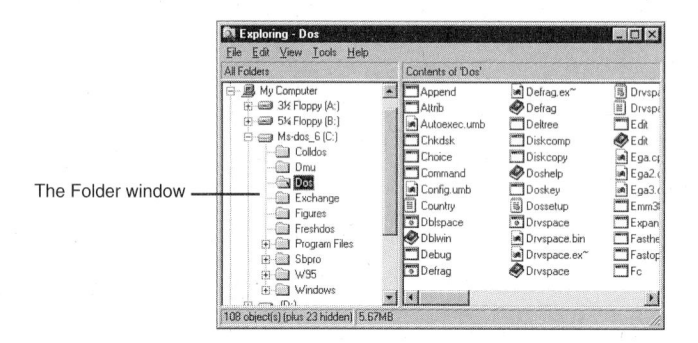

Fig. 3.2 The Folder window shows a logical outline of the information on your system.

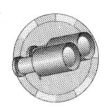

> **Note:** When you first start the Explorer, notice that your computer's A and B drives have a plus sign next to them, even if you don't have disks in those drives. This is because there *could* be additional information in those drives. Windows 95 doesn't actually check them unless you choose them; then it removes the plus sign if it detects no disk in the drives.

The Contents Window

The right side of the Explorer window, the Contents window, is used to show the contents of the drive or folder selected in the Folder window. Figure 3.3 shows what a typical Contents window looks like.

To specify how information is displayed in the Contents window, use the View menu. Options on this menu are used to control the display. You can display information displayed in the Contents window in any of four different formats:

➤ *Large icons.* The files and folders in the Contents window are displayed as large, easy-to-identify icons (see fig. 3.4). Because each icon takes up a larger percentage of the screen, this is a good choice if a lot of objects aren't on disk or in a folder.

68 Chapter 3: New Windows 95 Tools

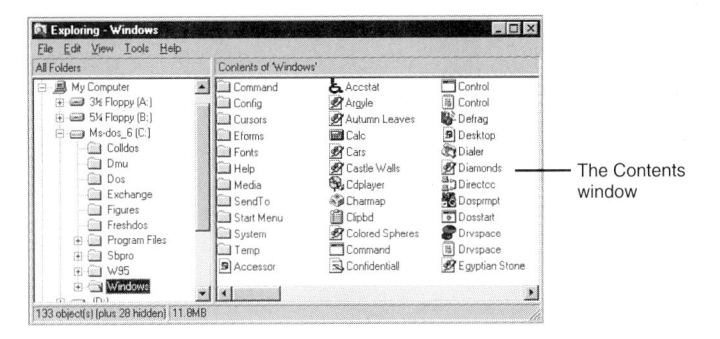

Fig. 3.3 The Contents window shows detailed information about what's in a portion of your system.

Fig. 3.4 You can display the Contents window with large icons for each file and folder.

➤ *Small icons.* The files and folders are displayed by using smaller icons and therefore can be closer together (see fig. 3.5). This is a good choice if you still like to see the icons but have quite a few files to display.

➤ *List.* Information in the Contents window is simply listed in columns with a small icon to the left of each name in the list. This is a good way to pack as much information in the Contents window as possible without having to scroll. Figure 3.3 shows what this type of display looks like.

Using the Explorer **69**

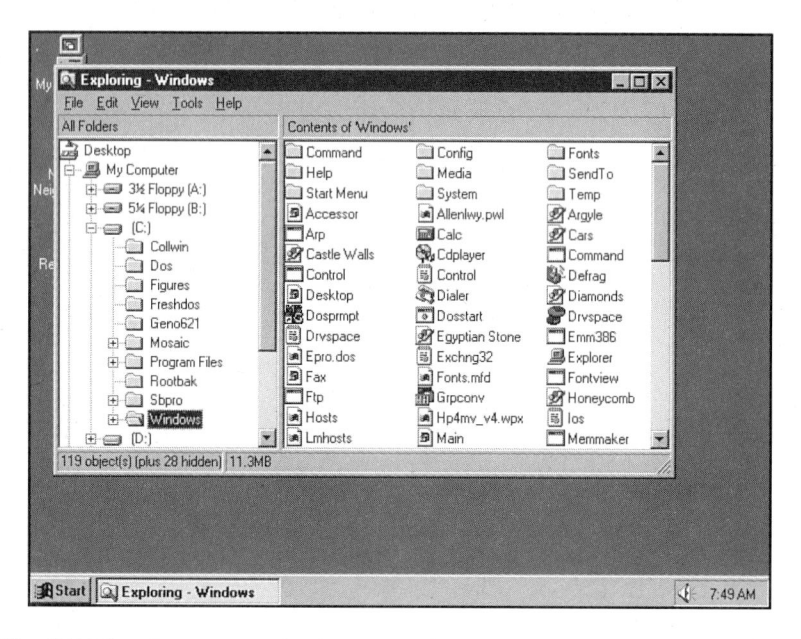

Fig. 3.5 The Contents window can display more information at a time when small icons are used.

➤ *Details.* This view provides the most information about individual files or folders in an object (see fig. 3.6). Each file or folder is shown on a separate line, along with its size, type, and last date and time it was modified.

Other Explorer Features

Besides the menu bar, Folder window, and Contents window, you can use two other features in the Explorer: the toolbar and the status bar. You can turn both of these optional features on or off by using the View menu. A check mark next to the option on the menu means that the feature is displayed. Selecting the menu option again turns the feature off and removes the check mark.

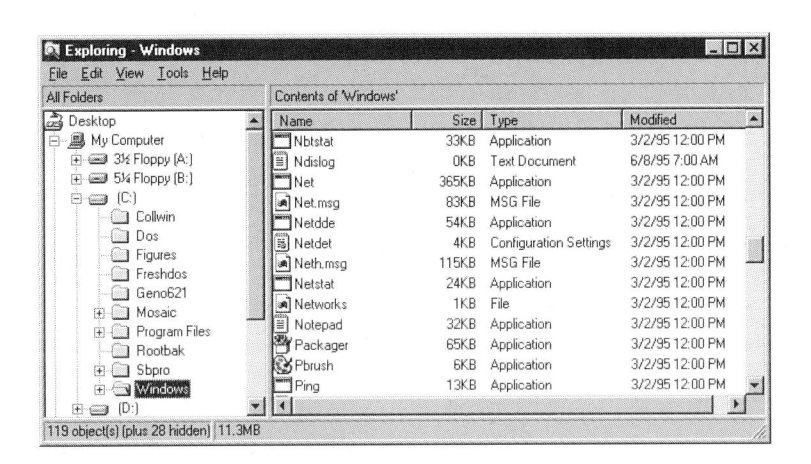

Fig. 3.6 The Contents window can show detailed information about the files on your system.

The Toolbar The Explorer's toolbar is similar to toolbars in most any Windows application. It's displayed just below the menu bar (see fig. 3.7).

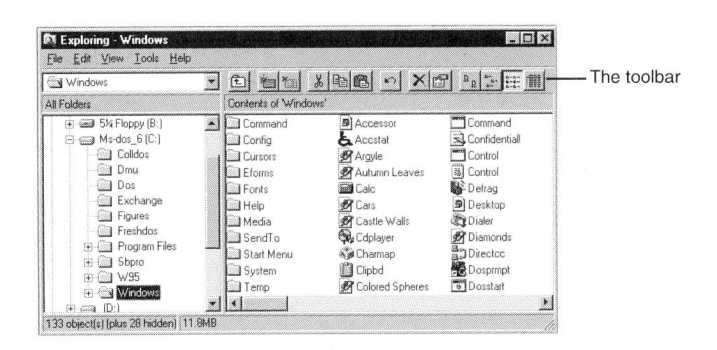

Fig. 3.7 The Explorer toolbar allows easy access to common functions.

The left-most part of the toolbar indicates what object you've selected in the Folders window. If you click the pull-down arrow next to the box, you see a list of drives and folders that looks very similar to what's in the Folders window.

Using the Explorer **71**

To the right of the current object indicator are the actual tools. To discover the purpose of a tool, move the mouse pointer over it and wait a moment (keep the mouse pointer over the tool); you'll see a tip that indicates what the tool is used for.

Notice that the tools are divided into groups, with a small space between each group of tools. The first group consists of a single tool that has a folder with an upward-pointing arrow on it. You use this tool to move back through the system hierarchy shown in the Folder window. Click it once to move up to the next highest folder level.

The next group to the right consists of two tools, both of which are used to work with objects on the network. If you used Windows for Workgroups, these tools probably look similar to icons you used in File Manager. The first one allows you to connect and map a network drive, and the second allows you to break a connection with a previously mapped drive.

The next group consists of three tools that are standard in many Windows applications. These tools allow you respectively to cut, copy, and paste information or objects (including files). For instance, you could copy a file and then paste multiple copies of it in different places on your hard disk.

To the right of this group is another group that consists of a single tool—Undo. This tool can be used, however, only to undo the previous action, not the last few actions.

> **Caution:** Some actions you accomplish with the Explorer can't be undone. While Undo provides some level of protection, the best rule is to make sure that you really want to perform an action before you do it.

The next group consists of two tools. The left-most tool, with a big × on it, is used to delete a file or folder. The other one is an icon you'll see in many places in Windows 95. It allows you to review or modify the properties of an object. Properties are characteristics of an object and can vary from object to object. For instance, the characteristics of a file include things such as file size, file type, and creation date, but these are slightly different from the properties associated with another object, such as a folder.

The final group of four tools are used to change how information is viewed in the Contents window. These tools allow you to quickly and easily switch between different program window views, as discussed earlier in this chapter in the section titled "The Contents Window."

> **Tip:** Remember that the toolbar is optional. You can accomplish the same functions provided in the toolbar by using the menu system.

The Status Bar The status bar appears at the bottom of the Explorer window. It's used to display additional information about objects selected in the Explorer, and about menu options. Figure 3.8 shows the position of the status bar in the Explorer window.

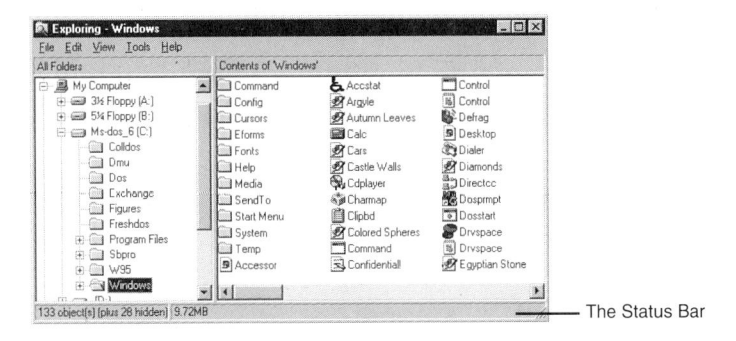

Fig. 3.8 The Explorer's status bar displays helpful information about menu options and objects in the Explorer.

As already mentioned, the Explorer allows you to turn the status bar on or off. Whether you use the status bar or not is strictly personal preference, but you should know that you can display a bit more information on the screen with the status bar turned off.

Using the Explorer **73**

Putting the Explorer to Use

You've already learned a bit about how you can use the Explorer. If you're familiar with using File Manager in previous versions of Windows, you'll quickly come up to speed with the Explorer.

Managing Files and Folders

The Explorer allows you to perform many different operations on individual files or entire directories. For instance, you can rename, delete, or copy them. You can also set properties for various objects.

The first step in working with a file or folder is selecting it. Then you can do any of the following:

- *Rename.* Choose File, Rename, or right-click and choose Rename from the context menu. The name right under the file or folder becomes active, and you can edit it in any way you want.

- *Delete.* There are four ways to delete an object. You can choose File, Delete; right-click and choose Delete from the context menu; click the Delete tool on the toolbar; simply press the Delete key, or press Shift+Delete (which deletes without moving the object to the Recycle Bin). Regardless of the method chosen, you're asked to confirm the deletion. When you click Yes, the file or folder is removed.

- *Move.* Use the mouse to drag the file or folder to where you want it moved. You can drag from the Contents window to the Folders window, or vice versa.

- *Copy.* Hold down the Ctrl key and use the mouse to drag the file or folder to where you want it copied. You can drag from the Contents window to the Folders window, or vice versa. If you prefer not to use the mouse to do the actual file movement, you can right-click on the file or folder, choose Copy from the context menu, and then enter the name of where you want the object copied.

- *Change properties.* Choose File, Properties; right-click and choose Properties from the context menu; or click the Properties tool on

74 Chapter 3: New Windows 95 Tools

the toolbar. The type of properties available depend on the type of object you select. For example, figure 3.9 shows the Properties sheet for a program file.

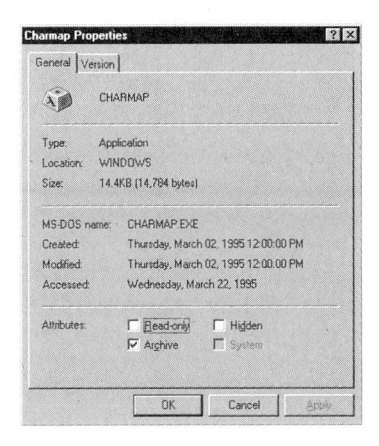

Fig. 3.9 This Properties sheet displays and allows changes to characteristics of a program file.

Sorting the Contents Window

Normally, the Explorer takes care of sorting the files displayed in the Contents window into alphabetical order. Sometimes, however, you may want to change how the information is presented. This is easily done by choosing View, Arrange Icons. This displays a menu with several arrangement choices:

➤ *Name.* Files are displayed in alphabetic order based on their name.

➤ *Type.* Files are sorted first by file type (such as DOC, GIF, BMP, and EXE) and then by name. This is handy when you want to view all files of the same type at once.

➤ *Size.* Files are sorted based on file size, from smallest to largest.

➤ *Date.* Files are displayed by when they were last modified. The most recently modified files are listed first.

At the bottom of the Arrange Icons menu is a final option, <u>A</u>uto Arrange. This option is available only if you're displaying icons (small or large) in the Contents window. When you select this option, a check mark appears next to it on the menu. You can remove the check mark by selecting the option a second time.

When selected, Auto Arrange ensures that the icons don't run off the right side of the Contents window unless absolutely necessary. Icons are rearranged in the best possible manner to make sure you can see as many of them as possible in the window size. If the window size is too small to display all the icons at once, then Windows adds a scroll bar so that you can easily access the additional icons. If you later change the window size, the icons are again rearranged to fill the window.

It is interesting to note that the Arrange Icons menu does not provide all the sorting options in which you may be interested. For instance, it does not provide a way to sort files in descending order instead of ascending order. You can increase the sorting flexibility by choosing the <u>D</u>etails option from the <u>V</u>iew menu. This displays detailed information about files and folders in the Contents window, as shown earlier in figure 3.6. Notice, as well, that column heads are shown at the top of each column in the Contents window. If you click on a column head, the files are sorted based on that column. Click on the column head a second time, and the sorting order for that column is reversed. For instance, the first time you click on the Size column head, the files are sorted in ascending order by size; click on the Size column head again, and they are sorted in descending order by size.

Creating Associations

As in earlier versions of Windows, Windows 95 allows you to define associations between data files and the programs used to control them. You do this by indicating the type of files created by the application, and then Windows 95 assumes that all files of that type can be manipulated by that application. For instance, you could associate all files with a DOC extension with Word for Windows, and all files with a GIF extension could be associated with a graphics program.

76 Chapter 3: New Windows 95 Tools

To work with file associations, choose View, Options. In the Options dialog box, click the File Types tab. The dialog box should now appear as shown in figure 3.10.

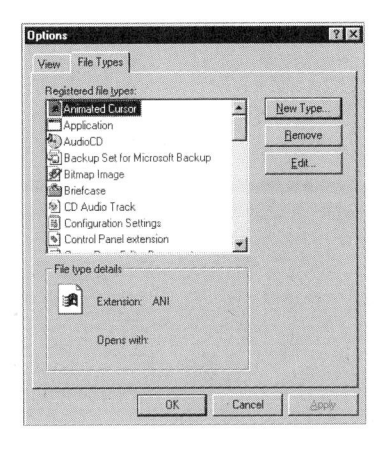

Fig. 3.10 The File Types tab in the Options dialog box shows the associations that exist between files and programs.

This dialog box contains a list of the associations that now exist. The list shows the icon associated with the file type and the name of the file type. If you want to edit an association, you can do so by selecting the existing file type, and then clicking Edit. Figure 3.11 shows an example of the dialog box used when you're editing an association.

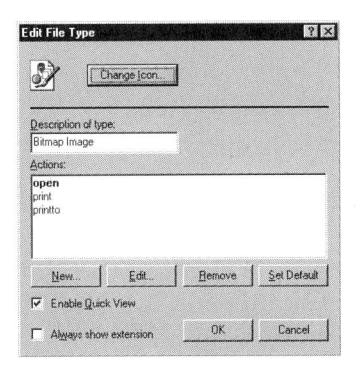

Fig. 3.11 Editing an existing association is done by using the Edit File Type dialog box.

Using the Explorer   **77**

The Edit File Type dialog box has three main parts. At the top of the dialog box, you can specify the icon that's used for this type of file. If you click the Change Icon button, you can select a different icon. Remember that the icon you choose here is used every time this type of file is graphically displayed on your system.

The second part of the dialog box is the field labeled Description of Type. This is simply a name used to describe the association. You can change this to anything; it shows up when you click the File Types tab in the Options dialog box.

The third and most important part of the editing dialog box is the Actions list. By using the four buttons that appear under the Actions list, you can change what appears in the list. *Actions* are nothing more than a definition of what can be done with the file. If you refer to figure 3.11, for example, notice that three actions are listed: open, print, and printto.

Actions are much more versatile than mere file-type associations, which were available in older versions of Windows. Actions allow you to define a wide range of functions that can be performed on a file. Once defined for a file type, actions then appear in the context menu for the file. Thus, you can use actions to define what appears in context menus.

Windows 95 allows you to define what application is used to perform any of a number of actions for a particular type of file. Say that you wanted to add an action for a type of file. All you need to do is click the New button. This displays the New Action dialog box (see fig. 3.12).

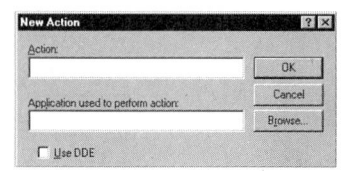

Fig. 3.12 The New Action dialog box is used to define actions for a file type.

All you need to do is to provide a name for the action in the Action field. This can be any name you want, such as *print*, *delete*, *process*, or whatever. There are no preset actions, so what you enter as an action is entirely up to you. You could even use multiple words in the Action field, such as Open with Word. Whatever actions you enter are shown in the context menu for the file.

In the next field, Application Used to Perform Action, you provide the complete command line that should be used to achieve the action (when the action is selected from the context menu). When you're satisfied with the action and the command used to carry out the action, click OK. The new action then appears in the Actions list of the Edit File Type dialog box (refer to fig. 3.11).

Note: Normally, applications use OLE (object linking and embedding) technology to work with files. This technology is common to many Windows applications, but some older Windows applications don't implement OLE; instead, many of these older applications use DDE (dynamic data exchange). If you choose an application but don't see any actions available for that application, click the Use DDE check box in the New Action dialog box. Actions may be available by using this older technology.

In the Edit File Type dialog box, actions are shown in the Actions list alphabetically. By default, the first action listed is used to control the icon displayed for the file type. You can modify the default action by choosing an action and then clicking the Set Default button. The selected action then appears in boldface in the Action list.

Using Quick View

Windows 95 incorporates a new feature that allows you to quickly view the contents of a file. This feature, known as Quick View, is available from virtually any place you can select files. You can use Quick View, for example, as you're browsing through the My Computer portion of your desktop, or you can use it from within the Explorer. Figure 3.13 shows an example of what you would see if you use the Quick View option to examine the PROTOCOL.INI file, found in the Windows folder.

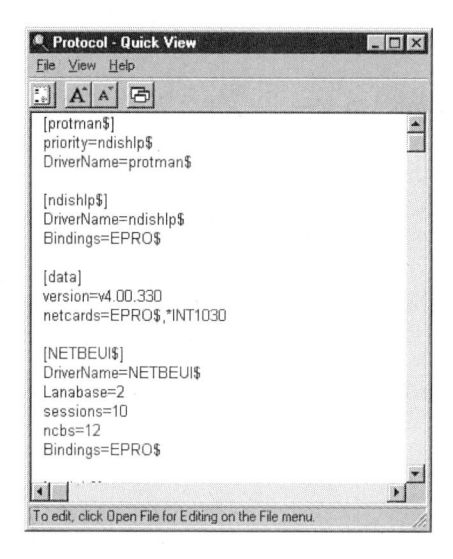

Fig. 3.13 Using Quick View to examine a text-based file is much like viewing it in the Notepad accessory.

Before you can use Quick View, you must select a file. Click the file's icon once to select it; the icon is then highlighted. You can then access the Quick View feature in two ways: from the File menu or from the context menu. Figure 3.14 shows an example of the context menu for a file. Notice that the third option on the menu is Quick View.

Not all files have the Quick View option available. Quick View requires a file type that Windows recognizes and can process. The ability to view a file with Quick View is dependent on the existence of a Quick View filter. Filters are used to define how a particular type of file should be translated and displayed. Table 3.1 lists the file types for which Windows 95 provides Quick View filters.

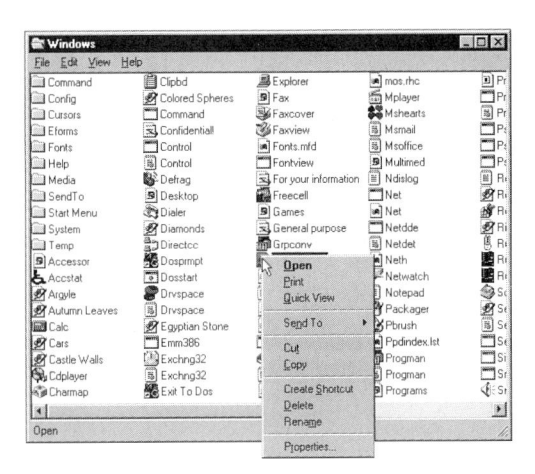

Fig. 3.14 You can access the Quick View feature of Windows 95 from the context menu for an object.

Table 3.1   File Types Supported by Quick View

File Type	Extension
Bit-map image	BMP
Setup information	INF
Configuration settings	INI
Registry files	REG
Rich Text Format file	RTF
Setup information	INF
Text documents	TXT
WordPad documents	DOC
Write documents	WRI

In addition to the file types listed in Table 3.1, the Quick View feature is available for other objects, such as disk drives and folders. It's also possible that Quick View filters are installed with some of your application programs so that their data files can be viewed quickly.

Using Quick View   **81**

Understanding Shortcuts

Now that the traditional Program Manager has been done away with, Windows 95 provides the capability to create *shortcuts*. These are nothing more than links to documents or programs that you can place on the desktop for quick and easy access.

Why would you use a shortcut to access a program, rather than run the program and minimize it to the taskbar? Because running the program, even if it's minimized, consumes valuable system resources such as memory and a portion of your CPU time. Creating a shortcut, on the other hand, doesn't consume resources, yet your program is still readily available for use at any time.

Creating a Shortcut

The easiest way to create a shortcut is to either browse through My Computer or your Network Neighborhood, or to use the Explorer. When you can see the icon for the program or document for which you want to create a shortcut, drag the icon onto your desktop. But rather than drag by using the left mouse button, you should perform the drag using the right mouse button. When you release the mouse button, a small menu appears with several options (see fig. 3.15). Choose the Create Shortcut(s) Here option.

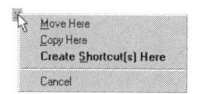

Fig. 3.15 Creating a shortcut is easy when you drag an object by using the right mouse button.

Windows creates a new icon on the desktop. You can tell that the icon is for a shortcut because it has a small diagonal arrow in the lower left corner of the original icon (the one that you dragged to the desktop). Figure 3.16 shows a comparison of the original icon for a program and the shortcut icon to the same program.

Fig. 3.16 A shortcut icon is the same as the original icon, except it has a small diagonal arrow in the lower left corner.

Another way to create a shortcut is to display the context menu for an object. One choice on the context menu is Create Shortcut. If you choose this option, the shortcut is created in whatever folder you're now working. You can then move the shortcut to wherever you want it, such as onto the desktop.

Renaming a Shortcut

Once you create a shortcut, you can treat its icon like any other icon in Windows. To rename the shortcut, simply display its context menu and choose the Rename option; Windows allows you to rename the shortcut to anything you desire.

> **Caution:** To avoid confusion with the original program or document icon, don't give the shortcut the same name as the original program or document.

Deleting a Shortcut

To delete a shortcut, select it and press Delete, or display the context menu for the icon and choose Delete. You're asked to confirm whether you really want to delete the icon; if you click Yes, the shortcut is deleted.

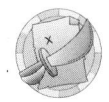

> **Tip:** Deleted shortcuts are moved to the Recycle Bin. If you later decide you want to salvage the shortcut, you may be able to find it in the Recycle Bin.

Understanding Shortcuts **83**

It's important to remember that shortcuts are nothing more than links to a program or document. When you delete a shortcut, you delete the link—not the original document or program. If you want to delete those, you need to search for the program files or documents and manually delete them.

> **Tip:** If you're deleting an application, the vendor sometimes provides an uninstall feature. Before you spend time searching for application files to delete manually, check the documentation to see whether there's an easier way to uninstall the program.

Searching for Files

As you work with your computer system, one thing you'll notice is that it's rather easy to collect a large number of files. Because it's virtually impossible to keep track of large numbers of files over a period of months, Windows 95 includes a tool that allows you to quickly and easily locate files on your system. You can access this tool by clicking the Start button and then choosing Find. This displays another menu that lists the types of searches you can perform. Since you want to find files on your system, choose the Files or Folders option. You then see the Find dialog box (see fig. 3.17).

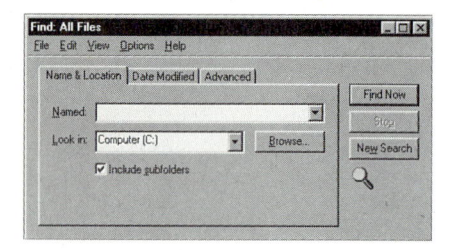

Fig. 3.17 You can quickly and easily search for files by using the Find dialog box.

Chapter 3: New Windows 95 Tools

Entering Your Criteria

Notice that the Find dialog box has three tabs, which allow you to specify the criteria that should be used when searching for a file:

➤ *Name & Location.* This tab is used to indicate where Find should start looking, how deep the search should go, and any hints on the file name. The Named field is used to specify a file name or partial file name. (You can use the ? and * wild-card characters to provide a partial file name.) The Look In field tells Find where to start looking, and the Include Subfolders check box indicates whether Find should look in any subfolders it encounters.

➤ *Date Modified.* This tab allows you to specify the age of the file you're looking for. You can specify a date range or a specific age for the files selected. The dates are based on when the files were either created or last modified.

➤ *Advanced.* Use this tab to specify a file type, text within a file, or a file size. If you're looking for a file that contains specific text, the search can take a while.

Find provides other ways to specify criteria as well. You can use the Options menu to specify this criteria. The choices on this menu are turned on and off every time they're selected. If the option is in effect, a check mark appears to the left of the option. Selecting the option again turns off the check mark and the option.

The first choice on the Options menu allows you to indicate whether the text you specify in your search should be considered Case Sensitive. If this option is selected, how you enter your text (including file names) matters as much as what you enter. For example, the text *Widget* is treated differently from *widget* or *WiDgEt*.

Starting a Search

Once you've specified the criteria for a search, you can start the search by clicking the Find Now button. Your criteria are analyzed, and the appropriate places on your system are searched. During the search, you see information on the status bar about the search's progress. When the search is complete, the files that were located are displayed at the bottom of the Find window (see fig. 3.18).

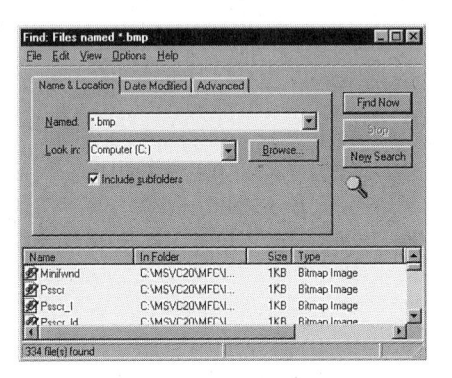

Fig. 3.18 After a search, the Find window lists the files that were located.

You can use the files located in the search in the same way as you would a file list in the Explorer. For instance, you can drag the file icons and drop them into another folder in the Explorer window (if the Explorer is running and open on your desktop), or you can rename or delete the file. What you do with files located by the Find tool is completely up to you.

Saving Your Search Criteria

It's possible to develop searches that are quite complex. In these instances, the Find tool provides a way to save your search criteria. To do so, simply choose Save Search from the File menu. Windows then creates a shortcut to the search, placing it on your desktop. You can then rename the shortcut to reflect a meaningful name.

Installing Windows 95

by Allen L. Wyatt

How you install Windows 95 will vary, to some extent, depending on the primary use for your system. Because of this variance, this chapter provides three different installation sections: installing Windows 95 on a home computer, an office computer, and a network workstation.

In addition to these install instructions, this chapter discusses the following topics:

- ➤ What to do before and after installation
- ➤ What setup type you should choose
- ➤ How to upgrade from a previous version of Windows
- ➤ How to configure your system for dual-boot between Windows 3.*x* and Windows 95

The Different Types of Systems

The proliferation of computers in the past few years has enabled many people to set up systems in their homes and offices, including systems attached to networking workstations. In the following sections, you'll learn a little about each of these areas.

What Is a Home Computer?

Depending on who is addressing the issue, a home computer can be many different things. The quick answer would be to say "a home computer is any computer you use at home." The complex and varied uses to which people put their computers makes this answer too simplistic, however.

Obviously, a computer used at home differs from traditional office-oriented systems because of the different workloads placed on it. Although there are exceptions, system components for the home computer typically consist of the following:

- 386- or 486-based computer
- 420M or smaller hard disk
- 4M RAM
- 14-inch SVGA monitor and graphics card
- Dot-matrix or ink-jet printer

In addition, more and more home machines are coming equipped with sound cards and CD-ROM drives. This is in recognition of the rapid growth of multimedia in computer systems in general, as well as the distribution of complex software on CD-ROM. Even Windows 95 is available on CD-ROM, which is definitely the easiest way to install the product.

Just a few years back, that seemingly modest 386 running at 33 MHz was the power user's dream machine. As of this writing, the Pentium has taken a stronghold with processor speeds up to 133 MHz. In general, home systems stay a step or two behind the "power machines" on the market. As the requirements for home-oriented software continue to increase, so will the specifications for home computer systems. In a couple years, when the Pentium has been superseded by a newer and faster CPU, it will probably become the mainstay of home systems. (Just take a look at Intel's TV advertising, which is focusing on using the Pentium in the home market.)

What Is an Office Computer?

An office computer typically differs from other systems because of the different workloads placed on it. Office systems tend to be used more often than other systems, and their successful use is often more critical to the productivity of the entire office. In addition, office computers may or may not include networking capabilities. Although there are exceptions, system components for the office computer typically (or should) consist of the following:

➤ 386- 486-, or Pentium-based computer

➤ 340M or larger hard disk

➤ CD-ROM drive

➤ 8M RAM

➤ 14-inch SVGA monitor and graphics card

➤ dot-matrix, ink-jet, or laser printer

If you haven't already browsed through Chapter 8, "Examining the Hardware You Need for Windows 95," you may want to do that now. As computer technology advances, so do the minimum system requirements. As mentioned earlier, just a few years ago, a seemingly modest 386/33 was the power user's dream machine. Now, the Pentium/133 has taken the lead. If the trend continues, in two years that Pentium will be yesterday's news.

What Is a Network Workstation?

By definition, a network workstation is any computer connected to a network. Further, the workstation specifically uses resources made available through the network. This means that in a client/server network, the client is synonymous with the workstation. In a peer-to-peer network, each peer on the network is a workstation.

When you look at individual workstations on a network, the capabilities of the machine probably don't differ that much from other stand-alone office systems. However, not all workstations are alike. For instance, some workstations are diskless PCs that provide a trouble-free and secure environment. Portable computers can also be considered workstations, even if they aren't connected to the network at all times. Other workstations may be desktop PCs with their own resources that are not shared over the network.

System Requirements to Install Windows 95

Before you install Windows 95, make sure that your computer system is up to the challenge. Few things are more frustrating than not having adequate hardware to install Windows 95—or your favorite application, for that matter.

According to product information, Windows 95 requires a minimum of a 386 processor with 4M of RAM and a 30M hard disk. This minimum will work, but programs (and Windows) will run very slowly using this configuration. You're better off with 8M or 16M of RAM and as big a hard disk as possible.

Next, do you have the appropriate media? You can install either from floppy disks or CD-ROM. Certainly, installing from CD-ROM requires less effort than swapping more than 20 disks over the course of 45 minutes.

Before You Install

Before you actually begin the installation process, consider what will take place. You're about to make some major changes in your computer system and the software that runs it. Because of this, you'll want to perform a few tasks before you even think of running the Setup program. These tasks are as follows:

- Defragment your hard drive
- Back up your system
- Disable your swap file
- Check your disk compression
- Disable your current programs

The following sections describe the reason for each task in a bit more detail, and some sections describe how to perform the task.

Checking Your Media

Windows 95 is available on either floppy disk or CD-ROM. If you have a CD-ROM drive on your system, it is a nice luxury to be able to install from CD-ROM. By doing so, you eliminate the swapping of about 20 disks over the course of 45 minutes. If you need to install Windows 95 on a number of systems in your office, the CD-ROM version is the only cost-effective method of installing the product.

Defragmenting Your Hard Disk

It is always wise to defragment your hard drive, but this becomes even more of a good idea as you're preparing to upgrade your system. A defragmented disk helps ensure that the installation process goes smoothly. With fragmented files, installation could take longer because it takes longer to read files that are scattered all over the disk. Besides, if the files on your hard disk are highly fragmented, Windows 95 will refuse to install until the disk is defragmented.

If you have MS-DOS (or PC DOS) version 6.0 or later, a defrag utility is included with the operating system. If you prefer, there are a number of third-party defragmenting utilities on the market such as *The Norton Utilities* from Symantec, or *PC Tools* from Central Point Software.

Backing Up Your System

As you install Windows 95, you're making a major upgrade to your system. This means that a new operating system is about to reorganize your existing system and overwrite some previously important files. Some files will be deleted and many new ones added. Consequently, it is in your best interest to perform a backup of your entire system. If you don't, you risk losing some information if something goes wrong with the installation process. It is rare to lose data during a Windows 95 installation, but "better safe than sorry."

If you don't want to back up everything, you should at least copy important files to a floppy disk. At a minimum these files would include the following:

- CONFIG.SYS
- AUTOEXEC.BAT
- Data files, such as word processing or spreadsheet documents

Once the files are copied to a disk, make sure you verify that the copy was accurate and that the disk can be read in another machine.

Disabling Your Swap File

If you're upgrading to Windows 95 (and not using the dual-boot feature), you should disable the permanent swap file used by your current version of Windows. If you're an avid Windows user, you may already be familiar with the term *swap file*. This is a special file, created on your hard disk, that serves as a memory overflow area. When a program needs more memory than is currently available, information is stored in the swap file on hard disk until it is needed later. In many ways, the hard disk serves as an extension of the RAM in your system. (With this understanding, you can envision how less RAM can slow down your system by requiring more swap file activity.)

Windows 95 does not use the same permanent swap file technology as Windows 3.*x*. As you learned in Chapter 2, "Under-the-Hood Improvements," the virtual memory manager within Windows 95 (which manages the swap file) has been rewritten entirely. It now uses more dynamic management, which means that the size of the swap file is adjusted, as necessary, to fit the needs of the operating system. Because a different swap file is used, any previous swap file just sits on your hard disk and wastes space.

To disable your permanent swap file in your current version of Windows, follow these steps:

1. Double-click on the Control Panel icon in the Main program group. The Control Panel appears.
2. Double-click on the Enhanced icon in the Control Panel. The Enhanced dialog box appears.
3. Click on the Virtual Memory button in the Enhanced dialog box. The Virtual Memory dialog box appears.
4. Examine the Swapfile Settings area of the Virtual Memory dialog box. If the Type field shows Permanent, click on the Change button. Otherwise, click on Cancel and exit from all dialog boxes. A permanent swap file is not present.
5. In the New Swapfile Settings area, choose None from the Type list box.
6. Click on OK to close the Virtual Memory dialog box.
7. When asked to confirm your change, click on the Yes button.

At this point, you'll need to restart Windows. When you've done so, your permanent swap file is disabled and deleted.

Checking Your Disk Compression

If you use disk compression, you'll want to make sure that it is compatible with Windows 95. The following disk compression utilities are compatible with Windows 95 and are fully supported:

- Microsoft DriveSpace
- Microsoft DoubleSpace
- Stac Electronics Stacker versions 3.0 and 4.*x*
- SuperStor

Windows 95 uses the DriveSpace utility in preference to the other compression methods that Windows 95 recognizes. Windows 95 includes some built-in utilities specifically designed to work with DriveSpace. For instance, the defragmenting and scanning utilities included with Windows 95 have been tuned specifically to work with DriveSpace. If you use a different compression utility, you may need to use whatever utilities are provided with that utility.

The point at which you upgrade to Windows 95 is a great time to decide if you want to switch over to DriveSpace. If you decide that it makes sense for you, then you'll need to decompress your drives before installing Windows 95. Exactly how you decompress depends on the compression utility you're using; you should consult the documentation for your utility to learn how to best do this.

Once you've installed Windows 95, you can use the DriveSpace utility to compress your hard drives. Full information on how to do this is contained in Chapter 10, "Optimizing Your Disk Drives."

Disabling Programs

Earlier versions of DOS relied heavily on TSR (terminate and stay resident) programs to add features to the operating system. Before installing Windows 95, be sure to disable any TSRs you've installed; these can conflict with the setup process. Examples of common TSR programs are the bill minder program in Quicken and some device drivers such as MOUSE.COM.

If you plan on installing Windows 95 from within your current version of Windows, be sure you close all open windows except for the Program Manager. Open program windows can slow down the installation process, and may stop necessary files from being copied to the hard disk.

Dual-Booting

Many people who are upgrading to Windows 95 want to set up their systems so they can boot to different operating systems. For instance, a user might want to use both OS/2 and Windows 95 at different times. In most office environments, you'll probably want to stay away from dual booting. Such installations are inherently more complex, and they can open up a technical support can of worms. For this reason, most offices do not implement a dual-boot setup for every Tom, Dick, and Mary in the office.

Instead, it is typically "power users" who choose to use dual-booting. By definition, however, these are the users who should need less technical support because they're more aware of the inner workings of their system.

There is one type of dual-boot situation that should be addressed, however. You may want to still be able to boot to your old version of DOS, as well as to Windows 95. Why? Because you'll need this capability if you want to still use an older version of Windows on your system. As an example, if you are a software developer, you may want both types of Windows systems available so you can test your product on both.

The preferred method of installing Windows 95 is to upgrade your old version of Windows to Windows 95. This upgrade ensures that all your settings, applications, and preferences migrate to Windows 95. However, if you're determined to maintain a previous version of Windows on your computer *in addition to* Windows 95, you can instruct Setup to install Windows 95 to a separate folder instead of overwriting the previous Windows version.

Ultimately, dual-booting enables you to choose which operating system you use to start your system. (More information is provided in Chapter 15, "Taking Control of Windows 95 Startup.") Some people view dual booting as "the best of both worlds." The drawback to dual-booting is that none of your existing Windows 3.1 settings and applications migrate to Windows 95.

The following questions can help you decide which installation method is best for you:

➤ **Do you want to be able to run Windows 3.1 and Windows 95 (dual-boot)?** If the answer is yes, then you should install Windows 95 to a folder other than C:\WINDOWS. If the answer is no, then you can allow Setup to install to the default folder and upgrade over the top of Windows 3.1.

➤ **Do you want Windows 95 to migrate (transfer) your existing Windows settings and applications?** If the answer is yes, then allow Setup to install to the default folder and upgrade over the top of Windows 3.1. If the answer is no, then install Windows 95 to a folder other than C:\WINDOWS.

➤ **Do you want to be able to load MS-DOS as well as Windows 95?** If the answer is yes, then install Windows 95 to a folder other than C:\WINDOWS. If the answer is no, then allow Setup to install to the default folder and upgrade over the top of Windows 3.1.

Installing Windows 95

More than with any previous version, the setup process for Windows 95 is simple and automatic. You only need to answer a few questions, then sit back and relax. Setup presents a wizard to guide you through the steps of installing Windows 95. When prompted, click on the appropriate buttons, typically either Continue or Next.

As a general rule, if you have Windows 3.1 or Windows for Workgroups 3.11 already installed on your system, you should install from within Windows. If you do not have Windows or if you have Windows 3.0 or earlier, you must install from MS-DOS.

Starting Setup from MS-DOS

If you don't have Windows 3.1*x* on your computer, or if you have an older version of Windows, such as 3.0 or earlier, you can install Windows 95 from the DOS prompt. Follow these steps to install from DOS:

1. If you're installing from a CD-ROM, insert the disc in your CD-ROM drive. If you're installing from a floppy, insert the first disk in your disk drive.

2. At the DOS prompt, type **d:\SETUP** and press Enter. (You should replace the letter *d* with the drive letter that represents the drive you used in step 1.) You'll see the following on your screen:

   ```
   Please wait while Setup initializes.

   Setup is now going to perform a routine check on your system.

   To continue, press ENTER. To quit Setup, press ESC.
   ```

3. Press Enter to continue with the setup. The program then runs ScanDisk to check the integrity of your disk drives.

4. When ScanDisk is complete, press X to exit the program.

At this point, a couple of files are copied to your hard drive in preparation for the rest of the setup procedure. Shortly, you'll see the welcome screen, as shown in figure 4.1. From this point forward, Setup is identical for DOS users as it is for Windows users. Click on the Continue button and proceed to step five in the next section to continue with the Windows 95 installation.

Starting Setup from Windows

During the installation phase, Setup detects whether you already have Windows installed and remembers its location. Setup later informs you where it was found. To install Windows 95 from Windows 3.1 or Windows for Workgroups 3.1*x*, follow these steps:

1. If you're installing from a CD-ROM, insert the disc in your CD-ROM drive. If you're installing from a floppy, insert the first disk in your disk drive.

2. Choose File, Run from Program Manager (not File Manager). This invokes the Run dialog box.

3. Enter **d:\SETUP** in the Command Line text box and click on OK. (You should replace the letter *d* with the drive letter that represents the drive you used in step 1.) In a moment, you see the Windows 95 Setup welcome screen (see figure 4.1). Click on Continue.

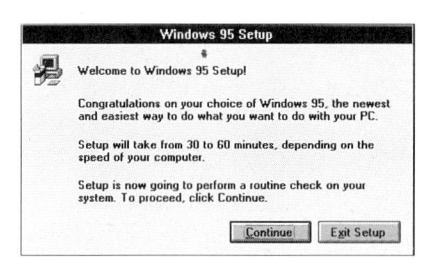

Fig. 4.1 Welcome to Windows 95 Setup.

4. Setup performs a behind-the-scenes ScanDisk. When it is finished, click on Continue. After you do, various files are copied to your hard disk in preparation for the Setup wizard.

5. When you see the software license agreement, read it, then click on Yes.

6. When you see the Setup Wizard shown in figure 4.2, you can see the number of steps required to complete the setup and what will occur. Click on Next.

7. As shown in figure 4.3, you now have the opportunity to specify where Windows 95 will be installed. If you currently have Windows installed and you want to update, you should accept the indicated folder. If you want Windows 95 installed in a different folder for whatever reason (including wanting to dual-boot

Chapter 4: Installing Windows 95

instead of upgrade), you should click on Other folder. When you have made your choice, click on the Next button.

Fig. 4.2 The Setup Wizard outlines what will occur during Setup.

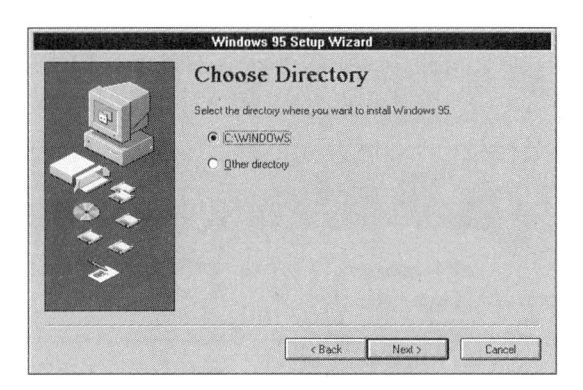

Fig. 4.3 Choose a folder where you want to install Windows 95.

8. If you indicated that you wanted Windows 95 installed in a different folder, you're asked to specify the folder. Pick a folder and click on the Next button.

9. When the Setup Options screen appears (see figure 4.4), choose a setup type. Most home computer users will choose Typical, but if you want to select extra options you can select Custom. (A full discussion of each setup type is found later in this chapter in the section titled, "Choosing a Setup Type.") Make your selection and click on Next.

Fig. 4.4 You can select from four setup types.

10. Enter your name in the User Information screen. You optionally may type the name of your company or organization, too. Click on Next.

11. You'll see the Analyzing Your Computer screen as shown in figure 4.5. If any of the devices are present in your system, and the devices are not Plug-and-Play compatible, choose them and click on Next.

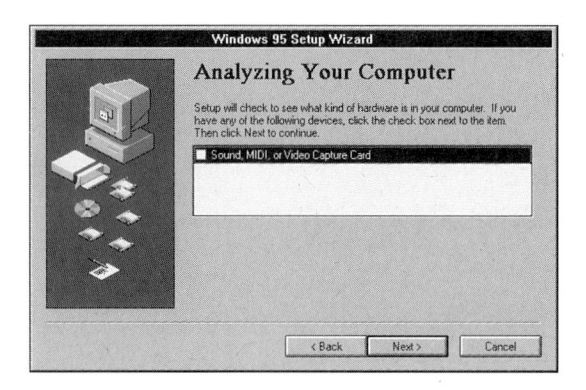

Fig. 4.5 The Analyzing Your Computer screen is used to specify the items present in your computer.

12. Setup now performs a complete hardware analysis, which may take up to five minutes (depending on the speed of your system).

13. After a time you'll see the Windows Components screen. Here you have two choices: you can accept the most common components for your type of installation (this is the recommended default), or you can indicate that you want to modify the components installed. Make your selection and click on Next.

14. If you chose to modify the components installed, you'll see the Select Components screen, as shown in figure 4.6. If you asked Windows to install the most common components, skip to step 16.

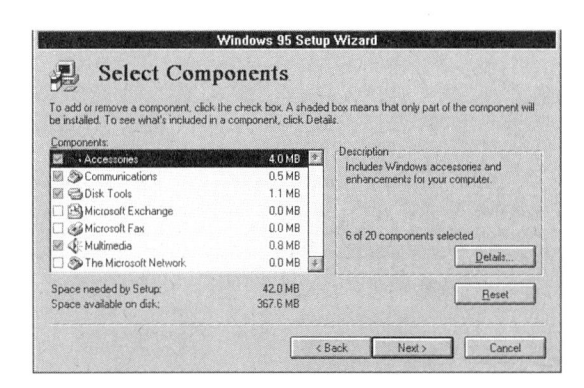

Fig. 4.6 Choose the options you want to install. Grayed entries indicate some components within the group are selected and some are not.

15. Select the options you want installed with Windows 95. If you want more options than are available in the Typical setup, you can pick from this list. Highlight a category and click on Details to choose individual items. To select all items in a component category, highlight it and press the spacebar. Click on Next when you're finished.

16. If your system is not 100 percent Plug-and-Play compatible, Setup may not be able to detect each item by name. If so, you may see the Computer Settings screen that you can safely ignore by clicking on Next. If you want Windows 95 settings to be a little more precise, scroll through the list and change any items marked Unknown to their proper setting. To do so, highlight the item and click on Change. Click on Next when you're finished.

17. Setup next asks if you want a startup disk. Choose Yes (the default) and click on Next. This disk serves as your bootable floppy in case of any future system trouble. Most of the time you'll never need it, but it is a good precaution. For information on how to use this disk, refer to the section titled, "Using the Emergency Startup Disk," later in this chapter.

18. The Setup Wizard displays the second phase of installation—the copying of files. Click on Next.

19. If you chose to create a startup disk, Setup prompts you to insert a disk and click OK. When Windows 95 has completed the disk, remove the floppy, label it clearly, put it in a safe place, and click on OK to continue.

20. Setup then copies the Windows 95 files to your computer; this step takes about 10 minutes. Click on Finish when prompted (see figure 4.7). When you do, the computer restarts and continues to configure Windows 95.

Fig. 4.7 After copying files, Setup is ready to restart your computer.

21. After several minutes of self-configuration, Setup requests your time zone (see figure 4.8). Click on the map to choose the appropriate time zone (or choose from the Time Zone pull-down list) and indicate whether you want to adjust for daylight savings time. Click on Next.

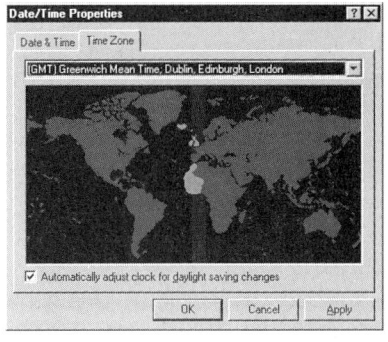

Fig. 4.8 Click on the map to choose your time zone.

22. If you chose to install the communications options, including Microsoft Exchange and Microsoft Fax, the Microsoft Exchange Setup Wizard intervenes, requesting information. For information on setting up Microsoft Exchange and its components, refer to Chapter 32, "Communicating with a Modem."

That's it! You've successfully installed Windows 95. The Welcome dialog box shown in figure 4.9 lets you see what's new in Windows 95. For a quick tour of Windows 95, choose Windows Tour. (The Windows Tour button may not be available if you did not explicitly install the feature.) Click on What's New to find out about the innovations and changes in the Windows interface. Online Registration enables you to dial into Microsoft to register your copy of Windows 95. When you're finished, click on Close. If your installation is unsuccessful, refer to Chapter 6, "Troubleshooting Windows 95 Installation and Startup," for help.

> **Note:** You're not limited to registering Windows 95 with a modem. If you don't have a modem, you can return the registration card provided with your Windows 95 software package.

Installing Windows 95   **103**

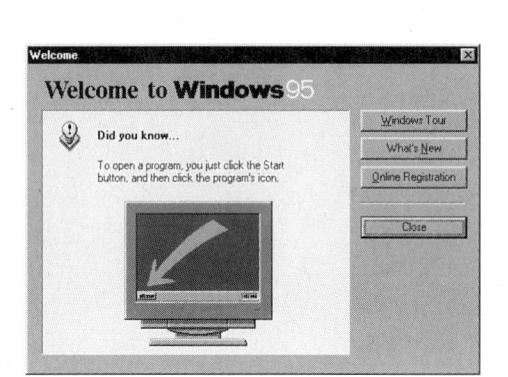

Fig. 4.9 Immediately after you install Windows 95, you see the Welcome dialog box. Choose an option and investigate.

Choosing a Setup Type

In the previous two sections, you learned how to install Windows 95 from start to finish. When performing step nine you learned that the Setup Wizard allows you to indicate what type of installation you want performed. Depending on the type of computer you have and its available resources, including hard disk space (or lack of it), you can select the type of installation you want. Windows 95 offers four distinct setup types—typical, portable, compact, and custom.

Different setup choices require different system resources. The most conservative choice is Compact, then Portable, Typical, and finally Custom. The biggest difference between each option is the number of tools (programs) that the option installs. The following is a quick overview of each installation type:

> **Typical Setup.** This setup type is a common approach for the home computer user, particularly if you have at least 100M of unused hard disk space. The only questions you must answer are to confirm the folder where Windows 95 files are to be installed and to specify whether to create a startup disk.

- **Portable Setup.** If you're a laptop, notebook, or subnotebook owner, this setup type installs the options most appropriate for your type of computer. The options installed with this setup type are geared toward a mobile computer user, basically installing fewer of the "bells and whistles" that accompany a typical setup and adding features that enhance portable computing.

- **Compact Setup.** This setup type installs only the bare essential files necessary to run Windows 95—a minimal installation. This is ideal for users with a small hard disk (less than 80M), and allows users to forego most of the Windows 95 options. Ultimately, this may save about 36M of disk space as opposed to a full Windows 95 installation.

- **Custom Setup.** This setup type lets you choose any or all options available in Windows 95. It is similar to walking through a delicatessen—you pick the pieces and parts you want included in your Windows 95 system. This type of setup is recommended for experienced users who want to control various elements of Windows 95 Setup.

The files installed on your hard drive will vary, depending on the type of setup you choose. Table 4.1 shows the different Windows 95 components that can be installed for each type of limited setup (typical, portable, and compact).

Table 4.1 How Windows 95 Components Are Installed for the Limited Setup Options

Component	Typical	Portable	Compact
Audio Compression	✓	✓	
Blank Screen Saver	✓		
Briefcase		✓	
Calculator	✓		
CD Player	✓	✓	
Disk Defragmenter	✓	✓	✓

continues

Table 4.1   Continued

Component	Typical	Portable	Compact
Document Templates	✓		
DriveSpace	✓	✓	✓
HyperTerminal	✓	✓	
Media Player	✓		
Notepad	✓	✓	✓
Object Packager	✓		
Paint	✓		
Phone Dialer	✓	✓	
Quick View	✓	✓	
ScanDisk	✓	✓	✓
Scrolling Marquee Screen Saver	✓		
Sound Recorder	✓		
Video Compression	✓	✓	
Volume Control	✓		
WordPad	✓		

If you choose the custom setup type, then you can install any or all of the Windows 95 components. Besides those that can be installed with one of the limited setups (as detailed in Table 4.1), there are a wide variety of other components you can choose:

➤ **Accessibility Options.** A collection of Control Panel tools designed to help people who are physically impaired.

➤ **Backup.** A disk tool used to back up your hard drive to floppy disks or tapes.

➤ **Character Map.** An accessory that allows you to access the entire range of Windows 95 characters. You can use Character Map to insert symbols and characters into documents created by other programs.

- **Clipboard Viewer.** An accessory that allows you to view the contents of the Clipboard, and to manage a Clipbook over the network.
- **Curves and Colors Screen Saver.** A screen saver you can use to customize your desktop.
- **Dial-Up Networking.** An accessory that allows you to connect with remote networks, such as the Internet.
- **Direct Cable Connection.** An accessory that allows two computers to be connected through a serial cable.
- **Flying Through Space Screen Saver.** A screen saver you can use to customize your desktop.
- **Games.** Five games that can be used for relaxation. Included are FreeCell, Hearts, Minesweeper, Party Line, and Solitaire.
- **Jungle Sound Scheme.** A collection of related sounds that can be assigned to different system events.
- **Microsoft Exchange.** A communications management accessory that combines e-mail and fax capabilities.
- **Microsoft Fax.** The fax portion of Microsoft Exchange (which is required for this option to be installed).
- **Microsoft Network.** The tools necessary to connect with the new Microsoft Network.
- **Mouse Pointers.** A collection of animated and nonanimated pointers that can be assigned to different mouse activities.
- **Multi-Language Support.** The files necessary to implement the international features of Windows 95.
- **Musica Sound Scheme.** A collection of related sounds that can be assigned to different system events.
- **Mystify Your Mind Screen Saver.** A screen saver you can use to customize your desktop.

➤ **Nature Sound Scheme.** A collection of related sounds that can be assigned to different system events.

➤ **NetWatcher.** A system tool that allows you to monitor the performance of the network.

➤ **Online User's Guide.** Tutorial information on how to use Widows 95.

➤ **Robotz Sound Scheme.** A collection of related sounds that can be assigned to different system events.

➤ **Sound and Video Clips.** Sample audio and video multimedia files that can be used with the Media Player accessory.

➤ **System Monitor.** A system tool used to troubleshoot and refine the performance of Windows 95.

➤ **System Resource Meter.** A system tool used to monitor the use of your system resources.

➤ **Utopia Sound Scheme.** A collection of related sounds that can be assigned to different system events.

➤ **Wallpaper.** Various bitmapped graphics files that can be used to customize your desktop.

➤ **Windows 95 Tour.** A guided on-screen tour of the newest features of Windows 95. (Available only on the CD-ROM version of Windows 95.)

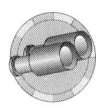

> **Note:** Windows 95 automatically installs four tools; there is no way to not install them. These tools are the Disk Defragmenter, DriveSpace, ScanDisk, and Notepad.

Remember, you can always add or remove options after Windows 95 is installed on your computer. For information on adding or removing options, refer to Appendix A, "Adding and Removing Windows 95 Components."

Choosing a Network Installation

There are countless network configurations and types that will ultimately challenge an upgrade to Windows 95. But, take heart—it's not as bad as it seems, particularly if you know what to expect and can plan in advance. Windows Setup is very flexible, whether you're installing on a network as small as two PCs or as large as 500 workstations. Each network environment requires a different approach to achieve a (relatively) quick, yet painless, installation.

Generally, there are two ways you can install Windows 95 on your network workstation:

- Connect to the network server and run Setup from a script (automated server-based setup).

- Perform a standard setup on individual workstations and connect manually to the network.

Method number one is the quickest and simplest route to pursue for networks with more than a few workstations, mainly because Setup can be automated with special INF batch (script) files. If you choose to install Windows 95 in this way, proceed to the following section, "Installing on a Client/Server Network."

The second method requires you to specify each setup option just as if you were installing on a stand-alone PC. The section "Performing a Standard Setup," later in this chapter, discusses how to perform a standard setup and afterward connect manually to the network.

Installing on a Client/Server Network

Installing Windows 95 on a client/server network is considerably different than a peer-to-peer network or standard setup. The latter two require you to run Setup from the PC and manually respond to the Setup prompts. In a client/server network, however, files must be copied in a special manner from the CD-ROM to the server's hard disk before installation can take place. This is mainly because, for some workstations, Windows 95 system files are shared either to save space on the workstation or to protect system integrity. Therefore, running Setup from the CD-ROM will not work.

Installation for a workstation can be handled from either the server or the client PC. Depending on the network configuration, an administrator can set up network workstations in a number of ways:

- Setup requires user response to all questions
- Setup is partially automated (minimal user interaction)
- Setup is completely automated (an unattended or *push* installation)

In any case, the administrator installs Windows 95 files on the server and then initiates the Setup command. This command can be issued from either the client workstation or from a special script created by the administrator. This type of arrangement gives the administrator complete control over how Windows 95 is installed. In addition, the ability to automate the setup procedure through scripts saves a great deal of time over installing Windows 95 on each PC one at a time.

To install Windows 95 on a workstation that is part of a client/server network, you must do the following:

- Run server-based Setup on the server.
- Define home folders for shared files, if necessary.
- Create batch scripts, if necessary.
- Run Setup from the workstation or through a batch script.

The next several sections explain each of these steps.

Running a Server-Based Setup

Before anything else can occur, the Windows 95 files must be copied to the server. Bear in mind that this does not, in itself, install Windows 95. Rather, it creates a location to which Setup (when run from a remote workstation) can look for the necessary installation files.

To give the administrator maximum flexibility and control, server-based Setup copies the files into a folder you specify. Within that folder, several folder hierarchies are constructed to mimic a real Windows 95 installation. This, in essence, serves as the installation files for the workstation. To copy Windows 95 files to the server, follow these steps:

1. Insert the Windows 95 CD-ROM in the CD-ROM drive that can be accessed from the server.

2. From the server, invoke the Run command. Windows NT users do this by choosing Run from the File menu. Windows 95 users select Run from the Start menu.

3. Click on Browse and change to the CD-ROM drive used in step 1. Navigate to the folder admin\nettools\netsetup and type **netsetup.** Click on OK.

4. The Server Based Setup dialog box appears, as shown in figure 4.10. Click on Set Path and provide a path on the server to which the Windows 95 files can be copied. Click on OK.

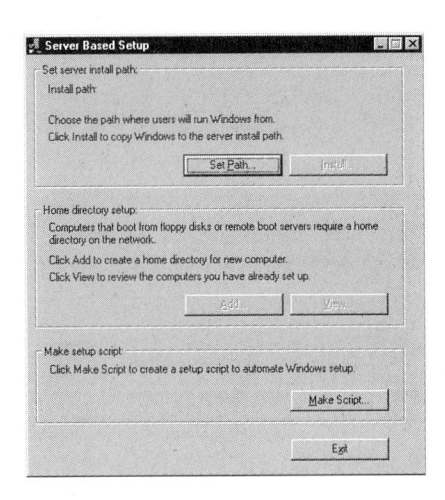

Fig. 4.10 Server-based Setup is the first step in performing a workstation installation.

Choosing a Network Installation **111**

5. Click on Install. This opens the Source Path dialog box (see figure 4.11) where you define *how* to copy the Windows 95 files to the path defined in step 4.

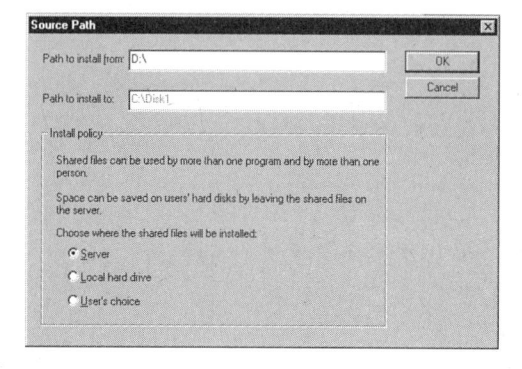

Fig. 4.11 Specify the source and destination of the Windows 95 files in this dialog box.

6. In the field labeled Path to install from, enter the drive letter assigned to the CD-ROM drive you used in step 1. For instance, you might use a location such as D:\ if the CD-ROM drive is drive D.

7. Specify the sharing properties of the files by selecting Server, Local hard drive, or User's choice. This determines how files are installed when a user runs Setup from the workstation. Keeping most files on the server saves space on the workstation, while installing the files on the workstation's local hard disk gives the user more flexibility. Click on OK to continue.

> **Tip:** If you have adequate hard disk resources on your workstations, you might want to always use the Local hard drive option. This cuts down on the amount of information that must be transferred over the network and results in faster response times at the local workstation.

112 Chapter 4: Installing Windows 95

8. To create an MSBATCH.INF batch script for you, click on Create Default to invoke the Policy Editor dialog box. Refer to the section "Creating a Batch Script" (later in this chapter) to learn to use the Policy Editor to create a batch script. If you select Don't Create Default, this dialog box does not appear and a script is not created.

If you choose Don't Create Default, server-based Setup begins copying the Windows 95 files to the folder you specified. Once these are copied, you can then perform the installation process for the workstation. However, if you set up any workstations to use shared files, such as when you keep most Windows 95 system files on the server, you must define the home folders that will be used by Windows after it is set up on the workstation.

Defining Home Directories for Shared Files

Once the Windows 95 files are copied to your computer via server-based Setup, you can define specific folders. As you learned earlier, an administrator can install Windows 95 on a workstation but retain most of the system files on the server in "shared" folders. Ultimately, the user really can't tell, yet the administrator can exercise firm control over the network.

To assign a home folder, click on Add in the Server Based Setup dialog box. In the Set Up Machine dialog box (see figure 4.12), you have a choice between defining a single workstation or many workstations. To set up a single machine, choose Setup one machine and enter the computer's name as you might see it on the network, then insert the UNC (Universal Naming Convention) of the path to be used as the computer's home folder.

To save time, the administrator can define a large number of machines at one time by creating a file that contains a list of machines to be processed. The file is a text file, created with a program such as Notepad. Each line in the file describes a single computer system, with the computer name separated from the UNC path for the computer's home folder, in this manner:

```
Marty's 486, \\OfficeServer\C\Marty
```

To indicate that Setup should use this file, choose Setup multiple machines and provide the name of the text file you just created. When you're finished specifying either a single machine or a text file, click on OK.

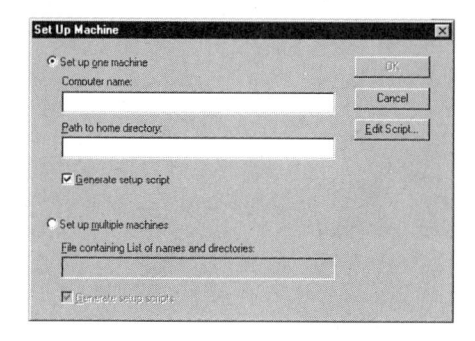

Fig. 4.12 The Home Directory Setup area becomes accessible after you copy Windows files to the server.

Creating a Batch Script

Installing Windows 95 on many computers throughout a network would be a nightmare without the ability to automate the process. A batch script allows you to specify in advance what responses Windows Setup will accept. This way you can invoke Setup on a workstation and effectively walk away from it—a big time-saver.

As Setup begins, it looks for a default batch script called MSBATCH.INF. However, you can specify any batch file you want as a setup parameter. For example, if you create a unique script for three workstations in a particular office, you would type the following at the command line prompt, or in the Run dialog box (accessed from the Start menu):

```
setup msbatch.inf.
```

If a script is differently named, such as station1.inf, provide that in place of MSBATCH.INF. Setup then executes the instructions in the batch script.

What is a batch script? A script is a plain text file consisting of nothing more than predefined responses to the questions asked by Setup. These responses are grouped in sections, similar to what you might find in the old Windows INI files. Individual parameters are followed by a specific value or description depending on the parameter type. For instance, the following are a few lines from a sample batch script:

```
[Setup]
Express=0                       ; allows user input
InstallType=1                   ; Typical Setup
EBD=1                           ; create startup disk
InstallDir=C:\WINDOWS
Verify=0
Detection=1
PenWinWarning=1
ProductID=999999999

[NameAndOrg]
Name="Martin R. Wyatt"
Org="Discovery Computing Inc."
Display=1           ; Display User Information dialog box

[OptionalComponents]
"Accessories"=1
"Communications"=1
"Disk Tools"=1
"Multimedia"=1
"Screen Savers"=1
"Disk compression tools"=1
"Paint"=1
```

In step 7 of the section "Running Server-Based Setup," you learned that clicking Create Default invokes the Policy Editor. Although you aren't really editing a policy (POL) file, you use the same interface to make script creation quick and simple. As you can see in figure 4.13, you specify which items you want included in the batch script by double-clicking on a section, such as Setup options, and choosing which parameters should be automated. When you enable a parameter, you must specify a value in the Settings for Automated Install near the bottom of the editing window. When you're finished, click on OK. This saves the batch script as msbatch.inf—the default batch script Setup expects when you run Setup from a workstation. You can later rename and edit this script file by using a program such as Notepad.

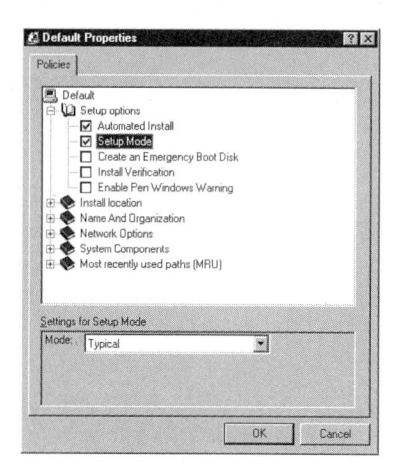

Fig. 4.13 Creating a batch script is as easy as clicking on options.

Granted, this isn't the only way you can create a script, but it's a good way to create your first one. This way, you can choose from all available elements to ensure that the script is complete with correct parameters and corresponding values. Later, you can create scripts with a simple text editor, such as Notepad, or you can modify existing scripts to suit a particular installation. Once the script is completed, you can begin the workstation setup.

Running Setup from a Workstation

Once you've completed the NetSetup installation of Windows 95 files on the server, you're prepared to run Setup. To do so, follow these steps:

1. At the workstation, log on to the network and connect to the server

2. Select the shared folder that contains the Windows 95 setup files.

3. From the command prompt type **setup**. If you're using a batch script you must instead type **setup msbatch.inf**, where msbatch.inf is the name of the script you previously created.

If the setup uses a batch script you created, Windows 95 will install with those parameters. Depending on the script's options, you may be required to respond to various questions Setup throws at you.

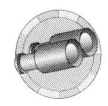

> **Note:** If a script named msbatch.inf exists, Setup will use it by default unless you specify the script to use.

Running Setup from the Server

Instead of formally running Setup from the workstation, the administrator can customize the batch scripts to automatically install Windows 95 on any number of remote workstations. Typically, this is beneficial if you're upgrading a large number of workstations, such as 50 or more. Of course, this can't occur magically during the night when the workstations are turned off or disconnected from the network. In actuality, this automated installation is automatic for the administrator, and depending on the batch script, is mostly automatic for the user.

For instance, the administrator may create a special logon script that triggers the setup script when the user logs on to the network. Therefore, the following circumstances must occur before an automated, or *push*, installation will work:

➤ The workstation must be on and connected to the network

➤ A setup script must exist for that workstation

➤ A logon script must also exist for that workstation

The logon script itself varies according to the network in place and the permissions and resources available to the user. For example, to upgrade Windows for Workgroups, you must create an empty, one-time Startup group with the Setup command as an icon inside it, then copy that STARTUP.GRP to the shared folder that the workstation accesses. Follow these steps to perform this procedure:

1. Modify the MSBATCH.INF file to ensure a one-time upgrade by adding the following sections to the file:

   ```
   [install]
   renfiles=replace.startup.grp

   [replace.startup.grp]
   startup.grp, startup.sav

   [destinationdirs]
   replace.startup.grp=10
   ```

2. Create an empty Startup group and place a new icon inside it that runs Setup off the server. In the Command Line field for Setup, enter the SETUP command that is valid for the workstation, followed by the batch script, if any. The following is an example:

   ```
   E:\SETUP E:\msbatch.inf.
   ```

3. Place the STARTUP.GRP file you just created in the shared folder on the server used by the workstation for the current version of Windows. Thus, if the workstation is running Windows for Workgroups and accesses a shared folder on the server, that is the folder in which the special Startup group file would be placed.

4. Delete the Startup group file from your computer after copying it to the server.

Now, when the user logs in to Windows for Workgroups, the new, special Startup group icon is opened and the Setup program is executed. When Setup is processing the commands in MSBATCH.INF, the sections you added will modify the Startup section of Windows 95 so that the Setup program is not run again.

Using Novell NetWare Servers

You learned in previous sections of this chapter how to place Windows 95's files on a server so that you can in turn install or run Windows 95 from that server. Because the networks in many companies include file servers that run Novell NetWare, you will likely not be placing your Windows 95 files on a file server running Novell NetWare. This section details the steps you follow to prepare to place Windows 95's files on a

Novell NetWare server. You also learn how to enable a Windows 95 workstation to log in to a NetWare server and how to assign drive letters to NetWare disk volumes.

When you prepare to place Windows 95's files on a server, you have to perform several preparatory steps:

➤ Create the folder or folders that will store the Windows 95 files

➤ Grant appropriate NetWare rights to the users who need to access those files

➤ Optionally use NetWare login scripts to automatically assign drive letters to the server-based Windows 95 folders

You learn about these steps in the following sections.

Limitations with a NetWare Server

Earlier in this chapter, you read about the benefits and liabilities of using Windows 95 from a server. When you share Windows 95's program files from a Novell NetWare server, there is another limitation to consider. Running Windows 95 from a server limits your choices for network card drivers and network clients.

What is the reason for this limitation? The situation is not unlike the age-old question: "Which came first, the chicken or the egg?" Because you have to log in to your server before starting Windows 95's graphical interface, you cannot use Windows 95's built-in 32-bit virtual network card drivers or clients. You must instead use DOS-compatible network card drivers and client software. If you're running Windows 95 from a Novell NetWare server, you'd typically need to load NetWare's ODI drivers and requester software in your workstation's AUTOEXEC.BAT file. You learn how to modify this file later in this section.

Creating Directories on a NetWare Server

Creating a folder on a NetWare server is just like creating a folder on a local hard disk, except that you have to log in to the server first and you also have to have sufficient rights to create the folder. Once you've logged in to the appropriate server and you've located the disk volume on which you wish to create the folder, you can use your favorite method to create the folder. With Windows 95, for example, you can use the Windows Explorer to create a folder by choosing File New Folder from the menu. With Windows 3.1*x*, you can use the File Manager's File Create Directory menu option, or, if you choose to be quaintly traditional, you can use the MD command from the DOS prompt.

Setting the Appropriate Access Levels

Once the required folders are created, you need to grant the appropriate rights, a step that requires a little forethought. If you're setting access levels for a Windows 95 installation folder, you probably want to limit to a chosen few the ability to add, delete, or modify the files in that folder. Users who will be installing Windows 95 from the folder should have the ability to use the files but not change them in any way.

The same sort of access applies for the folder from which users run a shared copy of Windows 95. Most users should have read-only access to the shared Windows 95 files, while the trusted few who are responsible for updating and maintaining the shared files should have the ability to make changes.

In those cases where users share a server-based copy of Windows 95 and also use server-based home folders to store their personal Windows configuration files, you also have to decide what access levels to provide for these home folders. In this situation, each user has a personal home folder, and should have full access to the files in that home folder.

The following table shows the NetWare rights that provide the access levels appropriate for the types of Windows 95 folders that you can create on a server.

Table 4.2 Netware Access Rights Guidelines

Directory Type	NetWare Rights to Grant for Normal Users	NetWare Rights to Grant for Users Who Manage the Folder
Shared installation files	READ, FILE SCAN	READ, WRITE, CREATE DELETE, MODIFY, FILE SCAN
Shared copy of Windows 95	READ, FILE SCAN	READ, WRITE, CREATE DELETE, MODIFY, FILE SCAN
Home folder for personal configuration files	READ, WRITE, CREATE, DELETE, MODIFY, FILE SCAN for personal home folder	READ, WRITE, CREATE DELETE, MODIFY, FILE SCAN for all home folders

Assigning Drive Letters Using Login Scripts

If you're going to provide the Windows 95 installation files on a server so that users can install Windows 95 from the network, you can make the installation process more convenient by automatically assigning a drive letter to the Windows 95 installation folder for users as they log in. You encounter a similar situation when the users on your network use a shared server-based copy of Windows 95. Those users need to have a drive letter assigned to the shared Windows 95 folder before they can run Windows 95. With Novell NetWare, you can use login scripts to create drive letters automatically at login time.

Providing a Drive Letter for the Installation Directory

You can include the following command in the server's system login script to automatically assign drive J to a Windows 95 installation folder called WIN95INS on the SYS disk volume of a server named SERV1:

```
MAP J:=SERV1/SYS:WIN95INS
```

When you place this command in the system login script (if you're using NetWare 3.*x* servers) in each user's container login script (if you're using NetWare 4.*x*), drive J is automatically assigned to the WIN95INS folder for each user at login time.

If you want to add a touch of elegance, you can also display a notice for each user that describes how to start the Windows 95 installation process. If you want to display the following login notice:

```
Windows 95 is now available for installation from the
network. Run the SETUP command from drive J to install
Windows 95 on your PC.
include these additional commands in the system login script:
WRITE "Windows 95 is now available for installation from the"
WRITE "network. Run the SETUP command from drive J to install"
WRITE "Windows 95 on your PC."

PAUSE
```

(see your NetWare reference manuals for information about creating and editing login scripts.)

Providing a Drive Letter for a Shared Copy of Windows 95

You can use similar techniques to create the proper drive letter assignments for users who need to share a copy of Windows 95. Each user who runs Windows 95 from a NetWare server must have a drive letter assigned to the folder that stores the Windows 95 program files. That drive letter also must be a *search drive*, which means that the files in the folder assigned to the drive letter are part of the PC's search path. (You can run an executable file in a search path folder even though the folder is not your current default folder.)

Place the following command in your login script to make the WIN95SH folder the first drive in your PC's search path:

```
MAP INS S1:=SERV1/SYS:WIN95SH
```

Notice that you follow the MAP command by INS (which stands for INSERT and means that the drive letter is added to the current list of search drives) and S1 (*s* stands for SEARCH and *1* indicates that you want the folder to be placed first in the search order—set this to any number from 1 to 16 to specify the place in the search order).

For complete details about assigning drive letters in login scripts, refer to your NetWare documentation.

Connecting to the Server

If you're running Windows 95 from a NetWare server, you must be sure that your PC's AUTOEXEC.BAT file connects you to the server before you start Windows 95's graphical interface. The following extract from a typical AUTOEXEC.BAT file shows the commands you use to load NetWare's ODI drivers and VLM requester and to then log in to the server:

```
;load ODI drivers
LSL
NE2000
IPXODI
;load VLM requester
VLM
;execute LOGIN command
F:
LOGIN
```

(See your NetWare documentation for complete details about using the ODI network card drivers, the VLM requester, and the LOGIN command.)

After You Install

Once you complete your Windows 95 installation, and if you have the CD-ROM version of Windows 95, be sure to take the Windows Tour. (This assumes, of course, that you selected an installation option in which the Windows Tour was installed.) It takes only a couple of minutes and introduces you to the new concepts you'll encounter by using this operating system.

In addition, you should run the ScanDisk utility to verify that all the files on your hard disk are intact. This also protects against any potential disk problems that might crop up. To start ScanDisk, follow these steps:

1. Select the Programs option from the Start menu.
2. Choose Accessories from the Programs menu.
3. Choose System Tools from the Accessories menu.
4. Choose ScanDisk from the System Tools menu.

When the program starts, choose the hard disk you want to scan and click on Start. For more information on using ScanDisk, refer to Chapter 10, "Optimizing Your Disk Drives."

Installation Problems

A nice feature of the Windows 95 Setup is that if something interrupts the installation, such as the power goes out, the hardware detection phase fails, or you intentionally cancel Setup, you can run Setup again and pick up where you left off. Setup calls it *Safe Recovery*.

In the event that you encounter a problem during installation, the Safe Recovery mode of setup is invoked the next time you attempt installation (see figure 4.14). When this appears, choose Use Safe Recovery and click Next. Setup proceeds as if nothing had happened. This is possible because Setup maintains special files during the setup process to guard against such events.

Additional information on how to overcome installation problems is covered in Chapter 6, "Troubleshooting Windows 95 Installation and Startup."

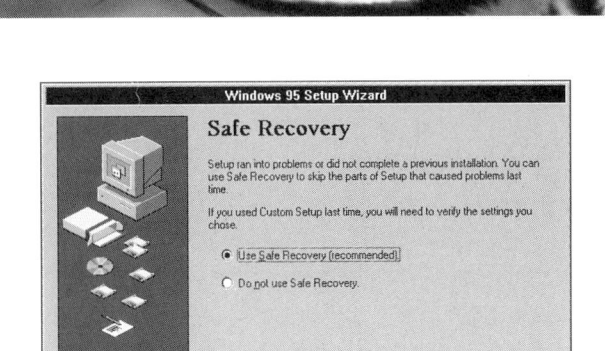

Fig. 4.14 Safe Recovery lets you salvage an aborted installation.

Using the Emergency Startup Disk

When you install Windows 95, you have the option to create a startup disk. This disk is nothing more than a Windows 95 boot disk with the basic system files and other programs such as the Registry Editor, disk utilities, and other useful files. Should your computer ever get corrupted and not boot properly, Windows 95 advises you and starts in a special "safe" mode. It is rare that you would need the startup disk, but it's available just in case of catastrophe.

For more information on the different Windows 95 startup modes and how you can troubleshoot a maligned system, refer to Chapter 6, "Troubleshooting Windows 95 Installation and Startup."

Changing Your Windows Configuration

If you've ever accidentally deleted an important system file in a previous version of Windows, you typically had one solution—reinstall Windows. Of course, if you knew the exact name of the file you deleted, you could copy it from the distribution disks and use the EXPAND command to decompress it, but that required knowing its compressed name and its location on your system.

Installation Problems **125**

Fortunately, Windows 95 resolves this dilemma. There is no real need to reinstall Windows 95 (unless you delete a substantial portion of the system files). System components can be reinstalled by doing the following:

1. Double-click on the Add/Remove Programs applet in the Control Panel.
2. Choose the Windows Setup tab.
3. Highlight and select any or all components and options you want to reinstall (or remove).
4. Click on OK.

Once you click on OK, Windows prompts you to shut down the computer. Confirm this action and Windows 95 will shut down and launch as normal. Additional information on adding and removing components is found in Appendix A, "Adding and Removing Windows 95 Components."

Installing Windows 95 on a Laptop

by Allen L. Wyatt

More and more, people on the road are using portable computers, particularly since they pack the same punch and carry the same load as a desktop computer. However, there are distinct differences between the two, which are mainly due to the compromises in technology made to optimize space.

As Windows 95 has evolved, the needs of the portable computer user have been kept in mind. Similar to its ability to easily adapt to the office computer user, Windows 95 makes portable computing painless. It has built-in features that integrate it with a remote network (if applicable) and accepts common features found on most laptops, notebooks, and subnotebook computers today.

Since networking is integral to the operating system itself, Windows 95 includes features that allow a portable computer user to dial into a remote network. Information can then be transferred to the portable (and vice versa), so that the user can stay in touch. Other improvements, such as deferred printing, file synchronization, and hot docking support, make Windows 95 a truly productive operating system for anybody on the road.

In addition to learning how to install Windows 95 on a portable computer, this chapter discusses the following topics:

- What to do before and after installation
- What setup type you should choose
- How to upgrade from a previous version of Windows
- Configuring your system for dual-booting between Windows 3.X and Windows 95
- Special Windows 95 features that are unique to portable computers

What Is a Portable Computer?

A portable computer is any unit designed to be easily moved from place to place and is primarily used by people on the go. The size and weight of portable computers vary, and their names are determined by their physical dimensions: subnotebooks are smallest, notebooks a bit larger, laptops larger still, and "luggables" are the largest.

Although it may act like a desktop computer, the portable differs from other systems simply because of size limitations. Manufacturers have incorporated proprietary designs and features into their units and, depending on the model you use, each portable may react differently with Windows 95. The system of a portable computer that is going to run Windows 95 should consist of the following components:

- 386-, 486-, or Pentium-based computer
- 170M or larger hard disk
- 4M RAM

➤ Dual-scan monochrome or color display

➤ PCMCIA port or internal modem

If you haven't already browsed through Chapter 8, "Examining the Hardware You Need for Windows 95," you may want to do that now. As computer technology advances, so do the minimum system requirements. The now modest 386 running at 33 MHz was, just a few years ago, the portable user's dream machine. As of this writing, the Pentium has taken a stronghold with CPU speeds of up to 133 MHz in desktop units and up to 90 MHz in portables. If the trend continues, in two years the Pentium will be yesterday's news.

System Requirements to Install Windows 95

According to product information, Windows 95 requires a minimum of a 386 processor with 4M of RAM and a 30M hard disk. This minimum will work, but programs (and Windows) will run very slowly. For a truly productive machine, you are better off with a system that has more resources (disk and memory) and a faster CPU. That is why the definition of a portable system in the previous section reflects higher requirements than the Windows 95 minimum system requirements.

For your system, you're better off with 8M or 16M of RAM and as big a hard disk as possible. (Even an 850M hard drive can be advantageous for the portable computer user.) The cost of disk drives has dropped to the point where you can specify huge drives at previously unheard of prices. In addition, a CD-ROM is a big plus for installing Windows 95—even on a portable.

Windows 95 readily supports PCMCIA cards, which are a feature in most portable computers. However, some older PCMCIA implementations may not be supported and may instantly become obsolete. (The newer, faster 32-bit elements in Windows 95 make this a possibility.) If you find yourself in this boat, you may want to see if you can either upgrade your system or find Windows 95 PCMCIA support from a third-party source, such as the manufacturer of your system.

Before You Install

Before you install Windows 95 on your portable computer, consider how you will use it to be most productive. Will the computer be networked with one or more Windows 95 computers? Do you want to share information while on the road? How and when will a printer be connected? Whatever your plan, Windows 95 is quite flexible in how it is implemented and is tolerant of any last-minute changes, such as inserting a PCMCIA modem or network card. But it is wise to plan in advance to save yourself from running around later.

In order to make your upgrade to Windows 95 as painless as possible, you will want to perform a few tasks before you even think of running the Setup program. These tasks are:

- ➤ Check your media
- ➤ Defragment your hard drive
- ➤ Back up your system
- ➤ Disable your swap file
- ➤ Check your disk compression
- ➤ Disable your current programs

The following sections describe the reason for each task, and some sections describe how to perform the task.

Checking Your Media

Windows 95 is available either on floppy disk or on CD-ROM. If you have a CD-ROM drive available for your system, it is a nice luxury to be able to install from CD-ROM. By doing so, you eliminate the need to swap about 20 disks during the course of an hour.

Defragmenting Your Hard Disk

It is always wise to periodically defragment your hard drive, but this becomes even more of a good idea as you are preparing to upgrade your system. A defragmented disk helps ensure that the installation process goes smoothly. With fragmented files, installation could take longer simply because it takes longer to read files that are scattered all over the disk. Besides, if the files on your hard disk are highly fragmented, Windows 95 will refuse to install until you remedy the situation.

If you have MS-DOS (or PC DOS) version 6.0 or later, you can use the defrag utility included with your operating system to defragment your hard disk. If you prefer, you can turn to any one of several third-party programs on the market, such as Symantec's The Norton Utilities or PC Tools from Central Point Software.

Backing Up Your System

As you install Windows 95, you are making a major upgrade to operating your system. This means that a new system is reorganizing your existing system and overwriting previously important files. Some files are deleted and many new ones are added. It is in your best interests to perform a backup of your entire system. If you don't, you'll risk losing some information if something goes wrong with the installation process. It is rare to lose data during a Windows 95 installation, but "better safe than sorry."

If you don't want to back up everything, you should at least copy important files to a floppy disk, including:

- ➤ CONFIG.SYS
- ➤ AUTOEXEC.BAT
- ➤ Data files, such as word processing or spreadsheet documents

Once the files are copied to a disk, make sure you verify that the copy was accurate and that the disk can be read by another machine.

Disabling Your Swap File

If you are upgrading to Windows 95 and not using the dual-boot feature, you should disable the permanent swap file used by your current version of Windows. If you're an avid Windows user, you may already be familiar with the term swap file. This is a special file created on your hard disk that serves as a memory overflow area. When a program needs more memory than is currently available, information is stored in the swap file on your hard disk until the information is needed. In many ways, the hard disk serves as an extension of the RAM in your system. (With this understanding, you can envision how less RAM can slow down your system by requiring more swap-file activity.)

Windows 95 does not use the same permanent swap-file technology as Windows 3.x. As you learned in Chapter 2, "Under-the-Hood Improvements," the virtual memory manager within Windows 95 (which manages the swap file) has been rewritten entirely. It now uses more dynamic management, which means the size of the swap file is adjusted, as necessary, to fit the needs of the operating system. Since a new swap file is used, any old swap file just sits on your hard disk and wastes space.

To disable your permanent swap file in your current version of Windows, follow these steps:

1. Double-click on the Control Panel icon in the Main program group. The Control Panel appears.

2. Double-click on the Enhanced icon in the Control Panel. The Enhanced dialog box appears.

3. Click on the Virtual Memory button in the Enhanced dialog box. The Virtual Memory dialog box appears.

4. Examine the Swap File Settings area of the Virtual Memory dialog box. If the Type field shows Permanent, click on the Change button. Otherwise, click Cancel and exit all dialog boxes. A permanent swap file is not present.

5. In the New Swap File Settings area, choose None from the Type list box.

6. Click on OK to close the Virtual Memory dialog box.

7. When asked to confirm your change, click on the Yes button.

At this point, you'll need to restart Windows. When this has been done, your permanent swap file is disabled and deleted.

Checking Your Disk Compression

If you use disk compression software—as many portable owners do—you'll want to make sure it is compatible with Windows 95. The following disk compression utilities are compatible with Windows 95 and are fully supported:

➤ Microsoft DriveSpace

➤ Microsoft DoubleSpace

➤ Stac Electronics Stacker versions 3.0 and 4.x

➤ SuperStor

Although Windows 95 recognizes several compression utilities, it includes some built-in utilities that are specifically designed to work with Microsoft DriveSpace. For example, the defragmenting and scanning utilities included with Windows 95 have been tuned specifically to work with DriveSpace. If you use a different compression program, you may not be able to take advantage of Windows' built-in utilities.

The best time to consider switching from the compression program you are now using to DriveSpace is when you upgrade to Windows 95. If you decide it makes sense for you to switch, then you will need to decompress your drives prior to installing Windows 95. Consult your utility's documentation to learn how to best decompress your files.

Once you have installed Windows 95, you can use DriveSpace to compress your hard drives. Full information on how to do this is contained in Chapter 10, "Optimizing Your Disk Drives."

Disabling Programs

Earlier versions of DOS relied quite heavily on TSR (terminate and stay resident) programs to add features to the operating system. Before installing Windows 95, be sure to disable any TSRs you have installed; these can conflict with the setup process. Examples of common TSR programs are those that aid in power management, the bill minder program in Quicken, and some device drivers, such as MOUSE.COM.

If you plan to install Windows 95 from within your current version of Windows, be sure to close all open windows except for the Program Manager. Open program windows can slow down the installation process, and may stop necessary files from being copied to the hard disk.

Dual-Booting

Many people who are upgrading to Windows 95 want to set up their systems so they can boot with different operating systems. For example, a user might want the ability to use both OS/2 and Windows 95 at different times. With most portable systems, you will probably want to stay away from dual-booting. Such installations are inherently more complex, and they can occupy more of your precious disk space (with files for both operating systems).

There is, however, one type of dual-booting that should be addressed. You may still want to be able to boot with your old version of DOS as well as with Windows 95. Why? You will need this capability if you want to use an older version of Windows on your system.

You should understand that the preferred method of installing Windows 95 is simply to upgrade your old version of Windows to Windows 95. This ensures that all of your settings, applications, and preferences are retained by Windows 95. However, if you're determined to maintain a previous version of Windows on your computer in addition to Windows 95, you can instruct Setup to install Windows 95 in a separate folder instead of overwriting the previous version of Windows.

Ultimately, dual-booting enables you to press F4 when you start your computer and choose between booting with Windows 95 and MS-DOS. If you choose DOS, you can use your computer as you always have. Some people view this arrangement as "the best of both worlds." The drawback of dual-booting is that none of your existing Windows 3.1 settings and applications migrate to Windows 95.

The following questions can help you make a decision for your company as to whether dual-booting is to be implemented:

- Do you need the capability to run both Windows 3.1 and Windows 95 (dual-boot)? If the answer is yes, then you should install Windows 95 in a folder other than C:\WINDOWS. If the answer is no, then you can allow Setup to install to the default folder and upgrade Windows 3.1 to Windows 95.

- Do you want Windows 95 to have the same settings and applications used in previous versions of Windows? If the answer is yes, then allow Setup to install to the default folder and upgrade Windows 3.1 to Windows 95. If the answer is no, then install Windows 95 in a folder other than C:\WINDOWS.

- Do you want to be able to load MS-DOS as well as Windows 95? If the answer is yes, then install Windows 95 in a folder other than C:\WINDOWS. If the answer is no, then allow Setup to install to the default folder and upgrade Windows 3.1 to Windows 95.

Installing Windows 95

The setup process for Windows 95 is simpler and more automatic than it was for any previous version of Windows. You only need to answer a few questions, then sit back and relax. Setup presents a wizard to guide you through the steps of installing Windows 95. When prompted, click the appropriate buttons, typically either Continue or Next.

As a general rule, if you have Windows 3.1 or Windows for Workgroups 3.11 already installed on your system, you should install from within Windows. If you do not have Windows or if you have Windows 3.0 or earlier, you must install from MS-DOS.

Starting Setup from MS-DOS

If your computer doesn't have Windows 3.1x installed, you can install Windows 95 from DOS without any problem. Follow these steps to install from DOS:

1. If you are installing from CD-ROM, insert the disc into your CD-ROM drive. If you are installing from floppies, insert the first disk into your disk drive.

2. At the DOS prompt, type **d:\SETUP** and press Enter. (You should replace the letter *d* with the drive letter that represents the drive you used in step 1.) You will see the following on your screen:

   ```
   Please wait while Setup initializes.

   Setup is now going to perform a routine check on your system.

   To continue, press Enter. To quit Setup, press Esc.
   ```

3. Press Enter to continue with the setup. The program then runs ScanDisk to check the integrity of your disk drives.

4. When ScanDisk is complete, press X to exit from the program.

At this point, a couple of files are copied onto your hard drive in preparation for the rest of the setup procedure. Shortly, you will see the welcome screen as shown in figure 5.1. From this point forward, the setup is identical for DOS users as it is for Windows users. Proceed to step five in the next section to continue with the Windows 95 installation.

Starting Setup from Windows

During the installation phase, Setup detects whether you already have Windows installed and, if so, remembers its location. Setup later informs you where it was found. All existing Windows settings will transfer to Windows 95 once the installation is complete. If you have a Windows-based network in place before installation, all the settings will convert without incident.

To install Windows 95 from Windows 3.1 or Windows for Workgroups 3.1x, follow these steps:

1. If you are installing from CD-ROM, insert the disc in your CD-ROM drive. If you are installing from floppies, insert the first disk in your disk drive.

2. Choose File, Run from Program Manager (not File Manager). The Run dialog box appears.

3. Enter **d:\SETUP** in the Command Line text box, and click OK. (You should replace the letter *d* with the drive letter that represents the drive you used in step 1.) In a moment, you see the Windows 95 Setup welcome screen (see figure 5.1). Click Continue.

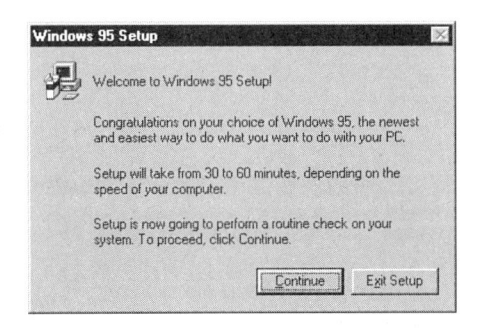

Fig. 5.1 Welcome to Windows 95 Setup.

4. Setup performs a behind-the-scenes ScanDisk procedure. When it is finished, click Continue. After you do, various files are copied to your hard disk in preparation for the Setup Wizard.

5. When you see the software license agreement, read it, then click Yes.

6. When you see the Setup Wizard shown in figure 5.2, you can see the number of steps required to complete the setup and what will occur. Click Next.

7. As shown in figure 5.3, you now have the opportunity to specify where Windows 95 will be installed. If you currently have Windows installed and you want to update, you should accept the indicated folder. If you want Windows 95 installed in a different folder for whatever reason (that is, to have dual-booting capability), you should click on Other folder. When you have made your choice, click on the Next button.

Fig. 5.2 The Setup Wizard outlines what will occur during setup.

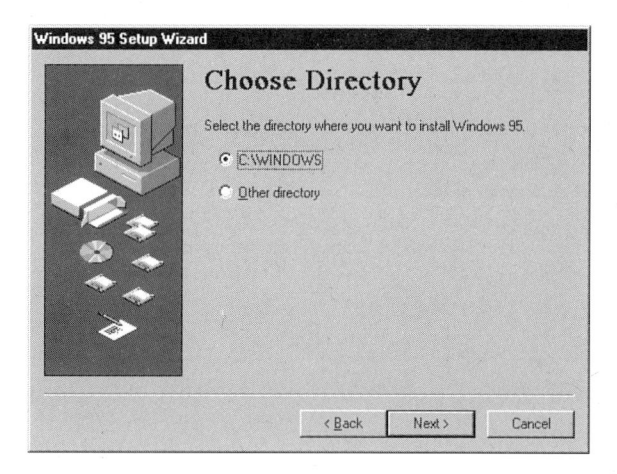

Fig. 5.3 Choose a folder where you want to install Windows 95.

8. If you indicated that you wanted Windows 95 installed in a different folder, you are asked to specify the folder. Pick a folder and click on the Next button.

9. When the Setup Options screen appears (see figure 5.4), choose a setup type. Most portable computer users should choose Portable. For most office installations, you will choose Typical. However, you may want to choose Complete, and tailor the

installation. A full discussion of each setup type (along with system suggestions) is found later in this chapter in the section entitled "Choosing a Setup Type." Make your selection and click on Next.

Fig. 5.4 You can select from among four setup types.

10. Enter your name in the User Information screen. Optionally, you may also type the name of your company or organization. Click Next.

11. You will next see the Analyzing Your Computer screen as shown in figure 5.5. If any of the devices listed are present in your system and if the devices are not Plug-and-Play compatible, then choose them and click Next.

12. Setup now performs a complete hardware analysis, which may take up to five minutes (depending on the speed of your system).

13. After a time, you will see the Windows Components screen. Here you have two choices: you can accept the most common components for your type of installation (the recommended default), or you can indicate that you want to modify the components installed. Make your selection and click on Next.

14. If you chose to modify the components installed, you will see the Select Components screen as shown in figure 5.6. If you asked Windows to install the most common components, skip to step 16.

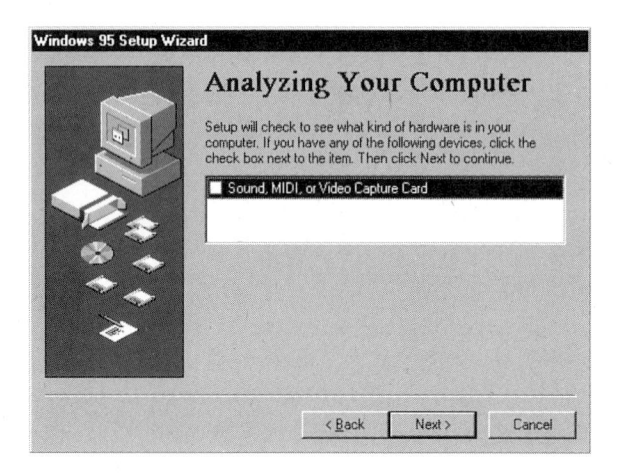

Fig. 5.5 The Analyzing Your Computer screen is used to specify the hardware components that are present in your system.

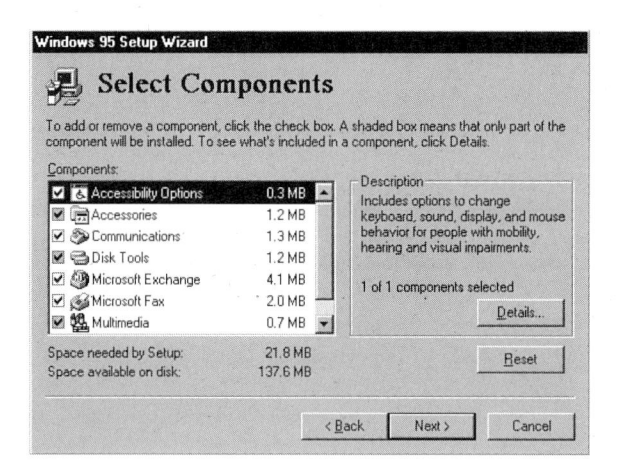

Fig. 5.6 Choose the options you want to install. Grayed entries indicate some components are selected.

15. Select the options you want installed with Windows 95. If you want more options than are normally available in your setup type, you can pick from this list. Highlight a category and click Details to choose individual items. To select all items in a component category, highlight it and press the spacebar. Click Next when you are finished.

16. If your system is not 100 percent Plug-and-Play compatible, Setup may not be able to detect each item by name. Consequently, you may see the Computer Settings screen, which you can safely ignore by clicking Next. If you want Windows 95 settings to be a little more precise, scroll through the list and change any items that are marked Unknown to their proper settings. To do so, highlight the item and click Change. Click Next when you are finished.

17. Setup next asks if you want a startup disk. Choose Yes (the default) and click Next. This disk serves as your bootable floppy in case of future system trouble. You may never need it, but it is a good precaution to create one. For information on how to use this disk, refer to the section "Using the Emergency Startup Disk," later in this chapter.

18. The Setup Wizard displays the second phase of installation—the copying of files. Click Next.

19. If you chose to create a startup disk, Setup prompts you to insert a disk and click OK. When Windows 95 has completed the disk, remove the floppy, label it clearly, put it in a safe place, and click OK to continue.

20. Setup then copies the Windows 95 files to your computer; this step takes about 10 minutes. Click Finish when prompted (see figure 5.7). When you do, the computer restarts and continues to configure Windows 95.

21. After several minutes of self-configuration, Setup requests your time zone (see figure 5.8). Click on the map to choose the appropriate time zone (or choose from the Time Zone pull-down list), and indicate whether or not you want to adjust for daylight savings time. Click Next.

22. If you chose to install the communications options, including Microsoft Exchange and Microsoft Fax, the Microsoft Exchange Setup Wizard intervenes and requests information. For information on setting up Microsoft Exchange and its components, refer to Chapter 32, "Communicating with a Modem."

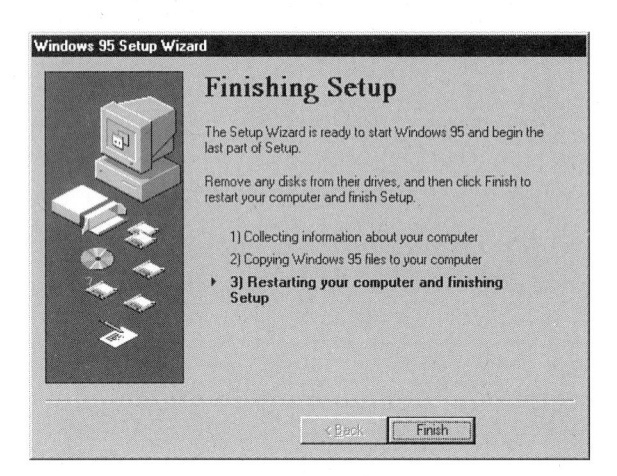

Fig. 5.7 After copying files, Setup is ready to restart your computer.

That's it! You have successfully installed Windows 95. The Welcome to Windows 95 dialog box shown in figure 5.8 lets you see what's new in Windows 95. For a quick tour, choose Windows Tour. (The Windows Tour button is available only if you installed from the CD-ROM and chose to explicitly install the feature.) Click What's New to find out about the innovations and changes in the Windows interface. Online Registration enables you to dial into Microsoft to register your copy of Windows 95. When you are finished, click Close.

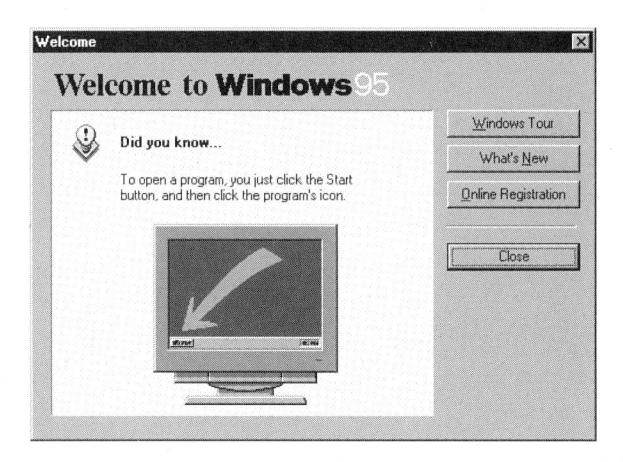

Fig. 5.8 Immediately after you install Windows 95, you see the Welcome dialog box. Choose an option and investigate.

Note: You are not limited to registering Windows 95 with a modem. You can mail the registration card provided with your Windows 95 software package.

Choosing a Setup Type

In the previous two sections, you learned how to install Windows 95 from start to finish. When performing step nine, you learned that the Setup Wizard allows you to indicate what type of installation you want, depending on the type of computer you have and its available resources, including hard disk space (or lack of it). Windows 95 offers four distinct setup types: typical, portable, compact, and custom.

Different setup choices require different system resources. The most conservative choice is compact, then portable, then typical, and finally custom. The biggest difference among the options is the number of tools (programs) that are installed. The following is a quick overview of each installation type:

➤ Typical Setup. This setup type is the most common installation selection, particularly for users who have at least 100M of unused hard disk space. The only decisions you must make are to confirm the folder where Windows 95 files are to be installed and whether to create a startup disk.

➤ Portable Setup. The options installed with this setup type are geared toward a mobile computer user. Basically, fewer of the "bells and whistles" that accompany a typical setup are installed, and features that enhance portable computing are added. If you have tons of available disk space and you want all the really cool features that a full Windows 95 installation has to offer, then you can safely choose Typical or Custom setup.

➤ Compact Setup. This setup type installs the bare essentials—only those files necessary to run Windows 95. A minimal installation that is ideal for those users with small hard disks (less than 80M), compact setup allows you to forego most of the Windows 95 options and may ultimately save about 36M of disk space.

➤ Custom Setup. This setup type lets you choose any or all options available in Windows 95, and thus is often appropriate in many office situations. It is similar to walking through a delicatessen: you simply pick the pieces and parts you want included in your Windows 95 system. This type of setup is recommended for experienced users who want to control the various elements of Windows 95 Setup.

The files installed on your hard drive will vary, depending on the type of setup you choose. Table 5.1 shows the different Windows 95 components that can be installed for each type of limited setup (typical, portable, and compact).

Table 5.1 How Windows 95 Components Are Installed for the Limited Setup Options

Component	Typical	Compact	Portable
Audio Compression	✔	✔	
Blank Screen Saver	✔		
Briefcase		✔	
Calculator	✔		
CD Player	✔	✔	
Disk Defragmenter	✔	✔	✔
Document Templates	✔		
DriveSpace	✔	✔	✔
HyperTerminal	✔	✔	
Media Player	✔		
Notepad	✔	✔	✔
Object Packager	✔		
Paint	✔		
Phone Dialer	✔	✔	
Quick View	✔	✔	

Component	Typical	Compact	Portable
ScanDisk	✔	✔	✔
Scrolling Marquee Screen Saver	✔		
Sound Recorder	✔		
Video Compression	✔	✔	
Volume Control	✔		
WordPad	✔		

If you choose the Custom Setup type, then you can install any or all of the Windows 95 components. Besides those which can be installed with one of the limited setups (as detailed in Table 5.1), there is a wide variety of other components you can choose:

➤ Accessibility Options. A collection of Control Panel tools that are designed to help those who are physically impaired.

➤ Backup. A disk tool used to backup your hard drive to floppy disks or tapes.

➤ Character Map. An accessory that allows you to access the entire range of Windows 95 characters. You can use Character Map to insert symbols and characters into documents created by other programs.

➤ Clipboard Viewer. An accessory that allows you to view the contents of the Clipboard and to manage a Clipbook over the network.

➤ Curves and Colors Screen Saver. A screen saver you can use to customize your desktop.

➤ Dial-Up Networking. An accessory that allows you to connect with remote networks, such as the Internet.

➤ Direct Cable Connection. An accessory that allows two computers to be connected through a serial cable.

➤ Flying Through Space Screen Saver. A screen saver you can use to customize your desktop.

- Games. Five games which can be used for relaxation. Included are FreeCell, Hearts, Minesweeper, Party Line, and Solitaire.

- Jungle Sound Scheme. A collection of related sounds that can be assigned to different system events.

- Microsoft Exchange. A communications management accessory that combines e-mail and fax capabilities.

- Microsoft Fax. The fax portion of Microsoft Exchange (which is required for this option to be installed).

- Microsoft Network. The tools necessary to connect with the new Microsoft Network.

- Mouse Pointers. A collection of animated and nonanimated pointers which can be assigned to different mouse activities.

- Multi-Language Support. The files necessary to implement the international features of Windows 95.

- Musica Sound Scheme. A collection of related sounds that can be assigned to different system events.

- Mystify Your Mind Screen Saver. A screen saver you can use to customize your desktop.

- Nature Sound Scheme. A collection of related sounds that can be assigned to different system events.

- NetWatcher. A system tool that allows you to monitor the performance of the network.

- Online User's Guide. Tutorial information on how to use Windows 95.

- Robotz Sound Scheme. A collection of related sounds that can be assigned to different system events.

- Sound and Video Clips. Sample audio and video multimedia files that can be used with the Media Player accessory.

- System Monitor. A system tool used to troubleshoot and refine the performance of Windows 95.

- System Resource Meter. A system tool used to monitor the use of your system resources.

- Utopia Sound Scheme. A collection of related sounds that can be assigned to different system events.

- Wallpaper. Various bit-mapped graphics files that can be used to customize your desktop.

- Windows 95 Tour. A guided, on-screen tour of the newest features of Windows 95. (Available only on the CD-ROM version of Windows 95.)

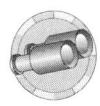

> **Note:** There are four tools that Windows 95 automatically installs: the Disk Defragmenter, DriveSpace, ScanDisk, and Notepad. There is no way to prevent their installation.

Remember, you can always add or remove options after Windows 95 is installed on a system. For information about adding or removing options, refer to Appendix A, "Adding and Removing Windows 95 Components."

After You Install

After you complete your Windows 95 installation, you should run the ScanDisk utility to verify that all the files on your hard disk are intact. This step also protects against any potential disk problems that might crop up. To start ScanDisk, follow these steps:

1. Select the Programs option from the Start menu.
2. Choose Accessories from the Programs menu.
3. Choose System Tools from the Accessories menu.
4. Choose ScanDisk from the System Tools menu.

When the program starts, choose the hard disk you want to scan and click Start. For more information on using ScanDisk, refer to Chapter 10, "Optimizing Your Disk Drives."

Special Portable Features

The characteristics of a portable computer are inherently different than your standard desktop computer, workstation, or server. If you have used a notebook computer for any length of time, you already know such computers are compact. You get most of the features of its desktop PC cousin, except in miniature. It's sort of like an RV with a miniature stove, rest room, and refrigerator. On a notebook you have a hard disk, albeit smaller and a bit slower. The LCD displays, even though they use color, are awkward at best. And forget about expansion unless you plug your notebook into a docking station. Still, even with these limitations, your portable computer gets the job done.

Windows 95 has several built-in features that only appear on specific types of equipment. It's as though the operating system is intelligent in the way it recognizes the needs and demands of your computer. The following sections describe these features and how you can best utilize them.

Power Management

Short battery life is forever the bane of portable computing. (Using a system that has a two-hour battery life on a four-hour plane flight is a real pain.) Someday, someone will develop a portable power source that will last for weeks at time. Until then, you must watch your remaining power until you can get a fresh battery charge or connect your system to AC power.

Windows 95 gives you some control over the battery's power management. It places a battery icon at the right side of the taskbar when you are mobile—that is, when you are using the battery and are disconnected from AC power. This icon notifies you of the remaining battery power in your system. Position the mouse pointer over the icon to see how much power really is left. Most modern portable computers have their own power management features, such as sleep mode and low battery meter. Of course, Windows 95 cooperates with these proprietary features.

You can instruct Windows to manage your precious battery power by shutting down energy-consuming devices, such as the display and the hard disk, until they are accessed. To modify these properties, do the following:

1. Choose Settings from the Start menu.
2. Choose Control Panel from the Settings menu.
3. Double-click on the Power icon in the Control Panel.
4. Choose Advanced, Standard, or Off from the Power Management list box.
5. Click on the OK button.

Standard power management provides sufficient energy conservation for most portables, while the Advanced setting is more beneficial for Pentium notebooks and CPUs with high-voltage consumption. The Advanced setting puts your devices into sleep mode every few seconds to save the most power possible.

If your battery power drops below 20 percent, Windows 95 alerts you with an audible beep and a message box. In addition, an exclamation mark appears next to the battery icon on the taskbar. Simply move your mouse pointer over the icon to see how much power remains.

PC Card (PCMCIA) Properties

PCMCIA, or the PC card, is most commonly used in notebook and subnotebook computers. Special slots accommodate these credit-card-sized devices as virtual hot-swapping mechanisms. This means that you can insert and remove cards while the computer is turned on and functioning without any adverse results. (Try this in a desktop computer with an adapter card, and you'll fry the components!)

As you add devices via the PCMCIA slots, you can view their status in the PC Card Properties sheet. Depending on your computer, you can also modify the card service's shared memory by specifying the exact starting and ending addresses. Normally, Windows 95 handles these addresses automatically, but you can override this by following these steps:

1. Choose Settings from the Start menu.
2. Choose Control Panel from the Settings menu.
3. Double-click on the PC Card (PCMCIA) icon in the Control Panel.
4. Choose the Global Settings tab.
5. Uncheck the Automatic selection check box.
6. Specify the Start address, End address, and Length as shown in figure 5.9.

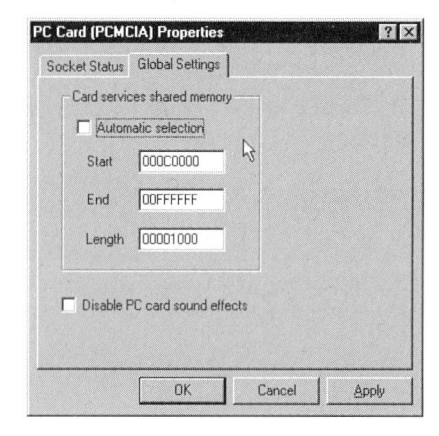

Fig. 5.9 You can change settings in the Global Settings page of this Properties sheet.

7. Click OK. You will be prompted to restart Windows based on your changes.

Tip: To disable the audible beep made by Windows 95 when you insert (or remove) a PC card, check the Disable PC card sound effects in the Global Settings tab (refer to figure 5.9).

Inserting a PCMCIA Card

Inserting a PC card is easy—just slide it into an available PCMCIA slot regardless of whether the computer is on or off. The instant you insert a PC card, Windows 95 recognizes its presence (assuming your computer is on), beeps to alert you, and configures itself accordingly. This action is instantaneous if the card has been previously configured. If the PC card has never been inserted in this computer before, Windows 95 assists you in the setup with the New Hardware Found Wizard, as shown in figure 5.10.

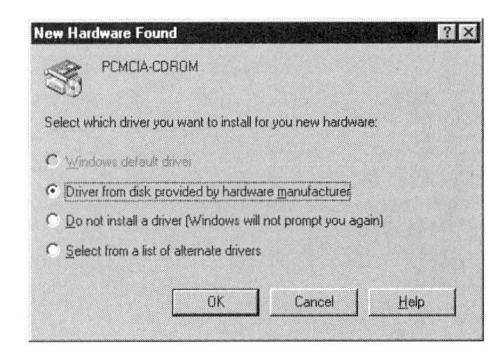

Fig. 5.10 First-time setup of a PCMCIA card is simplicity itself—just choose a driver in the dialog box.

Typically, you must install a driver for a new device, and Windows 95 lets you pick from several options. If this PC card is designed specifically for use with Windows 95, Windows may automatically detect it and install the appropriate driver(s). Otherwise, you have four options:

➤ Windows default driver. This option is available for only selected devices. In fact, with most PCMCIA devices, this option is not available.

➤ Driver from disk provided by hardware manufacturer. This is the default option, and should be selected if your vendor provided a disk containing Windows 95 device drivers.

Special Portable Features **151**

- ➤ Do not install a driver. Select this option if you don't want to use the new device you've just added.

- ➤ Select from a list of alternate drivers. This option should be used if you don't have a Windows 95 driver disk from the vendor. You can then scroll through a list of vendors and products to select the closest matching driver.

> **Tip:** If your PCMCIA card does not appear in the driver list, you can usually choose a generic substitute. If that doesn't work, call the PC card's manufacturer to obtain a Windows 95 driver disk.

Removing a PCMCIA Card

In previous versions of Windows, inserting and removing a PC card was as simple as sliding it in or out. The same is true for Windows 95, but bear in mind that some PC cards require special treatment. In general, you should disable any PC card via the PC Card Properties sheet before pulling it out of the slot. Granted, this is not mandatory, but for the more finicky devices (such as PCMCIA network cards), it makes the severing of resources a bit cleaner. Consider what would happen if you were connected to the network with your PCMCIA card, and you slid it out without thinking about it. Removing it is no big deal for you, but if someone else is accessing your computer, the removal of the card could be disastrous. Thus, properly disabling a card is desirable.

There are two ways to properly remove a PC card:

- ➤ Open the PC Card Properties sheet, highlight the desired card, and click Stop.

- ➤ Click (not right-click) on the PCMCIA tray icon on the taskbar and choose the device to stop (remove) from the pop-up menu (see figure 5.11).

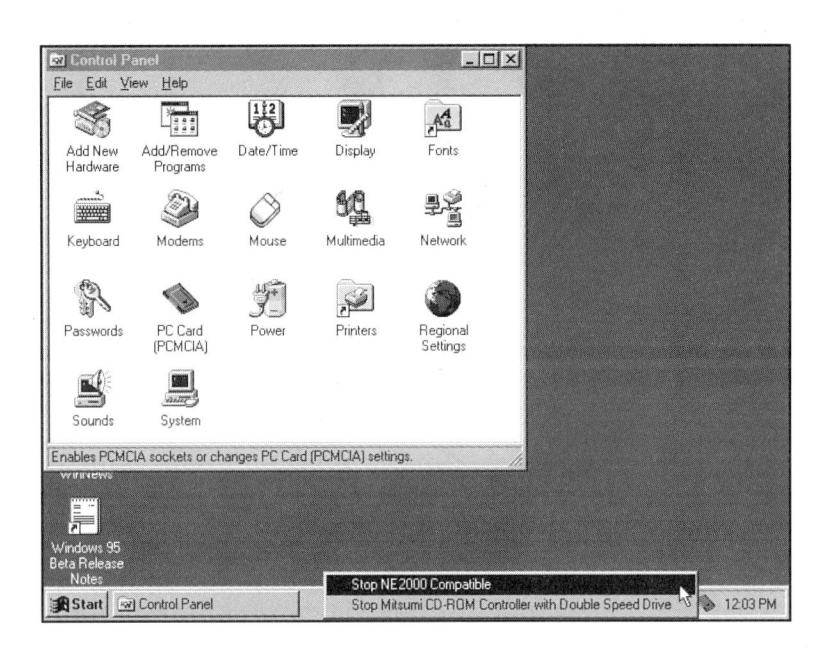

Fig. 5.11 A pop-up menu appears when you single-click the PCMCIA tray icon on the taskbar.

> **Tip:** If your computer has PCMCIA slots, the taskbar should display a PCMCIA tray icon. If the feature is not visible, you can enable it in the PC Card Properties sheet.

If you properly disable a PC card by following these instructions, Windows 95 informs you with a message box stating "You may safely remove this device." Click on OK. Once the card is properly disabled, you can remove it safely. If you don't follow this procedure when removing a PC card, Windows will warn you of your premature removal of the card as shown in figure 5.12.

Special Portable Features **153**

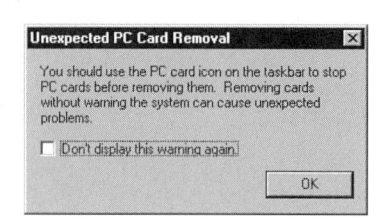

Fig. 5.12 Windows warns you when you remove a PC card without following the proper procedure.

Off-line Printing

Off-line printing, sometimes called deferred printing, is a way for mobile computer users to print documents while they are on the road, away from a printer. These documents are stored in a queue until you can again connect a printer to your computer. Ultimately, it's a time saver simply because you can issue the print command for any number of documents right away while you're thinking about it. The alternative is to wait until you get to a printer, summon the application, try to remember what you wanted to print, and then print.

Although this is not a feature specific to portable computers, it is significant. Desktop and portable computer users alike can use the deferred printing feature. However, off-line printing is automatically engaged when you are using a network printer, and you remove a PCMCIA network card from your system.

To manually enable off-line printing, follow these steps:

1. Choose Settings from the Start menu.

2. Choose Printers from the Settings menu.

3. Right-click on the printer icon you want to use for off-line printing.

4. From the context menu (see figure 5.13), click Work Offline.

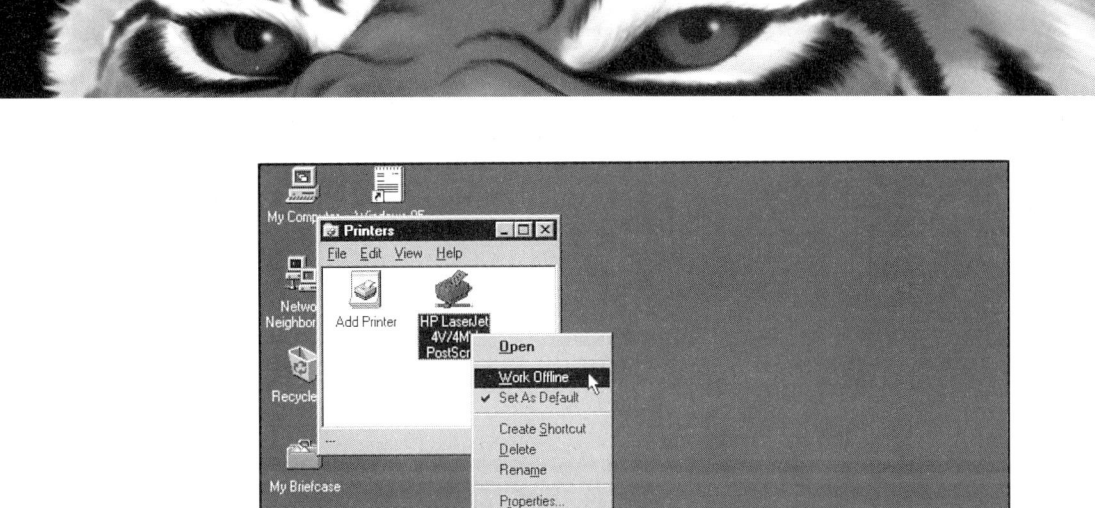

Fig. 5.13 To print without really being connected to a printer, choose Work Offline from the context menu.

Remember, off-line printing is engaged automatically for portable computer users when you remove a network PCMCIA card. A printer set to work off-line is displayed dimly in the Printers folder. Now, whenever you print, Windows creates a queue that holds all print jobs until you reconnect to the network. The instant you plug in the network PCMCIA card and the network printer is available, you get a message similar to figure 5.14. Click OK to print the jobs.

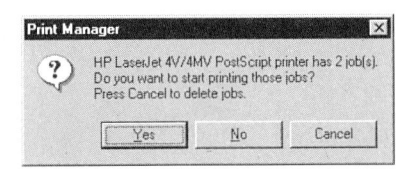

Fig. 5.14 When your printer is set to work off-line, print jobs are queued until you attach to a network or a printer.

Special Portable Features   **155**

Off-line E-mail

Since portable computers are mobile, they aren't always connected to a network or phone line. But you can still prepare e-mail when you're not connected. In fact, off-line e-mail works a lot like off-line printing in that you create your mail off-line via Microsoft Exchange, then when you reconnect your computer to the network (either directly or through Dial-Up Networking), your messages are automatically sent.

As you use Microsoft Exchange off-line, you won't have access to user names on the network (obviously), nor can you send mail into a queue like printer jobs in off-line printing. However, you still have your Personal Address Book from which you can select e-mail addresses. For example, when you attempt to open your Inbox (Microsoft Exchange), you see a screen similar to figure 5.15. When you see this, you can either choose Offline or Remote depending on how you want to work at that moment with Microsoft Exchange. Overall, e-mail functions the same as when you're connected, except you have to wait to connect before you can send e-mail. You can create it; you just can't send it until you connect to a network or the modem.

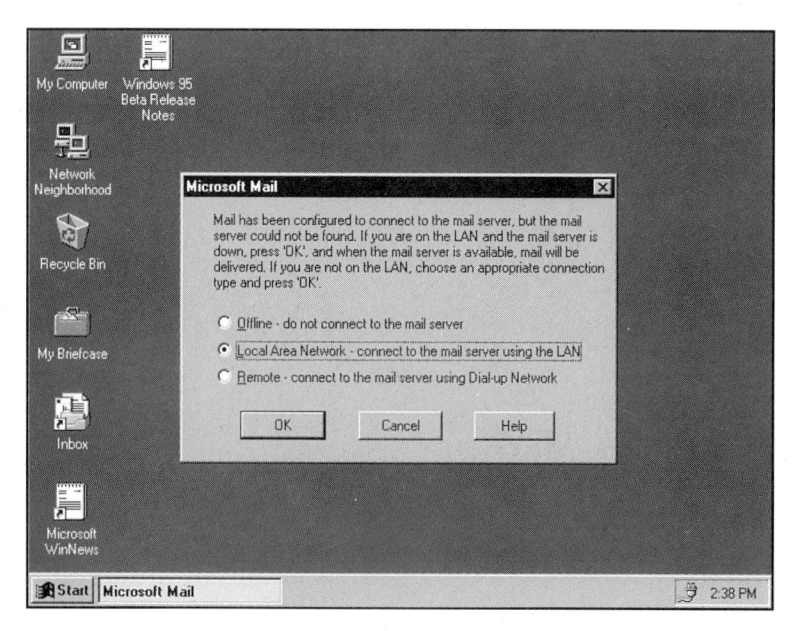

Fig. 5.15 You can work off-line with e-mail, too.

Installation Problems

A nice feature of the Windows 95 Setup is that if something interrupts the installation, such as if the power goes out, the hardware detection phase fails, or you intentionally cancel Setup, you can simply run Setup again and pick up where you left off. Setup calls it Safe Recovery.

If you have problems during installation, the Safe Recovery mode of Setup appears the next time you attempt installation. When this dialog box appears, choose Use Safe Recovery and click on Next. Setup will proceed as if nothing happened. This feature is possible because Setup maintains special files during the setup process to guard against such events.

Additional information on how to overcome installation problems is covered in Chapter 6, "Troubleshooting Windows 95 Installation and Startup."

Using the Emergency Startup Disk

When you install Windows 95, you have the option to create a startup disk. This disk is nothing more than a Windows 95 boot disk with the basic system files and other useful programs, such as the Registry Editor and disk utilities. Should your computer ever get corrupted and fail to boot properly, Windows 95 advises you and starts in a special "safe" mode. It is rare that you would need the startup disk, but it's available just in case of a catastrophe.

For more information on the different Windows 95 startup modes and how you can troubleshoot a damaged system, refer to Chapter 6, "Troubleshooting Windows 95 Installation and Startup."

Changing Your Windows Configuration

If you've ever accidentally deleted an important system file in a previous version of Windows, you typically had one solution—reinstall Windows. Of course, if you knew the exact name of the file you deleted, you could copy it from the distribution disks and use the expand command to decompress it. But that required your knowing its compressed name and its location on your system.

Fortunately, Windows 95 resolves this dilemma. There is no real need to reinstall Windows 95 (unless you delete a substantial portion of the system files). System components can be reinstalled by doing the following:

1. Double-click on the Add/Remove Programs applet in the Control Panel.
2. Choose the Windows Setup tab.
3. Highlight and select any or all components and options you want to reinstall (or remove).
4. Click OK.

Once you click OK, Windows prompts you to shut down the computer. Confirm this action, and Windows 95 will shut down and launch as normal. Additional information on adding and removing components is found in Appendix A, "Adding and Removing Windows 95 Components."

Troubleshooting Windows 95 Installation and Startup

by Allen L. Wyatt

To a degree not seen in any previous version, Windows 95 is a complex, robust operating system. Although well-hidden by the features apparent when you use Windows, the complexity of the operating system can raise problems. Ironing out these problems involves a process called *troubleshooting*.

This chapter attempts to address many of the troubleshooting issues that may arise as you use Windows. As you read through this chapter, pay close attention to the common threads that exist in all troubleshooting attempts. Regardless of the problem, you'll need to:

➤ **Analyze the symptoms.** Determine whether you can reproduce the problem or if it's random. If you can reproduce it, figure out exactly what steps lead up to the problem.

➤ **Identify the problem.** Once you know what creates the problem, you can generally figure out what the problem is. Is it due to a driver or a particular piece of hardware?

➤ **Determine a solution.** Find out what is necessary to correct the issue. Read through this chapter or related chapters. Refer to on-line help about the problem, if available. You may even need to contact a hardware or software vendor for assistance.

➤ **Resolve the problem.** Take the steps necessary to implement the solution. This typically involves using Windows to install a driver or make changes to properties. Make the changes.

➤ **Test the solution.** Once the solution has been implemented, you'll need to try to reproduce the problem again. If you can't after several attempts, and if additional problems don't arise, proceed to use your computer system as you intended.

Troubleshooting the Installation

Windows 95 has undergone extensive testing in order to make it work with virtually all hardware. This helps assure that the setup process for Windows 95 is simple and automatic. However, there is that occasional homemade computer that just isn't quite compatible or that network card that isn't supported (or manufactured) anymore. If you encounter problems during the installation of Windows 95, this section will help you locate and solve many of those problems.

Short of having defective media, it is unlikely that you will have any problem with beginning Windows 95 Setup. Once installation reaches the hardware detection phase, where Setup analyzes your existing hardware, your system may hang and force you to restart your computer. Setup has safeguards for such an event. If this does occur, simply run the Windows 95 Setup program again. This invokes Safe Recovery (see figure 6.1), which will then continue Setup from the point it failed. Safe Recovery consults the DETCRASH.LOG file (a file created during Setup that remains after a failed Setup), skips the conflicting device, and continues on its way. In such an event, you can later manually configure or install the offending device via the Add Hardware Wizard.

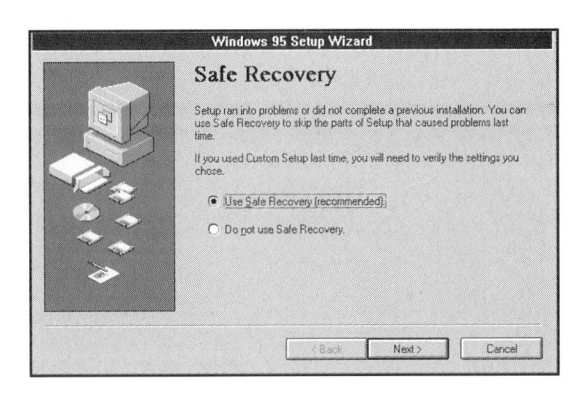

Fig. 6.1 Safe Recovery occurs when you run Setup after a failed installation.

Troubleshooting Startup

This section assumes that Windows is installed properly and, up to this point, everything is working as it should. There are times when you might have trouble launching Windows. Some of the more obvious causes might include:

- nonstandard hardware or devices
- corrupted system files (includes the Registry)
- hardware or device failure
- low disk space (not enough room for swap file activity)
- compromised disk integrity (fix with ScanDisk)
- excessive disk fragmentation (fix with Defrag)

A key feature of the Windows 95 startup is the ability to launch it in any of a number of modes. Some of these modes are designed specifically for troubleshooting your startup, while others simply let you access Windows in a different manner. The startup menu provides a menu of these different startup modes (see figure 6.2).

```
Microsoft Windows 95 Startup Menu
=====================================

    1. Normal
    2. Logged (\BOOTLOG.TXT)
    3. Safe mode
    4. Safe mode with network support
    5. Step-by-step confirmation
    6. Command prompt only
    7. Safe mode command prompt only
    8. Previous version of MS-DOS

Enter a choice: 1



F5=Safe mode   Shift+F5=Command prompt
Shift+F8=Step-by-step confirmation [N]
```

Fig. 6.2 The Startup menu for Windows 95 lets you control how the startup proceeds.

Isolating a Startup Problem

If you have trouble starting Windows, you can use these modes to help you troubleshoot the problem. But first, you must get an overall picture of how Windows is or isn't starting. To help isolate the problem, look through the following situations. In essence, you will isolate the problem by process of elimination.

Is It a Hardware or Software Conflict?

To find out whether the problem is related to hardware or software, try these steps:

1. Restart your computer. After the POST (power-on self test; the hardware check) is completed, you will see the phrase Starting Windows 95. The moment this displays, press the F8 key.

2. Choose Safe mode command prompt only. This does not load the Windows 95 GUI but takes you to the command prompt. This is equivalent to a bare-bones start without executing the AUTOEXEC.BAT or CONFIG.SYS.

If the computer boots to the command prompt, you can be certain the problem is a device driver or TSR in the startup files, and you can skip to the next situation. If the computer doesn't start properly, you have a hardware conflict or perhaps some defective hardware. Unfortunately, the only solution to this type of problem is discovered by process of elimination. If you've recently added a new piece of hardware, remove it and try to start the computer using the preceding steps.

Is It a Driver Conflict?

To determine which driver is conflicting with startup, you can have Windows launch a step at a time. This lets you see each driver load and discover if one is causing the problem. Refer to the section "Checking for Driver Conflicts" later in this chapter.

Are You Running Low on Hard Disk Space?

Windows needs a minimum of 8M of free disk space during normal use in order to operate correctly. This "extra" space is used for the swap file and should not be curtailed intentionally or otherwise. To display remaining disk space, boot to the command prompt (not a DOS window within Windows) and type **chkdsk**. If you are running low on disk space, remove some unnecessary programs, utilize DriveSpace, or upgrade to a larger hard disk.

Are Files Corrupted?

It is difficult to tell whether files have become corrupted. Your options include using the Emergency Boot Disk (startup disk), restoring from a backup, or reinstalling Windows. You can use the startup disk to help recover the Registry or perform limited diagnostics on a failing system. Refer to the section "Using the Startup Disk" later in this chapter.

Is the Hardware Malfunctioning?

If you have eliminated hardware, software, and driver conflicts, your hardware may be malfunctioning. You can remove some hardware from your computer to see if it starts properly. Other vital hardware, such as the hard disk, must be present in order to start Windows. Hardware diagnostics and repair is a complex, involved topic and is beyond the scope of this book. Discuss the problem with your hardware vendor.

Checking for Driver Conflicts

One of these modes is "Step-by-step confirmation." This mode takes you through each command in the Windows 95 startup and lets you selectively choose which to load. This is similar to the MS-DOS 6.X interactive startup. As you use this mode, pay close attention to the way in which each driver or device initializes. If one fails or loads incorrectly, you have identified the problem. To start Windows in this mode, follow these steps:

1. Restart your computer. Press F8 when you see the phrase Starting Windows 95.

2. Choose Step-by-step confirmation.

3. Just before each line in the startup files is executed, it will be displayed on your screen and you'll be asked whether you want to execute it. Press Enter if you do or Esc if you don't.

The value of starting Windows in this way is that you can see exactly where the startup hangs or where an error occurs. When you process a command, observe the result. If the computer hangs (stalls) after loading a specific driver or running a certain command, you've identified the problem. Reboot using the Safe mode startup, make the proper changes to CONFIG.SYS or AUTOEXEC.BAT (if they exist), and then restart Windows. You must realize that troubleshooting in this manner can be a time-consuming process—particularly if you are unsure which driver is the culprit. Generally, you can safely ignore the more common drivers in your AUTOEXEC.BAT and CONFIG.SYS, such as HIMEM.SYS or SETVER.EXE.

> **Don't Remove These Files**
>
> While you are working with your CONFIG.SYS or AUTOEXEC.BAT files, you may make changes to correct booting problems. The following files should not be deleted, since the drivers referenced must be present in order for Windows 95 to function properly:
>
> | | |
> |---|---|
> | AH1544.SYS | LDRIVE.SYS |
> | ASPI4DOS.SYS | NONSTD.SYS |
> | ATDOSXL.SYS | SCSIDSK.EXE |
> | DBLSPACE.BIN | SCSIHA.SYS |
> | DEVSWAP.COM | SKYDRVI.SYS |
> | DMDRVR.BIN | SQY55.SYS |
> | DRVSPACE.BIN | SSTBIO.SYS |
> | ENHDISK.SYS | SSTDRIVE.SYS |
> | EVDR.SYS | SSTOR.EXE or SSTOR.SYS |
> | FIXT_DRV.SYS | SSWAP.COM |
> | HARDRIVE.SYS | STACKER.COM |
> | ILM386.SYS | |

Troubleshooting Startup **165**

Using Safe Mode Startup

Choosing this mode forces Windows 95 to start without loading any device drivers or executing your CONFIG.SYS or AUTOEXEC.BAT (if they are on your system). This is useful when you need to determine whether the configuration files are causing problems. To start Windows in this mode, follow these two steps:

1. Restart your machine. After the POST (the hardware check) is completed, you will see the phrase `Starting Windows 95...`. The moment this is displayed, press the F8 key.

2. Choose Safe mode and press Enter.

Windows should start and display a screen similar to figure 6.3. Whenever you start Windows in Safe mode, it displays in the base 640 × 480 resolution, thereby avoiding any possible video conflicts. If Windows starts in this mode, you know that your startup problems lie within the startup files (CONFIG.SYS and AUTOEXEC.BAT). Examine the contents of these files to see if any troublesome commands are evident. You might even try changing the files to disable some statements, which may allow you to boot. If Windows doesn't start, even after bypassing the CONFIG.SYS and AUTOEXEC.BAT files, Safe mode will not do you much good. You must resort to generating a BOOTLOG.TXT file, as described in the section "Using BOOTLOG.TXT."

> **Tip:** Most driver problems occur in the CONFIG.SYS file, so examine that file first.

Of course, if your computer is connected to a network, you will have another option named "Safe mode with network support." When you troubleshoot such a computer, you can choose to let Windows 95 load the appropriate network drivers. This option assumes you have the proper networking hardware in place. To load Windows in this manner, do the following:

1. Restart your machine. After the POST (the hardware check) is completed, you will see the phrase `Starting Windows 95`.... The moment this is displayed, press the F8 key.
2. Choose Safe mode with network support and press Enter.

The screen displays the text `Safe mode with network` in all four corners (see figure 6.4), and it forces Windows to display in 640 × 480 resolution—just like Safe mode. When you start in this mode, check your device settings in the Device Manager to make sure your network settings are correct. If they are, you can rule out a conflicting network card.

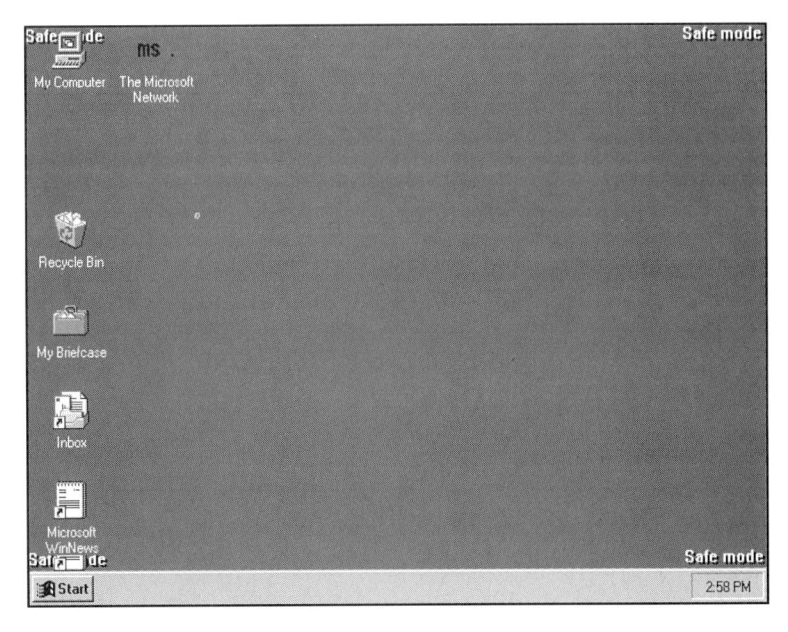

Fig. 6.3 Windows 95 displays the phrase "Safe mode" in all four corners of the screen.

Troubleshooting Startup **167**

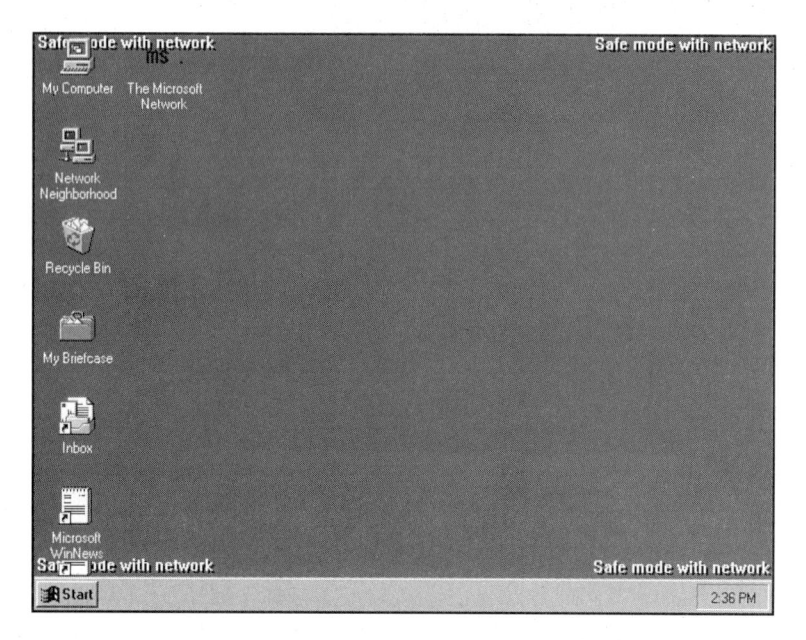

Fig. 6.4 Safe mode with network lets you load just the network drivers in Windows 95.

Using Command Line Switches

Other more technical issues surrounding system settings may cause Windows 95 to not launch properly. Or worse, it may function intermittently. You can force Windows to launch from the Windows 95 command prompt—not to be confused with the MS-DOS command prompt—and troubleshoot from there. Try these options if you can't get Windows 95 to launch properly.

To boot from the Windows 95 command prompt, do the following at startup:

1. Restart your machine. After the POST (the hardware check) is completed, you will see the phrase `Starting Windows 95...`. The moment this is displayed, press the F8 key.

2. From the Startup menu, choose 7, Safe mode command prompt only, and press Enter.
3. At the Windows 95 command prompt, type **win /d:** followed by a switch listed in Table 6.1.

For example, if you have a nonstandard disk controller, you'll want to make certain that 32-bit disk access is turned off. Otherwise, you could get intermittent results or Windows might not work at all. To run this command, type **win /d:f**.

Table 6.1 Command Line Switches

Switch	What It Does
f	Disables 32-bit disk access.
m	Starts Windows in Safe mode (same as Safe mode on the Startup menu).
n	Starts Windows in Safe mode with network support (if you have networking enabled). This is the same as Safe mode with network support on the Startup menu.
s	Instructs Windows not to use a ROM address space between F000:0000 and 1M for a break point.
v	Assigns ROM routines to handle hard disk I/O interrupts.
x	Prohibits Windows from searching for unused memory in the adapter area of memory.

Using the Startup Disk

When you first installed Windows 95, you had the option to create an Emergency Boot Disk (startup disk). You can troubleshoot Windows startup by using the utilities included on this disk. For example, if you get a message informing you of a missing operating system, use the SYS.COM command to restore these important files to the computer.

Troubleshooting Startup **169**

You can also edit, import, or export the Registry files from the command prompt, invoke ScanDisk on the suspect hard drive, or use various other commands provided on the startup disk. These utilities are placed on the startup disk:

- FORMAT.COM
- SYS.COM
- FDISK.EXE
- ATTRIB.EXE
- EDIT.COM
- REGEDIT.EXE
- SCANDISK.EXE

Using BOOTLOG.TXT

During the booting process, Windows becomes quite active loading drivers and other system files. This is particularly noticeable on slower computers. Most problems occur during this phase of startup. You can force Windows to keep a log of its boot processes, which is named BOOTLOG.TXT. This keeps a chronological account of each driver and system file it loads, and whether its loading was successful. To generate this file at startup, follow these steps:

1. Restart your machine. Press F8 when you see the phrase `Starting Windows 95...`.

2. Choose Logged (\BOOTLOG.TXT), which will start Windows and create the BOOTLOG.TXT file in the root directory. Chances are good that the startup will still be unsuccessful, but you now have a record of where the startup failed.

3. Reboot your computer following step 1 again. When you see the Startup menu, choose Safe mode command prompt only to boot to the command prompt. If this option works, proceed to step 5.

4. If step 3 did not work, use your Emergency Boot Disk (startup disk) to boot your system.

> **Tip:** If you don't have an Emergency Boot Disk, you can make a bootable floppy from a friend's or coworker's computer system.

5. Print out the file BOOTLOG.TXT, which is in your root directory.

When you examine the file, check to see what drivers were loaded and whether they were all loaded successfully. You'll notice that there are two entries for each device or driver that Windows 95 attempts to load. In the first entry, it attempts to load or initialize the driver. The second entry shows a message stating whether it succeeded or failed. The following is an excerpt from a BOOTLOG.TXT file:

```
[000F841B] Loading Device = C:\UTIL\ADAPTEC\ASPI4DOS.SYS
[000F8440] LoadSuccess    = C:\ADAPTEC\ASPI4DOS.SYS
[000F8441] Loading Device = C:\WINDOWS\HIMEM.SYS
[000F8445] LoadSuccess    = C:\WINDOWS\HIMEM.SYS
[000F8446] Loading Device = C:\WINDOWS\EMM386.EXE
[000F8452] LoadSuccess    = C:\WINDOWS\EMM386.EXE
[000F8453] Loading Device = C:\WINDOWS\DBLBUFF.SYS
[000F8456] LoadSuccess    = C:\WINDOWS\DBLBUFF.SYS
[000F8457] Loading Device = C:\WINDOWS\SETVER.EXE
[000F845B] LoadSuccess    = C:\WINDOWS\SETVER.EXE
[000F845C] Loading Device = C:\ADAPTEC\ASPICD.SYS
[000F846A] LoadSuccess    = C:\ADAPTEC\ASPICD.SYS
```

If a driver did not load properly, it may not exist (maybe it was deleted or moved elsewhere) or is corrupted. Try replacing the driver, and start Windows again in Logged mode (BOOTLOG.TXT). Then review the file to see if the driver loaded properly.

Hardware Troubleshooting

Although the Windows developers have made great strides in making Windows 95 compatible with almost every imaginable piece of hardware, it is possible that some hardware will not work. In such instances, all you can do is replace it with hardware that is compatible. If you believe that your hardware should work with Windows 95, then you must troubleshoot it.

Depending on the type of computer system you have, this could consume a lot of time. The newer Plug-and-Play-compliant systems allow for easy configuration—they automatically sense when you insert or remove a device. Resources are allocated on demand, and there is (usually) no conflict between devices. However, older devices (referred to as *legacy* devices) don't have Plug-and-Play capability. Many types of devices require resources in the form of IRQ lines (interrupt request lines) and DMA channels (direct memory access channels). The number of such resources is limited in your system. The more devices you install, the more likely you are to run into IRQ and DMA conflicts which arise when two or more devices try to use the same resources. If you have a non-Plug-and-Play computer, you'll want to follow these general guidelines for troubleshooting your system:

➤ Use the Device Manager to diagnose conflicting IRQ and DMA settings.

➤ If you have the stamina, use trial and error. (Don't underestimate its value.)

➤ Some older or nonsupported devices will not work with Windows 95. Generally, any device not detectable by Windows is not compatible.

The Device Manager gives you complete control over each piece of hardware you have installed in your system. All devices are diagrammed according to the information contained in the Registry (see figure 6.5), which is updated every time you restart your computer. From the Device Manager, you get a graphical representation of all devices attached to your computer, the device's complete (real) name, and more.

Consider how hardware configuration used to take place under DOS and previous versions of Windows. You would have to inventory the system to determine which IRQs were being used by existing hardware, then find a free DMA channel and reconfigure some other pieces of hardware (since one device was somewhat inflexible in how it could be set). Then came the trial and error of inserting it in the computer, slapping the case back on, switching the power on, and fainting as it hung up the system. Back to square one. Double-check dip switches, reconfigure other hardware, slap it back together, try it again.

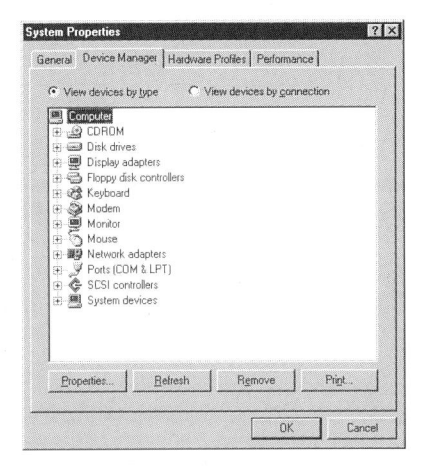

Fig. 6.5 Devices are listed in a diagram, which you can browse by pointing and clicking.

Windows 95 makes things much easier. The Device Manager is the tool which lets you configure the hardware in your system, including the IRQ and DMA channel each uses, and determine whether a device is currently active.

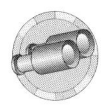

> **Note:** Although Windows 95 makes configuring easier, there still may be times when you must supply a driver on a floppy disk or set a dip switch on a card before inserting it into the computer. But instead of the trial and error method, as I previously described, the Device Manager will assist you.

To access the Device Manager, follow these steps:

1. Open the Control Panel by choosing Settings from the Start menu, and then select Control Panel.

Hardware Troubleshooting **173**

2. Double-click the System applet.
3. Choose the Device Manager tab to reveal a diagram of all the devices in your system.

As you can see, this diagram displays I/O addresses, IRQ settings, and DMA channels for every device. Each item is treated as a category for related items beneath it. Under the category of Mouse, for example, you will only find pointing devices. If you are familiar with the Explorer, you know that this diagram has a similar browse capability. Any icon with a plus (+) beside it indicates items that exist within that category. To view the contents of a category, simply double-click its icon. A closer inspection of an item can be done by highlighting it and choosing Properties.

When you are troubleshooting a device, locate it by its category in the diagram, then double-click on it to reveal its properties. In the properties dialog box, choose the View Resources tab. Figure 6.6 shows the Resources tab for a network card. For any device in question, examine the Interrupt Request (IRQ) and the Input/Output Range (I/O Address). The Device Manager will tell you if a device is conflicting with something else in the system. If you've just installed this device with the Add Hardware Wizard, you may also see suggestions for available jumper and hardware settings. Jot down any pertinent information, and proceed to change the hardware settings accordingly.

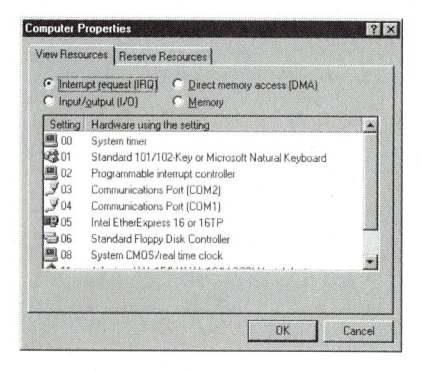

Fig. 6.6 In the View Resources tab, you can see if your device settings are in conflict with other system settings.

Chapter 6: Troubleshooting Windows 95 Installation and Startup

How Windows 95 Interacts with Your Hardware

by Allen L. Wyatt and Bill Lawrence

If you've been using DOS or Windows for some time, you're well aware of how they treated hardware. In most cases, the operating system was separate and distinct from the hardware—sort of an "interested bystander." This detached approach to hardware was fine, as long as everything was working the way it should. However, the operating system never was intelligent enough to recognize the presence or absence of a device, and so it mattered little whether your hardware was there or not. If it wasn't there, the worst case was that your system didn't work, and the best case was that you received an error message stating the obvious. Either way, you needed to resolve the conflict the "old-fashioned way," which of course meant manually.

Windows 95 takes an entirely different approach to the relationship between hardware and the operating system. In Chapter 2, you learned of one aspect of this difference—the Plug-and-Play system. Windows 95 is a Plug-and-Play operating system. The simple act of plugging in a card or other device triggers the reconfiguration process of Windows 95 (once the system is powered on). A database of all pertinent equipment is maintained and updated as changes are made to the system. Resources are reallocated if you remove a compressed drive; a driver is automatically loaded (usually without your knowing it) when you install a network card; and the chore of changing your video card's resolution—a relatively simple task—is taken care of quietly without the fanfare of disk swapping and searching for drivers.

Another aspect of the approach Windows 95 takes to hardware is that it continually attempts to communicate with the hardware. The principle behind Plug and Play dictates that the hardware must communicate with the operating system and BIOS, and vice versa. Of course, most of today's equipment does not comply with the Plug-and-Play standard and, consequently, does not "communicate" with anything—it does its own thing. For the most part, however, Windows 95 recognizes the presence of a great number of hardware items and can accommodate each, often without manual intervention.

In this chapter, you'll learn about the following:

- ➤ How device properties reflect the condition of your hardware, as well as help control it.
- ➤ How the Device Manager can be used to learn about your system.
- ➤ What Device Manager commands can be used to add or remove hardware from your system.
- ➤ How you can define hardware profiles to customize your use of Windows 95.
- ➤ How to add hardware devices to your system by using a wizard.

Understanding Hardware Properties

You already know that Windows 95 maintains a database of information about the components of your system. Part of this database is configuration information, attributes, or parameters that indicate how the device should be treated by the system. These parameters are referred to as *properties*. Every device in your system has properties you can view, and most devices have properties you can modify as necessary.

As an example, Windows 95 maintains a set of properties related to your entire system. To see your system's properties, right-click the My Computer icon on your desktop. From the context menu, choose Properties. The System Properties sheet appears, as shown in figure 7.1.

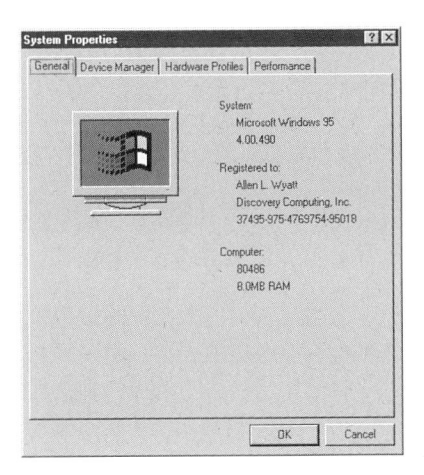

Fig. 7.1 The System Properties sheet is the gateway to the configuration of your entire system.

When you first display the System Properties sheet, the General tab is selected. This tab shows a summarization of several items, including the operating system and version, your registration information, and the computer's CPU type and installed memory.

The System Properties sheet acts as a gateway to several other important areas—areas that allow you to examine, in more depth, exactly how Windows 95 interacts with your hardware. The first of these areas is known as the Device Manager.

Using the Device Manager

The Device Manager is the place where you can monitor and change the properties of each device installed in your system. All devices are diagrammed according to the information contained in the Registry. The Registry is the unified database that contains all the configuration information for your system. The Registry replaces most of the INI files used in older versions of Windows; files such as SYSTEM.INI and WIN.INI. (The Registry is covered in detail in Chapter 17, "Fine-Tuning Windows 95 for Your Windows Applications.") The Registry database is updated every time you restart your computer, and sometimes during your Windows 95 sessions.

To view the Device Manager, start at the System Properties sheet (as described in the previous section), and then click on the Device Manager tab. The System Properties sheet appears, similar to that shown in figure 7.2.

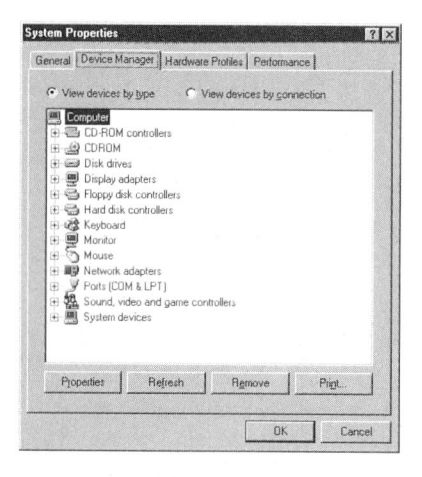

Fig. 7.2 The Device Manager allows you to see "the big picture" regarding your computer's components.

Chapter 7: How Windows 95 Interacts with Your Hardware

Note: Remember that every system is different. Thus, what you see when you use the Device Manager may be different in some ways from what is shown in figure 7.2.

The Device Manager allows you to see a graphical representation of the devices attached to your computer, the device's complete (real) name, and more. At first, "more" may not sound too exciting, but consider how device configuration used to take place under DOS and previous versions of Windows. Remember how tedious it was to install a network card? Before Windows 95, you would have to inventory the system to determine which IRQs were being used by existing hardware. Then you would find a free DMA channel and reconfigure a few pieces of hardware because the network card was somewhat inflexible in how it could be set. Next came the trial and error of inserting it in the computer, putting on the case, powering on, and fainting as it hung up the system. Back to square one. Double-check dip switches, reconfigure other hardware, put it back together, try it again.

Windows 95 makes things much easier. The Device Manager lets you configure the hardware in your system, including the IRQ and DMA channel each uses, and tells you whether a device is currently active.

Note: Although Windows 95 makes configuring easier, there still may be times when you must supply a driver on a floppy disk, or set a dip switch on a card before inserting it into the computer. But, instead of the trial and error method previously mentioned, the Device Manager can intelligently assist you in the process.

Inspecting Settings

The Device Manager is useful for configuring because of its accurate Registry list showing I/O addresses, IRQ settings, and DMA channels. It even shows devices that are using certain portions of memory. Each item shown in the Device Manager actually represents a category of related items. For instance, under the Mouse category, you find only pointing devices. If you're already familiar with the Explorer, this method of presenting information uses a similar browsing method. Any icon with a plus sign to the left of it indicates that items exist within that category. To view the contents of a category, click on the plus sign, or double-click on the category icon itself. In figure 7.3, the Ports category has been selected, revealing the available ports on the system.

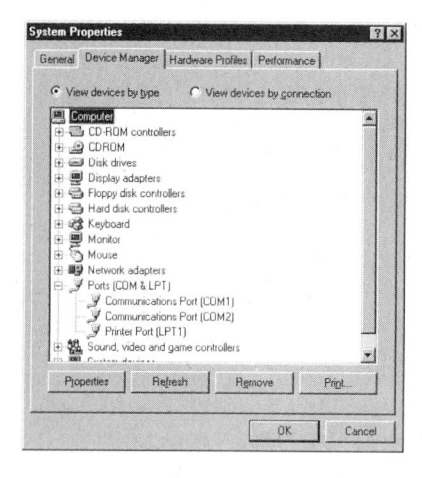

Fig. 7.3 Information in the Device Manager is presented in a hierarchical manner.

For a closer look at an actual device, highlight it and click on Properties. For instance, double-clicking on the first communications port (COM1) displays a properties dialog box for the device. Within the four tabs in the dialog box, you may activate or deactivate the device (discussed later in this chapter), view or change the device driver, or view and change the I/O address or IRQ settings. (The exact attributes and capabilities in the dialog box will depend on the device the dialog box represents.) Figure 7.4 shows the Resources tab for the COM1 port. Notice that the bottom of the dialog box indicates there are no conflicts for the port. Had there been a conflict (such as an internal modem using the same IRQ as the COM port), then this area would have indicated that information. The benefit over previous operating systems is that the Device Manager immediately notifies you if any of your changes conflict with existing devices in the system.

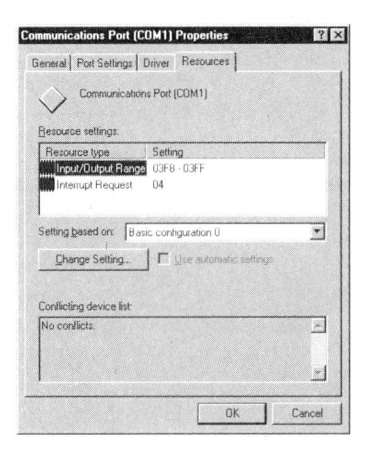

Fig. 7.4 In the Resources tab, you can see if your manual device settings are in conflict with other system settings.

The Device Manager and Adding New Hardware

All Plug-and-Play devices are switchless and jumperless because they're designed to automatically communicate with the operating system and BIOS and receive their configuration information from them. Therefore, there's no need to configure such a device manually. Many newer devices, which are not Plug-and-Play compatible, were designed to be software-configurable and are also switchless and jumperless. Windows 95 will also recognize and configure the majority of these without your intervention.

Older devices neither software configurable nor Plug-and-Play compatible are referred to as *legacy devices*. With these, you may have to manually set jumpers and/or DMA settings, or face potential device conflicts. Even with the inconvenience of having to manually change the jumper settings, Windows 95 helps you every step of the way. When you're ready to figure out which resources are available in your system, grab your device's installation manual and then do the following:

1. In the System Properties sheet, choose the Device Manager tab. (See figure 7.2.)

2. Click on the Computer icon in the device diagram (the one at the top of the diagram).

3. Click on the Properties button. The Computer Properties sheet appears. The Interrupt request (IRQ) radio button should be selected, as shown in figure 7.5.

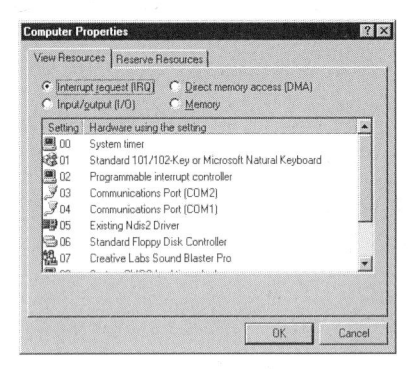

Fig. 7.5 The Computer Properties sheet displays resource information about your system.

4. Scroll through the IRQ list and view the resources allocated within the system. If an IRQ number is skipped (not listed), then it is available for use.

5. In the documentation for your device, find the possible IRQ settings it can use. Then set the jumpers or switches on the device for that IRQ.

6. You can also view the DMA channels currently in use by clicking on the the Direct memory access (DMA) radio button and performing similar setting adjustments as in steps 4 and 5.

7. Shut down your computer, install the device, and restart your system.

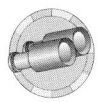

> **Note:** After restarting your system, Windows 95 may automatically recognize your addition of a new device and configure itself accordingly. Check the Device Manager and Computer Properties sheets to see whether Windows recognized the addition. If not, perform step 8.

8. Choose Add New Hardware in the Control Panel folder, and the Hardware Installation Wizard leads you through the installation of the device (discussed later in this chapter).

If you don't follow these steps, you risk a device conflict. If a device conflict occurs, Windows 95 will deactivate the device causing the conflict rather than hang the whole system. This action allows you to find out where the conflict resides and what setting(s) not to use. If a device has been deactivated, it will appear in the Device Manager diagram with a "slashed circle" over the device icon. View its properties to see what settings are conflicting and make the appropriate changes—or better yet, follow the preceding steps.

Deactivating a Device

With the Device Manager, you can deactivate some devices to free up system resources, or you simply may not want to use a particular device for a time. Activating and deactivating devices is related to device configurations, which are discussed later in this chapter.

In what circumstances would you want to deactivate a device? One time you might want to do this is when you have two network cards in your system, and you want to use only one at a time. If you deactivate one and activate the other, then Windows uses that configuration to communicate with the network. Another example might be if you suspect there may be a conflict between two devices in your system. You can deactivate one of them, restart your system, and perform your tests.

To deactivate (or later reactivate) a device, start at the Device Manager. Then display the Properties sheet for the device you want to modify. For instance, figure 7.6 shows the properties for a sound card.

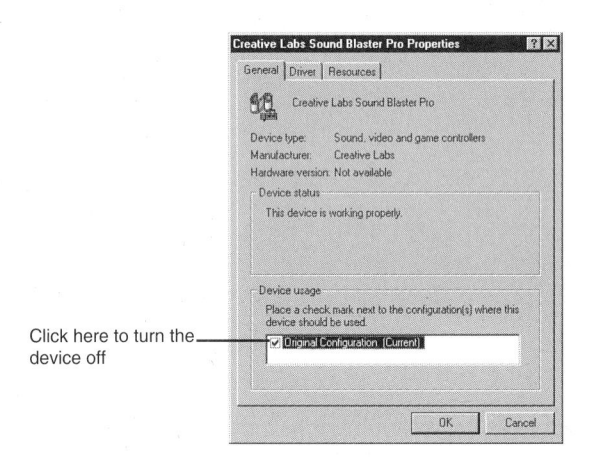

Fig. 7.6 You can turn a device on or off by using its Properties sheet.

To deactivate the device, examine the Device usage area of the sheet. This area lists the hardware configurations (again, discussed later in this chapter) in which this device is used. To turn the device off, clear the check box next to the current configuration. To turn the device back on, turn on the check box. Windows 95 allows you to control most other devices in the same manner, including the following device types:

- network cards
- sound cards
- pointing devices and the keyboard
- communications ports
- hard disk controllers
- monitors
- other system devices

Printing Resource Information

For your convenience, you can make a hard copy printout of your configuration for future reference. This is an excellent tool for troubleshooting and documentation of your system. Besides, if you must call Microsoft for technical support, this information is indispensable.

The first step in printing resource information is to decide exactly what you want to print. If you want to print a summary for your entire system, click on the Computer icon at the top of the device list. If you want to print information about a specific type of device in your system, click on that type of device. For instance, if you wanted to print information about your hard disk controllers, you would click on the hard disk controllers category in the device list.

Once you've selected an item in the device list, click on the Print button at the bottom of the Device Manager. The Print dialog box appears, as shown in figure 7.7.

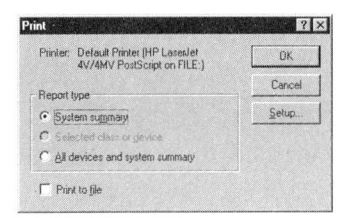

Fig. 7.7 The Device Manager provides an easy way for you to print your resource information.

From the Print dialog box, specify the type of report you want to print. You have three choices—a System summary, Selected class or device, or All devices and system summary. The length of each report depends on the configuration of your system, but the summary generally runs two pages and detailed information up to eight pages.

At the bottom of the dialog box is a check box labeled Print to file. If you click on this check box, then your printed output is sent to a disk file. When you're ready to print (either to a printer or to a disk file), click on the OK button. If you're printing to a printer, your report starts to appear. If you're printing to a disk file, you are asked to provide the file name that Windows 95 should use for the report. (The file name you pick is up to you.)

Removing Hardware

The time will come when you want to remove hardware from your computer. Or, you might need to replace a device. Perhaps you're upgrading to a 10baseT network card, or you just bought a quad-speed CD-ROM and 16-bit multimedia card to replace an old single-speed CD-ROM/Sound Card combo. Whatever the situation, it's going to involve removing and/or adding hardware as well as the corresponding drivers. One of the nice things about Windows 95 is the ease with which it lets you remove the old hardware, and, if you're replacing it, install the new. Another bonus is how it configures itself appropriately. Again, as mentioned previously in the section on "Adding New Hardware," you may be required to set a jumper setting or two on the device(s); that's not difficult if you follow the steps outlined in that section.

The Microsoft team members have worked hard to incorporate as many device definitions and drivers to automate the installation process as they could. It is likely that any product manufactured up to the point Windows 95 is shipped can be easily and automatically configured. Of course, your device comes with floppy disks containing the appropriate drivers, so if Windows 95 cannot configure itself for your particular device, you can follow the prompts for installing the device (as you'll see later in this chapter).

When you remove a device from your system, many times Windows 95 detects the change and automatically adjusts for it. This is particularly true with systems that are fully Plug-and-Play-compliant. With legacy systems, however, Windows 95 can't always be sure if a device was removed or if there is just a problem with the hardware. In these instances, the Device Manager can help you pinpoint the problem. For instance, say you remove a legacy network card from your system, and then you start up Windows 95. The operating system attempts to load the proper drivers for the card, and then initiate communication with it. Because it can't communicate with a nonexistent card, an error occurs.

Rather than make your entire system unusable, Windows 95 marks the device as defective and continues loading the operating system. When you open the Device Manager, the problem is highlighted. Figure 7.8 shows an example of how the Device Manager appears when a defective device has been detected.

There is a problem with this device

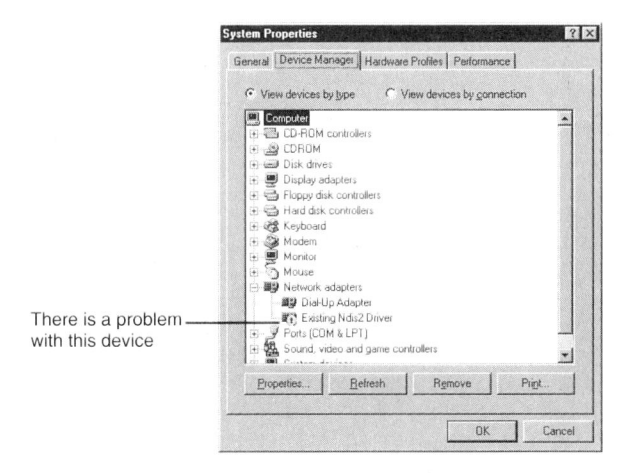

Fig. 7.8 The Device Manager informs you when there is a problem with a device in your system.

Notice that in the Network adapters group, the Existing Ndis 2 Driver device has an exclamation mark appearing over it. This mark tells you there is a problem with the device that Windows 95 cannot resolve. Had Windows 95 been able to determine that the card had been physically removed, it would have removed the device driver. Instead, it has marked the device, and you need to determine the cause of the problem. If you double-click on the device, you can get additional information in the Properties sheet, as shown in figure 7.9.

Using the Device Manager **187**

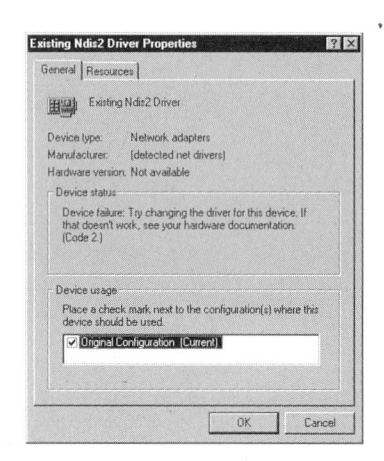

Fig. 7.9 The Properties sheet for a device can provide detailed information about the cause of an error.

In this case, where you know that you have physically removed the card, you have two choices. You can either leave the device driver intact or you can remove it. You would leave it in place if you had plans of adding the network card again at a later date. If you have no such plans, then you should remove the device from the Device Manager.

To remove a device from the Device Manager, highlight the device in the device list, and then click on the R<u>e</u>move button. You'll see a warning box asking you to confirm your action. When you click on OK, the device is removed. In most instances, you'll be prompted to restart your computer. Once this is done, the removal is complete.

Setting Up Hardware Profiles

There may be times when you might find it helpful to alternate between two or three different settings based on the hardware installed in your computer. For example, if you have a removable hard drive, an external tape drive that is moved between computers, or you have a laptop that uses a docking station, you can use different hardware configurations to instruct Windows 95 to load the appropriate drivers.

Once you "add" a new configuration, the next time you restart Windows 95, you'll be asked to select from a list of configurations. If your names are descriptive, you know immediately which configuration you need based on the changes you just made. When you select an option, Windows 95 will resume its startup with the chosen configuration.

Defining a Hardware Configuration

Windows 95 automatically has a hardware configuration created when you first install the operating system. The name of this configuration is Original Configuration. Defining another hardware configuration is easy. To start the process, follow these steps:

1. Right-click on the My Computer icon on your desktop.

2. From the context menu, choose the Properties option. The System Properties sheet appears.

3. Click on the Hardware Profiles tab. The System Properties sheet now appears, as shown in figure 7.10.

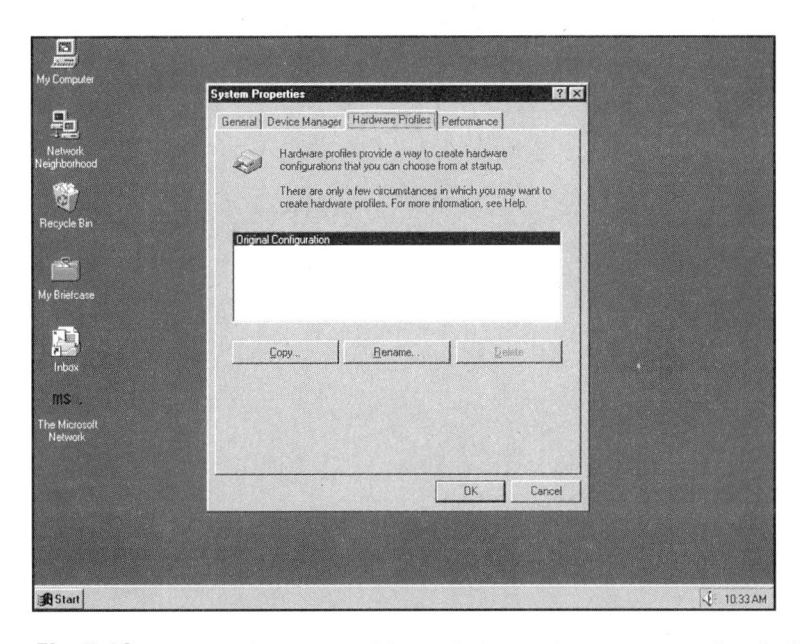

Fig. 7.10 The Hardware Profiles tab is used to manage the defined hardware profiles in your system.

Setting Up Hardware Profiles **189**

4. Make sure the Original Configuration profile is selected, then click on the Copy button. You're asked for a name to use for the new profile.

5. Provide a new profile name descriptive of the way in which the profile will be used. Then click the OK button. This adds the new profile to the list of profiles in the dialog box.

At this point, you can click on the Device Manager tab and make changes to the profiles. This is done as was explained earlier in the section titled "Deactivating a Device." When you next restart your system, you'll see a text screen that indicates the available configuration options (see figure 7.11). Make your selection, and Windows 95 will use it when starting the system.

```
Windows cannot determine what configuration your
computer is in.
Select one of the following:
  1. Original Configuration
  2. Backup capable configuration
  3. None of the above
  Enter your choice:
```

Fig. 7.11 Windows allows you to pick a configuration when you boot your system.

Note: If Windows 95 can make a configuration determination based on what it detects in your system, it will automatically make a profile choice without giving you the option. Typically, this happens with a portable computer with a docking station. You may have one configuration for the system out of the docking station, and another for when it is in the station. In such a case, Windows 95 can make an intelligent decision and will act accordingly.

Deleting a Hardware Configuration

To remove a hardware profile, follow these steps:

1. Right-click on the My Computer icon.
2. From the context menu, choose the Properties option. The System Properties sheet appears.
3. Click on the Hardware Profiles tab. The System Properties sheet appears, similar to what was shown earlier in figure 7.11.
4. Select the hardware profile you want to remove, making sure it is highlighted in the list of profiles.
5. Click on the Delete button. When asked to confirm your action, click on the Yes button.

The hardware profile is removed from the list of available profiles.

> **Note:** You cannot delete the original hardware profile created by Windows 95. When you choose the profile name (even if you rename it to something other than Original Configuration), the Delete button is no longer available.

Using the Add New Hardware Wizard

Integral to the Windows 95 operating system is the ability to quickly and painlessly install hardware. With several of its software products, Microsoft has introduced wizards to assist in creating or designing a spreadsheet, database, or letter. The idea is to make something that would normally be difficult, tedious, or time-consuming much faster. In this same vein, the Add New Hardware Wizard in Windows 95 helps you install hardware in your computer, basically by following the steps shown on-screen. If you have a Plug-and-Play system and you are adding a Plug-and-Play compatible device, this wizard is not necessary—devices are configured by the BIOS and operating system automatically. However, if you do not have such equipment, the Add New Hardware Wizard can be a great help.

> **Tip:** Any type of device, including a printer or mouse, can be installed from the Add New Hardware Wizard, even though you could install it also through another folder or program.

With the introduction of Plug and Play, hardware tends to take on a new classification depending on its construction. The devices that do not conform to the Plug-and-Play standard are called legacy devices, because they are (or soon will be) the older-style equipment, regardless of how easily they install. Chances are very good that you are using two types of legacy devices right now in your system—those with jumpers and those without. The hardware installation process you follow depends on which type of device you are installing.

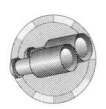

> **Note:** Keep in mind that most legacy cards function perfectly with Windows 95, but there are the occasional few that will behave erratically or won't function at all. These are typically identified, in advance, by Microsoft. Information on them is usually included on your installation disks or CD-ROM, as well as in Microsoft's electronic forums on various online services.

Legacy Devices with Jumpers

Jumpered devices can include any type of peripheral or add-on card, from sound to video to network cards. You set the jumpers manually to define which IRQ setting, DMA channel, and I/O address the card will use. To begin the installation process, you should follow the steps outlined earlier in this chapter in the section, "The Device Manager and

Adding New Hardware." Once you have followed those steps, you are ready to use the Add New Hardware Wizard. You can start the wizard in the following manner:

1. Choose the Settings option from the Start menu. The Settings menu appears.

2. From the Settings menu, choose the Control Panel option. The Control Panel window appears.

3. Double-click on the Add New Hardware applet. This starts the Add New Hardware Wizard, and you will shortly see the dialog box, as shown in figure 7.12.

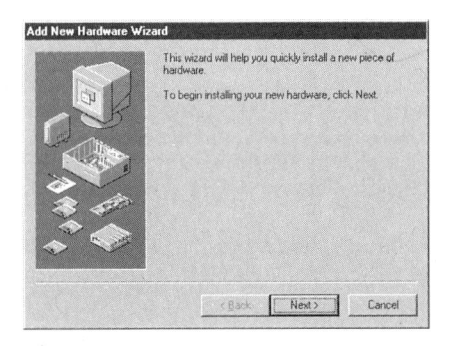

Fig. 7.12 The welcome dialog box is the start of the Add New Hardware Wizard.

Click the Next button to bypass the welcome screen. The next screen allows you to indicate whether you want Windows to automatically search for devices in your system. (See figure 7.13.) If you click on Yes, Windows assumes you've already installed the device inside your computer. It will attempt to identify the hardware, determine the driver to use, and what the device's default settings should be. Often with legacy devices this method produces conflicting settings that you can see by viewing the properties for the device in the Device Manager (as discussed earlier in the chapter).

Using the Add New Hardware Wizard **193**

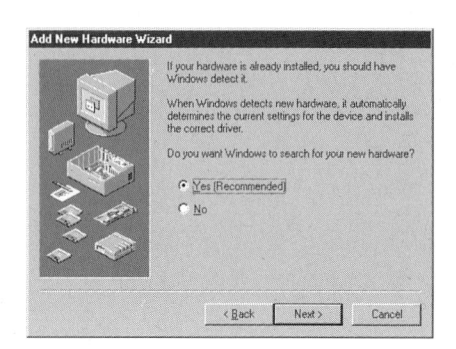

Fig. 7.13 The first step of the Add New Hardware Wizard is to select how you want the installation to proceed.

It is usually best to choose No at this point. When you do, you'll see a new dialog box that allows you to pick the type of hardware you want to install. Scroll through the list to identify the exact type of device you want to install. For example, if you want to install a sound card, you would scroll down until you find sound, video, and game controllers. Highlight the option and click on Next. The wizard then presents lists of the manufacturers and related models, as shown in figure 7.14.

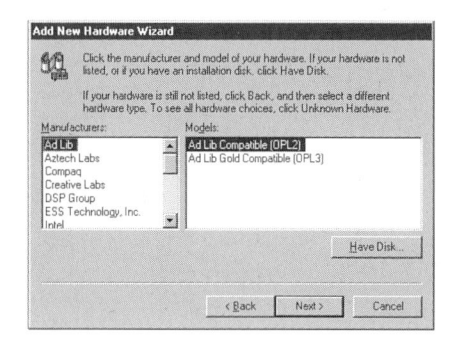

Fig. 7.14 Picking a manufacturer and model is essential to proper installation.

You should pick the manufacturer of your device (in this case, a sound card), and then the model of device. Make sure you pick the manufacturer first, as the choices in the model column will vary depending on the manufacturer. If you don't see a choice that matches your hardware, click Have Disk to install the drivers from a manufacturer's disk. When you're through selecting your hardware make and model, click on the Next button.

If your manufacturer and product model is not listed in the wizard, and you don't have a Windows 95 driver disk from the manufacturer, you should choose a make and model that is compatible with your product. If this is not possible (if nothing listed is compatible), then you have no choice—you'll need to get a Windows 95 driver disk before you can use the device in Windows 95.

If you have a device driver disk, and you click on the Have Disk button, you're asked to specify the disk drive where you have inserted the disk. Indicate the disk drive (and folder, if necessary), and then click on OK. The wizard will then indicate the names of the drivers on the disk, and you can pick the one that is appropriate for your needs.

After you've picked a product make and model or have picked a device driver from disk, the next dialog box informs you of the resources that Windows 95 will assign to the new hardware device. If Windows 95 suspects a conflict with existing device settings, the Add New Hardware Wizard will notify you and offer suggestions for properly setting up your device. Otherwise, it prompts you to mark down (or click Print to send to printer) the settings. When you have done this and click on the Next button, the correct drivers are automatically loaded and you're prompted to click on Finish to complete the installation process.

Your changes will not take effect until you shut down and restart your system. Essentially, the Add New Hardware Wizard is designed to remove the guesswork on the installation process and simplify it by asking a few simple questions.

Legacy Devices Without Jumpers

Because jumperless devices are software configurable, it is understandable that Windows 95 can communicate and configure them properly. In fact, next to Plug and Play, this type of device is the easiest to install. To install such a device into your computer with the Add New Hardware Wizard, do the following:

1. Insert or attach the device to your computer.

2. Start your computer to load Windows 95.

3. Choose the Settings option from the Start menu. The Settings menu appears.

4. From the Settings menu, choose the Control Panel option. The Control Panel window appears.

5. Double-click on the Add New Hardware applet. This starts the Add New Hardware Wizard.

6. Click on Next at the welcome screen, make sure Yes is selected, and click on Next.

At this point the wizard explains that Windows will detect newly installed hardware and may take a few minutes. When you click on Next, the wizard attempts to determine what hardware is attached to your system. Depending on the speed of your computer, this can take anywhere from a minute to five minutes. After it's completed, you can see a list of detected devices by clicking on the Details button, as shown in figure 7.15.

If everything looks OK, then click on Finish. If you are then asked to verify that the device actually exists, click on OK.

If everything does not look OK, then you only have one real option. You should click on the Back button to return to the previous dialog box in the wizard. This is the screen that allows you to indicate that you want to manually specify the hardware to install. If you choose this route, see the instructions in the previous section.

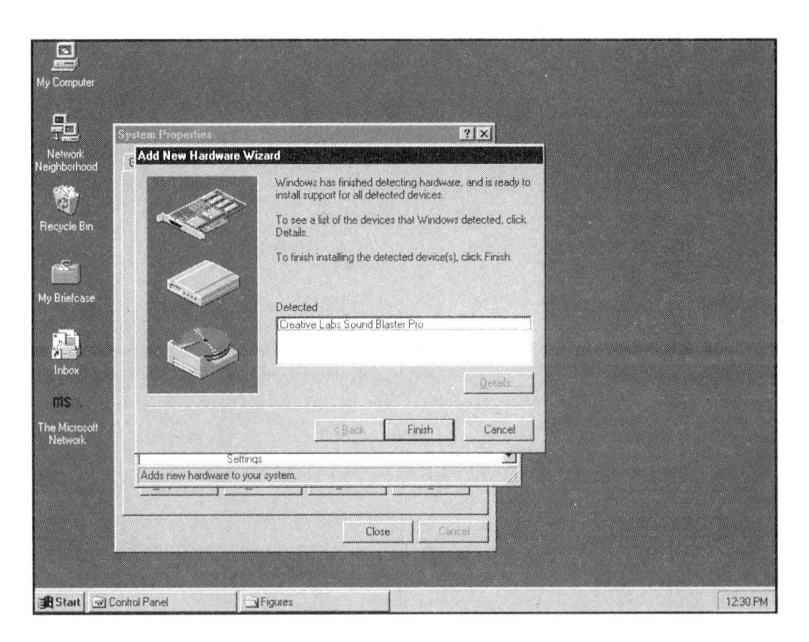

Fig. 7.15 With the Add New Hardware Wizard, Windows 95 automatically detects any new equipment you add.

Using the Add New Hardware Wizard   **197**

Examining the Hardware You Need for Windows 95

KILLER 8 WINDOWS 95

by Allen L. Wyatt

Windows 95 is a versatile operating system that demands far more of a computer system than any of its predecessors. The current low-end system for everyday use with Windows 95 is a 16MHz 386SX or better with 4M of RAM, a SuperVGA monitor and fast graphics adapter, and an 80M hard drive.

Evaluating Hard Drive Space

The more resources you can provide for Windows 95, the more satisfied you will be with its performance. If your system includes a small hard drive, the squeeze is on from the moment you install Windows 95. By itself, the operating system requires over 60M of hard drive space. The situation quickly gets out of hand as you add additional applications. For example, Word for Windows requires another 15M of disk space. The operating system and Word for Windows alone consume over 75M of space. If you have a smaller hard drive, you might be able to get by if you compress your disk drive, but the easiest solution is to run Windows 95 on a system with at least 150M.

Evaluating Graphics Capabilities

The need for a good monitor and a graphics accelerator board is equally compelling. When most programs were based on characters rather than graphics, users considered a .31 dot-pitch VGA monitor a luxury but made-do with EGA because that was all they really *needed*. Now, with the Windows 95 user interface and its bitmapped graphics, icons, menus, scroll bars, and What-You-See-Is-What-You-Get (WYSIWYG) display of documents, users need every bit of detail they can get. Furthermore, displays must be sharp if users are to work at monitors all day long and still be able to see well enough to drive home at night. A .28 dot-pitch monitor capable of 800×600 resolution and preferably 15 or 16 inches in size is rapidly becoming the minimum standard for a Windows 95 system.

Although Windows 95 is faster than earlier versions of Windows, it is much slower than older, character-based applications that ran under DOS, such as WordPerfect 5.1 and Lotus 1-2-3 version 2.2. You can run Windows 95 at speeds comparable to these applications, however, if you hook your monitor up to a graphics accelerator card capable of quickly displaying the huge amounts of graphics information presented by Windows 95.

Improving Hardware for Windows 95

Realistically, the high-end power system of yesterday is merely the adequate Windows 95 computer of today. If you're thinking about buying a new system, realistic low-end standards include a 66MHz 486 with 8M of RAM, a 300M 10-millisecond IDE hard drive, and a high-quality .28 dot-pitch 15- or 16-inch monitor with a graphics accelerator board. All the better if you can afford a faster CPU, more RAM, a larger hard drive, or a 17-inch monitor with a top-quality graphics accelerator.

The price difference between a 486SX/25 and a 486DX2/66 may be much less than you imagine, particularly if you buy from a top mail-order house like Gateway, Swan, Northgate, Dell, or Zeos. Given the consistent drop in computer prices, spurred by drastic price reductions in virtually every system component including CPU chips, computer RAM chips, hard drives, monitors, and graphics accelerator boards, even a 486DX2/66 is merely a mid-priced Windows 95 system.

Serious Windows 95 users benefit from their investment in good equipment. Windows 95's performance improves with every last bit of speed and capacity you can tweak from a system. Of particular benefit are a large, fast hard drive and a top-quality monitor with a graphics accelerator board.

This chapter covers the hardware essentials for running Windows 95 and, if necessary, for upgrading your system. It also tells you how to detect and correct incompatibilities between your system and Windows 95. The issues covered in this chapter include the following:

➤ Determining whether your computer is ready for Windows 95

➤ Checking system compatibility

➤ Looking at computers certified to run Windows 95

➤ Updating the BIOS

Consider the information in this chapter as a foundation for what is covered in Chapters 9 through 12 because this chapter provides an overview of the major parts of your computer system (CPU, hard drive, video system, and so on). In the following chapters you will learn the specifics of how you can improve the performance of each component of your Windows 95 system.

Getting Your Computer Ready for Windows 95

You can determine easily whether your computer is ready for Windows 95. If you have a 386 with a VGA monitor and card, only 4M of RAM, and a 40M hard drive, you really should buy a new system before you consider upgrading to Windows 95. Although it is possible to run Windows 95 on such systems, Microsoft acknowledges that it runs slowly and not very efficiently. The cost of trying to upgrade such a system to one capable of taking full advantage of Windows 95 is much greater than the cost of a new computer.

To evaluate whether your computer is up to the task of doing real work in Windows 95, remember this simple rule: a one-time hardware purchase is cheaper than the daily cost of you or your employees staring at a monitor in frustration as you wait for the computer to catch up. This rule is made particularly sound by the recent decline in the prices of computers, hard drives, RAM chips, and video subsystems.

Table 8.1 outlines the major system components that determine whether you can run Windows 95 on your 386SX or higher computer, or whether you need to upgrade some system components or purchase a new machine:

Table 8.1 Windows 95 Minimum Requirements

Component	Requires
RAM chips	Windows 95 can give users access to as much as 4G of RAM. Windows 95 and Windows 95 programs need a lot of RAM. The minimum for a 386SX or higher is 4M.
Hard drive	Windows 95 and its major applications each require many megabytes of hard drive space. The minimum reasonable requirement to run Windows 95 and more than one major Windows 95 application and to store their data files on-disk, is 300M of hard drive space. Even though you can run Windows 95 on a system with as little as 80M of space, the low cost of larger hard drives makes such a compromise unnecessary and unwise.
CD-ROM drive	While you don't absolutely need a CD-ROM drive to use Windows 95, it will come in handy. You can get a version of Windows 95 that installs from your CD-ROM drive, which makes installation and upgrading much faster and easier. (No diskettes to swap!) Any old CD-ROM will do, but if you can get one of the newer, faster models, so much the better. Investing in a triple- or quad-speed drive from a company like NEC or Mitsumi is well worth it.
Graphics accelerator card	Windows 95 is extremely slow unless you hook up your monitor to a graphics accelerator card designed to quickly display large amounts of video data. If you are purchasing a new system, make sure you get one with a PCI or VL-Bus; both will greatly speed up your graphics.
Monitor	With Windows 95, you need every bit of detail possible, displayed as sharply as possible. For Windows 95, the minimum recommended monitor is a .28 dot-pitch SuperVGA monitor capable of 800×600, preferably 15 or 16 inches in size. This resolution allows you the detail and clarity you need to be more productive.

If your system is at least a 386SX, but falls short in one or two of the preceding areas, you can consider upgrading your system hardware rather than buying a new computer. RAM chips currently sell for as little as $35 per megabyte from mail-order houses. Hard drive space now costs less than 50 cents per megabyte. Quality 15- or 16-inch monitors capable of non-interlaced resolutions up to 1024×768 range in price from $300 to $800, and 17-inch high-end monitors are available beginning at around $500. Top-rated graphics accelerator video cards with high resolution and color depth sell for as little as $250.

Note: Any prices noted here are for information purposes only, and reflect prevailing prices when this book was written. If you talk to a computer supplier and get a price within these ranges, make sure you get a another quote. Because computer prices continue to drop, chances are good that you will be able to get even better prices by the time you read this.

Adding RAM

Most motherboard manuals detail whether users can add more RAM to their system board, as well as the process for doing so. Basically, on most 386SX or higher systems, you can add 8M or 16M of RAM quickly and easily. Many computers enable you to add as much as 64M of RAM to your motherboard; a few allow you to add much more.

On most systems sold today, memory is easily added by plugging SIMMs into the motherboard. Anywhere from one to eight SIMMs can be added, depending on the motherboard. If you have an older system, you may not be able to use SIMMs. Instead, you will need to plug individual RAM chips into the motherboard.

If you need help adding RAM, your system manufacturer might be willing to give you step-by-step instructions on how to do so. Additionally, several books on the market can help. (You may want to refer to *Upgrading and Repairing PCs*, published by Que Corporation.) If you don't feel comfortable installing the memory yourself, a computer store in your neighborhood may be willing to sell and install the chips for slightly more than the mail-order cost.

Replacing Your Hard Drive

If you can remove your computer's cover and find the major pieces that make up your PC, you can replace your hard drive with a larger and faster model. Mail-order houses such as Hard Drives International or DC Drives specialize in helping novices upgrade their hard drives, and several books offering help are on the market. You can pay significantly more when you have a new hard drive installed by a neighborhood computer store than you do when you purchase the hard drive through mail-order and install it yourself.

Caution: Before attempting to change hard drives, you must do a full backup of your system, first to protect your programs and data, and second so that you can use the backup to restore these programs and data to the new hard drive. After you've installed a new hard drive, in most cases, you'll need to reinstall Windows 95. This reinstall will be necessary if your new hard drive is a different interface than the old one (for example, if you're replacing an ST506 drive with an IDE). Reinstallation is required because, in an effort to work with your system hardware, the Windows 95 Setup program detects the system's hard drive interface and bases Windows 95 configuration on it.

Types of Hard Drives

In general, Windows 95 works with the four hard drive types commonly used in the IBM-compatible personal computer market. These types are IDE, SCSI, ESDI, and ST506. The ST506 and ESDI drive interfaces are based on older technology and are rapidly being replaced by IDE and SCSI drives.

➤ *IDE* (Integrated Drive Electronics). IDE drives contain nearly all the electronics needed for operation, instead of major components being part of a separate controller card. In addition, IDE drives commonly are very fast and capable of storing large amounts of data. IDE hard drives capable of holding as much as 1G of data are easy to find, and even larger ones are making their way to the market. Because of the high degree of electronics integration and other refinements of hard drive technology, IDE drives can be small, which enables drives of large capacity to be installed in small computer systems. If you're considering a new hard drive for your system, consider an IDE drive.

> **Note:** Many computer systems that advertise IDE drives are actually using the newer generation EIDE (enhanced IDE) interface. While this provides greater throughput speeds and hard drive capacity, for the end user it is effectively the same as an IDE system.

➤ *SCSI* (Small Computer System Interface). SCSI drives typically are very fast high-performance devices, and many are very large capacity. SCSI drives capable of storing more than 9G (9,100M) are available, and often are used on network servers. Most of the electronics for SCSI drives are integrated into the drive itself, rather than major components being part of a separate controller card, although this integration is not as complete as with IDE drives. An additional feature of SCSI electronics is that several SCSI devices, such as a hard drive, CD-ROM drive, tape backup drives, scanner, and other equipment can be added to a single interface card. But because of variations in how the SCSI standard is implemented, not all SCSI devices will work with all SCSI interface cards. For this reason, it is important before buying SCSI devices to ensure that they are compatible with one another (or what you already have) by consulting with a knowledgeable technician or actually testing the device on your system.

➤ *ESDI* (Enhanced Small Device Interface). The ESDI interface is an enhancement of the original ST506 interface used in early XT, AT, and IBM PS/2 computers. Although the ESDI interface doubles the throughput of ST506 drives, and stores twice as much data per track as ST506 drives, it requires a separate drive controller and is considered slower and less reliable than IDE and SCSI drives.

➤ *ST506*. The ST506 interface is the original drive interface used in early XT, AT and IBM PS/2 computers. The ST506 was the common drive interface used in IBM-compatible personal computers for many years. The ST506-interface uses two common encoding formats: Modified Frequency Modulation (MFM), and Run Length Limited (RLL). (ST506 interface drives often are referred to as MFM or RLL.) The ST506 technology, which requires a separate drive controller, has been all but replaced by faster and more reliable IDE and SCSI interface drives.

If you're considering a new hard drive, you should probably purchase an IDE drive because of several factors, including price, availability, reliability, and storage capacity.

Controller Cards

If you need a great deal of speed and data throughput, you should consider souping up your IDE or SCSI hard drive with a hardware caching controller card. A caching controller card can greatly improve the effective access time of a hard drive.

The prices of caching controllers have plunged in recent months. Such cards once cost thousands of dollars (when equipped with 2M of RAM); they now add as little as $200 to the price of a new hard drive, making such cards a solid option for someone interested in a fast Windows 95 computer system.

It is now possible to find controller cards that plug into a PCI or VL-Bus slot. These types of controllers are cutting-edge, and offer the best overall performance. These bus slots, originally intended primarily for video controllers, are covered in Chapter 11, "Video Cards, Drivers, and Monitors."

Adding a CD-ROM Drive

Adding a CD-ROM drive to your computer system is relatively easy. In fact, in some ways it is easier than adding a disk drive. All you need to do is connect it to the power supply and the controller card. Windows 95 takes care of the rest.

Many new computer systems these days are being sold with CD-ROM drives installed right off the bat. When you buy your computer, it is generally best to get the CD-ROM right away. Many software products and references are now available on CD-ROM, and you will want access to this wealth of information. In addition, a version of Windows 95 is available on CD-ROM. Thus, instead of installing from a series of floppy disks, you could install or update directly from a single CD-ROM. (A single CD-ROM can contain up to 660M of information, as compared to 1.44M for a high-density floppy disk.)

When looking for a CD-ROM, remember that they are not all the same. While a basic CD-ROM is acceptable for multimedia use, for a few dollars more you can greatly improve the performance of the drive. All you need to do is get a triple- or quad-speed drive. (Some companies are even starting to bring out faster 6X drives.) These drives spin the CD-ROM at three, four, or six times the speed of the original drives. This means the data on the CD-ROM can be accessed faster by your computer.

Installing Graphics Cards and Monitors

As a rule, installing a graphics accelerator card is relatively simple. Installation of the hardware entails nothing more than turning off your computer, opening its case, removing the old video card, plugging the new card into the slot vacated by the old one, and reconnecting the monitor cable. After the card is installed, Windows 95 may recognize it automatically (if it is a Plug-and-Play card), or you may need to instruct Windows 95 to check out the new card for you (if it is not a Plug-and-Play card), or at worst you will need to install video drivers from the manufacturer.

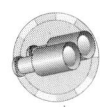

Note: Windows 95 requires that you use a VGA card. If you have an older system and are upgrading from an EGA to VGA, consult your system manual to determine how to reconfigure the system CMOS for the new card.

While the minimum requirements for Windows 95 only call for a VGA card, it is extremely slow unless you use a graphics accelerator card. These cards, which sell for as little as $250, are capable of running Windows 95 at speeds 25 times faster than traditional VGA cards. This entire area of picking a video adapter that takes advantage of graphics acceleration is discussed in depth in Chapter 11, "Video Cards, Drivers, and Monitors."

Installing a new monitor involves unplugging the old one from the computer and from the wall, and plugging in the new one. Remember, however, that the new monitor must be compatible with your video card.

Tip: Most mail-order houses gladly help with questions concerning the compatibility of a monitor and a video card. Furthermore, most of them have toll-free 800 numbers.

Checking System Compatibility

Windows, and in turn Windows 95, has driven the personal computer market to higher-powered hardware. The Windows family of operating systems has also spawned a curious change in terminology. Where computer manufacturers once claimed their systems were 100 percent "IBM-compatible," many now proclaim their systems "100 percent Windows-compatible."

Tip: The best way to ensure Windows 95 compatibility for a new computer is to buy from a well-known computer manufacturer that offers a lengthy warranty and a liberal full-refund return policy.

In truth, the Microsoft beta test program for Windows 95 involved more users running more brands and types of computers than any other software product in history. When the test revealed a compatibility problem that affected even a small segment of existing computers, Microsoft worked hard to fix it.

With few exceptions, Windows 95 runs well on most computer systems sold today, partly because many of these systems were designed with an eye toward maximizing the use of Windows and, in particular, Windows 95. If you have problems running Windows 95, contact your manufacturer for help. The popularity of Windows has forced hardware manufacturers to work hard to iron out compatibility problems in the models they have sold in the past two or three years.

Microsoft has compiled a list of computers it considers "Windows 95 compatible." To learn whether your computer or a computer you are considering for purchase is on that list, consult the Hardware Compatibility list included with the Windows 95 documentation. This list is also available in the Windows 95 forum on CompuServe.

More than 1,000 computer makes and models are included on the list of Windows 95 compatible machines, so little chance exists that your system is incompatible. If your computer is incompatible, check with your manufacturer to see if a fix has been developed. It is just good business for manufacturers to help their customers with problems using Windows 95.

The Hardware Compatibility list included with the Windows 95 documentation also details hundreds of printers, networks, video display types, keyboards, pointing devices, and other Windows 95-compatible hardware. To determine whether your hardware (or hardware you are considering for purchase) is Windows 95-compatible, consult the Hardware Compatibility list.

Plug-and-Play Equipment

In Chapter 2, "Under-the-Hood Improvements," you learned how Windows 95 supports Plug-and-Play devices. The Plug-and-Play standard allows you to add devices to your system and have them be automatically configured for you. This is a big advantage for users, one you will readily acknowledge if you have ever had the headaches associated with configuring a system manually.

If you are in the market to upgrade your system (by adding devices or even purchasing a new computer), it would be well worth your time and effort to look for devices that are Plug-and-Play compatible. They may cost a few dollars more (particularly in 1995 and early 1996), but they could save you hours of sheer frustration.

If you are adding Plug-and-Play devices to your existing computer, you could also benefit by upgrading the BIOS on your system. A BIOS that supports Plug and Play can be easily added to an existing system by changing a few chips on the motherboard. For information on doing this, contact your computer dealer directly.

> **Caution:** Some computers have the BIOS chips soldered directly to the motherboard. If your system is one of these, it is impossible to upgrade the BIOS. Before you invest in new BIOS chips, make sure you look at your motherboard to make sure it will accept the upgrade.

Exploiting Memory, Space, and Resources

by Allen L. Wyatt

Windows 95 has revolutionized the way many people use their personal computers because it has completely wiped out the historical 640K barrier that plagued earlier versions of PC operating systems. Windows 95 greatly expands the capabilities of the personal computer and also demands much more from the computer than DOS does. Most of the demands occur behind the scenes, automatically. However, you will find it useful to understand how Windows 95 uses virtual memory, a scheme in which hard drive space is used as if it were extra system RAM.

This chapter focuses on exploiting Windows 95 memory, disk space, and system resources. In this chapter, you learn how Windows 95 manages random-access and virtual memory.

This chapter discusses the following topics:

- How Windows 95 organizes system memory
- How Windows 95 manages virtual memory
- How you can change virtual memory settings
- How to determine when virtual memory settings should be changed
- How to control where Windows 95 stores temporary files

Understanding System Memory

To understand how Windows 95 uses memory on your system, you need to understand these terms related to memory:

- *Conventional memory* is system RAM below 640K.
- *Upper memory* is the area of memory above 640K and below 1M. This area is historically used by the system BIOS (basic input/output system), video BIOS, shadow RAM, and other system functions.
- *High memory* is the 64K area of memory immediately above the 1M mark.
- *Extended memory* is the area above high memory, up to the memory limit of the CPU.
- *Expanded memory* is memory above the 1M mark that conforms to the Lotus, Intel, Microsoft (LIM) specification. If your system contains expanded memory, you should reconfigure it as extended, using directions provided by the hardware manufacturer.
- *Virtual memory* is a scheme for using hard drive space as if it were system RAM.

In previous versions of Windows and under DOS, each of these memory areas played a critical role in the execution of programs under Windows. In Windows 95, several of these types of memory are no longer important. That is because of the way that Windows 95 views memory.

Under Windows 3.x, which operated in conjunction with DOS, memory was accessed by using a *segmented memory model*. (Sometimes referred to as 16-bit memory.) This meant that memory operations used two internal registers for addressing. One was the segment register, and the other an offset register. The combination of the segment and address register could be translated to a physical memory location within your system. The drawback to segmented memory is that you can only directly address 64K of memory—the largest number that can fit within the offset address register. After that, you need to change the segment register, recalculate a new offset register, and access memory again.

The use of segmented memory dates back to the earliest days of the PC. When the 8088/8086 CPU was introduced, it used segmented memory for a variety of reasons. The DOS operating system was based on the segmented model, which meant that DOS (and thus Windows) could only access memory in 64K blocks.

Windows 95 removes this barrier by using memory addressing capabilities that have been available in the CPU since the introduction of the 80386. This memory scheme views memory in a linear fashion, meaning that it is treated physically. To do this, Windows 95 uses a single 32-bit address register. Thus, Windows 95 uses 32-bit memory addressing, which allows 4G of memory to be addressed directly, without resorting to memory segments and offsets.

This change in memory models could be accomplished only by doing away with DOS, which historically has been the limiting factor. The benefit of this change is that programs written for Windows 95, using 32-bit addressing, can operate faster and more efficiently—there is less overhead in performing addressing manipulations.

Because memory is now treated in a linear fashion, historical constraints associated with conventional memory, upper memory, and high memory are done away with. Instead, you have only RAM and virtual memory; one is in your computer, and the other on your hard drive. The new memory manager in the Windows 95 kernel is charged with keeping things straight. It assigns memory areas to each procedure being executed, and the rest of memory is hidden from that procedure. This feature provides greater security and stability for both programs and the operating system itself.

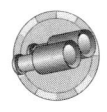

> **Note:** Windows 95 uses the same memory addressing techniques employed in Windows NT. Thus, any 32-bit programs written for Windows NT will operate just fine under Windows 95, and vice-versa.

As mentioned earlier, with a 32-bit addressing register you can directly address up to 4G of memory. Of this memory, 2G is reserved for use by the operating system, and the other 2G for use by programs. Thus, the largest program that can be run under Windows 95 requires 2G of memory—more than enough for anything that may crop up for the next couple of years.

Understanding Conventional Memory

Historically, conventional memory has been the bane of operating systems and programmers. This memory—the first 640K of memory in your system—was considered "prime real estate." This area is where parts of DOS, device drivers, and the like were all installed. If too much conventional memory was occupied before Windows executed, then Windows would perform sluggishly, or not at all.

Windows 95 does away with the conventional memory problem. The only time this memory comes into play now is when you're working with an MS-DOS window within Windows 95. When you open an MS-DOS window, the Windows 95 memory manager creates a "virtual machine" that behaves just like an old DOS system. There is only one difference—memory management is more secure, because any program running in the virtual machine cannot access memory used by other Windows programs. As far as any DOS program is concerned, however, it has complete use of all the resources in the machine. The application is completely oblivious to the fact it is working in a contrived and controlled universe created by Windows 95.

Using Expanded Memory

Expanded memory is a hardware-related standard, devised in the 1980s by Lotus, Intel, and Microsoft. It allowed older computer systems to add memory and make it accessible to programs. If you have not done so already, you should configure any expanded memory in your system as extended memory. This typically involves making some changes to the jumpers on your memory card; you should refer to your hardware documentation for more information.

> **Note:** Some DOS programs require your system to have expanded memory to run properly. If you must run such a program, Windows 95 provides support for you. For more information, refer to Chapter 19, "Fine-Tuning Windows 95 for Your DOS Applications."

Understanding Virtual Memory

You have already learned that Windows 95 allows direct addressing of up to 4G of memory. Building a PC with this much RAM would be prohibitively expensive, so most systems come with 4M, 8M, or 16M of memory. At first, this small amount of memory might seem like a restraint of the operating system.

To get around the disparity between actual RAM space and the 4G memory space of the operating system, Windows 95 employs a technique called *virtual memory*. This kind of memory is nothing new; virtual memory schemes have been around for years, and have been incorporated in previous versions of Windows.

Virtual memory uses hard drive space as if it were system RAM, temporarily storing information to free up system memory. This capability enables the computer to run more programs at the same time under Windows 95 than physical RAM alone would allow. Virtual memory functions are controlled by a virtual memory manager (VMM), a part of the Windows 95 kernel that handles swapping parts of memory to the disk and back again, as necessary. The area on disk into which memory chunks are stored is called a *swap file*.

Under previous versions of Windows, you had a large number of choices for managing your swap file. You could elect to use a temporary or permanent swap file, and you needed to determine the proper amount of memory to allocate to the file. This complexity is removed in Windows 95. There is no more decision to make about the type, location, or size of your swap file; Windows 95 can take care of all these matters automatically.

If you're familiar with the previous versions of Windows, you know that both temporary and permanent swap files had their advantages and drawbacks. Temporary swap files were dynamic, growing only as they were needed. Permanent swap files allowed faster access, because they were stored in a contiguous space on the disk. In Windows 95, there are no temporary or permanent swap files. Instead, a dynamic swap file is created and managed by the VMM, using 32-bit access. It could be said that the result is an optimized temporary swap file, with all the advantages of a permanent swap file.

Changing Virtual Memory Settings

Even though Windows 95 does an excellent job of managing virtual memory, there may be times you want to change the constraints under which it works. Windows 95 allows you to modify both the location and size of the virtual memory swap file. To do this, follow these steps:

1. Choose Settings from the Start menu. The Settings menu appears.
2. Choose Control Panel from the Settings menu. The Control Panel window appears.
3. Double-click on the System icon in the Control Panel. The System Properties dialog box appears.
4. Click on the Performance tab.
5. Click on the Virtual Memory button. The Virtual Memory dialog box appears, as shown in figure 9.1.

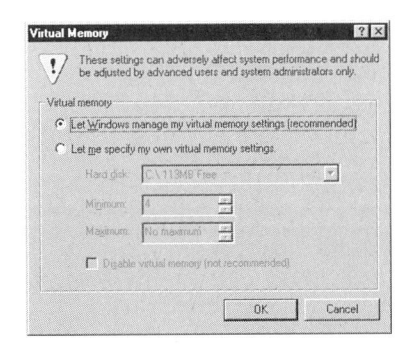

Fig. 9.1 The Virtual Memory dialog box allows you to control swap file settings.

6. Choose the virtual memory option that allows you to specify settings by clicking on the second radio button. The options in the middle of the dialog box then become available.
7. In the Hard disk drop-down list, select the hard drive where you want the swap file located.
8. In the Minimum area, indicate how small the swap file can be. (The smallest setting here is 4M.)
9. In the Maximum area, indicate how large the swap file can be. You can set any value, up to the current available space on your hard drive.
10. Click on OK.

At this point, when you exit from the System Properties dialog box, you'll be informed that you need to restart Windows in order for your changes to take effect. Once you do, the new virtual memory settings will be used.

Disabling Virtual Memory

If your hard drive space is at a premium, you can conserve disk space by preventing Windows 95 from swapping information to disk. To prevent Windows 95 from swapping, follow these steps:

1. Choose Settings from the Start menu. The Settings menu appears.
2. Choose Control Panel from the Settings menu. The Control Panel window appears.
3. Double-click on the System icon in the Control Panel. The System Properties dialog box appears.
4. Click on the Performance tab.
5. Click on the Virtual Memory button. The Virtual Memory dialog box appears, as shown earlier in figure 9.1.
6. Choose the virtual memory option that allows you to specify settings by clicking on the second radio button. The options in the middle of the dialog box then become available.
7. Click on the Disable virtual memory option.
8. Click on OK.

At this point, when you exit the System Properties dialog box, you will be informed you need to restart Windows in order for your changes to take effect. Once you do, the new virtual memory settings will be used.

> **Caution:** Turning off disk swapping can be detrimental to Windows—don't do it unless you absolutely have to. If you're running out of disk space, the better options are to delete files, compress your drive, or get a larger drive.

Optimizing Virtual Memory

Now that you know how to make changes to your virtual memory settings, you may wonder how you can determine whether you really should make a change. Windows 95 provides a diagnostic tool you can use to help make such a determination—System Monitor. If you installed the minimal system, System Monitor, along with many other options, is NOT automatically installed. However, you can install this program manually.

System Monitor is a program that allows you to analyze the performance of various parts of your computer system. Because the program is so comprehensive, full use of it is beyond the scope of this chapter. Portions of the program, however, can be used to determine the job your memory manager is performing.

To start the System Monitor, follow these steps:

1. Choose Programs from the Start menu. The Programs menu appears.

2. Choose Accessories from the Programs menu. The Accessories menu appears.

3. Choose System Tools from the Accessories menu. The System Tools menu appears.

4. Click on System Monitor. This starts the System Monitor program, as shown in figure 9.2.

The System Monitor features a menu, a toolbar, and a grid area. The grid area displays various performance statistics for your system. If you have not used the System Monitor before, the default area being monitored is the CPU usage on your system. The vertical axis on the grid shows the percentage of use, and the horizontal axis is time. Every few seconds, the usage of the CPU is calculated, and displayed on the graph. In figure 9.2, you can start to see some of the CPU usage being shown, at the lower-right corner of the grid. Over time, the percentage moves from right to left, and you can get an idea of your CPU use. Figure 9.3 shows an example of CPU usage after performing some typical disk operations (such as formatting a floppy disk or running the ScanDisk program).

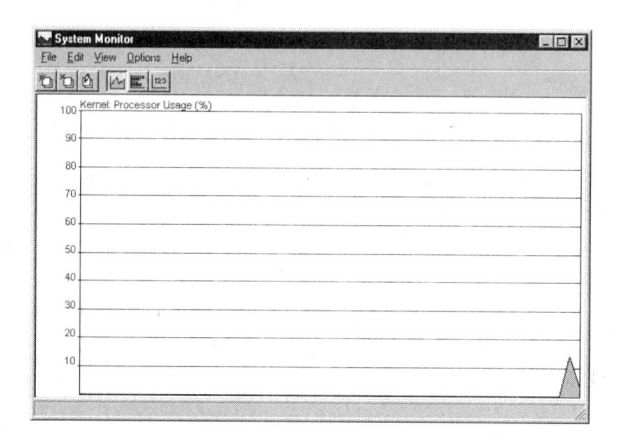

Fig. 9.2 The System Monitor is used to view the performance of your system components.

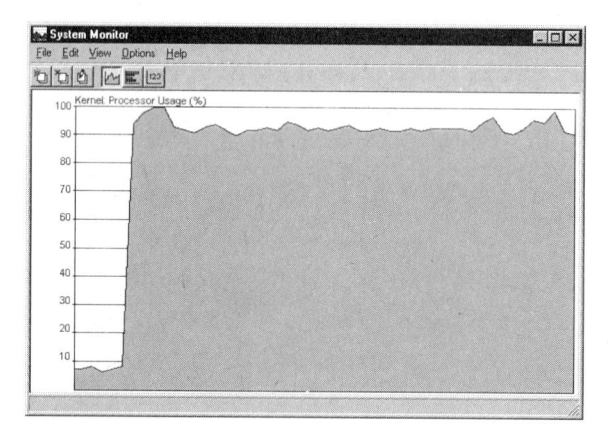

Fig. 9.3 After monitoring CPU usage for a few moments, you can get an idea of how your operations tax the CPU.

To change the performance area being monitored (which you need to do), choose Edit, Add Item. The Add Item dialog box appears, as shown in figure 9.4.

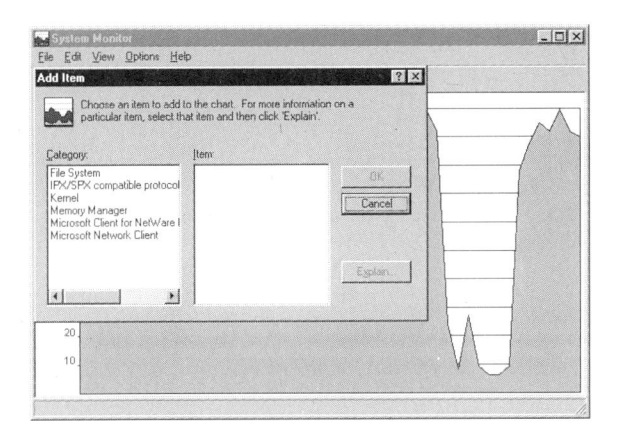

Fig. 9.4 The Add Item dialog box is used to select the performance areas you want to monitor.

This dialog box consists of two portions. The left side is where you select a category of performance items. Once you make a choice in this list, the items within that group will appear on the right side of the dialog box. To monitor items related to virtual memory, select the Memory Manager option in the Category list. The choices then displayed in the Item list are detailed in table 9.1.

> **Note:** The performance area categories listed in the Add Item dialog box will depend on the operating system components you have installed.

Table 9.1   Performance Items Related to Virtual Memory

Item	Meaning
Allocated memory	The amount of memory, in bytes, allocated by Windows to applications and operating system components.
Discards	Number of memory pages discarded per second.
Disk cache size	The size of the disk cache.

continues

Optimizing Virtual Memory   **223**

Table 9.1 Continued

Item	Meaning
Free memory	The amount of physical memory currently available.
Instance faults	Number of instance faults per second.
Locked memory	The amount of memory allocated and locked either by applications or the operating system.
Maximum disk cache size	The maximum disk cache size.
Minimum disk cache size	The minimum disk cache size.
Other memory	Memory that has been allocated, but cannot be stored in the swap file.
Page faults	Number of page faults per second.
Page-ins	Number of transfers from the swap file to physical memory, per second.
Page-outs	Number of transfers from physical memory to the swap file, per second.
Swapfile defective	Swap file bytes determined to be defective. This indicates bad sectors on the disk drive.
Swapfile in use	The memory in the swap file, in bytes, currently being used.
Swapfile size	The size of the swap file, in bytes.
Swappable memory	Memory that has been allocated from the swap file, in bytes.

Obviously, not all of the performance items listed in Table 9.1 are going to be meaningful to the average user. However, you can use some of the items to get a clearer picture of the performance offered by your swap file. As an example, you can use the Swapfile size and Swapfile in use items to monitor the dynamic growth of your swap file, as well as what portion of the swap file is being used. If you monitor this while you have a memory-intensive program running, you can see what sort of job the manager is doing.

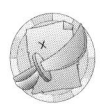

Tip: If you want to monitor how many times information is transferred to and from the swap file, you can use the Page-ins and Page-outs options.

Once you select the performance item you want to monitor, click on the OK button. The System Monitor screen is modified to display any existing performance items, in addition to the one you have chosen. Thus, if you choose the Swapfile size item, the System Monitor window would look similar to what is shown in figure 9.5.

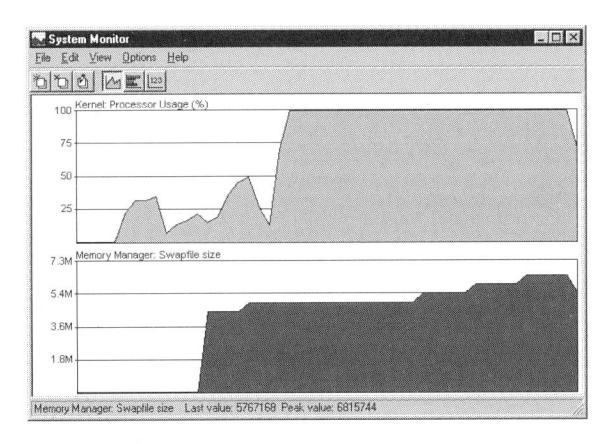

Fig. 9.5 Adding performance items modifies how the System Monitor grid area appears.

You can continue to add items to the monitor, or remove them, if desired. To remove an item, choose Edit, Remove Item, and then select the item to remove.

So how do you know when you should make changes? Simple. If you see that the swap file is maxing out the available space on the disk drive, then you may want to look at freeing up disk space. If you notice that the swaps are occurring slowly, you may want to get a faster hard drive, or change the swap file to another hard drive, which may be

Optimizing Virtual Memory **225**

faster. Selective and analytically using the System Monitor can help you tweak your virtual memory settings beyond what can be done automatically by Windows 95.

Understanding the TEMP Setting

Many programs use temporary files to store data while they're running. By swapping data to a disk in this manner, these programs are able to work more quickly and efficiently. By default, these temporary files are stored in the \WINDOWS\TEMP directory on your hard drive. This directory was created when you first installed Windows 95.

Notice that \WINDOWS\TEMP is a default directory for temporary files. You can change the location of the temporary files by modifying or creating your AUTOEXEC.BAT file, and setting the TEMP variable. This directory is read after Windows 95 is started, and temporary files are stored at the location you specify. For instance, adding the following line to your AUTOEXEC.BAT file instructs Windows 95 to store temporary files in the TEMP directory on the D drive:

```
SET TEMP=D:\TEMP
```

Some programs actually don't look for the TEMP variable. Instead, they look for a variable named TMP. This setting is particularly useful for DOS programs operating in an MS-DOS window. To set this variable, add a line such as the following to your AUTOEXEC.BAT file:

```
SET TMP=D:\TEMP
```

This command instructs the program to store the temporary files in the same location as you previously indicated for the TEMP variable.

Optimizing Your Disk Drives

by Allen L. Wyatt

In Chapter 8, "Examining the Hardware You Need for Windows 95," you learned that the absolute minimum system you need for Windows 95 is a 386SX with 4M of RAM and an 80M hard drive. If you're trying to run Windows 95 with a minimal system (one near the minimum requirements), this chapter presents valuable information about how you can get the most out of your system. In particular, this chapter focuses on maximizing performance of your disk drive systems.

This chapter discusses methods to access data more quickly, teaches you more about random-access memory (or RAM), and describes ways to increase the amount of data a small disk drive can hold. This chapter also provides housekeeping techniques that will help you keep your computer system streamlined, free up more disk space, allow you to install more programs, and give Windows 95 swap files more room to do their job.

If you try the suggestions in this chapter only to find that the improvement isn't enough, the last section of the chapter reviews what you can accomplish by upgrading your system. The review looks particularly at features that complement your system rather than conflict with it.

Whether you fine-tune or upgrade, many of the disk housekeeping suggestions in this chapter are necessary for maintaining optimum disk performance. This chapter presents many tips to simplify or automate disk cleaning.

Working with Caches

A cache is nothing more than a temporary storage area for information. In computer terms, a cache is a high-speed area used to store information until it can be processed by a slower device. Caches are used on computers to speed access to data stored on hard drives. As CPU speed continues to increase, the computer industry is relying more and more on caches to help data transmission by other components of the system keep pace with the CPU. Caches on the market today are of two basic types: RAM and disk. Each performs different—usually complementary—tasks, and this chapter reviews both. Although it may seem strange to be studying RAM in a chapter on disk drive performance, the best way to speed access to your drive is to move the data you're using to a faster location—that being RAM.

Examining RAM

The RAM installed in your computer is composed of dynamic RAM chips (DRAM), which are inexpensive but operate relatively slowly, at 130 to 200 ns (nanoseconds). This speed figure consists of access time (70 to 100 ns) plus the precharge time needed to refresh a RAM cell before data can be accessed again. The cycle of access and precharge time is improved by using a RAM design such as page mode or interleaved memory.

The RAM design used in a computer system is designed into the motherboard by engineers—you can't do anything to modify it. An understanding of how RAM can be designed can be beneficial if you're looking to upgrade or replace your system. The next two sections address two common methods of designing the RAM portion of your system.

Understanding Page Mode RAM Design

Page mode (and the similar static column access) design takes advantage of two aspects of computer design:

➤ Most of the time, computers read and write memory addresses that are clustered close together or sequentially.

➤ RAM chips are designed to store data in a matrix of rows and columns.

A page-mode DRAM chip includes a 2,048-bit buffer. When data is requested, the entire row of data represented by the first half of the address is read into the buffer. The second half of the address is then read, specifying the column where the bit of data is located. If the next request is for data located on the same row, the row is still in the buffer and the new bit can be accessed from the buffer. When the data is accessed from the buffer in this way, the precharge phase is unnecessary. This results in a page mode cycle, typically 40 to 60 ns, rather than a regular cycle of 130 to 200 ns.

Static column access design receives the second half of the address in a different but slightly more efficient manner. The advantage of both designs is that only a few additional RAM chips are required to implement them.

Understanding Interleaved RAM Design

Interleaved memory divides RAM into blocks (usually two or four). Memory addresses are assigned to the blocks sequentially, and data needed by the processor is written into each block of RAM in address order. Figure 10.1 shows a two-block arrangement of interleaved memory with address assignments appropriate for a 386 system with a 32-bit processor bus.

	Block 0	Block 1
Address Lines	16-19	20-23
	8-11	12-15
	0-3	4-7

Fig. 10.1 An interleaved memory layout featuring two blocks

When contiguous data is stored in RAM for use by the processor, that data is distributed in address order among the blocks of interleaved memory. If the processor needs this data again and the data is still stored in RAM, it's read from the blocks—alternately if using only two interleave blocks or sequentially if using four. Throughput is improved because data is accessed in one block while at least one other block is being precharged.

The more blocks of RAM used in an interleaved memory design, the less the chance of reading a block twice in a row. On the other hand, a drawback when upgrading interleaved memory is the need to add RAM to each block in equal amounts, often doubling or quadrupling the amount of RAM you must buy.

Effects of RAM Design

RAM design is incorporated into the motherboard of a system. A specific RAM design isn't a feature you can add as an easy upgrade. However, understanding how RAM design affects system performance gives you a starting point for evaluating ways to improve RAM access time as well as techniques that use RAM to speed access to disk data in Windows 95.

Consider how this information stacks up in relation to your present system. RAM access times range from 130 to 200 ns to a low in the neighborhood of 40 ns if one of the designs just discussed is implemented. A 33 MHz system has a clock cycle of 30 ns, and a 66 MHz system has a clock cycle of 15 ns. The specific CPU in a system affects the duration of the bus and instruction cycles of the system (which are linked to the clock cycles). In general, however, the bus cycles of the later chips (486 and Pentium) come closer to the actual clock cycles of the systems that use them. It's important to understand that it's possible for the effective speeds (throughput) of one generation of chips to overlap the throughput of the next generation of chips, depending on the clock speed. For instance, the performance of the fastest 486 systems (100 MHz) are just as great as the performance of the slower Pentium systems.

If the RAM design used in your system isn't tuned for optimal performance, it means that the CPU is automatically crippled. An efficient RAM design can deliver data at speeds equal to that of a fast processor. It's important to ensure that your system uses an efficient RAM design so that you can get the most performance possible from your system.

Processor performance isn't the only feature that depends on the manufacturer. The speed of the DRAM chips used in your system, for example, is an integral part of the system design. Refer to your operating manual or contact the motherboard manufacturer to see whether your system includes features such as adjustable wait-state settings or the capability to configure itself dynamically before you decide to buy and install faster DRAM chips.

Understanding RAM Caches

For speed faster than DRAM, static RAM (SRAM) chips are available. They boast access rates of 15 to 30 ns, with rates of less than 20 ns being most desirable. In addition to providing speed, static RAM doesn't need precharging or refreshing, as does dynamic RAM. This kind of speed is good enough to keep up with a fast CPU, but the memory chips are much more expensive (when compared to regular dynamic RAM). However, a small amount of SRAM (typically 16K to 256K) installed as a RAM cache can increase system performance substantially.

A RAM cache is managed by a cache controller circuit that acts as an intermediary between the CPU and regular RAM. It reads data from RAM that's requested by the processor, stores or tags the addresses of the data, places the information into the cache, and even prereads the next 8 to 16 bytes of data from RAM. The cache controller continues to intercept requests from the CPU, first checking its table of addresses to see whether the data is in the cache. If it is, the data is accessed at 20 ns speed or faster. If the data isn't in the cache, the cache controller reads the data from regular RAM, adds it to the cache, and then directs the processor to it. Most requests for data are channeled through the cache controller.

If the requested data is found in the cache, that bus cycle is referred to as a *cache hit*. If it's not found, the cycle is called a *cache miss*. Acceptable cache designs achieve a 95 percent hit rate, with 98 percent preferred, assuring that almost all data is delivered at the higher SRAM speeds.

A cache must be designed to read its address table and to discard old data efficiently. In a RAM cache, older data is discarded on a least recently used (LRU) algorithm. Efficient ways to read the address table is a more complex issue.

If you're shopping for a system with cache, you can choose from three designs used to organize the data in the cache:

➤ *Fully associative cache.* A fully associative cache allows data to be stored anywhere. The cache controller must then check the entire address table to find whether the data is in the cache. On many computers, the processor is giving the cache controller only 40 to 80 ns to do this, as well as to produce the data.

➤ *Direct-mapping cache.* A better design is a direct-mapping cache, where the cache is divided into address regions. This design allows the controller to check only a portion of the address table. The drawback is that a region can fill with continuous data while other regions remain empty.

➤ *Set-associative cache.* The most popular and efficient design is a set-associative cache. This system divides the cache into two to eight sets, or areas, and rotates the assignment of addresses among the sets in a fashion that somewhat resembles the way addresses are distributed in interleaved memory blocks (you may want to refer back to figure 10.1). All sets fill with data at a more balanced rate, which results in more hits, but the controller still must check two to eight entries in the address table. To avoid a slowdown at this step, the set-associative design also includes hardware that simultaneously checks all the addresses in a set.

None of these designs is inconsistent with the DRAM designs explained earlier in this chapter. Most cached systems use one of them, and their benefits are available whenever the cache needs to access RAM.

A larger cache doesn't necessarily mean faster performance, but it does mean a larger address table to read in the same amount of time. The efficiency of a system's cache controller and the system design can make a small cache outperform a large one. Similarly, an efficient, properly sized cache will show little performance increase if you add RAM to it. If you want to increase the size of a RAM cache, all you have to do is replace a set of chips on the motherboard and possibly change jumper settings. Manufacturers tend to increase cache size as processor speed is increased within a CPU family.

The 486 chip is designed with an 8K internal cache that uses a set-associative design with four sets. This cache is very efficient because it has a direct 128-bit data path to the chip's processing circuitry. Unfortunately, the size of the cache is small enough to reduce the hit rate to an unacceptable 90 percent. For this reason, a small on-board or external cache is usually included with 486 systems. For instance, a 486/33 system typically has a 64K cache.

The Pentium chip has two 8K internal caches, for a total of 16K of two-way set-associative caching. One cache is used for data and the other for code; both are software transparent to maintain compatibility with earlier CPU designs. Even though there's effectively twice the internal

Working with Caches **233**

cache in the Pentium when compared with the 486, many system designs include a small external cache as well.

Understanding Disk Caches

Disk caches come in two types: software and disk drive. Although both cache the same data, notable differences exist between the two. In some instances, the differences are incompatible.

Whereas a RAM cache speeds the rate of accessing whatever's in memory, a disk cache speeds disk access by holding frequently requested data in memory (again, either in the drive electronics or in an area of computer RAM). This action substantially decreases the number of times that the hard disk must be read. Since RAM can be read faster than a hard drive can be accessed and read, the overall system performance is increased substantially by proper use of a disk cache.

Software Caches

Software caches occupy RAM, offering high-speed access to data usually stored on disks. A software cache operates in much the same way as a RAM cache—the major difference is the amount of data that can be read ahead to improve performance. Not only can the software cache hold recently read data on the assumption that you'll need it again soon, but also the next clusters of data are read on the assumption that this data is what you'll need next.

The following steps illustrate the operating sequence:

1. When you boot the system, caching software sets up a buffer area in extended or expanded RAM in the amount you specify in the software command line, usually somewhere between 512K and 2M.

2. When the processor requires data from a disk, it sends a request to the drive where the data is stored.

3. If you have a RAM cache, the cache controller intercepts the request, checks to see whether the data is in its cache, and, if not, forwards the request.

4. The software disk cache (located in RAM) receives the request and checks to see whether the data is in its cache.

5. If the data isn't in the software cache, the data is located on the appropriate disk drive.

6. The data is read into the software cache buffer, where it's accessed by the CPU. If a RAM cache is on the motherboard, the data is read into the RAM cache and the CPU is directed to it.

7. During times when the CPU is idle, the cache reads sectors next to those just read (read-ahead feature), thus anticipating that the processor needs that data next. This tendency of computers to read clustered data was pointed out in the review of RAM earlier in this chapter. When reading from disks, the effect of this technique depends on how fragmented your disk is.

Adjusting Caching Parameters

Windows 95 includes built-in caching software designed to make your disk drives operate as efficiently as possible. For most users, this caching operates behind the scenes, with no input or configuration necessary on their part. Windows, however, does allow you to control both read-ahead and write-behind caching. (The pros and cons of write-behind caching are discussed shortly.)

To change read-ahead caching for your hard drive, follow these steps:

1. Choose Start, Settings, Control Panel.

2. In the Control Panel window, double-click on the System icon. The System Properties sheet appears.

3. Click on the Performance tab.

4. Click on the File System button. The File System Properties sheet appears, with the Hard Disk tab selected, as shown in figure 10.2.

Working with Caches   **235**

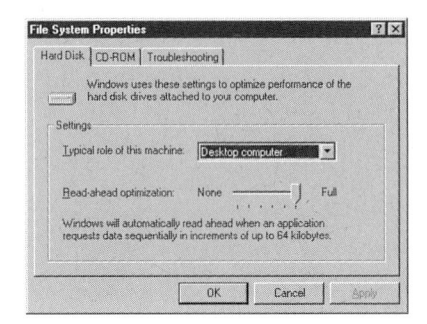

Fig. 10.2 Windows 95 allows you to modify how read-ahead caching is done on a hard drive.

There are two settings you can make in this sheet. The first is the pull-down list at the top of the Settings area. Here you can pick the typical use for your computer system, and then Windows will set the caching accordingly. There are three possible types of machines you can specify:

- **Desktop computer.** This setting is for an average system that is sitting on top of or beside your desk. Moderate-load caching is enabled when this machine type is selected.

- **Mobile or docking system.** You should select this as your machine type if you are running Windows 95 on a portable computer. Portable computers use their hard drives differently, and thus caching should be set accordingly. Windows does less read-ahead with this machine type so that there is not as much power drain (on the battery) through the hard drive.

- **Network server.** This type of machine typically has the highest disk performance requirements. The server basicly does nothing but access the disk to read and write information transmitted over the network. Because of this, the caching requirements are different than a single-user machine.

At the bottom of the Settings area is a slider control where you can indicate how big of read-ahead chunks you want Windows to use. Normally, at full read-ahead optimization, Windows will read up to the next 64K of information from the disk when your application is doing sequential data processing. You can set this cache amount to a lower value. Normally you should only do so if you have a very fast hard drive and your applications don't do much sequential processing of data.

Windows also allows you to set the same read-ahead caching parameters for your CD-ROM drives. To do this, follow these steps:

1. Choose Start, Settings, Control Panel.
2. In the Control Panel window, double-click on the System icon. The System Properties sheet appears.
3. Click on the Performance tab.
4. Click on the File System button, then on the CD-ROM tab. The File System Properties sheet appears, as shown in figure 10.3.

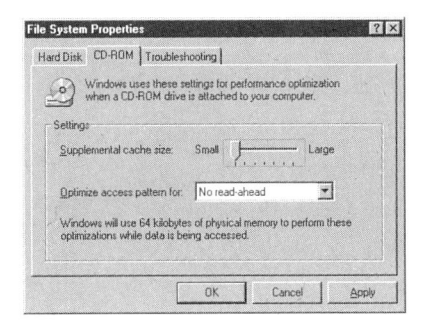

Fig. 10.3 Windows 95 allows you to modify how read-ahead caching is done on a CD-ROM drive.

Again, there are two settings you can make on this sheet. The first, at the top of the Settings area, is where you can set the supplemental read-ahead cache associated with the drive. Normally, this is set to the smallest setting possible. It is interesting to note that the smallest cache setting for the CD-ROM drive is the same value as the highest setting for the read-ahead cache on the hard drive—64K. This is because the CD-ROM is slower, and it is very conceivable you will want to set the cache to a larger value. If you find you do a lot of accessing of

Working with Caches

your CD-ROM drive, you can set the supplemental cache to a larger value by moving the slider control to the right.

At the bottom of the Settings area you can indicate how you want Windows to configure the read-ahead buffer for the CD-ROM. There are five possible settings accessed through the pull-down list:

> ➤ **No read-ahead.** This setting is the default, and means that Windows will do no read-ahead on the CD-ROM drive. Again, if you do a fair amount of processing from the drive, you'll want to choose one of the other optimization patterns.

> ➤ **Single-speed drives.** This setting is for conventional CD-ROM drives. With this pattern selected, you can specify a cache size (using the slider control) between 64K and 1,088K.

> ➤ **Double-speed drives.** This setting is for the popular double-speed drives. With this pattern selected, you can specify a cache size between 114K and 1138K.

> ➤ **Triple-speed drives.** Some systems come equipped with triple-speed drives. If so, you should select this pattern, which allows you to set a cache size between 164K and 1,188K.

> ➤ **Quad-speed or higher.** Most new high-performance systems sold today include a quad-speed CD-ROM drive, and some are coming equipped with a 6X drive. Selecting this option allows for cache sizes between 214K and 1,238K.

To change the write-behind cache used with disk drives (not CD-ROM drives, which are inherently read-only), follow these steps:

1. Choose Start, Settings, Control Panel.
2. In the Control Panel window, double-click on the System icon. The System Properties sheet appears.
3. Click on the Performance tab.
4. Click on the File System button and then the Troubleshooting tab. This displays the dialog box shown in figure 10.4.

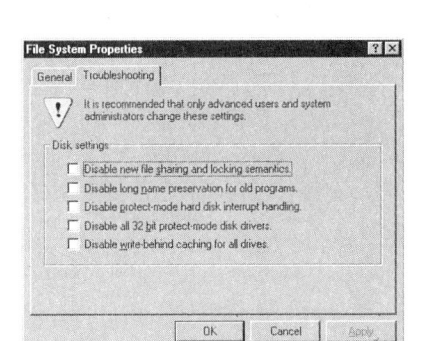

Fig. 10.4 Changing the file system properties is easy within Windows 95.

Notice that this dialog box has six check boxes. Each one allows you to control a different feature of the file system. The one you're interested in, however, is the final check box—Disable write-behind caching for all drives. If you select this check box, all information in Windows is written to the disk right away, rather than held in a software cache. While this provides for a greater degree of data integrity, it slows down your system a bit.

Using SmartDrive

In earlier versions of Windows that operated on top of the DOS operating system, it wasn't unusual to have a disk cache installed in the CONFIG.SYS file. These programs went by many different names, depending on the program vendor. One such program, provided with DOS and Windows, was SmartDrive. For many of the faster hard drives now available (particularly those with on-board caching), a software cache such as SmartDrive isn't necessary.

Many people think that Windows 95 has no need for the SmartDrive program. It's interesting, however, that a 32-bit version of SmartDrive is included with Windows 95. This new-and-improved caching program is loaded by Windows 95 if you had the older version of SmartDrive loaded in your CONFIG.SYS and/or AUTOEXEC.BAT files when you installed Windows 95. It's used primarily for DOS programs running under Windows 95.

> **Tip:** If you don't use DOS programs under Windows 95, remove the SmartDrive commands from your configuration files. SmartDrive isn't necessary for Windows programs, and you'll regain more memory for other programs.

The outward appearance of the Windows 95 version of SmartDrive is very similar to older versions of the program. Including the command line

```
C:\WINDOWS\SMARTDRV
```

in your AUTOEXEC.BAT file causes the following to happen:

➤ A disk cache is set up in extended memory. The size of the cache depends on the amount of extended memory on the system, as shown in the following table.

Extended Memory	InitCacheSize #	WinCacheSize #
Up to 4M	1M	512K
Up to 6M	2M	1M
6M or more	2M	2M

➤ All hard drives are read- and write-cached. Floppy drives and CD-ROM drives are read-cached only. Listing drive letters on the SmartDrive command line allows for the use of + and – to modify caching, as shown in the following list:

    d   Read-ahead-caching only

    d+   Both read-and write-caching

    d-   Don't cache

➤ The cache created will move 8,192 bytes at a time. You can specify 1,024, 2,048, and 4,096 by including **/e:ElementSize** after the driver letters on the command line.

➤ The read-ahead buffer is 16K but can be any multiple of ElementSize by adding **/b:BufferSize**.

> **Tip:** If your SCSI or ESDI disk controller uses bus mastering, you probably need to include the following line in your CONFIG.SYS file:
>
> DEVICE=C:\WINDOWS\SMARTDRV.EXE /DOUBLE_BUFFER
>
> Consult your disk controller manual, or type **SMARTDRV** at the DOS prompt and see a display of how SmartDrive is caching each drive. If yes appears under buffering in the line for your hard drive, you need double buffering.

The operation of SmartDrive allows caching of many drives such as Bernoullis, some hard cards, and many SCSI and WORM drives that require the use of device drivers. SmartDrive uses a FIFO (first in, first out) algorithm to determine what data to discard from the cache as new data is requested.

Write-Behind Caching

SmartDrive and the built-in Windows 95 caching software includes a write-behind feature that temporarily holds data to be written to disk in its cache. When a period of lower CPU activity occurs, the information held in the cache is written to the hard drive. The delay time isn't long—a maximum of 3 to 5 seconds. For some users, any write-behind delay time is unacceptable. For instance, you might want your changes committed to the disk immediately for security or data integrity reasons.

Earlier in this chapter you learned how you can turn off write-behind caching for Windows 95. SmartDrive also includes a way you can control write-behind caching. Unfortunately, the command syntax for SmartDrive is a bit vague. Here are some options:

Example: Set up only read-caching on all floppy drives and on hard drive C.

```
C:\WINDOWS\SMARTDRV C
```

Example: Set up read-caching on floppy drive A and the logical drive D.

`C:\WINDOWS\SMARTDRV a d`

Example: Disable caching your hard drive while defragmenting.

`C:\WINDOWS\SMARTDRV c-`

Testing Windows 95 with write-behind caching suggests that this feature is a major performance booster. If speed improvement is that important to you, look for other ways to protect your data from the write-behind feature. Delayed write caching provokes disagreement for some users. For users who might lose only a few numbers just entered on a spreadsheet or a few words in a document file, it's no big deal and might even be a help.

Power outages and freezing your system are examples of the disasters that loom when using the delayed write feature. You saved, the cache didn't. Some users complain about losses suffered when working with subroutines that write to multiple locations. Reconstructing that process may be impossible.

> **Tip:** When you exit from Windows 95 normally, all data stored in the SmartDrive buffers is written to disk; none is lost. If you're concerned about data loss from a power outage, invest in an uninterruptable power supply (UPS).

Hardware Caches

Most disks of 80M or larger with a built-in controller have a buffer of RAM on board. Also, internal and external disk caches, or hardware caches, are available. IDE and SCSI drives require a host adapter card for an external cache. ESDI drives have external controller cards.

At this point in the discussion, you'll benefit from knowing a few more definitions: A *buffer* is a holding tank for data read from the disk and awaiting transfer to the processor. A buffer can have read-ahead capability, reading neighboring data in case the system asks for the adjacent sectors. A variation of this is a full-track buffer, one that automatically reads the entire track containing the requested data. Although a buffer sounds like a cache, note that buffer activity doesn't require any logic to determine what is kept in the buffer and what is not. A cache may perform the same basic operations as a buffer, but algorithms are added to a cache to determine what data is replaced by incoming data.

Segmented caching technology is being adopted for internal caches, allowing greater speed and versatility. A segmented cache is divided into segments that store different types of data, and the size and contents of the segments can be automatically adjusted to match the way you work with your hard drive.

Hardware caches range in size from 256K to 64M, although caches of 1M or larger are disproportionately expensive compared to adding that much additional RAM to your motherboard. A large hardware cache can be advantageous on network servers, leaving system RAM free for multiuser applications. Possible software cache bottlenecks are thus eliminated, as are software conflicts.

Adding an external hardware cache if your drive has an internal cache isn't recommended. At some point, the housekeeping functions accumulate in various caches until they bog down. In fact, you may encounter similar problems with a software cache.

Using Compression Software

No matter how much you speed up your drive, if lack of space means you can't keep the applications and data files you need on your hard drive, all that speed won't do you any good. The idea of data compression started with the need to speed the process of downloading files from bulletin boards. Data compression has matured to become the easiest and least expensive way to increase space on your hard disk.

Archiving software has its roots in the DOS environment. These programs first appeared in 1985 in the form of ARC, created by System Enhancement Associates (SEA). Faster compression became available with Phil Katz's PKARC and PKXARC, which, after some legal scuffles, became the familiar PKZIP and PKUNZIP. Although PKWare is the standard for file archiving and a necessity if you want to download from bulletin boards, improved packages such as LHARC are being used by major software producers to compress their large applications onto a manageable number of floppy disks. When you install those applications after purchase, the install or setup program uses the LHARC or similar decompression program when transferring the application to your hard drive.

Refinements have been added to data compression software in the time since it was introduced, such as the capability to add a special header to a compressed file that makes it executable, or self-extracting. Some compression programs work better with one kind of data file than another. However, file compression programs don't save much disk space unless you use them to encourage the removal of unnecessary files to floppy disks. The capability to compress multiple, related files into one file, add identifying comments to each, and view an index and the individual files while still compressed makes the process of backing up and then deleting old files and programs from your drive more tolerable than backup methods previously available.

It's a tempting idea, to be sure, to compress that 300K monthly audit report form and a few other rarely used space hogs, decompressing a copy as needed. If your need for space is this serious, put the compressed file on a floppy disk instead. Although retrieving from a floppy disk is slow, don't forget that you're retrieving a compressed—and therefore much smaller—file. Retrieving the file and then decompressing it in faster RAM isn't as time consuming as copying the uncompressed version from a floppy disk. So, in addition to helping you better organize data you delete from the hard drive, file compression speeds the process of retrieving it when needed.

As of this writing, all the major compression programs are still DOS-based. You can run them under Windows 95 in an MS-DOS window, but you should be aware of two things:

➤ Switching to a DOS window to run the compression software can be a headache, although some Windows-based shells are available (such as WINZIP). While these shells are convenient, they still rely on the presence of the DOS-based compression programs on your system.

➤ Compression programs don't co-exist peacefully with long file names in Windows 95. If you're compressing files, make sure that you rename them or copy them to a file that conforms to the familiar 8.3 file name length limitation.

With the advent of long file names for all Windows users, it's likely that it won't be long before native compression software is available that won't limit how you work in Windows 95.

Using Swap Files

Windows 95 uses swap files to implement the virtual memory management made possible by the demand-paging capabilities of today's computer hardware. As the number of concurrent applications in memory increases, code and data that must remain in memory are swapped to the hard drive to make the space necessary to meet new demands.

If a request for information is made to a memory address and the information isn't in physical memory, the Windows 95 Virtual Memory Manager (VMM) steps in and retrieves the information from the swap file, swapping out other data if required. This step makes it possible for the computer to run more applications in memory than would otherwise be possible.

Unless you specify otherwise, Windows 95 creates a swap file named WIN386.SWP in the directory where Windows is installed. This swap file is dynamic in nature—it can grow, shrink, or disappear as dictated by Windows' swap-file needs. In this respect, Windows 95 swap files are similar to temporary swap files in older versions of Windows. However, the drawbacks historically evidenced in using temporary swap files (such as slow access) have been "weeded out" of Windows 95 through improved programming and logic in the VMM.

Even though the logic used in the VMM has been improved, you may want to explicitly specify the swap file parameters to be used by Windows 95. For instance, if you have a slow hard drive, you may experience faster swap file access if you specify a permanent area on your hard drive for the swap file. To modify the virtual memory settings, follow these steps:

1. Choose Settings from the Start menu.
2. From the Settings menu, choose Control Panel.
3. Double-click on the System icon in the Control Panel window.
4. In the Properties for System dialog box, click on the Performance tab.
5. Click on the Virtual Memory button to display the Virtual Memory dialog box (see fig. 10.5).

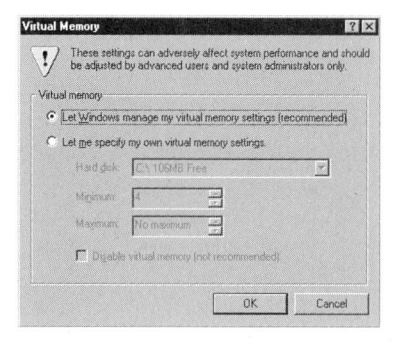

Fig. 10.5 The Virtual Memory dialog box allows you to specify how Windows 95 should manage its swap file.

246 Chapter 10: Optimizing Your Disk Drives

Normally, the first option in the Virtual Memory dialog box is selected. This allows Windows to manage virtual memory (disk swapping) as it sees best. If you choose the second option, you either can specify disable virtual memory support (which would severely cripple the performance of Windows), or you can specify three parameters concerning the swap file:

- Where it should be located
- What the minimum swap file size should be
- What the maximum swap file size should be

If you make the minimum and maximum sizes the same, you effectively are setting up a permanent swap file on disk. Unless you calculate (or guess) correctly as to the swap file size, you could slow down Windows' performance. Make sure that you specify only manual swap file parameters if you learn, through experience, that such settings are best for your system. You should also make sure that your disk is defragmented before you make such a change.

Defragmenting Your Disk Drive

Windows 95 derives its disk organization heritage from DOS. (You learned a bit about this in Chapter 2, "Under-the-Hood Improvements.") This means that the same disk structure is effectively maintained in Windows 95 that existed in previous versions of Windows and DOS. The disk is divided into tracks, each of which is divided into 512-byte sectors. On large hard drives, these sectors can't be accessed individually because of limitations in the File Allocation System (FAT). For compatibility reasons, this limitation also exists in the VFAT file system used in Windows 95. Instead of information being accessible as sectors, information is instead processed in *clusters*. These clusters are composed of anywhere from 2 to 4 sectors. Thus, a cluster can consist of anywhere from 1K to 2K of data.

Note: Clusters represent the minimum storage unit that can be allocated to a file. Thus, a small file can have quite a bit of wasted space at the end of it. This is one of the attractions of using compressed disk drives, as discussed earlier in the chapter—they allow you to pack information tighter, thereby reclaiming the space typically lost when storing small files in a FAT environment.

As information is first stored to a disk drive, the disk drive fills up in an orderly manner. As existing data is erased, the FAT is changed to indicate which disk clusters are empty. Later, when additional data is written to the drive, Windows starts writing in the nearest empty cluster as determined by the FAT, and when that cluster fills, moves on to fill the next empty cluster, skipping any occupied clusters along the way. As you continue to retrieve, edit, and save again and again, you end up with pieces of many files scattered across the entire drive. This condition is called *file fragmentation*. When data needs to be read from a disk, moving the read/write heads all around the disk to collect scattered parts of a file can be very time-consuming.

Windows 95 includes a disk defragmentation utility that you can use to correct this problem. *Disk defragmenting* is the process of analyzing a disk's file structure and making sure that each file on the disk occupies a series of contiguous disk clusters. You should periodically run the defragmentation utility, depending on how much you use your system. If you use your system only lightly, you should defragment your drives monthly. If you use it heavily, you probably want to defragment on a weekly basis. Using the utility is quick and easy, so you don't need to block large amounts of time to perform this bit of housekeeping.

To start the defragmenting utility, follow these steps:

1. Choose Start, Programs, Accessories.
2. From the Accessories menu, choose System Tools.
3. From the System Tools menu, choose Disk Defragmenter. This starts the defragmenting utility.

Now you need to choose which disk drive you want to defragment. Windows 95 displays the dialog box shown in figure 10.6.

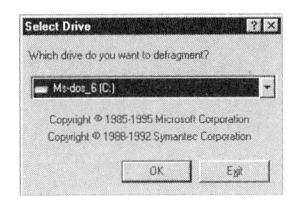

Fig. 10.6 Picking a disk drive is the first step in defragmenting.

You can pick any disk drive on your system, including floppy drives. (You can't, however, pick read-only drives such as a CD-ROM drive.) If you use the pull-down list in the dialog box, you can even pick the choice All Hard Drives, which runs the program on all the hard drives in your system. You should choose the disk drive (or drives) you want to defragment, and then click OK.

The program then checks to see how fragmented the disk already is. This is necessary so that the proper initialization areas can be set up. If the disk isn't very fragmented, you're advised of the fact, and you have the chance of forcing the defragmentation.

The amount of time necessary for defragmenting a drive depends on several factors, such as the size of your hard drive, how full it is, and how long it has been since you last defragmented. Defragmenting can take anywhere from several minutes to several hours to complete. As a result, you'll probably want to run the program when you know you'll have time to complete it. For example, run it as you are ready to quit work for the evening. That way, it can be done by the time you arrive at work the next morning.

When the program is done, you're given the opportunity to defragment another drive. You can select another one or close the program window.

Surviving with a Small Hard Drive

There are two major reasons to consider adopting the ideas presented in this section:

- You have an 80M or smaller drive with only 4M of memory and no data compression program.

- Your drive has reached its optimal speed, and you're ready to invest time to keep it that way.

There's no clear line dividing suggestions that increase speed and create extra space. You probably need to improve both because smaller drives are usually older drives using older technology that provide slow access times. Some of the following techniques have been discussed earlier in this chapter but are even more important for the small hard drive user to follow. Others are data management and housekeeping suggestions that help keep any disk in tip-top shape. All are designed to help you enhance the efficiency and effectiveness of your computer system.

Using Low-Level Formatting

Low-level formatting is a process that creates tracks and sectors on a disk. Many drives—such as those that use stepper motors—benefit from this process being repeated later in life. Low-level formatting addresses a frequent problem known as *alignment creep*. Alignment creep occurs as the stepper motor wears, which results in the sectors that pass under drive heads no longer being properly aligned with the heads. The low-level formatting process corrects this problem and also locates surface defects on the disks.

Many experts suggest that you low-level format your hard drive yearly. Most newer disk drives contain built-in utilities that allow you to perform a low-level format. Older drives may require a separate disk utility, which can be run from the floppy drive. All you need to do is boot to the floppy and run the formatting program.

Caution: Performing a low-level format too often can cause more harm than good. If you format more often than yearly, you run the risk of adding undue wear and tear on your drive.

Adjusting the Interleave

Older drives can't transfer disk data fast enough to be able to read the next sector before it's spun past the read/write head. To allow for this, sectors aren't numbered sequentially, but instead are numbered to skip every other one (2:1 interleave) or to skip 2 sectors (3:1 interleave), and so on. This allows time for the head to transfer data and be ready to read again. Older MFM and RLL drives were usually set with a 3:1 interleave, even though a 286 system could support a 2:1 interleaved drive.

Programs such as OPTune, SpinRite, Calibrate, and DiskFix can adjust the interleave without harming the data on your drive. When you're using Windows 95, these programs should be run after booting to a DOS diskette; you shouldn't run them from the Windows 95 command line.

Adjusting the disk interleave is a lengthy process, because each sector is renumbered and all data is transferred to new physical locations. The performance benefit of this one-time-only job is substantial.

Caution: Don't adjust the interleave on IDE or SCSI drives. Usually, optimizing software doesn't work on these drives, but some older IDE drives don't communicate their identity well. Refer to your owner's manual or obtain identifying data off the drive. Ask a dealer to look up the drive if you're unsure of the type of drive you have.

Cleaning Up Your Drive

All very small files waste space on your disk. This is because each file must occupy at least one cluster, even if the file isn't that large. For instance, a file that contains only 100 bytes of data still occupies an entire cluster of disk space; the rest of the cluster is simply wasted. If you can do without some of the smaller files, you should delete them. This has the potential of freeing up large amounts of disk space.

Also, many programs contain numerous files you don't need all the time. You can keep these files on floppy disks, which you can then use with your programs. For instance, programs such as Word for Windows allow you to specify the location of such files as clip art and templates. You can specify the new file location as the floppy drive. When it needs them, the program looks to the floppy drive. Database, desktop publishing, and some graphics programs might suffer an intolerable slowdown, but you won't notice a difference with other programs. If you need a directory display of a floppy disk often, set up a file manager window of the directory, and then switch back and forth as you need to view it.

Considering Hard Drive Upgrades

The final and most costly solution to the drive space crunch is to upgrade your hard drive. Many drives available feature access times of 10 milliseconds or less; you can easily find drives with access times of 8 ms. While small variations may not make much difference, jumping from a 16 ms drive to a 10 or 8 ms drive can make a large difference. Also, the faster your CPU, the faster access time you'll want for your disk drive.

Here are the questions you need to answer before selecting a specific drive (they aren't listed in any particular order):

➤ How much can you afford to pay? There's little difference in the price of drives of the same size.

- Does the price of the drive include everything, or do you need to buy a card or other items (such as a drive kit)?

- How much space do you need now and for the next two years? Windows 95 occupies about 60M. It's not uncommon for program sizes to double or triple from one major version to the next. Also, remember that as your expertise and ability increases, so does the number of programs you work with.

- What's compatible with your current system? What kind of drive is your system using now? Is the connector built into the motherboard?

- What peripherals are you using or wanting to buy?

The hard drives you need to consider for a Windows 95 system are those types large enough and fast enough to constitute a serious upgrade: a minimum size of 500M or larger at access speeds below 10 ms. As discussed in Chapter 8, "Examining the Hardware You Need for Windows 95," there are four types of hard drives: IDE, SCSI, ESDI, and ST506. However, IDE and SCSI are the only two generally available anymore due to the fact that ESDI and ST506 are older, slower, and less reliable technologies. Also, the older technology drives don't offer the speed and capacity of IDE and SCSI. There are pros and cons to both IDE and SCSI drives:

- IDE (Integrated Drive Electronics) drives range from 42M to more than 1G (1,000M). 230M and larger models consistently sport access times of 8 to 12 ms, with 10 and under readily available. Their transfer speeds have increased tremendously over the years.

  The name IDE comes from the fact that the controller electronics are built into the drive itself rather than on a separate card. Most of the systems being sold today feature an IDE drive for drives up to about 500M, and EIDE (an enhanced version of IDE) drives for larger capacities. Low-level formatting isn't needed, as the manufacturer precodes the drive's sector information.

➤ SCSI (Small Computer System Interface) drives are commonly available in sizes as large as 9G (9,100M). 500M and larger models feature access times of 8 to 12 ms. SCSI drives also have their controllers built into the drive.

The adapter card for the drive can support up to seven SCSI devices, such as tape backups and CD-ROM drives, and hard drives can be chained together to provide enormous amounts of storage. Because of this technology, SCSI drives are highly desirable for use with network servers. The large size, coupled with blazing transfer rates (40 to 80 megabits per second), can be combined with the more advanced system configurations found in network servers to give excellent performance.

> **Caution:** In the past, SCSI device drivers for host adapters suffered from chronic compatibility problems. To make your life easier, first find the other SCSI devices you want to use. Then ask what SCSI hard drives are compatible with them.

Hard drive technology is developing answers for more speed. One major area of change is in revolutions per minute. 3,600 rpm has long been the standard, and the ESDI interface is locked in to this speed. IDE and SCSI interfaces aren't, and 4,500 to 7,200 rpm drives are readily available. Another area of interest is in changing bus width from 8-bit to 16-bit or even 32-bit widths to increase data transfer rates.

> **Tip:** Most drives available today, including the drives discussed here, have a 1:1 interleave. You have one less thing to worry about while shopping, as they already will deliver maximum service.

Prices in the fall of 1994 were about $1 per megabyte for up to 150M, then dropping to $0.40 per megabyte for up to 1 gigabyte (1,000M), and as low as $0.35 per megabyte for the larger drives (those between 4G and 9G). That translates to about $175 for a 210M drive, $250 for the 340M that should keep many users happy for a few years, to $2,000 for 4 G (4,000M) for the power user. For drives over s4G, the cost ratio is somewhat lower.

Shopping for a hard drive can be a horrible experience. After you determine how much you can afford and how big a drive you want, figuring out what will really be compatible with your system can be a nightmare. Do your floppy drive cables plug into your present hard drive controller card? How much space do you have inside the box? What other peripherals are you using?

Get out your manual. Open the system and find all the numbers. Then sit down and start calling around. Hard Drives International at (800) 535-1506 is a reliable low-end price operation; Mega Haus at (800) 786-1185 is another good choice. Let them ask you questions and give you some options. Take a look at the Computer Shopper magazine for an extensive listing of equipment, best buys, and street pricing. Then call your local stores. If you've never installed a drive, you may want them to do it for you.

> **Tip:** If you're upgrading your entire computer system, make sure that you get one that has a PCI Bus or VL-Bus. These offer maximum performance, and you can even get hard drive controllers that use these faster buses.

Considering Hard Drive Upgrades **255**

Video Cards, Drivers, and Monitors

by Allen L. Wyatt

The video subsystem of your computer contains two different elements: the video adapter card and the video monitor. These elements work together to provide you a "window" into what your PC is doing. Windows 95 uses video drivers to communicate with the video subsystem. By using the right video drivers with a high-quality video card and monitor, you can greatly improve your productivity and limit fatigue and eye-strain.

This chapter discusses the various video elements you'll find in your Windows 95 system. In this chapter, you'll learn about video cards, monitors, and drivers. You'll also learn what to look for in both video cards and monitors, as well as how to configure Windows 95 for your video hardware. Finally, you'll receive a crash course in what you can do to improve the video processing speed of your system.

Video Cards

The root of your video system is the video card, sometimes called a video adapter or video adapter card. This card is either built into your computer's motherboard or installed in an adapter slot in your PC. The video card serves as an intermediary between your CPU and the monitor. It is perhaps the single most critical part of your computer system, outside of the CPU itself.

Types of Video Cards

The marketplace fields a number of different video standards used to define how information is displayed on a video screen. Some of these standards, although historically significant, are not really suitable for use in a Windows system. For instance, the following video standards have uses in some application areas, but not with Windows:

- **MDA.** The monochrome display adapter used with the original IBM PCs and XTs.

- **HGA.** The Hercules graphics adapter, which made monochrome graphics popular in the early days of the PC.

- **CGA.** The first color graphics adapter marketed by IBM.

- **EGA.** The enhanced graphics adapter, which brought higher resolutions and more colors to the PC.

- **MCGA.** The multi-color graphics array, introduced as one of two successors to the EGA, but primarily for the low-end of the PS/2 line of computers.

In the video arena, you already know that the minimum system requirement for Windows 95 is a video card that meets VGA standards. The VGA (*video graphics array*) was introduced by IBM when it first introduced the PS/2 line of computers. IBM used the VGA primarily in its high-end systems for the line, but the standard has since been adopted by a variety of companies as a common video standard for stand-alone video cards. The VGA is the absolute, rock-bottom minimum for a video system.

The VGA is rapidly becoming a thing of the past. Any computer system sold within the past two years most likely will have some sort of SVGA card installed. SVGA is an acronym for *super video graphics array*. It was given this name because it offers a super-set of the capabilities designed into the VGA standard. The problem is that there is not just one SVGA standard. Instead, there are two or three chip sets used to implement SVGA. These chip sets add different capabilities to the VGA standard, and they supply the capabilities in different manners.

If you have an MCA-based computer (some of the IBM PS/2 computers used MCA busses), then you could have other types of video adapters, as well. For instance, the 8514/A was distributed for a time. It provided greater resolution, colors, and throughput than the VGA adapter, but not as great as many of the SVGA cards on the market right now. After a couple of years, IBM stopped using the 8514/A and adopted the XGA standard. IBM introduced the XGA (*extended graphics array*) in 1990 as a successor to VGA (and the 8514/A). However, because of XGA's primary use in MCA systems, it was viewed as a proprietary system and was therefore not adopted by many third-party card vendors. In 1992, IBM introduced the XGA/2, which added to the XGA many of the capabilities of a bare-bones SVGA card. Again, the use of the XGA/2 has been limited largely to systems based on the MCA bus.

Windows 95 will support the following types of video adapters:

- VGA
- SVGA
- 8514/A
- XGA
- XGA/2

Graphics Accelerators

As a rule, the greater the graphics needs of a program, the slower it will run. This speed is directly related to the amount of data that must be updated on the video screen. When a full-screen, 256-color display is changed, the computer must send 640 × 480 or 307,200 bytes of data to the video display card. The situation gets worse when you use the SVGA modes; 800 × 600 mode requires 480,000 bytes and a 1,024 × 768 display needs 786,432 bytes. If you increase the number of possible colors in the display, the amount of information to be processed is increased further still. For instance, if you use a video card that supports 65,535 colors, then you double the amount of graphics information to be processed, and a video card that handles 1.5M colors must handle three times the information. Table 11.1 shows how the amount of information to be processed can vary, depending on the card's operating mode.

Table 11.1 The amount of information a video card can process

Resolution	16 Colors	256 Colors	64K Colors	1.5M Colors
640 × 480	307,200	307,200	614,400	921,600
800 × 600	480,000	480,000	960,000	1,440,000
1,024 × 768	786,432	786,432	1,572,864	2,359,296

Processing huge amounts of video information puts quite a high demand on the CPU and on the system bus in your computer. It's not that your computer can't handle it—it can, given enough time. That's why complex video displays can take a while to display all the information they're asked to process.

The solution to this "video bottleneck" is to use a graphics accelerator. In fact, many SVGA cards are marketed as graphics accelerators because they provide specialized circuitry that allows them to process information much quicker than standard VGA cards. The effect of using these cards is simple—if you speed up the video, you speed up the entire computer system. This is because you don't need to wait as long on what is typically the slowest part of your computer system. Many graphics accelerators that have been fine-tuned for use with Windows boast speed increases of from 50 percent to 100 percent.

Understanding Busses

Getting a faster video card, in the form of a graphics accelerator, is only half the story, however. Regardless of how fast a video card you get, the I/O bus (which is used to interface the adapter cards with the CPU) is still relatively slow—around 8 or 10 MHz with a 16-bit data path. This situation makes the I/O bus the weakest link in most systems, particularly those with demanding graphics needs. While the CPU is trying to push graphics data through the slow I/O channel, it can't be doing much else. The need for the I/O bus to remain at a lower speed was due to the huge installed base of adapter cards that could operate only at the slower speeds. Figure 11.1 shows a conceptual block diagram of the busses in a computer system.

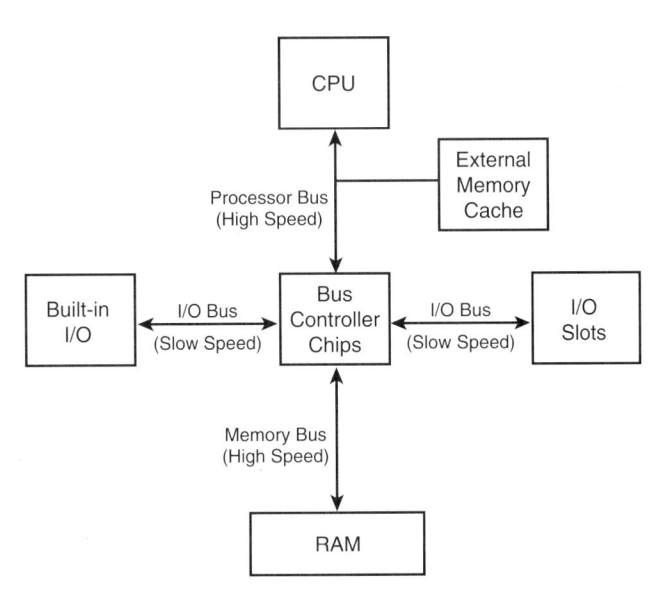

Fig. 11.1 The layout of a typical PC incorporates both high- and low-speed busses.

Video Cards **261**

To overcome this bottleneck, local-bus systems were developed. This bus gets its name from putting one or two bus connectors (or direct devices) on the bus used by the CPU. This bus is local to the CPU, thus the term *local bus*. This bus arrangement is shown in figure 11.2.

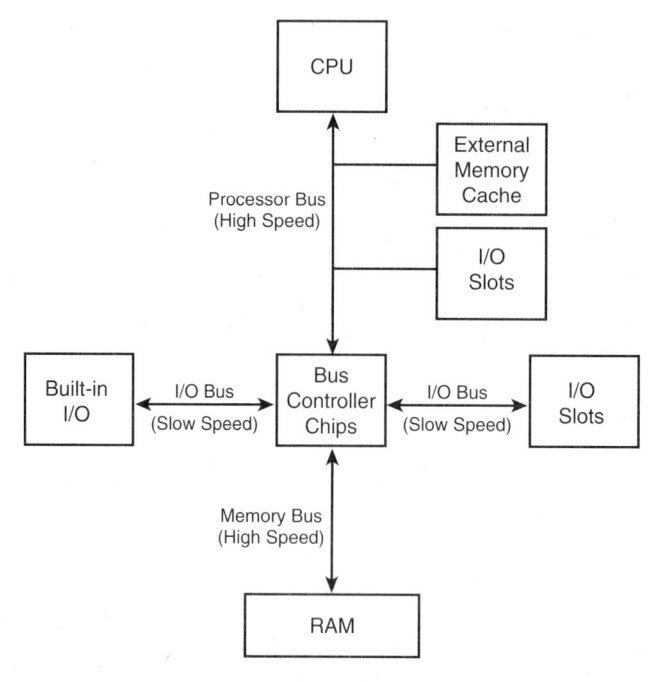

Fig. 11.2 A local-bus implementation includes I/O slots on both the normal I/O bus and the high-speed processor bus.

Note: It is important to note that local bus does not replace earlier bus standards, such as ISA or EISA. Instead, it complements them, which means that a system will typically be based on ISA or EISA, and have one or more local bus slots available as well. The result is that older adapter cards are still compatible with the system, but high-speed adapter cards can take advantage of the local-bus slots as well.

262   Chapter 11: Video Cards, Drivers, and Monitors

Primarily, the local bus is used for video subsystems and increasingly for disk drive controllers. To make your system as fast as it can be, you should look for a computer that implements one of the standard local busses. There are two such busses in wide use today—the VL-Bus and the PCI-bus. These are discussed in the next two sections.

VL-Bus

The initial implementations of local bus were designed to overcome video bottlenecks. The problem, however, is that there was no standard in these implementations. To overcome this oversight, the Video Electronics Standards Association (VESA) developed a standardized local-bus specification in 1992 and early 1993. This standardization became known as the *VESA Local Bus,* or simply as the *VL-Bus.* As with earlier local-bus implementations, the VL-Bus slot offers direct access to system memory at the speed of the processor itself. The VL-Bus can move data between the CPU and an adapter card 32 bits at a time—the full data width of the 486 chip. The maximum rated throughput of the VL-Bus is 128-132M/second. In other words, local bus went a long way toward removing the major bottlenecks existing in earlier bus configurations. The change made it possible to move enough data to refresh an entire 1,024 × 768 resolution screen, using 1.5M colors, many times per second.

Despite the benefits of the VL-Bus (and by extension, all local busses), there are a few drawbacks. These drawbacks are as follows:

> ➤ **486 CPU dependent.** The VL-Bus is inherently tied to the 486 processor bus. This bus is different from that used by the Pentium, and probably from those used by future CPUs. A VL-Bus that operates at the full rated speed of a Pentium has not been developed, although stop-gap measures (such as stepping down speed or developing bus bridges) are available.

- ➤ *Speed limitations.* The VL-Bus specification allows for speeds of up to 66 MHz on the bus, but the electrical characteristics of the VL-Bus connector limit an adapter card to no more than 50 MHz. If the main CPU uses a clock modifier (such as those that double clock speeds), then the VL-Bus uses the unmodified CPU clock speed as its bus speed.

- ➤ *Electrical limitations.* The processor bus has very tight timing rules, which may even vary from CPU to CPU. These timing rules were designed around only specialized circuitry being connected to the bus. As more circuitry is added (as with a VL-Bus), the electrical load on the bus is increased. If not implemented correctly, this increased load can lead to problems such as loss of data integrity and timing problems between the CPU and the VL-Bus adapter cards.

- ➤ *Card limitations.* Depending on the electrical loading of a system, the number of VL-Bus cards is limited. While the VL-Bus specification allows for as many as three cards, this can only be achieved at clock rates of up to 40 MHz with an otherwise low system-board load. As the system-board load increases and the clock rate increases, the number of cards supported decreases. Only one VL-Bus card can be supported at 50 MHz with a high system-board load.

These drawbacks should not dissuade you from investing in a VL-Bus system. Indeed, they provide an acceptable solution to the needs of high-speed computing. However, many critics complain that even though the VL-Bus is well suited to 486 systems, it is just that—a modified 486 system. They contend it is not adaptable or extensible, meaning it does not work well for non-video needs nor will it work well (without modification) for future generations of CPUs.

Note: Several implementations of local-bus video with proprietary graphics adapter cards do not include a VESA feature connector. When the local-bus video is implemented on the motherboard, some manufacturers sacrifice VESA feature connectors to reduce manufacturing costs. If you are considering purchasing a computer with a local bus and at some time will want to take advantage of full-motion video or even video frame-grabbers, make sure a VESA feature connector is provided.

Without the feature connector, you cannot add a conventional video-in-a-window card or an internal VGA-to-NTSC card to the system. In that case, to convert VGA output to NTSC television signals, you need an external scan converter. Scan converters with genlocking capability are considerably more expensive than their counterpart on an adapter card.

PCI Bus

In early 1992, an industry group (headed by Intel) was formed to overcome the bottlenecks imposed by earlier PC bus specifications. This group, the PCI Special Interest Group (PCI is an acronym for *peripheral component interconnect*), released its initial specification in June, 1992. The PCI bus redesigned the traditional PC bus by inserting another bus (referred to as a *bridge*) between the CPU and the native I/O bus. Rather than tap directly into the processor bus with its delicate electrical timing (as was done in the VL-Bus), a new set of controller chips was developed that extended the bus, as shown in figure 11.3.

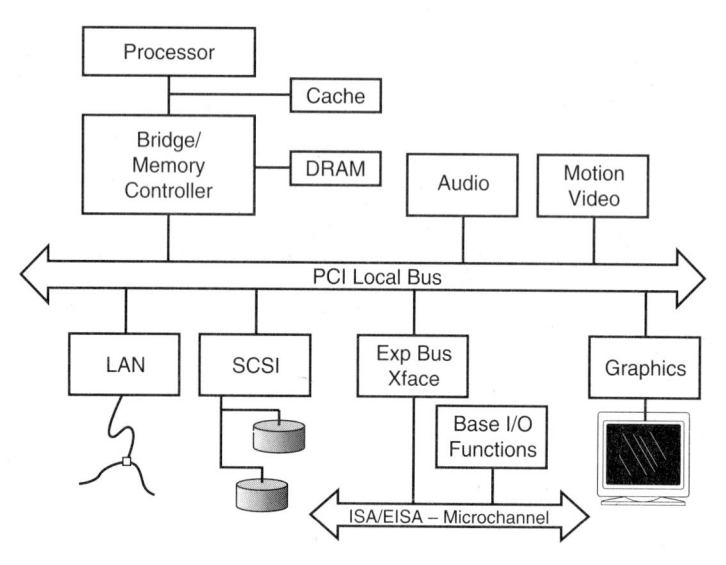

Fig. 11.3 The PCI bus adds another layer of busses to the traditional PC architecture.

PCI bypasses the standard I/O bus and uses the system bus to increase the bus clock speed and take full advantage of the CPU's data path. Systems integrating the PCI bus became available in mid-1993, and have since become the mainstay of high-end systems.

Information is transferred across the PCI bus at 33 MHz, at the full data width of the CPU. In addition, the PCI bus can operate concurrently with the processor bus; it does not supplant it. This means that the CPU can be processing data in an external cache while the PCI bus is busy transferring information between other parts of the system. This is a major design benefit of the PCI bus.

Monitors

The video monitor displays information sent to it by the video card. When examining a video subsystem, you don't want to spend all your time examining individual components without looking at the other components as well. In other words, you need to make sure that the video monitor you use is well matched to the capabilities of the video card you get. If a good match does not exist, then you won't be satisfied with the results achieved. In fact, if there is enough of a mismatch, it is possible to physically damage a monitor by connecting it to some video cards.

How can damage occur? Primarily by trying to "drive" a monitor beyond its design specifications. For instance, if you have a video card that sustains a high refresh rate, and the monitor does not, then damage can result. Thus, the best course of action is to make sure that the monitor you get has capabilities either matching or exceeding those of your video card.

How do you know which features to look for in a video monitor? The number of possible features is limited. The features include the following elements:

- Screen size
- Dot pitch
- Screen curvature
- Refresh rate
- Interlacing

There is no real hierarchy among these features; each is as important as the other. They do, however, tend to have a cumulative effect, from the perspective of the user. You should look for the monitor that has the best characteristics within each feature area, and then make your buying decision accordingly. The following sections address each of the features you should consider.

Screen Size

You already know that video monitors come in different sizes. You can find some that are small, and others that come packaged on their own shipping pallet. How do you know which size is right for you?

Screen size is based on the size of the image. To get the correct screen size, just measure diagonally across the image. Thus, a 14-inch monitor can produce an image that is 14 inches from top-left corner to bottom-right corner. If you remember your geometry from high school, and remember that monitors always have a 4:3 size ratio (horizontal to vertical), you can calculate the image width, image height, and screen area of a monitor. Table 11.2 shows these figures for a range of screen sizes.

Table 11.2   Specifications for Various Screen Sizes.

Screen Size	Width	Height	Screen Area
12-in	9.6-in	7.2-in	69.12 sq in
13-in	10.4-in	7.8-in	81.12 sq in
14-in	11.2-in	8.4-in	94.08 sq in
15-in	12-in	9-in	108 sq in
16-in	12.8-in	9.6-in	122.88 sq in
17-in	13.6-in	10.2-in	138.72 sq in
18-in	14.4-in	10.8-in	155.52 sq in
19-in	15.2-in	11.4-in	173.28 sq in
20-in	16-in	12-in	192 sq in
21-in	16.8-in	12.6-in	211.68 sq in

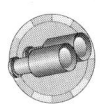

Note: Some monitor manufacturers have a tendency to exaggerate their monitor sizes. For instance, a 14-inch monitor may only produce a 13-inch (or less) image—cheaper video tubes tend to distort images near the corners of the image area. Manufacturers can get away with this exaggeration by quoting the unlimited image area instead of the actual image area, which should be the proper measure. Don't be afraid to take a ruler to the actual image area to determine the true image size. Use this measure for comparison.

In general, the screen size you use will depend on your personal preferences. If you work in a cramped area where space is scarce, then a larger screen is probably out of the question. However, if you do work in which higher screen resolutions are desirable or necessary, and work area is no problem, then you'll definitely want a larger screen.

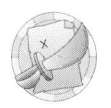

On a desktop computer system, at 640 × 480 resolution, a 14-inch monitor generally suffices. Anything smaller, and you might find it difficult to read some smaller text or make out detail in some icons. At the opposite end of the spectrum, if you're working at 1,024 × 768, then you'll find the 21-inch screen most satisfactory.

Tip: Before you purchase a monitor, if possible try out various sizes by using the software you work with most often. This way you can be sure you'll be happy with your monitor before you sign on the dotted line.

Dot Pitch

A video tube (CRT) used within a monitor is simple. It consists of three electron guns at the rear of the tube that shoot an electron stream at the front of the tube. This stream of electrons moves very rapidly across the screen. As it moves, it energizes a phosphor coating on the inside of the front of the tube. This illuminated phosphor is what creates the images you see on the monitor.

The phosphor is painted on the inside of the video tube in "groups." If you could get a powerful enough magnifying glass, you could actually see these groups on your screen. (This is why you can sometimes see color dots if there is a drop of water on your screen—the drop of water acts as a magnifying glass.) These groups consist of a red phosphor dot, a blue phosphor dot, and a green phosphor dot. The distance between these phosphor groups is termed *dot pitch*. The lower the dot pitch, the higher the picture quality that can be created on a monitor.

Monitors **269**

Dot pitch is provided in millimeters. Thus, a dot pitch of .30 means that there is .30 millimeters between phosphor groups on your. This translates to .011811 inches (1mm equals .03937 inches), or 84.67 dots per inch (approximately). If you look back at table 11.2, you'll see that a 14-inch monitor has an image that is 11.2 inches wide. This measurement means that there are approximately 948 phosphor groups across the width of the screen. Since each phosphor group can only be on or off at any given time, for the best picture, your horizontal resolution should not exceed the number of phosphor groups you have on a line.

You can also do the same calculations vertically, which for a 14-inch monitor would result in approximately 711 phosphor groups vertically. Thus, a 14-inch monitor would have 948 × 711 phosphor groups. For the best screen resolution, then, you should not exceed 800 × 600 resolution on a 14-inch monitor. If you use a higher resolution, you'll still be able to see an image, but not all the pixels will be displayed properly, and the picture might appear a bit fuzzy in places. Table 11.3 shows the approximate phosphor group configurations for the various monitor sizes at some popular dot pitches.

Table 11.3 Phosphor Group Configurations for Different Monitors

Screen Size	.31 Dot Pitch	.28 Dot Pitch	.25 Dot Pitch
12-in	787 × 590	871 × 653	975 × 732
13-in	852 × 639	943 × 708	1057 × 792
14-in	918 × 688	1016 × 762	1138 × 853
15-in	983 × 737	1089 × 816	1219 × 914
16-in	1049 × 787	1161 × 871	1300 × 975
17-in	1114 × 836	1234 × 925	1382 × 1036
18-in	1180 × 885	1306 × 980	1463 × 1097
19-in	1245 × 934	1379 × 1034	1544 × 1158
20-in	1311 × 983	1451 × 1089	1626 × 1219
21-in	1377 × 1032	1524 × 1143	1707 × 1280

When you look for a monitor, you should go for the lowest dot pitch you can find; the lower the dot pitch the sharper the image. Anything with a .28 dot pitch is considered a good monitor as of this writing. Higher dot pitches will not provide as good of an image as possible, and you should steer away from them.

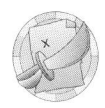

> **Tip:** Even though you can show a crisp 800 × 600 image on a 14-inch monitor with a .30 dot pitch, that doesn't mean you'll be happy with the size of the display. The best advice is still to try before you buy.

Screen Curvature

Earlier you learned that some monitor vendors frequently exaggerate the size of their screens. This exaggeration is caused by the distortion that affects many screens at the corners. The reason for this distortion is because many video tubes are curved at the front—just like your television screen at home. This curvature leads to the distortion. To overcome this distortion, many vendors offer flat-screen monitors. While the name may be a bit of a misnomer (since flat-screen monitors are still a bit curved, although not nearly as much as normal video tubes), these monitors provide a better image because the distortion inherent in the curved-screen models is removed. The trade-off is that flat-screen monitors cost more to produce, and therefore the price tag is higher.

Refresh Rate

The refresh rate refers to the frequency at which the electron guns in your monitor actually redraw the image on your screen. The higher the refresh rate, the crisper the image on your screen.

Refresh rates are determined by the two scanning frequencies of a monitor. The horizontal scanning frequency refers to the time it takes the electron gun to move all the way across the screen. The vertical scanning frequency refers to the time it takes to move the electron gun down the screen. Refresh rates are expressed in Hertz. A refresh rate of 60 Hz means that the image on the screen is redrawn 60 times a second. Likewise, a 72 Hz refresh rate means that the screen is redrawn 72 times a second.

It is important to match the refresh rates used by the monitor with the refresh rates produced by your video card. If the monitor expects a higher refresh rate than what the card produces, you won't see anything on the monitor. If the video card produces a higher refresh rate than the monitor can handle, then not only won't you see an image, but you can physically damage the monitor.

Interlacing

Interlacing refers to how the electron guns that "paint" the image on your screen actually do their job. You already know that the electron guns move back and forth, painting an image down the front of your video tube. In an interlaced monitor, the electron guns scan alternate lines. Thus, lines 1, 3, 5, 7, 9, and so on are scanned. When the bottom of the screen is reached, on the next pass the guns scan lines 2, 4, 6, 8, 10, and so on. This setup means that an interlaced monitor requires two complete vertical passes to create a complete image. A non-interlaced monitor does not do this. Instead, it scans lines consecutively, completing the screen in one pass.

Some users complain that interlaced monitors produce more flicker than non-interlaced, particularly at higher screen resolutions. Interlaced monitors typically cost less than non-interlaced models. Because they need to make two passes per screen, the refresh rates on interlaced monitors are also lower than on non-interlaced. If you spend a good deal of your time viewing high-resolution images, you'll definitely want a non-interlaced monitor.

Multisync Monitors

As you can imagine, the number of different video cards on the market means that there are a number of different specifications that a monitor must meet. This means that matching the proper monitor to the proper video card can be a time consuming and frustrating process.

Monitor vendors have a vested interest in making sure that their monitors will work with the widest variety of video cards. To address the many card specifications that exist, vendors have been (for the past few years) marketing multisync monitors. The primary feature of these monitors is that they can detect the frequencies used by your video card, and then adjust themselves to match. This feature makes matching up monitors to adapters much easier, and can prevent the damage possible if they should be mismatched.

Multisync monitors generally cost more than "monosync" monitors, but the investment is generally worth it. Why? Because there is a good chance that you'll upgrade your video card before you upgrade your monitor. If you don't have a multisync monitor, the chances are better that you'll need to change your monitor when you change the video card.

Video Drivers

You learned earlier that different video standards (such as VGA or XGA) have different specifications. You also learned that in the SVGA arena, different chip sets on the adapter cards accomplish video tasks in different ways. For Windows 95 to make the most use out of these video cards, it uses *video drivers*.

The use of video drivers is nothing new. Drivers have been used with different software (and Windows) for years. When you installed Windows 95, it attempted to determine what video card you have installed in your system. Most of the time, this testing is successful, and there is no problem. In some instances, however, the automatic testing could fail, in which case Windows 95 uses a generic driver for either the VGA, SVGA, or XGA cards.

In most instances, you (as a user) will never need to be concerned with which video driver is installed in your system. There are two instances where you need to be concerned, however:

- If your video card manufacturer provides an updated video driver specifically for Windows 95
- If you change the video card in your system

In this last instance, if you upgrade to a plug-and-play video card, you probably won't have any problem. If the card is not Plug-and-Play compatible, however, then you may need to manually change the driver. To change the video driver used by Windows 95, follow these steps:

1. Choose Settings from the Start menu. The Settings menu appears.
2. Choose Control Panel from the Settings menu. The Control Panel window appears.
3. Double-click on the Display icon in the Control Panel. The Display Properties sheet appears.
4. Click on the Settings tab.
5. Click on the Change Display Type button. The Change Display Type dialog box appears, as shown in figure 11.4.

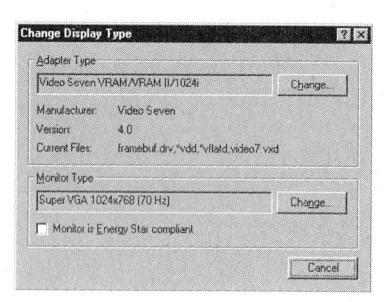

Fig. 11.4 The Change Display Type dialog box allows you to modify your video driver and monitor type.

You can change two settings from this dialog box. The first, at the top of the dialog box, is the type of video adapter card you have installed in your system. The second is covered in the next section. If the video adapter selected is incorrect, or if you have an updated video driver disk from the video card manufacturer, then click on the C*h*ange button. The Select Device dialog box appears, as shown in figure 11.5.

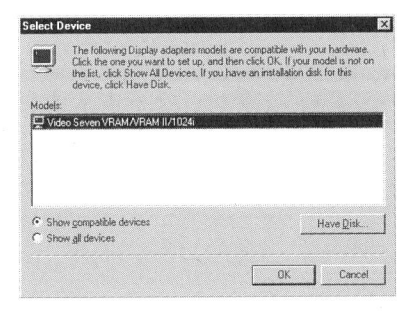

Fig. 11.5 The Select Device dialog box is used to select the video driver you want to use.

By default, Windows 95 lists in this dialog box only the video drivers it feels you can use. But what if you have an updated video driver disk? In this case (or if you want to try a different video driver), click on the Show *a*ll devices button at the bottom of the dialog box. Windows then lists all the video drivers that it knows about. You can select one of them, or click on the Have *D*isk button if you have a video driver disk from the manufacturer.

> **Caution:** You should only use the Have *D*isk button if you have a disk containing Windows 95 video drivers. Windows 3.1 drivers will not work properly with Windows 95.

When you're done specifying a video driver, click on the OK button. Your change is made either right away (if you choose a video driver compatible with your current driver), or you'll be prompted to restart Windows 95 before the change can occur.

Selecting a Monitor Type

Windows 95 also allows you to specify the type of monitor you have connected to your system. This setting acts as a modification to the video driver specification, and allows the video driver to interact properly with the monitor.

Unfortunately, Windows 95 cannot "reach out" and determine the type of monitor you have connected to your system. There is no interactive link between the video card and the monitor itself (all data travels one way—to the monitor). This means that you need to specify your monitor manually. To do this, follow these steps:

1. Choose Settings from the Start menu. The Settings menu appears.

2. Choose Control Panel from the Settings menu. The Control Panel window appears.

3. Double-click on the Display icon in the Control Panel. The Properties for Display dialog box appears.

4. Click on the Settings tab.

5. Click on the Change Display Type button. The Change Display Type dialog box appears, as shown earlier, in figure 11.4.

In the previous section you learned how to use the top portion of this dialog box, where you change your video driver. The bottom portion of this dialog box allows you to specify the monitor you have hooked up to your system. To change it, click on the Change button, and the Select Device dialog box appears, as shown in figure 11.6.

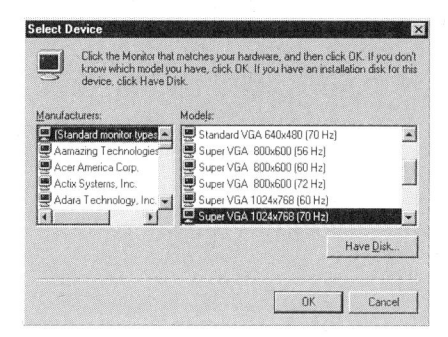

Fig. 11.6 The Select Device dialog box is used to select the monitor that is connected to your system.

You should pick a monitor vendor from the list at the left side of the dialog box. Your selection here controls what is then shown in the right side of the dialog box. Select a monitor model from the available list.

How do you determine the type of monitor you have? The easiest way is to look on the back of the monitor. Most monitors include some type of label that indicates the monitor manufacturer and model; this is the information you need. If such a label is not on your monitor, then you should refer to the documentation that came with the monitor or that came with your computer system. In some instances, you may even need to contact the vendor from which you purchased the monitor.

If you absolutely cannot determine the make and model of your monitor, you can select a generic monitor make and model. The first choice in the Manufacturers list is called Standard monitor types, as shown earlier in figure 11.6. You can select this manufacturer and then select the monitor resolution and refresh rate that works best for you. While this may take a bit of trial and error, going through the process of picking the monitor will provide the best display quality and least eye fatigue.

When you are through specifying a monitor, click on the OK button.

Selecting a Monitor Type   **277**

Changing Video Parameters

Earlier in this chapter you learned how different video cards support different types of displays. The video cards supported by Windows 95 can support a variety of display resolutions and colors. When you first install Windows 95, it sets your display parameters based on the following:

➤ If you updated from a previous version of Windows, then the same display parameters were used as you used in the previous version.

➤ If you installed Windows 95 on your machine without updating, then the display parameters are set to a default setting, namely 640 × 480 resolution and 16 colors.

You can change your display parameters to any values supported by your video card and monitor. To do this, follow these steps:

1. Choose Settings from the Start menu. The Settings menu appears.
2. Choose Control Panel from the Settings menu. The Control Panel window appears.
3. Double-click on the Display icon in the Control Panel. The Properties for Display dialog box appears.
4. Click on the Settings tab. The Properties for Display dialog box appears, as shown in figure 11.7.

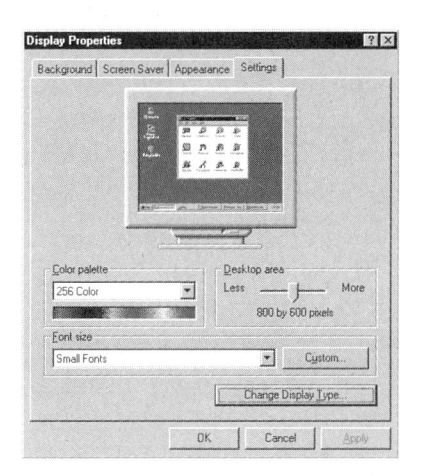

Fig. 11.7 The Properties for Display dialog box allows you to modify your video parameters.

The first setting many people like to change is the Desktop area setting, at the right side of the dialog box. This control contains a slider bar that specifies the screen resolution you want to use. The slider typically has three possible settings. The left-most setting is for 640 × 480 resolution, the middle one for 800 × 600, and the right-most for 1,024 × 768. Notice that as you make changes in the control, the sample display at the top of the dialog box also changes.

Now you can specify the number of screen colors you want to use. You do that in the Color palette area at the left side of the dialog box. If you display the pull-down list, you'll see the valid selections for your particular video card at the resolution you've specified.

Finally, at the bottom of the dialog box you can specify the Font size you want to use. This setting is a helpful one not necessarily related to your video card, but controls the size of font used by Windows to display information. Generally, the lower the resolution, the smaller the font you'll want to use. At higher resolutions you may want to use a larger font to make your displays more readable.

When you're done making changes to your display parameters, click on the OK button. Depending on your specifications, you may be asked to restart Windows in order for the changes to take effect, although this does not happen nearly as often as in earlier versions of Windows. Instead, you are informed that Windows 95 is about to make the changes, as shown in figure 11.8.

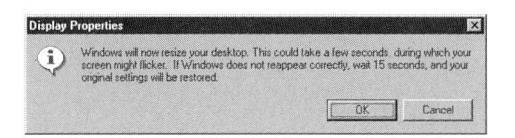

Fig. 11.8 Windows 95 allows you to change display properties on the fly.

When you click on the OK button, the display changes are made and you are asked to confirm the changes. If you don't confirm them within 15 seconds, your changes are abandoned, and you're returned to the Display Properties dialog box. This feature is a big improvement over earlier versions of Windows where it was possible to hang your system by choosing improper video settings.

Speeding Up Your Video

Now that you know the basics about video systems, you can turn your attention to speeding up your own system. If you want to increase the speed of your display, there are four primary methods you can use:

- Use fewer colors in your displays.
- Configure your software to place fewer demands on your video system.
- Install a graphics accelerator card.
- Buy a faster computer or motherboard, particularly one with high-speed local-bus video.

Using Fewer Display Colors

Perhaps the simplest way to increase your system speed is to change the number of colors you use in Windows 95. If you are currently using a 256-color or 65,535-color display, you can significantly increase the display refresh rate of Windows 95 by configuring Windows 95 so that you use only 16 colors. While you may not have as realistic a look to any exotic wallpaper or screen saver images you are using, the change won't hinder your use of most programs. In fact, most programs don't require more than 16 colors—unless you're using sophisticated graphics programs that rely on a high number of colors.

Many purchasers of SVGA cards use 256 colors (or more) because the card is capable of delivering the high number of colors, not because the extra colors are necessary. Computers purchased with Windows 95 preinstalled are almost invariably set up with the higher number of colors as the default. Sixteen colors are adequate for virtually all Windows 95 applications except those for image and video processing.

To change your display so it only uses 16 colors, take the following steps:

1. Choose Settings from the Start menu. The Settings menu appears.
2. Choose Control Panel from the Settings menu. The Control Panel window appears.
3. Double-click on the Display icon in the Control Panel. The Properties for Display dialog box appears.
4. Click on the Settings tab.
5. In the Color palette area of the dialog box, change the setting to 16 colors.
6. Click on the OK button.

Configuring Your Software

Another step you can take to improve your video performance is to configure your software so it does not perform as many graphics operations as it might otherwise. As an example, in Word for Windows you can turn on draft font and picture placeholders in the Options dialog box (on the View tab). This change will greatly improve the video performance of Word for Windows. Other Windows 95-based applications typically offer similar ways to speed up your video processing.

You can also use only standard fonts with your software. Processing will be fastest if you use one of the bit-mapped VGA-resident fonts supplied with Windows 95—MS Serif and MS Sans Serif—in one of their standard sizes (8, 10, 12, 14, 18, and 24 points) instead of TrueType or Adobe typefaces. VGA-resident fonts consist of individual bitmaps of the characters, so Windows doesn't need to convert the outline of a scaleable typeface to the size you specify. Even if the VGA-resident fonts do not appear in the list of fonts for your application, you can type their names (MS Serif or MS Sans Serif) into the text box of most applications' font selection combo boxes.

You can improve the graphics performance of some applications by allocating specific amounts of memory to store bitmaps. As an example, you can speed up the display of graphic images embedded in Word for Windows by making a change or two to the WINWORD6.INI file, which is located in your Word for Windows directory. You can add the line

```
BitMapMemory=nnn
```

to the [Microsoft Word] section of the file. The number you substitute for *nnn* specifies the amount of memory reserved in kilobytes, as shown in the following example:

```
[Microsoft Word]
BitMapMemory=512
CacheSize=128
```

This example allocates 512K of memory for bitmaps displayed in Word documents. Word normally allocates 1,024K (1M), so you free up half the memory normally reserved for this purpose. The second line, CacheSize=128, designates 128K of memory as a buffer area for storing documents. This is twice the default document cache size used by

Word. CacheSize is not related specifically to graphics, but usually improves the speed of paging through documents.

Only a few applications offer the ability to assign memory to store graphic images, and you might find it difficult to find the necessary instructions in the documentation. In some cases, the details are included in a README.TXT file on one of the distribution floppy disks and are not incorporated in the printed documentation.

The amount of memory (RAM) installed in your computer also plays an important role in graphics performance. If you use the preceding example to allocate blocks of memory to Word for Windows, the reserved memory will not be available to other applications while Word is running. Complex Windows applications, such as Microsoft Access, are resource-intensive; that is, the application consumes a substantial amount of memory when you launch it. Displaying large, bitmapped images adds to the amount of memory required. If you don't have enough RAM to store Windows itself, plus the application and the image, Windows uses the swap file on the disk as a substitute for RAM. If your disk activity light flashes constantly when you're using an application that involves graphics, you should consider adding 2M to 4M of RAM before investing in graphics hardware or software accelerators.

Installing Graphics Accelerator Cards

Earlier in this chapter, you learned about graphics accelerator cards, which can be plugged into local-bus slots in a computer. There is more to accelerator cards, however, than what has been presented so far.

Conventional VGA adapter cards are called *dumb frame buffers*. The cards store one display screen of data received from the computer's internal input/output (I/O) bus and convert the stored digital data to the RGB analog signals required by your monitor. (As you've already learned, the I/O bus runs at 8 MHz to 10 MHz, not at the speed of your computer's CPU chip.)

The amount of memory on the card determines the number of colors that can be displayed in the various operating modes supported by the card. Cards with 512K of memory can typically display 256 colors in 640 × 480 and 800 × 600 pixel modes but only 16 colors at 1,024 × 768 pixel resolution. You need 1M of memory to display 16 million colors at 640 × 480, 65,535 colors at 800 × 600, or 256 colors at 1024 × 768 mode.

> **Note:** Some people think that more memory on a video card means that the card will operate faster. This is not true. Memory is directly related to the number of colors that can be displayed. Thus, unless you have a need for millions of colors as high resolutions, chances are good that you may be wasting money by purchasing a video card that has 2M or 4M of memory installed.

Graphics accelerator cards require the same amount of memory as a conventional VGA card to display the same number of colors. Most accelerator cards use video random-access memory (VRAM), a special type of memory chip that, unlike conventional RAM, can be written to and read from at the same time. This feature speeds up video processing immediately. Some early graphic accelerator cards substituted VRAM for conventional RAM and achieved a moderate speed-up. Most graphic accelerator cards currently available are designed specifically for Windows-based systems (including Windows 95) and perform two specific functions:

➤ By using a separate processor dedicated only to graphics, accelerator cards execute at a much faster rate than many of the graphics calculations that would normally be performed by the computer's CPU. The cards achieve this rate by using a special driver that works closely with the operating system to process graphics information as quickly as possible.

➤ The cards eliminate the bottleneck that stems from sending streams of bytes to the graphics adapter card over the computer's relatively slow I/O bus. (The I/O bus connects the adapter cards to the CPU.) Because the graphics processor and the frame buffer memory are on the same card, the information does not have to travel over the computer's bus and can be stored in the VRAM at a faster rate.

Moderately priced Windows graphics accelerator cards (those priced around $200 or $300) provide a two- to five-fold improvement in overall system performance. The greatest benefit accrues in manipulating bitmapped images with a large number of colors at high resolutions, where you can realize improvements as great as 10-fold.

Under pressure to meet competitive prices, some manufacturers of Windows accelerator cards have chosen to omit the VESA feature adapter connector that is standard on virtually all conventional VGA and SVGA adapter cards. If the accelerator card you purchase does not have a feature adapter, you cannot connect it to most video-in-a-window and VGA-to-NTSC adapter cards used for displaying and generating standard NTSC video signals. Even if the accelerator card has a feature connector, its synchronization signal polarity and timing may not match that required by the video card you intend to attach to it. (Compatibility with video adapter cards is discussed in Chapter 28, "Understanding Full-Motion Video.")

Buying a Faster Computer

You can easily more than triple the speed of most Windows applications by replacing a 33 MHz 80386 system that has 4M of RAM with a 66 MHz 80486 DX2 computer with 8M of RAM, or with a Pentium system with the same amount of RAM. Many books are available that discusses what you should look for when buying a new computer. Also, it seems that every other month there is a feature article in computer magazines about the same topic. You should take your time and shop for the best system your budget will allow.

Using Mice and Other Pointing Devices

by Allen L. Wyatt

Windows 95 is a Graphical User Interface (GUI) that combines menus, icons, scroll bars, and windows into an elegant and efficient working environment. The most efficient way to manipulate and control this environment is with a pointing device, such as a mouse. Indeed, the growth of the Windows environment (including Windows 95) over the past several years has made the mouse an integral part of a computer system.

This chapter discusses pointing devices, and specifically the mouse. In this chapter you learn the following:

- Why you need a pointing device
- How to choose a pointing device
- What pointing devices that serve the same functions of a mouse are available
- How to install a mouse or other pointing device
- How to fine-tune the performance of your mouse

Most people are familiar with the mouse as a pointing device. In addition to the mouse, a variety of other pointing devices that perform the same function are available. Devices include trackballs, pens, touch tablets, and digitizing tablets with a mouse emulation mode. Throughout this chapter, the generic term *mouse* means any pointing device that serves the same purpose as a mouse.

Using a Mouse

Almost all Windows 95 features are available by using the keyboard as well as by using a mouse, so why use a mouse? As already pointed out, a pointing device is the most efficient way to control the Windows 95 environment. In some Windows 95 applications, not using a mouse causes severe usability limitations. In desktop publishing and graphics programs, a mouse or other pointing device enables you to move and resize items on-screen quickly. With drawing or paint programs, working without a mouse is practically impossible.

A mouse also enables a new user to learn programs more quickly. More programs are providing graphical representations of functions on-screen rather than forcing users to learn function keys or memorize commands. With a mouse, you click to perform a function, whether the function is simple or complex.

Imagine the mouse as an extension of your hand. With the mouse, you can point at items on-screen, then use the mouse buttons to perform a variety of actions. A mouse makes selecting these actions as natural as pushing a button with your finger.

All pointing devices enable you to move the pointer around the screen, pull down menus, select functions, and when used with a graphics program that supports it, do freehand drawing. However, the way each of the pointing devices operates and the added features they provide may differ quite a bit from the others. With the mouse, movement of the pointer occurs only when the mouse ball moves. Lifting the mouse and moving it (without the bottom of the mouse touching something) does not move the pointer.

Mice are manufactured in a variety of designs. Some have two buttons, some have three, and some have more. Also, mice can be connected to your computer in a variety of ways. Even infrared mice are available that allow the mouse to communicate with your computer without a wired connection.

Some functions can be performed faster with the keyboard; others faster with a mouse. You will be most efficient when you use a combination of the keyboard and mouse. With time, you'll know which functions you can do faster with the pointing device and which you can do faster with the keyboard. To select the proper pointing device, you must match what you do with your computer and the pointing technology available. What works best for you may not work best for someone else.

Understanding Mouse Sensitivity

In actual use, on a technical level, mice differ in one important point—*resolution*. Every time you move the pointing device, a series of pulses is sent to the computer. Resolution is the number of counts per inch (cpi) that a mouse can detect. The counts per inch are the number of those pulses sent by the pointing device to the computer in an inch of physical movement. The greater the resolution, the finer and more precise the movement the pointing device can sense. In addition to finer movement, the mouse pointer also appears to move more slowly across the screen, thereby providing greater control, particularly when working with detailed objects.

In many software setups for individual applications, you can adjust the mouse sensitivity for just that application. For instance, you can run WordPerfect for DOS from within Windows 95 and set WordPerfect's own mouse sensitivity without affecting Windows 95's mouse setting.

Using Mouse Shortcuts

In addition to standard mouse functions such as pointing, clicking, and dragging, most Windows 95 applications have shortcuts you can perform with a mouse that make the mouse even more useful. For example, double-clicking an item in a Windows 95 list box is usually the same as selecting the item and then choosing the default operation (often OK, Yes, or Select) for the dialog box. Selecting a figure in a graphics program normally is accomplished by clicking the item. After the item is selected, moving it is as easy as holding the mouse button while moving the mouse.

> **Caution:** Don't confuse the term *mouse shortcuts* with the new term making its debut in Windows 95—shortcuts. Shortcuts are described in detail in Chapter 3, "New Windows 95 Tools." Mouse shortcuts are those operations made faster by using a mouse rather than using the keyboard.

To show you how mouse shortcuts can help you use a Windows 95 application, Table 12.1 shows some of the mouse shortcuts used with WordPerfect for Windows. Many of the shortcuts also work with other Windows 95 applications.

Table 12.1 Typical Mouse Shortcuts in Windows 95 Applications

Action	Result
Click	Selects an object
Double-click	Selects and opens an object
Shift+click	Selects all items in a list from the previously selected item to the newly selected one
Ctrl+click	Selects an object in addition to all the other objects that may be selected
Click within a window	Makes that window active
Right-click	Displays a context menu for the object

Choosing a Pointing Device

After you decide to use a pointing device, you need to select the device that best meets your needs. Many newer systems come with a pointing device (such as a mouse), but you may want to replace it with one more suited to the work you do. With the variety of pointing devices available, plan on doing extensive research before you make your purchase—particularly if the purchase will cost a great deal of money. Each device may fit you differently or have different features that are important to you.

A large selection of alternative pointing devices is available. Trackballs have a ball held in a stationary holder that moves the on-screen pointer as you rotate the ball with your hand. Touch tablets enable you to run your fingers over a panel to move the pointer on-screen. A push on the panel sends the equivalent of the mouse click to the computer. You also have pointing devices that look like pens. The following section provides information to help you decide which type of device is best for you.

When choosing a pointing device, consider the following aspects:

➤ **Type.** The type of pointing device you select should reflect the type of work you plan to do. You can select a mouse or one of many alternative pointing devices. The most common types of pointing devices are the mouse, trackballs, touch tablets, light pens, joysticks, graphics tablets, and touch-screens.

➤ **Design.** The mouse and other pointing devices are manufactured in a variety of designs. Some devices have two buttons, and some have three or more. You also must consider how the design fits you physically and how comfortable you feel working with it. For instance, some mice are designed specifically for left-handed users.

➤ **Connection.** Make sure you know how the pointing device connects to your computer. The device may use a built-in connector, a serial port, or a special adapter card.

➤ **Compatibility.** Devices that are 100% compatible with a Microsoft mouse generally are easiest to install and run. Other devices may require their own drivers to work properly with your software. Make sure there is a Windows 95 device driver available before you commit to the device.

➤ **Resolution.** The resolution of a pointing device refers to how many times per second the device checks the position of the pointer or how small a movement the device can detect. The higher the resolution, the more precise operations you can perform with the pointing device.

To make sure the pointing device you select is best-suited for your needs, try to test the device before you make a final purchase. If possible, borrow a friend's pointing device and try it in your environment. You also can buy from a dealer who will allow you to return the pointing device if it doesn't meet your needs. Your pointing device must work well with your computer, your software, and you.

Getting Your Money's Worth

Nothing will sour you more quickly on using a pointing device than using one of poor quality. Poor devices hamper your efficiency, and you may find most functions faster with the keyboard. With a poor-quality mouse, fine movement may not be possible, the mouse may perform erratically, or the pointer may not move smoothly on-screen.

To help sell their products, some manufacturers frequently throw in a mouse for free or almost free. If the mouse provided is not good quality, you may be better off passing on the offer or purchasing a good-quality mouse and getting rid of the free one. A well-designed pointing device may cost a little more, but the investment pays dividends every time you use your system.

The Microsoft mouse is an example of a high-quality pointing device with good design. The device fits the hand comfortably. The ball, which records the movement of the mouse, is near the top of the mouse, by your fingers. This feature enables you to make very precise and accurate movements with the mouse. Other devices, like the IBM mouse, are high quality but fall short in design. The IBM mouse buttons are long and narrow and take quite a bit of pressure to click. The ball is farther away from the fingers. This condition can make fine movement more difficult than with the Microsoft mouse.

Understanding Connections

You can connect pointing devices to a computer through a dedicated mouse port, a serial port, or an adapter card plugged into the computer. Determine what type of connection your computer requires before you buy a pointing device. Some pointing devices come with the cables and electronics necessary to connect to a dedicated mouse port or a serial port. Other devices do not come with the necessary interface parts to work with all types of connections; you need to purchase these devices with the appropriate interface. After you have installed the mouse properly, the method of attachment makes no measurable difference in performance.

If your system has a dedicated mouse port, you may want to order a device that uses the port. This step saves you the expense of buying extra hardware or wasting a serial port or bus slot.

If your system doesn't have a dedicated mouse port, using a serial port probably is the least expensive way to proceed. Most systems have at least one serial port and often two. If one of your serial ports is available, then no additional hardware purchase (besides the mouse) is necessary. If you need to add a serial port, you generally can do so for under $25 through a mail-order company. (If you need assistance in this area, contact your local computer store.)

If your system does not have a mouse port and all the serial ports are in use, you may need to use a mouse with its own proprietary interface card that uses one of your computer's card slots. This device typically is called a *bus mouse*. It is also possible that some of the more exotic or esoteric pointing devices require their own special interface card. Because this type of pointing device comes with its own adapter card, it costs more than an equivalent pointing device that uses a built-in port or serial port. You also may have difficulty making the card work properly with the other equipment in your system. (For more information, see the section "Installing Your Pointing Device" later in this chapter.)

One last point about mouse ports. Some videoboards have mouse ports built into the board. If you want to utilize this special mouse port, make sure your mouse is compatible with such a port or that you can disable the port by some means. Otherwise, the port may not co-exist peacefully with the serial port mouse or bus mouse. Refer to the video board's manual or contact the video board's manufacturer for more details.

Examining Different Types of Mice

In general, there are three types of mice: the *mechanical mouse*, the *optical mouse*, and the *wireless mouse*.

The most common type of mouse is the mechanical mouse. It uses a hard rubber ball that rotates inside a compartment on the bottom of the mouse. Two or three capstans inside the mouse roll against the rubber ball as you move the mouse. One of the capstans translates horizontal motion into electrical pulses, and the second capstan does the same for vertical motion. On some mice there is an optional third capstan that acts as a stabilizer so the ball doesn't wobble. The mouse sends these electrical pulses from the first two capstans to the computer and, ultimately, to the software.

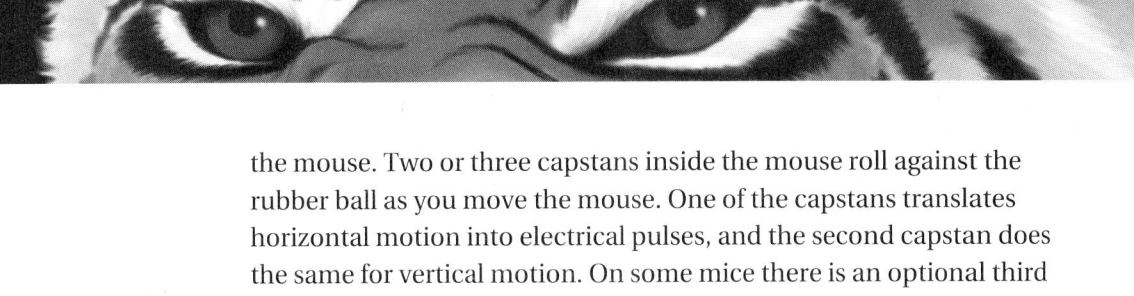

One of the drawbacks of the mechanical mouse is that it can pick up dust, dirt, and other debris you may have on your work surface. This material gets inside the mouse and can make the rolling ball sticky. You must clean the mouse from time to time. Except in the most serious cases, you can clean the mouse with little effort and time. Most manufacturers include cleaning instructions in the mouse owner's manual. Several companies even sell mouse cleaning kits.

> **Tip:** You can limit the amount of dust and dirt picked up by your mouse by using a good quality, lint-free mouse pad. These are available at any computer or office-supply store.

An optical mouse operates by shining a beam of light through the bottom of the mouse onto a reflective surface. As you move the mouse, the light reflects back to a sensor in the mouse. This sensor translates reflective differences into electrical pulses and sends them to the computer, like the mechanical mouse does.

> **Tip:** If you operate an optical mouse in direct sunlight or in a very bright light, it is possible it will not act reliably. The sunlight can interfere with the brightness of the light beam that is reflected from the glass pad used by the optical mouse.

You can roll a mechanical mouse on any surface that provides enough friction to move the ball, but you must use an optical mouse on a special surface. Typically you use a small glass pad, the size of a normal mouse pad, which provides the reflective surface the mouse needs to

Choosing a Pointing Device

operate properly. Because the optical mouse has no moving parts, it is less prone to picking up dirt and dust. The only cleaning an optical mouse requires is to periodically wipe off the glass pad and the sensor on the bottom of the mouse.

Finally, a wireless mouse is typically the same as a mechanical mouse, except no cable connects the mouse and the computer. Rather, the mouse transmits movement data to the computer through an infrared link or radio waves.

An infrared mouse works similarly to your television remote control. The mouse sends data by way of an infrared signal to a receiver connected to the computer. Reliable use of this kind of mouse depends on the positions of both the receiver and the mouse. If the mouse and the receiver have something between them (such as a stack of books), the mouse stops working. After you remove the obstruction and restore the line-of-sight positioning, the mouse starts working again.

The Logitech MouseMan Cordless mouse is a wireless mouse. Instead of using an infrared signal beamed at a receiver, the mouse functions by using radio signals to link the mouse to your computer. The MouseMan Cordless doesn't require line-of-sight positioning of the mouse and computer as does the infrared mouse. The computer even can be under a desk or located up to six feet away. The MouseMan Cordless can run on eight different frequencies, so you can use several mouse devices in close proximity without interference. The signals are also designed so they won't interfere with other devices that rely on radio signals.

Regardless of whether a mouse is mechanical, optical, or wireless, the number of buttons on the mouse is an open-ended issue. On the Macintosh computer, the mouse has only one button. Most mouse designs for the PC world have two or three buttons, although some designs have even more. Most PC applications utilize one or two buttons, although some packages (such as CAD programs) enable you to define additional buttons for your mouse.

Considering Mouse Alternatives

A mouse is not the only pointing device you can use in Windows 95. The variety of other devices includes trackballs, touch tablets, and pens. They all claim to make you more efficient. In the end, your comfort with the pointing device determines how efficient you are. The following information is provided to help you determine whether an alternative pointing device might work better for you than a mouse.

Trackballs

Compared with the surface area required to work with a mouse, trackballs require almost no desk space. Trackballs are very popular in any situation where space is at a premium. This feature makes trackballs the pointing device of choice for portable computers, laptops, or personal computers on a small desk.

One way to think of a trackball is it is an upside-down mechanical mouse. With a trackball, the case is stationary and a ball rests inside a compartment on top of the case. You move this ball with the palm of your hand, your fingers, or your thumb. Because the ball does not move around your desktop, it normally doesn't get dirty as fast as a mechanical mouse (unless you spill something on it).

Trackballs differ from one another in a number of ways, including the number of buttons, the arrangement of the buttons, the size of the ball, and the design of the case. The most common full-size trackballs have a billiard-size ball and two or three buttons.

As laptop computers become more popular, so do smaller trackballs. These trackballs normally clip to the right or left side of the keyboard and can be used easily in a very confined area. For more information about these smaller trackballs, read the section "Pointing Devices for Portable Computers" later in this chapter.

Pens

Today's market offers a number of pointing devices shaped like pens. Some of these devices are actually a mouse in a pen housing, and other devices are light pens.

One of the newer pointing devices on the market is the pointer pen or mouse pen. The mouse cable exits from the top of the pen; at the other end is a small ball. You hold the pointer pen like a regular pen and roll it around your desk as if you were writing with the pen. On the side of the pen are buttons used for performing the various mouse button functions.

Because the ball of the pen is so small, you can roll it on almost any surface, including a clipboard on your lap. These devices normally include some type of stand in which to rest the pen.

Light pens are fundamentally different from a mouse pen. You use a light pen to perform functions and move the cursor by pointing to your computer screen. Touch the screen with the pen, and the pen transmits the position to your software. Light pens typically are used with specialized software and CAD systems.

Touch Tablets

When referring to pointing devices, *tablet* normally refers to a digitizing tablet. You can think of these devices as electronic drawing boards. You use tablets most commonly with complex drawing programs and CAD packages. Digitizing tablets cost quite a bit more than mouse devices, trackballs, and pens, and tablets can be as small as a videotape or as large as a drafting table.

Rather than transmit movement information to the computer relative to where the on-screen pointer resides, tablets have a one-to-one correspondence to locations on your computer's screen. When you select a point on the digitizing tablet, the screen indicates the exact corresponding location. These tablets come with one of several types of pointing devices you use to change the location of the on-screen pointer. Some devices are plastic with buttons and a cross hair to enable you to select points on the tablet precisely (these devices are called *pucks*). Other tablet pointing devices are pens with one or more buttons. These tablets normally have a mouse mode that enables you to use them like a mouse.

Due to their cost and design, purchasing a tablet probably is not feasible unless you work with specialized applications that require a digitizing tablet. You probably would be more comfortable with one of the other pointing devices described in the preceding sections.

Another type of tablet is the touch tablet. Microtouch Systems, Inc., makes a touch tablet called the UnMouse. This tablet is very small, about three inches by five inches. With this touch tablet, you move the on-screen pointer by sliding your fingers over the glass panel. To click, you press on the glass. In the absolute mode, you can point to a location on the tablet, and the pointer instantly moves to the same place on-screen. By using a stylus (a pointer similar to a pen or pencil), you can use this device as a mini-graphics tablet.

A close relative to the touch tablet is the glidepoint. These devices are very small pads, with a surface area only a couple of inches wide and high. The pad on the glidepoint resembles the same shape as the video screen. You use the device by scooting your finger over the pad, which moves the pointer on-screen. There are buttons located in the housing of the glidepoint which perform the same function as mouse buttons.

Pointing Devices for Portable Computers

More and more computers are coming equipped with pointing devices already built in. For instance, the IBM ThinkPad includes what is called a Track Point, which is a small red-rubber button in the keypad. You can use your finger to wiggle the button in any direction, and the on-screen mouse pointer moves accordingly. While these built-in pointers conserve valuable space, they can be tricky to learn and master. Even with the built-in devices, many people prefer to add an external pointing device since they are a bit more comfortable to use.

The most common pointing device used with portable computers is the mini-trackball. Many people use portable computers in locations where they cannot use a traditional mouse—places like an airplane, airport, or automobile. Mini-trackballs come in a wide variety of shapes and sizes. Some trackballs are built into the computer, some are separate, and some clip onto the computer keyboard.

With a clip-on trackball, look for a breakaway mechanical design to prevent accidental damage to the mouse or keyboard if the computer is bumped. You normally can mount the clip-on trackballs on the left or right side of the keyboard and at a variety of angles. Some trackballs include software that enables you to calibrate which way is up before you use the device. Then the trackball works properly with your software in a variety of mounted positions.

Most pointing devices for portable computers are designed for use with the serial port because most laptops have a limited number of slots available for adapter cards. You probably would not want to devote one of those scarce slots to a pointing device. With graphic applications becoming so popular and laptop computers becoming more powerful, many laptops now have a built-in PS/2-compatible mouse port, leaving the serial port free for a printer, modem, or other serial device.

The cables connected to portable pointing devices are typically shorter than cables on devices designed for desktop use. Often these cables are only a couple of feet long. This setup enables you to use the pointing device more easily in close quarters. Extension cables sometimes are included or are available at an additional cost.

> **Note:** With most portable computers, the mouse pointer on-screen is difficult to see. Windows 95 has a solution for this problem, as described in the "Fine-Tuning Your Pointing Device" section later in this chapter.

Installing Your Pointing Device

After you have purchased a new pointing device, you need to install it. In most cases, the manufacturer provides detailed instructions for installing the pointing device.

Earlier you learned that there are several ways you can connect a mouse (or other pointing device) to your computer. The actual steps you follow when installing your pointing device depend, in large part, on the type of connection the device requires. Read the instructions provided with the device to learn how to successfully perform an installation.

If you are using an adapter card to install your pointing device, the card needs its own *interrupt* to communicate with your computer. No other hardware device may share this interrupt. If the pointing device is sharing an interrupt with another device, the pointing device may work erratically or not at all.

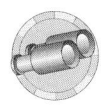

Note: If your mouse and the adapter card support Plug and Play, then you do not need to worry about interrupt conflicts. These will be resolved automatically by your system.

Your pointing device and computer documentation can help you from the System Tools menu determine what interrupt your device is using and what alternatives are available. You can change most device interrupt settings by moving jumpers or switches on the device's adapter card. Try the default settings first; they work in the widest range of computers.

Tip: If you plan to change any of the settings or switches in your system, make sure you write down the current settings before making any changes. This precaution enables you to easily change to the original settings if necessary.

Windows 95 includes utilities that provide a wealth of information about your system. For example, you can view information about your mouse and the hardware interrupts. To access this information, right-click the My Computer icon on your desktop. From the context menu, select the Properties option. You then will see the System Properties sheet. Click the Device Manager tab, and your screen will appear as shown in figure 12.1.

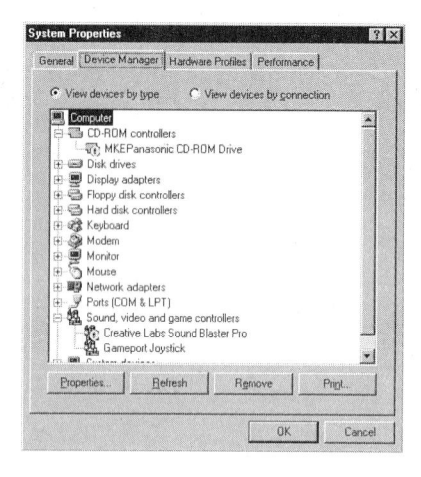

Fig. 12.1 The System Properties sheet, with the Device Manager tab selected, displays information about devices on your system.

This sheet shows all of the devices attached to your system, categorized by type. Notice that one of the devices listed, about two-thirds of the way down the list, is Mouse. Remember that this is a category of device; if you double-click it, you can find out what mice Windows 95 thinks are connected to your system. Double-clicking the mouse name itself displays a sheet similar to what is shown in figure 12.2.

This dialog box will differ based on the capabilities of your mouse and its driver. If you close the mouse properties dialog box and return to the System Properties sheet, you can explore other information that is pertinent to your pointing device. For instance, you can look at your

COM ports (if your pointing device is hooked up through a COM port), checking to see if there is a conflict.

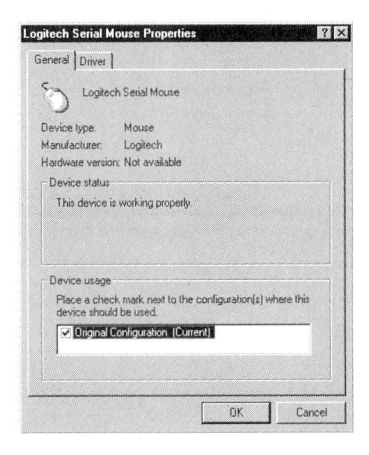

Fig. 12.2 Windows 95 provides a sheet that shows the properties associated with your mouse.

Likewise, you can check your system interrupts to see if there are conflicts. This is done by double-clicking the top-level Computer device in the System Properties sheet (refer to fig. 12.1; see the first item in the list). When you do this, a Computer Properties sheet appears, as shown in figure 12.3.

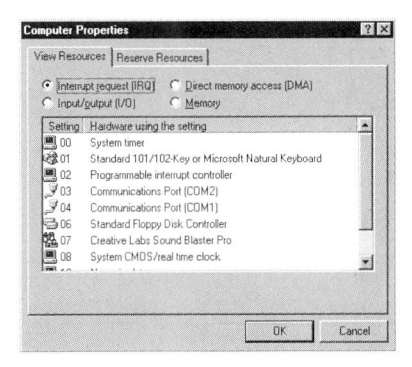

Fig. 12.3 The Computer Properties sheet, with the Interrupt request (IRQ) button selected, displays information about your system interrupts.

Installing Your Pointing Device **303**

This sheet enables you to review the different resources in your system. At the top of the sheet are four buttons that enable you to choose which category of resources you want to view. When you first display the sheet, Interrupt request (IRQ) is selected by default. You can scroll through the list of interrupts, seeing exactly which interrupts are used which way. If there is a conflict that Windows 95 can pinpoint, then the conflict is shown in the list as well. If an interrupt conflict exists, you should correct it (at the hardware level) as quickly as possible so that both devices use different interrupts. This then allows them both to work properly.

Selecting the Correct Driver

When you first installed Windows 95, it went through a detection phase in which it attempted to identify all the hardware connected to your system. During this phase, it is highly possible that it detected your pointing device and installed the proper driver. The driver enables Windows 95 to communicate properly with the pointing device. If the wrong driver is installed, or if you change your hardware and don't change the driver, it is very possible that your pointing device will not work as intended.

To check which driver is installed for your pointing device, or to change the driver, follow these steps:

1. Choose Settings from the Start menu. The Settings menu appears.
2. Choose Control Panel from the Settings menu. The Control Panel window appears.
3. Double-click the Mouse icon in the Control Panel. The Mouse Properties sheet appears.
4. Click on the General tab.
5. Click on the Change button. The Select Device dialog box appears, as shown in figure 12.4.

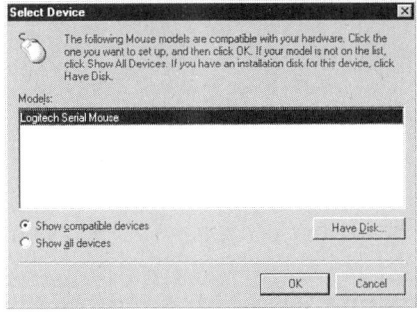

Fig. 12.4 This Select Device dialog box enables you to specify the mouse driver that Windows 95 should use.

At this point, the dialog box shows the different mouse models that Windows 95 feels are compatible with your hardware. If the information shown is not correct, you can click the Show all devices button at the bottom of the dialog box. The dialog box then changes so it displays two lists, as shown in figure 12.5.

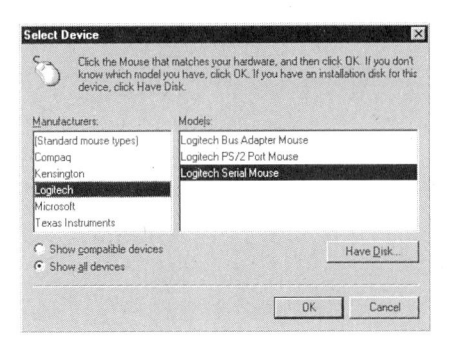

Fig. 12.5 In the Select Device dialog box you should pick both the vendor and the model of your mouse.

Your first task is to pick the manufacturer of your pointing device in the left-hand column. Based on the manufacturer, the information in the Models column changes. Pick the model of your pointing device, if it is shown. If it is not shown, and your vendor provided a Windows 95 driver disk, you can click the Have Disk button.

Installing Your Pointing Device   **305**

When you are done, click the OK button. This returns you to the Mouse Properties dialog box. At this point you can set other properties for your pointing device. This is done through the use of the other tabs in the dialog box. For instance, you can specify how the mouse buttons should be interpreted by clicking the Buttons tab. You also could change the way the mouse pointer looks and responds by choosing the Pointers tab. When you are finished, click the OK button to close the dialog box and effect your changes.

Troubleshooting Pointing Device Problems

If your mouse doesn't work, or if it operates erratically, you can take several steps to fix the problem. If the mouse won't work with Windows 95 applications, try the following things:

- If you can see a pointer on-screen but it won't move as you move your mouse, Windows 95 might have detected an unused mouse port and might be expecting it to have a mouse connected to it. If this is the case, contact the manufacturer of your computer or the device that has the unused mouse port to find out how to disable the extra mouse port.

- If you're using a serial mouse, make sure you've connected the pointing device to a properly configured serial port.

- Make sure the mouse cable is firmly connected to your PC. You may also want to make sure the connecting screws, if any, are tightened.

- Make sure the mouse driver being used by Windows 95 is the proper one for the pointing device being used.

- Determine which interrupt the mouse is using and make sure it is not sharing it with another hardware device.

- If the pointer moves erratically, the pointing device may need to be cleaned. See the documentation that came with the device for information about cleaning.

With a Microsoft mouse and most similar mouse devices, you can tell if the mouse is dirty or defective by removing the ball and moving the rollers with your finger. Watch the pointer on-screen. If the pointer is jumpy in one direction, the problem probably is a dirty or defective mouse. If the pointer is jumpy in two directions, the problem probably is the software. When you use your fingers to move the rollers in the cavity where the mouse ball goes, you may leave a fine coating of oil from your skin. After checking the mouse operation, clean the rollers with a soft, lint-free cloth and rubbing alcohol.

> **Tip:** If you suspect your mouse is dirty, carefully examine the rubber ball. Picking up dirt or something sticky from a work surface can cause the ball to get hung up and cause erratic pointer movement.

If these actions do not cure the problem, then there may be a problem with the mouse cord or the mouse itself. Connect the mouse to another computer system to determine if the mouse is defective.

Pointing for Physically Impaired Users

In previous versions of Windows, Microsoft had add-ons available that could be used by individuals with disabilities to make using Windows easier. In Windows 95, these add-ons have been incorporated into the Control Panel so they are always available. The Accessibility Options of the Control Panel enable you to modify Windows rather dramatically for those with disabilities. Most of these options are covered in Chapter 14, "Tailoring Windows 95 and the Registry," but one option is more appropriately discussed here.

Many people have a hard time with the manual dexterity necessary to use a mouse. One of the Accessibility Options available is called MouseKeys, which enables a person to use the keyboard to control the mouse pointer. This feature makes the keys on your numeric keypad act like a built-in mouse. Each of the keys moves the mouse in a specific direction—just as if you were using a real mouse! The 5 key on the keypad serves as the primary mouse button (typically the left button); there is no secondary button.

To enable the MouseKeys option, follow these steps:

1. Choose Settings from the Start menu. The Settings menu appears.
2. Choose Control Panel from the Settings menu. The Control Panel window appears.
3. Double-click the Accessibility Options icon in the Control Panel. The Accessibility Properties sheet appears.
4. Click on the Mouse tab. The Accessibility Properties sheet appears, as shown in figure 12.6.

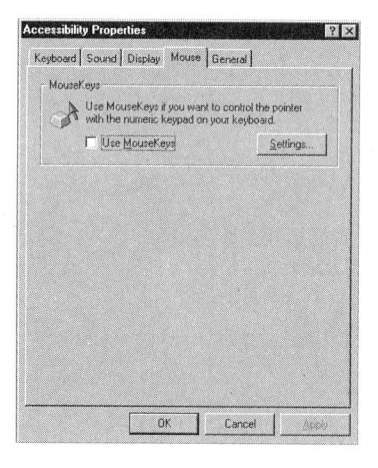

Fig. 12.6 The Accessibility Properties sheet, with the Mouse tab selected, enables you to enable or disable MouseKeys.

To turn on MouseKeys, select the check box next to the Use MouseKeys option. You also can click the Settings button to modify how MouseKeys functions.

With MouseKeys enabled, a small mouse icon appears on the status bar, near the right side. If you tap a mouse movement key (the arrow keys on the numeric keypad), the cursor moves one pixel in the specified direction. If you press and hold a movement key, the cursor moves continuously in the specified direction.

With MouseKeys turned on, you can use either the regular mouse or the keyboard as a mouse. The result is a system that is perhaps more accessible to those with disabilities.

How Windows 95 Interacts with Software

KILLER 13 WINDOWS 95

by Allen L. Wyatt

Any operating system provides a platform on which you can build and run applications. Windows 95 is no exception; it provides a robust and solid platform for a wide variety of applications. In this chapter you learn how Windows 95 interacts with software. Specifically, you learn the following:

➤ How the architecture of Windows 95 affects software

➤ What types of software can be installed on a Windows 95 system

➤ How to remove programs previously installed on your system

Understanding the Virtual Machine

To fully understand how Windows 95 interacts with software, you must understand a bit about the design of the operating system. Windows 95 includes a core service called *the Virtual Machine Manager.* The purpose of the VM Manager is to provide and manage the resources necessary to run both the operating system and the applications on your system. The environments created by the VM Manager are called *virtual machines.*

Think of a virtual machine as a logical computer within the physical computer. It is possible to have multiple virtual machines running within the same physical computer. From the perspective of an application program running within a VM, it is running within its own computer. It believes it has full access to the resources of the entire system, and that there are no other applications running within the system.

The resources (memory, disk space, I/O ports, and so on) needed by an application are made available to the application by the VM Manager. The VM where the operating system does its work is called the *System VM.* At any given time, there is only a single System VM in operation. In addition, you may have other DOS VMs also created within your system, as shown in figure 13.1. You'll learn more about the System and DOS VMs a little bit later in this chapter, in the section titled "Different Types of Software."

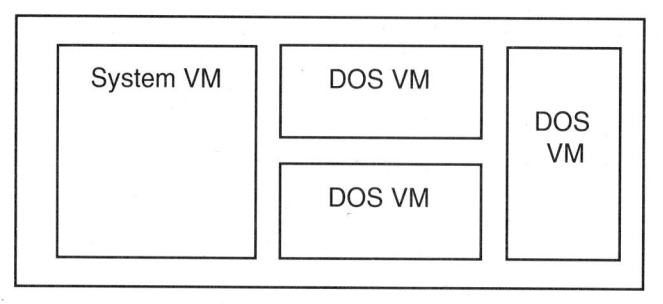

Fig. 13.1 Your Windows 95 system can have multiple virtual machines operating within it.

Chapter 13: How Windows 95 Interacts with Software

In administering your system, the VM Manager has three primary responsibilities:

- Process scheduling
- Memory paging
- MS-DOS Mode support

Each of these areas is discussed in the following sections.

Process Scheduling

A process is a task running on the computer. At any given time, you may have multiple tasks running on your system. A process can be either a portion of a program or the program as a whole.

The Process Scheduler is the portion of the VM Manager responsible for the following:

- Providing system resources to the processes running in the system
- Arbitrating between processes when they're competing for limited resources
- Scheduling which processes run in which order

System resources are provided to processes as they're requested. If there is a conflict (such as two applications that need to use the same resource), then whenever possible the resource is shared between the two processes. Some resources, such as memory or a disk drive, can be shared concurrently. Other resources, such as a printer, must be shared sequentially. Still other resources, such as a modem or an I/O port, must be shared exclusively. The Process Scheduler makes sure that processes do not "run over the top of each other" as they try to use resources that may be in short supply or in high demand.

The third responsibility of the Process Scheduler—scheduling—is the biggest responsibility of the three. This is why the Process Scheduler takes its name from this one aspect of its job. Scheduling concurrent tasks involves a process known as multitasking—the ability to run more than one task at the same time. This scheduling revolves primarily around the use of the CPU, and two forms of multitasking are used: cooperative and preemptive.

Cooperative Multitasking

The first type of multitasking is known as *cooperative* multitasking. This is the type of multitasking used in previous versions of Windows. It is included in Windows 95 for compatibility with older Windows software.

Cooperative multitasking relies upon the different processes within the system to cooperate with each other. Windows 3.1 basically trusted applications to periodically check a message queue to see what other tasks were waiting within the system. If no tasks were waiting, then the application could continue using the system.

If the operating system needed the application to relinquish control so that another process could use the CPU, then it would place a message in the queue. The next time the application checked the queue, it would cooperate by relinquishing control to the operating system, which would in turn pass control to the needy process waiting in the wings.

The problem with cooperative multitasking is that different programs would check the queue at different times. For instance, one application might check it every few milliseconds. Another application, however, might check it every five or 10 seconds. The result was "CPU hogs" that tried to use a disproportionately large amount of CPU time. This caused some programs to run slowly and others to run quickly, but all of them to run in a jerky stop-and-start manner.

Preemptive Multitasking

Windows 95 also implements a form of multitasking known as *preemptive* multitasking. In this scheme, the operating system acts as a traffic cop—it times each application and either takes control after a certain amount of time, or grabs control if a higher-priority event needs to occur right away. Examples of high-priority events would be attending to an I/O port or refreshing the video display.

Windows 95 is not the first operating system to use preemptive multitasking. Windows NT has been using it since it came on the market, and it is also used in multitasking schemes for larger mini and mainframe computers.

There are many benefits to preemptive multitasking:

➤ The applications don't need to check a queue. This means there is less management code necessary within the application itself.

➤ There is more even distribution of processing time to the various applications in the system. This means that applications run smoother with less "start and stop."

➤ Applications can use threads to enhance their own performance.

This last benefit may need some explaining. A thread is nothing but a portion of an application, running as a process within the system. An application can have multiple threads running at the same time. For instance, a spreadsheet might implement the recalculation function as a thread. This would allow lengthy recalculations to occur in the background, while a user input thread was running in the foreground accepting user input. If threads are effectively used within a program, the application makes better use of the time it is allotted by the operating system. For instance, if the same spreadsheet program used only a single thread at a time, each time it received a chunk of time from the operating system, it would need to check for user input. If there was user input, then the program would need to wait while the user typed his or her entries. Because humans type notoriously slowly (in computer terms), the time between keystrokes is wasted time. If the spreadsheet used threads, that time could be used for other processes that need to be done, but are not dependent on a specific sequence. For instance, recalculating or printing or automatically saving to disk or sending information to another application—the possibilities are almost limitless. The result is that the user becomes more productive with the application.

Understanding the Virtual Machine **315**

Memory Paging

The second task of the VM Manager is *memory paging*. This involves swapping information from physical memory to logical memory, as necessary. This involves moving memory around in RAM and also paging it to disk (and back) as necessary.

Every virtual machine within your system is composed of *address spaces*, as shown in figure 13.2. Each process running within a VM is granted an address space 4G in size. Half of this space is used for system management, and the other half by the process itself. Thus, a single process can address up to 2G of memory—more than enough for today's most demanding applications.

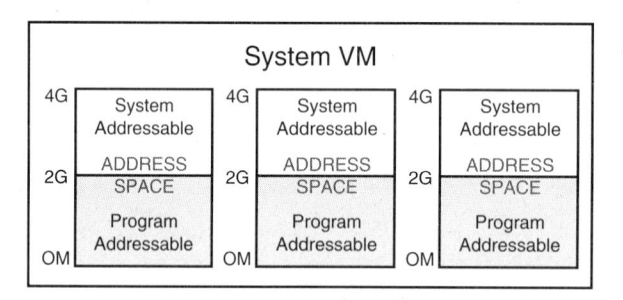

Fig. 13.2 A virtual machine is composed of processes running in address spaces.

It's pretty tough to find a machine that physically has 4G of memory installed (the RAM costs would be phenomenal, and the energy consumption huge). Thus, the address space is partly physical (the memory in the system) and partly virtual (what can be swapped to disk, as necessary). As far as the application running in the address space is concerned, the address space is *flat* and *linear*.

Flat and linear are characteristics of memory that mean it can be addressed with a single address register. This address register is 32-bits in size, which means it can hold an address between 0 and 4,294,967,295. (This is why there is a 4G address space assigned.)

Windows 95 uses a technique called *demand paging*. This refers to a method by which code and data are moved in pages from physical memory to a temporary paging file on disk. The Memory Pager portion of the VM Manager takes care of this process of moving memory pages within RAM and to and from the disk. As far as the application is concerned, however, the information (up to 2G) is available in RAM all the time.

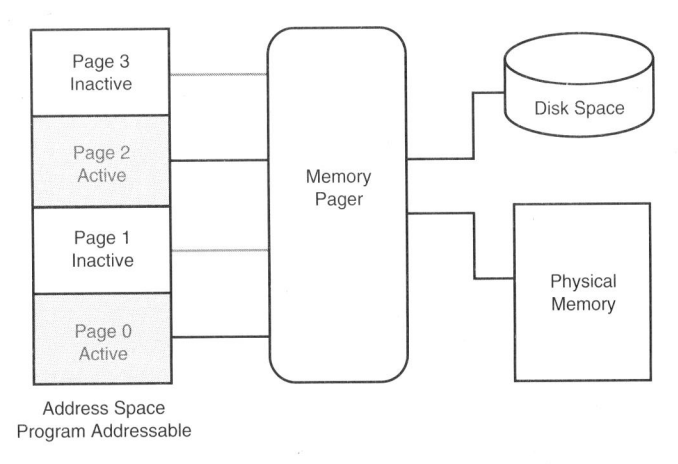

Fig. 13.3 The Memory Pager takes care of moving virtual memory to and from the disk.

The Memory Pager also takes care of mapping virtual addresses from the process's address space to physical pages in the computer's memory. In doing so, it hides the physical organization of memory from the application. This ensures that the application can access its memory as needed, but not the memory of other processes.

MS-DOS Mode

The final task of the VM Manager is to administer the system if it is required to operate in *MS-DOS mode*. This is a special mode of the operating system in which exclusive control of the entire machine and all its resources are given to a single MS-DOS task.

Understanding the Virtual Machine **317**

You should not confuse MS-DOS mode with opening an MS-DOS window on your system; they are not the same. MS-DOS mode is exclusive in nature, and an MS-DOS window can be used in a shared environment. MS-DOS mode is not required very often. In fact, most DOS programs can function quite well in the stable, isolated environment provided by an MS-DOS window in Windows 95. Some applications (very few, in reality) require the expanded and exclusive access to the system that can only be realized in MS-DOS mode.

When operating in MS-DOS mode, no other applications can be running in the system. Thus, the VM Manager takes care of shutting down all other processes when switching to MS-DOS mode. When the program running in this mode finishes running, the only way to exit from and reinitialize the system is to restart Windows.

Different Types of Software

Three general types of programs can be executed in Windows 95. Every program you run will fall into one of these categories:

- **Win32.** These are 32-bit Windows applications designed to take full advantage of the Windows 95 environment.

- **Win16.** These are traditional 13-bit Windows applications. They are carry-overs from earlier versions of Windows, but still operate satisfactorily in the Windows 95 environment.

- **MS-DOS.** These are programs designed to run in DOS, not in Windows. Windows 95 provides a suitable environment for running virtually any DOS program.

Both Win32 and Win16 programs occupy separate address spaces within the System VM, and each MS-DOS program runs concurrently within its own DOS VM. (This arrangement is shown in figure 13.4.) If a DOS program requires enough resources, then it is run in MS-DOS mode, where the DOS VM is the only VM defined in the machine.

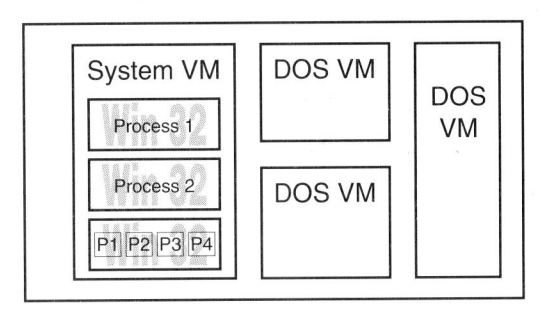

Fig. 13.4 Different program types reside in different VMs within your system.

Notice that each Win32 application occupies its own address space, while all Win16 applications share a joint address space. Every DOS application (every DOS window) occupies its own address space as well. In the case of DOS, however, the address space and the VM are the same.

If an application crashes for some reason, then the use of different memory areas protects the other applications (and the operating system) from being affected. The one possible exception is the Win16 programs. If one of these crashes, the crash may affect other Win16 applications because they're in the same address space. Improvements in Windows 95 resource management make such an occurrence less of a possibility than in earlier Windows versions.

If an application hangs, you can recover by pressing Ctrl+Alt+Del. This signals to Windows 95 that you want to end one of the applications—in effect recover either an address space or a VM (in the case of DOS). Windows displays a list of all applications in the system and asks which one you want to end. You can pick the offending application, and Windows 95 will close it after asking you to confirm your action.

Different Types of Software **319**

Removing an Application

Later in Part III, "Software," you learn how to install programs in Windows 95. Chapter 16, "Installing Windows Applications," and Chapter 18, "Installing DOS Applications," walk you through the procedures necessary to add software to your system. This section covers how to remove software you have previously installed.

Exactly how you remove a program depends on which type of program you're removing. Because there are three types of programs that can run in the Windows 95 environment, there are three corresponding ways to remove your software.

Removing a Win32 Program

There are two types of Win32 programs you can install on your system—one designed for Windows 95 or one designed for Windows NT. In the future, as more and more programs are designed to work with both operating systems, such distinctions will become less clear, but for the short term it can make a big difference.

A Windows 95-aware program is one that not only includes 32-bit support, but also comes with programs designed to uninstall the software. These programs work with the Add/Remove Programs Wizard in the Control Panel to allow you to easily remove the software. A Windows NT 32-bit program does not include such removal capability, so you must remove it according to the tried-and-somewhat-true methods of traditional Windows software. This process is described in the next section.

To uninstall Windows 95 software, start by following these steps:

1. Make sure that the program you want to remove is not currently running. Close any windows used by the program.

2. Choose Settings from the Start menu. The Settings menu appears.

3. Choose Control Panel from the Settings menu. The Control Panel appears.

4. Double-click the Add/Remove Programs icon. The Add/Remove Programs Properties sheet appears, as shown in figure 13.5.

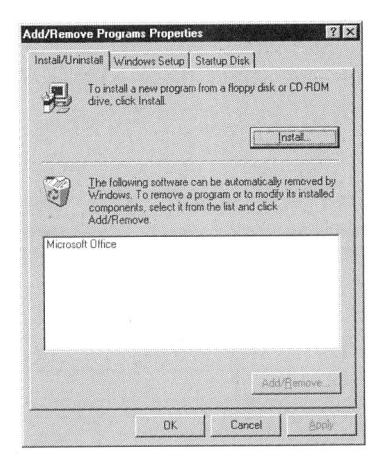

Fig. 13.5 The Add/Remove Programs Properties sheet is used to add or remove software from Windows 95.

5. At the bottom of the sheet is a list of installed software for your system. This is not all your software, just those programs designed to work with Windows 95. Click on the program you want to remove from your system.

6. Click on the Add/Remove button at the bottom of the sheet.

From this point, the software removal program for the application is actually running. Some programs include the removal as part of the setup program for the application, while others have a separate uninstall program. The steps you follow will vary based on how the setup or uninstall program was designed.

You should follow the instructions for the uninstall program for your application. You may need to refer to the documentation that came with your software for detailed instructions.

When the removal is complete, all elements of the application should have been removed. You may want to check to ensure that there are no shortcuts left over in places like the StartUp folder or in the Programs folder.

Removing a Win16 Program

People who have been around Windows for a while know that it can be difficult, at best, to remove Windows software. This is because the software almost becomes an extension of the operating system. It does not limit its effect to only a program folder, but instead may affect all of the following areas:

- DLL (dynamic link library) files may be copied into the Windows system folder

- INI files for the application are created in the Windows system folder

- Windows INI files (WIN.INI, SYSTEM.INI, and PROGMAN.INI)

- Program groups are modified to add program items for the software

Granted, not all of these are particularly germane under Windows 95. For instance, program groups no longer have applicability. However, the software you installed does not know that—it thinks it is still using the older Windows interface, and may have created program groups thinking they would be used by the operating system.

To remove Windows software, you should follow these steps:

1. Delete the folder(s) containing the application software.

2. Remove any shortcuts or menu items you had set up for the software.

3. Examine the INI files in the \WINDOWS folder to determine whether any of them belonged to the application. If you can clearly make such a determination, delete the file. Better yet, copy it to a floppy disk in case you're mistaken and need to restore the file.

4. Examine the WIN.INI and SYSTEM.INI files to see if there are any entries in them that clearly belonged to the application. If so, delete the entries.

5. Check the technical documentation for the program to see if it lists DLL files installed by the software. If so, you can remove the DLL files from either the \WINDOWS or \WINDOWS\SYSTEM folders.

This last step can be the trickiest. It is possible for more than one application to use a DLL file. If you remove a DLL file that you believe was used only by the application you are deleting, but it was instead needed by another piece of software, then the other piece of software will no longer function properly. If this occurs, the only option is to reinstall the software you still need so that the DLL files are restored.

When these steps are complete, you have probably deleted the program. No absolute can be given, however, because different programs have different impacts on a traditional Windows environment. There are, unfortunately, no absolutes with traditional Windows software. The Windows 95 improvement of clean uninstalls through effective use of the Registry is a long overdue change.

Removing an MS-DOS Program

Removing a DOS program is perhaps the simplest of all program removals in Windows 95. This is because DOS programs don't really manipulate the Windows environment like Windows applications do. They don't add DLL files or change the Registry or clutter the landscape with INI files.

To remove a DOS program, you need to follow these steps:

1. Delete the folder(s) containing the MS-DOS software.
2. Remove any Windows shortcuts you set up for your DOS programs.
3. Check to see if any residual commands were left in the CONFIG.SYS or AUTOEXEC.BAT files by the program.

This last step is the one that can potentially be the most confusing. It assumes you know what is in these files, and how the commands got there. Your MS-DOS program, not knowing or caring about Windows

95, could have added lines to the files to run programs like SHARE, to set BUFFERS and FILES to a certain level, or to include the SETVER program. None of these is necessary under Windows 95, so they can safely be removed.

Tailoring Windows 95 and the Registry

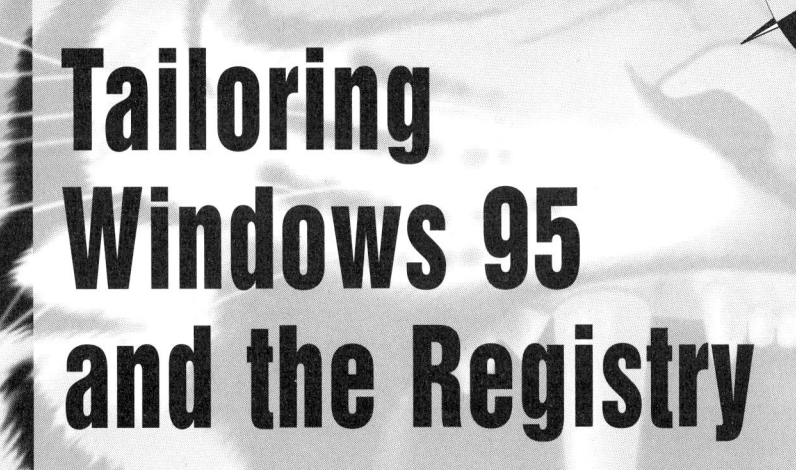

by Clayton Walnum

As you've undoubtedly found out, the Windows 95 operating system is extremely powerful and flexible. It's not simply another revision of a tired, old program, but a completely new and robust operating system brimming with friendly and easy-to-use features. A long-time feature of the Windows GUI has been the option to modify its appearance to suit your taste and needs. Although Windows 3.X was customizable for your needs, Windows 95 offers even more flexibility in the way you configure and use it. You can now change and customize individual elements however you want. Much of Windows ability to cope with such flexibility stems from its use of a centralized *Registry*, where virtually all pertinent information is stored about each component involved directly (and indirectly) with the operating system.

This chapter is designed for people who want to fine-tune Windows 95 for their needs. For those who want to become technically proficient with Windows, you can also learn to manage and troubleshoot most aspects of its daily operation. Unlike other Windows 95 books, this chapter is designed for people who are not yet Windows "experts."

Using This Chapter

If you're familiar with a previous version of Windows, you'll notice there are lots of changes. Some changes are subtle, while others are much different. For starters, the reliance on INI files has diminished greatly. In fact, Windows 95 hardly uses INI files, except where they are needed to maintain compatibility with previous versions of Windows and applications that just don't conform to the Windows 95 Registry structure.

This chapter addresses many aspects of configuring Windows for your specific needs. In addition, you'll learn about:

➤ The purpose of the Registry

➤ Editing the Registry

➤ Tuning Windows' Appearance

➤ Tuning Windows' Configuration

Several sections in this chapter have a short description of what you can expect to see in the Registry together with the location of the value in the Registry. For example, you might see:

```
Registry value: MouseTrails
Key location: MyComputer\HKEY_LOCAL_MACHINE\Config\0001
↪\Display\Settings
```

These show the Registry value and hierarchical location of that value. If you are viewing the Registry, simply navigate to the appropriate subfolder to view the current setting.

Understanding the Registry

One of the great improvements in Windows 95 from previous versions is the method in which it manages program and device information. This does not refer to the files you work with but the information that is automatically recorded by Windows 95 when you install or update a program or device. To understand the improvements that have been made, it is helpful to understand the way things used to be done in previous versions of Windows.

Until the advent of Windows 95, controlling information and parameters for the operating system were kept in a variety of INI files. These files controlled the look, behavior, and speed of Windows and the programs provided with Windows. Sure, you could quickly edit the files with any ASCII text editor, but just one typo or wrong deletion and you would spend more time than you intended just trying to fix it. In addition, information was spread all over the place (at least throughout different INI files) and became quite a nuisance if you wanted to "clean up" your system files.

Windows 95 has done away with this confusion, and has introduced the Registry. The Registry is a structured database describing information about your hardware, applications, and other Windows 95 settings. As you add or remove software and hardware, the Registry is dynamically updated so no "ghost" information lingers about recently removed applications or devices. If you run an application under Windows 95 that was designed to work with Windows 3.1, it continues to generate and maintain INI files, as if there had been no change. This is because 16-bit programs are not aware of the Registry, nor were they designed to take advantage of it. However, as new versions are released specifically for Windows 95, the reliance on INI files will be reduced drastically. Examine more closely how the Registry works.

How the Registry Works

The Registry's database approach to maintaining critical system and user information is very orderly and understandable compared to an

INI file. Technically speaking, the Registry consists of two files, *USER.DAT* and *SYSTEM.DAT*. Of course, both of these files are marked as hidden, so you won't see them (or inadvertently delete them) as you use the Explorer or work from the DOS prompt.

The file USER.DAT, which maintains information from the User Profiles, handles settings dealing with user preferences like screen type, size, file associations, network settings, and personal printer information. The information in USER.DAT varies, based on the users who are registered on the local machine.

The other file, SYSTEM.DAT, which tracks data from the Computer Profiles, maintains hardware settings including types of add-in cards, IRQ settings, and the like. SYSTEM.DAT maintains information that does not change based on who is using the machine.

Registry information is stored in separate files for a simple reason: You may want to store SYSTEM.DAT and USER.DAT in different places. The most common way to do this, in facilities that have large networks, is to keep the system-related information (SYSTEM.DAT) on the local system and the user-related information (USER.DAT) on a network server. This setup allows users to move from machine to machine and still have their preferences available wherever they work.

As you work with Windows 95 on a day-to-day basis, any changes you make to system settings are automatically recorded or updated in the Registry. It's easiest to imagine the Registry as a directory (or folder) structure, similar to the way Explorer displays the contents of your computer. The Registry consists of six keys, or groups, which comprise all aspects of the Windows operating system.

- ➤ **Hkey_Classes_Root.** OLE-related information, including shortcuts. This key is a pointer to the Key_Local_Machine\Software\Classes subkey. It is provided as a separate key for compatibility with older versions of the Windows registration database.

- ➤ **Hkey_Current_User.** User-specific settings, including preferences, color schemes, and so on. This key is nothing but a pointer to a subkey within the Hkey_Users key, representing the user currently logged into the system.

- **Hkey_Local_Machine.** Machine-related specifics, such as installed hardware and swap file settings.

- **Hkey_Users.** Additional user-specific information geared more toward the default settings before data is changed in the Hkey_Current_User key.

- **Hkey_Current_Config.** Configuration information about the current hardware settings, such as notebooks that plug into a docking station. This key is nothing but a pointer to a subkey within the Hkey_Local_Machine\Config key.

- **Hkey_Dyn_Data.** System information for various devices, including Plug-and-Play devices, which is updated each time you restart Windows.

Notice that of the six keys, three are actually pointers to identical data stored in other keys. The Hkey_Dyn_Data key is not actually a file, but is a branch of the Registry maintained in RAM. This key is created every time you start your machine, and is maintained in RAM for fast access. The upshot of all this is that there are really only two keys in the entire Registry that are stored on disk: HKey_Local_Machine (which is SYSTEM.DAT) and HKey_Users (which is USERS.DAT).

Each key plays an important role in how Windows operates and how the user accesses the computer. To many users, this structure can be a bit intimidating. This means that most users stick to simply making changes from the Control Panel, rather than editing the Registry.

If you're familiar with the INI structures found in older versions of Windows, you know that each major section started with a heading surrounded by brackets, such as [Enhanced] or [Desktop]. These groupings are analogous to the keys used within the Registry. A major difference between the two is that there could be dozens or hundreds of groups within the various Windows INI files, while there are only six major groups within the Registry.

Understanding the Registry **329**

The Registry is organized in a hierarchical fashion. Each key can contain either values or subkeys. These subkeys can then contain either values or subkeys, and so on. Just as hard disk directories can contain files or subdirectories, the six major keys can contain values or subkeys. (This is not to say that Registry values are the same as files; they are not. It is only to point out that there is a strong parallel in the structure of the Registry and the structure of a disk drive.)

Values within a key contain data. This is nothing but the current setting for the value; in effect, the "value of the value." Data can be of three types: binary, DWORD, or string. Binary and DWORD values both contain numeric data, but the difference is that binary data can be of any length, while DWORD data is limited to a single 16-bit value. The exact type of data maintained for a value is determined by the purpose for which the value is used.

Changes to the Registry

On a system level, values within the Registry and the structure of the Registry itself are changed all the time. For example, you learned in Chapter 2, "Under-the-Hood Improvements," that Windows 95 is a Plug-and-Play operating system. This means that when starting up, the operating system reads information from the Plug-and-Play BIOS and later from devices installed in the system. That information is compared with information in the Registry and, if differences are detected, Windows modifies itself and loads the appropriate drivers and adapts accordingly.

On a user level, there are two ways you can change the values of the Registry or its structure. The first method (and by far the easiest) is to use Windows tools such as those within the Control Panel. As documented throughout the rest of this book (and even within this chapter), the Control Panel allows you to add hardware or software, change the appearance of your system, or perform any of a score of other operations. Each time you perform such a task, you're editing the Registry—it may not appear as such on the surface, but that is where your changes are stored.

The other way you can change the Registry is through the use of the Registry Editor. This method is much more direct because you're working with the database itself. Software developers, technicians, and network administrators who must alter the Registry's contents will typically be the only ones to benefit from editing the Registry directly. For end users (you and me), editing the Registry directly offers no clear advantage.

Of the two ways you can change the Registry, using the Windows tools is much easier and faster than using the Registry Editor. As an example, consider the process of enabling the screen saver. You can either pick a screen saver from the list in the Display Properties dialog box, or run the Registry editor, search for the screen saver entry (there can be well over 100,000 lines of entries to search through), change one of the Registry values to 0 or 1 (whichever is appropriate), assign a screen saver, then save and exit the Registry editor. Which seems easiest to you?

Manually Editing the Registry

To manually modify the Registry, you must use the Registry Editor, or *Regedit*, program. (The Registry can't be modified with a standard text editor as the INI files could be in previous versions of Windows.) Of course, Regedit is not initially available on any Windows menu—after all, it isn't meant to be used on a regular basis. Regedit should be used only in special circumstances, such as when you are directed what to do by a technical support technician. For instance, you might need to manually update an application's registration information after being directed to do so. In such a case, you must explicitly follow the technician's instructions on proper Registry editing.

To manually invoke the Registry editor, follow these steps:

1. Choose Run from the Start menu. The Run dialog box appears.
2. In the Open field, type **regedit**.
3. Click on the OK button or press Enter.
4. The Registry editor appears, as shown in figure 14.1.

Understanding the Registry **331**

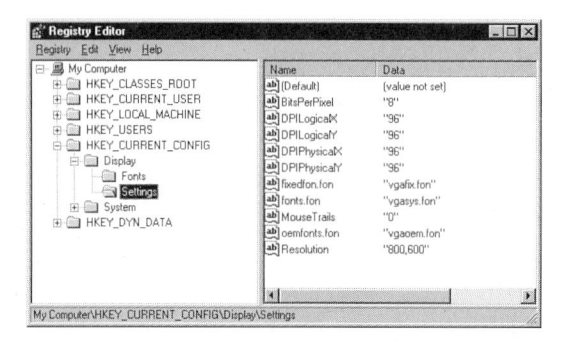

Fig. 14.1 The Registry editor shows keys in a hierarchical manner.

Notice the hierarchical structure of the Registry is similar to that in the Explorer. But beware—that's where the similarity ends. The Registry is divided into six major keys, as described in the previous section:

- Hkey_Classes_Root
- Hkey_Current_User
- Hkey_Local_Machine
- Hkey_Users
- Hkey_Current_Config
- Hkey_Dyn_Data

If you're familiar with modifying INI files in Windows 3.X, you won't see many similarities in editing the Registry. Again, the purpose of the Registry is to bring order to the chaos of Windows configuration and relieve users from endless tweaking to get Windows to act just the way they want.

Finding Information in the Registry

Editing the Registry requires knowing precisely what you want (or need) to edit. Typically, the advanced documentation or developer's kit for an application will document the area and value of the Registry entry should you need to modify a setting. There is no concise, comprehensive guide to Registry valid entries for Windows 95. The Registry was first used in Windows NT, and such a guide for NT did not become available for several years after it was introduced. When it did finally become available, it was several hundred pages long and was part of a larger documentation kit that cost around $150!

What can you do if you want to find something in the Registry and you don't have documentation or guidance available? Fortunately, the Registry Editor includes a search tool to find text anywhere within the database. Press Ctrl+F, or choose Edit, Find and enter the text for which you want to search (see fig. 14.2). For example, if you want to find where the entry for MouseTrails is located, enter that text and click on Find Next.

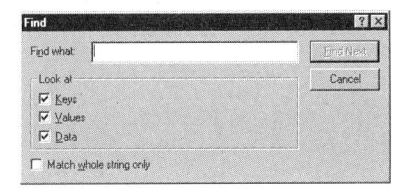

Fig. 14.2 You can use the Find dialog box to locate settings in the Registry.

If you use the search tool, it will locate any text matching the parameter you specify. This means the text may be in a key or subkey (displayed in the left pane of the Registry) or in Registry values (shown in the right pane).

Editing Value Data

Most editing tasks take place in the values shown in the right pane. To begin editing a value, either double-click on it or make sure it is highlighted and then press Enter. Depending on the specific value you are changing, a dialog box will appear that allows you to change the current value. Enter the appropriate value and click OK.

Caution: You should be forewarned that if you inappropriately change Registry values with the Registry Editor, your system may be rendered unstable or unusable. This is because the Registry Editor does no syntax or propriety checking—it blindly lets you do the editing and assumes you know what you are doing. Regedit will not stop you from shooting yourself in the foot.

As an example, say you wanted to edit the screen saver entry in the Registry—you know, the one that controls which screen saver is displayed. The first thing you need to do is open the Registry Editor and search for a term you think might be in the entry. If you search for Screen, you'll find a possible entry, as shown in figure 14.3.

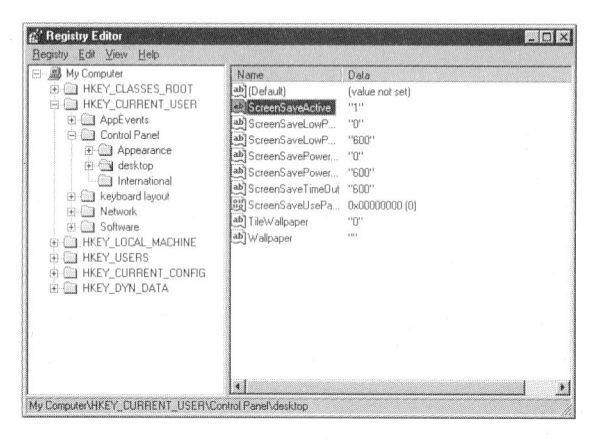

Fig. 14.3 The results of searching in the Registry Editor.

If you don't find such an entry, or if you find a different entry altogether, don't be concerned. About 10 entries in the Registry have the word *Screen* in them. Some of them deal with the screen saver; some do not. In fact, you might not find an entry related to the screen saver unless you've activated the screen saver in your system—this activation is what triggers Windows 95 to create the screen saver entries in the first place.

After you locate an entry, carefully examine it in the context of what you understand about the Registry structure, and then make an educated guess as to whether it's the key or value you want. For instance, from figure 14.3 you can see that the ScreenSaveActive value is within the HKEY_CURRENT_USER key (several subkeys down, but still there). Because the screen saver has to do with the appearance of the screen, and these types of settings are user-related, there is a very good chance that this is the value you are looking to change. The problem, however, is that you never are really sure unless you try things out. Thus, in many respects, working with the Registry Editor is a trial-and-error proposition unless you're given a detailed reference.

To change the value you've located, double-click on the ScreenSaveActive value. A dialog box appears, as shown in figure 14.4, prompting you for the new data to be stored in the value.

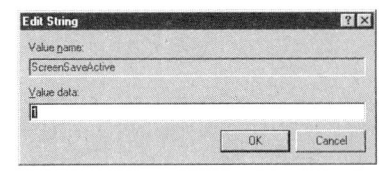

Fig. 14.4 When you change a value, Regedit prompts you for the new data.

The type of editing dialog box that appears depends on the type of value you're changing. If the value contains a string, then you see a dialog box like that shown in figure 14.4; other types of data require different types of dialog boxes. Regardless of the type, you can enter new data for the value, and then click on the OK button.

> **Caution:** Any changes you make to the Registry are instantly saved and permanent. There is no formal Save option or dialog box that asks whether you want to save or abandon changes. Neither is there an undo feature that lets you backtrack on your edits.

Adding Keys or Values

The Registry Editor allows you to add either new keys or values to existing keys. The worth of such additions will depend on whether the key or values will be used by software or the system. This presupposes that you know the proper syntax to make such an addition worthwhile; if you don't, then the software or Windows 95 itself will not know what to do with your entry.

To add a key, all you need to do is position and select, in the left pane, the key under which you want your new subkey to appear. For instance, if you want to add a subkey to the Hkey_Current_User\ControlPanel key, you expand the Hkey_Current_User key, and then select the ControlPanel key. Next, choose Edit, New, Key. The new key appears in the key tree, and you can change its name right away.

To add a value to an existing key, select the key to which you want to add the value, and then choose Edit, New. A submenu appears from which you can select the type of value you want to add: string, binary, or DWORD. You should make your selection based on the type of data you want the value to contain, as described earlier in this chapter. The new value then appears in the right-hand pane of the editor, and you can modify the name assigned to the value.

Deleting Keys or Values

The easiest way to delete a key or value is to select it in the Registry Editor, and then press the Delete key. You're asked if you really want to delete the object; if so, it is removed from the screen and from the Registry.

> **Caution:** There is no undo feature in the Registry Editor. Once you delete a key or value, it is gone for good. Remember, as well, that your deletions can make your system unusable, as can any edit to the Registry. Proceed with extreme caution.

Importing and Exporting the Registry

The data contained in the Registry can be imported or exported to text files. Why would you want or need to do this? In general, you may find it useful to move the entire Registry or parts of the Registry from one system to another. For example, say you've received 27 machines at your office for your employees. Instead of setting up each machine individually, you can configure one of them exactly the way you want. Then, in a stroke of time-saving genius, you can export the Registry to a text file on a floppy disk. Then, go to each of the other machines and import the Registry from the floppy disk. Viola—each of the other machines is a configured duplicate of the original machine.

> **Note:** If you copy the Registry to configure machines, make sure that you also copy supporting files to the other machines. This may include special drivers, screen savers, sound files, or wallpaper files. In short, whatever files you copied to the original machine should also be copied to the clone machines. Copying the Registry just precludes the need of going through the detailed configuration steps.

If you want a hard copy of the Registry, you can print it by choosing Print from the Registry menu. A hard copy lets you see the exact contents of a certain key or the entire database, depending on your print scope. The printed copy also provides a great way to see an "initial condition" of the Registry before you make any changes.

Emergency Registry Recovery

Despite all the warnings about how messing with the Registry can bring your system to its knees, you might still find yourself in that position some day. Fortunately, you can take one of several remedial actions to restore the Registry.

Understanding the Registry **337**

One action involves a backup copy of the Registry. If you have a recent copy of the Registry (one you created by exporting it), you can import the copy to reset everything back to its original state. This step presupposes, however, that you can at least get Windows 95 started. What happens if you cannot even get to that point?

Every time you start Windows 95, it creates a backup copy of both the SYSTEM.DAT and USER.DAT files. As you'll recall, these two files comprise the Registry. If you cannot successfully start Windows, you can follow these steps to restart your system:

1. Use a DOS disk or emergency boot disk to start your system.

2. Change to the directory in which Windows 95 is installed. Typically, this is the WINDOWS directory.

3. Use the following DOS commands to make the Registry files (and their backups) visible and to delete the original Registry files:

   ```
   attrib -s -h -r system.da?
   del system.dat
   attrib -s -h -r user.da?
   del user.dat
   ```

4. Use the following DOS commands to rename the backup Registry files:

   ```
   ren system.da0 system.dat
   ren user.da0 user.dat
   ```

5. Use the following DOS commands to set the newly renamed files to their proper condition:

   ```
   attrib +s +h +r system.dat
   attrib +s +h +r user.dat
   ```

6. Restart your system.

At this point, your system should restart properly. If it does not, you may have a more serious problem (such as a scrambled hard drive) for which more drastic measures would be necessary. At this point it would be best to consult a technician.

Accessing a Registry on a Remote System

People who administer large numbers of computers face a particularly tough job. One way to make that job easier is to access the Registry on a remote computer, over the network. This capability allows troubleshooting or checking to occur without having to be physically in front of the machine.

Accessing the Registry on a remote machine cannot be done unless the remote machine is first running the Microsoft Remote Registry service. Unfortunately, activating this on the remote machine requires that someone be at the remote machine. However, this service could be part of the normal setup of the machine before it is ever put into everyday use. To start this service, follow these steps:

1. Choose Start, Settings. The Settings menu appears.
2. Choose Settings, Control Panel. The Control Panel appears.
3. Double-click on the Network icon. The Network Properties sheet appears.

Tailoring Windows 95's Appearance

As you've learned already, the Registry is a complex and finely-tuned database maintained by the Windows 95 operating system. The majority of the time you'll never have need to poke around inside it via the Registry Editor. Indeed, there are less messy ways of getting Windows to look and act just the way you want.

Perhaps no other aspect of Windows 95 attracts as much attention as its appearance. The colors, combined with the attractive three-dimensional look of icons, buttons, and windows are enough to draw anyone away from a strictly DOS environment. To date, Windows lovers spend great amounts of time carefully changing colors, the screen saver, even the bitmap background graphics fondly referred to as "wallpaper." Interestingly enough, virtually all screen elements in Windows 95 can be changed by using the various tools in the Display Properties sheets. This section focuses on how to use the Control Panel to take full advantage of Windows 95's appearance.

Video Card and Monitor Settings

Changing the appearance of your Windows 95 system depends on the capabilities of both your video card and monitor. To a large degree, Windows can automatically detect the type of video card you have, and sometimes can discern your monitor. It cannot, however, determine the resolution at which you want to do your work, nor can it figure out which color palette you want to use.

The best thing to do is set these items by using the Control Panel. In most instances you should have to set them only once, unless you like to use different settings with different programs. To set the video card and monitor properties, click on the Settings tab of the Display Properties sheet. The sheet appears, as shown in figure 14.5.

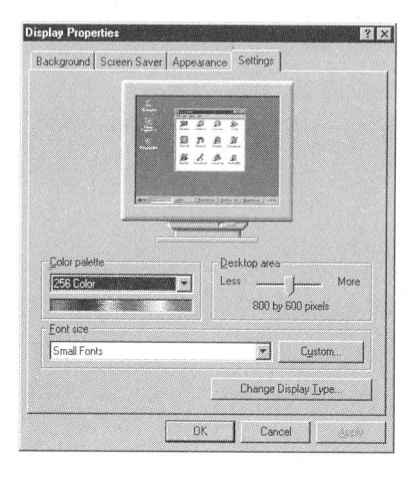

Fig. 14.5 Windows allows you to control how your video card and monitor are used.

You can make three settings on this page. The first, at the left side of the sheet, is the Color palette. Indicate the number of colors you want to use, from those available on your video card. At the right side of the sheet you can specify the resolution you want to use. Finally, at the bottom of the sheet you can pick the Font size you want to use. Each of these items is a matter of personal taste, and you should experiment to find the combination most pleasing and productive for you.

Also at the bottom of the sheet is a button, Change Display Type, which can be used to modify the type of monitor and video card installed in your system. If you click on the button, you will see the Change Display Type dialog box, as shown in figure 14.6.

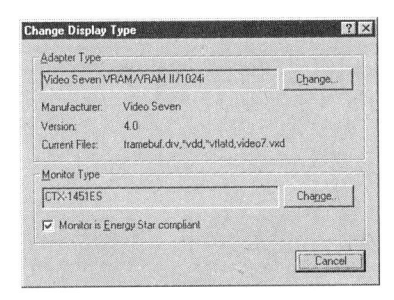

Fig. 14.6 The Change Display Type dialog box is used to specify both your video adapter and monitor.

Typically, you won't need to change your video card type; Windows 95 detects and sets this automatically. You should, however, set your monitor type by clicking on the Change button and then selecting a monitor make and model.

> **Note:** When you make changes in either the video adapter or the monitor, you should also make sure that your color palette and resolution are set the way you like them. These settings are sometimes made by Windows when you change the hardware on which they are based.

In the Registry, the video adapter and monitor information are considered part of the local machine key. As such, you can find the video adapter information in the first of the following two keys, and the monitor information in the second:

```
MyComputer\HKEY_LOCAL_MACHINE\System\CurrentControlSet\Services\
➥Class\Display\0000
MyComputer\HKEY_LOCAL_MACHINE\Enum\Monitor\Default_Monitor\0001
```

Modifying Your Background

Windows allows you to configure your desktop in virtually any manner you can imagine. One way you can do this is through the use of patterns and wallpaper. Both are available by using the Background page of the Display Properties sheet, as shown in figure 14.7.

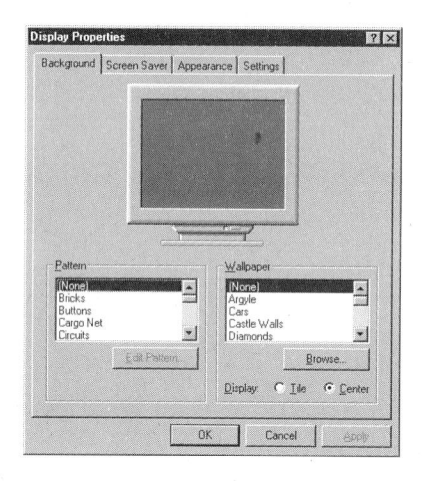

Fig. 14.7 You can change the appearance of your desktop by using the Background page of the Display Properties sheet.

Patterns refer to small bit-mapped images repeated over and over across your desktop; using patterns is similar to adding a texture to your desktop. The wallpaper setting controls the display of a graphic image on your desktop. This image can either be tiled (repeated to cover the entire desktop) or shown once (centered in the middle of the desktop).

Tip: If you're short on system resources, don't use wallpaper. It can quickly consume precious resources and slow down the overall performance of your system.

In the Registry, the values concerning both patterns and wallpaper are in the following key:

    MyComputer\HKEY_CURRENT_USER\ControlPanel\desktop

Changing Windows Colors and Styles

The easiest way to change colors in Windows 95 is to use the Display applet in the Control Panel. The applet lets you change the color of nearly any element of Windows 95, from the open background referred to as the *desktop*, to window borders, styles, and the fonts used in each window and title bar. As you make changes, you may notice that just a slight variation on the default is what you need to make Windows 95 even more pleasant. Color changes made in the Display applet also affect the colors used for Windows programs. Gone are the days of editing WIN.INI to get just the color scheme you want.

You can change the appearance of Windows 95 by using the Display Properties sheet. To display the proper sheet, follow these steps:

1. Choose Start, Settings. The Settings menu appears.
2. Choose Settings, Control Panel. The Control Panel appears.
3. Double-click on the Display icon. The Display Properties sheet appears.
4. Click on the Appearance tab. The Display Properties sheet appears, as shown in figure 14.8.

Tip: A shortcut for accomplishing the first three steps is to right-click on a vacant area of the desktop and choose Properties from the context menu.

Tailoring Windows 95's Appearance **343**

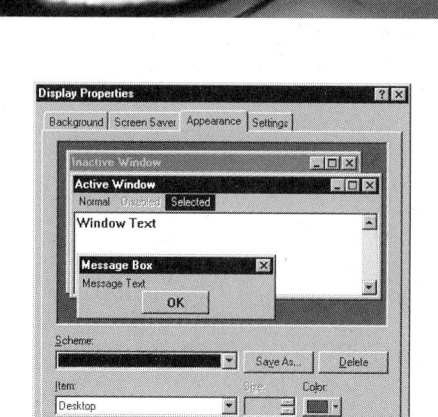

Fig. 14.8 The Appearance tab of the Display Properties sheet allows you to modify how Windows 95 looks.

Each of the following sections shows how to change specific items in the appearance of Windows 95.

Working with Schemes

Information about the appearance of Windows 95 is stored in schemes. These are nothing but named profiles that define specific colors and fonts for the objects used by Windows 95 to communicate information. You can pick an existing scheme by selecting it in the Scheme field—Windows 95 includes 27 different schemes, as follows:

- Brick
- Desert
- Eggplant
- Flat
- Flat (large)
- High Contrast Black
- High Contrast Black (large)
- High Contrast White
- High Contrast White (large)
- Lilac
- Lilac (large)
- Maple
- Marine (high color)
- Plum (high color)

- Pumpkin (large)
- Rainy Day
- Rose
- Rose (large)
- Slate
- Spruce
- Stars and Stripes (VGA)
- Storm (VGA)
- Teal (VGA)
- Wheat
- Windows Standard
- Windows Standard (extra large)
- Windows Standard (large)

As you pick a different scheme, the sample display at the top of the dialog box changes to show what the scheme will do to your desktop. If you don't like the way a scheme appears, you can modify it to your heart's content. (The next two sections discuss how to change elements of a scheme.)

Before modifying an existing scheme, save it under a new name, and then make changes to the copy. This method leaves the original intact in case you want to use it later. To save a scheme under a new name, click on the Save As button at the right of the scheme names. Windows asks you for the name of the new scheme, offering the current scheme name as a default. If you click on OK, the changes you have made overwrite the current scheme. If, however, you supply a new name, then it is saved as a new scheme and appears in the scheme list.

Schemes are stored in the Registry by using a single value for each scheme. These appear in the following Registry key:

```
MyComputer\HKEY_CURRENT_USER\ControlPanel\Appearance\Schemes
```

Figure 14.9 shows an example of what these schemes look like in the Registry. Notice that the data for the scheme values are stored in hexadecimal notation.

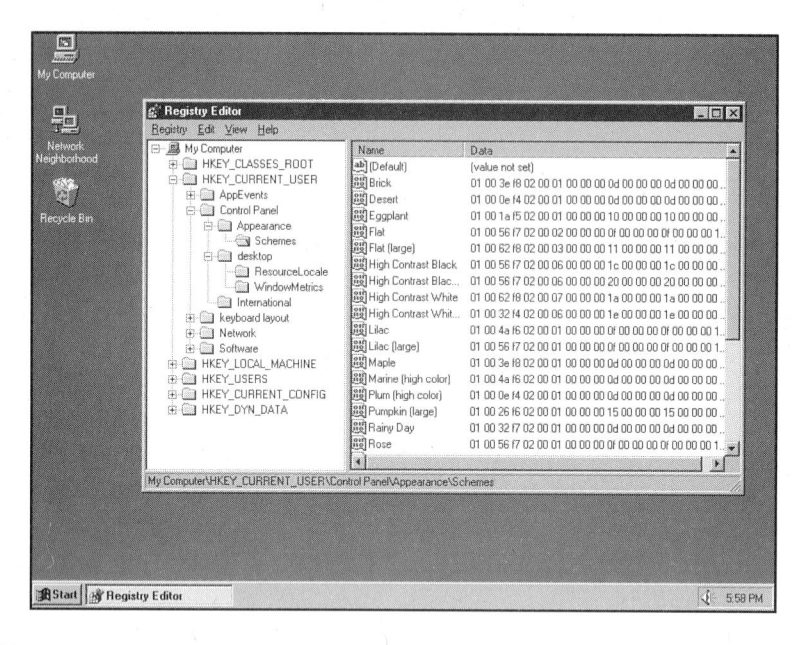

Fig. 14.9 Colors are stored under scheme names in the Registry.

Changing Item Color and Size

Part of the lure of Windows 95 is its ability to allow users to express their individuality. The next time you're near someone else's computer, take a look at the colors used in the color scheme. To you, the choice may be unappealing, but it suits the user just fine. Many users even modify their colors on a regular basis to liven things up. Windows 95 lets you use the Appearance tab in the Display Properties sheet (shown earlier, in fig. 14.5) to choose the precise color you want applied to various desktop items.

To change the colors associated with an object, you can take two approaches. First of all, you can select the item from the Item pull-down list, or you can simply use the mouse to click on the item in the sample desktop at the top of the sheet. Windows lets you modify the size and color of any of the screen elements listed in Table 14.1.

Table 14.1 Items Whose Size and Color Can Be Changed

Item	Size	Color
3D Objects		✔
Active Title Bar	✔	✔
Active Window Border	✔	✔
Application Background		✔
Caption Buttons	✔	
Desktop		✔
Icon	✔	
Icon Spacing (Horizontal)	✔	
Icon Spacing (Vertical)	✔	
Inactive Title Bar	✔	✔
Inactive Window Border	✔	✔
Menu	✔	✔
Palette Title	✔	
Scrollbar	✔	
Selected Items	✔	✔
ToolTip		✔
Window		✔

As you can see from Table 14.1, you cannot modify the size and color of all items. Once you have selected the object, you can modify the appropriate attribute—size or color. You modify the size by adjusting the Size value at the right side of the item name. Likewise, you modify the color by changing the Color field to the right of the item name.

The colors assigned to various elements of the desktop are stored in the following Registry path:

```
MyComputer\HKEY_CURRENT_USER\ControlPanel\Colors
```

Within this key are a large number of values that allow you to specify the colors of individual desktop items. The data assigned to each value consists of three numbers, separated by a space. The values of these

Tailoring Windows 95's Appearance   **347**

individual numbers range from 0 to 255. These numbers represent the amount of red, green, and blue (the primary colors) which, when combined together, represent a color blend from a 256-color palette.

The size of desktop elements are stored in the values in the following Registry path:

```
MyComputer\HKEY_CURRENT_USER\ControlPanel\desktop
➥\WindowMetrics
```

Colors are also stored in the WIN.INI file, as in previous versions of Windows. They are in a section labeled [colors] with various entries which appear similar to:

```
[colors]
Scrollbar=192 192 192
Background=0 128 128
ActiveTitle=0 0 128
InactiveTitle=192 192 192
Menu=192 192 192
Window=255 255 255
WindowFrame=0 0 0
MenuText=0 0 0
WindowText=0 0 0
TitleText=255 255 255
ActiveBorder=192 192 192
InactiveBorder=192 192 192
AppWorkspace=128 128 128
Hilight=0 0 128
HilightText=255 255 255
ButtonFace=192 192 192
ButtonShadow=128 128 128
GrayText=128 128 128
ButtonText=0 0 0
InactiveTitleText=0 0 0
ButtonHilight=255 255 255
ButtonDkShadow=0 0 0
ButtonLight=192 192 192
InfoText=192 192 192
InfoWindow=0 0 0
```

Each entry in the [colors] section consists of a name representing a desktop element, followed by an equal sign and three numbers. These three numbers have the same purpose as the color numbers stored in the Registry. You can edit this file with a text editor, but doing so offers no benefit over making changes via the Control Panel.

You may ask yourself why these are included in both the Registry and WIN.INI. The purpose behind this, as well as other seemingly duplicated entries, is compatibility. Many 16-bit (Windows 3.X) applications aren't conversant with the Registry—they expect to retrieve and place information in the WIN.INI, among other INI files. Ultimately, this forms a compromise so that 16-bit programs can function normally in a 32-bit (Windows 95) environment.

Changing Font Color and Size

In your schemes you can change the font used quite a few items. Fonts can be any typeface installed on your system, whether ATM (Adobe) or TrueType. This flexibility enables you to make system fonts easier to read and to customize the look of the desktop to suit your style and needs. In addition to changing the font used for an item, you can also change the font size and apply attributes such as bold or italic. Table 14.2 shows the desktop items whose fonts, font sizes, and font colors you can change.

Table 14.2 Items Whose Font Size and Color Can Be Changed

Item	Size	Color
3D Objects		✔
Active Title Bar	✔	✔
Icon	✔	
Inactive Title Bar	✔	✔
Menu	✔	✔
Message Box	✔	✔
Palette Title	✔	
Selected Items	✔	✔
ToolTip	✔	✔
Window		✔

Notice that for some elements you can't change the color of the fonts because their colors are self-changing depending on the style of other items. For example, a lighter Desktop color changes the Icon color automatically to black text.

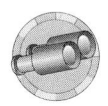

> **Note:** For the sake of aesthetics, use a simple sans serif font like MS Sans Serif—the default Windows 95 system font. Some fonts that appear nice in a heading or on paper take on a bizarre appearance when you have to stare at them on a screen.

As far as the Registry is concerned, information about the color and size of fonts used in the desktop is stored in a number of places. Text colors are stored in the first of the following keys, and sizes are stored in the second:

```
MyComputer\HKEY_CURRENT_USER\ControlPanel\Colors
MyComputer\HKEY_CURRENT_USER\ControlPanel\
desktop\WindowMetrics
```

Configuring the Screen Saver

The Windows screen saver fills the monitor screen when the computer has been free from any mouse or keyboard activity for a specified period of time. In the past, a continuous image left on a computer monitor would burn the image into the screen's phospors. Screen burn-in doesn't occur on today's VGA monitors mostly because of improvements in monitor technology. Screen savers are used mainly for amusement and, interestingly enough, security. The password protection feature of Windows 95 screen saver can protect your sensitive data from prying eyes. This section shows you how to configure the screen saver and use password protection.

The screen saver is controlled in the Display Properties sheet. To display the proper sheet, follow these steps:

1. Choose Start, Settings. The Settings menu appears.

2. Choose Settings, Control Panel. The Control Panel appears.

3. Double-click on the Display icon. The Display Properties sheet appears.

4. Click on the Screen Saver tab. The Display Properties sheet appears, as shown in figure 14.10.

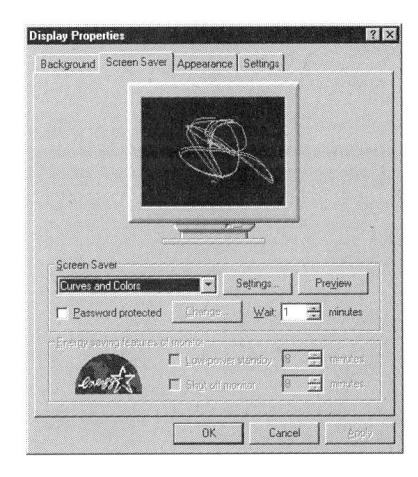

Fig. 14.10 The Screen Saver tab of the Display Properties sheet allows you to control the Windows 95 screen saver.

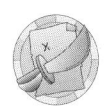

> **Tip:** A shortcut for accomplishing the first three steps is to right-click on a vacant area of the desktop and choose Properties from the context menu.

Each of the following sections shows how to change specific items related to the screen saver.

Activating the Screen Saver

You activate the screen saver by specifying a screen saver in the Screen Saver field of the Screen Saver tab of the Display Properties sheet. (Whew! Who said these things were easy?) All you need to do is pick a screen saver from the drop-down list. As you pick a screen saver, you'll notice that it shows up in the preview monitor in the top part of the sheet.

Tailoring Windows 95's Appearance **351**

Once you've decided on a screen saver, you can click on the Preview button to see how it will appear over your entire screen—not just the small preview monitor. Any keypress or movement of the mouse returns you to the dialog box. Click on OK when finished.

The screen saver is controlled by the ScreenSaveActive value in the following key in the Registry:

    MyComputer\HKEY_CURRENT_USER\ControlPanel\Desktop

Setting the Screen Saver's Options

Windows 95 has a group of options you can set for every screen saver. These options include items such as how long before the system should be idle before the screen saver is invoked and a host of Energy Star options. These latter options are available only if both your video card and your monitor are Energy-Star compliant, meaning that they have incorporated the energy-saving guidelines published by the EPA.

Each screen saver included with Windows (except Blank Screen) also has configuration settings which you can modify. To change or view these settings after choosing a screen saver from the list, click on the Settings button. Because each screen saver is different, the settings for each will also vary. Figure 14.11 shows the settings for the screen saver module *Curves and Colors*.

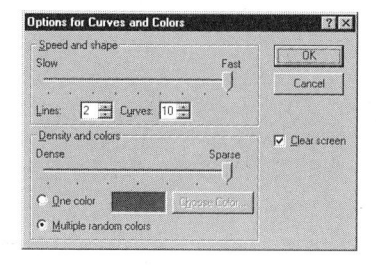

Fig. 14.11 The options for this screen saver offer a great deal of control over the image's shape, color, and speed.

352   Chapter 14: Tailoring Windows 95 and the Registry

A variety of values in the Registry control the screen saver. The values available will generally vary, depending on the type of screen saver you've selected. All of the values, however, are stored in the following key:

```
MyComputer\HKEY_CURRENT_USER\ControlPanel\Desktop
```

Some of the common values in this key, along with their meanings, are shown in Table 14.3.

Table 14.3   Common Screen Saver Registry Values

Registry Value	Meaning
ScreenSaveLowPowerActive	Determines whether low-power standby is enabled. This is an Energy-Star option.
ScreenSaveLowPowerTimeout	Specifies, in seconds, how long before the low-power standby signal is sent from the video card to the monitor. This is an Energy-Star option.
ScreenSavePowerOffActive	Determines whether shutting off the monitor is enabled. This is an Energy-Star option.
ScreenSavePowerOffTimeOut	Specifies, in seconds, how long after the monitor is in low-power mode that it should be turned off. This is an Energy-Star option.
ScreenSaveTimeOut	Specifies, in seconds, how long the system is idle before the screen saver is displayed.

Using Password Protection

The password protection option gives you the freedom to walk away from your computer without fear that someone will peek at your screen or access data from your computer. In fact, unless the correct password is entered, nobody can access the computer, including you.

In the Display Properties sheet, enable the Password protected check box and click on Change button to provide your password. Enter the password and, immediately below it enter it again to confirm, then click on OK. Your changes are enabled once you click OK in the Display Properties sheet. Now, if your computer is idle for the time you specified, any keypress or mouse movement will invoke the sheet shown in figure 14.12 requesting your password.

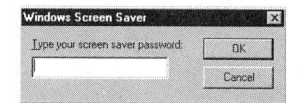

Fig. 14.12 To return to Windows you must enter the correct password and click on OK.

To remove password protection, remove the check from the Password protected check box and click on OK.

The Registry value ScreenSaveUsePassword controls the password. If you set the data for the value to 0, then the password is disabled, whereas setting it to 1 enables the password. The complete Registry path for this value is:

```
MyComputer\HKEY_CURRENT_USER\ControlPanel
➥\Desktop\ScreenSaveUsePassword
```

The password itself is also saved in the Registry, but it is encrypted. The exact encryption algorithm is unknown, but it appears that two bytes are stored for every single character of the password (this is consistent with the use of Unicode instead of ASCII in Windows 95). Rather than trying to change the password in the Registry, it is much more efficient to delete it and change the Registry values that control the use of the password. The following is the path of the Registry value used to store the screen saver password:

```
MyComputer\HKEY_CURRENT_USER\ControlPanel\Desktop\ScreenSave_Data
```

Tip: If you forget your screen saver password, you can get around it by turning off the computer and then turning it back on. After you log into Windows 95, edit the Registry to get rid of the screen saver password protection.

Setting the Date and Time

Your computer may not have the correct time and date. For a variety of reasons, many computers aren't set correctly. Perhaps the computer was purchased from a different part of the country, or maybe you just moved and haven't changed its clock, or perhaps you forgot to instruct Windows 95 to automatically adjust the clock for daylight savings time. It's important to make sure that your computer maintains the correct date and time because every file you create, update, or otherwise change gets "stamped" with whatever date and time are on your computer.

Windows 95 combines the date and time function into one convenient location. You can access this feature either by choosing Start, Settings, Control Panel, and selecting the Date/Time applet or by double-clicking on the clock on the taskbar. Choose the Date & Time tab and the Date/Time Properties sheet appears, as shown in figure 14.13.

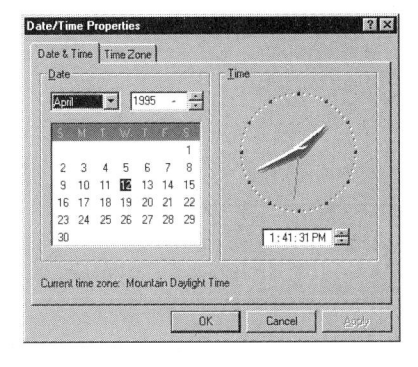

Fig. 14.13 You can adjust the date and time with a point and click.

Tailoring Windows 95's Appearance **355**

The date is displayed in a calendar representation, so choosing the correct date is as simple as picking the date and year from the corresponding fields. You change the time somewhat differently by clicking in the hour, minute, second, or AM/PM designator and then changing the value with the buttons to the right of the time field.

If you inspect the Time Zone tab, you'll notice Windows 95 can automatically adjust for daylight savings time. This feature means that rather than manually setting your clock ahead or back by one hour for daylight savings time, Windows can handle this automatically. To use this feature, choose the Time Zone tab and check the box labeled `Automatically adjust clock for daylight saving changes`. Remember, if you ever relocate your computer to another part of the country (or the world), be sure to select the appropriate time zone by clicking directly on the map. This ensures that your computer clock is accurate year-round.

As with every other configuration option, the Registry maintains information related to system date and time. Information about various time zones is stored in a number of subkeys under the following Registry key:

```
MyComputer\HKEY_LOCAL_MACHINE\SOFTWARE\Microsoft\Windows
➥\CurrentVersion\TimeZones
```

Information about which time zone is applicable to your machine is stored in the following Registry key:

```
MyComputer\HKEY_LOCAL_MACHINE\System\CurrentControlSet
➥\control\TimeZoneInformation
```

Configuring the Mouse

Among the hardware items in your computer system, besides the computer itself, your mouse is the most important device. Without it, you could not productively access Windows. So, your mouse must be installed and configured properly to get the most out of Windows. This section takes a close look at the various mouse settings in Windows.

All mouse changes are done through the Mouse Properties sheet, accessed by choosing Start from the taskbar, Settings, Control Panel, and clicking on the Mouse applet. Figure 14.14 shows what this sheet looks like.

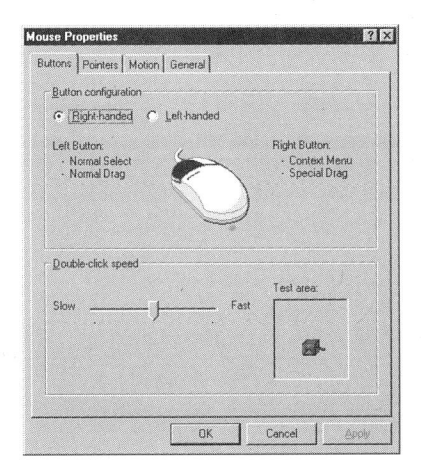

Fig. 14.14 Changing mouse settings is done in the Mouse Properties sheet.

Setting the Mouse Double-Click Speed

Double-clicking is the most common way to select items in Windows and Windows applications. A double-click occurs when you click a mouse button two times in quick succession. It's important to set the speed of the double-click properly, otherwise Windows will interpret your double-clicks inaccurately. Windows measures the time between each click and, if the value is less than the double-click setting, accepts it as a double-click.

To change the mouse double-click speed, select the Buttons tab in the Mouse Properties sheet and drag the slider control in the Double-click speed section either left (slower speed) or right (faster speed).

A slower setting increases the number of milliseconds you must wait between clicks while a faster setting requires you to double-click faster since there are fewer milliseconds between clicks. This setting has a value between 100 and 900 milliseconds.

In the Registry, the mouse double-click setting is stored in the following value:

    MyComputer\HKEY_CURRENT_USER\ControlPanel\Mouse\DoubleClickSpeed

Enabling Pointer Trails

If you have a hard time spotting the mouse pointer or just watching it move across the screen, you can enable *pointer trails*. This option makes the pointer image remain on-screen as you move the mouse, giving the effect of a pointer trail. To enable this option, double-click on the Mouse applet in the Control Panel, select the Motion tab, and check the Show pointer trails box. If you want to adjust the length of trails displayed on-screen, move the slider control. Click on OK to close and accept your changes.

The Registry value that controls this setting is located as follows:

    Registry value: MouseTrails
    Key location:
    MyComputer\HKEY_LOCAL_MACHINE\Config\0001\Display\Settings

Setting Mouse Acceleration

Mouse acceleration means how fast the pointer moves across the screen when you physically move the mouse. Depending on how you use your mouse and your current screen resolution, you may find that adjusting the acceleration can make using the mouse more comfortable.

At its most basic setting, the pointer moves across the screen as quickly as you move the mouse. Generally, this speed is fine for low resolutions such as 640 × 480, but as you increase the resolution, the distance the pointer must traverse the screen increases. This is due largely to the number of pixels visible at one time on your screen. For example, a resolution of 640 × 480 displays relatively few pixels, so a mouse appears to move more quickly. On the other hand, a resolution of 800 × 600 crams more pixels into the same screen area, so a mouse will appear to move a little slower. The higher resolution settings may cause you to move the mouse across the mouse pad several times before your pointer reaches a desired location on-screen.

To compensate for the screen resolution you are using, Windows lets you change the pointer speed. To do so, choose the Motion tab in the Mouse Properties sheet (see fig. 14.15). Click and drag the slider control to the desired setting and click Apply to test it. Basically, there are seven possible settings that determine how fast the pointer moves.

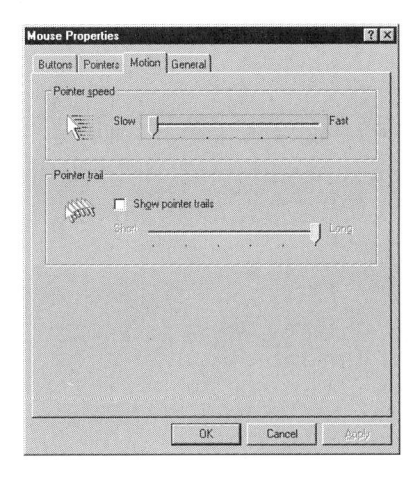

Fig. 14.15 Using the Mouse Properties sheet to adjust the speed of the pointer across the screen.

Technically speaking, mouse movement is based on specific settings: mouse speed and threshold. Windows sets these according to which of the seven settings you choose from the slider control. Table 14.4 shows the possible values placed into the Registry when you choose a pointer speed setting. The threshold values represent the number of pixels the pointer must traverse before acceleration kicks in. As you can see, when all parameters are set to zero, the mouse moves the slowest and does not accelerate as you move it. However, move the slider control to the fastest setting and the pointer will double its speed as you exceed the Threshold1 value. If you also exceed the Threshold2 value, the pointer will quadruple its speed.

Table 14.4 Mouse Acceleration Settings

	Slower				Faster		
Mouse Speed	0	1	1	1	2	2	2
Threshold1	0	10	7	4	4	4	4
Threshold2	0	0	0	0	12	9	6

The Registry value that controls this setting is located as follows:

```
Registry value: MouseSpeed, Mouse Threshold1, Mouse
Threshold2
Key location: MyComputer\HKEY_CURRENT_USER\ControlPanel\Mouse
```

Changing the Mouse Driver

When you install Windows 95, it automatically detects the kind of mouse you have and loads the appropriate driver. However, you may later upgrade your mouse driver or use a different pointing device altogether. To change the mouse type, perform the following steps:

1. Double-click the Mouse applet in the Control Panel folder.

2. Select the General tab and click on Change. The Select Device dialog box appears.

3. Choose the Show all device radio button and pick the corresponding manufacturer and model of your mouse or pointing device.

4. Click on OK.

If you have an unlisted mouse type, you can install your own mouse driver by placing a mouse driver disk in the floppy drive, clicking on Have Disk, and following the instructions.

The Registry value that controls this setting is located as follows:

```
Registry value:
Key location:
MyComputer\HKEY_LOCAL_MACHINE\System\CurrentControlSet\
Services\Class\Mouse\0000
```

Configuring Your Keyboard

Because the keyboard is one of the primary input devices for your system, you must be able to adjust its settings for maximum productivity. This section covers the various ways to change keyboard settings. In Windows 95, you change the keyboard settings by following these steps:

1. Choose Start, Settings. The Settings menu appears.

2. Choose Settings, Control Panel. The Control Panel appears.

3. Double-click on the Keyboard icon. The Keyboard Properties sheet appears, as shown in figure 14.16.

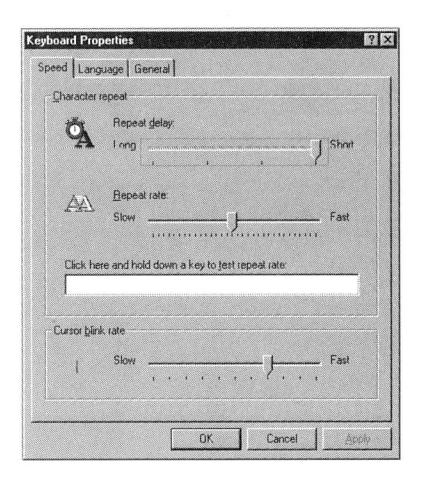

Fig. 14.16 Changing keyboard settings is done in the Keyboard Properties sheet.

Tailoring Windows 95's Appearance **361**

Controlling the Cursor Blink Rate

Windows displays the cursor as a thin, black line that flashes nearly once each second. For some users, changing the cursor blink rate makes it easier to spot the cursor on-screen. To change the cursor's blink rate, move the slider control in the Keyboard Properties sheet to a slow or fast setting. Although the default cursor blink rate setting is 530 milliseconds, or one blink every 1/2 second, it can range from 100 (fast) to 1,200 (slow).

The Registry value is located as follows:

```
Registry value: CursorBlinkRate
Key location: MyComputer\HKEY_CURRENT_USER\Control Panel\Desktop
```

Configuring the Keyboard Speed

Next to the actual quality of the keyboard itself, the keyboard's speed determines your productivity and comfort. By changing the keyboard's speed you can quickly enter or delete repetitive characters by holding down a key for a designated period of time. Also, you can move around in a document much faster—particularly when you use the directional keys. To change the keyboard's speed, make sure that the Speed tab is displayed in the Keyboard properties sheet (refer back to fig. 14.16). Then, modify the Repeat delay and Repeat rate settings as desired.

The Repeat delay specifies the length of time you must hold down a key before it begins repeating, and the Repeat rate controls how quickly the key repeats. Often, setting the keyboard to a short delay and a fast repeat rate is common. If a key repeats too soon after pressing it, move the Repeat delay slider one notch to the left. The default Repeat delay time is 2 milliseconds. The default Repeat rate is 31 milliseconds.

The Registry values for these two settings are located as followings:

```
MyComputer\HKEY_CURRENT_USER\ControlPanel
\Keyboard\KeyboardDelay
MyComputer\HKEY_CURRENT_USER\ControlPanel
\Keyboard\KeyboardSpeed
```

Picking a Type of Keyboard

You can use virtually any keyboard with Windows, so long as you choose the correct keyboard driver. When you first install Windows, the install process identifies your current keyboard. However, you might want to install a newer keyboard or resort to an old relic you found in your closet. To do so, follow these steps:

1. Double-click on the Keyboard applet in the Control Panel.
2. Choose the General tab in the Keyboard Properties sheet.
3. Click on the Change button and highlight the Show all devices button.
4. Select the appropriate keyboard and click on OK.

If your keyboard isn't listed, you can click on Have Disk and insert a disk containing the keyboard driver into the floppy drive.

In the Registry, the keyboard driver information is located in the following key:

```
MyComputer\HKEY_LOCAL_MACHINE\System\CurrentControlSet\Services\Class\Keyboard\0000
```

Controlling Application Icons and Folders

As you learned earlier, part of the Registry is the USER.DAT file. If two users share the same computer at different times, one might prefer a blue background while the other enjoys a green background. Windows 95 accommodates both (or more) users by maintaining separate subkeys for each user in the Hkey_Users key of the Registry, which is stored in the USER.DAT file. When a user logs on to the system, the pointer responsible for the Hkey_Current_User key is updated to point to the proper subkey in Hkey_Users. Some of the adjustments and options unique to each user profile include the following:

➤ Location, size, and characteristics of the Taskbar

➤ Icon and applet size/arrangement

- Which programs launch automatically at startup
- Other user-related options such as screen saver, mouse settings, and sound events

Automatically Arranging Icons

Due to the nature of a graphical user interface like Windows, icons tend to become jumbled. Of course, trying to organize them manually is tedious. Fortunately, Windows can automatically arrange your icons for you. In fact, you can instruct Windows to arrange icons in a variety of ways.

To arrange a group of icons one time, right-click anywhere in the window and choose Arrange Icons from the context menu. Icons can be organized in one of four ways:

- **Name.** Arranged alphabetically in ascending order.
- **Type.** Arranged alphabetically by extension (file type).
- **Size.** Arranged by size in ascending order.
- **Date.** Arranged by date, most recent first.

To have Windows automatically arrange icons for a particular window, choose Auto Arrange from the context menu. Once enabled, any time you delete or add an icon, the icons are automatically arranged—no more jumbled icons. If you have a difficult time using the context menu, you can choose Arrange Icons from any window's View menu.

Controlling Program Applets

If you're familiar with a previous version of Windows, you'll recall how you could group applications within Program Groups. Now you have the option of maintaining your applications in any way you choose. For example, in Windows 95 you can place individual application icons (actually "shortcut" icons that act as pointers) anywhere—even on the desktop.

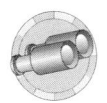

> **Note:** *Applet* is a term coined by Windows users to refer to small applications; not full-blown in their own right, but a smaller parts of the operating system.

When you install a program in Windows 95, it is stored in a single folder or folder structure. You can create any number of shortcut icons that "point" to the application, however. When you click on that specific icon, the program launches. For example, if you install an application like CorelDRAW!, the program files are stored in the folder Corel50, but the shortcuts for that application are kept in the \Windows\Start menu\Programs\Corel 5 folder. As such, you can put a shortcut on the desktop, in another folder, or virtually anywhere you like. You can even have shortcuts for the same application in multiple locations. So, instead of starting a program in the traditional way (navigating through the Start menus), place a shortcut on the desktop and double-click on it.

Tuning Windows Configuration

In addition to making changes to its appearance, you also need to understand the behind-the-scenes activity of Windows to gain maximum usefulness of the operating system. Indeed, Windows is installed according to the hardware it detects and other criteria you specify. However, there are a number of settings you can make based strictly on personal preference, including choosing startup preferences, reorganizing program groups, assigning sounds to certain events, and designating file associations.

Choosing Startup Preferences

Windows 95 allows you complete control over how you start the operating system. You can control not only how Windows 95 itself starts, but also which programs are run automatically after startup is complete. Settings related to these options are stored in the user information maintained by Windows 95.

You can find complete information on how the startup procedure can be modified in Chapter 15, "Taking Control of Windows 95 Startup."

Reorganizing Program Groups

You can easily change the location of programs in the Start menu. This feature lets you modify the default placement of program shortcuts and group them in a manner that suits your particular tastes. For example, one simple change might be to add a commonly accessed program directly to the Start menu (the menu that appears when you first click on the Start button). Or, you might have a number of the same categories of program, such as three word processors, three spreadsheets, two DTP programs, and so on. Rather than having each listed within the Programs menu, you can create submenus to contain them. This method would give you a Word Processor folder, a Spreadsheet folder, a DTP folder, and so on. Another situation might require that you rename a program group, such as when you want to maintain two versions of an application that install into the same folder. Also, you may want to rename a program name listed in the Start menu.

To add a program directly to the Start menu, you perform steps similar to adding a program to the Startup menu:

1. Choose Start from the Taskbar, Settings, Taskbar. The Taskbar Properties sheet appears.

2. Select the Start menu Programs tab and click on the Add button.

3. Type the program's executable file name (typically an EXE extension) in the Command line text box. If you're not sure where it is or what it's called, click on the Browse button instead to find the correct folder and file and click on Open to select it.

4. Click on Next, highlight the Start menu folder, and click on Next.

5. Provide a descriptive name for this program. Typically, Windows inserts the name of the executable file but you can retype it to display whatever you wish.

6. Click on Finish to complete the Start menu modification, then click on OK.

> **Tip:** If you've created a shortcut for a program, you can move it to the Start menu by dragging the icon for the shortcut and dropping it on the Start button.

Removing a program from the Start menu is just as easy. Open the Taskbar Properties sheet as mentioned previously, select the Start menu Programs tab, and click on Remove. Highlight the program and click on the Remove button, then click on Close.

To add new folders to the Start menu, take these steps:

1. Choose Start from the Taskbar, Settings, Taskbar. The Taskbar Properties sheet appears.
2. Select the Start menu Programs tab and click on the Advanced button.
3. Highlight the Programs folder, then choose File, New, Folder from the menu bar.
4. Give the new folder a descriptive name, such as Word Processors.

Now, click and drag the application folder, such as Winword, to the newly created Word Processors folder. Remember, the programs you see in the Winword folder are shortcuts, not the actual programs. These shortcuts are small files that point to the real location of the original application. Close the Explorer window and click on OK in the Taskbar Properties sheet.

You can rename a program group through the Explorer or through the Taskbar Properties sheet. From the Explorer or Taskbar Properties sheet, navigate to the appropriate folder (begin looking in the Windows\Start menu\Programs hierarchy). Right-click on the desired folder, choose Rename from the context menu, and enter a new name.

Tuning Windows Configuration **367**

There are a few things you can't change about the Start menu and its program groups. First, the Start menu items themselves are unchangeable. There will always be the Programs, Documents, Settings, Find, Help, Run, and Shut Down options. Of course, as you just learned, you can add a number of programs—even new folders—above these defaults. Also, program groups and names within those groups are always displayed in alphabetical order.

Assigning Sounds to Windows Events

Windows lets you assign sounds to common events such as when you launch a program or exit from Windows. In fact, you can enable or disable sounds at your discretion so that, for example, the computer only makes a sound when an error occurs. All sounds are controlled from the Sounds Properties sheet. To assign sounds to events, open the Control Panel and double-click on the Sounds applet. This displays the Sounds Properties sheet, as shown in figure 14.17.

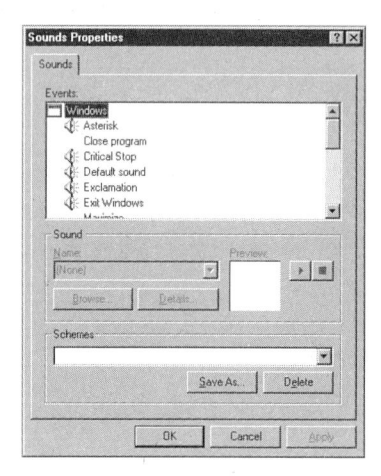

Fig. 14.17 Changing sound associations is done in the Sounds Properties sheet.

To change a sound event, all you need to do is highlight it in the list and choose a sound from the Name list. The Name list details all the sound files located in the Windows\Media folder.

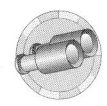

> **Note:** If no sound card is present, Windows sounds a beep through the internal speaker.

The Sounds Properties sheet lists all applicable sound events on your system. Some events are applicable to Windows as a whole, and others are applicable to specific programs. Table 14.5 lists the sound events applicable to Windows as a whole, as well as what causes the events.

Table 14.5   Sound Events in Windows 95

Sound Event	How It Is Produced
Asterisk	Occurs when an informational message box appears
Close program	Occurs when an application is closed
Critical Stop	Occurs when a message box appears with a stop sign in it
Default sound	The default beep for system events
Exclamation	Occurs when a message box appears with an exclamation point in it
Exit from Windows	Occurs when you shut down your system
Maximize	Occurs when you maximize a window
Menu command	Occurs when you select a command from a menu
Menu popup	Occurs when a menu is displayed
Minimize	Occurs when you minimize a window
Open program	Occurs when you launch a program by double-clicking on it
Program error	Occurs when an application encounters a program error
Question	Occurs when an application needs information from the user, such as "Save changes to QUESTION.DOC?"

continues

Table 14.5 Continued

Sound Event	How It Is Produced
Restore Down	Occurs when restorint a window from its maximized state
Restore Up	Occurs when restoring a window from its minimized state
Start Windows	Occurs when Windows is first started
Empty Recycle Bin	Occurs when you empty the Recycle Bin

In addition to assigning sound events, Windows includes several *sound schemes* that contain numerous preassigned sound events. With these, you can pick a scheme and all sounds change accordingly. You can save various sound settings into your own sound scheme, too, by making the sound changes, clicking on Save As, and providing a name for the scheme.

Defining File Associations

Although the term seems unfriendly, *file association* is what helps make Windows user-friendly. Here's how it works. Most files on your system have some sort of extension that serves to classify the file. For example, files that have an extension such as EXE or BAT are considered in the category of executable files, and they are run automatically when you double-click on them in the Explorer. Typically, when you install an application, it automatically updates the Registry with pertinent file associations. For example, Windows associates the extension BMP with the Paint program, the extension TXT with Notepad, as well as the extension WAV with Sound Recorder. A double-click on any of these files automatically loads the associated program. A file extension such as XLS, which is an Excel file, is not native to Windows. However, when you install Excel, you update the Registry with certain file associations. From that moment on, if you double-click on a file with the extension XLS, Excel loads and displays the document.

To associate a file with a particular application, use the Explorer. Highlight the file, select Open With from the File menu, and choose the program with which you want to associate the file. Click on OK when you are finished.

You cannot have the same file extension associated with more than a single program. However, if you later want to change the association between file types, you can do so easily. Start at any browser or Explorer window and follow these steps:

1. Choose Options from the View menu. The Options dialog box appears.
2. Click on the File Types tab.
3. In the Registered file types list, highlight the type of file whose association you wish to change.
4. Click on the Edit button. The Edit File Type dialog box appears, as shown in figure 14.18.

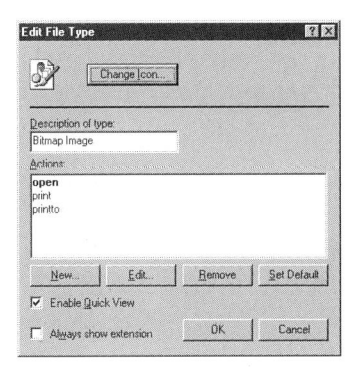

Fig. 14.18 The Edit File Type dialog box allows you to modify actions that can occur to a particular type of file.

5. In the middle of the dialog box is an Actions list. This list describes the actions that can be done with this file. Highlight the open action.
6. Click on the Edit button. A dialog box appears that allows you to change the application, which will be used to open the file type.

Tuning Windows Configuration **371**

7. In the Application used to perform action field, specify the name of the program (along with its path) you want to use to open this type of file.

8. Click on OK.

9. Click on Close.

10. Click on Close again.

Changing the Name of the StartUp Folder

As you learned previously, you can automatically launch programs when you start Windows by placing application shortcuts in the StartUp folder. You can change this default startup folder by directly editing the Registry; Windows 95 does not provide a way to change it in a "user friendly" manner such as through the Control Panel.

The value controlling this part of your system is located in the Registry as follows:

```
Registry value: Start menu
Key location:
MyComputer\HKEY_USERS\Default\Software\Microsoft\Windows\
CurrentVersion\Explorer\ShellFolders
```

Most users have little reason to change the default Windows StartUp folder. Adding a program to the StartUp folder is a simple process as described earlier in this chapter, so this is not a recommended option.

Taking Control of Windows 95 Startup

by Allen L. Wyatt

Many people probably start Windows without even thinking about what is going on behind the scenes. In reality, there is quite a bit going on to get the operating system prepared to enable you to do your daily work.

If you're familiar with the DOS-based system, which may be rendered obsolete by Windows 95, you know that configuring your system can be a time-consuming process. When you configured your DOS system, it seemed you were subject to endless tweaking to get things "just right." Only the masochists at heart truly enjoyed going through this process. Windows 95 has eliminated much of the tweaking that used to be necessary. There is still tweaking that can be done, however, and much of that is covered in this chapter. Here you learn the following:

- How to control the startup process
- How to control the various system menus
- How to run programs when you start Windows 95

➤ How to make the most out of system resources

As stated earlier, DOS may be obsolete after Windows 95 is released. Although this is true to an extent, DOS still lurks in the background and under the new, fancy covers provided by Windows 95. Nowhere is this more apparent than during the startup process. As you read through this chapter, you'll find many references reminiscent of the days when DOS ruled the roost. Although these remnants hang on, belying the claim that DOS is dead, they are included primarily for compatibility with the DOS hand-me-down programs that still exist on many computer systems.

Controlling the Startup Process

In the "old days" of computers, systems went through a booting process. Windows 95 documentation no longer refers to booting, but to *startup* (as opposed to shutdown). It seems that the folks at Microsoft limit booting to what is done before their software takes over, which means that booting is limited to what the BIOS does. After control is passed to the operating system loaders and various components, then the startup has begun in earnest.

Many aspects of Windows 95 startup could be discussed, although many of the aspects would only have meaning to a systems programmer. There are facets, however, that are important for you, the user, to understand. In the following sections you learn what goes on in the startup and how you can exercise some degree of control over it.

Understanding the Startup

From a user's perspective, the startup process used by Windows 95 is remarkably similar to that used by previous versions of Windows. Whenever you boot your system, the following steps are followed.

1. If the system is a Plug-and-Play compatible system, then the BIOS performs its analysis of the various cards in the system, making

resource allocations as necessary. (See Chapter 2, "Under-the-Hood Improvements," for more information on Plug-and-Play systems.)

2. The system BIOS performs its power-on self test (POST). The POST is a preliminary check of the hardware, to make sure that the base system elements (keyboard, video adapter, and so forth) are responding properly.

3. The CONFIG.SYS file, if any, is processed. This file is provided for compatibility with older real-mode drivers that may not be supported directly by Windows 95.

4. The AUTOEXEC.BAT file, if any, is processed. Again, this file is provided for backward-compatibility purposes.

5. Protected-mode 32-bit drivers needed by Windows 95 are loaded, even though the system has not been switched to protected mode.

6. The CPU is switched to protected mode, in preparation for the final phases of booting.

7. Plug-and-Play device conflicts are resolved, using information gathered by the BIOS, if it is available.

8. Main protected-mode subsystems, such as the kernel, graphics interface, user interface, fonts, and so forth, are loaded.

9. You are prompted to log in, if network support has been installed.

10. The StartUp folder (described later in this chapter) is processed.

Considering the amount of work required during the startup, most Windows 95 computers are able to breeze through it fairly quickly. After all ten steps are completed, you're able to do your normal work with Windows 95.

Modifying the Startup

Normally when you start your computer, Windows 95 starts running right away, and the first opportunity you have to interact with Windows is when you are asked to log in (if you're connected to a network).

You can "grab control" of the booting process, however. This can be helpful for troubleshooting purposes, or if you want to load DOS without using Windows.

To grab control of the booting process, first reboot your machine. After the POST is completed (the hardware check), and before the first Windows screen appears, press the F8 key. You'll see the Startup menu, shown in figure 15.1.

```
Microsoft Windows 95 Startup Menu
=====================================

    1. Normal
    2. Logged (\BOOTLOG.TXT)
    3. Safe mode
    4. Safe mode with network support
    5. Step-by-step confirmation
    6. Command prompt only
    7. Safe mode command prompt only
    8. Previous version of MS-DOS

Enter a choice: 1

F5=Safe mode   Shift+F5=Command prompt
Shift+F8=Step-by-step confirmation [N]
```

Fig. 15.1 The Startup menu for Windows 95.

The actual contents of the Startup menu will vary, depending on how certain startup options have been set and what is installed in your system. For instance, if you don't have network support in your system, then option 4 is not available, and all subsequent options are moved up one position in the menu.

Notice that this menu provides several different options. If you want a normal Windows 95 startup, you should choose option 1. Options 2 through 5 and 7 are used for troubleshooting the startup. Options 6 and 8 accomplish essentially the same tasks, but do it quite differently. In each case, you'll see the DOS command prompt after booting is complete. The difference is that option 5 uses the MS-DOS files provided with Windows 95. Thus, much of the Windows 95 code is running in the background. Option 8 bypasses Windows 95 entirely and boots the version of DOS you had installed on your system when you first installed Windows 95.

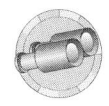

> **Note:** Your ability to begin DOS assumes that it was installed on your machine before you installed Windows 95. If it was not, you will not be able to run DOS unless it is within an MS-DOS window.

Startup Option Keys

In the previous section you learned that you can press F8 to display the Startup menu. The F8 key is only one of several startup option keys available in Windows 95. The following are the startup keys you can use after the POST is completed:

Key	Function
F4	Loads the previous version of DOS. Same as selecting the "Previous version of MS-DOS" option from the Startup menu.
F5	Starts Windows 95 in Safe mode. Same as selecting the "Safe mode" option from the Startup menu.
Shift+F5	Starts Windows 95 at the command prompt. Same as selecting the "Safe mode command prompt only" option from the Startup menu.
F6	Starts Windows 95 in Safe mode with network support. Same as selecting the "Safe mode with network support" option from the Startup menu.
F8	Displays the Startup menu.

In addition to these option keys, if you hold down the Shift key and press any function key (except F5), Windows 95 starts in Safe mode. This is the same effect as pressing the F5 key during startup.

Controlling the Startup Process **377**

Changing Startup Options

Internally, Windows 95 maintains options that modify how the startup process occurs. You can modify these options to affect the startup. These options are stored in a file called MSDOS.SYS, located in the root directory of the boot drive (typically C). The following is what the contents of this file may look like on your system:

```
[Options]
BootGUI=1

[Paths]
WinDir=C:\WINDOWS
WinBootDir=C:\WINDOWS
HostWinBootDrv=C
```

The organization of the MSDOS.SYS file is consistent with the organization structure used in most other INI files. The file is divided into sections, designated by section names in brackets. There are two possible sections in the MSDOS.SYS file. One of these is [Paths], which is used to maintain path information that Windows 95 needs to boot properly. If you change the settings in this section, it is highly possible you could stop Windows 95 from starting at all.

The other section, [Options], is used to set startup options. You can modify this section to contain any of 16 different options, as listed in Table 15.1. The options are entered as a keyword, followed by an equal sign, and then a value. Table 15.1 also lists the defaults for the options; these can be assumed to be in force unless you explicitly place a different option value in the [Options] section.

Table 15.1 MSDOS.SYS Option Keywords and Settings

Keyword	Default	Meaning
BootDelay	2	Number of seconds to delay before booting. This is the pause period after the POST but before the operating system loads. Longer delays allow the user a longer time in which to press a startup option key. This option has no meaning if BootKeys is disabled.

Keyword	Default	Meaning
BootFailSafe	1	Indicates that Fail-Safe Startup can be used. Set to 0 to disable.
BootGUI	1	Indicates that the normal Windows interface should be used. Set to 0 to start at the command prompt instead of Windows. Same as selecting the "Start only the command prompt" option from the Startup menu.
BootKeys	1	Controls whether startup option keys can be used. Set to 0 to disable.
BootMenu	0	If set to 1, then the Startup menu is displayed whenever the computer is booted. If set to 0, then the user must press F8 after the POST to see the Startup menu.
BootMenuDefault	1	The Startup menu option to use as a default.
BootMenuDelay	30	When displaying the Startup menu, indicates the number of seconds to delay before the default selection (BootMenuDefault) is automatically executed. Only has effect if BootMenu is set to 1.
BootMulti	1	Indicates whether dual booting capabilities are enabled. If set to 0, then user cannot use the F4 startup option key, and the "Start the version of MS-DOS previously installed on this computer" option on the Startup menu is not displayed.
BootWarn	1	Controls how the Fail-Safe mode is displayed by Windows. If set to 0, then Fail-Safe mode is disabled.
BootWin	1	Indicates the default operating system to use. If set to 1, Windows 95 is loaded. If set to 0, DOS is loaded. Similar to pressing the F4 startup option key or choosing the "Start the version of MS-DOS previously installed on this computer" option from the Startup menu.
DblSpace	1	Controls automatic loading of the DoubleSpace driver. If set to 0, driver is not loaded, even if needed.

continues

Table 15.1 Continued

Keyword	Default	Meaning
DoubleBuffer	0	Indicates whether a SCSI adapter in your system needs double buffering for caching. If set to 1, double buffering is enabled.
DrvSpace	1	Controls automatic loading of the DriveSpace driver. If set to 0, driver is not loaded, even if needed.
LoadTop	1	Indicates how COMMAND.COM or DRVSPACE.BIN should be loaded. If set to 1, they are loaded normally at the top of conventional memory. If set to 0, they are not. Some network operating systems may require setting this option to 0.
Logo	1	Controls display of the Windows 95 animated logo that is used when booting. If set to 0, logo is not displayed.
Network	0	Indicates whether network drivers are installed. If set to 1, then the "Start Windows, bypassing startup files, with network support" option is available on the Startup menu.

Note: MSDOS.SYS is stored as a hidden, read-only system file. If you want to change it, you need to change its read-only attribute first. Remember to change the attribute back after you have changed the file.

Controlling Menus

The Start menu is at the heart of Windows 95. Positioned at the left edge of the taskbar, the Start menu enables you to easily access programs, documents, and configuration settings for your entire system.

Windows 95 enables you to easily modify what appears on your Start menu. For instance, you could place the names of your favorite programs in the menu, or you could put them in the Programs menu, or you could put commonly accessed documents in the Documents menu. Each of the following sections explains how to accomplish these tasks.

Changing the Start Menu

You are already familiar with what the Start menu looks like. It contains commonly used programs and folders. You can modify the appearance of the Start menu any time you want. For instance, you might want to add your most-used programs (such as your spreadsheet or word processing programs) to the menu. This is easy to do if you follow these steps:

1. Right-click on the Start menu button. A context menu for the Start menu button appears.

2. From the context menu, choose the Open option. The Start Menu folder appears.

3. Create a shortcut for the program you want listed in the Start menu, placing the shortcut in the Start Menu folder window.

4. Close the Start Menu folder window.

If you now display the Start menu, you will notice that your shortcut is listed at the top of the menu. Figure 15.2 shows an example of a modified Start menu.

From these steps you might assume that the Start menu is nothing but a graphic representation of the structure of a folder on your disk drive. This is absolutely correct. Anything that appears within the Start Menu folder is shown on the Start menu; it is that simple.

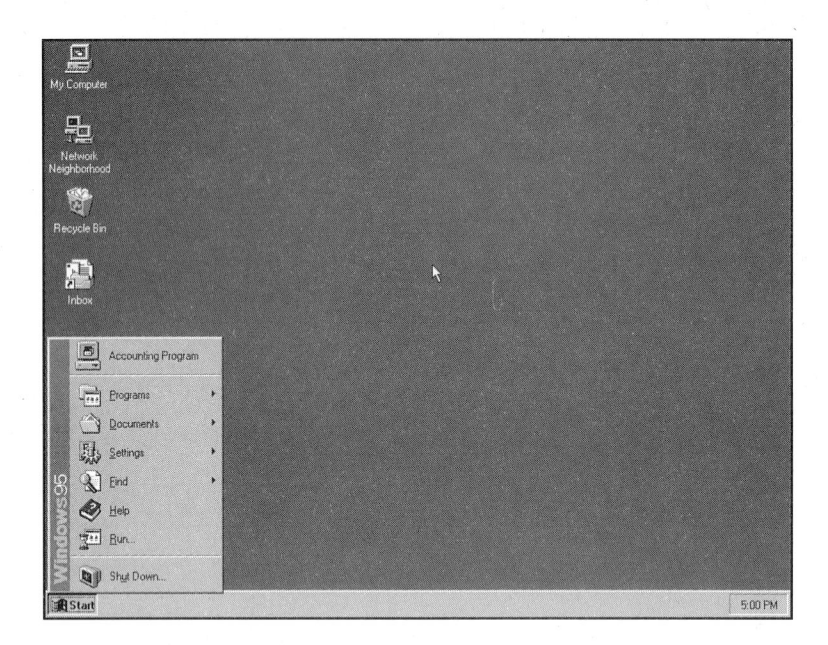

Fig. 15.2 Changing the Start menu is easy in Windows 95.

> **Note:** Even though you can install actual programs in the Start Menu folder and have them appear on the Start menu, this is not necessarily a good idea. If you do this, chances are good that your Start menu will quickly become cluttered with useless files. Instead, install the program in its own directory and place a shortcut to the program in the Start Menu folder. In this way you won't see all the ancillary files that are associated with an application; you will only see the icon for starting the application itself.

You also can add a new folder to the Start menu by following the same steps (just described), but creating a folder in the Start Menu folder instead. For instance, you might have several different but related programs you want grouped together. Placing them at the top of the Start menu would start to clutter the screen. Placing them in their own folder, however, makes more sense. Making the folder accessible from the Start menu makes sense, as well.

As an example, let's say you are working on the budget forecasts for your company. You spend a good part of each day working with them, using three different programs. You want the programs easily accessible, so you follow these steps to create a new folder in the Start menu:

1. Right-click on the Start menu button. A context menu for the Start menu button appears.

2. From the context menu, choose the Open option. The Start Menu folder appears.

3. In the Start Menu folder window, click File and then New. This displays a menu showing the types of objects you can create.

4. Choose Folder. A new folder appears in the Start Menu folder window.

5. Rename the folder to a descriptive name, such as Corporate Budget.

6. Close the Start Menu folder window.

Now the folder appears in the Start menu, as shown in figure 15.3. Whenever you select the folder from the Start menu, the contents of the folder are shown in menu form, as well. In this way, you quickly and easily can build your own menu structure for Windows 95.

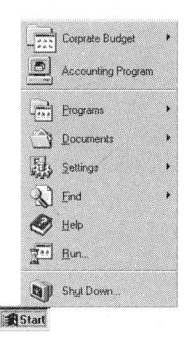

Fig. 15.3 Adding folders to the Start menu enables you to build your own menu structure.

Controlling Menus **383**

> **Tip:** If you have an existing folder or shortcut you want added to the Start menu, you can do so by using the mouse to drag the object to the Start menu button. When you drop the item on the button, it appears in the Start menu.

Changing the Programs Menu

In the previous section you learned how you can add both programs (shortcuts to programs) and folders to the Start menu. You probably noticed that the icon for the Programs menu (visible on the Start menu) is a folder, as well. This would imply that, from a purely hierarchical perspective, the Programs menu is nothing more than a folder within the Start Menu folder. This implication is correct—in fact, adding programs to the Programs menu is as easy as copying them into the Programs folder. To accomplish this, follow these steps:

1. Right-click on the Start menu button. A context menu for the Start menu button appears.

2. From the context menu, choose the Open option. The Start Menu folder appears.

3. Double-click the Programs folder. This opens a window that shows the contents of the Programs folder, as shown in figure 15.4.

Fig. 15.4 The Programs folder window shows the contents of the Programs folder.

Notice that there are already six objects in the Programs folder window. These objects are the same choices you see when you select the Programs menu from the Start menu (see fig. 15.5).

Fig. 15.5 The choices on the Programs menu are the same as the objects in the Programs folder.

You can modify the Programs menu by modifying the contents of the Programs folder. For instance, you could add your own shortcuts to programs or add additional folders. As you do, the Programs menu is automatically changed.

Changing the Documents Menu

The Documents menu is not as easily changed as the Start menu and Programs menu. In fact, many times the Documents menu seems to have a mind of its own.

In theory, the Documents menu is supposed to be the 15 most recently accessed documents—in other words, the 15 data files, spreadsheets, or word processing documents that you last accessed. The concept behind the Documents menu should be familiar to those who have been using Windows applications for some time. Many Windows applications include a list, at the bottom of the File menu, of the most recently used files. In this way, you easily and quickly can recall a file you recently worked on.

Controlling Menus   **385**

The Documents menu serves the same purpose. The 15 files it maintains are shown in alphabetical order; they are shortcuts to the documents themselves. If the menu contains 15 files, and you open a new file that is not already on the list, then the shortcut that has been on the menu the longest, without being accessed, is removed and replaced by the new file.

Exactly what mechanism is followed to determine what appears on the Documents menu is unclear. Files that you wouldn't assume to be "documents" often show up (like DLL files accessed through a file browser), while other files that could be assumed to be document files (such as the Registry accessed with the Registry Editor) don't show up.

You cannot explicitly force something onto the Documents menu without opening the document itself. Likewise, you cannot force something to stay on the Documents menu without periodically accessing it. You can, however, clear the entire Documents menu if (for some reason) you want to "start over." To clear the Documents menu, follow these steps:

1. Choose Settings from the Start menu. The Settings menu appears.
2. Choose Taskbar from the Settings menu. The contents of the Taskbar Properties sheet appear.
3. Click the Start Menu Programs tab. The sheet now appears as shown in figure 15.6.
4. Click the Clear button near the bottom of the sheet.
5. Click OK to close the sheet.

After following these steps, if you take another look at the Documents menu, you see that it is empty. It again starts to fill up as you access other documents.

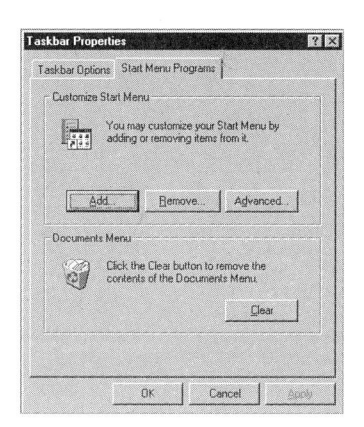

Fig. 15.6 The Clear button is used to delete all the Documents menu options.

Automatically Running Programs

If you are a long-time Windows user, you have probably already taken advantage of the StartUp program group. This powerful feature enables you to run programs whenever Windows is started. In previous versions of Windows, any program icon that was in the StartUp program group was automatically started whenever Windows was started.

Windows 95 also continues this feature. With Windows 95, you have complete control over what programs run whenever you boot your system. If you installed Windows 95 as an upgrade to an existing version of Windows, then the programs in your old StartUp group were automatically placed in the new version of the StartUp group. (It is not called a StartUp group any more; it is now called the StartUp folder.)

Since there is no real Program Manager in Windows 95, it may be a bit confusing to figure out where the StartUp folder is located. In reality, there are now two ways you can add or remove programs from your StartUp folder: either manually or through the use of a wizard.

Using a Wizard to Change the StartUp Folder

Perhaps the easiest way to add or remove things from the StartUp folder is by using a configuration wizard. To start the wizard, follow these steps:

1. Choose Settings from the Start menu. The Settings menu appears.
2. Choose Taskbar from the Settings menu. The Taskbar Properties sheet appears.

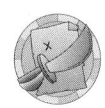

> **Tip:** A quick way to accomplish the first two steps is to right-click the taskbar and then choose Properties from the context menu.

3. Click the Start Menu Programs tab. The Taskbar Properties sheet should appear as shown earlier, in figure 15.6.
4. Click the Add button in the Customize Start Menu area. This starts the wizard, and you see the dialog box shown in figure 15.7.

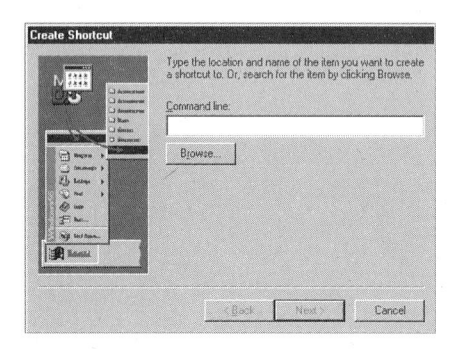

Fig. 15.7 The Create Shortcut Wizard can be used to add items to the StartUp Folder.

At this point, all you need to do is specify the program you want started when Windows starts. (You can click the Browse button, if desired, to

388 Chapter 15: Taking Control of Windows 95 Startup

help locate the program.) When you have provided the path and name of the program, click the Next button. You then see the dialog box shown in figure 15.8.

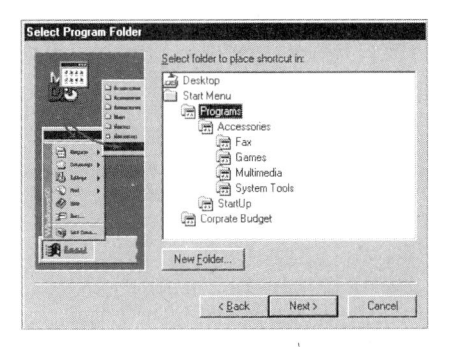

Fig. 15.8 The second step of the wizard is to specify where you want the shortcut stored.

The Select Program Folder dialog box is used to specify where the shortcut is to be placed. You should click the StartUp folder, shown at the bottom of the folder tree in the dialog box. Once you have highlighted the folder, you can click the Next button.

> **Note:** If you select a folder other than the StartUp folder, the shortcut you are creating appears in the menu constructed from the folder you select. The concepts behind this were covered earlier in this chapter in the section titled "Controlling Menus."

You now should see the dialog box shown in figure 15.9. From this dialog box you specify the name of the shortcut you are creating. This can be any name you desire; it appears in both the StartUp folder listing and under the icon for the shortcut. When you have provided a name, click the Finish button.

Automatically Running Programs **389**

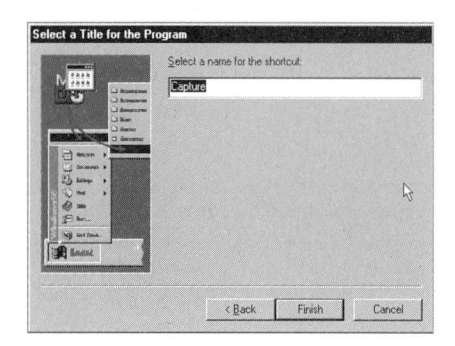

Fig. 15.9 The final step in the wizard is to specify a name for the new shortcut.

At this point, you are returned to the Taskbar Properties sheet, as shown earlier in figure 15.6. From here you can add more shortcuts to the StartUp folder, if you desire. When you are through, click OK to close the sheet. The next time you start Windows 95, the shortcuts in the StartUp folder are executed.

Manually Changing the StartUp Folder

Earlier in this chapter you learned how to change the Start menu and Programs menu by changing the contents of the proper folders. The same can be done with the StartUp folder. This manual process is closely related to how you managed the StartUp program group in older versions of Windows—you placed program items in the StartUp group.

To change the StartUp folder manually, follow these steps:

1. Right-click on the Start menu button. A context menu for the Start menu button appears.

2. From the context menu, choose the Open option. The Start Menu folder appears.

3. Double-click the Programs folder. This displays a window that shows the contents of the Programs folder.

4. Double-click the StartUp folder. This displays a window that shows the contents of the StartUp folder.

5. Create shortcuts for the programs you want run when Windows 95 starts. Place these shortcuts in the StartUp folder window.

6. Close the folder windows on your desktop.

The next time you start Windows 95, the shortcuts in the StartUp folder will be executed.

If you place a new folder in the StartUp Folder, that folder is opened and displayed when you start Windows 95. The contents of the folder are not executed; they are simply displayed. Only the following types of shortcuts are executed, and then only if they are located in the StartUp folder:

➤ Shortcuts to programs

➤ Shortcuts to documents associated with programs

➤ Actual program files

Conserving System Resources

Windows uses hard drive space as a general system resource. In addition to storing data files in hard drive space, Windows uses hard drive space as an extension of your RAM (random access memory) by means of the virtual memory management features discussed in Chapter 9, "Exploiting Memory, Space, and Resources." If you run short of hard drive space, you can delete nonessential Windows components (such as help files and dynamic-link libraries) from your system.

Caution: Many Windows applications rely on dynamic-link library (DLL) files to operate properly. Before you delete such files willy-nilly, make sure you don't need them for your applications. You could also copy them to a floppy disk and make note of the original directories in which they belong. In this way you could later restore them if a problem arises.

Windows includes many different components, some of which you can remove from your system without disabling Windows. By deleting different components as you don't need them any more, you can free quite a bit of hard drive space. Windows 95 includes an easy way you can delete components from your system. To do so, follow these steps:

1. Choose Settings from the Start menu. The Settings menu appears.

2. Choose Control Panel from the Settings menu. The Control Panel window appears.

3. Double-click the Add/Remove Programs icon in the Control Panel. The Add/Remove Programs Properties sheet appears.

4. Click the Windows Setup tab. The sheet now appears as shown in figure 15.10.

In this sheet you can see the different Windows 95 components, as well as which ones are installed on your system. (Those that have a check mark in the box to the left of the component are installed.) To the right of the component is an indication of how much hard drive space is used by the component.

To delete a component from your system, simply clear the check box to the left of the component. When you are through, click the OK button, and Windows may ask you to confirm your action (depending on what you are removing). Once confirmed, the components are removed and you are returned to the desktop.

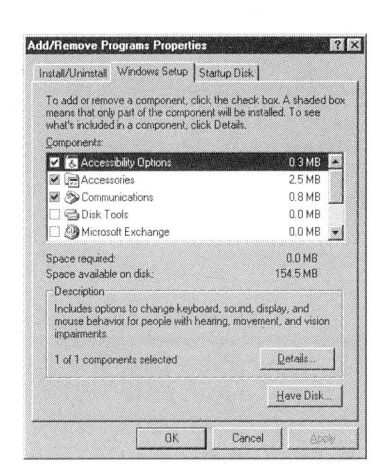

Fig. 15.10 Windows 95 enables you to easily add or delete different system components.

To later reinstall a component, repeat the steps previously listed. Instead of clearing a check box, however, you should select the check box. When you click the OK button, Windows prompts you for the Windows 95 program disks or CD-ROM. (This is necessary because you physically deleted the components from your disk drive.) When you have complied with the disk request, Windows copies the files to your hard drive.

Installing Windows Applications

by Allen L. Wyatt

Installing Windows applications is easier than ever with Windows 95. The operating system includes a new software installation wizard that can make adding software (or removing it later) as easy as clicking on a button. The following topics are covered in this chapter:

- ➤ How to install Windows applications by using the Add/Remove Software Wizard
- ➤ How to install Windows applications manually
- ➤ Differences between 16-bit and 32-bit Windows applications
- ➤ How to overcome compatibility issues for older 16-bit programs

In addition, you'll find tips explaining how to troubleshoot any glitches that may crop up as you install your applications.

Installing with a Wizard

Windows 95 includes a software installation wizard you can use to add software to your system. This wizard, located in the Control Panel, is the preferred method of adding software to Windows 95. As the wizard installs the software, it updates the Registry with the information related to the program. This step ensures that the system resources required by the software will be available.

If the application you're installing was created for Windows 95 (it has the Windows 95 logo on the software package), it will also update the Registry with additional information. For instance, the Registry will contain information about the following:

- Which components can be added to the software. For instance, you might have installed only a portion of the software package, and the Registry will contain information about what else is possible to install.

- Which parameters are needed by the application in order for it to run properly.

- Which files can be deleted from Windows 95 if the application is removed from the system.

Running the Installation Wizard

To run the software installation wizard, follow these steps:

1. Choose Settings from the Start menu. The Settings menu appears.

2. Choose Control Panel from the Settings menu. The Control Panel appears.

3. Double-click on the Add/Remove Programs icon. You'll see the Add/Remove Programs Properties sheet appear, as shown in figure 16.1.

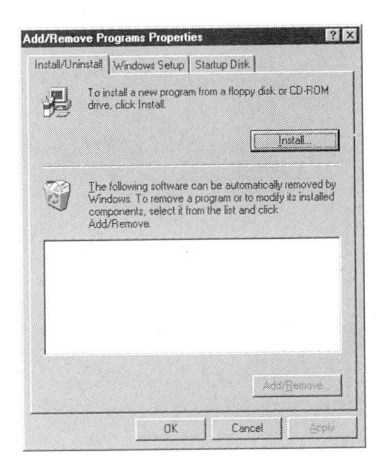

Fig. 16.1 The Add/Remove Programs Properties sheet is used to add or remove software from Windows 95.

4. Click on the Install button. This starts the wizard and displays the first screen, as shown in figure 16.2.

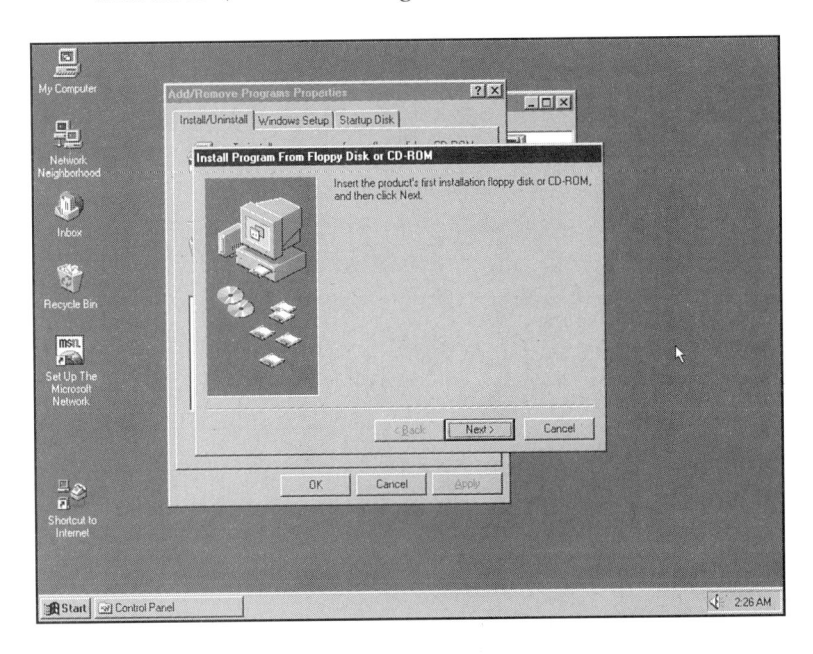

Fig. 16.2 Windows 95 includes a wizard that is used to install software from a floppy disk or CD-ROM.

Installing with a Wizard **397**

Make sure that either the installation floppy disk for the software or the CD-ROM containing the installation files is inserted in a disk drive. When you're ready to proceed, click on the Next button. The wizard proceeds to look through your disk drives (and CD-ROM drives) to find a setup disk. It looks for program names, such as SETUP.EXE or INSTALL.EXE. When it finds a disk or CD-ROM that contains what it believes to be setup files, a new dialog box appears, which shows what was found.

The command line field in the middle of the sheet should reflect the command line necessary to install the software. You may want to check the command line against the command line indicated in the documentation for the software. If you need to, you can click on the Browse button to locate a different program to use in the installation routines.

When you're finished with the command line, click on the Finish button. This step ends the wizard and starts the setup program for your software. The steps you follow from this point depend on the software you're installing. Different applications have different setup programs that require different user input.

> **Tip:** If you're having trouble installing your software, refer to the manual that came with it. If that doesn't help, you may need to contact the vendor's technical support department.

Installation Wizard Problems

You probably will not encounter problems with the Add/Remove Programs wizard. If you have problems, but they occur after you click on the Finish button of the wizard, then the problem may lie with your program's ability to work with Windows 95. Later in this chapter, you'll learn what you can do in some of these instances.

The best solution if you have a problem is to contact the software vendor to see if the company has any other reported problems in using their software with Windows 95. If they do, you can request a new version of the program or the steps to follow to install the software manually.

Installing Manually

Microsoft does not suggest that you install your software manually. By *manually* is meant two common ways of installing software:

➤ Directly running the installation program supplied with the software

➤ Copying the program files to a folder and running the program

In previous versions of Windows, there was very little problem in doing either of these actions. The problem under Windows 95 is related to the new Registry. If you are installing older 16-bit Windows applications, there is little chance that they are designed to recognize or take advantage of the Registry. Without using the Add/Remove Programs wizard, the Registry will not have a chance to be updated properly. This could lead to problems down the road when you want to remove the software or if you install other software that requires the application to be present.

There are a few cases when you can add software manually. You should be safe in directly running the installation program provided with your software if the program was created to be Windows 95 compatible. If it was, there is a good chance that it will update the Registry automatically during installation.

The other exception is if you have a very small program that doesn't require any special installation program. For instance, you may download a small utility program from a BBS system. This utility is designed to be run "as is." It doesn't have an installation program, and it doesn't really modify any INI files or the Registry. If this is the case, feel free to copy the file to a folder on your hard disk. You should remember the following when installing in this manner:

➤ If you install the program to a folder within the Start Menu folder (\Windows\Start Menu), then the program or folder will appear on the Start menu itself.

➤ If you install the program to a folder within the Programs folder (\Windows\Start Menu\Programs), then the program or folder will appear within the Programs option of the Start menu.

If you have problems with the application after you install it manually, remove it from your system and contact the program vendor. They may have an update or a setup disk available that will work properly with Windows 95.

32-Bit versus 16-Bit Windows Programs

There are two types of Windows applications you can install. The first type, sometimes called "legacy applications," are programs designed for older versions of Windows. These applications have been designed to work with 16-bit API (application program interface) functions. These programs will work just fine under Windows 95, but they're inherently less stable than their 32-bit counterparts.

The second type is a 32-bit application. These applications are called 32-bit because they use the Win32 API functions and are designed to run under a 32-bit operating system. These applications will work under both Windows NT and Windows 95, because both systems use the Win32 API.

> **Caution:** Windows NT applications, which take advantage of NT-specific API functions, will not work under Windows 95. These functions include security- and NTFS-related functions.

All things being equal, 16-bit applications will run as well (if not better) under Windows 95 as they would under Windows 3.1x. They run well because, as you learned in Chapter 2, "Under-the-Hood Improvements," significant parts of the operating system have been rewritten. The improved management algorithms and the 32-bit architecture ensures that while the operating system is running, it is running as efficiently as possible.

Windows 95 provides the same operating system resources to both 32-bit and 16-bit applications. However, 16-bit applications cannot use preemptive multitasking. They also use a shared memory pool and a common message queue, and their processes are scheduled cooperatively. 32-bit applications are designed to take full advantage of all of the Windows 95 performance enhancement features. These applications offer the following advantages when compared to 16-bit legacy applications:

- Preemptive multitasking
- Threaded operation
- Separate message queues
- Flat address space
- Memory protection
- Long file name support

Preemptive Multitasking

Under previous versions of Windows, control was passed from one application to another cooperatively. This meant that when one application gained control of the system, no other application could gain control until the running application became "cooperative" and relinquished control. At best, this situation led to sluggish performance in some applications.

Under Windows 95, preemptive multitasking is supported. This means that Windows 95 schedules the time allotted for running applications in the system. When the time allotted to an application is done, the operating system "preempts" the running application and passes control on to the next scheduled task. This results in smoother concurrent processing and prevents any one application from using all system resources without permitting other tasks to run.

One of the reasons that 32-bit applications can run faster than 16-bit operations is that they don't need to have any scheduling routines built in to the application. For instance, 16-bit applications needed timers and the like to determine when it was appropriate to pass control back to the operating system. No such gymnastics are required of 32-bit applications because they rely on the operating system to take care of scheduling.

Threaded Operation

This feature is available to 32-bit applications, but not all of them may take advantage of it. Threaded operation means that different parts of the application can execute at the same time, resulting in better performance and use of resources. This feature is closely akin to multitasking.

Whereas multitasking generally means that multiple applications can be executing at the same time, threaded operation means that a single application creates multiple tasks, which are then simultaneously executed. It is a fine point, to be sure, but one that is not available to 16-bit applications.

Separate Message Queues

You've already learned that Windows 95 uses preemptive multitasking for managing the affairs of applications running on the system. One feature implemented as part of this is that each 32-bit application on the system has its own "messaging queue." This queue is used to pass information between the application and the operating system or between the application and other tasks running on the system.

16-bit applications are written to take advantage of the old way that Windows used messaging queues. In previous versions of Windows, a single messaging queue was used for all applications running in the system. This worked fine, as long as the running application allowed other applications to check the queue. If this was not allowed (such as when the running application was ill-behaved or when it locked up), then the other applications locked up as well because they could not check the queue.

The result of independent message queues is that the operating environment is more stable than was previously possible. Each 32-bit application can check its own queue whenever deemed appropriate by the application, and is not affected by how other applications may check the queue.

Flat Address Space

Windows 95 looks at and manages memory differently than in earlier versions of the operating system. Instead of dealing with segmented memory, the operating system treats all of memory as a flat address space, meaning that larger memory operations can occur in a faster time frame.

32-bit applications are written to take advantage of APIs that use the flat memory space paradigm. The older 16-bit applications are written to an older API standard that relies on segmented memory access. The result is that 16-bit applications require additional code overhead and run slower than 32-bit applications.

Memory Protection

In previous versions of Windows, memory was allocated from a giant pool that could be used by all applications. The result, while very dynamic in nature, was not always very stable. People who have used Windows quite a bit are no doubt well acquainted with the dreaded GPF (general protection fault), which meant that some program mucked about in some other program's memory area. More often than not, the program being mucked with was Windows itself. The result was not only that the application that generated the error was shut down, but also that the resources used by the program were not always released back to the pool. This meant that the best way to handle a GPF was to exit from Windows and restart—a tiresome procedure, at best.

Under the 32-bit environment created by Windows 95, there are two categories of memory:

- 32-bit application protected memory
- 16-bit application pooled memory

32-bit programs—those designed to use Windows 95—pull their memory from the first category. Older 16-bit programs are lumped together in the second category.

The memory area used by 32-bit applications is sequestered from memory used by other applications. This means that the application cannot be interfered with by other applications, nor can it interfere with other applications (or the operating system itself). The result is a more stable program.

16-bit programs all share the same pooled memory space, as in previous versions of Windows. Thus, it is still possible to get a GPF if you are using an old application. The benefit under Windows 95, however, is that if the program crashes, it affects only the other 16-bit programs running at the time. The 32-bit applications and the operating system itself remain unaffected.

Long File Name Support

You learned in Chapter 2, "Under-the-Hood Improvements," how Windows 95 implements long file names. Applications written to the legacy 16-bit guidelines don't take advantage of long file names. On the other hand, 32-bit applications designed for Windows 95 can freely take advantage of long file names.

Note: 32-bit applications written for Windows NT do not necessarily recognize the long file names supported by Windows 95. The long file name algorithms used under Windows NT (for NTFS partitions) are different than the algorithms used to support long file names in a FAT partition (as is done in Windows 95).

16-Bit Application Problems

Some 16-bit applications may not run well under Windows 95 because they were designed with older operating systems in mind. For instance, a 16-bit application may take advantage of known quirks in previous versions of Windows, or it may count on the user interface appearing a certain way. The following sections address potential problem areas and how you can solve them.

Note: The best way to solve 16-bit application problems is to get an upgrade to your old program. You should use the workarounds described here only if you cannot get an upgrade.

User Interface Problems

Some 16-bit software is written to take great advantage of the older Windows user interface. For example, an application could use the title bar to add a special icon to a window, or it could place its own toolbar at the bottom of the desktop.

The problem with this is that Windows 95 has significantly changed the user interface. Now title bars are formatted differently, and the taskbar appears at the bottom of the desktop. These changes can cause information to appear "funny" when displayed under Windows 95. Information may be overwritten, or it may appear behind desktop objects.

These problems should not cause critical errors; you should still be able to use your software, although you may not be able to use the features not supported by the Windows 95 user interface. The only way to really cure this problem is to upgrade your software to a Windows 95 version.

Undocumented Features

A couple of years ago there were some books on the market that touted the discovery of "undocumented" features and functions (from a programmer's perspective) in Windows. Although these books caused quite a stir for a while, some programmers began to rely on the newly uncovered functions. Microsoft suggested they not do it, but some programmers persisted.

With the introduction of Windows 95, the old Windows is done away with; this is to be expected with the complete redesign of the operating system core. While Microsoft supports most of the long-established programming functions, it does not support all of the undocumented functions. Thus, if you have a 16-bit program that uses any of these undocumented functions, it will not work under Windows 95. The results of trying to run them will depend on the function calls being used. In some cases, certain program features may not work correctly or may not be available. In other cases the program could crash entirely, refusing to continue.

There is absolutely no way around this sort of problem short of getting a new version. Until you get a new version of your program, you should not run the old version because the results are so hard to predict.

Version Number Errors

Older applications can have two types of problems in regard to version numbers. Some applications may incorrectly check for the version number, and others may refuse to work if the Windows version number is not 3.1x.

If the application checks the version number incorrectly, it is usually because it "mixes up" the version information. For instance, the program may check the version number and see it as 10.3 instead of 3.10. Because most programs check for a minimum version number to ensure compatibility, Windows 95 always reports its version number as 3.95. In this way, if your application compares 3.95 to 3.10 (its base version requirement), it should conclude that it is OK to proceed. Even if the software reverses the version numbers, it is still comparing 95.3 to 10.3, and should still conclude that it is safe to continue.

Some applications check for the version number and refuse to proceed if the reported number is not exactly the same as what it expects. Thus, a program may falter if it does not believe it is running under Windows 3.1x. Windows 95 provides a way you can fool the older application into thinking it is running under Windows 3.1x. Believe it or not, this fix uses the WIN.INI file. (And you thought WIN.INI was a thing of the past.) All you need to do is edit the [Compatibility] section of the file by using a regular text editor, such as the Notepad accessory. The following is a portion of the contents of the [Compatibility] section on a newly installed version of Windows 95:

```
[Compatibility]
_3DPC=0x00400000
_BNOTES=0x224000
_LNOTES=0x00100000
ACAD=0x8000
ACT!=0x400004
ACROBAT=0x04000000
AD=0x10000000
ADW30=0x10000000
ALARMMGR=0x0040000
ALDSETUP=0x00400000
WPWIN60=0x00000400
WPWIN61=0x02000400
WSETUP=0x00200000
XPRESS=0x00000008
ZETA01=0x00400000
ZIFFBOOK=0x00200000
```

The left side of each entry in the [Compatibility] section contains information derived from the header of the executable program file; it is referred to as the compiled module name of the program. Most of the time you can find the compiled module name of an executable file by using the DOS TYPE command to view the contents of the file (the name will be in the first couple of lines of what you see on-screen).

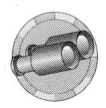

> **Note:** If you cannot determine the compiled module name of the program by using the TYPE command, you should call the vendor and talk through the fix with them. They should be able to provide you with the name you need.

Create a new entry in this section for the application with which you're having version number problems. On the left side of the equal sign, place the compiled module name; on the right place the value 0x00200000. For example, if the compiled version name of the program was MYPROG, then the entry would look like this:

```
MYPROG=0x00200000
```

Save the file and restart Windows 95. This should fix the compatibility problem. If it does not, you'll need to contact the vendor agents to see if they have a fix for their program.

Fine-Tuning Windows 95 for Your Windows Applications

by Allen L. Wyatt

The operating environment provided by Windows 95 is more stable and robust than ever before. People who have been using Windows for a while immediately recognize the performance and stability improvements when they start using Windows 95. For most Windows programs, there is little you'll need to do to make your software "run better." In this chapter, you'll learn about the few improvements you can make, including the following:

- Changes you can make to your operating environment
- How you can set working folders in Windows 95
- What performance improvements can be made to 16-bit programs
- How the improved resource management in Windows 95 affects your programs

Changing Your Environment

If you've ever installed MS-DOS software under Windows 95, you know that there is quite a bit you can do to affect the operating environment of the software. (See Chapter 19, "Fine-Tuning Windows 95 for Your DOS Applications.") This is because, as you learned in Chapter 13, "How Windows 95 Interacts with Software," Windows 95 creates a Virtual Machine for each DOS program you run. When you change the environmental properties, you're modifying how that VM is created.

On the other hand, Windows programs (16-bit or 32-bit) operate within a single VM. There is little you can do to affect the environment created by Windows 95 for these applications. Instead, you can only adjust parameters that affect all Windows programs (these will be covered shortly).

Windows 95 does not allow you to individually change the operational environment of a Windows program. If you right-click on the program icon for a Windows program, and choose the Properties option from the context menu, you can modify the attributes of the file (read-only, hidden, and so on), but there are no environment-related properties to change as there are with DOS programs.

Improving Video Performance

To improve the performance of your video system, you may want to refer to Chapter 11, "Video Cards, Drivers, and Monitors." Windows 95 does a good job of optimizing the performance of your video system, within certain constraints. It allows you to pick operational parameters for your video card that can affect the overall performance of your system.

If you notice that your system is giving sluggish performance, and you suspect that your video system is the culprit, follow these steps:

1. Choose <u>S</u>ettings from the Start menu.
2. Choose <u>C</u>ontrol Panel from the Settings menu.
3. Double-click on the Display icon. The Display Properties sheet appears.
4. Click on the Settings tab.
5. In the <u>C</u>olor palette pull-down list, choose the 16 Color setting.
6. Move the <u>D</u>esktop area slider bar all the way to the left, so it is set to 640 by 480 pixels.
7. Click on OK.
8. Restart your computer, if necessary. (A dialog box may appear informing you that this is necessary.)

With these settings, your video system will operate as fast as possible (for the hardware). This is because the video settings have been placed at their least-demanding state. If this improves the speed of your software, then you're home free. Some software, however, doesn't work well at these low-level settings. For instance, some multimedia software is designed to work with at least 256 colors displayed on-screen. In such a case, you can try stepping up the number of colors used by your video card, but that may slow down your system a bit. If the speed reduction is not acceptable, the only solution you have is to upgrade your video card to a newer, faster model.

If the performance of your system does not improve, even with your video settings set as low as possible, then perhaps any perceived slowdown in your system is not due to the video system. You may want to reset the video settings back to their original values and see whether adjusting other performance factors affects your system more favorably.

Improving Disk Performance

Windows 95 works with a wide variety of disk drives, but not all disk drives have the same capabilities. As you learned in Chapter 10, "Optimizing Your Disk Drives," there is much more to the performance of a disk system than just the capacity of the hard drive.

If you're using software that uses the hard disk quite a bit, you can use the following tips to maximize the performance of your hard drives:

- Defragment your disk drives
- Adjust your disk cache size
- Disable DriveSpace or other disk compression

Detailed information on each of these steps is included in Chapter 10, but the quick information in the following sections may help you accomplish your goals in this area.

Defragmenting Your Drives

If your software uses the disk drives heavily, your drives may become fragmented quickly. You may even want to defragment your drives as often as once every other week. The defrag utility, included with Windows 95, is an excellent choice for performing this task. To start this utility, follow these steps:

1. Choose Programs from the Start menu.
2. Choose Accessories from the Programs menu.
3. Choose System Tools from the Accessories menu.
4. Choose Disk Defragmenter from the System Tools menu.
5. Select the disk drive you want to defragment, then click on OK.

Changing Your Disk Cache Size

The disk cache used by Windows 95 is geared toward normal disk-usage requirements. If you use software that relies heavily on the disk drive, you may want to adjust the cache size by following these steps:

1. Right-click on the My Computer icon on your desktop.
2. Choose Properties from the context menu.
3. Click on the Performance tab.
4. Click on the File System button at the bottom of the page.
5. In the pull-down list beside the Typical role of this machine field, select the setting Network server.
6. Make sure the slider for Read-ahead optimization is slid all the way to the right (toward Full).
7. Click on the OK button.
8. Click on the Close button.
9. Restart your computer, if necessary. (A dialog box may appear, informing you that this is necessary.)

Disabling Disk Compression

Any disk compression software, including the DriveSpace feature of Windows 95, adds overhead to your operating system. This overhead can introduce a slight performance penalty in accessing your drives. For your operating system to operate as quickly as possible in relation to your drive, you may want to remove the compression. To do this, follow these steps:

1. Choose Programs from the Start menu.
2. Choose Accessories from the Programs menu.
3. Choose System Tools from the Accessories menu.
4. Choose DriveSpace from the System Tools menu.
5. In the drive list, choose the disk drive you want to uncompress.
6. Choose Uncompress from the Drive menu.

This starts the uncompression portion of DriveSpace. You should follow the instructions as they appear on your screen as this process continues.

If you're using a different disk compression utility, you should refer to the instructions for your software to learn how to disable disk compression.

Improving CD-ROM Performance

More and more software is relying on the storage capacity and convenience of CD-ROM drives. If you use software that frequently accesses the CD-ROM drive, you can benefit by checking the performance settings of your CD-ROM. Do this by following these steps:

1. Right-click on the My Computer icon on your desktop.
2. Choose Properties from the context menu.
3. Click on the Performance tab.
4. Click on the File System button at the bottom of the page.
5. Click on the CD-ROM tab. The File System Properties sheet appears as shown in figure 17.1.

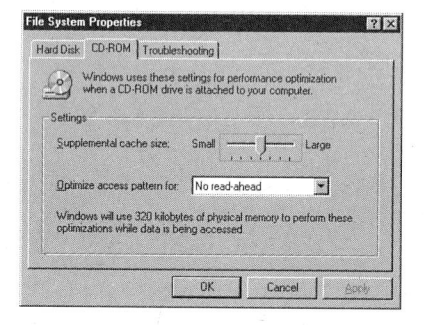

Fig. 17.1 The File System Properties sheet, with the CD-ROM tab selected, allows you to modify how Windows 95 uses the CD-ROM drive.

6. In the pull-down list beside the Optimize access pattern for field, select the setting that best matches the rated speed of your CD-ROM drive—single speed, double speed, and so on.

7. Move the slider for §upplemental cache size toward the right (toward Large).

8. Click on the OK button.

9. Click on the Close button.

10. Restart your computer, if necessary. (A dialog box may appear informing you that this is necessary.)

In general, the access pattern for your CD-ROM should be set to match the speed rating of your drive. If you use the CD-ROM a lot, then you should also increase the supplemental cache size until the performance of your system more closely matches your expectations.

Working Directories

If you're familiar with previous versions of Windows, you may remember that you were able to specify working folders for program items (these would be called working folders in Windows 95). This means that you could indicate the initial folder for a program to use when it first started. Unlike Windows 3.x, Windows 95 does not allow you to specify working folders for programs.

The stated reason for not permitting you to assign a working folder to a program is that there are links which Windows 95 sets up to the program, and these links expect very few changes to the program properties (which is where a working folder would be maintained). There is a way around this shortcoming, however—through the use of shortcuts.

In Chapter 2, "Under-the-Hood Improvements," you learned about shortcuts and how they're created in Windows 95. You can set working folders for shortcuts, even though you cannot for programs. While at first this may seem awkward, it is really more flexible. This means you can create shortcuts for different uses of the same program, and each shortcut can start the program by using a different working folder. For instance, you could have three shortcuts for your spreadsheet program:

- The first shortcut is labeled "Budget Figures" and uses the C:\BUDGET folder.

- The second shortcut is labeled "Tax Information" and uses the D:\FINANCE\TAXES folder.

- The third shortcut is labeled "Family Finances" and uses the C:\PERSONAL\FINANCES folder.

To set the working folder for a shortcut, follow these directions:

1. Right-click on the shortcut icon (the icon with a small arrow in the bottom left corner) you want to change.

2. Choose Properties from the context menu.

3. Click on the Shortcut tab. You'll see the Shortcut Properties sheet, similar to figure 17.2.

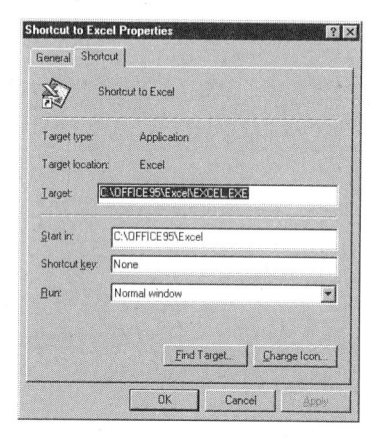

Fig. 17.2 The Shortcut Properties sheet allows you to modify how a shortcut starts a program.

4. In the Start in dialog box, indicate the working folder you want used when the program is started.

5. Click on the OK button.

The next time you use the shortcut to start the program, the folder you specified is used as the working folder.

16-Bit Program Performance

The best way to improve the performance of your 16-bit programs is to replace them with 32-bit versions, particularly if the 32-bit versions are optimized for Windows 95. If you do this, you'll be able to realize all the performance benefits covered in Chapter 16, "Installing Windows Applications." In addition, you'll be able to more easily remove the application if you ever need to.

If you must keep 16-bit applications on your system, remember the following pointers:

- 16-bit applications know nothing about the Windows 95 Registry. Thus, they still save their information in the various INI files for which Windows 3.x was famous. Windows 95 even includes abbreviated WIN.INI and SYSTEM.INI files for compatibility with older 16-bit programs. Do not delete INI files relied upon by your programs, including WIN.INI and SYSTEM.INI.

- Don't edit WIN.INI and SYSTEM.INI directly unless you absolutely have to. These files are updated automatically with some variables every time you modify the Registry. Thus, if you need to change a variable that affects your entire system (such as your display settings or the like), it is better to make the changes in the Registry (using the Control Panel) and let Windows take care of modifying the older WIN.INI and SYSTEM.INI files.

- Steer clear of 16-bit disk utilities designed for Windows. These rely on the outdated FAT file structure used in Windows 3.x. *Using such programs could wipe out any long file names you've used under Windows 95.*

System Resources

Under Windows 3.x, it was easy to crash your system. All you needed to do was have a program or two crash, and the resources in your system would be eaten up. All of a sudden, other programs were refusing to load or were running short on memory.

Under Windows 95, your 16-bit applications will automatically run better because the entire resource structure of Windows has been revamped. Now there are greater resources available to all programs, including 16-bit holdovers from Windows 3.x.

Under Windows 3.x, the operating system used 64K memory heaps for different system components. This memory area was used to store information about objects used in system function calls by both the operating system and the applications running in the system. When you looked at the percentage of system resources in the About box of the Help menu in any application, you were looking at how much of the 64K heap was left available. The closer this percentage got to zero, the closer you were to crashing your system.

To overcome this problem in Windows 95, many of the resources that used to quickly consume memory in the 64K heap have been reallocated to a new 32-bit heap. This means that there is much more room for tracking system objects and performing system function calls. The net result is that more resources are available, and programs are less likely to exhaust them.

For a comparison of the improvements, take a look at the information shown in Table 17.1. This shows the increases in limits on all aspects related to running 16-bit applications under Windows 95.

Table 17.1 Windows Resource Limits

System Resource	Windows 3.1 Limits	Windows 95 Limits
COM ports	4	Unlimited
Device contexts	Approx. 175	16,000
Edit control data	64K	Unlimited
Installed fonts	Approx. 250	1,000
Listbox data	64K	Unlimited
Listbox items	8K	32K
Logical fonts	64K local heap	Approx. 750
Logical objects	64K local heap	64K local heap

System Resource	Windows 3.1 Limits	Windows 95 Limits
LPT ports	4	Unlimited
Menu handles	Approx. 299	32K each
Physical objects	64K local heap	Unlimited
Regions	64K local heap	Unlimited
Timers	32	Unlimited

Installing DOS Applications

by Allen L. Wyatt

Microsoft has made more of a concerted effort to make Windows 95 compatible with MS-DOS programs than they have with any previous version of Windows. This is understandable, because you can't exit out of Windows and run your MS-DOS application, as you could previously. The result of this effort is a stable and robust environment for your MS-DOS programs. In this chapter you'll learn the following about installing your DOS applications:

- ➤ How to install a DOS program by using the Add/Remove Programs wizard
- ➤ How to manually install a DOS program
- ➤ What you should do after you've installed the software
- ➤ How Windows 95 uses the APPS.INF file to aid in running MS-DOS programs

Installing a Program

Most DOS programs know little about Windows. Some do, it is true, but by and large, they assume that you'll be running the program outside of Windows. Because of the stability of the Virtual Machine created for a DOS application, you can generally install directly from within Windows. There are two ways you can install your programs: by using the wizard supplied by Windows, or by manually installing. The following sections describe both approaches.

Using the Wizard

Windows 95 includes a software installation wizard you can use to add software to your system. This wizard, located in the Control Panel, is typically used to add Windows software, but it is also the preferred method of adding MS-DOS software. As the wizard installs the software, it checks in a special information file to determine whether there are any special configuration needs for the software. This special information file, APPS.INF, is fully described later in this chapter. If you don't use the wizard for installing, then the APPS.INF file is not consulted and the installation might not occur correctly.

To run the software installation wizard, follow these steps:

1. Choose Settings from the Start menu. The Settings menu appears.

2. Choose Control Panel from the Settings menu; the Control Panel appears.

3. Double-click on the Add/Remove Programs icon. You'll see the Add/Remove Programs Properties sheet appear, as shown in figure 18.1.

4. Click on the Install button. This starts the wizard and displays the first screen, as shown in figure 18.2.

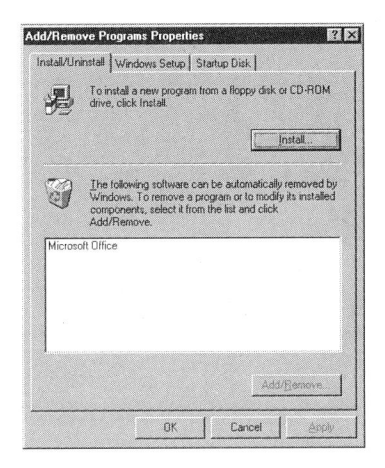

Fig. 18.1 The Add/Remove Programs Properties sheet is used to add or remove software from Windows 95.

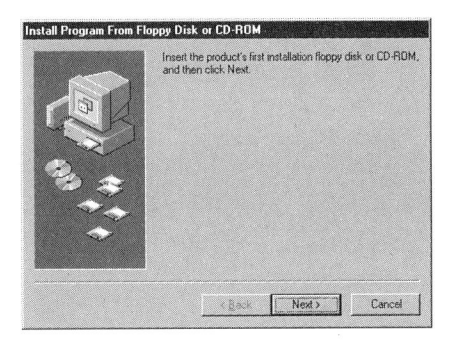

Fig. 18.2 Windows 95 includes a wizard used to install software from a floppy disk or CD-ROM.

Make sure that either the installation floppy disk for the software or the CD-ROM containing the installation files is inserted in a disk drive. When you're ready to proceed, click on the Next button. The wizard proceeds to look through your disk drives (and CD-ROM drives) to find a setup floppy disk. The wizard also looks for program names, such as SETUP.EXE or INSTALL.EXE. When it finds a disk or CD-ROM that contains what it believes to be setup files, a new dialog box appears that shows what was found (see figure 18.3).

Installing a Program **423**

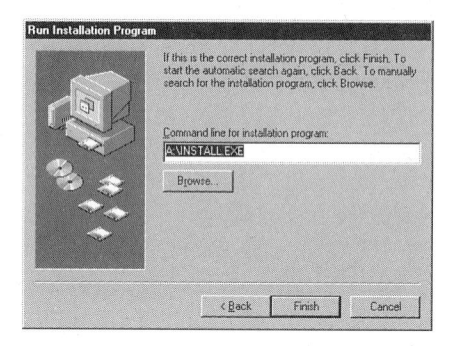

Fig. 18.3 When Windows 95 detects a setup disk, it displays information to let you know what it found.

The command line field in the middle of the dialog box should reflect the command line necessary to install the software. You may want to check the command line against the command line indicated in the documentation for the software. If you need to, you can click on the Browse button to locate a different program to use in the installation routines.

When you're finished with the command line, click on the Finish button. This ends the wizard and starts the setup program for your software. The steps you follow from this point depend on the software you're installing. Different applications have different setup programs that require different user input.

Manually Installing

Whenever possible, you should use the Add/Remove Programs wizard to install a DOS program. There may be times, however, when this is not feasible—for instance, if you get a shareware program from a friend or from a BBS, or you need to install a program you wrote. In most cases, you can directly run the setup or installation program, and Windows will configure an environment just fine. Although this may work in 90 percent of the installations you do, it is not necessarily the safest way to do the installation. In addition, your DOS application may be small enough that it doesn't even have an installation program.

In instances where you must install manually, it is a good idea if you follow these general steps:

1. Create a folder for the DOS program.
2. Copy the files from the floppy disk to the folder.
3. Determine which executable files are in the folder; write down their names on a piece of paper.
4. Right-click on the icon for an executable file.
5. Choose Properties from the context menu; the Properties sheet appears for the application.
6. Set the memory, screen, and other attributes particular to this executable file.
7. Click on the OK button.
8. Repeat steps 4 through 7 for every executable file in the folder, even the setup program and any batch files.

To complete step 6, you may need to refer to your program documentation for information about special needs of the program. Such information could be in the system requirements, technical notes, or troubleshooting sections of the manual. If you need help with setting the properties for the files, you can refer to Chapter 19, "Fine-Tuning Windows 95 for Your DOS Applications."

Once these steps are complete, you have a good chance of successfully running both the setup program (if there is one) and the application itself.

After Installation

After you're through installing your DOS software, and it has been copied to your disk drive, you're ready to use it. You may want to take the time to create a shortcut to access the program, however. Regardless of whether you install by using the wizard or do it manually, Windows 95 doesn't create shortcuts for DOS programs, nor does it make them available through the Start menu.

To make your DOS programs available through either shortcuts or the menu system, refer to Chapter 3, "New Windows 95 Tools," and Chapter 15, "Taking Control of Windows 95 Startup," for information on how to take advantage of these features.

The Application Information File

When you run an MS-DOS program for the first time, including any DOS setup programs, Windows checks the contents of a file called APPS.INF. This file, supplied with Windows 95, is located in the \WINDOWS\INF folder. It contains information on over 400 executable DOS programs, and supplies Windows with the environmental parameters that will allow the program to run the best.

The file is organized the same as any other Microsoft INF file. It contains sections, denoted by key words enclosed in brackets, and each section contains a series of individual entries. The file is divided into three groups of sections, and you can examine it with the WordPad accessory, if you desire. The groups of sections are:

- [PIF95]
- Applications
- [Strings]

Each of these is detailed in the following sections.

The [PIF95] Section

The first section, [PIF95], contains a master list of all the programs for which APPS.INF contains information—over 400 in all. For example, the following is the first part of the [PIF95] section:

```
[PIF95]
123.COM=%123.COM%,moricons.dll,50,,123.COM
123.EXE=%123.EXE.1%,moricons.dll,51,,123.EXE.1,WYSIWYG.APP
123.EXE=%123.EXE.2%,moricons.dll,51,,123.EXE.2,L123SMP3.RI
1942.EXE=%1942.EXE%,moricons.dll,1,,1942.EXE,MPSCOPY.EXE
1942.BAT=%1942.BAT%,moricons.dll,1,,1942.BAT,1942
```

```
ACAD.EXE=%ACAD.EXE%,moricons.dll,16,,ACAD.EXE,ACAD386.BAT
ACAD386.BAT=%ACAD386.BAT%,moricons.dll,16,,ACAD386.BAT,ACAD.EXE
ACCESS.COM=%ACCESS.COM.1%,moricons.dll,95,,ACCESS.COM.1,SYMPHONY.EXE
ACCESS.COM=%ACCESS.COM.2%,moricons.dll,101,,ACCESS.COM.2,ACCESS.MDM,1
ACROBAT.EXE=%ACROBAT.EXE%,moricons.dll,1,,ACROBAT.EXE,ACROMAIN.EXE
AEGIS.EXE=%AEGIS.EXE%,moricons.dll,1,,AEGIS.EXE,ARCTAN.TAB
AEGISV.EXE=%AEGISV.EXE%,moricons.dll,1,,AEGISV.EXE,ARCTAN.TAB
```

Notice that each entry in the section follows a specific format. To the left side of the equal sign is the executable file for the application, and to the right is information about that application. Notice, as well, that there can be more than one entry for a specific executable file. For instance, there are two entries for 123.EXE and for ACCESS.COM. The reason is that different DOS software packages can use the same executable file names for their products.

The information to the right of the equal sign can consist of up to seven fields. These fields, in order, are as follows:

➤ **Title key.** This is a string identifier that Windows uses to look up the wording that will appear in the title bar of the program's window. The title key is enclosed in percent signs, and ties to an entry in the [Strings] section, as described later.

➤ **Icon file.** The name of the file from which the icon for the program should be selected. More often than not, this is MORICONS.DLL, the catch-all icons file in Windows.

➤ **Icon index.** The number of the icon within the icon file. This is an offset within the file, starting at 0. Thus, a value of 51 means that the 52nd icon in the file is used for the program. The default value is 0. When the icon file is MORICONS.DLL, then the default setting appears to be 1 when a specific icon for the application is not available.

➤ **Working folder flag.** This is a flag that indicates whether Windows 95 can automatically set the working folder for the program. If set to 0 (the default), then setting is allowed; if set to 1, then the folder cannot be set automatically.

➤ **Section.** This is the name of the section (again, within brackets) of APPS.INF that contains detailed information about the application. The section name is often the same as the executable name that appears to the left of the equal sign, but not always. For instance, the section names for the two ACCESS.COM entries are ACCESS.COM.1 and ACCESS.COM.2. The individual application sections start immediately after the [PIF95] section, and will be discussed shortly.

➤ **Key file.** This is the name of a file within the program folder that identifies exactly which application this is. For instance, where the executable file can be duplicated (as with 123.EXE), the key file is checked. If a file of the same name is found in the folder, then Windows 95 knows that this is the correct entry for the application, because the two files match.

➤ **PIF flag.** This is a flag that indicates whether Windows 95 can create a PIF file for the application. If 0 (the default), then a PIF can be created; if 1, then it cannot be created.

The Applications Sections

Immediately following the [PIF95] section is the start of the applications sections. This part of the file consists of multiple sections, one for each application on which information is maintained. The section names are tied to the section field in individual entries within the [PIF95] section. Thus, if the section field within the [PIF95] section is LEARN.EXE.4, then the corresponding section within this part of the file will be [LEARN.EXE.4].

The section for each application contains three or four settings, all of which are optional. The purpose of the section is to indicate special environmental settings that need to be made in order for the program to run correctly under Windows 95. In addition, execution parameters can be indicated for the program.

Entries again consist of a key word, followed by an equal sign, and the settings related to that key word. For instance, the following is a small portion of the applications section:

```
[CCHELP.EXE]
LowMem=524
Enable=dos
Disable=win

[CHART.COM]
LowMem=256
Disable=win

[CKTEST.EXE]
LowMem=512
XMSMem=None
Enable=lml,rvm,dos,gmp
Disable=win,dit,hma,asp,aen

[CHECKIT.EXE]
LowMem=512
XMSMem=None
Enable=lml,rvm,dos,gmp
Disable=win,dit,hma,asp,aen

[CL.EXE.1]
Params="?"
LowMem=384
Enable=dos
Disable=win
```

The key words that can appear to the left of the equal sign can be any of the following:

- AppHack
- BatchFile
- Disable
- DPMIMem
- EMSMem
- Enable
- LowMem

The Application Information File **429**

- Params
- XMSMem

Not all key words need to be set for each application. Only those that vary from the default DOS window settings need to be noted. The following sections describe each of the key words.

AppHack

The exact purpose of this setting is not known. It is included in APPS.INF for only seven applications out of over 400. The apparent possible settings for the key word are the numeric values 4, 8, or 16.

BatchFile

This is the name of any batch file that must be run before the program is actually executed. In reality, this can be the name of a batch file or a DOS command that must be executed. There is only one application that has this key word used—for the program MenuWorks, as shown in the following application section:

```
[MW.EXE]
BatchFile="cls"
LowMem=512
Enable=cwe
Disable=win,hma
```

Microsoft indicates that the purpose of the batch file should not be to run the program, but instead to set up the environment in which the program will subsequently run. For instance, you may have a batch file that loads a TSR program necessary for the DOS program. If you were setting the batch file name manually, you would do so in the Properties sheet for the executable file, on the Program tab. The Batch file field on that tab should contain the same information as the BatchFile key word.

Disable

This key word defines attributes of the environment that must be disabled in order for the application to run. These are the same attributes you can control manually in the Preferences dialog box for the application. (See Chapter 19, "Fine-Tuning Windows 95 for Your DOS Applications.") The attributes to be disabled are listed to the right of the equal sign, separated by commas and no spaces, as in the following application section for the Rules of Engagement 2 program:

```
[RULES2.COM]
LowMem=542
XMSMem=1024
Disable=win,hma
```

The possible attributes that can be used with the Disable key word are shown in Table 18.1. The other information shown in the table is the Property tab used to manually set the attribute, along with the setting on the tab.

Table 18.1 Attribute Meanings for the Disable Key Word

Attribute	Property Tab	Setting
aen	Misc	Alt+Enter
aes	Misc	Alt+Esc
afp	Misc	Fast pasting
aps	Misc	Alt+PrtSc
asp	Misc	Alt+Space
ata	Misc	Alt+Tab
bgd	Misc	Always suspend (Background)
ces	Misc	Ctrl+Esc
dit	Misc	Idle sensitivity
emt	Screen	Fast ROM emulation
hma	Memory	Uses HMA
psc	Misc	PrtSc
win	Screen	Full-screen / Window

The Application Information File

DPMIMem

This is the setting for how much DPMI memory should be set aside for the program. It corresponds to the same setting on the Memory tab of the Properties sheet. If not specified, the value defaults to Auto; if set to -1, then the value corresponds to Auto.

EMSMem

This is the setting for how much EMS memory should be set aside for the program. This value can be manually changed on the Memory tab of the Properties sheet, provided there is EMS software installed for Windows 95. For more information, refer to Chapter 9, "Exploiting Memory, Space, and Resources."

Enable

This key word defines attributes of the environment, which must be enabled in order for the application to run; these are attributes that would otherwise be disabled. These are the same attributes you can control manually in the Preferences dialog box for the application. (See Chapter 19, "Fine-Tuning Windows 95 for Your DOS Applications.") The attributes to be enabled are listed to the right of the equal sign, separated by commas and no spaces, as in the following application section for the CheckIt! program:

```
[CHECKIT.EXE]
LowMem=512
XMSMem=None
Enable=lml,rvm,dos,gmp
Disable=win,dit,hma,asp,aen
```

The possible attributes that can be used with the Enable key word are shown in Table 18.2. The other information shown in the table is the Property tab used to manually set the attribute, along with the setting on the tab.

Table 18.2 Attribute Meanings for the Enable Key Word

Attribute	Property Tab	Setting / Meaning
cwe	Program	Close on e‌xit
dos		Real mode
eml	Memory	EMS memory locked
gmp		Global memory protection
lie		
lml	Memory	P‌rotected (conventional memory)
rvm	Screen	Dynamic m‌emory allocation
uus		
xml	Memory	XMS memory locked

LowMem

An indication of how much conventional memory should be set aside for the program. This value can normally be set in the Memory tab of the Properties sheet. If not specified, the value defaults to Auto. The following is an example for BASICA, where the conventional memory is set to only 80 bytes. (BASICA is built in to the ROM on some systems.)

```
[BASICA.EXE]
LowMem=80
Disable=win
```

Params

This key word indicates any command-line parameters needed for the executable file. The parameters are enclosed in quote marks, as in the following example for the Folder Maintenance portion of PCTools:

```
[DM.EXE]
Params="/nf /ngm"
LowMem=330
Disable=win,afp,asp
```

The Application Information File **433**

If the parameter is a question mark, then Windows will ask for parameters when the program is run. The following is an example for QuickBASIC:

```
[QBASIC.EXE]
Params="?"
LowMem=330
EMSMem=None
XMSMem=None
Disable=win
```

XMSMem

This is the setting for how much extended (XMS) memory should be set aside for the program. It corresponds to the same setting on the Memory tab of the Properties sheet. If not specified, the value defaults to Auto; if set to -1 then the value corresponds to Auto.

The [Strings] Section

For the purposes of the APPS.INF file, the [Strings] section is used to define the wording that will appear in the title bar of a window. The section consists of a string identifier on the left side of the equal sign, and the actual string on the right side. The following is a small portion of the [Strings] section of the file:

```
[Strings]
123.COM="Lotus 1-2-3"
123.EXE.1="Lotus 1-2-3   2.3 WYSIWYG"
123.EXE.2="Lotus 1-2-3 version 3"
1942.EXE="1942: The Pacific Air War"
1942.BAT="1942: The Pacific Air War"
ACAD.EXE="Autocad"
ACAD386.BAT="Autocad"
ACCESS.COM.1="Symphony (Access)"
ACCESS.COM.2="MS Access for DOS"
ACROBAT.EXE="Adobe Acrobat"
AEGIS.EXE="Aegis: Guardian of the Fleet"
AEGISV.EXE="Aegis: Guardian of the Fleet"
AOD.EXE="Aces of the Deep"
AOD.BAT="Aces of the Deep CD"
ARCHON.EXE="Archon Ultra"
```

```
ARMADA.EXE="Wing Commander - Armada"
ADMIN.EXE="Microsoft Mail - Admin"
AFS.EXE="Chuck Yeager's FlightSim"
AFS.BAT="Chuck Yeager's Flight Simulat"
AFRAID.BAT="Are You Afraid of The Dark?"
AGENDA.EXE="Lotus Agenda"
ARCADE.BAT="Pinball Arcade"
```

Within APPS.INF, the string identifier is used in the [PIF95] section of the file. Each entry there has a title key, which is nothing but a string identifier. The title key points to a string identifier in the [Strings] section, and the corresponding string value is what is used in the title bar text for the application. As an example, the entry for RISE.EXE in the [PIF95] section has a title key of %RISE.EXE%. In the string section, the %RISE.EXE% string identifier corresponds to the text "Rise of the Robots." This is the text that will be used in the title bar.

Fine-Tuning Windows 95 for Your DOS Applications

by Allen L. Wyatt

When you install your DOS applications, Windows 95 creates an environment in which they can run. You can modify this environment rather easily through adjusting the attributes assigned to a program. This chapter covers the ways you can modify the environment in which your DOS programs are run. Here you will learn the following:

➤ What happened to the ever-present PIF files used in previous versions of Windows

- How you can change the way the DOS environment is initialized
- What you can do to modify the memory settings for a DOS program
- How the screen settings can be modified
- What tips you can use to avoid problems when running DOS programs

What About the PIF?

In previous versions of Windows, the PIF (program information file) was an integral part of making your DOS programs work correctly within Windows. It was used to define operational parameters for the DOS window created for the program.

The PIF file has not gone away; its maintenance has simply been "absorbed" into the mainstream Windows 95 interface. For instance, there is no longer a PIF Editor program in Windows. Instead, the functions of this program have been assumed by the PIFMGR.DLL, which is called when you choose to edit the properties of either a DOS window or an MS-DOS executable file.

The PIF file is created automatically when you first run a DOS program, and it is assumed to be in the same folder as the executable file. If the PIF file cannot be located, Windows creates one. When creating a PIF file, Windows first checks the APPS.INF file to see if information on the executable file is included there. (Detailed information on APPS.INF is included in Chapter 18, "Installing DOS Applications.") If it is, then the settings there are used for the PIF. If there is no information in APPS.INF on the executable file, then a default PIF is created, based on the file MS-DOS~1.PIF (MS-DOS Prompt.pif).

After the PIF file is created, you can modify it through either of these methods:

- Right-click the icon for the executable file, and then choose Properties from the context menu.

➤ While the DOS program is running, right-click the title bar for the program window, and then choose Properties from the context menu.

Either method displays the Properties sheet for the program. You can make any changes you want; they will be used the next time you run the program.

Program Initialization

When you open a DOS window, either manually or by running a DOS program, Windows 95 creates a complete environment for that window. You learned about this environment (referred to as a *Virtual Machine*) in Chapter 13, "How Windows 95 Interacts with Software."

While Windows 95 does an admirable job setting up a DOS environment, you can also take charge and configure the environment to your liking. The following sections describe how you can change the way a DOS program is initialized into its environment.

Changing the Environment Variables

Many programs require that environment variables be set in order to work properly. For instance, you may have a DOS program that requires the TEMP variable to be set to a specific location, or the LIB variable to be set to the folder where special library files are located. The easiest way to set environment variables is to follow these steps:

1. Create a batch file that contains the commands to set the necessary environment variables.

2. Open the Properties sheet for the DOS program icon. Make sure that the Program tab is selected, as shown in figure 19.1.

3. In the Batch file field, indicate the path and name of the batch file you created in step 1.

4. Click the OK button.

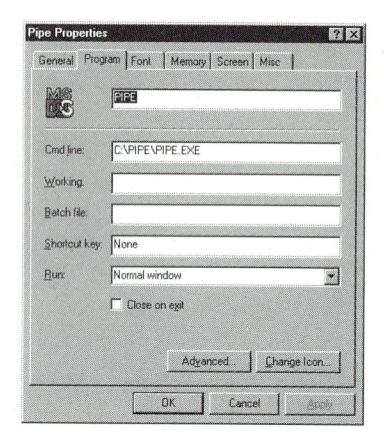

Fig. 19.1 Windows 95 enables you to run a batch file before executing a DOS program.

The next time you run the DOS program, the batch file you created will be run automatically, prior to running the program itself. When you close the DOS window, the environment variable values are discarded.

If you set too many environment variables, you might actually run out of environment space. This condition occurs when the number of DOS environment variables exceeds the amount of memory initially set aside for those variables. In older DOS-based systems, this was overcome with a change to the CONFIG.SYS file. In Windows 95, you can change it by following these steps:

1. Display the Properties sheet for the DOS program in which you want to increase the environment space.

2. Click the Memory tab. The dialog box will look similar to what you see in figure 19.2.

3. In the Initial environment field, use the pull-down list to select the number of bytes to allocate to the environment space. The minimum is 256 bytes; the maximum is 4,096 bytes. If you select Auto, then Windows 95 attempts to make an educated guess as to how much space to allocate.

4. Click the OK button.

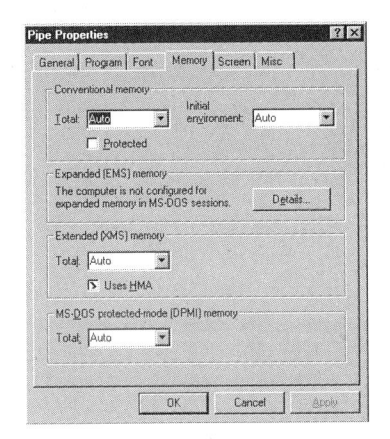

Fig. 19.2 You can use the Memory tab to change the amount of memory dedicated to the environment space in a DOS VM.

Setting the Path

There are two ways you can specify a DOS path. The first is to do it globally, and the other is to do it temporarily. The steps you follow for each of these are covered in the following sections.

Globally Setting the Path

The default path used by Windows 95, whenever you open the MS-DOS window or start a DOS program, is the following:

```
PATH=C:\WINDOWS;C:\WINDOWS\COMMAND
```

Obviously, if you installed Windows 95 in a folder other than C:\WINDOWS, that folder will instead appear in the path command. You can modify this default path by simply adding a path command to the AUTOEXEC.BAT file stored in your root folder. This file will be appended to the default path whenever you start Windows 95, and it becomes the default path for all DOS windows you open after that.

Program Initialization **441**

After you have changed the path, restart Windows 95. You can then open an MS-DOS window to make sure that the change has indeed occurred. For instance, I changed my AUTOEXEC.BAT file so that it contained a single line:

```
path=d:\
```

When I restarted Windows, opened an MS-DOS window, and issued the path command, the following was shown as the path:

```
PATH=C:\WINDOWS;C:\WINDOWS\COMMAND;D:\
```

Temporarily Setting the Path

You can temporarily set the path used with a particular program by setting it within a batch file that is run prior to running the program. To do this, follow the steps outlined earlier in this chapter, in the section "Changing the Environment Variables." The batch file you create should contain the proper path command to set the path as you need it.

After the batch file is in place and you have set the correct attribute in the Properties sheet, the batch file is executed by Windows 95 just before the corresponding DOS program is run. When the window is closed, the value to which you set the path is discarded.

Setting a Working Folder

Many programs enable you to work faster if you can start the program in a specific folder. For instance, if you are using a DOS word processor, you may want it to start in a folder where your files are located. Windows enables you to specify the folder where the DOS program should begin. To do this, simply display the Properties sheet for the program. Make sure that the Program tab is selected, as shown in figure 19.3.

The Working field is where you specify the path of the working folder you want to use. Simply enter the path of an existing folder, and then click the OK button. The next time you start the DOS program, it will start in the specified folder.

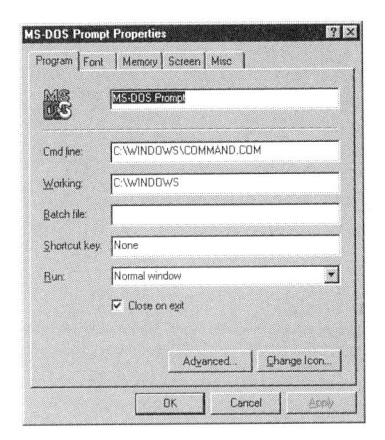

Fig. 19.3 Use the Program tab to indicate the working folder for a DOS program.

> **Note:** If the DOS program enables you to specify an initial folder within the program, that is where you should set the working folder. If the folder specified in the program is different from the one you specify in the Properties sheet, then the one in the program will be used.

Fine-Tuning Memory

Memory allocation and use for DOS programs can be confusing, to say the least. It is beyond the scope of this chapter to explain the different types of memory which DOS programs can use when running in real mode, but you can refer to Chapter 9, "Exploiting Memory, Space, and Resources," for additional information on the subject.

Windows 95 enables you to have complete control over the type and amount of memory you allocate to a DOS Virtual Machine. The next several sections explain how you can modify each type of memory.

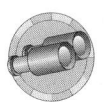

Note: If the PIF file for your DOS program was set up automatically by Windows 95, there is probably very little you need to do to optimize memory. Memory settings are automatically configured when you first run the DOS program. For more information on how this happens, refer to Chapter 18, "Installing DOS Applications."

Conventional Memory

Conventional memory is where the majority of DOS programs actually execute. The reasons for this are long and involved, but suffice it to say that you can consider conventional memory to be "prime real estate" in the memory market.

Windows 95 enables you to allocate various amounts of conventional memory to your DOS applications quickly and easily. You can do this through the Memory tab of the Properties sheet for the application. You can set conventional memory to any multiple of 40K bytes, between 40K and 640K. You can also set the conventional memory to Auto, which means that Windows 95 makes the decision about what setting to use.

To change the conventional memory setting, follow these steps:

1. Display the Properties sheet for the DOS program in which you want to change conventional memory allocation.

2. Click the Memory tab. The dialog box will look similar to what you see in figure 19.4.

3. At the top of the dialog box, in the Total field, set the amount of conventional memory to use for the program. If you are in doubt, set it either to Auto or to 640.

4. Click on the OK button.

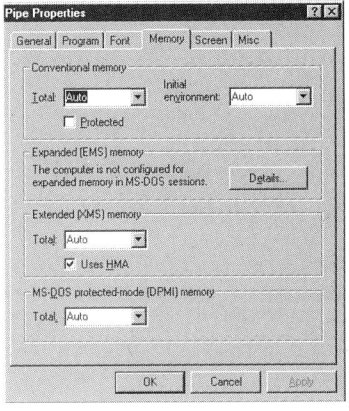

Fig. 19.4 Use the Memory tab to change the memory configuration for a DOS program.

Expanded Memory

Expanded memory (EMS) is a type of memory used by some older DOS programs. Typically it is used for large blocks of data that cannot fit into the 640K maximum of conventional memory. Special accessing functions were used to work with this memory, and special drivers or memory managers were required.

To use EMS memory with Windows 95, you must have a real-mode memory manager installed in the system. You must perform this installation according to the instructions of your memory manager software. It will involve changing or creating the CONFIG.SYS file and then restarting your system. After the memory manager is correctly installed, Windows will automatically make EMS memory available as your DOS programs need it.

Extended Memory

Extended memory (XMS) is a memory specification that came into popularity about two years after EMS. Most of the DOS programs in use today will utilize XMS memory in preference to EMS memory. The

XMS specification is more flexible in how it allows memory to be accessed, and to what uses the memory can be put.

To change the amount of XMS memory allocated to the DOS Virtual Machine by Windows 95, follow these steps:

1. Display the Properties sheet for the DOS program in which you want to change XMS memory allocation.

2. Click the Memory tab. The dialog box will look similar to what is shown earlier in figure 19.4.

3. Toward the bottom of the dialog box, in the Total field, set the XMS memory limit to impose on the program. You can pick any value between 1M (1024K) and 16M (16384K) in 1M increments. You can also set the value to None or Auto. If you choose the latter, then Windows 95 places no limit on the amount of XMS memory used by the program.

4. Select the Uses HMA check box if your program utilizes the high memory area just under the 1M memory boundary.

5. Click on the OK button.

If your program seems to be having problems working with extended memory, change the XMS setting to a value such as 8192 or lower. (Some programs have a hard time utilizing more than 8M of XMS.)

DPMI Memory

As hardware advances became more frequent, and memory more prolific in the advanced machines, a new memory specification emerged which allowed DOS to take advantage of protected mode operation. This specification was called DPMI, or DOS protected-mode interface. This specification was supported in Windows 3.x, as well as several commercial memory managers.

Some software on the market required the presence of DPMI functions in order to work. This is particularly true of high-end software such as CAD software. If your software requires such memory, then you should try to leave the setting at Auto (the default). With this setting, Windows 95 makes up to 16M of DPMI memory available to a DOS program, as needed.

It is possible that your software will not work properly with an essentially unlimited supply of DPMI memory. If this is the case, you can change the DPMI setting by following these steps:

1. Display the Properties sheet for the DOS program in which you want to change DPMI memory allocation.

2. Click the Memory tab. The dialog box will look similar to what is shown earlier in figure 19.4.

3. Toward the bottom of the dialog box, in the Total: field, set the DPMI memory limit to impose on the program. You can pick any value between 1M (1024K) and 16M (16384K) in 1M increments.

4. Click on the OK button.

Video Memory Use

Your video system uses memory routinely to display graphics, text, and other information in the DOS window. You can modify the way your video system uses video memory by displaying the Properties sheet and then clicking the Screen tab. The dialog box should appear as shown in figure 19.5.

At the bottom of the dialog box, in the Performance area, are two check boxes. These settings come into play when you are not running the DOS program in full-screen mode; in other words, it is running in a window on your desktop. The first setting, Fast ROM Emulation, causes Windows 95 to move the ROM instructions into faster RAM memory. This utilizes a few more memory resources, but it also causes text and some graphics to be displayed faster; how you set the option is up to you.

The other setting, Dynamic Memory Allocation, controls how Windows allocates screen display memory. If the check box is selected, then Windows is free to use the screen memory area as necessary (and as appropriate) for the DOS program. If the check box is cleared, then the maximum amount of memory necessary for the screen display is always reserved for the program, and is therefore not available to other programs. Clearing this check box may speed up the DOS program running in the window, but it may also slow down any other programs you have running in Windows 95.

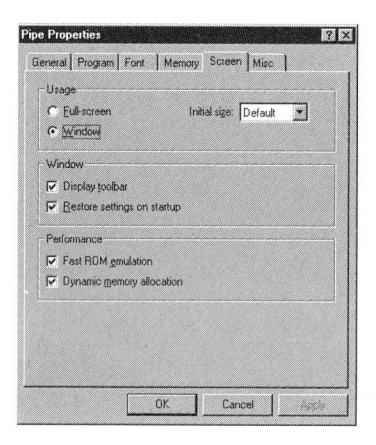

Fig. 19.5 The Performance area of the Screen tab enables you to control how Windows 95 uses video memory.

Fine-Tuning the Screen

One of the traditional areas where DOS programs have had problems in Windows is in displaying all text and graphics faithfully and without problem. Windows 95 has solved the traditional problems; you can now display virtually anything in a DOS window with no adverse side effects.

Windows 95 gives you a great deal of control over how the display screen is used in a DOS window. The following sections discuss how you can configure Windows 95 in order to get your DOS displays exactly the way you want them.

Changing Fonts

Windows includes fully scaleable windows for running DOS programs. This means that you can pick any size window you want; Windows will simply modify the size of the font to fit the requested information in the available space. Conversely, if you pick a different font size, then Windows adjusts the size of the DOS window so that all the information can be displayed.

The easiest way to change fonts in a DOS window is to simply select a font from the pull-down list on the toolbar. Both bitmapped system fonts and TrueType fonts are displayed. You can pick the one you want, and Windows makes the change right away. (For more information on how the font technology works, refer to Chapter 22, "Working with Fonts.")

You can also change fonts by using the Properties sheet. This dialog box enables you to indicate the default font (and subsequent window size) that should be used when you first start a DOS program. To change fonts in this manner, follow these steps:

1. Display the Properties sheet for the DOS program.
2. Click the Font tab. The dialog box will look similar to what you see in figure 19.6.

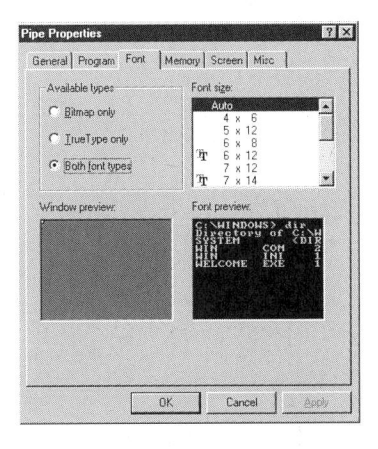

Fig. 19.6 Use the Font tab to specify the initial font used in a DOS window.

Fine-Tuning the Screen **449**

3. In the Available types area (upper-left corner of the dialog box), select the type of fonts that Windows should make available.

4. In the Font Size list, select the font size to use. The numbers indicate the number of pixels used to make each character. A TT symbol to the left of a particular font size indicates that the font is a TrueType font.

As you make changes, you can see at the bottom of the dialog box how text will appear within the DOS window. When you are satisfied with your changes, click the OK button.

Text-Mode Lines

Some text-based DOS software is designed to run best in a "nonstandard" screen size. The standard text screen is 80 characters wide by 25 lines deep; Windows 95 enables you to specify that a different line count should be used. You can pick from four settings:

➤ **Default.** Windows 95 will use whatever it detects as the value the program uses. Typically, this is the best choice to make.

➤ **25 lines.** The initial screen size is set to 25 lines deep. This is the normal size of a DOS text screen.

➤ **43 lines.** The initial screen size is set to 43 lines. This allows 72% more information in the DOS window at a time.

➤ **50 lines.** The initial screen size is set to 50 lines, which is 100% more information than normal.

To change the initial line count used by Windows 95, follow these steps:

1. Display the Properties sheet for the DOS program.

2. Click the Screen tab. The dialog box will look similar to what you see in figure 19.7.

3. Change the Initial Size field to reflect the number of lines you want Windows 95 to use in the DOS window.

4. Click the OK button.

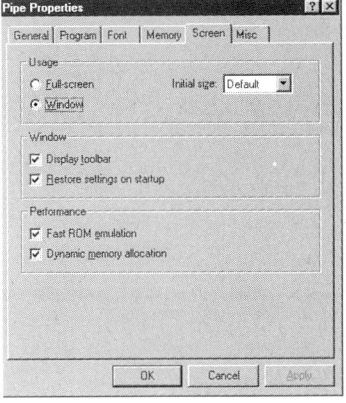

Fig. 19.7 Use the Screen tab to modify the initial screen settings for the DOS window.

When you are through changing the initial number of lines on the screen, you may want to change the font size. Different font sizes look different with various line counts.

> **Note:** Understand that regardless of what you instruct Windows 95 to set as the initial line count, it is possible that your DOS software could reset the value to some other size.

Adjusting Screen Size

As you may already have surmised, Windows 95 provides you with complete control over the size of your DOS window. You can indicate an initial screen size in the Properties sheet, and then you can modify the screen size while you are using the program.

To set the initial screen size, open the Properties sheet for the program. Make sure that the Program dialog box is displayed, as shown in figure 19.8.

Fine-Tuning the Screen   **451**

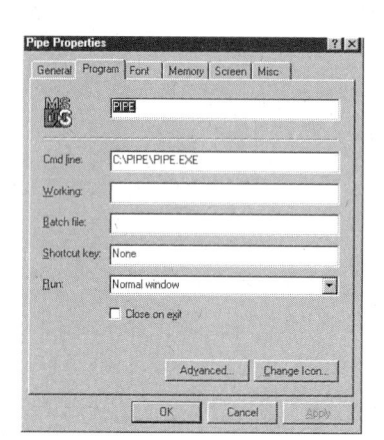

Fig. 19.8 The Program tab is where you indicate how the DOS program should initially run.

In the Run field, at the bottom of the dialog box, use the pull-down list to indicate how you want this DOS window to be opened. There are three choices:

- **Normal window**. The DOS window will simply be another window on the desktop.

- **Minimized**. The DOS window will be minimized to a button on the taskbar.

- **Maximized**. The DOS window will occupy the entire screen.

Notice that this is for the initial size of the screen; you can always change it after Windows 95 has created the DOS window. There are other settings, however, that enable you to indicate how the DOS program should use the DOS window. You can access this configuration area by clicking the Screen tab of the Properties sheet. (This tab was shown earlier in figure 19.7.)

At the top of the dialog box are two buttons in the Usage area; one is Full-screen, and the other is Window. These are mutually exclusive buttons—you can pick only one or the other. If you pick the Window button, then the DOS program can run in a window on the desktop, and the settings you made on the Program tab will be meaningful.

This setting is best for programs that use predominantly text screens. The other setting, Full-screen, is best for graphics programs, such as games. With this setting selected, the DOS window takes the entire screen, and you cannot reduce the window to take only part of the screen.

Finally, in the Window portion of the Screen tab you can indicate whether the DOS window toolbar is visible. If you clear the Display Toolbar check box, then the toolbar is not available. You may want to do this if you need the maximum window area for your program, or if you simply do not use the toolbar.

Other Fine-Tuning

The final group of DOS program settings is a hodgepodge of miscellaneous items. This is not to say that they are unimportant; on the contrary, these settings can greatly affect the use of your DOS programs. The following sections take a look at each of the other settings you can make to change your DOS window configuration.

Adjusting Multitasking

In the system architecture used by Windows 95, a DOS window normally receives as much attention as any other program window. You can modify how the operating system treats your DOS program, however. You do this from the Properties sheet for the program. Simply display the dialog box, and then click the Misc tab. The dialog box appears as shown in figure 19.9.

The first item you should pay attention to is the Always Suspend check box. Normally this check box is cleared, which means that when the window in which the DOS program is running is not in the foreground, it is treated like any other program window. If you select the check box, then whenever the program window is not in the foreground, the DOS program is suspended. In other words, this check box is a way to pause your DOS program whenever its window is not active.

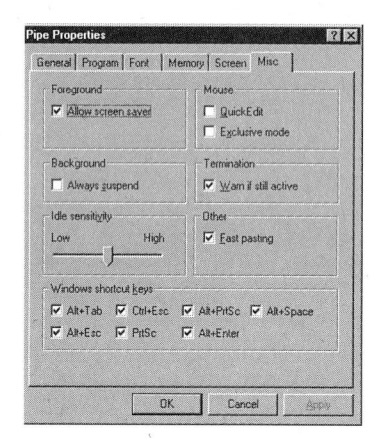

Fig. 19.9 You can use the Misc tab to control the multitasking attributes of a DOS program.

Also on this tab is the slider bar labeled Idle Sensitivity. This slider bar controls how Windows treats the DOS program when it is waiting for keyboard input. The lower the idle sensitivity, the longer the DOS program can run before Windows starts allocating resources to other tasks. Conversely, the higher the idle sensitivity, the shorter the time allowed before reallocation occurs.

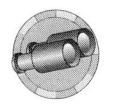

> **Note:** You should only adjust the idle sensitivity if you feel the program in the DOS window is not executing fast enough. When you move the slider toward the Low setting (meaning your DOS program holds on to resources longer when it is idle), your other Windows programs may run slower than otherwise.

The final setting that affects the multitasking rules which Windows applies to the DOS program is the Fast Pasting check box. This setting controls how Windows pastes information into the DOS window. If the check box is selected, then Windows pastes information into the DOS window just as fast as it does in any other program window. Most DOS programs can accept information at this rate, but some cannot. You should clear this check box if you try pasting something into your DOS program and it does not paste properly.

Using a Mouse Under DOS

Normally, the mouse works just about the same in a DOS window as it does in any other window. I say "just about" because there are a few subtle differences that can affect how you work. The first involves using the mouse for editing.

In a Windows program, you can generally use the mouse to do editing tasks. Primarily, you can use the mouse to select text for a subsequent action (such as cutting or copying to the Clipboard). By default, you cannot use the mouse to select text in a DOS window. Instead, you must use the Mark command from the DOS window toolbar. The reason for this is that most DOS programs do not recognize the use of the mouse for this purpose. However, if you find yourself copying a lot of information within a DOS window or between a DOS window and another program, you can instruct Windows 95 to allow the mouse to be used for selecting text. To do this, follow these steps:

1. Display the Properties sheet for the DOS program in which you want this mouse capability enabled.

2. Click the Misc tab. The dialog box will look similar to what you see in figure 19.10.

3. Select the QuickEdit check box.

From this dialog box you can also modify whether the mouse should work only in the DOS window or whether it can be used in other windows, as well. If you select the Exclusive Mode check box, then the mouse will be available only in this program window, and in no others. This seems like an odd attribute because using Windows 95 without the mouse is even harder than in previous versions of Windows.

When you finish configuring your mouse, click the OK button to close the dialog box.

Other Fine-Tuning **455**

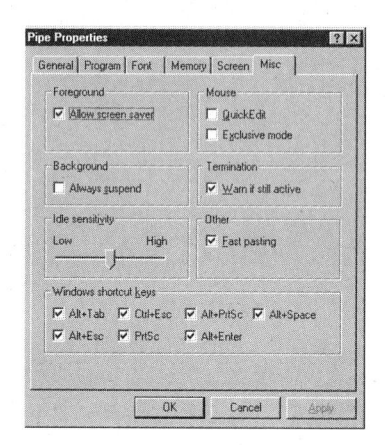

Fig. 19.10 Use the Misc tab to change the settings for how the mouse is used in a DOS window.

Shortcut Keys

Windows 95 uses a standard group of shortcut keys for system operations, which are used for moving between windows, controlling windows, and similar functions. These shortcut keys and their purposes are listed in Table 19.1.

Table 19.1   Windows 95 Shortcut Keys

Key	Purpose
Alt+Tab	Switch between Windows 95 tasks
Alt+Esc	Cycle through tasks in the order they were started
Ctrl+Esc	Display the Start menu
PrintScreen	Copy contents of the screen to the Clipboard (screen capture)
Alt+PrintScreen	Copy contents of the active window to the Clipboard
Alt+Enter	Switch between full screen and window operation
Alt+Spacebar	Display the window's System menu

While these shortcut keys work great in Windows programs, they can cause conflicts in some DOS programs. Normally, the purpose of the shortcut keys according to Windows takes precedence. However, you may want some of these keys to assume their designed purpose within the DOS program. To control how these keys work for your DOS program, follow these steps:

1. Display the Properties sheet for the DOS program in which you want to modify the shortcut keys.

2. Click the Misc tab. The dialog box will look similar to what you see in figure 19.11.

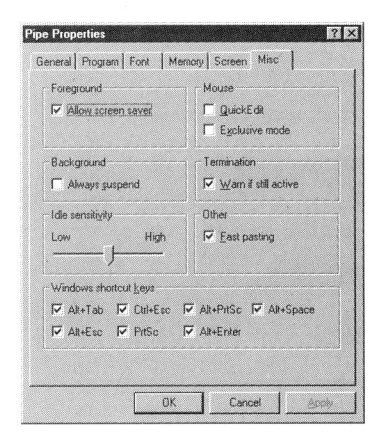

Fig. 19.11 You can use the Misc tab to modify how shortcut keys behave in a DOS window.

3. At the bottom of the screen is an area called Windows Shortcut Keys, which contains check boxes for seven keys. If a check box is selected, Windows rules take precedence; if it is cleared, then the DOS program's rules are in effect.

4. Change the settings for the shortcut keys as desired.

5. Click the OK button to close the dialog box.

Other Fine-Tuning **457**

MS-DOS Safety Tips

If you run MS-DOS programs under Windows 95, the relationship between the program and the operating system is strange and sometimes twisted. Granted, many of the quirks and work-arounds necessary in previous versions of Windows have been eliminated, but there are still some present. When you run MS-DOS programs, there are some pointers you will still want to keep in mind. The following sections address some potentially thorny issues.

The Registry

It is safe to say that DOS applications know nothing about the Windows 95 Registry. The Registry is so new that even "Windows aware" DOS programs have not had time to catch up. This may change in the future, but in the short term could cause a problem or two.

If you use a DOS program that was designed to work with a previous version of Windows, it may save some of its configuration information in the various INI files for which Windows 3.x was famous. Likewise, the program may count on finding some information in those files.

You should become familiar with how the DOS program interacts with Windows INI files. If DOS saves information in the INI files, you will not want to delete them, even though Windows 95 does not need them. To get around the problem of the program expecting to read information from the INI files, Windows 95 includes abbreviated WIN.INI and SYSTEM.INI files. These files contain only a limited amount of information, such as settings for the screen colors or the display resolution. If your program expects more information than this, chances are good that it will not work properly under Windows 95.

Disk Utilities

There are hundreds, if not thousands, of disk utilities that run under DOS. These do everything from defragmenting your disk to adding long file name capabilities. You should not run any such program under Windows 95. If you do, you run the risk of damaging the file system.

The biggest potential for corruption is with long file names. Windows 95 uses a new method of storing long file names, as described in Chapter 2, "Under-the-Hood Improvements." Your DOS program knows nothing about the changes necessary to implement the long file names. If you run the program, it may see the changes and assume that they are errors in the file structure. If the program "fixes" the perceived errors, then you will lose all your long file names.

Managing Your Printers

by Allen L. Wyatt and Bill Lawrence

Perhaps you are using Windows 95 in a single-user environment, where you are simply working with your computer in your home office. You have an inkjet printer, and you spend your day writing letters and preparing proposals. Or, perhaps you work in a large office, with your own printer and access to three other printers over a network. Either way, you need to be concerned with an important task—*managing your printers*.

Windows 95 makes it easy to manage printers. In fact, it is a much easier task than it used to be in previous versions of Windows. Now you can perform all your management chores from a single area, with only a few commands. This chapter will teach you the skills you need in order to manage your printers. Here you will learn the following:

➤ How to use the Printers folder

➤ How to add printers to Windows 95

- How to change printer properties
- How to remove a printer from Windows 95
- How to make your printer available over a network

Using the Printers Folder

Within Windows 95, all printer management occurs in the Printers folder. This folder is a special area that contains the printer drivers for your system. You can access the Printers folder by choosing Settings from the Start menu. This displays the Settings menu, from which you should choose the Printers option. You will then see the Printers folder window, similar to what is shown in figure 20.1.

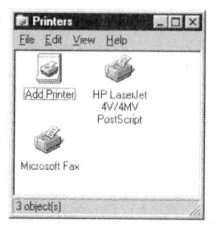

Fig. 20.1 The Printers folder is where you manage your printers.

Notice that the Printers folder contains icons. At a minimum, it will contain one icon—the one for Add Printer. The number and type of other icons it contains will depend on which printers you have installed for use with your system.

At the top of the Printers folder is a menu. Using the options in this menu, you can control how information within the folder appears. If you have used Windows for any length of time, many of these menus and their options should already be familiar:

- File. These options enable you to control a printer. You can delete or rename a printer, as well as change a printer's properties. This is the menu that is displayed as the context menu for a printer icon (when you right-click a printer icon).

➤ <u>E</u>dit. These options are basic editing options that apply to what you do within the Printers folder. The options deal with undoing an action, as well as cutting, copying, pasting, and selecting icons.

➤ <u>V</u>iew. The <u>V</u>iew options control how information is displayed within the Printers folder. You can change the size of icons, arrange them, turn the toolbar and status bar on and off, and access the properties for an icon.

➤ <u>H</u>elp. The <u>H</u>elp menu displays the various Help options for the folder.

Understanding Printer Drivers

Windows 95 actually prepares printer output using what is called a *printer driver.* Printer drivers contain the specifications and instructions necessary to communicate properly with a printer. These drivers essentially act as intermediaries between your applications, Windows 95, and the printer itself. They work to translate information from the format produced by the application into a format that the printer can understand.

Windows 95 provides direct, out-of-the-box support for over 700 different printers. For those printers that are not supported directly by Windows 95 (such as new printer models that have just entered the market), you can often get a printer driver from the printer manufacturer. Later in this chapter, you will learn how you can use such a disk when installing your printer.

Printer drivers are essential to the proper operation of Windows 95; without them, you could not use your printer with Windows at all. When you add or install a printer, you are actually adding or installing printer drivers. If you later delete a printer, you are deleting nothing but a printer driver. In the next several sections, you will learn how to perform these operations.

Adding a Printer

Adding a new printer in Windows 95 is quite easy. You accomplish this task by using the Add Printer Wizard, whose icon is located in the Printers folder. (In fact, on some systems it may be the only icon in the Printers folder.) To start the Add Printer Wizard, double-click the Add Printer icon.

> **Note:** The Printers folder is not the only place you can start the Add Printer Wizard; it is also indirectly available through the Control Panel. To do this, choose the Add New Hardware applet in the Control Panel, which starts the Add New Hardware Wizard. If you choose to add a printer from within this wizard, the Add Printer Wizard automatically starts.

After you start the Add Printer Wizard, you will see the dialog box shown in figure 20.2. If you were the person who installed Windows 95 on your system, this dialog box may look familiar. The Windows 95 Setup program uses the Add Printer Wizard so that you can specify a printer.

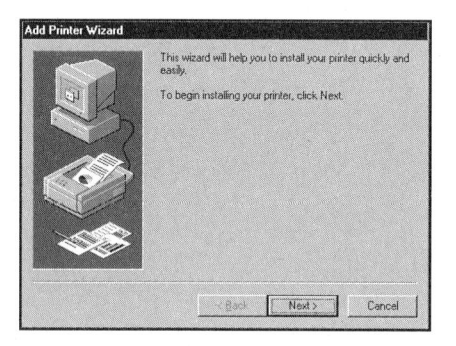

Fig. 20.2 You may already be familiar with the dialog boxes used in the Add Printer Wizard.

The first dialog box in the Add Printer Wizard is nothing more than a welcome screen. Read the information on the dialog box and click the

Next button. This displays the dialog box shown in figure 20.3, where you are asked to specify the type of printer you are adding.

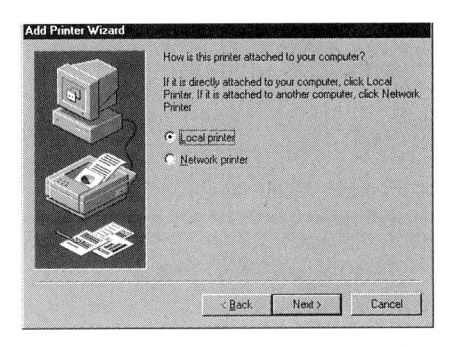

Fig. 20.3 If you're connected to a network, you can specify how your printer connection is made.

If your system is not connected to a network, or you do not have the networking capabilities installed on your system, then you will not see this dialog box. It is only shown if you are connected to a network. With Windows 95, you can print either to a local computer or to one you can access through a network. You should make your choice based on the type of printer you want to install:

➤ Choose Local Printer if the printer is physically connected to your computer via one of your parallel or serial ports, or if you will be printing to a disk file.

➤ Choose Network Printer if the printer is connected to a different computer that you can access through a network, or if the printer is connected directly to your network.

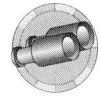

> **Note:** The rest of this section assumes you are adding a local printer. If you are connecting to a network printer, you should skip the rest of this section and refer to the following section.

Picking a Type of Printer

After you have indicated whether your printer is connected locally or through a network, you can click the Next button to proceed to the next step. Shortly you will see a dialog box (shown in figure 20.4) that lists the types of printers directly supported by Windows 95.

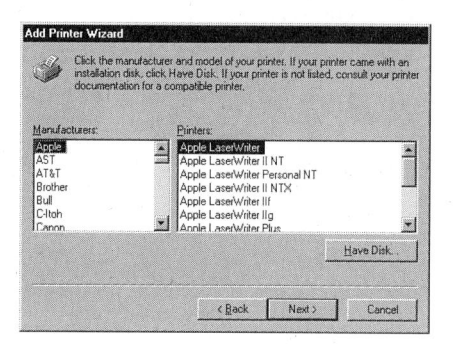

Fig. 20.4 Windows 95 directly supports a wide variety of printers.

In the Manufacturers list of this dialog box, select the manufacturer of your printer. In the Printers list, select the model of printer you want to install. Make sure that you select the manufacturer first, because the information in the Printers list of the dialog box changes whenever you pick a different manufacturer.

Windows 95 directly supports hundreds of different printers. It is possible, however, that you may have a new printer that just came on the market, or one that Windows 95 does not directly support. In this case, you should get a Windows 95 printer driver disk from the company that made your printer. With the disk, you can click the Have Disk button, which enables you to install a printer driver that Windows 95 does not have listed in the dialog box.

Go ahead and make your printer selection based on what is appropriate for your needs. For instance, if you are installing a Lexmark ValueWriter 600, you should choose IBM/Lexmark in the Manufacturers list, and Lexmark ValueWriter 600 in the Printers list.

Picking a Printer Port

Now that you have specified the type of printer you want to install, click the Next button. The Add Printer Wizard then displays the dialog box shown in figure 20.5.

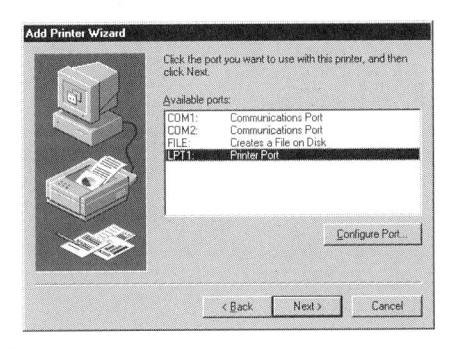

Fig. 20.5 You need to specify how your printer is connected to your system.

In this dialog box you are asked to specify how your printer is connected to your system. Although there are four possible connections listed in this example, your system may have other connections available. Typically, there will be connections for your serial ports (these begin with COM), connections for your parallel ports (these begin with LPT), and a choice for information to be sent to a disk file (FILE).

> **Caution:** Depending on how you have set up your system, you may also have the connections labeled FAX or PUB. These are visible if you have added the Microsoft Exchange portion of Windows 95. You should not choose either of these as your printer connection. Instead, let Microsoft Exchange manage these connections.

The choice you make at this dialog box depends on how your printer is connected to your system. If you are installing a printer that is physically connected to your computer, you should highlight the appropriate port name.

Using the Printers Folder **467**

Configuring Your Printer Port

In most instances, you will not need to configure your printer port. The Add Printer Wizard enables you to either check or change the configuration by clicking the Configure Port button. For instance, figure 20.6 shows the dialog box displayed when you have selected LPT1 as your port and you click the button.

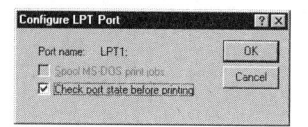

Fig. 20.6 There are not many configuration options available for a parallel port.

Here you can specify whether Windows 95 should use the spooler in managing this printer port when it is used from the MS-DOS window. With the Windows spooler, you can store information in a disk file until it is ready to be received by your printer. By storing information, you can "free up" the computer so that you can get back to using your applications quicker. (The spooler is covered in detail in Chapter 21, "Printing from Windows 95.") In most cases you will want to have the spooler active for DOS print jobs, so you should leave this option selected.

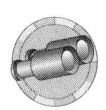

> **Note:** Remember that at this point in the Add Printer Wizard you are configuring the port, not the printer connection. If you make a change in a port's configuration, it is also changed for other printers using the same port. You should only make changes in the default port settings if you have a well-defined need to do so.

You can also specify whether Windows should check the status of the printer port before printing begins. With parallel ports, this is a good idea. For instance, if the printer is off-line, then by forcing Windows to check before printing, you are aware of this fact sooner (and can hopefully correct it).

If you instead are connecting your printer to a serial port, there are quite a few additional configuration options available. Figure 20.7 shows the dialog box displayed when you specify a serial port and click the Configure Port button.

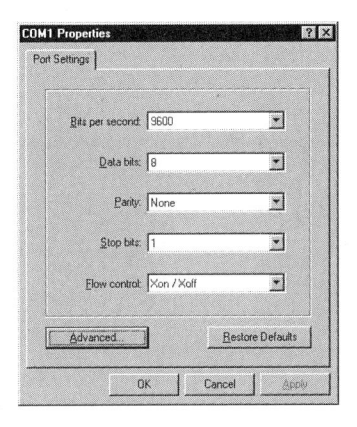

Fig. 20.7 When you connect to a serial port, you must specify how your printer expects communication to occur through the port.

The settings for configuring a serial port relate to how the communications channel should be maintained. In-depth information on serial ports is provided in Chapter 31, "Serial Communications Basics," but there are basically five settings you can control from this dialog box:

- **Bits per second.** This refers to how fast your printer can accept information. Most serial printers operate at 9600 bps, but you should check your printer manual to determine the data rate used by your printer model.

- **Data bits.** When information is sent over a serial connection, it is sent in packets. These packets contain a certain number of data bits, which convey the information to be printed. Normally, PC-based equipment uses eight data bits.

- **Parity.** Some serial connections use a parity bit to provide rudimentary error detection. Possible settings are Even (parity is based on whether there is an even number of data bits set to 1), Odd (opposite of Even), None (parity is not used), Mark (parity bit

Using the Printers Folder   **469**

is always set to 1), or Space (parity bit is always set to 0). The default is None, which is appropriate for most PC-based equipment.

- ➤ **Stop bits.** A communications packet also contains stop bits that mark the end of the packet. Some equipment uses 1.5 or 2 stop bits, but most use the default of 1.

- ➤ **Flow control.** This determines how the flow of information over the communications link is managed. The default of Xon/Xoff means that a software signal is used by the printer to indicate when it does not want to receive information, and another software signal to indicate when communication should resume. Hardware flow control means that dedicated wires in the serial cable are used for the same signals. Finally, if None is selected, then information is sent to the printer without pausing. You should check your printer manual to see which type of flow control the printer uses. (Xon/Xoff is the most universal, but Hardware is the most efficient.)

If you are using a serial printer, you should check with your printer manual to see which settings you should use. This is the easiest way, because the number of possible combinations of these five settings is quite high (2,925 possibilities, to be exact). If you do not have the information, then try the default settings (click Restore Defaults); these are the most common serial port settings.

If you click the Advanced button, you will see additional properties available for the serial port, as shown in figure 20.8. This dialog box only has meaning if your serial port uses an advanced UART chip that utilizes a FIFO (first in, first out) buffer. In most instances, you do not need to change these settings. More information on these settings is provided in Chapter 31, "Serial Communications Basics."

When you finish configuring your printer port, you can click the OK button to return to the Add Printer Wizard.

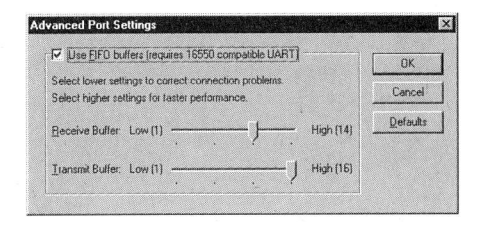

Fig. 20.8 The advanced serial properties control the features of the serial chip used for the port.

Finishing the Installation

When you finish specifying how the printer is connected to your system, click the Next button. The Add Printer Wizard asks you to provide a name for this printer (as shown in figure 20.9). This name can be anything you want, up to 31 characters in length.

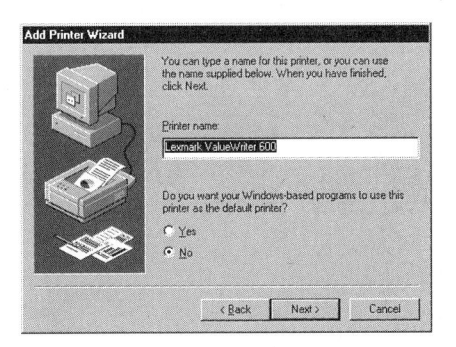

Fig. 20.9 You can specify any name you want for the printer you are adding.

After you have provided a name for your printer, click the Next button. This displays the final dialog box for the Add Printer Wizard, as shown in figure 20.10.

Using the Printers Folder **471**

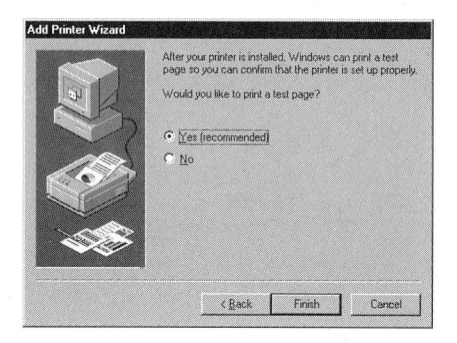

Fig. 20.10 Indicating whether Windows 95 should print a test page is the final step in adding a printer.

In this dialog box, you can indicate whether or not you want Windows to print a test page. If the printer you are installing is connected to a port on your system, you will probably want to click Yes. On the other hand, if your printer output is directed to a file, you will want to select No.

After you click the Finish button, the necessary printer driver is added to Windows 95. You may be asked at this point to supply the Windows 95 program diskettes or CD-ROM. When the driver installation is complete, the test page is generated, if you chose to print one.

When you have completed your printer installation, an icon appears in the Printers folder for your new printer. You can then use the icon to manage the printer, as described later in this chapter.

Adding a Network Printer

Earlier in this chapter, you learned how you can start to add a printer, using the Add Printer Wizard. The second step in the wizard enables you to indicate whether the printer is connected to your computer, or whether you will be accessing it through the network. If you selected the Network printer option, and clicked the Next button, you are ready to continue adding your printer. At this point, you will see the dialog box shown in figure 20.11.

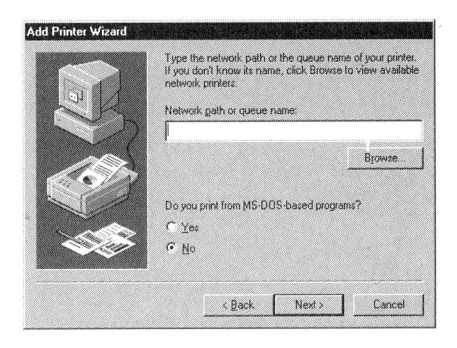

Fig. 20.11 If you are printing through a network, you need to indicate where the printer is located.

In this dialog box you should provide the name of the printer you will be using on the network. This network path is referred to as a *fully qualified network name*. It starts with two backslashes, and describes the route to follow to the printer. For instance, the following is a proper network path name for a printer:

    \\Allen's Pentium\HPLJ_Net

If you do not know the exact path, you can click the B<u>r</u>owse button, and choose the printer as you would choose a file in the Explorer.

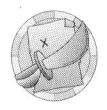

> **Tip:** If you are still unsure about which printer you should use, check with your network administrator for help.

At the bottom of the dialog box is a place to indicate whether you want to print to this particular network printer from your DOS programs. Normally, DOS programs can only print to local printers—those connected to an LPT or COM port. If you do not use DOS programs, then you can accept the default of <u>N</u>o. If you do use DOS programs, then you will want to change the setting to <u>Y</u>es. This causes Windows 95 to map the network printer to a local port. If you fail to do this, you will not be able to access the network printer from within an MS-DOS window.

Using the Printers Folder **473**

When you finish providing a path for the printer, click the Next button. The wizard then checks to make sure that the printer you have specified can be selected. What happens next depends on whether the wizard can access the printer:

- If the wizard can access the printer, the wizard attempts to determine information about the printer, which it then uses in the setup steps that follow.

- If the wizard cannot access the printer right away, you are asked if you want to continue. Assuming you do, you are asked to specify the manufacturer and type of printer you are installing.

At this point, the installation procedure continues in a manner very similar to what you have already learned about local printers. When you finish installing the printer, it appears as an icon in your Printers folder. The only difference is that the icon has a network symbol over it, indicating that the printer is not attached to your local computer.

Understanding Printer Compatibility

If you do not have a printer driver available from your printer's manufacturer, and your printer is not directly supported by Windows 95, you may be able to select a different printer driver which is, in fact, compatible with your printer. For instance, many PostScript printers can use the generic PostScript printer driver provided with Windows 95. Likewise, many inkjet or dot-matrix printers provide compatibility with Epson printers.

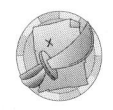

> **Tip:** Your printer manufacturer, if it cannot provide a printer driver, should be able to direct you as to which compatible printer driver you can use.

Determining printer compatibility is a major source of frustration for many Windows users. For every printer recognized as a standard, you can have even more emulations from which to choose, complicating the process of configuring and using printers. Novice and experienced users alike will eventually need help to properly install, configure, and troubleshoot a printer driver.

Hewlett-Packard LaserJet and compatible printers normally include Courier and Line Printer typefaces in portrait and landscape orientations. Printers emulating the LaserJet, however, may have not only those customary fonts and sizes, but also a selection of proportional typefaces and additional Courier and Line Printer type sizes.

Some printers even have additional fixed-pitch fonts (such as Prestige Elite and Letter Gothic) not found in standard LaserJet printers. And other laser printers may even emulate dot-matrix printers such as those from Epson or the IBM ProPrinter.

For dot-matrix printers, Epson's FX-86 printer or IBM's ProPrinter are the most common standards emulated by other printers. However, many dot-matrix printers can emulate more than one printer and offer enhanced features above and beyond the level offered by the printer being emulated.

When choosing a printer driver, if the Add Printer Wizard does not specifically list your printer, observe the following guidelines:

➤ If your laser printer is compatible with Hewlett-Packard's Printer Control Language (PCL) codes, choose the HP LaserJet+ driver.

➤ If your PostScript laser printer is compatible with the Apple LaserWriter (35-font PostScript Page Description Language or similar emulation built-in), choose the Apple LaserWriter or the Apple LaserWriter II driver.

➤ If your 9-pin dot-matrix printer is IBM-compatible, try using the IBM/Lexmark ProPrinter or Epson FX-80 drivers.

➤ If your 24-pin dot-matrix printer is IBM-compatible, try using the IBM/Lexmark ProPrinter X24 or the Epson LQ-1500 drivers.

➤ You can define your printer in Windows by using the Generic/Text Only driver or the Unlisted Printer driver. Using these drivers provides plain text printing when you do not have a basic driver available to you for your printer. You can also use these generic drivers in Windows applications for draft printing so that you can quickly print a hard copy of your document or file.

When you are installing a printer driver, and if you are choosing a compatible printer, you may want to specify a printer name that lets you know you chose a compatible driver rather than a native one.

Understanding Printer Icons

After you add printer drivers to Windows 95, they appear as icons in the Printers folder. The appearance of these icons is a big clue to the connection used by the printer. Some of the icons may look familiar, but others may not. There are basically five ways an icon can look in the Printers folder:

- A local printer, connected to either a parallel (LPT) or serial (COM) port.

- A local printer, with output directed to a disk file (FILE).

- A local printer, connected to either a parallel (LPT) or serial (COM) port, that has been shared over the network.

- A printer that is accessed through the network, and is available.

- A printer that is accessed through the network, and is unavailable.

Setting Up Your Printer

After you have installed the printer driver for your printer, you may need to set the parameters by which the printer will operate. Typically, you will only need to set most parameters once, and then Windows will remember them from there on. Other parameters, however, may need to be set based on the type of information you will be printing in the next job.

To set printer properties, open the Printers folder and right-click the printer icon. This displays the context menu for the printer. From this list you can select the P̲roperties option, after which the Properties sheet for the printer will be displayed. Exactly what is included in the dialog box depends on the printer. For instance, figure 20.12 shows an example of how the Properties sheet looks for an HP LaserJet 4V/4MV PostScript printer.

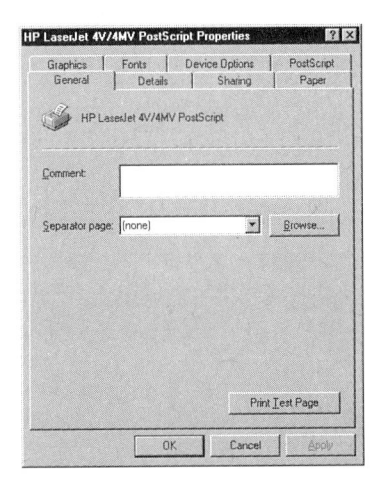

Fig. 20.12 The Properties sheet enables you to set configuration properties for a printer.

This Properties sheet may look rather complex (there are seven tabs for this printer), but remember that the properties displayed for your printer will probably vary. Figure 20.13 shows an example of the same dialog box, but for an IBM ProPrinter XL II.

In general, there are only a limited number of tabs that appear in printer Properties sheets. These tabs represent the general classifications of properties you can control. While the information on each tab may vary, the tabs themselves are fairly constant. (The tabs available may vary, based on your network environment, however.) The following sections cover some of the more common Properties tabs and what you use them for.

Setting Up Your Printer **477**

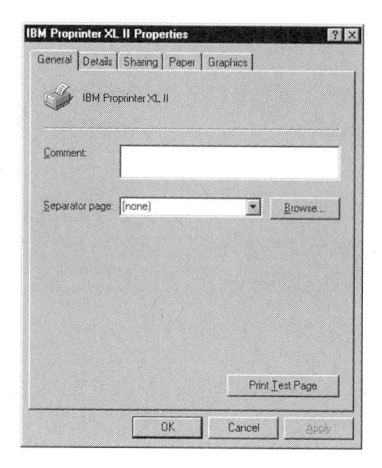

Fig. 20.13 The tabs displayed in the Properties sheet differ widely for different printers.

The General Tab

The General tab is visible when you first open the Properties sheet (as shown in figure 20.13). You use this tab to specify general printer information. For instance, you can indicate comments about your printer in the Comment field. These comments serve two purposes. First, they act as a memory jogger for you about the purpose or setup of a printer driver. Second, the printer comments are transferred over a network to a remote computer if the following conditions are met:

➤ The printer has been shared on the network.

➤ The remote user has set up the printer by using the Point and Print feature. (Point and Print is covered in Chapter 21, "Printing from Windows 95.")

This behavior is ideal, then, for supplying printer comments such as the rules under which the printer is available and who the remote user should contact for more information about the printer.

The other primary purpose of the General tab is to indicate whether you want to use a separator page. Separator pages are printed out at the start of each print job, and are used in busy environments to differentiate between jobs from different users. You can only specify this option for local printers attached to your computer. There are four options you can specify for this setting:

- **None.** No separator page is printed.
- **Simple.** A short and sweet separator page that consists of information such as the user's name, the date and time, and the application used to create the print job.
- **Full.** Same as the Simple selection, except more detail about the print job is provided. In addition, some graphic elements are added to the page.
- **Custom.** You can choose a custom separator page by clicking the Browse button and selecting a Windows metafile (.WMF extension) that contains the separator page information.

Clicking the Print Test Page button causes Windows 95 to print a test page to the printer. This test page is the same one you had the opportunity to print when you first installed the printer.

The Details Tab

The Details tab is the nuts and bolts of the printer definition. When you click this tab, the printer Properties sheet appears as shown in figure 20.14. This information in this tab consists of the specifications you made when you first installed the printer driver.

At the top of the dialog box, in the Print to the Following Port field, you can specify how this printer is connected to your system. Earlier in this chapter you learned about the various ports that you can specify for a printer; if you make a change here, you can easily modify the place where printer information is sent.

Setting Up Your Printer **479**

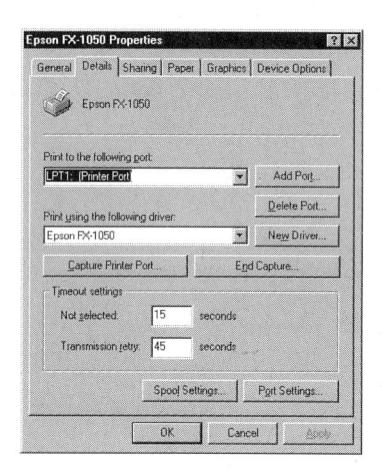

Fig. 20.14 The Details tab is the nuts and bolts of the printer definition.

Adding Ports

On most systems, the ports defined for the computer are fairly stable. Periodically you may add a new printer card or upgrade your serial ports. In such an instance, Windows 95 recognizes the change and modifies your system automatically. However, you may need to physically create a port, such as when you are printing over a network to a remote printer. For instance, suppose that you are working in a networked office environment, and you have been printing to a printer connected to your local printer port (LPT1). If this printer is taken from you and instead connected to a coworker's system down the hall, you need to change the printer port for your printer. To do this, you would click the Add Port button and then you would see the dialog box shown in figure 20.15.

Here, you simply need to click the Browse button and locate the remote printer. Alternatively, you could simply provide the path to the network printer in the field. When you click the OK button, the port is added to the list of available ports on your system.

Chapter 20: Managing Your Printers

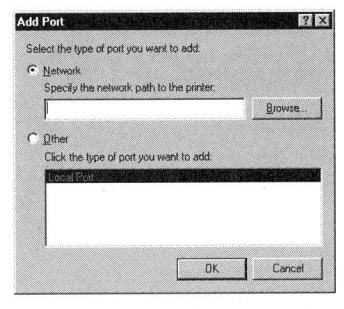

Fig. 20.15 Define a network port with the Add Port dialog box.

Picking a Printer Driver

The Details tab also enables you to indicate which printer driver is used for your printer. (The printer driver was specified when you first installed the printer and indicated a printer make and model.) You can either select from a driver already installed on your system, or click the New Driver button to select a printer make and model.

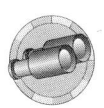

> **Note:** If you pick a different printer driver, the properties for the printer will change to reflect the characteristics of the new printer driver.

Mapping Ports

In the center of the Details tab are two buttons: Capture Printer Port and End Capture. These buttons control the mapping of individual ports to specific network printers. For instance, you can use the Capture Printer Port to capture information destined for LPT1 and redirect it to a remote network printer. When you click the button, you will see the dialog box shown in figure 20.16.

Select the parallel port you want to redirect, and then choose a network path at which the remote printer is located. You can redirect up to nine parallel ports (LPT1 through LPT9). If you do not click the Reconnect at logon check box, then the mapping you are creating is maintained only for your current computer session.

Setting Up Your Printer **481**

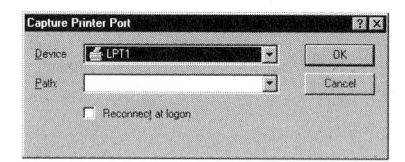

Fig. 20.16 You can redirect up to nine parallel ports in Windows 95.

For much of the software you use under Windows, you will never need to worry about capturing printer ports. Where this comes into play is with DOS programs that do not recognize network ports, but only recognize local ports such as LPT1 or LPT2. In this instance, you will need to redirect the printer information.

If you later want to disassociate a port with a network printer, you would click the Release Printer Port button and select the parallel port you want to disconnect.

Timeout Settings

If you are working with a local printer, you may want to modify the timeout settings at the bottom of the Details tab. There are two settings that indicate, in seconds, how long Windows should wait before it informs you something is wrong. The Not Selected timeout value is used when Windows detects that a printer is off-line. The default value is 45 seconds, which means that Windows will wait 45 seconds before letting you know that the printer is off-line. It is good to have some sort of time lag in here; otherwise Windows gives you no time at all to check and switch the printer status.

The second setting, Transmission Retry, is used to indicate how long Windows should wait before assuming that there is something wrong with the printer. The default, 260 seconds, means that Windows will wait 4 minutes and 20 seconds before determining that the printer is not working. If you know you have a fast printer, then you may want to set this value lower. However, if you get timeout errors periodically because your printer is taking too long to chunk away at a complex file, then you may want to increase the value in this field.

Spool Settings

If you click the Spool Settings button at the bottom of the Details tab, you can modify how this printer functions in relation to the Windows spooler. Detailed information about controlling the spooler is provided in Chapter 21, "Printing from Windows 95."

Port Settings

If you click the Port Settings button at the bottom of the Details tab, you can modify the configuration of your system ports. These are the same settings discussed earlier in the chapter, in the section entitled "Configuring Your Printer Port."

The Device Options Tab

Device options are those features of a printer that make it unique. This tab, more than any other, is intimately tied to the capabilities of the printer. Because of this, the contents of the tab can vary greatly from printer to printer. For instance, figure 20.17 shows an example of this tab for an HP LaserJet 4V/4MV PostScript printer.

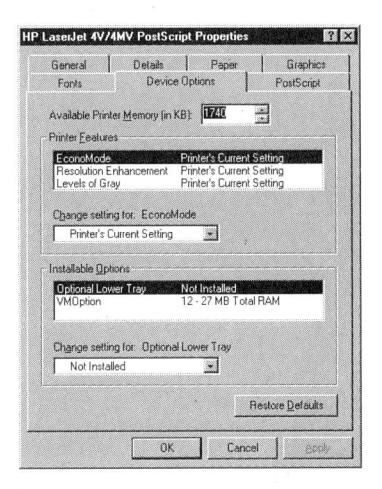

Fig. 20.17 The Device Options tab can vary greatly from printer to printer.

Setting Up Your Printer **483**

In this particular example, the Device Options tab enables you to indicate the amount of memory in the printer, how EconoMode, Resolution Enhancement, and Levels of Gray are implemented, and what options are installed in the printer. On a different printer, the information available will be different.

The best bet when working with the Device Options tab is to change the settings in it after you understand what your printer can really do. You should review your printer manual and make the changes based on how you want to take advantage of specific features and options.

The Fonts Tab

The purpose of the Fonts tab is to specify how you want TrueType fonts handled by the printer driver. The appearance of the tab will vary, depending on whether the printer is a graphics printer (such as a dot-matrix), a PCL printer (such as an HP), or a PostScript printer. Figure 20.18 shows how this tab appears for a Lexmark ValueWriter 600.

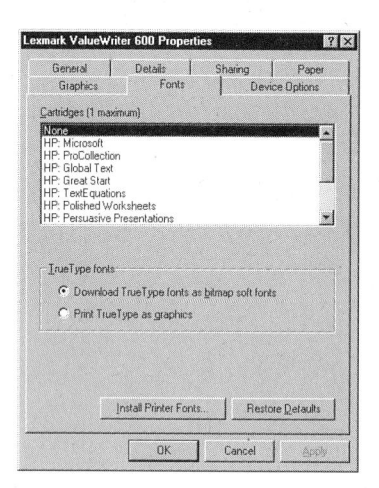

Fig. 20.18 The Fonts tab can differ based on the capabilities of your printer.

At the top of this dialog box you can indicate any font cartridges you have installed in your computer, in the middle you can specify how you want TrueType fonts handled by Windows, and at the bottom is a button that enables you to install printer fonts. Details on how to use the various settings in this tab are covered in Chapter 22, "Working with Fonts."

The Graphics Tab

If your printer is capable of generating graphics, the Graphics tab enables you to specify the quality of the graphics created. Because different printers differ in their graphics capabilities, the appearance of this tab also differs. For instance, figure 20.19 shows how this tab appears for an Epson FX-1050 printer.

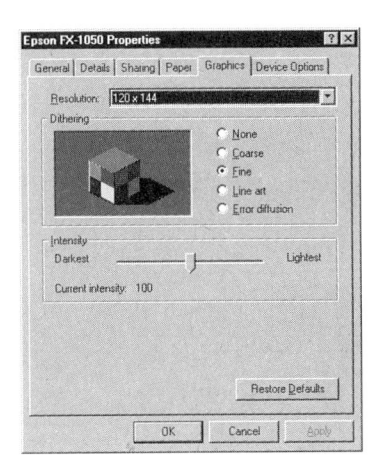

Fig. 20.19 Use the Graphics tab to control how graphics images are printed.

Notice that the graphics resolution indicated at the top of the tab is not real huge; this is a simple dot-matrix printer. In general, the tab enables you to indicate the resolution, dithering (color blending or shading), and the shade intensity for the printer. On PostScript printers, additional high-power settings such as lines per inch and half-tones

Setting Up Your Printer **485**

are also provided. Graphics under Windows 95 is covered in detail in Chapter 23, "Handling Graphics."

The Paper Tab

You use the Paper tab to indicate the type and characteristics of paper used by the printer. For instance, figure 20.20 shows an example of the Paper tab for an HP LaserJet III Si, which is a high-powered network laser printer.

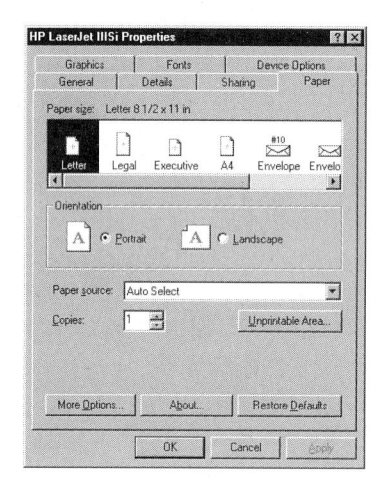

Fig. 20.20 Use the Paper tab to specify the type of paper used by a printer.

The appearance of this tab will vary widely, based on the printer you are using. For instance, some printers can handle 11×17 paper, while others can only handle letter size. Also, notice in figure 20.20 that there is a More Options button at the bottom of the dialog box. With this button, you can specify how options such as duplexing (two-sided printing) should be handled. Because these sorts of options are not available on all printers, they are likewise not available on the Paper tab on some printers.

Chapter 20: Managing Your Printers

Most of the settings on the Paper tab are handled automatically by your application software. For instance, if you are using Microsoft Word, it can automatically switch between landscape and portrait printing modes. Thus, there are only a few items that you might manually change on this tab.

One option you might want to change is displayed when you click the Unprintable Area button, as shown in figure 20.21.

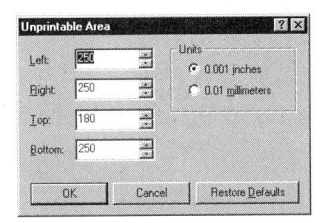

Fig. 20.21 Windows 95 printer drivers enable you to specify the unprintable margins for a piece of paper.

Most printers have an area around the outside of the paper where it is physically impossible for the printer to print. For instance, laser printers typically cannot print within 1/4-inch of the edge of the paper because this is where the printer's paper-handling mechanism grabs and transports the paper. For common printers, Windows 95 already knows what the unprintable area is, but you may need to modify the settings just a bit to get a better quality image. (This will take some trial and error on your part.)

The PostScript Tab

This tab appears only if the printer uses the PostScript language. When you select the tab, you will see the dialog box shown in figure 20.22.

The information on the PostScript tab is used to indicate how PostScript is to be generated for the particular printer, as well as how PostScript errors should be handled. There are several sections to this tab, as described in the following sections.

Setting Up Your Printer **487**

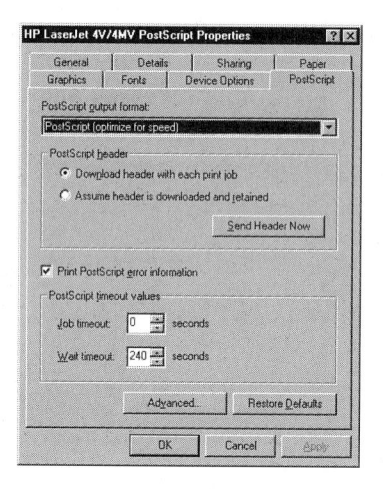

Fig. 20.22 The PostScript tab appears only for printers using the language.

PostScript Output Format

At the top of the tab you can indicate what output format should be used by the printer driver. There are four common formats you can specify in the PostScript Output Format field:

➤ **PostScript (Optimize for Speed).** This is the default setting, which is most appropriate for printing a document directly on a printer.

➤ **PostScript (Optimize for PortabilityADSC).** This option is intended for when you are printing to an output file instead of a printer. It utilizes the Adobe Document Structuring Conventions (ADSC), which means that the document is portable from one PostScript device to another. Each page in the output file is a self-contained object that can be processed independent of all others.

➤ **Encapsulated PostScript (EPS).** This option is intended for use when printing to a file, as well. The output file is in a format suitable for inclusion in other PostScript files; it is essentially a picture that you can use in other documents.

488 Chapter 20: Managing Your Printers

➤ **Archive Format.** This PostScript format is perhaps the most generic available. It utilizes none of the options of the local output device, so you can use it on differing PostScript equipment quite easily.

PostScript Header

Every PostScript job you print includes a header that has information about the page being printed. The header also includes information about the parameters of the job, the application that created the job, and the fonts being used. In most instances, you only need to download the header at the beginning of a print job; this is the safest way to print a PostScript document, because the information needed for the print job is included with the job.

Even though the default specifies that the header is downloaded for each job, you can indicate that you do not want it downloaded. For instance, you may have an application that sent specialized header commands with a previous print job, and you know they are still retained in the printer. In such a case, you can get faster printer performance by turning off header downloading.

There is also a button in this section of the tab (Send Header Now) that you can use to download the generic header information. It is a good idea to do this at the beginning of a series of similar print jobs, unless you are sure that the header was previously downloaded.

> **Tip:** If you are printing to a networked PostScript printer, you should download the header with each print job. Other people may print jobs in between your jobs, and that can play havoc with the secondary jobs. Downloading the header with the print job overcomes this potential problem.

Setting Up Your Printer **489**

PostScript Errors

PostScript is a page definition language that only works in full page increments. If you are printing a page, and an error occurs within the middle of the page (for instance, a command is used that your printer does not understand), the normal recourse is for the printer to flush the buffer and discard the page. In such a case, you will not see anything print out. To overcome this, some PostScript printers have the capability to print out the error messages when they occur. Windows 95 also includes such a capability, even if your printer does not.

By default, printer drivers will print error information. If you want, you can turn off the capability by clearing the check box entitled Print PostScript Error Information.

Just below this check box is an area where you can indicate timeout values. The Job Timeout value indicates how long the printer should wait for a print job to be completed before it assumes something is wrong and flushes the job. It is typically best to set this value to 0, which means the printer will wait indefinitely for a job (however long it takes).

The second timeout value is the Wait Timeout. This value specifies how long the printer should wait between pieces of a print job. For instance, if a part of the print job is sent, and then your computer pauses because it is busy doing something else, the idle time is what this timeout value measures. If you are printing complex print jobs, you should set the value fairly high. It is not a good idea, however, to set the Wait Timeout to 0. If you do, the printer will wait forever on a job, even if you have interrupted it (such as by unplugging the printer cable or turning off your computer).

> **Tip:** You should always set the PostScript timeout values lower than the timeout values specified in the Device Options tab.

490 Chapter 20: Managing Your Printers

Advanced Settings

You can access Advanced PostScript settings by clicking the Advanced button at the bottom of the PostScript tab. Doing so displays the Advanced PostScript Options dialog box, as shown in figure 20.23.

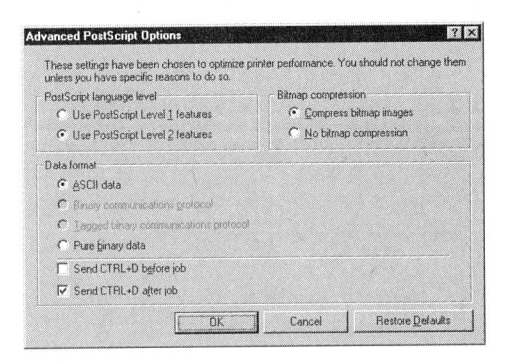

Fig. 20.23 The Advanced PostScript Options dialog box enables you to control low-level PostScript formatting.

In most instances, you should never have to change these options. They are set up for optimal use of your printer when you install the printer driver. When would you need to change them? A good time would be if you upgrade the firmware in your printer. For instance, you may have a printer that Windows 95 believes only understands PostScript Level 1. If you later upgrade your printer to PostScript Level 2, then you should change the language level in the Advanced PostScript Options dialog box. (Doing so will provide better compatibility and greater throughput.)

You may also want to change information when you have a need to create a peculiar PostScript file format. For instance, at the bottom of the dialog box you can indicate when the Ctrl+D character should be sent by the driver. This is the character that signals the end of a printer job, and most often in the PC environment it is sent at the end of the PostScript file. In the UNIX environment, however, the Ctrl+D is expected at the *beginning* of a job. Thus, if you are creating a file that will be used in such an environment, you will need to make the change here.

Setting Up Your Printer **491**

The Sharing Tab

If you are changing the properties of a local printer and you can share printers over your network, the Sharing tab is available. The tab appears as shown in figure 20.24.

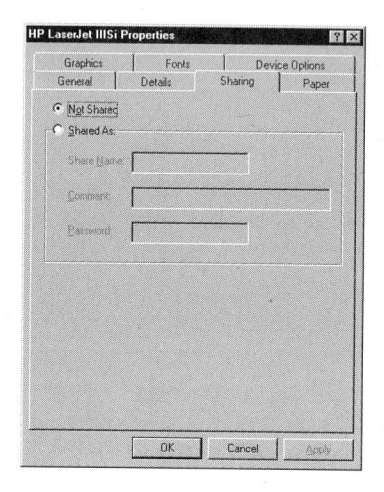

Fig. 20.24 Use the Sharing tab to set up rules for how you want your local printer shared over the network.

There are two primary options on this tab: You can specify that the printer is Not Shared (the default), or choose Shared As, which enables you to specify other sharing options. For instance, you can provide a name for your printer (such as Allen's Printer). This is the name that others will see when they are browsing the network. You can also specify a comment for the printer, which other people also see when browsing through the network. Finally, you can indicate a password that is needed to access the printer over the network.

Information about using a printer over the network is covered later in this chapter.

Deleting a Printer

From time to time you may have a need to delete a printer you previously installed. With Windows 95, deleting a printer is quite simple. All you need to do is follow these steps:

1. Open the Printers folder.
2. Select the icon for the printer you want to delete.
3. Press the Delete key, or choose File, Delete.

At this point, Windows asks you if you really want to delete the printer. If you choose Yes, you are asked another question, as shown in figure 20.25. Although the printer's availability is removed, Windows 95 can still keep the printer driver and related files on your hard disk. Click Yes to remove the driver and related files or No to keep them. Even though you may keep the files, you cannot print to that printer until you reinstall it.

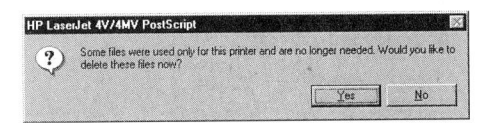

Fig. 20.25 Before actually deleting a printer, Windows asks you whether you want the driver file deleted.

Click Yes, and the files used for the printer driver are removed from your system.

> **Caution:** After you delete a printer, it is deleted for good. The only way to access the printer again is to reinstall it using the Add Printer Wizard, as described earlier in this chapter.

Special Network Considerations

If you have connected to a printer over a network, there are some extra steps and considerations that you may have. Before jumping into these, however, it should be pointed out that printing over a network is no different (from a program's perspective) than printing to a local printer.

The differences that come into play are because network printers are shared resources. This means that there may be a set of rules that govern the use of the resource. For instance, whoever is responsible for the printer may have placed usage restrictions on it. This means that the printer may only be available between certain hours of the day, or that you may need a password to access the printer. If you want a copy of the rules defined for a certain printer, you will need to get them from the person responsible for it.

> **Note:** The types of restrictions that can be placed on a printer depend entirely on the capabilities of the network operating system being used.

This brings us to another topic—what if *you* are the person responsible for a shared printer? How can you share your local printer, and how do you set up rules?

Sharing a Printer

The first step in making your printers available over the network is to make sure that you have installed your printer driver correctly. After installing, you should print a few documents to make sure that everything is working well on the printer.

When you are satisfied with the performance of your printer, you are ready to share it with others. You do this by first opening the Printers folder, and then right-clicking the icon for the printer you want to share. From the context menu, select the Sharing option. This displays the Sharing tab on the Properties sheet for the printer, as shown in figure 20.26.

> **Note:** If there is not a Sharing option on the context menu, or if there is no Sharing tab in the Properties sheet for your printer, then you cannot share printers. Either networking has not been enabled on your computer, or you have not chosen to be able to share printers over the network. For more information, refer to Chapter 37, "Using Windows 95 on a Network."

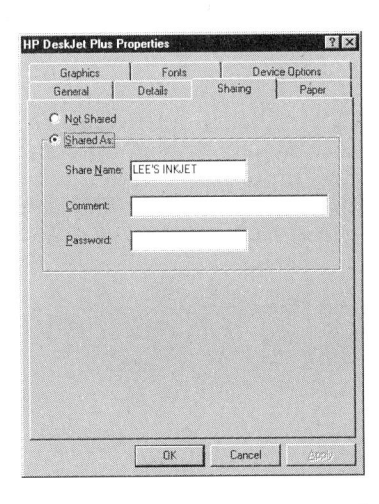

Fig. 20.26 Sharing a printer over the network is an easy task.

At this point, you only need to accomplish two steps. First, click the Shared As radio button. This enables the options in the middle of the dialog box. You can now provide a name, in the Shared Name field, that you want your printer known as on the network. When you finish, click the OK button. Your printer is now available on the network.

Special Network Considerations   **495**

Network Printer Properties

After you have made your printer available to others on the network, you have complete control over who can access the printer. With Windows 95, you can specify a password that users must know before they can connect to your printer.

Access restriction is controlled from the Shared tab on the Properties sheet for the printer. Display this by right-clicking the printer icon, and then choosing S_h_aring from the context menu. Shortly, you will see the dialog box, similar to what is shown in figure 20.27.

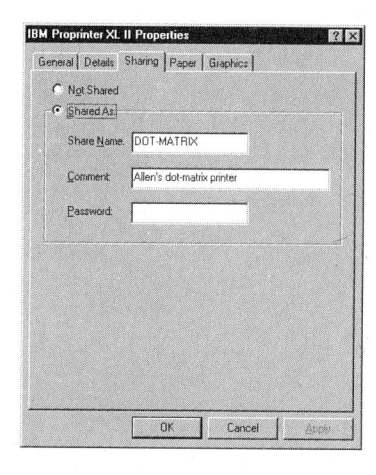

Fig. 20.27 Sharing a printer over the network is an easy task.

Notice that this printer has previously been shared on the network, but there is no password in the Password field. If you enter a password here, then users attempting to connect to the printer will be prompted for a password. If they do not know it, they cannot print to the printer.

Tuning Printing Performance with Shared Printers

When you send a print job to a shared printer, the print job makes a few stops before finally arriving at the printer. By default, the print job first goes to the print spooler on your Windows 95 workstation. The print spooler quickly captures your print job as a file on your hard disk so that your wait time is minimized while the job is printing. Next, the job travels over your network cable system to the print spooler on the workstation where the printer is attached. If you are printing to a dedicated server, this spooler is often called a *print queue*. In the print spooler or queue, the print job is again captured as a file. When the printer is available to print your job, the print job file in the spooler or queue is sent to the printer.

When to Bypass the Local Print Spooler

Windows 95 enables you to control these steps to customize printing performance. Open your printer Properties sheet and click the Details tab. Click the Spool Settings button to display the Spool Settings dialog box. If you want to bypass the local print spooler on your PC and print directly to the print spooler or queue on the PC or server connected to the shared printer, choose the Print Directly to the Printer option. This is a wise choice under two circumstances. When your network is fast and the print queue or spooler for the device connected to your shared printer is also fast and introduces minimal delays, printing directly to the printer will not noticeably slow down the time it takes for your print jobs to finish at your workstation and will result in jobs reaching the shared printer more quickly. The Print Directly to the Printer option also makes sense if most of the programs that you use to print have their own internal background printing feature (this is the case with most Windows-compatible word processors and spreadsheets).

Special Network Considerations **497**

When to Use the Local Print Spooler

If you need your print jobs to finish more quickly at your workstation and are less concerned about how quickly they reach the network shared printer, choose the Spool Print Jobs So Program Finishes Printing Faster setting. When you choose this setting, print jobs go first into the local spooler on your PC before going to the network printer. You can choose two options to customize the behavior of your local spooler. Select Start Printing After Last Page Is Spooled to specify that your spooler will wait until the print job is complete before releasing it to the network printer. Choose Start Printing After First Page Is Spooled to specify that the print job will be released to the network printer as soon as the first page is received. The former option is the safest—some types of graphical jobs may not print correctly if you do not choose this option.

Network Responsibilities

Sharing your printer on the network involves a bit more work than if you are the only one using the printer. If you have shared your printer, then you need to expect that others may use it from time to time. You should expect the following:

- **Delays.** There may be times when you cannot print for a while because someone else's print job is coming through your printer.

- **Interruptions.** If the printer is located in your office, then you will need to put up with people stopping by to pick up their print jobs.

- **Frustration.** There aren't many frustrations associated with having a printer all to yourself. You should expect that you will become frustrated periodically when someone leaves draft copies of documents laying around the printer, or a print job goes unclaimed for a few days. You will need to resist the urge to snap at other people because they do not treat your printer the same way you do.

➤ **Service needs.** Because there will be more print jobs going through your printer, it will need to be serviced more often. This includes adding paper and changing ribbons, toner, or ink more frequently.

Despite these points, you may still need to share your printer. Simple math lets you know that it is cheaper to share a printer (particularly an expensive or exotic printer) than it is to put that printer on all your co-workers' desks.

Printing from Windows 95

by Allen L. Wyatt

In the previous chapter you learned how you can set up printers in Windows 95. Setting up printers is only half the story, however. After setup, you must also learn how to use your printers (within Windows 95) on a daily basis. This chapter provides information you need in order to put your printers to work. Here you will learn the following:

- ➤ How the print spooler works to increase your productivity
- ➤ How you can create a print job in Windows 95
- ➤ How you can manage your print jobs after you create them
- ➤ The basics of printing to a network
- ➤ What the Point and Print feature of Windows 95 means to network users
- ➤ How improvements in Windows 95 benefit your DOS applications.

Using the Print Spooler

If you are familiar with older versions of Windows, you are already familiar with a print spooler—the Print Manager. In Windows 95, the printing process has been completely revamped and rewritten by using 32-bit code. This allows true behind-the-scenes print spooling, improved overall printing performance, and more intelligent management of print jobs.

From a user's perspective, there are many different components in the Windows 95 printing system besides a simple spooler. These components are illustrated in figure 21.1.

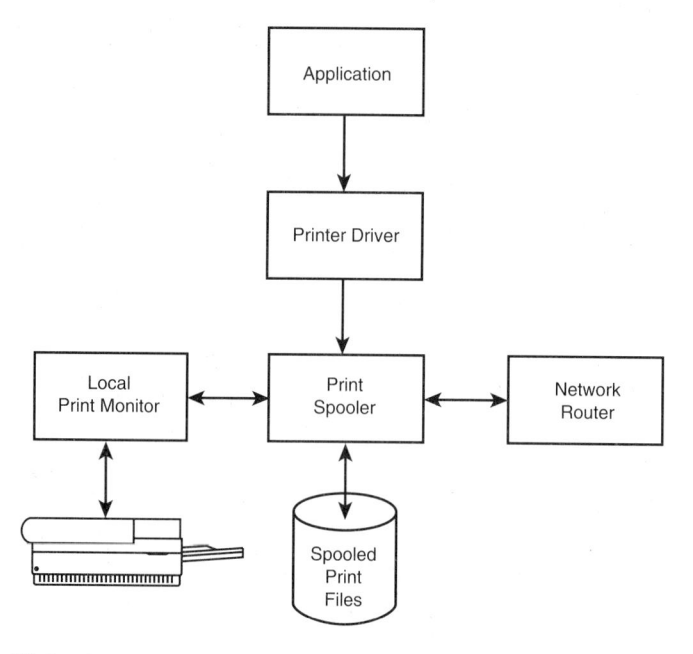

Fig. 21.1 The Windows 95 printing system consists of several major components besides a print spooler.

In effect, when you print from an application, the printer driver creates a print job (which you learned about in the last chapter). The printer driver then hands this print job to the print processor, which in turn works with the print request router to determine where the print job

502 Chapter 21: Printing from Windows 95

should be routed. If the print job is to be handled on a local printer, then it is routed to the local print spooler. If the print job is destined for a printer available through the network, then it is routed across the network to the appropriate destination where it is processed.

How the Print Spooler Works

Windows 95 uses a fully integrated 32-bit print spooler. The purpose of this spooler is to queue up print jobs destined for a particular printer. You are well aware that with the speed of today's computer systems, the printer is often much slower than the computer. The spooler acts as an intelligent buffer between your computer and a printer. In effect, when you print, you are printing to the spooler, not to the printer. The spooler can accept information as quickly as your software can send it. The information is then stored in print jobs and doled out to the printer as fast as the printer can handle it. All of this happens in the background, of course, in a manner that is completely transparent to the application you are using.

In older versions of Windows, the Print Manager was a spooler. With the Print Manager activated, you would print to it, and then the Print Manager would take care of sending your information to the printer. This enabled you to work on other tasks while information was being sent to your printer. Due to the way the Print Manager was implemented, Windows itself was often slowed down, and working on a different task while the Print Manager was busy was very disconcerting. Often, the process was jerky and disruptive, with the operating system being unresponsive while the Print Manager was doing its work.

In Windows 95, the Print Manager has been replaced with a more robust spooler that is a fully preemptive 32-bit application. This means you will no longer notice jerky responses while the spooler is working. Instead, printing is a true background process that will not interfere with whatever application you are using in the foreground.

Later in this chapter, you will learn how you can control both the printer and the print jobs that have been submitted to the spooler.

Controlling Print Spooling

Any print job you send to your printer under Windows is automatically spooled (placed in a queue) and printed in the background while you continue to work. For most users this is the most efficient way to print. Without a print spooler in place, Windows must wait until the printer has finished accepting the print job before it returns control of the computer back to you.

Spooling is printer-dependent, so if you have two (or more) printers defined in Windows, one printer might have spooling enabled while the other does not. To control how Windows 95 spools information to a printer, follow these steps:

1. Open the Printers folder by choosing Settings from the Start menu, and then choosing Printers.

2. Right-click the icon for the printer you want to change.

3. Choose Properties from the context menu. This opens the Properties sheet for that printer.

4. Select the Details tab.

5. Click the Spool Settings button. This displays the Spool Settings dialog box, as shown in figure 21.2.

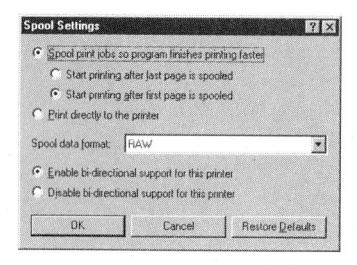

Fig. 21.2 The Spool Settings dialog box enables you to control spooling for a printer.

504 Chapter 21: Printing from Windows 95

The Spool Settings dialog box presents you with several options, each of which affects how Windows 95 sends information to your printer. At the top of the dialog box there are two main options. The first (which is selected in figure 21.2) enables the print spooler. With this option selected, you have two ways that the spooling can occur. The first option, Start Printing After Last Page Is Spooled, causes the spooler to hold all information until it receives the entire print job from your application. Choosing this option can cause a disconcerting delay before you get the first page from your printer. The second option, Start Printing After First Page Is Spooled, causes information to be sent from the spooler to the printer as quickly as possible.

Because printing quickly is typically a good thing, why would you ever want to choose the first option? The biggest reason is if your printer is used by an application that "prints as it goes." For instance, suppose that you are creating a report from a database program, and after processing a record for a time, it prints a line or two of information. If it takes 15 seconds to process each record, then it could be 10 or 15 minutes before a completely printed page has been created—that's 10 or 15 minutes for each page of the report. If the spooler is set to start printing after the first page is ready to be printed, all other people wanting to use the printer will be waiting while the second and subsequent pages are assembled and printed by the database program. If you have an application similar to this, you will want the print spooler to hold the job until it is complete, and only then release it.

The second option at the top of the Spool Settings dialog box enables you to turn print spooling off. The Print Directly to the Printer option bypasses the spooler altogether, sending information to the printer in the old-fashioned way. This type of printing can be slow, because you are tied to the speed of the printer instead of the speed of your computer.

> **Tip:** If you have a printer that you have shared over the network, do not turn off print spooling for that printer. Because your printer will be handling jobs from many sources, print spooling is necessary.

In the middle of the dialog box is an option called Spool Data Format. This option enables you to specify how you want information stored in the spooler. RAW is the most likely format choice, which means that the information is stored in the format that is native to the printer. The other option, EMF, stores information in a metafile format (an intermediary format) that conserves on disk space.

Another advantage of EMF print files is faster apparent printing. The operative word here is "apparent." If you set the spooler to use EMF files, then much of the printer-dependent translation takes place in the background rather than as your document is printing. For instance, if your document requires a large rectangle to be printed, and you have EMF enabled, then the rectangle command is stored in the spool file and later translated to the printer-driver level. If you turn EMF off, then the rectangle is converted into a format the printer understands at print time. This process is more time-consuming (depending on the document), and can slow down the overall performance of Windows 95. The upshot is that you should choose the EMF format if at all possible.

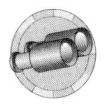

> **Note:** Spool settings are printer dependent. If you are changing settings for a PostScript printer, the EMF format option is not available. The only option available to PostScript printers is RAW.

The two options at the bottom of the Spool Settings dialog box enable you to indicate how the spooler should expect to communicate with the printer. Both serial and parallel ports now support bidirectional communication, which can greatly increase the amount of information you get back from your printer. For instance, over a bidirectional communications link, your printer can inform the operating system that it is out of paper, that the toner is low, or that there is a paper jam.

You seldom need to change the default setting for the printer, except in one situation. If you have an older system that does not have a bidirectional parallel port, then you should turn off the bidirectional feature. This choice will not necessarily slow down your printer, but it does inform Windows about the capabilities of the communication channel between your system and the printer.

When you are through changing the spooler settings, click the OK button. Your changes are saved and implemented immediately.

Creating a Print Job

In Windows 95, application programs create print jobs. For instance, you can create print jobs with your word processor or your spreadsheet program. The amount and type of programs that can create print jobs are almost innumerable.

Exactly how you print from an application will depend, in large part, on how the application was developed. While there are broad guidelines for how an application should appear and behave, the specifics of "how things look" are left up to the individual or company creating the software.

> **Tip:** Before you try to print with an application, you should make sure that you have installed the necessary printer drivers as described in Chapter 20, "Managing Your Printers."

Many Windows users do not install a single printer driver. This is particularly true in office environments, but may also apply to solitary users. Many applications send printer output to whatever you have set as the default printer. For instance, most of the accessories supplied with Windows 95 send information to the default printer. Thus if you have installed more than one printer driver, make sure that you select the proper printer driver before you start to print.

There are two ways you can select the default printer. Some applications provide a way to do this, typically through the Print command, itself. You can always use the Printers folder to set the default printer, however. To do this, follow these steps:

1. Open the Printers folder by choosing Settings from the Start menu, and then choosing Printers.

2. Click the icon for the printer you want to use as the default printer. This highlights the printer icon.

3. Choose the Set as Default option from the File menu.

When you set the default printer, there is no change in the appearance of the Printers folder. Instead, Windows 95 knows where to send printer information, unless your application specifies a different printer. You can only tell which printer has been selected as the default by highlighting the printer and pulling down the File menu. If the highlighted printer is the default printer, a checkmark will appear next to the Set As Default option, as shown in figure 21.3.

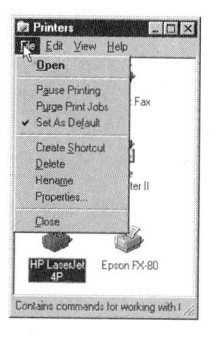

Fig. 21.3 A checkmark beside the Set As Default option indicates that the selected printer is the default.

When you are ready to create your print job, all you need to do is choose the Print command or follow the print procedure specific to your application. In general, if the program has a toolbar, you can find a print tool that will send your document to the printer. You can also typically find a Print option under the File menu for the application. For instance, figure 21.4 shows the dialog box that appears when you choose Print from the File menu in Microsoft Word for Windows.

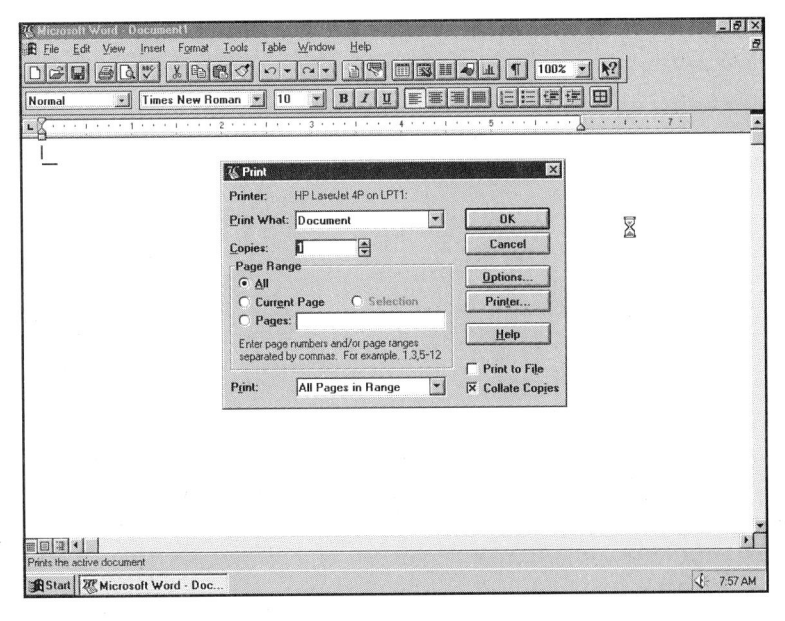

Fig. 21.4 Applications such as Word for Windows enable you to print from a toolbar or a menu option.

The Print dialog box is similar to the Print dialog boxes in many other applications. It enables you to specify what you want to print, as well as modify how it should be sent. Notice that the dialog box has information that indicates which printer driver will be used for this print job. In the case of figure 21.4, the printer is named HP LaserJet 4P on LPT1. If this is not the printer you want to use, click the appropriate button to change the printer. The exact button you use will vary from program to program; in the case of Word for Windows, it is the Printer button.

Creating a Print Job **509**

When the printer options are set correctly for your application, click the OK or Printer button. The application is instructed to compose the print job and send it to the printer driver. This information is then handed off to the spooling system, as described earlier in the chapter.

Managing Your Print Jobs

After you have created a print job and have sent it to the spooler, Windows 95 provides you with a great degree of flexibility in controlling the job. To manage the print job (as well as the printer), you use the printer icon in the Printers folder. To see how a printer is doing with the jobs it has to process, simply double-click the printer icon. You will see a window similar to the one shown in figure 21.5.

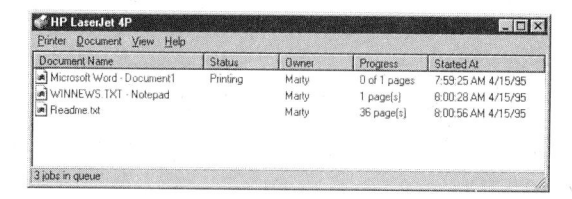

Fig. 21.5 Printer control windows enable you to manage both printers and print jobs.

> **Note:** If you are using a printer that sends information to a disk file, you cannot pull up a printer control window by double-clicking the printer icon. That is because the print job is sent to the output file immediately; there are no print jobs to manage.

The printer control window lists print jobs being worked on by the spooler. You can see information on the print job, as follows:

➤ **Document Name.** The name assigned to the print job by the application that created it. This may be the name of the document, the name of the application, or a combination of both.

➤ **Status.** The status of the printer in relation to this job. Typically, this is a single word, such as *Spooling, Printing,* or *Error.*

➤ **Owner.** The name of the user that sent the job to the printer. This is either the name of the person to whom Windows 95 is registered (in the case of a single-user system) or the name the person used when he or she logged on to the network.

➤ **Progress.** Information on either the size of the pending print job or the status of the print job being processed. Whenever possible, information is provided in terms of pages, although the veracity of this information may (at times) be questionable.

➤ **Started At.** The date and time the print job was created.

If there are quite a few print jobs in the queue (there could be if the printer is a heavily used network printer), you may want to sort the jobs in different ways. You do this by clicking the column header by which you want to sort. Thus, if you want to view the print jobs by who created them, just click the Owner column header. The print jobs are rearranged and shown in the order requested.

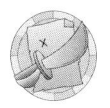

> **Tip:** If you want to display jobs in their original order, click the Started At column header. This displays jobs in the order in which they were submitted to the spooler.

Pausing Print Jobs

There are two ways you can pause print jobs, and the one you choose depends on the effect you want to have. If you want to pause all the print jobs at a printer, you pause the printer itself. If you want to pause a specific job, then you simply pause that individual print job.

To pause the entire printer, just choose P<u>a</u>use Printing from the <u>P</u>rinter menu. As an alternative, you can also right-click anywhere in the printer control window (except on the name of a pending print job). This displays the context menu for the printer control window, which is the same as the <u>P</u>rinter menu.

Managing Your Print Jobs **511**

When you choose to pause a printer, all output to the printer is immediately halted. The print jobs are not deleted; they are simply suspended. The title bar for the window is also changed to indicate that the printer has been paused. Figure 21.6 shows an example of a paused printer.

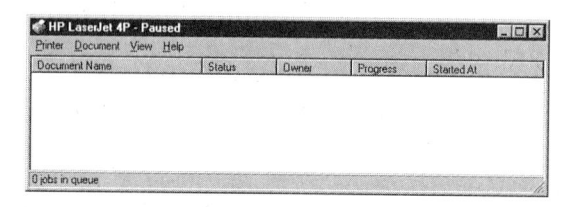

Fig. 21.6 The title bar tells you that the print jobs have been suspended.

If you want to individually pause a print job, follow these steps:

1. Display the printer control window containing the print job you want to pause.

2. Right-click the name of the print job to pause. This displays the context menu for the print job. (You could also select the print job and pull down the Document menu.)

3. Choose the Pause Printing option.

At this point, the spooler suspends the print job. If there are any other pending print jobs, they are sent to the printer normally; only the one single print job is affected. The paused job is indicated by the word Paused appearing in the Status column for the job (see figure 21.7).

Fig. 21.7 Pausing a print job causes it to be suspended; all others are unaffected.

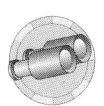

Note: Pausing a print job that is currently printing may have undesired effects. If you pause the job too long, your printer may timeout, which means what you have sent so far is flushed from the printer buffer. If this happens, you will need to delete the print job and start it again.

Resuming Print Jobs

If you know how to pause a print job, the chances are good that you also know how to resume one. Again, how you perform this task depends on whether you want to resume all print jobs (resume the printer) or resume individual print jobs.

To resume or unpause a printer, select the P<u>a</u>use Printing option from the <u>P</u>rinter menu or from the context menu for the printer control window. The spooler immediately begins sending any pending information to the printer, and the title bar for the window is changed so the `Paused` notation no longer appears.

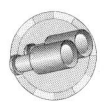

Note: Unpausing a printer has no effect on any individual print jobs that may be paused. If individual print jobs have been paused, you will need to individually unpause them.

To resume an individual print job, follow the same steps you used to initially pause the job:

1. Display the printer control window containing the print job you want to resume printing.
2. Right-click the name of a print job that was previously paused. This displays the context menu for the print job. You could also select the print job and pull down the <u>D</u>ocument menu.
3. Choose the P<u>a</u>use Printing option.

This releases the print job so it is processed normally by the spooler. The word `Paused` is removed from the Status column, and the job resumes its priority in the print queue based on the time the job was originally started.

Deleting Print Jobs

Windows 95 makes deleting an individual print job very easy. Just follow these steps:

1. Display the printer control window containing the print job you want to delete.
2. Click the name of the print job you want to delete. This highlights the print job.
3. Press the Delete key on your keyboard.

The print job is deleted, and its name removed from the printer control window.

> **Caution:** After a print job is deleted, you cannot resurrect it. Unlike deleted files (which are moved to the Recycle Bin), deleted print jobs are gone for good. The only option is to re-create the print job.

There are other ways to delete an individual print job, but pressing the Delete key is the easiest. For instance, you could right-click the name of the print job and choose Cancel Printing from the context menu, or you could choose the same option from the Document menu.

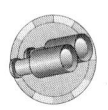

> **Note:** Deleting a print job that is in progress could have unwanted side effects. This is because even though you have deleted the job, your printer does not know this action has been taken—it can only tell that the data flow stopped. The result at your printer depends on the type and capabilities of your printer. In some rare instances, you may need to turn your printer off and back on or reset it.

If you want to delete all the print jobs queued up for a printer, you could delete them individually, but there is an easier way. Deleting all print jobs in a queue is called *purging*. You accomplish this by choosing Purge Print Jobs from the Printer menu or from the context menu for the printer control window. All print jobs for the printer are immediately deleted, regardless of their status.

Printing to a File

In Chapter 20, "Managing Your Printers," you learned that you can direct printer output to any number of devices. Normally, if you are using a local printer, you would print to either a parallel (LPT) or serial (COM) port.

Windows 95 also enables you to print to a file instead of a physical printer. This means the printer output is stored in a disk file, and you can later direct the file to the printer. The next section describes how to change the printer output to a file, and the following section teaches you what to do with the printer file once you have it.

Changing the Output Device

To print to a file, define the file as the destination of your printed output. You typically do this when you are preparing output for a printer make and model that you do not have physically connected to your system or available through your network. For instance, you might set up a printer definition for a printer you use at a service bureau. When the print files are created, the files can be taken to the service bureau for processing.

As an example, assume that you want to take advantage of the Linotronic 500 at the local print shop. All you need to do is install the printer driver for this printer, as described earlier in the chapter. When you are asked for the port used by the printer, choose the FILE option.

You can also change an existing printer driver so it is directed to a file, by following these steps:

1. Double-click the My Computer icon on your desktop.
2. Double-click the Printers icon. This displays the Printers folder.
3. Right-click the icon for the printer whose output you want directed to a file. This displays the context menu for the printer.
4. Choose the Properties option from the context menu. This displays the Properties sheet for the printer.
5. Click the Details tab.
6. In the Print To the Following Port field, choose the FILE option.
7. Click the OK button.

The icon for the printer is changed to indicate that the printer's output is directed to a file. Now, when you print by using this printer you are asked for a file name in which the output should be stored. When you supply the file name, the file is created and the print job is stored in the file.

Copying a Disk File to a Printer

When you have your printer output in a disk file, you are then faced with the problem of getting it to the target printer. This is most often a simple task of copying the file to a floppy disk, and then physically taking the disk to the computer connected to the target printer. For instance, if a service bureau operates the target printer, then you would take the disk file to the service bureau.

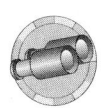

> **Note:** A printer output file does not contain plain text. Instead, it contains the control codes and commands necessary for the printer to process the print job. This means that a printer output file is intrinsically different from the original document used to create the file. It is important to understand these differences when you send your output to a disk file.

The most efficient way to send the file to the target printer is to do it from a DOS prompt. How you get to the DOS prompt depends on the type of machine connected to the target printer.

➤ If the system is running DOS, then you are set; the DOS prompt should be visible on the screen.

➤ If the system is running an older version of Windows, then you will need to either exit Windows or choose MS-DOS prompt from the Main program group.

➤ If the system is running Windows 95, then you will need to select Programs from the Start menu, and then choose MS-DOS prompt.

When the DOS prompt is visible, you can follow these steps:

1. Insert the transfer disk (the one containing the print file) into a disk drive. Make a note of which disk drive it is (A: or B:).

2. Make a note of which printer port the target printer is connected to. Typically this is a port such as LPT1 or LPT2.

3. At the DOS prompt, enter the following command line, replacing *d:* with the disk drive in which your diskette is located, *file* with the printer file name, and *dest* with the printer port to which the target printer is connected.

```
copy d:\file dest
```

This copies the printer file to the target printer. Soon you should start to see your output appear on the device. If you do not, you will want to check the command line to make sure that you used the proper information: disk drive, file name, and destination printer port.

Printing on a Network

For all intents and purposes, printing to a network printer functions just the same as printing to a network printer. All you need to do is set up a printer driver for the network printer, and then send your print jobs to that printer. The printer driver for the network printer can be set up either as described in Chapter 20, "Managing Your Printers," or by using the Point-and-Print feature, which is described later in this chapter.

> **Note:** For specific information on printing over networks, you can also refer to Chapter 37, "Using Windows 95 on a Network."

To gain maximum efficiency when printing to a network printer, implement these suggestions:

➤ Configure your printers to use direct network connections whenever possible. This provides fast throughput and flexible printer placement. It also removes the need for a dedicated printer server.

➤ If your printer does not have direct network connection capability, use a *parallel port* rather than a serial port. This avoids bottlenecks common to serial printers and networks.

➤ For slower laser printers designed primarily for text output, use the lowest print resolution, typically 75 or 150 dpi.

➤ Do not enable spooling for a network printer if you are using a separate spooling program provided with the network software.

You can perform each of these tasks from the Properties sheet for your printers. You can find information on the settings for the Properties sheet in Chapter 20, "Managing Your Printers."

Point-and-Print Capabilities

Windows 95 includes a new feature called *Point and Print*. This feature comes into play if you are connected to a network, and it allows simpler printing to a network printer.

In past networked versions of Windows, you needed to know quite a bit about a network printer before you could actually print to it. You needed to know what type of printer you were connecting to so that you could install the necessary printer drivers at your computer. This could cause problems, because it was not always easy to determine the characteristics of a remote printer.

In Windows 95, Point and Print removes this necessity. Now you need to know very little about the remote printer. Windows 95 will take care of determining what type of printer it is, and installing the proper printer driver on your computer. This driver is transferred across the network, so you do not need to worry about having the Windows 95 installations disks or CD-ROM at your computer.

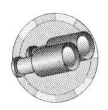

> **Note:** The Point-and-Print feature of Windows 95 attempts to determine the type of remote printer you want to use. If it cannot discern the information it needs, you will still be asked for the printer manufacturer and model, as in previous versions of Windows. In such an event, you will actually need your Windows 95 diskettes or CD-ROM in order to install the proper printer driver.

The Point-and-Print feature functions by using the Registry. When you install a new printer driver on your system, the information about that printer is stored in the Registry. If you share the printer on the network, then others have access to the printer. When another network user attempts to print to your printer, his or her Windows 95 queries your Windows 95 about the printer. Your system then retrieves the information about the printer from the Registry, and sends it to the remote user's computer. If the remote system determines that it needs the printer driver, your system takes care of sending it over the network, where it is installed on the remote user's system and used to send information to your computer. All of this is done without intervention from either you or the remote user.

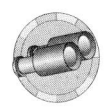

> **Note:** Point and Print will only function fully on Windows networks (Windows 95 and Windows NT) and on NetWare networks.

Point-and-Print Capabilities **519**

To enable Point and Print on your system, follow these steps:

1. Double-click the My Computer icon on your desktop. This opens a window showing the contents of your system.

2. In the My Computer window, double-click the C: drive icon (or whatever other drive contains your Windows folder). This opens a window for your disk drive.

3. In the disk drive window, double-click the Windows folder. This opens a window showing the contents of the Windows folder.

4. In the Windows folder window, right-click the System folder icon. This displays a context menu.

5. From the context menu, select the Sharing option. This displays the System Properties sheet with the Sharing tab selected.

In this dialog box, you set how you want others on the network to have access to your System folder. You do not need to fully share the folder, but you do need to give others read-only access to the folder. The only people that need to have access are those who you want to have Point-and-Print capabilities to your shared printers. Read-only access means they can read things from your System folder, but they cannot change them. They need to be able to read the folder in order to gain access to your printer drivers and the information in your Registry.

To use Point and Print, just browse through Network Neighborhood to find the printer you want to use. When you find it, simply drag the printer icon from the remote system, dropping it in your Printers folder window. The necessary printer driver information is transferred automatically, and the printer is set up. All you need to do is provide a name for the new printer driver on your system.

Printing from a DOS Application

If you have been using Windows for any length of time, you already know that printing from an MS-DOS window can be frustrating. This is because printing from an MS-DOS window went directly to the printer port, bypassing the Print Manager altogether. This could present problems, for instance, when you needed to print something from the Print Manager and from DOS at the same time.

Windows 95 has solved the historical problems in this area. All printing from the MS-DOS window is now routed through the print spooler, meaning that DOS printing jobs are handled the same as any other printing job.

One of the side benefits of this design change is the fact that you can now do work quicker in an MS-DOS window than you could in previous versions of Windows. This is because, previously, any MS-DOS printing went directly to the printer port. That meant that you needed to wait for the entire print job to be complete before returning to your application. With print jobs now routed through the regular print spooler, your application's output is accepted by the spooler instead of directly by the printer. The result is you are returned to the DOS application before your printed output is completed—the same benefit that has been inherent in Windows applications for some time.

Working with Fonts

by Allen L. Wyatt

You already know that Windows is a graphical user environment, based on the concept of WYSIWYG—what you see is what you get. That means that what you see on-screen should also represent what you see on printed output, or on a screen on a different system. While this is a great design concept, it unfortunately means that computer users must be concerned with details that users of less sophisticated systems don't need to pay attention to. Primarily, you need to be concerned with fonts.

This chapter discusses, in detail, how Windows 95 works with fonts. You learn not only what they are, but what types of fonts are available. You also learn how to install them in Windows and use them in your applications.

What Are Fonts?

A *font* is a collection of characters and symbols with a related design. The design itself is referred to as a *typeface*. A set of typefaces designed to be used together is a *typeface family*. For instance, common typeface families would be Times or Helvetica; these families can be found on many computer systems. Within these families, specific designs, or typefaces would be Times Roman or Times Italic (within the Times family) and Helvetica Narrow or Helvetica Bold (within the Helvetica family).

In effect, a font is a particular implementation of a typeface. These implementations vary from vendor to vendor. Thus, the Times Roman typeface from Adobe would be one font, while the Times Roman typeface from Bitstream would be another font.

In many instances (including within this chapter), the terms *typeface* and *font* are used interchangeably. This is not meant to cause confusion, it is just an indication of the reality that there is typically not much difference between implementations of the same typeface.

To understand fonts fully, you need to understand a few other key terms. It is not my intention to provide a complete tutorial on type design or layout, but a few key terms are appropriate to the discussion later in this chapter.

Type is composed of uppercase letters (ABC), lowercase letters (abc), numbers (123), and some symbols (such as punctuation marks). When type is placed on a page, there are three main parts to it. The x-height, or type body, is the height of a lowercase X, and it is also the height of the main part of every other letter. Ascenders are the parts of the letter that extend above the x-height, and descenders are those parts that fall below the x-height. Figure 22.1 shows an example of type, with the appropriate terms marked.

ascender →
x-height or body →
descender →

Extremely

Fig. 22.1 There are three basic elements to a font.

The dividing line between the x-height area and the descender area is called the *base line*. This is the line on which the type is aligned vertically; it is the path your eye follows when you read text.

The size of a font is measured in points. A point is approximately 1/72 of an inch. Thus, a 10-point type is ten points high, and a 48-point type is 48 points high. This can be a bit misleading, however. Point sizes, as a scientific measurement, are a hold-over from the days when type was cast in lead and manually placed on a wooden rack. The point size of a font referred to the height of the lead block on which the actual letter was placed; it had nothing to do with the height of the actual letters in the font. Take a look at the different letters shown in figure 22.2.

Baseline → A A ℋ A I A a A A

Fig. 22.2 All these letters from different fonts are the same point size, but different actual sizes.

Every one of the letters in figure 22.2 is considered 30-point type. They appear different on the page, however, because the point size has no relevance to the height of the actual characters in the font. In general, you should use point sizes as a guide to the relative sizes of fonts, not to their absolute size.

Purposes for Fonts

Fonts are created for many different purposes. In the computer world, fonts are typically designed based on the output device on which they will be used. In a Windows system, there are generally two font formats: printer fonts and display fonts. These two classifications are discussed in the following sections.

Printer Fonts

Fonts have been inextricably associated with printing since Gutenberg fired up his press. Fonts are the character applied to the content of what we read. In many cases they affect—either positively or negatively—our perception of what we are reading. Many times this effect is very subtle; we may not even be aware of it. Thus, fonts are very important to how we print and to what we print.

Printer fonts are used by a printer to control how text is formed on the printed page. They are stored in disk files on your computer, but if you use them in a document and then print the document, they are automatically downloaded to the printer so they can be used there. Downloaded printer fonts are often referred to as *soft fonts*, since they reside in software. When the printer is done using the fonts and your print job is complete, the fonts are erased from the printer's memory. They continue to reside on your computer, awaiting the next time they are needed by Windows to complete a print job.

Display (Screen) Fonts

The video display (along with the keyboard) is the primary interface device between you and the computer. On the display is where you do your work and view many of your results. Today's computer displays are more complex and capable than those of yesterday, and this trend will probably continue into the future.

Windows 95, being a graphical user interface, allows information to be displayed in virtually any way that program designers can create. One outgrowth of this is that the display of textual information has come very close to what we are used to seeing on the printed page. This capability necessitates the use of *screen fonts*, which control how different typefaces appear on a video display.

When you install a font in Windows 95, typically you are thinking in terms of final printed output—how the font will appear when the document is printed. The installation process typically also installs display fonts which correspond to the printer fonts. This is done so that what you see on-screen corresponds to what is printed on the printer.

Types of Fonts

After a typeface has been designed, it must be stored in a disk file, in a format which can be understood by the computer. There are typically two ways in which fonts can be stored: as bitmaps or as outlines.

Bitmap Fonts

Bitmap fonts represent the oldest computer font technology. A *bitmap font* is nothing but a graphic representation of a series of characters. These are stored in a file in the same way that bitmapped graphics are—each bit in the definition represents a single dot on the output device. If a bit is on (set to 1), then a dot is printed; if a bit is off (set to 0), then a dot is not printed. As you might guess, the smaller the character, the fewer bits it takes to define it. Conversely, the larger the character, the more bits it takes. This means that the larger the point size of the font, the more space it can take to store the font both on disk and in a device such as a printer. Since the font takes more space, that also means that it takes longer to transfer and manipulate the font.

One drawback of bitmap fonts is that they cannot be displayed well at different resolutions. For instance, if you have a 10-point bitmapped font, and you enlarge it quite a bit, the quality of the font deteriorates. The most easily recognized deterioration is "jaggies," which appear around the edges of the characters. Outline fonts, described in the following section, do not have this limitation.

Outline Fonts

The other format for fonts is outlines. An outline font is nothing but a mathematical description of a series of characters. Since the outline is based on math, it easily can be manipulated mathematically. Also, regardless of the point size of the font, the outline description is consistent in space requirements. Thus, it takes the same amount of time to manipulate or transfer an outline font, regardless of its point size.

How can you tell the font types apart if you are using Windows? Later in this chapter you will learn about the Fonts window and how you can use it to manage the fonts on your system. If you look at the Fonts window (see figure 22.3), you see that there are two types of fonts displayed. Those that use an icon with the letter A in it are bitmap fonts; those that have the TT symbol are TrueType fonts, which are stored in an outline format.

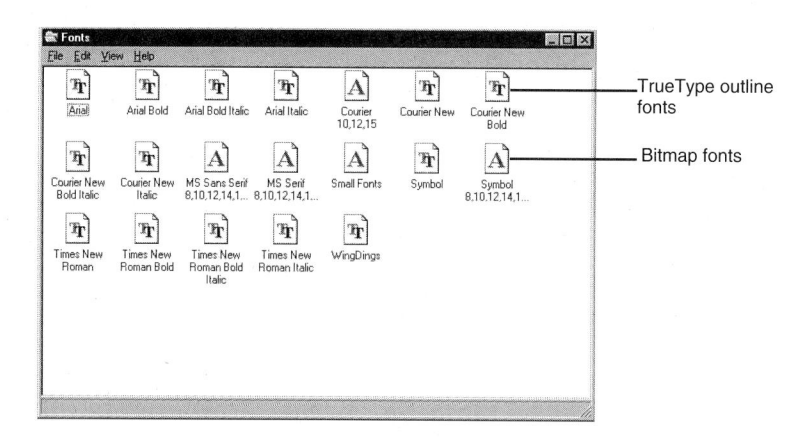

Fig. 22.3 There are two types of font file icons used in this Fonts folder window.

Notice, as well, that the names for the bitmap font files include numbers such as 8, 10, 12, 14, and so forth. These numbers represent the point sizes for each font within the file. If you use the font for a point size that is different from these, the font will be manipulated to that

528 Chapter 22: Working with Fonts

size, but it will not be as crisp or clear as if you used the bitmap font at one of the sizes it is designed for.

There are a variety of fonts available on the market. Each of these fonts come in any number of formats. The two most common types of fonts used in Windows systems are TrueType and PostScript fonts. These (as well as a few others) are discussed in the following sections.

TrueType Fonts

When you install Windows 95, several different fonts are automatically installed. These fonts are in the TrueType format, which was originally developed by Microsoft and several other vendors. In many ways, TrueType fonts are competitors to PostScript fonts, which are described in the following section.

Windows can scale TrueType fonts to any size. These fonts can be used with any graphic video adapter and any printer, provided that Windows 95 drivers exist for the devices. This capability alone is a boon to network users. In many environments, users may work from a variety of machines and use a variety of printers. Windows enables the same fonts to work anywhere.

The scaleable nature of the fonts makes them economical in their disk space requirements. Each TrueType font file occupies between 9K and 72K, and each typeface (bold, italic, condensed, and so on) requires a separate file. In contrast, bitmapped files would require separate files for each size of the same typeface, thereby occupying quite a bit more disk space.

> **Tip:** If you are running Windows 95 on a network, store your TrueType fonts in your master Windows directory on the server. This allows everyone to access the fonts and cuts down on redundant files on the network.

True Type Fonts Are Embedded into the File

TrueType fonts can be embedded in a document so that other users can print the document and still get the fonts printed properly, even if the original font is not on their system. TrueType fonts are encrypted when they are embedded into the document, which allows the font to be sent with the file, permitting the end-user recipient to view and print the file. The encrypting prevents the recipient from copying the font itself without licensing the font.

Font vendors have three levels of font embedding from which to choose. The most restrictive method doesn't permit the font to be embedded in a document. Instead, the document's recipient must substitute an available font for the original used to create the document. The second level only permits a recipient to view and print the document containing the font, but cannot affect the font itself. Recipients also cannot edit the document without deleting the font information first. The third type of embedding allows the recipient to edit and save the document without deleting the font information. This type of embedding permits the recipient to extract the font for personal use.

Printing TrueType Fonts

When printing a document containing TrueType fonts on a standard Hewlett-Packard compatible laser or ink-jet printer, Windows scans the first line printed and downloads only the characters needed. Then Windows scans the next line and downloads any additional characters needed for the next line. This process continues until the entire document is printed. This on-the-fly, download-if-needed strategy means that TrueType fonts print reasonably fast in spite of having several sizes and font styles in a document. Windows clears the printer's memory at the end of the print job and repeats the process afresh for new print jobs. To work in a networked environment, soft fonts need to be downloaded in this way. This method of downloading soft fonts is not a new idea. For years, soft fonts from SWFTE (Rockland, MD) have worked this way for DOS-based versions of Word and WordPerfect. For

Windows users, SWFTE has released its whole font series as TrueType fonts in a product called Typecase.

With PostScript laser printers, Windows converts TrueType fonts into Adobe Type 1 outline fonts or Adobe Type 3 bitmap fonts (both of these font types are discussed in the following section). If the point size you are printing is 8 points or smaller, you might find that printing them as Type 3 is faster because less data is required for a bitmap at this small size than is required for an outline font at this size. You can control the type of conversion you want to use for each printer installed on your system. How you do this is covered later in this chapter, in the section "Sending TrueType Fonts to a PostScript Printer."

On dot-matrix printers, TrueType fonts print as bitmapped graphics, and the quality is surprisingly good, even on the less sophisticated 9-pin printers.

PostScript Fonts

PostScript fonts have been around longer than TrueType fonts, and have many of the same benefits. They were originally developed by Adobe Systems, the developers of the PostScript language. Since they have been around longer, and since Adobe has done a wonderful marketing job, they are available in a wider array of high-quality printers and output devices.

There are two types of PostScript fonts on the market: bitmap and outline. Earlier in this chapter you learned the differences between these font formats. Bitmap fonts represent an older technology, and are often referred to as Adobe Type 1 fonts. Outline fonts, which are newer, are referred to as Adobe Type 3 fonts. All PostScript devices can handle Type 3 fonts, but some older PostScript devices cannot handle Type 1 fonts. This is because the older devices also use an older PostScript *interpreter*, which is the computing engine that processes the font information sent to it by the computer.

Note: If you are creating a document that is ultimately intended for a high-quality output device, such as an imagesetter, check with the people that run the imagesetter to determine which types of fonts you should use. Typically, most imagesetters are intimately tied to PostScript fonts, and you should not use fonts in other formats (including TrueType). Using the wrong type of fonts can make your output job unsatisfactory or completely unusable.

Other Types of Fonts

Besides TrueType and PostScript fonts, there are a wide variety of other fonts available on the market. These fonts are available from vendors such as Bitstream, SWFTE, and others. Some of these font packages are available in TrueType format, some in Adobe Type 1, and still others in Adobe Type 3.

This does not mean that all fonts are in Type 1, Type 3, or TrueType formats. Indeed, there are other formats available, although they are not nearly as popular or pervasive as the font types already mentioned. Typically these font formats, such as Bitstream's QEM format, are a variation on the bitmap formatting already mentioned. These "other" types of fonts are typically not managed directly by Windows, but instead require a Windows font management program provided by the font vendor.

Installing Fonts

Installing a font in Windows 95 is quite easy. In Chapter 23, "Managing Your Printers," you learned how Windows 95 uses the Printers folder as a place to organize all your printer drivers. Likewise, the Fonts folder is used by Windows 95 as a place to hold all your fonts.

The first step in installing fonts is to display the Fonts folder window. To do this, follow these steps:

1. Choose Settings from the Start menu. The Settings menu appears.
2. Choose Control Panel from the Settings menu. The Control Panel window appears.
3. Double-click on the Fonts icon in the Control Panel. The Fonts folder window appears, as shown in figure 22.4.

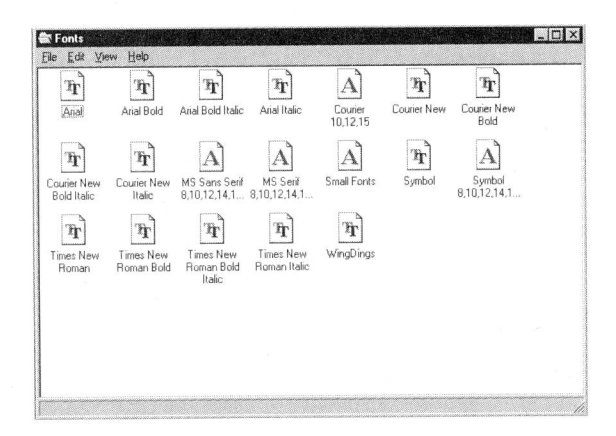

Fig. 22.4 The Fonts folder window shows all the fonts you have installed in your system.

Take another look at the Fonts icon in the Control Panel. Notice that this icon is actually a shortcut, as indicated by the arrow in the bottom-right corner of the icon. The Fonts folder physically resides in the Windows folder of your C: drive. If you browse through your system (possibly using the Explorer), you can open the Windows folder and then the Fonts folder. Regardless of whether you get to the Fonts folder window by browsing or through the Control Panel, you will see the same display and be able to take the same actions.

To install a font in your system, simply choose the Install New Font command from the File menu. This displays the Add Fonts dialog box, as shown in figure 22.5.

Installing Fonts 533

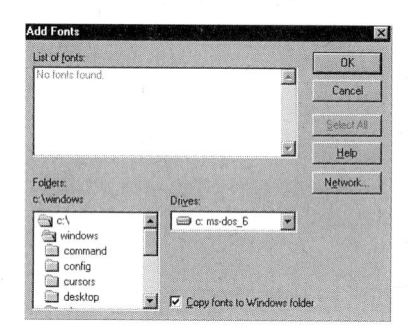

Fig. 22.5 The Add Fonts dialog box enables you to add fonts to Windows 95.

If you have been using Windows for any time, this dialog box should look somewhat familiar. It is similar to the dialog boxes used in previous versions of Windows to add fonts. All you need to do is select the drive and directory (folder) from where you are installing fonts. Typically, you will install fonts from either a floppy drive or a CD-ROM drive. When you specify where the fonts are located, the dialog box shows a list of the fonts available on the drive. For instance, figure 22.6 shows the fonts available on a CD-ROM that contains fonts.

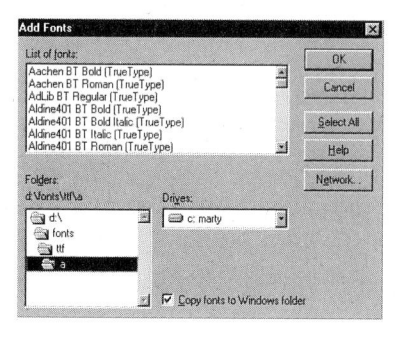

Fig. 22.6 When you have selected a drive and folder containing fonts, the fonts are listed in the Add Fonts dialog box.

To install one of the listed fonts, simply highlight the font name and click the OK button. You can select more than one font by using regular

Windows techniques: hold down the Shift key to select a consecutive series of fonts, or hold down the Ctrl key to select different, non-consecutive fonts.

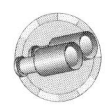

> **Note:** There are literally thousands of fonts available on the market. Just because a font is available doesn't mean you should install it on your system. Too many fonts will slow down the performance of even the best Windows software, in addition to needlessly occupying disk space. Be selective and install only those fonts you need.

Once the fonts have been installed, an icon for the font appears in the Fonts folder window. These fonts will also appear the next time you start an application that uses fonts.

Controlling How TrueType Fonts Print

Earlier in this chapter you learned what TrueType fonts are. Depending on your printer type, Windows allows you quite a bit of control over how TrueType fonts are printed. If you have installed a dot-matrix printer, there is no real control over how TrueType fonts are printed—they are always printed as graphics characters. This allows the best reproduction of what you see when you use TrueType fonts on your screen.

If you have installed a printer that uses PCL (an acronym for Page Control Language, a page definition language used in HP and compatible printers) or one that uses PostScript, Windows allows you to send the fonts in different ways. Regardless of the printer type, you can specify how TrueType fonts are to be handled by displaying the Properties dialog box for the printer. To do this, follow these steps:

1. Double-click on the My Computer icon on your desktop.

Controlling How TrueType Fonts Print **535**

2. Double-click on the Printers icon.

3. Right-click on the icon for the printer whose properties you want to change. The context menu for the printer appears.

4. Choose Properties from the context menu. The Properties dialog box for the printer appears.

5. Click on the Fonts tab. Figure 22.7 shows an example of the Properties dialog box for the HP LaserJet 4V, which is a PCL printer.

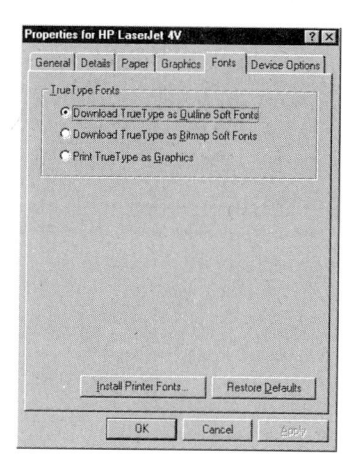

Fig. 22.7 The Fonts tab in the Properties for printer dialog box enables you to control how TrueType fonts are printed.

Notice that this dialog box provides three options for how TrueType fonts are printed. You can print them as an outline font, as a bitmap, or as graphics. Notice, also, that the default is the first option, to print them as outline fonts. This is because this choice typically provides the best quality output at a wide range of type sizes. Since different printers provide different quality output, you may want to experiment by selecting the other options here, as well.

If you have a PostScript printer installed, you have many of the same options in printing TrueType fonts. Figure 22.8 shows the Properties for HP LaserJet 4V/4MV PostScript dialog box, which represents a PostScript printer. Again, you have three options in this dialog box.

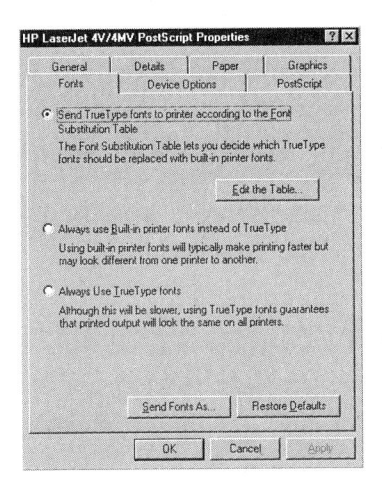

Fig. 22.8 The Fonts tab for a PostScript printer appears more complex than the same tab for a PCL printer.

TrueType Printer Options

The first option, which is the default, causes fonts to be sent according to what is called a font substitution table. This table is discussed in the next section.

The second option instructs Windows to always use built-in printer fonts rather than TrueType fonts. Printing with this option selected can be much faster than normal printing, since Windows does not need to download fonts with each print job. However, unless the printer contains fonts comparable to the TrueType fonts you are using, it will not produce satisfactory results every time. This is because the printer, if it cannot locate a requested font, substitutes its own fonts. If the printer cannot locate a font with the same name, the Courier font is often substituted. Thus, unless you know that all the fonts you will use are also available on the printer, you shouldn't choose this printing option.

The third option instructs Windows to always use TrueType fonts. This, in reality, is at the opposite end of the spectrum from the previous option. If you choose this, then your printing time can be increased

Controlling How TrueType Fonts Print **537**

tremendously, depending on how you use TrueType fonts in your document. This is because all the TrueType fonts must be downloaded every time they are used. The flip side of this, however, is that you will get the best match between what you see on your screen and what you see on your output. You can control how the fonts are sent by clicking the Send Fonts As button; using this feature is described later, in the section entitled "Sending TrueType Fonts to a PostScript Printer."

PostScript Font Substitution Table

If you have a PostScript printer, and you choose the first method of printing TrueType fonts (Send TrueType fonts to the printer according to the Font Substitution Table), then you may be interested in modifying the table itself. This allows you control over which fonts are substituted and which aren't. Depending on how many fonts are included with your PostScript printer, as well as how they are implemented, you may need to make extensive changes in the table.

To see the font substitution table, display the Properties for printer dialog box (refer to figure 22.8), and then click the Fonts tab. Finally, click the Edit the Table button. This displays the dialog box shown in figure 22.9.

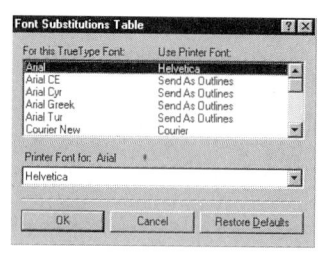

Fig. 22.9 The Font Substitutions Table dialog box enables you to control which PostScript fonts are substituted for which TrueType fonts.

There are two columns in the table. The left column shows all the TrueType fonts installed in your system. To the right of each font, in the right column, is the name of the PostScript font that will be substituted for the TrueType font. You can change the font to be substituted by following these steps:

1. Click the name of a TrueType font. This highlights in the table the row that you want to change.

2. In the drop-down list at the bottom of the dialog box, select a PostScript font to substitute. If you don't want the TrueType font sent without substitution, select the Send As Outlines option from the top of the list.

You can repeat these two steps for as many of the table entries as desired. When you are done making changes, click the OK button at the bottom of the dialog box. Your changes are saved, and are used the next time you print a document.

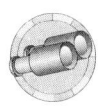

> **Note:** TrueType fonts won't show up in the Font Substitution Table until you have installed them in your system. Installing fonts is covered earlier in this chapter in the section titled "Installing Fonts."

Sending TrueType Fonts to a PostScript Printer

If you have a PostScript printer installed in your system, and you chose the third method of how TrueType fonts should be handled (Always Use TrueType fonts), you can control how Windows sends the fonts to the printer. This is done by displaying the Properties for printer dialog box, clicking the Fonts tab, and then clicking the Send Fonts As button at the bottom of the dialog box. This displays the dialog box shown in figure 22.10.

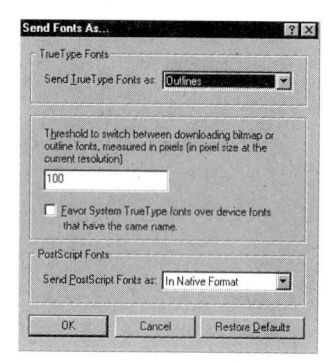

Fig. 22.10 The Send Fonts As dialog box controls how TrueType fonts are sent to a PostScript printer.

At the top of the dialog box, in the TrueType Fonts area, you can select how the fonts are to be sent. There are three possible selections in the drop-down list:

- ➤ **Outlines.** This option sends TrueType fonts as Adobe Type 1 font outlines. This font format is optimized for both speed (the fonts typically require less space than bitmaps) and scaleability (the outlines are easier to manipulate).

- ➤ **Bitmaps.** This option results in the TrueType fonts being converted to Adobe Type 3 fonts, which are scaled bitmaps. On some older PostScript printers this limitation may be required, since they might not understand Adobe Type 1 fonts.

- ➤ **Don't Send.** This option means that TrueType fonts are never sent to the printer. How the printer handles the font information is up to the printer, but typically a different font will be substituted by the printer itself.

You should select the option which is most appropriate to your printer. You also can adjust the parameters by which Windows makes a judgment between when Adobe Type 1 and Type 3 fonts are sent. For instance, you might select bitmaps as the way you typically want to send fonts to the printer, but then have Windows start sending outline fonts when it makes more sense. This adjustment is made in the T̲hreshold area, in the middle of the dialog box.

For example, in the Threshold area, you can specify a point size at which Windows will switch from bitmap to outline format. Why would you want to do this? Simply because outline fonts are fairly stable in their size requirements; after all, they are nothing but mathematical descriptions of the outline of a font. Bitmap fonts, on the other hand, can grow or shrink in size based on the point size of the typeface. Thus, a 6-point typeface takes less space than a 25-point typeface. It is very possible that the 6-point bitmap typeface will take less space than a 6-point outline typeface.

Exactly where the threshold should be set will vary, based on the resolution of your printer. This makes sense, since a 600 dpi printer requires four times the dots (vertical and horizontal) than a 300 dpi printer does to cover the same area. In general, there is an inverse relationship between the resolution of your printer and the threshold you should set. Thus, the higher the resolution of your printer, the lower the threshold should be. You will probably need to experiment with this setting to see if it offers noticeable results in your printing environment.

In the center, T̲hreshold area of the dialog box, there also is a check box. This check box controls how Windows reacts when it determines that there is a font in your printer that has the same name as a TrueType font you are using. Normally, Windows will use the built-in printer font instead of downloading the TrueType font. If you select this check box, however, you force Windows to always download the TrueType font, regardless of what it detects on the printer.

Finally, at the bottom of the Send Fonts As dialog box is a control that indicates how native PostScript fonts should be handled. There are two settings here, the default being to send the PostScript fonts in their native format (this is the setting you will want most of the time). The other possible setting is Don't Send, which stops Windows from downloading PostScript fonts entirely.

Changing the Fonts Used by Windows

Windows 95 allows you a great deal of control over what fonts you use in the operating system itself. You can change fonts used in title bars, messages, status bars, and other desktop items. To make your own changes, follow these steps:

1. Choose Settings from the Start menu. The Settings menu appears.
2. Choose Control Panel from the Settings menu. The Control Panel window appears.
3. Double-click the Display icon in the Control Panel. The Properties for Display dialog box appears.
4. Click on the Appearance tab. The dialog box appears as shown in figure 22.11.

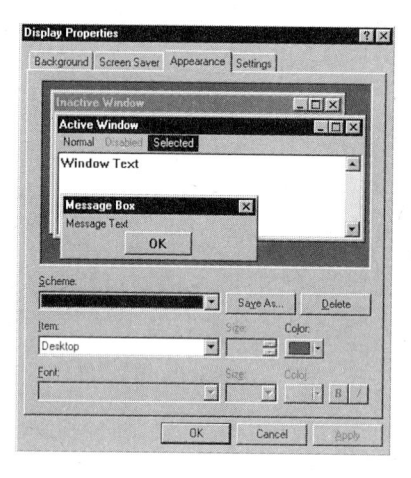

Fig. 22.11 With the Appearance tab selected in the Properties for Display dialog box, you are ready to change the fonts used by Windows.

This dialog box should look familiar if you have used Windows in the past. The dialog box enables you to change color schemes used when displaying the desktop. However, Windows 95 also enables you to modify fonts used in the display. Notice at the bottom of the dialog box there is a selection labeled Font. To change a desktop item, just click it in the Appearance box example of the desktop. If the desktop object you have selected in the Item box uses text in any way, then the Font area is active and you can modify the font used. You also can change the font attributes, such as size, color, and style (bold, italic, or both).

Windows enables you to change fonts for the following objects:

- Active title bar
- Icon title
- Inactive title bar
- Menu
- Message box
- Palette title
- Selected items

After you select the item whose font you wish to change, you can select any TrueType or system (bitmap) font you desire. As you make changes in the display fonts used, notice that they are updated at the top of the dialog box. When you are satisfied with your changes, click the OK button and your changes are made system-wide.

Changing Fonts in Applications

Earlier in this chapter, you learned that when you install a font it is available for use in your applications. This is true for the next time you start the application. This means if the application is running when you install a font, the chances are good that the font will not be available until you close the application and restart it.

There is a problem with this, however. Application programs typically maintain a font list of their own, usually in some kind of INI file for the application. If the application is using the INI file at the time the fonts are being installed, it might not get updated properly during the font's installation process. Because of this, it is generally a good idea to close all your applications before you install a font. When you later start the application, the new font should be available in your font list.

How you actually use fonts in an application is beyond the scope of this chapter, since it can vary tremendously. You should refer to your application's manual or online help system to discover exactly how to put the new fonts to use.

Handling Graphics

KILLER 23 WINDOWS 95

by Ewan Grantham

In this chapter, you learn how to set up Windows 95 to make the most of the graphics you have, or are creating. If you're creating a business presentation, the right graphics can mean a more effective sales pitch, as well as making it easier to "sell your point." Regardless of what you use your system for, graphics can make it more entertaining, and even make it easier to get around.

Windows 95 incorporates a number of changes to take advantage of the improvement in video cards and displays. Whether you're a game designer working with WinG, or a casual user trying to set up a nice background, taking advantage of these changes can result in a more productive environment.

This chapter covers the following issues to help you get the most out of your Windows 95 graphics:

- ➤ How to associate your graphics applications in Explorer
- ➤ How to change your printer handles graphics
- ➤ How to identify and know when to use different graphics file types

➤ How to use the new Windows 95 features to adjust your system for its best graphics performance

➤ How to use Paint to create your own graphics

Properties for Graphics

One of the big changes in Windows 95 is the addition of the *Properties* setting to almost every object you can access. This means that you can adjust almost every part of your system to allow for greater customization, and make those adjustments without spending a lot of time changing device drivers or rebooting your computer. Graphics are no exception.

If you right-click on your desktop and select Properties, you get the Display Properties sheet, which has several tabs. The first tab that can affect your graphics is the Settings tab, which allows you to set your resolution and color depth as shown in figure 23.1.

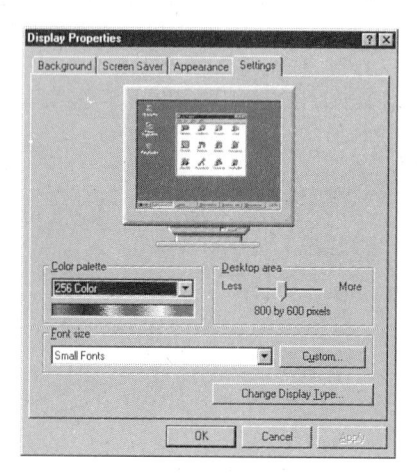

Fig. 23.1 The Display Properties Settings tab allows you to set your resolution and color depth.

With Windows 95, you can make most of these changes "on the fly" — in other words, without having to reboot your machine. This makes it easier to run in different resolutions and different color depths as your programs require.

Depending on what you're doing, you'll find that various settings have different effects. For example, if you're playing a digital video you'll discover that you want a resolution of 640 × 480 to make the image take up as much of your screen as possible, while your color depth will be either 256 colors (which plays back faster but doesn't look quite as good) or 16-bit color. On the other hand, if you're drawing a complex graphic, say of a gear assembly, you will probably want a resolution of 1024 × 768 to give you as much room on the screen as possible to work.

System Properties for Graphics

Just as you can change the screen settings, you can also change how graphics are treated at the system level. To do this, go to the Start menu, select Settings, Control Panel, and then double-click on the System icon. A window with four tabs appears. Select the Performance tab and you'll notice in the Advanced Settings box a button labeled Graphics. Click on the button and the window shown in figure 23.2 appears.

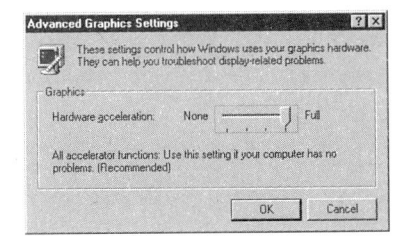

Fig. 23.2 The Graphics window set to its default values

The Graphics window shows you any problems the system has noticed with your graphics setup. It also has a default setting for the "acceleration" of graphics on your system based on the type of video card you have. In general, you want to leave the acceleration setting alone, as Windows has already tested your card when it did the hardware setup. Changing the values on this may speed your system up, but may also cause video problems to occur.

There are a few other places where working with the Windows 95 settings for graphics and graphics files can make using your system easier. To begin with, look at setting up associations for your graphics files.

Types of File Formats

When you work with graphics, you need to know the two basic graphics categories—*raster* and *vector*. You also need to know the various formats you might want to use, as well as their strengths and weaknesses.

Raster Graphics

Raster graphics (or *bit maps*) are graphics images composed of small dots (called *pixels*). The pixels can be simple *on-or-off bits* as in a black and white image, or represent various colors. Generally you will work with four levels of raster images: black and white (1 bit per pixel), 16-colors (4 bits per pixel), 256-colors (8 bits per pixel), or 16-million colors (24 bits per pixel, also called *Truecolor* mode). Raster graphics do not generally scale to larger sizes very well; the dots become squares or rectangles and the image appears grainy. Raster graphics also use lots of disk space and memory. However, they generally display faster than vector graphics and can show much more true-to-life detail than vector graphics. Examples of raster graphics are GIF files and BMP files. Following is a list of the major raster formats:

Extension	Type
BMP, DIB, RLE	**Windows bitmap files.** This is the standard bitmap format supported by Microsoft Windows in programs such as Paint. Unlike many other formats, BMPs and DIBs have no compression options, so even simple pictures can be quite large.
GIF	**CompuServe Graphics Interchange Format files.** The GIF format was developed by CompuServe to provide good file compression and relatively fast decompression speed— important criteria for pictures designed to be passed around electronically. The GIF format is a

Extension	Type
	very popular format for online services, but is limited to a maximum of 256 colors. Two standards have been developed: 87a and 89a.
JPG, JFI, JIF	**JPEG compressed files**. The JPEG format was developed to provide a high degree of compression for images. It is a "lossy" compression method, meaning that some color information from the original is lost. JPEG is generally appropriate for photographed and scanned images, and works best if the images originate from 24-bit sources. JPEG is generally inappropriate for any type of line-drawn art.
PCX	**ZSoft picture files**. PCX files are a fairly early PC graphics format, which has been extended over the years to support more and varied color depths. PCX files may or may not be compressed. For example, PCX is the standard used for submission of graphic files to be incorporated in Que books.
TIF	**Tagged Image Format files**. The Tagged Image Format was developed by several companies, including Aldus, to be the "be-all" and "end-all" of image file formats. Because of its scope and extensibility, it is an extremely complex format. It also is an example of a standard that has as many exceptions as it does requirements, thus making it a clear example of the danger of design by committee.

Vector Graphics

Vector graphics are graphics objects composed of the definition of drawn shapes and lines—rectangles, arcs, ellipses, curves, and so on. Because they are descriptions of shapes rather than a collection of individual dots (pixels), vector graphics may be scaled more readily and more accurately than raster graphics. This also means that they tend to be smaller. However, they often are slower to display than raster graphics because of the need to "calculate" the picture each time. The CGM and WPG files are examples of common vector graphics.

The vector formats you're most likely to work with are listed here:

Extension	Type
CDR, PAT, BMF	**CorelDRAW and CorelGALLERY**. These formats are used by Corel products and are a proprietary standard.
CGM	**Computer Graphics Metafile**. CGM files are vector graphic files that have been designed to be useful as clip art. They scale (grow larger or smaller) well and have the distinction of being the only ANSI standard graphic format. There are many flavors of CGM files as the original format was adopted, then "enhanced," by several different vendors. Although this is primarily a vector format, certain forms can also incorporate raster data.
EPS	**Encapsulated PostScript files**. EPS files are PostScript language files, created for PostScript printers. Many programs that understand PostScript (particularly from Adobe) will also use this format.
GEM, IMG	**GEM metafiles and GEM image format**. GEM metafiles are vector graphic files that include drawing commands for rendering pictures. They are similar to CGM files. GEM files originated on the Amiga, and have gone through several enhancement periods. The IMG format, on the other hand, was originally designed for the Atari computers, and then migrated to PCs for several GEM-based products, such as Ventura Publisher. IMG files may also be embedded in GEM metafiles.
WPG	**DrawPerfect graphics files**. WPG files are a vector format that WordPerfect Corporation developed for use with its word processing products. Like other formats, WPG has evolved over the years.

The particular image format you use depends on the tools you have available, what format any existing images you use come in, and what you're planning to use the images for.

Note: One format not listed in the preceding table, but expected to become a major player soon, is the new graphics format that CompuServe has developed to replace the GIF standard. This new, enhanced 24-bit lossless (meaning that the image doesn't allow any bits of information to be lost to improve compression)

> specification will offer the professional graphics community a significant enhancement to the earlier GIF 89a specification while also eliminating the proprietary LZW software, replacing it with compression technology compliant with the PNG (pronounced *ping*) specification. At this time it has not been announced whether this graphics format will be called PNG or will simply be referred to as a new version of GIF.

Setting Associations for Graphics Files

After you've had a computer for a while, you tend to have a number of graphics in different formats scattered around the system. Not only do you have the graphics that you have obtained or created, but also you have the graphics that various programs have loaded. One way to speed the process up is to set up associations in the Registry for various types of graphics files. This way, when you see a graphics file listed in the Explorer, you can double-click on it and have the appropriate graphics application display the file.

You can set up this association two ways. The first is to go into Explorer and right-click one of the graphics files you see listed. When the pop-up menu appears, choose Open With to bring up the Open With window. Type in the full path to the graphics application you want to use, or click on the Other button to bring up a File Open requestor for finding the graphics program you want.

A more direct way is to open an Explorer window and choose View, Options. From the two tabs that appear, select the File Types tab in which you can select a known program, or use a File Open requestor to specify what program will be used to view this type of image. An example is seen in figure 23.3.

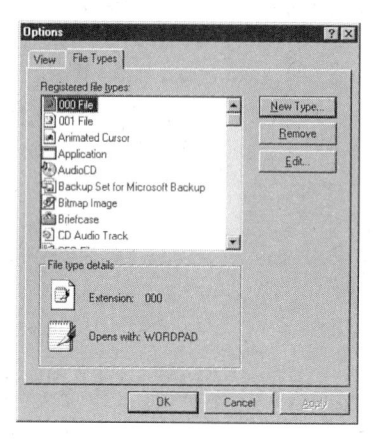

Fig. 23.3 Graphics extension assignment in Explorer using the File Types tab.

You can find more information about both of these methods in Chapter 3, "New Windows 95 Tools." With graphics files it is important to know these options because many graphics programs will try to change the association when they're installed. In other words, you may normally use a small viewer for your JPEG files, and then, after installing a graphics program, discover that it now gets loaded when you double-click on the graphics file. By using one of these methods, you can change things back to the way they were.

You can drag a graphics file from Explorer to the desktop for easy access. Double-clicking on the file will automatically start the application you "tied it to" in the Explorer association and then display the graphics file.

The Graphics Tab for Printing

Printers under Windows 95, as with Windows 3.11 before it, can use one of the Microsoft printer drivers, or a custom driver developed by the vendor. If your printer uses one of the Microsoft drivers, editing its properties will give you a screen with four tabs for controlling how it is used. The easiest way to get to these properties is to go to the Start menu and select Settings, Printers. Right-click the printer you want to edit, and the Properties sheet for that printer appears. Depending on the type of printer you have, the number of tabs available here will vary, but most printers will have a Graphics tab. Figure 23.4 shows what the Graphics tab looks like for the Fax printer in Windows 95.

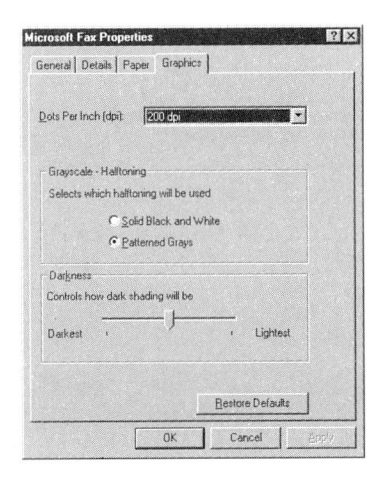

Fig. 23.4 Graphics tab showing settings for the Fax printer.

The setup for this is similar to what you would use for any dot-matrix or ink-jet printer that did not support color. DPI (dots per inch—how many bits will represent each inch of your image) should usually be adjusted to the highest number supported by the printer (in the case of a fax, it should be the highest number you think the fax on the *other* end will support). If you're working with graphics images, you almost never want to use the Solid Black and White option; however, if you're printing text only, it can save you a little speed. The Darkness option should be somewhere toward the middle of the scale unless your printer needs servicing. Otherwise your image will either look washed out (like an overexposed picture) or too dark (like an underexposed picture).

A color printer has many more options to consider, and almost always has a custom setup for this reason. For example, see figure 23.5, which shows the setup for an HP 560c (a color inkjet printer from Hewlett-Packard) in Windows 95.

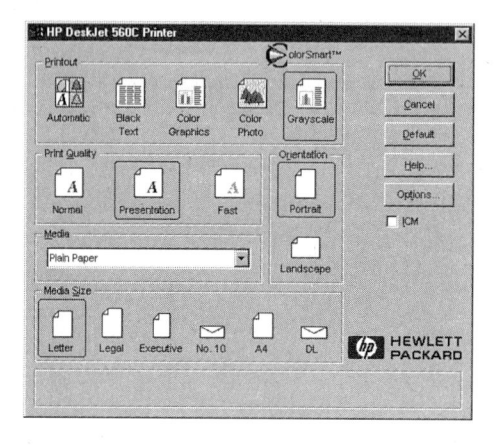

Fig. 23.5 Setup for an HP560c printer.

As you can see, you have many different options. These options give you the flexibility of having the best results for any type of graphic, whether a scanned photo or some black and white piece of clip art.

Using Windows 95 Paint

As you may know, Windows 3.1 came with a simple, yet useful graphics program called *Paintbrush*. Windows 95 comes with a graphics program called *Paint*. The big difference is the added functionality in the Windows 95 Paint program.

Figure 23.6 shows what many people think Paint is good for—drawing squiggly lines. Well, obviously you can do that, but at least you can draw them in several colors. Paint also prepares you for using the other tools.

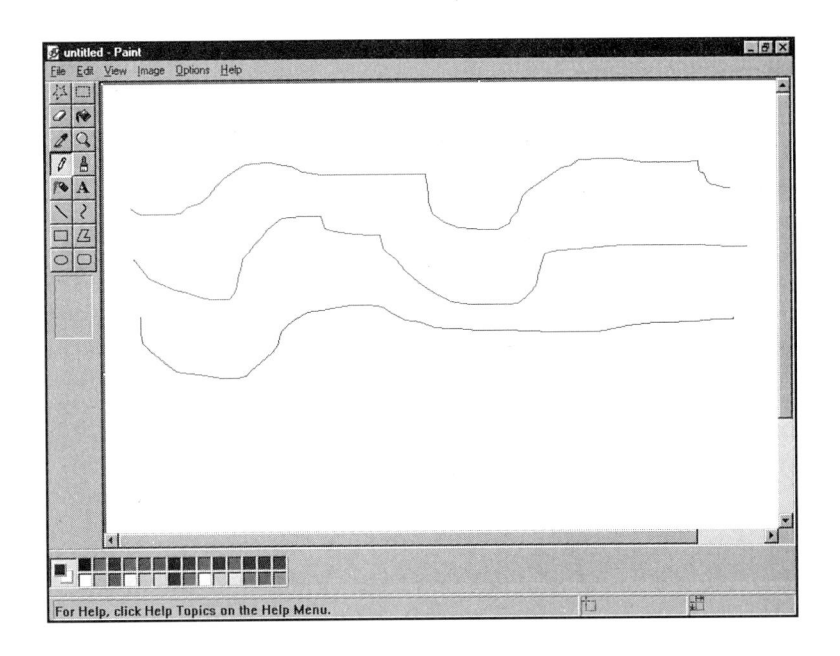

Fig. 23.6 Using Paint to draw squiggly lines.

Starting with the same line, you can use a different tool to create a very different effect. Figure 23.7 shows how you can use the Airbrush tool to create a squiggly line that has quite a bit of character. Notice how selecting each of the three different "dispersal" options affects the look of the lines. From a design aspect, also notice how using multiple lines in different weights gives a feeling of texture to a simple graphic.

Another useful tool is the Fill tool (which looks like a paint can). Normally you would think of using it to fill in a solid area (such as a square), but by using the lines you had earlier, you can get an abstract, *posterized* (also sometimes called solarized, referring to an image that looks like it was overexposed and then colored) effect by doing a fill of the background with a color. Look at figure 23.8, and you notice how certain areas remain unaffected, adding to the overall feel.

Using Windows 95 Paint   **555**

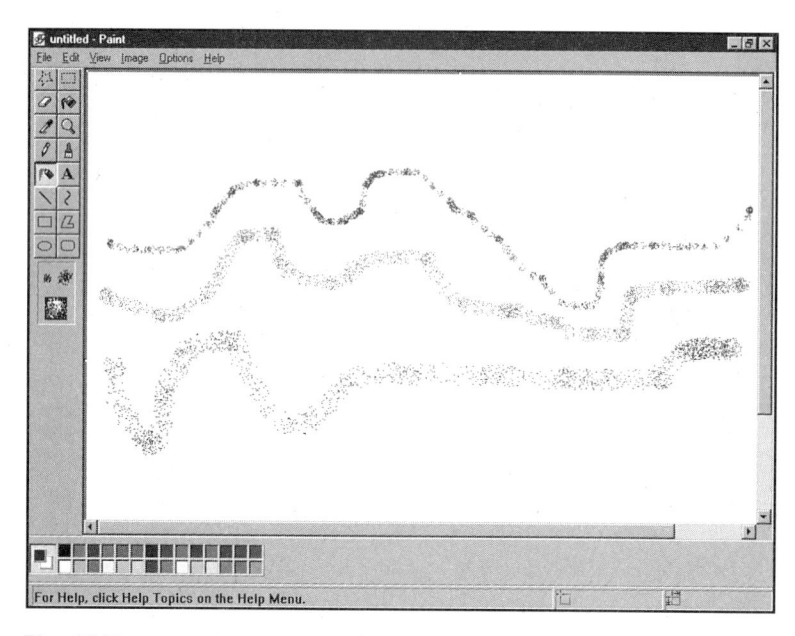

Fig. 23.7 Using the Airbrush tool to draw some lines in Windows 95 Paint.

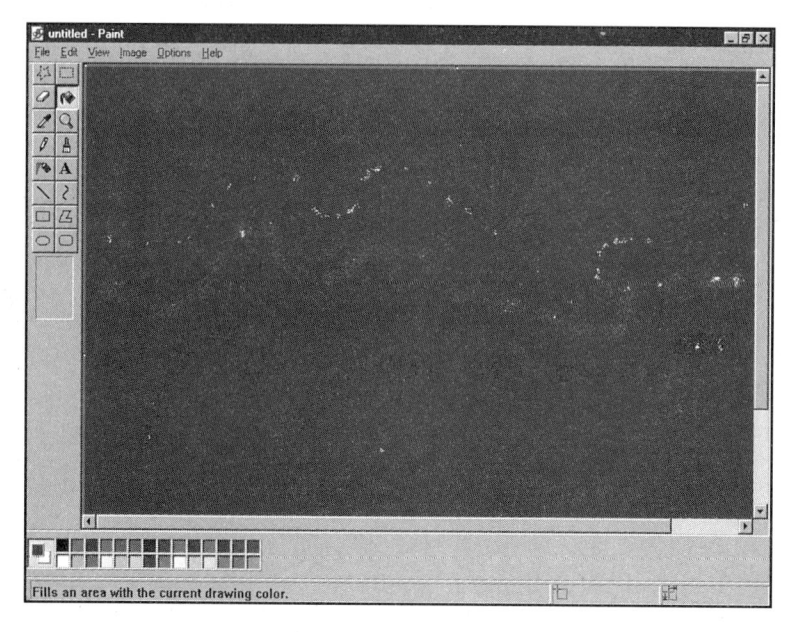

Fig. 23.8 An unusual use for the Fill tool.

556 Chapter 23: Handling Graphics

While you drew a squiggly line earlier with the Pencil, going back and doing the same thing with the Paintbrush by using the various point options can give you many interesting variations. Figure 23.9 shows how the different strokes can give a variety of weights and textures to the end result.

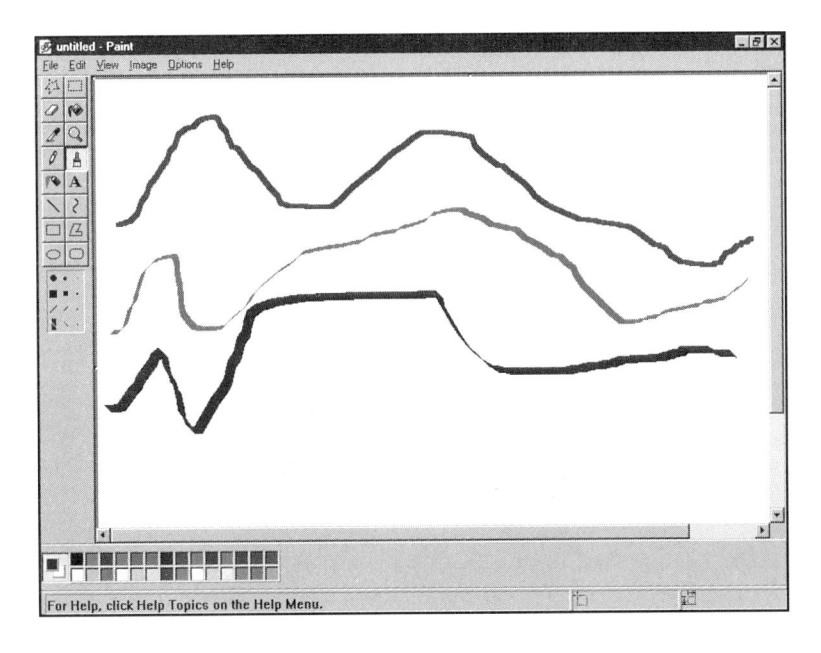

Fig. 23.9 Different types of lines drawn with Paint.

Finally, as an example of quickly building something attractive, look at figure 23.10, which is a sunset (sort of) that took under 10 minutes to create. In addition to the tools mentioned earlier, the Ellipse tool was used to create the sun and its companion.

One thing that many people do with the images they've created or modified is to use them as their desktop wallpaper. Formerly, you used Paintbrush (the Windows 3.x drawing applet) to create the image, and then used the Control Panel to set up your wallpaper. Because setting an image up as wallpaper is done so often, in Paint you can do this without leaving the program. If you look at the File menu, you will see

Using Windows 95 Paint **557**

two options for this, one called Set as Wallpaper (Tiled) and one called Set as Wallpaper (Centered). If you've already saved the loaded image, choose the appropriate menu selection. If you haven't saved the image yet, save it and then choose one of these wallpaper selections from the File menu.

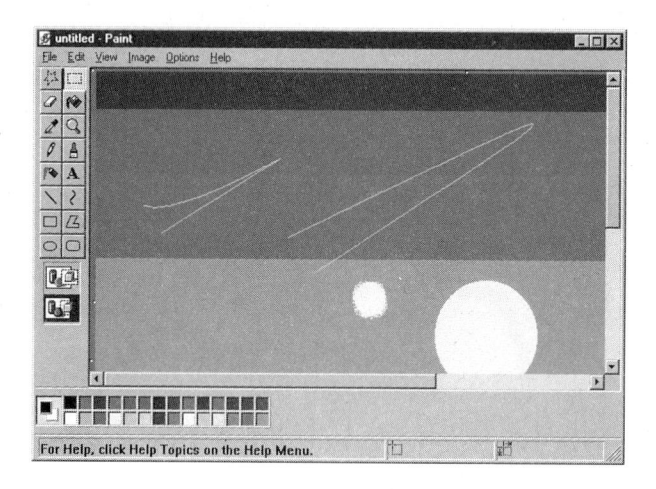

Fig. 23.10 Stylized sunset using several tools from Paint.

Looking at the Options menu, you can also work with what colors are available by using the Edit Colors option. This option gives you a color table with a slider that can be used to find the particular color you're interested in, and then add it to your palette.

Now that you've seen some of what Paint can do, you should think about using it the next time you need a quick, custom 2-D graphic.

Getting the Most from Your Printer

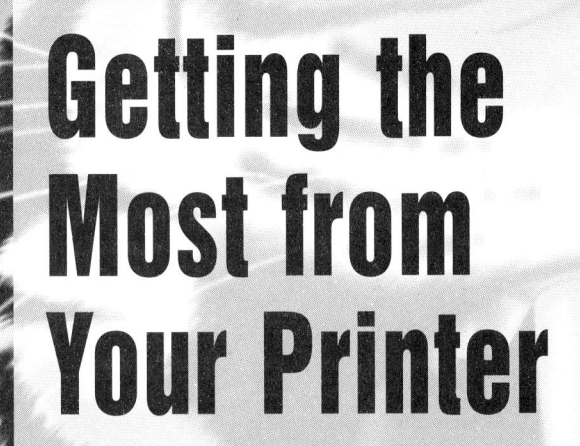

by **Allen L. Wyatt**

Now that your printer is installed, you understand how the print spooler works, and your fonts are in place, you can use your printer with no problems, right? In most cases, the answer is yes. There are a few times, however, when things don't quite go as planned. The purpose of this chapter is to discuss ways you can get the most from your printer. Specifically, you will learn the following:

➤ How to speed up your printer

➤ What the solutions are to common printing problems

➤ How you can use the built-in Windows 95 Print Troubleshooter to help solve your printing problems

Speeding Up Your Printer

Printers come in a wide variety of shapes, sizes, and capabilities. This last attribute—capabilities—is the one that most affects your everyday use of the printer. Printing capabilities can dramatically affect the speed at which your print jobs are processed.

Regardless of the type of printer you use, you can put a multitude of tricks to work to improve the speed at which your printer operates. You can approach the issue from three directions: the Windows 95 side, the printer side, and the computer side.

The Windows 95 Side of the Fence

You can do a variety of things in Windows 95 to speed up your print jobs. The choices you make, however, often affect the quality of the output you receive. Before looking at those choices, however, look at what you can do without affecting quality.

If your computer has multiple hard drives, make sure Windows 95 is set so the swap files are stored on the fastest hard drive. This will improve performance when it comes to storing print jobs on the hard drive and later retrieving them. To change where the swap file is located, follow the directions in Chapter 9, "Exploiting Memory, Space, and Resources."

So there is no possibility of slowing down your print job, you can disable the print spooler altogether. This means your print job is sent directly to the printer, without an intermediate stop on your hard drive. Turning off print spooling is explained fully in Chapter 21, "Printing from Windows 95," but you can follow these steps as well:

1. Open the Printers folder and right-click on the icon for the printer you'll be using. This displays the context menu for the printer.

2. Choose the Properties option from the context menu. The Printer Properties sheet appears.

3. Make sure the Details tab is selected, and then click on the Spool Settings button. The Spool Settings dialog box appears.

4. At the top of the dialog box, select the Print directly to the printer option.

When you close the dialog boxes, any print job for that printer will bypass the print spooler entirely.

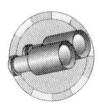

> **Note:** Although printing directly to the printer may make the print job go faster, it can decrease your productivity in the long run. While Windows 95 is waiting on your printer, you can't do any other work with the program that is printing. Make sure you temper your printing needs with the need to continue working on other projects.

To really speed up your print jobs, the trick is to make them as simple as possible. You can do a variety of things in Windows 95 to make the jobs simpler, but these also typically affect the quality of the print job. Try one or more of these suggestions:

➤ *Turn off graphics output.* Many programs allow you to control exactly what is sent to the printer. If you turn off graphics, the print jobs will be smaller. This is great for draft or intermediate printings of a document.

➤ *Turn on draft quality.* Some application programs allow you to enable a setting that turns on draft quality. This means the program uses fonts native to the printer, which decreases processing time. With some printers, you can change the printer properties to use a draft quality built in to the printer itself.

➤ ***Reduce resolution.*** Some printer drivers allow you to control the resolution at which graphics are printed. Printing at a lower resolution can speed processing time. This is covered in Chapter 23, "Handling Graphics."

➤ ***Turn off font downloading.*** If your printer has built-in fonts, you can use them instead of downloading TrueType fonts. You do this on the Fonts tab of the printer Properties sheet, as discussed in Chapter 22, "Working with Fonts." If you don't download fonts, the printer substitutes a font it has available, and processing of the print job takes less time.

The Printer Side of the Fence

With many printers, there is not much you can do to speed them up. This is particularly true with dot-matrix printers, which are limited by the speed at which the print head can travel across the page. There is one area you can check on your dot-matrix printer, however. Check to make sure that bidirectional printing is turned on. Many printers allow this to be controlled via a dip switch or a jumper setting. Bidirectional printing means that the print head can print as it moves in either direction on the page. Some printers come configured for only unidirectional printing, meaning that the print head wastes movement in one direction.

If you have an ink jet or laser printer, you typically have greater control over the performance of the unit. The first item to check is the amount of memory in the printer. If the printer understands some form of page description language (such as PCL or PostScript), then the entire page is constructed in the printer's memory before it is placed on the page. Thus, memory becomes particularly critical if you're printing large or complex print jobs—the printer needs more memory for these types of print jobs. Most printers come with a base amount of memory (such as a megabyte or two), but can be upgraded. Some printers can actually contain quite a bit of memory (24M or 32M). If you're working with complex print jobs, you should consider upgrading to 12M or more of printer memory.

Another area that can generally be improved on faster laser printers is the interface used for the printer. Some already come configured with two or three types of interfaces. Choosing the wrong interface can slow down your printer—in effect, the interface acts as a bottleneck. The laser printer could go faster, but it has to wait for information to arrive through the interface. When it comes to the interface, keep the following in mind:

➤ In most instances, the serial interface is the slowest you can choose. Only choose the serial interface when distance between the printer and your computer is excessive and speed is not an issue.

➤ The parallel interface is perhaps the most common interface used with printers. Make sure your computer and printer are using the highest-capability parallel settings possible. For instance, if your printer can handle bidirectional parallel communications, you should make sure your computer can as well. These types of parallel connections often have operational modes that are superior to the older IBM PC parallel interface.

➤ If you're printing over a network, consider getting a native interface for the network. For instance, if you have an Ethernet network, you can often get a 10BaseT interface that fits directly into the printer. This allows information to be transferred to the printer at the speed of your network—typically 10 Mbps or greater.

On most printers you can select the fonts or print mode that will be used by the printer. For instance, you can instruct the printer to use a draft font or a lower resolution when printing. While this may work for some jobs, other programs may override your settings by sending commands that change the font or resolution to higher settings.

Finally, some top-of-the-line laser printers have the capability of installing a hard drive. This disk is either contained within the printer itself, or sits externally, next to the printer. The hard drive is used to store printer fonts and predefined forms. Taking advantage of such a device can greatly increase the speed at which your print jobs are processed. The reason is quite simple—the font or form does not have to be downloaded from the computer with every print job. Instead, the command to use the font or form is downloaded, and the actual image is retrieved from the printer's hard drive. This can result in much faster performance of the printer.

Your Computer's Role

Believe it or not, your computer has a role in how quickly your printer can do its work. Many of today's printers are quite capable, and they can print pages very quickly. If your computer is not quite up to snuff, the printer could actually be waiting on your computer. The best way to make sure that your computer is not slowing down your printer is to check three areas: your CPU, RAM, and hard drive.

If your CPU is an older model (meaning 386), then it is very possible that your computer cannot perform all the tasks expected of it in an efficient manner. If you have print spooling turned on, your print job is in the spooler, and you're doing other work, then time is taken from your print spooler by a CPU that is not as quick at switching between tasks as it could be. If you print a lot of large print jobs, you may want to consider a faster CPU.

The amount of RAM in your computer determines how many things Windows 95 can do at once without resorting to the hard drive. Although print jobs are almost always spooled to the hard disk, there comes a time when they must be moved through memory to go to the printer. If memory is limited and you're running other programs, chances are good there is little free memory available for other operations. This means that virtual memory must be used, which slows down the overall speed of your system—including printing. This becomes particularly critical if you have only 4M of memory. In such an instance, consider upgrading to at least 8M, and possibly more.

Under Windows 95, your hard drive always gets a good workout. This is particularly true when using virtual memory or when printing large documents. Virtual memory results in RAM information being written to the swap file, on disk, for short periods of time. Print jobs, when they're spooled, are always stored on your hard disk. If the amount of space on your hard drive is limited, then the size of print jobs you can handle is also limited. If your hard drive is slow (14 ms or greater), then sending print jobs to and from the hard drive is slow, as well. If you routinely process large print jobs or a large quantity of small print jobs, consider upgrading to a newer, faster hard drive. You'll see an immediate improvement not only in your print speeds but also in your overall Windows performance.

Troubleshooting Common Problems

It never fails. Just when you thought you had everything under control, a new problem crops up. Printing is no exception. You are bound to run into glitches that will frustrate you until you discover the solutions. Your first step in determining where your problem lies is to find out if the printing problem is evidenced only in a particular application, or globally throughout Windows 95. The best way to discover this is to print a test page for the printer. To do this, follow these steps:

1. Display the Printers folder, and then right-click the printer you want to test. A context menu appears.

2. From the context menu, select Properties. The printer Properties sheet for the printer appears.

3. Click the Print Test Page button at the bottom of the sheet.

You should see a printout appear on your printer. If you do, and it appears properly, the printing problem probably lies with your application. If it does not print properly, you have a global problem you need to address within Windows 95. Many Windows 95 printing problems can be boiled down to a few common maladies. The following sections discuss common printing problems and what you can do to correct them.

Driver Problems

Printer drivers are at the heart of how Windows 95 uses printers. If you have the wrong printer driver installed, or you have the wrong printer driver settings, at best you won't be able to use your printer fully, and at worst you won't be able to use the printer at all.

Make sure the printer driver you have selected matches the printer actually connected to the printer port. If you can't find the proper printer driver, contact the vendor for a driver disk. Alternatively, you could select a compatible printer driver, but only if you're sure it can be used by the printer you have. Remember that if you choose a compatible printer driver (instead of one specifically for your printer), some printer options may not work from within Windows 95.

The Wrong Font Prints

If the fonts printed on paper don't match those you selected in your application, there could be several reasons. The first thing to check is to make sure you've installed the fonts correctly in your system. You should be able to select the desired fonts, and they should appear on-screen. For some types of fonts, you need to install both a screen and printer version. If you've installed the screen font, but not the printer font, this can lead to mismatches.

To install printer fonts, you have two options. You can use either the font installer program that was supplied with the fonts package, or Windows 95 capabilities. The latter can be accomplished if you're using a PCL printer that allows you to download soft fonts. To do this, follow these steps:

1. Display the Printers folder, and then right-click on the printer you want to use from DOS. A context menu appears.

2. From the context menu, select P<u>r</u>operties. The printer Properties sheet for the printer appears.

3. Click on the Fonts tab, and then on the <u>I</u>nstall Printer Fonts button. The font installer dialog box appears, shown in figure 24.1.

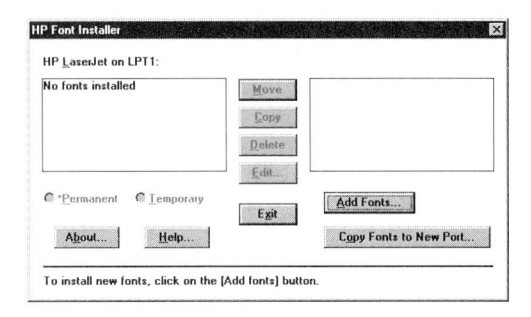

Fig. 24.1 The Fonts tab of the printer Properties sheet for a PCL printer allows you to install printer fonts.

Troubleshooting Common Problems **567**

4. Click on the Add Fonts button. You're asked where the fonts are located that you want to install.

5. Supply the drive and path to where the printer fonts are located. Typically this will be on a floppy disk provided with your printer or from the font provider. Once you have provided this information, click on OK.

6. In the right side of the font installer dialog box, select the fonts you want installed on the printer. Click the Move or Copy button to transfer the fonts.

7. Repeat steps 4 though 6 until you're satisfied with the fonts installed.

8. Click the Exit button when you're done.

Another item to check is that font downloading has not been disabled for the printer. Check the Fonts tab in the printer Properties sheet to make sure the fonts are being handled the way you expect.

Finally, check to make sure the printer driver you're using is the proper one for your printer. If you have substituted a different printer driver, then you can experience unexpected results. The printer driver, for instance, may believe the printer has a certain set of fonts. The printer, on the other hand, has a different set of fonts. Only those fonts indicated in the printer driver will show as available on the printer (even though they may not, in reality, be there).

TrueType Fonts Won't Print

You probably are using a printer that uses the PostScript page description language. You need to make sure you've enabled TrueType fonts in the printer driver. If you have not, then other fonts will be substituted for the TrueType fonts, or you won't see any output at all.

To enable printing of TrueType fonts on a PostScript printer, follow these steps:

1. Display the Printers folder, and then right-click the printer you want to use from DOS. A context menu appears.

2. From the context menu, select P<u>r</u>operties. The printer Properties sheet for the printer appears.

3. Click the Fonts tab. The dialog box shown in figure 24.2 appears.

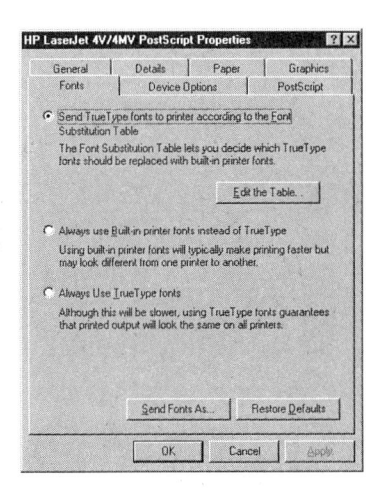

Fig. 24.2 The Fonts tab of the printer Properties sheet for a PostScript printer allows you to change how TrueType fonts are handled.

From this dialog box you can indicate how you want TrueType fonts to be handled by your printer. Make sure you're using settings consistent with both your desires and the capabilities of your printer. For a

Troubleshooting Common Problems **569**

complete discussion of how TrueType fonts are handled in various printers, refer to Chapter 22, "Working with Fonts."

Another possible cause of the problem is that your printer is incapable of printing TrueType fonts. Not all printers can print TrueType fonts. Older models of LaserJet printers, for example, cannot understand the PCL commands enabled in the LaserJet Series II and Series III printers, and other laser printers cannot accommodate downloadable fonts. Check your printer documentation to determine the capabilities of your individual printer.

You Can't Print in an MS-DOS Window

Printing in an MS-DOS window is a bit different than printing in Windows itself. Where Windows allows you to set up a wide variety of printers, DOS expects that you have only one or two printers connected to your system, and that they be connected to a parallel port. To use specific printers from DOS, you must map them to different ports. For instance, you might have five different printers defined within Windows, but you want to print to only one of them in a DOS window. So the print system knows which printer should be used, mapping the port is necessary. To map a printer to a port, follow these steps:

1. Display the Printers folder, and then right-click on the printer you want to use from DOS. A context menu appears.

2. From the context menu, select Properties. The printer Properties sheet for the printer appears.

3. Click on the Details tab, and then on the Port Settings button. The dialog box shown in figure 24.3 appears.

4. Make sure the Spool DOS Print Job check box is selected.

When you close the dialog boxes and open an MS-DOS window, you will be able to print to the port from your DOS programs.

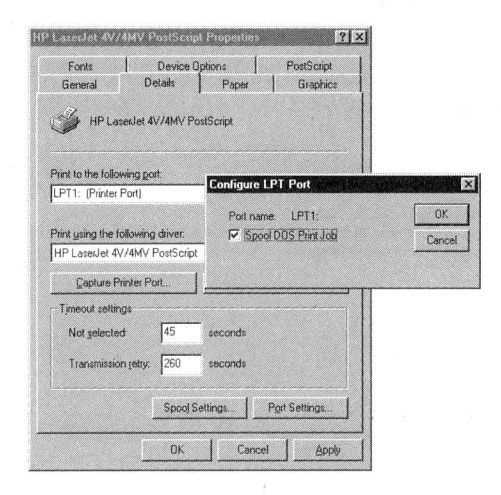

Fig. 24.3 The Configure LPT Port dialog box allows you to indicate if DOS printing is available from the port.

Your Print File Is Too Big

When trying to print a huge document, you might get an error indicating that your disk is full. What is happening is that the print spooler is trying to write the print job to the disk, and it cannot; it has run out of room. There are three solutions to this problem:

➤ *Chop your printing job into smaller portions.* Perhaps you can print only certain pages, or don't print the entire thing at once.

➤ *Move your swap file so it is on a disk drive with more space.* How you can do this is covered in Chapter 9, "Exploiting Memory, Space, and Resources."

➤ *Print directly to your printer.* Turn off the print spooler (as covered earlier in this chapter) so the job goes directly to the printer instead of being written to a disk file.

Incomplete Printing

If only part of a page is printed from your printer, chances are good it is because of the complexity of the page. Start by determining if the page had a lot of graphics or type fonts. If the answer is yes, then your printer may not have enough memory to handle the demands of the print job.

There are several ways you can work around the problem:

➤ *Decrease the print resolution.* If your printer allows you to select different print resolutions (for instance, 300 dpi vs. 600 dpi), try the lower setting. The quality of the output won't be as good, but you may be able to get the entire page out.

➤ *Decrease the complexity of the job.* Reduce the number of fonts or the size or quantity of graphics on the page. This, in turn, requires less printer memory, and you may be able to print the page.

➤ *Print to another printer.* You may know of another printer that has the resources to print your job. If you can reach the printer through your network, redirect the job. If the printer is located elsewhere and cannot be reached from your computer, print the job to a disk file. You can then take the disk file to the printer and output it there.

➤ *Add memory to your printer.* This is the best long-term solution, particularly if you'll be printing quite a few print jobs at this resolution or complexity. In order to do this, you'll need to refer to your printer documentation to determine what is possible and how to go about adding the memory.

Your Print Job Disappears

You've pressed the Print button in an application, and printing seems to go OK from your computer, but nothing comes out of the printer. Typically, this is the result of the printer being directed to the wrong printer port. Check to determine what printer port the printer is physically connected to. Then, open the Properties sheet for the printer and make sure (in the Details tab) that the printer is using the same port.

It may also be that your printer is "confused" for some reason. The easiest way to see whether this is the issue is to turn the printer off and back on. After the printer warms up and comes on-line (the on-line or ready light is illuminated), try printing your job again.

Printing Is Slower Than Normal

If you've been using your printer for some time, but lately it is printing a bit sluggishly, here are a few things you should try:

- Turn the printer off and back on. It may be that memory used in a previous print job was not released properly. Restarting the printer should clear the memory and make it all available again.

- In the Properties sheet for the printer, click on the Details tab and then on Spool Settings. Make sure the Spool data format is set to EMF. Enhanced Meta Files take less room and are faster to process than raw data files.

- Make sure that the printer driver you have loaded for the printer is the proper printer driver. Using a compatible printer driver instead of the matching printer driver can slow down your print jobs.

➤ Run the Disk Defragmenter to clean up the hard disk that contains your swap file. It is possible that the disk is very fragmented, and thus slower when retrieving your print job.

Using the Print Troubleshooter

Windows 95 includes a new feature that can help you determine the best solution to your printing woes. This feature is called the Print Troubleshooter. It is part of the Help system built in to Windows. To use the Print Troubleshooter, follow these steps:

1. Choose Help from the Start menu. The Help Topics dialog box appears.
2. Click on the Index tab. The dialog box changes to what is shown in figure 24.4.

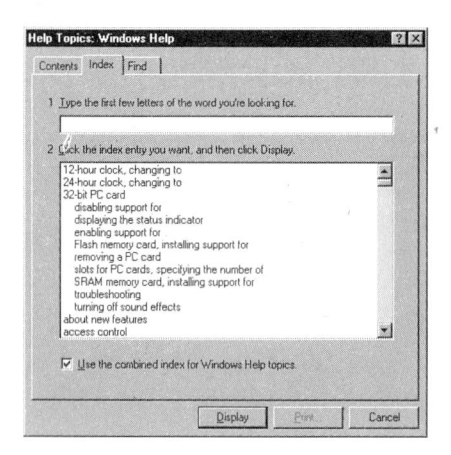

Fig. 24.4 The Help system Index tab allows you to search for topics of interest.

3. In the top portion of the dialog box, enter the word **Print**. The topics at the bottom portion of the dialog box will change accordingly.

4. In the bottom portion of the dialog box, click the print troubleshooting entry.

5. Click the <u>D</u>isplay button. The Print Troubleshooter dialog box appears, as shown in figure 24.5.

From this point, you can read the questions presented in the dialog box and make your choices from the options available. For instance, if you are having problems getting any output from your printer, the questions would lead you through printing a test page and determining where the problem lies.

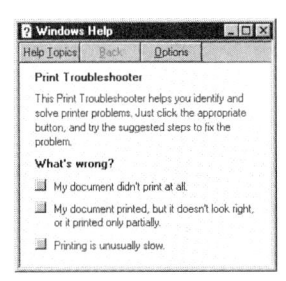

Fig. 24.5 The Print Troubleshooter is part of the Windows 95 Help system.

Using the Print Troubleshooter **575**

Adding Multimedia Capability to Your Computer

KILLER 25 WINDOWS 95

by Clayton Walnum

Perhaps no computing term has been thrown around more lately than "multimedia." A good portion of the software at your local computer store boasts multimedia features, and salespeople at computer stores use the term multimedia in much the same way snake-oil salesmen used the words "miracle cure." What exactly is multimedia? Is it really the big deal some people would like you to believe? Can multimedia make your computing experience more productive and gratifying?

How can you make your computer multimedia capable? In the discussions to follow, you'll get the answers to these questions (and many more!). In this chapter, you learn:

- What multimedia means
- How to interpret the multimedia standards
- The best systems for multimedia
- What to look for in a sound card
- How to install a sound card and CD-ROM drive

Understanding the Multimedia PC

There are almost as many definitions of the term *multimedia* as there are pages in this book. This is because multimedia is a general term, rather than something specific. Literally, multimedia means nothing more exotic than "many media." In other words, a multimedia application presents its information by using more than one type of media. For example, a slide show accompanied by a recorded voice is a multimedia presentation because it uses two types of media to present its information: slides and recorded tape.

Obviously, multimedia is nothing new. In fact, adding multimedia capabilities to a computer doesn't make the computer some sort of digital wonder of the future; it simply makes your computer able to do things that the rest of the world has been doing for decades. So much for all those Flash Gordon images that have been flitting through your head!

So, what's the big deal? In the early days of computing, computers presented information only as text on a screen. There's nothing wrong with text, of course. After all, the world's greatest thinkers presented their ideas to the brain-challenged masses in only text form. Pythagoras sure didn't have access to a CD-ROM player! Nowadays, though, computers use not only text, but also photographic-quality images, digitized sound, and full-motion video to present information. And, in case you haven't guessed, such a computer is a multimedia computer.

The fact is that a multimedia PC is basically little more than a computer that's been equipped with a sound card and a CD-ROM drive. But, in order to acquire the coveted multimedia title, the computer has to perform to a specific set of standards created by some folks who know exactly what it takes to run today's (and tomorrow's) multimedia applications. You discover these standards in the next section.

Upgrading Your Hardware to MPC Standards

In order to be sure that the multimedia computer you buy performs well enough to run multimedia software, the Multimedia PC Marketing Council created the Multimedia PC (MPC) specifications. These specifications dictate minimum requirements for every component of your system that affects multimedia. Many older computers do not comply with these standards. If you can remember using your computer while watching first-run episodes of *Family Ties*, chances are good that you're due for a system upgrade! To help you decide how to best go about upgrading your computer, the MPC standards come in two levels.

The Level-1 Multimedia Standard

The Level-1 MPC standard is the absolute minimum requirements for a multimedia system. However, because the Level-1 requirements were determined way back in 1990, they are outdated. While you can run some types of multimedia software on a Level-1 MPC system, most of today's multimedia titles run too slowly, or not at all, on such a system. The Level-1 requirements are listed in Table 25.1.

Table 25.1 The Level-1 MPC Minimum Requirements

Device	Requirements
CPU	16-MHz 386SX
Operating system	Windows with Multimedia Extensions
Memory	2M
Hard disk	30M
Floppy disk	1.44M (high-density)
CD-ROM drive	Single speed with 150K transfer rate and one-second average seek time.
Sound card	8-bit digital sound, 11.025 KHz sampling rate, 8-note synthesizer, MIDI playback, microphone input, and speakers or headphones
Video	640x480 with 16 colors.
Ports	Joystick, MIDI I/O, serial, and parallel
Input	101-key keyboard and a two-button mouse

The Level-2 Multimedia Standard

As hinted at previously, the Level-1 MPC requirements are almost obsolete. If you're planning to upgrade your system for multimedia, you should shoot for at least the Level-2 requirements. This ensures that you'll be able to run most of the latest software. Of course, a Level-2 MPC system is more expensive to put together than a Level-1 system. Just remember the old saying: You get what you pay for! Table 25.2 lists the Level-2 MPC minimum requirements. These days, a Level-2 MPC system goes for about $1,000.

Table 25.2 The Level-2 MPC Minimum Requirements

Device	Requirements
CPU	25-MHz 486SX
Operating system	Windows 3.1 or later
Memory	4M

Device	Requirements
Hard disk	160M
Floppy disk	1.44M (high-density)
CD-ROM drive	Double-speed with 300K transfer rate and 400-ms average seek time.
Sound card	16-bit digital sound, 44.1 KHz sampling rate, stereo channels, 8-note synthesizer, and MIDI playback
Video	640 x 480 with 65,536 colors
Ports	Joystick, MIDI I/O, serial, and parallel
Input	101-key keyboard and a two-button mouse

Beyond Level-2

Keep in mind that although the Level-2 MPC requirements are the newest specifications, they represent only a minimum Level-2 MPC system. To get a truly worthwhile MPC system, you're going to have to boost some of the minimum requirements listed in the Level-2 standard. Table 25.3 shows the average MPC requirements for today's MPC systems. If you upgrade your system to meet Table 25.3's specifications, you'll be able to get satisfactory results with virtually any MPC software package on the market today.

Table 25.3 Recommended Average MPC Requirements

Device	Requirements
CPU	66-MHz 486
Operating system	Windows 95
Memory	8M
Hard disk	500M
Floppy disk	1.44M (high-density)

continues

Table 25.3 Continued

Device	Requirements
CD-ROM drive	Quad speed with 600K transfer rate and 250-ms average seek time
Sound card	16-bit digital sound, 44.1 KHz sampling rate, stereo channels, 8-note synthesizer, and MIDI playback
Video	640 x 480 with 65,536 colors
Ports	Joystick, MIDI I/O, serial, and parallel
Input	101-key keyboard and a two-button mouse

As you can see, the preceding recommended system requirements up the ante on the CPU, operating system, memory, CD-ROM drive, and hard disk. Many of today's multimedia software packages run sluggishly on anything less than a 60-MHz 486 with 8M of RAM. Also, because today's multimedia titles include so many audio and graphics files, they consume a great deal of hard disk space. A 500M hard disk drive is the minimum you should consider. Quad-speed CD-ROM drives are rapidly becoming the standard, so you shouldn't settle for less. Finally, Windows 95, which provides almost automatic configuration of multimedia devices, provides significantly better support for DOS programs as well. The system outlined in Table 25.3 goes for about $1,700.

Getting the Top of the Line

You say that you want a state-of-the-art system? How thick is your wallet? If you can pinch an inch or more of that folding green stuff, you might want to consider the powerhouse system recommendations listed in Table 25.4. Such a system not only runs today's multimedia software at blazing speeds, but also ensures that your system remains viable for a couple of years to come. Be prepared to pay around $3,500 or more for such an electronic marvel.

Table 25.4 State-of-the-Art MPC Recommendations

Device	Requirements
CPU	100-MHz Pentium
Operating system	Windows 95
Memory	16M
Hard disk	1G
Floppy disk	1.44M (high-density)
CD-ROM drive	Quad-speed with 600K transfer rate and 250-ms seek time
Sound card	16-bit digital sound, 44.1 KHz sampling rate, stereo channels, 32-note synthesizer, wavetable synthesis, and MIDI playback with General MIDI or Roland MT-32 sound sets
Video	800 x 600 with 16 million colors
Ports	Joystick, MIDI I/O, serial, and parallel
Input	101-key keyboard and a two-button mouse

The major differences in this system are the super-fast Pentium processor, an additional 8M of memory, and a 1G hard drive. If you really want the absolute, absolute best, you can substitute a 133 MHz Pentium and get a 6X CD-ROM rather than a 4X (quad speed). Now you're talking really big bucks!

Upgrading an Existing System

Of course, you don't necessarily have to run out and buy a new system in order to use today's multimedia software. You might be able to upgrade your existing system by adding and replacing components. In order to upgrade an existing system, though, it's highly recommended that you at least have a system that meets the CPU and video requirements you're shooting for. Replacing motherboards (the part of the system that holds the CPU) and matching up monitors and video cards can be a frustrating experience, one that is best left to a technician.

Moreover, when you add up the prices of several separate components, you may discover that it's actually wiser to buy a whole new system.

The bottom line is that the only components you should probably try to upgrade yourself is the CD-ROM drive and the sound card. The remaining sections of this chapter give you some general guidelines and instructions for accomplishing these relatively simple upgrade tasks. Keep in mind, though, that PCs are complex machines that come in an almost unlimited number of configurations. Often, even the easiest upgrades lead to complications that you must be prepared to handle. If the thought of opening up your system and poking around inside gives you dizzy spells and cold sweats, you should probably ask a qualified technician to do the upgrade for you.

How much will an upgrade cost? That depends on the number of components in your system that need to be replaced. The cheapest way to add (or replace) a CD-ROM drive and sound card is to purchase one of the many multimedia upgrade kits (figures 25.1 through 25.3) that are available at your local software store or by mail order. Such upgrades usually cost between $200 and $500, the price being based on the quality of the components and the extras that are included with the package.

A minimum multimedia upgrade kit includes a double-speed CD-ROM drive, a 16-bit sound card, and speakers. Most upgrade kits also come with a library of multimedia software to get you started.

You can also buy the CD-ROM drive, sound card, and speakers separately. However, because sound cards are often matched with a CD-ROM drive, you could run into configuration problems if you don't know exactly what you're doing. Moreover, you may end up having to buy both a sound card and a separate CD-ROM interface card, which adds to the cost. One of the big advantages of a complete multimedia upgrade kit is that the CD-ROM drive's interface is usually built in to the matching sound card, ensuring few configuration problems and eliminating the need to buy expensive interface cards that take up an extra slot in the back of your computer.

Fig. 25.1 A Sound Blaster multimedia upgrade kit from Creative Labs.

Learning About Sound Cards

Probably the most important multimedia component you can add to your system is a sound card. Virtually all modern software packages use sound extensively, for everything from digitized voices to explosions, gun shots, and roaring engines. Although you can sometimes get by without a CD-ROM drive (a lot of so-called multimedia software comes on floppy disks, as well as on CD-ROMs), you cannot get full value from your software purchases unless you have a quality sound card.

Unfortunately for the sound shopper, sound cards come in dozens of types, all the way from the very basic for about $70 to the fabulous for around $500 or more. No matter what price range you have in mind, though, there are some common specifications you should look for when choosing a sound card. These specifications are presented in the following sections.

Sound Blaster Compatibility

Over the years, the Sound Blaster sound card has become the industry standard. Virtually every piece of software supports Sound Blaster cards, so if you want to be able to run all software that requires a sound card, you should choose a Sound Blaster-compatible sound card.

A word of warning to folks who want to use their sound cards under DOS as well as under Windows 95: Many sound cards boast 100 percent Sound Blaster compatibility, but don't deliver it. Once you get the card home, you'll discover that some software simply won't work with the sound card. When you call for technical help, you'll get all kinds of technical excuses why the sound card doesn't work with certain software packages. Often, they'll blame the software, in spite of the fact that the software runs perfectly on a real Sound Blaster card.

How do they get away with claiming a sound card is 100 percent Sound Blaster compatible when it's really not? There is no way to really fully tell. But the reality is that supposedly 100 percent Sound Blaster-compatible cards are really only about 50 to 75 percent compatible. So, the fact is that the only way you can be 100 percent sure that your sound card will work with all software is to buy an actual Sound Blaster card.

The downside of this choice is that you may want sound features not available on a Sound Blaster-brand sound card. In this case, you'll just have to decide how much you want the additional features and balance that need against the possibility that some of your programs may have to run without sound.

Sound Cards and Windows

The preceding discussion about Sound Blaster compatibility is really only applicable to DOS software. If you're running your multimedia software under Windows, the Sound Blaster compatibility issue disappears, and you're free to choose any sound card that is Windows compatible. This is because every sound-card manufacturer who wants his product to work properly under Windows must supply a Windows sound driver. Because this sound driver is written by the manufacturer specifically for that one sound card, compatibility problems rarely crop up under Windows.

And, unless you've been living in a submarine for the last few years, you've noticed that DOS programs are starting to disappear, being slowly replaced with Windows versions. In fact, currently only game software is still clutching to the DOS era, due to the sluggishness of Windows graphics capabilities. Recently, however, Microsoft has gone to great lengths to make Windows a viable gaming operating system. Even such CPU-intensive games as the ever-popular DOOM are being ported to Windows. It won't be too long before DOS is a thing of the past.

What's my point? Thanks to Windows, the Sound Blaster standard is about to become a non-standard. Any sound card that comes with a Windows sound driver is a solid choice for your Windows system. Dropping the Sound Blaster compatibility issue opens up all kinds of new possibilities, because almost every sound card in existence includes drivers for Windows.

Sampling Quality

Currently, the most common sound cards provide 8-bit or 16-bit sampling. As you can see in the Level-2 MPC requirements back in Table 25.2, you should consider no less than a 16-bit sound card. The more bits used to sample sounds, the higher quality the result. Make sure that your 16-bit sound card provides 16-bit sound for both playback and recording. Sometimes, so-called 16-bit sound cards offer 16-bit sound only for playback, meaning that, if you want to record your own sounds, you'll have to live with reduced quality. Also, make sure that the sound card provides stereo sound in both playback and recording modes.

FM Synthesis versus Wavetable Synthesis

Sound cards produce instrument sounds in various ways, using an onboard synthesizer. The most common and least expensive synthesizer uses something called FM synthesis to produce sounds using formulas. The resulting sound has a kind of toy-like quality, often not sounding much like the instruments it's intended to mimic. On the plus side, a card that offers only FM synthesis is usually inexpensive. So, if you're not fussy about the music produced by your sound card, you can save some bucks by going with FM synthesis.

If you'd like your music to sound like the real thing, then you should look for wavetable synthesis in your sound card. (Such a sound card usually offers FM synthesis as well, so you don't have to give up anything to get wavetable synthesis.) The advantage of wavetable synthesis is that actual instrument sounds have been recorded and stored in the sound card's memory. The result is stunningly realistic music that sounds almost as if it were being played from a CD. Of course, wavetable cards are much more expensive, often twice as much as cards offering only FM synthesis.

General MIDI MPU-401

MIDI, which stands for Musical Instrument Digital Interface, is a way of transferring performance information between a musical instrument and computers. You don't have to know how to play a musical instrument to take advantage of MIDI on your computer. Often, your sound card acts as the musical instrument, playing back the music that's been stored in files for whatever program you're currently running. If you examine the files on your hard disk, you may find some with an MID extension. These are Windows MIDI files that you can play on a MIDI-capable sound card.

To be sure that all MIDI equipment is compatible, the General MIDI standard specifies the type of commands that can be sent between MIDI devices. It also specifies that a MIDI device must support 16 channels, each of which can play back a different instrument sound.

Because the General MIDI standard specifies 128 instrument sounds (or "patches," as they're called by the experts), a MIDI-capable sound card can reproduce just about any kind of music you can imagine, from Beethoven to Nirvana.

Besides the 16 channels and 128 patches, a MPC-compliant sound card must also be able to play at least three instrument sounds simultaneously with at least six simultaneous notes on each instrument. For good quality, however, you should look for a card that can play 16 instrument sounds simultaneously, with as many as 24 simultaneous notes on each instrument. Such a card is said to be 16-voice multitimbral and 24-note polyphonic.

For extra fun, you can pick up a MIDI-compatible keyboard, which you can plug into your sound card's MIDI ports. (You may need a MIDI adapter for your sound card in order to do this.) Then, you can play music directly into your computer and even record it by using a sequencer application (figure 25.2). Of course, if you can't play keyboards, you probably won't be doing yourself or anyone else any favors by trying to create your own music!

Fig. 25.2 A sequencer is an application that records and plays back MIDI information.

Learning About Sound Cards **589**

Adding a Sound Card to Your PC

Whether you buy a complete multimedia upgrade kit or buy your sound card separately, you must install the sound card into your computer. Although you should follow the installation instructions that come with your sound card, most sound-card installations require that you follow a basic set of procedures, which are:

- Configuring the sound card's IRQ, DMA, and I/O settings
- Inserting the card into your computer, by placing it into an empty expansion slot
- Attaching speakers, a CD-ROM drive, an amplifier, or headphones to the sound card
- Installing any software that came with the sound card
- Adding the new device to the Windows 95 system

Depending on what type of sound card you bought, the preceding steps can be easy or hard. The three main types of sound cards are as follows:

- Plug-and-Play sound card
- Sound card without jumpers
- Sound card with jumpers

Plug-and-Play Sound Cards

The Plug-and-Play type of sound card is the easiest to install, because Windows 95 can take care of all the configuration tasks for you. You insert the sound card into an expansion slot in the computer (figure 25.3), connect any external devices (figure 25.4), and reboot the computer. The operating system then senses that a new device has been installed and communicates with that device to ensure that it's configured properly. But in order to take full advantage of Plug-and-Play devices, your computer must also have a Plug-and-Play BIOS (Basic Input/Output System). Check your system's literature to see whether your system can accommodate such devices. Most newer systems can.

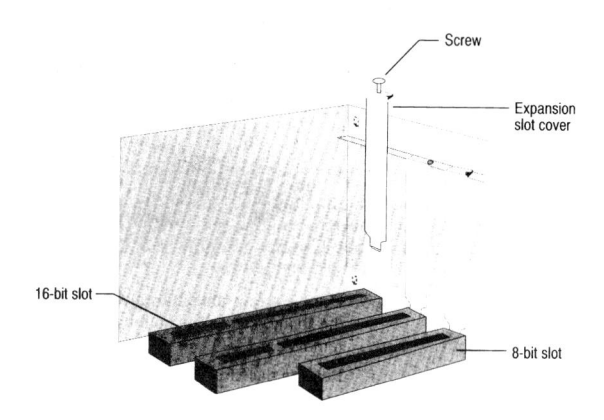

Fig. 25.3 You place a sound card into an empty expansion slot located at the back of your computer's system unit.

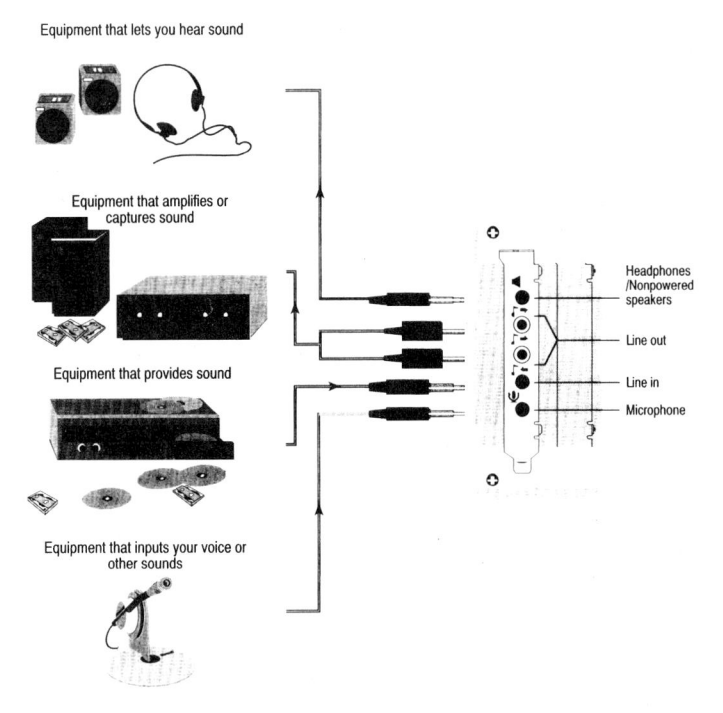

Fig. 25.4 You can connect many types of external devices to a sound card.

Adding a Sound Card to Your PC **591**

Jumperless Sound Cards

If you didn't get a Plug-and-Play sound card (there aren't too many of them around at this point), you can still get a lot of configuration help from Windows 95. The next easiest type of card to add to your system is the jumperless card. Because such a card can be configured by sending commands to the card, Windows 95 is likely able to set up the card for you, almost as if the card were Plug-and-Play.

As with the Plug-and-Play card, you first have to insert the card into one of your computer's expansion slots and then connect any external devices you need (speakers, CD-ROM, and so on). Then, close up the computer and turn it on. When Windows 95 appears on-screen, follow the instructions given in the next section, "Adding New Hardware."

Note that you can change the settings on a jumperless sound card, too, just as easily as Windows can. And you can change the settings without touching the card or even having to open your computer. Usually a jumperless device comes with a configuration program that, when started, enables you to change the device's settings right on the screen. This sure beats the old method of manually placing jumpers on the circuit board!

Sound Cards with Jumpers

The last type of sound card requires that you set the card's IRQ, DMA, and I/O settings right on the card itself. You do this by positioning jumpers on the appropriate jumper pins (figure 25.5). Which settings should you use? That's the hard part! You should first try the default settings, which should already be set when you buy the card. You can find these default settings listed in the sound card's manual.

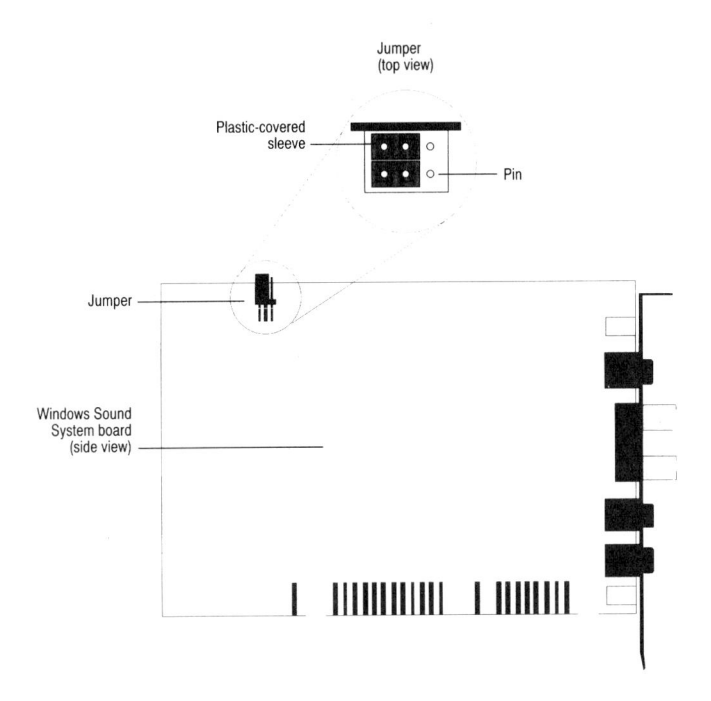

Fig. 25.5 Some sound cards require that you set jumpers on the circuit board.

Once you know what the default settings are, run Windows 95. Then, take the following steps:

1. Find Control Panel in the Settings section of the Start menu.
2. Run Control Panel by clicking on its entry in the Settings menu.
3. Click on the System icon to bring up the System Properties sheet. Make sure the Device Manager tab is selected (see figure 25.6).

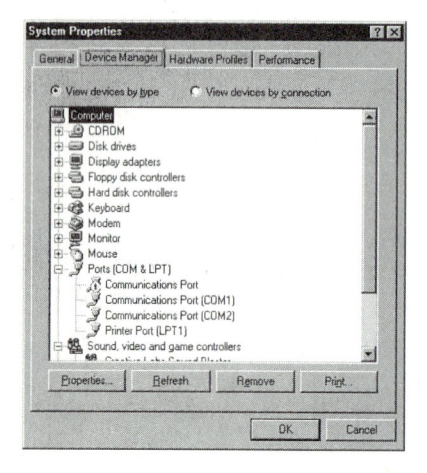

Fig. 25.6 The System Properties sheet with the Device Manager tab selected.

4. Click the Properties button, and then select the Interrupt Request (IRQ) option. You then see a list of interrupts currently being used by your system (figure 25.7).

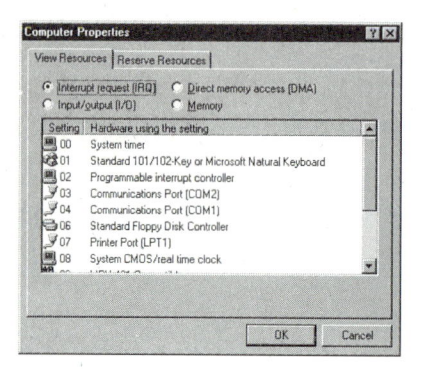

Fig. 25.7 The interrupt list in the Computer Properties sheet.

5. Make sure that the default IRQ on the sound card is not already being used. If the IRQ is in use, make note of an unused IRQ that's compatible with your card, and then change the card's jumper to the unused IRQ.

594 Chapter 25: Adding Multimedia Capability to Your Computer

6. Follow the same procedure to set the card's DMA channel. Figure 25.8 shows the Computer Properties sheet with the Direct Memory Access (DMA) option selected.

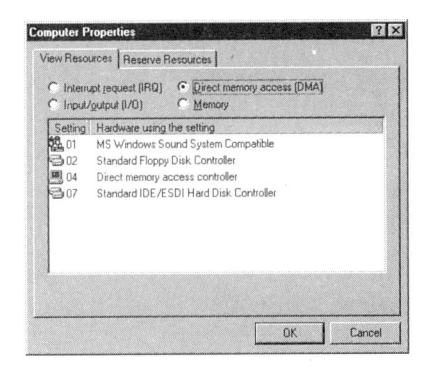

Fig. 25.8 The DMA list in the Computer Properties sheet.

Now that you have your sound card configured so that it doesn't conflict with other devices in the system, you can insert the card into one of the empty slots in your computer. (Turn off the computer first, of course.) If you made a mistake in the configuration process, and there is still a conflict in the system, Windows will not allow the device to operate, thus ensuring that the system doesn't lock up. You can solve your problem by using Windows 95's troubleshooting help. See this chapter's "Troubleshooting Your Sound Card" section for further information on this handy feature.

Adding New Hardware

Now that you have your sound card configured and installed in your computer, it's time to add the new hardware to Windows 95. You do this by using the Add New Hardware Wizard, as described in the following steps:

1. Restart Windows 95, run Control Panel, and select the Add New Hardware icon. When you do, you see the Add New Hardware Wizard, as shown in figure 25.9.

Adding a Sound Card to Your PC **595**

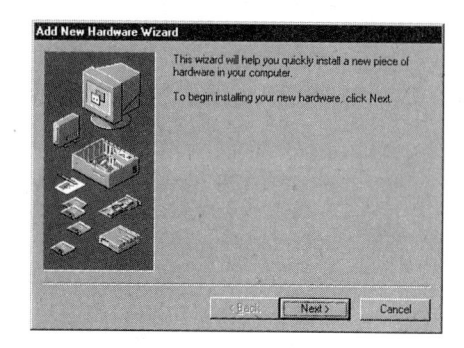

Fig. 25.9 The Add New Hardware Wizard helps you set up new devices.

2. Click on the Next button to start the wizard. When you do, you see the window shown in figure 25.10, which lists the various types of hardware you can add to your system.

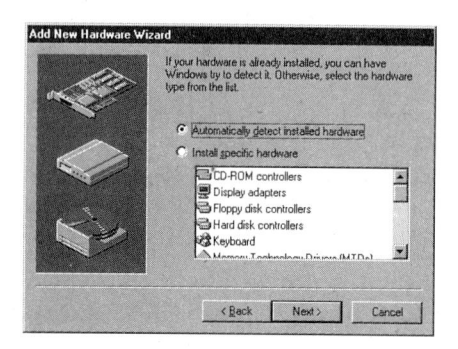

Fig. 25.10 The Add New Hardware Wizard's hardware list.

3. Click on the Install Specific Hardware button, and select Sound, video and game controllers in the hardware list (figure 25.11).

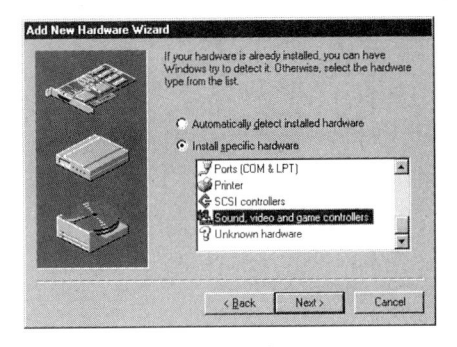

Fig. 25.11 Selecting the Sound hardware from the hardware list.

4. Click on the Next button to see a list of supported sound cards (figure 25.12).

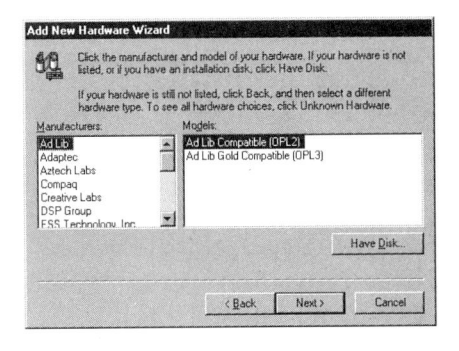

Fig. 25.12 The list of supported sound cards.

5. In the Manufacturers list, select the manufacturer of your sound card. In the Models list, select the sound card's model. Figure 25.13 shows the MediaVision sound cards selected. (If your sound card isn't listed, you need to have a driver disk from the manufacturer. Click the Have Disk button to load the drivers from the disk.)

Adding a Sound Card to Your PC   **597**

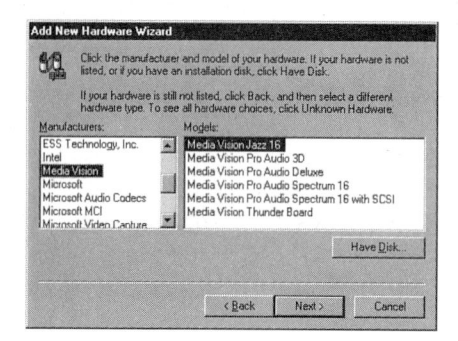

Fig. 25.13 Selecting the sound card's manufacturer and model.

6. Click on the Next button, and you see the window shown in figure 25.14. Click on the Finish button to install your new sound card into Windows 95.

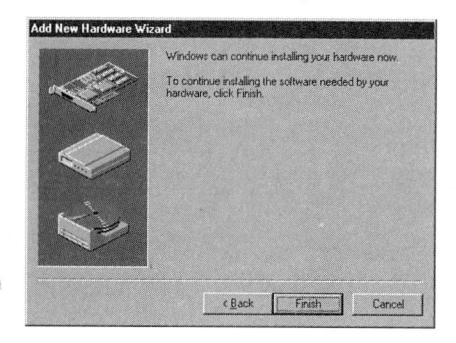

Fig. 25.14 Finishing the sound-card installation process.

Testing Your Sound Card

Once you have your sound card installed, it's time to see whether it's working properly. First, you want to be sure that it can play back both waveform files (digital sound effects) and MIDI files (MIDI music). To do this, select the Media Player entry from the Start/Programs/Accessories/Multimedia menu. When you do, you see the Media Player accessory, which looks like figure 25.15.

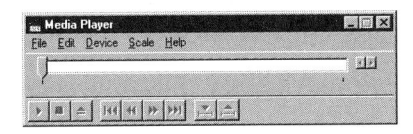

Fig. 25.15 Finishing the sound-card installation process.

Select the Open command from the File menu, and select a waveform Sound file. After loading the sound file, test the sound card by clicking on the Media Player's Play button (the first button at the bottom of the window). If you hear the sound effect, your sound card is playing Sound files properly.

Next, you want to be sure your sound card can handle MIDI files. Select the Open command from the File menu, and select a MIDI file. As you can see from figure 25.16, a MIDI file has an icon with two notes on it. (If you have Windows 95 set to display file extensions, you can also identify a MIDI file by its MID extension.) After loading the MIDI file, click on the Media Player's Play button. If you hear the song, your sound card is playing MIDI files properly.

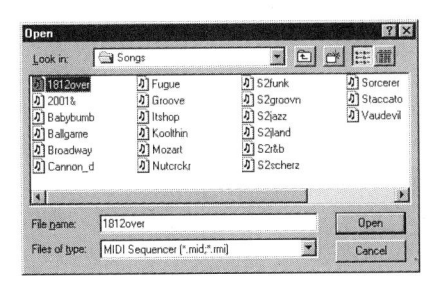

Fig. 25.16 Loading a MIDI file into Media Player.

Troubleshooting Your Sound Card

If you run into conflicts when trying to set up your sound card, you'll probably see a window like that shown in figure 25.17. Here, Windows warns that there is a conflict, but still allows you to proceed in order to troubleshoot the problem.

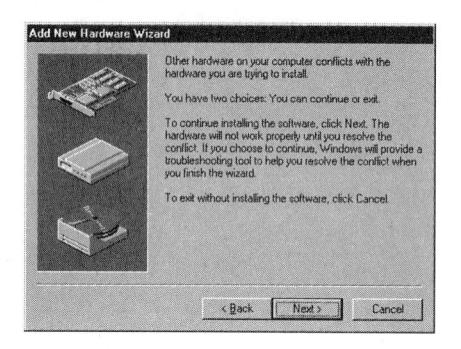

Fig. 25.17 Windows warns of conflicts in the system.

After installing the device drivers for the sound card you selected, Windows displays the dialog box shown in figure 25.18. When you click the Start Conflict Troubleshooter button, Windows guides you through the troubleshooting process, as shown in figure 25.19. Just follow the step-by-step instructions in each window.

Along the way, Windows has you check whether the device is installed twice, whether other devices are conflicting with the device you're trying to install, whether there are other settings you can use to get rid of any conflicts, and more. The detailed questions and answers guide you painlessly through the steps.

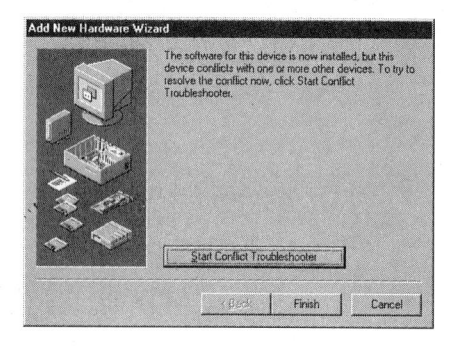

Fig. 25.18 This window gives you access to Windows device troubleshooter.

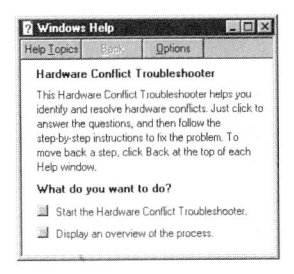

Fig. 25.19 The first troubleshooter window.

Installing a CD-ROM Drive

As mentioned previously, if you're going to add a CD-ROM drive to your system, your best bet is to get a multimedia upgrade package that includes both the CD-ROM player and the matching sound card. This ensures that the sound card includes the right interface for the CD-ROM drive. If you choose to buy a CD-ROM drive separately from a sound card, you must be sure that you also purchase the appropriate interface card.

While every CD-ROM drive comes with its own specific installation instructions, there are several basic steps that apply to all installations. Those steps are:

➤ Install the CD-ROM drive into an empty drive bay in your system unit.

➤ Install the CD-ROM drive's interface card. (This is often the sound card.)

➤ Connect the power, audio, and data cables.

➤ Use Control Panel's Add New Hardware option to install the new device into Windows 95.

The instructions that come with your specific CD-ROM drive or multimedia upgrade kit will provide detailed instructions for installing your CD-ROM drive into the computer. However, the instructions may not include detailed instructions for adding the device to Windows 95. Luckily, you already know most of what you need to know to get your CD-ROM to perform under Windows 95. Just refer back to this chapter's "Adding New Hardware" section. In step 3 of the instructions, however, you should select CD-ROM controllers instead of Sound, video and game controllers (figure 25.20).

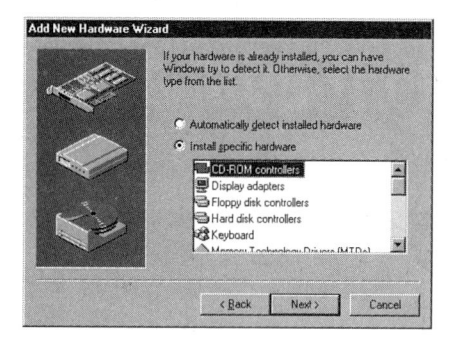

Fig. 25.20 Adding a CD-ROM drive to Windows 95.

Just as with a sound card, if you have trouble getting your CD-ROM to work under Windows 95, you can use Windows troubleshooting help to find the solution to your problem.

Using Multimedia on Your Computer

KILLER 26 WINDOWS 95

by Clayton Walnum

Now that your multimedia devices are installed and chugging along nicely, it's time to see a few things you can do with those devices under Windows 95. Keep in mind that this chapter only gets you started with multimedia. There are so many multimedia applications out there that it would take an entire book (or more!) to cover all the great stuff you can do with a multimedia system. But every journey begins with the first step. So, in this chapter, you learn the following:

- How to customize the sounds your computer makes
- How to create sound schemes
- How to play an audio CD with your CD-ROM drive and sound card
- How to personalize the CD Player application
- How to make Windows 95 remember the titles of CDs and songs from one session to the next

Assigning Sounds to Windows Events

If you're a Windows user, you've noticed how Windows plays sound effects whenever you do such things as click outside of a dialog box, bring up a system-alert message box, or exit from Windows. All of these sound effects are attached to the events by the Sounds Properties sheet. In this section, you learn how to use Sounds Properties to customize your Windows 95 sound.

Understanding the Sounds Properties Sheet

To view the Sounds Properties sheet, bring up the Control Panel, located in the Start/Settings menu. Then, double-click on the Sounds icon. When you do, you see the dialog box shown in figure 26.1.

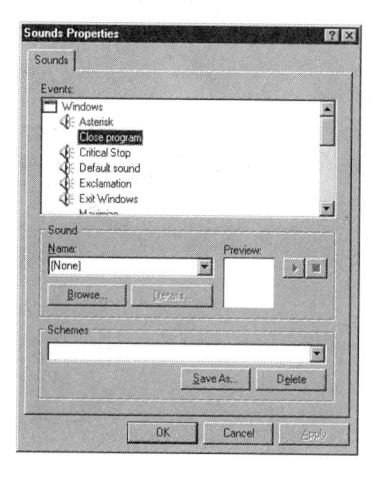

Fig. 26.1 The Sounds Properties sheet enables you to match sound effects to Windows events.

At the top of the dialog box, you see the list of Windows events to which you can attach sound effects. Some events are already associated with a sound, as you can tell by the speaker icon next to the entry.

604 Chapter 26: Using Multimedia on Your Computer

Other events have no sounds attached to them. You can add whatever sounds you like to these events, as well as change the sounds associated with events that already have sounds. In the next section, you learn how to assign sounds to Windows events.

Viewing, Selecting, and Listening to Sounds

To see the sound that's already associated with an event, just click on the event in the window. When you do, the name of the sound file associated with the event appears in the Name list box.

To hear the selected sound effect, click on the play button just to the right of the Preview speaker icon. If you want to change the sound effect, you have a couple of choices. The easiest way to change the sound effect is to select one from the Name drop-down list box, as shown in figure 26.2. When you first bring up the Sounds Properties sheet, the sound effects shown in the drop-down list are found in your Windows\Media folder on your hard drive. If you change the current folder by using the Browse button (see the next paragraph), the drop-down list shows the sounds in the newly selected folder.

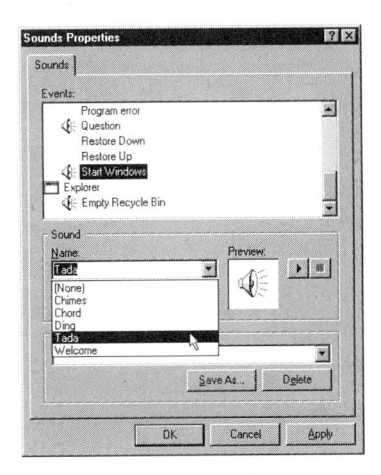

Fig. 26.2 You can select a new sound effect from the Name list box.

Assigning Sounds to Windows Events **605**

If you want to use a sound effect that's stored somewhere else on your hard disk, click on the Browse button. When you do, the Browse dialog box appears (figure 26.3), which enables you to search your entire system for the sound effect you want. Notice also that you can preview sound effects by selecting them in the window and then clicking the play button located near the bottom of the window, just to the right of the word "Preview."

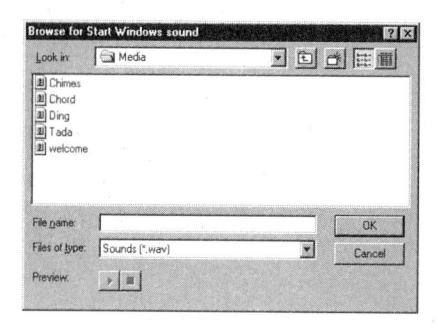

Fig. 26.3 You can use the Browse dialog box to find a sound effect.

Saving Sound Schemes

Once you have your sound effects set up the way you want them, you can save the "sound scheme" (as they call a collection of sounds) to disk along with the default sound schemes and any other sound schemes you may have created. To do this, click on the Save As button near the bottom of the Sounds Properties sheet. When you do, you see the Save Scheme As dialog box. Just type a name for your sound scheme and press Enter. Windows 95 then adds your sound scheme to the others listed in the Schemes list box (figure 26.4). The sound scheme you just saved will be active the next time you start Windows. (The new sounds won't take effect until then.)

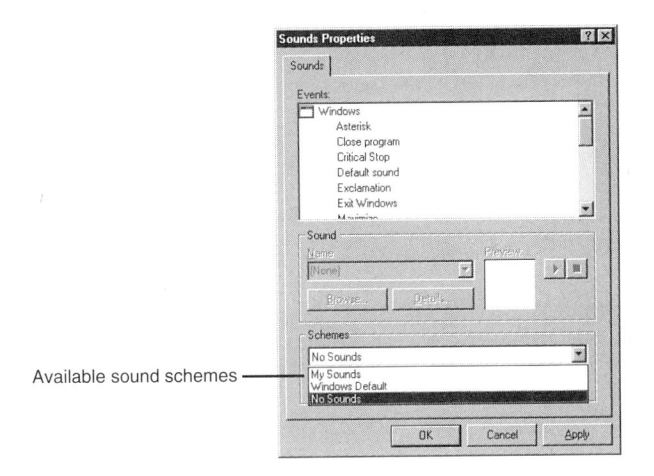

Fig. 26.4 The Schemes list box enables you to select whatever sound scheme you want.

Playing an Audio CD with CD Player

One of the coolest things you can do with your multimedia Windows 95 computer is play CDs while you work. In many cases, all you need to do is put an audio CD in your CD-ROM player, and Windows 95 automatically starts up the CD-ROM Player application. This little trick is accomplished by Windows' new AutoPlay function that'll also automatically start up games on CD-ROM. You can disable the AutoPlay feature, if you like, by following these steps:

1. Open Control Panel's System icon. The System Properties sheet appears.

2. Click on the Device Manager tab to display the Device Manager page.

3. Double-click on CD-ROM in the device list. Your CD-ROM driver appears in the list.

4. Click your CD-ROM driver to select it.

5. Click the Properties button to display the CD-ROM Properties sheet for your driver.

6. Click the Settings tab to display the Settings page.

7. Turn off the Auto Insert Notification option by clicking it with your mouse.

If you want to start CD Player "by hand," you can find this handy mini-application in the Start/Programs/Accessories/Multimedia folder. When you click on its entry in the menu, you see the window shown in figure 26.5. As you can see in the figure, CD Player has many of the same controls that a regular CD player has, and you use them in exactly the same way. For example, to start playing a CD, you click on the play button. When you want to pause the CD, click on the pause button. The other buttons also work just as you'd expect on a real CD player.

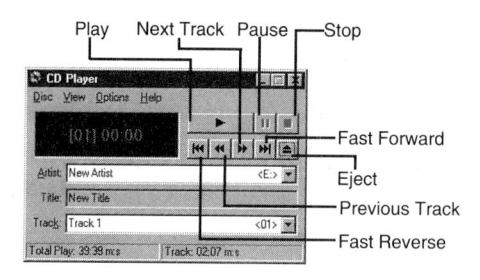

Fig. 26.5 CD Player has many of the same controls that a regular CD player has.

Creating a Play List

Although you can use CD Player just to play whatever CD happens to be in your computer's CD-ROM drive, you can do tons more. For example, look at the Artist, Title, and Track boxes in figure 26.6. You can edit the information shown in these boxes so that they show specific information about any CD. That is, you can have CD Player automatically recognize the CD in the drive and display the CD's artist and title, and the title for each track. How? Just follow these steps to create something called a play list:

608 Chapter 26: Using Multimedia on Your Computer

1. Make sure that you have an audio CD in your CD-ROM drive, and then select the Edit Play List command from the Disc menu. When you do, you see the Disc Settings window as shown in figure 26.6.

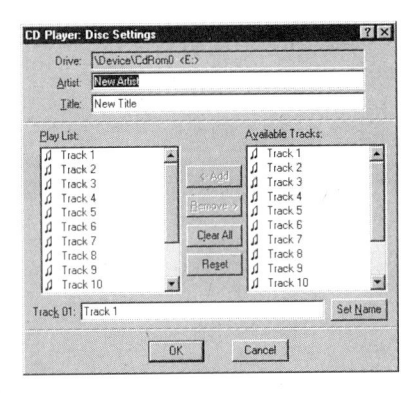

Fig. 26.6 The Disc Settings window.

2. Type the artist's name in the Artist box and the CD's title in the Title box.

3. Click on Track 1 in the Available Tracks list box, and then type the track's title into the Track text box, as shown in figure 26.7.

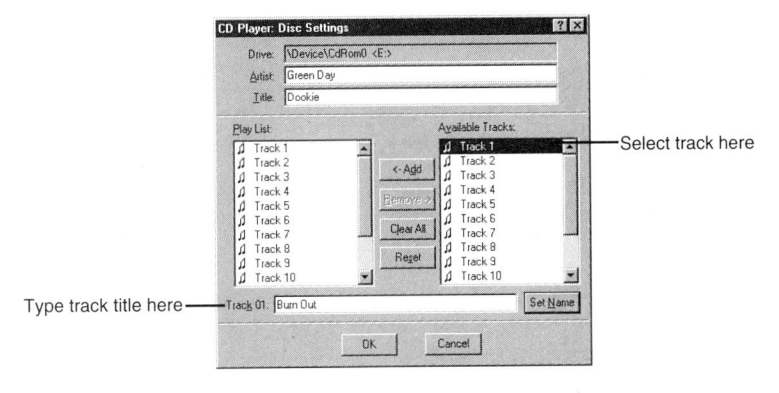

Type track title here

Select track here

Fig. 26.7 Typing a title for track 1.

Playing an Audio CD with CD Player **609**

4. Press Enter, and CD Player adds the new track title to the Available Tracks list, as well as sets up track 2 for editing.

5. Repeat step 4 until you've entered all the CD's track titles, at which point the Disc Settings dialog box will look something like figure 26.8.

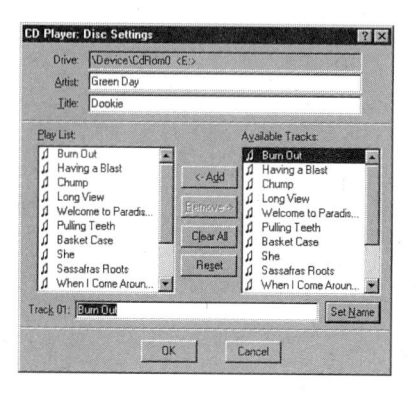

Fig. 26.8 The Disc Settings dialog box with all track titles entered.

6. Click on the OK button, and CD Player now shows the information for the new CD, as shown in figure 26.9.

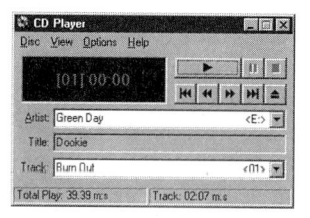

Fig. 26.9 CD Player with the new CD ready to play.

Notice that the Disc Settings dialog box has Add and Remove buttons that you can use to select exactly the tracks you want to play, as well as the order in which to play them. Don't like track 4? Just highlight the track in the Play List and click on the Remove button to zap it from the list. Conversely, the Add button enables you to move tracks from the Available Tracks list to the Play List.

After you complete the preceding steps, CD Player not only plays your CD but also displays the name of the artist, the title of the CD, and the title of the currently playing track. Best of all, CD Player saves all this information so that the next time you insert the CD, it will automatically find and display the correct information for the CD. Switch CDs, and *presto!*, CD Player finds and displays the new information (assuming, of course, that you previously entered the information).

If you click on the little arrow next to the Track list box, CD Player displays your play list (figure 26.10). You can instantly play any track in the list just by clicking on its name. Similarly, if you have a multi-disc CD-ROM drive (a special CD-ROM drive that can hold more than one disk), you can select different CDs by using the Artist list box.

Fig. 26.10 You can easily select songs from your play list.

Accessing CD Player's Toolbar

CD Player offers plenty of other options besides editing a play list. For example, if you select the View menu's Toolbar command, a toolbar appears in CD Player's window (figure 26.11). This toolbar provides quick access to most of the options available in CD Player's menus. Just click on a button to choose a command. If you want to see what a command button does before selecting it, just place your mouse pointer over the button for a second or two. When you do, a command tip appears.

Playing an Audio CD with CD Player **611**

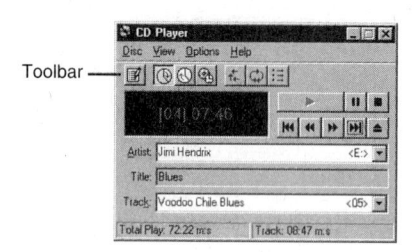

Fig. 26.11 The toolbar makes command selection as easy as a button click.

Setting CD Player's Options

Under the View menu, you'll also find commands for hiding and showing the track info and the status bar. In addition, you can set the time display to show elapsed track time, remaining track time, or remaining disc time. Finally, the View menu enables you to bring up Windows 95's volume control (figure 26.12), with which you can adjust the balance of the various sound devices operating on your system.

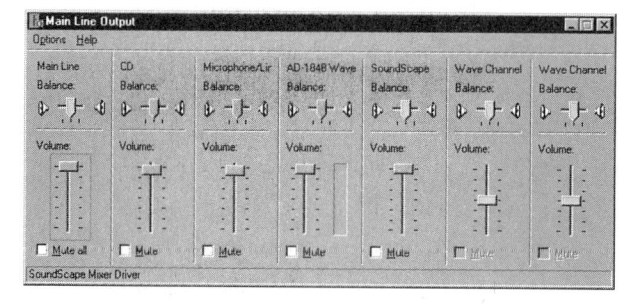

Fig. 26.12 The Volume Control accessory enables you to balance sound sources.

The Options menu, too, contains several handy commands. By selecting the Random Order command, you can have CD Player play the tracks on the CD in a random order. (This command is often called "shuffle" on real CD Players.) The Continuous Play command, on the other hand, causes the CD to play over and over, from beginning to

612 Chapter 26: Using Multimedia on Your Computer

end. Finally, when you select the Intro Play command, CD Player plays only the first few seconds of each song. When you find the song you want, just turn off the Intro Play command to hear the entire song.

Setting CD Player's Preferences

Finally, the View menu's Preferences command brings up the Preferences dialog box (figure 26.13), from which you can control several aspects of CD Player's operation. If the Stop CD Playing On Exit option is checked, the CD will stop playing when you exit from the program. If this option is not checked, you can close the CD Player application without stopping the CD; the CD continues to play in the background, although you no longer have control over it. (You can regain control just be restarting the CD Player application. When you do, CD Player determines the CD's current status and displays the appropriate information.)

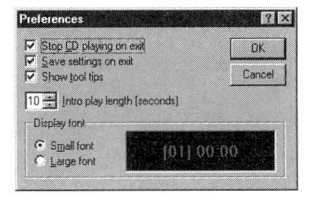

Fig. 26.13 Use the Preferences dialog box to set several aspects of CD Player's operation.

The Save Settings On Exit option ensures that CD Player remembers how you have it set up. The Show Tool Tips option controls whether tool tips (those tiny windows that tell you what buttons do) appear when you hold your mouse pointer over a button. If you like, you can change how much of a track the Intro Play command plays. To do this, just change the number of seconds displayed in the Intro Play Length box. Finally, you can change the size of the time display by selecting either the Small Font or Large Font option. The time display to the right of the options shows the selected font size.

Getting the Most out of Multimedia

by Clayton Walnum

Although Windows 95 makes using multimedia features as easy as possible (for example, by automatically playing an audio CD when you place it in your CD-ROM drive), there are many things you can do to customize your system's use of multimedia. By customizing how your system uses its multimedia features, you can make your system easier to use. In this chapter, then, you learn:

- Where to find your system's multimedia settings
- How to safely set the properties of audio and video devices
- How to add a MIDI keyboard to your system
- How to control and balance the volume of audio devices
- How to calibrate and test a joystick

Understanding the Multimedia Properties Sheet

As you now know, a multimedia computer contains many devices that work together to present information in many exciting ways. These devices include not only sound cards, but also video boards and CD-ROM players. Moreover, a couple of these devices do double duty. For example, a CD-ROM player can load a program from a CD-ROM or play music from an audio CD. In addition, a sound card can usually play back digital sound effects, as well as MIDI music files.

Each of your computer's multimedia features is controlled by a *driver*, which is a piece of software that matches Windows' multimedia system up with the specific devices you have on your computer. For example, a Sound Blaster sound card requires a different driver than a sound card from MediaVision. Similarly, different video cards and CD-ROM players also require specific drivers for the models you have installed on your system.

Luckily, when you installed Windows 95, Windows took care of matching up drivers with your devices. You probably didn't have to lift a finger to get everything working. (However, if you install new hardware that's not Plug-and-Play capable, you do need to inform Windows of the change. See the section "Adding New Hardware" in Chapter 25, "Adding Multimedia Capability to Your Computer," for more information on how to do this.)

Although different drivers control how your devices work with Windows, there are a number of device characteristics (or *properties*, as they're called in Windows 95) that you can set yourself. To do this, first click on Control Panel's entry in Windows' Start/Settings menu. When you do, the Control Panel appears on your screen. Next, double-click on the Multimedia icon to display the Multimedia Properties sheet (figure 27.1).

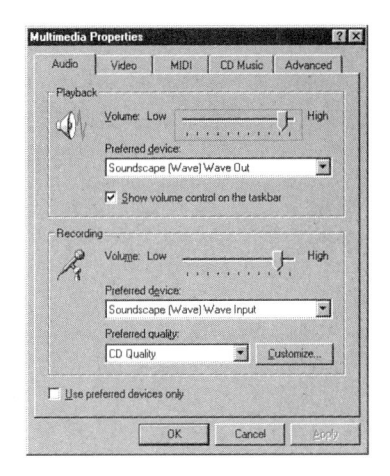

Fig. 27.1 The Multimedia Properties sheet enables you to fine-tune your multimedia devices.

As you can see by looking at the tabs across the top of the windows, the Multimedia Properties sheet provides pages for Audio, Video, MIDI, and CD Music devices, as well as a special Advanced page. Each page holds controls that you can use to fine-tune how a particular device works. To select a page, just click the appropriate tab. In the sections that follow, you learn how to use the various settings on each of the Multimedia Properties sheet's pages.

Setting Audio Properties

When the Multimedia Properties sheet first appears, the Audio tab is selected. The Audio page of the dialog box enables you to set several properties that determine how your system plays back and records sound. The upper part of the dialog box, labeled Playback, controls your system's playback properties, of course, whereas the Recording section controls recording properties.

Both sections enable you to set the volume for the device. In the playback section, the volume control determines how loudly your system plays sound effects, including the system effects that you hear when you do things like start Windows, exit from Windows, or bring up a system alert box. (See the section "Assigning Sounds to Windows Events" in Chapter 26, "Using Multimedia on Your Computer," for more information on how to attach your own sound effects to Windows events.)

The Recording volume determines the level of input that Windows receives from your microphone or other input device. For example, if you have the recording volume set low, when you try to record a sound effect, it will come out very quietly. On the other hand, if you try to record a sound effect with the recording volume set all the way up, you'll probably end up with sound that's distorted. (See the section "Recording Sound" in Chapter 29, "Fine-Tuning Your Windows 95 Sound Card," for more information on how to create your own sound effects.)

Both the Playback and Recording sections of the Audio dialog box enable you to select the devices used to play back or record sound. You make this selection by using the Preferred Device list boxes. Normally, these list boxes should be set to your main sound card. In figure 27.2, you can see that the playback and recording devices are set to a Soundscape card.

In the Playback section, you can also find an option labeled Show volume control on the taskbar. When this option is checked, you'll have a small speaker icon in your Windows taskbar, as shown in figure 27.3. When you single-click on the speaker icon, the volume control window appears. You can use the slider in this window to set the volume of your sound card. If you click on the Mute option in the volume control, all sound is set to the minimum level until you uncheck the Mute option.

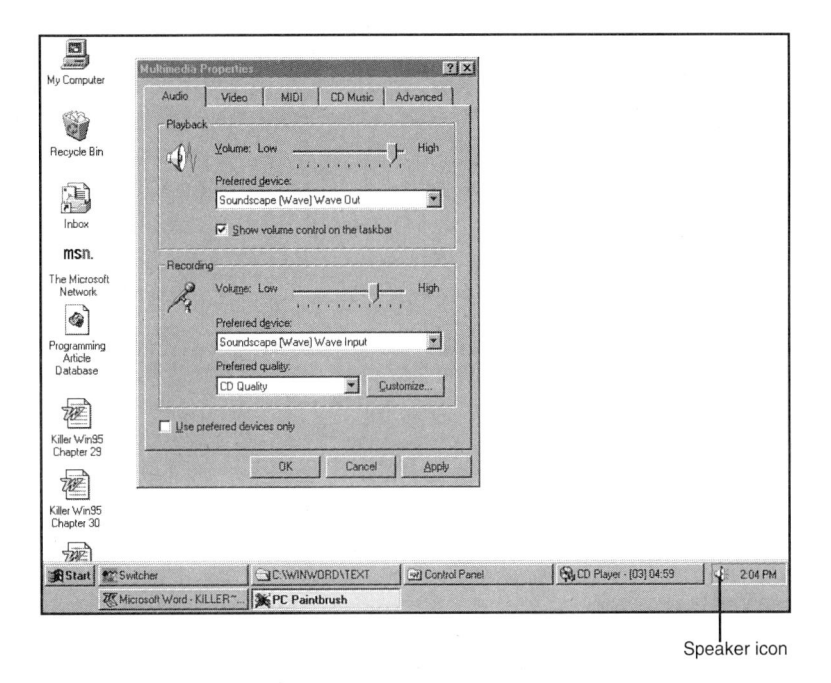

Fig. 27.2 The speaker icon on the taskbar gives you control over sound volume.

Finally, if you double-click on the speaker icon in the taskbar, you bring up the full volume-control accessory, which acts as a mixer for the various sound sources in your system. See the section "Using Volume Control" later in this chapter for more information on this handy accessory.

Getting back to the Audio page of the Multimedia Properties sheet, besides the other settings already discussed, the Recording section enables you to set the recording quality of sound. The easiest way to do

Setting Audio Properties   **619**

this is to select a setting from the Preferred Quality list box, as shown in figure 27.4. CD Quality is the absolute best sound you can record, with Radio Quality yielding less quality, and Telephone Quality being the worst of all.

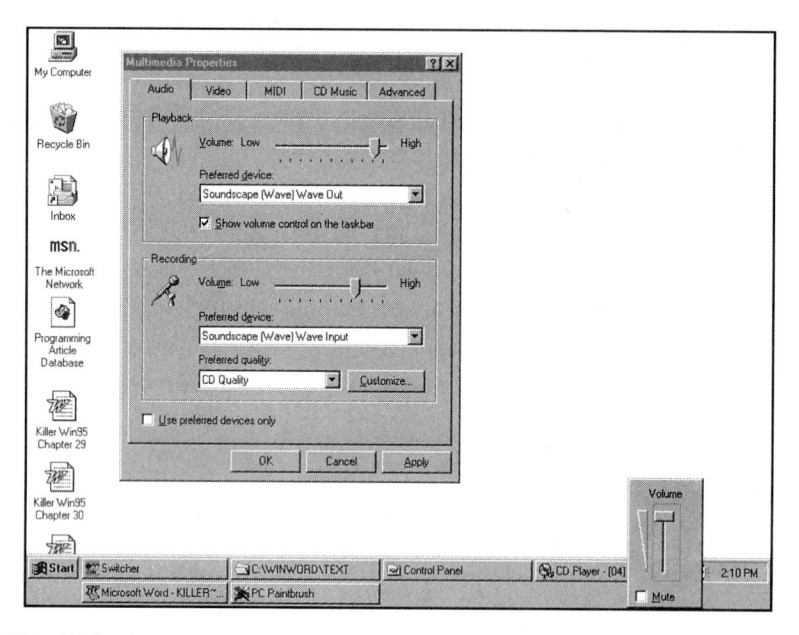

Fig. 27.3 The volume control enables you to set a volume level or mute sound.

If you want more control over the recording quality, click on the Customize button to display the Customize dialog box (figure 27.5). In this dialog box, the Name list box holds the names of the currently available quality settings. At first, this list box contains only the CD Quality, Radio Quality, and Telephone Quality entries. Using the Customize dialog box, you can add your own settings to the list. Please refer to the section "Setting Recording Quality" in Chapter 29 for more information on how to do this.

620 Chapter 27: Getting the Most out of Multimedia

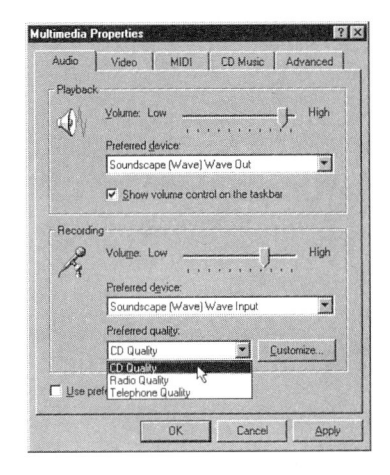

Fig. 27.4 Use the Preferred Quality list box to quickly set recording quality.

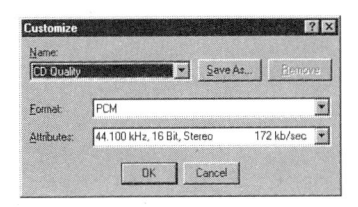

Fig. 27.5 Use the Customize dialog box to create your own record-quality settings.

Setting Video Properties

A multimedia computer is capable of displaying something called *full-motion video*, which is a lot like having a TV set right on your screen. Although full-motion video is a great way to present information, this multimedia feature is still in its infancy. If you run a video clip, for example, you'll see that the quality of the video isn't going to keep network executives up nights worrying about losing their market share to computers!

Still, full-motion video is an exciting multimedia feature of which you'll want to take full advantage. The Video page of the Multimedia Properties sheet (figure 27.6) lets you select the quality of the video presentation by controlling the size of the video image.

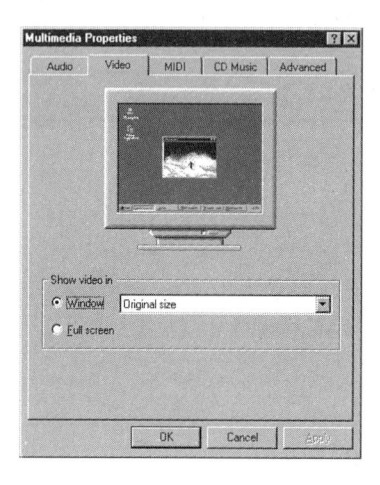

Fig. 27.6 The Video page of the Multimedia Properties sheet controls the size of the video image.

In most cases, you'll want to leave the video set to the Original Size setting, as shown in figure 27.7. This allows Windows to display the video at the same size with which it was created (figure 27.8). However, if you like, you can change the size of the video window. You do this by selecting a size from the list box (figure 27.9). As you can see, you have six different choices. If you don't want to have the video appear in a window at all, just click the Full Screen option. Then, the video will fill your entire screen. Keep in mind, though, that the bigger you make the video image, the slower it runs and the blockier the image looks.

Fig. 27.7 The Skiing video clip at its Original Size setting.

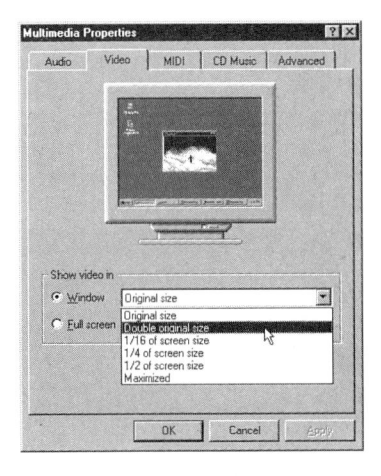

Fig. 27.8 Selecting a new video image size.

Setting MIDI Properties

Besides creating digitized sound effects and adding voice-overs to presentations, your sound card can play back MIDI files, which are files that contain commands that control MIDI synthesizers. The quality of the MIDI playback depends on the quality of your sound card (please see Chapter 29, "Fine-Tuning Your Windows 95 Sound Card," for more information about sound cards); but, in most cases, MIDI can provide the highest quality music of which your sound card is capable.

Setting MIDI Properties **623**

As you may have guessed, the MIDI page of the Multimedia Properties sheet (figure 27.9) provides controls for customizing how your system uses its MIDI features. The Single Instrument setting controls which instrument will receive MIDI commands when you play a MIDI file. In most cases, the MIDI "instrument" will be your sound card.

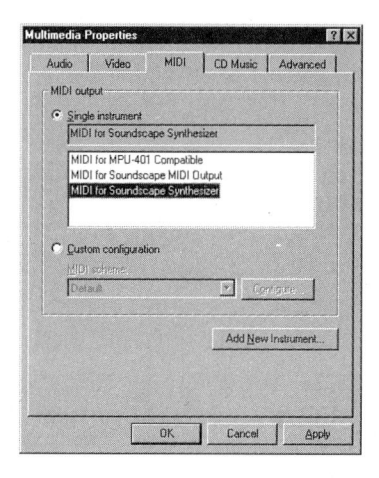

Fig. 27.9 The MIDI page of the Multimedia Properties sheet enables you to set your system's MIDI properties.

In figure 27.9, there are three instruments listed: MIDI for MPU-401 Compatible, MIDI for Soundscape MIDI Output, and MIDI for Soundscape Synthesizer. When you bring up the Multimedia Properties sheet on your system, you'll have a list of MIDI settings that match the sound card you've installed.

The MIDI for MPU-401 Compatible is a general MIDI standard that most sound cards support. This entry will probably appear for your sound card, too. You can have your MIDI for Soundscape MIDI Output setting send MIDI commands to your sound card's MIDI output port rather than to the sound card's on-board synthesizer. This will enable you to play MIDI files on a MIDI device, such as an electronic keyboard, attached to the sound card's MIDI output port.

Finally, the MIDI for Soundscape Synthesizer setting sends MIDI commands to the Soundscape sound card's on-board synthesizer. Again, your sound card may have a similar setting, although it may only have the MPU-401 Compatible setting. To select an instrument, just click on its entry in the list, and then click on the dialog box's OK button.

The MIDI page of the Multimedia Properties sheet also enables you to set up a custom configuration. To do this, click on the Custom Configuration option to enable the MIDI Scheme and Configure controls. The MIDI Scheme list box holds any configurations that you've created for your system. The first time you see this control, it'll probably only contain the Default entry. To create your own configuration, click on the Configure button. (For more information about creating a MIDI configuration, refer to the section "Creating a MIDI Configuration" in Chapter 29.)

The last thing you can do with the MIDI page is set up a new MIDI instrument that you've connected to your sound card's MIDI output port. This can be any MIDI-compatible instrument from a drum machine to a full-featured electronic keyboard and synthesizer. To add such an instrument to your system, you must first connect it to your sound card's MIDI port. To do this, you probably need special MIDI cables that are usually sold separately. Contact the company that made your sound card for more information.

Once you have the instrument physically connected to your sound card, you can use the MIDI page of the Multimedia Properties sheet to tell Windows 95 about the new instrument. To do this, click on the Add New Instrument button. You then see the first page of the MIDI Instrument Installation Wizard (figure 27.10).

This page enables you to select the MIDI port to which your instrument is attached. In figure 27.10, the Soundscape card's MIDI output port is selected. This is the port to which Windows 95 will direct MIDI commands when a MIDI file is played or some other sort of MIDI application is used, such as a sequencer program. (A sequencer program can do anything from play back MIDI files to let you compose music in an on-screen studio.)

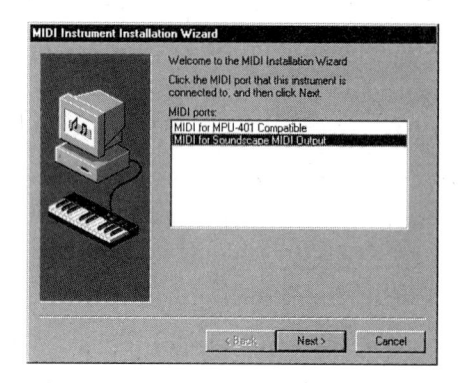

Fig. 27.10 Selecting a MIDI output port.

After selecting the MIDI port, click on the Next button to move to the next page (figure 27.11), where you can select the type of instrument you're installing. In most cases, the instrument will be a General MIDI Instrument, which is an instrument that conforms to the MIDI standard. Some special instruments—like drum machines, for example—may fit a different category. If you were installing a drum machine, you'd select the Percussion on Channel 16 option.

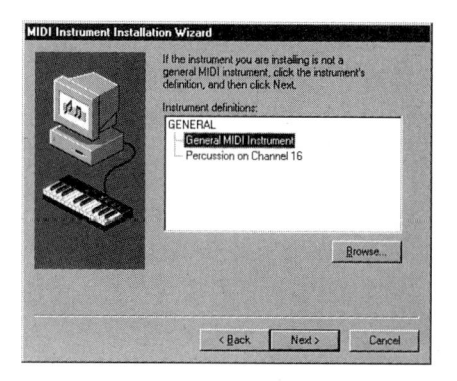

Fig. 27.11 Selecting the MIDI instrument type.

After selecting the instrument type, click on the Next button. The next page of the MIDI Instrument Installation Wizard (figure 27.12) gives you a chance to name the new instrument. You can type anything you want into the Instrument Name box, or just stick with the default name. When you're finished typing, click on the Finish button. When you do, Windows 95 adds the new instrument to your MIDI configuration, as you can see in the Multimedia Properties sheet (figure 27.13).

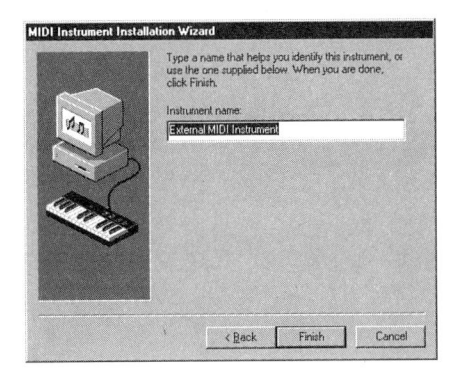

Fig. 27.12 Naming the new MIDI instrument.

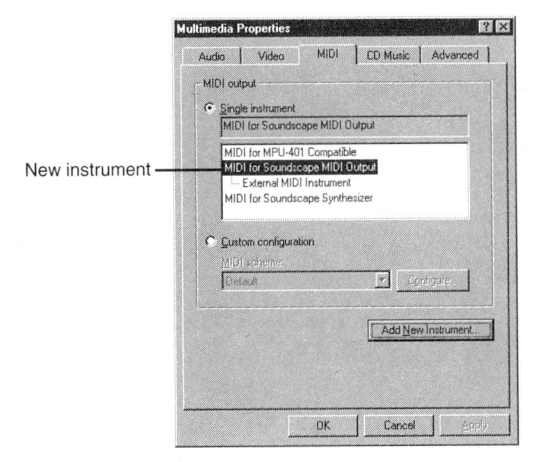

Fig. 27.13 The new MIDI instrument listed in the Multimedia Properties sheet.

You might expect that you can delete a MIDI instrument as easily as the wizard lets you install it. Unfortunately, to delete a MIDI instrument, you must access the Advanced page of the Multimedia

Setting MIDI Properties **627**

Properties sheet, as shown in figure 27.14. To get to this page, which lists all the multimedia devices in your system, click on the Advanced tab of the Multimedia Properties sheet.

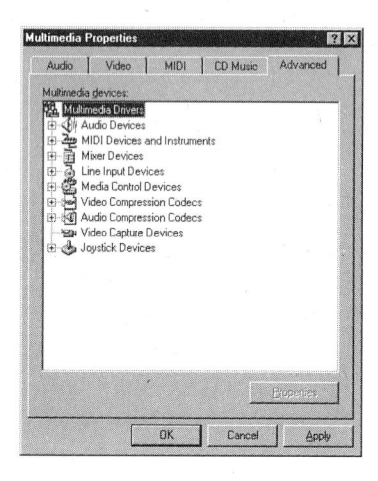

Fig. 27.14 The Advanced page of the Multimedia Properties sheet.

Once you have the Advanced page on-screen, click on the plus sign (+) next to the MIDI Devices and Instruments entry. You can then see the MIDI devices that are active on your system. To get to the instrument, click on the plus sign next to the MIDI device to which you added the instrument. Windows then displays the list of instruments for that device, as shown in figure 27.15.

To delete the instrument, click on its entry to highlight it. Then, click on the Properties button to display the External MIDI Instrument Properties sheet (figure 27.16). Click on the Remove button to remove the instrument from your system. When you do, the Advanced page of the Multimedia Properties sheet appears, this time with the deleted instrument removed from the instrument list.

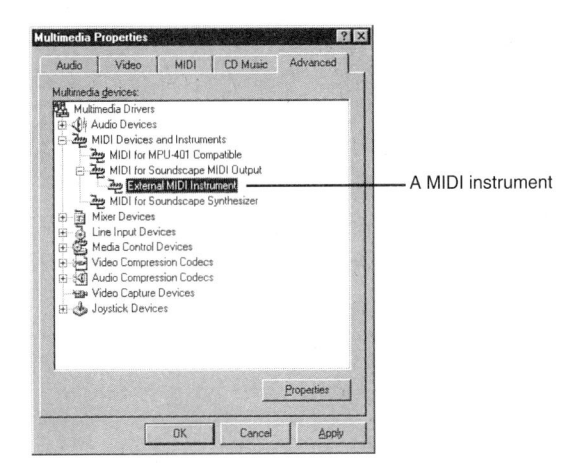

Fig. 27.15 Selecting an instrument in the Multimedia Properties sheet.

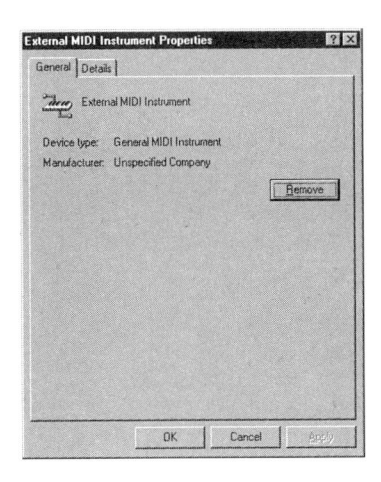

Fig. 27.16 The Remove button deletes a MIDI instrument from your system.

Setting CD Music Properties

The CD Player application enables you to play audio CDs with your CD-ROM drive. Most of the configuration tasks involved in using audio CDs are handled by that program. However, the Multimedia Properties sheet does have a page that lets you select a CD-ROM drive (if you happen to have more than one in your system) and adjust the volume control of the CD-ROM drive's headphone jack. To see the CD Music page (figure 27.17), just click on the CD Music tab in the Multimedia Properties sheet.

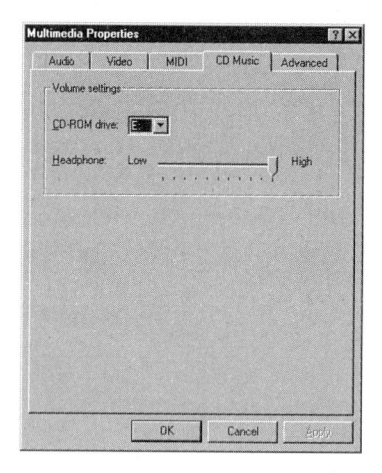

Fig. 27.17 The CD Music page of the Multimedia Properties sheet.

To change the volume of a CD-ROM drive's headphone jack, select the CD-ROM drive in the CD-ROM Drive list box. (Most people have only one drive listed.) Then, use your mouse to adjust the Headphone slider volume control. When you do this, you'll probably want to be playing an audio CD through your headphones so that you can hear the volume change.

630 Chapter 27: Getting the Most out of Multimedia

Using the Advanced Page

The Multimedia Properties sheet has one final page called Advanced. As you may suspect, you shouldn't fiddle with the entries on this page unless you're sure you know what you're doing. Basically, this page enables you to view the properties of devices or to delete devices. While it's usually safe to view the properties of any device, you shouldn't delete any entries from the Advanced page unless you're positive you understand the results of the deletion.

To get to the Advanced page, click on the Advanced tab on the Multimedia Properties sheet. When you do, you see the window shown in figure 27.18. To view the properties of a device, first click on the plus mark next to the device category. Then select a device from the list that appears, and click on the Properties button. You then see a display that lists the properties of the selected device, as well as provides a Remove button for deleting the device from the list.

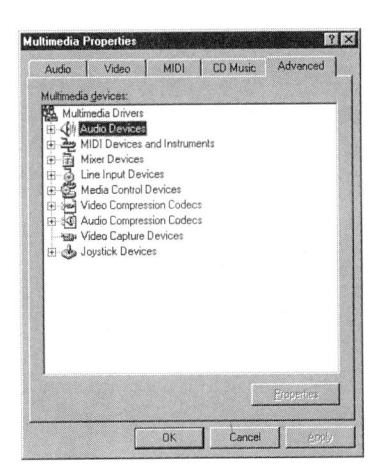

Fig. 27.18 The Advanced page of the Multimedia Properties sheet.

As you can see, the device's properties display provides option buttons to turn the device on or off. In addition, the device properties display may have enabled the Settings button, which lets you change the hardware settings for the device. When you click on this button, you see a window something like that shown in figure 27.19. Obviously, unless you understand I/O ports, interrupts, and DMA channels, you shouldn't change these settings. If you do change the settings, the device will probably stop working or even cause other devices to malfunction.

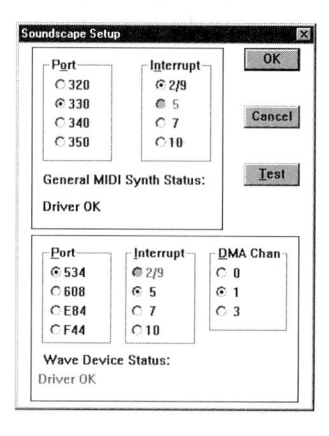

Fig. 27.19 Viewing a device's hardware settings.

Using Volume Control

Previously, in the "Setting Audio Properties" section, you learned about the volume-control accessory that you can access from the taskbar. To learn how to make the volume-control accessible from the taskbar, refer back to the "Setting Audio Properties" section. To bring up the volume-control accessory, double-click on the speaker icon found on the right side of the taskbar. You can also access the volume control from the Start/Programs/Accessories/Multimedia menu. When you run the volume-control accessory, you see a window something like that shown in figure 27.20.

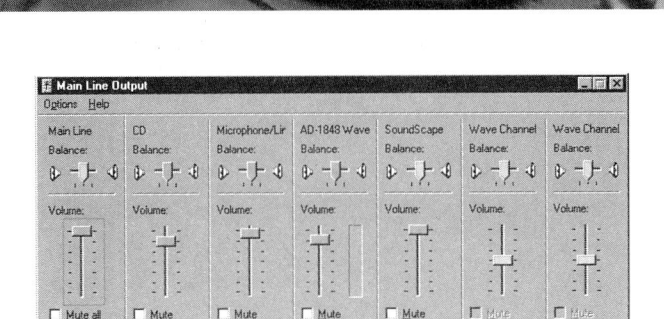

Fig. 27.20 The volume-control accessory is a sound mixer for balancing the volumes of various audio devices.

Exactly how the volume-control accessory looks depends on the devices attached to your computer and the program's options settings. As you can see, though, changing a device's volume is a simple matter of using your mouse to reposition the Volume slider for the device. For example, to lower the volume of your CD-ROM drive, slide the CD Volume control down. On the other hand, if you want to change the volume of digitized sound effects, you should use the Wave device's slider. To learn more about volume control and its many options, please refer to Chapter 29.

Configuring a Joystick

Many people use their multimedia computers for games. In fact, games were probably the first multimedia applications, using sound and animation long before the term *multimedia* was even coined. Most games these days can be controlled from your keyboard or by using your mouse. However, some games—especially arcade-type games—are easier to play by using a joystick.

Luckily, most sound cards include a port to which you can attach a joystick. However, because of the way joysticks work, they need to be calibrated before you use them in a game. Windows 95 probably already took care of this calibration, but to check your joystick or to change its calibration, you can follow the instructions given in this section.

You calibrate a joystick by using the Joystick Properties sheet, which you can access from the Control Panel. First, bring up Control Panel, and then double-click on the Joystick icon. When you do, you see the Joystick Properties sheet.

Although most systems have only one joystick connected to them, Windows can handle up to 16. Before calibrating or testing a joystick, you must select the joystick in the Current Joystick list box. If you have only one joystick, the Current Joystick box should already be set properly.

Because joysticks come in many varieties, the Joystick Properties sheet enables you to select a type that matches your particular joystick device. You select the joystick type from the Joystick Selection list box (figure 27.21). This list box contains many types of joysticks, even many types with which you may not be familiar. Chances are you have a 2-axis, 2-button joystick. Other types of joysticks include gamepads, which look like the controllers that come with video-game consoles (Nintendo, Sega, and so forth), and light yokes, which look like airplane controls and are used mainly for flight simulators and racing games.

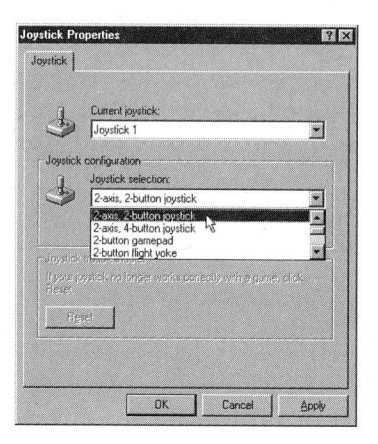

Fig. 27.21 Selecting the joystick type.

634 Chapter 27: Getting the Most out of Multimedia

Once you have the joystick type set, click on the Calibrate button to bring up the first Joystick Calibration window, as shown in figure 27.22. Follow the instructions in the window. When you're done, you'll see a window that gives you a chance to test your joystick.

To test your joystick, click the Test button, which brings up the Joystick Test window, as shown in figure 27.23. Watch the small cross in the Position section while moving your joystick's handle. The cross should match the handle's movement. Finally, press the joystick's buttons to make sure that the appropriate button indicator in the Buttons section lights up. To complete the calibration, click on the Joystick Test dialog box's OK button, and then click on the Joystick Calibration dialog box's Finish button.

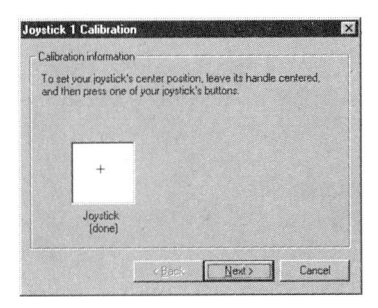

Fig. 27.22 The first step in calibrating a joystick.

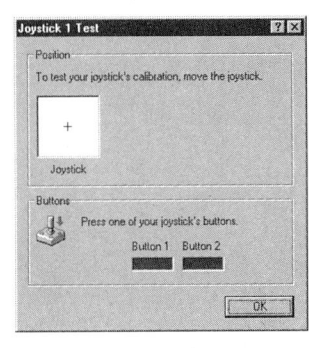

Fig. 27.23 The Joystick Text window gives you a chance to test your joystick's motion and buttons.

Configuring a Joystick **635**

Checking CD-ROM Settings

When Windows 95 first configures your system, it does its best to identify and set up your hardware, including your CD-ROM drive. However, sometimes Windows 95 is unable to identify a CD-ROM drive and so uses less-efficient, default settings for that device. For this reason, you should check your CD-ROM settings to ensure that your CD-ROM is operating at peak efficiency.

Checking the CD-ROM's performance settings is easy. The trick is finding the settings in the first place, because they are deeply buried in the Windows system. Of course, discovering such hidden secrets is exactly why you bought this book, right? Follow these steps to find your CD-ROM's performance settings:

1. Right-click on the My Computer icon on your desktop, and select properties from the menu that pops up. The System Properties sheet appears.

2. Click on the Performance tab on the System Properties. The Performance page appears.

3. Click on the File System button. The File System Properties sheet appears.

4. Click on the CD-ROM tab. The CD-ROM page (figure 27.24), which contains your CD-ROM's performance properties, appears.

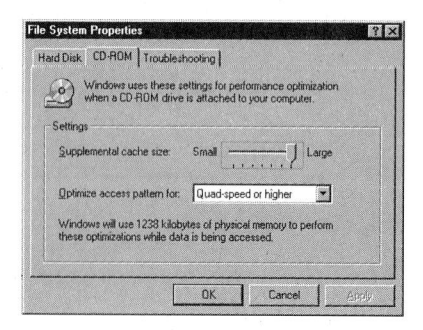

Fig. 27.24 The CD-ROM performance properties are well hidden in the Windows 95 system.

As you can see in figure 27.24, you can change two performance settings for your CD-ROM: the cache size and the access pattern. If you have 8M or more of memory in your computer, you should set the cache size to Large. With less memory, you'll have to experiment with the cache size to find the largest cache that doesn't adversely affect your system's performance.

The access pattern should be set to the type of CD-ROM drive you have. For example, if you have a quad-speed drive, you should set the access pattern setting to "Quad-speed or higher," whereas if you have a double-speed CD-ROM drive, the access pattern should be "Double-speed drives."

Understanding Full-Motion Video

KILLER 28 WINDOWS 95

by Robin Hohman

There are two kinds of video signals: analog and digital. Camcorders, VCRs, televisions, and laser discs transmit analog video, which is stored on videotape or videodisc. Digital video is made up of analog signals converted into bits and bytes that can be stored as a computer file.

The quality of analog video is higher than that of digital video, but the push is on to make digital video signals as seamless and color-rich as what you see on a TV screen.

In this chapter, you learn about the following:

- ➤ Video for Windows
- ➤ Hardware requirements for video
- ➤ Software requirements for video
- ➤ Video compression

- Video formats, such as MPEG and JPEG
- How to play video files

Video for Windows

Desktop digital video first debuted with QuickTime for the Macintosh, but didn't take off until Microsoft and Intel unveiled Video for Windows software in 1992.

QuickTime, and then Video for Windows (VfW), changed the way people thought about video production. As employed by TV stations and video houses, video production requires expensive tape and editing equipment. The standard method is to take video from one or more sources and copy it to a single videotape. The production has to be sequential, meaning you have to lay in shot A before shot B, and so forth. Each time you create a videotape from another tape, you lose quality. Each succeeding generation is subject to an increasing loss of quality.

The Video for Windows software converts the analog signal into a computer file, which is then stored on a hard disk, tape drive, floppy, or CD-ROM. That makes the video easily accessible for playback and editing. There is no generational loss of quality, because each time you view the video it comes from the original files. VfW also makes video a true hypermedia, because you can quickly retrieve the video shots in any sequence for any number of times.

Being hypermedia enables products that are created from digital video to be interactive, because the sequence of shots (and audio) is not limited to one person's design. For example, the popular CD-ROM Myst requires the user to choose different paths to follow during the course of the game. That's only possible with digital video. The game is programmed so that when the user makes a choice, the program searches the CD-ROM until that choice is found and presented on the screen. If the medium was videotape, you would have to go back and forth on the tape to access the desired sequence.

Most CD-ROM games don't employ *full-motion video*. Full-motion video is defined as stills displayed at 30 frames (still shots) per second (fps). At that rate, the human eye perceives the motion to be fluid and natural.

Digital video ranges from 10 to 30 fps, but it has two major drawbacks: it takes up huge amounts of storage space, and the quality and synchronization is dependent upon the speed and power of the computer. Uncompressed 30 fps video uses gigabytes of space per minute of video. It can also take up to 30M per second to transfer the data to display on a monitor.

Until huge hard drives and very fast computer chips became available, digital video remained a distant dream for most people. With the advent of the Pentium and other very fast chips, and the drop in prices and availability of 1+gigabyte hard drives, digital video came down to the masses.

Windows 95 makes video even more accessible because it includes VfW, which was formerly only available as an add-on development kit.

However, even with huge drives and faster computers, digital video must be compressed somehow to make PC video a realistic delivery tool for presentations, games, and even movies.

There are two ways to compress video for storage and playback: with video compression boards and with software. To capture video from an analog source, you must have a video capture board. To play video files, you can use a board or software that decompresses video files.

Video Hardware

Video capture boards grab raw analog video and convert it to digital data. The best rate for full-motion video is 30 fps, but not all cards can operate at that speed. Many capture 15 fps. The lower the fps, the less fluid the motion will seem. However, depending on what kind of video you're capturing and how you intend to distribute it, the lower fps may be suitable. The lower the fps, the less space needed to store it.

> **Tip:** Some video capture boards don't have the ability to display the incoming signals. If you want to display the data as it is captured, make sure the board supports that.

If you want to capture video, you must have a special board. If you only want to display and manipulate digital video, you have another choice: decompression software. Since there are many pitfalls inherent in adding internal hardware—it's expensive, time-consuming to install, and raises compatibility issues—software may be the better choice for people who don't need to capture their own video.

> **Caution:** Compatibility is the biggest problem with video capture boards. Before you buy and attempt to install a board, make certain it will be compatible with your system. Also make sure you can return it if it's not.

Video Software

Video software uses compression *codecs* (*co*mpression and *dec*ompression algorithms) that provide a shorthand for storing and playing the video. It's easier, cheaper, and more portable than hardware-assisted compression.

However, the same software used to compress the video must be used to decompress the video. That's where Video for Windows comes in.

Video for Windows

The single most important feature of VfW is the inclusion of a runtime engine, which allows people to play digital video on a PC without special hardware.

As of this writing, the VfW included with Windows 95 contains compression codecs for Cinepak, Indeo, YUV, RLE (Run Length Encoding),

642 Chapter 28: Understanding Full-Motion Video

and Video 1. These codecs allow you to play most files, but not MPEG (Moving Pictures Experts Group). The way people talk about it, MPEG is the most important development in desktop video since the Macintosh. Before you can understand what a big leap MPEG is, you have to first understand what came before it.

> **Tip:** The version of Cinepak that ships with Windows 95 (and Windows NT 3.5x) has an error in it that disables support for YUV. You can get the corrected software, version 1.10.0.6, from CompuServe's MS Win Multimedia forum in the Video for Windows library.

Compression Schemes

Video files would be unmanageable without compression. Remember, uncompressed 30 fps video uses more than a gigabyte of space per minute of video. Video files are compressed with so-called *lossy* compression. It means you will lose certain (perhaps unnoticeable) details in order to compress the file.

Compression works in one of two ways. Interframe works on the differences between similar frames. For example, a video of someone running along a beach would have many frames that are similar, with fewer that are different. Interframe compression captures key frames as whole frames, and only the differences in the delta frames.

Intraframe compression schemes work only within individual frames. Pixels are converted into mathematical formulas.

Lossy compression schemes sacrifice detail to compression ratio. That is, with lossy compression, you lose some of the original video frame, but fit more images in a smaller file.

The YUV compression scheme, for example, results in very high quality images, but the compression ratio is only 2:1. That is, two images in the original video are represented as one in the compressed video. You can have compression ratios as high as 200:1, with a resulting loss in picture quality. Obviously, the lower the compression ratio, the bigger the file.

You can choose the amount of compression you're willing to put up with. Codec compression methods vary widely, and certain codecs might not be the best for particular tasks. For example, the RLE scheme only works with blocks of color, so you wouldn't want to use it for a close-up that demanded great detail.

The codecs vary in compression rate, compression ratio, file size, and quality. You can't determine the quality of the video by compression ratio alone. The quality of the video is highly dependent upon the types of images you're looking to compress.

The good news about Windows 95 is that, since several codecs are included, you can experiment without incurring additional expense.

Descriptions of the codecs included with the final beta release of Windows 95 follow.

Cinepak

Cinepak is an efficient, 24-bit codec designed to handle high compression rates without degrading the image quality. It uses an asymmetrical compression scheme, which means it compresses and decompresses images at different speeds, and takes a relatively long time to compress.

Intel Indeo R3.1 and R3.2

Intel's Indeo is slower than Cinepak, and it depends heavily upon the speed of the CPU running the software. However, Indeo has a somewhat better color quality than Cinepak, and you can enhance the speed with hardware-assisted compression/decompression.

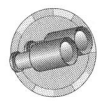

> **Note:** Both Cinepak and Indeo will be available in 32-bit versions, which will considerably speed up the compression/decompression process. They're slated to ship with Windows 95.

YUV9

This is the encoding standard used by the broadcast industry. Many capture cards employ the YUV standard. YUV, which is also called component video, splits a video signal into two chroma signals and one brightness signal. The quality is very high, but the compression ratio is only 2:1.

RLE

RLE is a simple but not dazzling compression scheme. It uses *banding* techniques to encode the video; that is, rows of pixels are grouped together to portray the image. It's mainly used for animation.

Video 1

Video 1 was created by Microsoft and distributed with the Video for Windows Developer's Kit, so it automatically had a chance to be among the most popular schemes. Now that Microsoft is distributing other codecs as well, which codec you choose might just come down to personal preference. One thing that might limit the appeal of Video 1 is that it works as software only; that is, you can't enhance its performance with a video board as you can with Indeo.

MPEG-1

MPEG-1 is undoubtedly the way to squeeze full-screen, high-quality audio and video for wide distribution. MPEG-1, and its subset JPEG (Joint Photographic Experts Group), compress and decompress digital video in a new, more manageable way. Both are high-quality standards for compressing video signals.

MPEG-1 uses a technique called *transform coding*. That means it transforms all the time-based information for frequency components and looks for redundancies in the frequency domain to compress the video. It has a lower *compression ratio* than earlier codecs (50:1) because it treats every frame as a key frame. MPEG-1 compression is done in two phases: in the spatial direction and also in the conception of motion.

Earlier techniques such as Indeo and Cinepak use *vector quantization*, which is like sending a secret code from one place to another. If you know the code, you can decipher the content.

With Indeo and Cinepak, the information is coded into a *codebook*, and the codebook itself is transmitted. On the decompression side, the codebook is used to create the decoded (decompressed) video signals.

MPEG files are popping up everywhere, most visibly on World Wide Web pages on the Internet. University home pages in particular, but other pages as well, increasingly include hypertext links to nearly real-time full-motion videos.

Until recently, MPEG-1 was a hardware-dependent codec, which meant that you had to have an MPEG compression/decompression board to play MPEG files. Now there are codecs that allow you to play MPEG without special hardware.

There is one major advantage to hardware compression/decompression over software-only routines: you will get full-motion video at 30 fps regardless of the speed or power of your computer.

Software fps scales directly with CPU performance. In fact, a leading company marketing MPEG-1 software recommends no less than a 486DX2-66 for playing MPEG files. Even with that CPU, the computer won't be able to reach the maximum of 24 fps, but will hover around 10 fps—not enough speed to look like full-motion video.

> **Note:** Standard broadcast video is shown at 30 fps; movies are shown at 24 fps and codecs range from 15-30 fps.

Several companies are now marketing MPEG software, but one company has become the front-runner due to a deal with Microsoft. In early June 1995, Microsoft signed a deal with Santa Clara, Ca.-based Mediamatics, a three-year-old software company, to include its MPEG Arcade Player software with future releases of Windows 95 and Windows NT. The deal was struck too late for inclusion in the premiere August release of Windows 95, but will be included in the add-on developer's kit.

MPEG Arcade Player allows you to display MPEG files without any special hardware. The software is now included with some graphics cards, such as Western Digital, Diamond Multimedia, and Brooktree cards. But if you use Windows 95, you can use any graphics card. Depending on your needs, however, a high-end graphics card may still be the way to go.

However, all is not rosy in the MPEG video world. Software-only MPEG video won't run on less than a 90MHz Pentium, and at that all you'll get is 24 fps.

MPEG-2

The latest entry into digital video is MPEG-2, which can yield a 200:1 *compression ratio.* MPEG-1's best ratio is 6:1. As with all compression techniques, the actual ratio depends on the playback quality and content.

Another advantage MPEG-2 offers over MPEG-1 and other codecs is the *screen resolution rate.* Screen resolution describes the amount of detail within a shot. Without scaling, MPEG-1 offers a resolution of 352 by 240 pixels. MPEG-2 offers a resolution of 720 by 480 pixels at 30 fps, with high-quality audio.

MPEG-2, however, takes a great deal of time to compress even one second of video—sometimes at rates of hundreds of seconds to compress each second of video. New fast encoding chips will bring that time down considerably.

MPEG-3

There was an MPEG-3 designed to handle *HDTV (High Definition Television)*, but it's been dropped in favor of the MPEG-2 codec.

MPEG-4

MPEG-4 isn't scheduled to debut until 1998. It will use video synthesis, fractal geometry, and artificial intelligence to encode and decode video. As the technology improves, MPEG-4 will undoubtedly provide higher-quality video at perhaps higher compression ratios. The initial cost, however, may be a drawback.

Windows 95 Codecs

The codec you want to use must be installed in Windows 95. To view the codecs included with Windows 95, do the following:

> **Tip:** You can also take advantage of Windows 95's interactive help to find and configure most options. To use help, click on Start, Help, Index. Type in the word you're looking for and click on the entry. An interactive help screen will guide you to the right place to change settings.

If you have no programs open, click on My Computer, Control Panel to get the Multimedia Properties window.

If you have one or more open programs, click on Start, Settings and Control Panel.

Double-click on the Multimedia icon to display the Multimedia Properties window. Click on the Advanced tab to display the Multimedia devices list shown in figure 28.1.

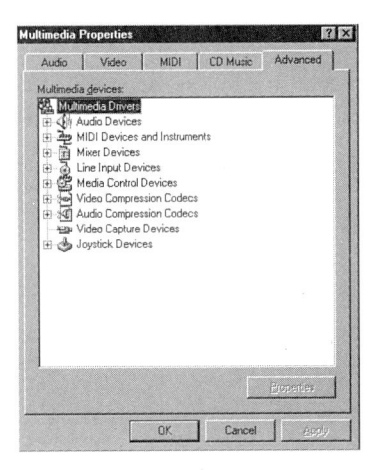

Fig. 28.1 The Advanced tab under the Multimedia Properties window lets you choose a codec for compressing/decompressing video.

Click on the + to the left of the Video Compression Codecs for a full listing of available schemes (see figure 28.2).

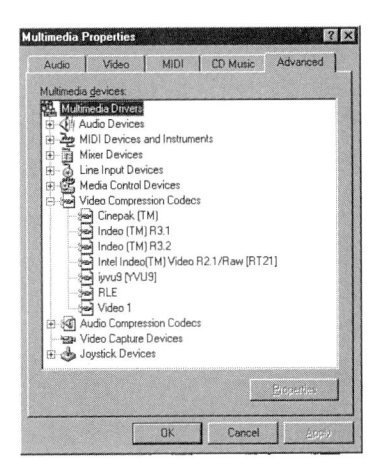

Fig. 28.2 Windows 95 ships with various codecs for working with video.

Windows 95 Codecs **649**

Click on any of the codecs (Cinepak, Indeo, Video 1, etc.) to make the Properties option available. Click on the <u>P</u>roperties button to display the tab for that coding (figure 28.3).

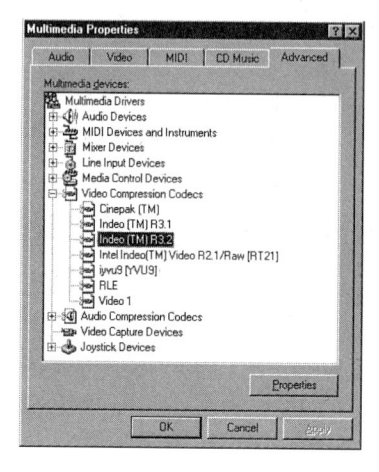

Fig. 28.3 Each codec has its own settings tab to customize it for your needs.

Click <u>S</u>ettings to customize it for your use. To save space or to install an updated codec, click on <u>R</u>emove to delete a codec from your computer.

Viewing AVI Files

Audio Video Interleaved (AVI) files contain synchronized video and sound. Windows 95 supports AVI, MIDI (Musical Instrument Digital Interface), and audio waveform (WAV) files. See Chapter 25, "Adding Multimedia Capability to Your Computer," and Chapter 26, "Using Multimedia on Your Computer."

Windows 95 comes ready with AVI files and the codecs needed to play them. All you need is a sound card (although a CD-ROM drive and speakers or headphones are nearly a must as well).

Media Player

You can use the Media Player (figure 28.4) to play AVI files by doing the following:

Click on Start, Programs, Accessories, Multimedia, Media Player to display the Media Player.

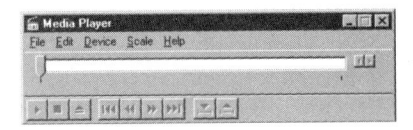

Fig. 28.4 The Media Player comes ready-made to play digital video.

To play AVI files, do the following:

1. With the Media Player open, click Device.
2. Click 1, Video for Windows.
3. Enter a File name or browse through the folders for the file you want to play.
4. Click on the file.
5. Click Open. You'll get the screen shown in figure 28.5.

> **Tip:** Look in the Media folder in the Windows folder to find multimedia files that come with Windows 95.

The Media Player will become active with an audio-tape-like panel on-screen, as in figure 28.5.

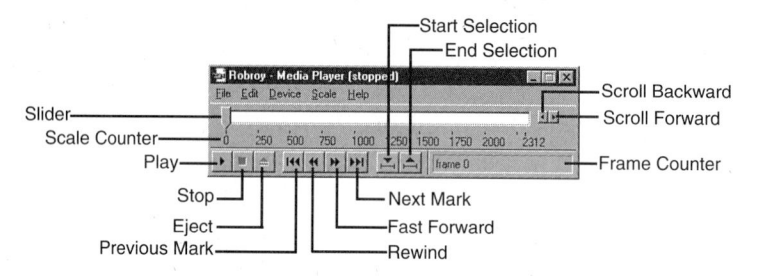

Fig. 28.5 Once enabled, Media Player displays control buttons.

6. Click the play button to play the video.

Scale: Frames

You can set the scale that is displayed; you have a choice between *frames* and *time*. That is, you can track the video frame by frame, with each frame counting as one, or you can count how long the video takes to run (see figure 28.6). To set the scale to frames, click on Scale, Frames.

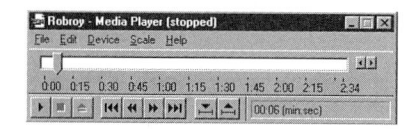

Fig. 28.6 You can view the video by frame or by second.

When the scale is set to frames, you can move ahead frame by frame by clicking on the Scroll Forward and Scroll Backward buttons. The frame number will appear in the frames box.

If you click the Fast Forward or Rewind buttons, the video will move by 12-frame increments.

Scale: Time

There may be times when you want to work with seconds instead of frames. Set the scale to time by clicking on Scale, Time.

When you click the Fast Forward or Rewind buttons, the video display moves in increments of roughly .70 of a second.

Playing the File

Click and hold on the slider to move the video forward or backward. You can click the Play button at any time to start the video. It will begin at the slider point. You can click on the Stop or Pause buttons at any time.

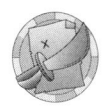

> **Tip:** The Pause button replaces the Play button whenever Play is activated.

Selection Points

When you're working with video, you often have to use a small bit of the file to edit it or to synchronize the audio. You can choose selection points to make it easier to find or to skip over specified areas in the video. There are two ways to set the selection points:

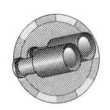

> **Note:** You can only create one set of selection points at a time. You can expand or decrease the selection, but the first set will disappear if you create a second set.

1. Move the slide control to the point you want to mark, and click on the Start Selection button. A small caret appears at that point on the scale line.

2. Drag the slide control to the point where you want to end the selection. A blue bar appears on the viewing line, and a small caret appears at that point on the scale line.

3. You can now use the Previous Mark and Next Mark to navigate back and forth in the video.

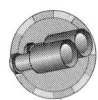

> **Note:** The selection doesn't carry over from time to frames or vice versa.

You can also set the selection points in a more precise way by using the Set Selection dialog box.

To use the Set Selection dialog box, do the following:

1. Choose frame or time mode.
2. Select Edit, Selection to get the screen shown in figure 28.7.

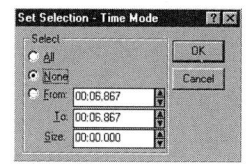

Fig. 28.7 The Set Selection Frame Mode lets you group a block of frames.

3. Select All, None, or From. To specify a sequence of frames (or time), either click the scroll buttons to get to the desired numbers, or type in the numbers.
4. You can instead choose a size (frames or seconds) by using the scroll button in the Size box or by typing in a number.
5. Click OK to mark the selection.

Properties

Setting the Properties is the most important parameter for the quality of the playback video. Properties allows you to choose what size the video plays back.

Select Device, Properties, and the Video tab to get the screen shown in figure 28.8.

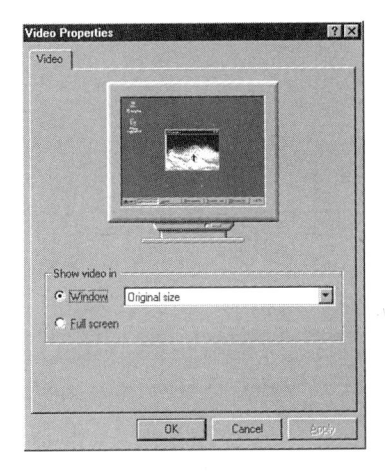

Fig. 28.8 You can select a playback size in the Video Properties sheet.

Take a look at the different ways you can play an image. Figure 28.9 shows a sample avi file.

Fig. 28.9 Using Windows 95's Media Player, the CBT_demo.avi file included with Asymmetrix Multimedia Toolbook authoring software.

The default window size is quite small but offers the least distortion of color or image. The screen can be resized by dragging on its borders. Notice what happens when the screen is resized to roughly twice its original size, as in figure 28.10.

Fig. 28.10 An AVI file increased to about double its size loses a lot of quality.

The quality is far more grainy than the original size, and it's plagued by the blockiness that results from reducing frames to color blocks in a run through the codec.

The default size is the original size. You have the following options:

- Original size
- Double original size
- 1/16 of screen size
- 1/4 of screen size
- 1/2 of screen size
- Maximized

The following five figures illustrate the difference in size and quality:

Fig. 28.11 Original size.

656 Chapter 28: Understanding Full-Motion Video

Fig. 28.12 Double original size.

Fig. 28.13 1/16 of screen size.

Fig. 28.14 1/4 of screen size.

Properties **657**

Fig. 28.15 1/2 of screen size.

A maximized, or full-screen, size is about twice the size of figure 28.15, but looks considerably more distorted.

OLE

Perhaps the most outstanding result of the video capabilities of Windows 95 is that you can easily use OLE (object linking and embedding) to drop video clips into presentations, word processing documents, spreadsheets, and many other Windows programs.

The instructions are similar for most Windows programs. I'm going to drop a video clip into Microsoft Word for Windows:

1. Open a Word document and position the cursor where you want the clip to go.
2. Select Insert, Object to get the Object dialog box.
3. Click the Create New tab.
4. Highlight and click Media Clip.
5. Click OK. In the document, you'll get the Media Clip placeholder as shown in figure 28.16. You'll also get a modified form of the Media Player box.

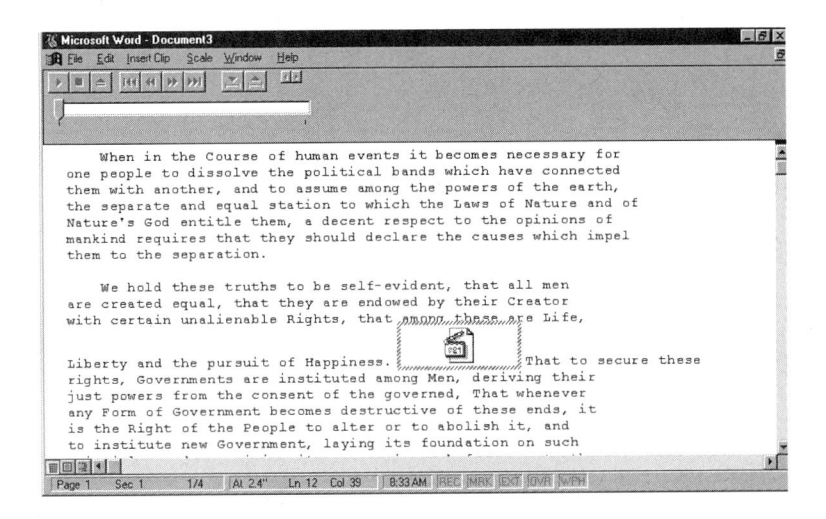

Fig. 28.16 The Media Clip placeholder points the way to the OLE clip.

6. Select Insert Clip.

> **Tip:** If you go to another task and lose the modified version of the Media Player, double-click on the placeholder shown in figure 28.17 to get it back.

7. Select 1, Video for Windows.
8. Choose a folder and a file name.
9. Click Open. The file will open within the document, as in figure 28.17.

OLE **659**

Fig. 28.17 The media clip appears where the placeholder was inserted.

10. Select Insert Clip, Properties and set a size.
11. Click OK.
12. If you only want a portion of the clip to play, select Edit, Selection.
13. Specify a range.
14. Click OK.
15. If you want to control the volume, select Insert Clip, Volume Control and set the volume.

    Click Options, Exit.

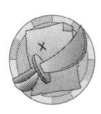

> **Tip:** Play the clip before you close it to verify that you've chosen the right one.

16. Click anywhere else in the document to close the play panel.

> **Tip:** To move the clip within the document, click once on it to define it, and then drag and drop it to the desired place.

To play the clip, double-click on it.

660 Chapter 28: Understanding Full-Motion Video

Options

There are seven different options you can set for the clip. To see the options, select Edit, Options to get the screen shown in figure 28.18.

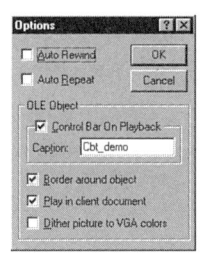

Fig. 28.18 You can set different options for the media clip.

You can choose to have the clip Auto Rewind or Auto Repeat after it plays.

If you're linking and embedding the clip in another Windows application, you can choose to display the control bar on playback. You can also designate a caption or choose not to have one. The default caption is the clip's file name.

DCI

In mid 1994, Microsoft released the *Display Control Interface* (DCI) display driver development kit, which was developed along with Intel. DCI enables Windows to implement advanced hardware features to speed up the way games and digital video read and write to disc. DCI allows the following features:

- Overlay
- Color-space conversion
- Double buffering
- Chroma key
- Asynchronous drawing
- Stretching

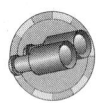

> **Note:** You need a high-quality graphics adapter card to make these features work.

As of this writing (early summer 1995), Microsoft planned to drop support for DCI for the first release of Windows 95. It will be included in later versions.

Just how much that would affect developers and end users is disputed. Microsoft anticipates no problems, but some companies expressed concerns about compatibility with multimedia software. Mostly, it will affect packages that need software MPEG, Apple QuickTime for Windows, and hardware enhancement to run.

Fine-Tuning Your Windows 95 Sound Card

KILLER 29 WINDOWS 95

by Clayton Walnum

At this point, you've got your multimedia system all set up and ready to go. All your devices are installed and configured, and you've even had some time to experiment a bit, playing audio CDs or MIDI files, or maybe even watching full-motion video clips. Although you've had a chance to use many of your multimedia devices, you've yet to learn how to really control your sound card. Because a sound card is probably the most complicated device in your new multimedia system, it gets an entire chapter of its own!

In this chapter, you learn the following:

➤ How to mix sounds with the Volume Control accessory

➤ How to set recording levels

➤ How to add or remove the volume control from the taskbar

➤ How to set your sound card's recording quality

➤ How to record sound effects for use with Windows

➤ How to assign sound cards and instruments to different MIDI channels

Using Volume Control

Back in Chapter 27, you used the Multimedia Properties sheet to customize how some of your multimedia devices work. However, much of the details of dealing with a sound card were left to this chapter. One of the topics that got skipped over was the Volume Control accessory. In this section, you make up for that lack, by learning the details of using Volume Control with your sound card.

To start Volume Control, you can select it from the Start/Programs/Accessories/Multimedia menu. When you do, Volume Control's main window appears on-screen, as shown in figure 29.1. As you can see, this window contains various controls for mixing the sound sources installed in your system.

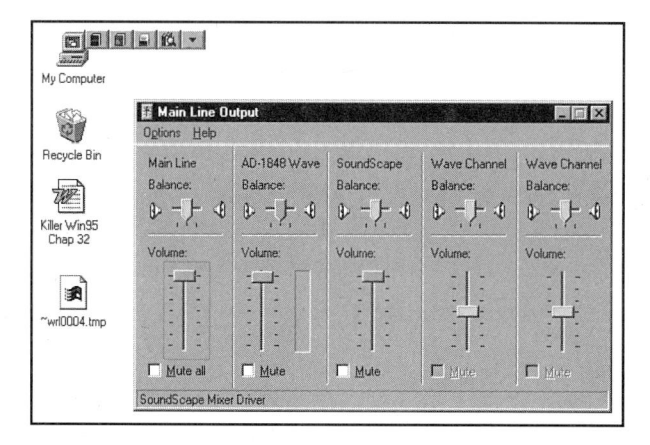

Fig. 29.1 Volume Control's main window looks like a studio-style mixer.

Choosing Which Channels to Display

When you first run Volume Control, you may notice that not all your audio devices are represented by a channel on the mixer. You can remedy this situation by selecting the Properties command from the Options menu. When you do, you see the Properties sheet (figure 29.2).

At the bottom of the dialog box is a list of available devices. To expand the Volume Control window so that it provides a channel for each device, just make sure there's a check mark in each box in the list. To remove a channel from the main window, remove its check mark from the list. In this way, you can display channels for only those devices you need. Figure 29.3 shows a typical Volume Control, with a channel displayed for every device.

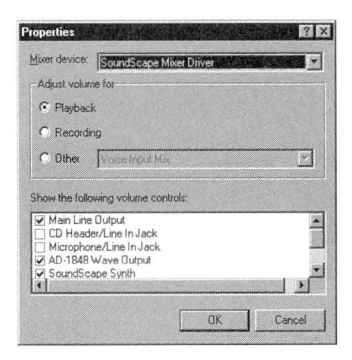

Fig. 29.2 The Properties sheet enables you to customize the Volume Control accessory.

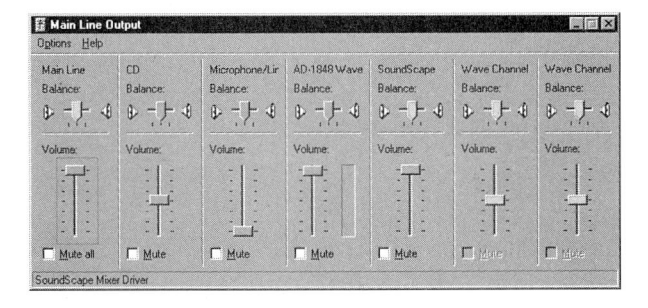

Fig. 29.3 You can display as many or as few channels as you like.

Using Volume Control **665**

Mixing Sound

How do you control sound with Volume Control? A good question! Notice that the first channel in the mixer is called Main Line. (Your version of Volume Control may look different, depending on the type and capabilities of your sound card.) Like all the other channels, the Main Line channel has a balance control, a volume slider, and a mute box. Unlike the other channels, however, the Main Line channel controls the sound of every device simultaneously. That is, the Main Line controls are the master controls.

To reduce the volume of every sound device, drag the Main Line volume slider down. To increase the volume of every channel, you would, of course, drag the slider back up. Dragging the Balance slider left or right changes the amount of sound that comes from the left or right speakers. When the slider is all the way to the left, only the left speaker produces sound. Similarly, when the slider is all the way to the right, only the right speaker produces sound. In most cases, you'll want the Balance slider exactly in the center, so your speaker can produce the best stereo effect.

Finally, you can instantly bring every channel down to its minimum volume by clicking the Mute all box. When you do, a check mark appears in the box, which indicates that every channel is at its minimum level. To turn all channels back on, click on the Mute all box again to remove the check mark.

Each of the other device channels works similarly to the Main Line channel, except they control only the specific devices that are marked at the top of the channel. For example, to change the volume of the CD device, you would adjust the volume slider in the CD channel. Likewise, the Balance and Mute controls in the CD channel only affect the CD device.

By setting the channels in various ways, you can achieve some interesting results. You can, for example, set the Wave channel's balance control all the way to the left and the Microphone channel balance all the way to the right. Then, digitized sound effects will come from the left speaker, while at the same time, someone speaking into the microphone will be heard in the right speaker. You can, of course, shut off any individual channel by clicking its Mute box.

Notice that the Main Line controls always affect all the other channels. For example, the setting of the Main Line volume slider sets the maximum sound level attainable by any other channel. If you have the Main Line volume slider set at its halfway point, all the other volume sliders must work within the set range. That is, if you drag a device's volume slider to its maximum position, the volume of the device will be the Main Line's volume setting, with lower device volume settings representing a volume level somewhere between off and the Main Line's volume setting.

Setting Record Levels

In the previous section, you used Volume Control's Properties sheet to determine which devices have channels displayed in the mixer. What you may not have realized at the time was that you were controlling which playback channels were to be displayed. *Playback channels* control sound being played back by a sound device. For example, when you play an audio CD or listen to a digitized sound effect (a wave file), you're using a playback channel. The opposite of playback is record, and Volume Control also has a set of *record channels*, which control the sound being recorded. (When you record sound, you're storing it for later playback. You learn to record sounds later in this chapter, in the section titled, "Recording Sound.")

If you have a cassette deck in your home, you know that you can change the volume of a tape by turning up the volume on your stereo. This is the equivalent of manipulating Volume Control's playback channels. You probably also know that you can capture a radio broadcast to tape by recording the radio with your cassette deck. You control the volume of the recording by turning up your cassette deck's record level. This is the equivalent of manipulating Volume Control's recording channels.

Using Volume Control **667**

To access the recording channels, you must first display the Properties sheet, which you do by selecting the P_roperties command in the Options menu. As you saw back in figure 29.3, the Properties sheet contains a section with three option buttons labeled Playback, Recording, and Other. When the dialog box first appears, the Playback option is selected, which means that you're setting the properties for the playback channels. To change to the recording channels, click the Recording option button.

When you click the recording option button, the devices listed at the bottom of the dialog box change to show the recording devices. Use this list to select the devices for which you want a channel in the mixer. To select a device, place a check mark in its box, by clicking on the box. To deselect a device, remove its check mark, by clicking on the box again. When you're finished selecting recording devices, click on the dialog box's OK button. You'll then see that Volume Control now displays the recording channels you selected (figure 29.4). You can tell that you're now dealing with recording channels because the window is labeled "Record Input Mix."

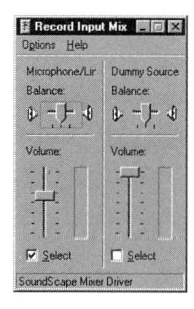

Fig. 29.4 Volume Control can also display recording channels.

Just as the playback controls affect how sounds are played, the controls on the recording channels change how sound is recorded. The Balance control determines how much of the sound is recorded for the left and right speakers. The volume slider determines how loudly the sound is recorded. Finally, the S_elect option determines which channel is the source of the sound to record.

If you look in the Options menu, you may find that the Advanced Controls command is enabled. If it is, you can click on it to display the Advanced button in the Volume Control window, as shown in figure 29.5. Clicking on this button displays the Advanced Controls dialog box for the channel (figure 29.6). The controls in this dialog box enable you to modify such settings as tone (treble and bass) for sound devices that support such functions. Because every sound card is different, you should check your sound card's manual to determine what the advanced controls do for your sound card.

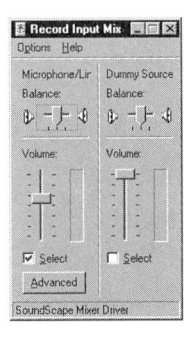

Fig. 29.5 The Advanced button provides access to advanced controls for a specific device's channel.

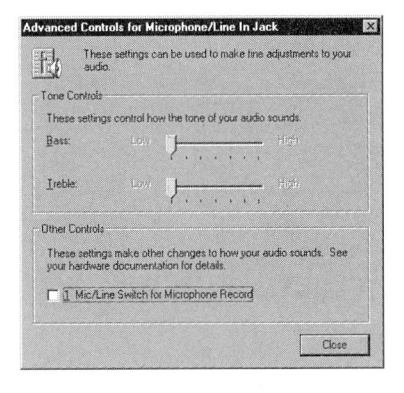

Fig. 29.6 The Advanced Controls dialog box contains extra controls that may be supported by a sound device.

Using Volume Control **669**

Accessing Volume Control from the Taskbar

In its default state, the taskbar displays a speaker icon that represents the Volume Control accessory. As you learned in Chapter 27, "Getting the Most out of Multimedia," if you single-click on the speaker icon, a small volume control appears (figure 29.7). This miniature version of the Volume Control accessory determines the volume for all sound channels in your system. In that way, it acts just like the Main Line volume slider in the full-featured version of the Volume Control accessory. (If the speaker icon does not appear on your taskbar, refer to the next paragraph to learn how to enable and disable this option.)

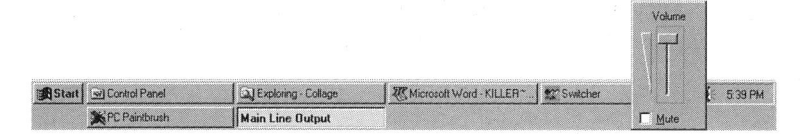

Fig. 29.7 The miniature version of Volume Control sets the volume for every sound channel simultaneously.

If you double-click on the speaker icon, Windows displays the full version of the Volume Control accessory, which you can use as described earlier in this section. If you'd rather that the speaker icon not appear in the taskbar, you can remove it with the Multimedia Properties sheet. (You can also add the speaker icon to the taskbar with the Multimedia Properties sheet.) To display this dialog box, double-click on the Multimedia icon in the Control Panel window. When you do, Windows displays the Multimedia Properties sheet, as shown in figure 29.8. To remove the Volume Control icon from the taskbar, remove the check mark from the Show Volume Control on the taskbar option. Another way to access the Show Volume Control option is to right-click the speaker icon in the taskbar and select the Adjust Audio Properties option in the pop-up menu.

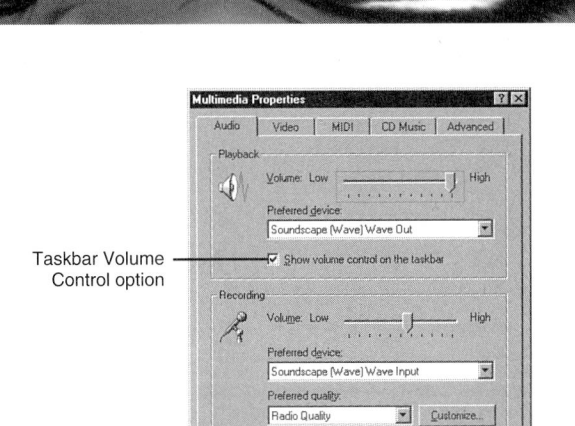

Fig. 29.8 The Multimedia Properties sheet enables you to add or remove Volume Control from the taskbar.

Setting Recording Quality

The Multimedia Properties sheet also enables you to set the recording quality of your sound device. As you learned back in Chapter 27, "Getting the Most out of Multimedia," the easiest way to set the recording quality is to select a setting from the Preferred Quality list box, as shown in figure 29.9. However, if you want more control over the recording quality, click on the Customize button to display the Customize dialog box.

In the Customize dialog box, the Name list box holds the names of the currently available quality settings. At first, this list box contains only the default CD Quality, Radio Quality, and Telephone Quality entries. Using the Customize dialog box, you can add your own settings to the list.

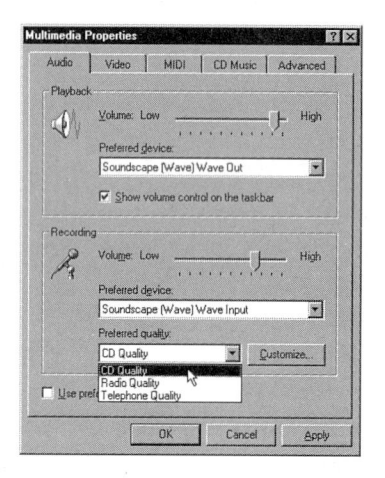

Fig. 29.9 The Preferred Quality list box enables you to set recording quality quickly and easily.

Unless you really know what you're doing, you should probably leave the Format box set just as it is. You can safely experiment with the Attributes list box, though, which displays the various sound-quality settings you can use, as shown in figure 29.10. The four values displayed in each list entry contribute to the quality of the recording; the higher the number, the better the quality.

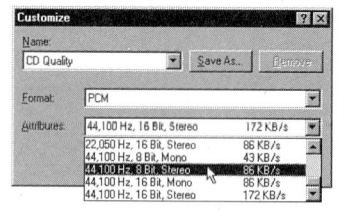

Fig. 29.10 Use the Customize dialog box to create your own recording-quality settings.

The first number (for example, 44,100 Hz) is the sampling rate, the second is the sampling size (for example, 16 bits), the third setting selects between mono and stereo sound, and the last setting (for example, 172 kb/sec) shows how much memory or disk space is required for each second of sound. Notice that the higher the sound quality, the more memory and disk space required to store the sound.

When you select a new sound setting from the Attributes list box, the Name list box shows the name [untitled]. To make use of your new setting, you should give the setting a name and then save it to disk. You do this by clicking on the Save As button, entering a name into the dialog box that appears, and then clicking on the dialog's OK button. When you finish the Save As procedure, your new sound setting appears in the Name list box, where it will be whenever you display the Audio page of the Multimedia Properties sheet.

Figure 29.11 shows a new sound format, My Sound Format, in the Name list box. Notice that, when a custom sound format is displayed in the Name box, Windows enables the Remove button. This is so you can remove from the Name list any custom sound formats that you've created. To remove the format, first make sure that the sound format you want to remove is displayed in the Name box; then, just click the Remove button.

Recording Sound

If you've never recorded sound effects under Windows before, you're in for a treat. Not only is the job easy, but it's also fun. Besides Sound Recorder, which comes with Windows, most sound cards also come with the software you need to create sound effects for any application that can handle wave files. Moreover, many of these sound-recording programs can edit sounds in various ways, from clipping unwanted noise to adding echo or even reversing a sound effect.

On some systems, for example, you can have an Ensoniq Soundscape Wavetable sound card. It comes with a sound recording, editing, and playback program called Audiostation (figure 29.11). This program can do everything from record WAV files to play your favorite CD.

Fig. 29.11 The Audiostation sound application not only looks cool, but works great, too.

If you have a Sound Blaster 16 sound card, you might have a program called WaveStudio, which, although not as elaborate as Audiostation, provides all the basic editing features you need to create sound effects for use under Windows. Other types of sound cards come with similar sound-editing programs.

No matter what sound card you have and what software you'll be using to record and edit sound effects, the first step is to plug a microphone into the sound card. Then, whatever sounds the microphone picks up are transmitted to the sound card and on to whatever sound-editing program you're running. In this book, you learn about the Sound Recorder accessory that comes with Windows, but most of what is discussed here, you can apply to any sound-recording application.

Once you have the microphone plugged in, start Sound Recorder by clicking on its entry in the Start/Programs/Accessories/Multimedia menu. When you do, you see the window shown in figure 29.12. To start recording, just click on the Record button. When you do, the time in the Position box starts counting upward and any sound picked up by your microphone is stored in the computer's memory.

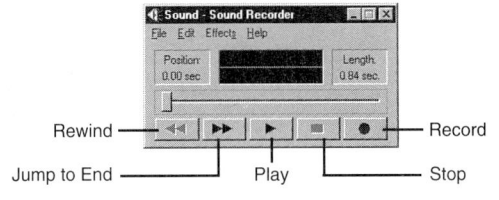

Fig. 29.12 The Windows Sound Recorder records sound effects.

For example, suppose that you want to record the words *Welcome, Master*, to be used as a greeting when you start Windows (replacing the famous *tada*). After plugging in your microphone, starting Sound Recorder, and clicking the Record button, just speak into the microphone. When you're done speaking, click on the Stop button. To hear what you've just recorded, click on the Play button. The rewind and jump-to-end buttons bring you to the very beginning or end of the sound effect, respectively. (If you like, you can drag the slider control to position yourself at any point in the sound effect you want.)

When you have your sound effect recorded just the way you want it (it'll probably take a few tries unless you're a professional announcer), you must save it to disk so that other programs can use it. To do this, click on the File menu's Save As command, enter a name for the file into the Save As dialog box, and click on the dialog box's Save button. Notice that you don't need to add the WAV extension (normally used for sound files) to the sound name. Sound Recorder does this for you.

Now, your sound effect is safely stored on disk, and you can use it with any application that can play wave files. If you want to attach your sound effects to Windows events (such as replacing that aforementioned *tada* sound), use the Sounds Properties sheet. For more information on the Sounds Properties sheet, see Chapter 26, "Using Multimedia on Your Computer."

A final note: If your sound effects don't seem to be recording as loudly as they should be, remember that you can use the Volume Control accessory to change the recording volume. Refer to this chapter's "Setting Record Levels" section for more information.

Recording Sound

Editing Sounds

Once you have a sound effect recorded, you'll almost always need to edit it somehow. Different sound programs have different editing features, but most of them let you delete various portions of the sound, as well as change the volume of the sound.

One piece of editing you'll almost certainly have to do is delete part of the beginning and end of the sound. This is because you're going to have a second or two of silence before the actual sound wave you want. Why? It takes a second or two for you to go from turning on the sound program's record function to actually creating the sound you want to record. Similarly, you may not get to the stop button as quickly as you'd like.

As you can see from figure 29.13, Sound Recorder's Edit menu contains a number of commands that you can use to clean up your sound recordings. To delete the beginning portion of a sound effect, drag the slider control to the end of the area that you'd like to delete, and then select the Edit menu's Delete Before Current Position command. Similarly, to delete an ending portion from the sound effect, drag the slider to the start of the area that you want to delete, and then select the Delete After Current Position command. (You can also position the slider by playing the sound effect and then clicking the stop button at the appropriate point.)

Fig. 29.13 Use Sound Recorder's Edit menu to clean up your sound effects.

Another thing you may have to do is increase the volume of the sound effects. For some reason, they never seem to record loud enough. In Sound Recorder, you can increase the volume of the sound effects by selecting the Effects menu's Increase Volume command (figure 29.14). If you need to reduce the sound effects' volume, select the Effects menu's Decrease Volume command.

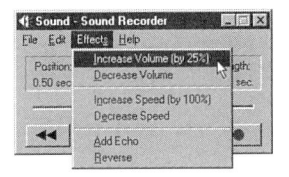

Fig. 29.14 Sound Recorder's Effects menu offers interesting ways to modify a sound effect.

Notice that these commands do not change the volume of your playback or record channels. Instead, they increase the amplitude of the sound itself. *Amplitude* is the height of a sound wave. The higher a sound effect's amplitude, the higher its volume. Figure 29.15 shows a sound effect's waveform before the volume has been increased. Figure 29.16 shows the same waveform after the volume has been increased. Notice how the waveform is higher.

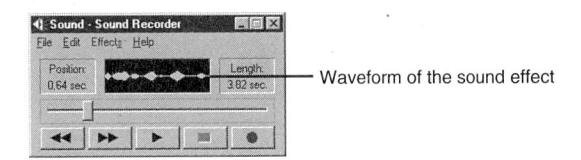

Fig. 29.15 The waveform in this window is shown at its normal amplitude.

Editing Sounds **677**

Fig. 29.16 This is the same waveform, but with its amplitude increased.

Other commands on the Effects menu let you increase or decrease the sound effect's speed (which has the effect of speeding or slowing a tape), add echo to the sound, or even reverse the sound so that it plays backward! With all these tools at your command, you should be able to come up with some strange and interesting effects.

Creating a MIDI Configuration

In Chapter 27, "Getting the Most out of Multimedia," you learned to add MIDI instruments to your system. As you discovered, these instruments can be anything from electronic keyboards to drum machines and any other type of sound module that responds to MIDI commands. What you didn't know then was that MIDI commands can be sent on any of 16 different channels. This means that you can route MIDI commands to as many as 16 different instruments just by assigning each instrument to its own MIDI channel.

The MIDI page of the Multimedia Properties sheet enables you to assign instruments to channels by setting up a custom MIDI configuration. To do this, first display the Multimedia Properties sheet by clicking on Control Panel's Multimedia icon. Then, select the dialog box's MIDI tab to display the MIDI page, as shown in figure 29.17.

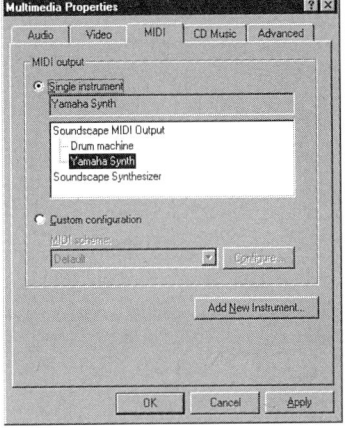

Fig. 29.17 Use the MIDI page of the Multimedia Properties sheet to set up a custom MIDI configuration for your sound card.

As you can see, the list box on the MIDI page shows the instruments installed on your system. You can select any single instrument to receive MIDI commands by clicking on the instrument in the box. But, if you'd like to have different instruments on different channels and thus use many instruments simultaneously, click on the Custom Configuration option to enable the MIDI Scheme and Configure controls. Then, click on the Configure button, which displays the MIDI Configuration dialog box (figure 29.18).

Fig. 29.18 The MIDI Configuration dialog box assigns MIDI channels to specific instruments.

Creating a MIDI Configuration **679**

In the MIDI Configuration dialog box, the Schemes list box holds any configurations that you've created for your system. The first time you see this control, it'll probably only contain the Default entry. Your task now is to add your own custom MIDI configuration to the list. To do this, first click on the channel with which you want to associate one of your MIDI instruments. Then, click the Change button to bring up the Change MIDI Instrument dialog box (figure 29.19).

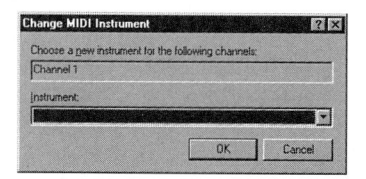

Fig. 29.19 The Change MIDI Instrument dialog box lets you associate an instrument with the selected MIDI channel.

The upper box in the dialog shows the channel that you're currently assigning. The list box in the lower part of the dialog box holds all the MIDI instruments attached to your system. Just select an instrument from the list and *presto!* that instrument is assigned to the selected channel. If, for example, you assign MIDI channel 1 to an electronic keyboard and MIDI channel 2 to your sound card, any MIDI commands targets for channel 1 go to the keyboard and commands on channel 2 go to the sound card.

After you've set up your MIDI configuration, you'll want to save it for future use. To do this, click on the Save As button, enter a name for the configuration into the dialog that appears, and then click on the dialog's OK button. You can delete any custom MIDI configurations you add to the list by selecting the configuration in the Schemes list box and then clicking on the MIDI Configuration dialog box's Delete button.

Using OLE to Communicate with Other Applications

KILLER 30 WINDOWS 95

by Allen L. Wyatt

Through your computer experience, you've learned that you generally perform a specialized type of work with a given application. For example, for word processing, you use a word processing application. For spreadsheets, you switch to a spreadsheet application, and so on. But the programming wizards at Microsoft have visualized a completely different way to use computers.

In tomorrow's computers (and to a degree, in Windows 95), the emphasis on individual applications will slip into the background, and instead the focus will be on documents. You'll use more than one application to create a single document, and as you do, a variety of application tools will be instantly available for your work. You'll draw on word processing tools to create text, presentation graphics tools to create a chart, and font-design tools to create an attractive document title. Moreover, data entered into one document will be automatically and dynamically linked with similar data in another document so that changes made to the source document are automatically and instantly reflected in all the copies. When you receive notice that a correspondent's address has changed, for example, you'll type it once, and the computer will take care of updating every last copy you've made of that address, regardless of the application in which the address is used.

Sound futuristic? Tomorrow isn't all that far off, as you will find out by working with Windows 95. The foundation for this new way of using computers was laid with Windows 3.1, and has been strengthened and enhanced with the introduction of Windows 95. Incorporated into the operating system are two sets of standards that permit *interprocess communication,* which is the sending of messages from one application to another.

The first (and earliest) of these standards is *dynamic data exchange* (DDE). This standard establishes the basis for linking, in which the changes you make to a source document are automatically updated in copies you've made of this document and inserted in other documents, even those of other applications. Linking closely resembles Clipboard copying, except that the copy is dynamically updated when the original changes. With many applications, you can display and edit the source data just by double-clicking any of the copies you've made of this data.

Windows has included DDE capabilities since version 2.0; however, before Windows version 3.1, DDE was hard to use: you had to write complicated commands to create DDE links. For example, Word for Windows and Microsoft Excel have both, for some time, allowed you to type external reference commands that create DDE links.

Because DDE command syntax is difficult to master, few Windows users (or programmers) took advantage of DDE. Interprocess communication started to take off, however, with the introduction of a new standard called *object linking and embedding* (OLE) in Windows 3.1. OLE (pronounced *olay*) has been strengthened with the release of OLE 2.0, and it has been fully integrated into Windows 95.

In brief, OLE provides easy-to-use menu commands so anyone can create links just by choosing options from menus. OLE also makes possible a new kind of application integration called *embedding*. With embedding, you can create a compound document in which the various parts are created by different applications. Such a document could contain text created by Ami Pro for Windows, a beautiful title created by Microsoft WordArt, a presentation-quality graphic created by Microsoft Excel, and a spreadsheet table created by Quattro Pro for Windows. To edit such a document, you just place the cursor in the portion you want to edit, and Windows starts the application that created the object.

Linking and embedding may sound futuristic, but you can put it to work right now. If you spend a little time learning how to create links and embed objects, you'll ensure that every copy you make of authoritative source data, such as a price list, is always up to date and correct. And what's more, you'll find it much easier to locate and edit this source data, should changes become necessary. With Windows 95 and OLE-capable applications, the source document—and the application that created it—is no more than a double-click away.

> **Note:** OLE makes enormous demands on your computer system's microprocessor. Although you can link and embed with any system on which you can run Windows 95, some operations may take a few seconds to a minute or more. If you plan to use interprocess communication extensively, you should plan to upgrade to an 80486DX-based computer running at 33 MHz or better, and preferably with at least 16M of memory.

Understanding OLE

OLE is sufficiently unfamiliar that some introduction and terminology will prove helpful. In this section, you learn the difference between linking and embedding, and you learn when to choose one over the other. In any discussion of OLE, however, you will find a knowledge of some basic terms useful. The following terms have special meaning in relation to OLE:

➤ An *object* is a whole document or part of a document, such as part of an Excel spreadsheet or Paintbrush drawing, produced by a particular application. For OLE and DDE purposes, then, you'll encounter references to Excel objects, Ami Pro objects, and the like. Here, *objects* just means "documents" or "selected portions of documents."

➤ A *server application* is a Windows application capable of creating an object that can be used by other Windows applications. For example, Ami Pro objects are created by Ami Pro, which is the server application. Not all Windows applications are capable of performing as a server application.

➤ A *client application* is a Windows application capable of using an object created by a server application. As an example, Word for Windows can incorporate objects created by server application. In this instance, Word for Windows is the client application. Not all Windows applications are capable of performing as client applications. Some applications, however, can function as both servers and clients.

➤ The *source document* is the document from which you copy an object. You create a source document with a server application. For example, if you create a chart with Excel that you intend to incorporate into a document created with a client application, then the chart is the source document.

➤ The *destination document* is a document into which you paste or embed an object. You create a destination document with a client application. Continuing the example, if you create a document with Word for Windows and link the source document created by Excel (the chart mentioned in the previous definition), then the Word for Windows document is the destination document.

➤ An *OLE-capable application* is one that can function as a server application, as a client application, or as both. All of the applications mentioned in each of the foregoing definitions refer to OLE-capable applications.

Understanding Linking

When you link one document with another, you copy a document or part of a document by using the Clipboard. The only difference between ordinary Clipboard copying and linking is what happens when you paste.

With linking, you choose a special Edit menu command. Applications vary in the name they use for this command; examples are Link, Paste Link, or Paste Special. But they all share the same function: they paste the Clipboard object into your document, and they create the dynamic link between the server and client applications. The result is a *hot link,* which means that the link between client and server is active and dynamic—it is automatically and instantly updated when you make changes to the source document.

To illustrate linking, consider the Excel worksheet shown in figure 30.1. This worksheet calculates the monthly principal plus interest (P&I) payment needed to amortize a mortgage.

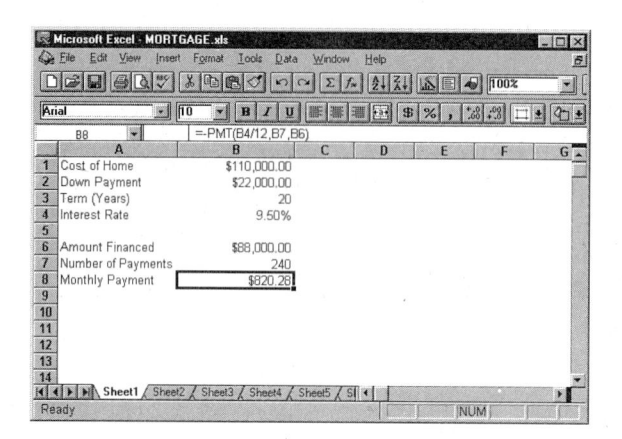

Fig. 30.1 A spreadsheet can be used to calculate a mortgage payment.

Say you wanted to create a link between this spreadsheet and a letter that will contain the figures created in the spreadsheet. To do this, follow these steps:

1. In the Excel spreadsheet, select the cells you want included in the letter.

2. Copy the cells to the Clipboard, using the Copy command from the Edit menu, or by pressing Ctrl+C.

3. Open the Word for Windows document in which you want to place the figures.

4. Within the document, position the cursor at the point where you want the figures placed.

5. Choose the Paste Special command from the Edit menu in Word for Windows. The Paste Special dialog box appears, shown in figure 30.2.

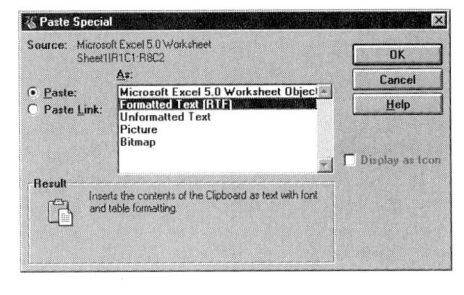

Fig. 30.2 The Paste Special dialog box allows you to perform different types of pasting in a document.

6. Choose the Paste Link button at the left side of the dialog box.

7. In the As list, choose the first option, Microsoft Excel 5.0 Worksheet Object.

8. Click on OK. Word inserts the object at the cursor's location.

After pasting the object into Word, it appears just as it would if you had performed the paste by using ordinary Clipboard techniques (see figure 30.3), but there's a big difference. If you make a change to the source document (the Excel worksheet), Windows automatically updates the object you've placed in the Word document. In figure 30.4, the home's cost has been changed to $99,500, causing the down payment, amount financed, and monthly payment to change accordingly. When you switch to Word, you will see that the altered figures have been immediately and automatically posted to your Word document (see figure 30.5).

Understanding OLE **687**

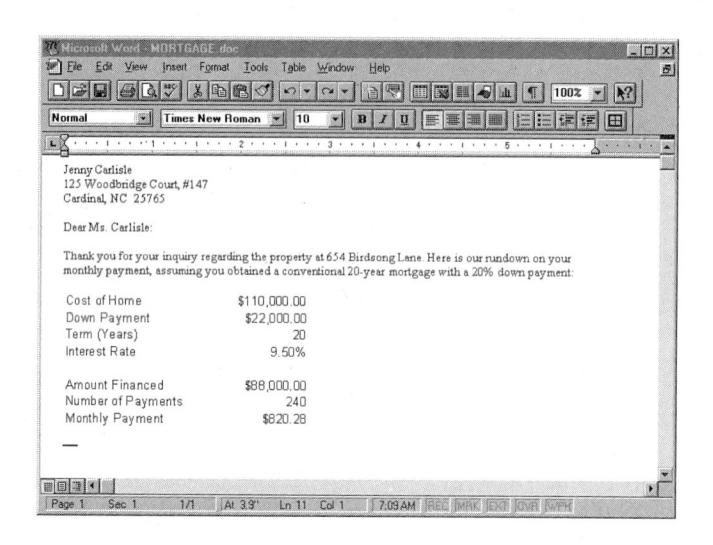

Fig. 30.3 After pasting and establishing a link, the information appears in the document as if you had pasted it normally.

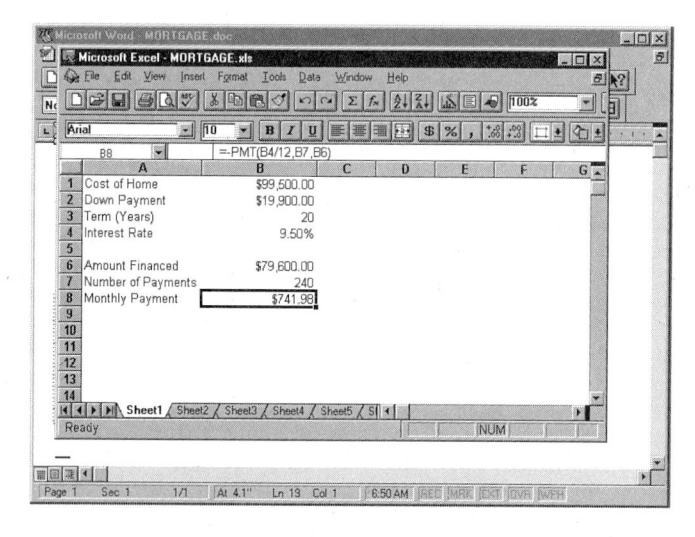

Fig. 30.4 Changes can easily be made to the original spreadsheet in Excel.

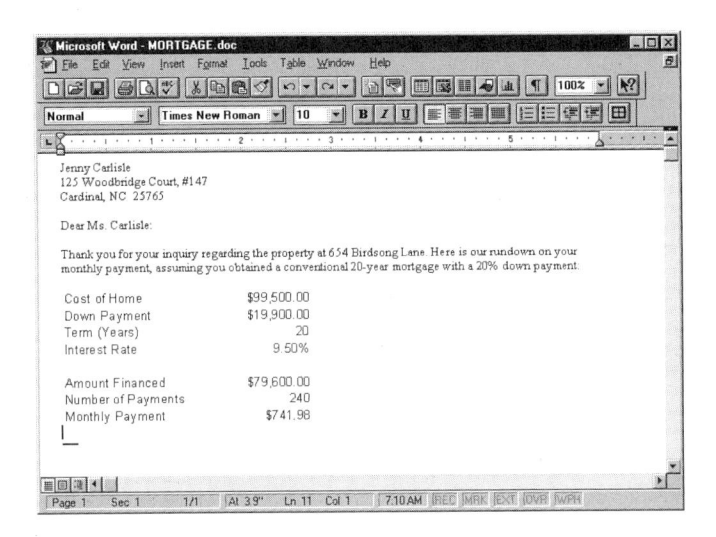

Fig. 30.5 After changing the original spreadsheet, the linked information in the Word for Windows document is automatically updated.

In a real estate office, the letter shown in figures 30.3 and 30.5 could be saved as a template document, which contains the body text, but not the address. To create a version of the letter quickly, open the template, add the name and address, switch to Excel, type in the required data (cost of home, and so forth), switch back to Word, and print.

You can automate this process even more by using a Word for Windows macro. When you open the template, the macro will display a dialog box that prompts you to supply the name and address of the correspondent, the cost of the home, the down payment, the interest rate, and the payment period. After you choose OK, the macro inserts the name and address in the letter. Then it automatically opens Excel, displays the Mortgage worksheet, inserts the altered variables in the correct cells, and prints the updated letter.

If linking seems like magic, you're wrong—it's just good technology. Knowing more about how linking works will help you work with it more successfully. When you use a linking command, (such as Link, Paste Link, or Paste Special) to paste the object in your document,

Understanding OLE   **689**

Windows stores hidden information about the source of the file. This information includes the name and location of the source document. If you make changes to the source document, the client application detects these changes and recopies the information. In short, linking really is an automated version of Clipboard copying. The only real difference between Clipboard copying and linking is that the client application can automatically detect a change in the source document. When it does, it recopies the information automatically.

After you create a link, often you can edit the linked object directly. But it doesn't make much sense to do so. After all, when the client application (in this case, Word for Windows) detects a change in the source document (the Excel spreadsheet), the client application will recopy the object, thus wiping out all your changes. Notice, though, that some client applications will retain the formatting you do to the linked object. Word for Windows, for example, preserves fonts, font sizes, type styles such as bold or italic, and other formats, even if the linked data are repeatedly updated.

To edit the linked object, the best course of action is to edit the source document directly. In applications that do a good job of implementing OLE, you can quickly access the source document from the destination document. You just double-click on the linked object, and the source document appears on-screen. After you make and save changes to the source document, these changes are automatically reflected in the destination document.

You can create links that involve more than two documents, if you want. For example, an Excel worksheet containing quarterly sales report figures could be linked to a memo, a report, and a letter. In addition, you can include as many links as you want within a destination document, subject to the limitations of your computer's memory and processing prowess. These links can involve more than one server application.

In summary, linking provides one of the pathways toward Microsoft's vision of future computing. Within your destination document, you can place objects that were created by different applications. To edit these objects, you just double-click on the object, and the server application appears on-screen, with the source document displayed. You use the server application's tools to edit the source data. When you switch back to the client application, you see that your changes appear there, too. Soon, you stop thinking, "I'm working with a word processing program—I can write, but I really can't do anything else." You start focusing on your document, and on all the varied types of data you can include—databases, spreadsheets, graphics, and more.

> **Caution:** After you start linking information in your OLE-aware programs, don't delete your source documents or move them to different directories. Client applications record links with hidden information about the source document's location. If you erase the source document or move it out of its original directory, the client application won't be able to locate it, and you'll see an error message. You'll learn subsequently how to fix this problem, but the best practice is to leave your documents where they are.

Understanding Embedding

When you link an object, you establish links between the source document and the linked object (or objects, if you made more than one copy). The linked object is just an on-screen simulation of the information in the source document. It doesn't contain the programming code necessary to alter the source document. For this reason, the copied object isn't really editable. It just seems to be, because when you double-click on the object, Windows starts the server application, displays the source document, and allows you to edit the source document. When you switch back to the destination document, you find that the client application has deleted the old object, overwriting it with the new, updated version.

Embedding is different. When you embed an object, Windows actually physically includes, within the destination document's file, all the information that the server application requires to let you edit the object—not just a link to the source document. The result is a *compound document*, a document that contains supporting information for more than one application. For example, suppose you embed a Microsoft Graph column chart into a Word for Windows document. (Microsoft Graph is a business graphics package included with Word for Windows) The result is a compound document (see figure 30.6) that contains some parts created by Microsoft Graph, and other parts by Word for Windows.

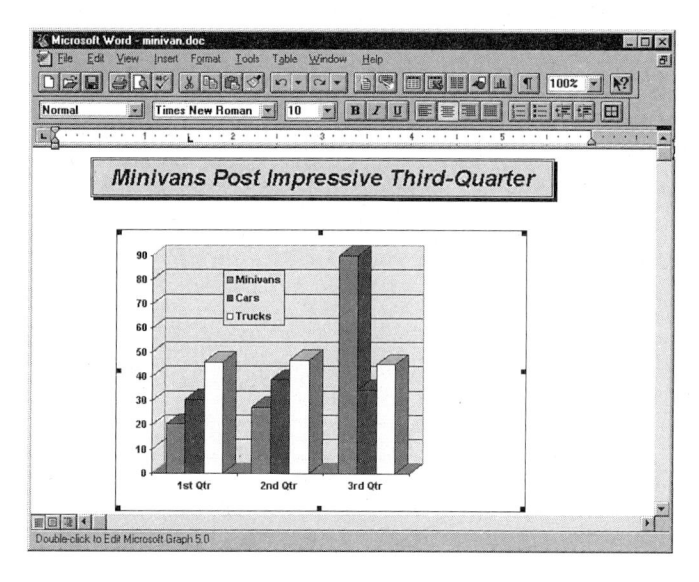

Fig. 30.6 Word for Windows also allows you to embed objects in a document.

Now suppose you want to edit the embedded object. You double-click the object, and Windows starts the server application—Microsoft Graph, in this case. You see the object in the application's workspace, with the tools applicable to that application enabled, as shown in figure 30.7. The embedded object contains all the hidden information required by the server application. When you double-click on the embedded object to edit it, Windows starts the server application, and you actually edit the embedded object, not the source document.

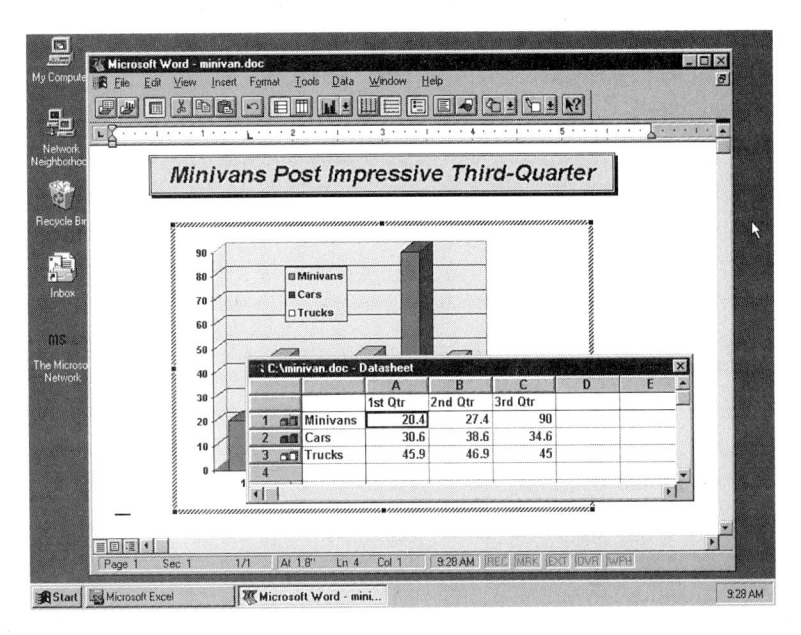

Fig. 30.7 Double-clicking on an embedded object allows you to edit the object by using all the tools appropriate to the object.

The major difference is that, with embedding, no link is created between the source document and the destination document—the embedded object stands on its own. When you make changes to the embedded object, the changes do not affect the source document.

If you do not create a link between the source document and the destination document, why bother with embedding? Why not just use the regular Clipboard methods? Embedding creates a fully editable copy of the original document; you can modify this copy as much as you like without worrying about modifying the original. And as you modify the embedded object, you have available to you all the tools and resources of the application that created it. Suppose that you've created a fantastic graphic with Paintbrush and you want to keep the graphic just the way it is. But you're creating a Write document that calls for a slight modification to the graphic. After embedding the object in the Write document, you can modify the embedded graphic without affecting the original.

Understanding OLE **693**

In summary, embedding gives you a way of adding a fully editable but unlinked copy of an object to your destination document. You can change the object as you please without affecting the original.

> **Note:** Compound documents take much more disk space than documents that contain linked objects. When you embed rather than link, Windows places into the destination document all the hidden information needed to let you edit the object. This information takes up much more disk space than a simple link.

Choosing Between Linking and Embedding

Both linking and embedding facilitate the editing and updating of copied information placed in a destination document. With either technique, you just double-click on the object to have Windows start the server application, display the object, and give you all the tools you need to make the needed change.

Both techniques increase the amount of application computing power available to you as you work with documents. You can bring all the tools of two, three, or more applications to bear on the work you're doing in a single document. When you need text processing power, you have a word processing program. When you need number-crunching power, you have a spreadsheet. And when you need graphics capabilities, you have graphics programs. With linking and embedding, you can use all these tools, and more, to create a single document. The programs themselves seem to recede into the background; what counts is your document, not the applications used to create those documents. To shape your document just as you like, you have a wide range of tools readily available. Many users find that this sensation of power is thrilling and satisfying—and, once experienced, it is close to impossible to go back to less technologically advanced systems.

The difference between linking and embedding is simple. With linking, you can create two or more dynamically linked copies of the source object. A change to any one of them is reflected automatically in all the others. With embedding, editing is convenient, but the changes affect only the embedded object.

Linking is useful when you want to maintain one authoritative version of an object, which you might want to copy many times. This object could be an entire document, a portion of a document, or just a tiny little cell that happens to contain the bottom line result of a huge worksheet. Here's an example of when keeping an authoritative version of a file would be useful: Suppose that you keep your firm's price list in an Excel worksheet. You often copy all or part of this price list to Word documents, such as reports or proposals. You always want a change in the Excel worksheet to be reflected automatically in all the copies you have placed in Word documents. After all, you wouldn't want to quote the wrong price. In such a case, you would choose linking.

Embedding is useful when you want to place just one copy of an object in a file, and you don't want the changes you make to this object to be reflected in the original or in any other copies. For example, suppose you embed your firm's price list in a proposal. Just for this one client, and this one only, you want to cut all your prices by 10 percent. You don't want this change to be reflected in the original Excel worksheet, do you? You choose embedding. After embedding the object, you double-click on it. Windows starts Excel and displays the embedded object, not the source object. You can use all of Excel's number-crunching prowess to cut the prices by the requisite 10 percent, without affecting the original Excel worksheet. Here, embedding is the best choice.

Understanding Packaging

Windows includes a feature called Object Packager that adds a new wrinkle to linking and embedding. With Object Packager, you can

Understanding OLE **695**

insert a linked or embedded object from virtually any other application that has OLE capabilities. In many respects, the Object Packager provides another way to add objects to your documents.

Packaging is useful if you're inserting or embedding a very lengthy object, or one so complex that it takes a long time for your computer to scroll through it. While you're editing the document, you can package all the objects, displaying them as icons, which speeds scrolling considerably. Then you can unpack them when you're ready to print.

Another nifty way to use packaged objects is in a document that your correspondent can read on-screen, with the same application that created it. For example, suppose that your friend Robin has Word and Excel. You can send her a Word document with an Excel object packaged in it, as shown in figure 30.8. When (and if) Robin wants to examine or work with the original document, all she has to do is double-click on the object icon, and the Excel object is "unpackaged" on her machine.

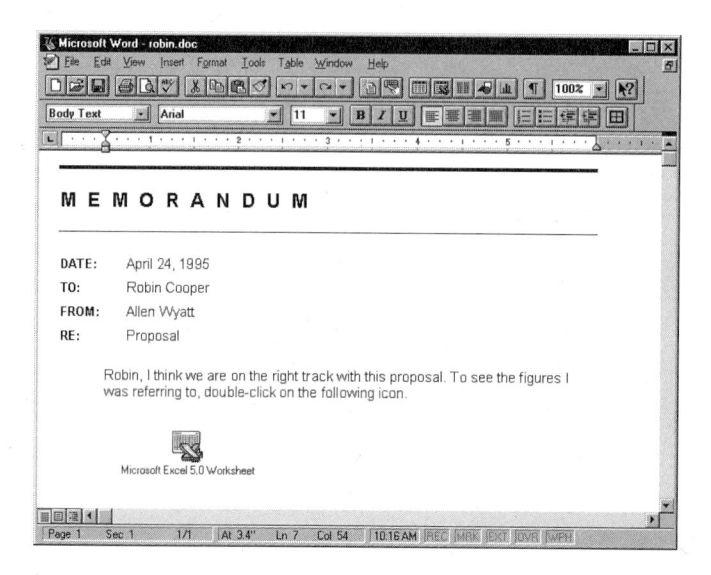

Fig. 30.8 Packaged objects appear only as icons in an OLE-capable application, which allows the destination document to be quickly displayed and scrolled.

Creating and Managing Links

Earlier in this chapter you learned how to paste information into a document so it is linked to the original document, created by a different application. Linking is almost as easy as copying with the Clipboard. The underlying differences between ordinary Clipboard copying and linking aren't apparent to the user—until you see that the copied data is dynamically updated.

Links are easy to create. As in all outstanding technology, the user need not learn the technical details—and, for the most part, isn't even aware of them. With linking, though, you must manage the links, after you've created them. That's where some of the following complexities creep in:

➤ Links aren't always automatically updated. In some cases, you may have to update the links manually. In Word for Windows, links between Word documents must be manually updated—automatic updating is available only for links with external documents (documents created by another OLE-compatible application).

➤ You may need to choose the appropriate data type (such as Rich Text Format [RTF] or unformatted text) for the paste operation. In some applications, linking is available only when you choose the correct data type. (The term *data type* refers to the format, such as RTF, Picture, or Bitmap, used to transfer the data via the Clipboard.)

➤ Applications vary in the linking features they provide. Some do not implement linking completely, and a few provide no linking capabilities at all.

➤ After creating the link, you must learn special procedures for redirecting the link, repairing broken links, and breaking existing links.

➤ When working with a document containing links, you may encounter error messages informing you that Windows couldn't find the server application or the source document.

In short, there's plenty to learn about linking. This section demonstrates the procedures you'll use to create links, edit linked documents, open documents that contain links, control existing links, and troubleshoot linking problems.

> **Note:** Linking procedures vary among applications. There are, as yet, no hard-and-fast rules about how linking commands should be located on menus—it's true even for applications created by the same software publisher. Despite such variations, the underlying concepts of linking are the same for all OLE-capable Windows applications, and the general procedures apply well enough that you can learn all the fundamentals of linking. The information in this chapter provides a good understanding of what's involved in creating links and keeping them operating smoothly.

Creating Links Between Windows Applications

The most common use of linking is to link one application's source document with another application's destination document. In this section, you learn how to create a dynamic link between two applications.

When establishing any link, one application acts as a server, and the other as a client. The server is the application that created the source document, and the client is the one used for the destination document. To create a dynamic link between two applications, follow these general steps:

1. Start the server application, and display or create the source document.

2. Save the source document in a disk file, using the steps customary for the server application. For example, if the server application was Excel, you would choose File Save and provide a name for the document (workbook) you were saving.

3. Open the client application and display or create the destination document.

4. Switch to the server application, and select the data you want to link into the destination document.

5. Copy the data to the Clipboard. This is done in different ways from different applications. For example, you might need to choose Copy from the Edit menu, or press Ctrl+C.

6. Switch to the client application, and position the cursor at the point where you want the information placed and the link established.

7. How you proceed from this point can vary widely by application. Generally, some sort of special pasting feature should be available on the Edit menu. Look for options such as Paste Link, Paste Special, or Links. Choose the option appropriate for the application you are using.

The client application inserts the information into your document and creates the link.

Editing Linked Documents

If properly implemented, a client application's linking capabilities should enable you to edit the source document with ease. (That's not always the case with all client applications.) Ideally, you should be able to edit the linked object without having to leave the client application. If your application is capable of editing linked objects, you can correct the linked data.

Follow these steps to edit the linked object:

1. In the client application, double-click on the linked object.

2. In the server application, make the needed change to the source document.

3. Save the source document. (If you don't save the document, Windows can't update the destination document.)

4. Close the server application. The destination document will reflect the change you've made.

As an example, say you have a Microsoft Word document that contains a business proposal. Besides text explaining a new service your company is offering, it also contains charts and figures showing sales forecasts. These figures and charts are from different Excel workbooks, but are linked into the Word document. When you want to update the sales figures while you're using Word, all you need to do is double-click on the figures. Excel appears (Windows even starts the application, if necessary), and you can make your changes. When you're done in Excel, save your changes and exit from the program. That's it; your changes have been made in both the source and destination documents.

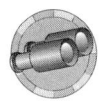

> **Note:** If you see an alert box that informs you that the server isn't available, don't panic; the server application might be busy performing some task. Wait a few moments, and try again. If you still get this message, switch to the server application and close all open dialog boxes or text response fields. You might also have to wait until it completes the operation that's consuming its attention, such as printing or recalculating.

Opening Documents that Contain Links

How a client application behaves when you open a document containing links depends on the application. In some applications, the links might be updated without any intervention necessary on your part. In some applications, you may be asked if you want to update links.

In general, if you see a dialog box asking whether you want to update links, you should choose Yes if you want the links updated, or No if you don't need to update at the moment. (For instance, you might not be ready to print yet, and so the updated information is not relevant yet.)

As the client application goes through the process of updating links, you may see additional dialog boxes. Read each one carefully, and make your choices based on your needs at the time.

Editing Multiple Links

One advantage of linking is that you can create multiple links. In a multiple link, one source document is linked to two or more destination documents. In a multiple link, as in an ordinary (single) link, any changes you make to the copied objects do not affect the source (or any other copies). If you want the changes to be made consistently to all copies of the source object, switch to the source document and make the change.

Controlling Update Frequency

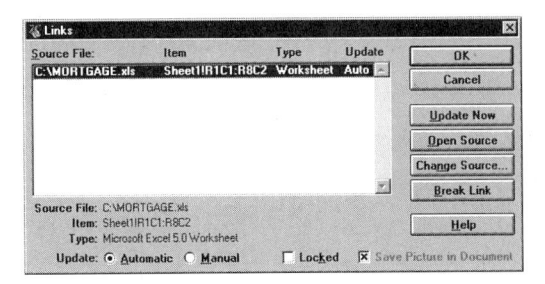

Most client applications let you choose between automatic updating (the default) and manual updating. If you want to change the update type, you must usually do so after you've created the link. You use an Edit menu command (typically Edit Link or Link) that displays a list of all the links in your document, together with their current settings. Figure 30.9 shows Word for Windows link list (produced by choosing Links from the Edit menu).

Fig. 30.9 The Links dialog box in Word for Windows allows you to modify properties associated with individual links.

Why choose manual updating, when the whole point of linking is to create dynamic links between the source and destination documents? After you've edited a document with many links in it, you'll understand why. Automatic links make heavy demands on your computer's microprocessor, which is constantly comparing the two documents to see whether they're the same. If you're editing a destination document

Creating and Managing Links **701**

that has many links, switch them to manual until you're finished editing, and then switch back to automatic. Your application will display and scroll the document more quickly.

Choosing Manual Updating

To choose manual updating, follow these steps:

1. In the destination document, choose the command that lets you edit the links in the document. This command is usually found in the Edit menu and is called Links or Edit Links. After you choose this command, you see the link list (see figure 30.9). The link list dialog box indicates the source of the link and whether the link is set to automatic or manual.

2. Select the link you want to change.

3. Choose Manual. This will be some type of control, such as a button, radio button, or check box.

4. Click on the OK button.

To switch back to automatic updating, repeat the steps just given, but in step 3 choose Automatic instead.

Updating Manual Links

If you've chosen manual updating for any of the links in your destination document, the client application will not automatically update this document when you change the source document. To update the destination document, you must choose an update command. In most Windows applications, the update command is available as an option in the link list.

To update the manual links in a document, follow these steps:

1. In the destination document, choose the command that lets you edit the links in the document. This command is usually found in the Edit menu and is called Links or Edit Links. This displays the link list (see figure 30.9). The link list dialog box indicates the source of the link and whether the link is set to automatic or manual.

2. In the link list, highlight the manual link you want to update.

3. Click on the Update or Update Now button.

4. Click on the OK button.

Breaking the Link

If a dynamic link no longer serves any need, you can break the link. Doing so does not erase the object that you've pasted into your document; it just erases the hidden information that specifies the source file's location.

To break a link, follow these steps:

1. In the destination document, choose the command (such as Edit Link, Edit Link Options, or Edit Link Delete) that displays the document's link list so that you can break a link.

2. In the link list, highlight the link you want to break.

3. Choose the button that cancels the link. This button is variously called Cancel Link, Delete, or Break Link.

4. Choose OK to confirm the deletion.

Some applications display an alert box warning you that you are about to sever a link. If you're certain you've broken the correct link, choose OK. To cancel the break, choose Cancel.

After you break the link, you still see the formerly linked information in your document. However, the client application will not update this information if you make changes to the source document.

> **Note:** Some applications, such as Word for Windows, let you lock linked objects. If you lock an object, Windows cannot update the link, even if it is set to automatic linking. However, you can still modify the linked object within the destination application, and the destination will retain all the link information. Locking is preferable to breaking the link because, should you change your mind and wish to restore dynamic linking, you can do so easily.

Creating and Managing Links **703**

Restoring a Broken Link

You can break a link in two ways: deliberately (as just described), or accidentally. Accidental breaks result when you move the source document after creating the link. After the move, Windows can't find the source document, so you see an alert dialog box informing you that the source document is missing or, worse, corrupted.

Follow these steps to restore the broken link:

1. Choose the command that displays the link list (such as Edit Link, Edit Link Options, Edit Link Edit, or File Links). You see the link list in a dialog box.

2. Choose the option that lets you change the link. In Word for Windows, for example, you click the Change Source button.

3. In the dialog box that appears, carefully change the part of the link command that lists the source document's location.

4. Click on the OK button.

Embedding Objects

Embedding differs from linking in two very important ways.

- When you embed an object, you actually put into the destination document all the information that the application requires for you to edit the object. The result is a compound document, a document that contains supporting information for more than one application.

- Embedding creates no links, dynamic or otherwise. You can embed an object by copying data from one document to another, as you learned earlier in this chapter, but Windows will not update the copy if you make changes to the original.

What follows from these two differences is simple: use embedding when ease of object editing is your chief concern and you don't care about automatic updating. Figure 30.10 provides an example of an embedded object that wouldn't need updating (but might need different formatting): the company name that has been incorporated into a Word for Windows document. (Why doesn't this object need updating? Company names don't change very often.) The handsome type was created in Microsoft WordArt, an OLE-capable application packaged with Word for Windows.

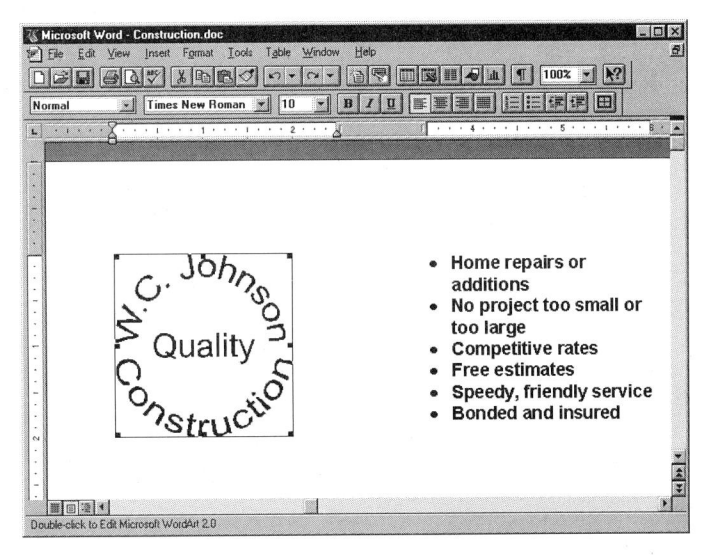

Fig. 30.10 An embedded object, created with WordArt, probably wouldn't need updating that often—at least not as a source document.

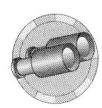

Note: Embedding creates fewer editing problems than linking. You can run into problems editing a linked object because Windows must locate the source document as well as the server application, starting from the client application. With embedding, editing is faster, easier, and less prone to error. If you want to include an object in your document and don't care about dynamic updating, embedding is an excellent choice.

Embedding Objects **705**

After you have embedded an object into your document, you have a compound document, a document created by more than one application.

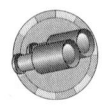

> **Note:** Compound documents are longer than normal documents. They must contain all the information for editing needed by the applications that contributed the objects. If you're short on disk space, you might want to link instead of embed. Linking requires much less disk space because when Windows links, you see only a picture of your data (or unformatted text) in the destination document.

Properly implemented, an application with embedding capabilities seems to have an endless set of alternative command menus, serving to expand its functionality to an amazing degree. With Word for Windows, for example, you can switch almost instantly to applications that create graphs, drawings, artistic typography effects, and mathematical equations.

Choosing the Correct Embedding Procedure

You can embed an object in two ways. The first way is to create the object (such as a chart or drawing) in the server application, and then copy the object to the destination document by using the Clipboard. So far, this procedure is identical with linking. However, you insert the object by displaying the link list and choosing the Object data type instead of the usual linking data type options (Formatted Text, Picture, and so on). When you choose the Object data type, the Paste Link button grays, informing you that linking has become unavailable. The client application inserts the object, but no link is created.

The second way to embed an object is to start from the client application. You choose a command (named Insert Object or Insert New Object) that displays a list of OLE-capable applications (see figure 30.11).

You choose an application, and Windows starts it, displaying a blank workspace with all the server application's commands available. You can open an existing document or create a new one. To exit, you choose Update from the File menu; the server application quits, and you see the object in the destination document.

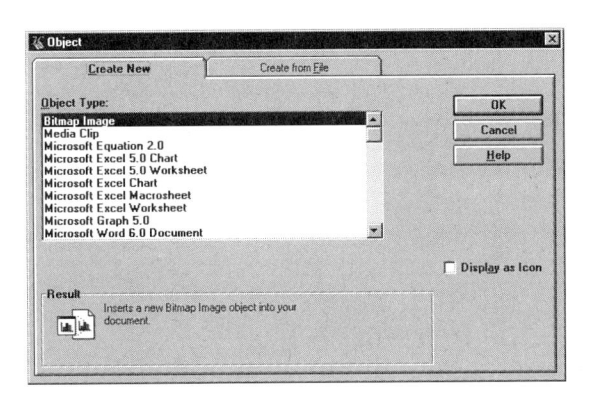

Fig. 30.11 Creating an embedded object can be done from within the client application.

Creating an Embedded Object

As you've just learned, you can use two methods to embed objects in an OLE-capable client application. You can start from the server application, which is the best technique to use when you want to embed part of a document you have already created and saved with the server application. You can also start from the client application. This technique is the best to use when you want to create the object from scratch. The following sections detail both techniques.

Starting from the Server Application

This technique, which closely resembles linking by using the Clipboard, is best used when you want to embed some information from a server application document you've already created. For example, you would use this technique when you want to embed into a Word for

Embedding Objects **707**

Windows document a portion of an Excel worksheet you have already created and saved.

To embed an object from the server application, follow these steps:

1. Open the server application and the document that contains the information you want to embed.
2. Select the information you want to embed.
3. Choose Copy from the Edit menu.
4. Switch to the client application, and place the cursor where you want the object to appear.
5. Choose the Edit menu command that lets you choose the data type as you paste (typically, this command is called Paste Special). This should display a dialog box.
6. Select the object type (such as ObjectLink, Embedded OLE, Native, or Paste), which ensures that the data will be imported as an embedded object.
7. Choose Paste or OK.
8. Save the destination document.
9. Switch back to the server application, and save or discard the source document.

Yes, you read that correctly. Discarding the source document is indeed an option. When you inserted the object into the client application, you created a compound document. This document contains all the information the server application needs to open the object and allow you to edit it. When you saved the destination document in step 8, you saved all your work, including the work you did to create the object.

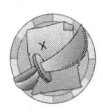

> **Tip:** After you insert the object, you can size and scale it by dragging the handles that appear when it is selected. However, it's best to edit the object in its server application, as described later in this chapter. The next time you update the object by editing it with the server application, you may lose the changes you made directly to the object.

Starting from the Client Application

The preceding technique employs the familiar Clipboard method of copying and uses Edit menu commands. When you create an embedded object starting from the client application, however, a new command (called Object or Insert Object) comes into play. In both Word and Excel, you find this command on the Insert menu.

This technique is best used when you need to create the embedded object from scratch. When Windows switches to the server application, you see a new, blank workspace. You create the new object there.

Follow these steps to embed an object starting from the client application:

1. Choose Object from the Insert menu. (If such a menu choice is not available in your application, look for one called Insert Object, or for an object-related command under the File or Edit menus.)

2. Choose the server application you want to use, and click on OK. You will see the server application.

3. Create the object.

4. Choose Update from the File menu. (This command appears only when you are using the server application to create an embedded object.)

5. Close the server application. This step isn't necessary in some applications; the application closes automatically after you choose Update from the File menu.

6. Save the destination document.

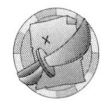

> **Tip:** If you decide that you don't want to embed the object after creating it, choose Close in the server application's File menu. You'll see a dialog box asking whether you want to update the destination document. Choose No.

Embedding Objects **709**

Editing Embedded Objects

Editing an embedded object is simplicity itself. You don't need to worry about whether the source document has moved; the source document is part of the document that contains the object!

To edit an embedded object, follow these steps:

1. Double-click on the embedded object, or choose the object editing command from the Edit menu.
2. Edit the object within the workspace.
3. Choose Update from the File menu.
4. Close the server application. (This step isn't necessary in some applications; the application closes automatically after you choose Update from the File menu.)

Note: Some embedded objects are designed to perform actions when you double-click on them. For example, Sound Recorder objects produce a sound when double-clicked. For these objects, you must choose the Object command from the Edit menu to initiate editing.

Deleting an Embedded Object

To delete an embedded object, select it and choose Cut or Clear from the Edit menu, or press the Delete key. Before doing so, bear in mind that there may not be any other copy of the object on disk. The following procedure shows you how to save an embedded object in a separate file before you delete the object from the source document.

To save an embedded object in a separate file follow these steps:

1. In the destination document, double-click on the embedded object or choose Object from the Edit menu.
2. In the server application's workspace, choose Save As or Save Copy As from the File menu and save the object.

3. Choose Exit from the File menu. When you're prompted to update the destination document, choose No.

Canceling Embedding Without Deleting the Object

In a compound document, embedded objects take up lots of space. If you want to cut down on the amount of space a file consumes, you can convert objects into pictures or unformatted text. After you've done so, the object becomes a static object rather than a dynamic one. You can't edit the object, and double-clicking on it won't start the server application. But it will take up much less room, and with most applications, it still looks exactly the same.

The procedure you follow to cancel embedding without deleting the object varies widely from application to application. For example, in Word for Windows you highlight the embedded object, and then press the Unlink Field key (Ctrl+Shift+F9). You can also choose WordArt Object from the Edit menu, and then choose Convert. To discover the steps to follow in your application, you will need to consult your applications on-line help or documentation.

Serial Communications Basics

by Allen L. Wyatt

Serial communications can be both a rewarding and frustrating experience. As a computer without a printer is nothing more than a fancy game machine, a computer without a modem keeps its user in a prison of only his or her ideas. More than one user likely has given up on using a modem because of problems encountered while trying to "make it work."

There are many factors that, when done properly, combine to make data communications work. In this chapter you'll learn the basics of data communications. Here you will learn the following:

➤ What serial communications is and how it works

➤ What modems do, how they do it, and what their capabilities are

➤ How serial ports relate to modems, and what makes for the best serial port

➤ What place communications software has in data communications

➤ How you can set up Windows 95 to use a modem

Understanding Serial Communications

Data communications, through a modem, is often referred to as *serial communications*. The word serial is used because the data sent through your communications port to your modem is sent in a serial, or bit-by-bit, format. Data inside your computer is moved around in a parallel format using 16, 32, or 64 bits at a time. Serial ports are typically used for modems (although there are parallel modems) because you need only one wire to send the actual data. Parallel ports require one wire per data bit, and normally have eight data bits per port. Besides the wires used to transmit data, both serial and parallel connections have additional wires that are used for tasks such as handshaking signals. *(Handshaking* refers to an agreed-upon method of synchronizing the two ends of a connection.)

All IBM-compatible serial ports use the RS-232 standard, which allows serial signals to go much further than is possible in a standard parallel connection. Your computer uses a UART (universal asynchronous receiver/transmitter—discussed later in this chapter) to convert the internal parallel data used by your computer to a serial format that can be used by the modem. One UART will exist on both the sending and receiving ends of a serial connection. Using a serial port connected to a modem has become the standard way to communicate.

You may understand serial communications better if you first step back and look at the big picture. For example, consider the following three elements:

1. You must have a computer system with a properly configured serial port.
2. You need a modem of sufficient speed to perform the required tasks. This modem is connected to your serial port (if it is an external modem) or includes the serial port (if it is an internal modem).
3. You need a software communications program capable of managing your modem. This marriage of hardware and software permits you to communicate within your local area and beyond.

Understanding Modems

You probably already know how to use your PC for word processing, spreadsheets, and information management. Certainly, you are familiar with telephones. Learning to use a PC to communicate over telephone lines would seem a logical next step. The problem, however, is that telephones are designed to transmit sound, and computers use different types of signals based on digital technology. Much of the complexity of telecommunications comes down to this dichotomy.

Analog and Digital Signals

Understanding a little bit about how telephones transmit sound signals can help you comprehend how computer data is sent. When you use your voice, your vocal chords cause the air to vibrate in a wave-like motion. The vibrating air, called a *sound wave*, causes a listener's eardrum to vibrate, enabling the listener to hear the sound you make. The frequency of the sound wave (the number of wave cycles in a given period of time) is heard as pitch. The amplitude (size) of the wave is heard as volume.

When you speak into your telephone, the telephone electronically converts the sound wave into an electromagnetic wave that can be transmitted over telephone lines. The frequency and amplitude of this electromagnetic wave correlate directly to the frequency and amplitude of the sound wave—your voice. As the sound wave's frequency varies up or down, the electromagnetic wave's frequency varies up or down in the same proportion. As the sound wave's amplitude varies, so does the electromagnetic wave's amplitude. In other words, the electromagnetic wave is an analog representation of the sound wave. The signal your telephone sends over the telephone lines often is referred to as an analog signal (see figure 31.1). When this signal reaches the other end of the line, the phone at that end converts the signal back into a sound wave.

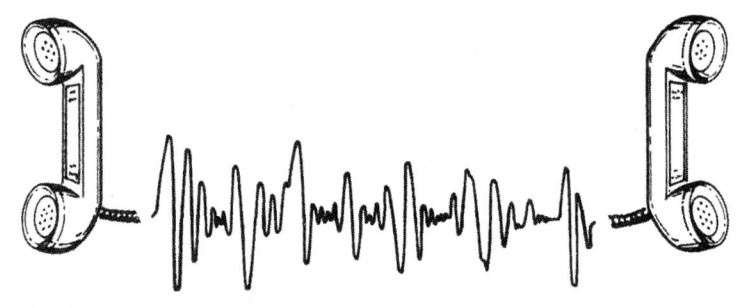

Fig. 31.1 The signal transmitted by telephones is analog in nature.

Computers do not, however, communicate by sound waves. They use discrete electrical pulses that represent numbers. All data is encoded as a stream of 1s and 0s called *bits*. A bit (short for *binary digit*) is the most basic form in which a PC stores information. To transmit a bit with a value of 1, for example, the computer may set the line voltage to –12 volts (direct current) for a set length of time. This set length of time determines the transmission speed. The computer may transmit a bit with a value of 0 by setting the voltage to +12 volts for a set length of time. A typical transmission speed is 1,200 bits per second. At that speed, each voltage pulse is 1/1,200th of a second in duration. Some PCs and compatibles can send as many as 115,200 bits per second with each pulse lasting only 1/115,200th of a second.

When one of the communicating computers needs to send the code 01001011, for example, the computer sets the voltage to +12 volts for one unit of time, –12 volts for one unit of time, +12 volts for two units of time, and so on. (The unit of time can be any set length of time agreed on by the two computers.)

The square-shaped waves shown in figure 31.2 show the voltage pulses that the computer uses to transmit this code. Because a signal of this sort is transmitting bits, it usually is called a digital signal.

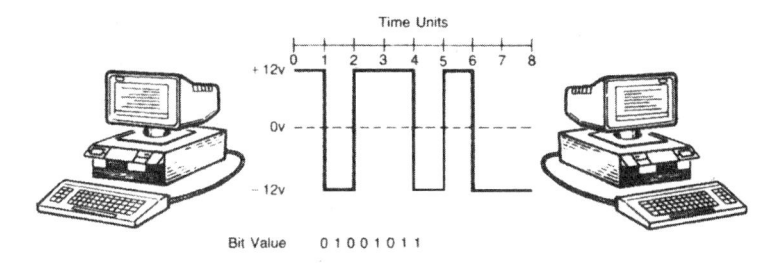

Fig. 31.2 Signals are transmitted directly between and within computers in a digital form.

In some areas of the country, Integrated Services Digital Networks (ISDNs) are available, and should be available most everywhere before the end of the century. These networks are slowly replacing the traditional analog phone networks, and are able to carry simultaneously voice, data, and image transmissions. Until ISDNs are more widely available, however, you must convert your PC's digital signal to an analog signal—a process known as *modulation*—in order to be sent over the phone lines. The analog signal then must be converted back to a digital signal—known as *demodulation*—before your PC can communicate with another computer at the other end. The piece of hardware that accomplishes both modulation and demodulation is the modem, short for modulator-demodulator (see figure 31.3). Without a modem at each end of the phone line, the two computers cannot communicate.

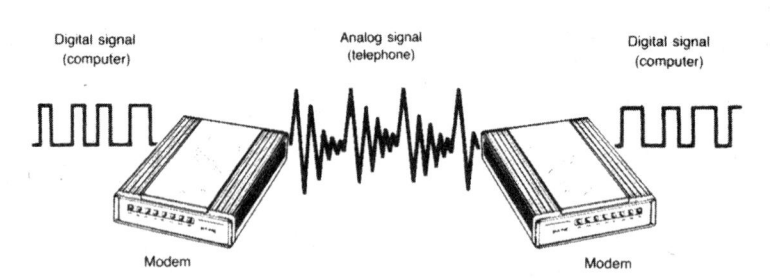

Fig. 31.3 Modems convert digital signals into analog signals, and vice-versa.

Modem Speed

Although all modems modulate and demodulate transmitted signals, all modems are not equal. The most important difference among the various types of modems is the maximum speed at which they can transmit data.

Only a few years ago, communications programs used modems that sent data at a maximum rate of 300 bits per second (bps). To put this transmission rate into perspective, consider the number of bits required to represent meaningful information. All information stored and used in your PC is represented by combining eight bits—called a *byte*—at a time.

When you are transmitting text or typing at your keyboard on-line (connected to another computer), each character sent to the other computer is represented in ASCII (American Standard Code for Information Interchange). The IBM version of ASCII uses a single byte to represent each character.

At eight bits per character and 300 bits per second, you may think the modem can transfer 37.5 characters per second, or 375 five-letter words per minute. PCs, however, normally add to each byte two extra bits, called start and stop bits (see "Understanding Serial Ports" later in this chapter). Consequently, a single character requires 10 bits of data when transmitted through a modem. Thus, a speed of 300 bps results in a data-transmission speed of approximately 30 characters per second, or about 300 five-letter words per minute. In comparison, a fast typist usually averages less than 80 words per minute.

This 80-word rate is fast enough when you want to type an instruction to a remote computer or chat (type messages back and forth) on-line with another user. This rate is not adequate, however, when you are sending a large document you already have typed. At about 1,000 words per page, sending a 10-page document can take nearly 30 minutes. If you send the document over long-distance lines, use of a 300-bps modem can translate into expensive telephone bills.

In recent years, modem speeds have increased and prices have decreased. Soon after IBM introduced the PC in August 1981, the Smartmodem 300 and Smartmodem 1,200 by Hayes Microcomputer Products became the standard modems for business use. More recently, a growing number of users are using 14,400 bps and 28,800 bps modems. Technological advances in the manufacture of integrated circuits and fierce competition have brought the prices of modems down so far that you have little, if any, reason to buy a less capable modem.

You sometimes may hear the term *baud* used synonymously with bits per second, but they are not the same. Although 300-bps modems also are referred to as 300-baud modems, 1200-bps modems do not operate at 1,200 baud; they usually operate at 600 baud.

Baud is a technical term that means the number of symbols per second sent over a communication line. (The term is named after J.M.E. Baudot, a French telegraphy expert.) Each symbol may be represented by a certain voltage, a certain combination of frequencies (tones), or a certain wave phase (angle). Each symbol may be able to represent more than one bit. In 2,400-bps modems, for example, each symbol represents four bits. Although the modem transmits only 600 symbols per second (600 baud), data is transmitted at 2,400 bits per second.

The term baud is misused so often that its technical meaning largely is ignored. You, therefore, can assume that the salesperson who wants to sell you a 9,600-baud modem means a 9,600-bps modem (and that he should be selling you a faster modem).

Modem speed can have a great impact on productivity (how much work can be done in a given period of time). For example, say you need to transmit a document across the country, and the file containing the document occupies 20,000 bytes on your disk. Table 31.1 shows how long it would take to transmit the file at various modem speeds, assuming there are no errors during transmission. Notice how much time is spent at the slower speeds—time that could productively be spent doing other work.

Table 34.1   Modem Speed Comparison When Transmitting 20,000 Characters

Speed	Time to Transmit
300 bps	11 minutes, 7 seconds
1,200 bps	2 minutes, 47 seconds
2,400 bps	1 minute, 23 seconds
9,600 bps	21 seconds
14,400 bps	14 seconds
28,800 bps	7 seconds

Modulation Standards for Modems

The speed at which modems communicate is one of several attributes that must be consistent between two modems in order for them to be able to send and receive data reliably. These attributes are referred to collectively as *modulation standards.*

Bell 103 is the U.S. and Canadian modulation standard used by 300-bps modem connections. This standard uses Frequency Shift Keying (FSK) modulating at 300 baud and sends one bit per baud. Even though this speed is the slowest, most modems work at 300 baud.

Frequency shift keying toggles between two different audio tones in response to the data being sent. The transitions between these two tones are used to represent the data. Differential Phase Shift Keying changes the phase of an audio signal in relation to reference audio signal. The toggling in phase (0–180 degrees) between the signal and its reference is used to represent the data.

Bell 212A is the U.S. and Canadian standard for 1200 bps transmissions. This standard uses Differential Phase Shift Keying (DPSK) working at 600 baud and sends out two bits per baud.

The CCITT (Consultative Committee on International Telephone and Telegraph) is an international communications standards organization and an agency of the United Nations. CCITT V.22bis is the data transmission standard used by 2,400 bps modems in the United States. V.22bis is an improved standard of V.22 that is used outside the United States. V.22 was never used much in the United States. CCITT V.22bis is an international standard for 2,400 bps communications. V.22bis operates by using quadrature amplitude modulation, known as QAM. It works at 600 bps and can transmit four bits per baud. Four bits times 600 produces the 2,400 bps rating.

CCITT V.32 is the standard for full duplex communications at 9600 bps. CCITT V.32 includes full forward error-correction and echo cancellation. Using 9,600 bps connections often works when 2,400 bps does not. Recent advances in modem chip sets make this a relatively inexpensive modem speed to use. The actual transmission uses Trellis Coded Quadrature Amplitude Modulation (TCQAM) working at 2,400 baud to send 4 bits per second. Four times 2,400 gives the effective 9,600 bps.

CCITT V.32bis is an improvement over V.32 and can send data at a full duplex rate of 14,400 bits per second. CCITT V.32bis modems also use TCQAM, working at 2,400 baud, to send six bits per second. The effective rate is six times 2,400 or 14,400 bits per second. This protocol defines a method to fall back to CCITT V.32 if the phone line is impaired. According to many experts in the industry, this modulation standard is the best you can buy for standard phone line modems that meet international standards.

V.34 is the newest modulation standard to be approved. It is an extension of V.32 and V.32bis and offers a higher transmission speed of 28,800 bits per second. This standard is widely recognized as the fastest

Understanding Serial Communications

and most advanced that data communications can get over regular analog phone lines. V.34 is probably the last analog-based transmission scheme, since most telephone systems will be converted to digital (ISDN) in the not-too-distant future.

While all this talk of modulation standards may sound confusing, most of the details can be safely ignored. You should recognize what the current standards are, however, and look for modems that support them. Thus, you should now look for modems that comply with the V.34 standard. In this way, you will be able to communicate at the fastest speeds possible (provided the modem at the other end is also capable of communicating at V.34 speeds).

Hayes-Compatible Modems

The series of software commands that activate the Hayes Smartmodem's smart features usually begin with the letters AT (short for attention). This command set therefore has come to be known as the *AT command set*. To dial a telephone number by using touch-tone signals, for example, communications software typically sends the modem the command sequence ATDT, followed by the telephone number.

The prefix of ATDT instructs the modem what to do with the phone number that follows. The AT part gets the modem's attention, and then the DT instructs it to dial a number using tone signals. The phone number is sent out after the ATDT and ends with a carriage return (CR).

There are a wide variety of commands in the AT command set, and most of them are now set up and used automatically by your communications software. The majority of modems on the market today follow this same command set. Virtually every modem manufacturer has adopted the AT command set as the de facto standard command language for modems intended for use with PCs. Modems that recognize this command set often are called *Hayes-compatible modems*. Not all so-called Hayes-compatible modems, however, implement the entire command set. In this sense, some modems are more compatible than others.

When Hayes introduced the Smartmodem 2400, the company also introduced new commands to the AT command set. Other manufacturers have implemented this *extended AT command set* to varying degrees. You can use most Windows communication software effectively, regardless of whether your modem supports the extended AT command set. Using a modem that supports the AT command set, however, is the most convenient.

Error-Control

To be effective, computer data must be transmitted error-free. The detection and elimination of errors in computer data transmissions usually is called *error-checking,* or *error-control.* Although a telephone line doesn't have to be perfectly clear of static or interference for effective voice transmission, a slight variation or interruption of a computer signal can change completely the meaning of the data the signal carries.

Many communications programs can run checks on incoming data to determine whether any errors were introduced into the data during transmission. The techniques used to perform this error-checking are called *error-checking protocols.* (A *protocol* is a set of agreed-on rules.)

Instead of requiring that the communications software perform error-control, most modem manufacturers now produce modems that do this chore automatically. When compared to the results of software error-checking, error-detection and the overall speed of transmission improve when the modem handles error-control. For this feature to work, however, the modems on both ends of the connection must be using the same error-control protocol.

Two types of error-control protocols have developed a significant following. Fortunately, an industry standard has emerged that incorporates the following two competing error-control schemes:

➤ Hayes Microcomputer Products produces a line of modems called the Hayes V-series modems. At the low end of this line is a 2400-bps modem that performs error-control by using a method called Link-Access Procedure for Modems (LAPM).

> Nearly all other PC modem manufacturers produce modems that support a different set of error-control protocols—the Microcom Networking Protocol (MNP) Classes 1 through 4, developed by Microcom, Inc. The MNP protocols are progressive. A modem can support Class 1, Classes 1 and 2, Classes 1 through 3, or Classes 1 through 4. The higher the class, the faster the transmission. These protocols are not compatible with LAPM.

Two 2,400-bps modems using the two different standards can still communicate, but only as 2,400-bps modems without modem-based error-control. (In this case, your software must take care of error detection to ensure that line impairment during transmission doesn't corrupt the transmitted data.)

In 1989, the CCITT established an error-control standard called V.42. This standard includes the protocol used by Hayes V-series (LAPM) as well as MNP Classes 1 through 4 error-control protocols, with a bias toward LAPM. When connected to another modem, a V.42-compliant modem attempts to use the LAPM protocol. If this approach fails, the V.42 modem then attempts to use the MNP protocols. If the other modem supports neither of these error-control protocols, the V.42 modem acts like a standard modem, without error control.

When using a V.42 compliant modem, using software error-correction increases overhead, and therefore slows down transmission. Selecting a file transfer protocol that does not use error correction increases overall throughput. This step leaves error-correction to the two connecting modems.

Data Compression

Many modems that provide built-in error-control also compress the data as it is sent. A compatible modem on the other end decompresses the data. Compressing data is similar to sitting on a loaf of bread; you squeeze out the air but leave the nourishment.

A modem compresses data by matching long strings (sequential patterns) of characters in the data with entries in a dictionary of known strings. Each entry in the dictionary has an index value, or code. The sending modem finds a code for each string of characters in the data and transmits only the codes. The receiving modem in turn converts these codes back into the original data.

By reducing the number of characters the modem has to send, this process often can more than double the effective transmission speed. In other words, a 4,800-bps modem using data compression sometimes can send as much information in the same length of time as a 9600-bps modem not using data compression.

As with error-control methods, two data-compression standards have developed in the PC modem market. This time, however, a CCITT standard replaces them both (it does not incorporate them). Hayes Microcomputer Products V-series modems perform data compression by using a proprietary algorithm. Many other PC-modem manufacturers follow Microcom's lead and use the MNP Class 5 data-compression algorithm. Again, these two competing data-compression methods are not compatible.

In September 1989, the CCITT ratified the V.42bis standard, which adds data compression to the existing V.42 error-control standard. The data-compression scheme included in this new standard is neither the Hayes algorithm nor the MNP algorithm. The CCITT V.42bis proposes, instead, the use of an algorithm known as the British Telecom Lempel-Ziv (BTLZ) compression algorithm.

The V.42bis standard does not include MNP data compression (MNP Class 5). Many manufacturers, however, produce modems that support V.42bis data compression as well as MNP data compression. Hayes has upgraded its V-series modems to include V.42bis and MNP Class 5.

External Versus Internal Modems

In addition to modems capable of transmitting data at different speeds, manufacturers often produce modems in external and internal versions. Each type offers several advantages.

An external modem typically is a metal or plastic box about 10 inches by 6 inches by 2 inches, with a panel of LED (light emitting diodes) on the front. The modem is connected to your PC by a serial cable and powered by an AC adapter. The external modem has at least one telephone jack for connecting the modem to the telephone line and often a second jack for connecting a telephone.

Many vendors also produce a small external modem that can be called a pocket modem. These are small enough to fit in your pocket and can run on batteries. These types of modems typically plug directly into a serial port on your computer and are particularly handy for laptop computer users who don't have the newer PCMCIA slots on their systems.

An external modem has the following advantages:

- You can move it easily from one computer to another.
- You can use it with nearly any type or brand of computer that has an asynchronous serial port (see "Understanding Serial Ports," later in this chapter).
- It can be shared by several computers through a serial switch box, but, only one computer at a time can use the modem.
- You often can stash it under your desk telephone or on top of your PC.
- If it's a pocket-sized modem you usually can plug it directly into a serial port, taking up no room on your desk.
- It usually has a panel of LEDs (light-emitting diodes) that enable you to monitor continuously the state of certain modem parameters.

Table 31.2 lists the meanings of the LEDs on the front panel of external Hayes modems and many external Hayes-compatible modems.

Table 31.2 Hayes Smartmodem LEDs

LED	Meaning
HS	High Speed
AA	Auto-Answer
CD	Carrier Detect
OH	On Hook
RD	Receive Data
SD	Send Data
TR	Terminal Ready
MR	Modem Ready

On the negative side, an external modem usually is a little more expensive than an internal modem with otherwise identical features from the same manufacturer. An external modem also requires your computer to have an available serial port and a serial cable.

Each internal modem is built on a circuit board that plugs into an empty expansion slot inside your PC, and thus takes up no room on your desk. Some internal modems are long enough to fill up a long expansion slot; others need only a half-size slot.

Because an internal modem is designed to work only with a PC, internal modems usually are bundled and sold with PC communications software. This setup is an advantage, unless you don't like the software.

The major disadvantage of an internal modem is that it is inconvenient to use with several different computers. If you need to move a modem among several computers or want to share a modem, an external modem is the better choice. For some users, the lack of status LEDs also is an annoyance.

Telephone Line Requirements

Both external and internal modems must be connected to a working telephone line. The modems, however, do not require a special type of telephone line; a voice-quality line is sufficient. You can use touch-tone or pulse dial service because nearly all auto-dial modems can dial either type of signal.

> **Caution:** One type of special telephone feature can cause problems for modem transmission. The feature, usually known as *call waiting*, is available from most telephone companies. Call waiting uses an audible click or beep to alert you to an incoming call while you are talking on the line. If your modem is on the line, this call-waiting signal may disrupt and even disconnect your transmission. If you have this type of service and plan to use your modem during periods when you might receive incoming calls, consider removing the service. In some areas, you can disable the feature temporarily by entering a special code on your telephone keypad or by transmitting the code in a software dial command. Check with your local telephone company to determine whether such a code is available and how to use it.

Understanding Serial Ports

Before your modem can transmit data, your PC must send the data from your keyboard or disk to the modem. The computer sends data to the modem through a serial port in your PC. A serial port, or COM port, is an outlet through which your computer can send data as a stream of bits, one bit at a time (that is, in serial). Data normally moves around the computer eight bits at a time—referred to as in parallel.

You can think of the internal modem as having its serial port built in. When you use an internal modem, you don't connect the modem to a serial port. A special chip on the modem, called the UART (universal asynchronous receiver/transmitter), performs the same function as a serial port; it converts the parallel signal into a serial signal. When you install the modem, you must configure it as one of your computer's COM ports.

Most PCs come with one or two serial ports already installed. The single most common device to use a serial port is a mouse. The modem comes in second, and possibly a serial-driven printer third. You can identify serial ports because they use the logical device names of COM1, COM2, COM3, and COM4.

Every serial port has a UART, and it is one of the following four types, or a clone of one of these:

- The 8250 was the original IBM PC and XT UART. Although most software works with the 8250 UART, the 8250 is not recommended for high-speed serial communications.

- The 16450 is the UART the IBM PC/AT computer system uses and is what you find on almost all computers using the Intel 80286 CPU or better. It is more suited to high-speed serial communications than the 8250, but it looks almost the same as an 8250 to your software.

- The 16550 was the first UART used in the IBM PS/2 computers. The 16550 was the first UART to include a 16-byte FIFO (first in first out) buffer. However, the FIFO buffer in this chip is defective and you cannot use it reliably. Because the FIFO buffer is defective in this chip, do not enable it or attempt to use it; loss of data is the result.

- The 16550A UART was released by National Semiconductor as a replacement for the 16550 and includes a working FIFO buffer. With the FIFO buffer, very high baud rates can be supported without losing characters. This feature is very important in multitasking environments like Windows 3.1. Some software may not work correctly if the FIFO buffer is turned on and your software expects only an 8250 or 16450 to be present.

The easiest way to identify the type of serial ports in your system is to use the MSD program, which is distributed with Windows 95. If you have been using DOS or Windows for some time, you're probably already familiar with this program. If not, you can follow these steps to start it:

Understanding Serial Communications **729**

1. Choose <u>P</u>rograms from the Start menu. The Programs menu appears.

2. Choose MS-DOS Prompt from the Programs menu. This choice opens an MS-DOS window on the desktop.

3. At the command line, type **MSD** and press Enter. This step starts the Microsoft Diagnostics program.

4. Choose the COM Ports option from the menu.

At this point, you'll see a display about the serial ports installed in your system. At the bottom of the display you can see the types of chips installed in your PC. When you are done, you can exit the program and close the DOS window.

Adding a 16550A UART

To add a 16550A UART to your system, you typically need to purchase a new serial card. When you get ready to purchase, you will need to examine the card or ask the salesperson whether it features a 16550A UART. If the salesperson cannot answer your question, don't make any assumptions—find a vendor who can answer the question.

The 16550A UART provides an extra margin of safety in Windows multitasking environment; it makes sure that no characters are lost because of high baud rates or switching between various applications. Losing data is still always possible, but the 16550A provides a way to reduce that chance.

The Serial Connector

On IBM PC, PC/XT, and PS/2 computers, as well as on most compatibles, each serial port is a D-shaped connector that has 25 protruding metal pins and is located on the back of the computer. This type of connector is called a DB-25 M (male) connector. The connector on the serial cable that attaches the modem to this serial port has 25 holes to match the male connector's 25 pins. This connector is called a DB-25 F (female) connector.

The serial ports on IBM PC AT computers and most compatibles use D-shaped connectors with nine protruding pins, called DB-9 M connectors. To connect a serial cable to such a port, the cable must end in a DB-9 F connector.

Depending on the brand of computer, each port may be marked with the label COM, Serial, or RS-232. (RS-232 is a published communications hardware standard with which PC serial ports comply.)

Asynchronous and Synchronous Transmissions

Data sent through a serial port comes out as a stream of bits in single file, but each bit means nothing by itself. Because a PC stores information in eight-bit bytes, the receiving computer must be able to reconstruct the bytes of data from the stream of bits. Computers use two ways to identify clearly each byte of data sent through a serial port: *synchronous transmission* and *asynchronous transmission*.

When computers use the synchronous method of transmitting data, bytes of data are sent at precisely timed intervals. Both the sending and receiving modems must be synchronized perfectly for this method to work properly.

PCs typically use the asynchronous method to send data through a serial port. The sending PC marks with a start bit the beginning of each byte that is to be transmitted. This start bit informs the receiving computer that a byte of data follows. To mark the end of the byte, the PC sends one or two stop bits (the number of stop bits is a user option). The stop bits inform the receiving computer that it has just received the entire byte. Timing is not critical with this procedure.

When you set up PC communications software to communicate with another computer, you need to specify whether to use one or two stop bits. The number of stop bits used on your end must match the number used by the computer on the other end. When in doubt, use one stop bit. You seldom, if ever, find two stop bits used by another computer.

Because a PC uses the asynchronous method to send data through its serial port, a protocol converter is required for a PC to communicate with a computer using the synchronous method. The protocol converter converts the signal from asynchronous to synchronous. Many mainframe computers communicate only in synchronous mode, but they often have an asynchronous dial-in port with a built-in protocol converter. This design enables PCs and other computers to connect by using an asynchronous signal.

Synchronous transmission can achieve higher transmission rates, but it requires higher-quality telephone lines. Telephone lines used for synchronous transmission often are specially prepared and used exclusively for that purpose. These lines usually must be leased from the telephone company, making synchronous transmission extremely expensive for use in everyday PC communications.

Data Bits

As mentioned previously, the PC uses eight bits to represent a byte of data. Because exactly 256 ways are available to arrange eight 1s and 0s (2 to the 8th power), eight bits are needed to represent each of the 256 characters in IBM's extended ASCII character set. Many other types of computers—including mainframes used by on-line services—use only seven data bits per byte. The ASCII character set used by these computers includes only the first 128 characters of the IBM extended ASCII character set (2 to the 7th power). These 128 characters include all the numbers and letters (uppercase and lowercase), punctuation marks, and some extra control characters. Special characters, such as foreign letters and box-drawing characters, require all eight bits.

When you set up PC communications software to communicate with another computer, you need to specify whether data occupies the first seven bits or all eight bits of each byte. Some software calls this specification the number of data bits. Other programs may use the term *word length* or *character length* for the same specification. You sometimes may use your PC to communicate with another PC that needs eight data bits per byte. At other times, you may communicate with a type of computer that can use only seven data bits per byte. The only way to know for sure which setting you need is to ask the operator of the other computer.

A simple rule of thumb is to use eight data bits for PC-to-PC or PC-to-BBS connections. All PCs need eight-bit bytes to represent the full IBM character set and to transmit program files. When calling an on-line service, such as CompuServe, or another mainframe-based system, use seven data bits. Most such systems are run on computers that can handle only seven data bits per byte. CompuServe defaults to 7 data bits and even parity. You can change the default to 8 data bits and no parity if you like. File transfer requires using 8 data bits. If your software does not support auto switching of the data bit configuration from 7 data bits to 8 data bits during a file download, you need to use 8 data bits at all times.

Parity Checking

An error in transmission of even a single bit can change completely the meaning of the byte that includes that bit. To help detect these errors as they occur, some computers use the eighth bit of each byte as a *parity bit*. The parity of an integer (whole number) is whether it is odd or even. You can use a parity bit in two ways. Both methods add the other seven digits in each byte and check whether the sum is an even or odd number.

When using the *even parity method*, the computer sets the value of the parity bit (either 1 or 0) so that the total of all eight bits is even. If the sum of the first seven bits is odd, such as 0000001, the parity bit becomes a 1. The eight-bit byte transmitted is therefore 00000011. If the sum of the first seven bits is even, such as 0010001, the parity bit becomes 0, and the eight-bit transmitted byte is 00100010. In both cases, adding all eight bits results in an even number—2 in both examples. The receiving computer then adds the digits of each byte when it receives them. If the sum is odd, an error must have been introduced during transmission, so the computer software asks that the byte be sent again.

Similarly, the *odd parity method* assigns the value of the parity bit so that the sum of all digits in each byte always is an odd number.

One parity bit method, known as *mark parity,* always sets the parity bit to the value 1. Another method, known as *space parity,* always sets the parity bit to the value 0.

> **Note:** Parity-checking provides rather minimal error-checking when compared to the many other more sophisticated error-checking methods now available in software (see the "Transferring Files" section of this chapter) and hardware (see "Error Control," earlier in this chapter).

For PC-to-PC communication, including transmission to bulletin boards, use the None (no parity) setting. When connecting to an on-line service, you usually have to use Even parity. If you are connected to an on-line service and are receiving nothing but strange-looking characters, you probably have parity set to None. Try changing the parity to Even.

Interrupt Request Lines

Before any computer can operate a COM port at high speed or in a multitasking environment, it must make use of one of the hardware interrupt request lines (IRQs). By using an IRQ, the computer CPU is free to do other things until new data is received that must be processed. The interrupt triggers an interrupt handler in the PC that gets the data from the port and places that data in the correct location for the communications program to process when ready. The CPU then resets the interrupt and continues about its other business until another interrupt comes in.

A possible 17 interrupt request lines are available, numbered from 0 to 15 and one called Non-Mask Able Interrupt (NMI). The NMI is the only interrupt the CPU can never ignore or turn off. All other IRQs can be turned on or off depending on what the computer is doing. Table 31.3 shows the normal assignments.

Table 31.3 Standard IRQ Assignments in ISA and EISA Bus Systems

Interrupt Request Line Number	Normal Assignment
NMI	Memory Parity Errors
0	Internal Timer
1	Keyboard
2	Cascade to second 8259, IRQs 8 to 15
3	COM2,COM3 (also COM4 on MCA BUS PS/2s)
4	COM1,COM4 (no COM4 if on a MCA PS/2)
5	LPT2
6	Floppy disk controller
7	LPT1
8	Clock/Calendar (CMOS RTC)
9	Redirected IRQ2, used by many Network cards
10	Reserved (may be available)
11	Reserved (may be available)
12	PS/2 Mouse (may be available on ISA BUS)
13	Math Co-Processor
14	Hard disk controller
15	Reserved (may be available)

Windows uses the standard default IRQs for ISA, EISA, and MCA bus computers. The default IRQ settings for ISA and EISA computers are as follows:

Port	Interrupt Request Line (IRQ)
COM1	4
COM2	3
COM3	4
COM4	3

On an MCA computer, COM1 and COM2 use the same interrupts as ISA and EISA computers. COM3 and COM4, however, use IRQ3. In an MCA computer, default COM port IRQ settings are as follows:

Port	Interrupt Request Line (IRQ)
COM1	4
COM2	3
COM3	3
COM4	3

ISA computers support no more than two COM ports operating simultaneously by using the two default interrupt request lines. EISA and MCA computers, however, can support more than one port using the same hardware interrupt by permitting the ports to share the interrupt. If you own an EISA or MCA bus computer, Windows, by default, enables interrupts to be shared. Windows disables interrupt sharing for ISA machines.

To change Windows assignment of serial port IRQ settings, follow these steps:

1. Right-click on the My Computer icon on the desktop. The context menu for the object appears.

2. Choose Properties from the context menu. The System Properties sheet appears.

3. Click on the Device Manager tab. The System Properties sheet now appears, as shown in figure 34.4.

4. Double-click on the Ports (COM & LPT) in the lower portion of the device list. This expands the device list, showing all your serial and parallel ports.

5. Double-click on the serial port you want to change. The Communication Port Properties sheet appears.

6. Click on the Resources tab. The Communication Port Properties sheet appears as shown in figure 31.5.

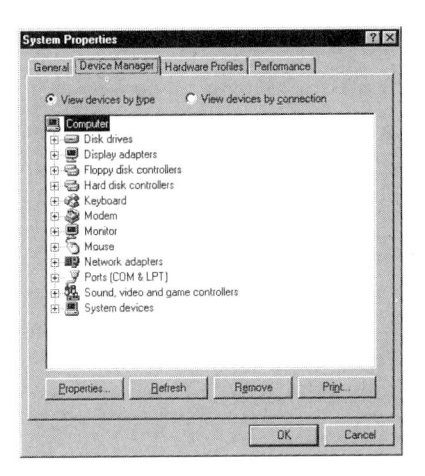

Fig. 31.4 The Device Manager tab in the System Properties sheet allows you to identify components in your system.

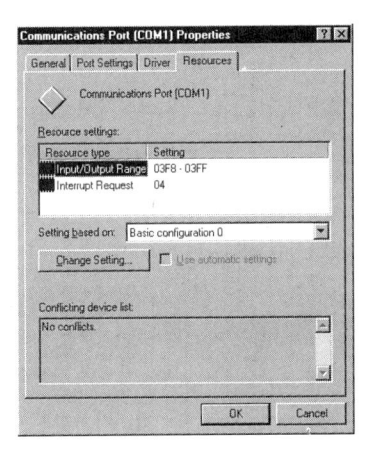

Fig. 31.5 The Communication Port Properties sheet allows you to configure your serial ports.

To use more than two COM ports on an ISA bus system, change the Interrupt Request setting to one of the other possible interrupt request lines. If your computer does not have an LPT2 (second printer) port, you can use IRQ5 for either COM3 or COM4 (assuming your serial card provides a method of selecting one of these interrupt request lines—

Understanding Serial Communications **737**

refer to your adapter card's documentation to find out the possible settings). IRQ5 is sometimes used by a BUS mouse and, therefore, may not be available. IRQ2 is also a possibility, but it serves as the cascade to interrupt lines 8 through 15. Sometimes trying to use IRQ2 can cause a problem, but it may be worth a try.

If only IRQ3 and IRQ4 are available for assignment to a serial port, make the assignments in only one of the following combinations.

> COM1 (IRQ4) with COM2 (IRQ3)
>
> COM1 (IRQ4) with COM4 (IRQ3)
>
> COM2 (IRQ3) with COM3 (IRQ4)
>
> COM3 (IRQ4) with COM4 (IRQ3)

Any combination of ports that puts two devices, being used at the same time, on the same IRQ almost certainly leads to problems.

Base Addresses

One other parameter of your serial ports that must be identified to Windows is the base address. This is a memory address used to transfer information between the CPU and the UART that comprises the serial port. In Windows 95, this base address is actually referred to as an input/output range. In most instances, this range is automatically identified by Windows 95 and will not need to be changed.

In an ISA system, there are four base addresses generally recognized as belonging to COM1 through COM4. These are:

Port	Base Address
COM1	3F8H
COM2	2F8h
COM3	2E8h
COM4	2E0h

Most PCs store COM port addresses in a table in the BIOS at memory address 40:00 hex; it is placed there during the boot process. Windows accesses this information, if it exists, to establish the base addresses used by the system. If your computer doesn't store COM port addresses in a BIOS table, you may need to manually adjust the input/output ranges within Windows 95. To do this, display the Communications Port Properties dialog box, as described in the previous section. The base addresses (input/output ranges) used by the serial ports are resources you can modify as you see fit.

Understanding Communications Software

To use a modem effectively, you need some sort of communications software. The purpose of the software is to facilitate routine communications and file transfer with a remote system, using your modem as the go-between.

In Chapter 32, "Communicating with a Modem," you'll learn how you can use specific software to communicate. Before jumping into that, however, there are some basics that apply to communications software, regardless of who makes it.

Understanding Terminal Emulation

Terminal emulation performs a function similar to that of a United Nations translator. If you've ever seen or read about the United Nations General Assembly, you probably know that an army of translators is always at work so that representatives of all nations can understand what is being said, regardless of the language spoken. All the representatives can listen with ear phones to a simultaneous translation of the proceedings into their native language.

When a communications program is emulating a particular type of terminal, the program is performing a simultaneous translation between different languages. However, the program translates in two directions at once. Each time you press a key on your keyboard, the program converts the keystroke into the code that would be generated by a real terminal; this code is the language the host minicomputer or mainframe computer expects to receive. This conversion of outgoing keystrokes is referred to as keyboard mapping. At the same time, the host computer is sending to your computer codes intended to control the screen and printer of a real terminal; these codes are in a language the terminal understands. The communications program also translates these incoming codes into codes your PC understands.

Just as the United Nations needs translators for more than one pair of spoken languages, your communications software also needs to emulate more than one type of terminal. Terminals from different manufacturers often don't speak exactly the same language, and not all host computers are designed to work with the same type of terminal. Unless your software emulates a terminal that speaks and understands the language spoken and understood by the host computer to which your computer is connected, effective communication cannot take place. Your communications program, therefore, typically gives you several terminal emulations from which to choose, in an effort to provide at least one emulation that each host computer can understand.

Each emulation maps your PC's keyboard in a different way and expects a different set of screen (and sometimes printer) control signals from the host computer. Standard typewriter keys—A through Z and 0 through 9—are understood universally by other computers, regardless of the type of terminal your software is emulating. This understanding is possible because all terminals emulated by your software send the generic ASCII character codes for these keys. The remaining, so-called special keys on the keyboard, however, are the crux of the issue. You can use these keys—alone, or with another key (Shift, Ctrl, or Shift-Ctrl)—to program (or map) so that you can send a different code to the remote computer for each different type of terminal emulation.

Your communications software maps your keyboard to act like the keyboard of a real terminal. Each time you press a mapped key, the software sends the code that would be sent by pressing a corresponding key on a real terminal's keyboard. Each terminal emulation uses a particular keyboard mapping specially designed to match the codes generated by a real terminal.

Always keep in mind that terminal emulation is never 100 percent effective. Just as all PCs are not alike, each type of terminal has its own special features and capabilities. Although the power and flexibility of your PC enables programmers to make it act like many different types of terminals, your PC cannot always perform every special function of every type of terminal.

Transferring Files

File transfer is a two-way street. Communications software enables you to send and receive computer files to and from the remote computer. The steps you take to send a file are similar to but not exactly the same as the steps necessary to receive a file.

Transferring files can be broken into several sections. You first need to know the basics of transferring files. To understand transferring files, you must be familiar with several of the *file-transfer protocols*, which define how the file is physically sent between two systems. Understanding file-transfer protocols is the key to successfully moving files to and from your system by modem.

Sending or Receiving a File

In most communications programs, the phrases *send a file, upload a file,* and *transmit a file* mean the same. They refer to the act of transferring a computer file from your computer to a remote computer. Sometimes new users are confused by the term upload. You may think, for example, that it refers to uploading a file to your computer, which is receiving the file. When used in most programs, however, the phrase upload a file means to send a file to another computer. This usage is easiest to understand in the context of sending files to a host computer, such as a bulletin board. When you send a file to the bulletin board, you are uploading the file to the host. Receiving a file from the host is called *downloading* a file.

Before you can use a Windows communications program to send or receive a file, you must be connected to the remote computer. If the remote computer is a PC that is not operating a bulletin board, you must inform the remote computer's operator that you are about to upload a file. For file transfer to occur, the remote operator must begin the appropriate download procedure soon after you execute your upload procedure.

When you're connected to a host system (an on-line service such as CompuServe, for example, or a PC bulletin board), you inform the host program that you intend to upload (send) or download (receive) a file by selecting an appropriate menu option or command. (The exact command depends on the host program with which you are communicating.) You usually have to type the name of the file (or select a file name from a file list) you're going to upload to the host or download from the host and indicate a file-transfer protocol.

A *file-transfer protocol* is an agreed upon set of rules that controls the flow of data between two computers. The agreed upon rules often screen transmitted data for errors introduced by the transmission process. As you learned earlier in the chapter, this error-screening process usually is referred to as *error checking* or *error control*. Using a file-transfer protocol that performs error checking ensures that the data received by the remote computer is the same as the data your computer sends. Like most other communication parameters, the file-transfer protocol you choose must match that used by the remote computer.

> **Tip:** If both your modem and the remote modem support error-correcting protocols at a modem level, it is redundant to choose a file-transfer protocol that includes error correction.

When the host (remote computer) instructs you to begin your transfer, you begin the upload or download procedure for your software.

Understanding File-Transfer Protocols

When you type a message to someone who is sitting at the keyboard of a remote computer, your communications software sends ASCII characters to the screen of the remote computer. The operator of the remote computer can detect transmission errors by reading the characters on-screen. If characters look like hieroglyphics, that condition reflects a transmission error. Most computer files, however, are not stored entirely as ASCII characters. Computer programs, most word processing files, spreadsheet files, database files, and other types of computer files contain data that cannot be displayed on-screen as transmitted. These non-ASCII files typically are referred to as *binary files*. To send binary files, you must use a file-transfer protocol that can send data without displaying it to the screen, and you must take steps through software or hardware to detect data errors that may be caused by degradation of the telephone signal.

Each time you begin uploading or downloading files by using your Windows communications software, you typically can choose among several file-transfer protocols. The following guidelines can help you decide which protocol to use:

➤ *Use matching file-transfer protocols.* The same file-transfer protocol must be used on the sending and receiving ends of the file-transfer process. This requirement limits the number of protocols available to you during any particular communication session to the protocols that your communications software and the remote program have in common.

➤ *Use the ASCII protocol only for ASCII files.* When sending or receiving a file that contains only printable ASCII characters, you have the option of choosing the ASCII protocol. This protocol sends data character by character, just as when you type a message at the keyboard.

➤ *Send and receive the largest blocks of data possible.* For maximum transmission speed when sending binary files, use the file-transfer protocol that sends blocks of the largest size. YMODEM, COMPUSERVE B+, YMODEM (Batch), and ZMODEM protocols can send blocks of 1,024 bytes.

However, if you're having a great number of data transfer errors, you might want to select a file-transfer protocol that uses a smaller block size. The smaller block size may allow you to sneak more blocks through between errors. This step can reduce the amount of data you must resend and avoid an ultimate file-transfer termination because of the total error count.

- ▶ **Send and receive multiple files.** Some file-transfer protocols enable you to send or receive multiple files with one command. This type of transfer often is called a *batch transfer*. Protocols that can send or receive multiple files include COMPUSERVE B+, KERMIT, YMODEM (Batch), YMODEM G (Batch), and ZMODEM.

- ▶ **Send and receive file characteristics.** Several file-transfer protocols also send with the file such file characteristics as file name, file size, and the date and time the file was last changed. When you are downloading a file, this information enables your communications software to display information about the progress of the file transmission. The protocols that transmit at least one of these file characteristics include YMODEM, YMODEM (Batch), COMPUSERVE B+, KERMIT, and ZMODEM.

- ▶ **Use sliding windows on PDNs and over long-distance lines.** When you connect to a host computer over a *public data network* (PDN), such as Tymnet and Telenet (or any other packet-switching network), or over long-distance telephone lines that may go through satellite relays, most file-transfer protocols can be slowed significantly. PDNs and satellite relays often cause an appreciable increase in the time needed for the receiving computer to reply to each block sent. The sending computer can spend a great deal of time just waiting. The KERMIT, ZMODEM, and CompuServe B+ protocols, however, take advantage of the full-duplex nature of your modem. Instead of waiting for a reply before sending another block, the protocols send blocks and simultaneously watch for the reply to previous blocks. These protocols send several blocks before requiring any reply. ZMODEM and CompuServe B+ probably are the best choices for use on public data networks.

- ▶ **Use appropriate protocols with error-control modems.** If you are using a modem that performs error control in hardware, such as a modem that supports MNP Classes 1 through 4 or CCITT V.42, use a protocol that sends data without doing any error checking in software. Two protocols in this group are YMODEM and YMODEM (Batch).

Some file-transfer protocols have the ability to restart a terminated file-transfer. Two such file-transfer protocols are ZMODEM and CompuServe B+. The ability to restart where the transfer was terminated could save considerable time depending on the size of the file.

Understanding XMODEM

The most widely available PC-based file-transfer protocol is XMODEM. Like so many other communications terms, XMODEM can mean different things to different people, so you need to understand a little about the background of this protocol.

As most broadly used, the term XMODEM refers to a file-transfer protocol included in the program MODEM2, written by Ward Christensen and introduced in 1979. This file-transfer protocol originally was called the MODEM protocol and was intended to transfer files between computers running the CP/M operating system. Over the years since 1979, however, the MODEM file-transfer protocol has become known as XMODEM and has been implemented in countless communications programs for use in transferring files between computers running many different operating systems. Virtually all popular communications programs for PCs include an implementation of XMODEM. Since its introduction, several new and improved versions of the protocol have appeared under various names.

The original XMODEM used the checksum error-checking scheme. This method of detecting errors is adequate for low-speed data transmission (300 bps or less) but can miss errors that are more likely to occur when you're sending data at higher transmission speeds (or over noisy phone lines). One popular variation of XMODEM adds the CCITT CRC-16 error-checking scheme, which is much more reliable than the checksum method at the higher transmission rates.

The CRC-16 version of XMODEM often is called XMODEM/CRC, but many programs refer to the protocol simply as XMODEM. Use of the name in this manner leads to no problems, however, because the CRC-16 version of XMODEM is backward compatible with the checksum version. In other words, you can use the CRC-16 version of XMODEM to send or receive a file to or from a computer that is using the original checksum version of XMODEM or the newer CRC-16 version.

Several other modified versions of XMODEM seem to have overtaken XMODEM in popularity. To varying degrees, these other protocols overcome XMODEM's recognized weaknesses: 128-byte blocks, no multiple file transfers, no file characteristics transferred, and no sliding windows. The 1K-XMODEM version of XMODEM is a CRC XMODEM with a 1,024-byte (1K) packet rather than the 128-byte packet. The 1K-XMODEM-G version of XMODEM is the same as the 1K-XMODEM but provides no software error detection and relies on the modem error-correction hardware to provide that function.

Other protocols that have evolved directly or indirectly from the original XMODEM protocol are SEALINK, TELINK, WXMODEM, YMODEM, and ZMODEM.

Understanding YMODEM

The YMODEM protocol was introduced in 1985 by Chuck Forsberg of Omen Technology, Inc., as an extension of Ward Christensen's XMODEM protocol. As implemented originally, Forsberg's YMODEM protocol includes CRC-16 error checking; 1,024-byte blocks; multiple file transfer; and transmission of file name, file size, and the date and time each file was last modified. Forsberg's YMODEM also includes an option called the G option, which enables you to take full advantage of modems that perform error control.

Understanding ZMODEM

The ZMODEM protocol also was developed by Chuck Forsberg of Omen Technology for the public domain under a Telenet contract in 1986. This protocol has rapidly become a favorite among many users.

ZMODEM was designed to eliminate many of the problems or limitations associated with older protocols such as XMODEM and YMODEM while taking advantage of new technologies in modem hardware. According to Forsberg, "The ZMODEM file-transfer protocol provides reliable file and command transfers with complete end-to-end data integrity between application programs. ZMODEM's 32-bit CRC catches errors that continue to sneak into even the most advanced networks."

Because ZMODEM has buffering and windowing modes, it can work efficiently on a number of data networks. ZMODEM provides faster transfers than other protocols—particularly with error-correcting modems—on timesharing systems (such as CompuServe), satellite relays, and any other kinds of packet-switched networks. The sophisticated error-correction capabilities make ZMODEM useful if you are transferring information over noisy telephone lines.

ZMODEM's benefits are not just limited to its technological advances. ZMODEM also is easy to use. Its Auto Download feature enables you to skip some of the steps necessary with other protocols. After you specify a download, for example, the ZMODEM transfer begins without you having to initiate the protocol (by clicking the Receive File Action icon) or having to type the file name again. Unlike many other protocols, ZMODEM can preserve a file's date and time stamp as well as the file's exact size during transmission, which eliminates the annoying problem of having unneeded characters at the end of a file—a common problem with some other protocols.

The Crash Recovery feature in ZMODEM is also impressive. If a download is interrupted before completion and is restarted, ZMODEM can pick up where the download left off, saving you valuable connect time. ZMODEM also has multiple-file capability, which means that you can specify file transfers by using global characters (such as *.DOC).

Of the many file-transfer protocols available in most Windows communications programs, ZMODEM probably is the best to use when transferring files to and from PC bulletin boards or on public data networks. The protocol's 1,024-byte block size, coupled with multiple-file-transfer capability, automatic transfer, and sliding windows, makes ZMODEM a fast protocol that also is easy to use.

Understanding KERMIT

KERMIT is the name of a program, a file-transfer protocol, and a famous frog. In fact, the program and protocol are named after the Jim Henson muppet, Kermit the Frog. Unless specifically noted otherwise, this section discusses the file-transfer protocol KERMIT rather than the KERMIT program.

KERMIT was developed in 1981 at Columbia University by Frank da Cruz and Bill Catchings and released into the public domain. In contrast to XMODEM, which requires eight data bits to operate, KERMIT can be used on computers that can handle only seven data bits (many mainframe computers, for example) and still can manage to transmit files that contain bytes made up of eight bits per byte. Since 1981, KERMIT has been implemented on countless brands and models of computers, from mainframes to microcomputers. Since its introduction, KERMIT has enjoyed numerous enhancements.

Transferring Files on CompuServe

Use the CompuServe B, B+, or QuickB file-transfer protocols when sending and receiving files over the CompuServe on-line service. The primary difference between the CompuServe B and CompuServe Quick B protocols is that Quick B has sliding windows. As implied by the name, CompuServe Quick B transfers files faster than CompuServe B. The B+ protocol introduces some new enhancements to the Quick B protocol, which gives CompuServe B+ some of the advantages of the ZMODEM protocol.

Setting Up Your Modem in Windows 95

Adding a modem in Windows 95 is much easier than in previous versions of Windows. In most instances, it is simply a matter of selecting your modem type from the list maintained by Windows.

Specifying the type of modem installed in your system allows Windows to automatically configure it for any communications needs you may have. To specify a modem, display the Control Panel, and then double-click on the Modems icon. You'll shortly see the sheet shown in figure 31.6.

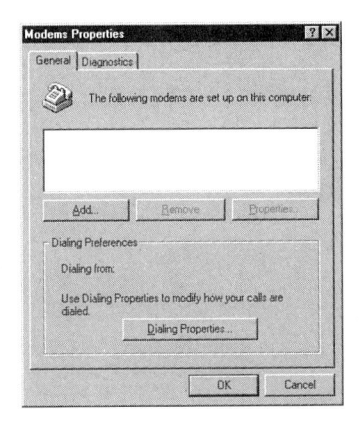

Fig. 31.6 The Modems Properties sheet allows you to configure your modem.

Selecting a Modem

The General tab within the Modems Properties sheet is where you specify the types of modems you use in your system. You can have Windows 95 configured for more than one modem, if desired. For instance, if you use external modems, you may want to switch between different modems from time to time, depending on what's available at the time.

To add a modem, click on the Add button. This action starts the Install New Modem Wizard, as shown in figure 31.7.

By default, the Wizard attempts to automatically determine the type of modem in your system. It does this by analyzing all your serial ports to see whether there are any devices attached. If so, and the device appears to be a modem, the Wizard sends commands to the modem to see if it can identify itself. (Most modems now marketed provide information that can help an operating system or communications software identify the modem.)

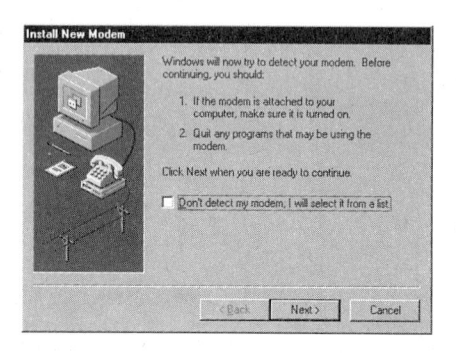

Fig. 31.7 Windows 95 provides a Wizard to help with the installation of a new modem.

At this first Wizard dialog box, you can indicate whether you want Windows to automatically try to detect the modem. In most instances, you should allow automatic identification. If you would rather specify the modem yourself, then you can click on the Don't detect check box.

At this point, you should click on the Next button. If you're allowing the Wizard to automatically identify the modem, there will be a delay as the identification is attempted. If you want to pick the modem yourself, or if the Wizard can't determine which modem you have installed, you'll see the dialog box in figure 31.8.

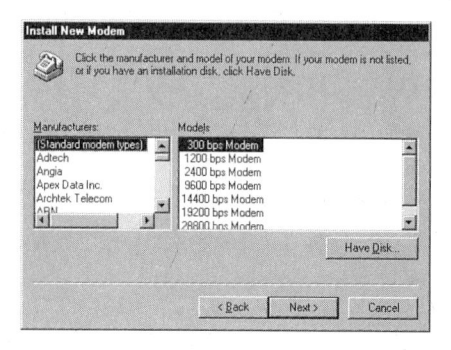

Fig. 31.8 Picking a modem type is similar to installing other types of devices in Windows 95.

From the list of manufacturers and models, you should select the modem installed in your system. Make sure you pick the manufacturer first, as the available models will vary by manufacturer. When you're done, click on the Next button, and you'll see the dialog box in figure 31.9.

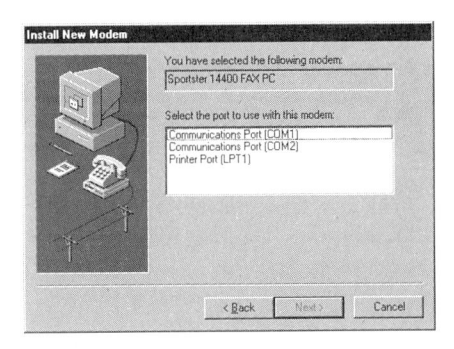

Fig. 31.9 After picking a modem type, you need to specify where it is connected within your system.

At this dialog box, you can pick how the modem is connected to your system. If your modem was automatically detected, this step is taken care of automatically. Pick the port to which the modem is connected, and then click on the Next button. The proper settings for your modem are then recorded in the Registry, and you'll shortly see the dialog box shown in figure 31.10.

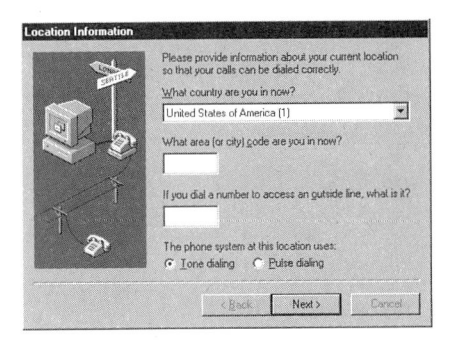

Fig. 31.10 Windows 95 keeps track of where you live in order to make calls on the modem correctly.

Setting Up Your Modem in Windows 95 **751**

There are four settings you can make on this dialog box. The first is the country in which you are using the modem. (If you use the pull-down list, over 230 different countries are available.) The second setting is where you indicate the area (or city) code in which you are located. For instance, if you were making your calls from Wyoming, you would enter a 307 area code.

The third setting is used if you must dial a number to get an outside line. Typically, this setting is used only in offices, where it is common to dial 9 or some other number to get an outside line.

> **Tip:** You may want to put a comma after the access number (such as 9,). This action causes your modem to wait two seconds after dialing the access number before it dials the rest of the phone number.

The final setting is used to indicate whether your phone uses tone or pulse dialing. If you work in an office, and you must dial 9 to get an outside line, it is a virtual certainty that you use tone dialing. On other phones, you can tell if you use tone dialing by listening to the sounds your phone makes as you dial a number. If you hear "beeps," then you use tones. If you hear any "clicks," then you use pulses. (In a pulse-dial system, you hear a click for every number being dialed. For instance, if you dial the number 5, you will hear five clicks.)

When you have completed making your choices, click on the Next button. This displays the final dialog box in the Wizard, which informs you that the installation is completed. At this point, click on the Finish button.

Configuring Your Modem

Once your modem is set up, you can make changes to its configuration any time you desire. You do this by double-clicking on the Modems icon in the Control Panel. The Modems Properties sheet appears, as shown in figure 31.11.

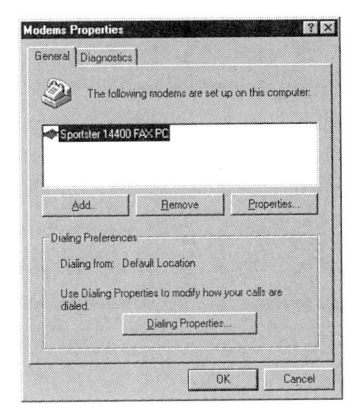

Fig. 31.11 To change modem configuration, you start at the Modems Properties sheet.

On your system, the Modems Properties sheet may show more than one modem installed. If this is the case, you should select the modem whose properties you want to change. Then click on the Properties button. You will shortly see the dialog box shown in figure 31.12.

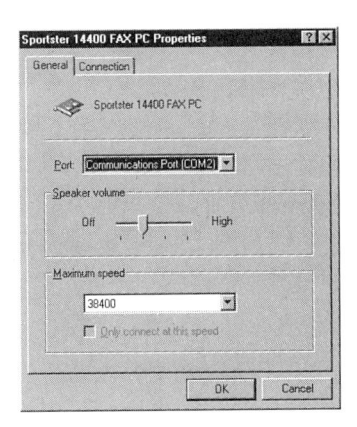

Fig. 31.12 A properties dialog box for individual modems allows you to change their configuration.

The exact appearance of this Properties sheet may differ from modem to modem, depending on the capabilities of the modem. In this instance, for this modem, there are two tabs in the dialog box. The first tab, General, allows you to change the port assignment for the modem, the speaker volume, and the speed at which the modem communicates.

The Connection tab is a bit more complicated. This is where you specify the default communications parameters for the modem. Figure 31.13 shows an example of the sheet with the Connection tab selected.

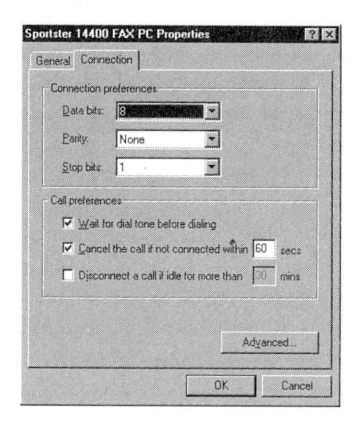

Fig. 34.13 The Connection tab is used to modify default communications parameters.

In the Connection Preferences area at the top of the sheet, you can set parameters you learned about earlier in the chapter. Here you set the default data bits, parity, and stop bits. Remember that these are default values, and can be overridden by whatever communication software you're using.

The next area of the dialog box allows you to indicate, in general, how a call should be handled. You can indicate whether the modem should wait for a dial tone before dialing (typically a good idea), and how long the modem should wait (in seconds) before giving up on making a connection. Notice that there is also an option (not selected by default) which allows you to specify how long a connection should be held if there is no activity. If you do quite a bit of unattended modem work, you may want to select this option and choose an inactivity time, in minutes.

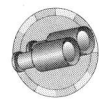

> **Note:** If you're using a modem to directly connect your PC to another PC (not going through the phone system), then you should turn off the Wait for dial tone option. In this instance, waiting for a dial tone would stop you from ever establishing a connection.

Notice that there is an Advanced button at the bottom of the dialog box. If you click on this button, you'll see the dialog box shown in figure 31.14.

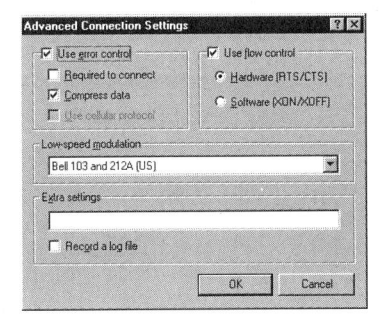

Fig. 31.14 Advanced modem settings are used to control behind-the-scenes aspects of a connection.

When you display this dialog box, it may not appear exactly the same as what is shown in figure 31.14. The settings available on this dialog box depend on the capabilities of your modem, and can vary accordingly. The upper-left corner is where you indicate whether your modem should use error-control and data compression. You learned about these two topics earlier in the chapter. If your modem supports these capabilities, by default Windows 95 will use them. You can turn off support for these features in this area. (You can also indicate whether such capabilities are required by both modems before a connection can be established.)

Setting Up Your Modem in Windows 95   **755**

Note: The error-control area of the dialog box also allows you to indicate whether your modem should use cellular protocols. Only certain modems have these capabilities—typically if the modems are used in mobile computing. If your modem does have these capabilities, and you will be using it for an extended time over regular phone lines, you may want to disable this feature. It will help improve connection time and possibly data speed.

In the upper-right corner of the dialog box you can indicate how you want to handle the data flow between your computer and the modem. You need flow control any time the modem sends or receives data faster than the modem or the computer can deal with it. When a data buffer becomes full, for either the modem or the computer, some method must be present to tell the other end to stop sending data.

Windows 95 supports two types of flow control, or you can turn flow control off altogether.

➤ If you turn off the Use flow control option, then none is done, and data is sent or received without regulation.

➤ Hardware (RTS/CTS) is the most common choice when using the serial port to communicate with a modem. You must use hardware flow control when you are using a high-speed error-checking modem to get optimum throughput.

➤ Software (XON/XOFF) works best when you are connecting your computer to dumb text-based systems by modem, typically at lower speeds.

In the middle of the dialog box is the Low-speed modulation specification. Here you indicate how you want the modem to communicate when working at 300- and 1200-bps connections. Typically, this will not be an issue; most modem connections these days are handled at rates of 9,600 bps or greater. The default setting (Bell 103 and 212A) should generally be left undisturbed, but you can change it to another communications standard if there is a compelling need. The only times this should be necessary is if you are communicating with computers outside the U.S.

At the bottom of the dialog box is a field called E_xtra settings. This field is used to send special initialization strings to the modem after the initialization information from Windows 95 has been sent. You create these initialization commands with commands from the AT command set described earlier in the chapter. If you need to enter any such commands, you should refer to the user's guide that came with your modem for information on proper command syntax.

Finally, at the very bottom of the dialog box is a check box labeled Record a log file. If this check box is selected, Windows 95 will keep a record of all modem commands and responses. This is helpful if you're trying to trouble-shoot what is happening with a modem. The log file is named MODEMLOG.TXT, and is stored in the Windows directory. When you are done troubleshooting your modem, don't forget to turn the log file off, as it can quickly become very large.

Configuring Dialing Properties

Dialing properties refer to the parameters that govern how Windows 95 will actually dial a phone call. These properties are related to the modem, but only indirectly. In reality they are influenced more by the location from where you are making your call.

To specify your dialing parameters, again display the Modem Properties sheet, as shown earlier in figure 31.11. Click on the Dialing Properties button at the bottom of the sheet. You will then see the Dialing Properties sheet, as shown in figure 31.15.

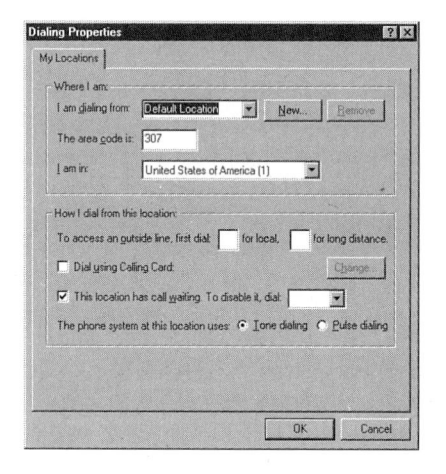

Fig. 31.15 The Dialing Properties sheet allows you to specify how your outgoing calls should be placed.

Dialing Locations

At the top of the Dialing Properties sheet you can specify originating locations for your calls. The first field, titled I am dialing from, is where you specify a location. For most people who use a computer in the same location every day, you can leave this set to the Default Location setting. If you're using Windows 95 on the road, however, you can set up dialing profiles for each location from which you might place calls. The exception to this is if you have different ways to place calls from the same location. For instance, if you're using a computer at work, you might want to define a location that reflects parameters for your work-related calls and another location with parameters for personal calls.

If you want to add a new location, click on the New button to the right of the location name. You're asked what you want the location called, after which the name is added to the location list.

Pick the location for which you want to define properties from the list of available locations. You then need to supply an area code and country for this location. If you're setting up dialing properties for outside the United States, you should use the city code in place of the area code.

If you have defined multiple locations, at some time you may want to remove a location profile. This is done by choosing the location name at the top of the Dialing Properties sheet, and then clicking on the Remove button. You are asked to confirm your action, after which the profile is erased. Windows 95 will not allow you to remove the Default Location profile.

How Calls Should Be Placed

At the bottom of the Dialing Properties sheet, you can specify how the call is to be made. The first two fields are used to indicate prefacing numbers you may need dialed in order to get an outside line for both local and long distance calls. For instance, in some offices, you may need to dial 9 before you get an outside dial tone. In some hotels, you may need to dial 9 for a local call or 8 for a long-distance call.

> **Tip:** It's a good idea to place a comma after the outside line number. This forces your modem to wait two seconds before dialing the rest of the phone number. This pause should accommodate any delays introduced by the office or hotel switching system.

The next option has to do with calling cards. Windows 95 allows you to dial the modem by using calling card information, as well as direct dialing. Most often, calling card information will come in handy for those traveling on the road. Calling cards are covered in detail in the next section.

The third option allows you to specify what Windows 95 should do about call waiting. Earlier in the chapter you learned that call waiting can disconnect a modem call (which can be quite frustrating). If you click the check box in the call waiting area, you can indicate the proper numbers to use to disable it. Windows 95 includes three different codes in the pull-down list for this option: *70, 70#, and 1170. You can also define custom sequences that disable call waiting simply by typing them into the field. Each sequence can be up to five characters long.

Setting Up Your Modem in Windows 95 **759**

> **Tip:** The exact sequence to disable call waiting varies from phone system to phone system. Check with the local phone company for the location you're defining to determine the proper sequence you should use.

The final option on the Dialing Properties sheet refers to the type of phone service you have. There are two different phone service types: tone and pulse dialing. With tone dialing, the phone equipment generates "beep tones," which are understood by the phone company's switching equipment. Older systems, still used in many parts of the country, do not use tone dialing. Instead, they use pulse dialing which relies on a series of clicks for each number dialed—when you dial 3, the equipment generates three clicks, for 7 there are seven clicks generated, and so on.

You can find out which type of service you have by listening on your phone as you dial a number. If you hear tones only, then you have a tone dialing system. If you hear any clicks at all (with or without tones), then you have a pulse dialing system. You should set this property according to your needs at the location whose properties you are defining.

Using Calling Cards

Calling cards have become a way of life, especially for travelers. Windows 95 supports the use of calling cards when placing a modem call. To specify that calls made from a specific location should use a calling card, enable the Dial using Calling Card option on the Dialing Properties sheet. You should then see the Change Calling Card page appear, as shown in figure 31.16. (If it does not appear, click on the Change button to the right of the Calling Card option.)

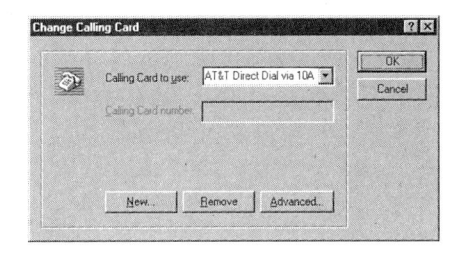

Fig. 31.16 The Change Calling Card page is where you pick the type of calling card to use from a given location.

At the top of the dialog box you can specify which calling card you want to use. Windows 95 already includes definitions for 22 of the most common calling cards:

- AT&T Direct Dial via 10ATT1
- AT&T via 1-800-321-0280
- AT&T via 10ATT0
- British Telecom (UK)
- Calling Card via 0
- Carte France Telecom
- CLEAR Communications (New Zealand)
- Global Card (Taiwan to USA)
- MCI Direct Dial via 102221
- MCI via 1-800-674-0700
- MCI via 1-800-674-7000
- MCI via 1-800-950-1022
- MCI via 102220
- Mercury (UK)
- Optus (Australia) via 008551812

- Optus (Australia) via 1812
- Telecom Australia via 1818 (fax)
- Telecom Australia via 1818 (voice)
- Telecom New Zealand
- US Sprint Direct Dial via 103331
- US Sprint via 1-800-877-8000
- US Sprint via 103330

To use one of these pre-defined cards, select the card, enter the calling card number in the appropriate field on the dialog box, and then click on OK—Windows 95 will take care of the rest. There may be a specialized calling card you want to use, however. If this is the case, you can click on the New button at the bottom of the dialog box. You are then asked for the name of the calling card. (You can provide a descriptive name, as the preceding list shows.) Once provided, the descriptive name is added to the list, and then you can click on the Advanced button to change the rules by which the calling card operates. The Dialing Rules dialog box appears, as shown in figure 31.17.

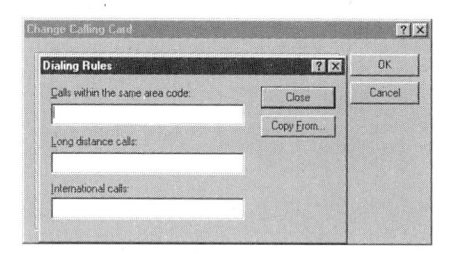

Fig. 31.17 The Dialing Rules dialog box allows you to specify exactly how your calling card should be used.

This dialog box contains three fields, each of which can contain a dialing rule. The first field is for long-distance calls within the current area code (or city code), the second is for domestic long-distance, and the third for international long-distance. You can fill each of these fields with a character sequence that describes how the calling card is to be used. Don't confuse this sequence with the modem commands you can use in your modem properties. While there are similarities, those are based on the Hayes AT command set, whereas dialing rules are constructed from characters that have different meanings. Table 31.4 shows the characters you can include in a dialing rule, along with what they mean.

Table 31.4 Dialing Rule Characters and Their Meanings

Character	Meaning
!	Generate hook-flash
#	Pound key
$	Wait for calling card prompt tone
*	Star key
,	Pause for two seconds
?	Pause for user input during dialing sequence
@	Wait for ringback followed by five seconds of silence
0-9	The digit is dialed
E	Country code
F	Area or city code
G	Local number
H	Calling card number
P	Switches to pulse dialing
T	Switches to tone dialing
W	Wait for second dial tone

As an example, if you entered a rule such as 0FG$TH, then Windows would perform the following steps when placing the call:

1. Dial 0 (zero).
2. Dial area or city code.
3. Dial the phone number.

4. Wait for the calling card prompt tone (that strange "bong" sound you hear when dialing with a 0).

5. Switch to tone dialing (in case pulse dialing was used so far).

6. Dial the calling card number.

As you can see, dialing rules can be powerful. In fact, they can be used for other specialized dialing needs instead of just calling cards. Using the characters in Table 31.4, you can create any type of calling sequence you desire.

Checking Out Your Modem

If you ever suspect that your modem is not working properly with Windows 95, you can get information about how the modem is working by starting at the Control Panel and double-clicking on the Modems icon. The Modems Properties sheet appears, where you should click on the Diagnostics tab. The sheet will then appear similar to what is shown in figure 34.18.

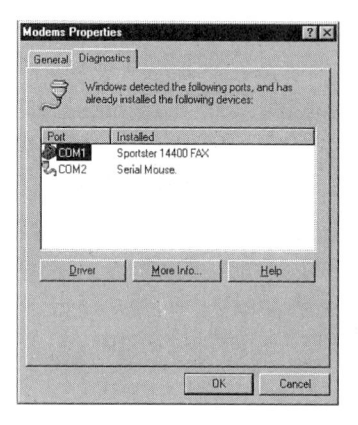

Fig. 31.18 The Diagnostics tab of the Modems Properties sheet allows you to check the connection to your modem.

Here you should highlight the port to which your modem is attached—in this instance, COM1—and then click on the More Info button.

Windows 95 then attempts to interrogate the modem, to see what information it can determine. After a few moments you will see a dialog box similar to what is shown in figure 31.19.

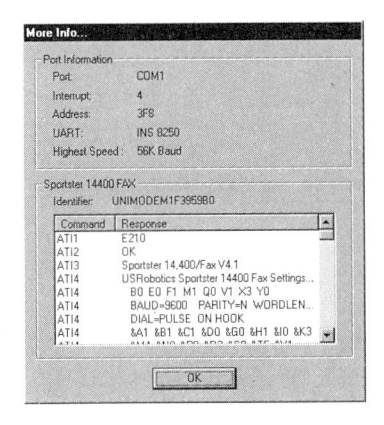

Fig. 31.19 Windows 95 can determine quite a bit of information about a modem.

The amount of information derived by Windows 95 depends solely on the capabilities of the modem. This information not only tells you about the modem and the connection, but also lets you know that Windows 95 can, in fact, communicate with the modem. Thus, if you continue to have problems establishing a communications link with a remote system, the chances are good that it is not because of your system or modem.

Communicating with a Modem

KILLER 32 WINDOWS 95

by Yvonne Johnson

The previous chapter, "Serial Communications Basics," explained the ins-and-outs of communications hardware and software settings. In this chapter, the rubber meets the road, so to speak. All the hardware and software specifications and setup are put into action with the features discussed here.

Several features in Windows 95 use the modem as the hardware vehicle, including the Phone Dialer, HyperTerminal, Dial-Up Networking, Microsoft Network, and Microsoft Exchange. The dialing properties used by the communications features are all organized in one central location: the Dialing Properties sheet.

The Basis of Communications in Windows 95

Windows 95 provides extensive and consistent support for telecommunications based on the Telephony API (TAPI), a standard by which communications programs can control transmission of data, fax, and voice calls. TAPI manages all the signaling between a computer and a telephone network, and it arbitrates among the communications programs that want to share communications ports and devices. TAPI manages the basic functions of establishing, answering, and terminating a call, as well as supplementary functions, such as hold, transfer, conference, and call park. In addition, TAPI also accommodates features that are specific to certain service providers. TAPI's built-in extensibility will accommodate future telephony features and telephone networks as they become available.

TAPI's arbitration among communications programs allows the computer to simultaneously run several communications programs (that is, it eliminates the need to perform only one telecommunications task at a time). For example, you can send a fax at the same time that Dial-Up Networking waits for an incoming call. There is no need to terminate Dial-Up Networking to send the fax, because TAPI allows programs to share the same device in a cooperative manner.

Setting Dialing Properties

Dialing properties govern the way outgoing calls are made. You can access the Dialing Properties sheet from the Control Panel, but because dialing properties are used by all the communications features of Windows 95, you also can access the Dialing Properties sheet from any of the features.

The following steps show you how to access the Dialing Properties sheet from the Control Panel:

1. Click Start, point to Settings, and click Control Panel.

2. Double-click the Modems object to display the Modems Properties sheet (figure 32.1).

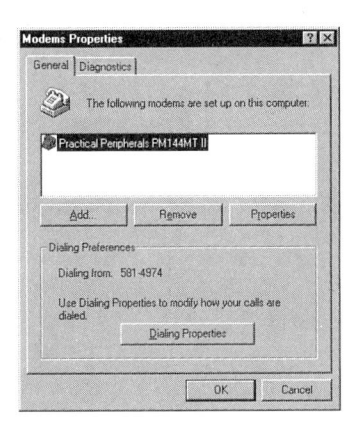

Fig. 32.1 The Modems Properties sheet is one place that you can access the Dialing Properties.

3. If there is more than one modem listed, select the one you want to configure and then click the Dialing Properties button. The Dialing Properties sheet appears (figure 32.2).

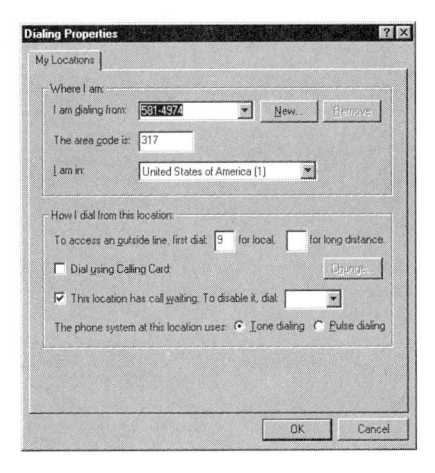

Fig. 32.2 The Dialing Properties sheet has settings for two broad categories: where you are and how you want to make the call.

Setting Dialing Properties **769**

4. Select the correct location from the drop-down list. If you want to create a new location name, click New, type a new name, and click OK. (Notice that you can also delete a location by selecting the location, clicking Remove, and choosing Yes.)

5. Enter the correct area code if the correct area code is not displayed by default. (Some settings in the Dialing Properties sheet—location, area code, and country code—are obtained by Windows 95 when you set up the modem initially.)

6. Verify that the I am in location is correct, or select a location from the drop-down list. The location that you select determines the international country code used for dialing international calls.

7. In the How I dial from this location section of the dialog box, specify the numbers you have to dial (if any) to get an outside line for local or long-distance calls (usually 9 for local calls and 8 for long distance).

8. If you want to dial using a Calling Card number, select Dial using Calling Card. The Change Calling Card dialog box opens as shown in figure 32.3. Choose a calling card from the drop-down list, or click New, enter your Calling Card number, and click OK. Then click OK to close the Change Calling Card dialog box. (If Dial using Calling Card is already selected, you can display the Change Calling Card dialog box by clicking Change.)

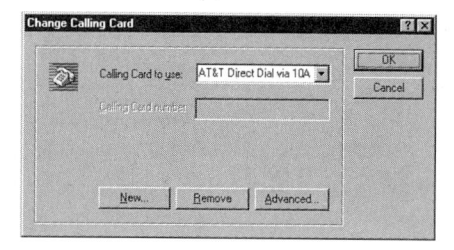

Fig. 32.3 You can add or remove Calling Card numbers in the Change Calling Card dialog box.

770 Chapter 32: Communicating with a Modem

9. If you have call waiting, you certainly want to disable it because receiving a call waiting signal during a fax or modem transmission will break the connection. Choose This location has call waiting, and then enter the number that suspends call waiting.

> **Note:** Different areas of the country have different numbers that you dial before making a call to suspend the call waiting feature. The feature is only suspended during the next call that is made. As soon as the call is disconnected, call waiting is automatically reactivated. To obtain the number, look in the information pages of your local telephone book, or check with your local phone company.

10. Select the type of dialing system you have: Tone dialing for Touch-Tone or Pulse dialing for rotary dial.
11. Click OK to close the Dialing Properties sheet. Click OK to close the Modems Properties sheet.

> **Note:** The Dialing Properties that you set are stored in the TELEPHON.INI file instead of the Registry to ensure backward compatibility with Windows 16-bit communications applications.

Defining Dialing Rules. To be more specific about how a number is dialed, you can define dialing rules. The dialing rules tell the modem exactly what to dial based on the criteria you specify.

To define dialing rules, follow these steps:

1. Display the Dialing Properties sheet. Display the Change Calling Card dialog box and click the Advanced button. The Dialing Rules dialog box displays as shown in figure 32.4.

Setting Dialing Properties **771**

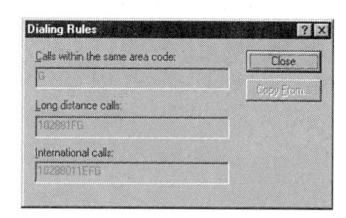

Fig. 32.4 By specifying dialing rules, you can specify the exact numbers that should or should not be dialed.

2. Fill in each box with the appropriate codes and numbers. To see a list of the codes, click the What's This button, and then click one of the text boxes. The codes are listed in Table 32.1.

3. When finished, click Close.

Table 32.1 Codes Used for Dialing Rules

Code	Description
0 - 9	Dialable digits
ABCD	Dialable digits
E	Country code
F	Area code
G	Local number
H	Calling Card number
*, #	Dialable digits
T	The following digits are tone
P	The following digits are pulse
,	Pause for a specified period of time
!	Hookflash (used, for example, to answer a call if you have the call waiting feature
W	Wait for second dial tone
@	Wait for ringback followed by five seconds of silence
$	Wait for Calling Card prompt tone
?	Ask for input before dialing continues

In the following example, which might be used on a PBX system, the modem would dial only the local number for calls in the same area, only the area code and local number for long distance (the mandatory 1 would not be dialed because the PBX takes care of it), and 011 plus the country code, area code, and local number for international calls.

Calls within the same area	G
Long-distance calls	FG
International calls	011EFG

Using Phone Dialer

The Phone Dialer is an accessory that dials phone numbers for voice telephone calls. It is used in conjunction with a telephone that is plugged into the phone jack (not the telecom jack) of the modem card. The Phone Dialer includes a telephone dial pad, user-programmable speed dialing, and a call log that tracks both incoming and outgoing calls.

Opening the Phone Dialer

These steps open the Phone Dialer:

1. Click Start, point to Programs, and click Accessories.

2. Click Phone Dialer. The Phone Dialer opens as shown in figure 32.5.

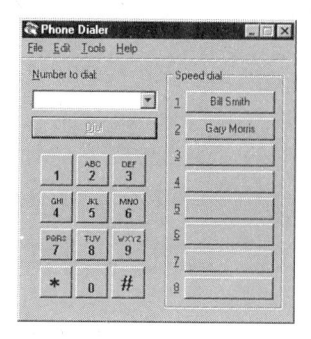

Fig. 32.5 The Phone Dialer makes outgoing voice calls and logs both outgoing and incoming calls.

Dialing a Number

With Phone Dialer, you can use several different methods to dial a number, including:

- Clicking a speed-dial button.
- Typing the phone number and clicking Dial.
- Clicking the numbers on the Phone Dialer numeric pad and clicking Dial.
- Selecting a number from the drop-down list, which contains the most recently used numbers.

After you dial the number, lift the receiver and click Talk. (The party that answers will not be able to hear you until you click Talk even though you have lifted the receiver.) If desired, type a name to place in the call log that is kept automatically by Phone Dialer. When finished with the call, replace the receiver in the cradle and click Hang Up.

Storing a Number on a Speed Dial Button

To store a number on a speed dial button, click an empty speed dial button and type a name. Type the number and click Save. The name appears on the speed dial button.

Note: You can type as many as 40 characters in the number text box, so you have plenty of room to type even an international phone number. All non-numeric characters that you type in the number are ignored except the plus sign (+) if it is typed at the beginning of the number. International format for a number begins with a plus sign and requires parentheses around the area code, for example: +1 (206) 555-8080.

Editing Speed Dial Buttons

To change the name or number associated with a speed dial button, choose Edit, Speed Dial. The Edit Speed Dial dialog box displays as shown in figure 32.6. Select a button and enter a new name or number. Edit as many buttons as necessary, and then click Save.

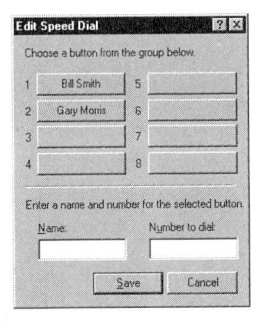

Fig. 32.6 In the Edit Speed Dial dialog box, you can modify speed dial buttons that you have previously defined, and you can define empty speed dial buttons.

Using the Call Log

Phone Dialer keeps a log of the calls that are made using Phone Dialer as well as the calls received on a telephone that is connected through the computer. By default, it logs both incoming and outgoing calls. To view the log of calls, choose Tools, Show Log. The log displays in the Call Log window as shown in figure 32.7.

Using Phone Dialer   **775**

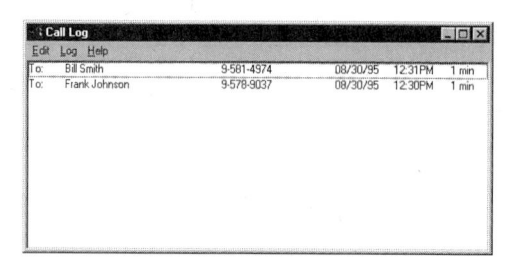

Fig. 32.7 The calling log can be set up to show incoming calls, outgoing calls, both types of calls, or no calls.

Both incoming and outgoing calls can be kept in the log. To specify the types of calls, choose Log, Options in the Call Log window. Choose the type of calls you want to log and click OK.

> **Tip:** To call a number that is listed in the log, simply double-click the number in the log.

To delete entries in the log, first select the entries by dragging the mouse over them if the entries you want to select are listed contiguously, or by pointing to an individual entry and pressing Ctrl while you click. Then choose Edit from the menu bar and choose either Cut or Delete.

Although there is no option to print the log, you can easily do so with some quick maneuvering. First select the entries in the log and choose Edit, Copy. Then open a text editor, such as WordPad or your favorite word processing program, and choose Edit, Paste. Then print the document.

Using HyperTerminal

The HyperTerminal accessory is a telecommunications program that connects you with a remote computer via a modem. Once connected, you can type messages back and forth or send and receive files. You can save the communication settings that you use in a session so you can use them again. HyperTerminal is a 32-bit application that replaces the 16-bit application, Terminal, which was provided in Windows 3.x.

HyperTerminal is not installed by default. If it is not installed on your system, open the Add/Remove Programs object in the Control Panel and go to the Windows Setup page. HyperTerminal is listed in the Communications category.

Starting the HyperTerminal Program

To start the HyperTerminal program, click Start, point to Programs, point to Accessories, and click HyperTerminal. The HyperTerminal folder opens in a window. Double-click the icon for Hypertrm.exe. The HyperTerminal program starts and displays the Connection Description dialog box as shown in figure 32.8.

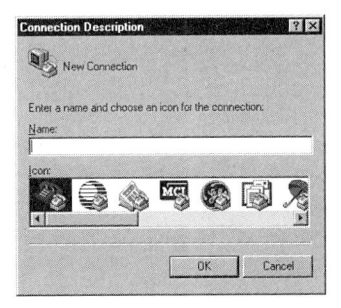

Fig. 32.8 The Connection Description dialog box gathers information about the communications session that will be retained if the session is saved.

Making a Connection with a Remote Computer

After starting HyperTerminal, follow these steps to make a connection with a remote computer:

Using HyperTerminal **777**

1. In the Connection Description dialog box, type a name for the connection. The name should describe the location or type of connection in some way, such as *Sales Office, ABC Company,* or *Monthly Upload.*

2. Select an icon to represent the connection.

3. Click OK. The Phone Number dialog box displays as shown in figure 32.9.

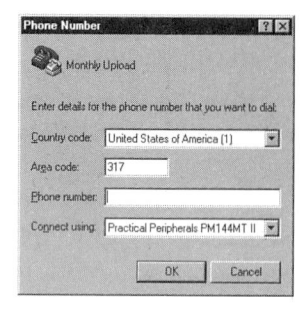

Fig. 32.9 The Phone Number dialog box collects information about the remote PC's telephone number and the modem that you are using.

4. Select the appropriate Country code from the drop-down list.

5. Enter an area code in the Area code text box.

6. Enter the phone number in the Phone number text box.

7. Select the modem you will use from the drop-down list.

8. Click OK and the Connect dialog box displays (figure 32.10).

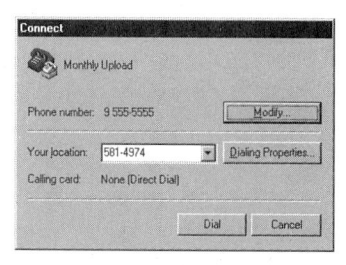

Fig. 32.10 The Connect dialog box contains the information about the number from which you are calling and the way in which you want to make the call.

9. At this point, it is a good idea to check the dialing properties. Although you probably will use the same dialing properties all the time, you may need to change some of the properties for a particular connection. For example, you might need to use a special Calling Card that you are only allowed to use when you make this connection. Enter the appropriate information and make the appropriate selections to describe the way you will make this call. Then click OK. (See "Setting Dialing Properties" earlier in this chapter.)

> **Caution:** If you change the dialing properties, the changes will stay in effect for all other communications, so you may need to change them back to the way they were after you make the connection.

10. Click Dial. The modem dials the number. If a connection is made, connection information is displayed in the HyperTerminal window. If there is no answer or the line is busy, the dialog box displays the word Busy and changes the Dial button to Dial Now.

> **Tip:** If you plan to connect with the same computer repeatedly, save the session so you can use it each time you want to connect.

Disconnecting and Saving a Session

To disconnect, choose Call, Disconnect, or simply click the Disconnect button in the toolbar. HyperTerminal asks if you want to save the session. Click Yes, and the icon will be placed in the HyperTerminal folder automatically. If you want to save the session before you actually make the connection, choose File from the menu bar and choose Save.

Using HyperTerminal **779**

Making a Connection with a Saved Session

Use these steps to connect with a remote computer using a saved session.

1. Click Start, point to Programs, point to Accessories, and click HyperTerminal. The HyperTerminal folder opens. Double-click the icon for the session you want to start. The HyperTerminal program starts and displays the Connection dialog box for the selected session.

2. Click Dial. The modem dials the number. If a connection is made, connection information is displayed in the HyperTerminal window. If there is no answer or the line is busy, the dialog box displays the word Busy and changes the Dial button to Dial Now.

Chatting

Once you are connected with another user at a remote PC, you can engage in a real-time conversation (*chatting*) by typing messages back and forth to each other. To send a message to the remote, type the text and press Enter. (The text that you type appears on your screen.) Wait for a response. When the remote user types text and presses Enter, the text will appear on your screen.

Saving or Printing the Text of a Session

Sometimes it is helpful to save the text that appears on your screen during a telecommunications session. For example, if you connect with an unfamiliar bulletin board, you can save both the text that you see and that you type while exploring it. Later you can review the file so that you will be able to maneuver more quickly the next time you connect with the bulletin board. You also can send the text to the printer instead of saving it as a file.

To save the text of a session, choose **T**ransfer from the menu bar. Choose **C**apture text, type the location and name of a file, and click Start. To print the text, choose **T**ransfer, Capture to **P**rinter. (This option is a toggle and should be turned off when you no longer want to use it.)

Sending a File

Before you can send a file to a remote computer, the remote must prepare for receiving the file. If the remote PC is using Windows 95 HyperTerminal, the remote user prepares to receive the file as described in the next topic. If the remote is using bulletin board software or some other type of telecommunications software, it will have its own routine for preparing to receive a file. Usually, when you upload to a bulletin board, you must select the Upload task from a menu, and then the bulletin board responds by telling you when it is ready.

These steps send a file to the remote computer after a connection has been made.

1. Choose **T**ransfer from the menu bar.
2. Choose **S**end File.
3. Type the path and name of the file.
4. Select a protocol from the drop-down list. (For information about protocols, refer to Chapter 31, "Serial Communications Basics.")

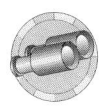

> **Note:** Both computers must use the same protocol.

5. Click **S**end.

Receiving a File

In order to receive a file from a remote PC, the user of the receiving PC must perform these steps:

1. Choose <u>T</u>ransfer from the menu bar.
2. Choose <u>R</u>eceive File.
3. Specify the location where the file will be stored.
4. Select a protocol from the drop-down list. (As when sending a file, both computers must use the same protocol when receiving a file.)
5. Click <u>R</u>eceive.

Using Terminal Emulation

To communicate with some remote systems, you must have a specific type of terminal because the keys are mapped differently on the terminal than the way the keys are mapped on a PC. HyperTerminal can emulate several different types of terminals including ANSI, Viewdata (for the United Kingdom), Minitel (for France), DEC VT 100, Auto Detect, VT 52, and TTY.

Before starting a telecommunications session that requires a different type of terminal, you can choose the terminal you want HyperTerminal to emulate by choosing <u>F</u>ile, <u>P</u>roperties. Click the tab for the Settings page, and choose an emulation from the drop-down list (see figure 32.11).

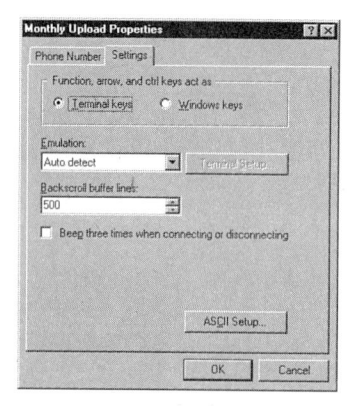

Fig. 32.11 On the Settings page of the Properties sheet, you can choose a different kind of terminal to emulate.

Once a terminal type is selected, click Terminal Setup and choose the appropriate options to set up the terminal. Each terminal uses different options. Options for the VT100, a common terminal, are shown in figure 32.12. The options for the VT100 terminal determine the appearance of the cursor and the way the keypad keys and cursor keys are used, divide the screen into 132 columns instead of 80, and specify the character set that will be used.

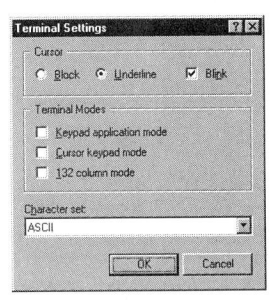

Fig. 32.12 The options for the VT100 terminal direct how your PC should function when emulating a VT100.

Additional options on the Settings page include the following:

➤ Terminal keys. Uses the terminal functions for the function, arrow, and Control keys.

➤ Windows key. Uses Windows functions for the function, arrow, and Control keys.

➤ Backscroll buffer lines. Determines the number of lines that you can scroll to with the PgUp key.

➤ Beep three times when connecting or disconnecting. Causes your computer to beep three times when it receives a bell signal from the remote.

If you click the ASCII Setup button, the dialog box shown in figure 32.13 displays. Options in this dialog box include:

➤ Send line ends with line feeds. Sends a carriage return to the remote each time you complete a line by pressing Enter.

Using HyperTerminal **783**

➤ Echo typed characters locally. Displays commands on your computer as you type them.

➤ Line delay. Specifies the number of milliseconds that a line is delayed before being sent to the remote. (This is an Xon/Xoff-type of control.)

➤ Character delay. Specifies the number of milliseconds that characters will be delayed before being sent to the remote. (This is another type of Xon/Xoff-type of control.)

➤ Append line feeds to incoming line ends. Inserts a carriage return at the end of every line that you receive from the remote.

➤ Force incoming data to 7-bit ASCII. Forces 8-bit ASCII to be translated to 7-bit ASCII.

➤ Wrap lines that exceed terminal width. Wraps text to the next line if it will not fit in the width used by your PC.

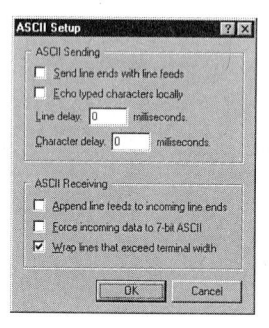

Fig. 32.13 The ASCII Setup dialog box determines how ASCII text is sent and received.

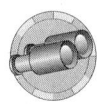

Note: Another way to change the emulation setting is to point to the icon for the session in the HyperTerminal folder, and click the secondary mouse button. Choose Properties, click the tab for the Settings page, and then select the emulation type from the drop-down list.

Using Third-Party Communications Software

Many third-party communications software packages are available for use with modems and fax/modems. Many of these programs do little more than HyperTerminal, while other programs are more sophisticated. Some allow you to set up telecommunication scripts to automate telecommunication sessions by making connections, sending and receiving files, etc., without the intervention of the user.

Any telecommunications software that works with Windows 3.1 should work with Windows 95; however, you can expect to see 32-bit upgrades made to work specifically with Windows 95 to take advantage of preemptive multitasking, as well as other features. Preemptive multitasking is particularly important in the realm of telecommunications, where uploading and downloading files tie up the system.

Understanding Online Services

"Online services," "surfing the information highway," and "cyberspace"—terms that crop up in TV commercials and are casually bandied about by many computer users—still hold a mysterious meaning for many people. These terms are all associated with the new "electronic frontier," in which every home will be wired to online services that let you make bank transfers, purchase groceries, reserve airline tickets, rent movies, video-conference, get sports scores, buy and sell stock, etc., etc. The system that will magically provide all these services will somehow be bound up with a television, a computer, the phone lines, and some other microcombobulator that is not in production yet, but undoubtedly is already in the mind of Bill Gates or one of his cronies.

Many online-service providers are already in place and doing well. The five major commercial services (listed in alphabetical order) are America Online, CompuServe Information Service, Dow Jones News/Retrieval, GEnie, and Prodigy.

Then there's the prodigious Internet, which is not a commercial service at all, but a worldwide network of millions of computers located at universities, government offices, research institutions, and corporations. (For more information about the Internet, see Chapter 35, "Internet Communications.")

A newcomer (but sure to be well-known and popular in a hurry) to online services is Microsoft Network (MSN). The Microsoft Network provides or has plans to provide all the services currently being provided by the established services, and its front-end software is include in Windows 95. (For more information about the MSN, see Chapter 33, "The Microsoft Network.")

If you are a true "killer" computer user, you already know that the online services offer e-mail, downloadable information and software, information forums, chat rooms for real-time conversations, and other miscellaneous services, such as online shopping. In fact, you probably subscribe to several of these services and surf the Internet on a regular basis. For those readers who aspire to the killer-computer-user status, it is mandatory that you get connected. Prodigy, America Online, GEnie, and CompuServe are all favorites of home users.

Most of the online services have several different pricing structures based on the amount of usage and sometimes the speed of the modem. Other costs that may be incurred when using an online service include long distance charges (if you are in an area where a local number cannot be provided) and the cost of front-end software to navigate the service.

> **Note:** Many times, if you buy the front-end program that is sold by the online system, the cost of the software is credited back to you in free connect time.

All of the 16-bit front-end software currently designed to connect with online services works with Windows 95. Soon you can expect to see new 32-bit programs designed to work with Windows 95. You also can expect the online services to provide MAPI drivers to allow them to interact with Microsoft Exchange (i.e., store messages in the Microsoft Exchange universal Inbox). CompuServe already has such a driver, which is included in Windows 95.

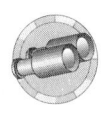

> **Note:** Almost all online services have forums on Windows 95. It is a great place to get information and get help with problems.

Using Microsoft Exchange

Microsoft Exchange is a new network feature of Windows 95. It sends and retrieves messages for members of a Windows workgroup and connects them with many kinds of information services, including Microsoft Mail, Microsoft Fax, and the Microsoft Network. Microsoft Exchange provides one location for all user mail and provides efficient ways to organize and store mail.

> **Note:** If you install Windows 95 over Windows or Windows for Workgroups, Microsoft Exchange automatically replaces Microsoft Mail or Windows for Workgroups Mail, but it retains your old post office and converts all mail to the new Microsoft Exchange format.

Two important components of Microsoft Exchange are the *Personal Address Book* (PAB) and the *Personal Information Store* (PST). Individual users can set up and maintain their own Personal Address Book, which contains names, phone and fax numbers, mailing addresses, personal contact information, and multiple electronic mail addresses (for different services). Through MAPI interfaces, a PAB can be used by a wide variety of applications.

The Personal Information Store is a database that stores messages, forms, documents, and other information in folders. It functions as the user's local mailbox and organizes and sorts messages.

Starting Microsoft Exchange

There are several ways to start Microsoft Exchange. You can double-click the Inbox on the Windows 95 desktop, select Microsoft Exchange from the Programs menu, or double-click the envelope icon that appears on the Windows 95 taskbar when you get a message. The Microsoft Exchange is shown in figure 32.14.

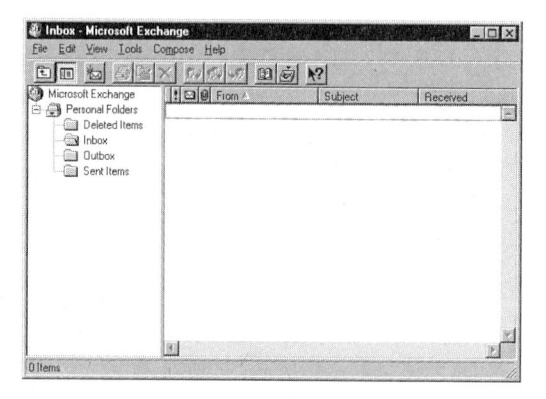

Fig. 32.14 The Microsoft Exchange window is very similar in design to Windows Explorer.

Reading Mail

To read a message that has been sent to Microsoft Exchange, open Microsoft Exchange, click the Inbox in the left pane, and double-click the message that you want to read in the right pane.

Composing and Sending Mail

To compose a new message and send it, follow these steps:

1. Choose Co*m*pose, *N*ew Message from the menu bar, or click the New Message icon in the toolbar. A screen like the one in figure 32.15 displays. Type the name of the recipient, or click the T*o* button and choose the address name from a list. Click OK.

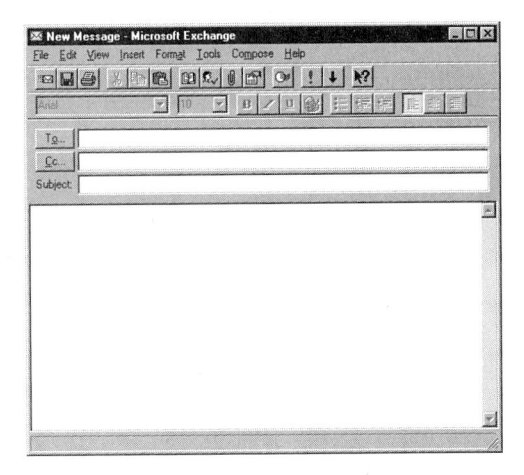

Fig. 32.15 The message screen contains areas for addressing the message, and sending "carbon copies," a subject, and the text of the message.

2. To send copies of the message, type the address names of the recipients, or click the *C*c button and select the names from a list. Click OK.

3. Type the subject.

Using Microsoft Exchange **789**

4. Type the message.

5. Choose File, Se<u>n</u>d from the menu, or click the Send button in the toolbar.

The Microsoft Network

KILLER 33 WINDOWS 95

by Yvonne Johnson

The Microsoft Network (MSN) is the newest entrant in the international electronic information service market. Although it is a new service, it breaks on the scene full-blown. As with CompuServe, Prodigy, and America Online, it has e-mail, product forums, special interest groups, bulletin boards, chat rooms, file libraries, and online shopping, and, of course, it is the single best place to get information and support for Microsoft products. You can also connect with information services that provide news, sports, weather reports, stock information, and so on.

In May of 1995 Microsoft and NBC announced a broad multimedia alliance. As part of the alliance, the announcement said that NBC would build new online services for MSN encompassing all NBC content areas, including NBC Entertainment, NBC Sports, NBC Productions, CNBC, America's Talking, NBC's international ventures, and NBC-owned stations. Additionally, NBC's advertisers and its more than 200 affiliates would be invited to participate in NBC's service on MSN. The prospects of what the MSN will eventually become are overwhelming.

Before the May 1995 announcement, Microsoft already had an impressive list of companies committed to offering content and services on the MSN. The list is too long to enumerate, but it's filled with names you would recognize immediately, such as American Greetings; Borland International, Inc.; C-SPAN; Corel Systems Corporation; Epson America Inc.; Gateway 2000 Inc.; Hayes Microcomputer Products Inc.; Hewlett-Packard Company; Lotus Development Corporation (now a part of IBM); New York Times Sports Leisure Magazines; Toshiba America Information Systems, Inc.; US News & World Report; and Ziff-Davis Interactive, to name only a few.

Connecting to and Disconnecting from MSN

Before you can connect to MSN, you must install the software. If you did not install MSN in the initial installation, you can do so by using the Windows Setup tab of Add/Remove Programs in the Control Panel dialog box. Of course, you must also have a modem to connect with MSN.

Becoming a Member of MSN

The first time you connect with MSN you'll have the opportunity to become a member. Follow these steps to sign on to MSN and become a member:

1. Double-click on the MSN icon on the desktop. The screen shown in figure 33.1 appears. Click on OK to continue.

2. Enter the area code (if it is not displayed) and the first three digits of the telephone number used by your modem and click on OK. The screen shown in figure 33.2 shows the local access number you'll use to call MSN.

Fig. 33.1 This screen appears the first time you attempt to log on to MSN.

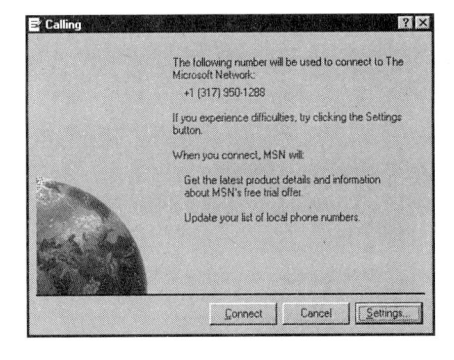

Fig. 33.2 After you have entered your area code and the first three digits of your phone number, you're given an access number.

3. Click on Settings to verify your access numbers, dialing properties, and modem settings as shown in figure 33.3.

   Click on Access Numbers to see the primary and backup numbers that Windows 95 will use to connect you with MSN. If you want to change either the primary or backup number, click on the Change button for either number. Choose the country, state/region, and the access number from the appropriate lists. Click on OK twice.

Connecting to and Disconnecting from MSN   **793**

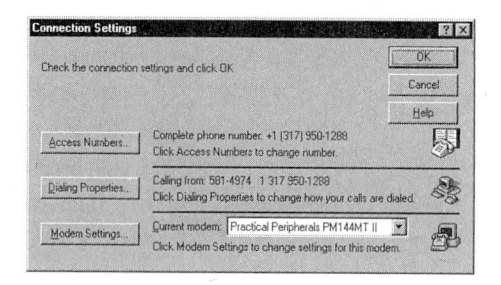

Fig. 33.3 Before logging on, you can change or verify the settings for the access number, dialing properties, and the modem.

>Click on <u>D</u>ialing Properties to display the Dialing Properties sheet. Make any changes that you want on this sheet; but remember, these dialing properties are used for all programs that use the modem, including the Phone Dialer, Hyperterminal, third-party software, and so on. When finished, click on OK.
>
>To use a different modem, select a modem from the <u>C</u>urrent modem drop-down list. Then click on <u>M</u>odem Settings to verify or change the modem configuration. If you make changes to the modem configuration, remember that these settings will be used by any telecommunications program that uses the modem. When finished, click on OK.
>
>Click on OK to return to the Calling window.

4. Click on <u>C</u>onnect. Before you start the process, click on the <u>D</u>etails button and read the information there about what the MSN contains. Click on Close and then click on <u>P</u>rice. Read the pricing information. When finished, click on Close.

   Click <u>T</u>ell for your name and address. Fill in the appropriate information about yourself, click the box in the bottom-left corner if you don't want to receive special promotions from Microsoft, and click on OK.

Click on Next, select a way to pay. Select a credit card from the list, fill in the card number, expiration date, and name on the card, and click on OK.

Click on Then. Read the rules and click on I Agree if you want to continue.

5. Click on Join Now; then click on OK; and finally, click on Connect.

> **Note:** If more than one person uses the PC, you can apply for multiple memberships and each member will be billed as a separate account. To sign up more than one member on one computer, open the Program Files folder, double-click on the Microsoft Network folder, and double-click on the MSN Signup icon. Follow the directions and provide the information about the new member.

Connecting to MSN

You connect to MSN by double-clicking on either the MSN icon on your desktop or on a shortcut to an area of the MSN (see "Getting There the Fastest Way," later in this chapter). The Sign In dialog box appears as shown in figure 33.4. If you have previously signed on to MSN and entered your member ID and password, your member ID appears by default. If Remember my password is marked, the password (represented by asterisks) is also displayed by default. If Remember my password is not selected, you must enter your password each time you log on to MSN. (If other people use your computer, you may not want to select Remember my password.) Click on Connect. The screen called MSN Central appears, as shown in figure 33.5.

Connecting to and Disconnecting from MSN **795**

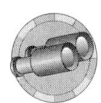

> **Note:** Your password must be at least eight but no more than 16 characters long. Passwords may use only the following characters: A through Z (upper- or lowercase), 0 through 9, and a hyphen (-).

Fig. 33.4 The Sign In dialog box lists the password (with asterisks) by default because Remember my password is checked.

When you dial into MSN, you're actually dialing the number of a network provider. Network providers have local nodes all over the world that allow users to connect to MSN by making a local phone call. After you're connected to the network provider, the provider further connects you to the MSN Data Center by using a high-speed network that is much faster than phone lines. The MSN Data Center is where the actual exchange of information between your computer and the network takes place.

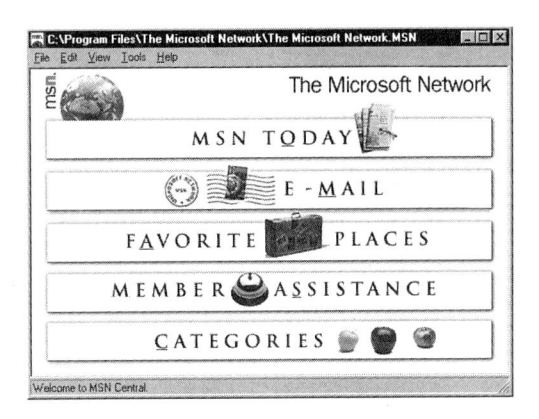

Fig. 33.5 The MSN Central screen displays when you connect with MSN.

> **Note:** From time to time, Microsoft will upgrade the MSN software. When you log on to MSN, the system checks your network software version in the Registry to see whether it's the latest version. If it isn't, you're prompted to upgrade. You must accept the upgrade, or you won't be able to log on to MSN. After you click on Yes, the files download and you must restart the PC to complete the upgrade.

Changing Your Password

To change your password, log on to MSN and choose Tools, Password. Type your current password, type your new password, type your new password again, and then click on OK.

Disconnecting from MSN

There are several ways to initiate disconnecting from the network:

- Click on the Sign Out button in the toolbar.
- Choose File, Sign Out from the menu bar.
- Point to the Connection Indicator (MSN) in the status bar (next to the time) and click the secondary mouse button. Choose Sign Out.
- Close all windows.

If you choose any of the preceding methods, MSN displays a prompt asking if you want to disconnect from the network. Select Yes.

Exploring MSN Central

The MSN Central screen has a menu bar, five categories, and a toolbar. The categories include MSN Today, E-Mail, Favorite Places, Member Assistance, and Categories. Each category is covered in the following sections.

MSN Today

MSN Today is an information screen that changes from day to day. It usually has an inviting tidbit about something you can access on the network and a shortcut that will take you right to it. MSN Today may have daily highlights, tips, links to other MSN services, and previews of upcoming services. To see what's scheduled on MSN for the week, click on Calendar of Events. The calendar shows dates, times, and places for scheduled events. Examples include Bi-weekly Moderated Comedy Chats in LuLu's Lounge, OS/2 Chat in the OS/2 chat room, and Recovery Chat: Getting Free of Nicotine in the Recovery chat room.

E-Mail

E-Mail starts Microsoft Exchange, which enables you to send or receive e-mail messages to and from MSN members or anyone with a mailbox on the Internet (if you have the Plus Pak). Although Microsoft Exchange also provides other services, such as faxing, you would not want to use valuable time online to do anything with Microsoft Exchange except exchange e-mail. For more information about the capabilities of Microsoft Exchange, see Chapter 34, "Using Microsoft Exchange."

Favorite Places

Favorite Places is empty when you first sign on to MSN. It is a location where you can store shortcuts to your favorite places on the network.

Member Assistance

Member Assistance has topics to help you get started using the MSN. It has a user's guide, billing information, frequently asked questions (FAQs), and so on. Member Assistance is a good place to start if you're unfamiliar with online services or you have a particular question about using the service.

Categories

Categories is a list of the broad general categories of services and information on the network. Another name used for a broad general category is *forum*. Each category has several subcategories, which may also have several subcategories, and so on. The structure of the network is just like the hierarchical structure of a hard disk. In fact, if you use the explore mode, as explained later in this chapter, the structure of MSN is represented by folders.

The Menu Bar

The menu bar has five options: File, Edit, View, Tools, and Help. The options in these drop-down menus vary depending on where you are in MSN.

The Toolbar

The toolbar found on the MSN Central screen has the following drop-down list and buttons: Go to a different folder (drop-down list), Up One Level, Go to MSN Central, Go to Favorite Places, and Sign Out. Table 33.1 shows the buttons and what they do.

Table 33.1 Buttons on the Toolbar

Icon	Name	Description
	Go to a different folder	Displays the hierarchy of folders on MSN.
	Up One Level	Move up one level in the hierarchy. (MSN Central is as high as you go in the hierarchy, so this button has no use on the MSN Central screen unless you are using the Windows Explorer mode.)
	Go to MSN Central	Takes you back to the MSN Central screen.
	Go to Favorite Places	Opens Favorite Places.
	Sign Out	Logs off the network.

Navigating the Network by Using My Computer

Microsoft provides two interfaces for the Microsoft Network. One is similar to My Computer—this is the default—and the other is similar to Windows Explorer. Because both interfaces should be familiar to Windows 95 users, navigating the Microsoft Network is relatively easy.

When you connect to MSN by double-clicking on the MSN icon on the desktop, the MSN Central screen appears. This is the My Computer mode. To open any of the five areas on the MSN Central screen, click anywhere inside the rectangle that borders the title. For example, to open Categories, click inside the rectangle at the bottom of the screen. A window (like My Computer) opens that contains icons for the various forums offered. (An icon that leads to other topics is represented by a folder. An icon that opens a service has an appropriate symbol, like an "i" in a blue circle for information kiosk.)

You'll notice that a forum window also has a toolbar with the same buttons found on the MSN Central screen plus these additional buttons: Properties, Add to favorite places, Large icons, Small icons, List, and Details.

Graphic	Name	Description
	Properties	Displays the Properties sheet.
	Add to Favorite Places	Adds a shortcut for the selected item in the Favorite Places area.
	Large icons	Changes the icons to large icons.
	Small icons	Changes the icons to small icons.
	List	Changes the icons to a list.
	Details	Changes the icons to a list with details.

To show how easy it is to navigate the network, click on Categories on the MSN Central screen. The Categories window opens, as shown in figure 33.6. Double-click on Business & Finance and a window appears as shown in figure 33.7. Double-click on Small Office/Home Office and a window appears as shown in figure 33.8. Double-click on SOHO Advisors and a window appears as shown in figure 33.9. Double-click on Janet Attard Business Know-How and a window appears as shown in figure 33.10. Double-click on Business Know-How Reports BBS, and the topics posted on the bulletin board appear as shown in figure 33.11. You can move back up a level in the hierarchy at any time by clicking the Up One Level button, or you can return to MSN Central by clicking the Go to MSN Central button.

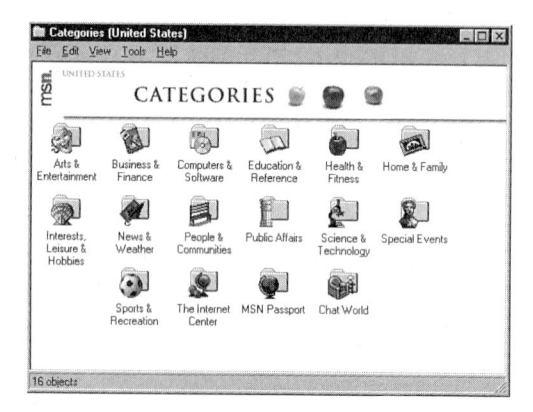

Fig. 33.6 The Categories window shows the broad, general topics on MSN.

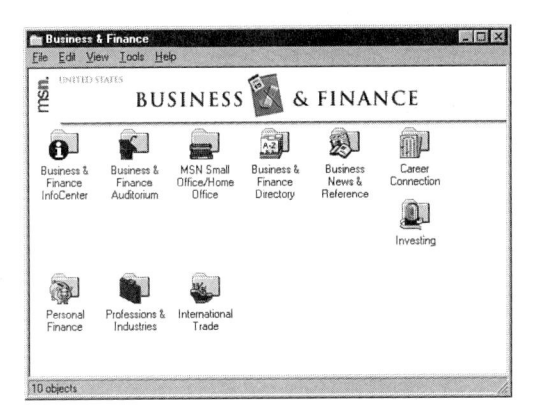

Fig. 33.7 The Business and Finance window shows a variety of topics.

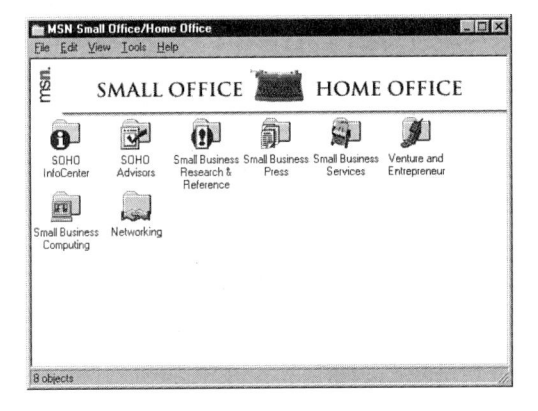

Fig. 33.8 The Small Office/Home Office window has topics specific to starting a new business, business services, education, and so on.

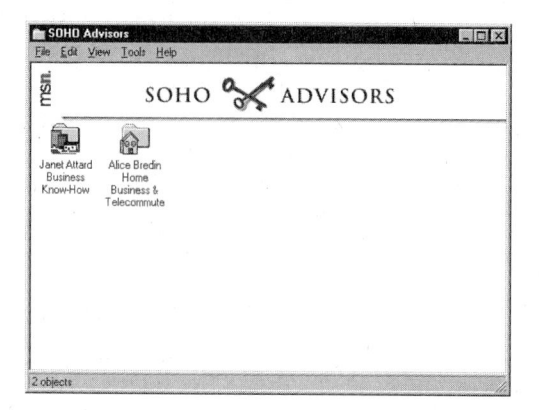

Fig. 33.9 The SOHO Advisors window lists two sources of information for small offices and home offices.

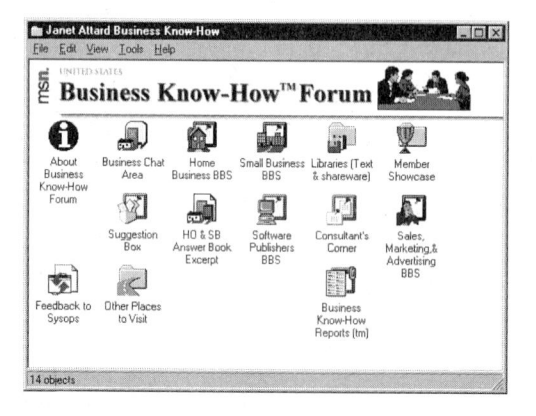

Fig. 33.10 The Janet Attard Business Know-How window lists the topics covered by the author, Janet Attard, in her Business Know-How forum.

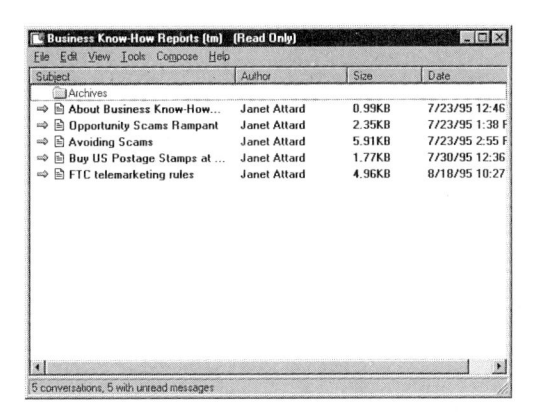

Fig. 33.11 The messages on the Business Know-How Reports bulletin board are listed in order by date.

Navigating the Network by Using the Explorer

To start MSN in the Windows Explorer mode, point to the MSN icon on the desktop and click the right mouse button. Choose Explore. When the Sign In screen appears, enter your password if necessary and then click on Connect. The MSN Central screen looks like figure 33.12. Now, take the same route through the hierarchy to get to the Home Business by using the left pane of the window. First, click on the plus sign (+) beside Categories in the left pane. Then click on the plus sign (+) beside Business and Finance. Click on the plus sign beside Small Office/Home Office. Click on the plus sign beside SOHO Advisors. At this point, you might want to make the left pane wider so you can see all the text. Click on the plus sign beside Janet Attard Business Know-How. Click Home Business BBS. The messages posted on the bulletin board appear in the right pane as shown in figure 33.13.

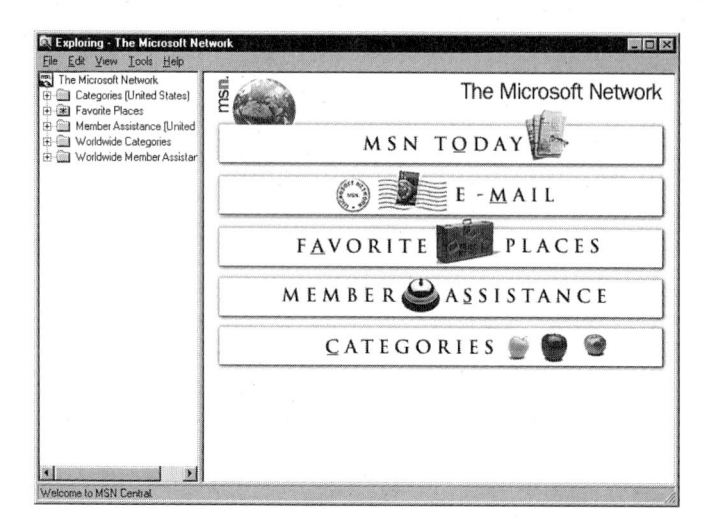

Fig. 33.12 The Windows Explorer mode for MSN uses the familiar two-pane view.

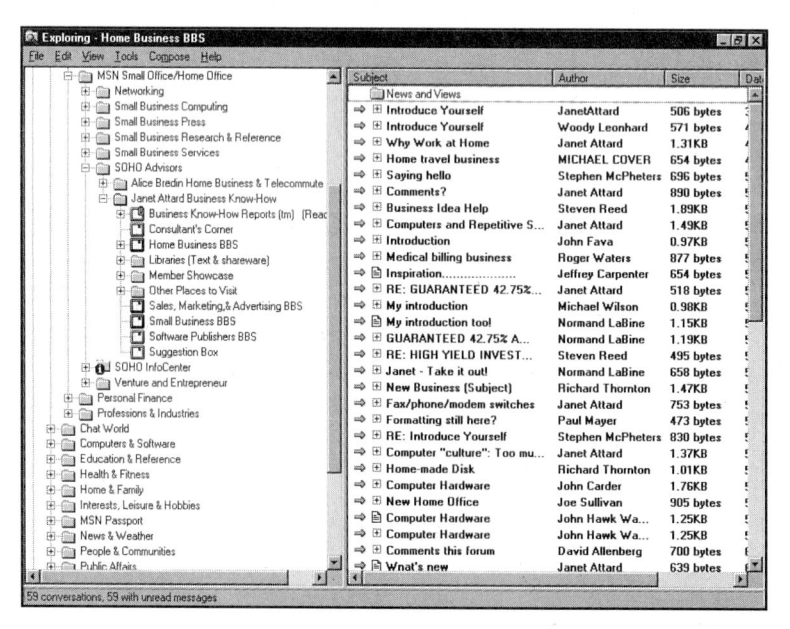

Fig. 33.13 Messages in the Home Business bulletin board appear in the right pane.

Getting General Information about Forums and Services

Because Windows 95 now uses long file names, the names of forums and services are usually very explanatory. However, if the name does not give you a good clue to the content of the folder or service, you can look at the Properties sheet. To view the Properties sheet, right-click on the icon for the folder or service and click on the Properties button in the pop-up menu. Figure 33.14 shows the Properties sheet for the Science and Technology category. It lists the scope of the forum as math, science, biology, engineering, and so on.

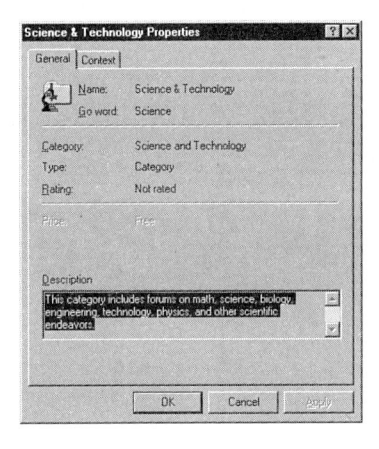

Fig. 33.14 The Properties sheet for the Science and Technology category describes the scope of the category.

Getting There the Fastest Way

Whenever you find a place or a program that you want to return to frequently, you'll want some way to get there quickly. You can do so by choosing one of three methods: adding the folder or service to Favorite Places, creating a shortcut, or using a Go word.

Adding to Favorite Places

It's simple to add an area to Favorite Places; just select the icon and click on the Add to Favorite Places button in the toolbar. The next time you return to the MSN Central screen and click on Favorite Places, you'll see an icon for the favorite place you added. When you double-click on the icon in Favorite Places, the folder or service opens. When the folder or service is open, you can click on the Up One Level button in the toolbar, to return to Favorite Places, not to the parent folder of the folder or service.

> **Note:** If you want to delete one of your favorite places, select the icon and choose File, Delete. The original icon from which the favorite place came is NOT deleted—only the favorite place icon is removed.

Creating a Shortcut

To create a shortcut, select the folder or service and choose File, Create Shortcut. A verification message appears telling you that a shortcut has been successfully created and placed on your desktop. Click on OK. Alternatively, you can just drag the icon for the MSN folder or service to the desktop.

Double-clicking the shortcut displays the MSN sign on-screen. When you click on Connect, the folder or service opens immediately, bypassing the MSN Central screen.

> **Note:** To delete a shortcut on the desktop, use one of these three methods: point to the shortcut, click the right mouse button, choose Delete, and then click on Yes; click on the shortcut to select it, and press Delete; drag the shortcut icon to the Recycle Bin icon.

Using a Go Word

A Go word takes you directly to a folder or service on the network. Go words are listed on the folder or services' Properties sheet. To see the properties sheet, select the folder or service, and click on the Properties button in the toolbar.

To use a Go word, choose Edit, Goto, Other Location. Type the Go word and click on OK.

> **Note:** When you first go to an area in MSN, the icons used in that area download to a file in Program Files\The Microsoft Network\Cache. The next time you go to that area, the service will be faster because it accesses the files in the cache.

Setting Up MSN

You have only a few options for setting up the Microsoft Network. To locate these options, choose View, Options from the menu bar. The Options dialog box displays with the General tab selected as shown in figure 33.15.

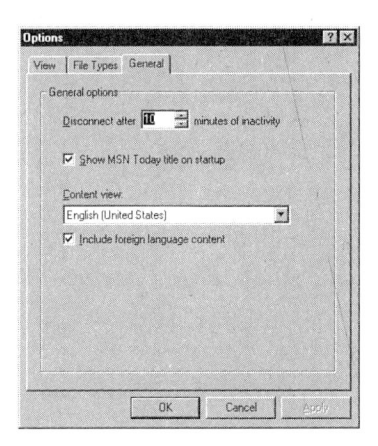

Fig. 33.15 Set the idle time in the Microsoft Network Options dialog box so that you are prompted at a reasonable time before MSN automatically disconnects.

Notice that the options include the amount of time that MSN can be inactive before you're prompted to disconnect, whether you want to see the MSN Today screen when you start MSN, what language to use for the content, and whether or not you want to include foreign language in messages, chat rooms, and so on.

Other pages in the Options sheet include View, File Types, and Folder. These properties sheets should be familiar to you because they are the same ones used by My Computer and Windows Explorer. Figure 33.16 shows the View page.

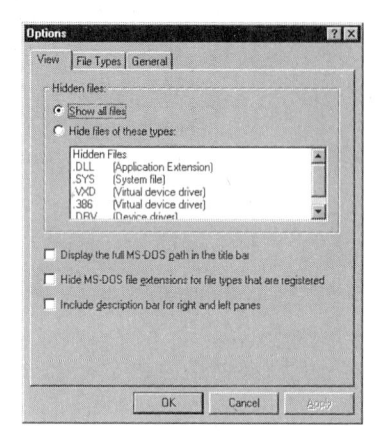

Fig. 33.16 The View page of the Options Properties sheet is just the same in MSN as it is on the Windows 95 desktop.

Exploring Kiosks

A *kiosk* is a read-only file that has information about a particular area. The file may include a summary of what is in the category, information about updates, what's new, and so on. The file is always represented by a blue circle with a white letter "i" icon. For example, the Albion Channel kiosk explains what the Albion Channel is, who is hosting the online service, and what its goals are. The Albion Channel is hosted by Albion Books, a San Francisco-based publisher of computer

810 Chapter 33: The Microsoft Network

networking books and related online services. When you open a kiosk, it opens a document in WordPad or, if Microsoft Word is installed, in Word.

Exploring Bulletin Boards

In addition to its own bulletin boards, MSN also provides access to the Internet bulletin boards (called newsgroups). MSN carries two kinds of bulletin boards:

➤ Read-only boards that do not allow you to post messages or replies.

➤ Read-write boards that allow you to post messages and replies. Most MSN bulletin boards fall into this category.

> **Tip:** You can recognize an Internet bulletin board by its name. The name (always lowercase) has a period in it, as in misc.biz.

A file library is a special kind of bulletin board that has files, such as useful software programs, that you can download. There may be a fee for copying some files. Be sure to check the file's properties before downloading to see if there is a charge.

Every MSN bulletin board has a manager who monitors and maintains the board. If you need to discuss an issue about the way a bulletin board is being run, you can send messages directly to the manager. If the bulletin boards are Internet bulletin boards, they may or may not have a manager.

Reading Messages

By default, messages are listed on a bulletin board in ascending order by date, but you can sort on any column (subject, author, size, or date) by clicking on the column heading. Click on the column heading again to sort in the other direction. Also by default, the bulletin board window shows only the messages that have accumulated since the

Exploring Bulletin Boards **811**

most recently read message. If you want to see all the messages, choose Tools, Show All Messages. The number of messages displays in the status bar.

Messages with a plus sign (+) beside them have replies. This is called a conversation or a thread. To see all the replies in a conversation, press Shift and click on the plus sign to expand the message. To expand all messages, choose View, Expand All Conversations.

To open a message on a bulletin board, double-click on the message. (You may have to scroll through the list of messages if it is long.) Figure 33.17 shows an open message. Notice that message screens have their own toolbar. See Table 33.2 for an explanation of the buttons in the toolbar.

> **Tip**: Press Home to go to the first message in the list and End to go to the last message.

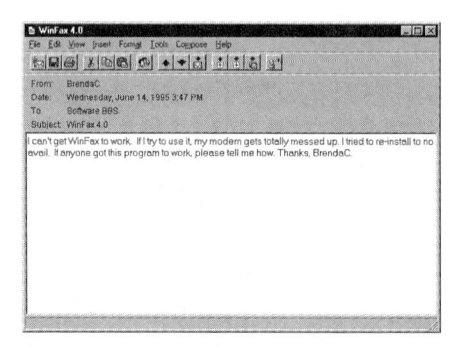

Fig. 33.17 This message is a request for help in a software forum.

Table 33.2 Buttons on Message Screens

Graphic	Name	Description
	New Message	Opens a screen for creating a new message

812   Chapter 33: The Microsoft Network

Graphic	Name	Description
	Save	Save the current message as a file
	Print	Prints the current message
	Cut	Cuts the selected text to the Clipboard
	Copy	Copies the selected text to the Clipboard
	Paste	Pastes the contents of the Clipboard at the cursor location
	Reply to BBS	Opens a screen for creating a reply to the current message
	Previous	Displays the previous message
	Next	Displays the next message
	Next Unread Message	Displays the next unread message
	Previous Conversation	Displays the previous conversation
	Next Conversation	Displays the next conversation
	Next Unread Message	Displays the next unread message
	File Transfer Status	Displays the status of a file transfer

Tip: To find out more about the sender of a message, open the message and choose Tools, Member Properties. Or just double-click on the sender's name.

Exploring Bulletin Boards **813**

Replying to a Message

You can post a reply to a message on the bulletin board, or you can send the reply directly to the author of the message by e-mail. To send a reply to the bulletin board, open the message and click on the Reply button in the toolbar (or choose Compose, Reply to BBS). Type the reply in the space provided and then click on the Post button.

To send a reply by e-mail, open the message and click on Compose, Reply by E-mail. Type the reply and click on the Send button.

To forward a message to someone else, open the message and click on Compose, Forward by E-Mail. Type the recipient's name and click the Send button.

Posting a New Message

When you want to post a new message on a bulletin board, open the board and click on the New Message button. Type the message in the space provided and click on the Send button. You may not see your message posted immediately—posting sometimes takes a few minutes.

> **Note:** The Microsoft Network does not notify you when you receive a reply to a message you've posted. You must physically check the bulletin board for a reply. If you've left several messages at different times on the same bulletin board, you can sort the messages by author so that all your messages are listed together.

Downloading Files

To download a file from a bulletin board message, follow these steps:

1. Open the message that contains the file you want to download.
2. Click on the file's icon. Choose Edit, File Object, Properties to see how large the file is, how long it will take to copy, and whether there is a fee for copying the file.

3. Click on the Download File button. The File Transfer Status dialog box appears. This dialog box has a progress bar that shows how much of the file has been downloaded and tells approximately how much time remains until the remainder of the file is downloaded.

> **Tip:** You also can copy a file by dragging the file icon in a message to your desktop or to a window or folder on your desktop.

Setting Options for Downloading

By default, files are downloaded to \Programs Files\The Microsoft Network\Transferred Files. You can specify the path for downloaded files and other options for downloading files by choosing Tools, File Transfer Status. Choose Tools again and then choose Options. The download options include:

➤ Pause files as they are queued. If this option is selected, you must select each file in the queue and click Pause to start the download. If this option is not selected, files in the queue are downloaded automatically.

➤ Delete compressed file after decompressing. Deletes zipped files after they are downloaded and decompressed.

➤ Automatically decompress files. Decompresses zipped files automatically when they are downloaded.

If you click on Browse, you can select a different folder for the default download folder.

Exploring Chat Rooms

A chat room (see figure 33.18) is an area where a "live" conversation takes place on a particular subject. However, because chat rooms are live conversations, they are just as likely to stray into other subjects as a conversation at a party. If a chat room is monitored, it has a host. The host, if there is one, is indicated in the list on the right side with a gavel icon, and he or she can designate members as participants or spectators. If there is no host, all members who join a chat room are participants. Their names are also listed on the right.

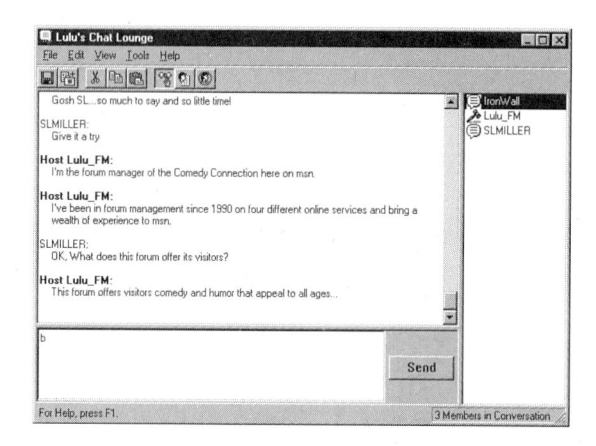

Fig. 33.18 This chat room is called LuLu's Lounge and currently has several participants as well as a host.

When you join a chat room, people who are already in the chat room see your name on the list. If a member of the chat has set the option to be notified when someone joins the chat, the member will see a message on the screen that says you've joined the conversation. To find out more about people in the chat room, you can view the person's properties. Double-click on the person's name in the list (or select the name in the list and then click on the Member Properties button).

To send a message, type the message in the lower pane and click on Send (or press Enter). If you type a message that exceeds the maximum number of characters, the computer will beep.

If a chat member sends you a message filled with question marks, the chat member is using a language (like Kanji, for example) that uses the

Double Byte Character Set (DBCS). English-speaking chat rooms use the Single Byte Character Set (SBCS). When a DBCS text string is sent into an SBCS chat session, MSN converts all the characters to question marks.

> **Note:** The DBCS was introduced to handle languages that have too many characters to be defined by the standard ASCII and ANSI character sets.

Setting Chat Options

To set the options for a chat room, choose Tools, Options. The Options dialog box has the following settings:

- Join the chat. Displays a message when a person joins the chat.
- Leave the chat. Displays a message when a person leaves the chat.
- Save chat history before clearing or exiting. Prompts you to save the chat if you try to clear or exit without saving.
- Insert blank line between messages. Inserts a blank line between the messages.

Saving a Chat

If you're involved in a particularly interesting chat or a chat with a famous person, you may want to save the chat. To save a chat, choose File, Save History. Type a name for the file and click on Save. You can start saving a chat at any point during the chat.

To make sure that you don't forget to save a chat, choose Tools, Options, and make sure that Save chat history before clearing or exiting is checked. Then if you try to exit without saving, you will be reminded to save with a prompt.

Exploring Chat Rooms **817**

Scheduled Chats with Famous People

Quite often chats will be scheduled with well-known people, including authors, actors, O.J. Simpson's attorneys, Microsoft moguls, and so forth. Look for these chats in the Calendar of Events on MSN Today as well as in the forum most closely associated with the subject. If you can't participate in the chat because it's scheduled at a bad time for you, you usually can get a transcript of the chat by downloading a file that is posted in a given area.

Sending E-Mail

To send an e-mail message, click on E-Mail on MSN Central. The Microsoft Exchange opens. Compose and send the message as you normally would. (See Chapter 34, "Using Microsoft Exchange.")

Finding Topics of Interest

The Find command, located in the Tools menu of MSN or on the Start menu, helps you locate topics of interest on the MSN. Figure 33.19 shows the Find: All MSN services dialog box. In Containing, type a keyword for the topic you want to find, such as "communications." Select one or all of the In options (Name; Topic, place and people; or Description). To select a type of service, click on the Of type drop-down list. When you've specified the search criteria, click on Find Now. The results of the search appear in the pane at the bottom of the window. To go to a location listed in the pane, double-click on the pane.

> **Note:** If you use the Find command when MSN is not open, the Sign In screen appears and you'll have to log on to MSN before the search can be started.

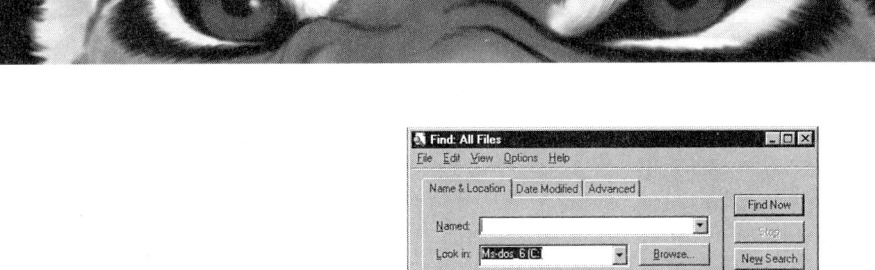

Fig. 33.19: The Find: All MSN services dialog box allows you to specify a keyword to search for on the network.

Problems You Might Encounter

If you boot Windows 95 in the Safe mode, you won't be able to connect to the MSN because the path to the MSN is not set up. The message `Modem is busy or cannot be found` will appear. To solve the problem, reboot Windows 95.

If you connect to another computer in a LAN that has MSN, you won't be able to run MSN from that computer. MSN components don't support being shared across LANs. You must run MSN locally.

Finally, don't drag the MSN icon from the desktop to the Start menu. If you do, MSN will not start, and you'll have to reinstall it.

Checking Your Bill

To see the charges on your bill, choose Tools, Billing, and Summary of Charges. Click on the Get Details button. Select the billing period and click on OK. When you're finished looking at your charges, click on the Close button.

To change the billing information, choose Tools, Billing, Payment method. Click on Name and address. Make changes as needed to your name, address, and phone number and click OK.

To change the billing method, choose Tools, Billing, Payment method. Click on Payment method. Choose the credit card you want to use from the drop-down list. Fill in the card information (card number, expiration date, and name on the card) and click on OK.

KILLER 34 WINDOWS 95

Using Microsoft Exchange

by Yvonne Johnson

Microsoft Exchange is a new network feature of Windows 95 that replaces Windows for Workgroups Mail and Microsoft Mail. It has been dubbed "the universal inbox" because you can communicate (send and receive messages) with members of a Windows workgroup as well as with many kinds of information services, including Microsoft Mail, Microsoft Fax, Internet Mail, and the Microsoft Network (MSN). In addition, Microsoft Exchange is able to communicate with other online services like CompuServe if they have MAPI (Messaging API) drivers. A MAPI driver, like a gateway, specifies all the connection and addressing settings needed to communicate with a network on one end and with Windows 95 on the other end. The MAPI drivers must be obtained from the online services; they are not provided by Microsoft.

Microsoft Exchange takes the place of third-party software that accesses, schedules, routes, and organizes e-mail. Microsoft Exchange does it all. You can send messages to anyone with an online address, schedule logons to services like CompuServe, route your mail with address books, and view various information about incoming mail.

If you install Windows 95 in the former Windows or Windows for Workgroups folder, Microsoft Exchange automatically replaces Windows for Workgroups Mail or Microsoft Mail 3.2, and all MMF files are automatically converted to the Microsoft Exchange format (PST). Additionally, if you install Windows 95 over Windows for Workgroups, the workgroup postoffice is retained for use with Microsoft Exchange.

When you install Microsoft Exchange, either during the initial installation or as an add-on later, the Microsoft Exchange Setup Wizard guides you in configuring Microsoft Exchange and setting up a profile.

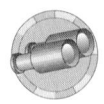

> **Note:** If you install Microsoft Exchange during the initial installation of Windows 95, the Microsoft Exchange Setup Wizard appears at the end of Setup. Unless you already have a postoffice created from Windows for Workgroups, you will not have had an opportunity to create a postoffice, and when you're prompted to enter the path for the postoffice, you'll have to cancel the wizard. When you cancel, the wizard tells you that you can set up the postoffice and then configure Microsoft Exchange any time by double-clicking on the Inbox icon on the desktop.

Setting Up the Microsoft Exchange Postoffice

The Microsoft Workgroup Postoffice Admin Wizard helps you configure the postoffice; but before you start the Wizard, you should decide where the postoffice will be stored. It can reside on any computer in the workgroup, but the computer should have at least 2M of storage space and more than 4M of memory. The disk space available on the postoffice PC should be expandable because more space will be needed as the number of users and messages increases.

Tip: If you have more than 20 users, consider using a dedicated PC for the Postoffice. If you have more than 100 users, you should upgrade to the full Microsoft Mail Server.

Creating the Postoffice

To set up a postoffice, follow these steps:

1. Open the Control Panel and double-click on the Microsoft Mail Postoffice icon. The Microsoft Workgroup Postoffice Admin Wizard appears.

2. In the Microsoft Workgroup Postoffice Admin dialog box, click on Create A New Workgroup Postoffice and then click on Next.

3. Specify where you want the workgroup postoffice to be located and click on Next.

4. The wizard displays the path and asks you to verify the path. Accept or change the path (as needed) and click on Next. The Enter Your Administrator Account Details dialog box appears.

5. Type information about the postoffice administrator, including name and mailbox name, and a password to restrict administration of the postoffice to the administrator. Click on OK to finish creating the postoffice. A message appears that advises you to make sure the folder that contains the postoffice is a shared folder. Click on OK.

Caution: If you create more than one postoffice for your workgroup, the users will not be able to send mail to each other.

Sharing the Folder That Contains the Postoffice

1. Open Windows Explorer or My Computer, point to the folder for the workgroup postoffice, and click on the right mouse button. Choose S_haring. The Sharing page of the Properties sheet appears. It looks like figure 34.1 if access control is set on user-level.

> **Note:** If no S_haring option appears on the shortcut menu, you have not enabled the network property of file sharing. Open the Control Panel, double-click on Network, click on the F_ile and Print Sharing button, and mark I want to be able to give others access to my f_iles.

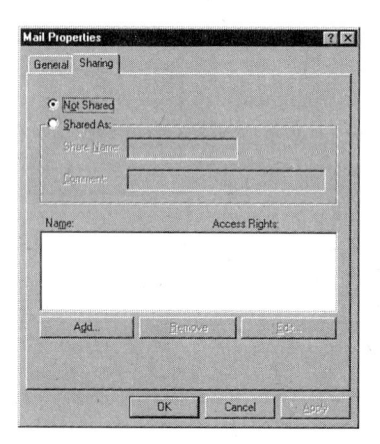

Fig. 34.1 The Sharing page of the postoffice folder Properties sheet allows you to specify the names of users if access control is set on user-level.

2. In the Sharing folder, click on S_hared As and verify the name of the postoffice in the Share N_ame field. You can also add a comment in the C_omment field. The comment shows when you open

Chapter 34: Using Microsoft Exchange

Network Neighborhood and look at a list of computers on the network (if you're using the Detail view).

3. If access control is set on share-level, choose the Access Type that you prefer.

   ➤ **Read Only**—Allows users to read and copy files.

   ➤ **Full-Access**—Allows users to read, copy, change, add, and remove files.

   ➤ **Depends on Password**—Allows you to specify different types of access for different users.

   Type the passwords that you require in the Read-Only Password field and/or the Full-Access Password field. Click OK.

   If access control is set on user-level, click on the Add button to add people to the access list.

4. Click on OK.

> **Note:** Although Microsoft Exchange can send and receive messages in the same postoffice, it cannot communicate between postoffices; that is, it cannot communicate with another workgroup. The full Microsoft Mail Server is required for this.

Setting Up Profiles for Users

Before you can use Microsoft Exchange, you must have a profile, and every person who uses the PC should have a unique profile. The profile includes the location of a user's postoffice, Personal Address Book, and Personal Information Store, and the types of services available to the user, such as Microsoft Mail, the Microsoft Network, faxing, and so on. When Microsoft Exchange is set up initially, the Setup Wizard creates a profile at the end of the setup routine; however, it is necessary to set up another profile if there is another user on the machine.

To create another profile, follow these steps:

1. Open the Control Panel and double-click on the Mail and FAX icon. The MS Exchange Settings Properties sheet appears showing the Services page, which lists the services for the default profile.

2. Click on §how Profiles. The Microsoft Exchange Profiles dialog box appears with a list of all the profiles defined on the computer. (You can see what a profile includes by selecting a profile and clicking on Properties.)

3. Click on A_dd. The Microsoft Exchange Setup Wizard starts.

4. Make selections as prompted and click on Next to advance to the next screen. The prompts vary depending on which information services you add to the profile, but they'll include user name, mailbox name, user password, and the locations of the Personal Address Book and the Personal Information Store. (The properties of all services are discussed later in this chapter if you have any questions about what settings you should make for a service.)

After the profile is created it is listed on the General page of the Microsoft Exchange Profiles dialog box. You should select the profile and click on P_roperties to configure the services included in the profile. To configure a service, select the service and then click on the P_roperties button.

Specifying Internet Mail Properties

Internet Mail is offered as a service only if you've installed the Internet Jumpstart Kit in Microsoft Plus! When you install the Internet Jumpstart Kit, a wizard helps you configure it at that time. To reconfigure the Internet Mail Properties after the installation, choose the service in the desired profile and click on the P_roperties button. The Properties sheet for Internet Mail has two pages: General and Connection.

Network Neighborhood and look at a list of computers on the network (if you're using the Detail view).

3. If access control is set on share-level, choose the Access Type that you prefer.

   ➤ **Read Only**—Allows users to read and copy files.

   ➤ **Full-Access**—Allows users to read, copy, change, add, and remove files.

   ➤ **Depends on Password**—Allows you to specify different types of access for different users.

   Type the passwords that you require in the Read-Only Password field and/or the Full-Access Password field. Click OK.

   If access control is set on user-level, click on the Add button to add people to the access list.

4. Click on OK.

> **Note:** Although Microsoft Exchange can send and receive messages in the same postoffice, it cannot communicate between postoffices; that is, it cannot communicate with another workgroup. The full Microsoft Mail Server is required for this.

Setting Up Profiles for Users

Before you can use Microsoft Exchange, you must have a profile, and every person who uses the PC should have a unique profile. The profile includes the location of a user's postoffice, Personal Address Book, and Personal Information Store, and the types of services available to the user, such as Microsoft Mail, the Microsoft Network, faxing, and so on. When Microsoft Exchange is set up initially, the Setup Wizard creates a profile at the end of the setup routine; however, it is necessary to set up another profile if there is another user on the machine.

To create another profile, follow these steps:

1. Open the Control Panel and double-click on the Mail and FAX icon. The MS Exchange Settings Properties sheet appears showing the Services page, which lists the services for the default profile.

2. Click on Show Profiles. The Microsoft Exchange Profiles dialog box appears with a list of all the profiles defined on the computer. (You can see what a profile includes by selecting a profile and clicking on Properties.)

3. Click on Add. The Microsoft Exchange Setup Wizard starts.

4. Make selections as prompted and click on Next to advance to the next screen. The prompts vary depending on which information services you add to the profile, but they'll include user name, mailbox name, user password, and the locations of the Personal Address Book and the Personal Information Store. (The properties of all services are discussed later in this chapter if you have any questions about what settings you should make for a service.)

After the profile is created it is listed on the General page of the Microsoft Exchange Profiles dialog box. You should select the profile and click on Properties to configure the services included in the profile. To configure a service, select the service and then click on the Properties button.

Specifying Internet Mail Properties

Internet Mail is offered as a service only if you've installed the Internet Jumpstart Kit in Microsoft Plus! When you install the Internet Jumpstart Kit, a wizard helps you configure it at that time. To reconfigure the Internet Mail Properties after the installation, choose the service in the desired profile and click on the Properties button. The Properties sheet for Internet Mail has two pages: General and Connection.

The General Page has options for Personal information and mailbox information. The personal information you must supply is your full name and your e-mail address. The mailbox information required is the name of the Internet mail server, your account name, and your password. You may enter either the name or the IP address of the mail server, but the mail server must be running POP3 (Postoffice Protocol version3) to receive mail, and SMTP (Simple Mail Transfer Protocol) to send mail. If the POP3 and the SMTP server are not the same, click on the Advanced Options button on the General page to specify the SMTP server.

Click on the Message Format button on the General page to specify a character set and message format. Choose Use MIME when sending messages to use a rich text format. (MIME stands for Multipurpose Internet Mail Extensions.) Click on Character Set to choose a character set. Click on OK twice to return to the General page.

The Connection Page has options for connecting to Internet Mail and transferring Internet mail. For the connection you can choose Connect using the network or Connect using the modem. If you choose, Connect using the modem, you must specify the connection name (used in Dial-Up Networking). If you want to create a new dial-up connection, click on the Add Entry button to start the Make New Connection Wizard. To edit the dial-up connection, click on the Edit Entry button. To see the login information for the dial-up connection, click on the Login As button.

To receive only the headers of mail messages, that is, the information on the top of a message, such as To, From, and Subject, choose Work off-line and use Remote Mail. If you do not choose this option, you can click on the Schedule button and set a time interval for receiving messages. To keep a log of mail sessions, click on Log File and specify the level of logging you want (basic to log time of logon and logoff and errors, or troubleshooting to record all session events) and specify a location for the log file.

Specifying Microsoft Fax Properties

To configure the Microsoft Fax Properties, choose the service in the desired profile and click on the Properties button. The Properties sheet for Microsoft Fax has four pages: Message, Dialing, Modem, and User. Most of the settings on the Dialing, Modem, and User page are taken from other setup routines.

The Message Page

The options on the Message page (see figure 34.2) include selections for the time to send the message, the message format, and the default cover page. In addition, an option allows you to edit the subject line of new faxes received.

The Time to Send options are as follows:

➤ **As soon as possible**—Sends the FAX as soon as the modem is free.

➤ **Discount rates**—Sends the FAX during the time that is specified as the discount period. To specify the discount period, click on the Set button and enter a Start and End time.

➤ **Specific time**—Specifies the exact time the FAX should be sent.

The options for the message format are as follows:

➤ **Editable, if possible**—Sends editable faxes if the recipient has Microsoft Fax. If the recipient does not have Microsoft Fax, the faxes are uneditable bitmaps.

➤ **Editable only**—Sends faxes only to recipients that have Microsoft Fax.

➤ **Not editable**—Sends bitmap faxes only.

If you want to include a cover page with a FAX, select Send cover page and then select the name of the cover page you want to use. (You also can create a new cover page, open an existing cover page, or browse the system to find a different cover page. Additionally, you can modify an existing page.)

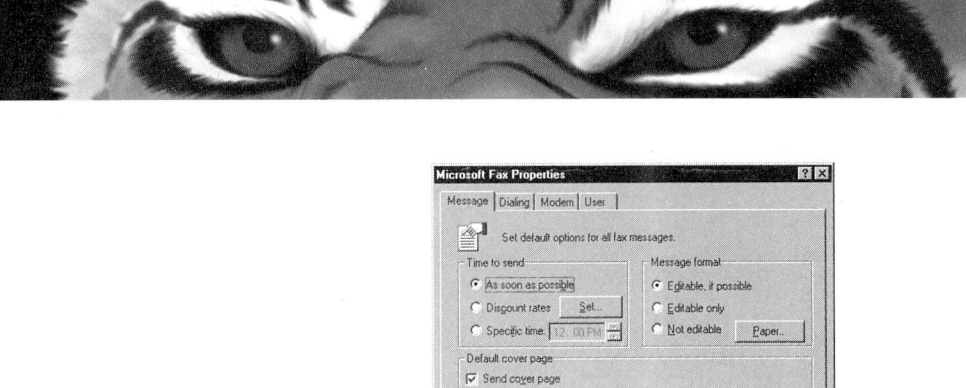

Fig. 34.2 The Message page of the Microsoft Fax Properties sheet has options for the time the message is sent, the format of the message, and the cover page.

The Paper button on the Message page displays the Message Format dialog box, which has options for the paper size, the image quality (in terms of dpi or resolution), and orientation.

The Dialing Page

The Dialing page (see figure 34.3) includes a Dialing Properties button, a Toll Prefixes button, the Number of retries (defaults to three), and the Time between retries (defaults to two minutes). If you've set up a modem for any other purpose, the Dialing Properties are already set up for you.

If you want to change any of the dialing properties, click on the Dialing Properties button, make the desired changes, and then click on OK. The Dialing Properties sheet includes these options that describe your dialing location:

➤ **I am dialing from**—Describes your location, like "Office."

➤ **The area code is**—Displays the area code of your calling area.

Specifying Microsoft Fax Properties **829**

➤ **I am in**—Specifies your country so Windows 95 can determine the international code.

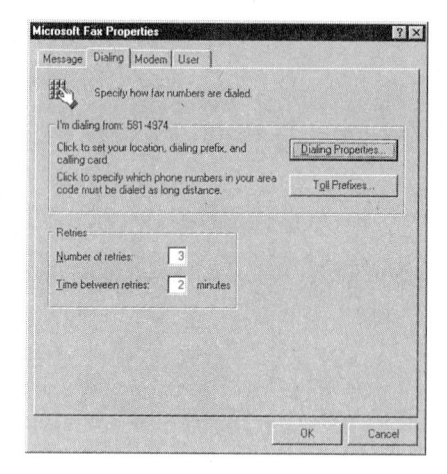

Fig. 34.3 The Dialing page gives information about your location and dialing properties as well as how many times to retry the fax and how often.

The following options describe how you dial:

➤ **To access an outside line first dial**—Specifies the number to dial for local and long distance.

➤ **Dial using Calling Card**—Specifies whether you want to use a Calling Card or not. If you select this option, the Change Calling Card dialog box appears and you can specify the Calling Card to use and the Calling Card number. (To make a change to the Calling Card information, click on the Change button to display the Change Calling Card dialog box.

➤ **This location has call waiting**—Allows you to specify the number that you can dial before making a call to disable call waiting (which can break a telecommunication connection).

➤ **The phone system at this location uses**—Provides an option for Tone dialing or Pulse dialing.

To specify the prefixes that require long-distance dialing in your area, click on T*o*ll Prefixes button. A list of local phone numbers appears in a list box on the left (see figure 34.4). Select a local phone number that requires you to dial 1 + the area code and then click on the *A*dd button. Add each local number that requires long-distance dialing and then click on OK.

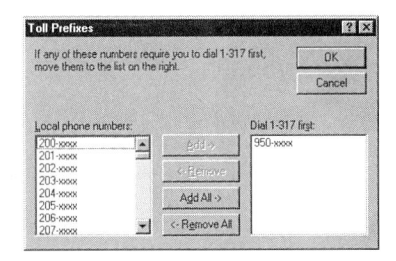

Fig. 34.4 The Toll Prefixes dialog box allows you to specify which area codes must be dialed.

The Modem Page

The Modem page (see figure 34.5) lists the available modems and allows you to select one as the active fax modem. You also can choose to let other people share your modem.

To configure a modem, select the modem in the A*v*ailable fax modems list and click on the *P*roperties button. The Fax Modem Properties sheet appears (see figure 34.6). You can set the answer mode for the fax to answer after three rings, wait until you answer it manually, or not answer at all. (You would disable answering if you were using a program that used the same COM port as the fax modem.) A slider bar allows you to set the volume of the speaker, and the *T*urn off after connected option turns the speaker off after a connection is made if it is selected. Call preferences include *W*ait for dial tone before dialing and *H*ang up if busy tone. Additionally, you can specify the number of seconds to wait for an answer after dialing.

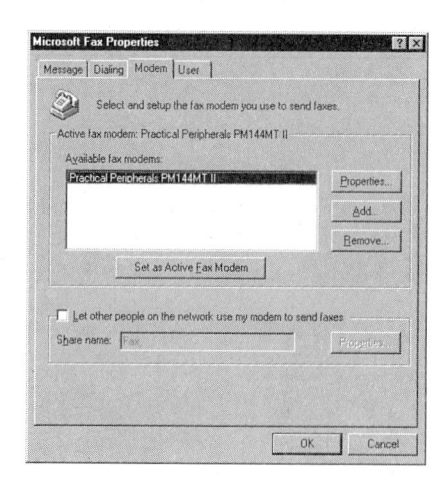

Fig. 34.5 The Modem page specifies the modem and how it is used.

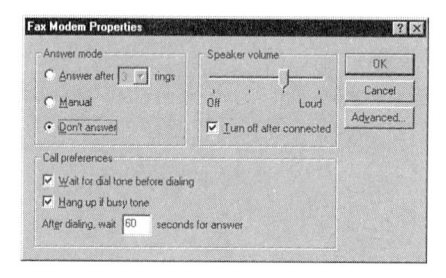

Fig. 34.6 The Fax Modem Properties sheet allows you to configure the modem.

If you click on the Advanced button, you can set these additional options:

- **Disable high speed transmission**—Disables transfers at speeds higher than 9600 baud. This option is selected only if your fax modem is unreliable at high speeds.

- **Disable error correction mode**—Disables error correction when you're sending uneditable file formats (bitmaps).

- **Enable MR compression**—Compresses fax files when they're sent. This option makes fax transmission faster, but a compressed file is more susceptible to line noise.

➤ **Use Class 2 if available**—Specifies the modem as a Class 2 device. You cannot send or receive editable faxes or use error correction if this option is selected.

➤ **Reject pages received with errors**—Will not accept pages with too many errors. The error tolerance is set in the Tolerance list box. Tolerances include high, medium, low, and very low.

If you select the option on the Modem page to let other people share your modem to send faxes, you can set the properties of sharing by clicking on the Properties button. The NetFax Properties sheet displays the same options that you see for sharing a printer or a folder. The options are determined by the type of access control that is enabled for the network (share-level or user-level).

The User Page

The User page (figure 34.7) includes information about you that you can use on the fax cover sheet. (The default cover sheets do not use every field of information on the User page, but you can add any of these fields to the default cover sheets). Additionally, you can create your own cover sheet that uses any of the fields from the User page.

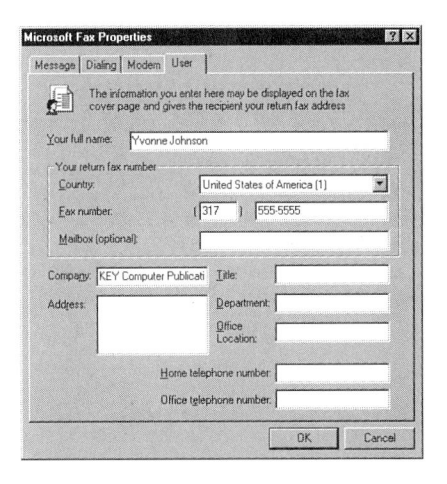

Fig. 34.7 The User page gives information about the user that may appear on the cover page of the fax.

Specifying Microsoft Mail Properties for Local Use

To configure the Microsoft Mail Properties, choose the service in the desired profile (on the General page) and click on the Properties button. The Properties sheet for Microsoft Mail has five pages for local properties: Connection, Logon, Delivery, LAN Configuration, and Log. Additionally, there are three pages for remote properties.

The Connection Page

The Connection page (figure 34.8) includes the following options:

- **Enter the path to your postoffice**—Specifies the network location of your postoffice.

- **Select how this service should connect at startup**—Specifies the way you're connected to your postoffice. If you select Automatically sense LAN or Remote, Windows 95 senses whether your computer is connected to your postoffice by a LAN connection or a modem. If your postoffice cannot detect a connection type, Microsoft Mail prompts you for one. If you select Local Area Network, you're connected via the LAN. If you choose Remote using a modem and Dial-Up Networking, you're connected via a modem, and you can store mail in your Outgoing folder and then send and receive mail when you connect to your postoffice. If you select Offline, you're not connected to the postoffice, and you cannot send or receive mail, but you can compose mail and store it in the Outbox folder.

The Logon Page

The Logon page (figure 34.9) has the following options:

- **Enter the name of your mailbox**—Specifies the name of your mailbox.

- **Enter your mailbox password**—Specifies the password. (The password does not appear, but is represented by asterisks.)
- **When logging on, automatically enter password**—Enters your password for you so you don't have to type it each time you log on. If you use this option, anyone can log on to your mailbox from your PC if you have logged on to the system already.

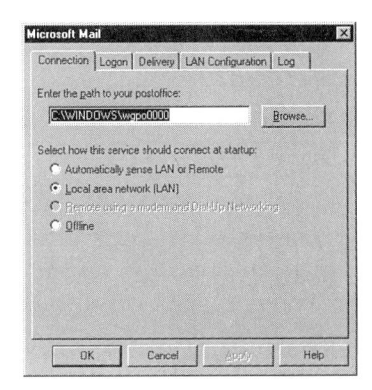

Fig. 34.8 The Connection page specifies how you're connected to Microsoft Mail.

Fig. 34.9 The Logon page specifies how you log on to Microsoft Mail.

Specifying Microsoft Mail Properties for Local Use **835**

To change the mailbox password, click on the Change Mailbox Password button. The Change Mailbox Password dialog box appears. By entering your old password and then a new password and verifying the new password, you can change your mailbox password.

The Delivery Page

The Delivery page (figure 34.10) includes these options:

- **Enable incoming mail delivery**—Delivers mail from the postoffice to your inbox.

- **Enable outgoing mail delivery**—Sends mail to your postoffice.

- **Address types**—Clicking the Address types button displays a list of mail types that you can select. Types that are not selected cannot be delivered.

- **Check for new mail every *n* minutes**—Sets the interval (in minutes) for mail delivery.

- **Immediate notification**—Notifies you of the arrival of mail and notifies the recipient of your mail's arrival (if this option is marked). This option requires NetBIOS.

- **Display Global Address List only**—Displays only the global address list, reducing the size of the name list.

The LAN Configuration Page

The LAN Configuration page (figure 34.11) has only these three options:

- **Use Remote Mail**—Displays mail headers instead of downloading mail.

- **Use local copy**—Uses the Address Book stored on your computer instead of the Address Book for your postoffice.

- **Use external delivery agent**—Uses an external delivery mail program to deliver mail.

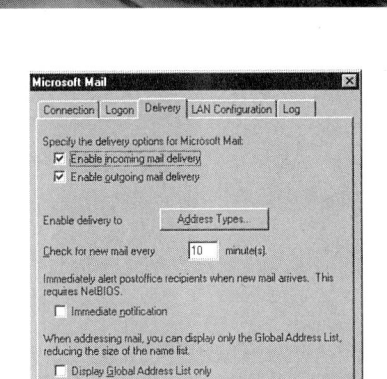

Fig. 34.10 The Delivery page specifies how mail is sent and received.

Fig. 34.11 The LAN Configuration page specifies how you use the LAN.

The Log Page

The Log page (figure 34.12) includes the name of your mailbox and your password. The option, When logging on, automatically enter password eliminates the need for you to enter your password each time you open Microsoft Exchange. The Change Mailbox Password button allows you to change your password.

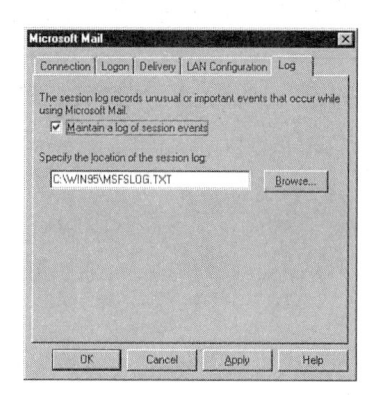

Fig. 34.12 The Log page contains settings that you use to log on.

Specifying Personal Address Book Properties

The Personal Address Book properties specify the name and path of the address book and how to display names, by first name first or by last name first. A Notes page allows you to enter any comments you may have about the address book.

Specifying Personal Information Store Properties

The properties of the Personal Information Store include the path and name of the store and the type of encryption selected when the store was created. The Properties sheet also allows you to change the password used with the store, compact the store so it takes up less disk space, and enter comments about the store.

Specifying Microsoft Network Online Service Properties

If you want to use the Microsoft Network Online Service (MSN) to exchange mail, you must establish an account with MSN. The Microsoft Network Properties sheet (figure 34.13) has two pages: the Transport page and the Address Book page. The Transport page has the following options:

- **Download mail when e-mail starts up from MSN**—Copies your e-mail to your mailbox as soon as you start Microsoft Network (MSN).

- **Disconnect after Updating Headers from Remote Mail**—Copies the subject lines of your e-mail to your Inbox and disconnects from MSN. You can screen your e-mail this way and use Remote Mail to copy only the messages you want and delete the others.

- **Disconnect after Transferring Mail from Remote Mail**—Copies your e-mail to your mailbox and disconnects. This saves you connect time because you can read your e-mail off line.

The Address Book page has only one option: Connect to MSN to check names. If you do not select this option, you can compose mail messages offline. If you select this option, when you address an e-mail message, you'll be connected with MSN so that the address can be verified (if you're using an MSN address).

Configuring the Options of Microsoft Exchange

The Microsoft Exchange has many options that control the way the program works. Options are divided among the General, Read, Send, Spelling, Services, Delivery, and Addressing pages. To see these pages, start Microsoft Exchange and choose Tools, Options.

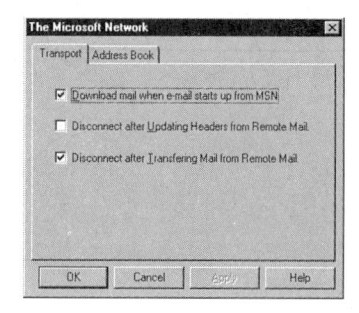

Fig. 34.13 The Transport page specifies how mail will be received from Microsoft Network.

The General Page

The General page (see figure 34.14) contains options for the general operation of Microsoft Exchange, such as what to do when new mail arrives, what to do with deleted items, what profile to use, and so on.

When new mail arrives, you can specify that the system do any or all of the following: play a sound (specified by the New Mail Notification setting in Control Panel), briefly change the pointer to the shape of an envelope, or display a notification message.

When deleting an item, you can have the system warn you before permanently deleting the item and have the Deleted Items folder emptied automatically when you exit from Microsoft Exchange.

When starting Microsoft Exchange, you can use a default profile or have the system prompt you for the profile you want to use. If several people use the same PC, you should choose Prompt for a profile to be used so that each person can use his or her own profile. You cannot switch between profiles while you're running Microsoft Exchange. You must exit and choose a different profile.

Additional options on the General page include Show ToolTips on toolbars and When Selecting, Automatically Select Entire Word (which selects an entire word when you drag the pointer).

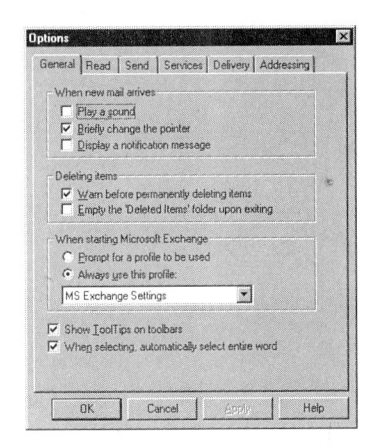

Fig. 34.14 On the General page, you can set options to control what happens when mail arrives.

> **Note:** Some users have experienced problems and degradation of speed when using a profile with two or more dial-up services. If you run into a similar situation, try creating a separate profile for each dial-up service. Then choose the Prompt for a profile to be used option on the General page so you can choose the profile you want to use.

The Read Page

The Read page (figure 34.15) sets options for reading messages and formatting replies and forwards.

The category After Moving Or Deleting An Open Item includes these options:

- **Open the item above it**—Opens the previous item in the folder.
- **Open the item below it**—Opens the next item in the folder.
- **Return To Microsoft Exchange**—Returns to the Inbox window.

Configuring the Options of Microsoft Exchange   **841**

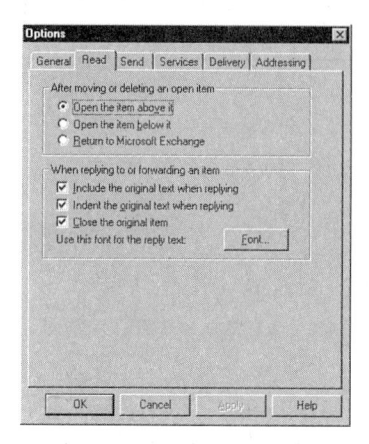

Fig. 34.15 The Read page has options that control what happens next when you are reading mail and decide to delete or move the message to a different folder.

The category When Replying To Or Forwarding An Item includes these options:

➤ **Include the original text when replying**—Includes the text of the original message below the text of your reply.

➤ **Indent the original text when replying**—Includes the text of the original message and indents it below the text of your reply.

➤ **Close the original item**—Closes the item you're replying to or forwarding.

The Font button displays the Font dialog box in which you can select the default font, size, color, and so on, for the text used in replies and forwards.

The Send Page

The Send page (figure 34.16) sets options for sending and formatting new messages.

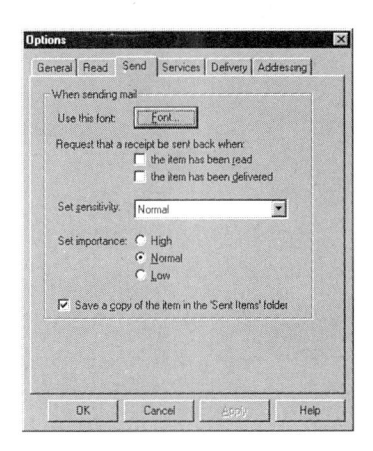

Fig. 34.16 Options on the Send page determine the appearance of messages that you sent.

The Font button displays the Font dialog box in which you can select the default font, size, color, and so on, for the text used in new messages.

You can request that a receipt be sent back to you when the item has been opened or delivered. This option provides assurance as well as documentation that your message has been received or read.

The Set sensitivity option assigns one of these sensitivity levels to outgoing mail: Normal, Personal, Private (prohibits the recipient from modifying your original message when it is replied to or forwarded), and Confidential. The sensitivity level appears in the Sensitivity column, if this column is used. The Sensitivity column will be blank for an item if the item has a normal sensitivity level.

You can set a default importance level for all outgoing mail by selecting High, Normal, or Low. If the Importance column is used, a message with a high importance level shows an exclamation point (!), and a message with a low level of importance shows a down arrow.

If you choose Save a copy of the item in the Sent Items folder, Microsoft Exchange saves a copy of every message that you send and stores it in the Sent Items folder.

Configuring the Options of Microsoft Exchange   **843**

The Spelling Page

The Spelling page specifies options for checking spelling. This page is not available unless you have a 32-bit Microsoft application installed that contains a spell checking feature.

The General options include Always <u>s</u>uggest replacements for misspelled words, and Always <u>c</u>heck spelling before sending.

When checking spelling, you can instruct Microsoft Exchange always to ignore words in <u>U</u>PPERCASE, words with <u>n</u>umbers, and the <u>o</u>riginal text in a reply or forward.

The Services Page

The Services page (figure 34.17) allows you to add and remove services to and from a profile. The services listed on the Services page depend on the services that you have installed. For example, they may include CompuServe Mail (if you have installed it with the CompuServe program that can be downloaded from the WINNEWS forum), Internet Mail (if you have installed it with Microsoft Plus!), Microsoft Fax, Microsoft Mail, Personal Address Book, Personal Information Store, and the Microsoft Network Online Service. It also allows you to copy a service in the existing profile to another profile, and it shows the properties of the services.

To add a service, click on the A<u>d</u>d button. Choose the service you want to add and click on OK. To remove a service, select the service in the list and click on the R<u>e</u>move button.

The A<u>b</u>out button displays the About Information Service dialog box, which lists the DLL files used by a service and gives other details about the service such as the description, company, version, language, creation date, and size.

The Delivery Page

The Delivery page (figure 34.18) sets the location where your incoming mail is delivered and the order in which your outgoing mail is sent.

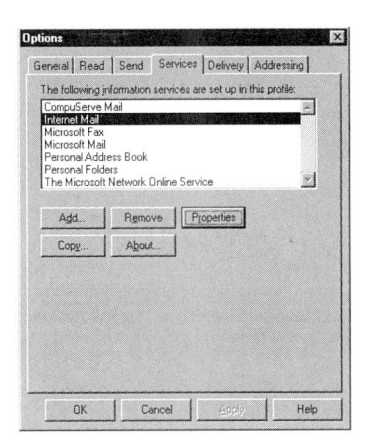

Fig. 34.17 The Services page lists all the services available to include in a profile.

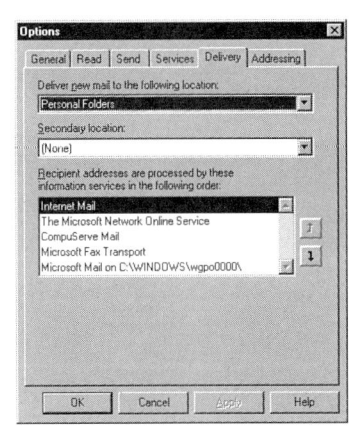

Fig. 34.18 Specify the default delivery location for mail on the Delivery page.

To specify the default location where new mail will be delivered, choose Deliver new mail to the following location and specify the location. Personal Information Store is selected by default. This location is created for you when you set up Microsoft Exchange. You can create your own Personal Information Stores, using different names, and they'll be listed in the drop-down list.

To specify an alternate location for mail delivery, choose Secondary location and specify the location.

The option, Recipient addresses are processed by these information services in the following order, lists the services in the profile in a particular order. You can change the order by clicking on the up or down arrow beside the list box.

The Addressing Page

The Addressing page (figure 34.19) sets options for using the Address Book.

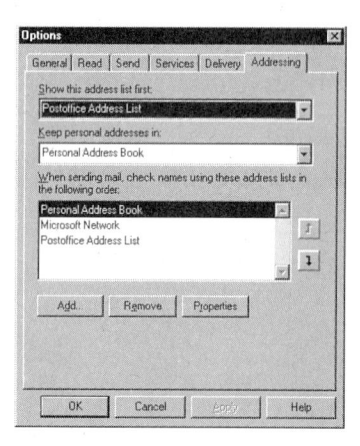

Fig. 34.19 To set defaults for your address lists, use the Addressing page.

To specify a default address list, choose a list from the Show this address list first drop-down list. To specify which address list to keep personal addresses in, choose an address book from the Keep Personal Addresses In drop-down list.

846 Chapter 34: Using Microsoft Exchange

The Addressing page determines the order of the address lists in which Microsoft Exchange will check names when sending mail. To change the order, use the up or down arrow keys next to the list box. The A<u>d</u>d button adds an address list to the list box and the Remove button removes an address list from the list. The P<u>r</u>operties button displays the properties of a list.

Using Microsoft Exchange More Efficiently

In Chapter 32, "Communicating with a Modem," you learned to use Microsoft Exchange to send and receive messages. In this chapter you'll explore two features of Microsoft Exchange that will help you use Microsoft Exchange more efficiently: the Personal Address Book and the Personal Information Store.

Using a Personal Address Book

The Personal Address Book (PAB) is an important component of Microsoft Exchange that is used when addressing mail messages. When you create the first profile, Microsoft Exchange automatically creates a Personal Address Book, which is maintained by the user, and a Postoffice Address List, which is maintained by the postoffice administrator. An address book contains names, phone and fax numbers, mailing addresses, personal contact information, and multiple electronic mail addresses (for different services). When you address a message, you can select the recipient from the address book to ensure that the message goes to the right place.

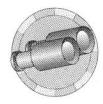

> **Note:** Users can copy addresses from the postoffice address book to their own PAB.

Selecting a Name from a PAB

When you compose a new message, you can type the name of the person you want the message to go to, but using the PAB to supply the name ensures that the message is addressed correctly. To select a name from the PAB, follow these steps:

1. Start a new message in Microsoft Exchange (Co<u>m</u>pose, <u>N</u>ew Message).

2. Click on the Address Book button on the toolbar. The Address Book dialog box appears as shown in figure 34.20.

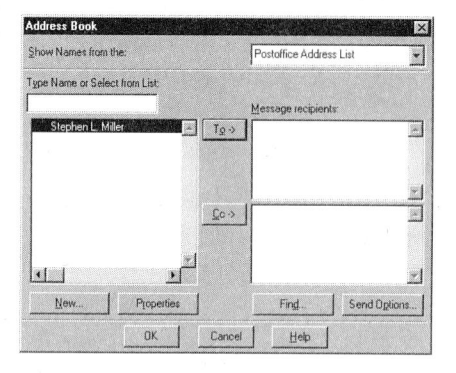

Fig. 34.20 The Address Book dialog box shows the names in the specified address list.

3. Select the address list you want from the drop-down list.

4. Click on the name you want, and then click on <u>T</u>o or <u>C</u>c. Click OK. The name appears in the To line (or Cc line) of the message.

Adding a Name to a PAB

You can add names to your PAB by using the Address dialog box, or you can add names to the PAB "on the fly" when you're creating a message. To add names to the PAB by using the Address Book dialog box, follow these steps:

1. Open Microsoft Exchange. Choose <u>T</u>ools, <u>A</u>ddress Book or click on the Address Book button in the toolbar.

2. Choose File, New Entry or click on the New Entry button in the toolbar. The New Entry dialog box appears (figure 34.21).

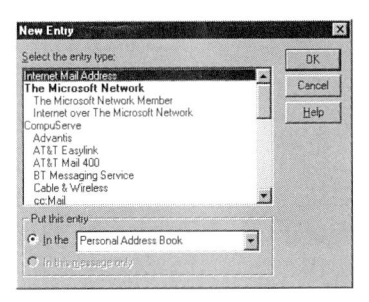

Fig. 34.21 The New Entry dialog box allows you to add new entries in an address list.

3. Choose the type of entry and the place where you want to put the entry and click on OK. An appropriate dialog box appears. For example, if you select Other Address, the dialog box shown in figure 34.22 appears.

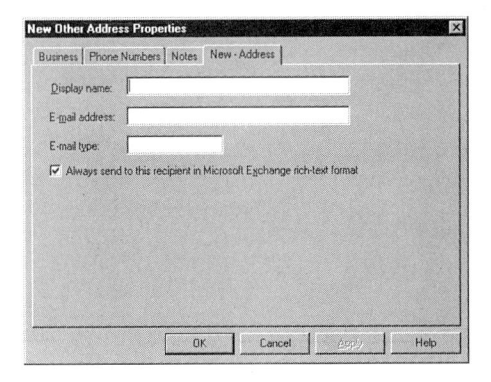

Fig. 34.22 The Other Address dialog box has the same pages as all the address lists' dialog boxes, but the first page of each dialog box has options specific to the type of address book.

4. Fill in the appropriate information on each page of the dialog box and click on OK.

Using Microsoft Exchange More Efficiently **849**

To add a new address when you're composing a message, follow these steps:

1. On the new message screen, click on the To button or the Cc button. The Address Book dialog box appears.

2. Select the address book you want to add the new name to and click on New. The New Entry dialog box appears.

3. Choose the type of entry and the place where you want to put the entry, and click on OK. An appropriate dialog box appears. Fill in the information (there may be more than one page) and click on OK.

> **Tip:** If you have an e-mail message open, you can add an address to the PAB directly from the message header by double-clicking the From name, clicking on Personal Address Book, and clicking on OK.

Keeping the PAB Up-to-Date

It is a fact of life that people leave an organization, new people are hired, and people change their phone numbers and e-mail addresses. To keep the PAB updated, follow these steps:

1. Display the Address Book dialog box in Microsoft Exchange. Double-click on the name that you need to update.

2. Make the appropriate changes and click on OK.

Using the Personal Information Stores

A Personal Information Store (PST) is a database that stores mail messages, forms, documents, and other information in these specific folders: Deleted Items, Inbox, Outbox, and Sent Items. These folders are visible in the left pane of Microsoft Exchange as shown in figure 34.23. The Personal Information Store stores messages for all the information services you're connected to through Microsoft Exchange. It functions as the user's local mailbox and organizes, sorts, and filters messages.

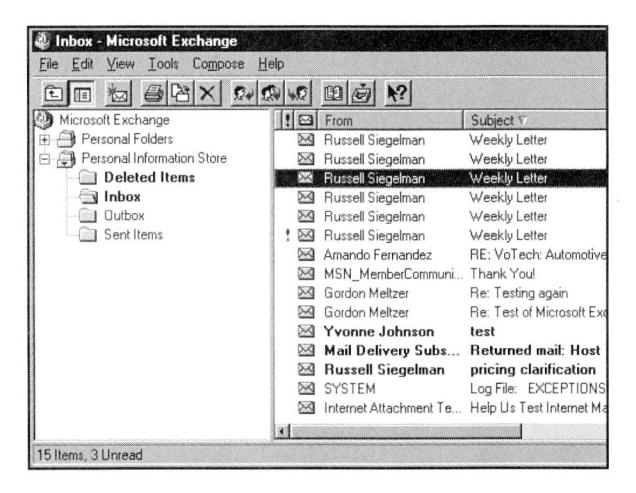

Fig. 34.23 The Microsoft Exchange displays the Personal Information Store in the left pane.

Adding Personal Folders

In addition to the PST, you can have personal folders. For example, you may want to add personal folders to hold old messages or messages from different services. To add a personal folder, follow these steps:

1. Open Microsoft Exchange and choose Tools, Services.

2. Click on the Add button. The Add Service to Profile dialog box appears.

3. Select Personal Folders and click on OK. The Create/Open Personal Folders File dialog box appears.

4. Type a name for the file and click on Open. The Create Microsoft Personal Folders dialog box appears (see figure 34.24).

Using Microsoft Exchange More Efficiently **851**

Fig. 34.24 Set the encryption method and password in the Create Microsoft Personal Information dialog box.

5. Type a name for the set of personal folders. This name will appear in the Services list and in the left pane of the Inbox.

6. Select an encryption setting. Because a personal folder file can be opened and read in other programs (even if it is password-protected) you should secure the file by encrypting the information. If you select Compressible Encryption, your files are encrypted as well as compressed. If you choose Best Encryption, your files are encrypted in an uncompressible format. This option provides the greatest degree of protection, but the files occupy more room on the disk.

7. Enter a password in the Password text box. Enter the same password in the Verify Password text box. If you want, choose Save this password in your password list. Click OK.

The new Personal Information Store appears in the left pane of Microsoft Exchange.

Arranging and Finding Messages

By default, certain categories of information are displayed for each message in the Microsoft Exchange window, and messages are arranged in order by the date received. You can choose the columns of information you want to display about messages, sort messages by the column of your choice, and find messages based on specific criteria.

Selecting the Columns of Information That Are Viewed

If you're using the default settings for Microsoft Exchange, the right pane of the Microsoft Exchange displays the following columns of information about messages: Importance, Item Type, Attachment, From, Subject, Received (date), and Size. Other columns such as Application Name, Category, Keywords, and Number of Words, also are available.

To add or remove columns from the display, choose View, Columns. The Columns dialog box appears as shown in figure 34.25. To add a column, select a column you want from the list on the left and click on Add. To remove a column, select a column from the list on the right and click on Remove. To arrange the columns in the list on the right, select the column and click on Move Up or Move Down. To set the width of each column, select the column in the list on the right and specify the number of pixels in the Width text box. If you want to return the display to the default settings, click on Reset. When you have the columns selected and arranged the way you want them, click on OK.

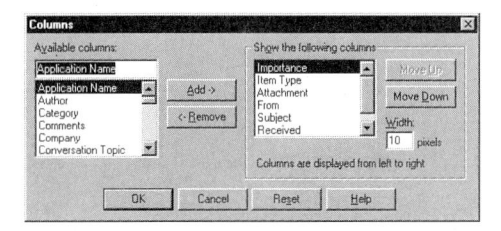

Fig. 34.25 The Columns dialog box lists the available columns on the left and the columns that you want to display on the right.

Sorting the Information

To sort messages by a particular column, click on the heading for the column. That column will display a triangle that points up (if the sort is ascending) or down (if the sort is descending). To change the order of

Arranging and Finding Messages **853**

the sort, point to the column heading, click on the right mouse button, and choose the sort that you want.

Finding Messages

The Find dialog box finds messages based on criteria that you specify. To find a particular message, follow these steps:

1. In the Microsoft Exchange window, choose Tools, Find. The Find dialog box appears (see figure 34.26).

2. Click Folder to specify a different location for Look in.

3. Specify the criteria necessary to find the messages including From, Sent To, Sent directly to me, Copied (Cc) to me, Subject, and Message body.

4. Click on Advanced to specify additional criteria such as size, date, importance, sensitivity, unread items, items with attachments, and items that do not match the criteria. Click on OK to close the Advanced dialog box.

5. Click Find Now to activate the search.

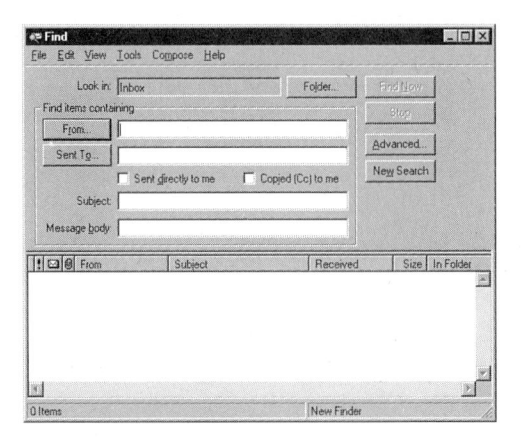

Fig. 34.26 The Find dialog box can find messages based on many different criteria.

854 Chapter 34: Using Microsoft Exchange

Messages that meet the criteria appear in the bottom pane of the dialog box. You can open a message displayed in this pane by double-clicking on it.

Attaching Files, Messages, and Objects to Messages

A common practice among users is to send files to each other. Attaching a file to a message is one way to send a file; however, if most of the messages sent on a network have files attached to them, large amounts of disk space will be used. To conserve disk space, it is better to link a file to a message. A link is a pointer to the file that works like a shortcut. The user can double-click on the pointer to open the file. In addition to attaching files, you can attach other messages as well as objects to messages.

To attach a file to a message, by simple attachment or by link, follow these steps:

1. In the message screen, choose Insert, File. The Insert File dialog box appears. (See figure 34.27.)

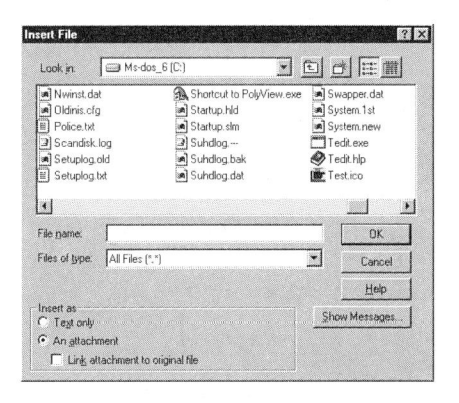

Fig. 34.27 The Insert File dialog box allows you to attach or link a file to a message.

Arranging and Finding Messages **855**

2. Double-click on the folder that contains the file, and then click on the file you want to attach.

3. Click An <u>a</u>ttachment if you want to attach the file.

   If you want to link the file, click on An <u>a</u>ttachment and Lin<u>k</u> attachment.

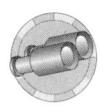

> **Note:** To attach a message link to a file, the file must be in a shared folder on a computer that is part of the network.

4. Click on OK. An icon appears in the body area of the message.

> **Note:** You also can attach a file to a message by dragging the file to the message, if the file supports OLE.

To attach an existing message to a new message, follow these steps:

1. In the message screen, choose <u>I</u>nsert, <u>M</u>essage. The Insert Message dialog box appears. (See figure 34.28.)

2. Double-click on the folder that contains the message you want to attach, and then click on the message you want to attach.

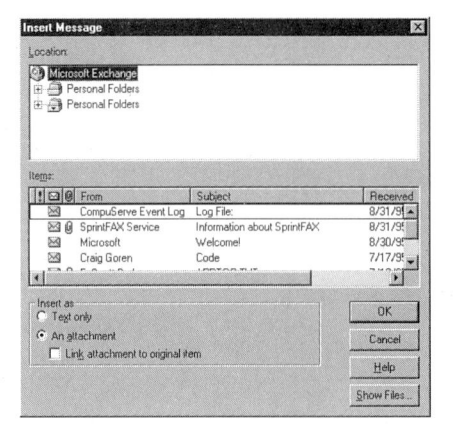

Fig. 34.28 The Insert Message dialog box allows you to attach or link existing messages.

856 Chapter 34: Using Microsoft Exchange

3. Click on An **a**ttachment if you want to attach the message.

   If you want to link the message, click on An **a**ttachment and Lin**k** attachment.

4. Click on OK. An envelope icon appears in the body area of the message.

To insert an object in a message, follow these steps:

1. In the message screen, choose **I**nsert, **O**bject. The Insert Object dialog box appears. (See fig. 34.29.)

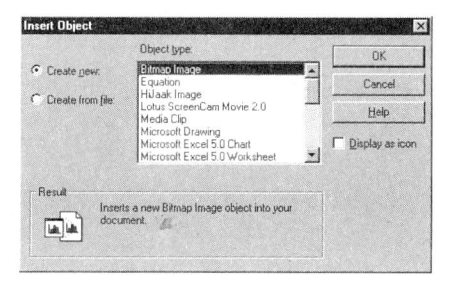

Fig. 34.29 The Insert Object dialog box allows you to embed or link an OLE object.

2. Choose Create **n**ew, select an object type from the list, and click on OK. The program that creates the object opens. Create the object and choose **F**ile, E**x**it & Return to Mail Message.

   Or choose Create from **f**ile. Specify the file and, if desired, choose **L**ink. Click on OK.

KILLER 35 WINDOWS 95

Internet Communications

by Yvonne Johnson

The Internet is undoubtedly the most famous network in the world today. It has tens of thousands of computers connected to each other using a common protocol called TCP/IP (Transmission Control Protocol/Internetwork Protocol). Some estimates say that over 30 million users have e-mail addresses on the Internet. The fact that the Internet has evolved to its current state without central planning or a controlling body is truly mind boggling.

What Can You Do on the Internet?

You can find every imaginable kind of information on the Internet, from cookie recipes to the North American Free Trade Agreement. You can even contact Rush Limbaugh, but rumor has it he never reads mail from an Internet address. (I sent him a message on CompuServe, but he didn't answer that either.) The problem is, how do you access all the information you desire on the Internet?

The information flows across the Internet as e-mail, in newsgroups and mailing lists, in World Wide Web documents, in FTP files, and via Telnet. First we'll examine each of these methods of acquiring information. Later in the chapter, you will learn exactly how Windows 95 fits into the picture.

E-Mail

E-mail is the most popular activity on the Internet. To send and receive mail on the Internet, you must have an Internet e-mail address.

E-mail addresses use the Domain Name System (DNS). A typical e-mail address from another country might look like this:

mhampton@hum.rhodes.edu.uk

The address begins with the user's or organization's name (mhampton). The at sign (@) connects the name of the user with the identification of his location. This particular address has two descriptors and two extensions. The descriptors are *hum* (humanities department) and *rhodes* (Rhodes College); the second descriptor (rhodes) is the domain. The two extensions are *edu* (educational institution) and *uk* which denotes the country (United Kingdom). E-mail addresses in the United States usually omit the country extension. Table 35.1 lists several of the most commonly used extensions and their descriptions.

Table 35.1 Commonly Used Extensions

Extension	Meaning
ca	Canadian domain
com	commercial organization
edu	educational institution
fr	French domain
gov	U.S. government network or organization
int	international organization
mil	U.S. Department of Defense network or organization

Extension	Meaning
net	network or organization running a network on the Internet
org	research or non-profit organization
uk	United Kingdom domain
us	United States domain

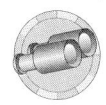

Note: Don't send unsolicited e-mail messages. Many Internet users must pay a fee for each piece of e-mail they receive.

An e-mail address, also known as a DNS address, is really an alias for a numeric string that is used to connect to the Internet. DNS numbers are kept in databases, and DNS servers translate a DNS address into the numeric string called an IP address. An IP address might look like this:

198.79.88.20

Newsgroups and Mailing Lists

Newsgroups, collectively referred to as *USENET*, are similar to Microsoft Network bulletin boards. The USENET newsgroups are all loosely organized around seven topics: comp (computer), misc (miscellaneous), news (news), rec (recreation), sci (science), soc (social), and talk (talk). These seven hierarchies follow a specified set of rules, and you should not start posting to these newsgroups until you become familiar with their rules.

In addition to USENET newsgroups, there are other newsgroups (the most notable of which is the alt group) that follow very different rules from each other and from USENET newsgroups.

Newsgroup messages can include attachments, which are binary files, but the attachments must be encoded when they are sent and decoded when they are received. Two popular programs used for encoding and decoding attachments are UUencode and UUdecode. Both of these files can be downloaded from various sites on the Internet as well as from MSN.

Mailing lists are managed by list servers. When a member of the mailing list sends an e-mail message, the list server sends the e-mail message to every member on the mailing list. To join a mailing list, you must send an e-mail that includes your Internet e-mail address. The exact syntax of the message varies with the list server. When your message has been successfully accepted, you'll receive a reply that confirms your acceptance and contains valuable information about how to *unsubscribe* to the list. Be sure to keep this information on file for future reference. You may tire of the list or find that you have subscribed to a list that does not have the content you want.

> **Note:** Mailing list members can receive hundreds of e-mail messages a day.

World Wide Web

The World Wide Web (WWW) is a network of servers that provide multimedia "publications" that use hypertext links to jump from file to file. You can be in a file located on a server in the United States, click a hypertext link (which might be an underlined word, an icon, a graphic, and so on), and jump to another file located on a server in a country that is on the other side of the globe.

WWW servers use HTML (Hypertext Markup Language) documents that are very similar to Windows help files in the way they work. For example, when you click on an underlined word or phrase in a help file, you jump to the help topic that explains that word or phrase. The underlined word is the hypertext link.

WWW was started by CERN European Particle Physics Laboratory, and their Web pages are a great source of information about the WWW itself (http:www.cern.ch). *PC Magazine* is another example of a WWW server on the Internet (http:www.pcmag.ziff.com/~pcmag).

To use the WWW you have to have a tool called a *web browser*. Mosaic, one of the first Web browsers that is still widely used, was developed by the National Center for Supercomputing Applications at the University of Illinois at Champaign-Urbana. This program has probably done more to popularize the Internet than any other program. Mosaic accesses WWW as well as other services on the Internet. It is free and can be downloaded from many sites on the Internet as well as MSN. Many commercial programs, like Internet in a Box, include enhanced versions of Mosaic.

Another popular Web browser, Netscape, is also available for downloading from many sites. This Web browser offers more features than the original Mosaic and has become widely used.

Web sites have a home page that is displayed when you connect with the site. Each WWW home page has a unique Uniform Resource Locator (URL) that serves as its address. For example, the URL for the Macmillan home page is http://www.mcp.com.

Gopher

The Gopher system was developed by the University of Minnesota. A Gopher is a hierarchical menu system that tunnels deeper and deeper into the Internet. The top level Gopher at the University of Minnesota is gopher.micro.mnu.edu. Many Gopher servers have joined the ranks of the university, including the InterNIC gopher (gopher.internic.net), the official source of information about the Internet.

Windows 95 does not provide Gopher software, but you can download many different Gophers from various places. The University of Minnesota is a good place to find Gopher software.

Veronica (Very Easy Rodent-Oriented Netwide Index to Computerized Archives) is a utility program that searches Gopher sites. A Veronica search produces a menu of Gopher items, each of which is a direct pointer to a Gopher data source. Because Veronica is accessed through a Gopher client, it is easy to use, and gives access to all types of data supported by the Gopher protocol.

The following is a list of Gopher sites accessible to the public at large (these addresses are subject to change or termination):

Hostname	IP Address	Area
consultant.micro.umn.edu	134.84.132.4	North America
ux1.cso.uiuc.edu	128.174.5.59	North America
panda.uiowa.edu	128.255.40.201	North America
gopher.msu.edu	35.8.2.61	North America
gopher.ebone.net	192.36.125.2	Europe
gopher.sunet.se	192.36.125.10	Sweden
info.anu.edu.au	150.203.84.20	Australia
tolten.puc.cl	146.155.1.16	South America
ecnet.ec	157.100.45.2	South America
gan.ncc.go.jp	160.190.10.1	Japan

FTP Sites

FTP (File Transfer Protocol) refers to a protocol as well as to a program that uses the protocol to transfer files. The Internet has thousands of anonymous servers with a variety of files available for downloading. The servers are called anonymous because the user is allowed to log on as "anonymous" and use his or her e-mail address as a password.

> **Caution:** Lots of freeware and shareware is downloadable from FTP sites, but many are not checked for viruses, so be careful.

To use FTP sites effectively, you must have an FTP program (one is supplied by Windows 95). The commands used by the FTP program are very similar to UNIX commands. If you're not familiar with UNIX commands, you can display the list of commands that FTP uses once you have started FTP. (See "Using FTP" later in this chapter for more information about FTP commands.)

Unless you know something about the FTP site and the files that exist there, it helps to use a tool, such as Archie, that searches for the information you want. FTP sites are indexed by title and keyword on a regular basis, sometimes every day. Archie searches these indexes for the files you want based on the title or key word that you specify.

Here are some FTP sites you might want to explore:

Microsoft: ftp.microsoft.com

University of Illinois: ftp.ncsa.uiuc.edu

Indiana University: ftp.cica.indiana,edu

Project Gutenberg: ftp.mrcnet.cso.uiuc.edu

InterNIC: ftp.internic.net

Telnet

Telnet is probably the least exciting feature of the Internet. This service allows you to log on to a remote network using terminal emulation (most commonly VT100 and VT320). Once logged on, you can perform any task that the network can perform.

WAIS

WAIS (Wide-Area Information Server) is a server system used for searching databases (referred to as sources) that contain mostly text, but may also contain sound, pictures, or video. You can find WAIS servers listed on many Gopher menus. The WAIS databases may be organized in different ways, using various query languages and syntax, but using a WAIS client, the user can type natural language queries to find relevant documents.

Connecting to the Internet

Before examining the way Windows 95 connects to the Internet, let's look at the traditional ways of connecting to the network. There are three possibilities; you can connect via:

- a network
- a SLIP/PPP connection
- an online service

Network Connection

A network is the fastest and most complete type of connection to the Internet. It is also the most expensive. For a dedicated 56 Kbps line, prices start at about $2,000 per month. (Prices vary by bandwidth, or speed, of connection.) LAN-based connections also require routers at the local site.

With a network connection, your network is connected directly to the Internet using TCP/IP. Your computer must be connected to your network with a network adapter card and be running either ODI (Open Data-link Interface) or NDIS (Network Driver Interface Specification) packet drivers. (Both drivers allow multiple transport protocols to run on one network card simultaneously.) If you are running any version of Windows, you need Winsock support. Winsock is an API that allows Windows applications to run over a TCP/IP network.

With a network you have access to everything the Internet has to offer.

SLIP/PPP Connection

With a SLIP (Serial Line Interface Protocol) or PPP (Point-to-Point Protocol) connection, you must connect with a service provider that lets you dial into a SLIP or PPP server. Service providers generally include service for networks as well as stand-alone PCs. Prices are based on bandwidth and the hours of usage.

For a stand-alone PC using Dial-Up Networking, the fee for using a service provider will range from about $10 to $150 a month (based on the number of hours of usage and the locality). The bandwidth for this kind of service is typically 14.4K to 56K. If you have an ISDN adapter, you can connect at a bandwidth of 64K, and you might pay $50 to $300 a month depending on the number of hours of usage and the locality.

For a network connection the prices may range from $200 a month to $2000. Most network connections are full-time—that is, not based on hours of usage—and the bandwidth may range from 64K to 128K to a T-1 connection, which is 25 times faster than 64K.

> **Note:** Microsoft plans to provide PPP connection through the Microsoft Network, but rates and speeds are unknown at this writing.

With a SLIP or PPP connection you are a full peer on the Internet and have access to everything the Internet has to offer. The only drawback is speed. A direct connection is much faster than a SLIP or PPP connection. Modems below the speed of 14.4 Kbps are too slow to use on the Internet.

> **Note:** SLIP and PPP providers are easy to find in magazines about the Internet. You can also download a list of service providers called PDIAL from many Internet sites. Of course, if you can't get on the Internet, you can't download the list, so have a friend do it for you or see if your online service has it.

Online Connection

If you connect to the Internet with an online service, all you need is a modem and an account with an online service. All the major online services—America Online, CompuServe, Delphi, GEnie, Prodigy, and so on—give you access to the Internet. It varies with the online service, but many give you access to WWW, e-mail, FTP, Telnet, and Gopher. Charges for these services also vary.

Connecting to the Internet with Windows 95

Now that you know the three ways to connect to the Internet, all you have to know is that Windows 95 uses all three types of connections. You can install TCP/IP (it's supplied with Windows 95) and a network adapter, connect to a network that is connected to the Internet, and you're off and running. Secondly, you can install TCP/IP, SLIP or PPP software (supplied by Windows 95), and Dial-Up Networking (also supplied by Windows 95), subscribe to a SLIP or PPP service provider, and you're off and running again. Finally, if you are connected to the Microsoft Network, you don't have to do anything special to connect with the Internet, but you are limited to e-mail and newsgroup services (at this time). Microsoft plans to add other Internet services in the future.

Installing and Configuring TCP/IP

Installing TCP/IP is the first step you must take toward setting up a connection with the Internet, regardless of whether you'll be connecting through your network or though Dial-Up Networking on a stand-alone PC. Windows 95 provides TCP/IP, so there is nothing extra you have to purchase. To install TCP/IP, follow these steps:

1. Open the Control Panel and double-click the Network icon. Then click the Add button. The Select Network Component Type dialog box displays. (See figure 35.1.)

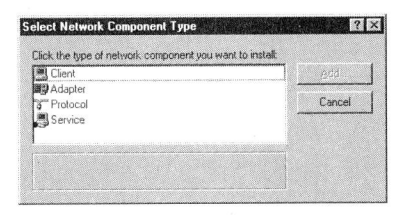

Fig. 35.1 The Select Network Component Type lists the network components.

2. Double-click Protocol. The Select Network Protocol dialog box displays as shown in figure 35.2.

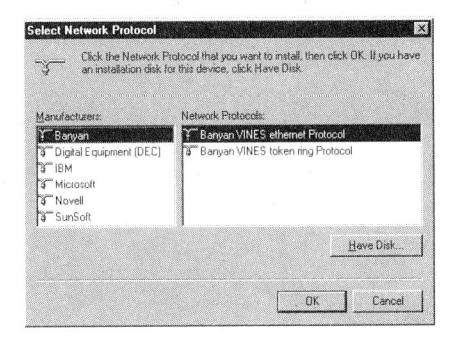

Fig. 35.2 The Select Network Protocol dialog box lists the network protocols that Windows supports.

3. In the Manufacturers box, click Microsoft, and click TCP/IP in the Network Protocols list. Click OK.

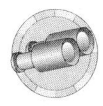

> **Note:** Make sure that the TCP/IP protocol is bound to the dial-up adapter or network card by checking the Binding page of the adapter's Properties sheet.

Installing and Configuring TCP/IP **869**

Understanding the Properties of TCP/IP

If installing the TCP/IP were all you had to do to connect to the Internet, life would be so good. Unfortunately, you also have to configure TCP/IP. This is where things might begin to get a little complicated, so dig in. Before going through the steps to configure the properties of TCP/IP, you must know what information you need for proper configuration.

To configure TCP/IP you have to configure a DNS server, and possibly an IP address, a subnet mask IP address, and a gateway IP address. You will need an IP address, subnet mask IP, and a gateway IP only if your provider does not have Dynamic Host Configuration Protocol (DHCP). With DHCP, the provider can dynamically assign you these three addresses each time you connect to the Internet. Regardless of whether or not the addresses are assigned dynamically, the TCP/IP protocol relies on the IP address, subnet mask IP, and gateway IP to receive and deliver data packets between hosts (nodes on the same network).

IP Addresses

Every node on a TCP/IP network has a unique IP address. Earlier you learned that an e-mail address is really an alias for a numeric string which is the IP address. An IP address is a 32-bit address. The four 8-bit bytes are represented in dotted decimal notation like this:

    102.54.94.97

Each octet (byte) of the address is represented by its decimal value and separated from the other octets with a period. The IP address contains two pieces of information: the network ID and the host ID. Here network is defined as a group of computers and other devices that are all located on the same logical network (which may be interconnected by routers). Host is defined as any device attached to the network that uses TCP/IP. A unique network ID must be obtained from the InterNIC. The unique host IDs are assigned by the network administrator.

The first octet in the IP address always refers to the network ID. The remaining octets may refer to the network ID or the host ID as explained in Table 35.2.

The first octet in the IP address identifies the class of the network as defined by the InterNIC. See Table 35.2. Class A, the class that contains the largest networks, has only 126 IDs reserved by the InterNIC. IBM and Hewlett-Packard both have addresses in this "elite neighborhood." Each network in a class A network can have 16,777,214 hosts per network. Class B has 16,384 available network addresses, with 65,534 hosts available per network. Class C has 2,097,151 network addresses available, with 254 hosts per network.

Table 35.2 IP Addresses

Class	Values of 1st Octet	NetworkID	Host ID
A	1-126	First octet	Remaining 3 octets
B	128-191	First 2 octets	Remaining 2 octets
C	192-223	First 3 octets	Remaining 1 octet

DNS Server

You also learned earlier that e-mail addresses are translated into numbers by DNS servers. The DNS server itself has a DNS address. For example, the server named rex.isdn.net has the numeric address of 198.79.88.10. When you configure the DNS server in the TCP/IP Properties sheet, you need to know both the server name and the numeric character string for the DNS server.

Subnet Mask IP

A subnet mask distinguishes the network ID portion of an IP address from the host ID portion so that recipients of IP packets can recognize a node on the same system. Subnet masks are also used to split network addresses into subnetwork addresses so you do not have to apply for additional network IDs. For example, if the logical network is composed of 12 LANs, you can apply for one network ID and then subdivide the network ID with subnets to provide 11 more addresses.

Gateway IP

A gateway is a connection between two networks that would otherwise be incompatible, such as between a LAN and a WAN. The gateway IP is just like the IP address in that it is a 32-bit address that uses dotted decimal notation.

Configuring TCP/IP

Regardless of whether you're connecting to the Internet via a network or a dial-up connection, you must configure TCP/IP. Before setting the properties of TCP/IP, make sure you know the following information:

- What is the name and IP address of the DNS server?
- Does the DNS server use DHCP?
- If the DNS server does not use DHCP, what is the IP address, the subnet address, and the gateway address?

Additionally, if you'll be connecting to the Internet via Dial-Up Networking, you need to obtain the following information from your service provider:

- access phone number
- logon name
- logon password

Configuring DNS

To configure DNS, open the Network Properties sheet and display the properties for TCP/IP. Click the DNS Configuration tab to display the properties page and follow these steps:

1. Choose Enable DNS unless you are on a network that uses a WINS (Windows Internet Naming Service). If your network uses a WINS, choose Disable DNS and click OK. Then click the WINS Configuration tab and see "Configuring the WINS" later in this section.

2. Type the name for the Host (the name of your computer) and the name for the Domain (the name of the DNS server).

3. Type the address of the DNS server and click Add. The address appears in the list box. See figure 35.3.

4. If additional server addresses are available, type each one, clicking Add for each. (Server addresses should be entered in the same order in which you want the servers to be searched.)

5. If you have a domain suffix, type it and click Add. (A domain suffix is used in conjunction with your host name to further identify your computer.)

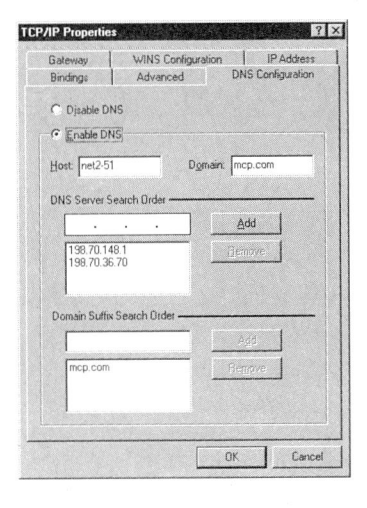

Fig. 35.3 The DNS configuration shows that the host name is "yvonne" and the domain name is "isdn.net."

Installing and Configuring TCP/IP **873**

Configuring the IP Address

The IP address is specified on the IP address page of the TCP/IP Properties sheet. Display the page (see figure 35.4) and follow these steps if you are connected to a server that does *not* use the DHCP protocol:

1. Choose Specify an IP Address.
2. Type the IP Address (given to you by your service provider).
3. Type the Subnet Mask (given to you by your service provider).

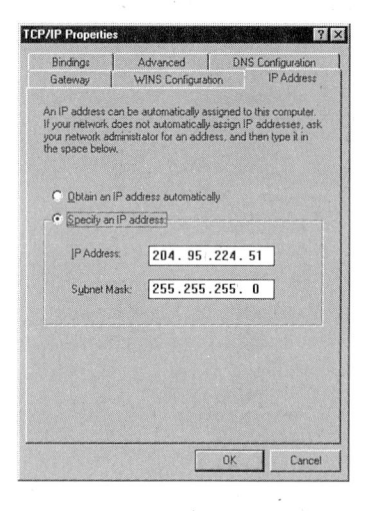

Fig. 35.4 The IP Address page allows you to specify the IP address and the subnet mask.

If you use a server that dynamically assigns IP addresses and subnet masks, choose Obtain an IP address automatically on the IP page.

Additional TCP/IP Settings for a Network

If you're connecting to the Internet via a network, you may also have to configure the Gateway and the WINS (Windows Internet Naming Service). If you are using Dial-Up Networking, you do not need to be concerned with a gateway or WINS.

Configuring the Gateway

You need to configure the gateway **only** if you are using a server that does not have DHCP. Click the gateway page of the TCP/IP Properties sheet, type the gateway address, and click Add. Since this is the last setting you have to make in the TCP/IP Properties sheet, click OK to close the TCP/IP Properties sheet and then click OK again to close the Network Properties sheet.

Configuring the WINS

You need to configure the WINS **only** if your network uses WINS, which is similar to a DNS server. WINS requires that one or more Windows NT servers be configured as WINS servers, and that they contain a dynamic database for mapping computer names to IP addresses. DNS servers are generally used for Internet communications rather than WINS servers, but you can use either.

Click the WINS Configuration tab and choose Enable WINS Resolution or Use DHCP for WINS Resolution if you have this protocol to supply the WINS configuration dynamically. If you choose Enable WINS Resolution, then enter the address of the primary and secondary WINS servers. Enter the Scope ID, if there is one. A scope ID identifies a group of computers on the network that recognize a registered NetBIOS name. These computers can "hear" each others' messages. When finished, click on OK.

Installing and Setting Up Dial-Up Networking

If you're using a network, no other configuration is needed. You're ready to use the Internet with whatever tools you have installed on your system. However, if you are using Dial-Up Networking, you have more configuration to do. Your next step in connecting with the Internet is configuring Dial-Up Networking.

Installing Dial-Up Networking

If you have not installed Dial-Up Networking, follow these steps to do so:

1. Open the Control Panel and double-click Add/Remove Programs.
2. Click the Windows Setup tab.
3. Click Communications and then click Details.
4. Click Dial-Up Networking and click OK. Click OK again. If prompted, insert the Windows installation disk or CD.

Creating a Connection

Once Dial-Up Networking is installed, follow these steps to create a new connection for the Internet:

1. Double-click My Computer and then double-click the Dial-Up Networking icon.
2. Double-click Make New Connection. The Make New Connection Wizard starts (see figure 35.5).

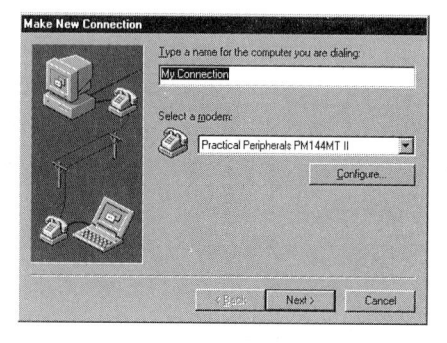

Fig. 35.5 The Make New Connection Wizard displays the modem that is installed.

3. Type a name for the connection (like Internet) and click Next.
4. Type the area code (if not a local number) and the phone number given to you by the service provider.
5. Choose the correct country and click Next.

6. Click Finish. The new connection displays an icon in the Dial-Up Networking window.

This may be all you need to do to configure Dial-Up Networking, but if your service provider requires encrypted passwords, you will have to do some further configuration.

Configuring Encrypted Passwords

Encrypted passwords are required by servers that do not support the Password Authentication Protocol (PAP) or the Challenge-Handshake Authentication Protocol (CHAP). To enable encrypted passwords, right-click the dial-up icon for the Internet and choose Properties. Click the Server Type button to display the screen shown in figure 35.6. Choose Require encrypted password and click OK to close the Server Types dialog box. Then click OK to close the Properties sheet.

Note: If you are using a PPP provider, you will notice on the Server Type dialog box that the option Enable software compression is selected by default. This option specifies that your computer will try to compress information before sending it, but compression will occur only if the computer you are connecting to is using a compatible compression program. Compressing data improves the throughput and transfer times because it reduces the amount of information that needs to be transmitted over the modem.

Note: If you need to enter commands to control your modem, either before or after you dial your service provider, you must specify that a terminal window display. To do this, right-click the dial-up icon for the Internet, choose Properties, and click the Configure button. Click the Options tab (see figure 35.7). Choose Bring up terminal window before dialing or Bring up terminal window after dialing and click OK. Refer to the modem manual for the commands that you type to control the modem.

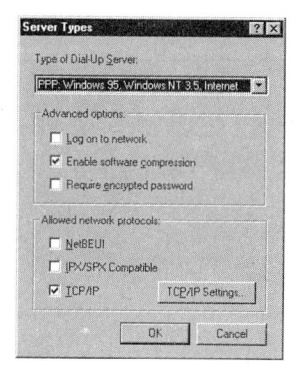

Fig. 35.6 Server types may be selected from the drop-down list at the top of the dialog box.

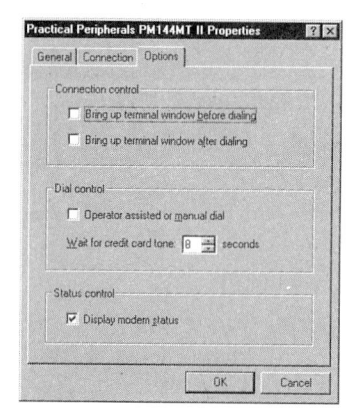

Fig. 35.7 You can display a terminal window for entering commands directly to the modem either before or after dialing the service provider.

Connecting to the Internet through PPP

You're getting close now! If you have a PPP provider, all you have to do to connect to the Internet is use your new dial-up connection. If you have a SLIP provider, this section does not apply to you. Skip to the next section, "Configuring and Using SLIP."

To connect, follow these steps:

1. Double-click My Computer and then double-click Dial-Up Networking.

2. Double-click the icon that represents your Internet connection. A Connect To dialog box displays as shown in figure 35.8

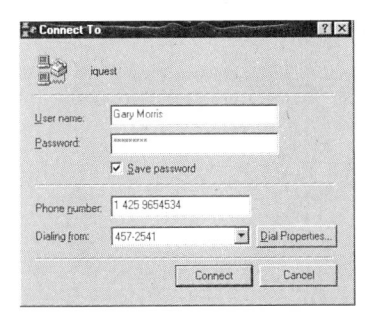

Fig. 35.8 Your user name will display in the Connect To dialog box by default after you have entered it the first time.

3. Type your user name and password. If desired, choose Save Password.

4. And now for the big moment—connecting to the Internet. Click the Connect button. The Connect To dialog box displays to show you the status. (See figure 35.9.) First the dialog box says it's dialing. (The anticipation is mounting.) Then it says it is verifying the user name and password. (You're bursting with anticipation now.) And finally the dialog box says that you are connected . Nothing else changes on the screen. You begin to wonder when something will happen. The duration field is ticking off the seconds and still nothing happens. You begin to say to yourself, "Is this all there is? This is the big Internet that everyone is so worked up over? Where's all the e-mail? Where are the newsgroups?" The pent up excitement turns to disappointment, and finally, in desperation, you click the Disconnect button.

Note: If you are experiencing this disappointment right now, see immediately "What to Do Once You Get Connected," later in this chapter.

Fig. 35.9 The connect dialog box shows what is happening while your modem tries to connect to the service provider.

Configuring and Using SLIP

SLIP is an older, less robust protocol than PPP and is used by some service providers if they have older UNIX servers. Only about one in a hundred service provider accounts is set up as a SLIP account. If you have a choice, you should always choose PPP over SLIP. If you have a PPP provider, skip this section; it does not apply to you.

Windows supports SLIP, but does not install it automatically. SLIP must be installed as a new program (using the Add/Remove Programs object in the Control Panel), and it is located on the CD in the ADMIN\APPTOOLS\DSCRIPT folder.

Once SLIP is installed, you must configure the dial-up connection so it displays a terminal logon after dialing. Additionally you will have to select SLIP as the type of server.

Specifying a Terminal Window after Dialing

To specify that a terminal window display after dialing your service provider, right-click the Internet connection icon in Dial-Up Networking. Choose P*r*operties and click the Options tab. Choose Bring up terminal window a*f*ter dialing and click OK to return to the General page of the Connection Properties sheet.

Specifying the Server Type

To specify SLIP as the server type, click Server *T*ype (on the General page of the Connection Properties sheet). Choose SLIP from the Type of Dial-Up *S*erver drop-down list. Click OK twice to close the Server Types dialog box and then the connection dialog box.

Connecting to the Internet through SLIP

To connect with a SLIP service provider, double-click the dial-up connection icon and enter your password. Click Connect. The terminal window displays. When you receive the TCP/IP address, press F7 to continue. The terminal window closes. Type the assigned address and click OK. You are connected to the Internet, but as you will see, nothing exciting happens. After waiting for a frustrating period of time for something (anything) to happen, you may eventually give up and click the Disconnect button.

What to Do Once You Get Connected

Now if you had just read a little further in this book, dear reader, you wouldn't have had such a disappointing first experience. After you get connected to the Internet, one of the first things you'll want to do is download a Web browser.

Probably the easiest way to download a Web browser is to connect to your own service provider's site. Ask your service provider the name of the file and the name of the folder that contains the file. Then use FTP to download the file.

Using FTP

Once connected to the Internet, open an MS-DOS Prompt window, change to the folder where FTP is stored (usually \Windows) and enter this command:

ftp

The prompt changes to ftp>.

Now suppose that the service provider's site is an anonymous server with this address: rex.isdn.net. Enter this command to connect to it:

open rex.isdn.net

When prompted, enter the user name *anonymous*. Then enter your Internet address as the password. If you are successfully connected, you can begin to enter commands to move around on the site and eventually download files.

To see a list of commands used by FTP, type **help** and press Enter. To get information on a particular command, type **help** followed by the command word and press Enter.

Common Commands

Look at the commands you might want to enter. To see the organization of folders at the site, enter this command:

dir

Figure 35.10 shows the output of this command.

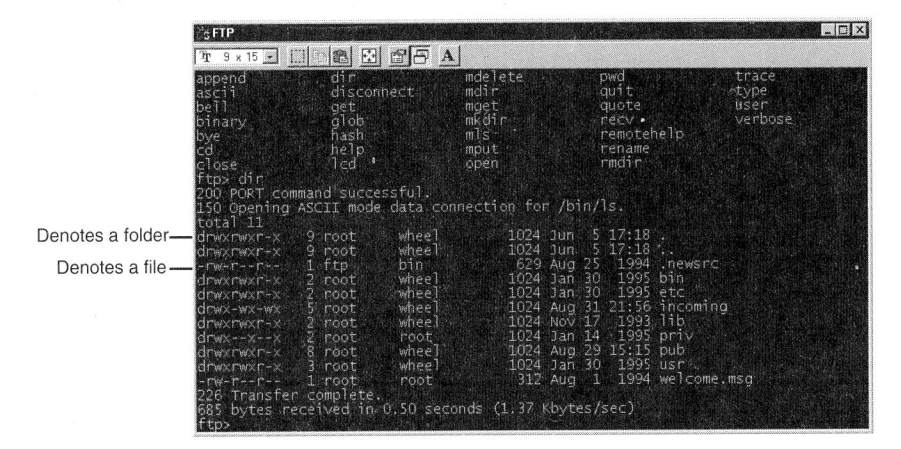

Denotes a folder
Denotes a file

Fig. 35.10 The listing of a folder at an FTP site uses "d" in the first column to designate a folder and an "r" to designate a file.

To change to a different folder, enter this command:

cd *foldername*

To see the files in the folder, enter the **dir** command again. When you see a file you want to download, change the folder on your computer so the file will be downloaded to the proper folder. Enter this command:

lcd *foldername*

If the file that you want to download is a binary file, enter this command to set the download mode to binary (as opposed to ASCII):

binary

To download the file, enter this command:

get *filename*

Tip: Most folders have "readme" files that you can download to get more information about the site, how it is organized, what's in the particular folder, and so on.

Disconnecting and Exiting FTP

When you want to disconnect from the FTP site, type the command **disconnect**. If you want to disconnect and exit FTP, type **bye** or **quit**. Be aware that disconnecting from the site does not disconnect you from the service provider. To disconnect from the service provider, return to the desktop and click Disconnect in the Connected to dialog box.

Using a Web Browser

Suppose that you download the 32-bit version of Netscape 1.1 to use as a Web browser. The file may be a self extracting file (with an EXE extension) or a zipped file (with a ZIP extension). Extract the file or unzip it and then install the file as you would any Windows program. The next time you dial up your service provider and connect to the Internet, start Netscape from the Programs menu. Then you will truly be impressed. This is what you were expecting! Figure 35.11 shows the home page of Netscape.

Notice the Netsite prompt at the top. If you know a location that you want to go to directly, you can type it in this prompt and Netscape will take you there. For example, to go to the home page of Macmillan Publishing, enter this URL in the Netsite text box:

http://www.mcp.com

Fig. 35.12 shows the Macmillan home page at this URL.

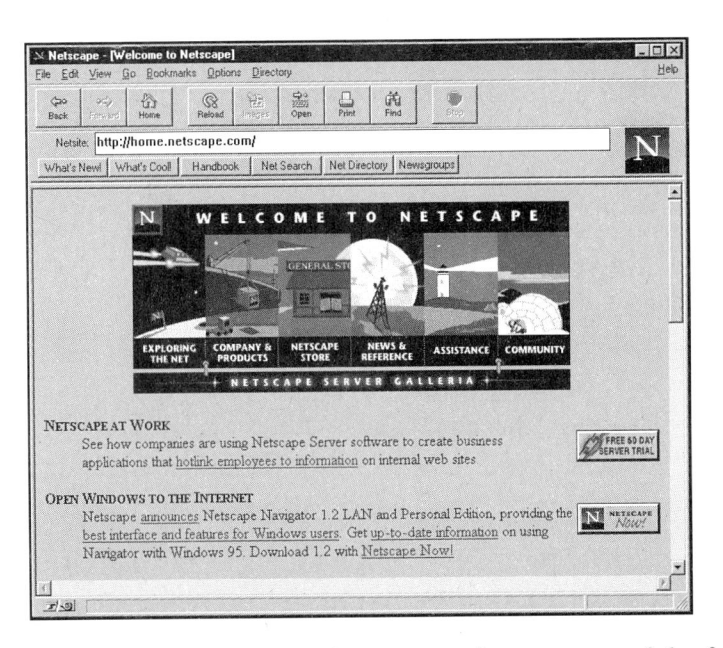

Fig. 35.11 The home page of Netscape shows many of the features that Netscape provides.

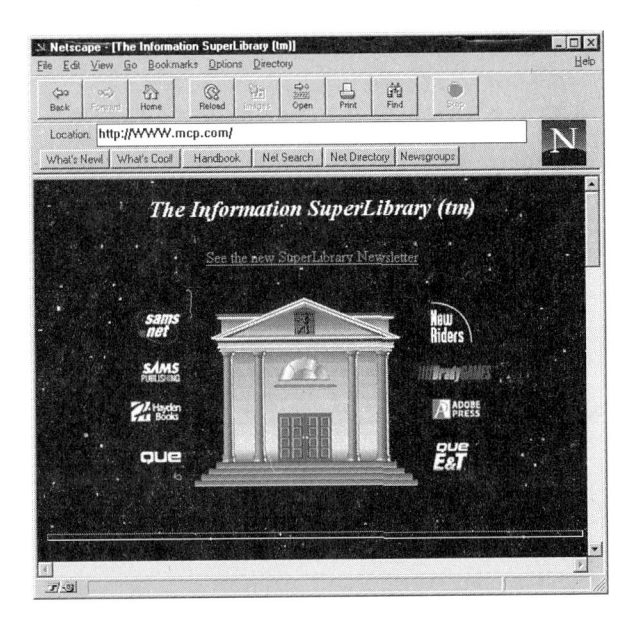

Fig. 35.12 The home page of the Macmillan site lists the publishing divisions you can go to by clicking on the name of the division.

What to Do Once You Get Connected **885**

Using a Windows Gopher

As mentioned previously, Windows 95 does not supply a Gopher. One of the best locations to download a Gopher is http://uts.cc.utexas.edu/~neuroses/cwa.html. This site contains one of the most complete lists of Winsock applications. The applications are listed by category (one category is Gophers) and each application is rated so you will have some idea of how good it is.

If you have downloaded a Gopher program, you can start it after making connection with the Internet. Figure 35.13 shows the gopher WSGOPHER.EXE and its main menu at the University of Illinois. A different Gopher program, BCGOPHER.EXE, connects to Boston College as shown in figure 35.14.

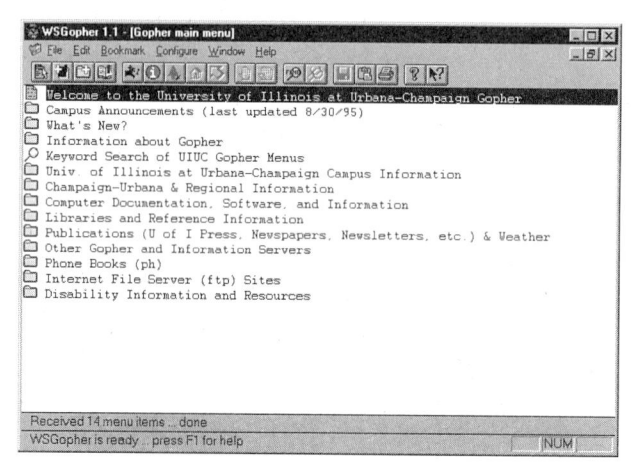

Fig. 35.13 The menu of the University of Illinois Gopher lists categories that pertain to the University.

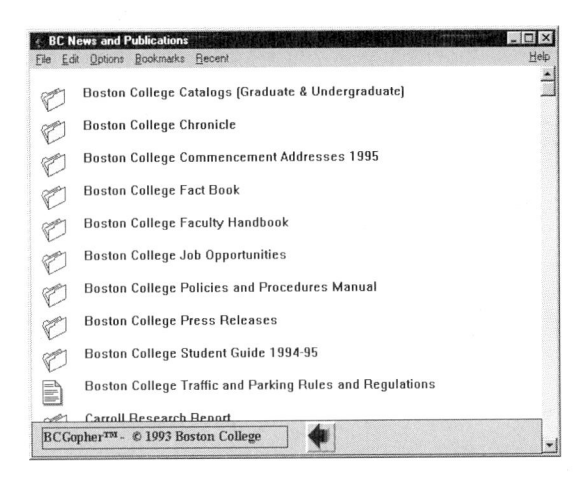

Fig. 35.14 The Boston College Gopher menu looks quite different from the University of Illinois Gopher, and, of course, the menu options are different.

Using Telnet

Windows 95 provides Telnet software. It should be stored in the Windows folder. To connect with Telnet, open an MS-DOS Prompt window, change to the folder that contains Telnet.exe, and enter the **Telnet** command. When Telnet opens, choose Connect, Remote System. Enter the name of the host, the port, and the terminal type and click Connect. Once connected, perform commands that you would if you were a node on the network.

> **Note:** You can enter the Telnet command and the connection address in one command from the DOS prompt.

If you would like to practice with Telnet and Gopher at the same time, change to the folder that contains Telnet and enter the following command at the DOS prompt:

    telnet consultant.micro.umn.edu

When prompted, logon as **gopher**.

> **Tip:** Maximize the Telnet window. Some logons display data at the bottom of the screen, and the data is not visible if the window is not maximized; therefore, you think nothing is happening.

Figure 35.15 shows the Telnet connection. To exit Telnet, choose Connect, Exit or close the Telnet window.

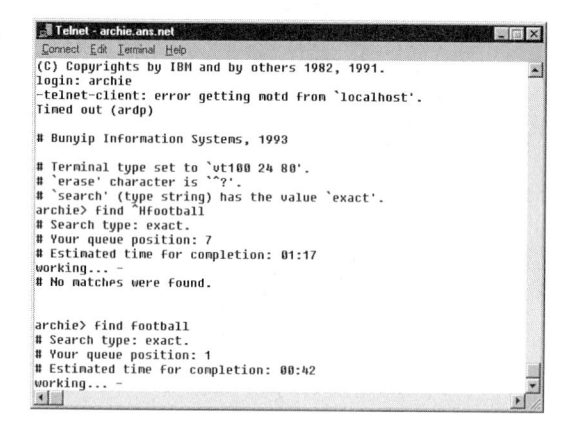

Fig. 35.15 This Telnet connection is logged on to the University of Minnesota Gopher.

Using Archie

Archie, as you may or may not recall (depending on how frazzled your brain is with all these acronyms), searches the indexes of FTP sites for files that match a title or key word that you specify. Figure 35.16 shows a Telnet connection with Archie at archie.ans.net. (The login is "archie.") The results of the command *find football* are shown on the screen.

888 Chapter 35: Internet Communications

```
Telnet - archie.ans.net
Connect  Edit  Terminal  Help
(C) Copyrights by IBM and by others 1982, 1991.
login: archie
-telnet-client: error getting motd from `localhost'.
Timed out (ardp)

# Bunyip Information Systems, 1993

# Terminal type set to `vt100 24 80'.
# `erase' character is `^?'.
# `search' (type string) has the value `exact'.
archie> find ^Hfootball
# Search type: exact.
# Your queue position: 7
# Estimated time for completion: 01:17
working... -
# No matches were found.

archie> find football
# Search type: exact.
# Your queue position: 1
# Estimated time for completion: 00:42
working... -
```

Fig. 35.16 This Archie search lists the sites that contain information about football.

> **Tip:** It is wise to choose Terminal, Start Logging before performing a search. This command creates a telnet.log file that contains the results of the search.

Archie is also found on many Gopher menus. Figure 35.17 shows the screen that displays when you initiate an Archie search from the WSGOPHER menu at the University of Illinois.

Using WAIS

WAIS client software is not provided with Windows 95, but you can download free WAIS programs from various locations. If you would like to practice with WAIS in an emulation mode, you can use Telnet and connect to sunsite.unc.edu, logging in as **swais**. Figure 35.18 shows what the WAIS looks like at this site. Notice the directions at the bottom of the screen that tell you how to select a database, how to enter a key word, and how to search.

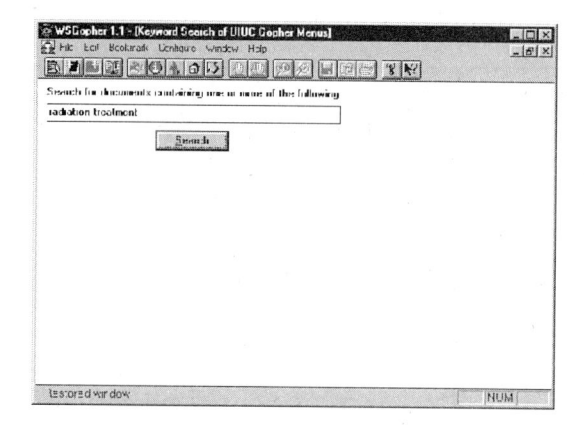

Fig. 35.17 The WSGOPHER menu displays a prompt for the key words to be used in an Archie search.

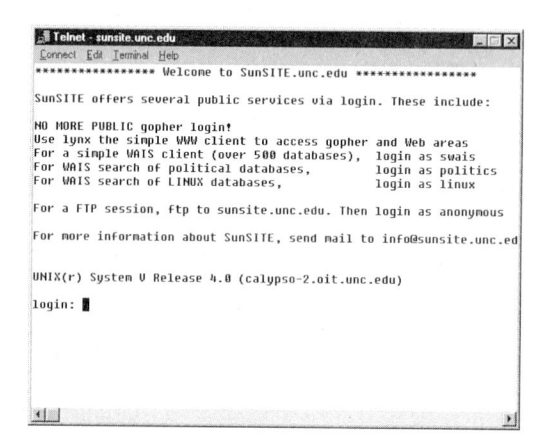

Fig. 35.18 This WAIS emulation is performed in the text mode because it originates in the Telnet window.

When you perform a WAIS search, you select a set of databases to be searched and then formulate a query consisting of key words. When the query is run, WAIS asks for information from each selected database. Headlines of documents satisfying the query are displayed, and the selected documents are ranked according to the number of matches.

To retrieve a document, you simply select it from the resulting list. The WAIS client retrieves the document and displays its contents on the screen.

Communicating with a Network

KILLER 36 WINDOWS 95

by Allen L. Wyatt and Bill Lawrence

Windows 95 has been written with networks in mind from the ground up. Throughout this book you have seen references to how you can use network resources as easily and conveniently as your local resources. You also know that Windows 95 provides much more network support than previous versions of Windows.

In this chapter you will learn more about how the network interfaces function. By learning this information you will be better able to understand what is going on "behind the scenes" and to make network-related adjustments to your system. In this chapter you will learn the following:

- ➤ How Windows 95 uses network components
- ➤ How you can change your network configuration
- ➤ How network identification and access control work

➤ How to configure your system for a Microsoft network

➤ How to configure your system for a NetWare network

➤ What the purpose of the PROTOCOL.INI file is

There is much, much more that could be written about networking. In fact, entire books have been written on this very subject. The information presented here provides a good user-oriented approach to the topic. When you combine this information with that in Chapter 37, "Using Windows 95 on a Network," you will be able to use your network connections like an expert.

Understanding Network Components

There are four types of components which combine to provide networking support to Windows 95. Think of these components as drivers, each providing a different layer of networking support. The types of components are:

➤ **Adapters.** These components enable you to communicate with the actual network interface card in your computer.

➤ **Protocols.** These components define the different communication methods that will be used over your network. These communication methods are comparable to languages, and the protocols provide the set of definitions necessary to use the languages.

➤ **Clients.** These components enable you to use devices available over the network. For instance, without clients you could not use disk drives or printers shared by other computers.

➤ **Services.** These components enable you to provide or use different services over the network. For instance, one service enables you to share files and printers, while another enables you to do automatic network backups.

To work with a network, at a minimum you need an adapter, a protocol, and a client; services are optional. In Windows 95 you can typically specify each of these components for use with your network. There are exceptions, however. If you have a Plug-and-Play system, and you use a Plug-and-Play network adapter, Windows 95 will detect the new network adapter right after you add it to your system. When you first boot, the new adapter components for that network card will be added, automatically, to the operating system.

To manually make changes to your network connection type, you simply add, remove, or make changes to the different components. You can do this from the Network dialog box. To access this dialog box, follow these steps:

1. Choose Settings from the Start menu.
2. Choose Control Panel from the Settings menu.
3. Double-click the Network icon in the Control Panel.

At this point you will see the Network dialog box, as shown in figure 36.1.

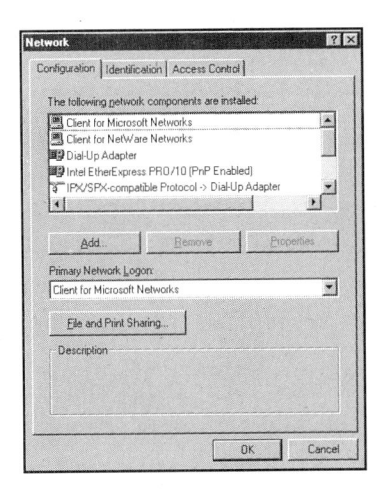

Fig. 36.1 Use the Network dialog box to control the configuration of your network.

Understanding Network Components 893

With the Configuration tab selected, you can see the different components installed for your network at the top of the dialog box, in the list area. Each component has an icon to the left of it which identifies the type of component category to which it belongs.

- Adapters
- Protocols
- Clients
- Services

You can select different components by scrolling through the list and clicking the component you want. Later in this chapter you will learn how to use the Network dialog box to modify the configuration of your network.

Your Initial Network Configuration

When you first install Windows 95, it attempts to determine your network setup. In reality, the extent of the attempts is limited to determining the type of network adapter you have installed in your system. Although Windows 95 does pretty well at determining hardware, the "automatic nature" of the operating system comes to a dead end. Windows cannot automatically determine the type of network you are using, nor can it determine which protocols you should install for your network.

Note: If you are upgrading to Windows 95 from a previous version of Windows or DOS that has networking enabled, Windows 95 can set up the proper network clients and protocols for your system. It does this by detecting the type of network that is currently configured on your system. The assumption is then made that you want to use the same network configuration under Windows 95.

After Windows 95 initially determines the type of network adapter installed in your system, and if you do not have networking installed with a previous version of Windows or DOS, it has to make a few assumptions. The safest assumption about your network is that you are using one of the two most popular networks on the market (Novell NetWare or a Microsoft network). It then loads the following two clients automatically:

➤ **Client for Microsoft Networks.** This client enables you to communicate with a Windows NT (client/server), LAN Manager (client/server), or Windows for Workgroups (peer-to-peer) network. If you are not using these types of networks, you can safely remove the client.

➤ **Client for NetWare Networks.** This client enables you to communicate with a NetWare 3.x or 4.x (client/server) network. If you are not using this type of network, you can safely remove the client.

Furthermore, Windows automatically assumes that you are using one of the network protocols most common to these two types of networks. The components for these protocols are automatically added to your system:

➤ **IPX/SPX-compatible Protocol.** This is the protocol used predominantly in NetWare environments. If you are not using this type of network, you can safely remove the protocol.

Understanding Network Components **895**

➤ **NetBEUI.** This term is a contraction for NetBIOS Extended User Interface. IBM introduced NetBEUI in 1985, and it has since been adopted by Microsoft for use in its networks. If you are not using a Microsoft network, you can safely remove the protocol.

The Purpose of Bindings

Bindings is just a fancy word to describe the links that exist between network adapters and network protocols. The bindings inform the operating system (Windows 95) which protocols should be used with which network adapters.

You can look at the listed network components in the Network dialog box to see which bindings are in effect. If you look at the protocol lines, you will see the name of the protocol followed by a right-pointing arrow and the name of an adapter, as shown in figure 36.2. These indicate the bindings in effect between a protocol and an adapter.

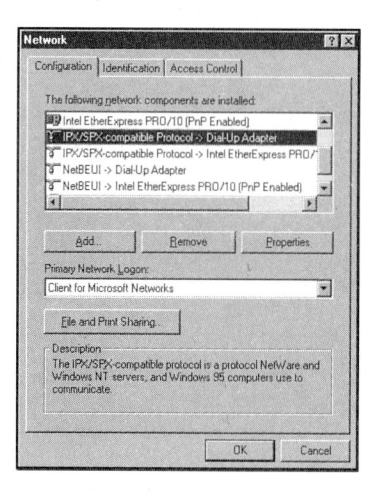

Fig. 36.2 Bindings are indicated in the list of network components on the Network dialog box.

If you have only one adapter card in your system, and you have only one or two protocols loaded, then each of the protocols will be bound to the adapter card you have installed. Later in this chapter you will learn how you can change bindings for your system.

Changing Your Network Configuration

You can change an existing network configuration from the Network dialog box. This is the same dialog box you accessed earlier in this chapter. To display the dialog box, follow these steps:

1. Choose Settings from the Start menu.
2. Choose Control Panel from the Settings menu.
3. Double-click the Network icon in the Control Panel.

> **Tip:** To quickly access the Network dialog box, you can right-click the Network Neighborhood icon on your desktop, and then choose Properties from the context menu.

At this point you will see the Network dialog box, as shown in figure 36.1 earlier in the chapter.

Now you can select different network components in the list at the top of the dialog box, and then you can use the other controls in the dialog box to change your configuration. The following sections describe the different actions you can take.

Adding Network Components

To add a component to your network, click the Add button in the Network dialog box. This displays the Select Network Component Type dialog box, as shown in figure 36.3.

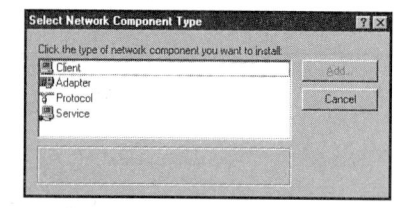

Fig. 36.3 The first step in adding a network component is to identify the type of component you want to add.

The four different network components are listed in this dialog box, and you can select the one you want to add. After you select the component type, simply click the Add button. The following sections describe the different aspects of adding each type of component.

Adding Clients

When you choose to add a network client, you are shown the Select Network Client dialog box which lists the different manufacturers and models of clients you can add (see figure 36.4). Select the make and model of your network.

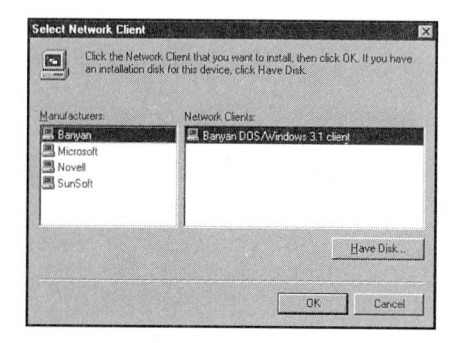

Fig. 36.4 Windows 95 enables you to specify a wide variety of network clients.

Windows 95 supports over six different network clients from four different manufacturers:

➤ **Banyan.** There is only one client available for this vendor. The Banyan DOS/Windows 3.1 client supports the Banyan Vines network configuration.

➤ **Microsoft.** There are two different Microsoft clients provided. These two clients, for Microsoft networks and for Novell NetWare, are the clients described earlier in the chapter as the default clients loaded by Windows 95.

➤ **Novell.** The Novell-specific clients are used if you are using real-mode network device drivers. One client interfaces with the Novell 3.x workstation shell, and the other with the 4.x shell. Microsoft suggests that you do not use these clients, as the real-mode drivers offer inferior performance when compared to the 32-bit support offered by the Microsoft client for Novell.

➤ **SunSoft.** A single SunSoft client is provided: SunSoft PC-NFS (version 5.0). This network client provides connectivity to SunSoft networks.

In addition, if you have an updated or different client from a network manufacturer, you can click the Have Disk button in order to install your client from a disk.

Adding Adapters

When you choose to add an adapter, you will see the Select Network Adapter dialog box, which enables you to select the vendor and adapter model used in your system (see figure 36.5).

When you specify a vendor in the Manufacturers list, the choices available in the Network Adapters list change to reflect the products from that vendor. Windows 95 supports over 248 cards from 50 different vendors, so the chances are quite good that you can find the adapter card applicable to your network.

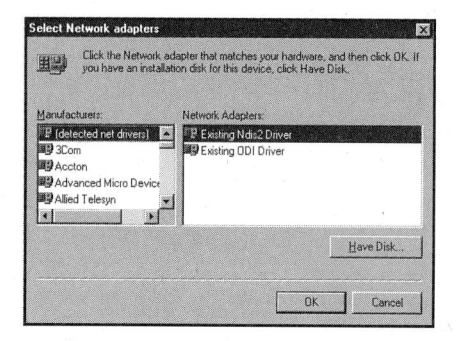

Fig. 36.5 Picking a network adapter is a simple matter of selecting a vendor and a card type.

> **Tip:** If you cannot determine what type of adapter you have, you should refer to the documentation for the card or contact your network administrator. If you do not have a network administrator, then contact the person that sold you the card or installed it.

If, for some reason, you cannot find your particular adapter in the list of those available, you can use the Have Disk button to load an adapter driver from disk.

Adding Protocols

When you choose to add a network protocol, you will see the Select Network Protocol dialog box, as shown in figure 36.6. Network protocols are closely related to the type of network client you have specified. All you need to do is pick a vendor (from the Manufacturers list) and then a protocol applicable to that vendor.

Windows 95 provides support for 14 protocols from 6 different vendors. In most cases you should select the same manufacturer as you did when you specified a network client. Then pick the protocol you want to use in your network. If you are connecting to an already established network, check with your network administrator to see what protocol is used on the network.

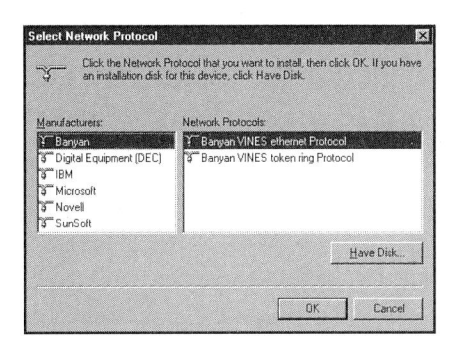

Fig. 36.6 You use network protocols to define communication procedures over the network.

> **Caution:** If you do not pick a compatible protocol when connecting to an existing network, you will not be able to communicate with other computers on the network. Furthermore, you may also stop other computers on the network from communicating properly.

If your network protocol is not available from the list, you can click the Have Disk button to add a protocol provided by your vendor.

Adding Services

Network services are used to provide well-defined features that other computers on the network can access. The two most common examples of network services are file sharing and printer sharing. The network service is the operating system component that enables a feature. For instance, if you don't load the printer sharing network service, you won't be able to share your printers on the network.

When you choose to add a service, you will see the Select Network Service dialog box shown in figure 36.7.

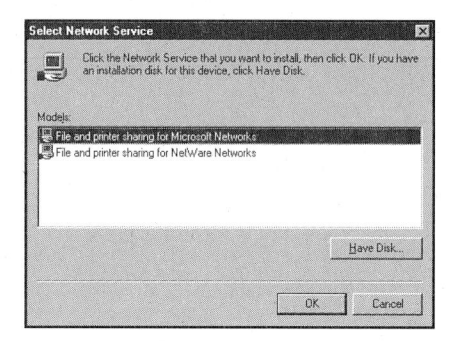

Fig. 36.7 Adding services allows you to offer resources to the network.

The Select Network Service dialog box is where you will most likely use the Have Disk button. For instance, you may purchase a network archival system that enables you to back up your entire network. The vendor may have supplied a Windows 95 disk that includes the service driver necessary to utilize its hardware.

Removing Network Components

To remove a network component, all you need to do is highlight it in the Network dialog box, and then click the Remove button. The component is immediately removed, without asking for confirmation. After it is removed, the only way to undo your action is to again add the component to your system.

Changing Bindings

You will remember from the discussion earlier in this chapter that bindings are the linking of a protocol with an adapter. If you have only one adapter card in your system, and you have only one or two protocols loaded, chances are good that you will never need to change bindings. If you have multiple adapter cards connected to dissimilar networks, then you may need to change bindings. For instance, if you have an adapter card used to connect to a Microsoft network and another loaded to connect with a NetWare network, then you will need to bind the proper protocols to the proper adapter cards for each type of network.

To change bindings, you can start with either the protocol or the adapter. If you want to change bindings from the aspect of the adapter, start with the Network dialog box displayed. Then, follow these steps:

1. In the list of network components, highlight the adapter for which you want the bindings changed.
2. Click the Properties button. You will see the Properties sheet for the adapter.
3. Click the Bindings tab. The dialog box now appears, as shown in figure 36.8.

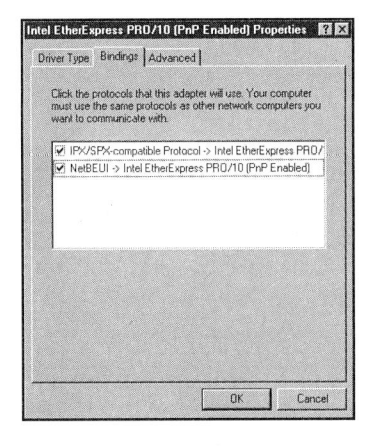

Fig. 36.8 Windows 95 enables you to easily change the bindings to an adapter.

The dialog box lists all the protocols that are loaded for your system. In the check box to the left of each protocol you can see whether it is bound to the adapter whose properties you are changing. To break the binding, simply clear the check box; to establish the binding, select the check box. When you are done, click the OK button.

You can also change bindings by starting with the protocol instead of the adapter. To do this, display the Network dialog box, and then follow these steps:

1. In the list of network components, highlight the protocol for which you want the bindings changed.

2. Click the Properties button. You will see the Properties sheet for the protocol.

3. Click the Bindings tab. The dialog box now appears, as shown in figure 36.9.

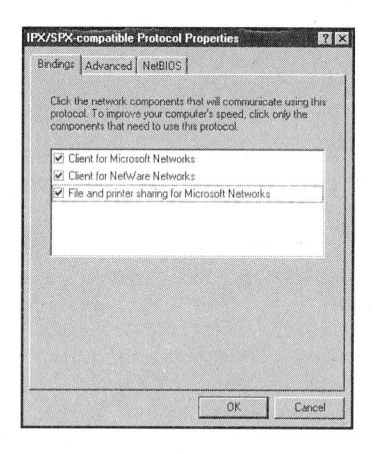

Fig. 36.9 Windows 95 enables you to easily change the bindings for a protocol.

Notice that the list in this dialog box is a bit different from the earlier list. Here you see a list of all the network components (clients and services) that can communicate using the protocol you have selected. By default, the protocol is bound to every component that can possibly use it.

Tip: To improve the performance of your system, disable the binding between the protocol and a component that you know will never use that protocol. To break the binding, simply clear the check box; to establish the binding, select the check box.

Remember that you should only have the network components loaded that you will actually be using in your network. To have extraneous components loaded can slow down the performance of your system in relation to the network. Therefore, delete the components you absolutely do not need, and then check your bindings to ensure they reflect the logical links appropriate for your network.

File and Print Sharing

Earlier in this chapter you learned that network services enable you to share both files and printers over the network. You can either add this service as you would any other network component (as described earlier in the section "Adding Network Components"), or you can simply use the shortcut that Windows 95 provides for this feature. At the bottom of the Network dialog box, first shown in figure 36.1, is a button labeled File and Print Sharing. If you click this button, you will see the dialog box shown in figure 36.10.

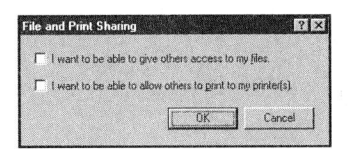

Fig. 36.10 The File and Print Sharing dialog box is a quick way to indicate what resources you want to share.

From this dialog box you can select the type of file and printer sharing you want done. Simply select the check box to the left of the option (or options) that expresses what you want to do. When you finish, click the OK button. If the File and Printer Sharing for Microsoft Networks service is not already installed on your system, it is added to fulfill your request.

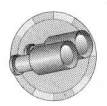

> **Note:** If you are using a Microsoft network under Windows 95, file sharing is actually a misnomer. In reality, you share folders, which in turn contain files. Thus, you cannot make an individual file available on the network, unless that file is the only one within a folder you have shared.

Your Primary Network Logon

Near the middle of the Network dialog box (shown in figure 36.1), you may have noticed a pull-down list entitled Primary Network Logon. This list enables you to specify the network definition to which you want to log on whenever you start Windows. The choices in this list are defined by which clients you have installed. For instance, if you are using a Microsoft network, and you have the client for Microsoft networks installed, this is one of the choices in the pull-down list.

The client you choose in this list defines how your logon process occurs. It is a safe bet that every network client requires that you provide a user ID and a password, but from the type of network you are connecting to these network clients will dictate what steps will occur. For instance, some clients may require you to identify a workgroup, domain, or server to use for your initial connection.

Regardless of the clients you have installed, there is one other choice always available in the pull-down list—Windows Logon. This option is used to log you on to Windows 95, but no network authentication is performed. Thus, if you type the wrong user ID or password, you can still receive access to Windows 95. Choosing this logon process (as opposed to a specific network logon) should only be used if your computer is physically disconnected from a network for a time.

For instance, you may be using a portable system that keeps getting network connection errors whenever you are on the road. To solve this problem, simply select Windows Logon as your logon process.

Network Identification

Regardless of the type of network you have installed, Windows 95 requires you to specify information that identifies your machine to your network. At the highest level, you can do this by using the Identification tab in the Network dialog box. To change your identification settings, follow these steps:

1. Choose Settings from the Start menu.
2. Choose Control Panel from the Settings menu.
3. Double-click the Network icon in the Control Panel.
4. Click the Identification tab. The Network dialog box appears, as shown in figure 36.11.

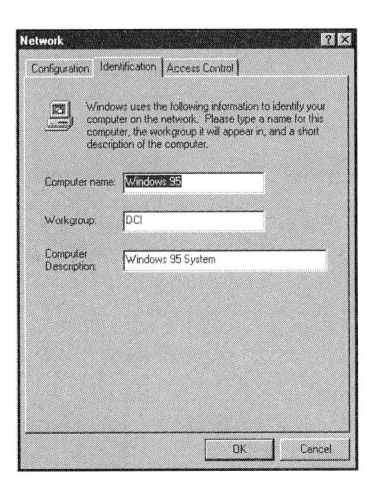

Fig. 36.11 Identification information is used to identify your machine on the network.

Depending on your network configuration, you can use the three pieces of information in this dialog box in different ways. For instance, if your network client and protocol require the use of domains or workgroups, then use the Workgroup setting in this dialog box to identify which one you belong to. If you enter the name of an existing workgroup, then you are grouped with that workgroup. If you enter the name of a new workgroup (even if it is by misspelling an existing name), then a new workgroup is created with you as the only member.

Regardless of your network type, the contents of the Computer name and Computer Description fields are used whenever you browse through the Network Neighborhood. The fields in this dialog box have the following constraints:

➤ **Computer name.** Any name used to identify your system. The name is required and can contain up to 15 characters. The name cannot contain any of the characters listed in Table 36.1.

➤ **Workgroup.** Any name that uniquely identifies the workgroup or domain to which you belong. The name is required and can be up to 15 characters long; it cannot contain any of the characters listed in Table 36.1.

➤ **Computer Description.** Any comment about your computer that you want displayed to other network members. This is an optional field, and can be as long as you want.

Table 36.1 Illegal Characters for Computer and Workgroup Names

Character	Name
!	Exclamation point
#	Pound sign
$	Dollar sign
%	Percent sign
&	Ampersand
'	Apostrophe

Character	Name
( )	Parentheses
-	Minus sign/dash
.	Period
@	At sign
^	Caret
_	Underscore
{ }	Braces
~	Tilde
	Space

It is very possible that your company already has some sort of identification system set up for computers on the network. You will want to check with your system administrator to see if you should include specific information in the identification fields. For instance, the rules of your network may require that a phone number, department name, or office number be included in the Computer Description field.

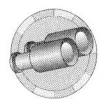

> **Note:** If you are using the TCP/IP protocol on your network, you will also be required to specify additional identification settings for your computer. You do this through the Properties sheet for the TCP/IP protocol. The exact details of TCP/IP settings are described in detail in Chapter 35, "Internet Communications."

Access Control

Access control refers to how other computers on the network can access resources attached to your computer, such as printers or files. Windows 95 enables you to specify the rules by which you want access to occur. To change the access control settings, follow these steps:

1. Choose Settings from the Start menu.
2. Choose Control Panel from the Settings menu.
3. Double-click the Network icon in the Control Panel.
4. Click the Access Control tab. The Network dialog box appears as shown in figure 36.12.

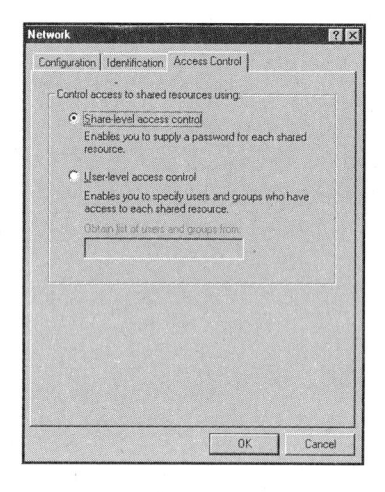

Fig. 36.12 You use access control information to control how your system resources are tapped.

You can pick either of two settings in this dialog box. The first setting (Share-level access control) is the default. With this option chosen, access is controlled on a printer-by-printer or file-by-file basis. When you share the printer or file, you have the opportunity to specify a password which is required for others to use the resource.

If you choose the second access option (User-level access control), then users or groups of users will always have access to your shared printers or files. A user who is not the one you specified (or, if you specified a group, in the group you specified), cannot access your resources. With this option selected, you must specify a server or domain where the list of authorized users is stored. You should note that

Underline-level Access Control is available only if you are using a client/server networking environment running under Windows NT (thus, the domain name requirement) or NetWare (the server name requirement).

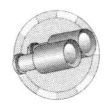

> **Note:** You can set the access control rules anytime you want, but they only have meaning if you have chosen to share files or printers for your system.

Configuring Your System for a Microsoft Network

After you have set up your Microsoft network for the first time, you will need to be concerned with how Windows 95 is configured to use the network. You do this by accomplishing the following three tasks:

- Specifying whether Microsoft network is the primary client for logging on your system.
- Specifying whether your system is part of a Windows NT domain.
- Specifying how network drives should be treated in relation to your system.

The order in which you perform these tasks is not important. Each task is covered in the following sections.

Setting the Primary Network

Specifying a primary network logon has already been touched on earlier in the chapter. To specify Microsoft network as your logon choice, follow these steps:

1. Choose Settings from the Start menu.
2. Choose Control Panel from the Settings menu.

3. Double-click the Network icon in the Control Panel. This displays the Network dialog box.

4. Click the pull-down control at the right side of the Primary Network Logon field. This displays a list of available network clients.

5. Select the Client for Microsoft Networks option.

If there is no Client for Microsoft Networks option in the pull-down list, then you have not installed the client. Refer to the section on adding a client, earlier in this chapter, for information on how to do this.

Specifying Domain and Network Drive Information

You can accomplish two of the steps in setting up a Microsoft network by changing the properties associated with the Microsoft networks client. To display this dialog box, follow these steps:

1. Choose Settings from the Start menu.

2. Choose Control Panel from the Settings menu.

3. Double-click the Network icon in the Control Panel.

4. In the list of network components at the top of the dialog box, choose Client for Microsoft Networks.

5. Click the Properties button. You should see the Properties sheet appear, as shown in figure 36.13.

To change the domain information, modify the information in the Logon validation area of the dialog box. If you select the check box, then anytime you log on to your system, you also automatically log on to your Windows NT network. The domain name you specify is checked for your user ID and password. If they are found, you are given the appropriate level of access to the network. (Your access level is determined and managed by the network administrator.) If either your user ID or password is incorrect, then you will not see any errors, but you will not have full access to the network.

912 Chapter 36: Communicating with a Network

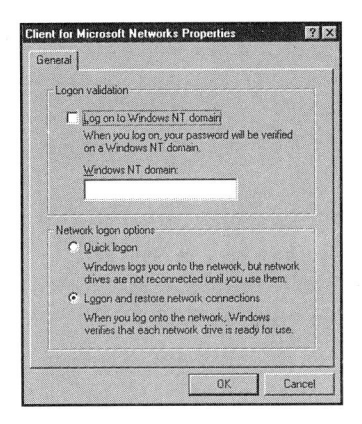

Fig. 36.13 You can modify the properties of the Microsoft network client.

If you are not part of a Windows NT network, but instead are using a peer-to-peer network consisting of Windows 95, Windows for Workgroups, or Windows NT workstation systems, then you should make sure that the Log on to Windows NT Domain option is not selected. Because a peer-to-peer network does not have a server used for centralized administration, checking the server is not necessary.

> **Note:** If you instruct Windows 95 to verify your account with a Windows NT server, but do not supply a domain name, then you will be asked for a domain name whenever you log in to the system.

At the bottom of the dialog box, in the Network Logon Options section, you can specify how you want your network drives treated during the logon process. If you select the first option, Quick Logon, then the validity of network drives is not checked during the logon process. Instead, network drives are only checked when you first attempt to use one. The other option, Logon and Restore Network Connections, causes a delay in logging on, but you are sure that the network drives are available right away.

Configuring Your System for a Microsoft Network

Most users should select the Quick Logon option. In many networks you could have drives coming on and off line all the time. Thus, even though the validity of a drive connection is checked when you first log on, it may change by the time you access the drive.

Running Windows 95 on a Novell Network

If you are running Windows 95 on a network where most or all of the servers are running Novell NetWare, you need to make some important choices. For starters, you have the choice of two network clients—Microsoft's NetWare client or the client that comes with Novell's workstation requester. Each client has its pros and cons, which you learn about later in this section. Your choice of clients also influences which tools you use to log in to servers, map drive letters, and connect to print queues.

Besides exploring the differences between the Novell and Microsoft NetWare clients, you also learn how to install the Novell client and how to configure the NetWare settings in Windows 95.

Choosing the Right NetWare Client

How do you choose between Microsoft's built-in NetWare client and the client that comes with Novell's DOS and Windows requester? It depends on what is important to you. Microsoft's client is a true 32-bit protected mode client and thereby holds an edge in terms of performance and tight integration with Windows 95. It is the client to choose if you never want to see the DOS prompt and you do not mind trading some compatibility for the privilege. Novell's client boasts complete compatibility with all NetWare versions and features, but requires that you use Novell's real-mode DOS-compatible network drivers.

As you weigh the pluses and minuses of each client, consider these factors:

- Do you need the client to be compatible with NetWare Folder Services (which comes with NetWare version 4.x)?

- Do you need or prefer to use the NetWare Windows utilities NWADMIN and NWUSER?

- Do you need to run protocols besides NetWare's IPX/SPX? Do you need to run the TCP/IP protocol, for example, to access the Internet?

- Is all the NetWare-aware software that you need to run compatible with the client you are choosing?

The Microsoft NetWare Client

You learned previously in this chapter how to install Microsoft's built-in NetWare client. Microsoft's Windows 95 NetWare client offers the following strengths:

- High performance and no DOS memory consumption because the client is a protected mode 32-bit application.

- Almost complete compatibility with NetWare 3.x and software that uses Novell's IPX/SPX protocol.

- Windows-based login including the ability to execute NetWare 3.x login scripts.

You will encounter the following drawbacks if you decide to use the Microsoft NetWare client:

- No compatibility with NetWare 4.x's NetWare Folder Services (NDS). NDS provides a global name and resource folder for a network comprised of NetWare 4.x servers.

- NetWare Windows utilities such as NWUSER and NWADMIN are not compatible with the Microsoft NetWare client.

Running Windows 95 on a Novell Network **915**

The Microsoft client for NetWare is worth a try if you want the highest performance and do not need NetWare 4.x or NetWare Folder Services compatibility. If you discover any serious compatibility issues with other software that you need to use, you can easily switch to Novell's Windows client.

Novell's NetWare Client

Windows 95 is fully compatible with Novell's DOS and Windows client (which is included as part of the NetWare DOS requester that comes with NetWare 3.12 and NetWare 4.x). Novell's client offers the following benefits:

➤ Complete compatibility with all NetWare versions and features and a long track record of compatibility and stability.

➤ All software that requires the IPX/SPX protocol should be compatible with the Novell NetWare client.

➤ NetWare's Windows utilities (NWADMIN and NWUSER) are fully supported.

➤ Novell's client can coreside with the Windows 95 client for Microsoft networks, so you can connect to both NetWare and Windows NT servers and also use Windows 95's peer-to-peer network features.

The Novell client is weak in the following areas:

➤ Because it uses real-mode DOS network card drivers, protocols, and a DOS requester (VLM.EXE), the Novell client consumes DOS memory and is not as fast as the Microsoft NetWare client.

➤ For best results and to execute your login scripts, you will need to log in from DOS before the Windows 95 graphical interface starts.

Table 36.2 details the differences between the Novell and Microsoft clients for Windows 95.

Table 36.2 Novell and Microsoft Client Feature Comparison

Feature	Microsoft Client	Novell Client
Real or protected mode?	Protected mode	Real mode
NetWare version	NetWare 3.x only	NetWare 3.x and 4.x compatibility
Logging in	Log in from Windows	Log in from DOS
Combined login and password with Windows and Microsoft networks?	Yes	No
Login scripts	Partial NetWare 3.x compatibility	Full NetWare 3.x and 4.x compatibility
Compatible with NWUSER and NWADMIN?	No	Yes
Can coreside with other protocols and other Windows 95 network clients?	Yes	Yes
Compatible with all built-in Windows 95 drive mapping and printer connection tools?	Yes	Yes

Installing Novell's client for NetWare is fairly simple but not quite as automatic as installing Microsoft's client for NetWare (a process that you learned about previously in this chapter). You need to start the Network dialog box (which you can open by right-clicking the desktop's Network Neighborhood icon and choosing Properties or by starting the Control Panel and clicking the Network icon). When the Network dialog box appears, choose the Configuration tab and click the Add button. Choose Client from the Select Network Component dialog box that appears, and then choose Novell from the client manufacturers that are listed.

When you select Novell from the list of client manufacturers, you can choose the version of the Novell client that matches the workstation requester or shell that you are using. After you have made your selection, click OK. Windows 95 prompts you to take the following steps:

1. Restart your computer (Windows 95 has modified your AUTOEXEC.BAT file so that your PC starts in DOS mode and displays special prompt messages about the following steps).

2. Run the NetWare DOS Requester installation program. This places the adapter drivers, protocol drivers, and NetWare requester files (DOS and Windows) on your PC.

3. Modify your AUTOEXEC.BAT to automatically load the network card and protocol drivers and requester files. Also modify your AUTOEXEC.BAT to execute NetWare's LOGIN command, which prompts you to log in. While you are modifying AUTOEXEC.BAT, remove the prompt messages referred to in step 1.

4. Restart your computer and log in. Then start Windows 95 by typing **WIN**.

5. Start the Control Panel and click the Network icon, or right-click the Network Neighborhood icon and choose P‍roperties. Windows 95 automatically updates your network configuration as required, and prompts you to restart your computer once more.

After you perform these steps, Windows 95 is configured to run Novell's client for NetWare.

Configuration Options for the Microsoft Client for NetWare

If you opt to use the Microsoft Client for NetWare, there are three options that you can configure after you install and activate the client. To set these options, start the Control Panel and click the Network icon or right-click the Network Neighborhood icon on the desktop and choose P‍roperties. The Network dialog box opens. Double-click the NetWare client listing in this box, and a dialog box appears that enables you to configure three options: your preferred server, the first network drive, and whether or not to process login scripts when you log in.

In the box labeled Preferred Server, enter the name of the NetWare server to which you want the NetWare client to connect at startup. In the First Network Drive box, choose the drive letter that should be assigned to the SYS volume on that server when you activate the NetWare client. Place a check mark in the Process Login Script box to execute your NetWare login script when you log in using the Microsoft client for NetWare. Click OK when you finish setting these options.

Understanding the PROTOCOL.INI File

Windows 95 includes a file called PROTOCOL.INI in the folder in which Windows is installed. You use this file for two purposes:

> As a configuration guide if you are using real-mode device drivers for your networking.

> If you ever boot your system in safe mode with networking support (as discussed in Chapter 6, "Troubleshooting Windows 95 Installation and Startup").

Caution: Use extreme care in modifying PROTOCOL.INI. Incorrect information in the file can cause unpredictable errors in running Windows 95, or can damage other Windows 95 configuration files. Always make a backup copy of the file before you make any changes.

The contents of PROTOCOL.INI are established by the Setup program when you first install Windows 95. Thereafter, the contents are modified as necessary by changes you make in the Network section of the Control Panel. It is possible that you may need to directly modify the information in PROTOCOL.INI if you are using real-mode network drivers and your system has a resource conflict for which Windows 95 cannot automatically compensate. As an example, if you have a network card that uses real-mode drivers, and the card conflicts with the

IRQs or I/O addresses used by your video card, then you may need to make changes in PROTOCOL.INI.

The following is an example of a PROTOCOL.INI file:

```
[protman$]
priority=ndishlp$
DriverName=protman$

[ndishlp$]
DriverName=ndishlp$
Bindings=EPRO$

[data]
version=v4.00.490
netcards=EPRO$,*INT1030

[nwlink$]
Frame_Type=4
cachesize=0
Bindings=EPRO$
DriverName=nwlink$

[NETBEUI$]
sessions=10
ncbs=12
Bindings=EPRO$
DriverName=NETBEUI$
Lanabase=1

[EPRO$]
INTERRUPT=11
ioaddress=0x240
DriverName=EPRO$
```

Notice that the file follows the traditional construction of an INI file. The file is a plain ASCII text file, major sections defined by a section name surrounded by brackets. Thus, [EPRO$] is a section within the PROTOCOL.INI file. The order of the sections within the file is not critical, but the composition of each section can be critical.

Individual sections are composed of entries that define settings. Each entry is composed of a setting name, an equal sign, and a value. The setting name is on the left side of the equal sign, and the setting value is on the right side. The major sections in PROTOCOL.INI are described in detail in the following sections.

In addition to major sections, there will also be other sections in the file that relate to each of the drivers' references in the major sections. For instance, in the listing of PROTOCOL.INI just provided, the first section, [protman$], is a major section. Within this section there is a reference to ndishlp$. Another section within the file actually defines the parameters of this driver.

The [protman$] Section

This section is used to provide settings for the protocol manager. There are two entries typically in this section, and their order does not matter. One entry, DriverName, is used to specify the device driver used for the protocol manager. The other entry is priority, which is used to specify the order in which incoming data frames are processed by the protocol manager.

The [NETBEUI$] Section

This particular section is named after the network protocol installed on the system—NETBEUI. There will be a corresponding protocol section in the file for each network protocol you have installed. Each protocol section will have, at minimum, the following types of entries:

- **Bindings.** This entry defines the network adapter cards to which the protocol is bound. In other words, if the protocol is used to communicate through the card, the card name is used in this entry. The card name is the same as the name of a card section defined elsewhere within PROTOCOL.INI. In the example file listed previously, the card cited in the entry is EPRO$, which is also the name of another section in the file. Because a protocol can be bound to multiple cards, you can include more than one card name for the Bindings setting. To do this, simply separate the card names with commas.

- **Lanabase.** This number is determined by the Setup program and specifies the binding between the network protocol and the network adapter.

Other settings within the protocol section can vary, depending on the protocol. For instance, the NETBEUI$ protocol section contains information on the number of sessions and ncbs for the driver.

The [nwlink$] Section

This is another protocol section, except this time it is related to the Client for NetWare Networks. The entries within the section define the parameters used by the NetWare protocol. The same comments made in the last section, in relation to NETBEUI, refer to this section of the file as well.

The [EPRO$] Section

The [EPRO$] section will not be available, by this name, in all PROTOCOL.INI files. Instead, a name will be used for this section that represents the actual card installed in the system. This particular PROTOCOL.INI file is from a system that has an Intel EtherPro PnP card. Other cards will have different names, but each card in a system will have a corresponding section within PROTOCOL.INI.

The entries within the card section define the various settings for the card. Because each network card varies, the contents of the section can vary as well. In the example file listed earlier, the settings define the IRQ used by the card (INTERRUPT=11), the I/O address used by the card (ioaddress=0x240), and the device driver used by the card (DriverName=EPRO$). In virtually all instances, if you compare the contents of this card section with what you know about the card from reading its manual, you can figure out what the entries represent.

Using Windows 95 on a Network

by Allen L. Wyatt

Networks can greatly increase your productivity, or they can present one more layer of complexity, thereby hindering productivity. The difference is in how the network is designed, administered, and used by all concerned. In this chapter, you will learn how you can use the network-specific features of Windows 95. Here you will learn the following:

- ➤ How you can share information on your system with others on the network
- ➤ How you can access information on other people's systems by mapping network drives

- Special network features when printing over a network
- How you can manage your network

Sharing Information

One of the primary purposes of a network is to facilitate the communal sharing of information. Windows 95 enables you to share information on your system and to access information that is on other people's systems. The next several sections describe how to both give and receive information.

Sharing Folders

When you are working in a networked environment, you may want to share information on your computer with another user on the network. This is easy to do using Windows 95 by simply sharing your folders. Shared folders and their contents are visible to other network users as they browse through the Net.

For example, let's assume that you are working with other people in your workgroup on a project. Your task is to come up with figures for a product manual being developed by your company. To keep the figures in a logical place, you have created a folder named FIGURES on your C: drive. To make this folder available to other network users, you would follow these steps:

1. Double-click the My Computer icon on the desktop. This displays the drives available on your system.
2. Double-click the C disk drive. This displays all the files and folders in your C drive, as shown in figure 37.1.

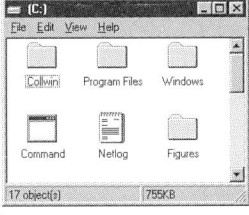

Fig. 37.1 The Figures folder is visible in the window that shows the contents of the C drive.

3. Right-click the Figures folder icon. This displays the context menu for the folder.

4. From the context menu, choose the Sharing option. This displays the Properties sheet for the folder, with the Sharing tab selected, as shown in figure 37.2.

> **Note:** If the Sharing option is not available from the context menu, then you need to set up file sharing as described in Chapter 36, "Communicating with a Network."

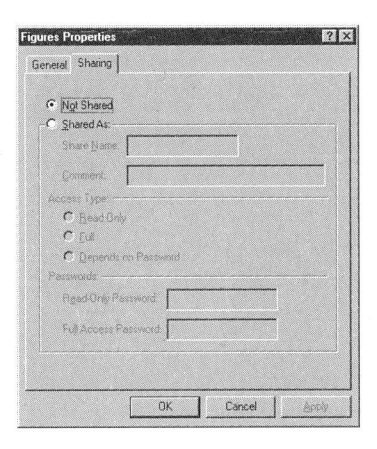

Fig. 37.2 The Sharing tab enables you to specify how a folder should be shared.

Sharing Folders **925**

At this point you can specify that you want to share the folder by simply clicking the Shared As option. You can then specify the name by which the folder should be shared, and the type of access you want to provide.

Naming a Shared Folder

After you have clicked the Shared As option, the Share Name field becomes active. In the Share Name field you can indicate the name you want to use for this folder when it is shared over the network. Windows 95 provides the actual name of the folder (Figures) as a default, but you can change it to any name you want.

Underneath the shared name for the folder is a field where you can include a comment. This comment has no value other than as a piece of information for whoever is browsing through the network. When the browser is looking through the detail for your computer, the comment appears to the right of the folder name.

Setting Access Rights

When you are sharing a folder, you can grant other people either read-only privileges (which means they cannot alter the files or the folder) or full privileges (which means they can do anything they want with the folder). To offer read-only privileges, click the Read-Only button; to offer full privileges, click the Full button.

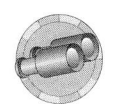

> **Note:** The access rights that you can grant to other people depends on the type of network client you are using. For instance, with NetWare you have a much finer level of control over access rights than with Microsoft networks.

There is a third access right available—Depends on Password. With this access right selected, what remote users can do to your folder depends on whether they know the proper password. Passwords are entered at the bottom of the Sharing tab. There are two passwords available—read-only and full. All you need to do is enter the passwords that you want associated with your folder.

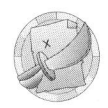

> **Tip:** If you are not concerned over the contents of your folder and who has access to it, simply leave the password fields blank. Without a password, anyone can access your system at the access level that you specify.

Determining Who Can Do What

By creatively mixing the settings of the access type and the passwords, you gain quite a bit of control over who can do what with your system. Table 37.1 shows how you can mix the settings to provide different types of access.

Table 37.1 Determining Types of Access

Type of Access	Access Type	Read-Only Password	Full-Access Password
Anyone can read	Read-only	Don't set	
Anyone can change	Full	Don't set	
Some people can read	Read-only	Set	
Some people can change	Full	Set	
Some people can read and change	Depends on password	Set	Set

Changing What Is Shared

After a folder on your system is shared on the network, you can modify the way in which it is shared at any time. To do this, simply select a folder you previously shared. You can tell which folders you have shared by the fact that they appear with a small hand holding them when you view the folder's icon (see figure 37.3).

Sharing Folders **927**

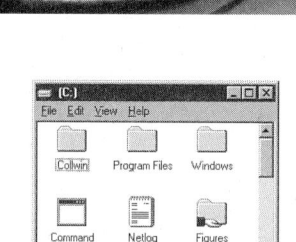

Fig. 37.3 A shared folder has a small hand under the folder icon.

Just right-click the shared folder and choose S<u>h</u>aring from the context menu. The Properties sheet for the folder appears, with the Sharing tab selected. At this point, you can change any aspect of the sharing you want. If you want to stop sharing the folder all together, simply click the N<u>o</u>t Shared option.

Accessing Other People's Data

The process of accessing data on other people's systems is called *mapping a drive*. This simply means that you create a drive letter on your system which is really a pointer to a folder on another system. This is the same process that other network users go through when they want to access information on your computer.

To map a drive to another person's system, you must first know the other system's UNC path.

Mapping a Drive

To map a drive on your system, follow these steps:

1. Right-click either the My Computer or the Network Neighborhood icons on your desktop. This displays a context menu for the object.

2. Select the Map N<u>e</u>twork Drive option from the context menu. This displays the Map Network Drive dialog box, as shown in figure 37.4.

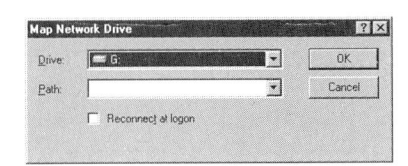

Fig. 37.4 You map a network drive by picking a drive letter and specifying a path to the remote folder.

3. In the Drive field, select a drive letter to use on your system when referring to the network drive. You can see the drive letters currently in use by clicking the arrow at the right side of the field.

4. In the Path field supply the full UNC path to the shared folder you want to access.

5. Select the Reconnect at logon check box if you want this network drive to be available every time you use Windows 95.

6. Click the OK button.

At this point, you can access the network drive as if it were a local drive on your system. Your ability to map a network drive depends on several points:

➤ The folder you want to access on a different system must have been shared by whoever controls that system.

➤ The remote system must be available on the network.

➤ You must know the passwords necessary to access the folder (if any) before mapping is complete.

While the mapping process just described is quick and easy, it assumes you know the system and folder name that you want to map. If you refer to figure 37.4, you will notice that there is no browse button on the Map Network Drive dialog box. There is one other way you can map a network drive. This method involves using either the browser or the Windows Explorer.

To illustrate, let's assume that you want to access a folder on a remote system that is used for budget data. You could double-click the

Accessing Other People's Data **929**

Network Neighborhood icon on your desktop, and then simply start looking through the different computers in the network. You only need to double-click a computer, and you will see the folders that have been shared on that system. When you find the folder you want, right-click the folder and choose Map Network Drive from the context menu. Figure 37.5 shows the results of going through this process.

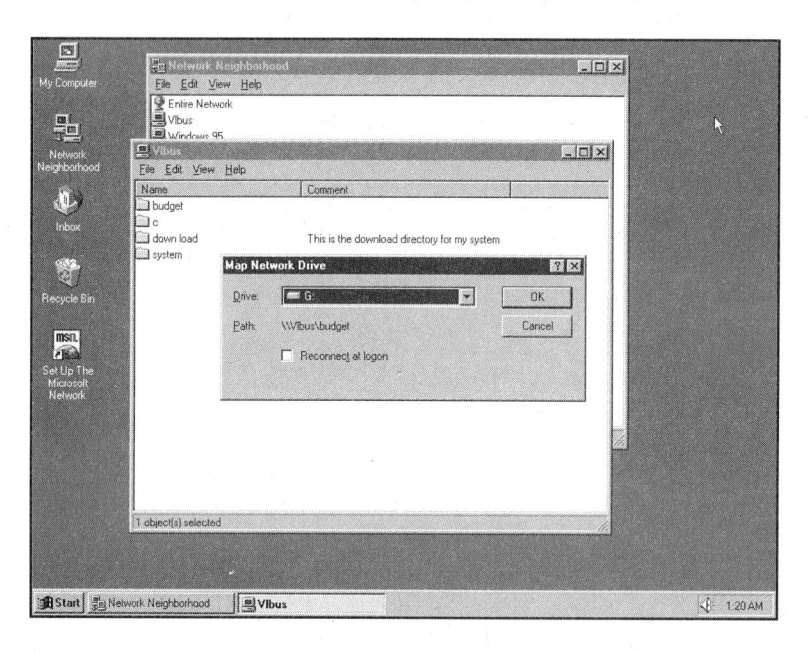

Fig. 37.5 Mapping a network drive is easy as you are browsing through the Net.

The Map Network Drive dialog box looks the same as shown earlier, except the Path field is filled in for you. All you need to do is confirm that the drive letter you want is selected, set the Reconnect at logon check box as desired, and then click OK.

Regardless of how you map a network drive, the drive shows up whenever you browse through My Computer, as shown in figure 37.6. You may wonder why the drives show up here rather than in the Network Neighborhood portion of your system. The answer is that the network drives are now assigned to local drive letters on your system, and disk resources on your system show up under the My Computer icon.

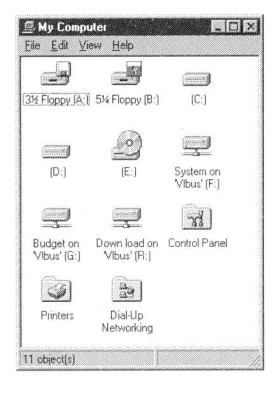

Fig. 37.6 Mapped drives show up in the My Computer window on your system.

Disconnecting a Network Drive

The point at which network drives are disconnected depends on their *persistence*. Persistence is a property that you set when you check or clear the Reconnec*t* at logon check box when originally mapping the drive. If you check the box, then the only way that the drive is disconnected is if you manually do it; if the check box is clear, then whenever you restart your system, the connection with the remote folder is broken.

To manually disconnect a previously mapped drive, follow these steps:

1. Double-click the My Computer icon on the desktop.

2. Right-click the icon for the drive you want to disconnect. This displays the context menu for the drive.

3. Choose *D*isconnect from the context menu.

At this point, the drive is disconnected, and you will no longer see the icon in the My Computer folder. If you later want to access the drive, simply go through the process of mapping the drive again.

Accessing Other People's Data **931**

Printing in a Networked Environment

In Chapter 20, "Managing Your Printers," and Chapter 21, "Printing from Windows 95," you learned the basics of using printers. Those basics are applicable to using printers whether you are printing to a local printer or through a network. There are a few other printing topics that are unique to the network environment which are addressed in the following sections.

Adding Separator Pages

Windows 95 enables you to add separator pages between print jobs you send to a printer. Separator pages print out between print jobs, making it easier in a shared-printer environment to determine to whom the printout should be sent. Although you can specify separator pages for a local printer, it does not make much sense because you are aware of everything you print on your own printer.

To instruct Windows 95 to use a separator page, follow these steps:

1. Choose Settings from the Start menu.

2. Choose Printers from the Settings menu.

3. Right-click the icon for the printer that needs a separator page. This displays the context menu for the printer.

4. Choose Properties from the context menu. This displays the Properties sheet for the printer.

5. Select the General tab. The dialog box should appear as shown in figure 37.7.

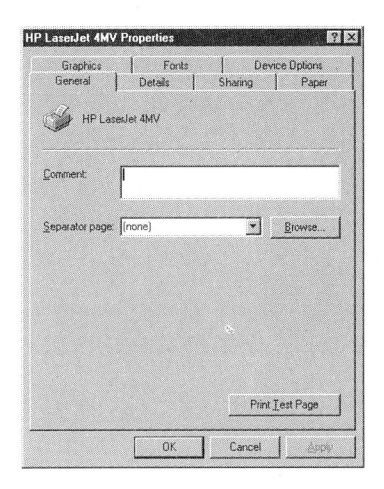

Fig. 37.7 You can specify a separator page for a printer using the General tab of the Properties sheet.

As you might surmise, the Separator page field controls the printing of a separator page. In this field you have three choices:

- **None.** No separator page is printed between print jobs. This is the default setting for each printer.

- **Full.** Prints a fancy page that includes graphics. Takes longer to process and print than a simple separator page.

- **Simple.** Prints a page that consists of text only. Prints faster than a full separator page.

In addition to the three basic choices, you can also pick a custom separator page to print. Windows 95 enables you to use any Windows metafile as a separator page. You can create these types of files with many types of graphics programs, such as the Paint accessory.

Printing in a Networked Environment **933**

Customizing Separator Pages for NetWare Printers

If the network printer you are configuring is serviced via a NetWare server, you have some additional options that you can customize when you set up the separator page. When you display the dialog box for a NetWare shared printer, click the Capture Settings tab. You can set NetWare-specific settings such as the form name or number, the timeout value, the name that appears on the separator page, and the number of copies of each print job that should be printed.

Using Fonts

One of the challenges that face network users is the issue of fonts. In Chapter 22, "Working with Fonts," you learned how you can use fonts effectively. While the instructions and guidance contained in that chapter are appropriate for a locally connected printer, there are some nuances that are applicable when printing in a networked environment.

The problem for network users is how to guarantee that the needed font is available and how you can downloaded it to the printer. This is particularly true when you are trying to print the documents you loaded from a network drive. If the fonts used in the document are also available on your local machine, you have no problem. This is not always the case, however.

One solution is to download fonts directly to the printer so that they are available there. In that instance, you would not need to worry about where the fonts resided; they would always be available on the printer. The danger in downloading fonts to the printer is that they are lost if someone shuts off the printer to clear a problem such as a paper jam. Some printers overcome this problem by adding a hard disk to the printer, on which you can store fonts until you need them. The number of printers with hard drives actually installed is rather low, however.

For a network, an obvious (and satisfactory) solution is to load your fonts onto a shared network drive. With Windows 95 you can treat the fonts as if they are loaded on your local system, even though they are actually on a remote system. To do this, the network administrator will need to install the fonts to the network drive. Do not use the Fonts folder in Windows 95 to do this; that is only helpful for loading fonts to your local computer. Instead, either use the font loader provided with the font collection, or simply copy the TTF (TrueType) font files to the shared network folder.

When you are ready to access the fonts from your local machine, follow these steps:

1. Choose Settings from the Start menu.
2. Choose Control Panel from the Settings menu.
3. Double-click the Fonts icon in the Control Panel. This displays the Fonts folder window.
4. Choose the Install New Font option from the File menu. This displays the Add Fonts dialog box.
5. Select the drive and folder for the network drive that contains the TTF files.
6. Clear the Copy fonts to Fonts folder check box at the bottom of the dialog box.
7. Select the fonts you want to use on your local system.
8. Click the OK button.

At this point, the Registry is updated so that it contains the pointers to the font files on the network drive, but the font files themselves have not been copied to your hard drive. When you look at the Fonts folder window, you can tell which fonts are not on your local system by the presence of a shortcut arrow on the font icon. This is illustrated with the Algerian font, in figure 37.8.

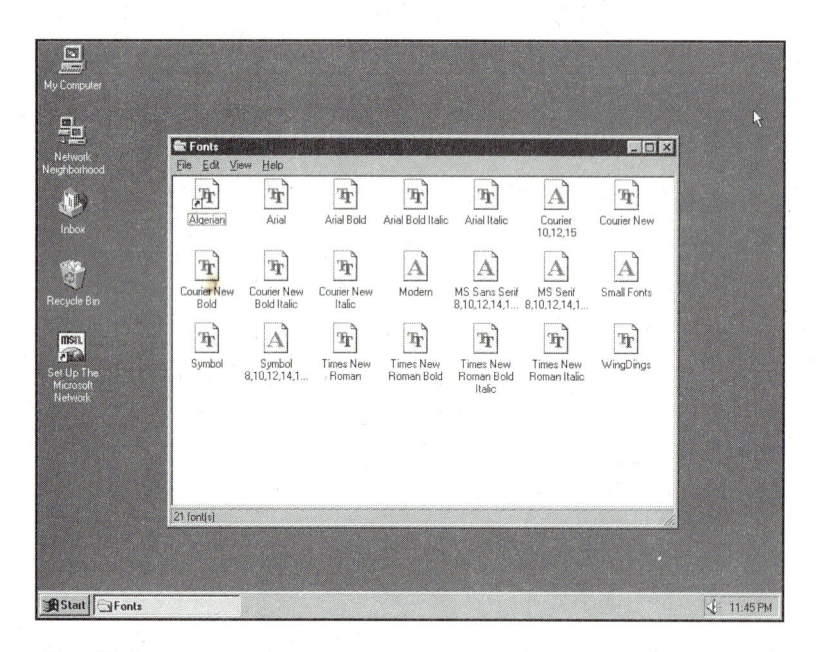

Fig. 37.8 Fonts not loaded on the local system are displayed with a shortcut arrow on the font icon in the Fonts folder.

Managing the Network

The amount of management done on a network depends on the type of network you are using. If you have a small peer-to-peer network (perhaps a couple of computers in your office), then there is not much management required. If you have a larger network (perhaps several hundred computers in a client/server network), then your network management tasks become much more complex and time-consuming.

In larger networks, the job of managing the network typically is the responsibility of a single person called the *network administrator*. In smaller or mid-size networks, the job of administering the network may be just one hat worn by a technician or a "power user" in the office. Regardless of the type of network you are using, there is always some sort of network management that must take place. The following sections describe some guidelines for managing your network.

Managing a Peer-to-Peer Network

Peer-to-peer networks are very simple in concept, and are intended for small offices and workgroups. They are characterized by the lack of a centralized file server and often lack a formal network administrator.

Peer-to-peer networking is built directly in to Windows 95. Managing such a network generally consists of the following tasks:

- Determining the location of network printers.
- Determining the location of centralized files.
- Setting workgroup standards.

Each of these topics is addressed in the following sections.

Network Printers

Adding printers to your network is a fairly easy task. You learned in Chapter 20, "Managing Your Printers," exactly how to add printers and make them available over the network. Many times the hard part is determining where network printers will be located. Wherever they are located, you know that there will be pretty high traffic to and from the printer. With this in mind, you could use the following guidelines in picking a location:

- Pick a location that is centrally located to the bulk of the printer users. This does not necessarily mean that the printer should be right in the middle of all the users. Instead, you should think through who will be using the printer the most, and then locate the printer in the middle of those people.

- Do not use network printers for sensitive data. It is not always a good idea for management or finance people to use the network printers. They are often printing sensitive information that is best not shared around the water cooler. For people who work with sensitive data, you may want to get local printers or special network printers that require passwords to use.

➤ If possible, place the printer near someone that will accept responsibility for it. Printers often need to be fed, and adding paper to a network printer can be frustrating if you need to walk to the other end of the building to do it. Instead, find someone near the printer who can watch it and change paper, toner, or ribbons if necessary.

Centralized Files

Because networks are designed to primarily share information, it is not unusual for even the smallest network to have files that are shared on a regular basis. These files might be something as simple as a common document repository, or as complex as the business accounting files.

Where you place common files has quite a bit to do with the productivity derived from your network. The following guidelines will help you make a sound decision in this area:

➤ Pick a computer system that has a large hard drive. Larger hard drives can accommodate more rapid growth in the quantity or size of shared files. In addition, the larger hard drives tend to have faster access rates, which can significantly boost throughput on network data.

➤ Pick a computer system that does not belong to a computer neophyte. There is less chance of accidentally deleting shared files or damaging them in some other way if the computer user is more comfortable with computers.

➤ Pick a system that has a fast CPU. If the system that has the shared files has a slow CPU, the user might notice a slowdown in the system as data is being accessed for users on the network. Faster CPU speeds mean less slowdown and less chance for developing bottlenecks.

➤ Pick a system that has at least 12M of memory. Actually, the more memory in the computer that has the shared files, the better. More memory means there is less disk swapping at the computer, and thus critical disk requests (such as those to send data over the network) can be processed faster.

➤ Pick a system that will not be turned off. Many people have a tendency to just flip their machines off at the end of the day. If you are dealing with files to be shared across the network, this can cause havoc. Make sure that the system with the files will be left on and available all the time.

Workgroup Standards

Workgroups (and the networks they use) have a tendency to grow over time. It seems that everyone on the network has a different way of doing things, as well. While this is acceptable for individual machines, it can quickly devolve into management anarchy when dealing with shared resources.

Early in the development of your network, you should develop a set of standards to which people on the network should adhere. For instance, you might develop the following:

➤ A shared folder structure. You should decide where common files will be placed on the network. For instance, you might place accounting data on one person's system and budget files on another person's system. Make sure that everyone maps the shared drives to the same letter.

➤ A common file-naming convention. When dealing with common documents, you should use a common naming standard that everyone can learn. With this system, you can recognize any file by its name. For instance, you might specify that any final documents begin with the word FINAL, or that spreadsheet names include both the responsible department and the quarter the spreadsheet represents.

➤ A standard device-naming method. As you share printers and folders on the network, you might want to require that the comments field include information that nails down the source of the resource. For instance, the field could contain a person's name, phone extension, or office number.

Managing the Network **939**

There are probably dozens of other ways you can think of to develop standards for your network. The whole idea behind developing workgroup standards is to increase productivity. If each computer on the network is set up to do the same tasks in a different way, then any given person will be completely lost if they switch to another workstation on the network.

As you develop standards, you should write them down and share them with others on the network. These could even become part of the employee manual or the information presented to the employee during training sessions.

Managing a Client/Server Network

Client/server networks differ from peer-to-peer networks primarily in one way: On a client/server network, dedicated servers provide shared disk space, processing capability, and printer management (unlike peer-to-peer networks where workstations double as disk and printer sharing devices). Dedicated servers are generally designed to provide high performance as well as near full-time availability. The most common server operating system for these dedicated servers is Novell NetWare, but Microsoft Windows NT and Banyan Vines are also popular operating system options.

The issues involved in managing shared resources in a client/server environment are similar to those with a peer-to-peer network, except that management responsibilities are often handled by a central group of network administrators. As with a peer-to-peer network, it is important that common and readily understandable naming conventions be used, and it is also important that shared resources such as servers and printers offer high performance and are available whenever users need them.

Client/server operating systems such as NetWare, Windows NT, and Vines offer greater capabilities in the areas of fine-tuning user access and managing shared printing.

Setting Up User Privileges

Your options for controlling user access levels are much broader when you work with a full featured client/server network operating system such as NetWare or Windows NT. With Windows 95's file and print sharing, you can grant others read-only or full-access, and you can optionally require users to enter a password to access a shared disk or folder. With a dedicated network operating system, you can grant and withhold a variety of user rights to fine-tune user access levels. Novell NetWare, for example, enables you to give or withhold the following eight rights to folders and files:

READ

WRITE

CREATE

ERASE

FILE SCAN

ACCESS CONTROL

MODIFY

SUPERVISOR

If you want users to be able to read from and write to a shared database file, but you want to be sure that those same users cannot accidentally or intentionally delete the file, you can grant the rights READ and WRITE but withhold the right ERASE.

Managing User Accounts

Full-featured network operating systems, such as NetWare and Windows NT, also enable you to provide users with individual accounts. When a user receives an account on a server, he or she has a unique login name. You can also require that each user have a password, and you can specify that those users change those passwords regularly. Because users have individual accounts, you can customize each user's access levels as required by granting each user an individual set of rights. If you want to provide each user with a private personal folder on a server, for example, you can do so by assigning to each user's account the rights that he or she needs to access his or her personal folder. For all other users, rights are withheld from that personal folder.

Using Resources on a NetWare Server

When you map drive letters to disks and folders or connect to shared printers on a server running NetWare, you must know how to translate the names that NetWare uses into the Universal Naming Convention (UNC) scheme used by Windows 95. With NetWare, a subdirectory on a server disk has been traditionally identified by the following name:

SERVER/VOLUME:FOLDER\SUBDIRECTORY

The folder structure \WPWIN\DOC on the SYS volume on the SERV1 server, for example, would be named SERV1\SYS:WPWIN\DOC. Using the UNC system, folders and subdirectories are named using this method:

\\SERVER\VOLUME\FOLDER\SUBDIRECTORY

The \WPWIN\DOC folder in the previous example would be named as

\\SERV1\SYS\WPWIN\DOC

using the UNC scheme.

NetWare print queues are named using this method:

\\SERVER\QUEUE

A queue named MRKTING-LJ on a server named SERV3 would be identified as

\\SERV3\MRKTING-LJ

Setting Up Remote Computing

by Gregory J. Root

Remote computing is becoming more and more a part of doing business today. As laptop computers are becoming more powerful, Windows 95 helps to further increase their power and to make connectivity easier than ever before.

Remote computing used to mean configuring IRQs and I/O ports, setting up cables, running arcane MS-DOS programs, and wasting altogether too much time transferring and updating files. Windows 95 running on your laptop will allow you to connect to your office without all these headaches. Almost any function you do on your desktop computer can be done on a remote computer with Windows 95.

With the advent of PC Cards (formerly known as PCMCIA cards), Plug-and-Play technology, and Windows 95, working away from your desk has never been easier. As you work, you can send faxes, print documents, or send electronic mail. You'll be able to quickly reconnect to your desktop workstation without reloading network drivers or restarting your computer. Once reconnected, Windows 95 will fax, print, and send everything you've done since you last connected.

In this chapter, you'll learn how to do the following:

➤ Extend your laptop's battery life

➤ Install the tools you need to remote compute

➤ Defer printing, faxing, and e-mail

Advanced Power Management (APM)

Keeping your laptop up and running while you're on the road is an important aspect of remote computing. Advanced Power Management (APM) lets you maximize the battery life of your laptop by suspending power usage of key components after a specified time period. As part of managing the remaining battery power, APM will stop your hard drive from spinning when you aren't accessing it. By doing this, APM puts a major source of battery drain in a state of suspended animation. The same is true for your display: APM will turn it off after a period of inactivity to save battery time. On some laptops, APM can even slow down your CPU to save a large amount of battery life. When you need to perform calculations, access the hard drive, or use the display, APM will quickly turn on the suspended devices for you.

Eventually, when your battery does become too low, APM intervenes. For example, if applications are running, APM automatically saves open files.

Most laptop manufacturers provide a program or keyboard combination to change the setup of the time-outs. These changes must usually be made from a DOS mode (see your laptop's manual for more details). By turning on APM, Windows 95 uses the values you specified when you configured your laptop's BIOS for APM.

To use APM, do the following steps. If you aren't sure if your laptop supports APM, try this procedure anyway; you'll be able to tell in the first few steps.

1. Right-click the My Computer icon on your desktop and choose Properties at the bottom of the menu. The System Properties sheet appears.
2. Click on the Device Manager tab.
3. Click on the + to the left of System devices.
4. Double-click on the Advanced Power Management support System device.

> **Tip:** If there is no listing for Advanced Power Management Support, your computer doesn't support it.

5. Click on the Settings tab in the Advanced Power Management dialog box, as shown in figure 38.1.
6. If it's not selected, click on the box next to Enable power management support.

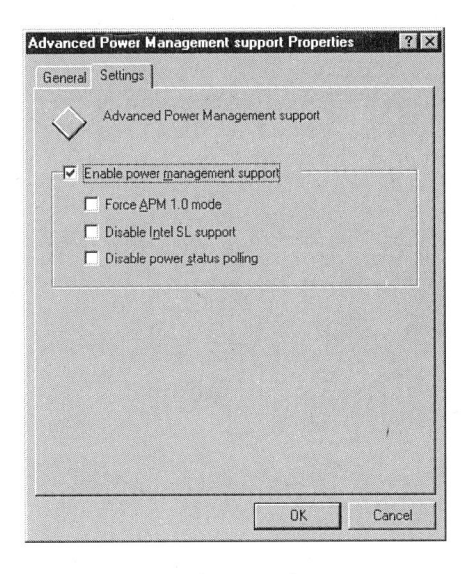

Fig. 38.1 You can enable Advanced Power Management by choosing Enable power management support.

Advanced Power Management (APM) **945**

If you want to force APM to use the mode compatible with Windows 3.1, place a check mark next to Force APM 1.0 mode. Microsoft and Intel originally developed the power management interface in your computer's BIOS for use under Windows 3.1. Since that time, advances have been made in BIOS technology. However, not all BIOS correctly handle the new features in APM 1.1. If you experience problems with your computer automatically moving into suspend mode, selecting this option may clear up those problems.

If your computer does not come out of suspend mode, try selecting Disable Intel SL support. This may allow your laptop to return from suspend mode without locking up.

If your computer spontaneously shuts down without your interacting with it, this may be caused by Windows 95 communicating with APM much more frequently than Windows 3.x would. If you have this problem, select Disable power status polling, which will disable the battery meter on the taskbar.

7. Click on OK to save your changes.

8. Click on OK to close the System Properties sheet. When asked if you want to restart your computer, click Yes. If you want to wait until later to restart your computer, click No. Be aware that APM won't become active until you restart.

Read the next section if you would like to learn how to add a status display that tells you how much battery power remains.

Showing the Battery Meter

When you use your computer away from an AC power source, battery life becomes an important factor in determining how much work you can accomplish. Windows 95 can assist you by displaying a battery meter, which can be displayed on the taskbar, so you're always aware of the status of your battery.

To display the battery meter on the taskbar, do the following:

1. From the taskbar, click Start, Settings, Control Panel.

2. Double-click the Power control panel icon in the Control Panel dialog box.

3. Click Enable battery meter on the taskbar if it's not already selected (see figure 38.2).

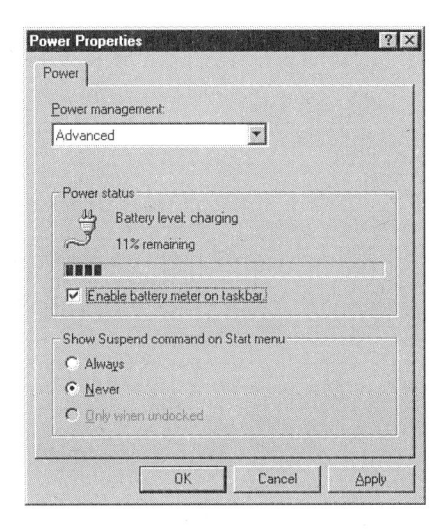

Fig. 38.2 You can choose to display the battery meter on the taskbar, so you're always aware of battery life.

4. Click OK at the bottom of the Power dialog box to save your change.

Now to check your battery supply, move the cursor over the battery symbol on the taskbar. As shown in figure 38.3, a box will pop up indicating the amount of power left. When the laptop is plugged into an AC adapter, a plug icon will display on the taskbar instead of the battery symbol, as shown in the second screen in figure 38.3.

Advanced Power Management (APM) **947**

Fig. 38.3 The battery icon in the tray on the taskbar shows how much battery remains when you move your mouse over it. If the battery is being charged, a power plug appears instead.

948 Chapter 38: Setting Up Remote Computing

Tip: If the battery meter shows that you're almost out of power, just plug in the AC adapter while the computer is running. The battery meter will show the plug icon to indicate that your battery is being recharged.

Finally, if you want to be notified that the battery is running out of power, you can turn on the low battery warning by following these steps:

1. Double-click the battery or power plug icon, as shown in figure 38.4. The Battery Meter dialog box appears.

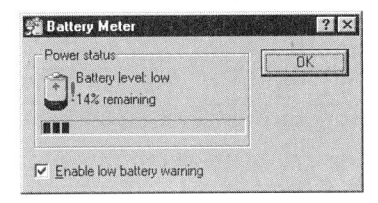

Fig. 38.4 The Battery Meter dialog box allows you to turn on a warning that notifies you when the battery supply is running low.

2. Select the Enable low battery warning check box.

3. Click OK to save your change.

Enabling Suspend Mode

When using your laptop away from an AC power source, every minute of battery power is valuable. As discussed earlier, Advanced Power Management will automatically suspend different functions of your computer based on your preferences. For example, you may have configured your laptop to go into complete suspend mode after 15 minutes. But if you know you're going to leave your laptop for a longer period, you can invoke suspend mode manually. This way, you won't have to shut all your programs down and then wait for Windows 95 to restart when you're ready to work.

When you manually activate the suspend mode, the current state of all your open programs and files is remembered, and your laptop will be placed in a mode that uses much less power. When you want to use the computer again, all your files and programs will be as you left them.

To immediately enable the suspend mode, do the following:

1. From the taskbar, click Start, Settings, Control Panel.

2. Double-click on the Power control panel icon in the Control Panel dialog box.

3. As shown in figure 38.5, choose Always under the Show Suspend command on the Start menu to have Suspend show on your Start menu every time.

   Choose Only when undocked to show the Suspend menu when you've taken your laptop out of the docking station.

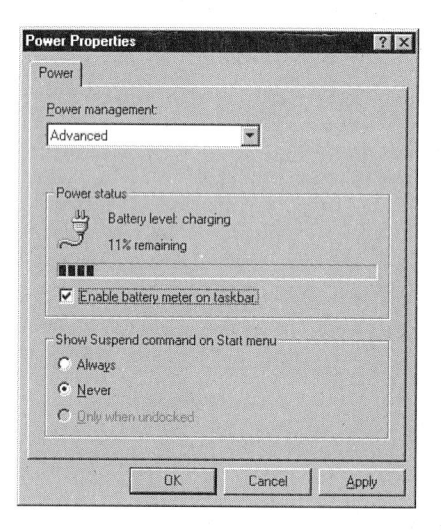

Fig. 38.5 You have to enable suspend mode to be able to access Suspend on the Start menu.

950 Chapter 38: Setting Up Remote Computing

> **Note:** If the Only when undocked option is disabled, this means that your laptop is unable to dock. Your best option, in this case, is to show the Suspend menu item Always.

4. Once you've made the appropriate choice, click on OK to save your changes.

Now when you click Start, depending on your choice, you'll have access to Suspend, as shown in figure 38.6.

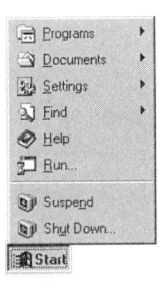

Fig. 38.6 Choosing Suspend on the Start menu immediately places your laptop in a state of low power usage.

To restore your computer, turn the power on. (Check with your laptop's documentation if that doesn't work. You may have to do something else.) All programs and files will be as they were before you initiated the suspend mode.

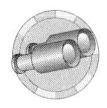

> **Note:** Your network connections may not be restored when the laptop comes out of suspend mode. Therefore, it's a good idea to save any documents that you have open from the network *before* you choose the Suspend mode.

Advanced Power Management (APM) **951**

Preparing to Connect a Laptop to a Desktop

With Windows 95, you can hook your laptop up to a desktop computer to print your documents, send your e-mail or faxes, or update your master files with the changes that you made while you were on the road. In the next section, you'll learn how to perform those specific tasks. Before you can go on the road, you may need to set up your laptop and desktop computer. The kind of setup depends on your hardware.

If your laptop normally docks at a docking station, uses PC Cards (PCMCIA cards), or communicates through standard ports on the back to access network, printer, and telephone services, you won't have to configure anything. Windows 95 automatically detects when your network, printing, and electronic mail services are available. In the case of a docking station, Windows 95 senses your docking state. If you use a 32-bit PC Card to access network services, Windows 95 automatically enables it without shutting down. Additionally, as you connect your local printer, Windows begins to send your documents when it comes online.

However, you'll need to install some additional Windows 95 components to store files and send electronic mail if you don't have a place to attach your laptop to a network. You'll also need these components if the printer you normally access is on the network and you don't have an extra connection to the network in your work area.

Installing Remote Networking

Windows 95 ships with two programs that allow your laptop to talk to other computers without a network between them: (1) Dial-Up Networking allows you to connect your laptop to other computers via a modem; (2) Direct Cable Connection allows you to connect your laptop to another computer through a parallel or serial port. These components give your laptop access to all the resources your desktop computer has. In other words, if your desktop computer has access to network servers, printers, and electronic mail, your laptop will too. In fact, the manner in which your laptop will access these resources is no different from using your desktop computer.

When you installed Windows 95 on your laptop by using the Portable installation type, the Direct Cable Connection and Dial-Up Networking components should have been installed for you. However, if you plan to connect to your desktop computer via a serial or parallel cable, you'll need to install the Direct Cable Connection on your desktop computer. If you aren't sure if everything is set up correctly, use these steps to install the required components for your laptop and desktop computers.

1. Insert the Windows 95 CD-ROM into your CD-ROM drive. If you're using a protected-mode CD-ROM driver, Windows 95 automatically displays the Windows 95 main installation menu window. Close the window for now.

2. From the taskbar, click Start, Settings, Control Panel.

3. Double-click on the Add/Remove Programs icon in the Control Panel dialog box to begin the installation.

4. As figure 38.7 shows, click on the Windows Setup tab to access the optional components of Windows 95.

5. Click on Communications. Notice that under Description, you're told two of four components are already installed (That's the default; it will be different if you've added others.)

6. Click on Details. The Communications dialog box appears (see figure 38.8).

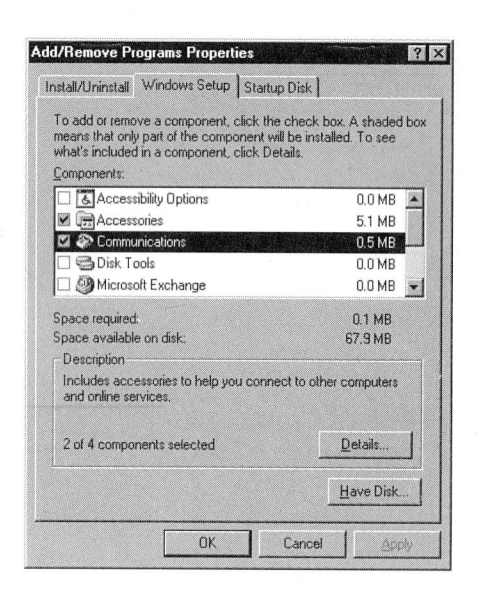

Fig. 38.7 Select the Communications component to access the Direct Cable Connection and Dial-Up Networking components.

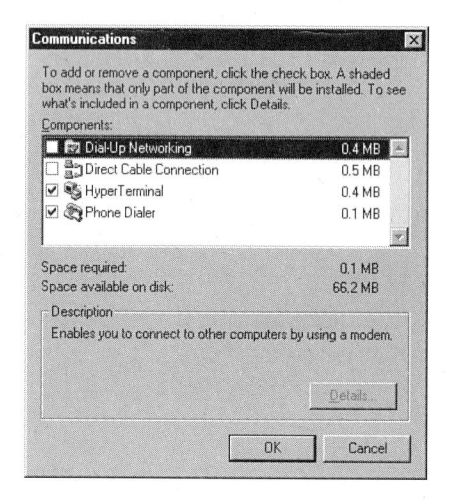

Fig. 38.8 To connect your computer to other computers, select the Dial-Up Networking and Direct Cable Connection components.

7. Select Dial-Up Networking and Direct Cable Connection by clicking on the box next to the options.

8. Click on OK to save your modifications. You'll be returned to the Add/Remove Programs Properties sheet.

9. Click on OK to finalize your changes. Windows 95 will now install the additional components from the CD-ROM.

10. A prompt tells you to enter the computer and workgroup name that will identify your computer. The computer name lets other people on the network find your computer. The workgroup identifies the group of computers to which you want to belong. Common examples of workgroups are departments or floors of a building. Click OK when you've entered them.

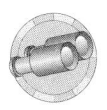

> **Note:** The computer name and workgroup name can't be the same.

> **Caution:** If you receive the following message, proceed with caution: A file being copied is older than the file currently on your computer. It is recommended that you keep your existing file. When in doubt, leave the existing version, especially if it's a DLL file.

A message appears stating that the system settings have been reconfigured.

You'll also briefly see a message that the system is updating shortcuts. The Dial-Up Networking and Direct Cable Connection options are being placed on the Start menu under Accessories.

11. Click on OK to restart your computer for the changes to take effect.

Preparing to Connect a Laptop to a Desktop **955**

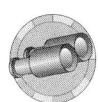

Note: The next time you turn on your computer, you will be prompted to enter a user name and password. If you are normally connected to a network, use your regular user ID and password, and click OK. To ignore it, click Cancel.

Caution: In order for the two computers to communicate, they must both have a common network protocol installed. Additionally, only shared resources using IPX/SPX and NetBEUI protocols are accessible to the laptop computer (the guest to the desktop). Even if TCP/IP is configured correctly on the desktop, the TCP/IP services are not passed on to the laptop.

Your computers are now ready to begin transferring information. To learn how to defer printing documents, sending faxes and electronic mail, and updating files, read the next few sections.

To learn how to actually transfer your work in progress between your laptop and the desktop computer, Chapter 39, "Seamless Remote Computing," instructs you for every type of connection.

Serial and Parallel Connections

You can connect your laptop to a stand-alone desktop or a workstation with a serial or parallel cable. Parallel cables are generally faster than serial cables. Additionally, if the two computers have ECP parallel ports, the speed is approximately four times that of a serial port connection.

Beware: Direct Cable Connection will *not* work with a plain parallel or serial cable. To run a parallel connection, the cable has to be a standard or basic 4-bit cable (also known as a Laplink or an Interlink parallel cable, or an ECP or UCM cable). To run a serial connection, you need a serial, null-modem RS-232 cable. It's not easy to get. You usually have to get it from a big computer dealer or a parts supplier, or by mail. Retail office-supply stores usually don't carry that item. In an emergency, you can buy a program—such as LapLink or FastMove!—that comes with the right parallel cables and is available at most software stores. It's an expensive option, though.

Installing Microsoft Briefcase

Windows 95 comes with a feature called Briefcase that synchronizes your laptop and desktop files. If your computer uses a docking station, a PC Card (PCMCIA), or Dial-Up Networking, Windows 95 will automatically begin synchronizing your files as soon as the connection is made to the network. If you connect to your desktop computer by a Direct Cable Connection, you manually initiate the synchronization process. If the program that created the files supports merging two revisions of a file (such as Microsoft Word for Windows), Windows 95 will try to use those features to update the files. However, not many applications provide this functionality yet. Instead, Briefcase will compare the dates of the files and keep the newest one.

You install Briefcase only on the computer that will modify the files. Therefore, you need to install Briefcase only on your laptop computer. You won't have to install it on your desktop computer.

To make sure Briefcase is installed on your laptop computer, right-click on a blank portion of the desktop and select New from the context menu. If Briefcase appears on the submenu, Briefcase is ready to go. If it doesn't appear, install Briefcase by following these steps:

1. Insert the Windows 95 CD-ROM in your CD-ROM drive. Windows 95 may automatically load the CD and bring up the main Windows 95 installation menu window. Close the window for now.

2. From the taskbar, click Start, Settings, Control Panel.

3. Double-click on the Add/Remove Programs icon in the Control Panel dialog box to begin the installation.

4. As figure 38.9 shows, click on the Windows Setup tab to access the optional components of Windows 95.

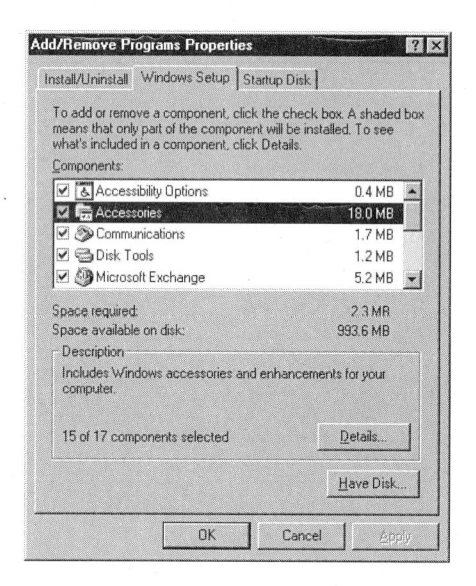

Fig. 38.9 Select the Accessories component to access the Direct Cable Connection and Dial-Up Networking components.

5. Click on Accessories. Notice that under Description, you're told 2 of 4 components are already installed (That's the default; it will be different if you've added others.)

6. Click Details. The Accessories dialog box appears (see figure 38.10).

7. Select Briefcase by clicking on the box next to the options.

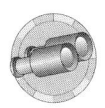

> **Note:** If Briefcase isn't listed in the components, it's already installed, and your computer is already set to use Briefcase.

8. Click on OK to save your modifications. You'll be returned to the Add/Remove Programs Properties sheet.

9. Click on OK to finalize your changes. Windows 95 will now install the additional components from the CD-ROM.

958   Chapter 38: Setting Up Remote Computing

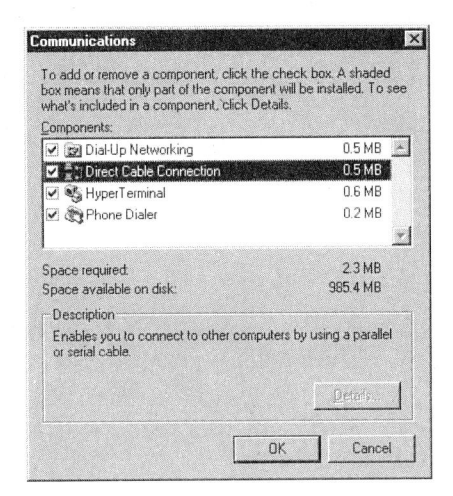

Fig. 38.10 To connect your computer to other computers, select the Dial-Up Networking and Direct Cable Connection components.

> **Caution:** If you receive the following message, proceed with caution: A file being copied is older than the file currently on your computer. It is recommended that you keep your existing file. When in doubt, leave the existing version, especially if it's a DLL file.

A message appears stating that the system settings have been reconfigured.

10. Click OK to restart your computer so that the changes take effect.

Deferring Communications on a Portable Computer

When you work at your desktop computer, printing is as easy as clicking on the Print button. When you worked remotely before Windows 95, you had to remember to print every file after hooking up your laptop. Or maybe you solved the problem by transferring your laptop files onto a floppy disk and then using the floppy in your desktop computer. Not only were those methods time-consuming, they were annoying. Furthermore, it wasn't possible to create electronic mail or faxes and store them until later. Previous versions of Windows required immediate access to a network to create these types of communications.

With the deferred communications features, Windows 95 keeps track of your outbound printing, mail, and faxes. Windows 95 automatically prints whenever the remote computer is hooked up to the network or direct cable connection. It also sends electronic mail and faxes when the connection is reestablished to the postoffice and a peer fax server.

Deferred Printing

You might want to use deferred printing on a laptop that doesn't have a printer installed. In that case, you'll have to install the same printer that's available on the computer to which you'll be connecting. To install the printer, follow the steps in Chapter 20, "Managing Your Printers."

Once you have your printer installed, you're ready to use deferred printing. You can defer your print jobs by doing the following:

1. Open the Printers folder by clicking on Start, Settings, Printers or double-clicking on My Computer on the desktop and double-clicking the Printers folder. Either way, the Printers window will be displayed similarly to figure 38.11.

2. Right-click the icon for your printer and check Work Offline. If your printer was originally defined as a local printer, Work Offline is replaced on the menu by Pause Printing. In our example above, this is a local printer that can be directly attached to the laptop computer.

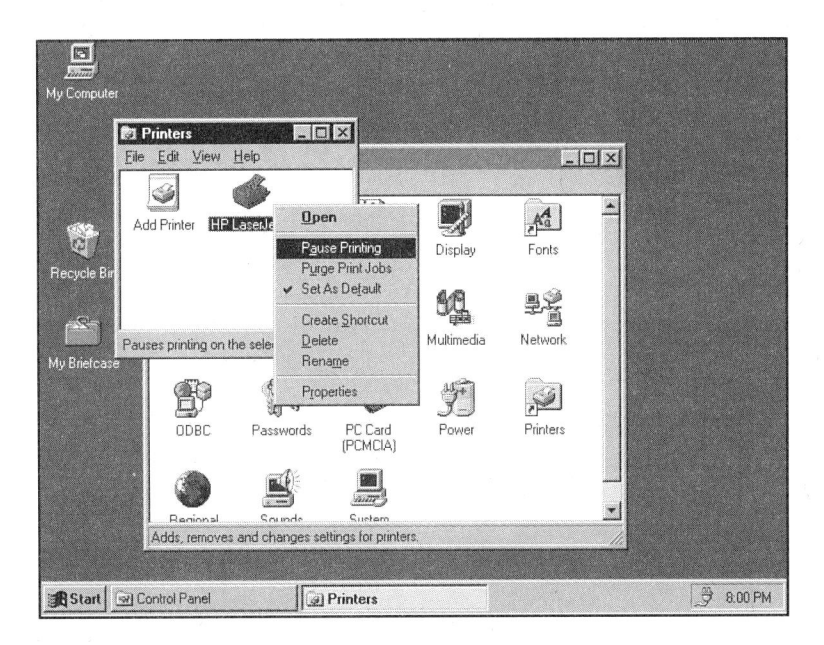

Fig. 38.11 The Printers window can be accessed via the Start menu or the My Computer dialog box.

That's all there is to it. Whenever you send a job to the printer, it will spool (store) instead of print.

As soon as your laptop is connected to the network containing the printer, Windows 95 will begin to print your jobs automatically. If you plan to use a Direct Cable Connection when you get back to your desktop, you'll need to uncheck manually Work Offline on the printer's context menu to begin printing (see figure 38.11).

Deferred Electronic Mail

If you want to create electronic mail to send when you get back to your office or send a fax, you'll need to have the Microsoft Exchange component installed on your laptop. If it's already installed, read through this section to verify that all the options are set correctly for remote computing.

Deferring Communications on a Portable Computer **961**

To install Microsoft Exchange as part of remote computing, follow these steps:

1. Connect your laptop to the network. The Microsoft Exchange client must be able to communicate directly with the postoffice to complete the installation.

2. From the taskbar click on Start, Settings, Control Panel.

3. Once the Control Panel dialog box appears, double-click the Add/Remove Programs icon.

4. Click on the Windows Setup tab to access the optional components of Windows 95.

5. In the Components list box, place a check mark in the box next to Microsoft Exchange, as shown in figure 38.12. Click OK at the bottom of the dialog box to begin the installation.

During this time, Windows displays the progress of installation and updating of the shortcuts. Once complete, you will be returned to the Control Panel dialog box.

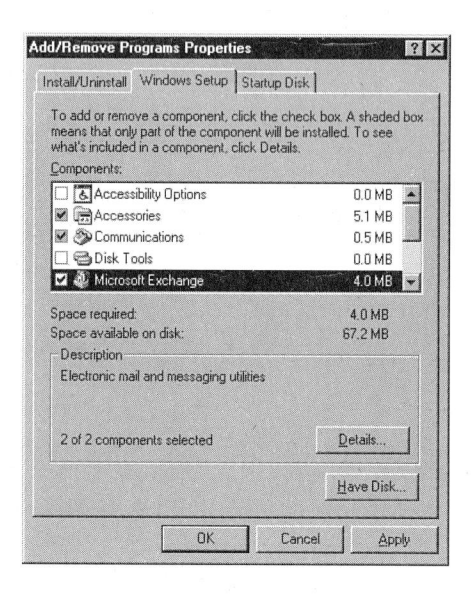

Fig. 38.12 Microsoft Exchange is added via the Windows Setup tab of the Add/Remove Programs Control Panel.

6. Once the Exchange client is installed, you need to modify its properties for remote computing. To do this in the Control Panel, double-click on the Mail and Fax icon. This will display the MS Exchange Settings Properties sheet, as shown in figure 38.13.

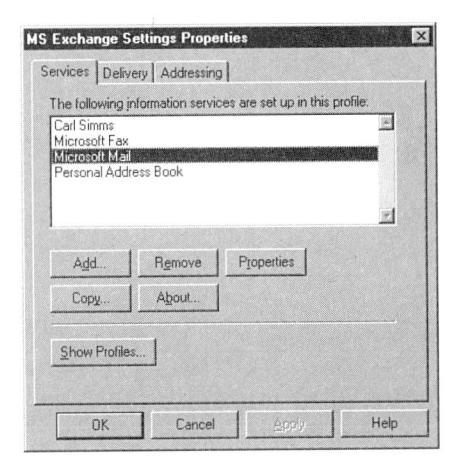

Fig. 38.13 Select the appropriate service for remote computing.

7. From the Services tab, double-click the information service to be used for remote computing on the laptop. The service configuration dialog box will appear (see figure 38.14).

8. Enter the location of the postoffice in the text box at the top of the dialog box. If you aren't sure where it is, click the Browse button to search for it.

9. Choose Automatically sense LAN or Remote option under Select to see how this service should connect at startup. Since you'll probably set up this information service only once, choosing this option will give you the most flexibility in the long term. In any case, if Windows 95 can't figure out which mode you're in, it will present you with a choice.

When you choose Automatically sense LAN or Remote, Windows 95 will use its capability to sense the correct choice of the three other options.

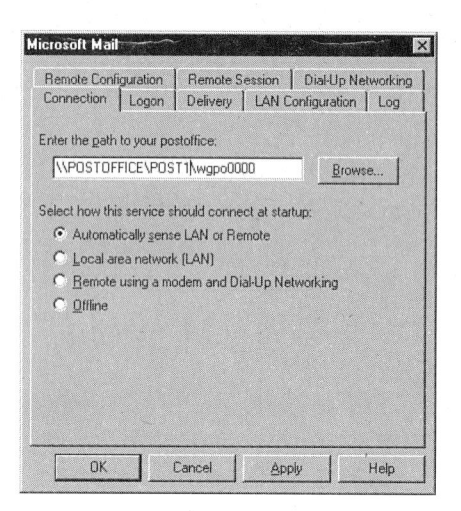

Fig. 38.14 The selected information service will display its Connection properties.

Selecting the Local area network option will cause Exchange to expect to find the postoffice using a network card or the Direct Cable Connection. It will also include the configuration choices you make on the LAN Configuration tab in this dialog box.

Clicking Remote using a modem and Dial-Up Networking will cause Exchange to look for the database over the dial-up connection. It will also use the configuration choices in Remote Configuration, Remote Session, and Dial-Up Networking tabs.

However, if you know the laptop will never directly connect to a local area network, then choose Remote using a modem and Dial-Up Networking.

10. On the Remote Configuration tab (see figure 38.15), make sure to select Use Remote Mail and Use local copy. Use Remote Mail will allow you to store your mail until you're ready to send it. Use local copy allows you to download a complete copy of the main Postoffice Address List to your computer. You'll need this list to address your messages while you're on the road.

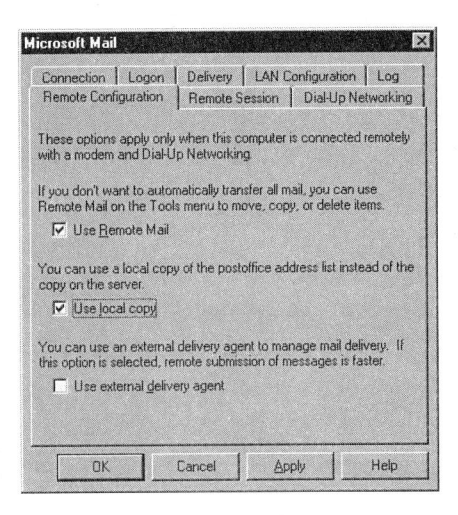

Fig. 38.15 Selecting Use local copy allows you to download a copy of the main Postoffice Address list.

11. Click on OK to save your changes. Click on OK in the MS Exchange Settings Properties to finalize your settings.
12. From the Inbox dialog box, choose Tools, Microsoft Mail Tools, Download Address Lists. This will place a copy of the main Postoffice Address list on your computer.

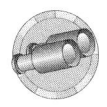

> **Note:** If you plan to send faxes as well, Microsoft Fax uses either the same address list as your electronic mail or a phone number you specify when you create the fax.

13. Click OK to save your changes.

If you want to send faxes while on the road, you must either have a fax modem in your laptop or set up your laptop to use a network fax modem. Chapter 34, "Using Microsoft Exchange," tells you how to configure Exchange to access the network fax. Once the network fax modem is configured, Microsoft Exchange takes care of the rest for you automatically. Exchange places the outbound fax in your Outbox.

Now you're ready to go on the road. Chapter 39, "Seamless Remote Computing," will show you how to seamlessly transfer your work from your laptop to your desktop in a remote computing environment.

Seamless Remote Computing

by Gregory J. Root

In the days before Windows 95, connecting to a host network or desktop computer was complicated and very technical. If you used MS-DOS 6.x, you were able to transfer files with Interlink but couldn't easily access printers and electronic mail. Windows 95 overcomes those obstacles by giving you full access to a network whether you're at home or on the road. What's more, your network doesn't have to run Windows 95; only your laptop does. Your access to the network is only limited by the privileges given to you. You can share files, print to the network printer, transfer documents, and send and receive e-mail. If you don't have a network, you can still access the same types of resources on a stand-alone computer.

The features added to Windows 95 make connections happen behind the scenes. With some minor setup dialog boxes, those connections allow you to interact with servers, printers, and other resources just as if they were actually connected to your laptop. A *host* provides the connection to those resources. With Windows 95 on your laptop, you can connect to many different types of hosts. You can connect to hosts using TCP/IP, IPX/SPX, and NetBEUI network protocols. To connect to a host, you can use any one of the connection protocols, such as PPP, RAS, SLIP, and NetWare Connect. The wide range of protocol support allows you to remotely connect to Windows NT, Novell NetWare, Banyan VINES, UNIX, DEC PATHWORKS, and SunSelect PC-NFS networks. If you have the Windows 95 Plus! Pack, you can even connect to your own desktop computer.

This chapter will show you the procedures to seamlessly connect your remote computer to your desktop or network. You will learn how to do the following:

- Establish a remote connection
- Keep your files in sync
- Transfer your deferred communications tasks

Establishing the Remote Connection

The connection from your laptop to the host is the most important part of remote computing. Therefore, understanding the capabilities and limitations of the network protocols, communication protocols, and connection types will help you correctly configure your remote access computing.

By default, Windows 95 installs several networking components when you install Dial-Up Networking and Direct Cable Connections. These are shown in figure 39.1.

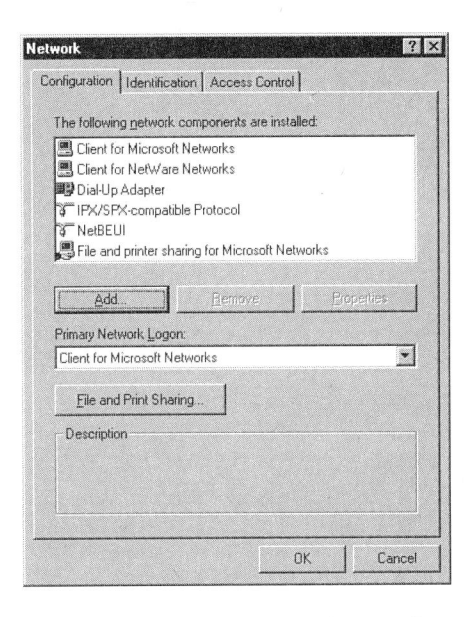

Fig. 39.1 The Network control panel shows the network components installed for Dial-Up Networking and Direct Cable Connection.

The following items are other useful components that may appear in your list, such as network cards or special services:

➤ **Clients.** Client software allows you to use files and printers shared by other computers on many different types of networks. Windows 95 ships with the clients for Microsoft networks and NetWare networks.

➤ **Adapter.** The adapter is the hardware that physically connects your computer to a network. The Dial-Up Adapter that comes with Windows 95 allows you to connect to PPP, RAS, NetWare Connect, and SLIP dial-up servers. You can connect by modem or directly with cables.

➤ **Protocol.** The protocol is the network protocol used to format the data being sent out through the adapter. By default, Windows 95 installs IPX/SPX-compatible Protocol and NetBEUI.

Choosing the Right Protocols

Windows 95 installs the protocols you'll most likely need to connect your remote computer to the host. However, you may have removed a network protocol or you'll need to add one based on the host with which you'll connect. A common protocol between your laptop and the host is necessary. Before you can decide which protocols to use, let's take a look at the important difference between network and communications protocols.

What's a Protocol?

A protocol is a set of formal rules to transmit data. The structure of the packets of information containing the data being transferred between two computers is called a network protocol. Some familiar network protocols include IPX/SPX, TCP/IP, NetBEUI, and NetBIOS. The methods and rules by which two computers pass the packets are called a communications protocol. NetWare Connect, PPP, RAS, SLIP, and CSLIP are well-known communications protocols.

As you can imagine, many combinations of network and communications protocols can exist. In the past, communications and network protocols were tightly integrated by the companies offering remote-networking solutions. Today, the combinations are becoming blurred with new advances in technology. Network administrators now want to select the best performing protocols for their network. Therefore, the companies that used almost-standard protocols have based their products on the true network and communication protocols. This allows network administrators to pick and choose the network and communications protocols best suited to the network users' needs for performance and functionality.

Remote Access Configurations

Windows 95 supports many different combinations of network and communication protocols. However, certain host types cannot understand specific network or communication protocols. To simplify what could be a complicated description, Table 39.1 shows the relationship between host type and the supported communications and network protocols.

Table 39.1 Supported Combinations of Host Types, Communication Protocols, and Network Protocols for a Remote Computer

Host Type	Communication Protocols	Network Protocol(s)	Remote Computer Can Share Its Own Resources
Internet, PPP server, Windows 95, Windows NT 3.x, Shiva LanRover, NetWare	PPP	IPX, NetBEUI, TCP/IP	Yes
Internet, UNIX, SLIP	SLIP, CSLIP	TCP/IP	No
Windows 95, Windows NT 3.x, Windows for Workgroups 3.11, LAN Manager	RAS	NetBEUI	Yes
NetWare Connect	NetWare Connect	IPX	No
Direct Cable Connection	Serial, Parallel	PPP	No

If you plan to use Dial-Up Networking, you should contact the administrator of the remote access host for the communication and network protocols used. These two pieces of information determine which remote computing component you'll use. Alternately, if you're using a direct-cable connection, you'll need to use a serial or parallel connection.

Choosing the Right Protocols   **971**

For example, say you have a Windows 95 computer at home and you want to connect to your Novell NetWare server at work to access files. The dial-up server at work is a Windows NT 3.5 Server running Remote Access Services. The preceding table shows that you'll need to use a PPP communications protocol with an IPX network protocol to access the NetWare server.

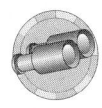

> **Note:** If you use the Microsoft Plus! pack to configure your Windows 95 desktop computer as a dial-in server, it will not pass data using TCP/IP to the remote computer.

Installing a Protocol

Windows 95 normally installs IPX/SPX and NetBEUI protocols for remote computing, which should be adequate for most needs. However, if you reviewed Table 39.1 in the previous section and discovered that you need to install a network protocol on your laptop or remote computer, follow these steps:

1. Open the Network components dialog box by right-clicking the Network Neighborhood and choosing Properties from the context menu.

2. Add a new network component by clicking Add under the list of network components. The Select Network Component Type dialog box is displayed, as shown in figure 39.2.

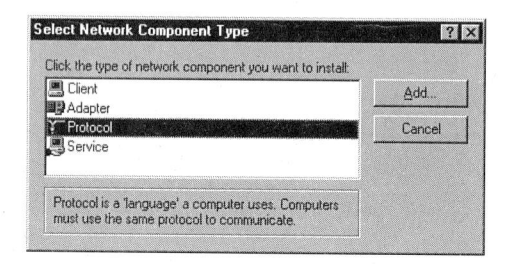

Fig. 39.2 Choose Protocol from the list of network component types.

Chapter 39: Seamless Remote Computing

3. Choose Protocol from the list of possible components types and then click <u>A</u>dd... to select the protocol.

4. As shown in figure 39.3, select the appropriate network protocol from <u>M</u>anufacturers and the list of Network Protocols. You'll be able to add only one new protocol at a time.

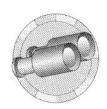

> **Note:** IPX/SPX, NetBEUI, and TCP/IP (the most common protocols) are available under Microsoft.

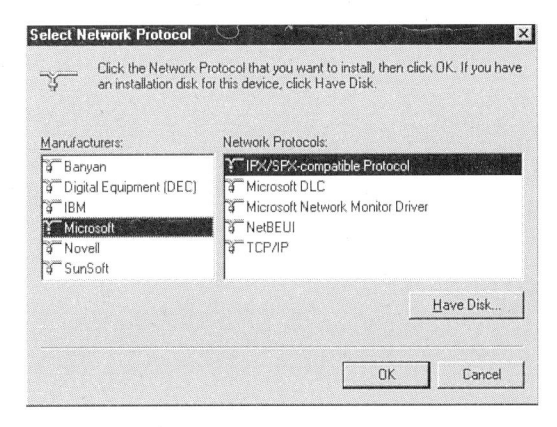

Fig. 39.3 Choose the manufacturer and then a protocol to install.

When ready, click OK to add the protocol to the network component list.

5. Click OK on the Network dialog box to begin installing the software for the new protocol. You will need your Windows 95 installation disks, CD-ROM, or a disk from the protocol manufacturer.

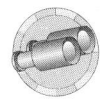

> **Note:** If you've chosen to install TCP/IP, it's very important that you contact your network administrator. He or she will tell you the exact configuration you'll need to set. For example, your network could use a *Dynamic Host Configuration Protocol* (DHCP) server instead of using a specific TCP/IP address.

Installing a Protocol **973**

6. When prompted, choose Restart to make the change take effect. Until you restart your computer, it will not know how to communicate using the new protocol.

From here, you'll want to establish the connection for your laptop to communicate via a Dial-Up Connection or a Direct Cable Connection. When you complete the connection, you'll be able to transfer files and access shared resources.

Dial-Up Networking

Once you've chosen the proper network and communication protocols, you have to configure the client software on your remote computer to access the host (server). To configure your computer to access resources on a dial-up connection, you'll need to perform some basic steps. Depending upon the type of host, specific tips will be identified as you progress.

> **Caution:** Using Dial-Up Networking requires that you have first configured a modem under Windows 95. To learn how to install one, see Chapter 32, "Communicating with a Modem," before you proceed.

Access the Dial-Up Networking folder from the Start menu. Click Start, Programs, Accessories, Dial-Up Networking. The Dial-Up Networking folder is just like any other folder. The menus are the same as other folders:

➤ **File**. These options allow you to control the set of dial-up connections. You can create a shortcut to a connection and delete, rename, or modify the properties of a connection.

➤ **Edit**. These options are normally used to cut, copy, and paste objects. However, dial-up connections are a special type of object and cannot be manipulated in this manner.

- ➤ **View**. These options control how connections are displayed within the Dial-Up Networking folder. You can change the size or arrangement of icons, and turn the toolbar or status bar on and off.

- ➤ **Connections**. These options allow you to perform the same tasks to initiate a connection or create a new connection by double-clicking on the icons in the folder. Additionally, you can configure settings for all your connections. As figure 39.4 shows, you can specify the number of times to redial and the amount of time between each attempt. When establishing a network connection, you can request Windows 95 to prompt you before beginning the process. Further, if you've installed the Windows 95 Dial-Up Server from the Microsoft Plus! pack, the server configuration can be modified from the Connections menu. Details on configuring this server can be found at the end of this section.

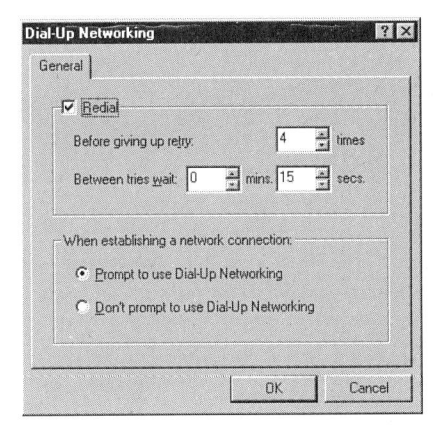

Fig. 39.4 Specify the Dial-Up Networking settings that are common to all connections from the Connection, Settings menu.

- ➤ **Help**. The Help menu displays the various help options for Dial-Up Networking.

Dial-Up Networking **975**

Creating the Connection

To begin creating a new dial-up connection, double-click the Make New Connection icon in the Dial-Up Networking window as shown in figure 39.5.

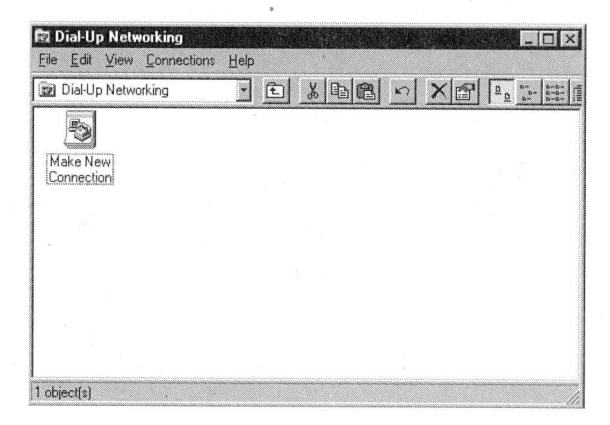

Fig. 39.5 Selecting Make New Connection will begin creating the connection to the host.

> **Tip:** If you haven't already installed the remote computing components, see Chapter 38, "Setting Up Remote Computing."

As seen in the next dialog box of the Make New Connection Wizard, Type a name for the computer that you are dialing. Then, click on Select a modem. Only those modems you've previously configured on this computer will be listed. Select Configure to check or modify the properties of the selected modem. If you do select Configure, you'll see the same Modem Properties sheet that appeared when you installed the modem. When you're ready to move to the next step, select Next.

To identify where your host can be reached, enter the Area code, Telephone number, and Country code, as shown in figure 39.6. Windows 95 uses the area code and country code to create the correct dialing string. Click Next to display the final dialog box for the Make New Connection Wizard. To complete the first phase of your configuration, click Finish.

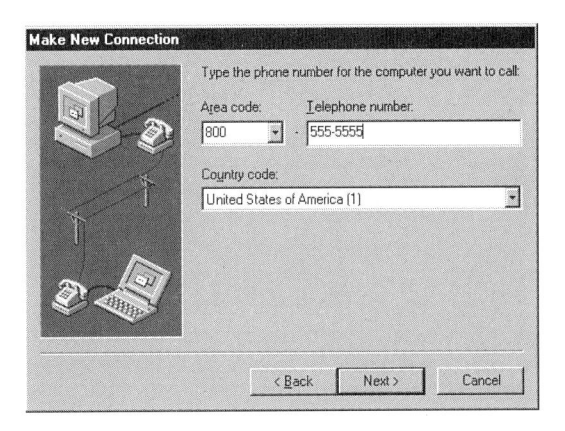

Fig. 39.6 Enter only the area code, telephone number, and country code of the dial-up network connection.

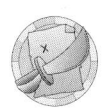

> **Tip:** When you enter these values, don't try to take into account your location by entering long-distance and outside line codes, credit card numbers, or area codes. You defined these local settings when you installed the modem.

Specifying a Server Type

You have to specify the type of server to which you're going to connect. Windows 95 needs to know the correct protocols to send and receive information. Review Table 39.1 in the previous section to determine the choice of server type.

To choose a server, open the properties of the connection you want to configure. To do this, access the Dial-Up Networking folder by clicking Start, Programs, Accessories, Dial-Up Networking. Then right-click the desired connection name and select Properties from the context menu.

From the Connection Properties sheet, you'll want to select the Server Type to specify the specific server type for this connection. The Server Types dialog box appears, as shown in figure 39.7.

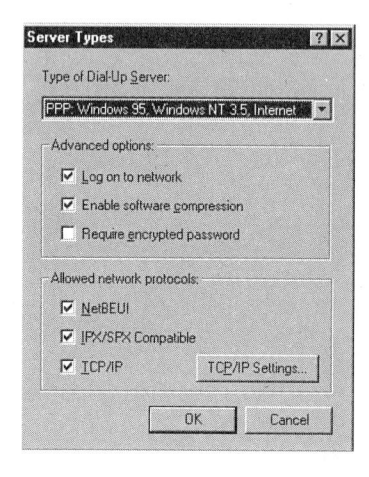

Fig. 39.7 You can choose the type of server to which you're going to connect.

From the Server Types dialog box, choose the Type of Dial-Up Server to which you're going to connect by clicking and holding the scrollable arrow. You have the following options:

- NRN NetWare Connect
- PPP: Windows 95, Windows NT 3.5, Internet
- Windows for Workgroups and Windows NT 3.1

Note that the options and allowed network protocols will change with each server type. For example, using NRN NetWare Connect, your only advanced option is Log on to network. The only network protocol allowed is IPX/SPX Compatible. For Advanced options, Windows will allow certain activities for the selected connection:

- Log on to network. When the connection is made to the host, Windows 95 will attempt to log onto the network that you are calling with the user name and password you used when you started your computer.

- Enable software compression. If both sides of the connection support compression, the data will be compressed before being sent over the connection to increase the transmission speed.

- Require encrypted password. If both sides of the connection support encryption, Windows 95 will encrypt the password you use for increased security against intrusion.

Windows 95 also permits you to limit the network protocols transmitted over the connection. You can set the connection to use or restrict NetBEUI, IPX/SPX, or TCP/IP protocols. If the host supports TCP/IP, you can specify additional settings for dynamic or manual TCP/IP configuration. As shown in figure 39.8, you can manually configure or allow the host to

- Assign an IP address
- Assign a name server address
- Use IP header compression to speed up the connection
- Use the default gateway on the remote network

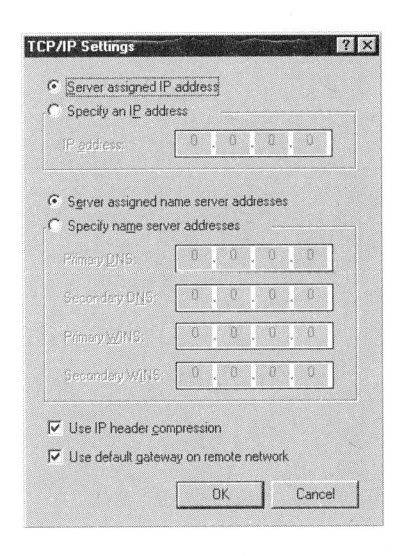

Fig. 39.8 If the host supports TCP/IP, additional configuration options can be specified.

Dial-Up Networking **979**

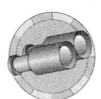

Note: Not all hosts support all the options. Unless these settings are correct, your connection may not work. Be sure to contact the administrator of the host for the correct values for all fields.

Once you've modified the settings to your liking, save your changes by selecting OK on each dialog box until you return to the Dial-Up Networking folder.

Establishing the Connection

Now that you've selected the right protocols and defined the server type, it's time to make the connection. To connect to the host, open the Dial-Up Networking folder if it isn't already open. Double-click on the name of the desired connection you wish to make.

As seen in figure 39.9, you'll be prompted to enter the User name and Password on the host. You can optionally Save the password in an encrypted format for the next time you connect to this particular host. Based upon where you are Dialing from, the Phone number contains area codes, credit card numbers, outside access line codes, or call waiting cancel codes. When you've verified all the information, select the Connect button to initiate the connection to the host.

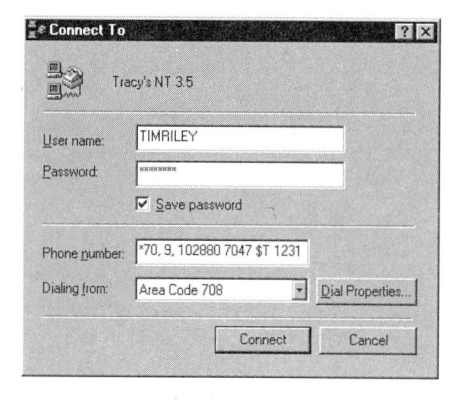

Fig. 39.9 Enter the user name and password, and select your location.

Tip: If you want to modify the Dialing from properties for the current location, select Dial Properties to edit these codes. For more details, see Chapter 32, "Communicating with a Modem," describing how to configure your modem.

You will see a series of messages, on a progress dialog box, similar to those at the left-hand side of figure 39.10. When the connection is ready for you to use, the dialog box changes, as shown at the right side of figure 39.10.

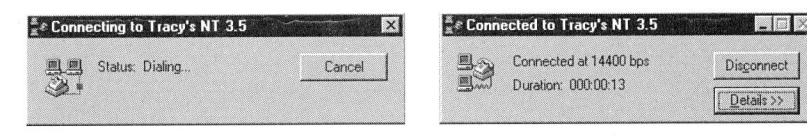

Fig. 39.10 Windows 95 shows you the progression and completion of the network connection.

Now that the connection is made, you have complete access to all the resources on the remote network. Additionally, your host may support the capability for your remote computer to share its resources with other network workstations. Table 39.1 in the previous section identifies which hosts support this.

Transferring Your Deferred Communications

If you deferred printing documents, sending faxes, or sending electronic mail, Windows 95 can begin the process of sending your communications once the network connection is made. If you've deferred printing, Windows 95 automatically detects when the printer is available and begins to send the print jobs to their destinations. If you've deferred faxes, just double-click on the Inbox icon on your desktop. Windows 95 detects when the network fax server is available and begins sending the stored faxes.

If you've deferred electronic mail because you specified the use of the Remote Mail tools for your mail service (as described in Chapter 38, "Setting Up Remote Computing"), you can selectively manipulate messages from the postoffice. However, here is an overview of the Tools menu, as shown in figure 39.11:

➤ Connect, Disconnect. You can selectively connect and disconnect from the postoffice. This allows you to determine when to receive and send mail.

➤ Update Headers. To check for new mail without being forced to receive its entire contents, select this option to preview the author, subject, priority, and other types of information about the messages.

➤ Transfer Mail. This option performs the actions specified for each message based upon how it was marked using the Edit menu.

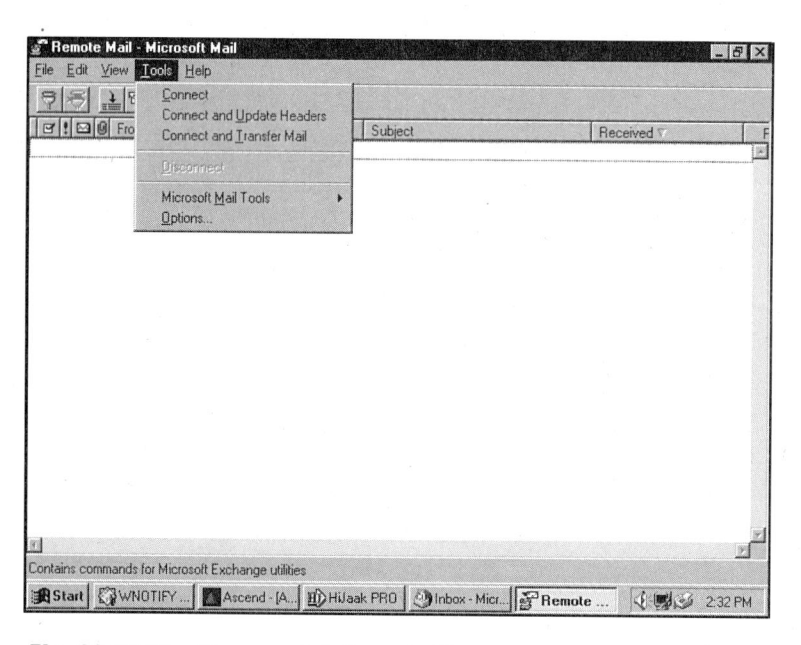

Fig. 39.11 The Remote Mail tool allows to you selectively transfer messages from the remote postoffice.

The Edit menu of the Remote Mail tool allows you to mark each message with an action to be performed. These actions include:

➤ Mark to Retrieve. By marking a message with this action, you will copy the message to your personal folders and then remove the copy on the postoffice. A return receipt will be generated at this time if the incoming message was marked as such.

➤ Mark to Retrieve a Copy. Marking a message with this action will copy the message to your personal folder without deleting it from the postoffice. A return receipt will be generated at this time.

➤ Mark to Delete. This action will delete the specified message from the postoffice when you select Transfer Mail from the Tools menu.

To establish a Remote Mail connection, choose Tools, Remote Mail from the Inbox dialog. From the Remote Mail dialog, choose Tools, Connect. Enter your user ID and password. By selecting Tools, Update Headers, choose one or more options to Send mail waiting to be distributed, Receive marked items from the list in the Remote Mail dialog, Update view of mail headers to show new mail in the Remote Mail dialog, Download address lists to show new potential recipients, or Disconnect after actions are completed. Once you've read your mail, created new messages, or deleted old ones, be sure to Update Headers one last time. You don't want to accidentally leave a message in your local mail file. When complete, select Tools, Disconnect from the Remote Mail dialog to finish your session.

Direct Cable Connections

Using a direct-cable connection allows you to transfer files and access resources on a desktop computer from a second computer with only a serial or parallel cable connecting them. In addition, if the desktop computer has access to network resources using IPX/SPX or NetBEUI, the second computer will too!

Once connected, no special programs (such as InterLink) are required to transfer files. You can perform almost any task on your laptop—just as if it were at your desktop machine. However, the link between your desktop and laptop computers is a one-way connection. Your laptop computer cannot share its resources with the desktop computer or other network workstations.

To establish a direct-cable connection, you should first install the Direct Cable Connection component and obtain the proper cable. Chapter 38, "Setting Up Remote Computing," shows you how to perform these tasks. Once completed, you're ready to set up the host and remote computers.

Setting Up the Host Computer

You have to designate one computer as the *guest* and one computer as the *host*. The guest computer is able to access the resources available to the host computer. The host computer cannot access the guest computer. For example, if I want to transfer files from my desktop to my laptop, I would designate my laptop as the guest and the desktop as the host.

To set up a host computer, you'll need to share a folder that the guest can access. By using the Windows Explorer or double-clicking on My Computer on the desktop, locate the folder you wish to share. Right-click the folder and select S*h*aring from the context menu.

> **Tip:** If the Sharing option does not appear on the context menu, you have not yet enabled file sharing. See Chapter 36, "Communicating with a Network," to use file sharing to its fullest.

The selected folder's Properties sheet shows the Sharing tab. If you enabled Share-level security in the Network Control Panel, the dialog box will look like the one on the left-hand side of figure 39.12. If you enabled User-level security, the dialog box will look like the one on the right.

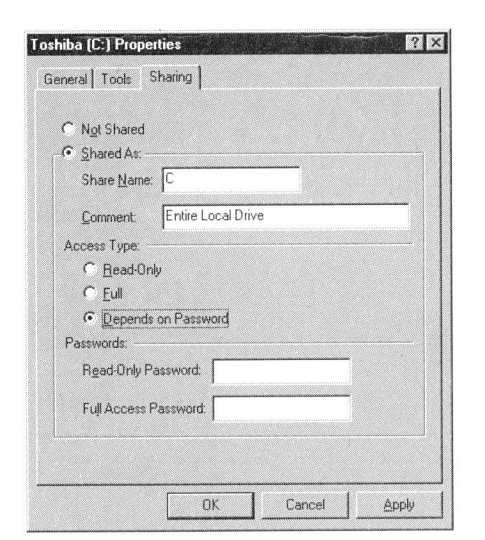

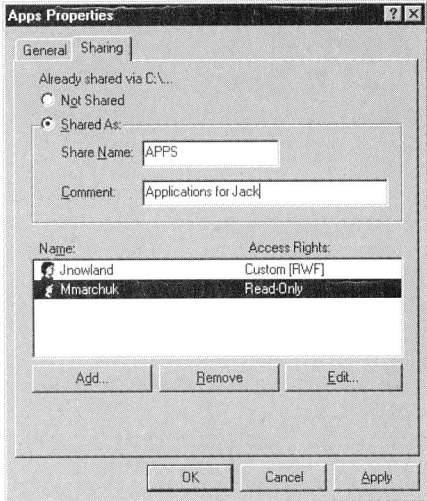

Fig. 39.12 You have to share at least one folder on the host computer for Direct Cable Connection to work.

Click S<u>h</u>ared As and provide a Share <u>N</u>ame. If you'd like, you may also enter a short <u>C</u>omment about the share. Since other network users don't know what you are sharing, placing a description of what can be found inside the folder is a good use for the comment field.

If you are using Share-level security, define what Access Type other users will have. There are three types of security:

- <u>R</u>ead-Only. This allows other users to view the contents and make copies of any file or folder in the drive or folder being shared. Other users will not be able to delete or rename files and folders.

- <u>F</u>ull. This allows other users to view the contents and make copies of any file or folder in the share. Additionally, other users will be able to delete or rename files and folders.

- Depends on Password. When users connect to your share, they will be granted either read-only or full access, depending upon which password they give. As you can see at the bottom of figure 39.12, you can enter passwords for both types when the <u>D</u>epends on Password option is selected.

Direct Cable Connections **985**

If you chose to set up your computer to use User-level access control, you'll need to add user or group names to the Name list. With the existing list of Names, you can perform three actions:

➤ Add. Allows you to specify a user name or group defined by the server you specified in the Access Control tab of the Network Control Panel. For each one, you can allow full access, read-only access, or a custom set of access privileges. A custom set can include one or more of the following privileges: Read Files, Write to Files, Create Files and Folders, Delete Files, Change File Attributes, List Files, and Change Access Control.

➤ Remove. For the selected name in the list, you can remove the access you've previously granted. Once you select the OK or Apply buttons, the change is permanent.

➤ Edit. For the selected name in the list, you can modify the current access privileges just as if you were adding the name for the first time.

> **Tip:** Notice in figure 39.12 the words "Already shared via C:\..." immediately under the Sharing tab. Windows 95 is telling you the folder has already been shared. If you specified User-level security, the names listed are those who already have access to this folder. For just this share, you may add, remove, or edit their access privileges.

Now that you've provided a share for the guest to access, initiate the connection on the host. On that computer, click Start, Programs, Accessories, Direct Cable Connection. If you haven't already set the computer to be a host, figure 39.13 shows the first step.

Select the Host option and click Next. Windows 95 will indicate that it's configuring ports. When prompted, select the port to which you've connected the cable. Figure 39.14 shows the selection of a parallel port. Click Next to accept your port selection.

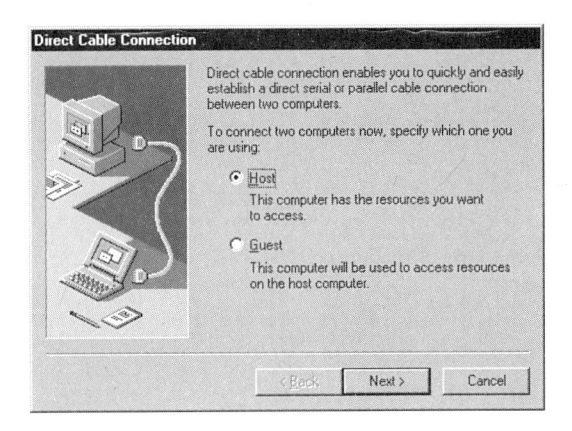

Fig. 39.13 You can access Direct Cable Connection through Accessories.

> **Tip:** The fastest type is a parallel *Extended Capabilities Port* (ECP) using a *Universal Cable Module* (UCM) cable. The BIOS in your computer defines the type of parallel port. Your local hardware dealer should be able to provide a UCM cable.

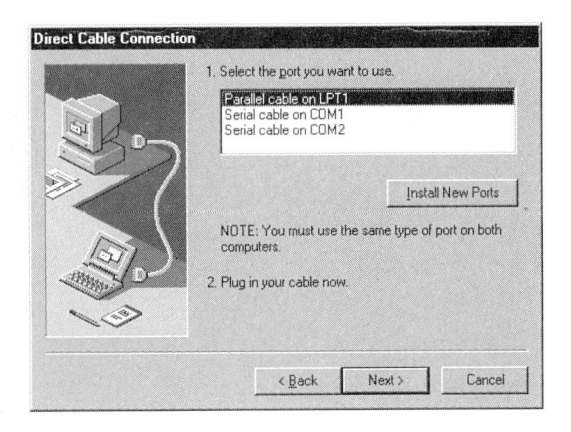

Fig. 39.14 Parallel ports run three- to four-times faster than serial cables.

Direct Cable Connections **987**

If you'd like to require the guest to enter a password when it connects to the host, click Use password protection and enter a password. In either case, click Finish to begin waiting for the guest to connect. If the guest computer isn't configured yet, see the following section, "Setting Up the Guest Computer." While you do this, the host will continue to wait for a guest connection.

Setting Up the Guest Computer

To access a host computer, you'll need to set up the guest computer in the Direct Cable Connection dialog box. On the computer you wish to designate as the guest, click Start, Programs, Accessories, Direct Cable Connection. Figure 39.14 is then displayed.

Select the Guest option and click Next. Windows 95 will indicate that it's configuring ports. When prompted, select the port to which you've connected the cable. Figure 39.15 shows the selection of a parallel port. Click Next to accept your port selection.

> **Tip:** The fastest type is a parallel *Extended Capabilities Port* (ECP) using a *Universal Cable Module* (UCM) cable. The BIOS in your computer defines the type of parallel port. Your local hardware dealer should be able to provide a UCM cable.

If the host computer requires a password to complete the connection, you'll be asked for it at this point. Enter it to complete the connection.

Using Direct Cable Connection

When you've installed Direct Cable Connection and established a connection, the guest computer has access to the shared resources on the host computer. If the host is connected to a network, the guest also has access to those resources (excluding those using TCP/IP protocol).

When the connection is established, Windows 95 will immediately open a folder on the guest computer. This folder (see figure 39.15) contains all the resources shared on the host computer, including shared folders and shared printers. Notice that it is just like any other folder on your desktop. If the host computer has access to other network resources, the Network Neighborhood will show those same resources on the guest computer.

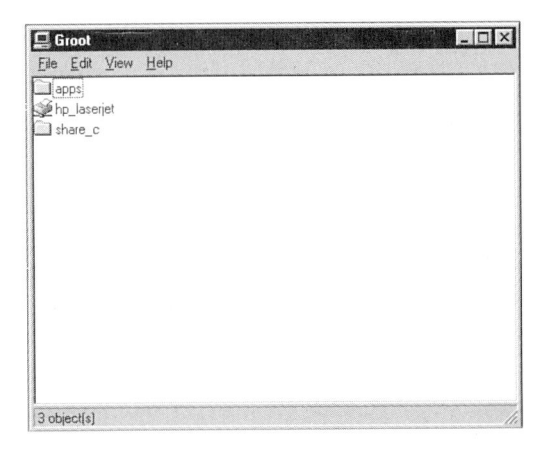

Fig. 39.15 The guest computer displays the folders and printers you have access to on the host computer.

> **Tip:** If you share a new folder from the host while you're connected, you have to refresh the guest computer. To do so, click View, Refresh.

If you shared access to individual folders within a drive, they'll be indicated separately. To view the contents of a folder, you can then double-click on it to open it.

To browse the entire network, double-click the Network Neighborhood icon on your desktop. If you don't have access to the whole network, you'll get an error message saying so.

> **Note:** The guest computer still has access to its own folders.

Direct Cable Connections **989**

Using Quick View you can access many files even if you don't have the program on the guest machine. Although you can run programs on the guest computer that are resident on the host, this procedure is very slow. As a rule of thumb, your guest computer should contain all the applications needed to do your work.

To disconnect, click on the Direct Cable Connection icon on the taskbar and click Close on each machine.

To transfer updated files in a Briefcase, see "Keeping Your Files in Sync," later in this chapter.

Changing from Guest to Host

If at any time you want to reverse the access capabilities between the guest and host, it's just a button click away. On each computer, click Start, Programs, Accessories, Direct Cable Connection. You'll get the Direct Cable Connection screen shown in figure 39.16. Select the Change button. By doing this, you restart (from scratch) the configuration of the computer as part of a Direct Cable Connection. If you want to configure the computer as a host, read the earlier section, "Setting Up the Host Computer." If you want to configure the computer as a Guest, "Setting Up the Guest Computer" will teach you.

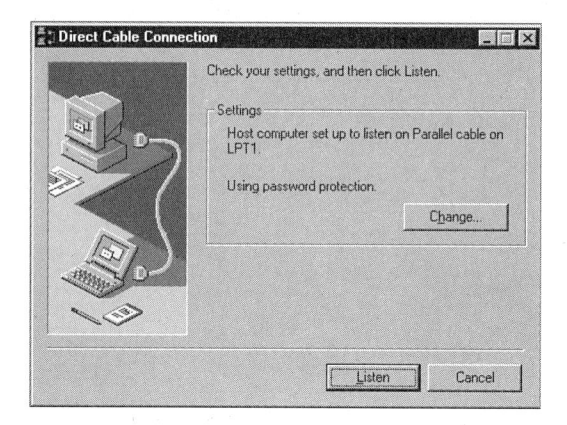

Fig. 39.16 You can change from host to guest or guest to host.

990 Chapter 39: Seamless Remote Computing

Troubleshooting a Direct Cable Connection

Here are some basic items to check if you are having problems establishing a Direct Cable Connection. Make sure you have

- Run Direct Cable Connection on both computers
- Set up one computer as the guest and one computer as the host
- Used the correct cable
- Secured the cable on both computers
- Given each computer a unique name
- Enabled sharing on the host computer

If these suggestions don't solve the problem, Windows 95's online help has an excellent interactive troubleshooting section for Direct Cable Connection. To access it, click Start, Help and type **Direct Cable Connection.** Choose the Troubleshooting option and click Display.

Hot-Docking

Because the three widely used protocols (IPX/SPX, TCP/IP, and NetBEUI) are Plug-and-Play enabled, the Windows 95 system runs even if the network becomes unavailable. That allows *hot-docking* for docking stations that support the Plug-and-Play BIOS. Without turning off the computer, the network is automatically enabled when it becomes docked. Windows 95 also notifies print, fax, and mail queues that the network resources are available to begin transferring deferred communications. When the computer becomes undocked, Windows 95 reconfigures the laptop's resources to conserve memory and power usage.

Note: If you use any real-mode network components, you will not be able to use hot-docking. Windows 95 only supports hot-docking with protected mode adapter cards, network clients, and protocols.

Caution: Be sure you confirm that your docking station is Plug-and-Play BIOS compliant. If not, it is possible to corrupt your open files. Without the application being notified that the network is no longer available, it may attempt to save the file and become confused. If your docking station isn't Plug-and-Play compliant, be sure to save and close your work before ejecting the computer.

Using Briefcase

When you work remotely, whether it's on a laptop away from home or on a desktop away from work, you often have to juggle multiple copies of the same file. With just a moment of carelessness, you can accidentally replace an updated file with an earlier version. Without a doubt, you're destined to print the wrong version at least once.

With the new Briefcase feature, you don't have to worry about any of that. Briefcase makes updating files a snap. If the program you used to create two versions of the same file supports merging file revisions (such as Microsoft Word for Windows), Briefcase will try to use the features provided by the program to merge the two versions together. However, not many applications provide this functionality yet. Briefcase will then compare the dates of the files and keep the newest one. You can use Briefcase with Dial-Up Networking and Direct Cable Connection, or move it to a floppy.

Briefcase prompts you to update files that have been changed since you copied them into the Briefcase. That way, you won't forget to transfer the latest version.

The Briefcase icon resides on your desktop. If it's not there, you need to create it. To create the Briefcase icon, do the following:

1. On the desktop, click the right mouse button.
2. Click on Ne_w_.
3. Click on Briefcase. The Briefcase icon appears.

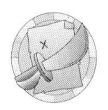

> **Tip:** If you share a Briefcase, you won't be able to synchronize any files that you drag-and-drop there while sharing is enabled. That means every document will display an *orphan status* and won't be updated.

To copy a file to Briefcase, do the following:

1. In the Windows Explorer, locate and click the icon for the file you want to update. (The file has to be closed.) This file can be located on any drive, folder, or shared resource to which your computer has access.
2. Reduce the size of the Explorer window so you can see the Briefcase icon.
3. Drag-and-drop the icon for the file you want to take with you into the Briefcase icon.

> **Tip:** If you know the name of the document but not the path, click Start, _F_ind, _F_iles or Folders. Type in the name of the file you want to find. You can then drag-and-drop the icon right from the Find window.

Using Briefcase **993**

The file will be copied into Briefcase. When you double-click on Briefcase, you'll get a window showing the large icons of all items copied inside. To view file details, click View, Details. You'll get a screen similar to the one shown in figure 39.17.

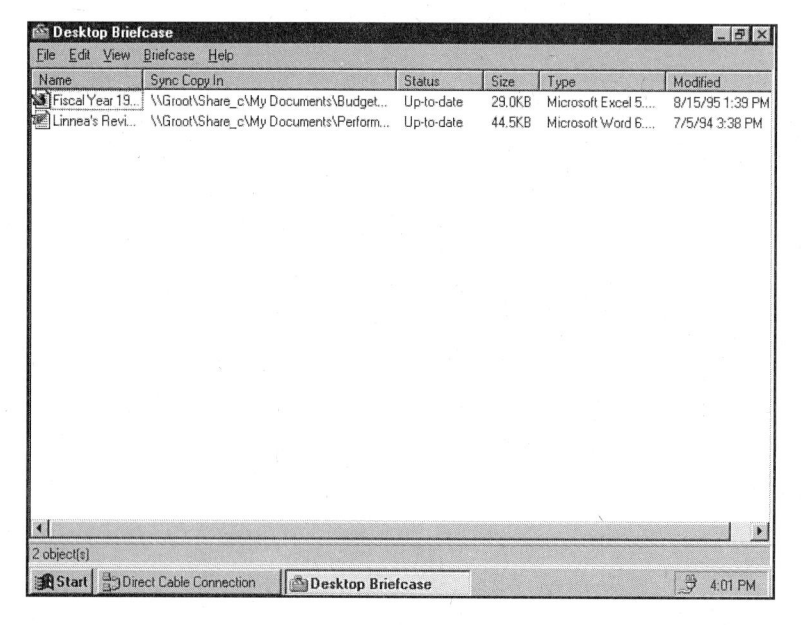

Fig. 39.17 A list view of Briefcase after two files have been copied into it.

Caution: You can change the name of the file in Briefcase, but if you do, you'll sever the link to the original file. Then Briefcase won't keep track of which file has changed.

Another way to copy a file into Briefcase is to click on the file's icon (the file has to be closed), and then click File, Send to, My Briefcase.

When you first copy a file into Briefcase, the status will indicate that it's Up-to-date. Whenever you save changes to the original file, the status will change to Needs updating.

Chapter 39: Seamless Remote Computing

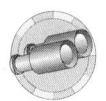

Note: If the Briefcase window is open when you save the original file, the status won't reflect the change until you close the window and open it again.

To update the Briefcase version of a file, do the following:

1. Double-click on the Briefcase icon to open the window.
2. Click on the icon of the file you wish to update.
3. Click Briefcase, Update Selection. You'll get a screen similar to the one shown in figure 39.18.

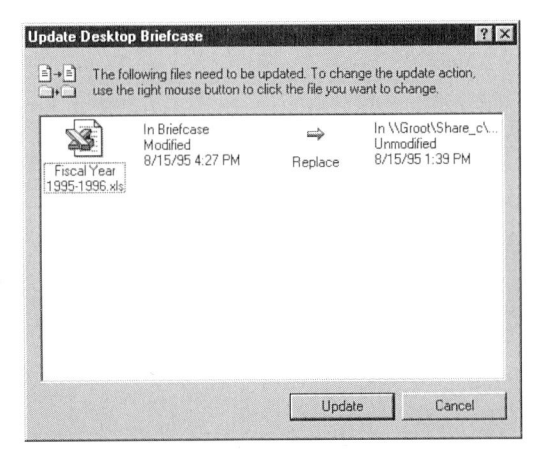

Fig. 39.18 Briefcase shows you the location of each file, and the date and time each file was modified, before it updates files.

4. Click Update.

The direction of the green arrow indicates which version of the file will be replaced. In this case, the file on the right, the one located in \\GROOT\Share_C, will replace the file on the left, which is an earlier version located in Briefcase.

If you want the earlier version of the file to replace the later version, do the following:

Using Briefcase **995**

> **Caution:** Replacing the latest version with an earlier version this way will backdate your original file. You will lose all revisions made since the Briefcase version. Make absolutely certain this is what you want to do before you do it. It cannot be reversed.

1. In the Update My Briefcase window, select the file you want to update (see the preceding instructions).

2. Move the cursor to the word Replace and right-click. You'll get the screen shown in figure 39.19.

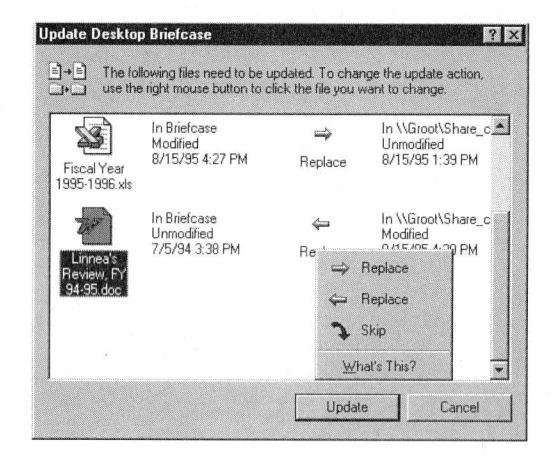

Fig. 39.19 You have the options to replace the latest version with the earlier version or to skip replacement altogether.

3. Click the green arrow to indicate the way you want the files updated.

4. Click Update.

If you aren't sure where the original file came from, Briefcase helps you find the original file. It also shows you all kinds of statistics about the versions.

Chapter 39: Seamless Remote Computing

To find the original file, do the following:

1. In the Briefcase window, click on the icon for the file you want to find out about.
2. Click File, Properties. You'll get the screen shown in figure 39.20.

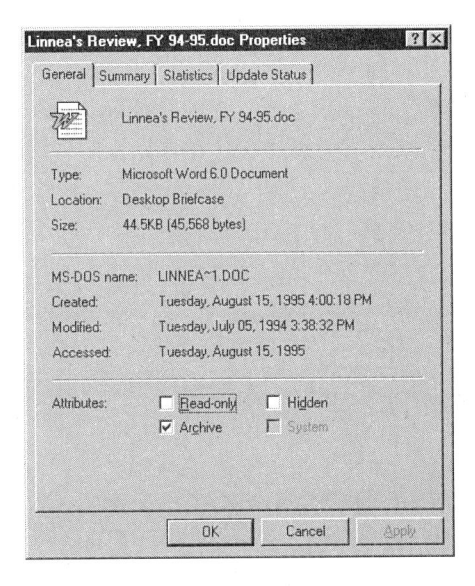

Fig. 39.20 The General Properties tab in Briefcase indicates the date the file was created, modified, and accessed. The accessed date tells you when Briefcase was opened.

3. Click the Update Status tab. You'll get the screen shown in figure 39.21.
4. Click Find Original to find the file. Briefcase will open the folder window.
5. Double-click on the file if you want to open it.

The easiest way to use Briefcase to synchronize files from one computer to another is to drag-and-drop the Briefcase to a floppy and take it with you. Then, when you get to your other computer, drag-and-drop the Briefcase onto the desktop and follow the preceding instructions for updating files.

Using Briefcase   **997**

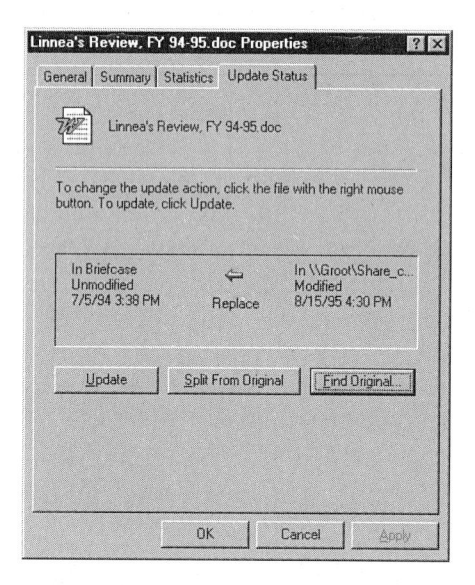

Fig. 39.21 Briefcase lets you find and access the original file.

You can use Briefcase to synchronize files with Direct Cable Connection or Dial-Up Networking, both described earlier in this chapter.

To use Briefcase to synchronize files on computers that are directly cabled or connected via a Dial-Up Connection, do the following:

1. Share the Briefcase from the computer with the updated files. (Click the Briefcase icon, click the right mouse button, click Sharing, click the Sharing tab, and click Shared As.)

> **Caution:** Remember to take sharing off the Briefcase icon after you've transferred it. Otherwise, you won't be able to save linked files and all files will be orphaned.

2. Connect the computers with a Direct Cable Connection or Dial-Up Networking. You'll get a screen similar to the one shown in figure 39.22.

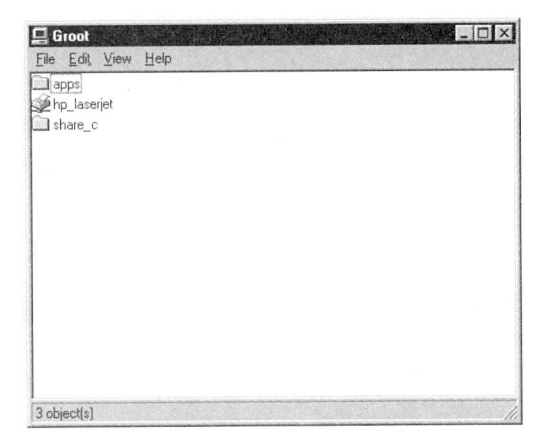

Fig. 39.22 The remote computer displays all of the shared folders from the host computer.

3. Double-click on My Briefcase from the host computer. You'll get a screen showing you the files.

4. Drag-and-drop the file you want to update from the host to the remote. (Or you can click on the file you want to copy, and click File, Properties, Send To My Briefcase.)

5. Click Yes.

To make sure you've copied the right file, double-click on My Briefcase on the remote computer. Click View, Details. Notice that under Sync Copy In there will be something similar to \\Robin\My Briefcase. That indicates the updated file came from a Briefcase folder on another computer.

If you don't want to bother connecting computers, you can simply copy the Briefcase to a floppy. Of course you can drag-and-drop the file, but there's an easier way to do it.

Using Briefcase **999**

To copy a file from Briefcase to a floppy, do the following:

1. Open the Briefcase window and click on the file you want to copy.
2. Click File, Send to, 3 1/2-inch Floppy (A).
3. Make sure you put the Briefcase back on your other computer.

You can also send files this way to a fax recipient or a mail recipient.

Operating in Windows 95 DOS

KILLER 40 WINDOWS 95

by Allen L. Wyatt

You have learned long ago that Windows 95 signals a change in the fundamental relationship between DOS and Windows. In previous versions of Windows, DOS was required because Windows ran as an adjunct to DOS. Now, DOS runs as an adjunct to Windows. Although DOS is still available, it is more "behind the scenes" than it has been historically.

This chapter covers information you need to know about using the MS-DOS command line. Here you will find the following:

➤ The historical DOS commands removed from Windows 95

➤ The new commands added to Windows 95

➤ How to use the command line interface

➤ How to change the properties of an MS-DOS window

This chapter does not present a complete list of commands available in the DOS window. Indeed, an effective discussion would take an entire book by itself. Instead, you should find a good DOS reference and use it as your basis for what you do in the DOS window. The information in this chapter will help you with the commands that have been deleted and added to Windows 95.

DOS Commands No Longer Available

If you have been using computers for a while, chances are good that you are already familiar with many DOS commands. The release of Windows 95 has meant a change in the way that DOS is both perceived and used. The DOS that you can use in Windows 95 does not include all of the commands you could previously use in DOS. Some commands have been replaced by integrated Windows utilities, but others are simply not needed anymore.

The DOS commands no longer available under Windows 95 are divided into several categories: disk commands, device drivers, file commands, memory management, printer management, and miscellaneous. Each of these categories is covered in the following sections.

Disk Commands

As you learned in Chapter 2, "Under-the-Hood Improvements," the disk access routines used by Windows 95 have been completely rewritten. In the process, a whopping 14 DOS commands were deleted from Windows 95. The following disk-related commands were deleted:

- **APPEND**. The APPEND command was used to link together different folders on a disk. Now that you can easily browse through your system (and other systems on the network), it is obsolete.

- **ASSIGN**. The ASSIGN command enabled you to create alias drive letters to refer to other drives. The same functionality is built in to the drive mapping capabilities of Windows 95.

- **BACKUP.** This DOS-based backup program has been replaced by the Windows 95 Backup utility.

- **FASTOPEN.** The FASTOPEN command provided for faster opening of disk files by keeping the disk folder in memory. The same functionality has been built directly in to the Windows 95 file routines.

- **INTERLNK.** The INTERLNK command was used to facilitate network communications in the DOS environment. Because Windows 95 has been built from the ground up with networking in mind, the INTERLNK command is obsolete.

- **INTERSVR.** The INTERSVR command was designed to work with the INTERLNK command to provide some networking capabilities. It has been rendered obsolete by Windows 95.

- **JOIN.** The JOIN command was used to provide an alias for different drives on your system. Originally provided as a work-around for software that could not easily access hard drives, the command is no longer needed. Some of the functionality of JOIN is provided by the drive mapping capabilities of Windows 95.

- **MIRROR.** The MIRROR command was used in conjunction with the UNFORMAT command. Because the UNFORMAT command has been deleted, MIRROR has been deleted as well.

- **MSBACKUP.** This is the DOS-based backup command. The capabilities of the MSBACKUP command have been replaced by the Backup utility.

- **MWBACKUP.** This is the Windows-based backup command included with previous versions of DOS. The capabilities of the MWBACKUP command have been replaced by the Backup utility.

- **RECOVER.** The RECOVER command was used to salvage data from a badly damaged disk. It is no longer necessary because of the improved filing system used in Windows 95. In addition, some of the remedial actions provided by RECOVER are now provided by the ScanDisk utility.

➤ **RESTORE.** The RESTORE command was used to restore information saved with the BACKUP command. It has been absorbed into the Windows 95 Backup utility.

➤ **SMARTMON.** The SMARTMON command was deleted because Windows 95 enables you to control disk caching and virtual memory settings directly from the Control Panel.

➤ **UNFORMAT.** It was easy in earlier versions of DOS to inadvertently format a disk by typing in the wrong drive letter; the UNFORMAT command helped undo such an error. With Windows 95, you can format disks from two places: from within Windows and from the MS-DOS command prompt. You can format floppies only from within Windows. If you issue the format command from the command prompt, you are asked to verify your action before it is executed. This double-checking makes it less likely you will need the UNFORMAT command.

File Commands

The improved file management capabilities of Windows 95 mean that some of the commands originally provided in DOS for this purpose are no longer necessary. The following file-related DOS commands were deleted in Windows 95:

➤ **COMP.** The COMP command was actually deleted in DOS 6.0, but it was still available on the Supplemental Disk. The COMP command is not available at all with Windows 95 because the FC command (available from the command line) provides a superset of COMP's capabilities.

➤ **MWUNDEL.** This Windows-based program enabled you to undelete files. With the introduction of the Recycle Bin, the MWUNDEL command was no longer necessary.

➤ **REPLACE.** The REPLACE command enabled you to selectively update files on a disk. Now you can update files through the Explorer.

- **SHARE.** The SHARE command was used to allow multiple programs to share information in the same file. The integrated networking capabilities of Windows 95 make SHARE obsolete.

- **TREE.** The TREE command enabled you to see a tree-type depiction of your folder structure. Such a command is redundant with the browsing capabilities of Windows 95, as well as the Explorer.

- **UNDELETE.** This DOS-based program was used for undeleting files. The same function is now provided through the use of the Recycle Bin on the Windows 95 desktop.

- **VSAFE.** The VSAFE program was used to ensure that data was written to disk immediately. The improved caching routines built in to Windows 95 make such a command unnecessary.

Memory Management

When you last saw DOS, the memory management capabilities could best be described as "tenuous." Management was effected through a collection of arcane commands and switches. After your memory configuration was set, you were often afraid to "mess with it" for fear it would cause your system to become unstable (or more unstable).

Windows 95 provides huge improvements in memory management. Most aspects of memory management are taken care of behind the scenes, without any human intervention. The biggest improvement of all was the removal of the 640K conventional memory barrier that was intrinsic to DOS. Now Windows 95 does virtually everything in protected mode or in *virtual real mode* in the case of DOS windows.

Because Windows 96 now handles memory management, the DOS MEMMAKER command was deleted. There is no longer a need for the program, which was used to automatically check various memory configurations and determine which was best for your system.

It is interesting to note that some commands which were related to DOS memory management are still available in Windows 95. Most notable is the LH or LOADHIGH command, which you use to load device drivers into upper memory. Because you may need to use some real-mode device drivers on your system, this command is still supported under Windows 95.

Printer Management

As you learned in Chapter 20, "Managing Your Printers," and Chapter 21, "Printing from Windows 95," the entire print spooler and printer management portions of Windows 95 have been rewritten. The new 32-bit subsystems now operate much more smoothly than in previous versions of Windows. The other big advantage is that printing from the DOS command line is routed through the Windows printer management subsystem. This feature allows for a more consistent approach to printer management, and fewer headaches reconciling Windows with DOS.

Due to the improved printer management, the following printer-related commands have been deleted from Windows 95:

- **GRAPHICS.** The GRAPHICS command was used so that the Print Screen key could be used to print the contents of screens displayed in graphics modes. With the printer drivers supplied with Windows 95, you can print graphics just as well as text, so the command is no longer needed.

- **PRINT.** The PRINT command implemented a print spooler for background printing. This task is now handled by the Windows 95 print spooler.

Device Drivers

Several device drivers have been deleted from Windows 95; they have been largely absorbed into the operating system itself. The following drivers used to be distributed with DOS, but are not distributed with Windows 95:

- **EGA.SYS.** The EGA.SYS driver was used in conjunction with the DOS Shell to correct problems that occurred when task switching on a system that used an EGA monitor. Because the DOS Shell is no longer necessary, and EGA cards will not work with Windows 95, the driver is not needed.

- **MONOUMB.386.** The MONOUMB.386 driver was used in previous versions of Windows to indicate when the DOS memory management functions had used the monochrome display region at B000h to B7FFh as upper memory. This is no longer necessary under Windows 95.

- **PRINTER.SYS.** The PRINTER.SYS driver provided international code page support for some IBM printers. The same capabilities are built-in as part of Windows 95.

- **RAMDRIVE.SYS.** The RAMDRIVE.SYS driver was used to create a RAM drive in memory. It is no longer supported under Windows 95.

- **VFINTD.386.** The VFINTD.386 driver allowed the Windows-based backup program (MWBACKUP.EXE) to access the floppy drives properly. Because this backup program has been deleted from Windows 95, the driver is no longer necessary.

- **WINA20.386.** The WINA20.386 driver was used to support some enhanced-mode device drivers in earlier versions of Windows. The functions it provided have been rendered obsolete by the newer sections of Windows 95.

As you can tell, most drivers have been deleted because they are simply no longer needed under Windows 95. The one surprise on the list may be the RAMDRIVE.SYS driver. The upshot of this is that you can no longer create a RAM drive after Windows 95 is installed on your system. Although this may seem to be a potential disadvantage, a look at the historical reasons for RAM drives may put this change in perspective.

When RAM drives were first introduced on PCs, there were two main reasons for their acceptance. First, RAM prices were much cheaper than hard drive prices, and second, RAM was much faster than hard drives. The former reason is no longer a big issue since the prices of hard drives have fallen through the floor. You can now find 1G drives for under $400. This means that the price is under 40 cents per megabyte—much cheaper than RAM prices.

The latter reason (speed) is also less of a concern. With the smart disk caching and fast disk speeds and transfer rates on today's disk drives, the speed differential is less of an issue than it used to be.

The final issue related to RAM drives is that whenever you use part of your memory for a dedicated purpose—such as a RAM drive—you cannot use it for something that may be more critical. In particular, the more memory you take for a RAM drive, the less memory Windows has to work with and the more likely it will need to swap memory to the hard drive. Thus, the use of a RAM drive could mean a slowdown in the performance of your system.

Miscellaneous Commands

A few DOS commands that have been deleted in Windows 95 do not readily fit into the other command categories. The following ten miscellaneous commands have been deleted from Windows 95:

- **DOSSHELL.** This is the graphical DOS Shell supplied with some versions of DOS. It would not make much sense to run the DOS Shell within a DOS window, so it was deleted.

- **EDLIN.** This is the venerable (and ancient) text editor available since the first version of DOS. It has been replaced by the EDIT command, which is still available from the DOS command line.

- **FASTHELP.** This method of getting help has been removed from DOS. Instead, you can use the /? switch on any command, or you can attempt to find DOS commands in the online help (the pickings are pretty sparse).

- **GRAFTABL.** The GRAFTABL command was used to support extended graphics characters on CGA graphics adapters. Because the CGA is not supported in Windows 95 (a VGA card is the minimum requirement), the command is no longer necessary.

- **HELP.** This was the full-blown help system available under DOS. It has been removed in favor of the command-oriented /? switch. You can also try to use the online help to find a few DOS commands.

- **MSAV.** The MSAV program was the DOS-based version of the Microsoft antivirus program. This feature has been deleted, with no explanation, from Windows 95.

- **MWAV.** The MWAV program was the Windows-based version of the Microsoft antivirus program. Like the MSAV program, it was deleted with no explanation.

- **MWAVTSR.** This was a TSR (terminate and stay resident) program that worked with the Windows-based version of the antivirus program. Because the antivirus program was deleted, there was no need for the TSR support.

- **POWER.** The POWER command provided support for the APM (advanced power management) specification in laptop computers. The functionality of this command has been built in to the Windows 95 Control Panel.

- **QBASIC.** This text-based version of BASIC apparently does not have a place in the fancy world of Windows-oriented graphics. It has been deleted, and wanna-be programmers will need to use a program such as Visual Basic to do their tinkering.

New Commands

The added capabilities of Windows 95 have meant that a few extra command-line commands have been introduced. This is understandable because there needs to be a way to access new features from the command line. The new commands fall into two categories: network commands and TCP/IP commands. Another major addition to the command line is the START command. Each of these areas is discussed in the following sections.

Network Commands

By this point in the book you have already learned that Windows 95 is a networking environment. This means that network resources are easily accessed both from within Windows 95 and from the DOS command line. Most operations enable you to utilize resources transparently. For instance, if you have mapped a network drive, calling it drive H:, you can simply use DOS commands at the command line to access drive H:. Windows 95 takes care of the rest, behind the scenes, to make sure that your commands are carried out as you intend.

To facilitate the use of the network, Windows 95 has included quite a few different network commands that you can use from the command line. These commands all consist of two keywords, and start with the word *NET*. The following are the different network commands:

- NET CONFIG
- NET DIAG
- NET HELP
- NET INIT
- NET LOGOFF
- NET LOGON
- NET PASSWORD
- NET PRINT
- NET START
- NET STOP
- NET TIME
- NET USE

- NET VER
- NET VIEW

These commands are intended to help you manage your network connections and network resources from the command line. In addition, there are two other network commands provided with Windows 95. The NETSTAT command (notice that it is one word, not two) is used to discover information about your network workstation and the network connections you have made. If you are using a network based on NetBIOS protocols (such as Novell), then you can use the NBTSTAT command, which provides much the same information, but procures it through NetBIOS functions.

The following sections detail the purpose and composition of each of the new DOS commands.

NET CONFIG

The NET CONFIG command displays information about your local workstation. You will see information about your computer name, user name, workgroup, root folder, and operating system version information, as shown in figure 40.1.

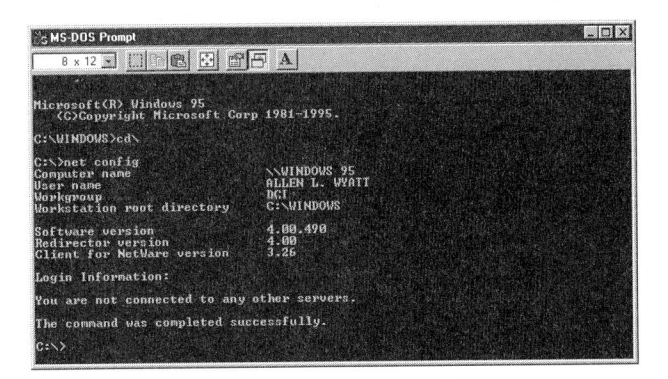

Fig. 40.1 The NET CONFIG command returns information about your network connection.

You can run the NET CONFIG command from the DOS command line in an MS-DOS window.

New Commands **1011**

NET DIAG

The NET DIAG command is used to troubleshoot the connection between two computers on your network. This command presupposes that there are at least two computers using the same command. When you first use it, it will search for another computer using the same program, and establish the link with it. If it cannot find another system using NET DIAG, then it will start to act as a diagnostics server, awaiting some other system on the network to run the same program.

When you have two computers running NET DIAG, you can view the statistics reported by the program. These statistics can help you diagnose where you may be having problems with the net.

NET HELP

The NET HELP command is used to get a short bit of information about the various network commands provided with Windows 95. For instance, figure 40.2 shows an example of the help information returned by the program for the NET PRINT command.

Fig. 40.2 The help information returned for the NET PRINT command.

> **Tip:** You can also get help on a network command by entering the command as you normally would, and then using a /? switch after the command.

1012   Chapter 40: Operating in Windows 95 DOS

In addition, you can use the NET HELP command to provide information about errors which may occur when using network commands. To use the command in this way, simply append the number of the error to the command.

NET INIT

The NET INIT command is used to load network drivers without binding them to the Protocol Manager. Typically, this command is used with third-party network drivers. You can use NET INIT in real-mode operation only. This means that you cannot use it in an MS-DOS window. Instead, you must restart your system at the command prompt. Afterwards, you can use it with no problem.

After using NET INIT, you can use the NET START NETBIND command to bind the drivers to the Protocol Manager. If you experience problems with some third-party networks, you might try using NET INIT with the /dynamic switch. This loads the drivers dynamically and may cure the problem.

NET LOGOFF

You can use the NET LOGOFF command in real-mode operation only. This means that you cannot use it in an MS-DOS window. Instead, you must restart your system at the command prompt. Afterwards, you can use NET LOGOFF.

The purpose of NET LOGOFF is to provide the same function in real mode that you would normally do within Windows 95. Using the command logs you off the network immediately, without any confirmation. You can use the NET LOGON command to again gain access to the network.

NET LOGON

The NET LOGON command is the opposite of NET LOGOFF. You can use NET LOGON in real-mode operation only, which means you cannot use it in an MS-DOS window. Instead, you must restart your system at the command prompt. Afterwards, you can use NET LOGON.

Normally, if you are using the Windows 95 graphical interface, you gain access to the network by logging on the system when you first start Windows. Similarly, you can use the features in the Control Panel to log on and off. In real mode you obviously do not have access to these features, so you must use the NET LOGON command to connect your system to the network.

When you use the command, you should follow it with your user ID, your password, an optional domain name, and an indication of whether you want the password saved. The syntax for the command is as follows:

```
NET LOGON user password /DOMAIN:name /yes /SAVEPW:NO
```

The /yes switch between the domain name and the save password flag is used if you want to carry out the logon process without asking for confirmation.

NET PASSWORD

There are three different forms of the NET PASSWORD command. Each of them is designed to help change your network password, but each is used in a different situation.

If you want to change your password on the current system, you can only do so from real mode. This means that you cannot have the Windows 95 graphical interface running. The best way to get rid of it is to restart the system at the command prompt. Then, when you are connected to the network, you can use the command as follows:

```
NET PASSWORD oldpw newpw
```

All you need to do is replace *oldpw* and *newpw* with your old and new passwords, respectively. The second form of the command enables you to change your password on another server. You can do this from the command line of an MS-DOS window. To use this form of the command, use the following syntax:

```
NET PASSWORD \\server user oldpw newpw
```

Notice that you must now include both the server address and your user ID. Similarly, you can use the third form of NET PASSWORD to change your password on a particular domain:

```
NET PASSWORD /DOMAIN:domain user oldpw newpw
```

Here you have replaced the server name with the /DOMAIN: key word and the name of the domain. You can also use this version of the command in an MS-DOS window.

NET PRINT

The NET PRINT command is used to control print jobs over the network or on your own system. In effect, the command provides a way to control a printer queue from the command line rather than using the Printers folder. Available options enable you to view the queue, as well as to pause, resume, and delete individual jobs.

The normal way you use the command is to first view the queue. This is done using the following command at the DOS command line:

```
NET PRINT location /yes
```

The location parameter is a port number (such as LPT1 or LPT2) or a UNC path for a network printer. The command returns a list of the print jobs currently in the queue. Associated with each print job is a job number. This number can then be used in a NET PRINT command that affects the individual job. For instance, if you want to delete print job 14, you would use the following command:

```
NET PRINT location 14 /DELETE /yes
```

Again, the location is the name of the printer whose queue you are modifying. NET PRINT recognizes two other commands as well—/PAUSE and /RESUME. You can use these commands on the command line in place of the /DELETE command.

Even though the NET PRINT command works just fine, it is much easier to use the Printers folder to manage individual printer queues. NET PRINT is provided primarily for the development of batch files that automatically manage the print queue.

New Commands **1015**

NET START

The NET START command is used to start different network services. You use this command after you have used NET INIT. You can use NET START in real-mode operation only, which means that you cannot use it in an MS-DOS window. Instead, you must restart your system at the command prompt.

To start a service, you use the following syntax:

    NET START service /yes /verbose /nondis

The last three parameters are optional. The /yes parameter carries out the startup process without asking for confirmation. The /verbose parameter indicates that you want detailed information about device drivers and services as they are loaded. The /nondis parameter starts the network redirector without loading any device drivers.

The *service* parameter is used to indicate the type of network service you want to start. Table 40.1 lists the different services you can specify on the command line.

Table 40.1   Network Services Used with the NET START Command

Service	Meaning
BASIC	Basic network redirector
NWREDIR	Microsoft Client for NetWare
WORKSTATION	The default redirector
NETBIND	Binds protocols and drivers
NETBEUI	Extended NetBIOS interface
NWLINK	IPX/SPX interface

If you want to list the active services on the workstation, you can use the following command:

    NET START /LIST

NET STOP

The NET STOP command is the opposite of the NET START command. It is used to halt network services, and can be used in real-mode operation only. This means that you cannot use it in an MS-DOS window. Instead, you must restart your system at the command prompt.

> **Tip:** It is a good idea to list the different active network services before you use NET STOP. You do this by using the NET START /LIST command.

To use the NET STOP command, all you need to do is append the name of the service you want to stop. You can use the service names detailed earlier in Table 40.1.

NET TIME

The NET TIME command is used to view the time on another computer in your workgroup or domain; it will work only on a Windows network. This remote computer is called a *time server*. You can also use the command to synchronize the time on your workstation with the time on the remote system.

To view the time on another system, use the following command:

    NET TIME location /yes

The *location* parameter indicates the name of the computer or workgroup you want to check. If you are checking a specific computer, a fully qualified UNC name must be provided. If you are checking the time on a workgroup, then the format is /WORKGROUP:*name*, where *name* is the name of the workgroup. You can only check the time of a workgroup if the workgroup has a defined time server for the group.

To set your system time based on the time on another system, use the following command:

    NET TIME location /set /yes

New Commands

The only change from the command to view the time is the inclusion of the /set switch, which tells NET TIME you want to set your local computer time.

NET USE

The NET USE command is used to manage your network connections with remote resources such as disks or printers. This command is similar in purpose to the network mapping functions of Windows 95. You can also use NET USE to display information about existing connections. You can see the currently defined network connections by entering the following command at the MS-DOS command prompt:

```
NET USE
```

To connect to a remote resource, you simply need to provide the name of the local device to which you want the resource mapped, and then provide the path to the network resource. For instance, if you wanted to map the printer at //Accounting/laser to your system, you would use the following command:

```
NET USE lpt2: //Accounting/laser Dollars /SAVEPW:NO
```

This example assumes that the password for the printer (if necessary) is *Dollars,* and that you do not care if the password is saved in the password file. You can also append a /yes or /no switch which is used to indicate how you want to answer any dialog boxes that may pop up. After this command is successfully completed, anything you print to LPT2 is automatically sent to the accounting department's laser printer.

Likewise, you can map a local drive letter to a network drive by using the same sort of command line (here the password is *Fiscal*):

```
NET USE G: //Accounting/Budget/New Fiscal /SAVEPW:NO
```

> **Tip:** If you use an asterisk (*) instead of a drive letter when mapping a network drive, the next available drive letter is automatically used.

To later disconnect the mapped resource, you would simply provide the local name you used for the mapping, and then use the /DELETE switch. For instance, if you wanted to delete the association between LPT2 and the accounting laser printer, you would use the following command line:

```
NET USE lpt2: /DELETE
```

NET VER

NET VER is a very simple command that displays the version number of your network redirector. If you are ever wondering what network redirector version is running on your workstation, type **NET VER** at the DOS command line; figure 40.3 shows an example of the output produced by the command.

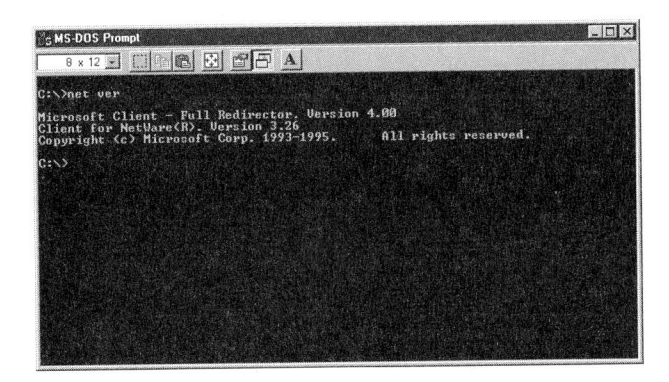

Fig. 40.3 The NET VER command indicates the version of your network redirector.

The NET VER command is typically used for diagnostic purposes. For instance, your network administrator may need to know your redirector version number to make sure that you are using the proper drivers.

NET VIEW

The NET VIEW command is used to determine which computers are available in a workgroup, or which resources are being shared by a specific computer on the network. To see a list of the computers in your workgroup, use the following at the DOS command prompt:

    NET VIEW

To see a list of computers in a specific workgroup on a Microsoft network, just append the name of the workgroup as follows:

    NET VIEW /WORKGROUP:*name* /yes

You must, of course, substitute the name of the workgroup for the *name* parameter. You can also use the NET VIEW command to see a list of the resources used by a specific workstation. You do this by including the UNC path to the workstation on the command line. For instance, if you wanted to see the resources on the production department's system (in the Acme domain), you would enter the following command:

    NET VIEW \\Acme\production /yes

NETSTAT

The NETSTAT command displays information and statistics about your current TCP/IP network connections. In many ways it is similar to the NBTSTAT command, described in the next section. Information displayed by NETSTAT includes the IP address and port number of a network connection, the IP address of your local system, the protocol used by a connection, and the status of a connection.

The format and exact content of the information displayed by NETSTAT can be modified by using command-line switches. Table 40.2 lists the different switches and their purposes.

Table 40.2 Command-line Switches for the NETSTAT Command

Switch	Meaning
-a	Shows all network connections.
-e	Shows only Ethernet statistics.
-n	Displays information in numerical form, as opposed to displaying name equivalencies.
-s	Displays statistics by protocol.
-p *protocol*	Indicates the protocols for which statistics should be displayed. Valid values for *protocol* without using the -s switch are tcp and udp. If you use the -s switch, valid values for *protocol* are tcp, udp, icmp, or ip.
-r	Shows the contents of the network routing table.
interval	Indicates the interval, in seconds, at which the requested statistics should be updated and redisplayed. Using this parameter places NETSTAT in a continuous updating mode; you can break the cycle by pressing Ctrl+C.

NBTSTAT

The NBTSTAT command displays network information, in table form, using NetBIOS protocols instead of TCP/IP protocols. This command is diagnostic in nature, and can be used to resolve network difficulties. Because it is a diagnostic tool, it is much more likely to be used by network administrators than by regular users.

You can enter the NBTSTAT command at the DOS command line. The switches for the command are listed in Table 40.3.

Table 40.3 Command-line Switches for the NBTSTAT Command

Switch	Meaning
-a *host*	Uses the name table from the specified host computer.
-A *address*	Uses the name table at the specified IP address.
-c	Lists the contents of the NetBIOS name cache.
-n	Lists local NetBIOS names.
-R	Purges the NetBIOS name cache and then reloads the LMHOSTS file.
-r	Lists name resolution information for Windows networking.
-S	Displays both workstation and server sessions, using IP addresses for remote hosts.
-s	Displays both workstation and server sessions, using host names for remote hosts wherever possible.
interval	Indicates the interval, in seconds, at which the requested statistics should be updated and redisplayed. Using this parameter places NBTSTAT in a continuous updating mode; you can stop the command by pressing Ctrl+C.

The NBTSTAT command relies on NetBIOS protocols to derive its statistics. This implies that you can only use the command with a network that uses NetBIOS (such as Novell).

TCP/IP Commands

When you configure Windows 95 for your network, you can install the TCP/IP client protocols. (Adding network protocols is discussed in Chapter 36, "Communicating with a Network.") If you do add TCP/IP, a group of network-related commands becomes available to you:

- ARP
- FTP

1022   Chapter 40: Operating in Windows 95 DOS

- PING
- ROUTE
- TELNET
- TRACERT

If you have worked on a UNIX system connected to the Internet before, some of these commands may look familiar. They should; they have been freely borrowed from the UNIX world. For instance, the FTP command starts the FTP utility program. Each of these commands is described in the following sections.

ARP

ARP is an acronym for *address resolution protocol*. This command enables you to modify the IP-to-Ethernet or Token Ring address translation tables used by the network services of Windows 95. You use the ARP command from the command line in an MS-DOS window. The switches you can use with ARP are detailed in Table 40.4.

Table 40.4 Command-line Switches for the ARP Program

Switch	Meaning
-a *address* -N *netaddr*	Displays information from the ARP table. If *address* is provided, then only information on that IP address is returned. If the -N option is used, then the ARP table from the server at the IP address *netaddr* is used.
-d *address netaddr*	Deletes the ARP table entry specified by the IP *address* provided. If *netaddr* is included, then the action is taken on the ARP table at that address.
-s *address physical netaddr*	Adds an ARP table entry. The IP *address* is associated with the physical Ethernet address specified by *physical*. If *netaddr* is included, then the entry is added to the ARP table at that IP address.

FTP

FTP is an acronym for *file transfer protocol*, and it is a command-line program for transferring files across TCP/IP networks. This utility started in the UNIX environment, but has migrated to other environments connected to the Internet. It is now available in Windows 95.

To start FTP, simply enter the command at a command prompt in an MS-DOS window. The FTP command can use any of the command-line switches listed in Table 40.5.

Table 40.5   Command-line Switches for the FTP Program

Switch	Meaning
host	Indicates the host name or IP address of the system to which you want to connect.
-d	Turns on debugging displays, which results in all FTP commands between your computer and the remote system being displayed, even if they would otherwise have been suppressed.
-g	Turns off ability to use wildcard characters in file name specifications.
-I	Turns off interactive prompts when transferring multiple files.
-n	Turns off auto-login when initially connected to a remote system.
-s: *filename*	Indicates the name of a text file from which FTP commands should be executed, rather than allowing command input from the keyboard.
-v	Turns off the display of the remote system's responses.

After you have used FTP to connect to a remote system, you are presented with the FTP command prompt. At this point there are many different commands that you can use with FTP. These commands, along with their meanings, are listed in Table 40.6.

Table 40.6 FTP Commands and Their Meanings

Command	Meaning
! *command*	Runs *command* on the local computer.
?	Displays a list of, or descriptions for, FTP commands. Identical to the help command.
append	Appends a local file to a file on the remote computer, using the current file type setting.
ascii	Sets the file transfer type to ASCII (the default).
bell	Toggles the bell setting. If the bell is on, a bell rings after each file transfer is completed; if off (the default), no bell is used.
binary	Sets the file transfer type to binary.
bye	Breaks the connection with the remote system and exits the FTP program. Identical to the quit command.
cd *folder*	On the remote computer, changes the working folder to *folder*.
close	Breaks the connection with the remote system and remains in the FTP program. Identical to the disconnect command.
debug	Toggles the debug setting. If on, messages between you and the remote system are displayed; if off (the default), messages are suppressed.
delete *filename*	Deletes the specified files on the remote system.
dir	Displays a folder on the remote system.
disconnect	Breaks the connection with the remote system and remains in the FTP program. Identical to the close command.
get *filename*	Copies *filename* from the remote system to your computer by using the current file transfer type. Identical to the recv command.
glob	Toggles the "globbing" setting. If on (the default), wildcard characters can be used in file names; if off, wildcard characters cannot be used.

continues

New Commands **1025**

Table 40.6 Continued

Command	Meaning
hash	Toggles hash setting. If on, a pound sign (#) is printed for each 2K bytes of data transferred with get or put; if off (the default), hash marks are not displayed.
help	Displays a list of, or descriptions for, FTP commands. Identical to the ? command.
lcd *folder*	On your system, changes the working folder to *folder*.
ls	Displays an abbreviated folder on the remote system.
mdelete *filelist*	Deletes multiple files on the remote system.
mdir *filelist*	Same as dir command, but allows multiple files or folders to be specified.
mget *filelist*	Copies the files in *filelist* from the remote system to the working folder on your computer by using the current file transfer type.
mkdir *folder*	Creates a folder on the remote system.
mls *filelist*	Same as ls command, but allows multiple files or folders to be specified.
mput *filelist*	Copies the files in *filelist* from your computer to the remote system by using the current file transfer type.
open *host*	Establishes a connection with the remote system whose host name or IP address is specified by *host*.
prompt	Toggles prompting setting. If on (the default), you are prompted during multiple file transfers about your desire to transfer each file; if off, no prompting occurs.
put *filename*	Copies *filename* from your computer to the remote system by using the current file transfer type. Identical to the send command.
pwd	Displays the name of the current folder on the remote system.
quit	Breaks the connection with the remote system and exits the FTP program. Identical to the bye command.

Command	Meaning
recv *filename*	Copies *filename* from the remote system to your computer by using the current file transfer type. Identical to the get command.
rename *file1 file2*	On the remote system, renames *file1* to *file2*.
rmdir *folder*	Deletes the specified *folder* on the remote system.
send *filename*	Copies *filename* from your computer to the remote system by using the current file transfer type. Identical to the put command.
status	Displays the current status of the connection with the remote system, as well as the settings of any toggles.
trace	Toggles the packet tracing setting. If on, the route of each data packet is displayed (between your system and the remote system); if off (the default), then routing is not displayed.
type *xfertype*	Sets or displays the file transfer type. Type binary is identical to the binary command; type ascii is identical to the ascii command. Without the *xfertype* parameter, the current transfer type setting is displayed.
verbose	Toggles verbose setting. If on (the default), all commands from your system or from the remote system are displayed; if off, no commands are displayed.

While the list of commands that you can use in FTP looks rather long, you will probably only use a couple of them. For instance, the most common commands are get (which transfers a file to your system) and bye (which disconnects you from the remote system).

Notice, as well, that many of the commands are simply synonyms for other commands. For instance, the get and recv commands do the same thing, as do the bye and quit commands. If the synonyms were removed, there would be approximately a third fewer FTP commands.

New Commands **1027**

PING

The PING command verifies an active connection with a remote computer by sending ECHO packets across the network. The remote computer, when receiving the packets, sends them back to your computer. This allows a response time to be calculated and displayed.

The PING command is used at the command prompt in an MS-DOS window. You can use the command-line switches shown in Table 40.7.

Table 40.7 Command-line Switches for the PING Command

Switch	Meaning
list	The list of host names or IP addresses to ping.
-a	Disables host name IP address resolution. Results in IP addresses being displayed rather than host names.
-f	Causes packets sent to the remote system to be unfragmented by intermediate gateways.
-i *ttl*	Indicates the value to use for the Time To Live field in the PING packets. Effectively limits the number of reroutings that the packets can make.
-j *list*	Indicates the route to be used as the PING packets are transmitted. The *list* consists of up to nine host names or IP addresses separated by spaces. The host list indicates that those hosts must be included in the routing, although additional intermediate hosts can also be used where necessary.
-k *list*	Same as the -j switch, except that no intermediate hosts can be used.
-l *length*	Indicates the amount of data (in bytes) to be included in each ECHO packet. The default length is 64, but you can specify any value between 1 and 8192.
-n *count*	Indicates how many ECHO packets to send in each PING. If omitted, the default count of 4 packets is used.
-v *tos*	Indicates the value to use for the Type of Service field in the PING packets.

Switch	Meaning
-r *count*	Indicates how many hosts should be recorded during the round-trip taken by the ECHO packets. You may specify a *count* between 1 and 9.
-t	Continuously pings the specified host until interrupted, by pressing Ctrl+C.
-w *timeout*	Indicates the timeout interval, in milliseconds.

When you are using PING, you can combine command-line switches as long as the switch does not require a value. For instance, either of the following would be a legal use of the PING command:

   ping -a -f

   ping -af

PING is generally viewed as a diagnostic command, used to make sure that a remote system really can be reached from your system. If you try PING with a DNS host name (such as foo.bar.net) and the PING does not work, try it using the IP address for the host (such as 147.192.40.2). If the IP address works, and you did not misspell the host name, then you have a problem with the DNS server you are using.

ROUTE

The ROUTE command is actually four commands in one. When used as the initial part of the command, it enables you to manage the routing table used by the networking services of Windows 95. The different forms of the command are:

> **ROUTE ADD.** Adds an entry to the routing table.

> **ROUTE CHANGE.** Changes an entry in the routing table.

> **ROUTE PRINT.** Prints the routing table.

> **ROUTE DELETE.** Deletes an entry from the routing table.

To add a gateway entry to the routing table, you would follow the command by the host name, the mask name, and the gateway to use, as in the following:

```
ROUTE ADD host MASK mask gateway
```

In this example, *host*, *mask*, and *gateway* should be replaced with their respective IP addresses. The syntax is the same if you are changing, printing, or deleting—the only change in the command is the second word.

You can also use the ROUTE command, with only the -f switch, to clear the entire routing table. You would enter this command as follows:

```
ROUTE -f
```

If you use the -f switch in a command line with any other ROUTE command, the clearing takes place before the other portion of the command line (add, change, print, or delete) is completed.

> **Caution:** Make sure that you have a printout of the routing table before you delete it using the -f switch. After it is deleted, you cannot undo your action without manually rebuilding the table.

TELNET

You can use the TELNET program to connect your computer to remote computer so that your computer can act as if it were a terminal for the remote system. This command originated in the UNIX environment, where all TELNET operations took place on the command line. The Windows 95 implementation of the program is quite different, however. If you enter the TELNET command at the DOS command line, a new window appears, containing a Windows-based version of the TELNET program (see figure 40.4).

With the menu choices in the TELNET window, you can connect to a TELNET server elsewhere on a network (such as the Internet) and behave as a terminal to that system. The Connect menu is used to control the connection with the remote system. This menu includes the following choices:

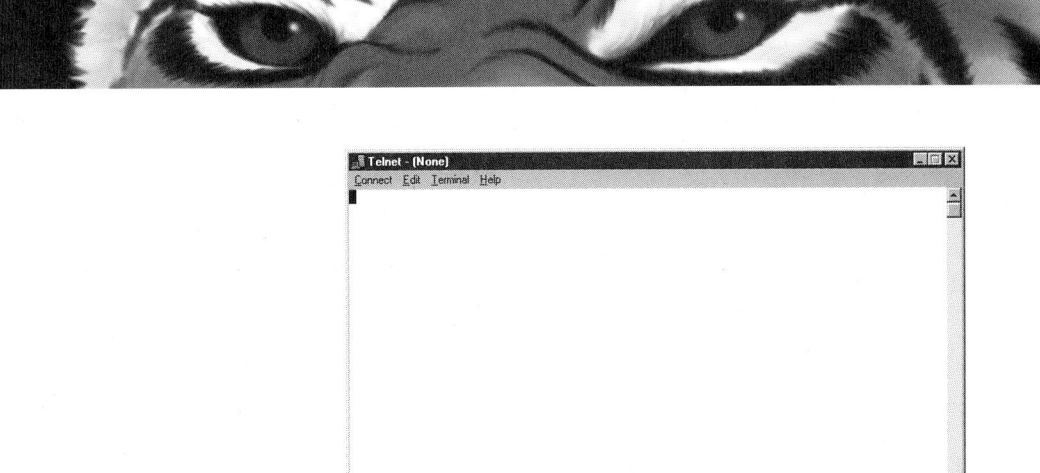

Fig. 40.4 The TELNET window is the result of running the TELNET command.

> ➤ **Remote System.** Used to specify the remote system with which you want a connection established. You can indicate the host name (or IP address), the port, and the terminal type to use.
>
> ➤ **Disconnect.** Used to break an established connection with a remote system.
>
> ➤ **Exit.** Used to exit the TELNET program.

The Edit menu serves much the same purpose as similar menus in other Windows programs. The choices on this menu are as follows:

> ➤ **Copy.** Used to copy the selected text into the Clipboard.
>
> ➤ **Paste.** Used to copy the contents of the Clipboard to the location of the cursor.
>
> ➤ **Select All.** Used to select all the text on the screen. (Provides a fast way to select everything before you use the Copy command.)

The Terminal menu is used to change the attributes of the TELNET window or the TELNET session. This menu also contains three choices:

- **Preferences.** Enables you to change the attributes of the TELNET window. Attributes include items such as terminal emulation, terminal options, background color, font, and buffer size.
- **Start Logging.** Saves the current TELNET session into a text file.
- **Stop Logging.** Stops saving information in a log file.

The final menu, Help, is used to get assistance in how to run TELNET.

TRACERT

TRACERT is a diagnostic utility that enables you to determine the network route between your system and a remote system. It does this by using much the same process as the PING command—sending out an ECHO packet to the remote host. The difference is that the ttl (Time To Live) field is manipulated by the TRACERT program to determine the route of the packet.

The first packet sent out has the ttl field set to 1, meaning that it will only go to the first gateway and then be returned. TRACERT then increases the ttl field by 1 (to 2) and sends out the packet again. This incremental approach is continued until the destination host is reached. At that point, the ttl field indicates how many steps the packet had to travel to reach the destination.

The TRACERT command is used from the MS-DOS command line. The switches you can use with the command are shown in Table 40.8.

Table 40.8   Command-line Switches for the TRACERT Command

Switch	Meaning
host	The host name or IP address of the ultimate target of the command.
-d	Disables host name IP address resolution. Results in IP addresses being displayed rather than host names.
-h *steps*	Indicates the maximum number of steps that the command should use before giving up.

Switch	Meaning
-j *list*	Indicates the route to be used as the ECHO packets are transmitted. The *list* consists of up to nine host names or IP addresses separated by spaces. The host list indicates that those hosts must be included in the routing, although additional intermediate hosts can also be used where necessary.
-w *timeout*	Indicates the timeout interval in milliseconds.

The route returned by the TRACERT command should not be considered an absolute. Routes may change over time, and the results of the TRACERT command depend on how well intermediate hosts follow accepted procedure. If a host does not return an indication of where a packet expired, then TRACERT has no way of reporting that host as an intermediate step on the route.

The Start Command

Perhaps the biggest addition to Windows 95 is the START command. This command, when entered at the command line, gives you a new way to execute a program.

Normally, all you need to do to run a program is simply enter the program name at the DOS command line. For instance, to run your favorite game, you might enter a command such as PLAY at the command line. This would search for a file such as PLAY.COM, PLAY.EXE, or PLAY.BAT, and then execute that file. You can still run programs this way at the Windows 95 command line. If you enter the program name, the program is run in the current window, and when you exit the program, you are returned to the command line. There is now another way, however.

If you preface the program name with the START command, the program will be run in a new DOS window. For instance, if you wanted to run your favorite game, you might enter the START PLAY command. Windows 95 then opens a DOS window for the program, and executes

PLAY within that window. When you exit the game program, the window opened for that program is automatically closed. All the while your original DOS window (the one in which you executed the START command) is still available for other purposes.

Using the Command Line

There are two main ways you can access the DOS command line in Windows 95. One involves working within Windows itself, and the other involves bypassing a normal Windows startup.

Using a DOS Window

To open a DOS window, follow these two steps:

1. Choose Programs from the Start menu.
2. Choose MS-DOS Prompt from the Programs menu.

Shortly you will see a DOS window appear, similar to what is shown in figure 40.5.

If you are familiar with using a DOS window under previous versions of Windows, you should feel right at home with using the Windows 95 DOS window. When you are at the command line you can go about business as usual and run the programs or other commands you want to use.

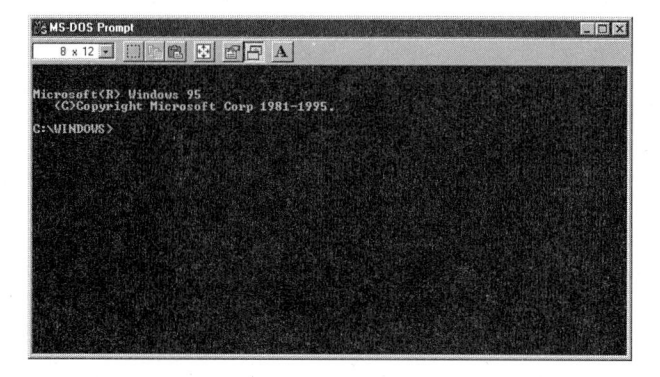

Fig. 40.5 The DOS window uses a command-line interface.

How DOS Windows Work Under Windows 95

You already know that Windows is a multitasking operating system. Depending on the amount of memory you have installed in your system, Windows 95 enables you to have many applications running at the same time—even multiple DOS applications.

When you open a DOS window under Windows 95, the operating system creates what is termed a *virtual machine,* or VM. A VM is maintained by Windows 95 in such a way that any application you run within a DOS window thinks it is actually running in DOS, without Windows or any other application being present. The side effect of using a VM arrangement is that your system is more stable—applications running in one DOS window cannot interfere with applications in another window, even if one of them crashes.

In Windows 95 you can have any number of DOS windows running concurrently, giving you the ability to multitask DOS applications. This is a huge improvement over previous versions of Windows. Again, this arrangement is enabled by the shift in the relationship between DOS and Windows. (Whereas Windows used to run under DOS, DOS now runs under Windows.)

Controlling the Appearance of the DOS Window

Notice that when you first open a DOS window, it does not occupy the entire screen. Depending on the size of your video monitor and the resolution of your video card, this may make the text in the window barely readable. You can increase the size of the window to occupy the entire screen by pressing Alt+Enter, or by clicking the maximize button in the upper-right window corner.

If you are working with a DOS window that does not occupy the entire screen, you will notice a toolbar at the top of the window. The addition of a toolbar to DOS windows is a departure from previous versions of Windows. The toolbar enables you to modify the appearance of what you see in the DOS window. You can modify the font and point size of text, copy and paste directly from the DOS window to a Windows 95 application, resize the window, and modify other performance settings of the DOS session.

> **Tip:** If the DOS toolbar is not visible, you can activate it by right-clicking the title bar of the DOS window and choosing <u>T</u>oolbar.

The controls on the DOS toolbar, from left to right, are as follows:

➤ **Font list.** This control shows the various fonts you can use to display text in the DOS window. You should pick the font that is best for your display environment. Both bitmapped screen fonts and TrueType fonts are included in the Font list. (See Chapter 22, "Working with Fonts," for more information on fonts.)

➤ **Mark.** This button enables you to mark text in the DOS window on which you want to take a subsequent action. After the text is marked, you can delete it by pressing the Delete key, or you can copy it to the Clipboard by clicking the Copy button.

➤ **Copy.** You use this button after using the Mark button to mark a block of text. Whatever you copy is placed in the Clipboard, where it can be used in other Windows applications.

➤ **Paste.** After you have copied or cut text within the DOS window (or from another window), you can paste it at the current cursor position by clicking this button.

➤ **Full screen.** This is the same as clicking the maximize button. The DOS window expands to fill the entire screen. To later reduce the window size, press Alt+Enter.

➤ **Properties.** Clicking here enables you to change the attributes used in this DOS window. The various properties are discussed later in the section entitled "DOS Window Properties."

➤ **Exclusive.** Clicking this button suspends operation of other Windows programs, turning full attention of the CPU over to the DOS program running in this window.

➤ **Background.** This button turns off exclusive mode. It allows the program in the DOS window to run in conjunction with other programs you are running. This is the normal operational mode for DOS windows.

➤ **Font properties.** Clicking here enables you to change other font properties, in addition to the font type (which can be changed from the Font list).

To close the DOS window, use the EXIT command at the command line. This closes the window and returns you to your Windows 95 desktop. If the command line is visible, you can also click the close icon in the upper-right corner of the DOS window.

Jumping to the Command Line

For some programs, operating within a DOS window simply will not do. You may have a DOS program that has exceptional memory requirements, or that needs tight control of other computer resources. In this case, you have two options. First, you can use a tried-and-true brute-force method of booting to a floppy disk and then running your software from there. A better solution, however, is to simply not load the Windows graphical interface. Windows 95 enables you to start the system and use only the command-line interface instead of the familiar graphical interface. To do this, follow these steps:

1. Shut down and restart your system.

2. After the initial system testing is complete, you will see a single-line message that says Starting Windows 95.

3. Press the F8 key. This displays the boot menu shown in figure 40.6.

4. Choose option 6, "Command prompt only."

This displays a screen that looks like a full-screen DOS window. The graphical Windows interface is not running, and you can work in this screen the same as you would have in regular DOS.

To run Windows from the command line, simply enter the WIN command. This starts Windows 95, the same as if you restarted your system.

Using the Command Line **1037**

```
          Microsoft Windows 95 Startup Menu
          ====================================

          1. Normal
          2. Logged (\BOOTLOG.TXT)
          3. Safe mode
          4. Safe mode with network support
          5. Step-by-step confirmation
          6. Command prompt only
          7. Safe mode command prompt only
          8. Previous version of MS-DOS

          Enter a choice: 1

          F5=Safe mode   Shift+F5=Command prompt
          Shift+F8=Stype-by-step confirmation [N]
```

Fig. 40.6 You can use the Startup menu for Windows 95 to access the command line.

DOS Window Properties

Earlier in this chapter you learned how you can access the properties of a DOS window—by clicking the Properties tool on the toolbar. Windows 95 enables you to modify quite a few properties of a DOS window. When you first display the MS-DOS Prompt Properties sheet, it looks similar to what is shown in figure 40.7.

There are five different tabs in the Properties sheet: Program, Font, Memory, Screen, and Misc. Each of these is covered in detail in the following sections.

Fig. 40.7 The MS-DOS Prompt Properties sheet enables you to modify how your DOS sessions are managed by Windows 95.

The Program Tab

The Program tab is the default tab displayed when you first open the MS-DOS Prompt Properties sheet (see figure 40.7). This tab enables you to change different aspects of how Windows 95 behaves when it opens the DOS window. At the top of the dialog box is a field where you can change the title bar wording for the DOS window. This effectively is the name of the program, and probably should not be changed for a generic MS-DOS window. You would normally change the title for windows used to run DOS-based programs.

You use the Cmd Line field to specify the command line used to run the program contained within the DOS window. Notice that the command line for the generic DOS window is the command interpreter (COMMAND.COM). If you were running a different program, then the name of the program's executable file would be in this field.

The Working field enables you to specify the working folder associated with this program. The default folder is C:\WINDOWS, or whatever folder it was in which you installed Windows 95.

DOS Window Properties **1039**

You use the Batch File field to specify the name of a batch file that should be run when the window is opened. For instance, you may need to run a batch file to run several programs in a row or to run some configuration programs before you run your DOS program.

You use the Shortcut key field to define a keyboard shortcut that you can use to switch to the window. The shortcut must consist of the Ctrl key (and optionally the Alt key) in addition to another key. For instance, you could define Ctrl+J or Ctrl+Alt+B to switch to the DOS window.

> **Caution:** You cannot use the Esc, Enter, Tab, Spacebar, Print Screen, or Backspace keys as shortcut keys for DOS windows. If the shortcut key is the same as something used in a Windows-based program, your shortcut key always takes precedence. In other words, the shortcut key in the Windows-based program will not work.

You use the Run field to indicate how the DOS window should be first run. If set to Normal window, then the window does not open in a full-screen mode, but instead opens on your desktop. If set to Minimized, then the window opens as a task on the taskbar (in a minimized condition). If set to Maximized, then the program starts in full-screen mode.

> **Tip:** To get out of full-screen mode, press Ctrl+Enter.

Finally, you use the Close on Exit check box to indicate how Windows 95 should treat the window when the program it is running is completed. Most of the time you will want to select Close on Exit, so that the window is eliminated when the program is over. If you clear the check box, then the window stays open even when the program is done; you are returned to the DOS command prompt.

If you click the Change Icon button, you can change the icon associated with the MS-DOS window. Normally this icon is automatically determined by Windows 95, based on the program you are running in the window.

If you click the Advanced button, you will see the Advanced Program Settings dialog box, as shown in figure 40.8.

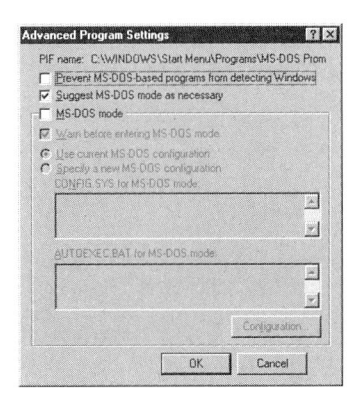

Fig. 40.8 The Advanced Program Settings dialog box enables you to configure the environment used by the DOS window.

You use the settings in this dialog box to determine the environment offered by the DOS window. In older versions of Windows, this type of information was contained within a PIF file (program information file). Windows 95 enables you to change the settings in a dialog box, instead.

Most of the time you will not need to change the settings in the Advanced Program Settings dialog box. Some programs, however, may benefit by tweaking some of the settings here.

Realistically, the first setting is the one you are most likely to change. It controls whether the DOS program can even detect the presence of Windows. Some older DOS programs refuse to run unless Windows is not running. If this is the case, selecting this check box can hide the presence of Windows completely.

DOS Window Properties **1041**

The next two check boxes determine the operating mode of the MS-DOS program you are defining. Microsoft suggests that you leave the first option, Suggest MS-DOS mode as necessary, selected. MS-DOS mode simply means that the program running in the DOS window displaces any other program running in your system. Some DOS programs work so closely to the hardware or require so many resources that it is impossible for Windows to effectively run. If you select the first option, and Windows detects that the DOS program would work best in MS-DOS mode, then it takes care of the transition for you.

If you select the other MS-DOS mode option, then the program you are defining will automatically kick your machine into MS-DOS mode. In this mode, all other Windows-based programs are closed, all DOS windows are closed, and the system starts in MS-DOS mode. The benefit to your DOS programs is that they are the exclusive program running on the system. The downside is that no other programs can run concurrently, and when the program is done, the system needs to be restarted to again use Windows 95.

If you choose MS-DOS mode, then you can also specify how the DOS-mode environment is configured. The first check box, Warn Before Entering MS-DOS mode, controls whether you will have a chance to back out of the DOS-mode switch. If the check box is selected (the default), then you are prompted before a switch is made. If the check box is clear, then the switch to DOS mode is done without any warning. Because this could play havoc with some other programs running on your system, you will probably always want to be warned.

Finally, you can specify whether Windows 95 should use the default DOS environment, or whether you want to define a special environment. If you choose the latter, you can indicate the contents of the CONFIG.SYS and AUTOEXEC.BAT files right in this dialog box. (You should consult a good DOS reference manual for information on putting together these special configuration files.)

The Font Tab

When you click the Font tab, the MS-DOS Prompt Properties sheet looks like what you see in figure 40.9.

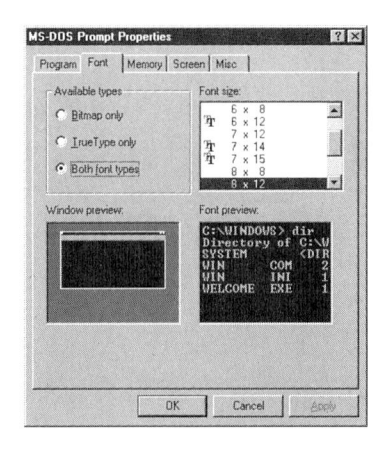

Fig. 40.9 The MS-DOS Prompt Properties sheet, with the Font tab selected, enables you to pick the display font for the DOS window.

This dialog box enables you to pick the font used to display information in the DOS window. At the upper-left corner you can specify the different types of fonts from which you can choose. (Fonts are covered in detail in Chapter 22, "Working with Fonts.")

At the upper-right corner you can pick the size of the font you want displayed. The font you choose will also result in a size change for the window, and can greatly affect the readability of the screen. You may need to play with different font sizes to find the one that is right for you. (I personally like the 8×12 font; it is crisp, clear, and easy to read.) Font sizes are indicated in pixels, so the smaller the numbers, the smaller the size of the characters on the screen.

As you modify the fonts and pick different font sizes, the preview screens (at the bottom of the dialog box) indicate the approximate appearance of your DOS window.

The Memory Tab

Clicking the Memory tab of the MS-DOS Prompt Properties sheet results in a window that looks like figure 40.10.

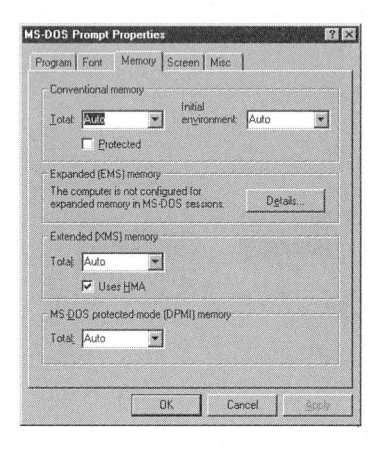

Fig. 40.10 The MS-DOS Prompt Properties sheet, with the Memory tab selected, enables you to configure the memory settings for the DOS session.

Even though Windows 95 does the vast majority of its work in protected mode, treating memory as a large contiguous block, older DOS programs have been written to a different standard. These programs may need special amounts of conventional, expanded, and extended memory. The settings in the Memory tab enable you to modify the memory portion of the DOS environment to suit the special needs of your programs.

> **Caution:** In most instances you should never need to change the memory settings in this dialog box. Do not make changes without being sure that you need the changes for a specific program. In other words, do not make the changes unless you are sure that your program will not work with the default Windows settings.

1044 Chapter 40: Operating in Windows 95 DOS

To make the settings in this dialog box properly, you should refer to your advanced documentation for your DOS program. In addition, you may want to read Chapter 9, "Exploiting Memory, Space, and Resources," for more information about memory settings.

The Screen Tab

With the Screen tab of the MS-DOS Prompt Properties sheet selected, you are ready to modify aspects of the DOS window's appearance. With the tab selected, the dialog box should appear as shown in figure 40.11.

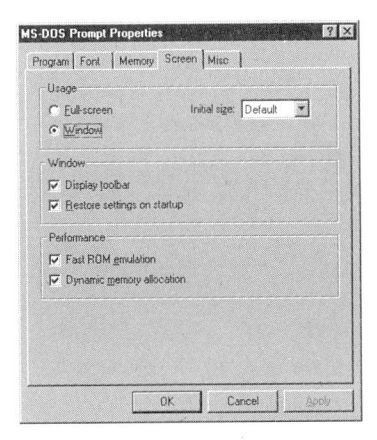

Fig. 40.11 The MS-DOS Prompt Properties sheet, with the Screen tab selected, is used to set aspects of the window appearance.

There are three sections to this tab. At the top of the dialog box you can indicate how you want the DOS window to appear when it is first opened. The Initial Size setting is the most important item here; it is used to indicate how many lines of text you want to appear in the DOS window. If you set it to Default, then the program running in the window controls the screen size. There are three possible settings in this pull-down list (besides Default): 25 lines, 40 lines, and 50 lines. The selection you make here affects the size of the DOS window, and if you make a change you will probably want to change the font selection as well.

DOS Window Properties   **1045**

At the left side of the Usage area is a place where you can select whether the DOS window should be functioning as a desktop Window or as a Full-screen application. Do not confuse this with the window size setting in the Program tab (discussed earlier); that setting refers to the initial condition of the DOS window, whereas this setting refers to the current condition.

In the middle of the dialog box you can specify the attributes of the DOS window. If Display Toolbar is selected, then the toolbar is shown at the top of the DOS window. If the Restore settings on startup check box is selected, then Windows 95 does not remember the DOS window appearance settings from one session to the next. For instance, the location of the DOS window will always revert to a standard position when this check box is selected. Clear the check box if you want Windows 95 to remember the settings.

Finally, at the bottom of the dialog box are two check boxes that control the performance of the DOS program when it is running within a window (less than full screen). The first setting, Fast ROM Emulation, causes Windows 95 to move the ROM instructions into faster RAM memory. This causes text and some graphics to be displayed faster. The other setting, Dynamic Memory Allocation, controls how Windows allocates screen display memory. If the check box is selected, then Windows is free to use the screen memory area as necessary (and as appropriate). If the check box is cleared, then the maximum amount of memory necessary for the screen display is always reserved for the program, and is therefore not available to other programs. Clearing this check box may speed up the DOS program running in the window, but it may also slow down any other programs you have running in Windows 95.

The Misc Tab

When you select the Misc tab, the MS-DOS Prompt Properties sheet appears, as shown in figure 40.12.

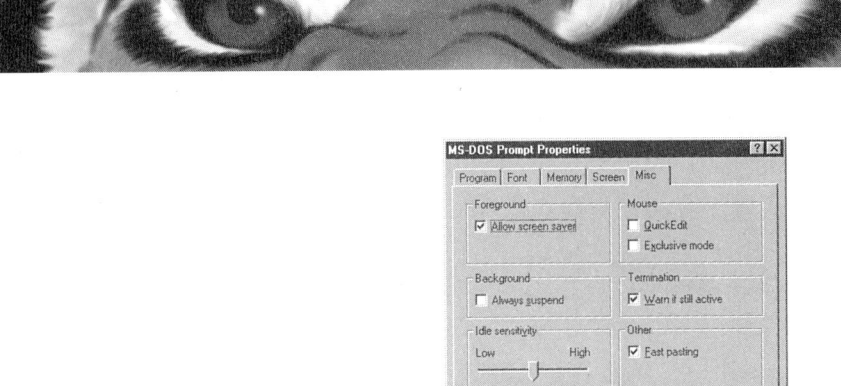

Fig. 40.12 The MS-DOS Prompt Properties sheet, with the Misc tab selected, is used to set various DOS window properties.

The Misc tab contains quite a few settings, evidently placed here because they are not readily categorized with the subjects of the other tabs. Each area is explained in the following sections.

Foreground. The Foreground area of the Misc tab contains only one setting, which controls how the Windows screen saver functions. If you clear this check box, then the Windows screen saver cannot start up when the DOS window is visible. Normally, you would only want to clear this if you are operating the window in full-screen mode.

If you select the check box, then the screen saver can work as required. You should note that this setting does not control whether the screen saver is enabled; that is controlled in the Display area of the Control Panel. You can find more information on the screen saver in Chapter 14, "Tailoring Windows 95 and the Registry."

Mouse. There are two check boxes in this area of the Misc tab. The first check box controls whether the mouse can be used for the QuickEdit feature. This feature is applicable only in DOS windows; it refers to the ability to use the mouse to mark text for subsequent editing. Without the check box selected, you must use the Mark tool on the toolbar in order to mark text.

DOS Window Properties **1047**

E_xclusive mode has to do with how the mouse behaves in relation to the DOS program. If selected, then the mouse will only work in this DOS window; it will not work in any other program under Windows 95. (Because Windows 95 is so difficult to use without the mouse, I can't think of a really good reason to enable this option.)

Background. Windows 95 usually shares system resources among all active programs as necessary. Each program, even though it is not currently active, continues to run in the background to complete whatever tasks are necessary. If you select the Always S_uspend check box, then when the DOS window is in the background, the program within it will not run. You should select this option only if you want the program to run while you watch it.

Termination. When you try to close a DOS window with an active program still running, Windows warns you that you are ending the program abnormally. The check box in this area controls this warning feature. If the W_arn If Still Active check box is cleared, then no warning is given and the program in the DOS window is terminated. You should only clear this check box if you are certain that the program running in the window will not be adversely affected by closing abnormally. For instance, some programs write configuration information to disk when you exit the program. It would not be a good idea for this type of program to be abnormally terminated.

Idle Sensitivity. This slider controls how much attention the DOS window receives from Windows 95. There is an inverse relationship between the amount of attention received and the slider setting. Thus, if the slider is moved toward the Low setting, then the program in the window receives more resources for a longer period of time. Conversely, if the slider is moved toward the High setting, then system resources are freed up more quickly and allocated to other programs.

You should only adjust this setting if you feel the program in the DOS window is not executing fast enough. When you do move the slider toward the Low setting, your other Windows programs may run more slowly than otherwise.

Other. The Fast Pasting check box controls how Windows pastes information into the DOS window. Most programs can accept information at the rate achieved with Fast Pasting enabled, but some programs cannot. You should clear this check box if you try pasting something into your DOS program and it does not paste properly.

Windows Shortcut Keys. Windows 95 uses a standard group of shortcut keys for system operations. The seven shortcut keys listed in this portion of the dialog box are those standard keys. If the check box beside the shortcut key is enabled, then the shortcut key will work as it should in Windows 95. You should only clear the check box associated with a shortcut key if that key combination is used by the DOS program for a different purpose. In that case, clearing the check box will disable the Windows use of the keys and allow the DOS program to use them.

> **Caution:** If you disable the Alt+Tab, Alt+Esc, and Alt+Enter shortcuts, and then switch the DOS window to full screen, there is no way to switch between the screen and the Windows programs running in the background. The only way around this problem is to exit the DOS program and thereby close the DOS window.

Monitoring Your Windows 95 Vital Files

by Ewan Grantham

When you're trying to determine what files to back up and maintain in your system, you want to start with files that affect the configuration and operation of your computer because, without them, your system will not run. These files are what constitute your system's vital files. For Windows 95, vital files include a group of files that control how the system is booted and operates. The files can be from previous versions of DOS and Windows that may still be important and INI files that affect your applications' configuration.

Knowing about these files can also help in determining what went wrong when a new application is installed and your system starts "acting funny." Being aware of these files and their role in your system's overall operation can also help you avoid doing anything to them yourself (such as deleting them) that will affect your computer's performance. In this chapter, you see what these files are and learn some ways to back up and maintain them.

In this chapter, you learn about the following:

- Important boot files
- Registry files
- DOS and Windows 3.x files still vital to Windows 95

Windows 95 Vital Files

Files that are vital to the configuration and performance of Windows 95 can be divided into two general categories:

- Files that affect how your system boots up after being turned on or rebooted. These files are referred to as *Boot files*.
- Files that affect how the system runs after Windows 95 has been started. These files are associated with the Registry.

In the following sections, you learn about both types of files and how to work with them.

Boot Files

With Windows 3.x, your computer relied upon five DOS files to manage booting after the computer was turned on or rebooted. Two of these files, IO.SYS and MSDOS.SYS, are hidden system files that told your system BIOS how to boot the operating system (OS) and work with the boot disk (either floppy disk or hard drive). Another file, COMMAND.COM, was used to support basic OS commands. The last two files, AUTOEXEC.BAT and CONFIG.SYS, loaded any special device drivers, configured the OS environment with commands such as FILES and COMSPEC, and specified any other programs or information the system needed to boot.

So, for example, your CONFIG.SYS might include lines such as:

```
device=c:\dos\ansi.sys
```

to make sure your screen display was compatible with programs that used ANSI escape sequences, while your AUTOEXEC.BAT almost certainly had the line:

```
PATH=c:\dos;c:\windows
```

to set the path that programs would use when searching for files.

In Windows 95, your computer needs only two files to boot, though you may need to add a version of your old AUTOEXEC.BAT and your CONFIG.SYS to get full functionality. The first file, IO.SYS, replaces the functionality of the old IO.SYS, most of the old MSDOS.SYS, and the old COMMAND.COM, but it is still a hidden system file. The second file, MSDOS.SYS, now contains information about where things are on your computer and some information about various boot options (see figure 41.1). This file is located in your root folder—C:\ (in most cases). In this way, the MSDOS.SYS file takes some of the functionality of the old CONFIG.SYS and AUTOEXEC.BAT files.

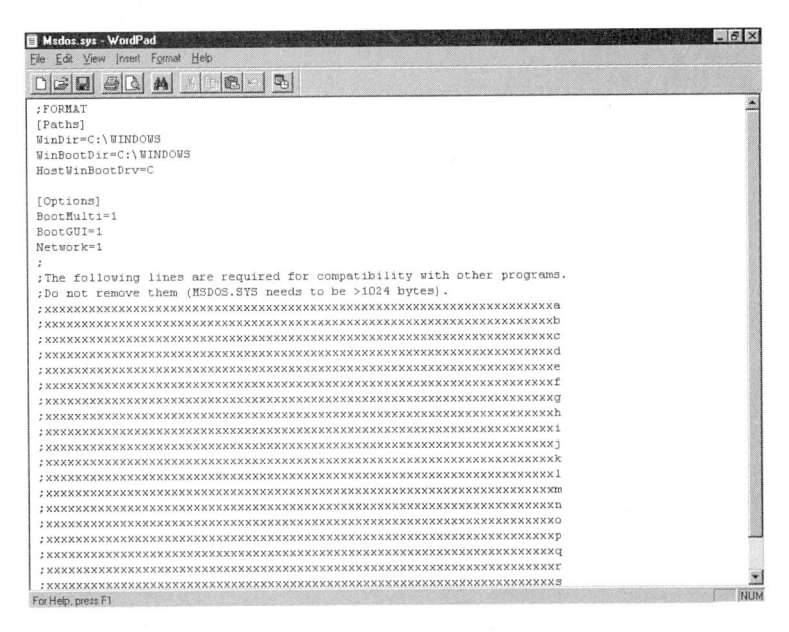

Fig. 41.1 What the MSDOS.SYS file contains.

Boot Files **1053**

Common MSDOS.SYS Elements

Although your MSDOS.SYS file may look different from the one shown in figure 41.1, this file usually contains several common entries on any system running Windows 95. The following is a list of these entries and what they do:

- **WinDir** This entry specifies the folder or subdirectory where Windows is located on the system.

- **WinBootDir** This entry controls where files that are needed for specifying how to bring up Windows 95 are located (almost always the same as WinDir).

- **HostWinBootDrv** This tells Windows which drive contains the essential boot files.

- **BootGUI** This is used to specify whether to boot into the Windows 95 interface (by using a 1 here), or into the command prompt interface (by using a 0).

- **Network** This entry is used to specify whether or not the computer is attached to a network. Even if all you use is Dial-Up Networking, your computer is considered part of a network. If you aren't part of ANY network, then this value should be a 0.

- **BootMulti** Used to specify whether or not to support booting into multiple operating systems (including old versions of Windows). Generally this won't be in the file unless you've specified to keep the old version of DOS/Windows when you installed Windows 95.

- **BootMenu** Specifies that a menu should be presented to users to allow them to select which OS they want to boot into, or which option for booting Windows 95 they want (similar to BootGUI). If this is a 1 they get a menu, if it's a 0 then they don't.

- **BootMenuDefault**   Says which menu option is the default selection. Use 7 for your old version of DOS, and 1 for Windows 95.

- **BootMenuDelay**   This specifies how many seconds the menu should be shown before the default value in BootMenuDefault is automatically selected.

Finally, it's important that when you modify the MSDOS.SYS file that you DON'T remove any of the x's from the lines in the bottom of the file. These HAVE to be there to ensure that MSDOS.SYS is at least 1,024 bytes long to remain compatible with previous versions of DOS.

Needing Your CONFIG.SYS and AUTOEXEC.BAT Files

Certain things may still require you to have a CONFIG.SYS and an AUTOEXEC.BAT file. The most common reason you still need CONFIG.SYS is to load a device driver for a piece of hardware that doesn't provide a version of its driver for Windows 95. You may still want an AUTOEXEC.BAT to set the PATH or have functions such as DOSKEY loaded and ready for your virtual DOS sessions.

Although you can back up these files, you usually need to have them available to help reload your system to start your backup program. In other words, having a backup made with either the backup applet or a third-party program will be no help for these files because you can't boot Windows 95 without them being present. The first two files (IO.SYS and MSDOS.SYS) are saved to the Emergency floppy created when you installed Windows 95. However, if you've made manual changes to your MSDOS.SYS since then, you lose those changes.

For this reason, it's often a good idea to go to a DOS session (either by booting to the command line, or by opening a DOS command line in Windows 95), and copy the MSDOS.SYS, CONFIG.SYS, and

AUTOEXEC.BAT files to a floppy disk. When you format the floppy it probably is a good idea to make it bootable by using the /s switch. So if your disk is in the A drive, you enter

```
FORMAT A: /S
```

It's also a good idea to copy other files to this floppy that you might need in an emergency, such as EDIT, FDISK, and XCOPY. Having all this on a floppy gives you added flexibility in case your hard drive breaks down or a virus infects your computer. A good way of doing this is to take the emergency disk that Windows 95 Setup creates for you, add your AUTOEXEC.BAT and CONFIG.SYS files to it with different extensions so that they aren't automatically loaded, and make sure that FDISK and XCOPY are on it. With this group of files, you can work around almost any software problem.

Setup Information in INF Files

In addition to these specific files, the group of files located in the C:\WINDOWS\INF folder contains setup information on any cards you may have. When doing a backup, you want to make sure you get the information that is in here as well.

While you will find INF files scattered throughout your system (they are information files created in a specific format for use by Windows 95 in setting up programs and peripherals), only the ones in the \WINDOWS\INF file are "vital." Losing the rest would be a nuisance, but not a major one.

The Registry Files

With your boot files safely stored, it's time to take a look at the files that make up the Registry. Most of the information is stored in two files: SYSTEM.DAT and USER.DAT. In addition, every time these files are updated, the old versions are saved as SYSTEM.DA0 and USER.DA0.

All four of these files are located in your main Windows directory. These files are hidden and read-only, so they won't normally show up under the Explorer. To make them show up, go into Explorer, select the View menu, then the Options choice. Next, select the View tab, and click on "Show all files."

You can use the Backup applet in Windows 95 to back up these files, but if they are damaged or corrupted, you may be unable to run Backup to restore them. The backup applet is located off the Start menu at Start>>Programs>>Accessories>>System Tools>>Backup. Because you may not be able to run a restore, there are a number of techniques you should be aware of for saving and restoring this vital information.

Using REGEDIT to Copy the Registry to a Text File

An option that can help you to better understand your system, as well as protect it, is to export the Registry to a text file. This gives you the opportunity to have a hard copy of the information by printing out the text file. You can also copy the text file to a floppy and then import it back into your system if it's needed.

To do this, you first need to start a program called REGEDIT located in your C:\WINDOWS folder (or wherever you have installed your Windows 95 files). REGEDIT (also known as the Registry Editor) is a program designed to make viewing and working with your Registry files easier—and safer. Figure 41.2 shows you what REGEDIT looks like when it has been started.

From here, you can export the Registry to a text file by following these steps:

1. From the REGEDIT menu bar, choose Registry, Export Registry File.

2. The Export Registry File dialog box appears (see figure 41.3).

The Registry Files **1057**

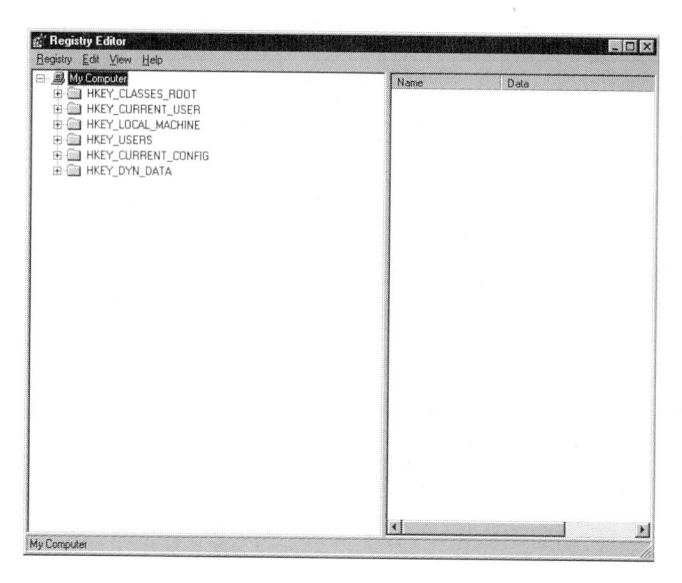

Fig. 41.2 The REGEDIT opening screen.

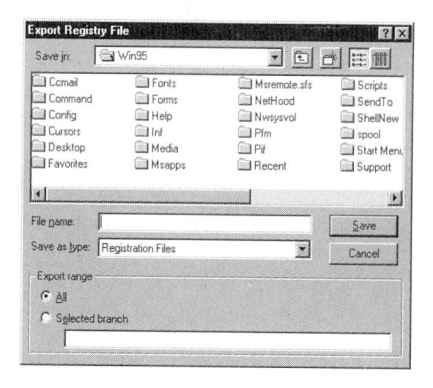

Fig. 41.3 The Export Registry File dialog box.

3. In the Export Range section choose All to back up the entire Registry or choose Selected Branch to back up only a particular branch of the Registry tree. If you're going to use Selected Branch, click on the folder at the level of the branch you want to start with.

Looking at figure 41.2 may lead you to think that there isn't much in the Registry. But if you look at figure 41.4 when you begin getting below the surface, you see that a lot of information is stored here. You'll also notice that values are not what come to mind if someone asks you for the settings of your system's audio.

To get to this point in the file, you start by double-clicking on HKEY_CURRENT_USER, then double-clicking on Software, then double-clicking on Microsoft, then double-clicking on Multimedia, and finally double-clicking on Audio. Not necessarily intuitive, but somewhat understandable. If you have a sound card on your system, try this and compare the values.

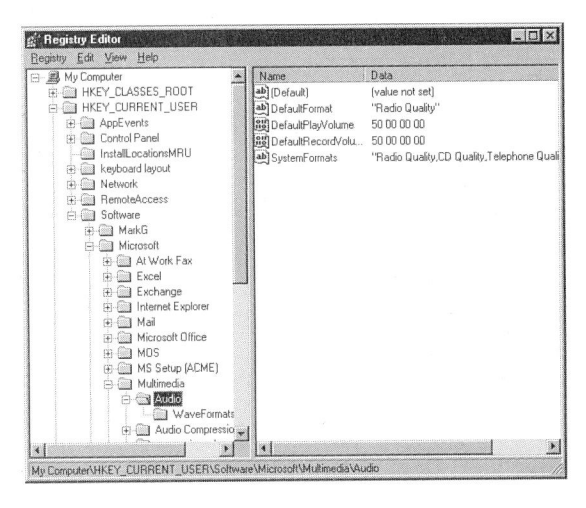

Fig. 41.4 Registry Editor values for Multimedia Audiox

You should note that the REG files created by doing this export can be edited by any text editor. The default place for placing the exported file is in your C:\WINDOWS folder, but you may want to have the file stored directly to a floppy disk instead. If you decide to store it to a floppy disk, make sure there is nothing else on the disk because these files can run as large as a megabyte each.

The Registry Files **1059**

If you want just a printed record of the Registry, you can use the following:

1. If you want to print only part of the Registry, click on the icon for the folder of the area you want to print.

2. Choose Registry, Print. If you want to print the entire Registry, select All here.

You want to be very careful about selecting All here. The standard Registry can take up to 200 pages and something with a lot of customization can go far beyond that.

Restoring the Registry

Somewhere down the line you might want to or have to restore the Registry settings using the information you exported. To do that, choose Registry, Import Registry File. The Import dialog box appears. Choose the file you want to import.

You may make a change in a value some day and then discover that Windows is behaving unusually or that something has stopped working. If you've backed up the Registry files, you have some options for repairing this. But there is also a fallback option. The most recent version before your change was saved with the DAO extension.

To restore the previous version of the Registry, follow these steps:

1. Shut down Windows by choosing the "Restart the computer in MS-DOS mode" option.

2. Once your machine returns with a DOS prompt, change to your C:\WINDOWS folder. For example, if your Windows folder is C:\WINDOWS, you enter

    ```
    CD C:\WINDOWS
    ```

3. Enter each of the following:

`ATTRIB -H -R -S SYSTEM.DAT`	Makes the System.DAT file visible (-H), editable (-R), and no longer having the system file attribute (-S). This is the same for the files below.
`ATTRIB -H -R -S SYSTEM.DA0`	
`COPY SYSTEM.DA0 SYSTEM.DAT`	Copies the old (good) System file over the new (bad) one.
`ATTRIB -H -R -S USER.DAT`	
`ATTRIB -H -R -S USER.DA0`	
`COPY USER.DA0 USER.DAT`	Copies the old (good) User file over the new (bad) one.

4. Reboot your computer.

Still Needed DOS and Windows 3.x Files

Although Windows 95 replaces much of what you used in DOS and Windows 3.x, some of your applications still rely on files that came with these earlier versions of Windows. This is particularly true of applications that don't currently have a Windows 95 version. For this reason, you probably want to use the Backup applet to back up these files or copy them to a floppy disk.

DOS files you want to keep an eye on are as follows:

➤ **Device drivers** The most common cards not supported directly by Windows 95 are scanner interface cards.

➤ **CONFIG.SYS** If this file is present, it's probably because you have a device driver that isn't supported or because a program you installed automatically wrote to this file.

- **AUTOEXEC.BAT**   You may have put this file in yourself to set the PATH environmental variable or to load other DOS utilities (such as DOSKEY) for your DOS sessions.

Windows 3.x files you want to keep an eye on are as follows:

- **WIN.INI**   This file contains setup information for older Windows programs that you may have on your system. Some Windows 3.x programs also store registration information. Generally, if the file exists, something is using it, and it should be backed up.

- **SYSTEM.INI and PROGMAN.INI**   These files are maintained for compatibility with older Windows programs that expect to be able to access them. You can remove them if you use only Windows 95 applications, but it is generally better to keep them for backward compatibility reasons.

It's hard to put any value in these three files that affect the running of Windows 95 directly, although it's always possible to confuse and crash an application.

Application INI File Considerations

Even though Windows 95 applications should be using the Registry to store setup information, old habits die hard, and many applications still create their own INI file that is placed in either the application's folder or the C:\WINDOWS folder. You generally don't have to worry about the contents of these files, unless you move the application. In that case you want to edit the file by using Notepad or WordPad to reflect the new location of files.

You do want to make sure that these files are safeguarded, however, because losing the file can often mean that you have to reinstall the application.

Dealing with Viruses and Security

by Glenn Fincher

The title of this book, *Killer Windows 95* takes on a more sinister meaning in terms of security. That there are "killers" out there waiting to invade your computer and ravage your data is certainly true when it comes to computer viruses. That there are likewise more personal "killers" wishing to gain unauthorized access to your data is also true. Many of the key features of Windows 95 are designed with security in mind even as they actually seem to offer new avenues for this security to be overcome.

The built-in peer-to-peer networking, Internet connectivity, Dial-Up Networking—both outbound and inbound—increases the potential for unauthorized access to your computer data. And though Windows 95 has built-in tools and features to assist you in protecting the integrity of your data, these tools will not help you defend your computer unless you know about them and know how to use these tools or features.

In this chapter, you'll learn about the following:

- Dealing with viruses and security
- Understanding the computer virus and Trojan horse
- Using effective antivirus strategies
- "Designed for Windows 95"—an antivirus example
- Backing up your system
- Using backup Agents

Windows 95 Virus Software

At the time of this writing, many antivirus software developers had announced that Windows 95-specific versions of their products were currently scheduled and would ship coincident with the release date or within 60 days of that date. Windows 95-specific versions of McAfee's ViruScan, Symantec's Norton Anti-Virus, and Datafellows F-Prot Professional will be available shortly after Windows 95 ships or possibly by the time this book is available. One example of what to expect of these "Designed for Windows 95" releases is shown in the following sections as you look at a pre-release version of VirusScan 95 by McAfee Associates.

> **Caution:** Previous versions of MS-DOS shipped with an antivirus utility named Microsoft Anti-Virus or MSAV. Microsoft does not ship a Windows 95 version of this utility. Additionally, the previous versions should not be used with Windows 95 because attempting to remove a virus may result in either Windows 95 disallowing the process, not working, or actually causing damage to the VFAT file system.

Why do you need a Windows 95-specific version? In short, the main reason is that Windows 95 is a 32-bit operating system, and the existing antivirus products are either 16-bit DOS or 16-bit Windows programs.

Written for DOS, these programs expect to have unlimited access directly to the hard drive using INT 13h or INT 21h. These programs depend on the ability to directly access the boot sector of the hard drive to disinfect certain types of viruses. Also, these programs may have a TSR component that expects to have access to all processes so that the processes can be examined for virus activity. Though not as robust as similar protection in Windows NT, Windows 95 virtualizes access to the hard drive, thus disallowing INT 13H and INT 21H, and will not allow programs direct access to processes as required to directly manipulate data on disk as antivirus programs are designed to do.

At best, the program may be able to identify a virus infection but will be incapable of removing the virus. In worse cases, the software may actually lock up your computer or cause file system damage if it tries to deal with the new long file name (LFN) feature of Windows 95. You may think that booting to DOS from a DOS floppy disk will do the trick, but even this may result in damage to a file or folder using an LFN. If you have installed Windows 95 into its own folder rather than in a pre-existing Windows 3.x folder, you will be able to boot to the DOS, and run your older 16-bit application. Be aware though that if the application attempts repairs that result in the file allocation table being changed that you may damage any long file or folder names. The best and really the last time you should use an older DOS or Windows 3.x antivirus program is before you install Window 95 for the first time. This should be one of the preparatory steps taken before installation, but remember that these programs cannot be depended on in Windows 95.

Dealing with Viruses and Security

Like its biological namesake, the computer virus is a plague of the computer age. Every user of a computer in today's environment has to pay at least cursory attention to the possibility of getting a virus infection. Because of the wide proliferation of viruses, it is likely that either you or someone you know will be hit with a virus attack. Though the avenues of attack are well known, it is the very nature of the computing world of the '90s that assist their proliferation. Computer users work in an increasingly network-connected environment. Whether it's the connectivity offered by a LAN, the Internet, online networks, or Bulletin Board Systems (BBS), there are more opportunities for viral infection than in the not so distant past. According to some experts in the field, there are around 5,000 known viruses including the miscellaneous virus strains or families. There are also more viruses being written and subsequently discovered in a seemingly endless cycle. Some have suggested that the virus writer and the antivirus software developer are in sort of a deadly symbiotic relationship with each depending on the other for existence. In this scenario, the user is the one in the middle, the unwilling victim of this quasi-biological menace.

A virus's ability to destroy your data is just one of the security problems you face with a virus infection. Even if the particular virus you encounter is one of the relatively docile ones, an infection will at the very minimum cause your system to slow down or use up an increasing amount of disk space. Though many of the reported 5,000 viruses are relatively docile. They may do no malicious damage like formatting your hard drive or rewriting your boot files, but the time you'll spend with a regular scan of your hard drive is time well spent to eliminate the possibility of an infection.

Understanding the Computer Virus

According to Dr. Fred B. Cohen's book, *A Short Course on Computer Viruses*, a computer virus is "a computer program that can infect other computer programs by modifying them in such a way as to include a (possibly evolved) copy of itself."

By this definition, a program doesn't actually have to do any damage at all to be considered a virus. If a program can replicate itself and infect other programs, you have a virus. And, even if it is a docile virus, if that docile virus interrupts a computer from its normal operation and that computer happens to be in use in a critical role, that docile virus suddenly becomes one of the killers. Any unsolicited invasion of your computer data by such a program is exactly that—an invasion—and it should be treated with no less concern than if it was an intruder in your home. It is the action you need to take to eliminate these killers that you learn about in this chapter.

Computer viruses take several recognizable forms. They may be the type of program commonly called a *worm*—a program with the ability to propagate itself across networks beyond the confines of the computer that it first attacks. The Trojan horse is so named because of its apparently useful facade, hiding the potentially malicious code within. Generally, viruses are categorized by their method of transmission. The most destructive are usually the *boot-sector viruses*, while others are called *file* or *program viruses*. The former attacks the boot sector of a hard or floppy drive, while the latter attacks individual files. There is also a *multipartite virus* that may be both a boot-sector and file virus. For the sake of precision, some may further define these into *parasitic*, *stealth*, or *polymorphic* viruses because of the peculiar propensity of some viruses to either directly attack specific types of files or the ability to mask their true nature to avoid detection.

> **Note:** Having more than one antivirus product in your antivirus suite is generally advised. One product may be particularly good at detecting certain strains of boot-sector viruses but not as good with other types of viruses. Another product may be particularly good at detecting previously unidentified viruses.

As mentioned earlier, the boot-sector virus is probably the most destructive because it replaces the existing Master Boot Record (MBR) or boot-sector of a hard disk or floppy disk with its own code and usually arbitrarily moves the original boot-sector to a fixed location. This relocation sometimes results in destroyed data because the original boot-sector is dropped over the file allocation table (FAT) or another file.

A drive's MBR is actually a special program executed when the computer's BIOS boots the system. This program is responsible for locating an active partition with the operating system (OS) files and

Windows 95 Virus Software **1067**

then passing control to the OS files. A boot-sector virus usually does the following:

- Checks whether it has already infected the disk
- Relocates the original boot sector
- Copies its own boot-sector replacement to the MBR or DOS boot sector
- Installs its memory resident portion
- Loads the original boot sector to continue the normal boot process
- Monitors floppy-disk access to infect the boot sector of additional floppy disks

For a boot-sector virus to infect an uninfected hard disk, an infected floppy disk's boot sector must be accessed. Note, however, that this floppy disk does not have to be a bootable floppy disk. When the BIOS searches for a bootable partition, the act of accessing the boot sector of an otherwise unbootable floppy disk can infect a hard disk with the virus. Thus an easy way to protect yourself from this type of virus is to avoid booting from a floppy disk of unknown origin. Also, many newer system BIOSs have an antivirus boot-sector setting that prohibits any direct writes to the MBR. Since this is a BIOS setting and the BIOS code executes before a disk is accessed, if your computer BIOS has this setting, this can be an added bit of security to prevent a virus infection.

> **Caution:** Be extremely careful when making changes in your computer BIOS. Make only those changes suggested or that you are absolutely sure of the effect. You can inadvertently disable your computer if you change the wrong setting.

The BIOS settings of your computer are commonly referred to as the CMOS, named so after the type of memory device originally used for this storage. Other CMOS or BIOS settings that may assist in preventing an infection are as follows:

- Disabling access to drive A at boot time
- Changing the normal boot sequence to boot from drive C before booting from drive A

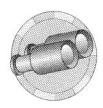

Note: If you enable the antivirus feature that prevents direct writes to the MBR before loading Windows 95, Windows 95's setup fails when attempting to write the Windows 95 boot sector. Setup will complain that your computer is running virus protection software. You must disable this setting for Windows 95 Setup to succeed. Setup will also generate the same error if you're running an older antivirus product when you attempt to install Windows 95. You may need to disable the software by remarking or commenting the lines in either your CONFIG.SYS or AUTOEXEC.BAT files to enable Windows 95 to complete its installation.

Understanding the Windows 95 Boot Sequence

You need to learn about the typical boot sequence of a PC to see exactly how a virus can gain such a vital hold on your computer. The Windows 95 boot sequence proceeds almost exactly as the DOS sequence with the important differences being the Windows 95 boot files, the addition of Plug and Play, and the necessary differences added by multiple hardware profiles, and so on. But the basic boot sequence that a virus exploits is the same. Look at the sequence to see the points that a virus can interject itself to infect your system.

When you first turn on your computer, it goes through a set sequence of steps. The first of these is the *Power On Self Test* (POST). This set of instructions is a step-by-step sequence that briefly checks each hardware subsystem for basic functionality. If you are fortunate enough to have a newer computer with Plug-and-Play BIOS, this sequence is considerably more involved than that found on older computers, but the results regarding the boot sequence are the same. The POST is followed by an initialization sequence, which involves setting up the different subsystems of the computer to default states. This initialization sequence may include setting registers, loading parameters, or establishing a more detailed list of the equipment present. After this BIOS initialization, any remaining BIOS routines, such as found on adapter cards, execute. At the end of the initialization sequence, the BIOS accesses the drives as it attempts to locate a valid bootable partition to continue booting the computer. Depending on the previously mentioned settings regarding the order of disk access, the BIOS attempts to locate a special kind of program called a *boot record*. This program is actually a small bit of executable code that further details the location of a valid operating system's boot files. When located, the initialization sequence passes control to this program and the boot process continues with this program now in control.

The initialization sequence locates and reads the contents of the first 512-byte sector of either a floppy disk or the first hard drive. This 512-byte sector is the MBR and contains program code to continue the remaining boot sequence. On a hard disk, the first 466 bytes of this sector is actually the program code, while the remaining bytes contain a two-byte header and four 16-byte entries defining up to four partitions. By definition, these partitions can be either four primary partitions or three primary partitions and one extended partition with logical drives. This *partition table* is used to locate an active partition to continue loading the OS. The first 512 bytes of the first primary partition that is marked "active" in the MBR is then loaded, and like the MBR itself, the executable code contained in these 512 bytes runs to complete loading the OS. This 512-byte sector is called the DOS boot record or simply the boot sector since you are no longer dealing with a necessarily MS-DOS structure. It is this boot sector that actually loads the OS boot files; thus until this step, a virus can interject itself and control what follows.

You can see why a virus attacking either of these boot sectors is potentially disastrous. This is why many of the most destructive viruses infect the MBR. The virus is loaded in memory before the OS loads, giving the virus an upper hand in either continuing to infect other programs or floppy disks when they are accessed and even resisting attempts to check for the presence of the virus in memory by redirecting such attempts. These programs can be killers indeed.

Boot-Sector Viruses

There are several viruses that have become well known because of their destructive potential. Probably the most well known of these is the virus that has been named Michelangelo. It is so named because the virus basically sits dormant until March 6, Michelangelo's birthday, and then activates and overwrites part of the hard disk with random information from memory, thus destroying any data that it overwrites. While it is dormant, it silently replicates itself to every floppy disk that is accessed, potentially spreading to other infected machines as these floppies are passed from one user to another. The Michelangelo virus remains a frequently reported virus, probably because it does no apparent damage unless you happen to boot up on March 6.

> **Tip:** One of the best defenses you have against a virus infection is frequent scanning of your hard drive. If you haven't already done so, create a Windows 95 boot disk by choosing the Add/Remove Programs applet in the Control Panel. Choose the Startup Disk tab. Copy your virus scanning software to the disk and then enable the write-protect tab on this diskette to protect it from infection. Clearly label this disk as an antivirus boot disk and keep it handy for a reassuring once a week scan.

Many of the boot sector viruses can be easily removed from your hard disk without using an antivirus product at all. Since MS-DOS 5.0, the FDISK program has had a command-line switch to rewrite the MBR. This feature of FDISK can be used to remove Michelangelo from your hard disk, as well as the 20 or so strains or *variants* of the Stoned virus. You cannot use this method to remove the virus from floppy disks because FDISK is only for fixed nonremovable media. To use this /mbr switch, follow these steps:

1. Use Start/Shut Down to shut down your computer before powering off. This step is required to ensure that the virus is not resident in memory.

2. Boot the computer from a write-protected floppy disk. The Windows 95 Startup boot disk you created when you installed Windows 95 has FDISK.EXE on the disk.

3. At the command prompt enter **FDISK /MBR**. This step will rewrite the Master Boot Record.

4. Turn off your computer and remove the floppy disk.

5. When you turn the computer back on, the virus should have been removed.

6. Use your antivirus software to scan and clean any suspect floppy disks that may have been used while the computer was infected.

> **Caution:** The primary use of FDISK is to initially prepare a hard disk by creating partition(s) prior to a "high-level" format. If used without the above /MBR switch, FDISK will present a menu that allows you to perform these functions. There should be no need to change the partition information on your hard drive unless you are initially preparing your drive. *Any changes made when running FDISK in it's interactive mode may render your hard drive unaccessible and unreadable.*
>
> Once your computer is infected with the Monkey virus, direct detection is almost impossible. It is called a stealth virus because it hides itself from detection by redirecting INT 12, which is used to determine the amount of free contigous memory, so that attempts to detect the virus in memory are turned away. It will also redirect attempts to read the MBR directly by presenting the "real" MBR to programs attempting to detect the virus. The MBR is encrypted so that unless the Monkey virus is resident in

memory, the data is unreadable. There are a couple of clues that you may have a Monkey virus infection though. Either of the following may indicate a Monkey virus infection:

➤ If after you boot from a floppy disk, attempts to change to the hard drive give you the error, Invalid drive specification, this may indicate a Monkey infection.

➤ When the Monkey virus is resident in memory, the MEM or CHKDSK command shows a decrease of 1,024 bytes in total available system memory.

Understanding Trojan Horses

The Trojan horse is another destructive virus that takes the particularly nasty form of a popular utility that may actually do something useful while it wreaks its hidden havoc. One of the common targets of Trojan horse writers is popular antivirus programs themselves. If the creator of a Trojan horse can successfully hide a destructive virus as a well-known antivirus program and advertise it as an important upgrade or patch release, many unsuspecting users can be tricked into attempting to use the program. Many writers of antivirus software refuse to classify Trojan horses as viruses. The argument is that since a virus is by definition a program that modifies another program and replicates itself; the typical Trojan horse does not fit this definition. Hence, some discussions of viruses do not mention Trojan horses at all. But since Trojan horses can actually be written to fit the strict definition of a virus, I mention them here.

A Trojan horse can be as simple as a program that is advertised for one purpose—say a calculator. But when the program is run, it may display offensive language or pictures on your screen. This type of program is not considered by most to be a virus. If this same program not only displays the offensive language but also seeks out other EXE or COM programs and infects these with the same code that caused the offensive display, this program is rightly called a virus. Recently an example of a Trojan horse was mentioned in the computer press and online forums. This Trojan horse, a bogus version of PKWARE's PKZIP product parading as version 3.00, was actually uploaded to PKWARE's own BBS as a file named PKZ300B.EXE or PKZ300B.ZIP. If either the PKZ300B.EXE file or the EXE contained inside the ZIP file is run, this Trojan horse formats your hard drive. Encountering this particular virus will be deadly. Preventing an attack by a virus or Trojan horse becomes a matter of following a few simple rules. Later on you'll look at effective antivirus strategies, but first look at a few examples of "File" viruses.

Understanding File Viruses

The type of virus that primarily infects other files is as equally dangerous as the ones already discussed. These viruses are the real parasites of the software world. They maliciously attach themselves to other program executables and wait for an opportunity to infect another program. A file virus may be as simple as the famous Lehigh virus that only infected COMMAND.COM but had the side effect of trashing the FAT after only four replications. Or a file virus may be one like the multipartite Natas virus that not only attacks files but also infects disk boot sectors.

You may first encounter a virus like Natas in an infected file, but once your computer is infected, your hard disk and any floppy disk accessed from the computer is also be infected. Natas also seeks out and infects all EXE and COM files by attaching itself to the file. Unfortunately, Natas also hides the subsequent size change in the folder. Thus when it's in memory, a folder listing shows no change in file sizes. While Natas is resident in memory, it decreases total system memory by 6K. A MEM check reveals 634K total memory. Natas contains a destructive routine that, when semirandomly activated, overwrites most of the first hard disk that it locates. If Natas is found on your system, you must make a thorough check of any floppy disks that you have used, as well as any files that you have shared with others by network.

Using Effective Antivirus Strategies

What kind of things do you need to do to ensure that your computer will not be the next victim of a virus? How can you protect your data from infection? The following simple guidelines are a start:

- Frequently scan your computer using a combination of at least two antivirus products preferably employing both scanners and an inoculator or integrity checker.
- Scan any floppy disk before installing any floppy-based software.
- Use BIOS settings to disable boot-sector writes.
- Use BIOS to disable booting from a floppy disk.
- Scan any downloaded software before use.
- Maintain a good backup strategy.

The preceding steps may cause you to ask a few additional questions. What do I mean by a *scanner* or *inoculator*? Do you have to scan each file separately; isn't there something to automate the process?

Current Virus Technology

The current level of virus activity worldwide is growing. By most people's estimation, the overall level of sophistication of virus developers is increasing. Because of the proliferation of tools like the "virus toolkit," virtually anyone with access to the Internet or a modem can actually download all the necessary tools to create a virus with only a nominal knowledge of the programming. The virus toolkit was created by the writer who calls himself the Dark Avenger, the notorious creator of one of the first *polymorphic viruses*. His creation has the ability to change its appearance with each subsequent infection, thus making it harder for antivirus software to detect the virus. His toolkit assists in the creation of whole new strains of virus all with polymorphic characteristics.

The stealth virus was mentioned earlier in this chapter. This type of virus technology has the capability of hiding from detection. A stealth virus may redirect DOS interrupts to avoid detection or a combination of both stealth and polymorphic technology to hide from antivirus software. Another common technique of a stealth virus is to alter folder listings to mask its change of an infected file.

Encryption is another technique commonly used by a virus developer. An encrypted virus encrypts its code while dormant. But to execute, it must decrypt itself; thus, these viruses are vulnerable to detection. The encrypted virus is particularly hard to detect while in memory or when it has infected a file or other portion of the data on a disk. Only when the virus activates can it usually be seen. Unfortunately, this may be too late.

Viruses may use events to trigger their activity—for example, the Michelangelo virus waiting for March 6. They may also wait for a number of keystrokes or invocations of a certain program before waging their havoc or wait for a combination of events to trigger, all the while silently infecting files or floppy disks as they are accessed. Because of all these different virus techniques, antivirus software must be increasingly updated to stay ahead of the virus. And antivirus software must use several techniques to defeat the different types of virus.

Current Antivirus Technology

To detect the many types of viruses, antivirus software typically uses a combination of methods. The methods used can help in categorizing the software, and most antivirus software packages employ several methods rather than depending on any one technique. The methods most commonly employed are as follows:

- Scanning and disinfecting
- Generic monitoring
- Inoculation
- Heuristics

Antivirus Scanning

Perhaps the most common method of the antivirus tool is the scanner. This tool is the one you use to check for the existence of a virus and may also be used to disinfect or remove a found virus. This tool is represented by VirusScan by the McAfee Corporation or F-Prot by Data Fellows, Incorporated. Typically you boot and run the software from a floppy disk and search for existing virus infections. If an infection is found, the scanner usually has a companion tool to remove the infection. It is this tool that requires frequent updates from the manufacturer. Most scanners work by containing data with actual binary strings of data identifying known viruses. These strings or *signatures* are used to identify suspected virus infections and thus require that whenever a new virus is discovered "in the wild," a new version of the scanning software must be released. Most commercial scanning software companies offer a subscription service for these updates or make updates available on a BBS or other online locations.

Monitoring Antivirus

Generic monitoring may be used in addition to a scanner or used as stand-alone program. Generic monitoring represents a logical addition to your antivirus arsenal. Most antivirus software developers have recognized the importance of this tool and include monitoring software as part of a total antivirus solution. Monitoring is usually accomplished by the use of a device driver in your CONFIG.SYS or AUTOEXEC.BAT file that loads every time you boot your computer. This software remains resident in memory and monitors every program loaded using scanning technology; the memory resident program also monitors potential "viral" activity; i.e., attempts to directly write to areas of the hard drive's boot sector or FAT or to write to other executable files. A monitor program may also look at every program's attempt to go resident in memory, giving you a chance to catch a program that is doing something that you do not expect. Most scanning software also has to include some mechanism for you to identify programs that routinely use any of these functions in their normal operation so that you don't have to always approve their use. One weakness of the monitoring program is that because it loads in one of your startup files, it cannot protect against a boot-sector virus that loads before these files are accessed. Another is that because a mechanism exists to bypass its checking function, many users may become lax and simply approve most or all of the program's prompts.

Inoculation or Integrity Method

Inoculation or integrity checking may be employed by a scanning program, used by monitoring programs, or simply used by itself. This technique is typically used in combination with other methods to improve the ability of detecting file infections. This usually is implemented as some type of CRC or CHECKSUM that is either kept in a database, separate files on the hard drive, or even attached to the file that is being inoculated. Once this CHECKSUM is computed, anytime the inoculated file is scanned or otherwise checked, any changes in the file are easily detected. Some of the more sophisticated inoculators actually store enough information about the file that a complete recovery of the file may be possible if the file is infected. One problem with an integrity checker is that some files are self-modifying, thus making them subject to change naturally. Like the monitor programs, inoculators usually have some facility to identify such programs so that false alarms won't be generated every time you run the program.

Rule-Based Antivirus Checking

Finally, a relatively modern advance in antivirus technology is the use of heuristics or rule-based detection of a virus. Heuristic technology relies on the fact that viruses of a specific type act the same or contain code that perform the same type of functions. Thus, heuristic searches can assist in determining whether a suspect program may be a virus. Heuristics may actually generate more false positives but are still quite useful in your antivirus arsenal.

The best defensive tool might employ several or even all of the above methods. It's not uncommon for a suite of tools to include a scanner, inoculator, and monitor utility and use heuristics in at least one of these tools. Your best bet to defeat a virus is to use a combination of these tools. When you do encounter an infection, it's usually wise to use a second product, possibly from another vendor, to verify and even increase the odds of locating a virus the first package may have missed. Even antivirus software can have blind spots that may miss an infection.

Controlling the Portals of Entry to Your Computer

One sure way to avoid a virus infection altogether is to control the ways a virus may enter your computer. The methods of entry are actually few: by floppy disk or network, whether the network is a BBS, a LAN, or other online resource. Another method of receipt may be an unsolicited attachment in a mail message. Like any other files or programs you receive, it is up to you to be sure that the software you are going to load to your computer does not contain a virus. Only you can guarantee that.

Watching Out for Dangerous Floppy Disks

Probably the single most common method of virus infection is by an infected floppy disk. It's not usually a malicious attack but rather an unsuspecting associate whose computer has already been infected who passes a virus along with the data that you are really expecting. This may even be a floppy disk that was formatted long before the actual infection was even suspected. It has also been a too frequent occurrence that commercial software has been inadvertently infected at some point in the manufacturing process, thus unknowingly infecting all the recipients of the software. Pirated software can be a source of a floppy infection as well. If a co-worker offers a copy of a program that you know to be a pirated version of software, "Just say No!" A pirate may not be anymore reticent to pass on a virus as to pass on a pirated piece of software.

Protecting Your Network from Viruses

In today's heterogeneous network environment, it may be harder to protect your computer network from a virus infection. Many antivirus companies have special network versions of their software to enable LAN-wide or even WAN-wide protection. This software may also employ one or more of the above techniques to offer real-time protection of individual computers or check each file that is written to a network drive for virus infections. In general, though, by using the same type of protection on a network that is used on the local computer, you'll not be likely to pick up an infection.

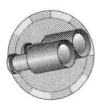

> **Note:** This section frequently mentions the Dial-Up Server, which is the Remote Network Access Server component delivered with Microsoft Plus! It is not delivered with the base Windows 95 product. Its inclusion here is to present the access control features of Windows 95 regarding dial-in access to your computer.

Another area of potential concern is when you have enabled either Windows NT Remote Access Services' (RAS) or Windows 95's own Dial-Up Server to allow remote computers access to your network. If you intend to allow remote access, be careful that you only allow specific users access to the network. Though the likelihood of someone accidentally gaining access from a remote node is limited, use the built-in security of the Dial-Up Server or RAS to define user access.

With Windows 95, the type of access restrictions you can set for the Dial-Up Server is the same access that you have set for the overall computer. Windows 95 allows you to use share-level or user-level access. Share-level access allows a per-share password, while user-level requires the pass-through validation of users from an NT Domain or NetWare Server. To check or configure your access control, open the Control Panel's Network applet. In the Network dialog box, choose the Access Control tab (see figure 42.1).

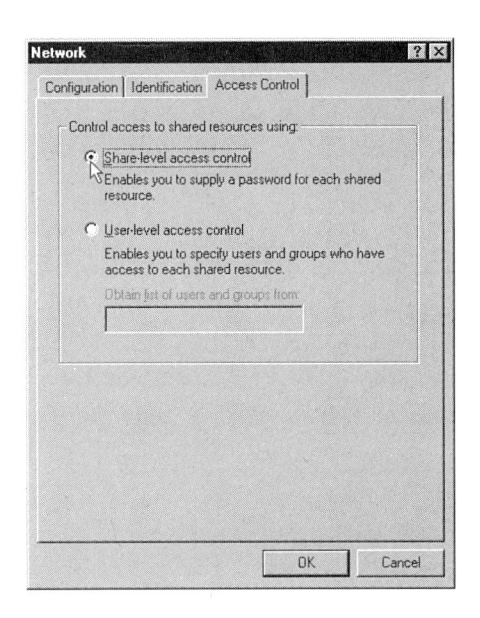

Fig. 42.1 The Access Control tab showing the selection of Share-level access control.

If you selected Share-level access control, when you configured the Dial-Up Server, you were allowed to set only a single password (see figure 42.2).

Fig. 42.2 This is how the Dial-Up Server dialog box appears when networking is configured for share-level access.

Controlling the Portals of Entry to Your Computer   **1081**

Note that this dialog box allows you to set a password for access and that this access is for anyone dialing in to the server. When you select the Change Pass<u>w</u>ord button, the Dial-Up Networking Password dialog box allows you to set the access password (see figure 42.3).

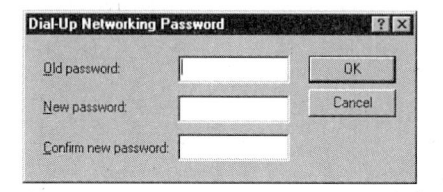

Fig. 42.3 The Dial-Up Server Networking Password dialog box allows setting or changing the server access password.

User-level access provides more security than share-level access because this method uses the advanced security of Windows NT or NetWare user account data. User-level access is only available when connected to a Windows NT or NetWare server. The Dial-Up Server approves or denies the request for access based on the "pass-through" account validation from the Windows NT or NetWare server. As previously mentioned, you configure the default access control using the Network applet in Control Panel. Figure 42.4 shows the <u>U</u>ser-level access control selected.

> **Note:** User-level access control requires a Windows NT or Novell NetWare Server for user authentication and that you define a valid domain controller or server in the Access Control dialog.

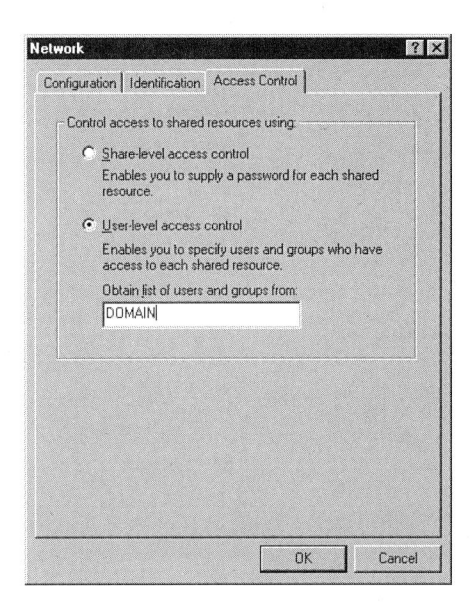

Fig. 42.4 The Access Control tab showing the selection of User-level access control.

Once you have set up user-level access control, you can configure the Dial-Up Server by selecting the Dial-Up Server from the Dial-Up Networking window (see figure 42.5).

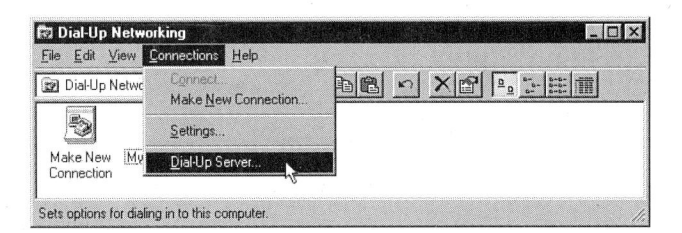

Fig. 42.5 Selection and configuration of the Dial-Up Server is done by using the Connections, Dial-Up Server selection in the Dial-Up Networking dialog box.

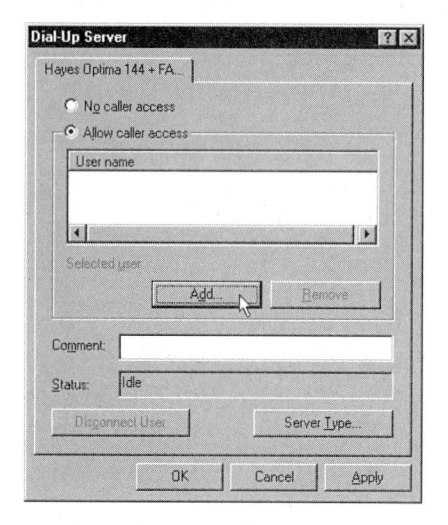

Fig. 42.6 The Dial-Up Server dialog box as it appears when configured for user-level access.

Now you can set up access using the advanced authentication of user-level access. Note that in figure 42.6, the Dial-Up Server dialog box looks different because it is user-based; when you click the Add button, you are allowed to choose users from the domain or server you selected in the Network dialog box (see figure 42.7).

With this type of access you have the added security of knowing exactly who is given access because the odds of someone gaining access to a specific user's name and password is less likely. With this method, you don't have to give access to everyone, but you do have the ability to assign access individually. With share-level access, anyone with the single password can gain access to your network.

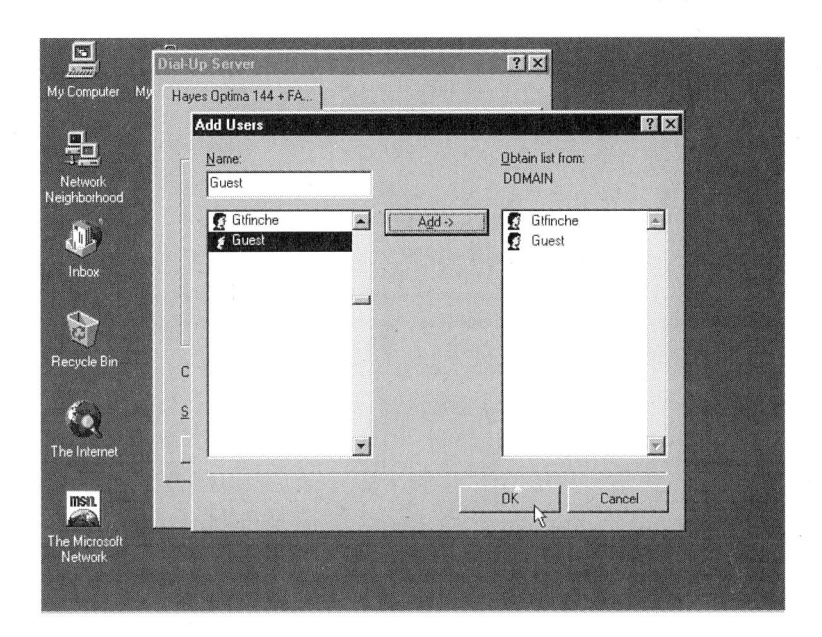

Fig. 42.7 The Dial-Up Server dialog box showing the Add Users access dialog box.

An additional item to consider is that Windows 95 will offer to save any password required in a dialog box which uses a password. These passwords are encrypted and saved in a PWL (password list) file named for the currently logged in user. If you elect to save these passwords and someone else uses your computer, that person can log on to your remote connections without having to enter a password (see figure 42.8). Unless you are very sure of the security of your computer, it is wise not to save these passwords.

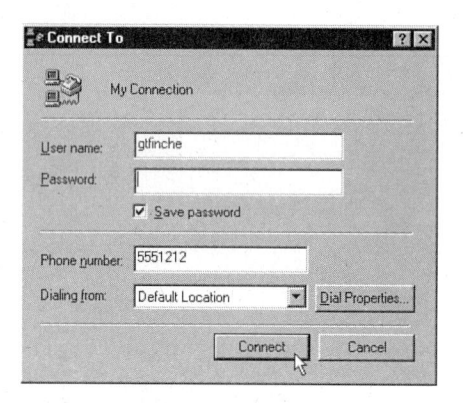

Fig. 42.8 This Dial-up Networking Connect To dialog box showing the Save Password selection enabled.

Knowing the Risks of Downloaded Software

There are risks involved in using downloaded software from any online source. It has been fashionable to routinely blame the BBS as the largest potential risk, but this simply is not the case. The majority of the operators of BBSs use a variety of techniques to assure their users that they are not going to download a virus. Most use a protected upload area where recent uploaded programs are "quarantined" until they have been verified. Also, popular shareware authors usually use one or more methods to ensure the validity of the archives that are commonly used for online distribution. Many shareware or commercial developers maintain dedicated BBS, FTP, or WWW locations for legitimate versions of their products. If you're downloading software, use either the author's own online point of distribution or another equally legitimate source like some of the larger BBSs or online collections available on the Internet. And always scan any downloads before using. It's your data you're protecting.

Online Sources for Antivirus Information

Probably the best defenses you can set up is increased awareness and knowledge of the changing virus landscape. There are a multitude of resources available to you, many of which are available on the Internet or by e-mail. Most vendors of antivirus software maintain BBSs, Wide World Web or FTP sites, or other electronic forums such as those on CompuServe, America Online, Prodigy, or the Microsoft Network. These can all be excellent sources of updated data. Whether your are looking for generic information about viruses, antivirus programs, or updates to a program, it is likely to be available online. Table 42.1 lists some of the sources that you may find helpful. Note that by listing these resources we're not endorsing any specific vendor or the sufficiency of the tools that may be listed nor have all the vendors announced Windows 95 versions of their software products.

Table 42.1 Online Antivirus Resources

Location	Identification
http://www.brs.ibm.com/ibmav.html	IBM Computer Virus Home Page
http://www.symantec.com/virus/virus.html	Symantec Anti-virus Reference Center
http://csrc.ncsl.nist.gov/virus/virusl/	VIRUS-L Forum
http://www.mcafee.com	McAfee software WWW page
http://www.sands.com/	Dr. Solomon's software
http://www.datafellows.fi/index.html	Data Fellows F-Prot software
http://www.icubed.com/ic.html	Sophos Intercheck software
http://www.nha.com/	NH&A software
http://www.thenet.ch/metro/av-links.html	MetroNet BBS—Anti-virus resources
http://ciac.llnl.gov/ciac/	Computer Incident Advisory Capability

Designed for Windows 95—An AntiVirus Example

As mentioned earlier, most if not all developers of antivirus software for the PC platform have announced that Windows 95 versions of their products will be available soon after the initial release of Windows 95. Each of these developers will take a slightly different approach to the task, and each program will certainly have its merits. Though you'll take a quick peek at one such program, McAfee Associates' VirusScan 95, you'll make no attempt here to gauge the relative performance of this or any other antivirus program. The preceding locations have a wealth of data, including performance comparisons that may help you in determining which program best suits your situation.

Shortly before this book went to print in September 1995, McAfee Associates released the first "External Test" Beta version of VirusScan 95 (first called "SCAN 95") to the McAfee FTP site and BBS. This release was one of the first glimpses of what a "Designed for Windows 95" antivirus product might be expected to look like. McAfee soon released a second version as a "Release Candidate" for a final scheduled release coincident with Windows 95's August 24, 1995 worldwide rollout. At this writing there is every indication that McAfee Associates intends to continue to offer this product as shareware, with evaluation versions available online at either of McAfee's WWW, FTP, or BBS locations. To locate the file on the McAfee Associate FTP site, you would look in either the /pub/antivirus or /pub/beta folder for a file called VS95.EXE or something similar. This file contains the complete program in a convenient self-extracting, self-installing format. You can install the program by running the executable directly or by using the Add/Remove Programs applet in Control Panel. As expected, once the program is installed, you can also remove the program by using the same Add/Remove Programs dialog box.

Once installed, VirusScan 95 is tightly integrated with Windows 95. The program will install the VSHEILD.EXE TSR in your AUTOEXEC.BAT file, and the VSHLDWIN.EXE program in the Start Menu/Startup folder; thus enabling the detection portion of VirusScan 95. This detection portion will attempt to prevent a virus from infecting your computer by preventing such activity as detailed in the preceding section. The main VirusScan 95 program is installed in the \Windows\McAfee folder or any other folder of your choice, and a corresponding McAfee VirusScan 95 shortcut menu is added as well. You can execute the program directly by using the VirusScan 95 icon in this group, but the best way to exectute the program is by using a file's context menu in Explorer. Figure 42.9 shows the Scan for Viruses selection that VirusScan 95 adds to this menu.

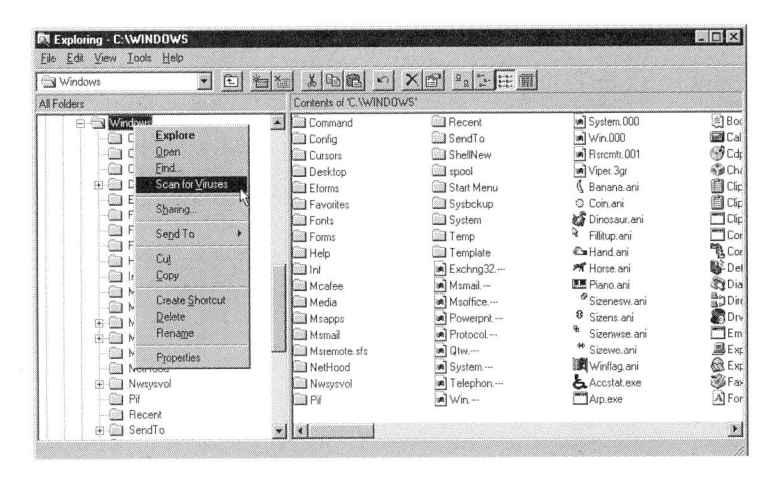

Fig. 42.9 The Explorer showing the addition of Scan for Viruses that VirusScan 95 adds to the context menu.

When you make this selection, the main VirusScan 95 dialog box opens (figure 42.10), which looks much like the Windows 95 Find Files dialog box (figure 42.11).

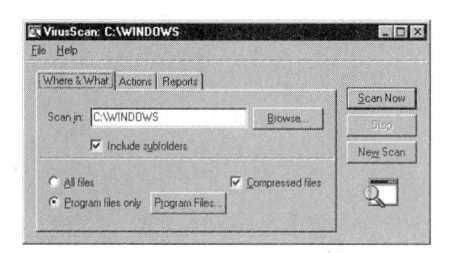

Fig. 42.10 The main VirusScan 95 dialog looks very much like the Windows 95 Find Files dialog box.

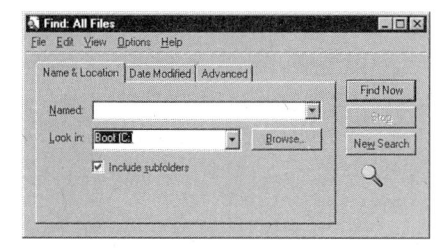

Fig. 42.11 The Windows 95 Find Files dialog box shown for comparison.

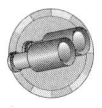

> **Note:** Notice that you can have either VirusScan 95 scan All files or Program files only or even scan inside compressed executable files. Also be aware that the New Scan button restores the programs defaults for a new scan selection.

If you want to immediately scan the selected file, folder, or drive, you click on Scan Now to begin the scan process. Because VirusScan is a 32-bit program, it can run in the background while you continue to work in another program. If a suspected virus is found, VirusScan will take whatever steps you have specified in the Actions tab (figure 42.12).

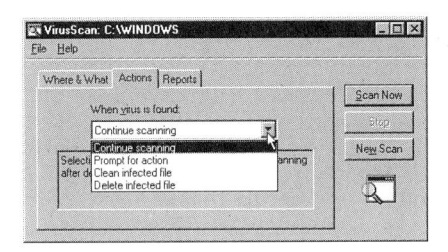

Fig. 42.12 The main VirusScan 95 dialog Action tab showing the possible actions that can be configured.

You use the Reports tab (figure 42.13) to display a message or sound an alert when a virus is found, or to log any results to a file.

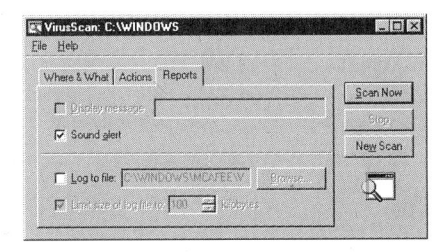

Fig. 42.13 The main VirusScan 95 dialog box Reports tab showing report functions that can be configured.

This has been a quick look at one developer's approach to Windows 95 antivirus protection. Fortunately, VirusScan 95 didn't find any virus' on your system. Following the recommendations you learned about earlier and those that follow should help you have similar results! Now, turn your attention again to backup—the best way *back* from an antivirus attack.

Backing Up Your System

Anytime the potential destruction or loss of data is mentioned, the issue of having a recent backup needs to be considered. Probably one of the most frequent mistakes of most PC users is that no backup plan is in place. Restoring lost data after a catastrophic occurrence like a virus infection may be the only way to recover from an infection like that caused by the Monkey virus. And other viruses equally destructive may result in significant loss of irreplaceable data. Many companies suffer financial damage when data is lost to a virus attack or to other catastrophic damage when no recent backup exists.

Windows 95 ships with several backup options. Microsoft Backup is used to back up to a local floppy, tape, or network drive. This application was developed by Colorado Memory Systems for Windows 95 and supports many well-known tape drives. The following tape drives are compatible with Microsoft Backup:

QIC 40, 80, and 3010 tape drives made by the following companies, and connected to the primary floppy-disk controller:

- Colorado Memory Systems
- Conner
- Iomega
- Wangtek (only in hardware phantom mode)
- Colorado Memory Systems QIC 40, 80, and 3010 tape drives connected through a parallel port

Windows 95 Microsoft Backup is very easy to use. It's so easy that if you have access to a local tape drive, I strongly recommend you use it. Figure 42.9 shows the main Microsoft Backup window.

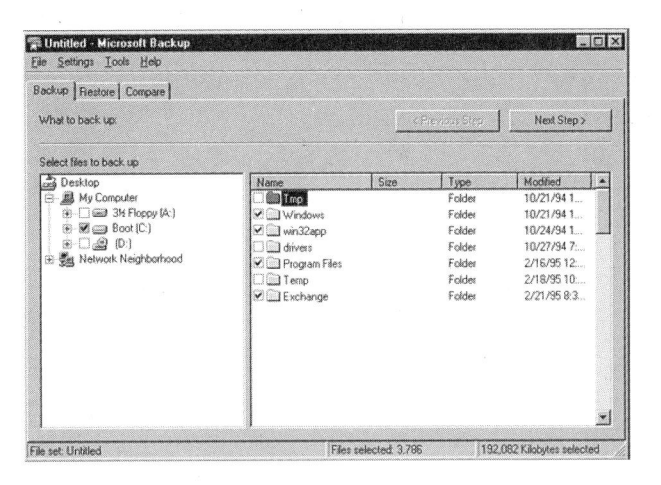

Fig. 42.14 The main Microsoft Backup dialog showing the selection of backup sources.

Selecting files to back up is a simple point-and-click operation. Once you have made your backup choices, you simply select Next Step to proceed with your backup. Figure 42.15 shows the destination window that you use to select a floppy disk, or tape drive, or a local or network drive for a backup destination.

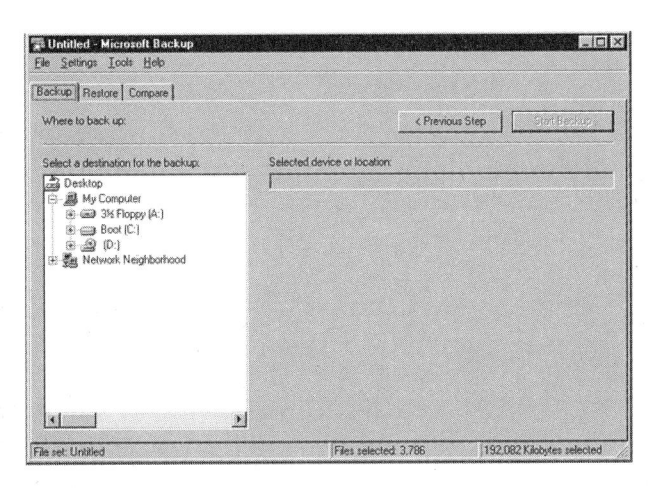

Fig. 42.15 The main Microsoft Backup dialog showing the selection of a backup destination.

You use the Microsoft Backup Settings, Options menu to modify your backup settings. You also use this dialog box to modify Restore options. Figures 42.16 and 42.17 illustrate the options for Backup and Restore.

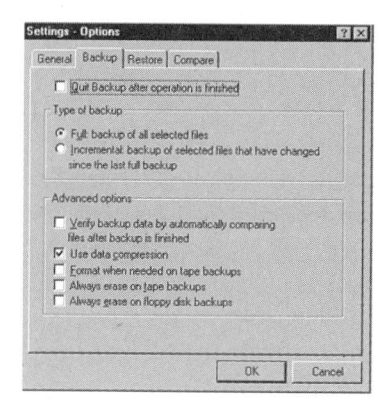

Fig. 42.16 The Microsoft Backup Settings, Options dialog box showing the Backup options page.

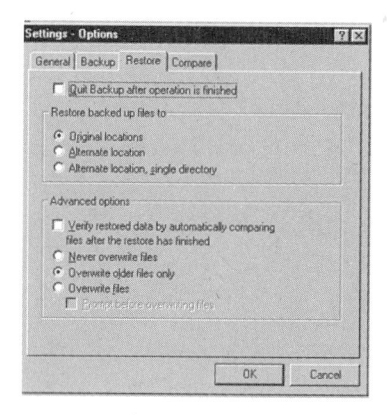

Fig. 42.17 The Microsoft Backup Settings, Options dialog showing the Restore options page.

Windows also includes Backup Agents to assist in remote backup of a Windows system to a network tape drive. These agents from Arcada (Backup Exec Agent) and Cheyenne Software (ARCserve Agent) assist in unattended backup to the corresponding network tape drive. Armed with the appropriate agent, an administrator can be sure that important data is regularly backed up to the network tape drive. The Arcada and Cheyenne backup agents require the corresponding server-based network backup software from either Arcada or Cheyenne. The server components are available for either Novell NetWare or Windows NT Servers.

Because these agents require network connections to a server, you use the Network dialog box to install the related software (see figure 42.13 and 42.14). Microsoft lists these as a service, so you choose A<u>d</u>d and double-click Service to open the Select Network Service dialog box. You then install the appropriate manufacturer's service and configure it for your backup server.

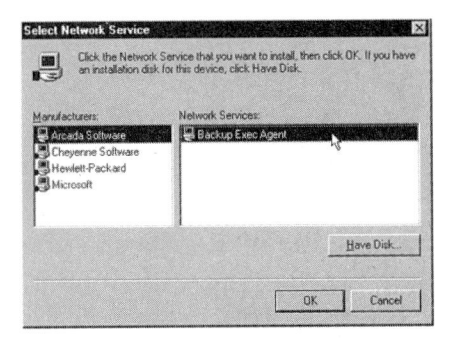

Fig. 42.18 The Select Network Service dialog box showing the selection of the Arcada Backup Exec Agent.

You'll step through a typical setup of Arcada's Backup Exec Agent to show the steps to take to enable a network backup. Remember, without one of these backup servers, you won't be able to use the agents.

The Arcada Backup Exec Agent delivered with Windows requires Arcada Backup Exec for NetWare, Enterprise Edition or Single Server Edition, version 5.01, or Arcada Backup Exec 6.0 for Windows NT. If your NetWare or Windows NT Server is running the appropriate Arcada products, you can use the Arcada Backup Exec Agent to regularly archive important data from your workstation. Installing the Backup Exec Agent is easy. Once you have located the service, you only need to click OK to install the software (refer figure 42.18). Then you have to configure the software by either double-clicking on Backup Exec Agent in the Network dialog box and then clicking on Properties to see the Backup Exec Agent Properties sheet for the agent (see figure 42.19).

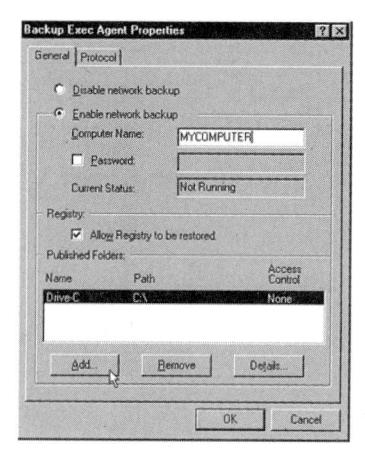

Fig. 42.19 The Backup Exec Agent Properties sheet showing the General page.

> **Note:** When you first install your software, Current Status indicates Not Running. After you install and configure the agent this status changes to Running.

When you enable the software, the NetWare or Windows NT Server software sees the Windows 95 computer as a backup source. The information that you need to pay careful attention to in this Properties sheet is as follows:

- You must enable the agent
- If needed, you must set a password

- Determine if you want the Registry to be restored
- Determine which folders need to be backed up using the Add, Remove, and Details dialog boxes

> **Caution:** If you mark the Allo<u>w</u> Registry To Be Restored check box, changes to the Registry you may have made explicitly or any that a program may have made since the last backup will be overwritten.

If you only want to back up your main Documents folder and your electronic mail Exchange folder, you use the Add dialog box, which opens the Select Folder to Publish dialog box (see figure 42.20) to select the folder you want backed up and then the Remove dialog box to remove any you don't want to back up.

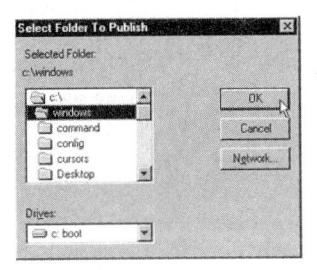

Fig. 42.20 The Backup Exec Agent's Select Folder To Publish dialog box showing the currently selected folders.

Click on the folders you want to add to the backup, click OK to bring up the Folders Details dialog where you can set any required passwords (see figure 42.21).

Backing Up Your System **1097**

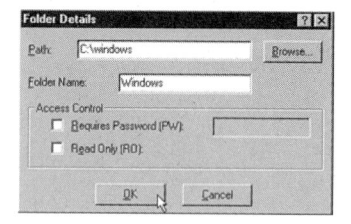

Fig. 42.21 The Folder Details dialog box allows you to assign appropriate access control.

Add any folders that you want to back up, and then check to see if you have set up the access control correctly. In this case, Read-Only access on the Windows folder was set up (see figure 42.22).

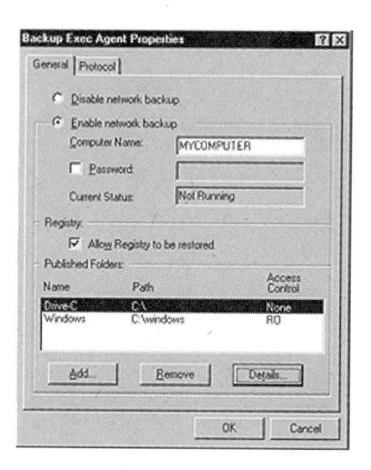

Fig. 42.22 The Backup Exec Agent General properties sheet showing the currently assigned access control.

You now need to set the appropriate protocol for the server. On the Protocol page, you find that you can use either the SPX/IPX or TCP/IP protocols (see figure 42.23). Also, if you select TCP/IP, you need to use either the correct TCP/IP address or server name. To add information, the Add button allows you to input the correct information. When you have made all the changes necessary, simply click the OK button to leave the Backup Exec Agent Properties sheet and click OK again to save the information. When you exit the Network dialog box, you are prompted to reboot the computer to accept the changes. Click the Yes button. When your computer is rebooted, you can visit these dialog boxes to see that the Backup Exec Agent is indeed running.

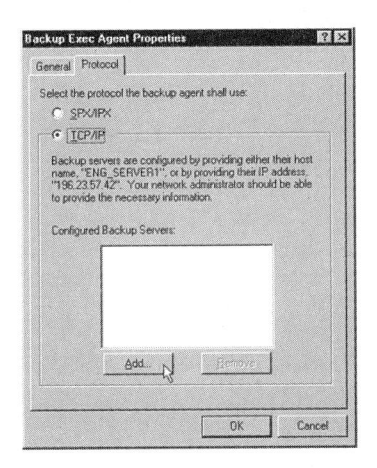

Fig. 42.23 The Backup Exec Agent Protocol Properties sheet showing the selection for the TCP/IP protocol.

If your server is running Cheyenne's backup software, you need to install the ARCserve backup agent which involves a similar set of steps.

System Agent

by Gordon Meltzer

The System Agent that is part of Microsoft Plus! is a powerful tool for scheduling applications and utilities. With System Agent, you can run other programs automatically, at certain preprogrammed times, in the background.

You can choose when to run the programs you schedule, and under what conditions they will start.

In this chapter, you learn about the following:

➤ How to use System Agent to schedule disk utilities

➤ The different kinds of programs you can launch with System Agent

➤ How to work with System Agent's optional settings

➤ How System Agent works with battery-operated computers

The programs that Microsoft pre-installs into System Agent are disk maintenance tools that, for now, seem to be the most useful types of programs to run in scheduled mode. They perform work that you should do regularly, but may often neglect. It's no surprise that these are the only pre-installed tools because, as you'll see, programs need to have settings configured to run properly in unattended mode. They also need settings that can alter the course of program execution, depending on the state of the computer at the time of scheduled execution.

Some programs that can benefit from scheduling, such as third-party backup solutions and third-party communications programs, already have scheduling built in. It would have been easy for Microsoft to build scheduling into Disk Defragmenter and the other applets, too.

Why then, did the system designers choose to put System Agent into the operating system itself?

The answer is simple. The answer builds on the premise established by Windows 1.0 back in 1985. The idea is to build uniform functionality for all programs into the operating system itself.

The first Windows was revolutionary, because it put printer drivers and display drivers into the operating system, and removed the need for these drivers to be part of Windows applications. Finally, video and printer drivers presented a universal interface to all programs. All Windows programs, for example, that used a printer used similar printer selection and setup dialog boxes, because the dialog box was really a part of the operating system.

In the same way, Microsoft designers decided to present a universal scheduling interface that would be available for designers of all programs to implement. No longer will the user have to remember a different set of scheduling commands for each program that can run unattended. The user interface and API in System Agent will be available to all program designers and coders.

This will make life easier for the user who wants to run a program in scheduled mode. Users can expect to see a large number of Windows 95 programs written to work with and take advantage of the power that is available in System Agent.

Exploring System Agent's Files

System Agent is a background scheduling application. It is implemented with several executables and a 32-bit virtual device, with a help system attached. The 10 files that collectively make up System Agent are as follows:

1. SAGE.EXE
2. SAGE.DLL
3. SAGE.VXD
4. SAGE.DEF
5. SAGE.DAT
6. SAGELOG.TXT
7. SYSAGENT.EXE
8. SYSAGENT.HLP
9. SYSAGENT.CNT
10. SYSAGENT.GID

System Agent starts when Windows 95 is loaded. It indicates that it is running by putting its icon in the system tray, next to the clock. It indicates its state by changing the properties of that icon.

> **Automatic Startup**
>
> The mechanism for automatically starting System Agent when Windows starts is new for Windows 95. You're used to seeing programs start automatically if they're listed on the RUN= or LOAD= lines of the WIN.INI file. You also know programs start automatically if they're in the STARTUP group on the Start button.
>
> System Agent starts in a different way. System Agent makes use of the new Registry automatic startup service. The Registry setting that provides the automatic startup service for System Agent is buried deeply at the following Registry location, which can be viewed or edited with REGEDIT.EXE:
>
> > HKEY_LOCAL_MACHINE, SOFTWARE, Microsoft, Windows, CurrentVersion, Run.

System Agent is designed by Microsoft to run programs in the background at certain times. In its default as-shipped configuration, System Agent is set to run the common disk utilities shown in figure 43.1. But it is capable of much more than this simple set of tasks.

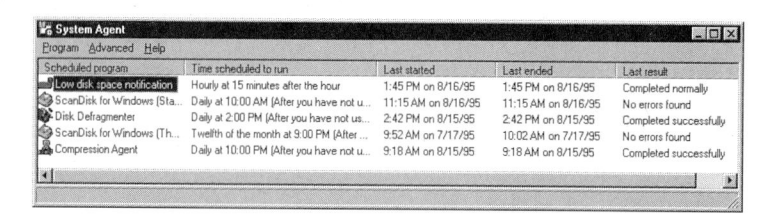

Fig. 43.1 Default System Agent configuration.

Understanding the System Agent File Functions

In the following sections, you take a look at how the 10 System Agent files work together, and examine the function of each.

The SAGE.XXX Files

SAGE.EXE is the background scheduler program engine. This program actually runs all the time in the background after you choose to install System Agent from PLUS! setup. SAGE.DLL is the library file for the scheduler engine. SAGE.DEF and SAGE.DAT are the data files containing the configuration of the System Agent. The DEF file is the default as-shipped configuration, and the DAT file is your user-modified System Agent configuration.

The SAGE.VXD is the virtual device driver that System Agent uses to take control of the system when it's time to run a scheduled program. This multitasking VXD will ensure that the scheduled program runs only if its tasking state conditions are met.

The SYSAGENT.XXX Files

These files are the front-end interface system for System Agent. When you use the interface to schedule a program, you're running SYSAGENT.EXE. This file also contains the icon image that you see in the system tray whenever you start a Windows 95 system that has Plus! installed.

SYSAGENT.EXE allows you to do the following:

- Schedule a new program
- Change a program's schedule
- Examine the properties of a scheduled program
- Run a scheduled program immediately
- Disable a scheduled program so it will not run on a schedule
- Remove a program from the list of scheduled programs

You'll also be using SYSAGENT.EXE if you want to do the following:

- Suspend the entire System Agent system

or

- De-install System Agent entirely

This program is also your interface to view the System Agent log file named SAGELOG.TXT.

The front end also includes the help system. SYSAGENT.HLP is the main help file, and SYSAGENT.CNT is the table of contents index for System Agent help. Finally, SYSAGENT.GID is the Windows 95 word index database file.

Working with System Agent's Defaults

By default, System Agent comes configured to run Low Disk Space Notification, ScanDisk for Windows, and Disk Defragmenter.

Look at the options System Agent gives you when working with these programs. You'll be able to schedule the programs and set some useful conditions for running them. These tasking state conditions can be modified by you to create an environment that works best for you. In determining how to set up System Agent, you'll want to consider whether your computer is left on all the time or only for a few hours a day. Your work schedule will also be important in determining how best to use the feature set.

Working with Low Disk Space Notification

System Agent calls DISKALM.EXE to run the Low Disk Space Notification. The default setting is to run this program once each hour, at 15 minutes past the hour, on local hard disk C, and notify you if disk space falls below 20M free.

You can alter the following settings for DISKALM.EXE:

➤ Change the schedule of activation

➤ Change the threshold of available disk space for notification

➤ Change the drives on which the program acts

Changing the Schedule

Figure 43.2 shows the basic options for running DISKALM.EXE. These settings apply also to any program that System Agent schedules. You have the option to change Run frequency, Start at time, and state dependence from this screen. Notice that the Start at option in the figure is tied to the Run Hourly selection in the same dialog box.

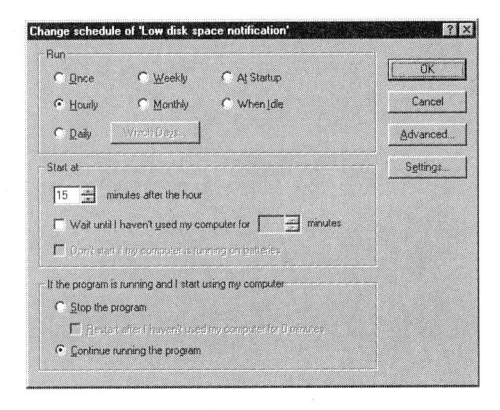

Fig. 43.2 System Agent's Change Schedule option.

The Change Schedule screen changes, depending on which Run frequency option you select. The Run frequency options to run the scheduled program are as follows:

- Once
- At Startup
- When Idle
- Hourly
- Daily
- Weekly
- Monthly

Click on one of the preceding options and then the Advanced button to configure when the low disk notification is to check whether one of

Working with System Agent's Defaults **1107**

your disks is low on available disk space. If you click on Advanced with Hourly selected, for example, the Advanced Options dialog box appears, as shown in figure 43.3. This dialog box gives you several options to configure the time intervals to check for low disk space. The first group of settings is called Deadline. Deadline settings let you tell the computer what to do if the computer is busy at the time low disk space notification is supposed to run. In the example shown in figure 43.3, System Agent will keep trying to start the program until 15 minutes after the hour. This 15 minutes past the hour setting is the deadline.

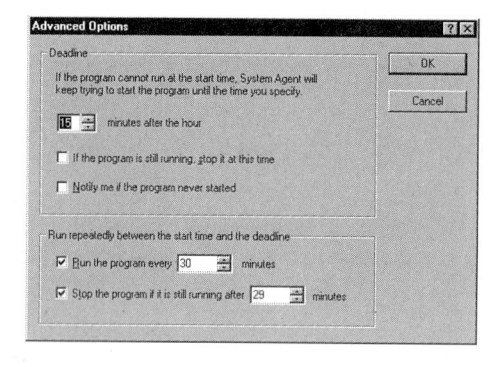

Fig. 43.3 The different Hourly Advanced options are shown here.

The idea in each case is the same. System Agent lets you choose when to start the program. If the program cannot start running in the background because your computer is in use, you choose a deadline time. This step creates a time window. The time window starts at the start time and ends at the deadline time. During this time, System Agent will try to run the program, and optionally notify you if it can't.

> **Note:** Programs scheduled to run At Startup or When Idle have no deadline options because they are not dependent on a set start time.

Changing the Settings

Although the Change Schedule dialog boxes and options are the same for any program scheduled by System Agent, the Settings dialog box shown in the preceding figures is tied tightly to the program being scheduled.

Keep working with the low disk space alarm. From the main System Agent screen, choose Program, Change Schedule, then choose Settings to display the Settings options shown in figure 43.4.

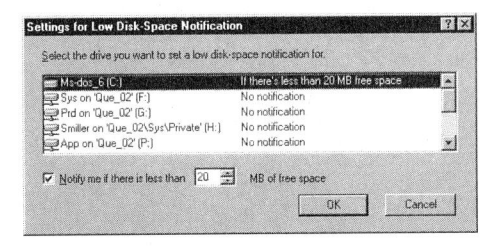

Fig. 43.4 System Agent's settings for low disk space notification.

The computer in use here has three disks eligible for examination by DISKALM.EXE. The local hard disk, drive C, is being examined, and the local CD-ROM, drive F, the compressed drive D, and host drive H are not. You can choose the amount of free disk space to set as a notification threshold in this dialog box.

> **Tip:** Set the low disk space notification threshold to no lower than 10 percent of total capacity on each monitored drive, or twice the amount of RAM, whichever is greater. This step will avoid virtual memory errors.

Changing the Low Disk Space Notification

You have access to the Properties sheet from the System Agent main screen. Highlight Low disk space notification, and right-click. Next, choose Properties.

Working with System Agent's Defaults   **1109**

The Low disk space notification Properties sheet will appear. You'll be able to make some major changes here, but be careful because you can change the executable associated with the description Low disk space notification. You can also change the description itself if you wish. In this dialog box you can also choose to log the results of DISKALM.EXE to disk. If you do this, you'll find the results in the SAGELOG.TXT file in the C:\Program Files\Plus! folder. You'll want to log the results of DISKALM.EXE if you're having intermittent problems with low disk space on a computer that is often unattended. When you look at the log, you'll know when disk space became low, and this can serve as a clue to solving the problem.

From this dialog box, you also have access to the Change Schedule and Settings dialog boxes covered in the earlier sections. Figure 43.5 shows how it looks on-screen.

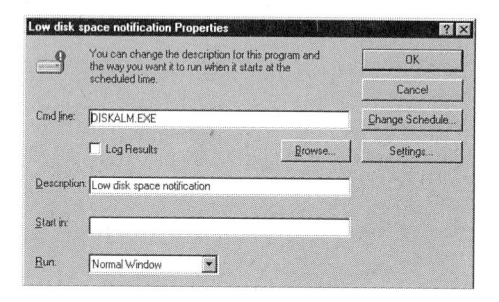

Fig. 43.5 Low disk space notification Properties.

Low Disk Space Notification Output

System Agent will run DISKALM.EXE in accordance with all the scheduling options and settings you've chosen. If disk space on the monitored drives is above the amount of free disk space you specify, no output will be written to the screen. The log file will be updated if you have *logging* enabled.

If disk space falls below your threshold setting, you'll see an alarm on-screen like the one shown in figure 43.6.

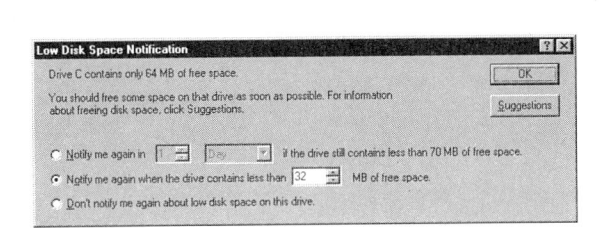

Fig. 43.6 The Low Disk Space Notification program alarm.

When disk space falls to a low level and the alarm is shown on-screen, you have five options to close the alarm dialog box. Figure 43.6 shows these options:

- Choose OK, which will not change DISKALM.EXE settings.
- Choose Notify me again in x days, which will change the scheduling options in System Agent.
- Choose Notify me again when the drive contains less, which will also change the scheduling options in System Agent.
- Choose Don't notify me again, which will disable the DISKALM.EXE program within System Agent.
- Choose Suggestions, which will open the Help Troubleshooter dialog box in figure 43.7.

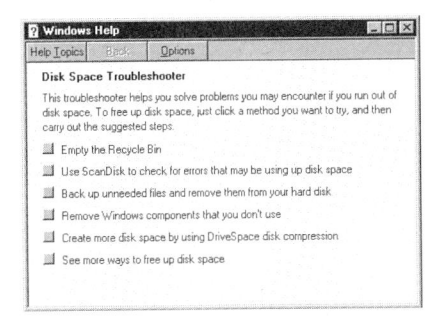

Fig. 43.7 Disk Space Troubleshooter.

Working with System Agent's Defaults

Working with ScanDisk for Windows

ScanDisk is a perfect candidate for scheduled operation. This tool can alert you to problems forming on the disk before they become critical.

ScanDisk can be configured around two types of operation:

- Standard test
- Thorough test

ScanDisk in Standard Configuration

The Standard test checks only for logical disk problems. First it verifies VFAT integrity and then looks at folders. It checks folders for common disk errors such as lost file fragments, crosslinking, and invalid file names, dates, and times. These errors can occur if a program crashes, or if you turn off your computer without going through the proper shutdown process.

ScanDisk in Thorough Configuration

The Thorough ScanDisk test adds a physical test of the disk surface to the Standard test, and takes much longer to perform. In the physical test, ScanDisk checks each sector of the disk to verify that good data can be read from each sector. This check is also called a surface test.

Physical errors are usually caused by defects in the surface of the disk platter. All disks have some physical surface defects when they come from the factory. During the low-level format of the disk, these bad spots are identified and marked *bad*. When a spot on the disk surface is marked *bad*, the sector or sectors located on that spot are locked out of the file allocation table by the operating system. No data can be written to those bad sectors.

Some physical surface defects don't exist when the drive comes from the factory, but are created later. These are called grown defects. Physical defects can grow on your disk if the drive head touches the spinning platter while the disk is running. The contact between the head and spinning disk can damage the disk surface and cause a grown defect.

The Thorough ScanDisk will find these physical defects and mark the sectors involved as bad, so no data can be written to them. If there is data in the damaged sector, ScanDisk will attempt to move the data to an undamaged area of the disk; but, since the source area is damaged, you can expect data loss.

Because it takes so much longer to do a Thorough ScanDisk test, System Agent by default schedules the Thorough test to run at night, after the computer has been idle for almost an hour. System Agent expects the computer to continue being idle under those conditions long enough to complete the surface test.

> **Tip:** Whichever ScanDisk option you select, make sure you check the Automatically fix errors option shown in figure 43.8 or System Agent will not be able to operate unattended. Do this through the Change Schedule or Settings dialog boxes, or on ScanDisk's main screen.

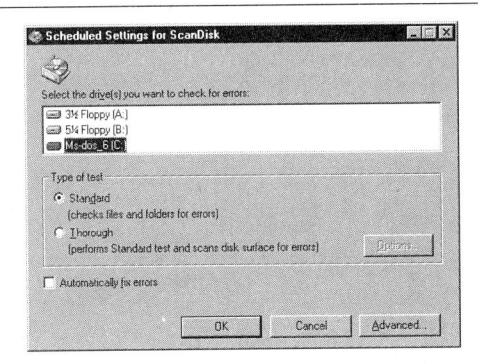

Fig. 43.8 The Scheduled Setting for ScanDisk for Windows dialog box.

Advanced ScanDisk Options

Chapter 10, "Optimizing Your Disk Drives," covers ScanDisk for Windows in a normal, stand-alone, unscheduled environment. With System Agent in control, it is important to remember that the system needs to be idle when ScanDisk executes. If there is other disk activity

Working with System Agent's Defaults 1113

while ScanDisk is running it will have to start over again, which it will do automatically up to 10 times. After 10 restarts, ScanDisk will halt, which means that ScanDisk can't complete automatically as it is intended to under System Agent's scheduled operation.

It's important then, that no other processes (like the screen saver or defrag) are scheduled at the same time ScanDisk wants to run. There are advanced settings you can use to tell ScanDisk what to do when it comes across disk errors.

You can reach the ScanDisk Advanced Options from the main System Agent screen. Highlight ScanDisk for Windows, double-click to display Scheduled Settings for ScanDisk, choose Settings, and then, choose Advanced. Figure 43.9 shows you the choices you can make.

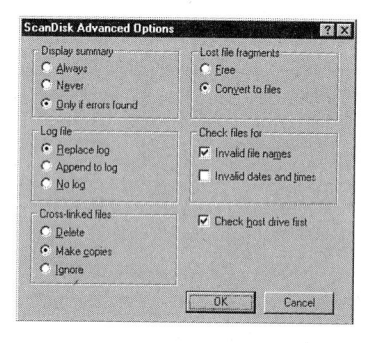

Fig. 43.9 The ScanDisk Advanced Options dialog box.

It's important to know that none of the advanced options will prevent ScanDisk from completing unattended, as long as you've chosen Automatically fix errors.

The advanced choices you make will affect how your disk looks after ScanDisk encounters errors, so you should know what they mean and what they do.

There are six groups of advanced options for ScanDisk.

- **Display summary.** The choices here are Always, Never, and Only if errors are found. Because System Agent is running ScanDisk in unattended mode, you'll probably want to select Never, so you won't have to manually close the summary display dialog box.

- **Log file.** You can choose to Replace log, Append to log, or No log. Choose Replace if you only want to keep results of the latest ScanDisk session in a file. Choose Append, and your log file will grow each time ScanDisk writes its results to the end of the log file. No log means that ScanDisk will not write a log of results. If you set enable logging in Advanced Options, ScanDisk will write a file in the root folder of your boot disk when it's finished running. The file name is SCANDISK.LOG. Figure 43.10 shows an example of this file.

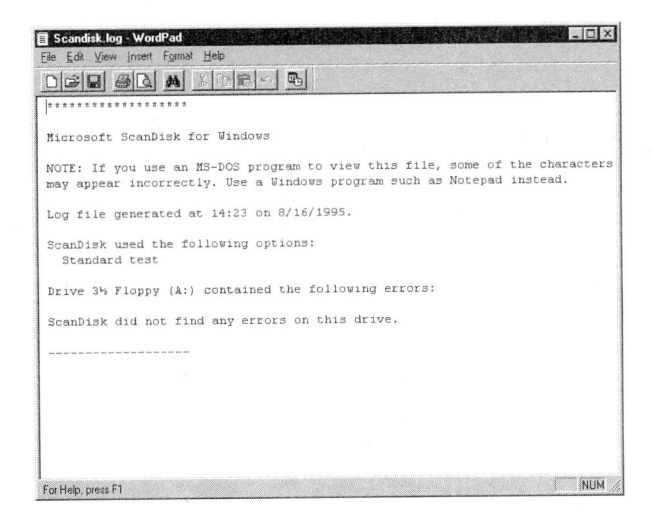

Fig. 43.10 An example of a typical ScanDisk log.

- **Cross-linked files.** If, due to an error, the operating system writes a file allocation table that says two or more different files occupy the same spot on the drive, the two or more files are said to be cross-linked. Cross-linked files cause problems for Windows, and constitute disk corruption. You can choose to Make copies of all the cross-linked files and have ScanDisk store the copies in proper, separate locations. You can choose to have ScanDisk delete all the cross-linked files. <u>D</u>elete is a good bet, because files that are cross-linked are usually damaged. The Make <u>c</u>opies option will probably make copies of damaged files that will do you no good. The only time you can benefit from Make <u>c</u>opies is when the files cross-linked are text files. Then, you can recover some of the text. If the cross-linked files are binaries, or program files, any small error will make the file useless. That's why <u>D</u>elete is recommended. You should ignore the <u>I</u>gnore option, since leaving cross-linked files on your drive will lead to bigger disk problems.

- **Lost file fragments.** These are harmless errors. See the section "ScanDisk in Standard Configuration" for more information on lost file fragments. The best choice is to <u>F</u>ree the disk space taken up by these lost fragments.

- You can, and should, check files for Invalid file na<u>m</u>es and Invalid dates and <u>t</u>imes. Letting ScanDisk correct any of these errors will help keep your disk tuned and in top shape.

- If your disk is compressed, you should Check <u>h</u>ost drive first. If there are errors on the compressed drive's host drive, they should be fixed on the host drive first. Fixing errors on the host may automatically correct errors on the compressed drive.

Working with Disk Defragmenter

The program described as Disk Defragmenter in System Agent is set by default to be DEFRAG.EXE. You can change the description as well as the program to be executed in the <u>P</u>rogram, Properties sheet in the main System Agent screen.

Continue looking at the default settings, and see how System Agent plans to schedule and run Disk Defragmenter.

Settings and Thresholds

Disk Defragmenter will run in different ways depending on its settings and threshold levels of fragmentation. You have the option, in stand-alone Defrag's settings dialog box, to choose from three modes of operation:

- Full defragmentation of both files and free space
- Defragment files only
- Consolidate free space only

The first option combines the functions of the second two. Choosing Defragment files only will ensure that all the files on the disk are contiguous but will leave small gaps of free space in between disk areas containing files. Choosing Consolidate free space only will close the gaps, making all the free space appear in one big section at the end of the drive, but will leave all files on this disk in whatever state of fragmentation they were previously. The Full option takes much longer to run than either of the other two.

When Disk Defragmenter runs in scheduled mode under the control of System Agent, another important option is added to Settings. You can choose the level of disk fragmentation necessary to cause Disk Defragmenter to run at all when scheduled. (See figure 43.11.)

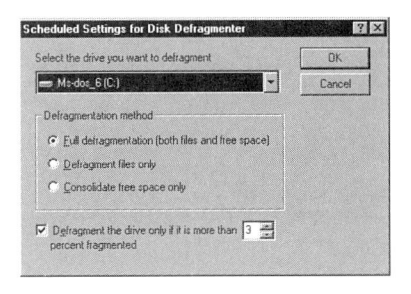

Fig. 43.11 The fragmentation threshold settings.

System Agent sets the fragmentation threshold to 3 percent by default. You'll want to adjust this percent depending on the type of work you do and the type and size of files you work with.

> **Tip:** If you commonly work with large files greater than 1M, set your fragmentation threshold to a lower level than the default, such as example 1 percent. This setting applies if you're installing and deinstalling large Windows applications, too.

The way Disk Defragmenter reads the level of fragmentation on a disk doesn't take into consideration the gaps between file areas. There can be many small free gaps in an otherwise defragmented disk. In this case, Disk Defragmenter will report that the disk is not fragmented and that Disk Defragmenter doesn't need to run. But this type of situation is a guarantee that future files written to the disk will in fact be fragmented, because Windows will try to write them in the small gaps, and will have to bridge those gaps with files larger than the gaps, writing the files into two or more nonsequential areas. This lack of intelligence is a limitation of the VFAT file system used in Windows 95.

This is exactly why you'll want to consider lowering the level of disk fragmentation needed to kick Disk Defragmenter into action.

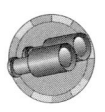

> **Note:** Running Disk Defragmenter in any mode other than Full defragmentation is really counterproductive. Although the other settings will complete faster, they leave gaps or fragmented files on the disk and thus are not useful. Running in those modes also guarantees that a full defragment will be needed more often than if you only run in Full mode.

Scheduling Options

All the standard System Agent scheduling options are active when scheduling Disk Defragmenter. The default setting is to run once daily after your computer has been idle for at least 10 minutes. You should pick a time when your computer will be on, but idle, for an extended time, to make Disk Defragmenter most useful. With modern hard drives of between 500M and 1G, allow at least 20 minutes for Disk Defragmenter to do a full defragmentation.

Interruptions and Restarts

Disk Defragmenter is very sensitive to other disk activity, just like ScanDisk for Windows. And like ScanDisk, if the disk state changes during operation, it will have to start over from the beginning. With all the things that can happen in the background affecting the disk, it's almost amazing that these types of programs can ever complete successfully. Everything from cache flushing to an incoming e-mail or fax can cause a running Disk Defragmenter session to have to restart.

This is taken into consideration in the scheduling dialog box. You should always schedule Disk Defragmenter to Continue running the program if the computer is used during its operation. Unlike ScanDisk, which will halt with a warning dialog after 10 restarts, Disk Defragmenter will start over an unlimited number of times until it is complete, while running in the background. This behavior ensures compatibility with a scheduler like System Agent.

Output and Logging

Unlike ScanDisk and Low Disk Space Notification, Disk Defragmenter creates no output, and writes no log. It doesn't even write to the SAGELOG.TXT file that the other programs record in.

The only way to see what Disk Defragmenter has done is to look in the main System Agent screen. You'll be able to see information on only the last run of the program. You'll see the last start time, the last end time, and whether the program completed successfully.

Working with System Agent Options

Until now you've looked at System Agent defaults, and worked with the default program installations. However, there are other options in the scheduling engine that you haven't worked with. These other options, which you'll cover in the next sections, are as follows:

- Running a scheduled program now
- Disabling a scheduled program
- Removing a scheduled program
- Suspending System Agent
- Stopping System Agent
- Scheduling a new program

Running a Scheduled Program Now

You can run any of the scheduled programs immediately. You might do this to get a quick handle on disk fragmentation levels or a quick look at free disk space on a local or network drive. To run the programs, select Program, Run Now from System Agent's main screen.

> **Caution:** Of the three default scheduled programs, only Low Disk Space Notification will operate on network drives. System Agent cannot ScanDisk or defragment a network drive.

Disabling a Scheduled Program

You can stop a scheduled program from running without shutting down all scheduled programs. To do so, highlight a program in System Agent, and choose Program, Disable. A check mark will appear in the drop-down menu next to Disable, and Disabled will appear in the Time Scheduled to Run column for that program. Figure 43.12 shows you what you can expect to see on-screen when you've disabled a scheduled program.

Chapter 43: System Agent

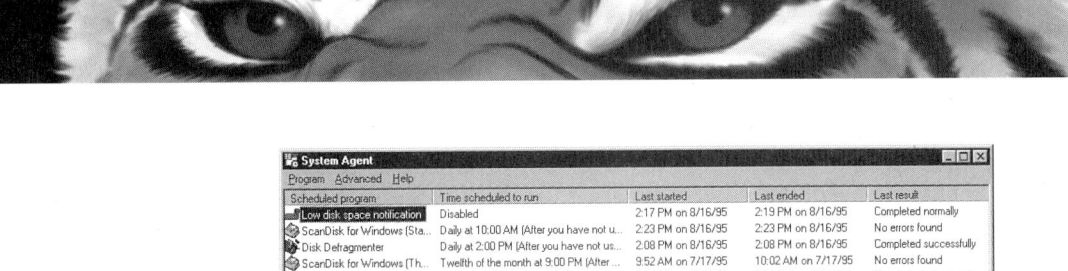

Fig. 43.12 The Disabled program display.

If you want to work with a scheduled program's settings, and if it is set to start running almost immediately, you can use Disable while you're adjusting the settings to prevent the program from running with the old parameters.

You'll notice that when a program is disabled, the Run Now option in the Program menu is grayed out.

Notice, though, that Disabled programs are reinstated with their last active settings, when you restart Windows.

Removing a Scheduled Program

Use the Remove a scheduled program option if you no longer want to schedule a certain program under System Agent control. To use this option from System Agent's main screen, highlight the program to be removed permanently, and choose Program, Remove. After a confirmation dialog box appears, choose Yes to delete the highlighted program from the list of scheduled programs. Of course, you can always add it back later as a new program.

Suspending System Agent

What if you temporarily want to stop all System Agent programs from running? You won't want to disable them individually because it's easier to suspend System Agent entirely for the amount of time you choose. This length of time is not programmable; it's handled by you manually.

Working with System Agent Options **1121**

Because the System Agent icon in the system tray is not active when right-clicked, you'll have to take this step, too. To do so, access System Agent's main screen, and choose Advanced, Suspend System Agent.

None of your scheduled programs will run at its scheduled time.

The System Agent icon in the system tray will appear with a large red X through it, indicating that it is disabled. However, the SAGE.EXE engine will remain loaded in memory.

Stopping System Agent

Stopping System Agent prevents the SAGE.EXE engine from loading when you start Windows 95. Of course, none of your scheduled programs will run. In fact, you won't have any scheduled programs any more.

Although stopping System Agent may have some minimal effect on the system performance by freeing up monitoring clock cycles, its effect on memory and system resources is negligible.

Scheduling a New Program

This option is found through System Agent's main screen, under Program, Schedule a new program. This is the way you'll schedule a program to run automatically under control of System Agent. The real question is what kind of programs are useful when run in scheduled mode, beside the three default programs that are pre-installed?

> **Note:** Compression Agent, which is covered in Chapter 44, is also installed by default into System Agent when you choose to install DriveSpace 3 disk compression.

1122 Chapter 43: System Agent

Backup Programs

Besides disk analysis and defragmenting, the function that most benefits from automatic scheduling is tape backup. You know that only certain types of programs really lend themselves to scheduling. These programs, such as ScanDisk for Windows, Low Disk Space Notification, and Disk Defragmenter, have hooks to settings that can be controlled by System Agent. These settings make it possible to have the programs' complete operation completely unattended.

Microsoft Backup comes bundled with Windows 95. Although Backup is not designed to run completely unattended, it can be scheduled by System Agent and you may find it useful, if your tape capacity is as large as your disk capacity. Of course, floppy backup will not be useful in unattended mode without a robotic floppy swapper, which is not bundled with the operating system.

Communications Programs

You may have a communications program that logs on to an online service and downloads information for you. Many such programs have built-in automatic scheduling features. Some, however, do not, and may be suitable for scheduling with System Agent.

System Agent and Portable Computers

System Agent operates differently when it's installed onto a computer that can be battery powered. Because any program running unattended can deplete batteries quickly, and disk intensive programs like Disk Defragmenter and ScanDisk for Windows especially so, System Agent includes an option named Don't start if my computer is running on batteries.

If you're using a desktop machine, or running your portable computer on AC power, that option will be grayed out as it is in figure 43.13.

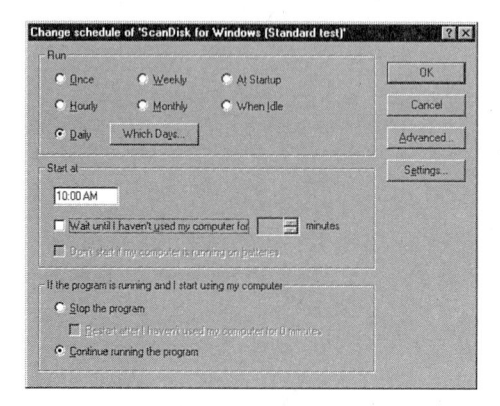

Fig. 43.13 The portable computer option.

You'll have this option for any scheduled program in System Agent on a computer that can sometimes be powered by batteries.

DriveSpace 3 and Compression Agent

by Gordon Meltzer

Compression Agent acts as an intelligent assistant to help you with compressed disk drives. Microsoft Plus! includes a new type of drive-compression program, DriveSpace 3. Once you've installed DriveSpace 3 and used it to compress your hard drive, Compression Agent works in the background to ensure that your compressed drive is always in its most efficient state of compression. This way, Compression Agent makes sure that you can fit as much information as possible on your drive. You won't have to perform analyses of your compression ratios and make adjustments to optimize your drive's compression. Compression Agent does it automatically for you in the background.

In this chapter, you learn how to

➤ Install DriveSpace 3 and Compression Agent

- Compress your disk drives to gain more free space
- Configure Compression Agent to keep your compressed drive in optimum condition

Understanding Drive Compression Compromises

Disk-drive compression technologies have been in use for several years. Several software publishers have tried their hand at writing useful disk-compression software. Microsoft includes a simple form of drive compression in Windows, called DriveSpace. In the past, disk compression always involved compromises. One compromise involved system speed, when using disk compression. As free disk space was gained by compressing data into a smaller space on the drive, system speed decreased because the CPU spent time compressing and decompressing data, instead of spending time running applications. Another compromise involved inefficient use of free space on the disk. In previous disk-compression technologies, if you wanted to compress a cluster that was larger than the available contiguous sectors, the cluster could not be compressed. Finally, earlier forms of disk compression limited a compressed disk to 512M.

DriveSpace 3, included in Microsoft Plus!, remedies some of the performance compromises earlier types of disk compression required.

Features of DriveSpace 3

DriveSpace 3 works in a multistep process. First, DriveSpace 3 creates a host disk drive that is, by default, mnemonically called drive H. (If drive H is already in use on your system, Windows will choose the next available drive letter, after H). Then DriveSpace 3 compresses all the data on your hard-disk drive C into one large compressed file on the host drive. Next, DriveSpace 3 swaps and interprets the large compressed file into uncompressed files as needed, and they appear as regular uncompressed files on drive C. When a file that has been uncompressed from the host drive for use as a regular file on drive C is no longer needed by an application program, it's stored in compressed form again. See Chapter 10, "Optimizing Your Disk Drives," for more information on drive compression software.

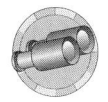

> **Note:** *Host drive* is a term used in connection with drive compression software. A host drive is an uncompressed disk drive that contains a compressed volume file (CVF). This large file appears to the user as a compressed drive. In fact, it is a single file on the host drive.

You can select whether the host drive should be visible or hidden during the DriveSpace 3 setup process. Typically, if there will be usable space left on the host drive after disk compression takes place, you'd choose to keep the host drive visible. If all free space on the host drive is used up during compression, you'd want to make the host drive invisible. You can also choose to hide or unhide the host drive at any time, as you'll see in the following sections.

DriveSpace 3 works with floppy drives, too.

The following section discusses how DriveSpace 3 has features that make drive compression work quickly and efficiently. It also explains some of the features that make it easier for you to work with your compressed drives.

DriveSpace 3 Performance Features

When you use DriveSpace 3 compression, your data is stored on your drive, compressed, with the following properties and features:

➤ Data can be stored in noncontiguous sectors with DriveSpace 3. This is an improvement over DriveSpace. DriveSpace requires a compressed cluster to be stored in contiguous sectors. If the drive is fragmented, there may not be enough contiguous sectors to hold a cluster. With the older DriveSpace, a cluster can take 16 sectors. With DriveSpace 3 however, a cluster can be split into whatever free sectors are available, and DriveSpace 3 keeps a list of where the data is stored. This list operates like a mini file allocation table and is responsible for DriveSpace 3's ability to store more data on the disk than its predecessor.

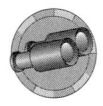

> **Note:** A sector in Windows is always 512 bytes. Clusters vary in size depending on the drive's size. The larger the drive, the larger the cluster size. In uncompressed drives 512M or over, the cluster size is 8K. This means any file, even a one-byte file, takes 8K on the disk, leading to wasted slack space. DriveSpace 3 uses the slack space to store files, increasing efficiency.

- ➤ DriveSpace 3 stores data on your drive in 32K blocks. The earlier form of DriveSpace used only 8K blocks. 32K blocks are more efficiently stored on your drive, and mean higher compression ratios, and higher compression ratios mean that more data can be compressed into the same disk space.

- ➤ DriveSpace 3 uses two new different compression formats. This means that data can be compressed to two different levels of compression, at your option. The two levels are called HiPack and UltraPack. You'll learn more about both of these compression formats and how to work with them in "Working with Compression Agent" later in this chapter.

- ➤ DriveSpace 3 can create compressed drives up to 2G in size. This is a fourfold improvement over previous versions of DriveSpace.

- ➤ DriveSpace 3 runs faster than earlier versions of DriveSpace on computers with a Pentium processor. DriveSpace 3 is one of the first Pentium-optimized programs available to computer users. Microsoft claims speed gains of up to 20% for DriveSpace 3 compared to standard Windows 95 DriveSpace on Pentium machines.

DriveSpace 3 Convenience Features

When you want to work with your compressed drives, DriveSpace 3 makes it easy with the following features:

- Each drive's Properties sheet includes compression statistics.
- When you've installed DriveSpace 3, you can compress uncompressed drives directly from their Property sheets.
- You have the option of working with an individual drive with its Property sheet or with all drives on the system using the DriveSpace 3 program.

Installing DriveSpace 3

To get started with DriveSpace 3 and Compression Agent, insert the Microsoft Plus! CD-ROM or installation disk. Then run the Setup program on the Microsoft Plus! CD-ROM or disk.

> **Caution:** If you are using Banyan Vines 5.5x or earlier as your network software, do not install DriveSpace 3. DriveSpace 3 and Vines both need large amounts of memory below 640K and cannot coexist. Contact Banyan for an updated Vines version that is compatible with DriveSpace 3.

You can choose either a Typical or Custom installation of Microsoft Plus! If you choose the Typical installation, DriveSpace 3 and Compression Agent are installed for you. If you choose the Custom installation, you'll have to make sure that DriveSpace 3 is checked in the Custom dialog box (see figure 44.1).

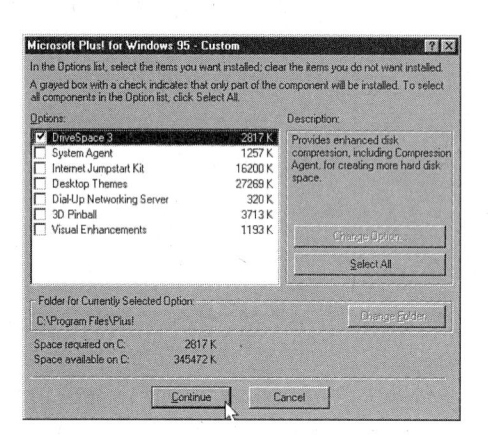

Fig. 44.1 Microsoft Plus! custom installation must include DriveSpace 3 to compress drives and work with Compression Agent.

After you've checked the DriveSpace 3 box in your custom installation, choose Continue. When Microsoft Plus! Setup has installed DriveSpace 3, Compression Agent will automatically be installed for you. Then Setup needs to restart your computer. When your computer restarts, Setup is finished, and you are ready to compress your drives. Setup will update the Start menu and add shortcuts to help you work with the compressed drives, as you'll see next.

Configuring DriveSpace 3

To get started working with compressed drives, choose a drive to compress. Or if you already have a drive that has been compressed with DriveSpace, choose a drive to compress with DriveSpace 3.

Running DriveSpace 3 on an Uncompressed Drive

To start Drivespace 3, follow these steps:

1. Open the Start menu and choose Programs, Accessories, System Tools, DriveSpace.

2. Choose a drive to compress by clicking on it in the DriveSpace 3 dialog box. The click will highlight the drive (see figure 44.2).

3. Choose Drive, Compress.

4. The Compress a Drive dialog box appears showing the amount free space and used space before and after compression (see figure 44.3). Choose Start.

5. The Are You Sure? dialog box gives you a chance to Cancel, Back Up Files using Microsoft Backup, or Compress Now (see figure 44.4). Choose Compress Now to continue. Before you do, you should perform the backup offered as a choice, for safety's sake. The tool you will be given to perform the backup is the Windows 95 accessory, Microsoft Backup.

6. The Compression Options dialog box appears to confirm the compression procedure. Choose Yes to proceed with DriveSpace 3 compression. Compression may take a very long time. You may measure the time in tens of hours, if you have a large drive and a slow system.

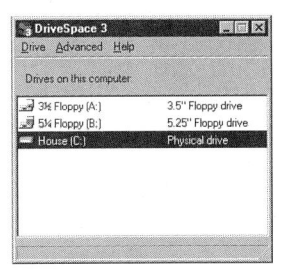

Fig. 44.2 The main DriveSpace 3 window where compression operations can be performed.

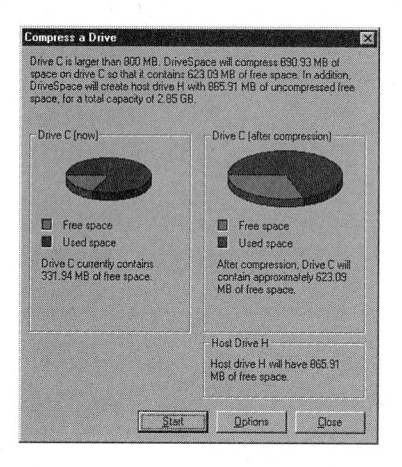

Fig. 44.3 The Compress a Drive dialog box shows before and after space estimates for your drive.

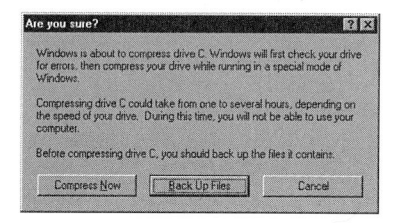

Fig. 44.4 The Are you sure? dialog box offers you a chance to back up your drive before compression.

When working with a disk drive under 800M, there are only 2M of uncompressed space left on drive H. In that case, you'll probably want to use the Compression Options dialog box in step 4 to Hide drive H. Hiding the nearly unusable 2M host drive H makes for simpler, cleaner displays for browsing in Explorer, My Computer, any dialog box, and any window. The 2M disk space is unusable because it is too small. If you use it, you will likely run out of space in the middle of a disk operation and lose data.

After DriveSpace 3 has finished compressing your hard drive, you will have to reboot your system. When your system reboots, the compression operation is finished, and you can examine the space gained by compressing your drive.

DriveSpace 3 Compression Information Screens

After DriveSpace 3 is implemented, it is easy to find out how much free space was gained. This information is gathered the same way for any drive you compress. For the rest of this chapter, you examine a system's C drive. Start My Computer, right-click on the icon for your C drive, and choose Properties. The C drive's Properties sheet appears. Choose the Compression tab (see figure 44.5).

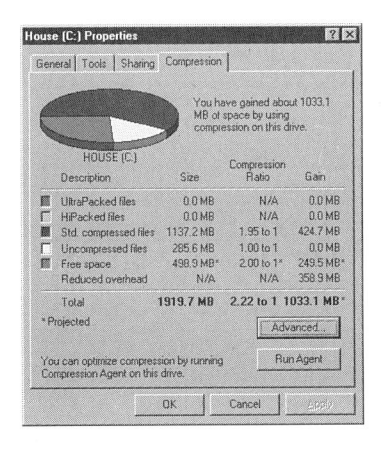

Fig. 44.5 The Compression page shows the results of DriveSpace 3 compression.

The pie chart in figure 44.5 shows how much free space you have on your drive after compression. In drive C, there were 332M free before compression. Now there are 498.9M free on drive C. There were 1137.2M of files on drive C before compression. These files have been compressed and now use only 424.7M of space, which is a compression ratio of 1.95 to 1.

In this page there is a Total row, and the text claims that you gained 1033.1M by compressing the drive. However, there are only 498.9M free on drive C, a gain of only about 150M from the starting free space of 332M. How does DriveSpace 3 claim a projected gain of 1033.1M?

Configuring DriveSpace 3   **1133**

To understand this, you have to look at drive C and the newly created host drive H. When you examine both drives together, the answer is clear. Right-click drive H's icon and choose Properties. Choose the Compression tab (see figure 44.6).

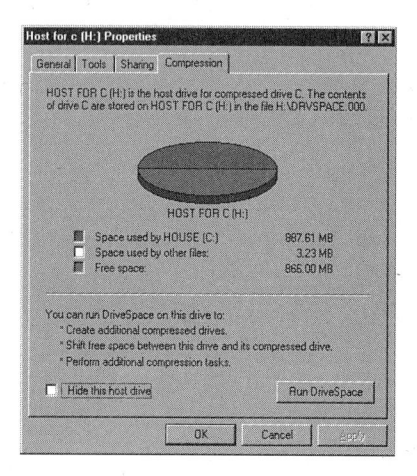

Fig. 44.6 Adding free space on drive C and on drive H shows the true free space on the physical disk drive that has just been compressed.

Figure 44.6 gives you very good information. Look at the information presented next to understand how DriveSpace 3 chooses projected space gain numbers.

➤ The contents of drive C are stored on the drive H, in a compressed file called DRVSPACE.000.

➤ Drive C uses only 887.61M of space.

➤ The free space on drive H is 866M. This space is not compressed and is fully available for your use.

When you look at the whole picture of drives C and H, the following facts show the value of DriveSpace 3.

The physical disk in question is 1800M.

Before compression, there were 1,137M of files. There were 332M free. Those figures only add up to 1,469M. The drive holds 1,800M. What happened to the other 331M that you'd expect the drive to hold? The answer is that the 331M is lost as slack space in the area holding files. That means there were 331M of wasted, slack space because of the use of 8K clusters in disks over 512M in size.

After compression, there are 500M free on drive C and 886M free on drive H. The total free space is now 1366M—hence, the explanation of the 1033M gain of free space.

Now that you've seen basic DriveSpace 3 compression at work on a real-world disk drive, you learn how DriveSpace 3 can get even more usable space from your drive using HiPack and UltraPack file formats. You also learn how Compression Agent squeezes more free room from your drive.

Notice the legend for the pie chart in figure 44.6 includes UltraPacked and HiPacked files, but no files of these types appear in the chart itself. This is because so far, DriveSpace 3 has only created Standard compressed files. DriveSpace 3 and Compression Agent can further optimize the drive, as you see in "Working with DriveSpace 3" and "Working with Compression Agent" later in this chapter.

Running DriveSpace 3 on a Drive Compressed with DriveSpace

When you run DriveSpace 3 on a drive that has already been compressed with an earlier version of DriveSpace, you perform an upgrade installation of DriveSpace 3.

To perform the upgrade, open the Start menu and Programs, Accessories, System Tools, DriveSpace 3. When the program starts, highlight the drive you want to compress with DriveSpace 3. Then choose Drive, Upgrade.

From here, the installation proceeds as if you were compressing an uncompressed drive in the previous section.

Adjusting DriveSpace 3's Settings

When you have created a compressed drive, you can manually make the following adjustments to its configuration:

- ➤ The amount of free space—balancing the available free space between your C and H drives.
- ➤ The estimated compression ratio.
- ➤ The compression method—using HiPack compression to generate more free disk space. (This method is only recommended for Pentium computers because on 386 and 486 computers HiPack compression is too slow to be useful.)

Adjusting Free Space

Compressing a disk drive certainly complicates the way drive statistics are presented to you. After compression, there are two drives where formerly one existed. You have to deal with free space on both of them. You should understand the relationship between the free space on both drives C and H.

The free space on drive H can be used for three purposes:

- ➤ File storage
- ➤ To create another empty compressed drive
- ➤ To allow drive C to grow and have more free space

The unused, free space on drive H can be used to resize drive C and make more free space available on drive C. Windows provides a set of graphical tools that make it easy to divide the free space between drives H and C.

From the main DriveSpace 3 program window, highlight compressed drive C, then choose Drive, Adjust Free Space. You see the Adjust Free Space dialog box (see figure 44.7).

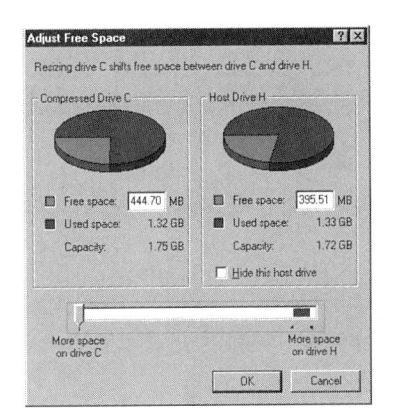

Fig. 44.7 Use the Adjust Free Space dialog box to divide the free space on your disk between drives H and C.

The settings shown in figure 44.7 are only one possible choice. Using the slider, you can divide the free space on your disk. At the left end of the slider, you can create the most free space possible on drive C. At the right end of the slider, you can give all the free space to drive H (see figure 44.8).

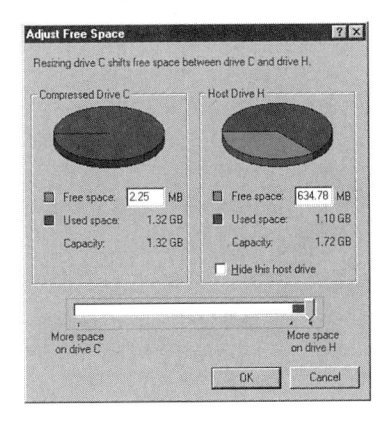

Fig. 44.8 All the free space has been given to drive H.

Notice with all free space given to drive H there is almost no space available on compressed drive C. This setting may not be very useful, so you may want to choose a balanced setting by dragging the slider to somewhere near the middle of the two drives.

A balanced setting allows drive C to continue operating normally, with enough free space to fill your immediate needs. With the slider set near the middle, you have more than 400M available on drive H. What can be done with those free megabytes? Before answering that question, choose OK to adjust the free space to the balanced setting somewhere near the middle.

Creating an Empty Compressed Drive

If you have space on your host drive left over after compression, you can compress this left-over space to form a new, empty, compressed drive that will hold much more than the left-over space would hold.

I said earlier that the free space on drive H can be used to create an empty, compressed drive. When you do this, you turn the more than 400M in the example drive into much more free space.

From the DriveSpace 3 window, highlight the drive H. Then choose Advanced, Create Empty.

You can take 485M of free space from drive H and create a new compressed drive D (pick any free drive letter). Based on the average, default compression ratio of 2:1 used for estimates by DriveSpace 3, the new, empty, compressed drive D contains 969M of free space.

Figure 44.9 shows the Create a New Compressed Drive dialog box. In this dialog box, you can choose the name for the new drive using the Create a New Drive Named drop-down list to choose any available drive letter.

You can also choose how much of the free space on the host drive to use for your new, empty, compressed drive by changing the space shown in the Using text box.

Tip: Don't use so much space on the host drive it runs out of space entirely.

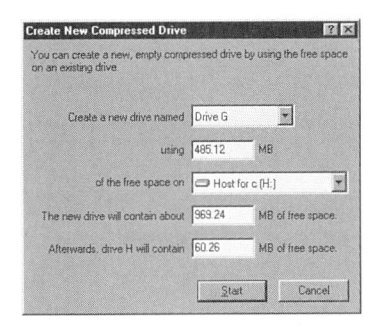

Fig. 44.9 You can create a new compressed drive from the free space on the drive H.

When you're ready to create a new, empty, compressed drive, choose Start. The host drive is checked for errors, and if any are found they will be fixed automatically if possible. Then the new compressed drive is created.

After the drive is created, double-click it in the DriveSpace 3 window, and you see your new drive's Properties sheet (see figure 44.10).

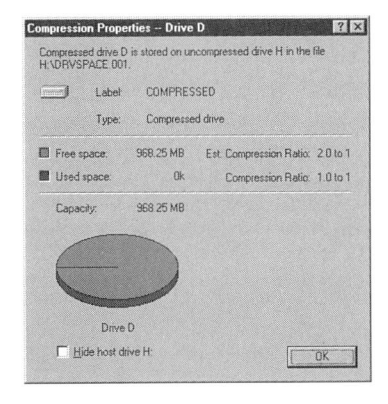

Fig. 44.10 You can see the compression properties of your new, empty, compressed drive.

Adjusting DriveSpace 3's Settings   **1139**

Drive D, like drive C, is stored on drive H, and all the drive D files are compressed into the DRVSPACE.001 file.

Choosing the Type of Compression

When DriveSpace 3 created your compressed drive C, it used the Standard compression file format. DriveSpace 3 can instead compress your files using the HiPack format. HiPack compression improves the speed at which your files are compressed and decompressed by using an improved lookup algorithm.

From the DriveSpace 3 window, choose Advanced, Settings. The Disk Compression Settings dialog box tells you that your files are compressed in the Standard format. If you have a Pentium microprocessor, you may want to use the Pentium-optimized code used for HiPack compression. To compress your files with HiPack, choose HiPack compression and then choose OK.

Working with Compression Agent

Compression Agent works in the background to ensure that your compressed drive is always in its most efficient state of compression. You won't have to perform analyses of your compression ratios and make adjustments to optimize your drive's compression.

Now that you have DriveSpace 3 installed and configured, you can use Compression Agent to gain more free space and make the files on your drives compress more efficiently. Using Compression Agent speeds up uncompressing files for use by applications.

To start Compression Agent, open the Start menu and choose Programs, Accessories, System Tools, Compression Agent.

When Compression Agent first starts, it asks you which compressed drive you want to work with. In this example, we'll continue with drive C. Next, you'll see the Compression Agent dialog box, and you'll have to make some choices before Compression Agent goes to work (see figure 44.11).

Choose the Settings button in the Compression Agent dialog box. Compression Agent lets you UltraPack your files. The UltraPack format gives the best compression, but your system accesses UltraPacked files more slowly than Standard compressed files.

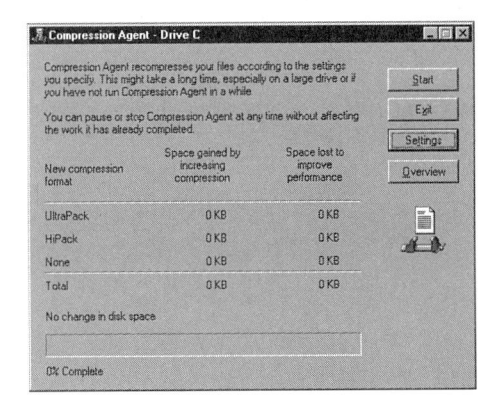

Fig. 44.11 Compression Agent is ready to run for the first time.

You can choose to UltraPack none or all of your files, or you can choose the default, which uses UltraPack on all files not accessed within the last 30 days. If you choose the default method, you can change the threshold value, from 1 to 999 days.

To choose the default, mark the UltraPack Only Files Not Used Within the Last 30 Days check box. To choose not to use UltraPack at all, mark the Do Not UltraPack Any Files check box. To UltraPack everything, mark the UltraPack All Files check box.

Working with Compression Agent **1141**

If you choose not to UltraPack anything or to UltraPack files based on date of last use, you have to decide how and if to compress the rest of your files that are not set to be UltraPacked.

You can choose to HiPack the rest of your files or leave them uncompressed. To HiPack the rest of your files, mark the Yes check box. To leave the rest of your files uncompressed, mark the No, Store Them Uncompressed check box.

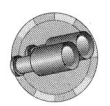

> **Note:** When you use Compression Agent on your compressed disk, the Standard compression format is no longer used. You can choose no compression, HiPack compression, or UltraPack compression.
>
> Remember, HiPack compression works best on Pentium computers.

Compression Agent Exceptions

In working with the Compression Agent Settings in the last section, you chose what compression method to use for certain groups of files. You can also choose how to compress particular files, folders, or types of files. The files and folders handled outside the rules set by Compression Agent Settings are called exceptions. To begin working with exceptions, choose the Exceptions button on the Compression Agent dialog box. Then on the Exceptions dialog box, choose Add. You'll see the Add Exceptions dialog box (see figure 44.12).

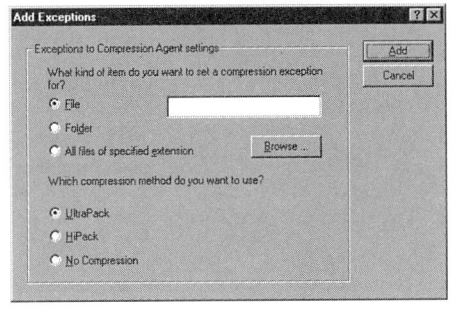

Fig. 44.12 Use the Add Exceptions dialog box to choose files to compress with special rules.

To choose a file as a compression exception, mark the File option button and enter the file name in the text box. You can also browse for the file you want with the Browse button. Next, choose how you want to compress the file. You can choose from UltraPack, HiPack, or No Compression. When you've chosen the file name and compression method, choose Add.

1. Choose either a file, folder, or file extension to compress. You can browse for a file name using the Browse button.

2. Choose the type of compression you want: UltraPack, HiPack, or No Compression.

3. Choose Add. Continue adding as many exceptions as you want. When you are finished adding exceptions, choose OK.

> **Tip:** To maximize system speed, choose all EXE and DLL files as exceptions and specify No Compression for them.

Advanced Compression Agent Settings

You may have told Compression Agent to use settings that reduce the free space on your drive. When you started Compression Agent for the first time, all your files were compressed using the Standard format. If you told Compression Agent that you didn't want to HiPack the rest of your files in "Working with Compression Agent," they were stored uncompressed. To do this, they are uncompressed by Compression Agent. This reduces the space available on drive C. To make sure you don't run out of disk space on drive C because you told Compression Agent to uncompress some files, choose the A_d_vanced button from the Compression Agent Settings dialog box, which displays the Advanced Settings dialog box (see figure 44.13).

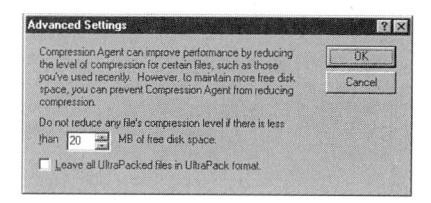

Fig. 44.13 The Advanced Settings dialog box prevents you from running out of space.

In its default, Advanced Settings does not uncompress any files if there are less than 20M free on the drive. You can change this value by entering the threshold megabyte size in the scroll box. Then, choose OK. If you want to leave all UltraPack files in UltraPack format regardless of how long it has been since they were accessed, check the Leave All UltraPacked Files in UltraPack Format check box.

When you've finished working with Compression Agent Settings, choose OK.

Running Compression Agent for the First Time

When you've configured Compression Agent settings, you'll be back at the Compression Agent dialog box seen in figure 44.11. Now, choose Start to have Compression Agent recompress your drive to match the settings you've chosen.

The recompression may take a long time. You may stop Compression Agent anytime. When you restart it, Compression Agent picks up right where it left off. No work is lost by stopping or pausing Compression Agent.

When Compression Agent has finished running, you see a report telling you how much space was gained through HiPack and UltraPack and how much space was lost because of the files you expanded.

Scheduling Compression Agent

The most useful way to use Compression Agent is to run it at a time you're not using your computer. To do this, you use System Agent and schedule Compression Agent to run at a time that is most convenient. The most convenient time may be at your lunch or late at night. System Agent gives you the flexibility to choose when, and how often, to run Compression Agent. The more frequently you run Compression Agent, the less time it takes to do its job. To learn how to schedule Compression Agent with System Agent, see Chapter 43, "System Agent."

Understanding DriveSpace 3's Memory Requirements

DriveSpace 3 uses about 150K of memory below 640K. The 150K is used by the DriveSpace 3 device driver and once you install DriveSpace 3 there is no way to eliminate this memory use. While this is not a problem for Windows applications and should not be a problem for

DOS applications running in a window or full-screen under Windows 95, it can be a problem when you run programs in MS-DOS mode. For information on MS-DOS mode, see Chapter 19, "Fine-Tuning Windows 95 for Your DOS Applications."

If you are running DOS applications or games that need over 500K of memory, and you are running them in MS-DOS mode, you may have a problem using DriveSpace 3. To work around this, set up your CONFIG.SYS file using HIMEM.SYS and EMM386.SYS. Also, set DOS=UMB and DOS=HIGH. Then use MEMMAKER.EXE to load as many of your startup files into the UMB area as possible. This may free up enough conventional memory so that your DOS application or game runs. Optimizing memory with MEMMAKER.EXE does not affect system performance under Windows 95.

> **Note:** If you installed Windows 95 as a stand-alone product rather than an upgrade to DOS and Windows 3.x, your system might lack a copy of MEMMAKER.EXE. If so, you must manually load the DriveSpace 3 compression driver in high memory. You do so in your CONFIG.SYS file, which is in the root directory of your boot disk.
>
> ```
> Insert the following three lines in your
> CONFIG.SYS file:
>
> DEVICE=C: \WINDOWS\HIMEM.SYS
>
> DEVICE=C:\WINDOWS\EMM386.EXE RAM NOEMS
>
> DEVICEHIGH=C:\WINDOWS\COMMAND\DRVSPACE>SYS /MOVE
>
> When you reboot your system, you'll be loading 113K
> compression driver into high memory, which will allow DOS
> programs that are memory hungry to run properly.
> ```

Desktop Additions

KILLER 45 WINDOWS 95

by Gordon Meltzer

Microsoft Plus! is a collection of utility groups. Not all the programs in Microsoft Plus! are productivity oriented. Some are just for fun, and to make using your computer a more relaxed experience. The Desktop Additions group of utilities contains programs to make Windows more fun to use by making it more visually attractive, and it also contains a great game, 3D Pinball. This game, besides being fun to play, is a programming tour-de-force. If Windows 95 is the family car, Desktop Additions make it look like the newest creation from the Ferrari factory.

The Desktop Additions group of utilities consists of separate programs in three groups: Desktop themes, 3D Pinball Game, and Visual Enhancements.

In this chapter, you cover the following:

- ➤ Visual enhancements Microsoft Plus! gives your system's desktop
- ➤ Various desktop themes in Microsoft Plus!
- ➤ Microsoft Plus! 3D Pinball

Installing Desktop Additions

To get started working with the desktop additions, install Microsoft Plus!. To do this, insert your Microsoft Plus! CD-ROM or setup disk, and run the Setup program for Plus!. Choose Custom Setup when prompted, and you will see a dialog box with an options list similar to the one shown in figure 45.1. Place check marks beside the boxes titled Desktop Themes, 3D Pinball, and Visual Enhancements. Then choose Continue.

After Setup checks for enough free disk space to install the options you have chosen, Desktop Additions will be installed. Finally, Setup will ask you to restart your computer. When you restart, installation of Desktop Additions will be complete.

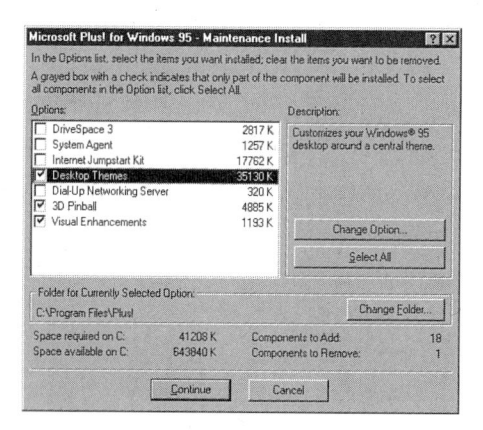

Fig. 45.1 Check these three items in Plus! custom setup to install Desktop Additions.

The disk space requirements for Desktop Additions are pretty extensive. Desktop Themes, if all themes are installed, uses 35M of disk space. 3D Pinball uses 4.5M, and the Visual Enhancements, if all are installed, uses about 1M.

The best approach to take in determining which of these modules to install is to install them all, if you have the space. Then, read the sections that follow, explaining Themes and Visual Enhancements. Get an understanding of what each theme does, and learn whether you can use each theme on your system. Next, experiment on your system. Try the Themes and Enhancements. It is easy to delete the ones you do not want, to reclaim lots of disk space.

If you decide to delete one of the Plus! modules, use the Control Panel. Then, choose Add/Remove Programs. Highlight Microsoft Plus! in the list of installed programs, and choose Add/Remove. When the Plus! setup dialog appears, choose Add/Remove. Put a check next to any modules you want to remove, and choose OK.

Visual Enhancements

The first thing you will notice after the installation of Desktop Additions is complete is the Visual Enhancements. As you begin to use your computer, your desktop and windows operate a bit differently and you will have access to new features that you will learn about in the next sections.

Full-Window Drag

Normally, when you move a window on your screen to a new position, the process works like this:

1. You choose a window to which you want to relocate.
2. You click the title bar of the chosen window and move your mouse toward the destination location for the window.
3. At the moment the window starts to move, the contents of the window disappear, and all that you see moving across your screen is an outline of the window.
4. When the outline of the window is in the destination location on-screen, you release the mouse button. The window contents reappear, inside the outline.

With Full-Window Drag enabled, the outline of the windows is not all you see, as you start to move the window across the screen. Instead, the entire window (with contents) moves as directed by your pointing device. This simple enhancement is very versatile. It is especially useful when the position of a window is critical. Seeing the contents of the window as it moves across the screen enables much more accurate window placement than working with the window outline alone.

Full-Window Drag is the kind of enhancement that you will appreciate every time you use your computer, because it seems to eliminate eyestrain. Moving a window complete with its contents across the screen is a natural mode of operation, and you will immediately see what a mediocre mode of operation outline dragging was.

The enhanced functionality of Full-Window Drag is not free. Like all the enhancements in the Microsoft Plus! product, there is a cost in processor cycles, which translates to a performance hit. With Full-Window Drag, the performance hit is minimal if your video card uses an accelerator chip. Using an accelerator on the card (such as an ATI Mach chip, or any of the S3 or Weitek video chips and others) transfers much of the processing burden required to move the image across the screen from the system CPU to the accelerator on the video card. If, however, your video card is not an accelerator, but simply a frame buffer, you will see a noticeable system slowdown when you are doing a Full-Screen Drag. Examples of the nonaccelerated, or minimally accelerated, video chips are the popular Tseng Labs ET4000 and the early Cirrus Logic chips.

Font Smoothing

Since Windows made the graphical user interface popular, users have been confronted with the *jaggies*. This well-known phenomenon shows up by making jagged edges on large fonts on-screen. You won't see jagged edges in the small fonts of menu bars and dialog boxes, but if you work with type sizes more than 24 points in your word processor, or in a page layout program, you've seen the jaggies.

In the past, users just had to put up with the jaggies. One video card maker, ATI, incorporated a proprietary technology in its Windows video drivers to reduce the jagged edges of screen fonts. This technology, which proved incompatible with many leading application programs, was called *Crystal Fonts*.

Microsoft has taken a font smoothing utility and integrated it into the Windows 95 operating system. This system-level integration of the smoothing feature ensures the smoothing technology is compatible with all Windows applications.

To put font smoothing to work, you must have a video card and monitor that can run in *High Color mode*. High Color mode is sometimes called *16-bit Color mode*, and sometimes called *64,000 Color mode*.

You must set your system to display in High Color mode to use Font Smoothing. To set up High Color display mode, follow these steps:

1. Right-click on an empty space on your desktop. A pop-up menu will appear.
2. Choose Properties from the list of choices.
3. Choose the Settings tab from the Display Properties sheet.
4. In the scroll list under Color palette, choose High Color.
5. Click OK to exit the dialog box.

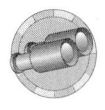

> **Note:** Font Smoothing requires at least High Color mode. It will also work in display modes with more color than High Color. In fact, Font Smoothing works best at 24-bit and 32-bit True Color modes.

Your system will now be in High Color mode. Before you enable Font Smoothing, look at some large text on-screen. The example shown in figure 45.2 is 132-point text. You can see the jagged edges on the fonts anywhere there is a curve in the shape of a letter. With Font Smoothing enabled, however, the jaggies are gone!

Visual Enhancements **1151**

Fig. 45.2 Before Font Smoothing, text looked jagged, like this.

To turn on Font Smoothing and make on-screen text look clean and sharp, follow these steps:

1. Right-click on an empty place on your desktop. A dialog box will appear.
2. Choose Properties from the list of choices.
3. Choose the Plus! page.
4. Put a check in the box called Smooth Edges of Screen Fonts.
5. Click OK to enable Font Smoothing. You will not have to restart your computer for smoothing to take effect.

The Plus! page dialog box for steps 4 and 5 is shown in figure 45.3.

How Font Smoothing Works

Font Smoothing looks like magic on-screen, but it uses a simple science to operate. Suppose that, as is usually true, your text is black and your background is white. The text is formed of black pixels which are square-like dots of a certain size. Because the letters are formed of these rather square-like dots, lining them up in a curve, as seen in all the letters with curves, results in a jagged collection of black dots, not a smooth line.

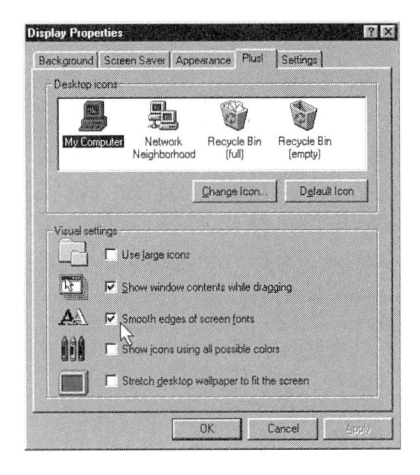

Fig. 45.3 Use the Display Properties Plus! page to enable Font Smoothing.

Because your monitor can have only about 72 of these dots per inch of screen space, the effect is amplified.

Font Smoothing fills in the white spaces, located between the jagged black squares, with barely visible intermediate shades of gray. These shades of gray are also made of square-like dots, but because they are halfway between paper-white and text-black, they blend in to make it seem as if the fonts are smooth. Font Smoothing is really an optical illusion, because if you look at the smoothed fonts on-screen really closely, or with a magnifying glass, you can see the gray dots all along the curved edges of the letters. The closer you look at the letters, the fuzzier the gray dots make the text look. At normal viewing distance, the letters look really sharp and clean, especially when you are used to looking at the jaggies.

Font Smoothing uses memory to calculate and display its dots. If your system is low on memory, you may want to turn off Font Smoothing. Try it, and see if it works for you as well as the Microsoft Plus! designers intended.

Enhanced MS-DOS Font

When you run a DOS window under Windows 95, you have a choice of fonts to use within the window. Windows 95 offers a selection of choices from both single size bitmapped fonts and scaleable True Type fonts.

There are eight bitmapped fonts supplied for use at the DOS prompt with Windows, and a single True Type font, which is available in an eight scale size.

While the bitmapped fonts are clear and easy to read, the True Type font supplied for the DOS box is thin and not very legible at any size.

Microsoft Plus! fixes that problem by including a special True Type font, called *Lucida*, and installing Lucida for use at the command prompt. When you have installed Desktop Additions, True Type Lucida becomes available for your use in DOS boxes.

Lucida is a clearer font than the standard Windows 95 DOS font, and you can scale it to a larger size. When you have installed Lucida (the enhanced MS-DOS font), you will have a choice of 16 different sizes. Figure 45.4 shows how clear Lucida appears in a DOS box under Windows 95, with Microsoft Plus! installed.

Animated Pointers

Windows 95 comes with a selection of mouse pointers, in addition to the standard arrow pointer, hourglass, and insertion bar that were included with Windows 3.x. Windows 95 supplies some dual purpose pointers that were inherited from Windows NT. Windows 95 comes with a Working in the Background pointer, which is half pointer arrow and half hourglass. Windows 95 also introduces a new type of mouse pointer, the animated pointer. Windows 95 comes with only one type of animated pointer, an animated hourglass that drops grains of sand, and spins, as you wait for Windows to finish a task.

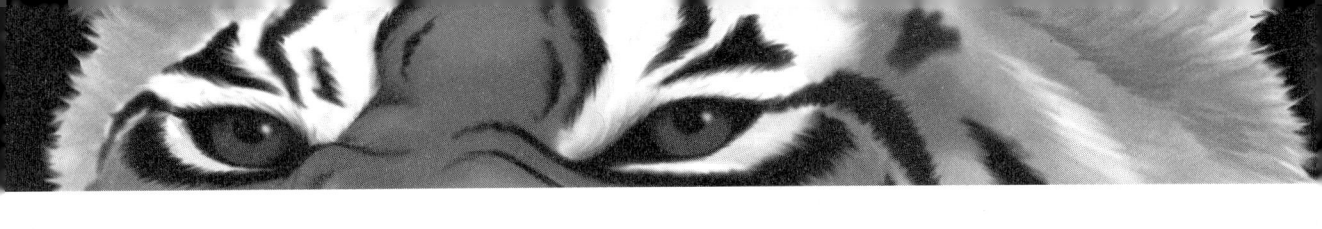

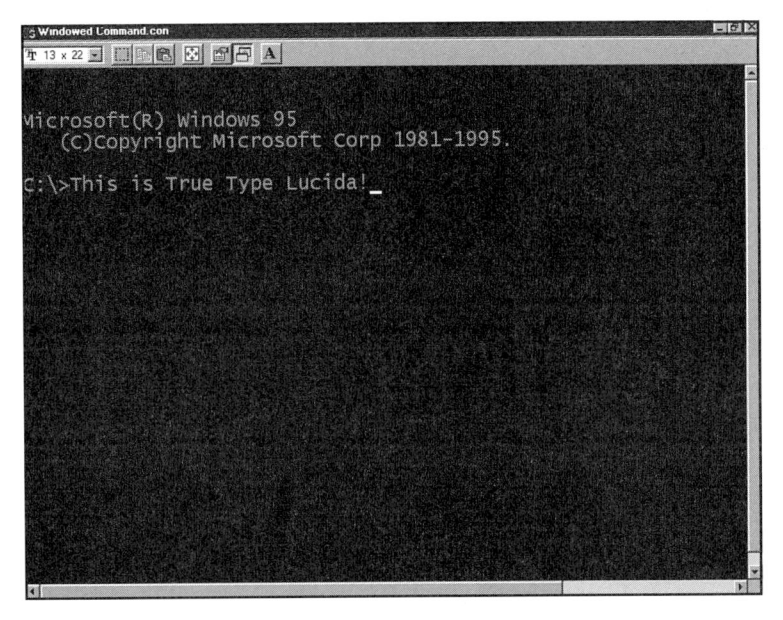

Fig. 45.4 Desktop Additions includes Lucida, the Enhanced MS-DOS Font.

You can see the animated hourglass by using Control Panel, Mouse, and choosing the Pointers page. Then, in the Scheme scroll box, scroll down and select Animated Hourglasses, as shown in figure 45.5. When you highlight the Busy pointer, the hourglass will perform its movements in a demonstration of the Animated Pointers feature.

The little spinning hourglass pales in comparison to the animated pointers included with Microsoft Plus!. You will learn about those animations in Desktop Themes, later in this chapter.

You can install an animated cursor without installing an entire desktop theme. To do this, follow these steps:

1. Use Control Panel, then double-click on Mouse.

2. Choose the Pointers page.

3. Highlight the cursor you want to replace with an animated cursor. Then, choose Browse.

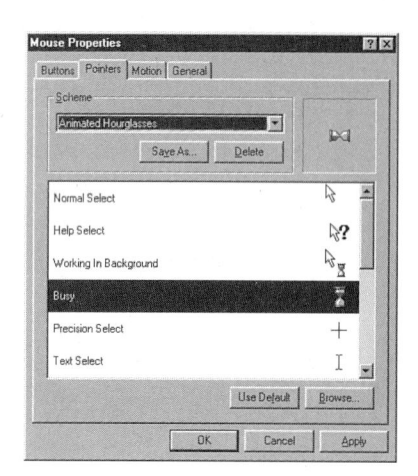

Fig. 45.5 Animated Pointers is a fun feature of Windows 95.

4. Using the browse tools, display the folder called C:\Program Files\Plus!\Themes. You'll see a large number of animated cursors displayed.

5. Highlight a cursor you'd like to use. When you highlight the cursor, you'll see an animated preview.

6. If you want to use the cursor you're previewing, choose Open, then choose OK.

If your animated pointers do not animate, check the following situations. Each of these situations is a potential cause for animated pointers that just do not move:

➤ If you have Windows 3.x remote control software installed, such as PC Anywhere or Laplink for Windows, you will lose your animated pointers.

➤ If you are using a video driver set to less than 256 colors, you will lose your animated pointers. Set the driver to at least 256 colors to make the animated pointers work.

Chapter 45: Desktop Additions

- If you are using an ATI Mach 8 Ultra, a Diamond Viper, or a VGA or Microsoft Super VGA video driver, your animated pointers will not animate.

- Finally, make sure that you are using 32-bit protected mode disk drivers. To check, use Control Panel, System, and choose the Performance tab. Then, choose File System, Troubleshooting. Make sure that Disable All 32 Bit Protect-mode Disk Drivers is NOT checked.

High Color Icons

The normal icons that Windows 95 scatters all over your desktop are VGA compatible, 16-color icons. They look the same on the lowliest 16-color VGA system as they do on a high-end true color graphics workstation. These default Windows 95 icons are all stored in two files called SHELL32.DLL and EXPLORER.EXE, which are found in your \WINDOWS\SYSTEM folder.

Microsoft Plus! Desktop Additions aims to eliminate the 16-color doldrums by supplying a collection of High Color icons you can use to replace the default set. The Microsoft programmers tell what they think of High Color icons by the name they gave the file that holds the High Color icons. It's called COOL.DLL, and you can also find it in the \WINDOWS\SYSTEM folder.

To use High Color icons, you first need to have a display card and monitor that is capable of displaying High Color, which is 64,000 on-screen colors at a time. High Color is also called 16-bit color. If your system is so equipped, use Control Panel, Display, and then click the Plus! page. Put a check in the box called Show Icons Using All Possible Colors. Then, click OK. You will have to restart your computer for the High Color icons to appear. The change is subtle, but it is a building block that adds to the overall polished effect of Desktop Additions.

While you are working with High Color icons, you can use the COOL.DLL file to change the default icons used for:

Visual Enhancements **1157**

- My Computer
- Network Neighborhood
- Recycle Bin (full)
- Recycle Bin (empty)

To change these icons, use Control Panel, Display, and choose the Plus! page, shown earlier in the chapter in figure 45.4. Highlight one of the four default icons shown in the preceding list. Highlight whichever icon you want to change first. Then, choose Change Icon, Browse. You can choose icons from EXPLORER.EXE, SHELL32.DLL, or COOL.DLL, by browsing for those file names, highlighting the file name, and choosing Open. Next, you will see a dialog box called Change Icon, similar to the one shown in figure 45.6. In this dialog box, you can choose an icon to replace one of the four in the preceding list.

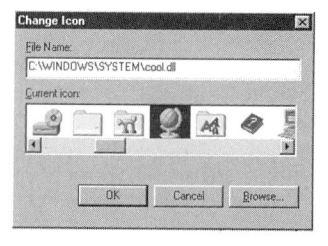

Fig. 45.6 Use the Change Icon dialog box to replace one of the major desktop icons.

Large Icons

Microsoft Plus! Desktop Additions contains a set of large icons you can use to replace the standard desktop icons. This set will be useful if you are running your screen at a very high resolution, 1024×768 pixel or higher. At those high resolutions, the normal icons supplied with Windows 95 are very small, and can be hard to interpret.

Another use for the large icons supplied with the Plus! product is to help a visually challenged user see the screen more clearly.

To enable large icons, use Control Panel, Display, and choose the Plus! page. Then, put a check in the box called Use Large Icons. Next, click OK. The icons on your desktop, and all through your system, will become twice as large as they were.

Figure 45.7 shows Control Panel with standard icons, and figure 45.8 shows Control Panel with the large icons that come with Desktop Additions.

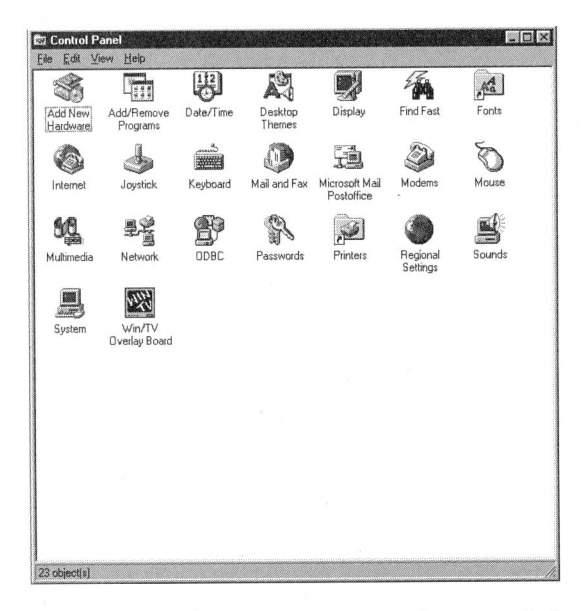

Fig. 45.7 Control Panel shown with Windows 95 default icons.

If you have installed Large Icons, some of the icons on your desktop may look very jagged and unclear. These icons come from programs whose maker has not supplied Windows 95 with compatible large icons. You can either contact the program's publisher for an update or stop using large icons.

Visual Enhancements **1159**

Fig. 45.8 Control Panel shown with large icons from Microsoft Plus!.

Taskbar Auto Hide

Desktop Additions includes two other minor enhancements. The first of these has no name, and is not even documented, but it adds polish to the operating system. If you set your taskbar to Auto Hide (Start button, Settings, Taskbar, Auto Hide), the taskbar will be hidden until you pass your mouse pointer over it; then, it will pop into visible position.

After you install Desktop Additions, the behavior of the taskbar is altered. When you pass your mouse pointer over the hidden taskbar, it will not pop into place, instead, it will gently glide into place. And when you move your pointer off the taskbar, it will gracefully retract into its hidden state. This little enhancement adds polish to the operating environment.

To enable this enhancement, use the Start button, then choose Settings, Taskbar. Check the Auto hide box, and choose OK.

Wallpaper Stretching

The last Visual Enhancement provided by Plus! is wallpaper stretching. Before the Plus! product, your options were to display desktop wallpaper bitmap files at original size, or tiled to fill the screen with repetitive displays. Plus! adds the option to stretch a single bitmap image to fill the entire screen.

To enable desktop wallpaper stretching, use Control Panel, Display, Plus!, and put a check in the box called Stretch Desktop Wallpaper to Fit the Screen. The Plus! dialog box for this operation is shown in figure 45.3, earlier in this chapter.

Desktop Themes

Desktop Themes is the heart of Desktop Additions. Themes are collections of screen elements, all installed together, based around a central theme.

The screen elements that are linked together to form themes are:

- Screen saver
- Sound events
- Mouse pointers
- Desktop wallpaper
- Icons
- Colors of fonts, menu bars, and all other screen elements
- Font names and styles
- Font and window sizes

When you install a Desktop Theme, every visual and sound element of your environment will change, to match the feeling of the theme.

Microsoft Plus! ships with the following themes:

- Dangerous Creatures

- Inside Your Computer (High Color)
- Leonardo da Vinci
- More Windows (High Color)
- Mystery (High Color)
- Nature (High Color)
- Science
- Sports
- The 60's USA
- The Golden Era (High Color)
- Travel (High Color)
- Windows 95

Each theme is only a starting point for you to customize the look, feel, and sound of your system. You can install a theme, then choose to change settings for any or all of the screen elements. You can mix and match elements of any theme with elements of another. For example, if you install the Travel theme, you may want to remove the mouse pointers that are part of Travel, and replace them with the nifty set of pointers from the Science theme. It is easy to get started with Desktop Themes. Each theme is a radical departure from the standard Windows blue-gray-white look and feel.

Starting with Themes

To install your first desktop theme, use Control Panel, Desktop Themes. You will see a screen similar to the one shown in figure 45.9.

In the scroll bar called Themes, choose a theme that appeals to you, and that is compatible with your video display.

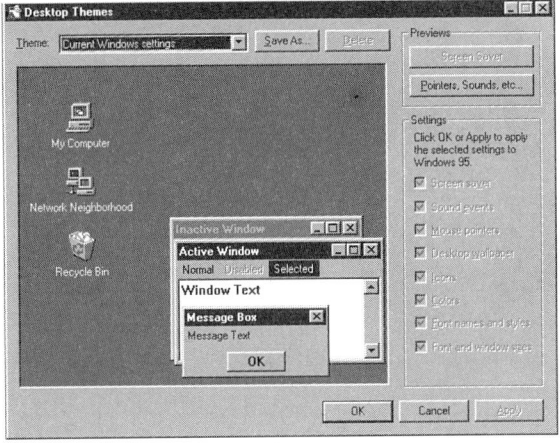

Fig. 45.9 Use the Desktop Themes dialog box to choose and customize a theme.

> **Note:** To use Desktop Themes, you must have your display driver set to use 256 or more colors. Some of the themes will not even work at 256 colors, and some will require (at minimum) a High Color driver to properly display. The themes that require a High Color display driver are listed in the preceding section followed by "(High Color)."

When you have highlighted the theme you want to try, click OK. For this example, choose the Dangerous Creatures theme. When you have highlighted the theme you want, in the Theme scroll box, the Desktop Themes dialog box changes to display the elements of your selected theme. This preview display, shown in figure 45.10, enables you to examine some of the properties of the theme you have selected, without actually installing it in your system.

Desktop Themes **1163**

Fig. 45.10 The Desktop Themes dialog box shows the elements of the Dangerous Creatures theme.

Previewing Theme Elements

You can see the desktop wallpaper, some new icons, and some dialog box fonts and styles in figure 45.11. You cannot see the screen saver that belongs to the theme, and you cannot see the animated pointers and sound events that belong to the theme. But the Desktop Themes dialog box provides gateways to preview the screen saver and the pointers and sounds.

To see the screen saver associated with the Dangerous Creatures theme, choose the Screen Saver button in the Desktop Themes dialog box. When you choose the button, your entire screen turns into a preview of the screen saver that is part of the Dangerous Creatures theme. This screen saver for Dangerous Creatures consists of swimming sting rays, floating bubbles, and gurgling sounds from an associated WAV file.

You can preview the mouse pointers associated with your selected theme, and preview the theme's sound events by choosing Pointers, Sounds, and so on, from the Desktop Themes dialog box. Then, the

Preview Dangerous Creatures dialog box will appear. Choose the Pointers page to see all the mouse pointers associated with the Dangerous Creatures theme.

In each Desktop Theme, some of the mouse pointers are going to be animated, and these are cleverly done. In Dangerous Creatures, the Working in Background pointer, normally represented by Windows' familiar arrow/hourglass icon, has changed to a color animation of a bee flying, complete with red wings and a yellow, striped body.

To hear a preview of the sounds associated with system events, choose the Sounds page, in the Preview Dangerous Creatures dialog box. The sounds chosen for this theme range from lions roaring (exit Windows) to a rattlesnake's rattle (program error). The programming of sounds is, at the least, creative.

When you have finished exploring the previews, click Close.

Running the Theme

When you have satisfied yourself that you do, in fact, want to inundate your desktop with a Desktop Theme, click OK from the Desktop Themes dialog box. In just a few seconds, you will be living amongst the Dangerous Creatures.

Screen Saver Hot Spots

Third-party screen savers have had hot spots for years. When you put your mouse pointer on a hot spot, the saver will either activate immediately, or not activate at all, depending on what kind of hot spot you have chosen. Now, Windows 95 has hot spots in screen savers.

In an example of Plus! components working together, you can only use hot spots if you have installed System Agent. This hot spot function relies on part of the SAGE.EXE scheduler for its engine. See Chapter 43, "System Agent," for more on SAGE.EXE.

To activate hot spots on your Plus! screen saver, use Control Panel, Display, Screen Saver. Then, choose Settings. In the Screen Saver Properties sheet, shown in figure 45.11, you can place a check mark in a corner of the screen. The check mark makes the corner act as a hot spot to activate the screen saver immediately. If you put a dot in a corner of the screen, the screen saver will never display, as long as your mouse pointer rests on that hot spot on-screen.

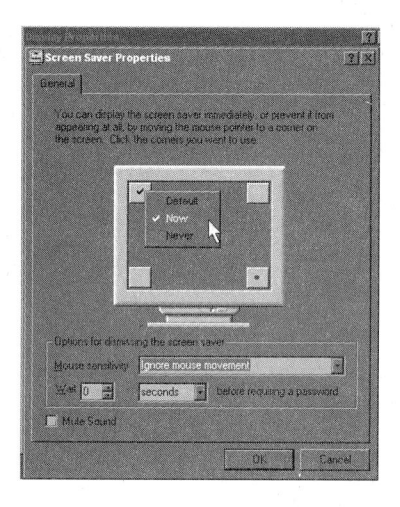

Fig. 45.11 You can select which corner to place your screen saver hot spot.

3D Pinball

When you have thoroughly explored all the Desktop Themes that come with Microsoft Plus!, it is time for a refreshing graphics game. Before Windows 95, you played PC action games in DOS. The game programmers needed the free-for-all DOS environment for their programming. They needed to interact directly with the video hardware in your computer, in order to make their games seem realistically fast and action packed.

Windows was never a good environment for game programmers. Windows graphics were too slow, and programmers working in Windows could not interact directly with the hardware. What games there were for Windows could never be described as action-packed.

Some time in 1994, Microsoft released a set of DLL and related files designed to make it possible for game programmers to work in Windows and still achieve acceptably fast graphics. Few have risen to the challenge up to this point. In fact, the Hover game that Microsoft wrote and shipped with Windows 95 has been the fastest game available for Windows. Then came 3D Pinball.

The programmers at Maxis wrote 3D Pinball for Microsoft. Only you can decide whether Hover, or Pinball, is the current Windows game champ. 3D Pinball is a very realistic simulation game. The programmers have achieved, in virtual form, an amazing degree of similarity to the functioning of a real pinball machine.

While the 3D in the game's name may come from the elevated ramps on the game's playing board, the three dimensionality is not the source of the game's most chilling realism.

The programmers have managed to duplicate, in code, the exact behavior of a metal pinball, as it hits thumper-bumpers and is sent flying; as the ball caroms off stretched rubber loops propelled by solenoid powered strikers, and as it sits, bouncing ever so slightly on rubber loop covered flippers, waiting to be sent back to the top of the board.

The degree of realism, in terms of ball behavior, in this simulation is totally uncanny. The sound effects are also pretty realistic. If you have ever played a real, mechanical pinball machine, you will be amazed. And, you may not go back to work for a long time.

Figure 45.12 shows the Pinball game table, but cannot begin to do justice to this awesome toy.

Fig. 45.12 3D Pinball is a very realistic pinball machine game included in Microsoft Plus!.

The sophisticated sound effects in Pinball have trouble with some Soundblaster clone sound cards. If you are having sound problems with 3D Pinball, run the program WMCONFIG.EXE. It is in the \Program Files\Plus!\Pinball folder.

When WMCONFIG is running, choose your sound card from the list shown in the scroll box. If your card is not shown by name, choose Generic Option One, and then choose Test. If the sounds are still not the way you want them, choose Generic Option Two, and so on, until you like the way that Pinball sounds.

Internet Explorer and Jumpstart Kit

KILLER 46 WINDOWS 95

by Benjamin F. Miller

The simplest way to connect to the Internet is by using the Internet Explorer. The Internet Explorer is a Web Browser that is part of Microsoft Plus! and is based on Spry's groundbreaking Mosaic Web Browser. Spry's Mosaic was the first Web Browser to catapult the world onto the Web, and set the standard for Internet browsers to come. The Internet Explorer makes it easy to get onto and surf the World Wide Web. Because the Explorer is designed as a Windows 95 application from the ground up, it takes full advantage of the advanced file management utilities and usability features of Windows 95.

In this chapter, you'll learn how to do the following:

➤ Use the Internet Setup Wizard

➤ Connect to the Internet with Internet Explorer

➤ Change Internet Explorer properties

- Use Internet Explorer with the Microsoft Network
- Use Internet Explorer to take full advantage of Windows 95. 2

Using the Internet Setup Wizard

When you install Microsoft Plus!, one of your options is Internet tools. When Microsoft Plus! has finished installing, it will place an Internet Tools folder inside your Accessories folder. To get to that folder, open Start menu, choose Accessories, and then Internet Tools. From there you'll have the option of either accessing the Internet Startup Wizard or Internet Explorer. Choose Internet Startup Wizard to begin configuring Internet Explorer. (See figure 46.1.) To get on the Internet by using the Internet Explorer, you need to do one of three things: establish an Internet Service provider, obtain a Microsoft Network account, or establish a LAN-based TCP/IP connection. Once that's done, you'll have the connectivity in place to get on the Web.

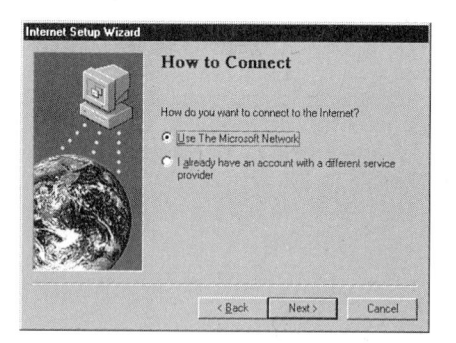

Fig. 46.1 The Internet Setup Wizard sets up your PC for the Internet.

The Setup Wizard is used to configure your dial-up Internet connection. The first question you're asked is whether you want to use the Microsoft Network as your Internet service provider or another service provider of your choice. The Internet Explorer will work with any Post

Office Protocol 3 (POP3) compliant Internet Service Provider. The Internet Setup Wizard will help you with whatever method you need in your particular setup. In the following section, you'll learn about the three different ways to access the Internet: via Microsoft Network, by using another Internet Service Provider, or through a local area network.

Connecting to the Internet Through Microsoft Network

If you choose the Microsoft Network as your service provider, you're asked if you're already a member of Microsoft Network. Whether or not you're a member, you see the Microsoft Network opening page. The opening page lets you know that the Internet Startup Wizard can identify Microsoft Network on your PC. Click on the connect button to log on. Microsoft Network is not required to use Internet Explorer to access the Web, but Microsoft has made it very easy to use Microsoft Network—setup requires only a few mouse clicks and you never have to worry about configuring TCP/IP networking.

Next, you'll see a dialog box that provides details on the Microsoft Network. After you click OK on the bottom of this dialog box, you'll see another dialog box that prompts you for your local area code.

Armed with your area code, the Internet Startup Wizard dials an 800 number that connects to a database that the Wizard searches for a local phone number you can connect to. Microsoft has set up local dial-up servers around the world so you don't have to call long distance to connect to either the Internet or the Microsoft Network. Once this has been done, Microsoft Exchange will be configured to call your local service number. Next, you'll see the Microsoft Network sign-on dialog box. If you're already a member, type in your name and password and press Connect. If you're using a different Internet Service Provider, you won't see any dialog box at all.

Using the Internet Setup Wizard **1171**

If you're the sole user of your computer, click on the box marked Remember My Password—it saves you the trouble of having to remember it. When Microsoft Network is finished researching your local access number, it automatically disconnects and displays a dialog box that offers you a choice of the best primary and backup phone numbers for your use. The backup number is used when you can't connect to the primary number.

There are a couple of telephone number access issues to keep in mind when using the Microsoft Network or any Internet Service provider to connect to the Internet:

- Access numbers change over time. If you use Microsoft Network regularly, the online service will notify you of phone number changes and even download the new numbers for you and automatically update your local database.

- The phone numbers you see listed will offer connection speeds from 9,600 to 28,800 bps. If the higher speed is offered in your area, take advantage of that phone number. If you upgrade your modem, you'll be able to take advantage of your faster modem without having to reconfigure your Internet connection. You will, however, have to make some changes to the Windows 95 modem control panel to take optimum advantage of your new modem. If you install one of the newer Plug-and-Play modems, Windows 95 will recognize the change in modems and make the configuration changes for you. Also, even with a slower modem, you'll be able to take advantage of the better data compression and error correction provided by those faster modems.

Now that your Internet connection has been configured, double-click on the Internet Explorer on your Windows 95 desktop and you'll be connected to the Internet. You can also drag the Internet Explorer icon onto the Start menu. This creates a shortcut to Internet Explorer on your Start menu so you can easily start it no matter what application you're in or where you are in Windows 95.

Connecting to the Internet Through a Service Provider

If you already have an Internet Service Provider and don't want to use the Microsoft network to connect to the Internet, click on the button `I already have an account with a different service provider` and then click on the Next button.

Later in the sign-up process you'll be asked questions about your service that you'll be able to answer only after you've contracted with that service. To connect to your service provider, you need to tell the Internet Setup Wizard the following:

- The name of your service provider
- IP address (if your service provider doesn't automatically assign it for you)
- The DNS address of your service provider
- Your Internet Service Provider's e-mail server [name]

If you are subscribing to a provider for the first time, don't use the Internet Setup Wizard to sign up.

Next, enter your Internet account name and password. If this is your first time using the Internet service, leave the password blank in case your Internet Service Provider assigns you a different password. This step will save you the trouble of having to change it later. Click on Next to continue.

The next dialog box, showing IP address, is very important. Depending on how your service provider configures itself, you may get an IP address you need to enter yourself. If this is the case, click on Always Use the Following and then enter the IP address in the IP Address box. If your service provider assigns an IP address each time you sign on, choose My Internet Service Provider Automatically Assigns Me One (see figure 46.2). This information will be given to you by your service provider when you first get an account. Most commercial Internet Service Providers use the latter method. Once you've entered the IP information, click on Next.

Using the Internet Setup Wizard **1173**

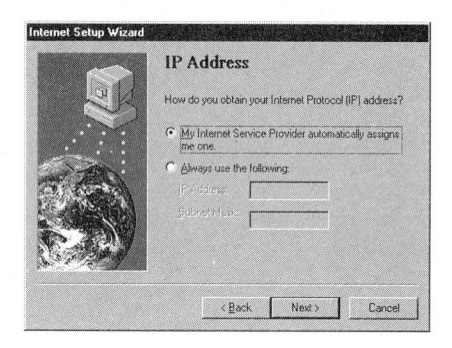

Fig. 46.2 Most Internet service providers automatically assign IP addresses.

You must also enter a DNS address for your service provider, which you need to obtain from your Internet Service Provider in advance. A standard DNS address comes in this format: 111.222.333.444 (see figure 46.3). Enter your DNS address and click on Next.

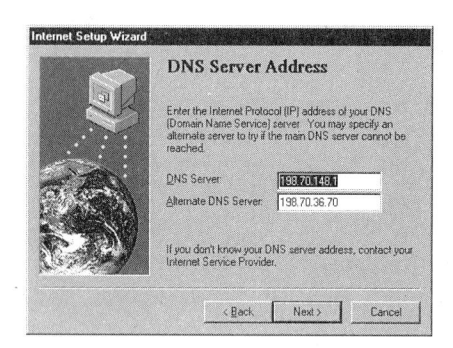

Fig. 46.3 Enter the DNS address in IP format.

The capability of sending and receiving e-mail is one of the most compelling reasons for getting on the Internet. Before you can send or receive e-mail, however, you must first enter the e-mail address assigned to you. You must also enter the name of your Internet Service Provider's e-mail server (see figure 46.4). If your provider assigns IP addresses dynamically, you may have to specifically request this information. Enter your service provider's e-mail address and the name of your Internet mail server and click on Next.

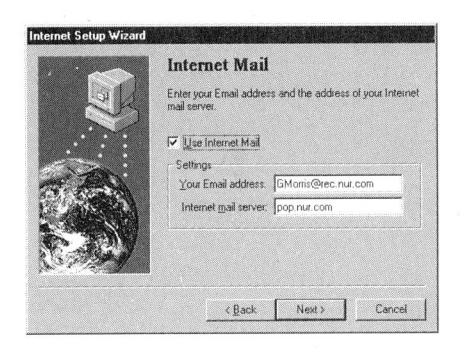

Fig. 46.4 You may have to specifically ask for the name of your Internet Service Provider's e-mail server.

You won't see anything about e-mail in the Internet Explorer; that will be handled by Exchange, Windows 95's universal inbox. The Internet Setup Wizard is just that, a place to configure Windows 95 to connect to the Internet. Although you're just going through the steps here to learn how to use the Internet Explorer, the Setup Wizard is a global routine for all the applications Windows 95 may use to communicate with the Internet.

Here are two tips to keep in mind when using your Internet e-mail:

➤ If you want to make any changes to your e-mail service later, choose Services (see figure 46.5) from the Exchange Tools menu, select the Internet Mail service, and click on the Properties button. You can use the Alt-T,V key combination to access your e-mail services.

➤ If you're using Microsoft Network as your Internet Service Provider, Microsoft Network Mail and Internet mail will be one and the same.

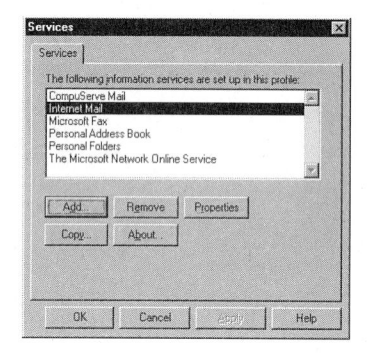

Fig. 46.5 Use Microsoft Exchange to send and configure your Internet mail.

The Internet Mail dialog box asks you to create an Exchange profile for your Internet mail. To create the profile, follow these instructions:

➤ Internet Mail is really useful only if you're attached to the Internet via a LAN or through an Internet Service Provider other than the Microsoft Network. The first filetab asks you for the name of your Internet server; that name usually looks something like "Microsoft.Com" and your user name and password. All of this information can be obtained from your network administrator or from your Internet Service Provider.

➤ The Connection tab configures your method for connecting to your Internet server, whether through modem or LAN.

➤ By clicking on the Schedule button on the bottom of this file tab, you can ask Exchange to look for your Internet mail at specified times. Perhaps even more helpful is the option to work off-line and use remote mail. Checking this box allows you to dial into your Internet server, see if there is mail waiting and, if so, determine the subject lines of your mail. You can then choose to download any or all of your messages. This feature can save you time and money if your Internet Service provider charges by the hour or if you're dialing long distance.

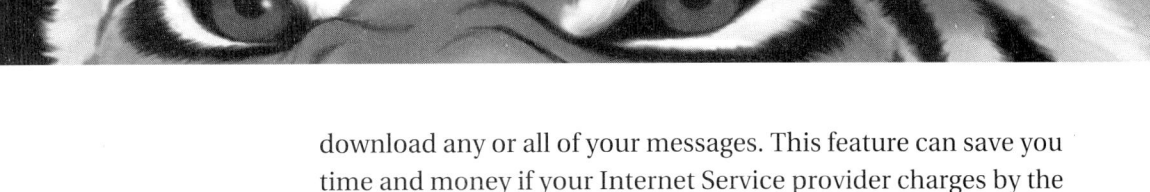

➤ Once you've set your Internet Mail settings, click on OK to close the Services dialog box. Then quit Microsoft Exchange so that your new mail service can take effect.

> **Caution:** If you have any other mail services to set up, create a new profile by clicking on the New button. Otherwise, your default settings will be overwritten to contain your new mail settings; any older mail configurations you have will be lost.

Connecting to the Internet Through a Network

You don't need the Internet Setup Wizard if you have a direct, network-based connection to the Internet. A direct connection means that an Ethernet or Token-Ring LAN is physically connected to the Internet. This connection can be through physical cabling or in some cases over a dial-up connection. If this is the case, the only thing you need to configure is your TCP/IP setting in your Network control panel. To do this, have your network administrator assign you an IP address, then configure your TCP/IP control panel as follows. Double-click on your network Control Panel. If you don't have TCP/IP installed, click on the Add button, double-click on Protocol, and then double-click on Microsoft. Choose TCP/IP and click on the Enter button. TCP/IP will appear in the main Network Control Panel window. Select and it and click on Properties to configure it. (See figure 46.6.)

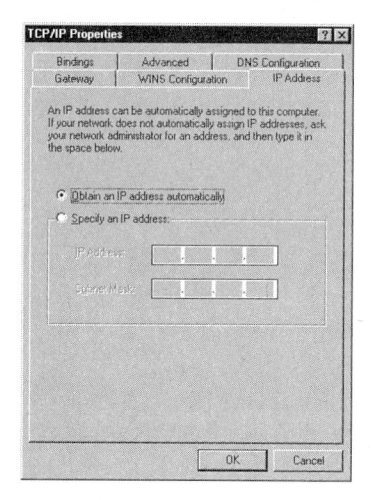

Fig. 46.6 IP addresses are needed for direct LAN Internet access.

Click on the IP address filetab to enter your IP address and your Subnet Mask. A Subnet Mask is a filter that distinguishes the network ID portion of an IP address from its host ID address.

If you're connecting to the Internet via Microsoft Network or another service provider, after you've set up your dial-in properties as outlined here, you're ready to surf the Net.

Working with the Internet Explorer

The Internet Explorer icon is on your desktop by default. Just double-click on the icon to start your connection to the Internet. The first screen you see after you double-click will vary depending on which of the following methods you use to access the Internet:

➤ **Microsoft Network as your service provider**—When you first launch the Internet Explorer, you see the Microsoft Network startup screen. Click on the Connect button and Microsoft Network connects you to an Internet dial-up server.

➤ **Your own service provider**—You see only a dialog box that tells you the modem is dialing.

➤ **Connected to the Internet via your LAN**—You won't see any new screens, just your home page as Internet Explorer loads it.

After the connection is established, you see the Microsoft homepage. Later, you'll see how to change your homepage so you don't have to start this way. After your homepage of choice is up and running, the World Wide Web is yours to explore. The following section provides several useful tips that will make using Internet Explorer a worthwhile experience.

Tips on Using the Internet Explorer

Text will always load onto the page you're downloading before graphics, which always takes much longer. As soon as the hyperlinked text is finished loading, you can click on your next destination and be speeding toward it long before the original page finishes materializing on-screen. This feature reduces your on-line charges and helps you avoid frustration while you're waiting to surf to the next page.

The Internet Explorer does an excellent job of giving messages about where you are and where you're going on the Internet. On the View menu, make sure that status bar is checked. The status bar is the strip at the bottom of the page that lets you know your status as you hop from one page to the next. Messages such as `opening`, `connecting`, and `accessing` tell you how close you are to arriving at a new Web page.

Once you're on the page, each time you move your cursor over an object you can connect to, the address or name of that object appears on the status bar. Anytime you download something, you see a progression of blue squares on the bottom right of the status bar. The farther the squares progress to the right, the closer you are to finishing your download.

Although the file menu in Internet Explorer may be what you would expect from a Windows 95 application, this file menu has the following subtle differences that add to the power of Internet Explorer:

- You can type any URL location in the address line or look at the pull-down list of recently accessed sites and choose a location from the list. Notice also the check box that says Open in New Window. This feature allows you to continue to download an image or information from one page while you access another. Only system resources and bandwidth limitations will stop you from opening successive windows.

- Internet Explorer also lets you open any file type supported by Internet Explorer such as JPEG, GIF, AU, WAV—in fact, any file type found in the Windows 95 Registry. If the application linked to a particular file type is located on your PC (Microsoft Word, for example), Internet Explorer will open the program as well as the file.

- Use the View menu to directly configure your Internet Explorer environment. The toolbar contains the typical Windows commands such as Cut and Paste. It also contains specific commands for going to a homepage, such as moving backward and forward. Finally, it has two buttons for accessing your Favorites folder and the Options dialog box.

- The Favorites menu makes it easy for you to create and use a hotlist of your favorite Web sites (more on Favorites later) as shown in figure 46.7.

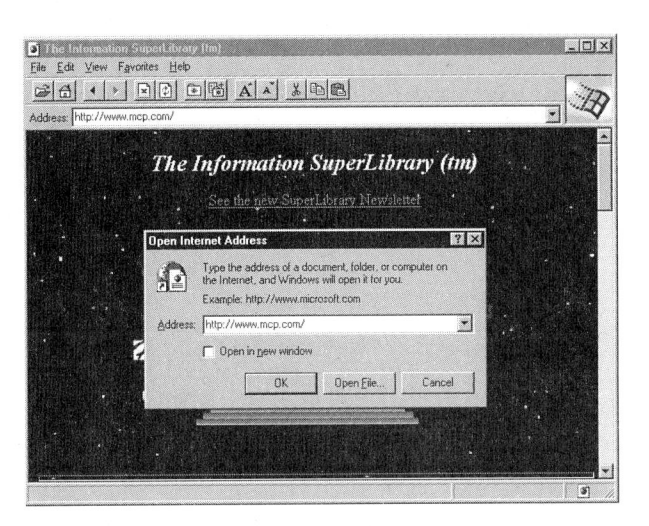

Fig. 46.7 You can open URL addresses or any other Internet file directly from Internet Explorer.

Setting Options

Use the Options selection in the View menu to configure the essential elements of Internet Explorer, such as Internet Explorer's appearance and where your Start page is located, so you can work in the most comfortable fashion for you.

The Appearance filetab of the Options dialog box (see figure 46.8) allows you to alter the way that text and graphics are displayed by Internet Explorer. You can toggle pictures on and off (displaying text without graphics makes things go much faster). Enabling custom colors allows you to change the colors of the text and background as Internet Explorer displays them. Another useful feature is the ability to change the colors of hypertext links that you either have or have not traveled to. This will make it very easy to remember where you've been on the World Wide Web—if you see a hyperlink on a Web page that is colored differently, you'll know you've been there.

Working with the Internet Explorer   **1181**

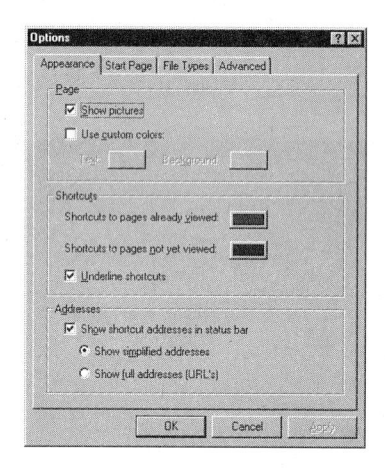

Fig. 46.8 You can easily change your startup home page.

The second filetab, Start Page, is very helpful if you don't want to log on to the Microsoft page every time you launch Internet Explorer. The trick here is that you have to be connected to the site you want as a homepage in order to set it that way. This can be helpful, though, if you frequently change your homepage whenever you find a new site that interests you.

The File Types filetab (see figure 46.9) allows you to associate different file types with the Internet Explorer. By associating files, you allow Windows 95 to recognize different files you may encounter on the Internet, and use them with different applications on your hard drive. There are a few exceptions to this, most notably AU files, which are UNIX sound files. Windows 95 Media Player doesn't understand the UNIX format, but Internet Explorer can play AU files for you upon downloading.

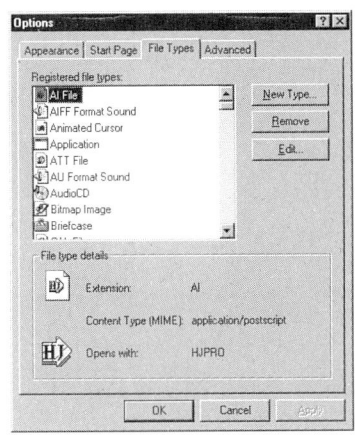

Fig. 46.9 By associating file types, you make it easier for Internet Explorer to work with Windows 95.

By associating file types, you enable Internet Explorer to instantly recognize files and either open them directly or call another application—for example, Microsoft Word—to open them. Associating a file means creating a link between Internet Explorer and a particular file extension (the three letters following the dot on a PC file name). To associate a new file type, click on the View menu and choose Options, then click on the File Type tab. Click on the New Type button and enter the required information. For example, on Description of type, enter a few words to remind yourself what this particular file type is used for. This has no bearing on the file association. In the Associated extension line, enter the three-letter file extension you want to associate (for example, MDF). The next line, Content_Type(MIME), is the Internet's way of determining what a particular file does (text, graphics, sound, and so on). Scroll down through the list menu provided and determine which description best matches your file type. To assign an application to the file type, click on the new button. This step opens a mini-Explorer. Navigate through the mini-Explorer until you find that application you want to associate and click on Enter. If you scroll down the list of associated programs, you should see your new association listed.

The Advanced filetab (see figure 46.10) is critical if you value your disk space. Internet Explorer increases its performance by caching recently accessed Web sites onto the hard drive in folders called History and Cache. Because you can visit Web sites differently, it makes sense to keep them stored in these two separate folders. But, if you keep too many sites on your hard drive, your hard drive space will erode away before you know it. Here are some pointers to help you preserve your disk space:

➤ The default number of sites visited and kept in History is 300. Unless you're a true Web wizard, this number is probably far more than you'll ever need. Try reducing it to no more than 150 sites. That number will free up disk space and enable you to continue surfing the Web quickly. There is also a button marked Empty, which works like a Delete button. Use this button regularly. In addition to saving you disk storage space, it will also weed out any repetitious Web sites that you may have stored.

➤ If you have a site in History that you want to keep, copy it out of the History folder before you use the Clear option. After your house cleaning is done, you can move the site back into History.

➤ In the Cache portion of the filetab, you can set the amount of hard disk you want to use to store Internet history. Again, unless you're an information hog, you probably don't need more than 10 percent of your hard drive set aside for caching. Use the Empty button as frequently as you can to keep a "clean house."

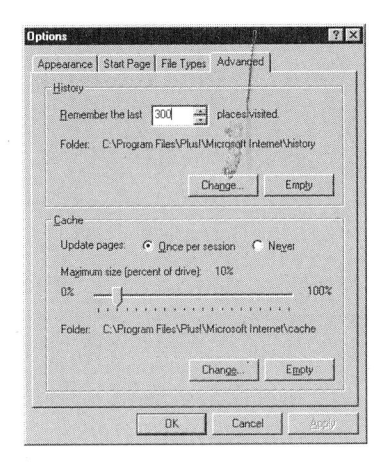

Fig. 46.10 Pay close attention to your cache settings, especially if you have limited hard drive space.

Favorites and Shortcuts

Internet Explorer borrows from a concept called Favorites, which is used by both Microsoft Network and Microsoft Office 95. But the Explorer takes the concept one step further. A Favorite can be any file, folder, or shortcut that you access frequently. Technically, a Favorite is any file, folder, or shortcut present in the Favorites folder, regardless of which application you use to open it. The idea behind this is that you should only be concerned with the task you want to accomplish, not the application you use to accomplish that task.

In the Favorites folder (see figure 46.11), notice that the shortcuts to Web sites share the folder with Word documents, an Access database, and even other folders. This sharing allows you to administer all of your favorite documents, whether they are Web shortcuts or otherwise.

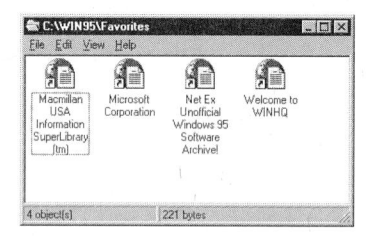

Fig. 46.11 Internet Explorer shares the Favorites folder with the rest of Windows 95.

Why shortcuts to Web sites and not actual files like the other members of the Favorites folder? Although Web sites exist on the Web, they may not be available the next time you try to connect to them. So, capitalizing on the shortcut technology used so well throughout Windows 95, Microsoft decided to implement shortcuts here as well. Like any other shortcut in Windows 95, there is a host of things you can do with your Internet Explorer shortcuts:

- **Put them anywhere you like.** For example, if you have a favorite Web site you visit every day, drag the shortcut to the desktop. Once there, just double-click on it. Internet Explorer will launch and take you straight to your favorite site.

- **Send them to a friend.** Using Microsoft Exchange as an e-mail client, you can drag the shortcut to an e-mail message and send it to a friend or co-worker. If your friends or co-workers also are using Windows 95 and Exchange, all they have to do is double-click on the shortcut when they open the message and they'll be led right to that Web site (see figure 46.12).

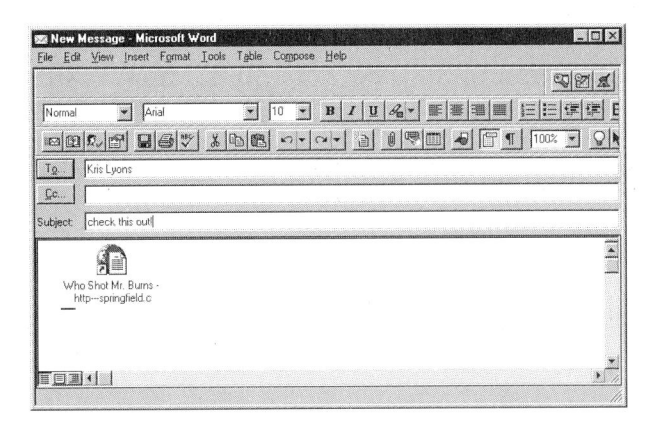

Fig. 46.12 E-mail Web site shortcuts to your friends and associates.

Internet Explorer and Microsoft Network

Neither Internet Explorer nor Microsoft Network offers everything a user needs. However, both programs working in tandem offer a complete set of online services and tools, as shown in the following:

- The Internet Explorer does not provide mail services. Any e-mail you want to send has to be sent through Microsoft Exchange, Microsoft Network, or through any other e-mail package.

- Newsgroups. Internet Explorer does not include a mail reader. Microsoft Network, however, does provide access to countless Internet newsgroups. If you have a Microsoft Network account and are using Internet Explorer on a dial-up connection, type **News:***newsgroup* in the URL line (see figure 46.13) and Microsoft Network will launch and open a window containing that newsgroup.

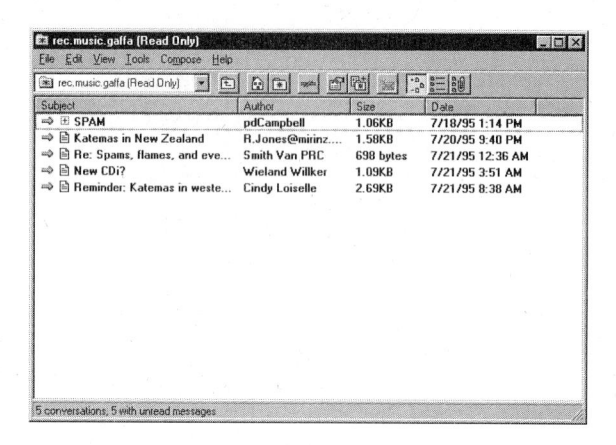

Fig. 46.13 Microsoft Network will bring your newsgroups right to you.

➤ Web pages on Microsoft Network. In several places on the Microsoft Network, you'll find Web pages (see figure 46.14). Although you can't read them on Microsoft Network, you can double-click on them and they'll instantly launch Internet Explorer and take you straight to that site.

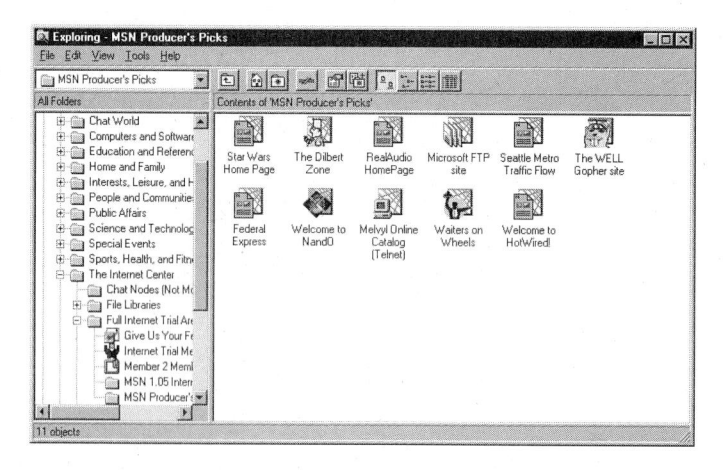

Fig. 46.14 Double-clicking on a Web page immediately starts Internet Explorer.

Internet Explorer and the Right Mouse Button

As with the rest of Windows 95, you can accomplish a lot with the right mouse button.

➤ You can cut, copy, and paste by using the right mouse button. This feature makes it easy to copy URL addresses from any other source and paste them directly into the address line. You'll never fuss with messy URLs again. Also, remember that you never have to type **http://** because Internet Explorer will add that for you.

➤ Any graphic you find can be saved as your Windows wallpaper (see figure 46.15). When you find a photo or graphic on the Web you think would make a nifty wallpaper for your PC, right-click on the graphic and choose Set As Desktop Wallpaper. Open the Display Control Panel and among the standard wallpaper files is one called Internet Explorer Wallpaper. You can center or tile it and treat it as you would any other wallpaper (BMP) file. Just remember that if you want to save the file, you'll have to rename it, because Internet Explorer will overwrite it the next time it grabs wallpaper off the Web.

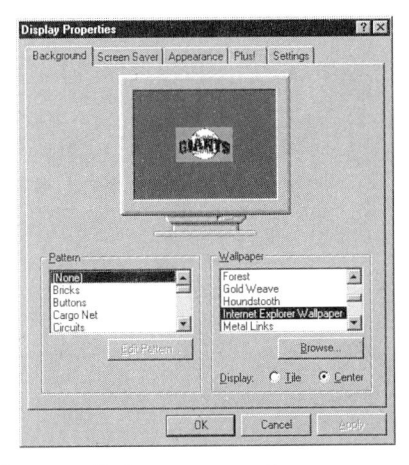

Fig. 46.15 With one click, you can change your Windows wallpaper to something new and exciting.

➤ Using the right mouse button, you can also copy images directly from a Web page onto your hard drive. Right-click and choose Save Picture As. A Windows 95 File Save dialog box will appear so you can choose a name for your file and pick a place on your hard disk where you want to store it. This is no different from managing a word processor or spreadsheet document.

Some Things to Remember While Surfing the Web

To put it poetically, the World Wide Web is a vast ocean of information, and, like the ocean, is constantly changing. Web sites spring into existence only to mysteriously vanish forever. Surfing the Web is really just what it sounds like, a journey over eddies and currents that may never take you to the same place twice, which is discussed further in the following:

➤ **Just because you accessed a Web site an hour ago doesn't mean that it will still be there an hour from now.**

A number of variables affect Internet availability, and speed as well. For example, Web servers are constantly going up and down, and when more people log on to a server than it can handle, it won't answer. Watch the status bar on the bottom of Internet Explorer. If the bar shows "opening" for a long time, cancel your trip to that page and try again later. This delay in responding usually means that your host server is having trouble negotiating a connection to the remote Web site, which further means that you could be waiting there a while only to get the inevitable `Sorry, this Web page doesn't exist` message. This tip is extremely useful if your Internet Service Provider charges by the hour.

➤ **Web Page locations vary wildly.**

Because anyone can create a Web page on the Internet, the information highway is saturated with thousands of Web pages. If you don't know the exact location of the Web page you want, be prepared to spend a lot of time searching for it. Several guides are available to help you search for Web sites. One of the first places to use as a guide should be WWW.Yahoo.Com. The folks at Yahoo do a tremendous job of listing and indexing Web sites by subject, category, and subcategory. This site is updated daily.

➤ **Your PC configuration can make a substantial performance difference in Internet Explorer and Microsoft Network.**

To effectively run any of the Plus! components, Microsoft suggests that your PC be a 486/50 with at least 8M of RAM. Even if your PC meets these requirements, if you run Internet Explorer and Microsoft Network together, be prepared to wait as you switch between the two applications. Particularly if you use large cache settings for Internet Explorer, a significant amount of file swapping takes place on the hard drive between these two applications. Unless you like the sound of your disk grinding away, the more memory you can throw at Internet Explorer, the faster it will run. This may be a truism for any software package, but it bears repeating.

Adding and Removing Windows 95 Components

by Allen L. Wyatt

When you first set up Windows, various accessories and components are installed along with it. These optional elements lend to the operating system's usefulness and contribute in varying degrees to your productivity. Components such as Disk Defragmenter and ScanDisk let you monitor your hard disk's health while the WordPad program gives you a simple, yet powerful, word processor.

This appendix shows you how to install and remove these optional components. In addition, you learn how to remove Windows 95 completely from your computer.

Understanding the Windows 95 Components

In an attempt to make Windows 95 more useful for everyone, Microsoft has included many accessories and utilities with the operating system. Now you can choose from a full array of options. These options can be logically separated into several categories as shown in Table A.1.

Table A.1   Windows 95 Components

Category	Component	Disk Space
Accessibility Options	Accessibility Options	300K
Accessories	Calculator	200K
	Clipboard Viewer	100K
	Desktop Wallpaper	600K
	Document Templates	100K
	Games	600K
	Paint	1.1M
	Screen Savers	100K
	System Resource Meter	100K
	Windows 95 Tour	2.5M
	WinPopup	100K
	WordPad	1.2M
Communications	Dial-Up Networking	400K
	Direct Cable Connection	500K
	HyperTerminal	400K
	Phone Dialer	100K
Disk Tools	Backup	1.0M
Microsoft Exchange	Microsoft Exchange	3.5M
	Microsoft Mail Services	600K
Microsoft Fax	Microsoft Fax Services	1.7M
	Microsoft Fax Viewer	300K
Multimedia	Audio Compression	200K
	Video Compression	400K
	Media Player	200K
	Sound Recorder	200K
	Volume Control	100K
The Microsoft Network	The Microsoft Network	2.0M

Note: The Windows 95 components that are available to you depend on whether you purchased the floppy disk or CD-ROM version. If you have the CD-ROM version, additional components are available that are not listed in Table A.1.

Depending on how Windows was installed on your computer, it's possible that not all available options were installed. For example, when you select Typical setup during the installation, only the most typical options are installed. But you might not be so typical—you might want more! This is no problem. Windows 95 gives you the ability to add or remove individual components at will. In fact, some users might have already squeezed Windows 95 onto their hard disk. In such a case, removing unwanted components is certainly desirable. On the other hand, the Portable setup installs only the options common to notebook and laptop users. What if you want the game Hearts, which isn't installed by default with Portable setup? Simply add it. The next section explains how to go about adding and removing Windows 95 components.

Adding and Removing Components

When you add components to Windows 95, the application or utility is installed and the menu is updated with the new icon(s). Conversely, removing a component deletes the programs or files and removes the icons from the menu. To add or remove a component, follow these steps:

1. Click on Start, Settings, then choose Control Panel
2. Double-click on the Add/Remove Programs applet.
3. Select the Windows Setup tab in the Properties sheet. This displays all possible components that you can add or remove (see figure A.1).

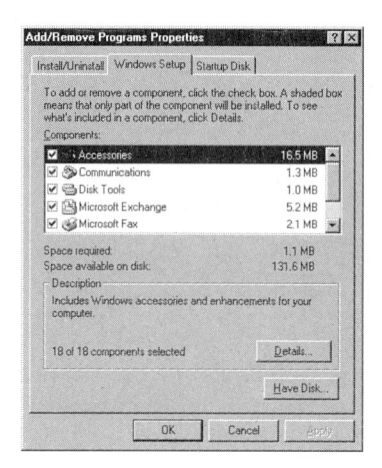

Fig. A.1 The Add/Remove Program Properties sheet shows which items are installed and those that aren't.

4. To add the item, highlight an unchecked component and click the check box beside it. Notice the size in megabytes to the right of the component—this is how much more disk space will be consumed. To remove the item, highlight a checked component and click on the check box to remove the check mark.

5. If you only want certain components added or removed from a group (such as Accessories), highlight the item and click on Details. A dialog box appears that lists individual components for that group (see figure A.2).

6. Choose the components you want to add or remove and click on OK.

7. Once you've selected all the components you want to add or remove, click on OK.

As soon as you choose OK, those components you selected will be installed and/or removed. In most cases, Windows will alert you to shut down and restart the computer.

Fig. A.2 Choose Details to select individual components from a group.

Depending on which components you already have installed, some items may not be selected in the Add/Remove Programs Properties sheet. (The check mark beside the component indicates it is installed.) Windows 95 components are grouped into eight categories (refer to Table A.1). Within these groups you can add or remove specific components. This allows you to pick only the options and accessories you'll really use. Remember these rules for adding and removing components:

➤ If you place a check mark beside an option, it will be installed.

➤ If you remove the check mark from an item, it will be removed.

Removing Windows 95 from Your Computer

When you install Windows 95, several transformations take place. Though many DOS files are deleted, some are replaced by newer versions adapted to Windows 95 and reside in the Windows\Command directory. The system files IO.SYS and MSDOS.SYS in your root directory are converted into Windows 95 system files. A few new directories are created including a hidden Recycled directory. Even a variety of hidden files are placed in the root directory. Indeed, removing Windows 95 from your computer can be fairly complex, but as long as you know what to expect, it's not too difficult.

> **Note:** Windows 95 includes an "uninstall" feature that can be used to restore a previous version of Windows or Windows for Workgroups. While this feature is nice, it assumes several things. First, that you made a backup of your old system as you installed Windows 95 (most people do not for some reason). Second, that you want to return to a previous version of Windows (many people prefer to start from scratch at a DOS level).

If you want to delete Windows 95—that is, completely remove it and return your system to its previous state—there are several items to consider *before* you set out to wipe it from the hard disk.

- **Backup.** You should back up your data before proceeding. Also, if you still have your backup before installing Windows 95, you're one step ahead in restoring your system exactly as it was before Windows 95 was installed.

- **Bootable floppy.** Make sure you always have a floppy disk with your MS-DOS system files on it. This means the files IO.SYS, MSDOS.SYS, DRVSPACE.BIN, and COMMAND.COM. The file SYS.COM is required for transferring these system files after you delete Windows 95. Of course, copies of your AUTOEXEC.BAT and CONFIG.SYS are a plus.

- **MS-DOS floppy disks.** You'll want to reinstall DOS after erasing Windows 95 because many of the files in your DOS directory will have been erased. This is why it's a good idea to copy the contents of your DOS directory to another unassuming location, such as a directory named C:\FRESHDOS.

Each of these items is necessary to smoothly and quickly remove Windows 95 from your computer. If you don't have them, you might be in for a frustrating experience. However, I'll assume you've done everything by the book and you now have each of these in front of you.

There are five basic steps in deleting Windows 95.

1. Boot to DOS.
2. Delete the directories associated with Windows 95.
3. Remove system files from the root directory.
4. If available, copy files to the DOS directory from a backup location.
5. Restart computer and transfer system files.

The following sections discuss each of these steps in greater detail.

Boot to DOS

You can't delete Windows 95 until you exit from its graphical interface. Hacking and cutting from the Explorer just won't suffice (although you can try it and really hang your system). You must boot to MS-DOS or the Windows 95 command prompt. It doesn't matter which you choose because the real MS-DOS system files aren't in the root directory.

For the quickest response time, make sure you have SmartDrive enabled. To do this, type **SMARTDRV** at the DOS prompt. With disk caching enabled, erasing complex directory structures such as the Windows 95 hierarchy will complete in 1/10 the time. Otherwise, you can expect to wait for five minutes while erasing files. Also, this is beneficial if you copy files to the DOS directory from another backup location.

Delete All Directories Associated with Windows 95

To delete a directory and its subdirectories in one fell swoop, use the DELTREE command. From the C:\> prompt, type the following:

```
DELTREE WINDOWS
```

> **Caution:** If your version of Windows 95 is installed in a directory other than WINDOWS, make sure you use the proper directory name with the DELTREE command. You want to delete the Windows 95 directory; nothing else.

This command removes the WINDOWS directory, and all subdirectories for WINDOWS. Windows 95 also creates several other root-level directories that you'll need to remove. You should look for each of the following on your system, and remove them if necessary:

- WINDOWS
- PROGRA~1 (known as Program Files in Windows 95)
- MYDOCU~1 (known as My Documents in Windows 95)
- RECYCLED (this is a hidden directory)
- EXCHANGE
- WININST0.400 (this is the Setup directory and is only available if you aborted a Windows 95 installation)

It's possible that one or more of these folders does not exist. For instance, if you haven't put any files in the Recycle Bin, the directory RECYCLED won't be there. Also, don't forget to delete Windows applications installed under the Windows 95 operating system. Leaving them is a waste of space because they won't work until you reinstall them under Windows 3.1.

Remove System Files

In the root directory are a number of hidden and visible files placed there by Windows 95. If you fail to remove these files, your computer will always boot to the Windows 95 command prompt instead of the MS-DOS prompt. So, to successfully delete all Windows 95 files, you must use the ATTRIB command to strip all attributes of these files.

Table A.2 lists the files added to your root directory or updated at one time or another when Windows 95 is installed. The attribute is shown to the right of the file name.

Table A.2 Root Directory Files

File Name	File Attributes
AUTOEXEC.BAT	
AUTOEXEC.DOS	
BOOTLOG.PRV	
BOOTLOG.TXT	Hidden
COMMAND.COM	
COMMAND.DOS	
CONFIG.DOS	
CONFIG.SYS	
DBLSPACE.BIN	System, Hidden, Read-only
DETLOG.OLD	
DETLOG.TXT	
DRVSPACE.BIN	System, Hidden, Read-only
IO.DOS	
IO.SYS	System, Hidden, Read-only
MSDOS.---	Hidden
MSDOS.BAK	System, Hidden, Read-only
MSDOS.DOS	
MSDOS.SYS	System, Hidden, Read-only
NETLOG.TXT	
SCANDISK.LOG	
SETUPLOG.OLD	Hidden
SETUPLOG.TXT	Hidden
SUHDLOG.---	Hidden, Read-only
SUHDLOG.DAT	Hidden, Read-only
SYSTEM.1ST	System, Hidden, Read-only

To change the files so they can be deleted, type the following at the command prompt:

```
ATTRIB -R -S -H *.*
```

This command will change the attributes of all the files in the root directory. If you want to change the attribute of an individual file instead, type the following:

```
ATTRIB -R -S -H IO.SYS
```

where *IO.SYS* is the name of the file.

> **Tip:** You may want to copy the few essential files such as AUTOEXEC.DOS and CONFIG.DOS to a floppy disk, remove the attributes of all files in the root directory, delete all the files, and then copy the files from the floppy disk. This saves time over erasing each individual Windows 95 file.

Whatever your method of removing these files, be sure to copy the AUTOEXEC.DOS and CONFIG.DOS files to the root directory after deleting all system files. When you install Windows 95, these two files are renamed with a DOS extension. You should then rename them to their proper file names AUTOEXEC.BAT and CONFIG.SYS, respectively.

Copy MS-DOS Files to DOS Directory

If you have another location where you copied the contents of your DOS directory before installing Windows 95, you should now go to the DOS directory and summon those files. For instance, you may want to keep a copy of the DOS files in a directory called FRESHDOS. These files represent DOS before it is modified by Windows 95. To copy the files from this directory to the DOS directory, enter the following at the DOS prompt:

```
COPY \FRESHDOS\*.*
```

You'll then be asked whether you want to overwrite files, to which you should type **A,** meaning you want to overwrite all files in the directory. This saves a great deal of time over installing DOS from scratch.

Transfer System Files

Finally, all files related to Windows 95 are now gone from your computer. But now you have no operating system files in the root directory. The quick fix for this dilemma is to insert your bootable MS-DOS floppy disk in the floppy drive and restart the computer. After your computer boots to the floppy disk, type the following at the DOS prompt:

```
SYS C:
```

This transfers the system files to your C drive. When the transfer is complete, you can restart your system. Thereafter, you should have a pristine DOS system just the way it was before you installed Windows 95.

Installing the Killer Windows 95 CD-ROM

by Stephen L. Miller

Before you can use the programs on the CD-ROM that comes with this book, you must first install the CD-ROM. This appendix helps you make that installation.

The Killer Windows 95 CD-ROM contains over 40 programs and games that represent some of the best shareware programs currently available for Windows 95.

Many of the applications are 32-bit, multithreaded, and use the Windows 95 interface, taking full advantage of the new power Windows 95 has to offer.

In this appendix, you learn how to do the following:

➤ Start the Killer CD-ROM Setup Program

➤ Find the programs you want to install

➤ Install the individual programs

➤ Exit from the Killer CD-ROM Setup Program

Starting the Killer 95 CD-ROM Setup Program

The Killer CD-ROM Setup Program (see figure B.1) makes selecting and installing the various shareware programs easy. You can start the setup program two ways. The following sections discuss both alternatives.

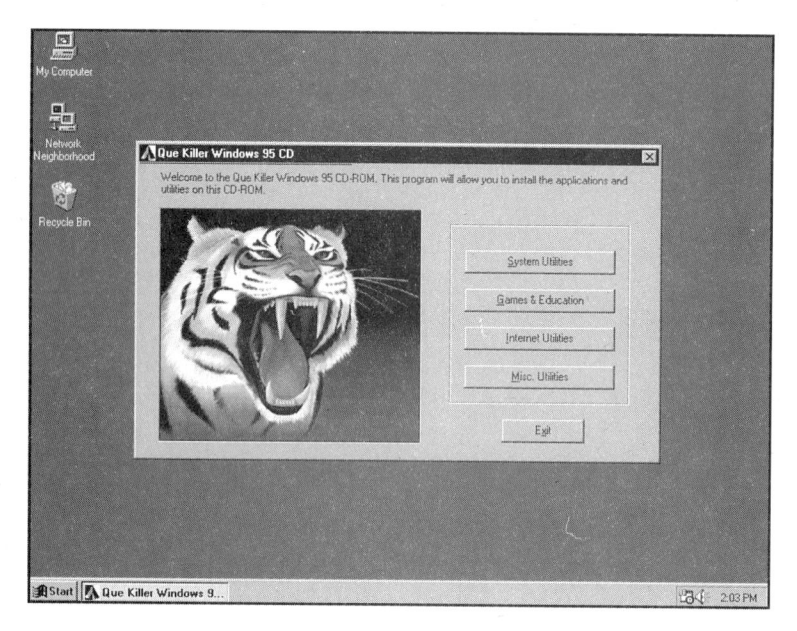

Fig. B.1 The Main Killer Windows 95 CD Setup Screen.

1206 Appendix B: Installing the Killer Windows 95 CD-ROM

Starting the Killer CD-ROM with AutoPlay

The Killer CD-ROM takes advantage of Windows 95's AutoPlay feature. The AutoPlay feature starts the CD-ROM as soon as the disc is inserted in the CD-ROM drive. No command, such as D:\INSTALL.EXE, is required.

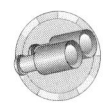

> **Note:** AutoPlay is a Windows 95 feature that can be turned on or off at any time, but the setting is a little hard to find. Here's how to set AutoPlay the way you want it on your system:
>
> 1. Right-click on My Computer, then select Properties.
> 2. Click on the Device Manager tab, then double-click on CD-ROM.
> 3. Click on your CD-ROM drive's description, then on the Properties button.
> 4. Click on the Settings tab.
>
>   If the "Auto insert notification" box has a check in it, AutoPlay is active on your system. If you want to turn AutoPlay off, click on the box and the check mark disappears, which turns off Autoplay.
>
> 5. Click on OK and the Properties sheet disappears.
> 6. Click OK on the Systems Properties sheet.
> 7. A page appears that tells you to restart your system in order for the new settings to take effect.
> 8. Click on OK. Your system reboots and the new AutoPlay setting is in effect.

Starting the Killer CD-ROM Manually

If you have AutoPlay turned off, the Killer CD will not start automatically. However, you can start the setup program manually, as you would any other program you need to start in Windows 95.

Starting the Killer 95 CD-ROM Setup Program **1207**

Here's how to manually start the Killer CD Setup Program:

1. Click on Start, then Run.
2. Type the letter of your CD-ROM drive, then type **:\INSTALL.EXE**. If your CD-ROM drive is D, for example, you type **D:\INSTALL.EXE**.
3. Click on OK.
4. The Killer CD Setup Program starts (see figure B.1).

The Different Killer Program Categories

Before you can start installing the programs, you need to know how to find them in the setup program. To make that task easier, the programs are divided into the following four categories:

- System Utilities
- Games & Education
- Internet Utilities
- Misc. Utilities

You'll use these categories in the next section to help you install the individual programs.

Installing the Individual Killer Programs

Now that you know how to start the setup program and find the programs you want to install, you may find it helpful to practice an example installation. (If you don't want to install a program at this time, click on the Exit button to end the setup program.) For instance, say you want to install a program from the Internet Utilities, such as Web Wizard: The Duke of URL.

To install this Internet program to your hard drive, follow these steps:

1. Start the Killer CD and click on the Internet Utilities button (see figure B.1). The Killer Windows 95 Internet Utilities dialog box appears.

> **Tip:** Double-clicking on the program's name also starts the install routine. This shortcut works for all installation types.

2. Click on Install Web Wizard: The Duke of URL (see figure B.2).

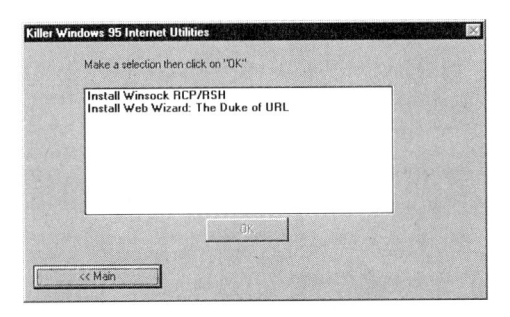

Fig. B.2 Select the program you want to install and click on OK.

3. Click on OK. A Welcome! dialog box appears, which tells you this is the install program for the Web Wizard.

4. Click on OK. The Select Destination Directory dialog box appears and asks you in which directory you want to install the Web Wizard (see figure B.3).

5. Click on OK to accept the default directory or type the directory of your choice and click on OK. The Make a Backup? dialog box asks whether you want to replace backups of the files you replace (see figure B.4).

Installing the Individual Killer Programs

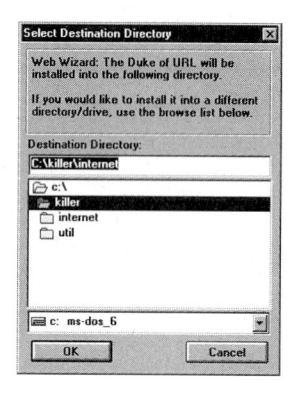

Fig. B.3 You can tell the setup program where to install the program files.

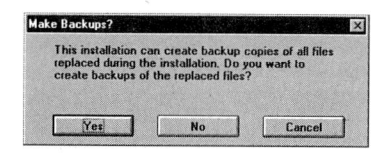

Fig. B.4 The setup program lets you back up any files your installation replaces.

6. If you need to save the original files, click on Yes. If you don't need to save the files being replaced with this installation, click on No.

The files are copied to your system's hard drive and the Killer Windows 95 Internet Utilities dialog box is available to install the next application or exit from the Killer setup program. Exiting from the setup program is covered in the next section.

Some of the programs on the Killer CD come with their own installation routines. This means that after you select the program to be installed and click on OK, the program automatically goes through whatever steps are necessary to complete its install routine. When the installation routine is complete, you're returned to the Killer CD Setup Program dialog box.

Quitting the Killer CD Setup Program

When you're done installing the various programs, you'll probably want to exit from the Killer CD Setup Program. If you practiced the example installation, then you're still in the Internet Utilities dialog box.

To quit the Killer CD Setup program, follow these steps:

1. Click on the << Main button in the Internet Utilities dialog box. This returns you to the setup program's main menu.

2. Click on Exit.

The program ends. You can now remove the Killer CD from your CD-ROM drive.

Index

Symbols

! command (FTP commands), 1025
(cpi) counts per inch (mouse), 289-290
.28 dot-pitch monitor, 200, 203
? command (FTP commands), 1025
123.EXE file, 427-428
16-bit architecture, 54
16-bit Color mode (High Color mode), 1151
16-bit memory (segmented memory), 215-217
16-bit programs, 400-405
 performance improvements, 417
3-D Pinball (Plus!), 1166-1168
 disk space requirements, 1148
300M 10-millisecond IDE hard drive (Windows 95 requirements), 201
.31 dot-pitch VGA monitor, 200
32-bit programs, 400-405
32-bit architecture, 54
33 MHz system, RAM clock cycles, 231
386 memory, 199
 adding, 204-205
386 chip (Windows 95 requirements), 202
486 bus cycles, 231
486 caches (RAM), 233-234
486 chips (Window 95 requirements), 201
60's USA theme, 1162
640 × 480 resolution (Safe Mode), starting, 166-168
64,000 Color mode (High Color mode), 1151
66 MHz system, 201
 RAM clock cycles, 231
8-bit architecture, 54
800 × 600 resolution monitors (Windows 95 standards), 200, 203
80386 memory, 215
8086 memory, 215
8088 memory, 215
8514/A video cards, 259

A

accelerating video systems, 280-285
acceleration (mouse), 358-360
access control (networks), 909-911
access levels (networks)
 client/server networks, 941
 Novell NetWare servers, 120-121
access rights, shared folders, 926-927

ACCESS.COM file, 427-428
Accessibility Options, MouseKeys, 307-309
accessing (remote accessing), Registry, 339
accessories (optional accessories), 1194-1195
    adding/removing, 1195-1197
Accessories command (Programs menu), 27
Accessories dialog box, 958
actions, 78-79
adapter cards, mouse, 294
adapters (networks), 892, 969
    adding, 899-900
    changing bindings, 902-905
Add dialog box, 1097
Add Fonts dialog box, 533
Add Item command (Edit menu), 222
Add Item dialog box, 222
Add New Hardware Wizard, 191-197
    installing
        legacy devices with jumpers, 192-195
        legacy devices without jumpers, 195-197
Add Printer Wizard, 464
Add/Remove Programs dialog box, 1088
Add/Remove Programs Properties sheet, 955, 958
Add/Remove Programs Wizard, 320, 424
    installation, 396-398
    problems, 398-399
adding
    optional Windows 95 utilities, 1195-1197
    printers, 464-465
Address Book dialog box (MS Exchange), 848-850
address books (e-mail), 838
address lists, Microsoft Exchange, 846-847
address (memory) programs, 16-bit vs. 32-bit, 403
address spaces (virtual machines), 316
    MS-DOS, 318
    Win 16, 318
    Win 32, 318

addresses
    e-mail addresses, 860-861
    I/O Device Manager, 179-181
    IP addresses, 861
        configuring TCP/IP, 874
        TCP/IP properties, 870-871
    memory, 215-217, 229-243
    Web addresses, 863
Adobe Systems, 531
Adobe Type 1 (bitmap) fonts, 531
Adobe Type 3 (outline) fonts, 531
Advanced Power Management dialog box, 945
Advanced Power Management, *see* APM
Advanced Program Settings dialog box, 1041
advanced settings (Compression Agent), 1144
Advanced tab (Find dialog box), 85
agents (backup agents), 1094
AH1544.SYS file, 165
Airbrush tool (Paint), 555
Albion Channel kiosk (MSN), 810
algorithms
    caches, 243
    encryption passwords, 354
    FIFO (first in, first out), 241
    LRU (least recently used), 232
alias file names, 53-54
alignment creep, 250
alt newsgroup, 861
America Online (AOL), 786
Amiga graphics files, 550
analog video, 639
Animated Pointers feature, 1154-1157
anonymous FTP servers, 864, 882
ANSI (American National Standards Institute), graphic files, 550
answering (replying), 814
AOL (America Online), 786
API (Application Program Interface) functions, 400
APM, 944-946
    laptop support, 944-966
APPEND (deleted DOS commands), 1002
append (FTP command), 1025
AppHack key word, 430
applets, 365
    controlling, 364-365

application information file, 426-435
applications
  16-bit performance, 417
  automatic running, 387, 1101-1103
    backup programs, 1123
    communications programs, 1123
    disabling scheduled programs, 1120-1121
    Disk Defragmenter, 1116-1119
    Low Disk Space Notification, 1106-1111
    portable computer option, 1123-1124
    removing scheduled programs, 1121
    running programs now, 1120
    ScanDisk, 1112-1116
    stopping schedules, 1122
    suspending schedules, 1121-1122
  client applications, updating links, 700
  communications applications
    Exchange, 787-790
    HyperTerminal, 776-784
    Microsoft Network, 807-809
    online services, 785-787
    Phone Dialer, 773-776
    TAPI, 768
    third-party communications programs, 785
  crashes, 319
  disabling, 94-95
    portable computers, 134
  DOS applications
    APPS.INF file, 426-435
    batch files, 439-443
    disk utilities, 459
    DOS VM, 318
    file names, long, 459
    folders, 442-443
    fonts, changing, 449-450
    initialization, 439-443
    installing, 421-426
    keys, shortcut, 456-457
    memory, 444-447
    multitasking, 453-457
    printing from, 520-521
    Registry, 458
    screen modifications, 448-453

    text-mode lines, 450-451
    variables, changing, 439-441
  font changes, 543-544
  group reorganization, 117-118, 366-368
  hung, 319
  INI files, 458
  installing, 395-408
    Killer CD-ROM, 1208-1210
    manually, 399-400
    wizards, 396-398, 422-425
  legacy, 400
  links, 698-699
  PIF Editor, 438
  removing, 320-324
    from Start menu, 366-368
  renaming, 366-368
  sequencer, 589
  shortcuts, 82-84, 364-365
  Start menu, adding to, 381-384
  switching between, 24-25, 32-33
  types, 318-319
  video clips, dropping, 658-660
  viruses, 1067, 1074
  Windows
    16-bit, 318, 400-405
    32-bit, 318, 400-405
    Windows NT, 400
APPS.INF file
  applications sections, 428-434
    key words, 429-434
  DOS programs, running, 426-435
  [PIF95] section, 426-428
    file fields, 427-428
  [Strings] section, 434-435
ARC, 243-244
Arcada Backup Exec Agent, 1094
  installing, 1095-1099
Archie, 865, 888
architecture, 54
archive software, 243-244
Arrange Icons command (View menu), 75
ascenders (type), 524
ASCII (American Standard Code for Information Interchange), 718
  character values, 49-54
  file names, 49-54
  file transfer protocol, 743

Index **1215**

ascii command (FTP), 1025
ASCII Setup dialog box, 784
ASPI4DOS.SYS file, 165
ASSIGN (deleted DOS commands), 1002
associations (file associations), 76-86, 370-372
    editing, 77-79
asynchronous data transmissions, 731-732
Atari graphics files, 550
ATDOSXL.SYS file, 165
attachments, newsgroup messages, 861
ATTRIB command (deleting system files), 1200-1202
ATTRIB.EXE file, 170
audio CDs, setting properties, 617-621, 630
Audio dialog box, 618
Audio Video Interleaved, *see* AVI files
Audiostation sound application, 673-674
Auto Arrange option, 76
Auto Hide feature (taskbar), 1160
auto-configuration, 60-64
AUTOEXEC.BAT file, 1052, 1055-1056, 1062
    caches (disk), 239-242
    DOS programs, removing, 323-324
    Novell NetWare servers (Windows 95 limitations), 119
        connecting, 123
    problems, 166-168
    restarting Windows 95, 164-165
    startup, 375
    TEMP setting, 226
automatic updating (OLE), 701-702
AutoPlay, 607
    starting setup program (Killer Windows CD-ROM), 1207
AVI files (Audio Video Interleaved)
    playing, 651-652
    viewing, 650

B

background (desktop), customizing, 342-343
Background control (DOS toolbar), 1036

BACKUP (deleted DOS commands), 1003
Backup applet, 1061
Backup dialog box, 1093
Backup program, 1092
Backup Settings, Options dialog box, 1094
backups, 205
    agents, 1094
    files, 92
    Registry, 338
    systems, 92
        portable computer, 131
    virus protection, 1091-1099
banding techniques (full-motion video), 645
bandwidth, service provider costs, 867
base addresses, 738-739
base line (type), 525
batch files (DOS), programs, 439-443
batch scripts, 117-121
    creating, 114-116
    INI files, 115
BatchFile key word, 430
Battery Meter dialog box, 949
battery meters, displaying (laptops), 946-949
baud rates (modems), 719-720
bell (FTP command), 1025
Bell 103 modulation standard, 720
Bell 212A modulation standards, 721
Billing command (Tools menu), 819
binary (FTP commands), 883, 1025
binary data (Registry), 330
binders (networks), 896-897
    changing, 902-905
BIOS (Basic Input/Output System)
    booting, 374
    Plug-and-Play, 61-63
        compatibility, 211
    settings, boot-sector viruses, 1067-1069
    startup, 375
    upgrading, 211
bit maps (raster graphics), 548-549
bitmap fonts, 527
Bitstream's QEM fonts, 532
blink rate (cursor), 362
blocks, interleaved RAM, 229-230

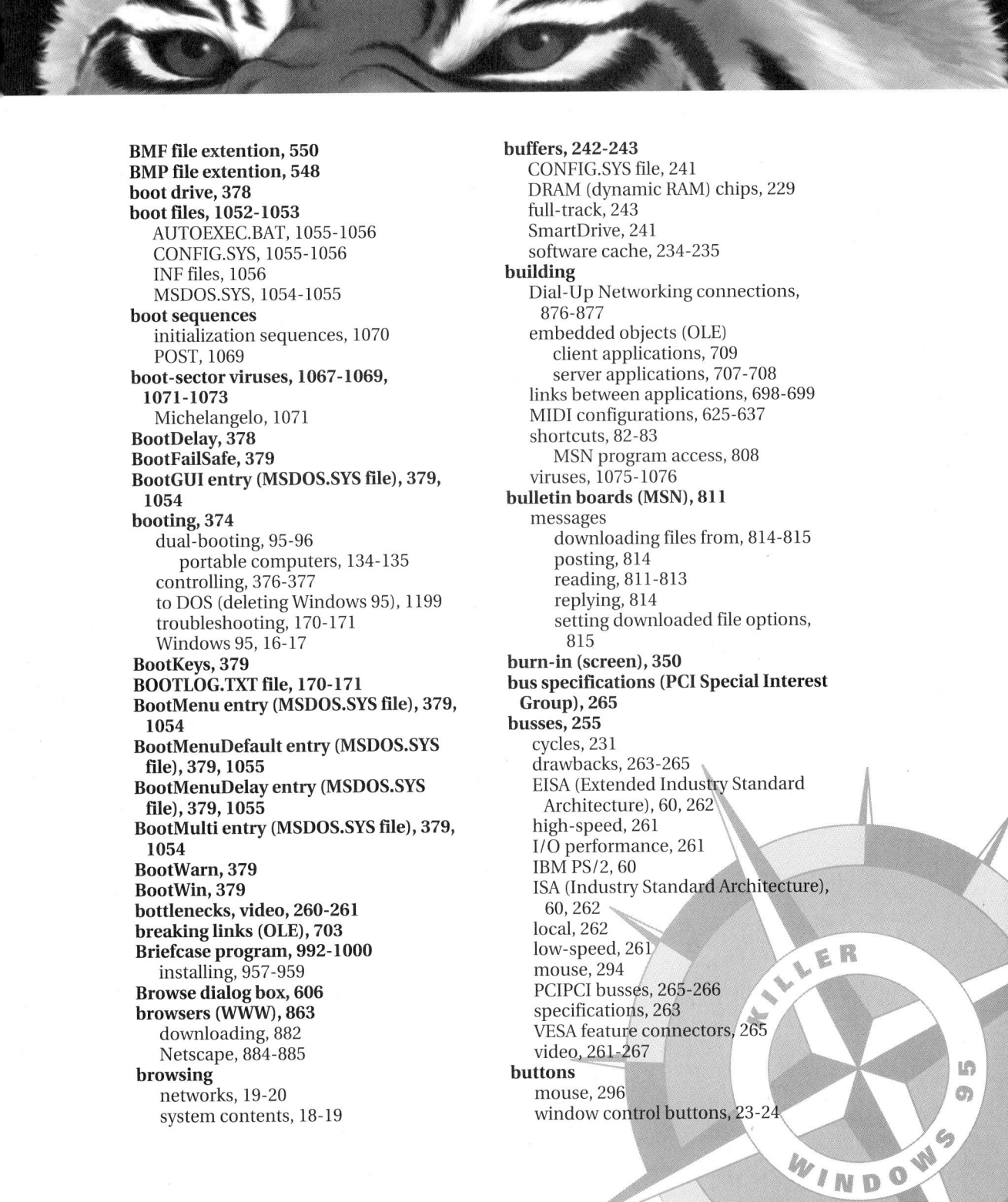

BMF file extention, 550
BMP file extention, 548
boot drive, 378
boot files, 1052-1053
    AUTOEXEC.BAT, 1055-1056
    CONFIG.SYS, 1055-1056
    INF files, 1056
    MSDOS.SYS, 1054-1055
boot sequences
    initialization sequences, 1070
    POST, 1069
boot-sector viruses, 1067-1069, 1071-1073
    Michelangelo, 1071
BootDelay, 378
BootFailSafe, 379
BootGUI entry (MSDOS.SYS file), 379, 1054
booting, 374
    dual-booting, 95-96
        portable computers, 134-135
    controlling, 376-377
    to DOS (deleting Windows 95), 1199
    troubleshooting, 170-171
    Windows 95, 16-17
BootKeys, 379
BOOTLOG.TXT file, 170-171
BootMenu entry (MSDOS.SYS file), 379, 1054
BootMenuDefault entry (MSDOS.SYS file), 379, 1055
BootMenuDelay entry (MSDOS.SYS file), 379, 1055
BootMulti entry (MSDOS.SYS file), 379, 1054
BootWarn, 379
BootWin, 379
bottlenecks, video, 260-261
breaking links (OLE), 703
Briefcase program, 992-1000
    installing, 957-959
Browse dialog box, 606
browsers (WWW), 863
    downloading, 882
    Netscape, 884-885
browsing
    networks, 19-20
    system contents, 18-19

buffers, 242-243
    CONFIG.SYS file, 241
    DRAM (dynamic RAM) chips, 229
    full-track, 243
    SmartDrive, 241
    software cache, 234-235
building
    Dial-Up Networking connections, 876-877
    embedded objects (OLE)
        client applications, 709
        server applications, 707-708
    links between applications, 698-699
    MIDI configurations, 625-637
    shortcuts, 82-83
        MSN program access, 808
    viruses, 1075-1076
bulletin boards (MSN), 811
    messages
        downloading files from, 814-815
        posting, 814
        reading, 811-813
        replying, 814
        setting downloaded file options, 815
burn-in (screen), 350
bus specifications (PCI Special Interest Group), 265
busses, 255
    cycles, 231
    drawbacks, 263-265
    EISA (Extended Industry Standard Architecture), 60, 262
    high-speed, 261
    I/O performance, 261
    IBM PS/2, 60
    ISA (Industry Standard Architecture), 60, 262
    local, 262
    low-speed, 261
    mouse, 294
    PCIPCI busses, 265-266
    specifications, 263
    VESA feature connectors, 265
    video, 261-267
buttons
    mouse, 296
    window control buttons, 23-24

bye (FTP commands), 884, 1025
bytes (file attributes), 49-53

C

cables
    parallel cables (laptop connections), 956-957
    serial cables (laptop connections), 956-957
    Universal Cable Module (UCM), 988

Cache folder (Internet Explorer), 1184-1185

caches, 228-243
    algorithms, 243
    controller cards, 207
    disks
        AUTOEXEC.BAT file, 239-242
        CONFIG.SYS file, 239-242
        DOS, 239-242
        size, 412-414
        SmartDrive, 239-242
        software, 234-242
        types, 234
    hardware, 242-255
        segmented, 243
    parameters, adjusting, 235-242
        CD-ROM drives, 237-238
    RAM, 231-234
        designs, 232-233
        hit, 232
        LRU (Least Recently Used) algorithm, 232
        miss, 232
        motherboard, 233
    read-ahead, 235-238
    write-behind, 238-239, 241-242

calibrating joysticks, 633-635
Call Log (Phone Dialer), 775-776
call waiting, disabling, 759-760
calling cards, 759, 760-764
cancelling embedded objects (OLE), 711
capstans (mouse), 295
Capture text command (Transfer menu), 781
Capture to Printer command (Transfer menu), 781
card drivers (Novell NetWare server), 119

cards
    adapter, mouse, 294, 300-301
    caching controllers, 207
    graphics accelerator, 203, 208-209
        color display, 284
        EGA, 209
        installing, 208-209
        VGA, 209
        video cards, 260-261
    interface, mouse, 294
    network, activating/deactivating, 184
    PCMCIA (PC card)
        beep, 150-154
        inserting, 151-154
        portable computers, 149-154
        removing, 152-154
    sound (Sound Blaster), 585-589
        activating/deactivating Device Manager, 184
        DOS compatibility, 586
        default settings, 592
        hardware, 595-598
        installing, 590
        jumperless, 592
        jumpers, 592-595
        MIDI, 598-599
        Plug-and-Play, 590-591
        sampling quality, 587
        Sound Blaster, 586
        synthesis, 588
        testing, 598-599
        troubleshooting, 599-601
        Windows 95 compatibility, 586-587
    video, changing settings, 340-342

Categories (MSN Central), 799
CCITT
    data compression standard, 725
    error control standard, 724
CCITT (Consultative Committee on International Telegraphs & Telephones), 721-722
cd (FTP commands), 883
cd folder (FTP commands), 1025
CD Player program, 607-613, 630
    Option settings, 612-613
    play list, 608-611
    Preference settings, 613
    toolbar, 611-612

CD-ROM
   audio discs, playing, 607-613
   caching parameters, 237-238
   drives
      adding, 208
      installing, 601-602
         performance settings, 636-637
      Windows 95 requirements, 203
   Killer Windows 95, installing, 1205-1211
   performance improvements, 414-415
CDR file extention, 550
CERN , 863
CGA video cards (Color Graphics Adapter), 258
CGM (Computer Graphics Metafile) file extension, 550
Change Calling Card dialog box, 770
Change Display Type dialog box, 274, 341
Change Icon dialog box, 1158
channels (DMA), Device Manager, 179-181
CHAP (Challenge-Handshake Authentication Protocol), 877
chat rooms (MSN), 815-817
   options, setting, 817
   saving discussions, 817
   scheduling discussions, 818
CHECKSUM, 1078
Cheyenne ARCserve Agent, 1094
chips
   386 chips, 199, 202
   486 chips, 201
      bus cycles, 231
      cache (RAM), 233-234
   Pentium
      bus cycles, 231
      cache (RAM), 233-234
   SRAM (static RAM), 231
CHKDSK command, 1073
Cinepak compression scheme (video), 644
Clear command (Edit menu), 710
client applications, 969
   configuring
      connections, 976-977
      dial-up properties, 974-975

      server types, 977-980
      user names/passwords, 980-981
   links, updating, 700
   OLE, 684
      embedding objects, 709
client/server networks, managing, 940
   access levels, 941
   NetWare server resources, 942
   user accounts, 941-942
clients (networks), 892, 895-896
   adding, 898-899
   NetWare, 119, 914-918
clock cycles (RAM design), 231
close (FTP commands), 1025
Close Program dialog box, 46
clusters, 247-249
CMOS settings, boot-sector viruses, 1068
codecs
   compression codecs (VfW), 642-643
   video compression
      Cinepak, 644
      Indeo, 644-645
      RLE, 645
      Video 1, 645
      viewing, 648-650
      YUV, 645
   video software, 642
codes, modem dialing rules, 772
color
   fonts, 349-350
   desktop elements, changing, 343-350
   display, changing, 281
COM (communications) ports, *see* **serial ports**
COM 1 serial port, 180-181
command line (DOS)
   accessing
      from command-line interface, 1037-1038
      from DOS window, 1034-1037
   switches, 168-169
COMMAND.COM file, 1052
commands
   ATTRIB command (deleting system files), 1200-1202
   CHKDSK, 1073
   Compose menu
      Forward by E-Mail, 814

New Message, 789
   Reply by E-mail, 814
   Reply to BBS, 814
Connect menu
   Exit, 888
   Remote System, 887
Context menu
   Properties, 177
   Scan for Viruses, 1089
DELTREE command (deleting Windows 95), 1199-1200
Device menu, Properties, 654
Disc menu, Edit Play List, 609
DOS commands, 1009-1010
   deleted commands, 1002-1009
   network commands, 1010-1022
   Start, 1033-1034
   TCP/IP, 1022-1033
DOS TYPE, 408
Edit menu
   Add Item, 222
   Clear, 710
   File Object, 814
   Goto, 809
   Links, 701
   Paste Special, 686
   Remove Item, 225
   Selection, 654
   Speed Dial, 775
File menu
   Create Shortcut, 808
   Delete, 74
   Empty Recycle Bin, 21
   Explore, 66
   Install New Font, 533, 935
   Properties, 74, 782
   Rename, 74
   Save History, 817
   Save Search, 86
   Send, 790
   Sign Out, 798
   Update, 709
File menu (Internet Explorer), 1179-1181
FTP commands, 882-884
Insert menu, Object, 658, 709
Insert menu (MS Exchange)
   File, 855-857
   Message, 856-857

MEM, 1073
Object menu, Edit, 710
Options menu
   Continuous Play, 612-613
   Intro Play, 613
   Random Order, 612-613
Programs menu
   Accessories, 27
   Netscape, 884
   StartUp, 27
Properties menu, Options, 881
Registry menu
   Export Registry File, 1057
   Import Registry File, 1060
   Print, 1060
Scale menu
   Frames, 652
   Time, 652
selecting, 26-27
   Programs menu, 27-28
   Settings menu, 29-31
   Start menu, 31-32
Settings menu
   Control Panel, 29
   Printers, 29
   Taskbar, 30, 1160
SETUP, 118
Start menu
   Help, 34
   Run, 31
   Settings, 29
   Show Suspend, 950
   Shut Down, 31
Terminal menu, Start Logging, 889
Tools menu
   Billing, 819
   File Transfer Status, 815
   Find, 818
   Member Properties, 813
   Microsoft Mail Tools, 965
   Options, 817
   Show All Messages, 812
   Show Log, 775
Tools menu (MS Exchange)
   Find, 854-857
   Services, 851-852
Transfer menu
   Capture text, 781
   Capture to Printer, 781

1220 Killer Windows 95

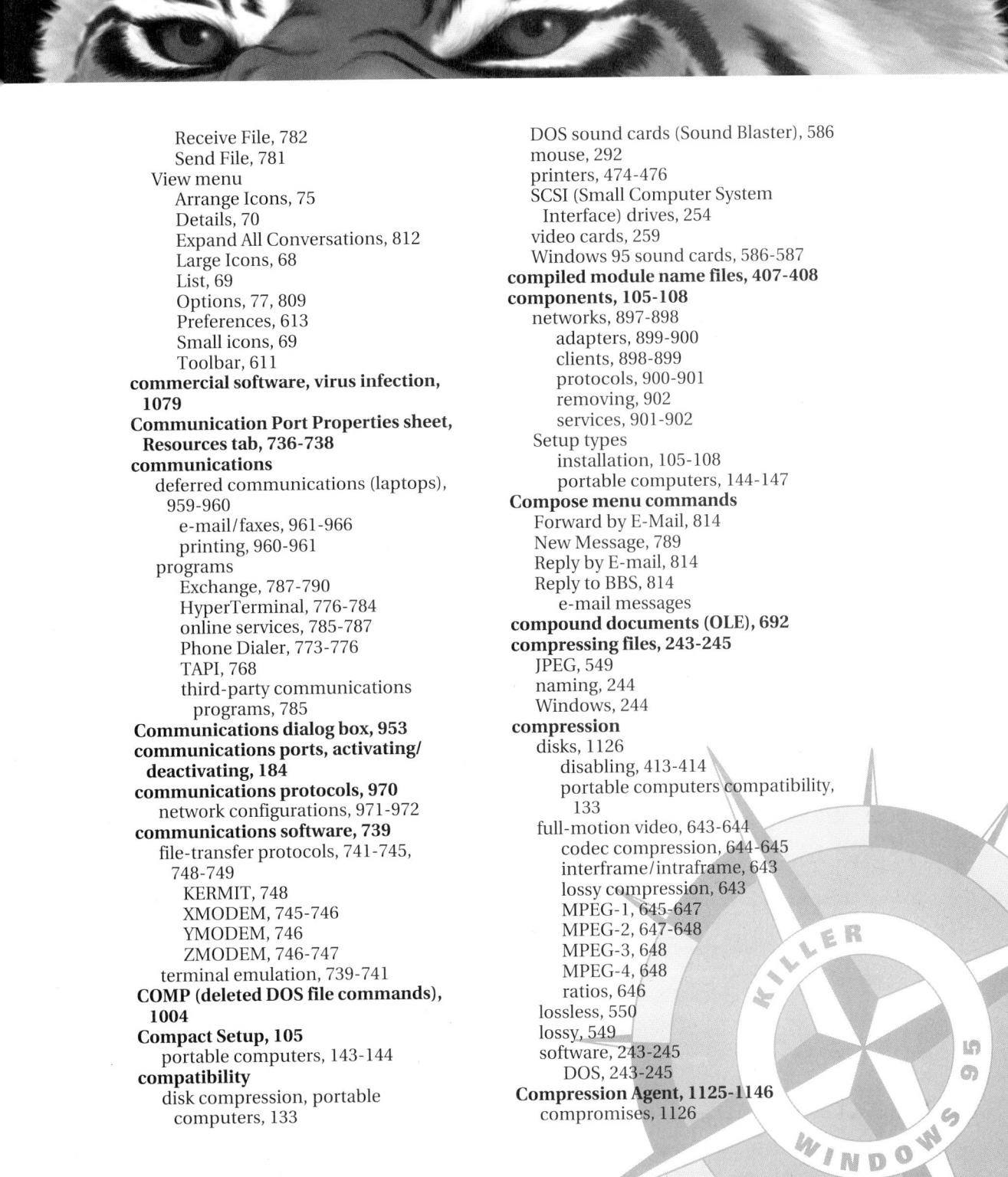

Receive File, 782
Send File, 781
View menu
Arrange Icons, 75
Details, 70
Expand All Conversations, 812
Large Icons, 68
List, 69
Options, 77, 809
Preferences, 613
Small icons, 69
Toolbar, 611
commercial software, virus infection, 1079
Communication Port Properties sheet, Resources tab, 736-738
communications
deferred communications (laptops), 959-960
e-mail/faxes, 961-966
printing, 960-961
programs
Exchange, 787-790
HyperTerminal, 776-784
online services, 785-787
Phone Dialer, 773-776
TAPI, 768
third-party communications programs, 785
Communications dialog box, 953
communications ports, activating/deactivating, 184
communications protocols, 970
network configurations, 971-972
communications software, 739
file-transfer protocols, 741-745, 748-749
KERMIT, 748
XMODEM, 745-746
YMODEM, 746
ZMODEM, 746-747
terminal emulation, 739-741
COMP (deleted DOS file commands), 1004
Compact Setup, 105
portable computers, 143-144
compatibility
disk compression, portable computers, 133

DOS sound cards (Sound Blaster), 586
mouse, 292
printers, 474-476
SCSI (Small Computer System Interface) drives, 254
video cards, 259
Windows 95 sound cards, 586-587
compiled module name files, 407-408
components, 105-108
networks, 897-898
adapters, 899-900
clients, 898-899
protocols, 900-901
removing, 902
services, 901-902
Setup types
installation, 105-108
portable computers, 144-147
Compose menu commands
Forward by E-Mail, 814
New Message, 789
Reply by E-mail, 814
Reply to BBS, 814
e-mail messages
compound documents (OLE), 692
compressing files, 243-245
JPEG, 549
naming, 244
Windows, 244
compression
disks, 1126
disabling, 413-414
portable computers compatibility, 133
full-motion video, 643-644
codec compression, 644-645
interframe/intraframe, 643
lossy compression, 643
MPEG-1, 645-647
MPEG-2, 647-648
MPEG-3, 648
MPEG-4, 648
ratios, 646
lossless, 550
lossy, 549
software, 243-245
DOS, 243-245
Compression Agent, 1125-1146
compromises, 1126

exceptions, 1142-1143
installing, 1129-1130
running initially, 1145
scheduling, 1145
settings, 1144
starting, 1141
UltraPack compression format, 1141-1142
CompuServe, 786
graphics files, 550
COMPUSERVE B+ protocol, 743, 744
Computer Profiles, SYSTEM.DAT file, 328
computers
buying, 285
portable, mouse, 299-300
CONFIG.SYS file, 1052, 1055-1056, 1061
buffers, 241
disk cache, 239-242
DOS, removing, 323-324
problems, 166-168
restarting Windows 95, 164-165
startup, 375
configurations, 58
capabilities, 60-64
defining, 189-190
deleting, 191
devices (Device Manager), 179
DriveSpace 3, 1130-1135
files, 58
problems, 166-168
hardware, 188-191
keyboard, 361-363
speed, 362
MIDI configurations, 625-637
modem, 752-757
MSN, 809-810
networks, 894-897
passwords (encrypted), 877-878
ports (printer), 468-471
resource information devices, printing, 185-186
screen saver, 350-355
SLIP (Internet connections), 880-881
software, 281-283
storage information, 58
TCP/IP, 872, 874-875
DNS servers, 872-873
gateways, 875

IP addresses, 874
WINS, 875
Windows 95, 365-372
changing, 125-126
Connect dialog box, 778
Connect menu commands, 1030-1031
Exit, 888
Remote System, 887
Connect To dialog box, 879
Connection Description dialog box, 777
connections
Internet, 866
networks, 866, 875-878
online connections, 868
PPP, 866-867, 878-880
SLIP, 866-867, 880-881
TCP/IP, 868-875
Windows 95, 868
Internet Mail, 826-827
Microsoft Mail, 834
MSN, inserting passwords, 795-797
networks, 893-894
Novell NetWare Server, 123
remote computers (HyperTerminal), 777-780
serial/parallel connections (laptops), 956-957
see also disconnecting
Connections menu commands (Dial-Up Networking), 975
connectors, serial ports, 730-731
Contents tab (Help topics dialog box), 35
Contents window (Explorer), 68-70
sorting, 75-76
Context menu commands
Properties, 177
Scan for Viruses, 1089
context menus, *see* pop-up menus
Continuous Play command (Options menu), 612-613
Control Panel, 343
Fonts icon, 935-936
Mail and FAX icon, 826
Microsoft Mail Postoffice icon, 823
Modems icon, 749
Network icon, 893-894
Control Panel command (Settings menu), 29

Control Panel dialog box, 792, 947
control-buttons (windows), 23-24
controller circuits, cache (RAM), 232
controller cards, SCSI drives, 206
controllers (hard disk), activating/
    deactivating Device Manager, 184
controls, DOS toolbar, 1036-1037
conventional memory, 214-216
    DOS programs, 444-445
conversations (MSN bulletin boards),
    812
COOL.DLL file, 1157
cooperative multitasking., 314
Copy command (pop-up menu), 74
Copy control (DOS toolbar), 1036
copying
    files, 74
        briefcases to floppy disks,
            999-1000
        disk files to printers, 516-517
        DOS files to DOS directory,
            1202-1203
        Registry files to text files,
            1057-1060
        to briefcases, 993-995
CorelDRAW files, 550
CorelGALLERY files, 550
costs
    online services, 786
    service providers, 866
cover sheets (faxes), 833
CPU (Central Processing Unit)
    startup, 375
    video cards, 258
Create Shortcut command (File menu),
    83, 808
Create Shortcut Wizard, 388
creating, *see* building
CRT (video tube), 269
CSLIP communications protocol,
    970-971
cursors, blink rate, 362
    see also pointers
Custom Setup, 105
    portable computers, 144
Customize dialog box, 620
customizing
    desktop background, 342-343
    Desktop Themes, 1162-1164

DOS window properties, 1038-1039
    Font tab, 1043
    Memory tab, 1044-1045
    Misc tab, 1046-1049
    Program tab, 1039-1042
    Screen tab, 1045-1046
separator pages, 934
sounds, 604-607
windows, DOS windows, 1035-1037
Windows 95, 325-372
    desktop, 339-365

D

Dangerous Creatures theme, 1161
Dark Avenger, 1075
data backups (virus protection),
    1091-1099
data bits (data communications),
    732-734
data compression, modems, 724-725
databases
    Registry, 178, 327-339
    searching, 865-866, 889-890
date settings, 355-356
Date Modified tab (Find dialog box), 85
DB-25 M/F connectors, 730
DB-9 M/F connectors, 731
DBLSPACE.BIN file, 165, 379
DCI (Display Control Interface),
    661-662
DDE (Dynamic Data Exchange), 79, 682
debug (FTP commands), 1025
decompression, full-motion video,
    645-647
default PIF (MS-DOS~1.PIF), 438
defaults
    directory files, temporary, 226
    sound card settings, 592
    System Monitor, 221-222
deferred communications (laptops),
    959-960
    e-mail/faxes, 961-966
    printing, 960-961
    tranferring, 981-983
deferred printing, *see* printing, off-line
defragmenting
    disk drives, 247-249, 412-414
    hard drive, 91-92

Index **1223**

DOS, 92
portable computer, 131
utilities, 92
Norton Utilities (Symantec), 92
PC Tools (Central Point Software), 92
Delete command (File menu), 74, 83
delete filename (FTP commands), 1025
deleting
Call Log entries (Phone Dialer), 776
Desktop Additions, 1149
embedded objects (OLE), 710-711
files, 20-21, 74, 417
MIDI instruments, 627
multimedia devices, 631-632
print jobs, 493, 514-515
shortcuts, 83-84
system files, 1200-1202
accidentally, 125-126
portable computers, 157-158
Windows 95, 1197-1203
booting to DOS, 1199
copying DOS files to DOS directory, 1202-1203
directories, 1199-1200
transferring system files, 1203
DELTREE command (deleting Windows 95), 1199-1200
demand paging, 317
descenders (type), 524
descriptors (e-mail addresses), 860
desktop, 343
background, customizing, 342-343
customizing
color, 343-350
fonts, 542-543
size, 346-349
styles, 343-350
icons, 17-18
Start button, 26-32
taskbar, 24-25
wallpaper, 558, 1161
stretching, 1161
Desktop Additions (Plus!), 1147
3-D Pinball, 1166-1168
Desktop Themes, 1161-1162
installing, 1162-1164
properties, 1164-1165
running, 1165

screen saver hot spots, 1165-1168
installing, 1148-1149
Visual Enhancements, 1149
Animated Pointers, 1154-1157
Font Smoothing, 1150-1153
Full-Window Drag, 1149-1150
High Color icons, 1157-1158
large icons, 1158-1160
Taskbar Auto Hide feature, 1160
True Type Lucida font, 1154
wallpaper stretching, 1161
desktop PCs
connecting to laptops, 952
file synchronization, 957-959
Desktop Themes (Plus!), 1161-1162
disk space requirements, 1148
installing, 1162-1164
properties, viewing, 1164-1165
running, 1165
screen saver hot spots, 1165-1166
Desktop Themes dialog box, 1163
destination documents (OLE), 685
Details command (View menu), 70
Details tab (Properties sheet), 479-484
DETCRASH.LOG file, 161
detecting viruses, 1076
generic monitoring, 1077-1078
heuristics, 1078-1079
inoculation/integrity checking, 1078
scanners, 1077
device drivers, 56-59, 1061
deleted DOS drivers, 1006-1008
installing, 195
portable computers, selecting, 151-152
Device Manager, 178-188
configurations
defining, 189-190
deleting, 191
devices
configuration, 179
conflicts, 183
deactivating, 183-184
installing legacy devices, 181-183
Plug-and-Play, 181-183
profile setup, 188-191
printing resource information, 185-186
removing, 186-189

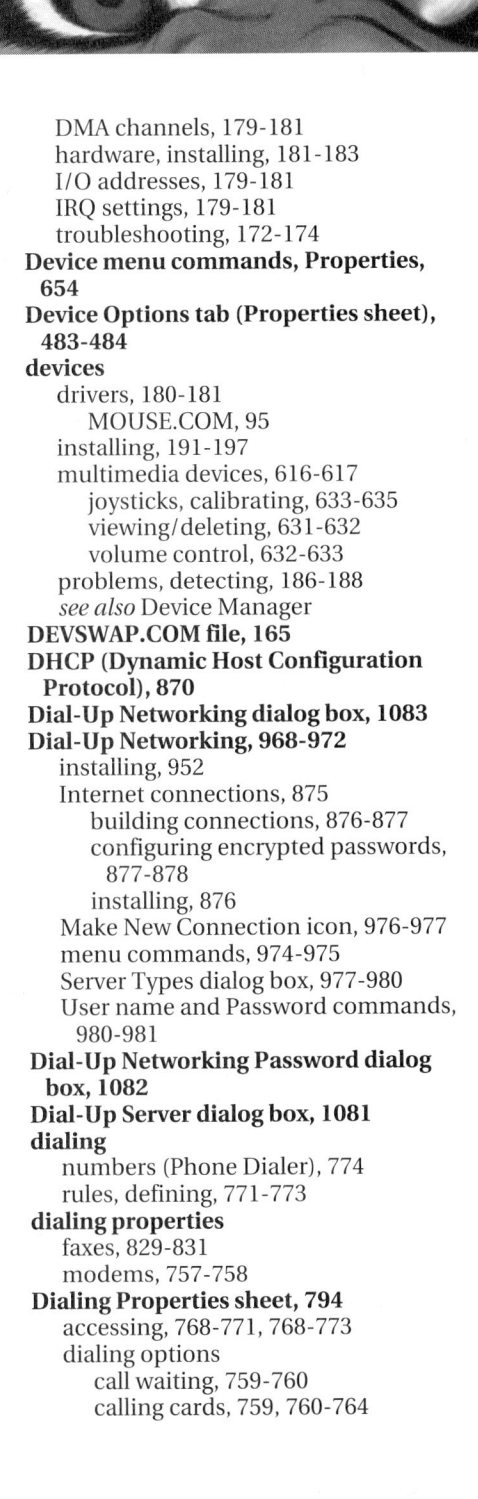

DMA channels, 179-181
hardware, installing, 181-183
I/O addresses, 179-181
IRQ settings, 179-181
troubleshooting, 172-174
Device menu commands, Properties, 654
Device Options tab (Properties sheet), 483-484
devices
drivers, 180-181
MOUSE.COM, 95
installing, 191-197
multimedia devices, 616-617
joysticks, calibrating, 633-635
viewing/deleting, 631-632
volume control, 632-633
problems, detecting, 186-188
see also Device Manager
DEVSWAP.COM file, 165
DHCP (Dynamic Host Configuration Protocol), 870
Dial-Up Networking dialog box, 1083
Dial-Up Networking, 968-972
installing, 952
Internet connections, 875
building connections, 876-877
configuring encrypted passwords, 877-878
installing, 876
Make New Connection icon, 976-977
menu commands, 974-975
Server Types dialog box, 977-980
User name and Password commands, 980-981
Dial-Up Networking Password dialog box, 1082
Dial-Up Server dialog box, 1081
dialing
numbers (Phone Dialer), 774
rules, defining, 771-773
dialing properties
faxes, 829-831
modems, 757-758
Dialing Properties sheet, 794
accessing, 768-771, 768-773
dialing options
call waiting, 759-760
calling cards, 759, 760-764

outside line dialing, 759
tone vs. pulse dialing, 760
location settings, 758-759
dialog boxes
Accessories, 958
Add, 1097
Add Fonts, 533
Add Item, 222
Add/Remove Programs, 1088
Address Book (MS Exchange), 848-850
Advanced Power Management, 945
Advanced Program Settings, 1041
ASCII Setup, 784
Audio, 618
Backup, 1093
Backup Settings, options, 1094
Battery Meter, 949
Browse, 606
Change Calling Card, 770
Change Display Type, 274, 341
Change Icon, 1158
Close Program, 46
Communications, 953
Connect, 778
Connect To, 879
Connection Description, 777
Control Panel, 792, 947
Customize, 620
Desktop Themes, 1163
Dial-Up Netwoking, 1083
Dial-Up Networking Password, 1082
Dial-Up Server, 1081
Disc Settings, 610
Edit File Type, 77
Edit Speed Dial, 775
editing (Registry), 335
Enhanced, 93, 132
Export Registry File, 1057
File and Print Sharing, 905-906
File Transfer Status, 815
Find, 84-85
Find (MS Exchange), 854-855
Find Files, 1090
Find: All MSN services, 818
Folders Details, 1097
Font Substitutions Table, 538
Help Topics, 35
Import, 1060

Inbox, 965
Insert File (MS Exchange), 855-857
Insert Message (MS Exchange), 856-857
Joystick Calibration, 635
Links, 701
Map Network Drive, 928-931
My Computer, 961
Network, 897, 1080
    Access Control tab, 909-911
    Add button, 897-898
    Client for Microsoft Networks option, 911-914
    Computer Name/Description fields, 907-909
    Primary Network Logon, 906-907
    Remove button, 902
Network components, 972-974
New Action, 78
Object, 658
Options, 77, 817
    MSN, 809
Options (Internet Explorer), 1181-1185
Paste Special, 686
Phone Number, 778
Plus! page, 1152
Plus! setup, 1149
Policy Editor, 113
Power, 947
Preferences, 613
Print, 185
Properties, 535
Properties for Display, 276, 542
Run, 114, 331
Save Scheme As, 606
Select Device, 275
Select Folder To Publish, 1097
Select Network Adapter, 899-900
Select Network Client, 898-899
Select Network Component Type, 869
Select Network Protocols, 869, 900-901
Select Network Service, 901-902, 1095
Select Program Folder, 389
Send Fonts As, 540
Server Based Setup, 111
Server Types, 881, 978-980
service configuration, 963

Set Selection, 654
Set Up Machine, 113
Sign In, 795
Source Path, 112
System Properties, 219
Virtual Memory, 93, 132, 219
VirusScan 95, 1089
Welcome, 103, 193
DIB file extension, 548
Differential Phase Shift Keying (DPSK) modulations, 721
digital signal modulation (modems), 715-718
digital video, 639, 640
digitizing tablets, 298
dir (FTP commands), 882, 1025
direct-cable connections, 968-970, 983-984
    briefcases, 992-1000
    Change button, 990
    connecting/disconnecting, 988-990
    guest computers, 988
    host computers, 984-988
    installing, 953
    reversing guests/hosts, 990
    Sharing commands, 984-988
    troubleshooting, 991
direct-mapping cache, 232
directories
    entries, 48-54
    files
        attributes, 49-53
        default, 226
    root, BOOTLOG.TXT file, 171
    subdirectories, filenames, 49
    Windows 95, deleting, 1199-1200
    see also folders
Disable key word, 430
disabling
    disk compression, 413-414
    Program Manager, 95
        portable computers, 134
    programs, 94-95
        portable computers, 134
    swap files, 92-93
        portable computers, 132-133
    TSR (Terminate and Stay Resident) programs, portable computers, 134

Disc menu commands, Edit Play List, 609
Disc Settings dialog box, 610
disconnect (FTP commands), 884, 1025
Disconnect command (Connect menu), 1031
disconnecting
   HyperTerminal sessions, 779
   MSN, 798
disk compression
   adjusting
      DriveSpace 3 settings, 1136-1140
      free space, 1136-1138
   disabling, 413-414
   compatibility, 94
      portable computers, 133
   Compression Agent, 1142-1145
      installing, 1129-1130
   compromises, 1126
   DriveSpace 3
      configuring, 1130-1135
      features, 1126-1129
      information screens, 1133-1135
      installing, 1129-1130
      memory requirements, 1145-1146
   empty compressed drives, 1138-1140
   HiPack compression, 1140
   portable computers, 133
   UltraPack compression format, 1141-1142
   upgrading compressed drives, 1135
Disk Defragmenter, automatically running, 1116
   interruptions, 1119
   output logging, 1119
   scheduling options, 1119
   settings, 1117-1118
disk drives
   contents, viewing, 68-70
   hard disk drives, scanning, 1071
disks
   cache size, changing, 412-414
   DOS commands, deletion of, 1002-1004
   drives
      defragmenting, 247-249, 412-414
      performance optimizing, 227-255
   files, copying to printers, 516-517
   performance, improving, 412-414
   printing problems, 570
   scanning, 124
   space, low, 163
   startup emergencies, 125, 157
   utilities, DOS programs, 459
Display applet, 343
Display Control Interface (DCI), 661-662
display fonts, 526-527
Display Properties sheet, 339, 1151
displaying
   battery meters (laptops), 946-949
   codecs, full-motion video, 648-650
   Desktop Themes properties, 1164-1165
   menus, 26-27
   multimedia device properties, 631-632
DLL (Dynamic Link Library) files, 392
   deleting, 322-323
DMA
   channels (Device Manager), 179-181
   settings (sound cards), 592-595
DMDRVR.BIN file, 165
DNS (Domain Name System), 860
   TCP/IP
      configuring, 872-873
      properties, 871
docking networked computers, 991-992
documents
   compound documents (OLE), 692
   help documents, viewing, 38
   linked documents, editing, 699-700
Documents menu, editing, 385-387
Domain Name System (DNS), 860
DOS (Disk Operating System), 44-45
   6.X interactive startup, 164
   applications, installing, 421-435
   booting to, 1199
   command line access, 1034-1038
   commands, 1009-1010
      deleted commands, 1002-1009
      network commands, 1010-1022
      Start, 1033-1034
      TCP/IP, 1022-1033
   compatibility, sound cards (Sound Blaster), 586
   device driver deletion, 1006-1008
   disk caches, 239-242
   files, 1061

Index **1227**

copying to DOS directory, 1202-1203
names, 47-54
hard drives, defragmenting, 92
memory, 215-217
memory management, 1005-1006
modifying, 437-459
Novell NetWare servers
   directories, 120
   Windows 95 limitations, 119
PIF (Program Information File), 438-439
platform, 44
Plug and Play, 64
printer management, 1006
programs, 446-447
   batch files, 439-443
   disk utilities, 459
   DriveSpace 3 memory requirements, 1146
   file names (long), 459
   folders, 442-443
   fonts, 449-453
   INI file interactions, 458
   initialization, 439-443
   installing, 422-426
   keyboard shortcuts, 456-457
   memory, 444-448
   multitasking, 453-457
   path settings, 441-442
   Registry, 458
   removing, 323-324
   running, 426-435
   screen modifications, 448-453
   screen size, 451-453
   text-mode lines, 450-453
   variables, 439-441
printing from, 520-521
   problems, 569-570
Setup
   portable computers, 136
   starting, 97
software compression, 243-245
startup, Windows 95, 373-374
temporary files, 226
toolbar, 1036-1037
TSR (Terminate and Stay Resident), 94-95
window properties (customizing), 1038-1039

Font tab, 1043
Memory tab, 1044-1045
Misc tab, 1046-1049
Program tab, 1039-1042
Screen tab, 1045-1046, 1047-1049
DOS protected-mode interface (DPMI) memory
DOS TYPE command, 408
DOS VM, 318
DOSSHELL (deleted DOS commands), 1008
double-click speed (mouse), 357-358
DoubleBuffer, 380
Dow Jones News/Retrieval, 786
downloading
   files, 741-742
      from MSN bulletin board messages, 814-815
      setting options (MSN), 815
      World Wide Web, 1179
   software, virus infections, 1086
   Web browsers, 882
DPI (dots per inch), 553
DPMI (DOS protected-mode interface) memory, 446-447
DPMIMem key word, 432
dragging windows, 1149-1150
DRAM (dynamic RAM) chips, 228
   buffers, 229
drawing program (Paint), 554-558
   tools
      Airbrush, 555
      Ellipse, 557
      Fill, 555
      Paintbrush, 557
      Pencil, 557
DrawPerfect graphics files, 550
drive letters
   installation dictionary, 121-122
   login scripts, 121-123
   Windows 95 shared copies, 122-123
drivers, 616
   32-bit protected-mode, startup, 375
   conflicts, 163-165
   device, 56-59, 180-181
      deleted DOS drivers, 1006-1008
      installing, 195
      MOUSE.COM, 95

portable computers, 151-152
keyboard, 363
MAPI, 821
mouse, 304-306
   changing, 360-361
printers, 463
printing problems, 565-566
sound, 587
video, *see* video drivers

drives
boot, 378
CD-ROM
   adding, 208
   checking performance settings, 636-637
   installing, 601-602
   Windows 95 requirements, 203
disk
   defragmenting, 247-249, 412-414
   optimizing performance, 227-255
hard, *see* hard drives
mapping, 928-931

DriveSpace 3 (disk compression), 1125-1146
adjusting
   free space, 1136-1138
   settings, 1136-1140
compatibility, 94
compromises, 1126
configuring, 1130-1135
empty compressed drives, designing, 1138-1140
features, 1126-1129
HiPack compression, 1140
information screens, 1133-1135
installing, 1129-1130
memory requirements, 1145-1146
starting, 1131-1132
upgrading compressed drives, 1135

DrvSpace, 380
DRVSPACE.BIN file, 165
dual-booting, 95-96
   portable computers, 134-135
dumb frame buffers, *see* **VGA video cards**
DWORD data (Registry), 330
Dynamic Data Exchange (DDE), 79, 682
Dynamic Host Configuration Protocol (DHCP), 870

dynamic links, building between applications, 698-699

E

e-mail
   addresses, 860-861
   attaching files to, 855-857
   deferred e-mail (laptops), 961-966
      transferring, 981-983
   information access (USENET newsgroups/mailing lists), 861-862
   messages
      finding, 854-855
      reading, 789
      sending, 789-790, 818
      sorting messages, 853-854
      viewing messages, 853
   Microsoft Exchange settings
      address lists, 846-847
      delivery locations, 844-846
      general options, 840-841
      online services, 844
      reading messages, 841-842
      sending messages, 842-843
      spelling checks, 844
   Microsoft Mail properties
      address books, 838
      automatic logon, 837-838
      connections, 834
      incoming/outgoing delivery, 836
      LAN configuration, 836-837
      logons, 834-836
      personal information stores, 838
   Microsoft Network, MS Exchange configurations, 839
   MSN Central categories, 799
   off-line, portable computers, 156
   Personal Address Book (PAB), 847
      adding names, 848-850
      selecting names, 848
      updating, 850
   personal folders, 851-852
   Personal Information Store, 850-851
Edit command (Object menu), 710
Edit File Type dialog box, 77
Edit menu commands, 1031
   Add Item, 222
   Clear, 710

    File Object, 814
    Goto, 809
    Links, 701
    Paste Special, 686
    Remove Item, 225
    Selection, 654
    Speed Dial, 775
Edit menu commands (Dial-Up Networking), 974
Edit Play List command (Disc menu), 609
Edit Speed Dial dialog box, 775
EDIT.COM file, 170
editing
    associations, 77-79
    files, 417
    links, 699-700
        multiple links, 701
    OLE objects,
        embedded, 692, 710
        linked, 690
    Registry, 331-332
        dialog boxes, 335
        value data, 333-335
    sound effects, 676-678
    speed dial buttons (Phone Dialer), 775
EDLIN (deleted DOS commands), 1008
EGA (Enhanced Graphics Adapter)
    monitor, 200
    video cards, 258
        graphics accelerators, 209
EGA.SYS (deleted DOS drivers), 1007
EIDE (Enhanced Integrated Drive Electronics)
    busses, 262
    hard drives, 206
EISA (Extended Industry Standard Architecture) bus, 60
    IRQ settings, 735
electronic mail, *see* **e-mail**
Ellipse tool (Paint), 557
embedded objects (OLE), 683, 691-694, 704-706
    building, 707
        client applications, 709
        server applications, 707-708
    cancelling, 711
    comparing to linking, 694-695

    deleting, 710-711
    editing, 710
    fonts, 530
Emergency Boot Disk (startup disk), 163-164
    troubleshooting, 169-170
emergency startup disks, 125, 157
empty compressed drives, 1138-1140
Empty Recycle Bin command (File menu), 21
EMS (expanded) memory (DOS programs), 445
EMSMem key word, 432
emulation (terminal emulation), 739-741, 783-784
Enable key word, 432
enabling
    Font Smoothing feature, 1152
    large icons, 1159
    low battery warning message, 949
    passwords, encrypted 877-890
    suspend mode option (laptops), 949-951
    Taskbar Auto Hide feature, 1160
    wallpaper stretching, 1161
encrypted
    passwords, 354
        configuring, 877-878
    viruses, 1076
Energy Star options, 352
Enhanced dialog box, 93, 132
ENHDISK.SYS file, 165
Ensoniq Soundscape Wavetable sound card, 673
environment (operating environment)
    DOS, modifying, 437-459
    changing, 410-415
    improving, 409-419
environment variables, changing in DOS programs, 439-441
EPS (Encapsulated Postscript) file extension, 550
error-checking protocols (modems), 723-724
ESDI (Enhanced Small Device Interface), hard drives, 207, 253
Ethernet, 1177-1178
EVDR.SYS file, 165
event-triggered viruses, 1076

events, 604
  sounds for, 369-370
exceptions (Compression Agent), 1142-1143
Exchange program, 787-788, 821-822
  address lists, 846-847
  attaching files to messages, 855-857
  deferred messages, 961-966
  faxes, deferred, 961-966
  finding messages, 854-855
  general settings, 840-841
  icon, 22-23
  installing, 822
  Internet Mail properties, 826-827
  message delivery locations, 844-846
  reading messages, 789
  sending messages, 789-790
  starting, 788
Exclusive control (DOS toolbar), 1036
Exit command (Connect menu), 888
exiting
  FTP, 884
  setup program (Killer Windows 95 CD-ROM), 1211
Expand All Conversations command (View menu), 812
expanded (EMS) memory (DOS programs), 214, 217, 445
expanding bulletin board messages (MSN), 812
Explore command (File menu), 66
Explorer, 66
  files
    associations, 551-552
    management, 74-75
    sorting, 75-76
  folder sharing, 984-988
  MSN navigation, 805-806
  network folders, creating, 120
  starting, 66
  status bar, 73
  toolbars, 70
  window components, 67
    Contents window, 68-70
    Folder window, 67-68
    menus, 67
EXPLORER.EXE file, 1157
Export Registry File command (Registry menu), 1057

Export Registry File dialog box, 1057
exporting
  Registry files to text files, 337, 1057-1060
extended (XMS) memory (DOS programs), 214, 217, 445-446
Extended Capabilities Ports (ECPs), 987, 988
extensions
  e-mail addresses, 860-861
  files, 370-372
    MID, 588
External MIDI Instrument Properties sheet, 628
external modems, 725-727
external scan converter, 265

F

f command line switch, 169
FASTHELP (deleted DOS commands), 1008
FASTOPEN (deleted DOS commands), 1003
FAT (file allocation table), 47-54, 1067
  access limitations, 247
  directories, entries, 48-49
Favorite Places (MSN Central categories), 799
Favorites (Internet Explorer), 1185-1186
faxes
  deferred, transferring, 981-983
    laptops, 961-966
  Microsoft Fax properties
    cover sheets, 833
    dialing, 829-831
    messages, 828-829
    modem settings, 831-833
FDISK program, 1071
FDISK.EXE file, 170
FIFO (first in, first out) algorithm, 241
file allocation table see FAT
File and Print Sharing dialog box, 905-906
File command (MS Exchange Insert menu), 855-857
File Manager, see Explorer

Index **1231**

File menu commands
    Create Shortcut, 808
    Delete, 74
    Empty Recycle Bin, 21
    Explore, 66
    in Dial-Up Networking, 974
    in Internet Explorer, 1179-1181
    Install New Font, 533, 935
    Properties, 74, 782
    Rename, 74
    Save History, 817
    Save Search, 86
    Send, 790
    Sign Out, 798
    Update, 709
File Object command (Edit menu), 814
file transfer protocols (FTP), 882-884
    commands, 882-884
        DOS, 1024-1027
    disconnecting/exiting, 884
    protocols, 742-745
        KERMIT, 748
        XMODEM, 745-746
        YMODEM, 746
        ZMODEM, 746-747
    sites, 864-865
        File Transfer Status command (Tools menu), 815
files
    123.EXE, 427-428
    access, 55
        levels, Windows 95, 120-121
    ACCESS.COM, 427-428
    AH1544.SYS, 165
    ANSI graphic, 550
    APPS.INF (application information), 426-435
        [PIF95] section, 427-428
        [Strings] section, 434-435
        applications section, 428-434
    ASPI4DOS.SYS, 165
    associations, 76-86, 370-372
        editing, 77-79
        Internet Explorer, 1182-1183
    ATDOSXL.SYS, 165
    attaching to e-mail messages, 855-857
    ATTRIB.EXE, 170
    attribute bytes, 49, 50-53
    AUTOEXEC.BAT
        caches, disk, 239-242

        Novell NetWare servers, 119
        problems, 166-168
        restarting Windows, 164-165
        server, connecting, 123
        startup, 375
        TEMP setting, 226
    AVI
        playing, 651-652
        viewing, 650
    backing up, 92
        portable computer, 131
    batch scripts, 114-116
    boot, 1052-1053
        CONFIG.SYS/AUTOEXEC.BAT, 1055-1056
        INF, 1056
        MSDOS.SYS, 1054-1055
    BOOTLOG.TXT, 170-171
    briefcase
        copying to, 993-995
        copying to floppy disks, 999-1000
        finding originals, 996-997
        synchronizing, 997-999
        updating, 995-996
    compiled module name, 407-408
    compressed, JPEG, 549
    compressing, 243-245
        naming, 244
        Windows, 244
    CONFIG.SYS
        buffers, 241
        cache, disk, 239-242
        problems, 166-168
        restarting Windows, 164-165
        startup, 375
    configuration problems, 166-168
    contents, viewing, 79-81
        DOS TYPE command, 408
    CorelDRAW, 550
    CorelGALLERY, 550
    corrupted, 163-164
    DBLSPACE.BIN, 165
    deleting, 20-21
    DETCRASH.LOG, 161
    DEVSWAP.COM, 165
    disk, copying to printers, 516-517
    DLL dynamic-link library, 392
    DMDRVR.BIN, 165
    DOS, 1061
        commands, deletion, 1004-1005

names, 47-54
downloading
    MSN bulletin board messages, 814-815
    setting options (MSN), 815
DRVSPACE.BIN, 165
EDIT.COM, 170
ENHDISK.SYS, 165
EVDR.SYS, 165
examining WordPad, 426
exporting Registry, 337
extensions, 370-372
    BMF, 550
    BMP, 548
    CDR, 550
    CGM (Computer Graphics Metafile), 550
    DIB, 548
    EPS (Encapsulated Postscript), 550
    GEM, 550
    IMG, 550
    INF, 1056
    JIF, 549
    JFI, 549
    JPG, 549
    LZW, 551
    MID , 588
    PAT, 550
    PCX, 549
    PNG, 551
    RLE, 548
    TIF (Tagged Image Format), 549
    WAV, 675
    WPG, 550
FDISK.EXE, 170
FIXT_DRV.SYS, 165
fonts, 527-532
FORMAT.COM, 170
fragmenting, 248
GIF (CompuServe Graphics Interchange Format), 548-549
graphics, 548-549
    Amiga, 550
    associations, setting, 551-552
    Atari, 550
    CompuServe, 550
    DrawPerfect, 550
    formats, types, 548-551
    Ventura Publisher, 550

    WordPerfect Corporation, 550
HARDRIVE.SYS, 165
hidden, 380
ILM386.SYS, 165
importing, Registry, 337
INI, 326
    batch scripts, 115
    deleting, 417
    DOS, interactions, 458
    programs, 16-bit, 417
    Registry, 327
    structures, 329
    laptop/desktop files, syncronizing, 957-959
LDRIVE.SYS, 165
management (Explorer), 74-75
MIDI, 598-599
MORICONS.DLL, 427
MSBATCH.INF., 114
MSDOS.SYS, 378-380
names
    16-bit vs. 32-bit programs, 404-405
    ASCII (American Standard Code for Information Interchange), 49-54
    DOS programs, 47-54, 459
    length, 47-54
    primary, 53-54
    secondary, 53-54
    Windows NT, 405
network sharing, 905-906
    centralized, 938-939
NONSTD.SYS, 165
PIFMGR.DLL, 438
POL (policy), 115
printing to, 515-517
    output devices, 515-516
protocols, transferring, 742-745
    KERMIT, 748
    XMODEM, 745-746
    YMODEM, 746
    ZMODEM, 746-747
    PROTOCOL.INI, 919-921
    [EPRO$] section, 922
    [NETBEUI$] section, 921-922
    [nwlink$] section, 922
    [protman$] section, 921
README.TXT, 283
receiving (HyperTerminal), 781-782

recovering, 20-21
REGEDIT.EXE, 170
Registry files, 1056-1061
    exporting to text files, 1057-1060
    restoring, 1060-1061
removal dangers, 165
SCANDISK.EXE, 170
scanning, 124
SCSIDSK.EXE, 165
SCSIHA.SYS, 165
searching, 84
    inserting search criteria, 85
    performing searches, 85-86
    saving search criteria, 86
sending (HyperTerminal), 781
shortcuts, 82-84
shared, home folders, defining, 113-114
SKYDRVI.SYS, 165
sorting
    Explorer, 75-76
SQY55.SYS, 165
SSTBIO.SYS, 165
SSTDRIVE.SYS, 165
SSTOR.EXE, 165
SSTOR.SYS, 165
SSWAP.COM, 165
STACKER.COM, 165
STARTUP.GRP, 117-118
structure, 47-54, 50-54
swap, 218, 245-247
    portable computers, disabling, 132-133
    settings, changing, 218-220
    VMM (Virtual Memory Manager), 245-247
SYS.COM, 170
system
    deleting, , 125-126, 157-158, 391-393
    reinstalling, 393
System Agent, 1103-1104
    SAGE.XXX, 1105
    SYSAGENT.XXX, 1105-1106
SYSTEM.DAT, 328
SYSTEM.INI
    deleting, 417
    editing, 417

programs, 16-bit, 417
Registry, 178
see also SYSTEM.INI file
temporary, DOS, 226
text files, exporting Registry files to, 1057-1060
transferring, 741-749, 748-749, 864-865
USER.DAT, 328
viruses, 1067, 1074
vital files, 1051, 1052
    boot files, 1052-1056
    Registry files, 1056-1061
WIN.INI
    [Compatibility section], version number errors, 407-408
    deleting, 417
    editing, 417
    programs, 16-bit, 417
    Registry, 178
see also WIN.INI file
WIN386. SWP, 245-247
Windows 3.x, 1061
Windows bitmap, 548
ZSoft picture, 549
Fill tool (Paint), 555
filters, Quick View tool, 80
Find command (MS Exchange Tools menu), 854-857
Find command (Tools menu), 818
Find dialog box, 84, 85
Find dialog box (MS Exchange), 854-855
Find Files dialog box, 1090
Find tab (Help topics dialog box), 36-38
Find: All MSN services dialog box, 818
finding
    e-mail messages, 854-855
    files, briefcase originals, 996-997
FIXT_DRV.SYS file, 165
floppy disks
    briefcase files copied to, 999-1000
    virus infection methods, 1079
FM synthesis (sound cards), 588
Folder window (Explorer), 67-68
folders
    \WINDOWS\INF, 426
    access levels, 120-121
    application, controlling, 363-365

C:\WINDOWS, 96
contents, viewing, 68-70
fonts, 533
History and Cache (Internet Explorer), 1184-1185
inserting, Favorite Places (MSN), 808
management (Explorer), 74-75
Novell NetWare servers, creating, 119-120
personal message, 851-852
Printers, 462-476
sharing, 924-926, 984-988
    access rights, 926-927
    modifying, 927-928
    naming, 926
Start menu, adding, 382-384
StartUp
    changing manually, 390-391
    names, changing, 372
    items, adding, 388-391
    items, removing, 388-391
    StartUp, changing wizards, 388-390
WIN95INS (installation), 121-122
working, setting, 415-416
see also directories

Folders Details dialog box, 1097
folders, working, setting DOS programs, 442-443
font engine, TrueType, 55-56
Font list control (DOS toolbar), 1036
Font properties control (DOS toolbar), 1037
Font Smoothing feature, 1150-1153
Font Substitutions Table dialog box, 538
Font tab, customizing DOS window, 1043
fonts, 523
    Adobe Type 1, 531
    Adobe Type 3, 531
    ascenders, 524
    base line, 525
    bitmap, 527
    Bitstream's QEM, 532
    changing
        in applications, 543-544
        in desktop items, 542-543
        programs, DOS, 449-450

color
    changing, 349-350
descenders, 524
display, 526-527
embedded, 530
encrypted, 530
engines, 55-56
files, 527-532
folders, 533
formats, 526-527
icons, 533
installing, 532-535
jaggies, 527
DOS
networks
    printing, 934-936
    storing, 529
outline, 528-529
points, 525
PostScript, 531-532
PostScript font substitution table, 538-539
printer, 526
printing
    controlling, 535-541
    problems, 566-567
size, changing, 349-350
soft, 526
substituting, 538-539
TrueType, 529-531
    Lucida, 1154
    PostScript printer, sending to, 539-544
    printer options, 537-538
    printing, 530-531
    printing problems, 568-569
typefaces, 524
types, 527-532
x-height, 524

Fonts icon (Control Panel), 935-936
Fonts tab (Properties sheet), 484-485
FORMAT.COM file, 170
formats
    encoding
        (MFM) Modified Frequency Modulation, 207
        (RLL) Run Length Limited, 207
    fonts, 526-527

formatting hard drives, low-level,
  250-251
Forward by E-Mail command
  (Compose menu), 814
forwarding messages, bulletin board
  (MSN), 814
fps (frames per second), 641
fragmenting files, 248
frames, tracking video, 652
Frames command (Scale menu), 652
frames per second (fps), 641
free space (disk compression)
    adjusting, 1136-1138
    DriveSpace 3 information screens,
      1133-1135
Frequency Shift Keying (FSK)
  modulations, 720
FTP (File Transfer Protocol), 882-884
    commands, 882-884
      DOS, 1024-1027
    disconnecting/exiting, 884
    protocols, 742-745
      KERMIT, 748
      XMODEM, 745-746
      YMODEM, 746
      ZMODEM, 746-747
    sites, 864-865
Full screen control (DOS toolbar), 1036
full-motion video, 641
    AVI files
      playing, 651-652
      viewing, 650
    capturing, 641-642
    clips
      dropping into programs, 658-660
      setting options, 661
    codec compression, 644-645
    compression schemes, 643-644
      interframe/intraframe, 643
      lossy compression, 643
      MPEG-1, 645-647
      MPEG-2, 647-648
      MPEG-3, 648
      MPEG-4, 648
    Display Control Interface (DCI),
      661-662
    playback, 653
      selection points, setting, 653-654
      sizing screen, 654-658
    properties, setting, 621-623

  software, 642
  tracking
    frames option, 652
    time option, 652-653
  viewing codecs, 648-650
full-track buffer, 243
Full-Window Drag feature, 1149-1150
fully associative cache (RAM), 232
function keys, startup, 377
functions, API (application program
  interface), 400

G

gamepads, 634
gateways
    TCP/IP properties, 872
    configuring , 875
GEM file extention, 550
General MIDI Instruments, 626
General tab (Properties sheet), 478-479
    drivers, printer, 481
    Port Settings, 483-484
    ports, printer
      adding, 480-481
      mapping, 481-482
    Spool Settings, 483
    Timeout Settings, 482
generic monitoring, virus detection,
  1077-1078
GEnie, 786
get (FTP commands), 883
get filename (FTP commands), 1025
GIF (CompuServe Graphics
  Interchange Format) files, 548-549
glidepoint (touch tablet), 299
glob (FTP commands), 1025
Go words (MSN program access), 809
The Golden Era theme, 1162
Gopher, 863-864, 886-887
Goto command (Edit menu), 809
GRAFTABL (deleted DOS commands),
  1009
graphics, 545-558
    acceleration setting, 547
    capabilities, 200
    color depth, 546-547
    creating, 554-558
    file formats, types, 548-551

files, 548-549
  associations, setting, 551-552
Paint, 554-558
properties, 546-547
raster, 548-549
resolution, 546-547
System properties, 547-548
tab, printing, 552-554
vector, 549-551
World Wide Web, 1189-1190
GRAPHICS (deleted DOS commands), 1006
graphics accelerator cards, 283-285, 260-261
  color display, 284
  EGA (Enhanced Graphics Adapter) cards, 209
  installing, 208-209
  HGA (Hercules graphics adapter)cards, 258
  VGA (Video Graphics Array) cards, 209
  Windows 95 requirements, 201-203
Graphics tab (Properties sheet), 485-486
guest computers (direct-cable connections), 988
  changing to host computers, 990
(GUI) Graphical User Interface, 287

H

hard drives, 200, 250-252
  alignment creep, 250
  backups, 205
  clean up, 252
  controllers, activating/deactivating, 184
  defragmenting, 91-92
    portable computer, 131
  formatting, low-level, 250-251
  IDE (Integrated drive Electronics), 242
    300M 10-millisecond, 201
  interleave, adjusting, 251
  replacing, 205-207
  scanning, 1071
  scrambled, 338
  SCSI (Small Computer System Interface), 242
  space
    storage, 391-393
    150M, 200
  types, 205-207
  upgrading, 252-255
  \WINDOWS\TEMP directory, 226
  Windows 95 requirements, 201-203
HARDRIVE.SYS file, 165
hardware
  caches, 242-255
  check, 163
  configurations
    defining, 189-190
    deleting, 191
  Device Manager, 178-188
  devices
    configuration, 179
    conflicts, 183
    deactivating, 183-184
    problems, detecting, 186-188
    profiles, setting up, 188-191
    resource information, printing, 185-186
    settings, 179-181
    startup conflicts, 162-163
    full-motion video, 641-642
  installation
    Add New Hardware Wizard, 191-197
    Device Manager, 181-183
    legacy devices with jumpers, 192-195
    legacy devices without jumpers, 195-197
    Plug-and-Play system, 60-64
  interaction, 175
  malfunctions, 164
  printers
    managing, 461-499
    performance, 562-564
  properties, 177-178
  removing, 186-189
  requirements, 199-211
  sound cards, 595-598
  troubleshooting, 171-174
  upgrading, MPC standards, 579-585
Hardware Compatibility list, 210-211
hash (FTP commands), 1026

Index **1237**

Hayes-compatible modems, 722-723
HDTV (High Definition Television), 648
heap (memory area), 58
deleted DOS commands, 1009
FTP commands, 1026
menu commands, 1032
    Dial-Up Networking, 975
    Start , 34
    system, 34-35
Help Topics dialog box, 35
    Contents tab, 35
    Find tab, 36-38
    Index tab, 35-36
Hz (hertz), refresh rates, monitors, 272
heuristics, virus detection, 1078-1079
HGA (Hercules graphics adapter) video cards, 258
hidden files, 380
High Color icons, 1157-1158
High Color mode, Font Smoothing feature, 1151
High Definition Television (HDTV), 648
high memory, 214
high-speed busses, 261
HIMEM.SYS driver, troubleshooting, 165
HiPack compression format, 1140
History folder (Internet Explorer), 1184-1185
home computers, 88-89
home folders, files, shared, 113-114
home pages (WWW), 863
    Microsoft, 1178-1179
host computers (direct-cable connections), 984-988
    changing to guest computers, 990
host disk drives (DriveSpace 3), 1126-1127
    empty compressed drives, 1138-1140
hosts (network)
    connections, 968-970
    IDs (IP addresses), 870
HostWinBootDrv entry (MSDOS.SYS file), 1054
hot links, 685
hot spots, screen savers, 1165-1166
hot-docking, 991-992
HTML (Hypertext Markup Language), 862

hung applications, 319
hypermedia, 640
HyperTerminal, 776-777
    files
        receiving from remote computers, 781-782
        sending to remote computers, 781
    remote computer connections, 777-779, 780
    sessions
        disconnecting/saving, 779
        text, saving/printing, 780-781
    starting, 777
    terminal emulation, 782-784
hypertext links (WWW), 862
Hypertext Markup Language (HTML), 862

I

IBM
    PS/2 bus, 60
    ThinkPad Track Point, 299-300
    video cards, 258
Icon index file field, 427
icons, 17-18
    application, controlling, 363-365
    arranging, 76
        automatically, 364
    Exchange, 22-23
    fonts, 533
    High Color, 1157-1158
    large, 1158-1160
    My Computer, 18-19
    Network Neighborhood, 19-20
    PCMCIA tray, 153
    printers, 476
    Recycle Bin, 20-21
    hard drives, 206
(IDE) Integrated Drive Electronics
    hard drives, 206, 242, 253
    interleave, 251
    Integrated Services Digital Networks (ISDNs), 717-718
identifications (network), 907-909
ILM386.SYS file, 165
images, drawing, 554-558
IMG file extention, 550

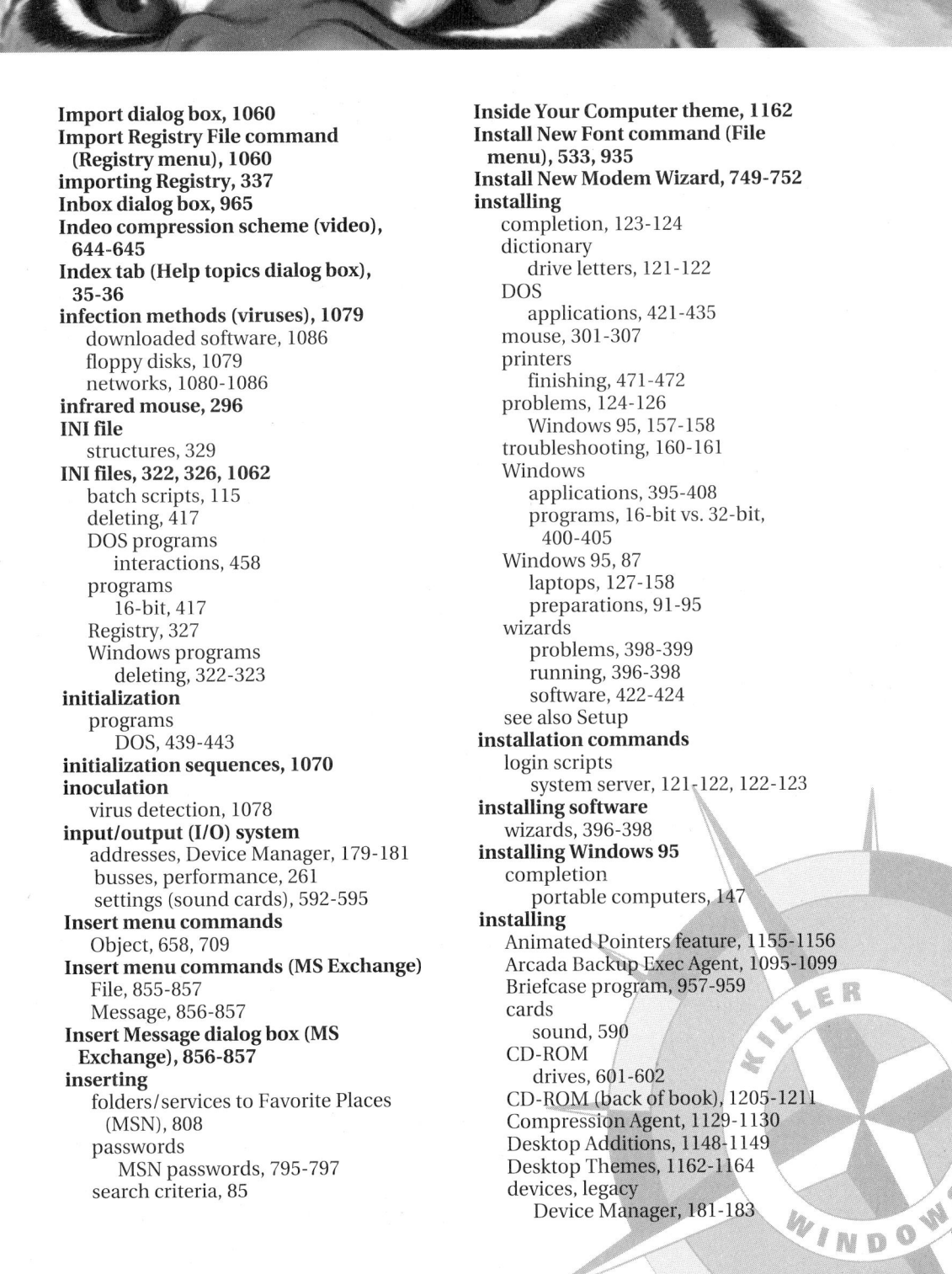

Import dialog box, 1060
Import Registry File command (Registry menu), 1060
importing Registry, 337
Inbox dialog box, 965
Indeo compression scheme (video), 644-645
Index tab (Help topics dialog box), 35-36
infection methods (viruses), 1079
    downloaded software, 1086
    floppy disks, 1079
    networks, 1080-1086
infrared mouse, 296
INI file
    structures, 329
INI files, 322, 326, 1062
    batch scripts, 115
    deleting, 417
    DOS programs
        interactions, 458
    programs
        16-bit, 417
    Registry, 327
    Windows programs
        deleting, 322-323
initialization
    programs
        DOS, 439-443
initialization sequences, 1070
inoculation
    virus detection, 1078
input/output (I/O) system
    addresses, Device Manager, 179-181
    busses, performance, 261
    settings (sound cards), 592-595
Insert menu commands
    Object, 658, 709
Insert menu commands (MS Exchange)
    File, 855-857
    Message, 856-857
Insert Message dialog box (MS Exchange), 856-857
inserting
    folders/services to Favorite Places (MSN), 808
    passwords
        MSN passwords, 795-797
    search criteria, 85

Inside Your Computer theme, 1162
Install New Font command (File menu), 533, 935
Install New Modem Wizard, 749-752
installing
    completion, 123-124
    dictionary
        drive letters, 121-122
    DOS
        applications, 421-435
    mouse, 301-307
    printers
        finishing, 471-472
    problems, 124-126
        Windows 95, 157-158
    troubleshooting, 160-161
    Windows
        applications, 395-408
        programs, 16-bit vs. 32-bit, 400-405
    Windows 95, 87
        laptops, 127-158
        preparations, 91-95
    wizards
        problems, 398-399
        running, 396-398
        software, 422-424
    see also Setup
installation commands
    login scripts
        system server, 121-122, 122-123
installing software
    wizards, 396-398
installing Windows 95
    completion
        portable computers, 147
installing
    Animated Pointers feature, 1155-1156
    Arcada Backup Exec Agent, 1095-1099
    Briefcase program, 957-959
    cards
        sound, 590
    CD-ROM
        drives, 601-602
    CD-ROM (back of book), 1205-1211
    Compression Agent, 1129-1130
    Desktop Additions, 1148-1149
    Desktop Themes, 1162-1164
    devices, legacy
        Device Manager, 181-183

devices, Plug-and-Play
　　Device Manager, 181-183
Dial-Up Networking, 876
DOS
　　programs, 422-426
DriveSpace 3, 1129-1130
fonts, 532-535
hardware
　　Add New Hardware Wizard, 191-197
　　Device Manager, 181-183
　　legacy devices with jumpers, 192-195
　　legacy devices without jumpers, 195-197
Microsoft Exchange, 822, 962-966
MIDI instruments, 625
modems, 749-752, 754-757
network protocols, 972-974
on networks
　　client/server, 109-119
programs (Killer CD-ROM), 1208-1210
programs, DOS
　　wizards, 422-424, 424-425
remote computing, 952-956
software
　　manually, 399-400
TCP/IP, 868-870
Windows 95, 96-108
　　portable computers, 135-147
　　system requirements, 90
　　see also Setup program
installing Windows 95
　　preparation
　　　　portable computer, 130-134
instruction cycles, 231
instruments
　　MIDI, 624
　　　　deleting, 627
　　　　installing, 625
　　　　naming, 626
　　　　selecting, 625, 626
Integrated Drive Electronics (IDE)
　　hard drives, 206, 242, 253
　　interleave, 251
Integrated Services Digital Networks (ISDNs), 717-718

integrity checking
　　virus detection, 1078
interface
　　DOS command line interface, 1037-1038
interface, see user interface
interfaces
　　cards
　　　　SCSI drives, 206
　　MSN
　　　　Explorer, 805-806
　　　　My Computer, 801-805
interframe compression
　　full-motion video, 643
interleave, 251
interleaved
　　RAM, 229-230
　　　　blocks, 229-230
INTERLNK (deleted DOS commands), 1003
internal modems, 725-727
Internet, 786
　　connections, 866
　　　　networks, 866, 875-878
　　　　online connections, 868
　　　　PPP, 878-880
　　　　SLIP, 880-881
　　　　SLIP/PPP protocols, 866-867
　　　　TCP/IP, 868-875
　　　　Windows 95, 868
　　FTP, 882-884
　　　　commands, 882-884
　　　　disconnecting/exiting, 884
　　Gopher, 886-887
　　information access, 859-860
　　　　e-mail, 860-861
　　　　FTP, 864-865
　　　　Gopher, 863-864
　　　　Telnet, 865
　　　　WAIS, 865-866
　　　　WWW, 862-863
　　Netscape, 884-885
　　Telnet, 887-888
　　WAIS, 889-890
　　Web browsers
　　　　downloading, 882
Internet Explorer, 1169-1170

1240　Killer Windows 95

associating files, 1182-1183
Favorites, 1185-1186
File menu commands, 1179-1181
Internet Setup Wizard, 1170-1171
    Microsoft Network option, 1171-1172
    network connections, 1177-1178
    Service Provider option, 1173-1177
Microsoft homepage, 1178-1179
    avoiding, 1182
Microsoft Network, 1187-1188
right mouse button operations, 1189-1190
setting options, 1181-1185
    custom colors, 1181
status bar, 1179
World Wide Web
    browsing, 1190-1191
    copying URL addresses, 1189
    downloading, 1179
    downloading graphics as wallpaper, 1189
    downloading graphics to hard drives, 1190
    hyperlinks, 1179
    shortcuts to, 1186-1187
    storing sites, 1184

Internet Mail (Microsoft Exchange), 826-827
Internet Setup Wizard, 1170-1171
    Microsoft Network option, 1171-1172
    network connections, 1177-1178
    Service Provider option, 1173-1177
InterNIC gopher, 863
interrupt request lines (IRQs), 734-738
INTERSVR (deleted DOS commands), 1003
intraframe compression
    full-motion video, 643
Intro Play command (Options menu), 613
I/O (input/output) system
    addresses, Device Manager, 179-181
    busses, performance, 261
    settings (sound cards), 592-595
    IO.SYS file, 1052, 1053
    Insert File dialog box (MS Exchange), 855-857

IP addresses, 861
    TCP/IP
        configuring, 874
        properties, 870-871
IPX/SPX network protocol, 970, 971, 972-974, 979-980
IRQs (Interrupt request lines), 734-738
    settings
        Device Manager, 179-181
        sound cards 592-595
ISA (Industry Standard Architecture) bus, 60
ISA bus computers
    IRQ settings, 735
ISA busses, 262
(ISDNs) Integrated Services Digital Networks, 717-718

J

jaggies, 1150
jaggies (fonts), 527
JFI file extention, 549
JIF file extention, 549
JOIN (deleted DOS commands), 1003
joining
    mailing lists, 862
Joint Photographic Experts Group (JPEG), 645
Joystick Calibration dialog box, 635
Joystick Properties sheet, 634
joysticks
    calibrating, 633-635
    selecting, 634
    testing, 635
JPEG (Joint Photographic Experts Group), 645
JPEG compressed files, 549
JPG file extention, 549
jumpers (sound cards), 592-595

K

KERMIT, 744, 748
kernel (operating system), 55
Key file file field, 428

Index **1241**

keyboard
    activating/deactivating
        Device Manager, 184
    configuring, 361-363
    cursor blink rate
        controlling, 362
    drivers, 363
    MouseKeys, 307-309
    speed
        configuring, 362

keyboards
    changing, 363
    MIDI, 589

keys
    function
        startup, 377
    Registry
        adding, 336
        deleting, 336
        operating system, 328-330
    Shift
        startup, 377
    shortcut
        DOS programs, 456-457
    startup option, 377

keystroke viruses, 1076
kiosks (MSN), 810-811

L

LANs (Local Area Networks)
    Microsoft Mail settings, 836-837

laptop computers
    direct cable connections, 983-984
        connecting/disconnecting, 988-990
        guest computers, 988
        host computers, 984-988
        reversing guests/hosts, 990
        troubleshooting, 991
        updating files, 992-1000
    network connections, 967-968, 968-970
        installing protocols, 972-974
        protocols, 970
        remote access configurations, 971-972
    System Agent options, 1123-1124

laptops, 128, 943
    APM (Advanced Power Management), 944-946
    battery meter, displaying, 946-949
    connecting to desktop PCs, 952
    deferred communications, 959-960
        e-mail/faxes, 961-966
        printing, 960-961
    file synchronization, 957-959
    remote computing
        installation, 952-956
    serial/parallel connections, 956-957
    suspend mode option, enabling, 949-951
    Windows 95
        installation, 127-158

large icons (Plus!), 1158-1160
Large Icons command (View menu), 68
lcd (FTP commands), 883
lcd folder (FTP commands), 1026
LDRIVE.SYS file, 165
legacy applications, 400
legacy devices
    installing
        Device Manager, 181-183

legacy devices with jumpers
    installing, 192-195

legacy devices without jumpers
    installing, 195-197

Leonardo da Vinci theme, 1162
Level 1 MPC standard, 579-580
Level 2 MPC standard, 580-581
    upgraded, 581-582

LHARC, 244
light yokes (joysticks), 634
lines, drawing, 554-558
Link-Access Procedure for Modems (LAPM), 723
linking
    OLE objects, 685-691
    vs. embedding, 694-695

links, 697-698
    DDE, 682
    hot links, 685
    multiple links
        editing, 701
    OLE
        breaking, 703
        building between applications, 698-699

editing, 699-700
restoring, 704
updating, 702-703
updating
in client applications, 700
Links command (Edit menu), 701
Links dialog box, 701
List command (View menu), 69
listing
codecs
video compression, 648-650
FTP commands, 882
multimedia device properties, 631-632
LOADHIGH command (DOS), 1006
LoadTop, 380
local bus, 262
locations, dialing, 758-759
log in
startup, 375
LOGIN command
servers
connecting, 123
login scripts
drive letters, 121-123
system server
installation commands, 121-122, 122-123
logins, 17
Logitech MouseMan Cordless mouse, 296
Logo, 380
logon scripts, 117-121
logons
Microsoft Mail, 834-836, 837-838
network, 906-907
see also connections
lossless (compression), 550
lossy (compression), 549
lossy compression (video), 643
Low Disk Space Notification
automatic running, 1106
alarm settings, 1110-1111
changing schedules, 1107-1108
notification changes, 1109-1110
settings, 1109
low-level formatting, 250-251
low-speed busses, 261
LowMem key word, 433
LRU (least recently used) algorithm, 232
ls (FTP commands), 1026
Lucida True Type font, 1154
luggables, 128
LZW file extention, 551

M

m command line switch, 169
Mail and FAX icon (Control Panel), 826
mailing lists, 862
Make New Connection icon (Dial-Up Networking), 976-977
Make New Connection Wizard, 876
managers
memory, 216-217
managing
memory, 58
resources, 57-58
managing networks, 936
client/server networks, 940
access levels, 941
NetWare server resources, 942
user accounts, 941-942
peer-to-peer networks, 937
centralized files, 938-939
printers, 937-938
workgroup management, 939-940
manual links (OLE)
updating, 702-703
manual startup
setup program (Killer Windows CD-ROM), 1207-1208
manual updating (OLE), 701-703
Map Network Drive dialog box, 928-931
MAPI drivers, 821
mapping drives (networks), 928-931
disconnecting, 931
Mark control (DOS toolbar), 1036
mark parity, 734
Master Boot Record (MBR), 1067
MBR (Master Boot Record), 1067
MCA bus computers
IRQ settings, 735
MCA computers
video cards, 259
MCGA (multi-color graphics array)
video cards, 258

MDA (monochrome display adapter)
   video cards, 258
mdelete filelist (FTP commands), 1026
mdir filelist (FTP commands), 1026
mechanical mouse, 295
media
   checking, 91
      portable computer, 130-134
Media Player, 598-599
   AVI files
      playing, 651-652
MEM command, 1073
Member Assistance (MSN Central categories), 799
Member Properties command (Tools menu), 813
members
   MSN chat rooms
      viewing properties, 816
membership
   MSN, 792-795
MEMMAKER (deleted DOS commands), 1005
memory, 213-226
   80386, 215
   8086, 215
   8088, 215
   adding, 204-205
      386, 204-205
      SIMMs, 204
   addresses, 215-217
   conventional, 214, 216
      DOS programs, 444-445
   DOS, 215-217
   DOS programs
      modifying, 443-444
   DPMI (DOS protected-mode interface)
      DOS programs, 446-447
   expanded, 214, 217
   expanded (EMS)
      DOS programs, 445
   extended, 214, 217
   extended (XMS)
      DOS programs, 445-446
   heap, 58
   high, 214
   management (DOS), 1005-1006
   managers, 216-217, 221-226

   Microsoft Exchange requirements, 822-823
   performance graphics, 283
   ROM (read only memory)
      Windows 95 requirements, 199
   segmented, 215-217
   swap file, 218
   swapping information, 316-317
   upper, 214
   video
      DOS programs, 447-448
   video cards, 284
   virtual, 214, 217-220
      disabling, 220-226
      settings, changing, 218-220
      settings, monitoring performance, 221-226
   VMM (virtual memory manager), 218
   Windows 3.x, 215-217
   Windows NT, 216
memory address
   Windows
      programs, 16-bit vs. 32-bit, 403
memory addresses, 229-243
memory management, 58
Memory Pager, 317
memory paging, 316-317
   demand paging, 317
memory protection
   Windows
      programs, 16-bit vs. 32-bit, 403-404
memory requirements
   DriveSpace 3, 1145-1146
Memory tab, customizing DOS window, 1044-1045
menus
   commands
      selecting, 26-27
   creating
      shortcuts, 380-387
   Documents, 28-29
      changing, 385-387
      clearing, 386-387
   Explorer window components, 67
   Gopher menus, 863-864, 886-887
   MSN Central, 800
   pop-up menus
      viewing, 40-41

Programs, 27-28
    changing, 384-385
Settings, 29-31
Start, 31-32
    changing, 381-384
startup, 162
Message command (MS Exchange Insert menu), 856-857
message queues
    Windows
        programs, 16-bit vs. 32-bit, 402-403
messages
    bulletin board messages (MSN)
        downloading files from, 814-815
        posting, 814
        reading, 811-813
        replying, 814
        setting downloaded file options, 815
    e-mail messages
        composing, 789-790
        reading, 789
        sending, 789-790, 818
    newsgroup messages, 861
    sending
        MSN chat rooms, 816-820
        to remote computers (HyperTerminal), 780
MFM (Modified Frequency Modulation) encoding format, 207
mget filelist (FTP commands), 1026
Michelangelo virus, 1071
Microcom Networking Protocol (MNP), 724
Microsoft DoubleSpace, 133
    see also DoubleSpace
Microsoft DriveSpace, 133
    see also DriveSpace
Microsoft Exchange, 821-822
    address lists, 846-847
    attaching files to messages, 855-857
    finding messages, 854-855
    general settings, 840-841
    installing, 822
    Internet Mail properties, 826-827
    message delivery locations, 844-846

Microsoft Fax
    cover sheets, 833
    dialing properties, 829-831
    message properties, 828-829
    modem settings, 831-833
Microsoft Mail
    automatic logon, 837-838
    connections, 834
    incoming/outgoing deliveries, 836
    LAN configuration, 836-837
    logons, 834-836
    Personal Address Book properties, 838
    Personal Information Store properties, 838
Microsoft Network configurations, 839
Personal Address Book (PAB), 847
    adding names, 848-850
    selecting names, 848
    updating, 850
personal folders, 851-852
Personal Information Store, 850-851
Postoffice
    setting up, 823
    sharing folders, 824-825
    system requirements, 822-823
    user profiles, 825-826
reading messages, 841-842
sending messages, 842-843
service options, 844
sorting messages, 853-854
spelling checks, 844
viewing messages, 853
Microsoft Exchange, see Exchange program, 22-23
Microsoft Fax
    properties
        cover sheets, 833
        dialing, 829-831
        messages, 828-829
        modem settings, 831-833
Microsoft homepage, 1178-1179
    avoiding, 1182
Microsoft Mail
    Personal Address Book properties, 838
    Personal Information Store properties, 838

Index **1245**

settings
    automatic logon, 837-838
    connections, 834
    incoming/outgoing deliveries, 836
    LAN configuration, 836-837
    logons, 834-836

Microsoft Mail Postoffice icon (Control Panel), 823

Microsoft Mail Server, 823, 825

Microsoft Mail Tools command (Tools menu), 965

Microsoft NetWare Client, 915-916

Microsoft Network
    Inernet connection, 1171-1172
    Internet connection, 1187-1188

Microsoft Network (MSN)
    Microsoft Exchange Inbox, 839

Microsoft network
    as primary network, 911-912
    domain information, 912-914

Microsoft Network, see MSN

Microsoft Plus!, 972
    DriveSpace 3 and Compression Agent
        installing, 1129-1130
    Internet Tools, 1170-1171
    see also Internet Explorer
    see also System Agent

Microsoft Plus!, see Plus!

Microsoft Remote Registry service, 339

Microsoft Workgroup Postoffice Admin Wizard, 823

Microtouch Systems, Inc., UnMOuse, 299

MID extension
    files
        hard drive, 588

MIDI, 598-599
    configurations
        creating, 625-637
    configuring MIDI instruments, 678-680
    instruments
        deleting, 627
        installing, 625
        naming, 626
        selecting, 625, 626
    keyboards, 589
    ports, selecting, 625
    properties, setting, 623-629

MIDI (Musical Instrument Digital Interface), 588

MIDI Instrument Installation Wizard, 625

mini-trackball, 300

MIRROR (deleted DOS commands), 1003

Misc tab, customizing DOS window, 1046-1049

mkdir folder (FTP commands), 1026

mls filelist (FTP commands), 1026

modems, 715
    communications software, 739
        Exchange, 787-790
        HyperTerminal, 776-784
        online services, 785-787
        Phone Dialer, 773-776
        TAPI, 768
        terminal emulation, 739-741
        third-party communications software, 785
        transferring files, 741-742, 748-749
    data compression, 724-725
    defining dialing rules, 771-773
    dialing properties
        call waiting, disabling, 759-760
        calling cards, 759, 760-764
        dialing locations, 758-759
        outside lines, dialing, 759
        tone vs. pulse dialing, 760
    Dialing Properties sheet access, 768-771, 768-773
    digital signal modulation, 715-718
    error-control, 723-724
    external vs. internal, 725-727
    fax, 831-833
    Hayes-compatible, 722-723
    Internet connection, 1172
    modulation standards, 720-722
    speed, 718-720
    telephone line requirements, 727-728
    troubleshooting, 764-765
    Windows 95 setup
        configuration, 752-757
        dialing properties, 757-764
        installation, 749-752, 754-757

Modems Properties sheet, 769
    Add button, 749-752
    Diagnostics tab, 764-765
    Properties button, 752-757

modes
  video cards, 260
modifying
  environment
    DOS, 437-459
  startup, 375-377
modulation standards (modems), 720-722
modulation/demodulation, 717
monitor
  settings, changing, 340-342
monitoring
  generic monitoring
    virus detection, 1077-1078
monitors
  .28 dot-pitch
    Windows 95 requirements, 200, 203
  .31 dot-pitch VGA, 200
  800 × 600 resolution
    Windows 95 standards, 200, 203
  activating/deactivating
    Device Manager, 184
  compatibility
    video cards, 209
  dot pitch, 269-271
  EGA, 200
  features, 267-273
  installing, 209
  interlacing, 272
  multisync, 273
  phosphor group configurations, 270-271
  refresh rate, 271-272
  resolution, 269, 270
  screen curvature, 271
  screen size, 267-269
  Super VGA monitor
    Windows 95 requirements, 199
  types
    selecting, 276-277
  VGA
    Windows 95 requirements, 202
  VGA (Video Graphics Array)
    screen burn-in, 350
  video cards, 258, 266-273
  Windows 95 requirements, 203
MONOUMB.386 (deleted DOS drivers), 1007

More Windows theme, 1162
MORICONS.DLL file, 427
Mosaic, 863
motherboard
  caches
    RAM, 233
  memory
    adding, 204-205
  RAM, 229
  SIMMs, 204
mouse, 287-309, 356-361
  (cpi) counts per inch, 289-290
  acceleration
    setting, 358-360
  alternatives, 297-299
  bus, 294
  buttons, 296
  buying, 291-296
  capstans, 295
  cards
    adapter, 294, 301
    interface, 294
  compatibility, 292
  configuring, 356-361
  connections, 293-294
  digitizing tablets
    pucks, 299
  double-click speed
    setting, 357-358
  driver
    changing, 360-361
  IBM, 293
  infrared, 296
  insertion point (blink rate), 362
  installation, 301-307
    drivers, selecting, 304-306
  mechanical, 294-295
    cleaning, 295
  Microsoft, 293
  optical, 295
  pads, 295
  pens, 298
  Plug and Play, 301
  pointer trails
    enabling, 358
  pointers
    animated pointers, 1154-1157
  portable computers, 299-300

adapter cards, 300
ports, serial, 300
ports
   dedicated, 294
   serial, 294
resolution, 289-290
sensitivity, 289-290
shortcuts, 290-292
touch tablets, 299
   digitizing, 298-299
   glidepoints, 299
Track Point, 299-300
trackballs, 297
   clip-on, 300
   mini, 300
troubleshooting, 306-307
types, 294-297
users, physically impaired, 307-309
   MouseKeys, 307-309
video boards, 294
wireless, 296
   MouseMan Cordless, 296
see also pointer

mouse operations
Internet Explorer, 1189-1190

Mouse Properties sheet, 357

MOUSE.COM
device drivers, 95

MouseKeys, 307-309

MouseMan Cordless mouse, 296

moving
files/folders, 74
video clips, 660
windows, 1149-1150

Moving Pictures Experts Group, see MPEG

MPC (Multimedia PC) standards, 579
Level 1, 579-580
Level 2, 580-581
   upgraded, 581-582
   state-of-the-art, 582-583

MPC standards
hardware
   upgrading, 579-585

MPEG

MPEG Arcade Player, 647

MPEG-1 compression scheme (video), 645-647

MPEG-2 compression scheme (video), 647-648

MPEG-3 compression scheme (video), 648

MPEG-4 compression scheme (video), 648

mput filelist (FTP commands), 1026

MS Exchange Settings Properties sheet, 963

MS-DOS, 318
see also DOS

MS-DOS Mode, 317-318

MS-DOS Prompt Properties sheet, 1038

MS-DOS~1.PIF
default PIF, 438

MSAV (deleted DOS commands), 1009

MSBACKUP (deleted DOS commands), 1003

MSBATCH.INF. file, 114

MSDOS.SYS file, 1052, 1053
entries, 1054-1055
option
   keywords/settings, 378-380
sections
   [Options], 378
   [Paths], 378
startup options, 378-380

MSN, 786, 791
billing information, 819-820
bulletin boards, 811
   downloading files from messages, 814-815
   posting messages, 814
   reading messages, 811-813
   replying to messages, 814
   setting downloaded file options, 815
chat rooms, 815-817
   options, setting, 817
   saving chats, 817
   scheduling chats, 818
configuring, 809-810
connections
   inserting passwords, 795-797
disconnecting, 798
e-mail messages, sending, 818
kiosks, 810-811
membership, 792-795
navigating
   Explorer, 805-806
   My Computer, 801-805

program access, 807
  building shortcuts, 808
  Go words, 809
  inserting folders/services to
    Favorite Places, 808
  Properties sheet, viewing, 807
  running, 819
  topics, searching, 818-819
MSN Central, 795
  categories, 798
    Categories, 799
    e-mail, 799
    Favorite Places, 799
    Member Assistance, 799
    MSN Today, 798
  menus, 800
  toolbar, 800
MSN Today, 798
multimedia
  (MPC) Multimedia PC standards,
    579-585
  adding, 577-602
  CD Player, 607-613
  devices, 616-617
    joysticks, calibrating, 633-635
    viewing/deleting, 631-632
    volume control, 632-633
  joysticks
    selecting, 634
    testing, 635
  music, 607-614
  properties
    audio CD properties, setting, 630
    audio properties, setting, 617-621
    CD-ROM performance properties,
      setting, 636-637
    MIDI properties, setting, 623-629
    video properties, setting, 621-623
  sound cards, 585-589
  sounds, 604-607
  system
    upgrading, 583-585
multimedia devices, 603-614
Multimedia PC Marketing Council, 579
Multimedia Properties sheet, 616
multipartite viruses, 1067
multitasking, 45-46
  adjusting
    programs, DOS, 453-457

cooperative, 45-46, 314-315
preemptive, 45-46, 314-315
  threads, 315
preemptive multitasking, 785
Windows NT, 315
multitasking, preemptive
  Windows
    programs, 16-bit vs. 32-bit,
      401-402
music, 607-614
  MIDI, 588-590
**Musical Instrument Digital Interface
(MIDI), 588**
MWAV (deleted DOS commands), 1009
**MWAVTSR (deleted DOS commands),
1009**
**MWBACKUP (deleted DOS commands),
1003**
**MWUNDEL (deleted DOS commands),
1004**
My Computer
  folder sharing, 984-988
  IRQ settings, 736-738
  MSN navigation, 801-805
My Computer dialog box, 961
My Computer icon, 18-19
Mystery theme, 1162

N

The Norton Utilities (Symantec), 92
n command line switch, 169
**Name & Location tab (Find dialog box),
85**
names
  changing
    StartUp folder, 372
  compiled module
    files, 407-408
  file, 47-54
naming
  files/folders, 74-86
  MIDI instruments, 626
  shared folders, 926
  shortcuts, 83
Natas virus, 1074
Nature theme, 1162

Index **1249**

navigating
  MSN
    Explorer, 805-806
    My Computer, 801-805
NBTSTAT command (DOS), 1021-1022
NCSA (National Center for Supercomputing Applications), 863
NDIS (Network Driver Interface Specification), 866
NET CONFIG command (DOS), 1011
NET DIAG command (DOS), 1012
NET HELP command (DOS), 1012-1013
NET INIT command (DOS), 1013
NET LOGOFF command (DOS), 1013
NET LOGON command (DOS), 1013-1014
NET PASSWORD command (DOS), 1014-1015
NET PRINT command (DOS), 1015
NET START command (DOS), 1016
NET STOP command (DOS), 1017
NET TIME command (DOS), 1017-1018
NET USE command (DOS), 1018-1019
NET VER command (DOS), 1019
NET VIEW command (DOS), 1020
NetBEUI, 896
NetBEUI network protocol, 970-974, 979-980
NetBIOS network protocol, 970, 971
Netscape, 863, 884-885
Netscape command (Programs menu), 884
NETSTAT command (DOS), 1020-1021
NetWare, 895
NetWare clients, 914-918
NetWare Connect communications protocol, 970, 971
NetWare servers
  client/server networks, 942
Network, 380
network cards
  activating/deactivating
    Device Manager, 184
Network components dialog box, 972-974
Network dialog box, 897, 1080
  Access Control tab, 909-911
  Add button, 897-898
  Client for Microsoft Networks option, 911-912, 912-914
  Computer Name/Description fields, 907-909
  Primary Network Logon, 906-907
  Remove button, 902
Network Driver Interface Specification (NDIS), 866
Network entry (MSDOS.SYS file), 1054
Network icon (Control Panel), 893-894
network IDs (IP addresses), 870
Network Neighborhood, 897
  Network components commands, 972-974
Network Neighborhood icon, 19-20
Network Properties sheet, 339
network protocols, 970
  configurations, 971-972
  installing, 972-974
network workstation, 90-91
networking, 58-59, 967-968
  access control, 909-911
  adapter/protocol binders
    changing, 902-905
  adapter/protocol bindings, 896-897
  client software configuration
    creating connections, 976-977
    dial-up properties, 974-975
    server types, 977-980
    user names/passwords, 980-981
  client/server networks, 940
    access levels, 941
    NetWare server resources, 942
    user accounts, 941-942
  components, 897-898
    adapters, 892
    adapters, adding, 899-900
    clients, 892, 895-896
    clients, adding, 898-899
    protocols, 892
    protocols, adding, 900-901
    removing, 902
    services, 892
    services, adding, 901-902
  configurations, 894-896
    new configurations, 897
  connection types, 893-894
  direct-cable connections, 983-984

connecting/disconnecting, 988-990
    guest computers, 988
    host computers, 984-988
    reversing guests/hosts, 990
    troubleshooting, 991
file and print sharing, 905-906
hot-docking, 991-992
identification, 907-909
Inernet connections, 1177-1178
logon, 906-907
managing networks, 936
    client/server networks, 940-942
    peer-to-peer networks, 937-940
mapping drives, 928, 928-931
    disconnecting, 931
Microsoft network
    as primary network, 911-912
    domain information, 912-914
Novell networks, 914
    configuration options, 918-919
    NetWare clients, 914-918
peer-to-peer networks, 937
    centralized files, 938-939
    printers, 937-938
    workgroup management, 939-940
printers, 937-938
printing
    fonts, 934-936
    separator pages, 932-933
PROTOCOL.INI files, 919-921
    [EPRO$] section, 922
    [NETBEUI$] section, 921-922
    [nwlink$] section, 922
    [protman$] section, 921
remote connections, 968-970
    installing protocols, 972-974
    protocol configurations, 971-972
    protocols, 970
Remote Mail connections, 983
sharing files
    centralized files, 938-939
sharing folders, 924-926
    access rights, 926-928
    naming, 926
transferring deferred
  communications, 981-983
updating files (briefcases), 992-1000

networks
    browsing, 19-20
    DOS commands, 1010-1022
    fonts
        storing, 529
    installing
        Windows 95, 109-118
    Internet connections, 866, 875
        building Dial-Up Network
          connections, 876-877
        configuring encrypted passwords, 877-878
        installing Dial-Up Networking, 876
    print spoolers, 497
    printers, 494-499
        adding, 472-474
        properties, 496
        sharing, 494-495
    printing, 517-518
        responsibilities, 498-499
    problems
        Safe Mode Startup, 166-168
    servers
        server-based Setups, 110-113
    virus infection, 1080-1086
    see also Dial-Up Networking, MSN
networks, client/server
    installing
        Windows 95, 109-119
New Action dialog box, 78
New Message command (Compose menu), 789
newsgroups, 861-862
Non-Mask Able Interrupt (NMI), 734
noncontiguous sectors (disk compression), 1127
notebooks, 128
Novell NetWare Server
    connecting, 123
Novell NetWare servers
    folders
        creating, 119-120
    installing
        Windows 95, 118-123
    Windows 95
        access levels, 120-121
        limitations, 119
Novell networks, 914
    configuration options, 918-919
    NetWare clients, 914-918

Index **1251**

numbers
dialing
Phone Dialer, 774
storing
on speed dial buttons (Phone Dialer), 774-775

O

Object command (Insert menu), 658, 709
Object dialog box, 658
object linking and embedding, see OLE
Object menu commands
Edit, 710
Object Packager program, 695-696
objects
embedded objects (OLE), 704-706
building, 707-709
cancelling, 711
deleting, 710-711
editing, 710
linked objects
editing, 699-700
OLE, 684
OLE objects
embedding, 691-694
linking, 685-691
packaged objects, 695-696
octets (IP addresses), 870
ODI (Open Data-link Interface), 866
ODI network card drivers (NetWare)
servers
connecting, 123
off-line e-mail
portable computers, 156
off-line printing
portable computers, 154-156
office computers, 89
OLE, 79
embedded objects, 704-706
building, 707-709
cancelling, 711
deleting, 710-711
editing, 710
linking vs. embedding, 694-695
links, 697-698
breaking, 703

building between applications, 698-699
editing, 699-700
manual/automatic updates, selecting, 701-703
multiple links, editing, 701
restoring, 704
updating, 700, 702-703
objects
embedding, 691-694
linking, 685-691
packaged objects, 695-696
terminology, 684-685
video clips, dropping into programs, 658-660
OLE-capable applications, 685
online antivirus resources, 1087
online help, 33-34
Tips, 34
Wizards, 39-40
see also Help system
online Internet connections, 868
Online Registration, 103
online service providers
Inernet connection, 1173-1177
online services, 785-787
Open Data-link Interface (ODI), 866
open host (FTP commands), 1026
opening
Dialing Properties sheet, 768-771, 768-773
DOS command line
from command-line interface, 1037-1038
from DOS window, 1034-1037
messages
bulletin board messages (MSN), 812
MSN programs, 807
building shortcuts, 808
Go words, 809
inserting folders/services to Favorite Places, 808
Phone Dialer, 773-774
operating environment
changing, 410-415
improving, 409-419
operating system
(VM) Virtual Machine Manager, 312-324

multitasking, 45-46
protected mode operation, 44-45
rebooting, 46-47
Registry
    keys, 328-330
software
    interaction, 311-324
space requirements, 200
System VM, 312
virtual machine, 312-318
operating system (OS)
    see also system
operating system, Windows 95
    DOS programs
        problems, 458-459
operating systems
    MS-DOS Mode, 317-318
optical mouse, 295
optimizing
    disk drives, 227-255
    virtual memory, 221-226
optional utilities (Windows 95), 1194-1195
    adding/removing, 1195-1197
options
    Energy Star, 352
Options command (Properties menu), 881
Options command (Tools menu), 817
Options command (View menu), 77, 809
Options dialog box, 77, 817
    MSN, 809
Options dialog box (Internet Explorer), 1181-1185

P

PAB (Personal Address Book), 788
packaged objects (OLE), 695-696
page mode (RAM), 229
Paint, 554-558
Paintbrush tool (Paint), 557
PAP (Password Authentication Protocol), 877
Paper tab (Properties sheet), 486-487
parallel cables (laptop connections), 956-957

parallel ports, 714-715
    direct-cable connection, 986-988
Params key word, 433
parasitic viruses, 1067
parity checking, 733-734
partitions, 1070
Password Authentication Protocol (PAP), 877
passwords
    encrypted passwords, configuring, 877-878
    encryption algorithms, 354
    MSN passwords, 795-797
    network passwords, 1085
    network server, 980-981
    security, 353-355
Paste control (DOS toolbar), 1036
Paste Special command (Edit menu), 686
Paste Special dialog box, 686
PAT file extention, 550
paths (DOS programs), 441-442
PC Card Properties sheet, 153
PC Cards, 943
PC Tools (Central Point Software), 92
PCI busses, 255, 265-266
    performance, 266
    Windows 95 requirements, 203
PCI Special Interest Group, 265
PCL (Page Control Language), 535
PCMCIA cards, 149-154
PCMCIA tray icon, 153
PCX file extension, 549
Pencil tool (Paint), 557
pens (mouse), 298
Pentium
    bus cycles, 231
    caches, 233-234
performance
    CD-ROM drives, 636-637
    improving
        16-bit programs, 417
        CD-ROMs, 414-415
        disks, 412-414
        video systems, 410-411
        printers, 559-575
Personal Address Books (PABs), 788, 838, 847
    adding names, 848-850

Index **1253**

selecting names, 848
updating, 850
Personal Information Store (PST), 788, 838, 850-851
Phone Dialer
  Call Log, 775-776
  numbers
    dialing, 774
    storing on speed dial buttons, 774-775
  opening, 773-774
  speed dial buttons, editing, 775
Phone Number dialog box, 778
phosphor group configurations (monitors), 270-271
pictures, drawing, 554-558
PIF (program information file), 428, 438-439
[PIF95] Section (APPS.INF) file, 426-428
PIFMGR.DLL file, 438
PING command (DOS), 1028-1029
pirated software (virus infections), 1079
pixels, 548, 1152
PKZIP/PKUNZIP files, 244
playback (full-motion video)
  selection points, setting, 653-654
  sizing screen, 654-658
playing
  AVI files, 651-652
  video clips, 660
Plug-and-Play, 59-64
  BIOS (Basic Input/Output System), 61-63, 375
  compatibility, 211
  devices, adding, 211
  DOS, 64
  graphics accelerator cards, 208
  hardware installation, 60-64
  mouse, 301
  network BIOS compliance, 991-992
  sound cards, 590-591
Plus! Desktop Additions
  3-D Pinball, 1166-1168
  deleting, 1149
  Desktop Themes, 1161-1166
    disk space requirements, 1148
    installing, 1162-1164
    properties, viewing, 1164-1165

    running, 1165
    screen saver hot spots, 1165-1166
  installing, 1148-1149
  Visual Enhancements, 1149-1161
    Animated Pointers, 1154-1157
    disk space requirements, 1148
    Font Smoothing, 1150-1153
    Full-Window Drag, 1149-1150
    High Color icons, 1157-1158
    large icons, 1158-1160
    Taskbar Auto Hide feature, 1160
    True Type Lucida font, 1154
    wallpaper stretching, 1161
Plus! page dialog box, 1152
Plus! setup dialog box, 1149
PNG file extention, 551
Point and Print, 518-520
Point-to-Point Protocol, *see* **PPP**
pointer trails, enabling (mouse), 358
pointers
  animated pointers, 1154-1157
  Device Manager, 184
points, 525
POL (policy) files, 115
Policy Editor, creating batch scripts, 115-116
Policy Editor dialog box, 113
polymorphic viruses, 1067
pop-up menu commands
  Copy, 74
  Create Shortcut, 83
  Delete, 83
  Properties, 74
  Quick View, 80
  Rename, 74
portable computers, 128-134
  disks (compression utilities), 133
  dual-booting, 134-135
  features, 148-156
  hard-drives, defragmenting, 131
  mouse, 299-300
  off-line e-mail/printing, 154-156
  PCMCIA (PC cards), 149-154
    inserting, 151
    removing, 152
  Power Management, 134, 148-149
  programs, disabling, 134
  Setup
    DOS setup, 136

options, 143-147
Windows setup, 136-143
swap files, disabling, 132-133
system
  backups, 131
  components, 128-129
  files, 157-158
  requirements, 129-130
TSR programs, disabling, 134
Typical Setup, 143
Windows 95
  configuration, 157-158
  installation, 127-158
  updating, 136-143
Portable Setup, 105, 143
ports
  communications ports (Device Manager), 184
  COM ports, 831
  MIDI ports, selecting, 625
  mouse, 293-294
  parallel ports, 714-715
    direct-cable connections, 986-988
  printers
    choosing, 467
    configuring, 468-471
  serial ports, 714-715, 728-730
    16550A UART, 730
    asynchronous vs. synchronous transmissions, 731-732
    base addresses, 738-739
    COM 1 ports, 180-181
    connectors, 730-731
    data bit identification, 732-733
    Interrupt Request Lines (IRQs), 734-738
    mouse, 300
    parity checking, 733-734
POST (Power On Self Test), 163, 375, 1069
posterized graphics, 555
posting bulletin board messages (MSN), 814
Postoffice (Microsoft Exchange)
  setup, 823
    sharing folders, 824-825
    user profiles, 825-826
  system requirements, 822-823
PostScript fonts, 531-532, 538-539

PostScript tab (Properties sheet), 487-491
POWER (deleted DOS commands), 1009
Power dialog box, 947
Power On Self Test (POST), 1069
PPP, 970-971
  Internet connections, 866-867, 878-880
preemptive multitasking, 785, 314-315
  threads, 315
  16-bit/32-bit programs, 401-402
Preferences command
  Terminal menu, 1032
  View menu, 613
Preferences dialog box, 613
pricing, see **costs**
primary file names, 53-54
PRINT (deleted DOS commands), 1006
Print command (Registry menu), 1060
Print dialog box, 185
print jobs
  creating, 507-510
  deleting, 514-515
  managing, 510-515
  pausing, 511-513
  resuming, 513-514
  searching, 571-572
print spoolers, 502-507
  networks, 497
Print Troubleshooter, 572-574
PRINTER.SYS (deleted DOS drivers), 1007
printers
  adding, 464-465
  compatibility, 474-476
  deleting, 493
  drivers, 463
  icons, 476
  installing, 471-472
  managing, 461-462
    DOS, 1006
  network, 494-499
    adding, 472-474
    peer-to-peer networks, 937-938
    properties, 496
    sharing, 494-95
  performance, 559-560
    hardware, 562-564

Index **1255**

software, 560-562
ports
    choosing, 467
    configuring, 468-471
Printers folder, 462-476
Properties sheet tabs, 477-492
set up, 476-492
troubleshooting, 559
    disk capacity, 570
    driver problems, 565-566
    performance, 572
types, selecting, 466
Printers command (Settings menu), 29
Printers folder, 462-476
printing, 56, 501-521
    Call log entries, 776
    deferred printing (laptops), 960-961
        transferring, 981-983
    DOS applications, 520-521
    files, printing to, 515-517
    fonts, 526, 535-541
    graphics, 552-554
    HyperTerminal sessions, 780-781
    network, 498-499, 517-518, 905-906
        fonts, 934-936
        separator pages, 932-933
    off-line, 154-156
    Point and Print, 518-520
    print jobs
        creating, 507-510
        deleting, 514-515
        finding, 571-572
        managing, 510-515
        pausing, 511-513
        resuming, 513-514
    Registry files, 337, 1060
    resource information, devices, 185-186
    spooling, 56, 502-507
    troubleshooting, 572-574
        DOS window won't print, 569-570
        font printing, 566-569
        incomplete printing, 571
        print jobs, finding, 571-572
        slow printing, 572
problems, *see* **troubleshooting**
Process Scheduler, 313-314
process scheduling, 313-315
    cooperative multitasking, 314

preemptive multitasking, 314-315
Prodigy, 786
PROGMAN.INI file, 322, 1062
    deleting, 322-323
Program Groups, 364
program information file (PIF), 438-439
Program Manager, disabling, 95
    on portable computers, 134
Program tab, customizing DOS window, 1039-1042
programs
    16-bit performance, 417
    automatic running, 387, 1101-1103
        backup programs, 1123
        communications programs, 1123
        disabling scheduled programs, 1120-1121
        Disk Defragmenter, 1116-1119
        Low Disk Space Notification, 1106-1111
        portable computer option, 1123-1124
        removing scheduled programs, 1121
        running programs now, 1120
        ScanDisk, 1112-1116
        stopping schedules, 1122
        suspending schedules, 1121-1122
    client applications, updating links, 700
    communications programs
        Exchange, 787-790
        HyperTerminal, 776-784
        Microsoft Network, 807-809
        online services, 785-787
        Phone Dialer, 773-776
        TAPI, 768
        third-party communications programs, 785
    crashes, 319
    disabling, 94-95
        portable computers, 134
    DOS programs
        APPS.INF file, 426-435
        batch files, 439-443
        disk utilities, 459
        DOS VM, 318
        file names, long, 459

folders, 442-443
fonts, changing, 449-450
initialization, 439-443
installing, 421-426
keys, shortcut, 456-457
memory, 444-447
multitasking, 453-457
printing from, 520-521
Registry, 458
screen modifications, 448-453
text-mode lines, 450-451
variables, changing, 439-441
font changes, 543-544
group reorganization, 117-118, 366-368
hung, 319
INI files, 458
installing, 395-408
Killer CD-ROM, 1208-1210
manually, 399-400
wizards, 396-398, 422-425
legacy, 400
links, 698-699
PIF Editor, 438
removing, 320-324
from Start menu, 366-368
renaming, 366-368
sequencer, 589
shortcuts, 82-84, 364-365
Start menu, adding to, 381-384
switching between, 24-25, 32-33
types, 318-319
video clips, dropping, 658-660
viruses, 1067, 1074
Windows
16-bit, 318, 400-405
32-bit, 318, 400-405
Windows NT, 400
see also software
Programs menu
changing, 384
commands
Accessories, 27
Netscape, 884
StartUp, 27
prompt (FTP commands), 1026
properties, 72
Desktop Themes, 1164-1165
DOS window properties, 1038-1039

Font tab, 1043
Memory tab, 1044-1045
Misc tab, 1046-1049
Program tab, 1039-1042
Screen tab, 1045-1049
downloaded file options (MSN), 815
full-motion video, 654-658
selection points, 653-654
IRQ Device Manager, 179-181
MIDI properties, 623-629
MSN chat rooms, 816-817
multimedia properties, 616-617
audio CDs, 617-621, 630
CD-ROM performance, 636-637
MIDI, 623-629
video, 410-411, 621-623, 661
viewing, 631-632
volume, 632-633
network printers, 496
switching, 74
TCP/IP, 870
DNS servers, 871
gateway IPs, 872
IP addresses, 870-871
subnet mask IPs, 871-872
Properties commands
Context menu, 177
Device menu, 654
File menu, 74, 782
Properties control (DOS toolbar), 1036
Properties dialog box, 538
tabs, 477-492
viewing (MSN), 807
Properties for Display dialog box, 276, 542
Properties menu commands, 881
protected mode operation, 44-45
PROTOCOL.INI files, 919-921
[EPRO$] section, 922
[NETBEUI$] section, 921-922
[nwlink$] section, 922
[protman$] section, 921
protocols, 970
CHAP, 877
DHCP, 870
file-transfer, 742-745
KERMIT, 748
XMODEM, 745-746
YMODEM, 746

Index **1257**

ZMODEM, 746-747
FTP, 864-865
installing, 972-974
network, 892
    adding, 900-901, 972-974
    IPX/SPX, 970-974
    NetBEUI, 970-974, 979-980
    NetBIOS, 970-971
    PROTCOL.INI files, 919-922
    TCP/IP, 859, 909, 970-74, 979-980
PAP, 877
PPP, 866, 878-880
SLIP, 866-867, 880-881
PST (Personal Information Store), 788
pucks (digitizing tablets), 299
put filename (FTP command), 1026
pwd (FTP command), 1026

Q

QBASIC command, 1009
queues, message, 402-403
Quick View command (pop-up menu), 80
Quick View tool, 79-81
QuickTime program, 640
quit (FTP command), 884, 1026

R

RAM (random access memory), 228-243
    access times, 230-231
    adding, 204-205
    caches, 231-234
        controller circuits, 232
        LRU (least recently used) algorithm, 232
        motherboard, 233
    clock cycles, 231
    DOS management, 1005-1006
    graphics performance, 283
    interleaved, 229-230
    motherboard, 229
    page mode, 229
    static column access, 229
    swap files, 93, 316-317
    Windows 95 requirements, 199, 202-203

RAMDRIVE.SYS (deleted DOS drivers), 1007
Random Order command (Options menu), 612-613
RAS (Remote Access Services), 1080
    communications protocol, 970-971
raster graphics, 548-549
rasterizer *see* **font engine**
ratios, compression, 646
read-ahead caching, 235-238
reading e-mail, 789
    bulletin board messages (MSN), 811-813
    e-mail messages, 789
    Microsoft Exchange, 841-842
README.TXT file, 283
rebooting, 46-47
    Compression Agent, 1145
    Windows 95, 338
Receive File command (Transfer menu), 782
receiving files (HyperTerminal), 781-782
recording sounds
    recording quality, 671-673
    sound effects, 673-675
        editing, 676-678
    volume control, 667-669
RECOVER commands, 1003
recovering
    files, 20-21
    Registry, 337-338
recv filename (FTP command), 1027
Recycle Bin icon, 20-21
Regedit (Registry Editor), 331-336
REGEDIT.EXE file, 170
registering Windows 95, 103
Registry, 58, 178, 327-339, 396, 1056-1057
    backups, 338
    DOS programs, 458
    editing, 331-336
        dialog boxes, 335
    exporting files, 337, 1057-1060
    font files, 935-936
    hard copy printing, 337
    importing, 337
    INI files, 327

1258 Killer Windows 95

keys
  adding, 336
  deleting, 336
  operating system, 328-330
modifying, 330-331
Regedit (Registry Editor), 331-336, 1057
remote accessing, 339
restoring, 337-338, 1060-1061
searching, 332-333
subkeys, 330
SYSTEM.DAT file, 328
SYSTEM.INI file, 178
USER.DAT file, 328
values, 330
  adding, 336
  binary data, 330
  deleting, 336
  editing, 333-335
  DWORD data, 330
  string data, 330
WIN.INI file, 178
Registry menu commands
Export Registry File, 1057
Import Registry File, 1060
Print, 1060
Remote Access Services (RAS), 1080
remote computing, 943
HyperTerminal connections, 777-780
installation, 952-956
Microsoft Exchange, installing, 962-966
receiving files, 781-782
sending files, 780-781
see also HyperTerminal; Microsoft Exchange
Remote Mail
connections, 983
Tools menu commands, 982-983
Remote System command (Connect menu), 887, 1031
Remove Item command (Edit menu), 225
removing
  applications, 320-324
  hardware, 186-189
  programs, 320-324
  utilities, 1195-1197
  Windows 95, 1197-1203

Rename command (File menu), 74
rename file1 file2 (FTP command), 1027
renaming, *see* **naming**
REPLACE command, 1004
Reply by E-mail command (Compose menu), 814
Reply to BBS command (Compose menu), 814
replying to messages (MSN), 814
resolution
full-motion video, 647
mouse, 289-290
resources
management, 57-58
Windows 95 limits, 418-419
restarting, 46-47
Compression Agent, 1145
Windows 95, 338
RESTORE commands, 1004
RLE (Run Length Encoding), 642
file extention, 548
video compression scheme, 645
RLL (Run Length Limited) encoding, 207
rmdir folder (FTP command), 1027
ROUTE command (DOS), 1029-1030
rule-based virus detection, 1078-1079
Run command (Start menu), 31
Run dialog box, 114, 331
Run Length Encoding (RLE), 642
file extention, 548
video compression scheme, 645
runtime engines, 642-643

S

s command line switch, 169
Safe Mode Startup, 164-168
640 × 480 resolution, 166-168
networks, 166-168
Safe Recovery, 124-125, 157, 160-161
SAGE.XXX file (System Agent), 1105
Save History command (File menu), 817
Save Scheme As dialog box, 606
Save Search command (File menu), 86
saving
  chats (MSN), 817

Index **1259**

embedded objects (OLE), 710-711
HyperTerminal sessions, 779-781
search criteria, 86
sound schemes, 606-608
Scale menu commands
Frames, 652
Time, 652
Scan for Viruses command (Context menu), 1089
ScanDisk, 124
automatic running, 1112
Advanced options, 1113-1116
Standard configuration, 1112
Thorough configuration, 1112-1113
SCANDISK.EXE file, 170
scanners (virus detection), 1077
scanning disk drives, 124, 1071
scheduling
chats (MSN), 818
Compression Agent, 1145
programs, 387, 1101-1103
backup programs, 1123
communications programs, 1123
disabling scheduled programs, 1120-1121
Disk Defragmenter, 1116-1119
Low Disk Space Notification, 1106-1111
portable computer option, 1123-1124
removing scheduled programs, 1121
running programs now, 1120
ScanDisk, 1112-1116
stopping schedules, 1122
suspending schedules, 1121-1122
schemes
sound, 370
Windows 95 color schemes, 344-346
Science themes, 1162
scrambled hard drives, 338
screens
burn-in, 350
Desktop Themes, 1161-1166
DOS program modifications, 448-453
fonts, *see* display fonts
sizing for video playback, 654-658
startup screen, 16

video resolution, 647
screen savers, 350-355
activating, 351-352
hot spots, 1165-1166
optional settings, 352-353
password protection, 353-355
Screen Saver Properties sheet, 1166
scripts
batch, 114-121
drive letters, 121-123
logon, 117-121
setup, 110, 117-121
SCSI (Smal Computer System Interface), 242
compatibility, 254
controller cards, 206
drive interleave, 251
hard drives, 206
interface card, 206
SCSIDSK.EXE file, 165
SCSIHA.SYS file, 165
SEA (System Enhancement Associates), 243-244
SEALINK protocol, 746
searching
databases, 865-866, 889-890
files, 84-86
FTP sites, 865
Gopher sites, 864
help topics
Contents tab, 35
Find tab, 36-38
Index tab, 35-36
MSN topics, 818-819
Registry, 332-333
secondary file names, 53-54
Section file field, 428
sectors, 247
security
network, 909-911
share-level, 985
virus security guidelines, 1075-1079
segmented
caches, 243
memory, 215-217
Select Device dialog box, 275
Select Folder To Publish dialog box, 1097

1260 Killer Windows 95

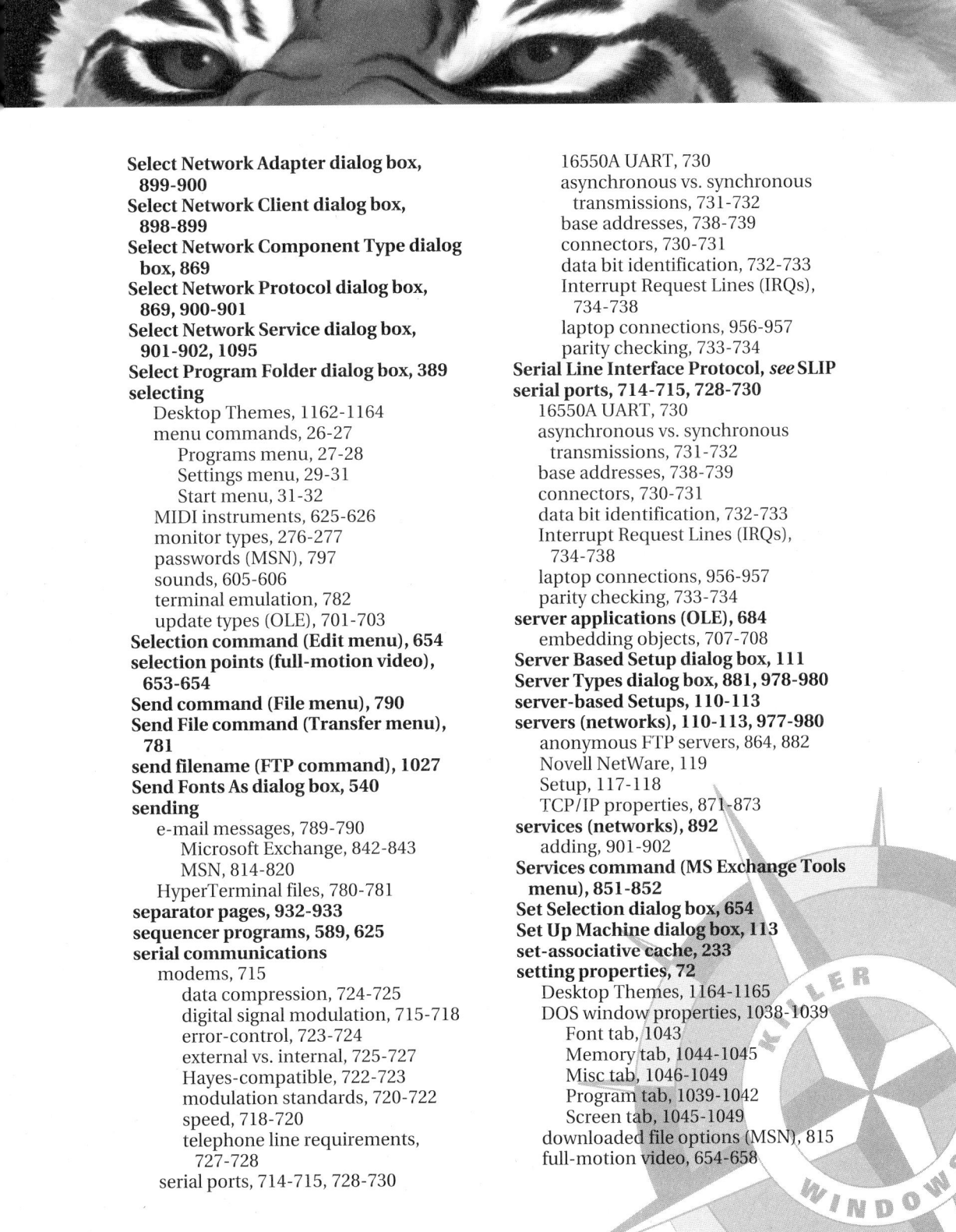

Select Network Adapter dialog box, 899-900
Select Network Client dialog box, 898-899
Select Network Component Type dialog box, 869
Select Network Protocol dialog box, 869, 900-901
Select Network Service dialog box, 901-902, 1095
Select Program Folder dialog box, 389
selecting
    Desktop Themes, 1162-1164
    menu commands, 26-27
        Programs menu, 27-28
        Settings menu, 29-31
        Start menu, 31-32
    MIDI instruments, 625-626
    monitor types, 276-277
    passwords (MSN), 797
    sounds, 605-606
    terminal emulation, 782
    update types (OLE), 701-703
Selection command (Edit menu), 654
selection points (full-motion video), 653-654
Send command (File menu), 790
Send File command (Transfer menu), 781
send filename (FTP command), 1027
Send Fonts As dialog box, 540
sending
    e-mail messages, 789-790
        Microsoft Exchange, 842-843
        MSN, 814-820
    HyperTerminal files, 780-781
separator pages, 932-933
sequencer programs, 589, 625
serial communications
    modems, 715
        data compression, 724-725
        digital signal modulation, 715-718
        error-control, 723-724
        external vs. internal, 725-727
        Hayes-compatible, 722-723
        modulation standards, 720-722
        speed, 718-720
        telephone line requirements, 727-728
    serial ports, 714-715, 728-730

16550A UART, 730
    asynchronous vs. synchronous transmissions, 731-732
    base addresses, 738-739
    connectors, 730-731
    data bit identification, 732-733
    Interrupt Request Lines (IRQs), 734-738
    laptop connections, 956-957
    parity checking, 733-734
Serial Line Interface Protocol, *see* SLIP
serial ports, 714-715, 728-730
    16550A UART, 730
    asynchronous vs. synchronous transmissions, 731-732
    base addresses, 738-739
    connectors, 730-731
    data bit identification, 732-733
    Interrupt Request Lines (IRQs), 734-738
    laptop connections, 956-957
    parity checking, 733-734
server applications (OLE), 684
    embedding objects, 707-708
Server Based Setup dialog box, 111
Server Types dialog box, 881, 978-980
server-based Setups, 110-113
servers (networks), 110-113, 977-980
    anonymous FTP servers, 864, 882
    Novell NetWare, 119
    Setup, 117-118
    TCP/IP properties, 871-873
services (networks), 892
    adding, 901-902
Services command (MS Exchange Tools menu), 851-852
Set Selection dialog box, 654
Set Up Machine dialog box, 113
set-associative cache, 233
setting properties, 72
    Desktop Themes, 1164-1165
    DOS window properties, 1038-1039
        Font tab, 1043
        Memory tab, 1044-1045
        Misc tab, 1046-1049
        Program tab, 1039-1042
        Screen tab, 1045-1049
    downloaded file options (MSN), 815
    full-motion video, 654-658

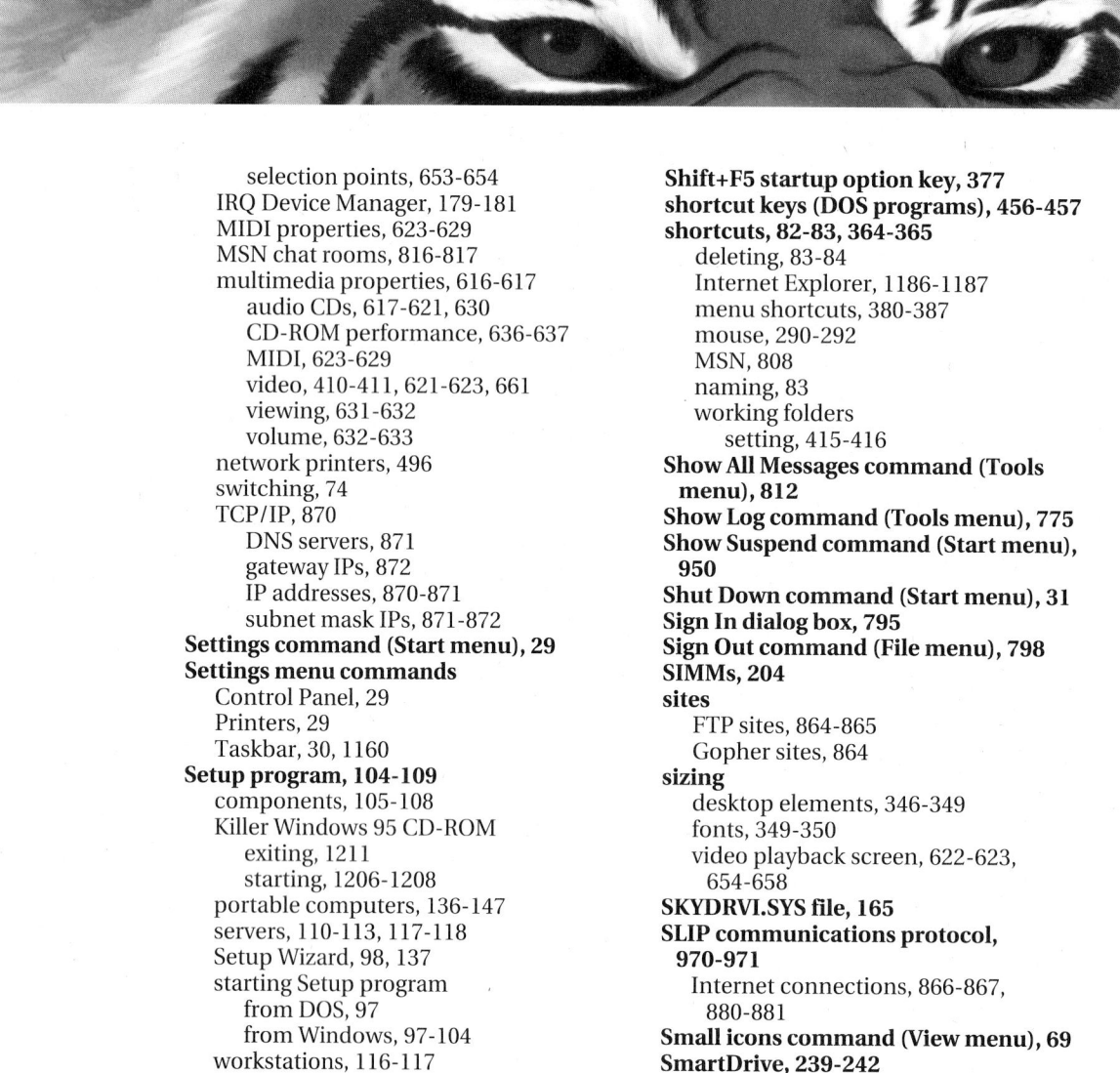

selection points, 653-654
IRQ Device Manager, 179-181
MIDI properties, 623-629
MSN chat rooms, 816-817
multimedia properties, 616-617
    audio CDs, 617-621, 630
    CD-ROM performance, 636-637
    MIDI, 623-629
    video, 410-411, 621-623, 661
    viewing, 631-632
    volume, 632-633
network printers, 496
switching, 74
TCP/IP, 870
    DNS servers, 871
    gateway IPs, 872
    IP addresses, 870-871
    subnet mask IPs, 871-872
Settings command (Start menu), 29
Settings menu commands
    Control Panel, 29
    Printers, 29
    Taskbar, 30, 1160
Setup program, 104-109
    components, 105-108
    Killer Windows 95 CD-ROM
        exiting, 1211
        starting, 1206-1208
    portable computers, 136-147
    servers, 110-113, 117-118
    Setup Wizard, 98, 137
    starting Setup program
        from DOS, 97
        from Windows, 97-104
    workstations, 116-117
SETUP commands, 118
setup scripts, 110, 117-121
SETVER.EXE driver, 165
SHARE (DOS command), 1005
sharing
    access rights, 926-928
    files, 984-988
    folders, 924-926
    Microsoft Exchange, 824-825
    naming shared resources, 926
    printers, 494-49
    see also networking
Sharing tab (Properties sheet), 492
SHELL32.DLL file, 1157

Shift+F5 startup option key, 377
shortcut keys (DOS programs), 456-457
shortcuts, 82-83, 364-365
    deleting, 83-84
    Internet Explorer, 1186-1187
    menu shortcuts, 380-387
    mouse, 290-292
    MSN, 808
    naming, 83
    working folders
        setting, 415-416
Show All Messages command (Tools menu), 812
Show Log command (Tools menu), 775
Show Suspend command (Start menu), 950
Shut Down command (Start menu), 31
Sign In dialog box, 795
Sign Out command (File menu), 798
SIMMs, 204
sites
    FTP sites, 864-865
    Gopher sites, 864
sizing
    desktop elements, 346-349
    fonts, 349-350
    video playback screen, 622-623, 654-658
SKYDRVI.SYS file, 165
SLIP communications protocol, 970-971
    Internet connections, 866-867, 880-881
Small icons command (View menu), 69
SmartDrive, 239-242
Smartmodem 2400, 723
SMARTMON (DOS command), 1004
smoothing fonts, 1150-1153
soft fonts, 526
software, 311-324
    archiving, 243-244
    caches, 234-242
    communications, 739
        terminal emulation, 739-741
        transferring files, 741-742, 748-749
    compression, 243-245
    configuring, 281-283
    conflicts, 162-163
    DOS, 318

full-motion video, 642
installing
    manually, 399-400
    wizards, 396-398, 422-424
printer performance, 560-562
types, 318-319
viruses, 1086
    software, 1064-1065
    detection methods, 1076-1079
Windows, 318
see also programs
sorting
    bulletin board messages (MSN), 811
    e-mail messages, 853-854
    files, 75-76
    icons, 76
sound, 604-614
    events, 369-370
    multimedia, 577-602
    schemes, 370
        saving, 606-608
Sound Blaster sound cards, 586, 674
sound cards
    activating/deactivating, 184
    editing sound effects, 676-678
    recording sounds
        recording quality, 671-673
        sound effects, 673-675
    Volume Control accessory, 664
        channel display, 665
        recording levels, 667-669
        taskbar access, 670-671
        volume control, 666-667
Sound Recorder
    Edit menu commands, 676-678
    editing effects, 676-678
    Record button, 674-675
sounds
    assigning to events, 368-370
    changing, 368-370
    customizing, 604-607
    editing sound effects, 676-678
    listening to, 605-606
    recording sound effects, 673-675
    selecting, 605-606
    viewing, 605-606
Sounds Properties sheet, 604
source documents (OLE), 684
Source Path dialog box, 112

space parity, 734
speed
    modem, 718-720
    Windows 95 requirements, 199-201
speed dial buttons (Phone Dialer)
    editing, 775
    number storage, 774-775
Speed Dial command (Edit menu), 775
spelling checks (Microsoft Exchange), 844
spooling print jobs, 56
Sports theme, 1162
SQY55.SYS file, 165
SRAM (static RAM) chips, 231
SSTBIO.SYS file, 165
SSTDRIVE.SYS file, 165
SSTOR.EXE file, 165
SSTOR.SYS file, 165
SSWAP.COM file, 165
ST506 hard drives, 207, 253
Stac Electronics Stacker, 133
STACKER.COM file, 165
Start button menus, 26-27
    Documents, 28-29
    Programs, 27-28
    Settings, 29-31
    Start, 31-32
Start command (DOS), 1033-1034
Start Logging command (Terminal menu), 889, 1032
Start menu
    adding
        folders, 382-384
        programs, 366-368, 381-384
    changing, 381-384
    controlling, 380-387
    removing programs, 367-368
Start menu commands
    Help, 34
    Run, 31
    Settings, 29
    Show Suspend, 950
    Shut Down, 31
starting
    Compression Agent, 1141
    DriveSpace 3, 1131-1132
    Exchange program, 788
    Explorer, 66
    HyperTerminal, 777

Killer Windows 95 CD-ROM,
   1206-1208
      AutoPlay, 1207
      manual startup, 1207-1208
   Windows 95, 16-17
Startup, 373-393
   Documents menu, 385-387
   DOS startup, 373-374
   modes, 162
      Safe, 164-168
      Step-by-Step Confirmation,
         164-165
   modifying, 365-366, 375-380
   option keys, 377
   Programs menu changes, 384
   screen, 16
   Start menu, 162, 376-377
      adding programs, 381-384
      changing, 381-384
      controlling, 380-387
   system resource conservation,
      391-393
   troubleshooting, 161-171
StartUp command (Programs menu),
   27
startup disks, 125, 127
   troubleshooting, 169-170
StartUp folder, 375
   changing
      manually, 390-391
      wizards, 388-390
   groups, 117-118
   programs
      adding, 388-391
      removing, 388-391
   name changes, 372
Startup menu, 376-377
STARTUP.GRP file, 117-118
state-of-the-art MPC standard, 582-583
static column access, 229
static objects (OLE), 711
statistics, disk compression, 1133-1135
status (FTP command), 1027
stealth viruses, 1067, 1075-1076
Step-by-Step Confirmation, 164-165
Stop Logging command (Terminal
   menu), 1032
stores, personal information, 838
storing speed dial numbers (Phone
   Dialer), 774-775

stretching wallpaper, 1161
strings
   APPS.INF file, 434
   Registry data, 330
styles (desktop elements), 343-350
subkeys (Registry), 330
submenus, creating, 366-368
subnet mask IPs, 871-872
subnotebooks, 128
subscribing to mailing lists, 862
subsystems, startup, 375
Super VGA monitor requirements, 199
SuperStor, 133
suspend mode option (laptops),
   949-951
SVGA (super video graphics array)
   video cards, 259
swap files, 218, 245-247
   disabling, 92-93
   portable computers, 132-133
   settings, 218-220
   WIN386.SWP, 245-247
switches (DOS commands)
   ARP, 1023-1033
   FTP, 1024
   NBSTAT, 1021-1022
   NETSTAT, 1020-1021
   PING, 1028-1029
   TRACERT, 1032-1033
switching
   applications, 24-25, 32-33
   passwords (MSN), 797
   properties, 74
   update types (OLE), 701-703
synchronizing
   briefcase files, 997-999
   laptop/desktop files, 957-959
synchronous data transmissions,
   731-732
SYS.COM file, 170
SYSAGENT.XXX file (System Agent),
   1105-1106
system, 88-89
   backing up, 92
   booting, 374
   browsing contents, 18-19
   components
      deleting, 391-393

portable computers, 128-129
reinstalling, 393
files
deleting, 125-126, 157-158, 391-393, 1200-1203
reinstalling, 393
hierarchy views, 67-68
multimedia upgrades, 583-585
network workstation, 90-91
office computers, 89
performance monitoring, 221-226
portable computer backups, 131
requirements
Microsoft Exchange, 822-823
portable computers, 129-130
Windows 95, 90, 202-209
resource conservation, 391-393, 417-419
server login scripts, 121-123
testing, 16
types, 88-90
video performance improvements, 410-411
System Agent, 1101-1103
backup program scheduling, 1123
Change Schedule option, 1107-1108
communication program scheduling, 1123
Disk Defragmenter scheduling, 1116
interruptions, 1119
output logging, 1119
scheduling options, 1119
setttings, 1117-1118
files, 1103-1104
SAGE.XXX, 1105
SYSAGENT.XXX, 1105-1106
Low Disk Space Notification scheduling, 1106
alarm settings, 1110-1111
changing schedules, 1107-1108
notification changes, 1109-1110
settings, 1109
options
dispabling scheduled programs, 1120-1121
removing scheduled programs, 1121
running scheduled programs now, 1120

stopping System Agent, 1122
suspending System Agent, 1121-1122
portable computer option, 1123-1124
ScanDisk scheduling, 1112
Advanced options, 1113-1116
Standard configuration, 1112
Thorough configuration, 1112-1113
System Monitor, 221-226
System Properties sheet, 177, 219, 636, 945
Device Manager tab, 736-738
System VM, 312
SYSTEM.DAT file, 328, 1056
SYSTEM.INI files, 58, 322, 1062
deleting, 322-323, 417
editing, 417
Registry, 178

T

TAPI program, 768
taskbar, 24-25, 32-33
Auto Hide feature, 1160
battery meter display, 946-949
Volume Control icon, 670-671
Taskbar command (Settings menu), 30, 1160
TCP/IP, 859
configuring, 872, 874-875
DNS servers, 872-873
gateways, 875
IP addresses, 874
WINS, 875
DOS commands, 1022-1023
ARP, 1023
FTP, 1024-1027
PING, 1028-1029
ROUTE, 1029-1030
TELNET, 1030-1032
TRACERT, 1032-1033
installing, 868-870
network protocol, 909, 970-974, 979-980
Internet connections, 1177-1178
properties, 870
DNS servers, 871
gateway IPs, 872

Index **1265**

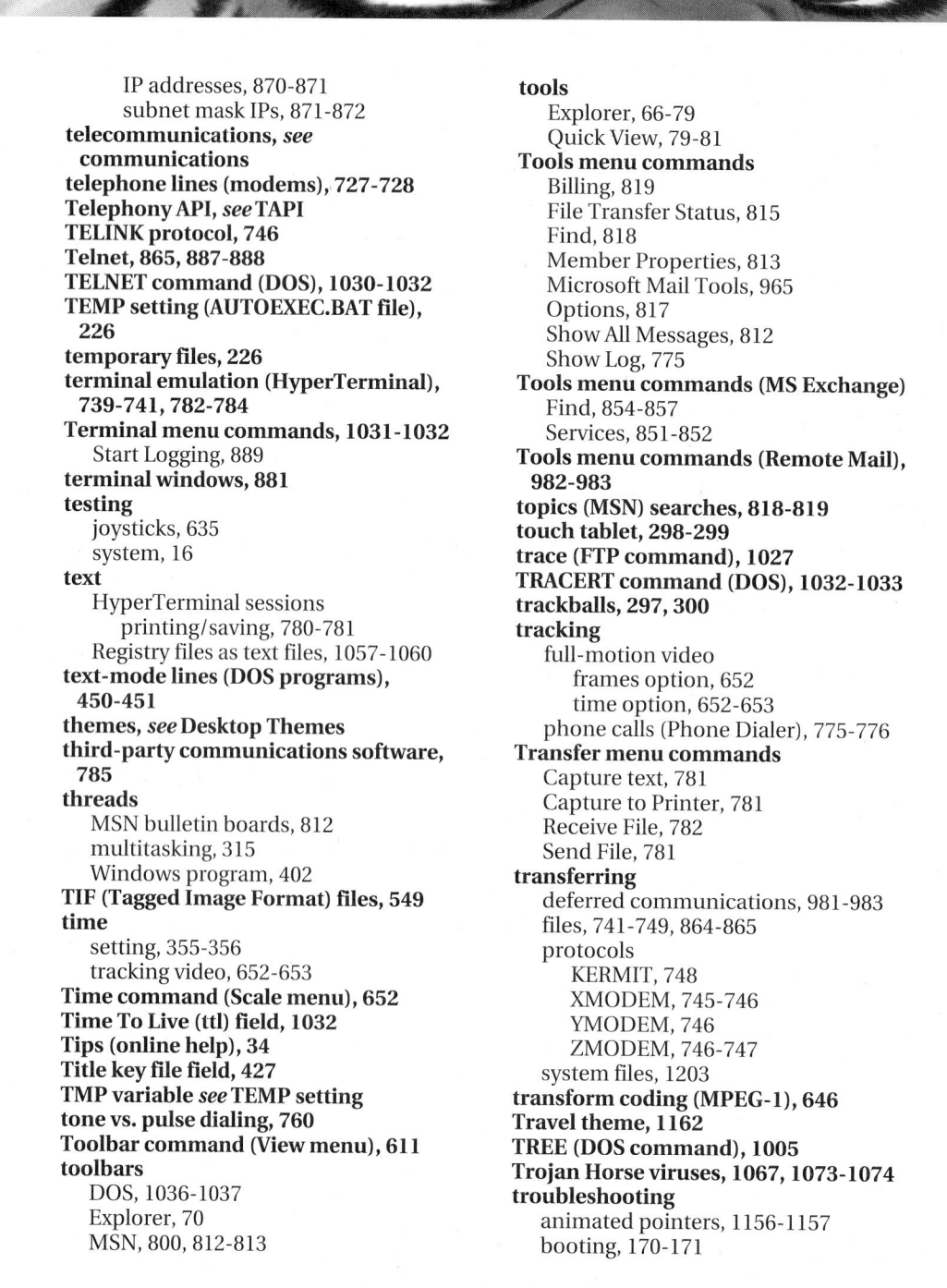

IP addresses, 870-871
subnet mask IPs, 871-872
telecommunications, *see* **communications**
telephone lines (modems), 727-728
Telephony API, *see* **TAPI**
TELINK protocol, 746
Telnet, 865, 887-888
TELNET command (DOS), 1030-1032
TEMP setting (AUTOEXEC.BAT file), 226
temporary files, 226
terminal emulation (HyperTerminal), 739-741, 782-784
Terminal menu commands, 1031-1032
Start Logging, 889
terminal windows, 881
testing
joysticks, 635
system, 16
text
HyperTerminal sessions
printing/saving, 780-781
Registry files as text files, 1057-1060
text-mode lines (DOS programs), 450-451
themes, *see* **Desktop Themes**
third-party communications software, 785
threads
MSN bulletin boards, 812
multitasking, 315
Windows program, 402
TIF (Tagged Image Format) files, 549
time
setting, 355-356
tracking video, 652-653
Time command (Scale menu), 652
Time To Live (ttl) field, 1032
Tips (online help), 34
Title key file field, 427
TMP variable *see* **TEMP setting**
tone vs. pulse dialing, 760
Toolbar command (View menu), 611
toolbars
DOS, 1036-1037
Explorer, 70
MSN, 800, 812-813

tools
Explorer, 66-79
Quick View, 79-81
Tools menu commands
Billing, 819
File Transfer Status, 815
Find, 818
Member Properties, 813
Microsoft Mail Tools, 965
Options, 817
Show All Messages, 812
Show Log, 775
Tools menu commands (MS Exchange)
Find, 854-857
Services, 851-852
Tools menu commands (Remote Mail), 982-983
topics (MSN) searches, 818-819
touch tablet, 298-299
trace (FTP command), 1027
TRACERT command (DOS), 1032-1033
trackballs, 297, 300
tracking
full-motion video
frames option, 652
time option, 652-653
phone calls (Phone Dialer), 775-776
Transfer menu commands
Capture text, 781
Capture to Printer, 781
Receive File, 782
Send File, 781
transferring
deferred communications, 981-983
files, 741-749, 864-865
protocols
KERMIT, 748
XMODEM, 745-746
YMODEM, 746
ZMODEM, 746-747
system files, 1203
transform coding (MPEG-1), 646
Travel theme, 1162
TREE (DOS command), 1005
Trojan Horse viruses, 1067, 1073-1074
troubleshooting
animated pointers, 1156-1157
booting, 170-171

command line switches, 168-169
Device Manager, 172-174
direct-cable communications, 991
disk space, 163
drivers, 163-165
Emergency Boot Disk (startup disk), 169-170
files
    AUTOEXEC.BAT, 166-168
    CONFIG.SYS, 166-168
    configuration, 166-168
    removal dangers, 165
files, corrupted, 163-164
hardware, 162-164, 171-174
installation, 160-161
modems, 764-765
mouse, 306-307
network computers, 166-168
printers, 559-575
    disk full, 570
    DOS window won't print, 569-570
    driver problems, 565-566
    fonts are wrong, 566-567
    incomplete printing, 571
    print job disappears, 571-572
    slow printing, 572
    TrueType fonts won't print, 568-569
Safe Mode Startup, 166-168
software, 162-163
sound cards, 599-601
Startup, 161-171
undocumented features, 406
Windows programs, 405-408
Windows 95, 159-174
True Type fonts, 529-531
    font engine, 55-56
    Lucida, 1154
    printing, 530-531
    troubleshooting, 568-569
TSR (terminate and stay resident) programs, 94-95, 134
ttl (Time To Live) field, 1032
type xfertype (FTP command), 1027
Typecase, 531
typefaces, 524
Typical Setup, 104
    portable computers, 143

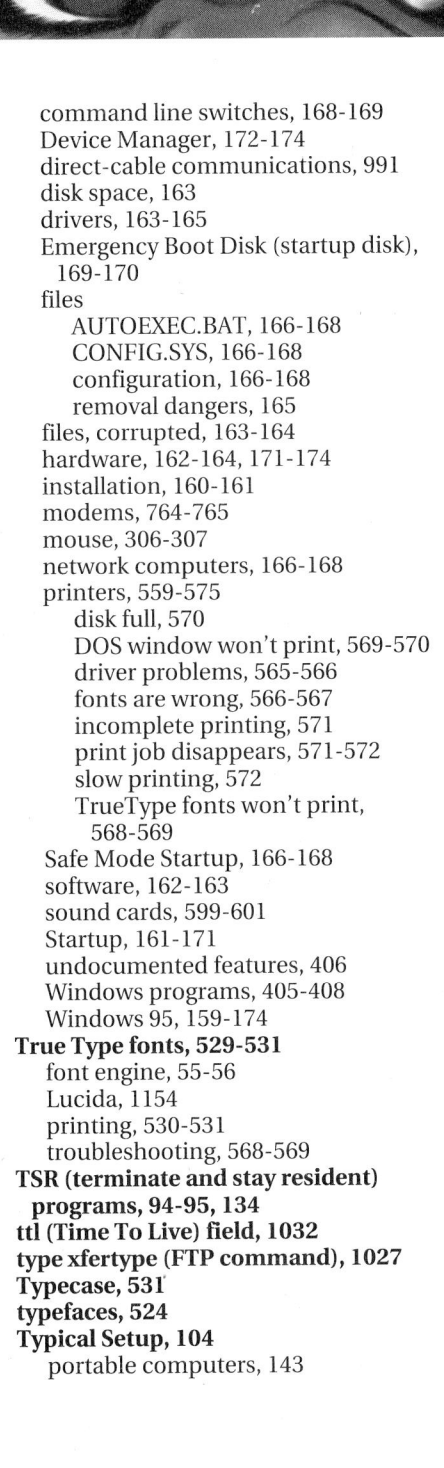

U

UART (universal asynchronous receiver/transmitter), 714, 729-730
UltraPack compression format, 1141-1142
UNC (Universal Naming Convention), 113
uncompressed disk drives, 1131-1132
UNDELETE (DOS command), 1005
UNFORMAT (DOS command), 1004
Unicode character set, 53
Uniform Resource Locators (URLs), 863
uninstall feature, 1198
Universal Cable Module (UCM) cable, 988
UnMouse, 299
Update command (File menu), 709
updating
    links
        client application, 700
        OLE, 701-703
    portable computers, 136-143
upgrading
    compressed drives, 1135
    hard drives, 252-255
    hardware
        MPC standards, 579-585
        Windows 95 requirements, 199-211
    multimedia systems, 583-585
    programs in Startup groups, 117-118
    Windows 95, 97-104
    Windows for Workgroups, 117-121
    Windows NT, 111-113
uploading files, 741-742
upper memory, 214
UPS (uninterruptable power supply), 242
URLs (Uniform Resource Locators), 863
USENET newsgroups, 861-862
user accounts (networks), 941-942
user profiles
    Microsoft Exchange, 825-827
    USER.DAT file, 328
user-level network virus protection, 1080-1086
USER.DAT file, 328, 1056
utilities, optional, 1194-1195
    adding/removing, 1195-1197

Index **1267**

V

v command line switch, 169
V-L busses, 263-265
values (Registry). 330
    adding, 336
    deleting, 336
    editing, 333-335
vector
    graphics, 549-551
    quantization, 646
Ventura Publisher graphic files, 550
verbose (FTP command), 1027
Veronica, 864
version number errors (Windows), 406-408
VESA (Video Electronics Standards Association)
    bus specifications, 263
    feature adapter connector, 265, 285
VFAT access limitations, 247
VFINTD.386 (deleted DOS drivers), 1007
VfW, 640-641
    compression codecs, 642-643
    runtime engines, 642-643
VGA (Video Graphics Array)
    adding accelerators, 209
    video cards, 258-259
    screen burn-in, 350
    Windows 95 requirements, 202
video
    bottlenecks, 260-261
    buses, 261-267
    capturing, 641-642
    cards, 258-266
        8514/A, 259
        buses, 261-267
        CGA (Color Graphics Adapter), 258
        color display, 281
        compatibility monitors, 209
        drivers, 273-276
        EGA (Enhanced Graphics Adapter), 258
        graphics accelerator cards, 260-261, 283-285
        HGA (Hercules Graphics Adapter), 258
        IBM PCs, 258
        IBM XTs, 258
        MCA computers, 259
        MCGA (multi-color graphics array), 258
        MDA (Monochrome Display Adapter), 258
        memory, 284
        modes, 260
        monitors, 266-273
        parameters, 278-280
        performance, 260-261
        PS/2 computers, 259
        settings, 340-342
        software configurations, 281-283
        SVGA (Super Video Graphics Array), 259
        system acceleration, 280-285
        types, 258-266
        VESA feature adapter connector, 285
        VGA (Video Graphics Array), 258-259
        VRAM video random-access memory, 284
        XGA (Extended Graphics Array), 259
    clips
        dropping into programs, 658-660
        setting options, 661
    DOS program memory, 447-448
    drivers, 273-276
    parameter changes, 278
    system performance, 280-285, 410-411
    tube (CRT), 269
    video boards mouse ports, 294
Video 1 compression scheme, 645
Video for Windows, *see* VfW, 640-641
Video Properties sheet, 655
View menu commands
    Arrange Icons, 75
    Details, 70
    Expand All Conversations, 812
    Large Icons, 68
    List, 69
    Options, 77, 809
    Preferences, 613
    Small icons, 69
    Toolbar, 611
View menu commands (Dial-Up Networking), 975

viewing
    AVI files, 650
    billing information (MSN), 819-820
    bulletin board messages (MSN), 811
    Call Log entries (Phone Dialer), 775
    codecs video compression, 648-650
    Desktop Themes properties, 1164-1165
    drive/folder contents, 68-70
    e-mail messages, 853
    file contents, 79-81
    FTP commands, 882
    full-motion video
        frames option, 652-653
        time option, 652-653
    help documents, 38
    member properties (MSN), 816
    menus, 26-27
    multimedia device properties, 631-632
    pop-up menus, 40-41
    Properties sheet (MSN), 807
    Registry files, 1057
    system hierarchy, 67-68
virtual machines, 312-318, 1035
    address spaces, 316
    System VM, 312
    VM Manager
        Memory Pager, 317
        memory paging, 316-317
        MS-DOS Mode, 317-318
virtual memory, 214, 217-220
    disabling, 220-226
    monitoring performance, 221-226
    optimizing, 221-226
    settings, 218-220
Virtual Memory dialog box, 93, 132, 219
viruses, 1065-1066
    backups, performing, 1091-1099
    boot-sector viruses, 1067-1069, 1071-1073
    detection methods, 1076
        generic monitoring, 1077-1078
        heuristics, 1078-1079
        inoculation/integrity checking, 1078
        scanners, 1077
    development techniques, 1075-1076
    encrypted viruses, 1076
    event-triggered/keystroke viruses, 1076
    file/program viruses, 1074
    hard disk drives, scanning, 1071
    infection methods, 1079
        downloaded software, 1086
        floppy disks, 1079
        networks, 1080-1086
    online antivirus resources, 1087
    PC boot sequences, 1069-1071
    security guidelines, 1075-1079
    software, 1064-1065
    stealth virus, 1075-1076
    toolkit, 1075-1076
    Trojan Horse virus, 1073-1074
    types, 1066-1069
    VirusScan program, running, 1088-1091
VirusScan 95, 1077, 1088-1091
Visual Enhancements (Plus!), 1149
    Animated Pointers, 1154-1157
    disk space requirements, 1148
    Font Smoothing, 1150-1153
    Full-Window Drag, 1149-1150
    High Color icons, 1157-1158
    large icons, 1158-1160
    Taskbar Auto Hide feature, 1160
    True Type Lucida font, 1154
    wallpaper stretching, 1161
vital files, 1051-1052
    boot files, 1052-1053
        CONFIG.SYS/AUTOEXEC.BAT, 1055-1056
        INF files, 1056
        MSDOS.SYS, 1054-1055
    Registry files, 1056-1057
        exporting to text files, 1057-1060
        restoring, 1060-1061
VL (VESA Local Bus), 255
    performance, 263
    Windows 95 requirements, 203
VLM requester servers, 123
VM (Virtual Machine Manager), 312-324, 1035
    Memory Pager, 316-317
    MS-DOS Mode, 317-318
    Process Scheduler, 313-315
        cooperative multitasking, 314

preemptive multitasking, 314-315
VMM (Virtual Memory Manager), 218, 245-247
Volume Control, 632-635, 664
    channel display, 665
    recording levels, 667-669
    taskbar access, 670-671
    volume control, 666-667
VRAM (Video Random-Access Memory), 284
VSAFE (DOS command), 1005

W

WAIS, 865-866, 889-890
wallpaper, 558
    stretching, 1161
    Paint, 558
    Web graphics as, 1189
    see also backgrounds
WAV files, 675
WaveStudio sound application, 674
wavetable synthesis (sound cards), 588
Welcome dialog box, 103, 193
What's New, 103
Wide-Area Information Server, *see* **WAIS**
\WINDOWS\TEMP directory (hard drive), 226
WIN.INI files, 58, 322, 1062
    deleting, 322-323, 417
    editing, 417
    Registry, 178
    version number errors, 407-408
Win16, 318
    removing, 322-324
Win32, 318
    removing, 320-321
WIN386.SWP file, 245-247
WIN95INS installation folder, 121-122
WINA20.386 (deleted DOS drivers), 1007
WinBootDir entry (MSDOS.SYS file), 1054
WinDir entry (MSDOS.SYS file), 1054
Windows 3.x
    files, 1061
    memory, 215

programs
    16-bit, 400-405
    32-bit, 400-405
    installation, 395-408
Setup
    portable computers, 136-143
    starting, 97-104
sound card compatibility, 586-587
windows
    control buttons, 23-24
    DOS window
        command line access, 1034-1037
        customizing, 1035-1037
        properties, customizing, 1038-1049
    Explorer, 67
        Contents window, 68-70
        Folder window, 67-68
        menus, 67
    moving, 1149-1150
    terminal windows, 881
    video window sizing, 622-623
Windows 95
    appearance schemes, 344-346
    booting, 16-17, 1069-1071
    compatibility, 94, 209-211
    configuration, 365-372
        changing, 125-126
    customizing, 325-372
        appearance, 339-365
    deleting, 1197-1203
        booting to DOS, 1199
        copying DOS files to DOS directory, 1202-1203
        system files, 1200-1202
        transferring system files, 1203
        Windows 95 directories, 1199-1200
    hardware
        interaction, 175, 210-211
        requirements, 199-211
    installing, 87, 96-108
        laptops, 127-128, 147
        networks, client/server, 109-119
        portable computers, 135-147
        preparations, 91-95
        problems, 124-126, 157-158
        system requirements, 90
        Windows NT, 111-118
    Internet connections, 868

modem setup
    configuration, 752-757
    dialing properties, 757-764
    installation, 749-752
networks
    installing, 109-118
    Novell NetWare servers, 118-123
Online Registration, 103
operating system, 43-64
    Plug-and-Play, 63-64
optional utilities, 1194-1195
    adding/removing, 1195-1197
platform, 44
registering, 103
requirements
    CD-ROM drives, 203
    graphics accelerator card, 203
    hard drives, 203
    RAM (Random Access Memory), 203
    upgrading hardware, 199-211
resource limits, 418-419
restarting, 338
software interaction, 311-324
speed, 200
system requirements, 202-209
theme, 1162
troubleshooting, 159-174
uninstall feature, 1198
upgrading, 97-104
virtual machine, 312-318
What's New, 103
Windows NT
    applications, 400
    file names, 405
Windows Tour, 103
Windows bitmap files, 548
\WINDOWS\INF folder, 426
Windows Explorer, 66
    files
        associations, 551-552
        management, 74-75
        sorting, 75-76
    folder sharing, 984-988
    MSN navigation, 805-806
    network folders, creating, 120
    starting, 66
    status bar, 73
    toolbars, 70
    window components, 67

    Contents window, 68-70
    Folder window, 67-68
    menus, 67
Windows for Workgroups, 58
    upgrading, 117-121
Windows Internet Naming Service, see WINS
Windows NT
    file names, 405
    installing Windows 95, 111-118
    memory, 216
    multitasking, 315
    removing programs, 320-321
    upgrading, 111-113
    Windows 95 applications, 400
Windows Tour, 103, 123, 142
WINS, 873, 875
Winsock, 866, 886
WINZIP, 245
wireless mouse, 296
wizards, 39-40, 388-390
    Add New Hardware Wizard, 191-197
    Add Printer, 464
    Add/Remove Programs, 320, 424
    Create Shortcut, 388
    DOS program installation, 422-425
    Install New Modem, 749-752
    installation
        running, 396-398
        software, 396-398, 422-424
    Internet Setup, 1170-1171
        Microsoft Network option, 1171-1172
        network connections, 1177-1178
        Service Provider option, 1173-1177
    Make New Connection, 876
    Microsoft Workgroup Postoffice Admin, 823
    MIDI Instrument Installation, 625
    Setup, 98, 137
    StartUp folder changes, 388-390
WMCONFIG file, 1168
WordPad files, 426
WordPerfect graphics files, 550
workgroups (network), 955
    managing, 939-940
working folders
    flag file field, 427
    setting, 415-416

Index **1271**

Working in the Background pointer, 1154
workstations, network, 90-91, 116-117
World Wide Web, 862-863
    associating files, 1182-1183
    browsing, 1190-1191
        downloading browsers, 882
        Netscape, 884-885
    copying URL sites, 1189
    custom colors, 1181
    downloading files, 1179
        graphics, 1189-1190
    Favorite sites, 1185-1186
    hyperlinks, 1179
    Microsoft homepage, 1178-1179
        avoiding, 1182
    shortcuts to sites, 1186-1187
    storing accessed sites, 1184-1185
worm viruses, 1067
WPG file extention, 550
write-behind caching, 238-239, 241-242
WXMODEM protocol, 746
WYSIWYG, 200, 523

X

x command line switch, 169
x-height type, 524
XGA (Extended Graphics Array) video cards, 259
XMODEM protocol, 743-746
XMS (extended) memory, 445-446
XMSMem key word, 434

Y

YMODEM protocol, 743-744, 746
YUV compression scheme, 643, 645

Z

ZMODEM protocol, 743-747
ZSoft picture files, 549

PLUG YOURSELF INTO...

THE MACMILLAN INFORMATION SUPERLIBRARY™

Free information and vast computer resources from the world's leading computer book publisher—online!

FIND THE BOOKS THAT ARE RIGHT FOR YOU!
A complete online catalog, plus sample chapters and tables of contents!

- **STAY INFORMED** with the latest computer industry news through our online newsletter, press releases, and customized Information SuperLibrary Reports.
- **GET FAST ANSWERS** to your questions about Macmillan Computer Publishing books.
- **VISIT** our online bookstore for the latest information and editions!
- **COMMUNICATE** with our expert authors through e-mail and conferences.
- **DOWNLOAD SOFTWARE** from the immense Macmillan Computer Publishing library:
    - Source code, shareware, freeware, and demos
- **DISCOVER HOT SPOTS** on other parts of the Internet.
- **WIN BOOKS** in ongoing contests and giveaways!

TO PLUG INTO MCP:

WORLD WIDE WEB: **http://www.mcp.com**

FTP: ftp.mcp.com

User-Friendly References for All Your Computing Needs

Using Windows 95
0-7897-0092-1, $19.99 USA
Publication Date: 8/95

Using The Microsoft Network
0-7897-0398-X, $19.99 USA
Publication Date: 9/95

Using PowerPoint for Windows 95
0-7897-0365-3, $19.99 USA
Publication Date: 11/95

Using Excel for Windows 95
0-7897-0111-1, $19.99 USA
Publication Date: 9/95

The new *Using* series gives readers just the information they need to perform specific tasks quickly and move on to other things. *Using* books provide bite-sized information for quick and easy reference, along with real-world analogies and examples to explain new concepts.

Que For more information on these and other Que products, visit your local book retailer or call 1-800-772-0477.

Copyright © 1995, Macmillan Computer Publishing-USA, A Simon & Schuster Company

Source code ISBN: 0-7897-0085-9

GET CONNECTED
to the ultimate source of computer information!

The MCP Forum on CompuServe

Go online with the world's leading computer book publisher! Macmillan Computer Publishing offers everything you need for computer success!

Find the books that are right for you!
A complete online catalog, plus sample chapters and tables of contents give you an in-depth look at all our books. The best way to shop or browse!

➤ Get fast answers and technical support for MCP books and software

➤ Join discussion groups on major computer subjects

➤ Interact with our expert authors via e-mail and conferences

➤ Download software from our immense library:
  - Source code from books
  - Demos of hot software
  - The best shareware and freeware
  - Graphics files

Join now and get a free CompuServe Starter Kit!

To receive your free CompuServe Introductory Membership, call **1-800-848-8199** and ask for representative #597.

The Starter Kit includes:
➤ Personal ID number and password
➤ $15 credit on the system
➤ Subscription to *CompuServe Magazine*

Once on the CompuServe System, type:

GO MACMILLAN

for the most computer information anywhere!

MACMILLAN COMPUTER PUBLISHING

CompuServe

Complete and Return this Card for a *FREE* Computer Book Catalog

Thank you for purchasing this book! You have purchased a superior computer book written expressly for your needs. To continue to provide the kind of up-to-date, pertinent coverage you've come to expect from us, we need to hear from you. Please take a minute to complete and return this self-addressed, postage-paid form. In return, we'll send you a free catalog of all our computer books on topics ranging from word processing to programming and the internet.

Mr. ☐ Mrs. ☐ Ms. ☐ Dr. ☐

Name (first) _____ (M.I.) ___ (last) _____
Address _____
City _____ State ___ Zip _____
Phone _____ Fax _____
Company Name _____
E-mail address _____

1. Please check at least (3) influencing factors for purchasing this book.

Front or back cover information on book .... ☐
Special approach to the content .... ☐
Completeness of content .... ☐
Author's reputation .... ☐
Publisher's reputation .... ☐
Book cover design or layout .... ☐
Index or table of contents of book .... ☐
Price of book .... ☐
Special effects, graphics, illustrations .... ☐
Other (Please specify): _____ ☐

2. How did you first learn about this book?

Saw in Macmillan Computer Publishing catalog ..... ☐
Recommended by store personnel .... ☐
Saw the book on bookshelf at store .... ☐
Recommended by a friend .... ☐
Received advertisement in the mail .... ☐
Saw an advertisement in: _____ ☐
Read book review in: _____ ☐
Other (Please specify): _____ ☐

3. How many computer books have you purchased in the last six months?

This book only .... ☐   3 to 5 books .... ☐
2 books .... ☐   More than 5 .... ☐

4. Where did you purchase this book?

Bookstore .... ☐
Computer Store .... ☐
Consumer Electronics Store .... ☐
Department Store .... ☐
Office Club .... ☐
Warehouse Club .... ☐
Mail Order .... ☐
Direct from Publisher .... ☐
Internet site .... ☐
Other (Please specify): _____ ☐

5. How long have you been using a computer?

☐ Less than 6 months   ☐ 6 months to a year
☐ 1 to 3 years   ☐ More than 3 years

6. What is your level of experience with personal computers and with the subject of this book?

	With PCs	With subject of book
New	☐	☐
Casual	☐	☐
Accomplished	☐	☐
Expert	☐	☐

Source Code ISBN: 0-7897-0001-8

7. Which of the following best describes your job title?

- Administrative Assistant ☐
- Coordinator ☐
- Manager/Supervisor ☐
- Director ☐
- Vice President ☐
- President/CEO/COO ☐
- Lawyer/Doctor/Medical Professional ☐
- Teacher/Educator/Trainer ☐
- Engineer/Technician ☐
- Consultant ☐
- Not employed/Student/Retired ☐
- Other (Please specify): _____ ☐

8. Which of the following best describes the area of the company your job title falls under?

- Accounting ☐
- Engineering ☐
- Manufacturing ☐
- Operations ☐
- Marketing ☐
- Sales ☐
- Other (Please specify): _____ ☐

9. What is your age?

- Under 20 ☐
- 21-29 ☐
- 30-39 ☐
- 40-49 ☐
- 50-59 ☐
- 60-over ☐

10. Are you:

- Male ☐
- Female ☐

11. Which computer publications do you read regularly? (Please list)

_____
_____
_____
_____
_____
_____
_____
_____

Comments: _____

Fold here and scotch-tape to mail.

BUSINESS REPLY MAIL
FIRST-CLASS MAIL PERMIT NO. 9918 INDIANAPOLIS IN

POSTAGE WILL BE PAID BY THE ADDRESSEE

ATTN MARKETING
MACMILLAN COMPUTER PUBLISHING
MACMILLAN PUBLISHING USA
201 W 103RD ST
INDIANAPOLIS IN 46209-9042

NO POSTAGE
NECESSARY
IF MAILED
IN THE
UNITED STATES